THE OXFORD HANDBOOK OF
THE LAW OF THE SEA

THE OXFORD HANDBOOK OF

THE LAW OF THE SEA

Edited by

DONALD R ROTHWELL
Professor of International Law, Australian National University

ALEX G OUDE ELFERINK
Professor of International Law of the Sea, University of Tromsø and Utrecht University

KAREN N SCOTT
Professor of Law, University of Canterbury

TIM STEPHENS
Professor of International Law, University of Sydney

Great Clarendon Street, Oxford, OX2 6DP,
United Kingdom

Oxford University Press is a department of the University of Oxford.
It furthers the University's objective of excellence in research, scholarship,
and education by publishing worldwide. Oxford is a registered trade mark of
Oxford University Press in the UK and in certain other countries

© The several contributors 2015

The moral rights of the authors have been asserted

First published 2015
First published in paperback 2017

Impression: 2

All rights reserved. No part of this publication may be reproduced, stored in
a retrieval system, or transmitted, in any form or by any means, without the
prior permission in writing of Oxford University Press, or as expressly permitted
by law, by licence or under terms agreed with the appropriate reprographics
rights organization. Enquiries concerning reproduction outside the scope of the
above should be sent to the Rights Department, Oxford University Press, at the
address above

You must not circulate this work in any other form
and you must impose this same condition on any acquirer

Published in the United States of America by Oxford University Press
198 Madison Avenue, New York, NY 10016, United States of America

British Library Cataloguing in Publication Data
Data available

Library of Congress Cataloging in Publication Data
Data available

ISBN 978–0–19–871548–1 (Hbk.)
ISBN 978–0–19–880625–7 (Pbk.)

Printed and bound by
CPI Group (UK) Ltd, Croydon, CR0 4YY

Cover illustration: Roger Coulam/Oxford Scientific/
Getty Images.

Links to third party websites are provided by Oxford in good faith and
for information only. Oxford disclaims any responsibility for the materials
contained in any third party website referenced in this work.

Preface

2014 marks the twentieth anniversary of the entry into force of the 1982 United Nations Convention on the Law of the Sea (LOSC). As such, this *Handbook* aims to provide a timely account of the law of the sea, that body of law applying to all activities in the oceans, which cover 70 per cent of the Earth's surface.

Some of the principles and concepts fundamental to the law of the sea—such as freedom of navigation—date back hundreds of years. Others—such as common heritage of mankind—are much more recent in origin and have evolved to meet new challenges and threats and, more fundamentally, to reflect changing attitudes in respect of the exploitation of natural resources, including the ocean's capacity to assimilate the detritus associated with human civilization.

The long-established tension between coastal and flag States and their respective rights and responsibilities continues to influence the evolution of the law of the sea. But today, of equal if not greater importance, is the recognition of the oceans as an inter-connected whole. This is now the dominating principle of oceans governance, taking the law of the sea forward into the twenty-first century.

This *Handbook* comprises 39 chapters that are arranged to guide the reader from an historical introduction to the law of the sea, through the principal maritime zones and key actors, to selected regional developments and cross-cutting issues such as security, resource management, and scientific research. Authors were encouraged to consider future challenges and developments in their assessment of individual topics and to identify future research agendas. As this was very much a collaborative project, authors also coordinated with one another in order to avoid unnecessary overlaps. In the style of Oxford Handbooks, each chapter is a free-standing scholarly essay, which is nevertheless intended to support the broader objectives of this project: a coherent and comprehensive exposition of the modern law of the sea.

In order to aid the reader treaties referred to in each chapter have been given a short form reference. Complete references to each treaty are to be found in the accompanying Table of Treaties. All URL references were accurate and complete as at December 2014. The law and literature reflects the position as at 1 January 2014, though in many instances it was possible to take into account subsequent developments.

The preparation of this *Handbook* would not have been possible without the contributions of the 35 chapter authors with whom we have been privileged to work. We acknowledge their enthusiasm for this project and sustained engagement between 2012 and 2014. We would also like to acknowledge their individual and collective contributions and to thank them for their flexibility as the book progressed through its various phases and a range of editorial comments were returned for their consideration.

We also acknowledge the contributions of our research and editorial assistants—Nina Ubaldi, Zoe Winston Gregson, and Connie Ye—who made significant contributions throughout 2014 as the book reached its final editing phases. Thanks are also extended to I Made Andi Arsana (Gadjah Mada University, Yogyakarta, Indonesia) for his contribution in the drawing of maps and figures.

The *Handbook* would not have been possible without the support of our home institutions, and we acknowledge the assistance provided to us by the ANU College of Law (Australian National University), Netherlands Institute for the Law of the Sea (Utrecht University), and KG Jebsen Centre for the Law of the Sea (University of Tromsø), School of Law (University of Canterbury), and Sydney Law School (University of Sydney). We particularly acknowledge the support provided to us by our academic and professional colleagues in those institutions, and their encouragement for us to engage in this project alongside our other teaching and administrative duties.

Last but by no means least we thank Oxford University Press who invited us to consider editing the *Handbook* in 2011 and have consistently supported us throughout this project. We especially extend our thanks to Merel Alstein (Commissioning Editor, Academic Law) for her sustained support and to the OUP production team that contributed to the final publication.

Canberra, Utrecht/Tromsø, Christchurch, and Sydney
15 October 2014

Table of Contents

List of Illustrations — xi
Table of Cases — xiii
Table of Treaties — xix
List of Abbreviations — xlvii
Notes on Contributors — lvii

1. Historical Development of the Law of the Sea — 1
   TULLIO TREVES

2. The 1982 United Nations Convention on the Law of the Sea — 24
   ROBIN R CHURCHILL

3. Between Stability and Change in the Law of the Sea Convention: Subsequent Practice, Treaty Modification, and Regime Interaction — 46
   IRINA BUGA

4. Baselines — 69
   COALTER G LATHROP

5. The Territorial Sea and Contiguous Zone — 91
   JOHN E NOYES

6. International Straits — 114
   DONALD R ROTHWELL

7. The Archipelagic Regime — 134
   TARA DAVENPORT

8. The Exclusive Economic Zone — 159
   GEMMA ANDREONE

9. The Continental Shelf — 181
   TED L MCDORMAN

10. The High Seas Douglas Guilfoyle	203
11. The Deep Seabed Michael W Lodge	226
12. Maritime Boundary Delimitation Malcolm D Evans	254
13. Port and Coastal States Erik J Molenaar	280
14. Flag States Richard A Barnes	304
15. Landlocked and Geographically Disadvantaged States Helmut Tuerk	325
16. The United Nations: A Practitioner's Perspective Hans Corell	346
17. The Law of the Sea Convention Institutions James Harrison	373
18. Courts and Tribunals: The ICJ, ITLOS, and Arbitral Tribunals Bernard H Oxman	394
19. The International Maritime Organization Aldo Chircop	416
20. Regional Fisheries Management Organizations Rosemary Rayfuse	439
21. Integrated Oceans Management: A New Frontier in Marine Environmental Protection Karen N Scott	463
22. Marine Living Resources Nele Matz-Lück and Johannes Fuchs	491
23. Science and the International Regulation of Marine Pollution Elizabeth A Kirk	516

24. Navigational Rights and Freedoms 536
    Yoshifumi Tanaka

25. Marine Scientific Research 559
    Tim Stephens and Donald R Rothwell

26. Maritime Security 582
    Natalie Klein

27. The Mediterranean Sea 604
    Irini Papanicolopulu

28. The South China Sea 626
    Keyuan Zou

29. North-East Atlantic and the North Sea 647
    Ronán Long

30. The Caribbean Sea and Gulf of Mexico 672
    David Freestone and Clive Schofield

31. The Indian Ocean and the Law of the Sea: A Work in Progress 701
    Alex G Oude Elferink

32. Polar Oceans and Law of the Sea 724
    Karen N Scott and David L Vanderzwaag

33. Conserving Marine Biodiversity in Areas Beyond National Jurisdiction: Co-Evolution and Interaction with the Law of the Sea 752
    Robin M Warner

34. Warming Waters and Souring Seas: Climate Change and Ocean Acidification 777
    Tim Stephens

35. Threatened Species and Vulnerable Marine Ecosystems 799
    Edward J Goodwin

36. Marine Bioprospecting 825
    Joanna Mossop

37. Piracy　　843
    ANNA PETRIG

38. Military Operations　　866
    JAMES KRASKA

39. Charting the Future for the Law of the Sea　　888
    DONALD R ROTHWELL, ALEX G OUDE ELFERINK,
    KAREN N SCOTT, AND TIM STEPHENS

Index　　913

List of Illustrations

4.1	Maritime Limits and Boundaries	73
9.1	The Continental Shelf	191
28.1	The South China Sea	630
30.1	Main Navigation Routes in the Caribbean Region	674
30.2	Fisheries Organizations in the Caribbean Region	685
30.3	Maritime Delimitation in the Caribbean Sea and Gulf of Mexico	694
31.1	The Indian Ocean	703
32.1	The Arctic	726
32.2	The Antarctic	727

TABLE OF CASES

Aegean Sea Continental Shelf (Greece v Turkey) (Provisional Measures)
  [1976] ICJ Rep 6 614
Aegean Sea Continental Shelf (Greece v Turkey) (Judgment) [1978] ICJ Rep 3 614
Aerial Incident at Lockerbie (Libyan Arab Jamahiriya v United Kingdom)
  (Provisional Measures) [1992] ICJ Rep 3 .... 35, 320
Air Transport Association of America and Others v Secretary of State for Energy
  and Climate Change (C-366/10) [2011] ECR I-13755 .... 284, 288
Air Transport Services Agreement between the United States of America
  and France [1969] 38 ILR 182 50
Al-Saadoon and Mufdhi v UK (2010) 51 EHRR 9 50
Alabama Claims of the United States of America against Great Britain (1872)
  1 Moore 495, (1872) XXIV RIAA 125 323
Alleged Violations of Sovereign Rights and Maritime Spaces in the Caribbean
  Sea (Nicaragua v Colombia), Order of the International Court of Justice
  (3 February 2014) 265
Andreou v Turkey, Judgment of the European Court of Human Rights,
  App No 45653/99 (27 October 2009) 858
Application for Revision and Interpretation of the Judgment of 24 February 1982
  in the Case Concerning the Continental Shelf (Tunisia v Libyan Arab
  Jamahiriya) [1985] ICJ Rep 192 612
ARA Libertad (Argentina v Ghana), Request for the Prescription of Provisional
  Measures by the International Tribunal for the Law of the Sea
  (15 December 2012) 873
ARA Libertad (Argentina v Ghana) (Provisional Measures) [2012]
  ITLOS Rep 21 .... 285, 312, 395, 401
ARA Libertad Arbitration (Argentina v Ghana), Republic v High Court
  (Commercial Division) Accra, Ex parte Attorney General, NML Capital
  and the Republic of Argentina, Civil Motion No J5/10/2013
  (Supreme Court, Ghana, 2013) 71
Arbitration between Barbados and Trinidad and Tobago (2006) XXVII
  RIAA 147; (2006) 45 ILM 798 (Barbados/Trinidad and Tobago) 44, 259, 263,
                                                              264, 265, 270, 275, 405, 693
Arbitration between Guyana and Suriname (2007) XXX RIAA 1
  (Guyana/Suriname) 44, 78, 256, 259, 401, 695
Arbitration between the United Kingdom of Great Britain and Northern Ireland
  and the French Republic on the Delimitation of the Continental Shelf (1977)

XVIII RIAA 3; (1979) 18 ILM 397 (Anglo-French Continental Shelf
  Arbitration) 22, 258, 273, 274, 276
'Arctic Sunrise' (The Netherlands v Russian Federation), Provisional
  Measures Order of the International Tribunal for the Law of the Sea,
  Case No 22 (22 November 2013) 173, 187, 399, 887, 892, 895
'Arctic Sunrise' Arbitration (Netherlands v Russian Federation), Permanent
  Court of Arbitration, Case No 2014–02 (pending) 187, 188, 201, 399, 407, 848, 895
'Arctic Sunrise' Arbitration (Kingdom of the Netherlands v Russian Federation)
  (Award on Jurisdiction) (26 November 2014) 407
Armed Activities on the Territory of the Congo (Democratic Republic of the
  Congo v Uganda) (Judgment) [2005] ICJ Rep 168 494
Arrest Warrant of 11 April 2000 (Democratic Republic of Congo v Belgium)
  [2002] ICJ Rep 3 860
A Salemink v Raad van bestuur van het Uitvoeringsinstituut
  werknemersverzekeringen, C-347/10, Judgment of Court of Justice of the
  European Union, 17 January 2012 172
Atlanto-Scandian Herring Arbitration (Denmark in respect of the Faroe
  Islands v EU) (Pending) 286, 409
Barbados/Trinidad and Tobago (2006) XXVII RIAA 147; (2006)
  45 ILM 798 . . . . 44, 259, 263, 264, 265, 270, 275, 405, 693
Barcelona Traction, Light and Power Company Ltd (Belgium v Spain)
  (Judgment) [1970] ICJ Rep 161 215
Bay of Bengal Maritime Boundary Arbitration (Bangladesh/India),
  Award of the LOSC Annex VII Tribunal (7 July 2014) 276–8, 410
Bering Sea Fur Seals (Great Britain v United States) (1893) 1 Moore 755 . . . . 441, 491
Castle John v NV Mabeco (1986) 77 ILR 537 847
Chile—Measures Affecting the Transit and Importation of Swordfish (2000)
  WTO Doc WT/DS1931/1 (request for consultations by the European
  Communities) (2000) WTO Doc WT/DS193/2 (request for the establishment
  of a panel by the European Communities) 60, 62, 286
Church v Hubbart (1804) 6 US (2 Cranch) 187 107
Clipperton Island (1932) 26 American Journal of International Law 390 631
Commission v Hellenic Republic (Case 62/96) [1997] ECR I-6725 309
Commission v Ireland (Mox Plant) (C-459/03) [2006] ECR I-4635 . . . . 403, 661
Conservation and Sustainable Exploitation of Swordfish Stocks in the
  South-Eastern Pacific Ocean (Chile/European Community) (Order)
  [2000] ITLOS Rep 148 . . . . 60, 286, 409
Continental Shelf (Libyan Arab Jamahiriya/Malta) (Judgment) [1985]
  ICJ Rep 13 . . . . 36, 69, 162, 199, 200, 258, 264, 274, 612, 615
Continental Shelf (Tunisia/Libyan Arab Jamahiriya) (Judgment) [1982]
  ICJ Rep 18 . . . . 258, 267, 272, 612, 615
Continental Shelf Between Iceland and Jan Mayen (Iceland v Norway)
  (1981) 20 ILM 797 658
Constitution of the Maritime Safety Committee of the Inter-Governmental
  Maritime Consultative Organization (Advisory Opinion) [1960] ICJ Rep 150 424
Corfu Channel (United Kingdom v Albania) [1949] ICJ Rep 4 . . . . . . 18, 114, 116–19, 121,
                                                   122, 129, 132, 133, 323, 540, 542, 545, 585, 882

'Cygnus Case', The (Somali Pirates), Rotterdam District Court, 17 June 2010,
    (2010) 145 ILR 491 225
Delimitation of the Border between Eritrea and Ethiopia (2002) XXV RIAA 110 50
Delimitation of the Continental Shelf (Nicaragua v Colombia) Application instituting
    proceedings file in the ICJ (16 September 2013) 411
Delimitation of the Maritime Boundary in the Bay of Bengal (Bangladesh/Myanmar)
    (Judgment) [2012] ITLOS Rep 4 (Bangladesh/Myanmar) 44, 65, 181, 184, 185,
                                    191, 192, 196, 200, 260, 265, 268, 270, 271, 274, 410, 411, 414, 696
Delimitation of the Maritime Boundary in the Gulf of Maine Area
    (Canada v United States) (Judgment) [1984] ICJ Rep 246
    (Gulf of Maine) 258, 266, 274, 275
Eastern Greenland (1933) PCIJ Rep Ser A/B No 53 631
El Salvador v Nicaragua (1917) 11 AJIL 674 . . . . 83, 107
'Erika' Case, Cour de cassation (France), No 3439 (25 September 2012) 177
Eritrea v Yemen (1999) XXII RIAA 335 258
European Union—Measures on Atlanto-Scandian Herring (2013)
    WTO Doc WT/DS469 (request for consultations by Denmark) 286
'Fast Independence' Case (2009) Bull Crim No 85 . . . . 176, 177
Fisheries (United Kingdom v Norway) (Judgment) [1951] ICJ Rep 116
    (Anglo-Norwegian Fisheries) 19, 20, 72, 79, 80, 85–7, 94, 136, 137, 140,
                                                                141, 143, 491, 653, 889, 906
Fisheries Jurisdiction (United Kingdom of Britain and Northern
    Ireland v Iceland) (Interim Protection Order) [1972] ICJ Rep 12 398
Fisheries Jurisdiction (United Kingdom of Britain and Northern Ireland v Iceland)
    (Jurisdiction) [1973] ICJ Rep 3, *(Merits)* [1974] ICJ Rep 3 . . . . 20, 21, 35, 161, 653
Fisheries Jurisdiction (Federal Republic of Germany v Iceland) (Jurisdiction)
    [1973] ICJ Rep 49, (Merits) [1974] ICJ Rep 175 . . . . 20, 161, 653
Gabčíkovo-Nagymaros Project (Hungary/Slovakia) [1997] ICJ Rep 7 . . . . 63, 323
German Piracy Trial, Judgment of the Regional Court of Hamburg,
    Germany (19 October 2012) 860
Grand Prince (Belize v France) (Prompt Release) [2001] ITLOS Rep 17 . . . . 248, 309, 407
Grisbadårna (Norway and Sweden) (1910) AJIL 226 274
Grisbadårna Arbitration (Norway v Sweden) (1909) XI RIAA 147 . . . . 183, 274
Hirsi Jamaa and Others v Italy, Judgment of the European Court of
    Human Rights, App No 27765/09 (23 February 2012) 104, 591, 857
Humane Society International v Kyodo Senpaku Kaisha Ltd [2004]
    FCA 15110; [2005] FCA 664; [2006] FCAFC 116; [2008] FCA 3 739
IATA and ELFAA (C-344/04) [2006] ECR I-403 661
Institute of Cetacean Research v Sea Shepherd Conservation Society (2012)
    860 F.Supp.2d 1216 847
Institute of Cetacean Research v Sea Shepherd Conservation Society (2013)
    725 F.3d 940 (9th Cir) 847
Inuit Tapiriit Kanatami and Others [2013] All ER (D) 246 670
Isaak and Others v Turkey, Judgment of the European Court of
    Human Rights, App No 44587/98 (2006) 858
Islamic Republic of Iran and United States of America, Interlocutory
    Award No ITL 83-B1-FT (9 September 2004), 2004 WL 2210709 50

Island of Palmas (1928) II RIAA 829 . . . . .631, 632
Kingdom of Denmark in respect of the Faroe Islands v European Union
   (Coercive Economic Measures in respect of the Shared Stock of Atlanto-Scandian
   Herring), Statement of Claim, 16 August 2013 286
Land and Maritime Boundary between Cameroon and Nigeria (Cameroon v
   Nigeria: Equatorial Guinea Intervening) [2002] ICJ Rep 303 . . . . 22, 259, 262, 275, 400
Land Reclamation by Singapore In and Around the Straits of Johor
   (Malaysia v Singapore) (Provisional Measures) [2003] ITLOS Rep 10 398
Land, Island and Maritime Frontier Dispute (El Salvador v Honduras:
   Nicaragua Intervening) [1992] ICJ Rep 351 . . . . 20, 262
Lauritzen v Larsen (1953) 345 US 571 . . . . 214, 306
'Le Louis', The (1817) 2 Dods 210 305
Legal Consequences for States of the Continuing Presence of South Africa in
   Namibia (Advisory Opinion) [1971] ICJ Rep 16 49
Legal Consequences of the Construction of a Wall in the Occupied Palestinian
   Territory (Advisory Opinion) [2004] ICJ Rep 136 49
Legality of the Threat or Use of Nuclear Weapons (Advisory Opinion) [1996] ICJ Rep 226 . . . 323
Legality of the Use by a State of Nuclear Weapons in Armed Conflict
   (Advisory Opinion) [1996] ICJ Rep 66 49
M/V *'Courier', Re* (2011) 25 K 4280/09 (Administrative Court of Cologne) 857, 862
M/V *'Courier', Re* (2014) 4 A 2948/11 (Higher Administrative Court of
   North Rhine-Westphalia) 862
M/V *'Elly Mærsk', Re* (2011) U.2011.3066H, TfK2011.923/1
   (Supreme Court of Denmark) 857
M/V *'Louisa' (Saint Vincent and The Grenadines v Spain)*, Judgment of the
   International Tribunal for the Law of the Sea (28 May 2013) 287, 623, 683
M/V *'Saiga' (No 1) (Saint Vincent and the Grenadines v Guinea)*
   (Prompt Release) (1997) 110 ILR 736 . . . . 169, 248, 403, 683
M/V *'Saiga' (No 2) (Saint Vincent and the Grenadines v Guinea)*
   (Provisional Measures) (1998) 117 ILR 111; (Judgment) [1999] ITLOS
   Rep 10, (1999) 120 ILR 143 . . . . .39, 44, 103, 169, 209, 215, 248, 297, 307–9,
                                                          313, 314, 398, 554, 555, 683, 856
M/V *'Virginia G' (Panama v Guinea-Bissau)*, Judgment of the International
   Tribunal for the Law of the Sea, Case No 19 (14 April 2014) 169, 179, 215,
                                                          216, 308, 309, 403, 555
Magda Maria, Netherlands Court of Appeal (1989) 20 Netherlands
   Yearbook of International Law 351 309
Mangouras v Spain, App No 12050/04, [2010] ECHR 1364 169
Marianna Flora, The (1826) 24 US 1 305
Maritime Boundary Dispute (Norway v Sweden) (Award) (1909)
   XI RIAA 155 (Grisbadarna Arbitration) 183
Maritime Delimitation and Territorial Questions between Qatar and Bahrain
   (Qatar v Bahrain) (Merits) [2001] ICJ Rep 40 . . . . . . 59, 74, 78, 81, 144, 256, 259, 262
Maritime Delimitation in the Area between Greenland and Jan Mayen
   (Denmark v Norway) [1993] ICJ Rep 38 (Jan Mayen) 50, 258, 262, 266,
                                                          274, 275, 281, 658, 659
Maritime Delimitation in the Black Sea (Romania v Ukraine) (Judgment) [2009]
   ICJ Rep 61 (Black Sea) 34, 44, 71, 259, 260, 262, 266, 267–71, 274, 275, 278, 696

*Maritime Delimitation in the Caribbean Sea and Pacific Ocean (Costa
    Rica v Nicaragua)*, Application Instituting Proceedings in the International
    Court of Justice (25 February 2014) 697
Maritime Dispute (Peru v Chile), Judgment of the International Court of Justice,
    General List No 137 (27 January 2014) 45, 199, 256, 259, 260, 262, 266, 269, 272, 615
McCulloch Case (1963) 372 US 10 312
Medvedyev and Others v France, Judgment of the European Court of Human
    Rights, App No 3394/03 (29 March 2010), [2010] ECHR 384 . . . . 225, 857, 858
*Military and Paramilitary Activities in and Against Nicaragua
    (Nicaragua v United States) (Merits)* [1986] ICJ Rep 14 . . . . 283, 284, 323
Molvan v Attorney General for Palestine [1948] AC 351, 369; (Privy Council)
    (1948) 15 ILR 11 218
MOX Plant (Ireland v United Kingdom) (Provisional Measures) [2001]
    ITLOS Rep 95, (2002) 41 ILM 405 . . . . 402, 403, 522, 524
*MOX Plant (Ireland v United Kingdom) (Suspension of Proceedings on
    Jurisdiction and Merits and Request for Further Provisional Measures)
    (Procedural Order No 3)* (2003) 42 ILM 1187 . . . . 62, 409, 414
Muslimin v The Queen (2010) 240 CLR 470 170
Munaf v Romania (2009) UN Doc CCPR/C/96/D/1539/2006 858
Muscat Dhows (France/Great Britain), PCA 1905 (1961)
    XI RIAA 83 . . . . 17, 209, 214, 306
Navigational and Related Rights (Costa Rica v Nicaragua) [2009]
    ICJ Rep 213 . . . . 50, 52
North Atlantic Coast Fisheries (Great Britain v United States) (1910)
    XI RIAA 167 . . . . 20, 82
*North Sea Continental Shelf (Federal Republic of Germany v Denmark;
    Federal Republic of Germany v The Netherlands)* [1969] ICJ Rep 3 . . . . . . 15, 21, 38, 49,
                                                            69, 184, 185, 190, 257, 259, 264, 269,
                                                            270, 274, 328, 656, 658, 707
Nottebohm (Liechtenstein v Guatemala) (Judgment) [1955] ICJ Rep 4 . . . . 215, 308
Nuclear Tests (Australia v France) (Interim measures) [1973] ICJ Rep 99,
    (Merits) [1974] ICJ Rep 253; *(New Zealand v France) (Interim measures)*
    [1973] ICJ Rep 135, *(Merits)* [1974] ICJ Rep 457 212
Öcalan v Turkey (2003) 37 EHRR 238; (2005) 41 EHRR 985 50
*Pulp Mills on the River Uruguay (Argentina v Uruguay) (Provisional
    Measures)* [2006] ICJ Rep 113; *(Judgment)* [2010] ICJ Rep 14 . . . . . 50, 323, 324, 482,
                                                            483, 497, 522
R v Musa Abdullahi Said & Six others, Judgment of Chief Magistrate's Court
    of Mombasa (6 September 2010) 848
R v Mills (1995) 44 ICLQ 949 111
R v Perry (2003) 222 Newfoundland and Prince Edward Island Reports 313 191
R v Secretary of State for Transport, ex parte Factortame (No 3) (C-221/89)
    [1991] ECR I-3905 . . . . 307, 339
Red Crusader Case (1962) 35 ILR 483 856
*Republic of Mauritius v The United Kingdom of Great Britain and
    Northern Ireland*, LOSC Annex VII Tribunal (Pending) 401
Republic of the Philippines, The v The People's Republic of China, Permanent
    Court of Arbitration (Pending) 630, 640

Request for an Advisory Opinion Submitted by the Sub-Regional Fisheries Commission
  (Pending), available at <http://www.itlos.org/index.php?id=252>
  (SRFC Advisory Opinion) 323, 324, 415, 893
Responsibilities and Obligations of States Sponsoring Persons and Entities with
  Respect to Activities in the Area, ITLOS Case No 17 (Advisory Opinion) [2011]
  ITLOS Rep 10 (Area Advisory Opinion) 63, 247, 248, 250, 274, 323, 324,
    414, 482, 483, 497, 520, 539, 764
Schooner Exchange, The v McFaddon (1812) 11 US (7 Cranch) 116 872
Soering v UK (1989) 11 EHRR 439 50
Somali Pirates see 'Cygnus Case'
Sonko v Spain (2011) Comm No 368/2008 (CAT Committee) 857
Southern Bluefin Tuna (New Zealand v Japan; Australia v Japan)
  (Provisional Measures) [1999] ITLOS Rep 280;
  [1999] 117 ILR 148 . . . . 63, 398, 402, 414, 449, 497
Southern Bluefin Tuna (New Zealand v Japan; Australia v Japan) (Jurisdiction
  and Admissibility) (2000) XXIII RIAA 1; (2000) 119 ILR 508 . . . . .396, 402, 445
SS 'I'm Alone' (Canada/United States) III RIAA 1609 856
SS 'Lotus' (France v Turkey) (Judgment) [1927] PCIJ Rep ser A no 10 . . . . . . 17, 18, 209, 218, 860
SS Wimbledon [1923] PCIJ Rep ser A no 1. 386
St Pierre and Miquelon Arbitration (1992) 95 ILR 645 274
Taba Arbitration (Egypt/Israel) (1988) 27 ILM 1421. 50
Territorial and Maritime Dispute between Nicaragua and Colombia
  (Nicaragua v Colombia) (Judgment) [2012] ICJ Rep 624 . . . . 36, 45, 95, 185, 254,
    259–63, 265–7, 270–3, 275–9, 410, 411, 696–9
Territorial and Maritime Dispute between Nicaragua and Honduras in the
  Caribbean Sea (Nicaragua v Honduras) (Judgment) [2007]
  ICJ Rep 659 . . . . 256, 259, 410, 695
Territorial Jurisdiction of the International Commission of the River Oder
  (Czechoslovakia, Denmark, France, Germany, Great Britain,
  Sweden/Poland) [1929] PCIJ ser A no 23
'Trans Arctic' Case (2009) Bull Crim No 85 . . . . .176, 177
Twee Gebroeders (1800) 165 ER 485 540
United States Diplomatic and Consular Staff in Tehran (United States of
  America v Iran) [1980] ICJ Rep 32 323
United States v Shi (2008) 525 F.3d 709 (9th Cir) 59, 860
Vassis and Others v France, Judgment of the European Court of Human
  Rights, App No 62736/09 (27 June 2013) 225
'Volga', The (Russian Federation v Australia) (Prompt Release) (2002)
  ITLOS Rep 10 318
Whaling in the Antarctic (Australia v Japan: New Zealand Intervening),
  Judgment of the International Court of Justice, General List No 148
  (31 March 2014) 169, 261, 496, 511, 561, 562, 565, 577, 581, 739, 895
Wildenhus (1887) 120 US 1 312
Women on Waves and Others v Portugal, Judgment of the European Court
  of Human Rights, App No 31276/05 (3 February 2009) 858

Table of Treaties

(listed chronologically excepting amending and supplementary instruments which follow the principal Treaty)

1856 Declaration Respecting Maritime Law 1856, OS—16 April 1856, EIF—16 April 1856, 15 Martens Nouveau Recueil Général des Traités 791 (Declaration of Paris) 871, 875

1884 Convention for the Protection of Submarine Telegraph Cables, OS—14 March 1884, EIF—1 March 1888, 163 CTS 391 208
  Art 2 208
  Art 10 208

1898 Treaty of Paris between Spain and the United States, OS—10 December 1898, EIF—11 April 1899, 187 CTS 100 139

1899 Hague Convention (III) for the Adaptation to Maritime Warfare of the Principles of the Geneva Convention of 1864, OS—29 July 1899, EIF—4 September 1900, 187 CTS 443 876

1900 Treaty between Spain and the United States for the Cession of Outlying Islands of the Philippines, OS—7 November 1900, EIF—23 March 1901, 189 CTS 108 139

1904 Convention for the Exemption of Hospital Ships, in Time of War, from The Payment of all Dues and Taxes Imposed for the Benefit of the State, OS—21 December 1904, EIF 26 March 1907, 197 CTS 331 876

1907 Hague Convention (VI) Relating to the Status of Enemy Merchant Ships at the Outbreak of Hostilities, OS—18 October 1907, EIF—26 January 1910, 205 CTS 305 876

1907 Hague Convention (VII) Relating to the Conversion of Merchant Ships into Warships, OS—18 October 1907, EIF—26 January 1910, 205 CTS 319 . . . . 871, 876, 877
  Arts 2–6 977

1907 Hague Convention (VIII) Relative to the Laying of Automatic Submarine Contact Mines, OS—18 October 1907, EIF—26 January 1910, 205 CTS 331 876

1907 Hague Convention (IX) Concerning Bombardments by Naval Forces in Time of War, OS—18 October 1907, EIF—26 January 1910, 205 CTS 345 876
  Arts 1–2 876

1907 Hague Convention (X) for the Adaptation to Maritime Warfare of the Principles of the Geneva Convention, OS—18 October 1907, EIF—26 January 1910, 205 CTS 359 876

1907 Hague Convention (XI) Relative to Certain Restrictions with Regard to the Exercise of the Right of Capture in Naval War, OS—18 October 1907, EIF—26 January 2010, 205 CTS 367 876

1907 Hague Convention (XII) Relative to the Creation of an International Prize Court, OS—18 October 1907, not in force, 205 CTS 381 876

1907 Hague Convention (XIII)
concerning the Rights and Duties of
Neutral Powers in Naval War, OS—18
October 1907, EIF—26 January
1910, 205 CTS 395 876
1909 Final Protocol to the Naval
Conference of London, OS—
26 February 1909, not in force, 208 CTS
338 (London Declaration) 876
1911 Treaty for the Preservation
and Protection of Fur Seals—
7 July 1911 816
1920 Treaty concerning the
Archipelago of Spitsbergen, OS—
9 February 1920, EIF—14 August
1925, 2 LNTS 7 . . . . 298, 732
Art 2 732
1923 Convention and Statute on the
International Regime of Maritime
Ports, OS—9 December 1923, EIF—
26 July 1926, 58 LNTS 287 (Maritime
Ports Convention) 284
Art 2 129
Art 4 129
Art 11 129
Art 13 284
Art 14 284
1924 Convention between the
United States of America and Great
Britain respecting the Regulation
of the Liquor Traffic, OS—
23 January 1924, EIF—22 May 1924,
27 LNTS 182 . . . . 6, 108
Art 1 6
1924 Convention between the
United States of America and Norway
respecting the Regulation of the
Liquor Traffic, OS—24 May 1924 6
Art 1 6
1926 Draft Convention on Oil
Pollution of Navigable Waters,
16 June 1926, not in force,
20 AJIL 555 871
1930 Convention between the
United States and Great Britain
Delimiting the Boundary between the
Philippine Archipelago and the State of
North Borneo, OS—2 January
1930, EIF—13 December 1932,
137 LNTS 297 139
1930 International Treaty for the
Limitation and Reduction of Naval
Armament, OS—22 April 1930, EIF—31
December 1930, 112 LNTS 65
(Treaty of London) 876
1936 Procès-Verbal relating to the
Rules of Submarine Warfare, OS—
6 November 1936, EIF—
6 November 1936, 173 LNTS 353
(London Protocol) 876
1936 Convention Regarding the
Regime of Straits, OS—20 July 1936,
EIF—9 November 1936,
173 LNTS 213 (Montreux
Convention) 116, 127, 296
Art 1 127
Art 2 127
Art 13 116
1937 Nyon Agreement, OS—
14 September 1937, EIF—14 September
1937, 181 LNTS 137 876
1937 Supplementary Agreement,
OS—17 September 1937,
EIF—17 September 1937,
181 LNTS 137 876
1941 Declaration of Principles,
OS—14 August 1941, EIF—
14 August 1941, 204 LNTS 381
(Atlantic Charter) 879
1942 Treaty between Great Britain
and Northern Ireland and
Venezuela Relating to the Submarine
Areas of the Gulf of Paria, OS—26
February 1942, EIF—
22 September 1942, 205
LNTS 121 . . . . 10, 15, 183
Art 1 692
1944 Convention on International
Civil Aviation—7 December 1944
Art 3(a) 872
Art 3(b) 872
1945 Charter of the United
Nations, OS—26 June 1945, EIF—24
October 1945, 1 UNTS XVI 35, 347,
494, 638, 642, 695,
867-9, 875, 881

Chapter VI	407
Chapter VII	35, 106, 370, 407, 565, 601, 854
Art 2	230
Art 2(3)	395, 397
Art 2(4)	869, 874, 884
Art 10	392
Art 25	320
Art 33	396
Art 33(1)	395, 397, 636
Art 41	601
Art 51	869
Art 58	392
Art 100(1)	390
Art 103	35

1945 Statute of the International Court of Justice, OS—26 June 1945, EIF—24 October 1945, 1 UNTS XVI

Art 34	399
Art 35	399
Art 36(2)	401
Art 38	258, 414

1946 Treaty of Friendship, Commerce and Navigation between the United States of America and the Republic of China, OS—4 November 1946, EIF—30 November 1948, 25 UNTS ... 69

Art XXI(2) ... 305

1946 International Convention for the Regulation of Whaling, OS—2 December 1946, EIF—10 November 1948, 161 UNTS 72 (ICRW) 484, 492, 561, 565, 739, 743, 804, 817, 895

Art I	509
Art VII(2)	510
Art VIII	510, 511, 561, 577, 739
Art VIII(1)	511, 817
Art VIII(2)	817
Sch	509
Sch para 7(b)	510
Sch para 7(c)	510
Sch para 10(e)	510
Sch para 13(b)	510

1948 Convention on the International Maritime Organization, OS—6 March 1948, EIF—17 March 1958, 289 UNTS 3 (IMO Convention) 417, 419, 424, 425, 427, 437

Art 1(a)	419
Art 1(b)	419
Art 1(c)	419
Art 1(d)	419
Art 1(e)	419
Art 2	420
Art 2(b)	420
Art 2(d)	421, 435
Art 15(j)	422
Art 15(k)	422
Art 15(l)	422
Art 17	422
Art 21	422
Art 26	422
Art 28(a)	424
Art 29(a)	424
Art 29(b)	424
Art 31	428
Art 33(a)	425
Art 34	425
Art 36	428
Art 38(a)	425
Art 38(b)	425
Art 41	428
Art 43(a)	425
Art 46	428
Art 48	425
Art 51	428
Art 66	425

1949 Geneva Convention II for the Amelioration of the Condition of Wounded, Sick and Shipwrecked Members of Armed Forces at Sea, OS—12 August 1949, EIF—21 October 1950, 75 UNTS 85 .... 16, 876

Art 17(4)	19
Art 52	876

1977 Protocol Additional to the Geneva Conventions of 12 August 1949, and relating to the Protection of Victims of International Armed Conflicts, OS—8 June 1977, EIF—7 December 1978, 1125 UNTS 3 (Additional Protocol I) 876

1951 Convention Relating to the Status of Refugees, OS—28 July 1951, EIF—22 April 1954, 189 UNTS 150 591

Art 31	104
Art 33	104

1967 Protocol Relating to the Status of
  Refugees, OS—31 January 1967, EIF—4
  October 1967, 606 UNTS 267 591
1952 Declaration on the Maritime
  Zone, OS—18 August 1952, EIF—18
  August 1952, 1006 UNTS 326
  (Santiago Declaration) 11–12
1952 International Convention for the
  Unification of Certain Rules relating
  to Penal Jurisdiction in matters of
  Collisions and other Incidents of
  Navigation, OS—10 May 1952, EIF—20
  November 1955, 439 UNTS 233
  Art 1 219
  Art 2 219
1954 International Convention for
  the Prevention of Pollution of the
  Sea by Oil, OS—12 May 1954,
  EIF—26 July 1958, 327 UNTS
  3 (OILPOL) 518, 531
  Art 1 311
1958 Convention on Fishing and
  Conservation of the Living Resources
  of the High Seas, OS—29 April 1958,
  EIF—20 March 1966, 559 UNTS 285
  (CFCLR) 14, 15, 28, 30, 37,
    114, 141, 161, 496, 518,
    561, 563, 889, 896, 904
  Art 2 496
  Art 6 161
  Art 7 161
  Art 7(2) 563
1958 Convention on the Territorial
  Sea and Contiguous Zone, OS—29
  April 1958, EIF—10 September 1964,
  516 UNTS 206 (TSC) 14, 28, 30, 37,
    73, 82, 87, 92, 93, 108–10,
    113, 114, 118, 141, 334, 518,
    545, 561, 563, 889, 896, 904
  Art 1 103
  Arts 1–2 96
  Art 2 .563
  Art 3 73
  Art 4 . . . . 19, 85, 87, 141
  Art 6 95
  Art 7 . . . . 20, 82
  Art 12 255
  Art 13 82
  Art 14(1) 540
  Art 14(4) 98, 543
  Art 14(5) 543
  Arts 14–23 . . . . .115, 118
  Art 15 18
  Art 16 . . . . 14, 15, 118
  Art 16(4) 19, 118
  Art 24 . . . . 109, 111
  Art 24(1) 108
  Art 24(3) 109
1958 Convention on the Continental
  Shelf, OS—29 April 1958, EIF—10
  June 1964, 499 UNTS
  311 (CSC) 14, 15, 28, 30, 37, 114,
    141, 183, 185, 186, 518, 561,
    563, 568, 707, 889, 896, 904
  Art 1 . . . . . . 36, 185, 186, 189, 190, 707
  Arts 1–3 21
  Art 2(3) 184
  Art 2(4) 183, 186
  Art 3 .186
  Art 4 .189
  Art 5(1) 563
  Art 5(8) 563
  Art 6 . . . . .21, 22, 256–8, 658
1958 Convention on the High
  Seas, OS—29 April 1958,
  EIF—30 September 1962, 450
  UNTS 11 (HSC) 14, 15, 28, 30,
    37, 58, 114, 141, 205, 306, 309,
    334, 335, 518, 561, 563, 843,
    863, 864, 889, 896, 904
  Art 1 . . . . .36, 205
  Art 2 206
  Art 3 .334
  Art 4 17
  Art 5 . . . . 17, 209, 215
  Art 5(1) 308
  Art 6 .214
  Art 8(2) 870
  Art 11 . . . . .18, 219
  Arts 14–22 844
  Art 15 . . . . .846, 859
  Art 18 861

TABLE OF TREATIES xxiii

Art 23 312
Art 24 518
Art 25 518
Arts 26–27 208
1958 Optional Protocol of Signature
  concerning the Compulsory
  Settlement of Disputes arising from
  the Law of the Sea Conventions,
  OS—29 April 1958, EIF—
  30 September 1962, 450 UNTS
  169 (OPSD) 14, 16
1958 ILO Convention (No 108)
  concerning Seafarers' Identity
  Documents, OS—13 May 1958,
  EIF—19 February 1961,
  389 UNTS 277 599
1959 Antarctic Treaty, OS—
  1 December 1959, EIF —
  23 June 1961, 402 UNTS 71 281 578,
        642, 740, 741, 743, 744, 761
  Preamble 211
  Art I 742
  Art II 840
  Art III 578, 742
  Art III(1) 840
  Art IV 211, 738
  Art VI 741, 742, 840
  Art VII 742, 745
  Art VII 742, 745
1991 Protocol on Environmental
  Protection to the Antarctic Treaty,
  OS—4 October 1991, EIF—
  14 January 1998, 30 ILM 1461 578,
                          741, 761, 840
  Art 2 741
  Art 3 . . . . 578, 743, 840
  Art 7 740
  Art 8 . . . . 578, 743, 840
  Annex I 743
  Annex II 578, 743
  Annex V 743, 750
  Annex V Art 2 743
  Annex V Art 6 750
1962 Convention on the Liability
  of Operators of Nuclear Ships—
  25 May 1962—57 AJIL 268 548

1963 Treaty Banning Nuclear Weapon
  Tests in the Atmosphere, in
  Outer Space, and Under Water, OS—5
  August 1963, EIF—10 October 1963,
  480 UNTS 43 212
1965 Convention on Facilitation of
  International Maritime Traffic, OS—9
  April 1965, EIF—5 March 1967, 591
  UNTS 265 425
  Art 3 871
1965 Convention on Transit Trade of
  Land-locked States, OS— 8 July 1965,
  EIF—9 June 1967, 597 UNTS 3 . . . 334, 335
  Art 1(a) 331
  Art 15 335
1966 International Convention for the
  Conservation of Atlantic Tunas, OS—14
  May 1966, EIF—21 March 1969, 673
  UNTS 63 (ICCAT Convention) . . . 621,
                                   667, 684
1966 International Convention on Load
  Lines, OS—5 April 1966, EIF—21 July
  1968, 640 UNTS 133 315
  Art 2 314
  Art 5 314
  Art 29 421
1967 Treaty of Navigation, OS—
  23 January 1967, EIF—14 March 1967,
  634 UNTS 181 341
1967 Treaty on Principles Governing
  the Activities of States in the
  Exploration and Use of Outer
  Space, including the Moon and other
  Celestial Bodies, OS—27 January 1967,
  EIF—10 October 1967, 610 UNTS 205
  Art 2 883
1967 Treaty on the Prohibition of
  Nuclear Weapons in Latin America
  and the Caribbean
  Protocol II 643
1969 International Convention on
  Civil Liability for Oil Pollution
  Damage, OS—29 November
  1969, EIF—27 June 1975, 973
  UNTS 319 (CLC) 431, 519, 531
  1984 Protocol, (1984) 23 ILM 177 531

xxiv   TABLE OF TREATIES

1992 Protocol, OS—27 November
  1992, EIF—30 May 1996, 1996
  UKTS 86 431 531
1969 International Convention on
  Tonnage Measurement, OS—
  23 June 1969, EIF—18 July 1982,
  1291 UNTS 3 315
  Art 4 .871
1969 International Convention Relating
  to Intervention on the High Seas in
  Cases of Oil Pollution Casualties,
  OS—29 November 1969, EIF—
  6 May 1975, (1969) 9 ILM 25
  (Intervention Convention) 519
1969 Vienna Convention on the Law
  of Treaties, OS—23 May 1969,
  EIF—27 January 1980, 1155 UNTS
  331 (VCLT) 34, 199
  Art 26 38
  Art 30(4)(b) 35, 58
  Art 31 47
  Art 31(1) 52
  Art 31(3) 110, 389
  Art 31(3)(a) 50
  Art 31(3)(b) 34, 49, 50
  Art 31(3)(c) 52, 61, 66
  Arts 31–32 199
  Art 32 . . . . 49, 426
  Art 34 444
  Arts 39–41 47
  Art 62(2)(a) 791
1971 Agreement on Cooperation
  in Taking Measures Against Pollution
  of the Sea by Oil—16 September
  1971 .663
1971 Convention on the Wetlands
  of International Importance,
  OS—2 February 1971, EIF—21
  December 1975, 996 UNTS 245
  (Ramsar Convention) 813, 814–15
  Art 1(1) 814
  Art 3(1) 815
  Art 3(2) 822
  Art 4 815
1971 International Convention on the
  Establishment of an International
  Fund for Compensation for Oil
  Pollution Damage, OS—18 December
  1971, EIF—16 October 1978,
  (1972) 11 ILM 284 (Fund
  Convention) 431, 519, 531
1992 Protocol, OS—27 November
  1992, EIF—30 May 1996, 1996
  UKTS 87 431 531
1984 Protocol (1971) 23 ILM 195 531
1971 Treaty on the Prohibition of the
  Emplacement of Nuclear Weapons and
  other Weapons of Mass Destruction on
  the Sea-Bed and the Ocean Floor and in
  the Subsoil Thereof, OS—11 February 1971,
  EIF—18 May 1972, 955 UNTS 115 (Sea-Bed
  Arms Control Treaty) 211,
                                    230, 643
  Preamble 211
  Art 1 211
  Art 5 211
  Art 8 211
  Art 10 211
1972 Convention for the Prevention of
  Marine Pollution by Dumping from
  Ships and Aircraft, OS—15 February
  1972, EIF—7 April 1974, (1972)
  11 ILM 262 (Oslo Convention) 520
  Art XIII 37
1972 Convention on the Conservation of
  Antarctic Seals—11 February 1972
  (London) (CCAS) 508, 743, 745
1972 Convention on the
  International Regulations for
  Preventing Collisions at Sea,
  OS—20 October 1972, EIF—15
  July 1977, 1050 UNTS 16
  (COLREG) 105, 315, 541
  r 3(a) 311, 314
  r 9 128
  r 10 .128
1972 Convention on the Prevention
  of Marine Pollution by Dumping of
  Wastes and Other Matter, OS—29
  December 1972, EIF—30 August 1975,
  1046 UNTS 120 (London
  Convention) 327, 520, 528, 529, 534,
                     535, 577, 717, 718, 763, 784
  Art 1 534

1996 Protocol to the London Convention
on the Prevention of Marine Pollution by
Dumping of Wastes and Other
Matter, OS—8 November 1996,
EIF—24 March 2006, (1997)
36 ILM 1 . . . . 327, 525, 528, 529,
535, 577, 581, 717, 718,
763, 784, 785
Art 14 528
Annex 2 483
Annex 4 785
1972 Convention on the Protection
of the World Cultural and Natural
Heritage, OS—16 November 1972,
EIF—17 December 1975, 1037 UNTS
151 (WHC) 813, 815–16
Art 2 816
Art 11(4) 823
1972 International Convention for
Safe Containers, OS—2 February
1972, EIF—6 September 1977,
1064 UNTS. 3
1973 Agreement on the Conservation
of Polar Bears, OS—15 November
1973, EIF—26 May 1976, (1974)
13 ILM 13 735
1973 Convention on International
Trade in Endangered Species of
Wild Fauna and Flora, OS—3 March
1973; EIF—1 July 1975, 993 UNTS
243 (CITES) 511, 818, 819
Art I(c) 819
Art I(e) 819
Art II 376
Art II(1) 819
Art II(2)(a) 819
Art III 819
Art III(5) 820
Art IV(2) 819
Art IV(6) 820
Art XIV(6) 37
Annex II 669
Annex V 820
App I 511, 819
App II 511, 819
1973 International Convention
for the Prevention of Pollution
from Ships, OS—2 November 1973,
as Modified by the Protocol of 1978
Relating Thereto, OS—17 February
1978, EIF—2 October 1983, 1340
UNTS 62 (MARPOL) 66, 99, 105,
106, 179, 285, 316, 327, 431, 432,
435, 436, 484, 530, 531, 548,
551, 728, 743, 745, 755,
763, 785, 898
Art 2(4) 311
Art 9(2) 37
Annex I 484, 683, 743, 755
Annex I reg 43 729
Annex II 484, 683, 743, 755
Annex III 755
Annex IV 755
Annexes IV–VI 484
Annex V 534, 683, 743, 755
Annex VI 179, 285, 755, 785
1973 Treaty establishing the
Caribbean Community, OS—
4 July 1973, EIF—1 August 1973,
946 UNTS 17 (CARICOM) 686
1974 Convention between
Government of the French
Republic and the Government
of the Spanish State on the
Delimitation of the Continental
Shelves of the Two States in the
Bay of Biscay (Golfe de Gascogne/
Golfo de Vizcaya), OS—29
January 1974, EIF—5 April 1975,
996 UNTS 333 658
Art 3 658
Annex 2 658
1974 Convention on the Protection
of the Marine Environment of
the Baltic Sea Area, OS—
22 March 1974, EIF—3 May 1980
(1974) 13 ILM 546 (1974
Helsinki Convention) 519, 526
1974 Convention on the
Prevention of Marine Pollution
from Land-based Sources,
OS–4 June 1974, EIF—6 May
1978, 13 ILM 352 (Paris
Convention) 519, 526

1974 International Convention for the
Safety of Life at Sea, OS—1 November
1974, EIF—25 May 1980, 1184 UNTS 278
(SOLAS) 105, 106, 315,
426, 431, 432, 436, 548,
551, 588, 599, 745
   Chapter XI-2 320
   Chapter V 432, 871
   Art XI-1(5) 314
   Art 8 421
1988 Protocol relating to the
International Convention for
the Safety of Life at Sea, OS—
11 November 1988, EIF— 3
February 2000, [2000] ATS 3 . . . .315, 551
1975 Treaty of Friendship and
Co-operation between the
Federative Republic of Brazil
and the Republic of Paraguay,
OS—4 December 1975,
EIF—17 September 1979,
1242 UNTS 174 . . . . .341, 343
1976 Convention for the Protection
of the Marine Environment and the
Coastal Region of the Mediterranean,
OS—16 February 1976, EIF—12
February 1978, amended and renamed
10 June 1995, EIF—9 July 2004,
1102 UNTS 27 (Barcelona
Convention) 477, 478, 528,
616–20, 624, 762
   Art 1(1) 618
   Art 1(2) 618
   Art 1(3) 618
   Art 3(4) 618, 619
   Art 3(5) 618
   Art 4(3)(a) 477
   Art 4(3)(c) 477
   Art 4(3)(d) 477
   Art 4(3)(e) 478
   Art 12 620
1976 Protocol for the Prevention and
Elimination of Pollution of the
Mediterranean Sea by Dumping
from Ships and Aircraft or
Incineration at Sea, OS—
16 February 1976, EIF—12 February 1978,
1102 UNTS 92 . . . . 478, 528
1980 Protocol for the Protection
of the Mediterranean Sea against Pollution
from Land-Based
Sources and Activities, OS—
17 May 1980, EIF—17 June 1983,
1328 UNTS 105, amended and
replaced by Protocol of same
name, OS—7 March 1996, EIF—
11 May 2008, (1999) OJ L322 18 478
1994 Protocol for the Protection of
the Mediterranean Sea against
Pollution Resulting from
Exploration and Exploitation of
the Continental Shelf and the
Seabed and its Subsoil, OS—
14 October 1994, EIF—
24 March 2011, (2013)
OJ L 4/15 . . . . 478, 619
   Art 27 619
1995 Protocol concerning
Specially Protected Areas and
Biological Diversity in the
Mediterranean, OS—10 June
1995, EIF—12 December 1999,
2102 UNTS 203 . . . . 478, 479, 528,
616, 618
   Preamble 479
   Arts 4–9 . . . . 477, 479
   Art 9(4)(c) 618
   Art 13 479
1996 Protocol on Prevention of
Pollution of the Mediterranean
Sea by Transboundary Movements of
Hazardous Wastes and their
Disposal, OS—1 October 1996,
EIF—19 December 2008,
12 IJMCL 474 478
2002 Protocol concerning Cooperation in
Preventing Pollution from Ships and,
in Cases of Emergency, Combating
Pollution of the Mediterranean Sea,
OS—25 January 2002, EIF—
17 March 2004, (2004)
OJ L 261/41 478

2008 Protocol on Integrated Coastal
  Zone Management, OS—21 January
  2008, EIF—24 March 2011,
  (2009) OJ L 34/19 . . . .478, 479, 617, 624
  Art 2(f) 478
  Art 3(1) 478
1976 ILO Convention (No 147)
  concerning Minimum Standards
  in Merchant Ships, OS—29 October
  1976, EIF—28 November 1981,
  1259 UNTS 335 506
1976 Trade and Payments
  Agreement between His Majesty's
  Government of Nepal and the
  Government of the People's
  Republic of Bangladesh with
  Protocol, OS—2 April 1976, EIF—
  2 April 1976, available at http://
  www.tepc.gov.np/tradeagreement/
  treagrebang.php 342
1978 Agreement on the Delimitation
  of the Marine and Submarine Areas
  and Maritime Cooperation between the
  Dominican Republic and the Republic of
  Colombia, OS—13 January 1978, EIF—15
  February 1979 693
1978 Kuwait Regional Convention
  for Co-operation on the Protection
  of the Marine Environment from
  Pollution, OS—24 April 1987,
  EIF—30 June 1979,
  1140 UNTS 133 718
1978 International Convention on
  Standards of Training, Certification
  and Watchkeeping for Seafarers,
  OS—7 July 1978, EIF—28 April 1984, 1361
  UNTS 190 . . . . 219, 315
1978 Treaty between Australia and the
  Independent State of Papua New
  Guinea concerning Sovereignty and
  Maritime Boundaries in the area
  between the two Countries, including
  the area known as Torres Strait,
  and Related Matters, OS—18
  December 1978, EIF—15 February
  1985, [1985] ATS 4 126

1979 Convention on Long-range
  Transboundary Air Pollution,
  OS—13 November 1979, EIF—
  16 March 1983, 18 ILM 1442 526
1979 Convention on the Conservation of
  Migratory Species of Wild Animals,
  OS—23 June 1979; EIF—
  1 November 1983, 1651 UNTS
  333 (CMS) 508, 717, 718, 757, 821
  Art I 821
  Art I(1)(i) 821
  Art III(4) 821
  Art III(5) 821
  Art IV(1) 821
  Art IV(3) 509
  Art IV(4) 509
  Art XII(1) 37
  App I 757, 821
  App II 757
1979 International Convention
  Against the Taking of Hostages,
  OS—17 December 1979, EIF—
  3 June 1983, 1316 UNTS 205
  (Hostages Convention) 862
  Art 5 862
  Art 8 863
1979 International Convention on
  Maritime Search and Rescue, OS—1
  November 1979, EIF—22 June 1985,
  1405 UNTS 97 . . . . 103, 315
1980 Convention on Future
  Multilateral Cooperation in
  North East Atlantic Fisheries,
  OS—18 November 1980, EIF—
  17 March 1982, 1285 UNTS 129
  (NEAFC Convention) 666
  Art 1(a) 667
  Art 1(1) 668, 769
  Art 1(2) 769
  Art 5 667
  Art 5(e) 667
  Art 6 667
  Art 6(1) 667
  Art 7(a)–(c) 770
  Art 7(e) 770
  Art 7(f) 770

1980 Convention on the
  Conservation of Antarctic Marine
  Living Resources, OS—20 May 1980,
  EIF—7 April 1982, 1329 UNTS 47
  (CCAMLR) 457, 459, 481, 484,
        704, 742, 743, 745, 761, 796, 840, 902
  Art I 742
  Art I(2) 493
  Art I(4) 704, 796
  Art II 450, 457
  Art XX 840
1981 Treaty establishing the
  Organization of Eastern Caribbean
  States, OS—18 June 1981, EIF—4 July
  1981, 1338 UNTS 97 (Treaty of
  Basseterre) 687
1982 Paris Memorandum of
  Understanding on Port State Control,
  OS—26 January 1982, EIF—
  1 July 1982, (1982) 21 ILM 1
  (Paris MOU) 282, 283, 291, 617, 664
1982 Regional Convention for the
  Conservation of the Red Sea and
  Gulf of Aden, OS—14 February
  1982, EIF—20 August 1985, (1983)
  22 ILM 219 718
  Art XI 523
1982 United Nations Convention on
  the Law of the Sea, OS—10 December
  1982, EIF—16 November 1994, 1833
  UNTS 397 (LOSC)
  Preamble 374
  Recital 1 27
  Recital 4 . . . . 27, 561
  Recital 5 27
  Recital 7 30
  Pt I 27
  Pt II 27, 28, 67, 149, 311
  Pt III 28, 36, 115, 118–20, 123,
              126, 133, 288, 550, 656
  Pt IV 28, 134, 135, 142, 144,
              154, 156–8, 553, 889
  Pt V 27, 62, 162, 163, 166, 170,
              300, 331, 431, 707, 833, 847, 891
  Pt VI 27, 28, 89, 170, 297, 500, 795,
              834, 891

Pt VII 28, 54, 62, 410, 501, 611,
              727, 755, 768, 804, 889
Pt VIII 28
Pt IX 28, 901
Pt X 28, 335, 339
Pt XI 26–9, 37, 45, 52, 53,
         207, 226–31, 233, 234, 240, 241,
         248–50, 252, 335, 347, 348–50, 385,
         386, 389, 399, 413, 486, 573, 676,
         740, 741, 755, 768, 836, 837, 909
Pt XII 28, 29, 36,
         54, 66, 163, 176, 206, 298, 300,
         394, 428, 498, 520–4, 528, 530,
         532, 533, 571, 717, 727,
         753, 771, 775
Pt XIII 29, 173, 207, 429, 561,
         562, 564, 566, 567, 569–75,
         579, 581, 742, 898
Pt XIV 29, 573, 574
Pt XV 29, 33, 249, 397–407,
         411, 413–15, 506, 586, 598, 885, 906
Pt XVI 29
Pt XVII 29
Art 1 . . . . 516, 909
Art 1(1) 190, 228, 281, 740
Art 1 (1)(1) 332
Art 1(1)(4) 783
Art 1(2) 95
Art 1(2)(2) 399, 412
Art 1(3) 230, 240, 573
Art 1(4) 809
Art 2 . . . . 91, 96, 103, 111, 399, 909
Art 2(1) 94, 95, 294, 537, 566
Art 2(3) 91, 97, 103
Art 3 . . . . 93, 114, 261, 296, 681
Art 4 . . . . 95, 681, 850
Art 5 . . . . .73, 76, 80, 294, 788
Art 6 . . . . .74, 788
Art 7 . . . . . 19, 59, 60, 70, 73, 80, 84–9,
         154, 155, 294, 590, 607, 708,
         792, 889, 906, 907, 909
Art 7(1) 86, 788
Art 7(2) 82, 87, 788, 789
Art 7(3)–(6) 86
Art 7(4) 788, 792
Art 8(1) 70, 294

Art 8(2) 70, 87, 295, 537, 538, 655	Art 21(1)(h) 111
Art 9 . . . . 80–2, 85, 88, 788	Art 21(2) 100, 105, 430, 543
Arts 9–10 294	Art 21(3) 100
Art 10 . . . . 20, 80, 82–5, 88, 788	Art 21(4) 105, 430, 541
Art 10(2) 82, 83	Art 21(g) 567
Art 10(3) 83	Art 22 99
Art 10(4) 83	Art 22(1) 544, 548, 549
Art 10(5) 83	Art 22(2) 105, 548, 549
Art 10(6) 82, 294, 406, 655	Art 22(3)(a) 105, 106, 430, 433
Art 11 . . . . 75, 85, 88	Art 22(4) 100, 544
Arts 11–12 281	Art 23 . . . . .99, 430, 548
Art 12 . . . . .75, 95, 283	Art 24(1) 100, 540
Art 13 . . . . .74, 95, 790	Art 24(1)(b) 100, 285
Art 13(1) 263, 788	Art 24(2) 100, 102, 540
Art 14 . . . . .74, 81, 788	Art 25 99
Art 15 . . . . 36, 256, 294, 406, 696	Art 25(1) 102, 544
Art 16 80	Art 25(2) 100, 101, 284, 544
Art 16(2) 100, 358, 793	Art 25(3) 100, 122, 127, 285, 544
Art 16(2)(k) 336	Art 26 . . . . 123, 540
Art 17 . . . . 60, 65, 70, 313, 334,	Art 26(1) 100
540, 545, 881	Art 27 . . . . . 99–101, 123, 404, 544, 586
Arts 17–26 98	Art 27(1) 101
Arts 17–32 115	Art 27(1)(b) 101
Art 18(1) 540	Art 27(1)–(2) 100
Art 18(2) 103, 428, 541	Art 27(2) 101, 102
Art 19 . . . . . .542, 543, 597, 833, 868, 885	Art 27(3) 105
Art 19(1) 98, 103, 541, 542	Art 27(4) 100
Art 19(1)(h) 102	Art 27(5) 101, 102
Art 19(2) 60, 98, 100, 541, 542,	Art 28 . . . . 99–101, 105, 123, 404
546, 881, 882	Art 28(1) 545
Art 19(2)(a) 99, 103, 542	Art 28(2) 101, 102, 545
Art 19(2)(b) 99	Art 28(3) 100–2, 545
Art 19(2)(c) 542	Art 29 870
Art 19(2)(h) 99	Art 30 . . . . 99, 547
Art 19(2)(i) 100	Art 31 . . . . 312, 547
Art 19(2)(j) 542, 567	Art 31(1) 103
Art 19(j) 570	Art 32 . . . . 99, 312, 586, 873
Art 20 . . . . . 60, 149, 541, 546, 594, 881	Art 33 . . . . . 92, 109, 111, 554, 586, 656, 681
Art 21 . . . . 99, 149, 432, 532, 885	Art 33(1) 108, 111, 537
Art 21(1) 100, 103, 543, 833	Art 33(2) 297
Art 21(1)(a) 105, 547	Art 34 404
Art 21(1)(b) 105	Art 35(c) 36, 120, 127, 296
Art 21(1)(c) 208	Art 36 . . . . 120, 296
Art 21(1)(e) 100	Art 37 . . . . 120, 132, 296, 882
Art 21(1)(f) 804	Arts 37–44 . . . . 98, 115
Art 21(1)(g) 570	Art 38 . . . . .313, 882, 883

Art 38(1) 120, 126, 127, 550, 552	Art 48 145
Art 38(2) 121, 284, 549, 550	Art 49 148
Art 39 . . . . . . .121, 122, 128, 130, 553, 567, 846, 882	Art 49(1) 294, 498
	Art 49(2) 148
Art 39(1) 124, 550, 585, 597	Art 50 . . . . 85, 148
Art 39(1)(c) 428, 550	Art 51(1) 148
Art 39(2) 105	Art 51(2) 148, 208
Art 39(2)(a) 31, 430, 551	Art 52 . . . . .149, 313, 552
Art 39(2)(b) 551	Art 52(1) 567
Art 39(3) 124	Art 52(2) 149, 553
Art 39(3)(a) 551	Art 53 . . . . 153, 295, 553, 567
Art 39(3)(b) 551	Art 53(1) 150
Art 40 . . . . .551, 553, 567, 570, 885	Art 53(2) 553
Art 41 . . . . 106, 128	Art 53(3) 149, 553
Art 41(1) 128, 551	Art 53(4) 149, 150
Art 41(3) 105, 551	Art 53(5) 150, 553, 554
Art 41(4) 105, 430, 433, 551	Art 53(8) 150
Art 41(5) 105, 433	Art 53(9) 150, 153, 430, 433
Art 41(7) 551	Art 53(12) 150
Art 42 . . . . 123, 125, 126, 129, 532, 553, 861	Art 54 . . . . .553, 567, 570
	Art 55 . . . . 114, 162, 165
Art 42(1) 551	Art 56 . . . . . . 165, 171, 176, 297, 440, 555, 584, 847, 885
Art 42(1)(a) 128, 552	
Art 42(1)(b) 552	Art 56(1) 199
Art 42(2) 551, 552, 883	Art 56(1)(a) 170, 171, 833
Art 42(3) 100	Art 56(1)(b) 165, 173
Art 42(4) 551, 552	Art 56(1)(b)(ii) 567, 885
Art 42(5) 129, 551	Art 56(1)(b)(iii) 804
Art 43 126	Art 56(1)(c) 165
Art 44 . . . . . . .122, 129, 550, 553, 883	Art 56(2) 30, 165, 213
Art 45 . . . . 98, 120, 127, 296, 883	Art 56(3) 199, 795
Art 45(1) 552	Art 57 681
Art 45(1)(b) 127, 296	Art 58 . . . . . . 121, 165, 205, 212, 555, 572, 584, 597, 884, 885, 889
Art 45(2) 127, 552	
Art 46 . . . . 88, 144, 145, 155	Art 58(1) 165, 208, 298, 554, 585
Art 46(2) 142	Art 58(2) 165, 212, 213, 847, 868, 884
Art 46(2)(a) 142, 295, 655	Art 58(3) 30, 317, 554
Art 46(2)(b) 142, 295, 627	Art 59 . . . . . . 165, 166, 179, 213, 297
Art 47 . . . . . 73, 80, 88, 89, 143, 145–8, 155, 156, 680, 708, 722, 788, 889	Art 60 . . . . . . 171–3, 188, 297, 430, 575
	Art 60(1)(b) 187
Art 47(1) 145, 147, 791	Art 60(2) 111, 172, 187
Art 47(1)–(6) 88	Art 60(3) 172, 431
Art 47(2) 145, 147, 791	Art 60(4) 75, 172, 187
Art 47(3) 146, 147	Art 60(5) 172, 187, 431
Art 47(4) 89, 95, 146, 147, 680	Art 60(6) 187
Art 47(5) 146	Art 60(7) 177
Art 47(9) 358	Art 60(8) 75, 95

Art 61 . . . . .166, 167, 332, 498,	Art 77 . . . . . . 172, 189, 296, 795, 834
576, 795, 833	Art 77(1) 186, 500
Art 61(2) 834	Art 77(3) 94, 184, 191, 656
Art 61(3) 54, 496, 498, 500, 806	Art 77(4) . . . 170, 186, 298, 500, 838, 839
Art 61(4) 481, 499, 806	Art 78 298
Arts 61–67 297	Art 78(1) 200, 538
Art 62 . . . . 166, 167, 332, 833	Art 78(2) 538
Art 62(2) 499	Art 79 . . . . 189, 208, 298
Art 62(3) 167, 290	Art 79(2) 189
Art 62(4) 555	Art 79(3) 178, 189
Art 63 . . . . .410, 500	Art 78(1) 186
Art 63(1) 286	Art 79(3) 213
Art 63(2) 317	Art 80 . . . . 171, 172, 187, 430, 575
Arts 63–67 167	Art 81 186
Art 64 . . . . 317, 410, 500	Art 82 . . . . .191, 192, 198, 199, 201, 229,
Art 64(2) 317	250–3, 265, 336, 337, 611, 891, 908
Arts 64–67 290	Art 82(3) 265
Art 65 508	Art 82(4) 231, 250, 337
Art 66 . . . . .443, 668	Art 83 . . . . 34, 406, 411
Art 67 668	Art 83(1) 44, 65, 258, 414
Art 68 . . . . .170, 199, 298, 500	Art 83(3) 586, 695
Art 69 . . . . 167, 332, 333	Art 84(2) 358
Art 70 . . . . 167, 332, 333	Art 86 212
Art 70(2) 331	Art 87 . . . . . . 121, 203, 206, 212, 287,
Art 72(1) 333	313, 334, 754, 829, 836
Art 73 . . . . 168, 170, 394, 403, 587	Art 87(1) 556, 742, 754
Art 73(1) 169, 505	Art 87(1)(a) 211
Art 73(2) 39	Art 87(1)(e) 501
Art 73(4) 169, 313	Art 87(2) 30, 211, 313, 486, 556, 754
Art 74 . . . . 34, 163, 406	Art 88 . . . . .210, 565, 868, 884
Art 74(1) 44, 65, 258, 414	Arts 88–115 847
Art 74(3) 586, 695	Art 89 . . . . 203, 565, 754
Art 75(2) 358	Art 90 . . . . .304, 313, 334
Art 76 . . . . 21, 39, 43, 45, 56, 66,	Art 91 . . . . 215, 216, 248, 755
70, 191–3, 195, 198, 201, 228,	Art 91(1) 217, 306, 308
298, 411, 412, 560, 569, 574,	Art 91(2) 306
707, 789, 834, 901, 907	Arts 91–92 17
Art 76(1) 36, 182, 185, 191, 261, 411	Art 92 . . . . 209, 214, 307, 447, 744
Art 76(2)–(7) 262, 264	Art 92(1) 851
Art 76(3) 182, 186	Art 92(2) 216
Art 76(4) 185, 186, 194, 411	Art 93 310
Art 76(4)(b) 194	Art 94 . . . . 206, 216, 309, 314,
Art 76(6) 195	394, 438, 447
Art 76(8) 39, 195, 196, 298,	Art 94(1) 314, 438, 874
352, 383, 410, 411, 739	Art 94(2)(a) 309
Art 76(9) 198, 358, 789	Art 94(3) 314, 430
Art 76(10) 196	Art 94(3)(b) 104

Art 94(4) 315	Art 119(3) 54, 285
Art 94(4)(c) 430, 755	Art 120 . . . . 207, 508, 727
Art 94(5) 31, 312	Art 121 . . . . . . 74, 95, 262, 659, 791
Art 94(7) 316	Art 121(1) 142, 791, 794
Arts 94–111 304	Art 121(3) 263, 272, 273, 791, 907
Art 97 18	Art 122 . . . . 281, 626
Art 97(1) 209	Art 123 . . . . 300, 332, 486, 606, 638
Art 97(2) 219	Art 123(d) 434
Art 98 . . . . 103, 206, 316	Arts 123–132 332
Art 100 . . . . 59, 860, 863	Art 124(1)(a) 331
Arts 100–107 844	Art 125 . . . . 334, 556
Art 101 . . . . . . 846, 848, 849, 859, 874	Art 125(2) 31
Art 101(a) 846–51, 853	Art 131 334
Art 101(a)(i) 850, 851	Art 132 335
Art 101(b) 846, 848–53	Art 133 . . . . 190, 836
Art 101(c) 846, 848, 849, 851, 853	Art 133(a) 230
Art 102 847	Arts 133–191 226
Art 103 . . . . 848–50, 852	Art 136 . . . . 37, 64, 190, 229,
Art 104 861	230, 740, 755, 836
Art 105 . . . . . . 57–9, 220, 587, 590,	Art 137 230
850–4, 861, 863, 874	Art 137(1) 229, 565
Art 106 856	Art 137(2) 755
Art 107 857	Art 139 240
Art 108(1) 221	Art 140 . . . . 230, 335
Art 109 220	Art 140(1) 335
Art 109(4) 220	Art 141 . . . . . . 210, 230, 335, 868, 884
Art 110 . . . . 220, 556, 587, 590,	Art 143 . . . . 207, 573, 829, 837
844, 851, 852, 853, 854, 874	Art 143(1) 210, 868, 884
Art 110(1) 506	Art 143(2) 231
Art 110(1)(e) 216	Art 143(3) 231, 573
Art 110(2) 220	Art 144(1) 231
Art 110(3) 852, 856	Art 144(2) 231
Art 111 . . . . 312, 556, 587, 875	Art 145 . . . . 755, 756
Art 111(3) 96	Art 145(a) 481
Art 112 208	Art 147(2) 884
Arts 113–115 . . . . 208, 219	Art 147(2)(d) 210, 868
Art 116 . . . . 54, 207, 444	Art 148 . . . . 332, 335
Arts 116–119 440	Art 152 . . . . 332, 335
Art 117 . . . . . . 31, 207, 209, 210, 317,	Art 153 . . . . 238, 247, 250
441, 448, 506, 727, 836	Art 153(2) 240
Art 118 . . . . . . 31, 207, 317, 441, 501,	Art 153(2)(b) 246
727, 754, 836	Art 153(3) 240
Art 119 . . . . 31, 207, 449, 501, 576,	Art 153(4) 38, 240, 908
727, 806, 836	Art 153(5) 38, 39, 908
Art 119(1) 496, 498	Art 153(6) 240
Art 119(1)(a) 54, 321, 449, 500, 806	Art 155(2) 210, 868, 884
Art 119(1)(b) 449, 481	Arts 156–185 231

Art 156(2) 231	Art 170(2) 239
Art 157 . . . . 231, 385	Art 186 249
Art 157(1) 230	Art 187 . . . . 249, 250, 412
Art 158 385	Art 188 399
Art 158(1) 385	Art 188(2) 249, 412
Art 158(4)(k) 332	Art 189 . . . . 249, 410
Art 159(10) 414	Art 190 250
Art 160(f)(ii) 44	Art 191 . . . . 250, 413, 414
Art 160(1) 232	Art 192 . . . . 54, 206, 212, 521, 750,
Art 160(1)(g) 908	753, 754, 783, 807, 829, 834
Art 160(2) 231	Art 193 . . . . 494, 498, 521
Art 160(2)(a) 232	Art 194 . . . . .66, 522, 535, 750, 807
Art 160(2)(b) 232	Art 194(1) 521, 783, 809
Art 160(2)(c) 232	Art 194(2) 521
Art 160(2)(e) 232	Art 194(3)(b) 206
Art 160(2)(f) 232	Art 194(4) 521
Art 160(2)(f)(i) 336	Art 194(5) 54, 481, 743
Art 160(2)(h) 232	Art 195 . . . . 521, 535
Art 160(2)(k) 332	Art 197 . . . . 434, 522, 660
Art 161(2)(a) 336	Art 198 433
Art 161(8)(d) 234	Art 199 . . . . 434, 522
Art 161(8)(e) 385	Art 200 . . . . 434, 522
Art 162 . . . . .234, 240	Art 201 . . . . 434, 522
Art 162(2)(a) 38, 234	Art 202 434
Art 162(2)(l) 38	Art 203 434
Art 162(2)(o) 242	Art 204 . . . . 434, 522
Art 162(2)(o)(i) 44	Art 205 . . . . 433, 522
Art 162(2)(o)(ii) 235	Art 206 . . . . .433, 483, 522, 743, 794, 829
Art 162(2)(y) 236	Art 207 . . . . 526, 727, 809
Art 162(2)(z) 39	Art 207(1) 31, 794
Art 163 235	Art 207(4) 430, 434
Art 163(3) 435	Arts 207–212 . . . . 31, 523
Art 163(8) 236	Art 208 727
Art 164 231	Art 208(1) 188
Art 165(2)(b) 235	Art 208(3) 404
Art 165(2)(c) 38	Art 208(5) 188, 430, 434
Art 165(2)(e) 235	Art 209(2) 756
Art 165(2)(f) 38, 235	Art 210 727
Art 165(2)(g) 235	Art 210(1) 102, 528
Art 165(2)(h) 235	Art 210(2) 528
Art 165(2)(i) 235	Art 210(4) 430, 434
Art 165(2)(k) 38, 235	Art 210(6) 102, 404, 430, 528
Art 165(2)(m) 38, 39	Art 211 . . . . 66, 99, 206, 430
Arts 166–168 385	Art 211(1) 301, 430
Art 169(1) 435	Art 211(2) 31, 102, 105, 177,
Art 169(2) 435	312, 316, 430, 532
Art 170 238	Art 211(3) 284, 433

Art 211(5)	105, 430	Art 240(a)	565, 884
Art 211(6)(a)	432	Art 241	564, 565
Art 211(6)(c)	105, 433	Art 242	565
Art 211(4)	102	Art 242(1)	210, 868, 884
Art 211(5)	31, 176, 430	Art 242(2)	565
Art 212	727	Art 243	435
Art 212(1)	31, 316, 783	Art 244	565, 832
Art 212(3)	430, 434, 783	Art 244(1)	435
Art 213	434, 526	Art 244(2)	435
Art 214	404, 434	Art 245	97, 566
Art 216	404	Art 246	174, 297, 567, 832
Art 216(1)	99, 434	Art 246(1)	834
Art 217	102, 312, 316	Art 246(2)	567, 834
Art 217(1)	430	Art 246(3)	207, 210, 435, 568, 574, 868, 884
Art 217(2)	316, 430		
Art 217(3)	430	Art 246(5)	174, 207, 435, 834
Art 217(4)	431	Art 246(5)(a)	568, 574
Art 217(7)	433	Art 246(5)(b)	568
Art 218	66, 290, 302, 430	Art 246(5)(c)	568, 574
Art 218(1)	431	Art 246(5)(d)	569
Art 219	206, 430	Art 246(6)	569, 834
Art 220	66, 587	Art 247	435, 569, 574
Art 220(2)	102, 544	Art 248	435, 569
Art 220(3)	430	Art 249(1)	435
Art 220(3)–(8)	102	Art 249(1)(a)	570
Art 220(5)	176, 290	Art 249(1)(b)	570
Art 220(6)	176, 290	Art 249(1)(e)	570
Art 220(7)	430	Art 249(1)(g)	570
Art 221	124	Art 249(2)	570, 575
Art 221(2)	219	Art 251	435
Arts 223–233	100, 102	Art 252	435, 569
Art 225	103	Art 253	435
Art 226(1)(c)	430	Art 254	337
Art 227	285	Art 254(1)	435
Art 228	176	Art 254(2)	435
Art 228(1)	176, 313	Art 254(3)	435
Art 233	123, 125, 130, 552	Art 254(4)	435
Art 234	734, 735	Art 255	284
Art 235(2)	394	Art 256	207, 435
Art 236	129, 618, 619	Art 257	207, 435, 572
Art 237	54, 66, 753	Art 258	574
Art 237(1)	36, 428	Art 259	95
Art 237(2)	36, 428	Art 261	572
Art 238	435, 564	Art 262	435, 572
Art 239	435, 564	Art 263	435
Art 240	188, 210, 564, 565, 572, 868	Art 263(2)	566
		Art 263(3)	566

Art 264 566	Art 308 26
Art 271 31	Art 308(1) 349
Art 279 397	Art 309 . . . . 33, 214, 405
Art 280 397	Art 310 . . . . 33, 34, 125, 214
Art 281 . . . . 401, 402, 408	Art 311 . . . . 35, 36, 385
Art 282 . . . . 401, 402, 408, 409	Art 311(1) 16, 35
Art 283 . . . . 397, 403	Art 311(2) 428, 740
Art 284 396	Art 311(2)–(6) 36
Art 286 . . . . 397, 400, 401, 403	Art 311(3) 64, 587, 740
Art 287 . . . . 399–401, 640	Art 311(6) 64, 229, 740
Art 288(2) 397, 400, 414	Art 312 . . . . 47, 57, 385
Art 288(3) 399	Arts 312–313 389
Art 288(4) 398, 886	Arts 312–316 43
Art 290 398	Art 313 . . . . 47, 57
Art 290(1) 398	Art 314 385
Art 290(5) 398, 399	Art 316 55
Art 290(6) 398	Art 316(5) 386
Art 292 . . . . 400, 408, 413	Art 319 . . . . .40, 360, 375, 376, 388
Art 292(2) 313, 895	Art 319(2)(a) 375
Art 297(2)(b) 566	Art 319(2)(e) 55, 360, 377, 894
Art 297(2)(i) 566	Annex I 500, 715
Art 297(2)(ii) 566	Annex II 197, 228, 410, 411
Art 292(3) 394	Annex II Art 2 . . . . 55, 351
Art 293 . . . . 65, 413	Annex II Art 2(1) 195, 383
Art 295 403	Annex II Art 2(2) 56
Art 296 398	Annex II Art 2(3) 56, 383
Art 297 . . . . 40, 403–5	Annex II Art 2(5) 195, 351, 383
Art 297(1) 404, 405	Annex II Art 3(1)(a) 383
Art 297(2) 405–7	Annex II Art 4 . . . . . . 56, 57, 192, 197
Art 297(3) 167, 405–7	Annex II Art 9 657
Art 297(3)(a) 334	Annex III 28, 226–8, 240, 241
Art 297(3)(b) 334	Annex III Art 3(5) 240
Art 297(3)(c) 167	Annex III Art 4(3) 246
Art 298 . . . 40, 403, 405–8, 614, 641, 886	Annex III Art 8 245
Art 298(1)(a) 400, 406, 586	Annex III Art 9 245
Art 298(1)(a)(i) 294	Annex II Art 13(15) 413
Art 298(1)(b) 211, 406, 407	Annex III Art 18 39
Art 298(1)(c) 407, 598	Annex IV 28, 238
Art 300 . . . . 97, 307	Annex V 167, 396, 405, 743
Art 301 . . . . 211, 230, 642, 742, 868, 884	Annex V Art 7(2) 396, 405
Art 302 597	Annex VI 29, 378
Art 303 . . . . 92, 108, 871	Annex VI Art 2(2) 379
Art 303(2) 297, 609	Annex VI Art 3(2) 379
Art 303(4) 623	Annex VI Art 4 55
Art 305 . . . . 32, 95, 412	Annex VI Art 4(2) 55
Arts 305–307 31	Annex VI Art 4(3) 55, 380
Art 306 231	Annex VI Art 4(4) 379

Annex VI Art 5 . . . . 379, 381
Annex VI Art 6 55
Annex VI Art 9 381
Annex VI Art 18 55
Annex VI Art 18(5) 381
Annex VI Art 18(5)–(6) 380
Annex VI Art 18(7) 380
Annex VI Art 19 . . . . 55, 387
Annex VI Art 19(1) 380
Annex VI Art 20 412
Annex VI Arts 20–22 400
Annex VI Art 21 414
Annex VI Art 28 398
Annex VI Art 33 398
Annex VI Art 38 413
Annex VI Art 39 395
Annex VI Art 40(2) 414
Annex VII 29, 188, 276, 399,
 400, 402, 408, 640,
 642, 695, 886
Annex VII Art 3 398
Annex VII Art 9 398
Annex VII Art 11 398
Annex VIII 29, 399, 886
Annex VIII Art 1 435
Annex VIII Art 2 416
Annex VIII Art 2(2) 436
Annex VIII Art 3 398
Annex VIII Art 4 398
Annex VIII Art 5 436
Annex IX 32, 412
Annex XI 231
1994 Agreement Relating to the
 Implementation of Part XI of the
 United Nations Convention on
 the Law of the Sea of
 10 December 1982, OS—
 28 July 1994, EIF—28 July 1996,
 1836 UNTS 42 (1994 Implementation
 Agreement) 27, 28, 43,
 52–5, 62, 227, 228, 231, 232,
 234, 238–41, 244–6, 250, 252,
 336, 350, 353, 359, 399, 408,
 654, 741, 763, 768, 909, 910
Art 2 . . . . .43, 227
Art 2(1) 53
Art 4 910
Art 4(1) 53
Art 5 910
Annex s 1(2) 53
Annex s 1(4) 53, 235
Annex s 2 . . . . .53, 246
Annex s 2(1) 239
Annex s 2(2) 239
Annex s 2(3) 53
Annex s 2(4) 239, 240
Annex s 2(15) 246
Annex s 3(1) 53
Annex s 3(2) 53, 234
Annex s 3(4) 232
Annex s 3(5) 53, 234
Annex s 3(7) 235
Annex s 3(8) 53
Annex s 3(11) 235
Annex s 3(15)(d) 336
Annex s 4 53
Annex s 4(1) 53
Annex s 5(2) 53
Annex s 6 244
Annex s 6(1)(a) 53
Annex s 6(7) 53
Annex s 7 . . . . .244, 763
Annex s 8 244
Annex s 8(1) 244
Annex s 8(2) 53
Annex s 9 . . . . 236, 237
Annex s 9(3) 237
Annex s 9(4) 237
Annex s 9(9) 236
Annex s 15(a) 233
Annex s 15(c) 233
1995 Agreement for the
 Implementation of the Provisions
 of the United Nations Convention on
 the Law of the Sea of 10 December
 1982 Relating to the Conservation and
 Management of Straddling Fish Stocks
 and Highly Migratory Fish Stocks,
 OS—4 August 1995, EIF—11 December
 2001, 2167 UNTS 88 (FSA) 43,
 53–5, 63, 167, 317, 354, 361, 410,
 412, 415, 441, 446, 481, 492, 506,
 587, 599, 654, 666, 754, 759,
 760, 806, 893, 910

Art 1(1)(c) 493
Art 1(1)(d) 502
Art 1(3) 310, 412
Art 2 . . . . .54, 502
Art 2(a) 502
Art 2(b) 502
Art 3 168
Art 4 . . . . 43, 909
Art 5 . . . . .449, 807
Art 5(b) 576
Art 5(d) 502
Art 5(e) 502
Art 5(d)–(f) 54, 63
Art 5(d)–(g) 481
Art 6 . . . . 168, 318, 497, 755
Art 6(2) 502
Art 6(3) 576
Art 6(7) 576
Art 7 . . . . 168, 460, 502
Art 7(5) 398
Arts 7–8 318
Art 8 . . . . .441, 446
Art 8(1) 502
Art 8(3) 290, 293
Art 8(4) 54, 313, 502
Art 10 457
Art 10(d) 450
Art 10(f) 576
Art 14 318
Art 16(1) 576
Art 16(2) 398
Art 17 502
Art 17(4) 447
Art 18 . . . . 446, 447, 453
Art 18(1) 317, 502
Art 18(2) 317
Art 18(3)(c)–(d) 318
Art 18(3)(e) 318
Arts 18–19 317
Arts 18–21 447
Arts 20–22 447
Art 21 . . . . 54, 303, 317, 456, 506
Art 21(17) 218
Art 22 . . . . 303, 456, 506
Art 22(1) 856
Art 23 . . . . 292, 507
Art 23(1) 290, 506

Art 23(4) 290
Art 26 447
Art 30(1) 403
Art 31(2) 398
Art 33(2) 503
1983 Agreement for
  Cooperation in Dealing with
  Pollution of the North Sea by Oil
  and other Harmful Substances,
  OS—13 September 1983, EIF—
  1 September 1989, 1605 UNTS
  39 (Bonn Agreement) 650, 663
Art 2 650
Arts 4–7 664
Arts 4–7 664
1983 Convention for the Protection
  and Development of the Marine
  Environment of the Wider Caribbean
  Region, OS—24 March 1983, EIF—
  11 October 1986, 1506 UNTS 157
  (Cartagena Convention) 479, 688
Preamble 479
Art 10 479
Art 12 . . . . .479, 688
Art 28(2) 689
1983 Protocol Concerning
  Co-Operation in Combating Oil
  Spills in the Wider Caribbean
  Region, OS—24 March 1983,
  EIF—11 October 1986,
  1506 UNTS 224 688
1999 Protocol concerning
  Pollution from Land-Based
  Sources and Activities, OS—
  6 October 1999, EIF—13 August
  2010, (1999) 93 AJIL 507, available
  at http://cep.unep.org/repcar/
  lbs-protocol-en.pdf . . . 479, 688, 689, 810
Art III.1 810
Art III.2 479
Art 7 689
1984 Convention against Torture
  and Other Cruel, Inhuman or
  Degrading Treatment or Punishment,
  OS—10 December 1984, EIF—26 June
  1987, 1465 UNTS 85
Art 3 104

1985 Nairobi Convention for the
Protection, Management and
Development of the Marine and Coastal
Environment of the Eastern African
Region (amended 2010), OS—21 June
1985, EIF—30 May 1996, 91 RGDIP
1122, (1993) UNEP Register 228
(Nairobi Convention) 479, 718–20
   Art 4 479
   Art 11 479
   Art 14 479
1985 Protocol Concerning Protected Areas
and Wild Fauna and Flora in the East
African Region, OS—21 June 1985,
EIF—30 May 1996, 985 IELMT 47
   Arts 8–11 479
1985 Northern Corridor Transit
Agreement, OS—19 February 1985,
EIF—15 November 1986, 7 DJI 169,
replaced by 2007 Northern Corridor
Transit and Transport Agreement, OS—6
October 2007, EIF—6 December 2012,
available at www.ttcanc.org/download.
php?docid=2 342
1985 South Pacific Nuclear-Free
Zone Treaty
   Protocol II 643
   Protocol III 643
1986 Convention for the Protection
of the Natural Resources and
Environment of the South Pacific Region,
Protocol Concerning Co-operation in
Combating Pollution Emergencies in
the South Pacific, and Protocol for the
Prevention of Pollution of the South
Pacific Region by Dumping, OS—24
November 1986, EIF—22 August 1990,
(1987) 26 ILM 41 761
1986 United Nations Convention on
Conditions for Registration of Ships,
OS—7 February 1986, not yet in force,
(1987) 26 ILM 1229 (Registration
Convention) 307
   Art 8 307
   Art 9 307
   Art 10 307
   Art 11(1) 314

1987 Agreement between the Government
of the Republic of Malawi and
the Government of the United
Republic of Tanzania concerning the
Malawi–Tanzania Transport System,
OS—15 August 1987, EIF—15 August
1987, 1552 UNTS 273 342
1988 Convention for the Suppression of
Unlawful Acts Against the Safety of
Maritime Navigation, OS—10 March
1988, EIF—1 March 1992, 1678 UNTS
221 (SUA Convention) 60, 319, 587,
                       595, 599, 848, 862
   Art 3 . . . . 319, 860
   Art 3bis 319
   Art 5 860
   Art 6 . . . . 591, 596, 862
   Art 6(a) 319
   Art 8bis(2) 319
   Art 8bis(5) 319
   Art 8bis(5)(c) 319
   Art 8bis(8) 319
   Art 8bis(10) 856
   Art 10 862
1988 Protocol for the Suppression of
Unlawful Acts Against the Safety
of Fixed Platforms Located on the
Continental Shelf, OS—10 March
1988, EIF—1 March 1992,
1678 UNTS 304 319
2005 Protocol to Convention for the
Suppression of Unlawful Acts
Against the Safety of Maritime
Navigation, OS—14 October
2005, EIF—28 July 2010,
1678 UNTS 304 . . . . . 223, 556, 557, 587,
                           591, 599, 856
1988 United Nations Convention
against Illicit Traffic in Narcotic
Drugs and Psychotropic Substances,
OS—20 December 1988, EIF—11
November 1990, 1582 UNTS 95
(Drugs Convention) . . . 221, 556, 587, 599
   Art 17 . . . . 599, 600
   Art 17(2) 218
1989 Basel Convention on the Control
of Transboundary Movements of

Hazardous Wastes and Their
 Disposal, OS—22 March 1989,
 EIF—5 May 1992, 1673 UNTS 57
 (Basel Convention) 429, 548, 549
 Art 4(12) 548
 Art 6(1) 548
 Art 6(4) 548
1989 Convention for the Prohibition
 of Fishing with Long Drift Nets in
 the South Pacific, OS—24 November
 1989, EIF— 17 May 1991,
 1899 UNTS 3 . . . . 503, 808
 Art 3(2) 503
1989 International Convention on
 Salvage, OS—28 April 1989, EIF—14
 July 1996, 1953 UNTS 165 315
1990 Protocol Concerning Specially
 Protected Areas and Wildlife to the
 Convention for the Protection and
 Development of the Marine
 Environment of the Wider
 Caribbean Region, OS—18 January
 1990, EIF—17 June 2000, 2180
 UNTS 101 (1990 Kingston SPAW
 Protocol) 688
 Art 3 688
 Art 11(1)(c) 689
 Annex I 689
 Annex II 689
 Annex III 689
1990 Accord de coopération en
 matière de transports et de transit entre
 le Burkina Faso et la République du
 Bénin, OS–13 September 1990, available
 at http://www.toefrank.net/textes/
 acc1990.htm 342
1990 Agreement on the Conservation
 of Seals in the Wadden Sea, OS—16
 October 1990, EIF—1 October
 1991 . . . . .509, 670
1990 Agreement for Cooperation in
 Protecting the Shores and Coastal
 Waters of the North East Atlantic Ocean
 from Accidental Pollution by Oil and
 Other Harmful Substances, OS—17
 October 1990, EIF—1 February 2014,
 (1993) OJ L 267/22 663

1990 Agreement on the
 Organization for Indian Ocean
 Marine Affairs Cooperation, OS—17
 September 1990, not in force, (1990)
 16 LOSB 57 710
1990 International Convention on
 Oil Pollution Preparedness, Response
 and Co-operation, OS—30 November
 1990, EIF—13 May 1995, (1991)
 30 ILM 735 (OPRC) 189
1990 Treaty between the Kingdom
 of Spain and the Italian Republic to
 Combat Drug Trafficking at Sea,
 OS—23 March 1990, EIF—7 May 1994,
 1776 UNTS 229 221
1991 Agreement between the
 Government of the Mongolian
 People's Republic and the
 Government of the People's
 Republic of China on Access to
 and from the Sea and
 Transit Transport by Mongolia
 through China's Territory, OS—26
 August 1991, EIF—
 26 August 1991 342
1991 Convention régionale relative à la
 coopération halieutique entre les Etas
 africains riverains de l'océan Atlantique
 (Convention on Fisheries Cooperation
 among African States Bordering the
 Atlantic Ocean), OS—5 July 1995,
 EIF—11 August 1995, 1912 UNTS 53
 Art 16 343
1991 Convention on Environmental
 Impact Assessment in a Transboundary
 Context, OS— 25 February 1991, EIF—11
 July 2010, 1989 UNTS 309 (Espoo
 Convention) 522, 523
1991 Treaty establishing the African
 Economic Community, OS—3 June 1991,
 EIF—12 May 1994, (1991)
 30 ILM 1241 340
 Art 4(2)(k) 340
1991 Treaty of Trade between the
 Government of India and His Majesty's
 Government of Nepal, OS—6 December
 1991, EIF—6 December 1991, revised

Indo-Nepal Treaty of Trade, OS—27 October 2009, EIF—27 October 2009, WTO Doc WT/COMTD/N/34 (3 August 2010), available at http://commerce.gov.in/trade/nepal.pdf. . . 342
1992 Agreement on Cooperation in Research, Conservation and Management of Marine Mammals in the North Atlantic, OS—9 April 1992, EIF—7 July 1992, 1945 UNTS 4 (NAMMCO Agreement) 510, 670
1992 Agreement on the Conservation of Small Cetaceans of the Baltic and North Seas, OS—17 March 1992, EIF—29 March 1994, 1772 UNTS 217 (ASCOBANS) 509, 670, 822
    Art 2.2 509
1992 Convention for the Protection of the Marine Environment of the North-East Atlantic, OS—22 September 1992, EIF—25 March 1998, 2354 UNTS 67 (OSPAR Convention) 327, 476, 525, 528, 530, 649, 660-3, 762, 769-71, 902
    Art 1(a)(i) 649, 769
    Art 1(a)(ii) 649, 769
    Art 2 660
    Art 2(1) 476, 661
    Art 2(2) 476, 660
    Art 4(1) 660
    Art 10 660
    Art 13(1) 660
    Annexes 1-5 660
    Annex 5 . . . . .476, 660
    Annex 5 Art 4 . . . . 477, 805
1992 Convention on Biological Diversity, OS—5 June 1992, EIF—29 December 1993, 1760 UNTS 79 (CBD) . . . 37, 466, 483, 485, 492, 534, 568, 663, 717, 719, 756, 765, 767, 775, 802, 805, 813, 825, 826, 829, 830, 833-6
    Preamble 494
    Art 1 . . . . 757, 830
    Art 2 . . . . 512, 756
    Art 3 830
    Art 4 . . . . 757, 830
    Art 5 . . . . 757, 830

    Art 6 835
    Art 6(a) 813
    Arts 7-10 835
    Art 8(a) 813
    Art 8(d) 481
    Art 8(j) 813
    Art 9 813
    Art 12 813
    Art 13 813
    Art 14 . . . . 483, 835
    Art 15 830
    Art 15(1) 835
    Art 15(7) 835
    Art 22 831
    Art 22(1) 62
    Art 22(2) 37
    Art 23 376
2010 Nagoya Protocol on Access to Genetic Resources and the Fair and Equitable Sharing of Benefits Arising from their Utilization, OS—29 October 2010, EIF—12 October 2014, UN Doc UNEP/CBD/COP/DEC/X1 (29 October 2010) 568, 831, 834
    Art 5 835
    Art 6 835
    Art 11 835
1992 Convention for the Conservation of Anadromous Stocks in the North Pacific Ocean, OS—11 February 1992, EIF—16 February 1993, (1993) 22 LOSB 21 (NPAFC Convention) 443
1992 Convention on the Protection of the Marine Environment of the Baltic Sea Area, OS—9 April 1992, EIF—17 January 2000, 1507 UNTS 167 (Helsinki Convention) 474, 521
    Art 3(2) 474
    Art 6 522
    Art 7 474
1992 Convention on the Protection of the Black Sea against Pollution, OS—21 April 1992, EIF—15 January 1994, 32 ILM 1110 (Black Sea Convention) 528
1992 Rio Declaration on Environment and Development, Report of the United Nations Conference on Environment

and Development, UN Doc A/Conf.151/
26/Rev.1, (1992) 31 ILM 874 (Rio
Declaration) 356
 Principle 2 494
 Principle 7 512
 Principle 15 . . . . 63, 496
 Art 4 495
1992 Framework Agreement between
the Government of Peru and the
Government of Bolivia on the 'Grand
Marshal Andrés de Santa Cruz'
Binational Project for Friendship,
Cooperation and Integration, OS—24
January 1992, (1992) 21 LOSB 87, (1993) 32
ILM 279 341
1992 International Maritime Organization
Protocol of 1992 to amend the
International Convention on Civil
Liability for Oil Pollution Damage of 29
November 1969, OS—27 November 1992,
EIF—30 May 1996, [1996] ATS 2 (1992
CLC) 531
1992 International Maritime Organization
Protocol of 1992 to amend the
International Convention on the
Establishment of an International Fund
for Compensation for Oil Pollution
Damage of 18 December 1972, OS—27
November 1992, EIF—30 May 1996,
[1996] ATS 3 (1992 Fund) 531
1992 Treaty on European Union, OS—7
February 1992, EIF—1 November 1993,
[2009] OJ C 115/3, as amended by
Treaty of Amsterdam Amending the
Treaty on European Union, the Treaties
Establishing the European Communities
and Certain Related Acts, OS—2 October
1997, EIF—1 May 1997, [1997] OJ C
340/1 (TEU)
 Art 21 661
1992 United Nations Framework
Convention on Climate Change,
OS—9 May 1992, EIF—21 March 1994,
1771 UNTS 107 (UNFCC) 728, 746,
         781–3, 798
 Art 1 786
 Art 2 . . . . 786, 812
 Art 4(1)(d) 786
 Art 7(2) 376
1997 Kyoto Protocol to the United Nations
Framework Convention on Climate
Change, OS—11 December 1997, EIF—16
February 2005,
2303 UNTS 214 . . . . 783, 798, 812
 Art 3(1) 786
1993 Agreement between Denmark,
Finland, Island, Norway and Sweden
concerning Cooperation in taking
Measures against Pollution of the Sea by
Oil or Other Harmful Substances—29
March 1993—Treaty No 146210 663
1993 Agreement for the Establishment of
the Indian Ocean Tuna Commission—25
November
1993—(1995) OJ L236/25 716
1993 Agreement to Promote Compliance
with International Conservation and
Management Measures by Fishing
Vessels on the High Seas, OS—24
November 1993, EIF—24 April 2003,
2221 UNTS 91 (FAO Compliance
Agreement) 307, 317, 446, 655
 Art II 447
 Art III 317, 507
 Art III(2) 507
 Art III(3) 307, 317
 Art III(6) 318
 Art III(7) 318
 Art III(8) 317
 Arts V–VI 318
1993 Convention for the Conservation
of Southern Bluefin Tuna, OS—
10 May 1993, EIF—20 May 1994,
1819 UNTS 360 716
 Art 9 577
1993 Djibouti Port Utilization
Agreement between the Transitional
Government of Ethiopia and the
Government of the Republic of
Djibouti, OS—12 December 1993,
(1998) 38 LOSB 56 342
1993 Maritime Delimitation Treaty
between Colombia and Jamaica—
12 November 1993 693

1994 General Agreement on Tariffs
and Trade, OS—15 April 1994, EIF—
1 January 1995, 1867 UNTS
187 (GATT) 409
Art I(1) 286
Art V(2) 286
Art V(3) 285
Art XI 285, 286
Art XX 285, 512
1994 Free Trade Agreement between
Azerbaijan, Armenia, Belarus, Georgia,
Moldova, Kazakhstan, Russian
Federation, Ukraine, Uzbekistan,
Tajikistan and the Kyrgyz Republic,
OS—15 April 1994, EIF—30 December
1994, WTO Doc WT/REG82/1
(1 October 1999) 341
1994 WTO Dispute Settlement
Understanding, Annex 2 to the
Marrakesh Agreement Establishing the
World Trade Organization, OS—
15 April 1994, EIF—1 January
1995, 1867 UNTS 3
Art 16(4) 382
Art 17(4) 382
1994 Convention on the Conservation and
Management of Pollock Resources in the
Central Bering Sea, OS—16 June 1994,
EIF—8 December 1995, (1995) 34 ILM 67
(CCBSP) 443
1995 Agreement on the Conservation of
African-Eurasian Migratory Waterbirds,
OS—16 June 1995, EIF—1 November
1999, (1995) 6 *Yearbook of International
Environmental Law* 907 757
1995 Convention for the Protection of
the Marine Environment and the
Coastal Region of the Mediterranean,
OS—10 June 1995, EIF—9 July 2004,
1102 UNTS 27 762
1995 Council of Europe Agreement on
Illicit Traffic by Sea, Implementing Article
17 of the United Nations Convention
against Illicit Traffic in Narcotic Drugs and
Psychotropic Substances, OS—
31 January 1995, not yet in force,
(1995) 29 LOSB 62 . . . . .221, 599

1995 Treaty on the South East Asia
Nuclear-Weapon-Free-Zone, OS—15
December 1995, EIF—28 March 1997,
(1995) 35 ILM 635 643
Art 1 643
1995 Washington Declaration on
Protection of the Marine Environment
from Land-Based Activities,
OS—1 November 1995 (1996)
31 LOSB 76 526
1996 African Nuclear-Weapon-Free
Zone Traety
Protocol I 643
Protocol II 643
1996 Agreement on the Conservation
of Cetaceans of the Black Sea,
Mediterranean Sea and Contiguous
Atlantic Area, OS—24 November 1996,
EIF—1 June 2001, (1997) 36 ILM 777
(ACCOBAMS) 509, 617, 822
Art II(1) 509
2000 Agreement between China and
Viet Nam on the Delimitation of the
Territorial Sea, the Exclusive Economic
Zones and Continental Shelves in Beibu
Bay/Bac Bo Gulf, OS—25 December
2000, EIF—30 June 2004, 2336
UNTS 179 (2000 China–Viet Nam
Agreement) . . . .|. 199
2000 Convention for the Conservation and
Management of Highly Migratory Fish
Stocks in the Western and Central Pacific
Ocean, OS—5 September 2000, EIF—19
June 2004, (2001) LOSB 79 (WCPF
Convention) 412
Annex 1(1) 310
Annex 1(3) 412
2000 Protocol Against the
Smuggling of Migrants by Land,
Sea and Air Supplementing the
United Nations Convention against
Transnational Organized Crime, OS—15
November 2000, EIF—28 January 2004,
[2004] ATS 11 (Migrant Smuggling
Protocol) 217, 587, 591, 599
Art 8 . . . . 217, 218, 591
Art 9 591

2001 Convention on the Protection of the
Underwater Cultural Heritage, OS—2
November 2001, EIF—2 January 2009,
(2002) 48 LOSB 29 . . . . . 609, 871, 908
   Art 3 62
   Art 6 623
   Art 8 609
2001 East African Community Tripartite
Agreement on Road Transport between
the Government of the United Republic of
Tanzania, the Government of the Republic
of Kenya and the Government of the
Republic of Uganda, A—29 November
2001 pursuant to Chapter 15 of the Treaty
Establishing the East African Community,
OS—30 November 1999, EIF—7 July
2000, 2144 UNTS 255 342
2001 International Convention on the
Control of Harmful Anti-fouling
Systems on Ships, OS—5 October
2001, EIF—17 September 2008,
[2008] ATS 15 . . . . 525, 763
   Art 1(3) 285
2001 International Treaty on Plant Genetic
Resources for Food and Agriculture,
OS—3 November 2001, EIF—29 June
2004, 2400 UNTS 303 839
   Art 1 839
2001 Revised Treaty of Chaguaramas
Establishing The Caribbean
Community Including the CARICOM
Single Market And Economy,
OS—5 July 2001, EIF—1 January
2006, 2259 UNTS 293 686
2001 Stockholm Convention on Persistent
Organic Pollutants, OS— 22 May 2001,
EIF— 7 May 2004, (2001) 40 ILM 531
(POPs Convention) 526, 528, 535,
                                  728, 746
2002 Agreement Establishing the
Caribbean Regional Fisheries
Mechanism, OS—4 February
2003, EIF—4 February 2002,
2242 UNTS 271 687
2003 Agreement Concerning Co-operation
in Suppressing Illicit Maritime and
Air Trafficking in Narcotic Drugs
and Psychotropic Substances in the
Caribbean Area, OS—10 April 2003,
EIF—18 September 2008, 2005
Digest 147, TRB 2010 No 253
(Treaty No 010467) 221, 623
2003 Convention for the Strengthening
of the Inter-American Tropical Tuna
Commission Established Between
the United States of America and
the Republic of Costa Rica, OS—14
November 2003, EIF—27 August 2010,
Senate Treaty Doc 109-2, (2006) OJ L
224/22 (Antigua Convention) 457
   Art XXVIII 310
2003 Framework Convention for the
Protection of the Marine Environment of
the Caspian Sea, OS—4 November 2003,
EIF—12 August 2006, (2003) 44 ILM 1
(Tehran Convention) 528
2004 Agreement on South Asian Free
Trade Area (SAFTA), OS—6 January
2004, EIF—1 January 2006, UN Doc
A/58/716-S/2004/122 (19 February
2004) Annex III 341
2004 International Convention for the
Control and Management of Ships' Ballast
Water and Sediments, OS—13 February
2004, not yet in force, IMO Doc BWM/
CONF/36, (2004) 19 IJMCL 446 (Ballast
Water Convention) 316, 525
2004 Regional Cooperation Agreement on
Combating Piracy and Armed Robbery
against Ships in Asia, OS—11 November
2004, EIF—4 September 2006, 2398
UNTS 199 (ReCAAP) 599
2004 Treaty between the Government of
Australia and the Government of New
Zealand Establishing Certain Exclusive
Economic Zone Boundaries and
Continental Shelf Boundaries, OS—25
July 2004, EIF—25 January 2006, [2006]
ATS 4 191
2005 Framework Agreement between
the UK and Norway Concerning
Cross-Boundary Petroleum
Cooperation—5 April 2005—
Cm 7206 658

2006 Agreement on Trade, Commerce
and Transit between the Government
of the Republic of India and the Royal
Government of Bhutan, OS—28 July
2006, EIF—29 July 2006, WTO Doc
WT/COMTD/N/28 (2 July 2008) . . .342
2006 Maritime Labour Convention,
OS—23 February 2006, EIF—20
August 2013, (2006) 45 ILM 792,
UNTS Reg No I-51299
  Art 2 311
2006 Memorandum of Understanding
for the Conservation of Cetaceans and
their Habitats in the Pacific Islands
Region, OS—15 September 2006, EIF—15
September 2006, available at <http://
www.pacificcetaceans.org/official_text.
php> 509
2006 Southern Indian Ocean Fisheries
Agreement, OS—7 July 2006, EIF—21
June 2012, (2006) OJ L196/14, UNTS Reg
No I-49647 759
2007 Memorandum of Understanding
Concerning the Conservation Measures
for the Eastern Atlantic Populations
of the Mediterranean Monk Seal,
OS—18 October 2008, EIF—18 October
2008, available at http://www.cms.int/
monk-seal/sites/default/files/basic_page_
documents/Monk_Seal_MoU_with_
signatures_En.pdf 509
2007 Nairobi International Convention
on the Removal of Wrecks, OS—18 May
2007, EIF—14 April 2015, IMO Doc LEG/
CONF.16/19 431
2007 Treaty of Lisbon amending the
Treaty on the European Union and
the Treaty establishing the European
Community—13 December 2007—
(2007) OJ C306/1 338
2008 CARICOM Maritime and Airspace
Security Cooperation Agreement, OS—3
July 2008, EIF—2 December 2010, (2008)
68 LOSB 20 599
2008 Treaty on the Functioning of
the European Union [2009] OJ C
115/199 (TFEU)

  Art 3(1)(d) 665
  Art 43(2) 661
  Art 49 307
  Art 91(1) 661
  Art 100(2) 661
  Art 173(3) 661
  Art 175 661
  Art 188 661
  Art 192(1) 661
  Art 194(2) 661
  Art 195(2) 661
2009 Agreement on Port State Measures to
Prevent, Deter and Eliminate
Illegal, Unreported and Unregulated
Fishing, OS—22 November 2009,
not yet in force, [2010] ATNIF 41
(PSM Agreement) 280, 282, 322,
                        507, 622, 624
  Art 1(g) 280, 281
  Art 4(1)(b) 284, 291, 302
  Art 4(2)–(3) 293
  Art 6 293
  Arts 7–9 284
  Art 9(4) 293
  Art 9(5) 291
  Art 10 284
2009 Convention on the Conservation
and Management of the High Seas
Fishery Resources of the South Pacific
Ocean, OS—1 January 2010, EIF—24
August 2012, [2012] ATS 28 (SPRFMO
Convention) 504
  Art 17 445
  Art 22 483
  Annex II 445
2009 Hong Kong International
Convention for the Safe and
Environmentally Sound Recycling
of Ships, OS—15 May 2009, not yet
in force, IMO Doc SR/CONF/45
(2009) (Hong Kong
Convention) 429, 431, 436
2010 Agreement between the Government
of the State of Israel and the Government
of the Republic of Cyprus on the
Delimitation of the Exclusive Economic
Zone—17 December 2010 614

2010 Amended Nairobi Convention for the Protection, Management and Development of the Marine and Coastal Environment of the Western Indian Ocean, OS—31 March 2010, not yet in force, UN Doc UNEP(DEPI)/EAF/CPP.6/8a (Amended Nairobi Convention) 523, 718
2010 Treaty between the Kingdom of Norway and the Russian Federation concerning Maritime Delimitation and Cooperation in the Barents Sea and the Arctic Ocean, OS—15 September 2010, EIF—7 July 2011, UNTS Reg 49095 730
   Art 3 299
   Art 4 730
   Art 5 730
   Annex I 730
   Annex II 730
2010 Transit Trade Agreement between the Governments of the Islamic Republic of Afghanistan and the Islamic Republic of Pakistan, OS—28 October 2010, EIF—12 June 2011 (APTTA) 342
2011 Agreement between the European Union and the Republic of Mauritius on the Conditions of Transfer of Suspected Pirates and Associated Seized Property from the European Union-led Naval Force to the Republic of Mauritius and on the Conditions of Suspected Pirates after Transfer, OS—14 July 2011, not yet in force, (2011) OJ L 254/3 862
2011 Agreement on Cooperation in Aeronautical and Maritime Search and Rescue in the Arctic, OS—12 May 2011, EIF—19 January 2013, (2011) 50 ILM 1119 (Arctic SAR Agreement). . . . 301, 736
2013 Agreement on Cooperation on Marine Oil Pollution, Preparedness and Response in the Arctic, OS—15 May 2013, not yet in force, (2013) 107 AJIL 661 (2013 Arctic MOPPR Agreement) 189, 301, 736
2013 Arms Trade Treaty, OS—2 April 2013, EIF—24 December 2014, (2013) 52 ILM 988
   Art 2(3) 223
   Art 7(2) 223
2013 Minamata Convention on Mercury, OS—10 October 2013, not yet in force, UN Depositary Notification No C.N.560.2014. TREATIES-XXVII.17 . . . . 527, 528
2014 Agreement between the Government of Ireland and the Government of the United Kingdom of Great Britain and Northern Ireland establishing a Single Maritime Boundary between the Exclusive Economic Zones of the two Countries and parts of their Continental Shelves, 21 UKTS 2014 Cm8933 659
2014 Association Agreement between the European Union and the European Atomic Energy Community and their Member States, of the one part, and the Republic of Moldova, of the other part, OS—27 June 2014, (2014) OJ L 260/4 (European Union–Republic of Moldova Association Agreement) 341

List of Abbreviations

A	adopted
ABNJ	areas beyond national jurisdiction
ABS	Access and Benefit Sharing
ACAP	2006 Agreement on the Conservation of Albatross and Petrels
ACCOBAMS	1996 Agreement on the Conservation of Cetaceans of the Black Sea, Mediterranean Sea and Contiguous Atlantic Area
ACS	Association of Caribbean States
AEC	African Economic Community
AEWA	African-Eurasian Migratory Waterbirds
AEWA Agreement	1995 Agreement on the Conservation of African-Eurasian Migratory Waterbirds
AIDCP	Agreement on the International Dolphin Conservation Programme
AJIL	American Journal of International Law
AMAP	Arctic Monitoring and Assessment Programme
AMSA	Arctic Marine Shipping Assessment
AOR	Arctic Ocean Review
APM	associated protective measure
App	Application
APTTA	2010 Afghanistan Pakistan Transit Trade Agreement
AR	Assessment Report
Arctic CAP	Arctic Contaminants Action Program
ASCLME	Agulhas and Somali Current Large Marine Ecosystems
ASCOBANS	1992 Agreement on the Conservation of Small Cetaceans of the Baltic and North Seas
ASEAN	Association of South-East Asian Nations
ASL	archipelagic sea lanes
ASLP	archipelagic sea lanes passage
ASMA	Antarctic specially managed area
ASPA	Antarctic specially protected area
ATA	Antarctic Treaty Area
ATCM	Antarctic Treaty Consultative Meeting
ATCP	Antarctic Treaty Consultative Party
ATNIF	Australian Treaties Not in Force
ATS	Antarctic Treaty System
AUNJ	areas under national jurisdiction

BAAP	Bonn Agreement Action Plan
BBNJ	biological diversity beyond areas of national jurisdiction
BGR	Federal Institute for Geosciences and Natural Resources (Germany)
BOBLME	Bay of Bengal Large Marine Ecosystem
BSPA	Baltic Sea Protected Area
Bull Crim	Bulletin des Arrêts de la cour de cassation rendus en matière criminelle
BVI	British Virgin Islands
CAFF	Conservation of Arctic Flora and Fauna
CAO	central Arctic Ocean
CAR/RCU	1981 Caribbean Action Plan Regional Coordinating Unit
CARICOM	Caribbean Community
CBD	1992 Convention on Biological Diversity
CCA	Causal Chain Analysis
CAMLR Convention	1980 Convention on the Conservation of Antarctic Marine Living Resources
CCAMLR	Commission on the Conservation of Antarctic Marine Living Resources
CCAS	1972 Convention for the Conservation of Antarctic Seals
CCBSP	1994 Convention on the Conservation and Management of Pollock Resources in the Central Bering Sea
CCSBT	Commission for the Conservation of Southern Bluefin Tuna
CDEM	construction, design, equipment, and manning
CEP	Caribbean Environment Programme
CFCLR	1958 Convention on Fishing and Conservation of the Living Resources of the High Seas
CFP	EU Common Fisheries Policy
CITES	1973 Convention on International Trade in Endangered Species of Wild Fauna and Flora
CJEU	Court of Justice of the European Union
CLC	1969 International Convention on Civil Liability for Oil Pollution Damage
CLCS	Commission on the Limits of the Continental Shelf
CLME	Caribbean Large Marine Ecosystem
CLR	Commonwealth Law Reports (Australia)
CMI	Comité Maritime International
CMS	1979 Convention on the Conservation of Migratory Species of Wild Animals
CNOOC	China National Offshore Oil Corporation
CO_2	carbon dioxide
COBSEA	Coordinating Body of the Seas of East Asia
COC	Code of Conduct
COLREG	Collision Regulation
COMESA	Common Market for Eastern and Southern Africa
COMRA	China Ocean Mineral Resources Research and Development Association

COP	Conference of Parties
COW	crude oil washing
CPUCH	2001 UNESCO Convention on the Protection of the Underwater Cultural Heritage
CRC	Consolidated Regulations of Canada
CRFM	Caribbean Regional Fisheries Mechanism
CSC	1958 Convention on the Continental Shelf
CTS	Consolidated Treaty Series
CUP	Cambridge University Press
DFO	Department of Fisheries and Oceans (Canada)
Digest	Digest of United States Practice in International Law
diss op	dissenting opinion
DJI	Documents juridiques internationaux (Montréal)
DOALOS	Division for Ocean Affairs and the Law of the Sea
DOC	2002 Declaration on the Conduct of Parties in the South China Sea
Dods	Dodson's Admiralty Reports
DPRK	Democratic People's Republic of Korea (North Korea)
DRC	Democratic Republic of Congo
DSU	Dispute Settlement Understanding
dwt	deadweight tonnage
EAC	East African Community
EAP	East Asian Seas Programme
EBM	ecosystem-based management
EBSA	ecologically or biologically significant area
ECCAS	Economic Community of Central African States
ECHR	European Convention on Human Rights
ECJ	European Court of Justice
ECOWAS	Economic Community of West African States
ECR	European Court Reports
ECtHR	European Court of Human Rights
EEA	European Environmental Agency
EEC	European Economic Community
EEZ	exclusive economic zone
EFPZ	ecological and fisheries protection zone
EFZ	exclusive fishing zone
EHRR	European Human Rights Reports
EIA	Environmental Impact Assessment
EIF	entry into force
EIFAAC	European Inland Fisheries and Aquaculture Advisory Commission
EPBC	Environmental Protection and Biodiversity Act (Australia)
EPL	Environmental Policy and Law
EPOCA	European Project on Ocean Acidification
EPPR	Emergency Prevention, Preparedness, and Response
EPZ	ecological protection zone
ER	English Reports

LIST OF ABBREVIATIONS

Espoo Convention	1991 Convention on Environmental Impact Assessment in a Transboundary Context
EU	European Union
EUNAVFOR	European Union Naval Force
Ex D	Law Reports, Exchequer Division
F.	Federal Reporter (United States)
FAD	fish aggregating device
FAL	IMO Facilitation Committee
FAO	United Nations Food and Agriculture Organization
FMA	Fisheries Management Act (Australia)
FPZ	fisheries protection zone
FSA	1995 Agreement for the Implementation of the Provisions of the UN Convention on the Law of the Sea relating to the Conservation and Management of Straddling Fish Stocks and Highly Migratory Fish Stock (Fish Stocks Agreement)
F. Supp.	Federal Supplement (United States)
GAIRS	generally accepted international rules and standards
GATT	1994 General Agreement on Tariffs and Trade
GDS	geographically disadvantaged States
GEF	Global Environment Facility
GESAMP	Joint Group of Experts on the Scientific Aspects of Marine Environmental Protection
GFCM	General Fisheries Commission for the Mediterranean
GHG	greenhouse gas
GIS	Geographic Information System
GPA	Global Programme of Action for the Protection of the Marine Environment from Land-Based Activities
GPASL	General Provisions on the Adoption, Designation and Substitution of Archipelagic Sea Lanes
HELCOM	Baltic Marine Environment Protection Commission (Helsinki Commission)
HFO	heavy fuel oil
HSC	1958 Convention on the High Seas
IACS	International Association of Classification Societies
IATTC	Inter-American Tropical Tuna Commission
IBRU	International Boundaries Research Unit
ICAO	International Civil Aviation Organization
ICCAT	International Commission for the Conservation of Atlantic Tunas
ICCAT Convention	1966 International Convention for the Conservation of Atlantic Tunas
ICES	International Council for the Exploration of the Seas
ICJ	International Court of Justice

ICJ Rep	Reports of Judgments, Advisory Opinions and Orders of the International Court of Justice
ICLQ	International and Comparative Law Quarterly
ICM	integrated coastal management
ICNT	Informal Composite Negotiating Text
ICP	Open-Ended Informal Consultative Process on Oceans and Law of the Sea
ICRW	1946 International Convention for the Regulation of Whaling
ICS	International Chamber of Shipping
ICZM	integrated coastal zone management
IELMT	International Environmental Legal Material and Treaties
IHL	international humanitarian law
IHO	International Hydrographic Organization
III Code	International Maritime Organization Instruments Implementation Code
IJMCL	International Journal of Marine and Coastal Law
ILA	International Law Association
ILC	International Law Commission
ILM	International Legal Materials
ILO	International Labour Organization
ILR	International Law Reports
IMCO	Intergovernmental Maritime Consultative Organization
IMDG	International Maritime Dangerous Goods Code
IMO	International Maritime Organization
IMP	Integrated Marine Policy
IMSO	International Mobile Satellite Organization
IOC	Indian Ocean Commission
IOComm	Intergovernmental Oceanographic Commission
IOM	integrated ocean management
IOMAC	Indian Ocean Marine Affairs Co-operation
IOR-ARC	Indian Ocean Rim-Association for Regional Co-operation
IORA	Indian Ocean Rim Association
IOTC	Indian Ocean Tuna Commission
IPCC	Intergovernmental Panel on Climate Change
IPOA-IUU	International Plan of Action to Prevent, Deter and Eliminate Illegal, Unreported and Unregulated Fishing
Iran–US CTR	Iran–United States Claims Tribunal Reports
IRGCN	Iranian Revolutionary Guard Corps Navy
ISA	International Seabed Authority
ISPS	International Ship and Port [Facility] Security
ITLOS	International Tribunal for the Law of the Sea
ITLOS Rep	Reports of Judgments, Advisory Opinions and Orders of the International Tribunal for the Law of the Sea
IUCN	International Union for Conservation of Nature
IUU	illegal, unreported, and unregulated
IWC	International Whaling Commission

JAPRA II	Japan's Second Phase of the Whale Research Program under Special Permit in the Antarctic
JOMSRE-SCS	Philippine-Vietnam Joint Oceanographic and Marine Scientific Research Expedition
JRA	Joint Regime Area
LBSP	land-based sources of pollution
LEG	IMO Legal Committee
LLS	landlocked States
LME	large marine ecosystem
LNTS	League of Nations Treaty Series
LNW	Law of Naval Warfare
LOMA	large ocean management area
LOSB	Law of the Sea Bulletin
LOSC	1982 United Nations Convention on the Law of the Sea
LRIT	long-range identification and tracking
MAP	Mediterranean Action Plan
MARPOL	1973 International Convention for the Prevention of Pollution, as modified by the Protocol of 1978
MEPC	IMO Marine Environment Protection Committee
MLR	marine living resources
MMO	Marine Management Organisation (UK)
Moore	John Bassett Moore, *History and Digest of the International Arbitrations to Which the United States has been a Party* (1898) vols I–VI
MOP	Meeting of States Parties
MOPPR	Marine Oil Pollution Preparedness and Response
MOU	Memorandum of Understanding
MPA	marine protected area
MPLBS/A	marine pollution from land-based sources and activities
MPS	Marine Policy Statement
MRCC	Maritime Rescue Coordination Centre
MSC	IMO Maritime Safety Committee
MSFD	Marine Strategy Framework Directive (EC)
MSP	marine spatial planning
MSR	marine scientific research
MSY	maximum sustainable yield
NAFO	Northwest Atlantic Fisheries Organization
NAMMCO Agreement	1992 Agreement on Cooperation in Research, Conservation and Management of Marine Mammals in the North Atlantic
NAP	national action programme
NASCO	North Atlantic Salmon Conservation Organization
NBSAP	National Biodiversity Strategies and Action Plan
NEAFC	North-East Atlantic Fisheries Commission
NGO	non-governmental organization

nm	nautical miles
NOC	National Ocean Council (USA)
NORDREG	Northern Canada Vessel Traffic Services Zone
NPAFC	North Pacific Anadromous Fish Commission
NPAFC Convention	1992 Convention for the Conservation of Anadromous Stocks in the North Pacific Ocean
OAU	Organization of African Unity
OECD	Organisation for Economic Co-operation and Development
OECS	Organisation of Eastern Caribbean States
OILPOL	1954 International Convention for the Prevention of Pollution of the Sea by Oil
OJ	Official Journal of the European Union
OLDEPESCA	Latin American Organization for Fisheries Development
OPRC	1990 Convention on Oil Pollution Preparedness, Response and Cooperation
OPSD	Optional Protocol of Signature Concerning the Compulsory Settlement of Disputes
OS	open for signature
OSPAR Convention	1992 Convention for the Protection of the Marine Environment of the North-East Atlantic
OSPESCA	Central America Fisheries and Aquaculture Organization
OUP	Oxford University Press
P-5	Permanent members of the United Nations Security Council
PAME	Protection of the Arctic Marine Environment
PCIJ	Permanent Court of International Justice
PCIJ Rep	Reports of Judgments, Advisory Opinions and Orders of the Permanent Court of International Justice
PEMSEA	Regional Programme on Partnerships in Environmental Management for the Seas of East Asia
pH	Potential for Hydrogen
PICES	North Pacific Marine Science Organisation
PLA	People's Liberation Army (China)
PNA	Parties to the Nauru Agreement
POPs	Persistent Organic Pollutants
POPs Convention	2001 Stockholm Convention on Persistent Organic Pollutants
ppm	parts per million
PSC	port State control
PSI	Proliferation Security Initiative
PSM	port State measures
PSSA	particularly sensitive sea area
QB	Law Reports, Queens Bench Division
RAC	Regional Activities Centre
Ramsar Convention	1971 Convention on the Wetlands of International Importance

ReCAAP	2004 Regional Cooperation Agreement on Combating Piracy and Armed Robbery Against Ships in Asia
RECOFI	Regional Commission for Fisheries
REEFVTS	Great Barrier Reef & Torres Strait Vessel Traffic Service
REMPEC	Regional Marine Pollution Emergency Response Centre for the Mediterranean Sea
Res	Resolution
RFB	regional fisheries body
RFMA	regional fisheries management arrangement
RFMO	regional fisheries management organization
RGDIP	Revue générale de droit international public
RIAA	United Nations Reports of International Arbitral Awards
RSC	Revised Statutes of Canada
RSO	regional seas organization
SAARC	South Asian Association for Regional Cooperation
SAC	special area of conservation
SADC	Southern African Development Community
SAFTA	South Asian Free Trade Area
SAP	Strategic Action Programme/Plan
SAR	search and rescue
SAR Convention	1979 International Convention on Maritime Search and Rescue
SBSTTA	1992 CBD Subsidiary Body on Scientific, Technical and Technological Advice
SBT	southern bluefin tuna
SDWG	Sustainable Development Working Group
SEAFO	South-East Atlantic Fisheries Organization
SEANWFZ	1995 Treaty on the Southeast Asia Nuclear Weapon-Free Zone
sep op	separate opinion
SICA	Sistema de la Integración Centroamericana (Central American Integration System)
SIOFA	2006 South Indian Ocean Fisheries Agreement
SOA	State Oceanic Administration
SOLAS	1974 International Convention for the Safety of Life at Sea
SPA	specially protected areas
SPAMI	specially protected areas of Mediterranean importance
SPAW	specially protected areas and wildlife
SPLOS	States Parties to the United Nations Convention on the Law of the Sea
SPRFMO	South Pacific Regional Fisheries Management Organization
SPRFMO Convention	2009 Convention on the Conservation and Management of the High Seas Fishery Resources of the South Pacific Ocean
SRFC	Sub-Regional Fisheries Commission
SUA	1988 Convention for the Suppression of Unlawful Acts against the Safety of Maritime Navigation
Suppl	Supplement
SWIOFC	Southwest Indian Ocean Fisheries Commission

TAC	total allowable catch
TCC	IMO Technical Cooperation Committee
TDA	Transboundary Diagnostic Analysis
TEU	1992 Treaty on European Union
TFEU	2008 Treaty on the Functioning of the European Union
TRB	Tractatenblad (Dutch Treaty Series)
TS	territorial sea
TSC	Convention on the Territorial Sea and the Contiguous Zone
TSS	traffic separation schemes
UK	United Kingdom
UKTS	United Kingdom Treaty Series
UN	United Nations
UNCED	1992 United Nations Conference on Environment and Development
UNCITRAL	United Nations Commission on International Trade Law
UNCLOS	United Nations Conferences on the Law of the Sea
UNCLOS I	First United Nations Conference on the Law of the Sea
UNCLOS II	Second United Nations Conference on the Law of the Sea
UNCLOS III	Third United Nations Conference on the Law of the Sea
UNCTAD	United Nations Conference on Trade and Development
UNDP	United Nations Development Programme
UNEP	United Nations Environment Programme
UNESCO	United Nations Educational, Scientific and Cultural Organization
UNFCCC	1992 United Nations Framework Convention on Climate Change
UNGA	United Nations General Assembly
UNGAOR	United Nations General Assembly Official Records
UNHCR	United Nations High Commissioner on Refugees
UNICPOLOS	United Nations Informal Consultative Process on Oceans and the Law of the Sea
UN-Oceans	United Nations Oceans and Coastal Areas Network
UNODC	United Nations Office on Drugs and Crime
UNOHRLLS	United Nations Office of the High Representative for the Least Developed Countries, Landlocked Developing Countries and Small Island Developing States
UNSC	United Nations Security Council
UNTS	United Nations Treaty Series
US	United States Reports
US / USA	United States/United States of America
USVI	United States Virgin Islands
VASB	Vision and Strategies around the Baltic Sea
VCLT	1969 Vienna Convention on the Law of Treaties
Virginia Commentaries	MH Nordquist et al (eds), *United Nations Convention on the Law of the Sea 1982: A Commentary* (Martinus Nijhoff The Hague 1985–2011), 7 vols

VME	vulnerable marine ecosystem
vol/vols	volume(s)
WCPFC	Western and Central Pacific Fisheries Commission
WCPF Convention	2000 Convention for the Conservation and Management of Highly Migratory Fish Stocks in the Western and Central Pacific Ocean
WECAFC	Western Central Atlantic Fishery Commission
WHC	1972 Convention Concerning the Protection of the World Cultural and Natural Heritage
WL	Westlaw
WMD	weapons of mass destruction
WMO	World Meteorological Organization
WTO	World Trade Organization
YbILC	Yearbook of the International Law Commission

Notes on Contributors

Editors

Alex G Oude Elferink is a professor at the KG Jebsen Centre for the Law of the Sea of the University of Tromsø, Norway, and the Director of the Netherlands Institute for the Law of the Sea at Utrecht University, The Netherlands. The focus of his research in public international law is on the law of the sea. He has written extensively on the law of the sea, covering such topics as the law of the sea in the polar regions, the South China Sea, the outer limits and delimitation of maritime zones, dispute settlement, fisheries, and the regime of marine areas beyond national jurisdiction. Among his most recent publications is *The Delimitation of the Continental Shelf between Denmark, Germany and the Netherlands: Arguing Law, Practicing Politics?* (CUP Cambridge 2013) that focuses on the impact of international law on State behaviour. His consultancy work is among others concerned with the outer limits of the continental shelf, maritime delimitation, and territorial disputes. He has acted as counsel before the ICJ and in arbitrations under Annex VII to the United Nations Convention on the law of the sea.

Donald R Rothwell is Professor of International Law, and Deputy Dean at the ANU College of Law, Australian National University (ANU) where he has taught since July 2006. His research has a specific focus on law of the sea, law of the polar regions, and implementation of international law within Australia. Since 2012, he has been Rapporteur of the International Law Association Committee on 'Baselines under the International Law of the Sea'. He was previously Challis Professor of International Law and Director of the Sydney Centre for International and Global Law, University of Sydney (2004–2006), where he had taught since 1988. He has acted as a consultant or been a member of expert groups for United Nations Environment Programme (UNEP), United Nations Development Programme (UNDP), International Union for Conservation of Nature (IUCN), the Australian Government, and acted as advisor to the International Fund for Animal Welfare (IFAW).

Karen N Scott is a Professor of Law at the University of Canterbury in New Zealand. Her research focuses on the areas of the law of the sea, the polar regions, and international environmental law. She has published over 50 journal articles and book chapters in these areas on issues such as ocean management, environmental governance, climate change, and geo-engineering. Recent publications include AD Hemmings, DR Rothwell, and KN Scott (eds), *Antarctic Security in the Twenty-first Century* (Routledge Abingdon 2012). From 2009 to 2012, Karen was General Editor of the *New Zealand Yearbook of International Law*. She is currently the Vice-President of the Australian and New Zealand Society of International Law (ANZSIL).

Tim Stephens is Professor of International Law and Australian Research Council Future Fellow at the Faculty of Law, University of Sydney. He teaches and researches in public international law, with his published work focussing on the law of the sea, international environmental law and international dispute settlement. Major works include *The International Law of the Sea* (co-authored with Donald R Rothwell, Hart Oxford 2010) and *International Courts and Environmental Protection* (Cambridge University Press Cambridge 2009). He has been a consultant for several non-governmental organisations, including a long association of work for the IFAW in relation to cetacean conservation. In 2014, Dr Stephens was appointed, on the nomination of the Australian Government, to the List of Experts for the South Pacific Regional Fisheries Management Organisation. He holds a PhD in law from the University of Sydney, an MPhil in geography from the University of Cambridge, and a BA and LLB (both with Honours) from the University of Sydney.

Chapter Authors

Gemma Andreone is a Senior Research Associate of International Law in the Institute of International Legal Studies of the Italian National Research Council (ISGI–CNR). She has been teaching International Law as an adjunct Professor at the University of Naples 'L'Orientale' from 2001 to 2013, and she obtained the National Scientific Qualification to Associate Professor of International law and European Law in Italian Universities on 24 January 2014. She obtained a PhD in Public and European Law at the Faculty of Law of *Seconda Università* of Naples in 2001 and an LLM in European Law and Economics at the University of Naples Federico II in 1998. She is Chair of the COST ACTION IS 1105 'MARSAFENET'—NETwork of experts on the legal aspects of MARitime SAFEty and security (http://www.marsafenet.org)—funded by the EU from March 2012 to March 2016. She is Treasurer and member of the Scientific Council of the International Association of the Law of the Sea. She is legal adviser and solicitor at the Bar of Rome, Italy. She is author of books, papers, and articles on many international law issues, and especially on the law of the sea, fisheries, and Mediterranean sea governance.

Richard A Barnes is Professor of Law at the University of Hull, United Kingdom, where he is Director of the McCoubrey Centre for International Law. He has lectured and written widely on the law of the sea and international law. Noted publications include *Law of the Sea: Progress and Prospects* (co-authored with David Freestone and David M Ong, Oxford University Press Oxford 2006) and *Property Rights and Natural Resources* (Hart Oxford 2008). The latter was awarded the SLS Birks Prize for Outstanding Legal Scholarship in 2009. More recent publications have focused on irregular maritime migration, search and rescue at sea, Arctic fisheries, control of offshore renewable energy, and the governance of areas beyond national jurisdiction. He has acted as an advisor for a number of governmental and private agencies on maritime and marine issues, including EU Parliament Committee on Fisheries, the UK Department for Environment, Food and Rural Affairs, the WWF, and the International Transport Workers Federation. He is an editor of the *International Journal of Marine and Coastal Law*, with responsibility for current legal developments, and sits on the editorial board of the *New Zealand Yearbook of International Law*.

Irina Buga is Doctoral Fellow in Public International Law at Utrecht University, and member of the Netherlands Institute for the Law of the Sea. She is an upcoming Associate in International Arbitration at De Brauw Blackstone Westbroek in Amsterdam. She has previously worked as Legal Assistant at the International Court of Justice in The Hague, and in the International Arbitration Group at Freshfields Bruckhaus Deringer in Paris. Her current research relates to treaty modification through subsequent practice, for which she has been awarded the François Prize by the Royal Netherlands Society of International Law. Irina completed the *Magister Juris* programme at the University of Oxford (Distinction; Clifford Chance Prize for Best Performance), following an honours BA at University College Utrecht, and a two-year Legal Research LLM at Utrecht University. She is also an alumna and prize recipient of the Rhodes Academy for Oceans Law and Policy. Irina has published articles in fields ranging from the law of the sea, international dispute settlement, and treaty law, to EU and commercial law.

Aldo Chircop was born in Malta and resides in Canada. He received the Doctorate in the Science of Law (JSD) from Dalhousie University in 1988. Dr Chircop is Professor of Law and is based at the Marine & Environmental Law Institute, Schulich School of Law, Dalhousie University. Over the course of his career, he was Chair in Marine Environment Protection at the International Maritime Organization's World Maritime University in Malmö, Sweden, and held directorships of the Marine Affairs Program and Marine & Environmental Law Institute at Dalhousie, International Ocean Institute, and the Mediterranean Institute in Malta. His teaching and research is in the fields of Canadian and international maritime law and the international law of the sea. Dr Chircop's current research addresses the development of Canadian maritime law and the international and comparative regulation of navigation and shipping in the Arctic. He chairs the International Working Group on Polar Shipping of the Comité Maritime International and is co-author and co-editor of 25 books (including 15 editions of the *Ocean Yearbook*, Nijhoff) and 80 articles and book chapters. Dr Chircop is a member of the Nova Scotia Barristers Society.

Robin R Churchill is Professor of international law at the University of Dundee (since 2006), and previously had held posts at Cardiff University and the University of Tromsö, and been a visiting fellow at the European University Institute in Florence and the University of Wollongong. His research interests include the law of the sea, international environmental law, EU fisheries law and human rights—on all of which he has published widely. He is the author (with Vaughan Lowe) of *The Law of the Sea* (3rd edn Manchester University Press Manchester 1999; 4th edn in preparation) and has also written books on the EU's Common Fisheries Policy and resource management in the Barents Sea, as well as numerous journal articles and book chapters on many different aspects of the law of the sea. Professor Churchill has acted as an adviser/consultant to various non-governmental organizations, a number of foreign governments, the European Commission, and the European Parliament. He is a member of the Scientific Advisory Board of the KG Jebsen Centre for the Law of the Sea, University of Tromsö, and the editorial boards of the *British Year Book of International Law* and the *International Journal of Marine and Coastal Law*.

Hans Corell was Under-Secretary-General for Legal Affairs and the Legal Counsel of the United Nations from March 1994 to March 2004. He was Ambassador and Under-Secretary for Legal and Consular Affairs in the Swedish Ministry for Foreign Affairs from 1984 to 1994. From 1962 to 1984 he served in the Ministry of Justice and in the Swedish Judiciary, where he was appointed Judge of Appeal in 1980. One of his responsibilities in the Ministry for Foreign Affairs was to serve as Chairman of the Swedish delegation in negotiations with the then Soviet Union, Poland, and Finland regarding marine delimitation in the Baltic. During his UN tenure he was responsible for supervising activities in connection with the entry into force of the LOSC, including the establishment of the International Seabed Authority, the International Tribunal for the Law of the Sea and the Commission on the Limits of the Continental Shelf. Since his retirement from public service in 2004 he is involved in many legal activities, including within the International Bar Association and the International Legal Assistance Consortium. With respect to the law of the sea he is also focusing on the Arctic Ocean within the framework of the Arctic Governance Project and Arctic Frontiers.

Tara Davenport is currently an instructor at the National University of Singapore (NUS). She is presently pursuing a JSD at Yale Law School on the NUS Overseas Graduate Scholarship. She holds a Bachelor of Laws from the London School of Economics, a Masters of Law in Maritime Law from the National University of Singapore, and a Masters of Law from Yale Law School. Prior to her graduate studies at Yale, she was a Research Fellow at the Centre for International Law at NUS where she was engaged in the research and teaching of oceans law and policy. Tara is also a Fulbright Scholar.

Malcolm D Evans is Professor of Public International Law at the University of Bristol. He is a member and Chair of the UN Subcommittee for the Prevention of Torture (SPT) and in 2014–2015 was Chair of the Meeting of Chairs of UN Human Rights Treaty Bodies. From 2002 to 2013 he was a member of the Organisation on Security and Cooperation in Europe's Advisory Council on the Freedom of Religion or Belief. From 2003 to 2005 he was Head of the School of Law and from 2005 to 2009 Dean of the Faculty of Social Sciences and Law at the University of Bristol. He is General Editor of the *International and Comparative Law Quarterly* and Co-Editor-in-Chief of the *Oxford Journal of Law and Religion*. Major published works include: *Relevant Circumstances and Maritime Boundary Delimitation* (Oxford University Press Oxford 1989), *Religious Liberty and International Law in Europe* (Cambridge University Press Cambridge 1997), *Preventing Torture* (Oxford University Press Oxford 1998), *Combating Torture in Europe* (Council of Europe Strasbourg 2002), *Manual on the Wearing of Religious Symbols in Public Areas* (Council of Europe Strasbourg/ Martinus Nijhoff Leiden 2009), *The Optional Protocol to the UN Convention against Torture* (Oxford University Press Oxford 2011). He is also Editor of *International Law* (4th edn, Oxford University Press Oxford 2014) and Blackstone's *International Law Documents* (11th edn Oxford University Press Oxford 2013).

David Freestone is the founding Editor of the *International Journal of Marine and Coastal Law*. He is a Visiting Scholar and Adjunct Professor at George Washington University Law School in Washington, DC and the Executive Secretary of the Sargasso Sea Commission established in 2014 pursuant to the signing by the governments of Bermuda, the Azores, Monaco, UK and USA of the *Hamilton Declaration on Collaboration for the Conservation of the Sargasso Sea*. From 1996 to 2008, he worked at the World Bank in Washington DC, first as Legal Adviser and head of the international environmental law group, and from 2004 to 2008 as Deputy General Counsel/Senior Adviser. He holds an advanced Doctorate in Law (LLD) from the University of Hull, UK, and an LLM from the University of London. He has published widely on law of the sea and international environmental law, his most recent books include *The 1982 Law of the Sea Convention at 30* (editor, Martinus Nijhoff Leiden 2013); *The World Bank and Sustainable Development* (Martinus Nijhoff Leiden 2012); *Legal Aspects of Carbon Trading: Kyoto, Bali and Beyond* (co-edited with Charlotte Streck, Oxford University Press Oxford 2009); *The Law of the Sea: Progress and Prospects* (co-edited with Richard Barnes and David Ong, Oxford University Press Oxford 2006).

Johannes Fuchs is a research fellow at the Walther Schücking Institute for International Law and he is associated with the interdisciplinary Cluster of Excellency 'The Future Ocean' at Kiel University. From 2009 to 2011, he worked as a research fellow for

Prof Rüdiger Wolfrum at the Max Planck Institute for Comparative Public Law and International Law, Heidelberg. His areas of research include the law of the sea, international energy law, and the law of State responsibility. He is currently pursuing a PhD, dealing with the topic of liability in international law.

Edward J Goodwin is Assistant Professor in Law at the University of Nottingham, United Kingdom. He is a graduate of the University of Oxford (BA (Hons)) and the University of Nottingham (LLM, PhD), and will be a Grotius Research Scholar at the University of Michigan Law School in 2015. He is the Book Reviews Editor for the *International Journal of Marine and Coastal Law*. His research interests include international environmental law, the law of the sea, international heritage law, and land law. In addition to a range of journal articles and contributions to collected works, he is the author of *International Environmental Law and the Conservation of Coral Reefs* (Routledge New York 2011) and the co-editor of the *Research Handbook on Biodiversity and Law* (Edward Elgar forthcoming 2015).

Douglas Guilfoyle is a Reader in Law at the Faculty of Laws, University College London, where he teaches public international law, the international law of the sea, and international criminal law. He is the author of *Shipping Interdiction and the Law of the Sea* (Cambridge University Press Cambridge 2009) and numerous articles on maritime security and law enforcement, naval warfare, and Somali piracy. He has acted as a consultant on piracy issues to the Contact Group on Piracy off the Coast of Somalia (Working Group 2), the Foreign Affairs Committee of the House of Commons and the UN Office on Drugs and Crime, and as an adviser to the government of Mauritius. He holds a PhD and LLM from the University of Cambridge, where he was a Gates Scholar, and undergraduate degrees in law and history from the Australian National University. Prior to graduate study, he worked as a litigation solicitor and as a judge's associate in Australia. From April 2015 he will be an Associate Professor at the Faculty of Law, Monash University.

James Harrison is a lecturer in public international law at the University of Edinburgh School of Law and he is currently Director of the Scottish Centre for International Law. He has written broadly in the field of public international law and he has particular interests in the law of the sea and international environmental law. James is the author of *Making the Law of the Sea: A Case Study in the Development of International Law* (Cambridge University Press Cambridge 2011) as well as several book chapters and journal articles focusing on questions of international law-making and dispute settlement. He is also the International Environmental Law Case Review Editor for the *Journal of Environmental Law*.

Elizabeth A Kirk is a Senior Lecturer at the School of Law, University of Dundee. She joined Dundee in 1995, having previously qualified as a solicitor in Scotland and worked as a Research Associate at the University of British Columbia. Elizabeth is the Western Europe representative on the Governing Board of the IUCN Academy of Environmental Law and sits on the Managing Board of the

European Environmental Law Forum. She is a member of the IUCN/Commission on Environmental Law Specialist Group on Ocean Law and a member of Council of the Society of Legal Scholars. Elizabeth is Joint Editor of the IUCN Academy of Environmental Law's journal—*The eJournal*—and on the Editorial Board of the *Journal of Water Law*. Elizabeth's research focuses on adaptability within legal regimes, in particular the ability of regimes to respond to changing circumstances, scientific understanding, or actors. Her work, which has been supported by a number of research grants from the Arts and Humanities Research Council, British Academy, Economic and Social Research Council, European Commission, Royal Society of Edinburgh and Society of Legal Scholars spans both the international law of marine governance (and marine resources) and domestic environmental law.

Natalie Klein is Professor and Dean at Macquarie Law School and acting Head of Macquarie's Centre for Policing, Intelligence and Counter-Terrorism. At Macquarie, she teaches and researches in different areas of international law, with a focus on law of the sea and international dispute settlement. Professor Klein is the author of *Dispute Settlement and the UN Convention on the Law of the Sea* (Cambridge University Press Cambridge 2005) and *Maritime Security and the Law of the Sea* (Oxford University Press Oxford 2011). She provides advice, undertakes consultancies, and interacts with the media on law of the sea issues. Prior to joining Macquarie, Professor Klein worked in the international litigation and arbitration practice of Debevoise & Plimpton LLP, served as counsel to the Government of Eritrea and was a consultant in the Office of Legal Affairs at the United Nations. Her masters and doctorate in law were earned at Yale Law School. In 2013, she was invited to become a Fellow of the Australian Academy of Law.

James Kraska is Professor of Oceans Law and Policy in the Stockton Center for the Study of International Law at the US Naval War College, where he served as Howard S. Levie Chair in International Law from 2008 to 2013. He is also a Distinguished Fellow at the Law of the Sea Institute, University of California Berkeley School of Law. His publications include numerous scholarly articles and books, including the treatise, *International Maritime Security Law* (with Raul Pedrozo, Martinus Nijhoff Leiden 2013). Dr Kraska is a retired US Navy lawyer and commander with more than 20 years of service, and conducted negotiations on international law and law of the sea issues with nations throughout the world and at the International Maritime Organization. He earned two doctorates in law from Indiana University and University of Virginia School of Law.

Coalter G Lathrop is principal and owner of Sovereign Geographic, an international boundary consultancy providing legal and cartographic services to clients throughout the world, including in the Middle East, Africa, Asia, South America, and North America. Lathrop has acted as counsel before the International Court of Justice and the International Tribunal for the Law of the Sea. He holds a Master of Marine Affairs from the University of Washington, and a JD and LLM in International and Comparative Law from Duke University. Lathrop is Editor of *International Maritime Boundaries* and a member of the extended faculty at Duke Law. He served as Rapporteur for the International Law Association Committee on Law of the Sea Baselines from 2008 to 2012. His research, writing, and speaking have focused on ocean law and the resolution of international disputes, including maritime boundary disputes.

Michael W Lodge is Deputy to the Secretary-General and Legal Counsel for the International Seabed Authority (ISA). He is a barrister of Gray's Inn, London. His professional experiences to date include serving as Legal Counsel to the ISA (2007–2010 and 1996–2003); Counsellor to the Round Table on Sustainable Development, OECD (2004–2007); and Legal Counsel to the South Pacific Forum Fisheries Agency (1991–1995). He has also held appointments as a Visiting Fellow of Somerville College, Oxford (2012–2013) and an Associate Fellow of Chatham House, London (2007). Currently, he is a member of the World Economic Forum Global Agenda Council on Oceans. Michael Lodge has authored over 25 published books and articles on law of the sea, oceans policy and related issues. Some of his significant achievements include his pivotal role in the ISA from its inception in 1996 and in helping to create and implement the first international regulatory regime for seabed mining. He also contributed to the future security of global fish stocks by leading the process to create the Western and Central Pacific Fisheries Commission from concept to its establishment as the largest regional fisheries management organization in the world.

Ronán Long holds a personal professorship and the Jean Monnet Chair of European Law at the School of Law, National University of Ireland Galway. He is the author/co-editor of several books on oceans law and policy issues including: *Enforcing the Common Fisheries Policy* (Blackwell Science Oxford 1998, reprint 2008, John Wiley); *Marine Resource Law* (Thomson Round Hall Dublin 2007); *Law, Science and Ocean Management* (co-edited with MH Nordquist, T Heidar, and J Norton Moore, Nijhoff Leiden 2007); *Legal Challenges in Maritime Security* (co-edited, Nijhoff Leiden 2008); *The Regulation of Continental Shelf Development: Rethinking International Standards* (co-edited, Nijhoff Leiden 2012); and *Freedom of Navigation and Globalization* (co-edited, Nijhoff Leiden 2014). He worked previously for the European Commission (1994–2002) and for the Naval Service in Ireland (1981–1994). He was the first recipient of the Michael Manahan Fellowship and held a Scholarship-in-Residence at the University of Virginia School of Law in the fall of 2007. Professor Long has participated in a broad range of EU marine research projects since the early 1990s and his current research focus is on the implementation of the ecosystem approach in the marine environment, the interface between the law of the sea and human rights, as well as energy law. Several of his current projects are focused on law reform in Africa and Central America and he is a long-standing contributor to the United Nations—The

Nippon Foundation of Japan Fellowship Programme. He is a keen sailor and has represented Ireland at the top competitive level in ocean racing.

Nele Matz-Lück, is Professor of the Law of the Sea and co-director of the Walther Schücking Institute for International Law at the University of Kiel since 2011 and a member of the Cluster of Excellency 'The Future Ocean'. She is adjunct professor at the KG Jebsen Centre on the Law of the Sea at the University of Tromsø since January 2014. From 2004 to 2011, she held a position as senior research fellow at the Max Planck Institute for Comparative Public Law and International Law in Heidelberg. She completed her PhD in 2003 at Heidelberg University Law School and holds an LLM degree in 'Environmental Law and Management' from the University of Aberystwyth (Wales). Her main areas of research and publications include the law of the sea, international environmental law, and fundamental questions of public international law.

Ted L McDorman is a Professor in the Faculty of Law at the University of Victoria, Canada. Before joining the University of Victoria in 1985, Professor McDorman was at Dalhousie University with the Dalhousie Oceans Studies Programme (DOSP). Since 2000, he has been the editor-in-chief of *Ocean Development and International Law*. From 2002 to 2004, and again from 2011 to 2013, Professor McDorman was 'academic-in-residence' in the Legal Affairs Branch of the Canadian Department of Foreign Affairs and International Trade where he was involved in a number of Arctic, law of the sea, and environmental matters and represented Canada at several international fora. For almost 20 years (1984–2002), Professor McDorman was involved with the Southeast Asian Ocean Law, Policy and Management Programme (SEAPOL) centred in Bangkok, Thailand and through this project had the opportunity to study and write about numerous Southeast Asian ocean law and policy issues. He has been a visiting professor at institutions in Thailand, Sweden, the Netherlands, and Canada. In 2007, Professor McDorman was the Fulbright Visiting Chair in Canada–US Relations at the Woodrow Wilson International Center for Scholars in Washington, DC.

Erik J Molenaar has been with the Netherlands Institute for the Law of the Sea (NILOS) at Utrecht University since 1994 and currently holds a position as Deputy Director. Since 2006, he has also been employed by the University of Tromsø, where he currently is a Professor at the KG Jebsen Centre for the Law of the Sea (JCLOS). After having completed his PhD on 'Coastal State Jurisdiction over Vessel-Source Pollution' (1998), he broadened his research field with international fisheries law and the international law relating to the Antarctic and Arctic. In addition to pure academic research, he also acted as a consultant for various governments, intergovernmental organizations, and private companies. His research and consultancy activities have led to, and benefitted from, his participation in various diplomatic conferences and other intergovernmental meetings, including the annual meetings of several regional fisheries management organizations.

Joanna Mossop is a senior lecturer in law at Victoria University of Wellington, New Zealand. Her research interests are in law of the sea and international environmental law. Recent publications have focused on a range of law of the sea interests including maritime security, marine mammals, and marine biodiversity. She has consulted with the New Zealand Ministry of Foreign Affairs and Trade, has been on the Council of the Australia New Zealand Society of International Law and is a member of the Commission on Environmental Law. She is co-editor of *Maritime Security: International Law and Policy Perspectives from Australia and New Zealand* (with Donald R Rothwell and Natalie Klein, Routledge New York 2009) and is a recipient of a New Zealand Law Foundation Research Award (2011) which is supporting the writing of a monograph on the regulation of the extended continental shelf.

John E Noyes is the Roger J Traynor Professor of Law at California Western School of Law in San Diego, California. He has also taught at the University of Connecticut School of Law, Wake Forest University School of Law, Roger Williams University School of Law, Suffolk University Law School, Victoria University (New Zealand), and the University of San Diego's Institute on International and Comparative Law. Professor Noyes is a past President of the American Branch of the International Law Association. A graduate of Amherst College and the University of Virginia School of Law, he has written extensively about the law of the sea, international dispute settlement, and other international law topics.

Bernard H Oxman is Richard A Hausler Professor of Law at the University of Miami School of Law, where he directs the Master of Laws Program in Ocean and Coastal Law. The author and editor of numerous books and articles on international law, he was co-editor-in-chief of the *American Journal of International Law* from 2003 to 2013, and was elected to the Institut de Droit International in 2011. He has served as judge ad hoc of the International Court of Justice and the International Tribunal for the Law of the Sea, as well as arbitrator and counsel in public and private international cases. He received his AB and JD degrees from Columbia University, New York, then served on active duty in the International Law Division of the Office of the Judge Advocate General of the Navy, after which he joined the US Department of State, where he was Assistant Legal Adviser for Oceans, Environment, and Scientific Affairs. He was United States Representative to the Third UN Conference on the Law of the Sea and chaired the English Language Group of the Conference Drafting Committee.

Irini Papanicolopulu is Associate Professor in International Law, University of Milano-Bicocca and Senior Lecturer in International Law, University of Glasgow, School of Law and Senior Research Fellow, Università di Milano-Bicocca (Italy). She holds a Doctorate in International Law from Università degli Studi di Milano, and has been a Marie Curie Fellow, University of Oxford, and a Visiting Fellow at St Peter's College. She is the author of a volume on maritime delimitation (*Il confine marino: unità* *o pluralità?*, Giuffrè Editore, 2005), is the editor or co-editor of four collections of essays and the author of numerous articles and book chapters on law of the sea, environmental law, human rights law, and international humanitarian law. Among others, she is a contributor to the *Max Planck Encyclopaedia of Public International Law* and the *International Maritime Boundaries* series. She has lectured in different States and institutions, including the Max Planck Institute for Comparative and International Private Law, the International Maritime Law Institute, the Institute for Advanced Defence Studies, Italian Ministry of Defence, and the San Remo International Institute of Humanitarian Law. She has been in-house Legal Advisor to the (Italian) Ministry of the Environment and has acted as a legal expert for the Italian Government and for a number of international governmental and non-governmental organizations.

Anna Petrig is a post-doc researcher at the University of Basel, Switzerland. She is a member of the Management Committee of MARSAFENET (network of experts on the legal aspects of maritime safety and security) and co-leader of its Working Group on *International Maritime Security and Boarder Surveillance*. Anna Petrig initiated the Sea Piracy Project of the Max Planck Institute for International and Foreign Criminal Law in Freiburg, Germany, in 2009 and managed it until the end of 2011. In 2013 she completed a research project on the transfer of piracy suspects at the University of Basel. Her major publications include *Piracy and Armed Robbery at Sea: The Legal Framework for Counter-Piracy Operations in Somalia and the Gulf of Aden* (with Robin Geiss, Oxford University Press Oxford 2011) and *Human Rights and Law Enforcement at Sea: Arrest, Detention and Transfers of Piracy Suspects* (Martinus Nijhoff Leiden 2014). Anna Petrig is a member of the Bar of the Canton of Berne, Switzerland, and the New York State Bar. She holds an LLM from Harvard Law School and a PhD from the University of Basel. Her broad legal experience includes work in private practice, the courts and the legal division of the International Committee of the Red Cross.

Rosemary Rayfuse is a professor of public international law in the Faculty of Law, The University of New South Wales (UNSW) Australia and holds a conjoint appointment as professor of international environmental law at Lund University and a visiting professorship in law of the sea at the University of Gothenberg. Her main fields of interest are oceans governance, high seas fisheries, protection of the marine environment in areas beyond national jurisdiction, and the normative effects of climate change on international law. Her books include *Non-Flag State Enforcement in High Seas Fisheries* (Martinus Nijhoff Leiden 2004); *Protection of the Environment in Relation to Armed Conflict* (Martinus Nijhoff Leiden 2014); *The Challenge of Food Security: International Policy and Regulatory Frameworks* (Edward Elgar Cheltenham 2012); and *International Law in the Era of Climate Change* (Edward Elgar Cheltenham 2012). She is also the author of numerous publications in these and other areas of international law including State responsibility, the law of treaties, international humanitarian law, use of force, international crimes and international dispute settlement. She is a member of the International Union for Conservation of Nature (IUCN) Commission on Environmental Law, Co-Chair of its Sub-Working Group on High Seas Governance, and a member of the International Law Association Committee on Sea Level Rise and International Law.

Clive Schofield is Director of Research at the Australian Centre for Ocean Resource and Security (ANCORS), University of Wollongong (UOW). He is also the Leader of the Sustaining Coastal and Marine Zones research theme within the UOW Global Challenges Program. He holds an Australian Research Council (ARC) Future Fellowship and is a former ARC QEII Fellow. He holds a PhD (geography) from the University of Durham, UK and an LLM from the University of British Columbia, Canada. Clive's research interests relate to international boundaries and particularly maritime boundary delimitation and marine jurisdictional issues. He has published over 200 scholarly publications including 22 books and monographs (including edited works) on these issues as well as on geo-technical aspects of the law of the sea and maritime security. Clive serves as an International Hydrographic Office (IHO)-nominated Observer on the Advisory Board on the Law of the Sea (ABLOS). He has also been involved in the peaceful settlement of boundary disputes, through the provision of advice and research support to governments engaged in boundary negotiations and in cases before the International Court of Justice and has been appointed as a Peacebuilding Adviser on behalf of the United Nations and World Bank.

Yoshifumi Tanaka is Professor of International Law with Specific Focus on the Law of the Sea at University of Copenhagen. He holds a DES and a PhD from the Graduate Institute of International Studies, Geneva (currently the Graduate Institute of International and Development Studies, Geneva) and an LLM from Hitotsubashi University, Tokyo. He is the single author of three books: *Predictability and Flexibility in the Law of Maritime Delimitation* (Hart Publishing 2006); *A Dual Approach to Ocean Governance: The Cases of Zonal and Integrated Management in International Law of the Sea* (Ashgate Farnham 2008); and *The International Law of the Sea* (1st edn Cambridge University Press Cambridge 2012).

Tullio Treves has had an academic career in Italy. He taught international law at the State University of Milano from 1980 until retirement in 2012. He has had international experiences as a member of the Italian Delegation to the Third United Nations Conference on the Law of the Sea, as Legal Adviser to the Italian mission to the UN in New York, and as Judge of the International Tribunal for the Law of the Sea from 1996 to 2011. He is author of numerous books and articles on public and private international law, focusing especially on the law of the sea and the settlement of international disputes. He pleaded in various cases before the International Court of Justice, and he is a member of international arbitration tribunals. He is a member of Institut de Droit International and of the Curatorium of the Hague Academy of International Law.

Helmut Tuerk has been a Judge of the International Tribunal for the Law of the Sea (ITLOS) from 2005 to 2015, serving as Vice-President of the Tribunal from 2008 to 2011. He is also a Conciliator under Annex V and an Arbitrator under Annex VII of the United Nations Convention on the Law of the Sea. For more than a decade, he served as the Legal Advisor of the Austrian Federal Ministry for Foreign Affairs as well as the Agent of the Austrian Federal Government before the European Commission and the European Court of Human Rights. He was subsequently appointed Ambassador to the United States of America, the Commonwealth of the Bahamas, Permanent Observer of Austria to the Organisation of American States as well as Ambassador to the Holy See, the Sovereign Military Order of Malta, and the Republic of San Marino. He was a member of the Austrian delegation to the Third United Nations Conference on the Law of the Sea, a delegate to the Preparatory Commission for the International Seabed Authority and the ITLOS, and served as President of the Meeting of States Parties to the United Nations Convention on the Law of the Sea.

David VanderZwaag holds the Canada Research Chair (Tier 1) in Ocean Law and Governance at the Marine & Environmental Law Institute, Dalhousie University, Halifax, Canada. He teaches international environmental law and is a former Co-director of Dalhousie's interdisciplinary Marine Affairs Program and a former Director of the Marine & Environmental Law Institute. Professor VanderZwaag is currently a member of the IUCN's World Commission on Environmental Law (WCEL) and Co-chair of the WCEL's Specialist Group on Oceans, Coasts & Coral Reefs. He is an elected member of the International Council of Environmental Law. Dr VanderZwaag has authored over 150 papers in the marine and environmental law field. His most recent book publications are: *Polar Oceans Governance in an Era of Environmental Change* (edited with Tim Stephens, Edward Elgar Cheltenham 2014) and *Recasting Transboundary Fisheries Management Arrangements in Light of Sustainability Principles: Canadian and International Perspectives* (edited with DA Russell, Martinus Nijhoff Leiden 2010). Professor VanderZwaag's educational background includes: PhD (1994, University of Wales, Cardiff), LLM (1982, Dalhousie Law School), JD (1980, University of Arkansas Law School), MDiv (1974, Princeton Theological Seminary), and BA (1971, Calvin College).

Robin M Warner is Associate Professor at the Australian National Centre for Ocean Resources and Security, University of Wollongong. She was formerly the Assistant Secretary of the International Crime Branch in the Commonwealth Attorney General's Department from 2002 to 2007 and Director of International Law for the Australian Defence Force from 1997 to 2001. Her current research interests include law of the sea, oceans governance, marine environmental law, climate law, and transnational criminal law. She is the author of *Protecting the Oceans Beyond National Jurisdiction: Strengthening the International Law Framework* (Martinus Nijhoff Leiden 2009) and editor of *Transboundary Environmental Governance: Inland Coastal and Marine Perspectives* (co-edited with Simon Marsden, Ashgate Burlington, VT 2012) and *Climate Change and the Oceans: Gauging the Legal and Policy Currents in the Asia Pacific* (edited with Clive Schofield, Edward Elgar Cheltenham 2012), as well as many book chapters and journal articles on oceans law and policy.

Keyuan Zou is Harris Professor of International Law at the Lancashire Law School, University of Central Lancashire (UCLan), UK. He is also Visiting Chair Professor at the Guanghua Law School of Zhejiang University, China. He specializes in international law, in particular law of the sea and international environmental law. Before joining UCLan, he worked at Dalhousie University, Peking University, University of Hannover, and National University of Singapore. He has published over 60 refereed English papers in 30 international journals. He is the author, among others, of *Law of the Sea in East Asia: Issues and Prospects* (Routledge New York 2005); *China's Marine Legal System and the Law of the Sea* (Martinus Nijhoff Leiden 2005); *China's Legal Reform: Towards the Rule of Law* (Martinus Nijhoff Leiden 2006); and *China–ASEAN Relations and International Law* (Chandos Publishing Online 2009). His recent co-edited volumes include *International Law in East Asia* (Ashgate Burlington, VT 2011); *Securing the Safety of Navigation in East Asia* (Chandos Online Publishing 2013); and *Major Law and Policy Issues in the South China Sea* (Ashgate Burlington, VT 2014). He sits on various editorial boards of academic journals, including, *inter alia*, *International Journal of Marine and Coastal Law*, *Ocean Development and International Law*, and *Chinese Journal of International Law*.

1
HISTORICAL DEVELOPMENT OF THE LAW OF THE SEA

TULLIO TREVES

1 INTRODUCTION

THE law of the sea is a branch of international law as old as international law itself. It emerges from the fact that States exercise sovereignty over territory and the conduct of activities taking place on or in the sea. Its historical development has been driven by political, economic, security, and, in more recent times, scientific and environmental interests. The evolution of technology and science plays a significant part. So, for instance, the law concerning fisheries has been influenced by the discovery of fish conservation techniques (salting and later freezing), and the law concerning the coastal State's rights on the seabed adjacent to its coasts has been influenced by progress in seabed drilling technology. The discovery of polymetallic nodules and of hydrothermal vents on the deep seabed has been at the root of the development of international law rules for areas and activities hitherto unregulated.

These interests and developments have given rise to competing claims to the freedom of the seas and to the exercise of exclusive (sovereign or jurisdictional) rights by States. The tension between, and the accommodation of, these competing claims is a recurrent theme of the historical development of the law of the sea. Writings by scholars have played an important part in this development, especially in early times, when most scholarly works were in fact briefs in favour of the interests of a State.

Up to the end of the nineteenth century, the international law of the sea was mainly customary in origin, to be ascertained on the basis of what States did and said, and basically from States' claims to exercise exclusive rights on portions of the sea and the reactions of other States to such claims. Later, other forms of international practice began to shape the evolution of the law. Collective endeavours by States to codify the international law of the sea spanned a half century of efforts, from the Hague conference of 1930 to the Third United Nations Conference on the Law of the Sea (UNCLOS III), and concluded in 1982 with the adoption of the United Nations Convention on the Law of the Sea (LOSC), presently in force for 166 States, while numerous treaties were concluded on specific matters (especially fishing, and later the protection of the environment). Moreover, international courts and tribunals made important contributions to the clarification and the progress of the law on various issues. Writings of individual scholars tried to adopt a scientific perspective independent of State interests, although influenced by their own political views, legal traditions, and cultural perspectives. The collective work by scholars became important in anticipation of, and in parallel with, the codification effort of States.

The aim of the present chapter is not to summarize in the small space allotted the history of the international law of the sea. Excellent work has been done by many scholars, to which reference should be made.[1] The perspective adopted is to highlight, in the historic development of the law of the sea, the roots of the law as it now stands and of the questions still open today. The early phases of the evolution of the law of the sea up to the end of the nineteenth century will be considered, followed by, in more detail, developments taking place within the twentieth century. This historical survey will, however, stop at the UNCLOS III. This fundamental event in the history of the law of the sea in the twentieth century is the basis of the international law of the sea of today, and is dealt with in subsequent chapters of this *Handbook*.

---

[1] RP Anand, *Origin and Development of the Law of the Sea* (Martinus Nijhoff The Hague 1983); T Scovazzi, 'The Evolution of the International Law of the Sea: New Issues, New Challenges' (2001) 286 *Recueil des cours* 39, chs I and II; A Kirchner, 'The Law of the Sea, History of' in R Wolfrum (ed), *Max Planck Encyclopedia of Public International Law* (Oxford University Press Oxford 2012) Vol VI, 732; DJ Bederman, 'The Sea' in B Fassbender and A Peters (eds), *The Oxford Handbook of the History of International Law* (Oxford University Press Oxford 2013) 359.

2 The Main Steps of the Evolution of the Law of the Sea between 1493 and the End of the Nineteenth Century

A convenient point of departure to trace the evolution of the law of the sea, in light of the tension between claims to sovereignty and to freedom, are two connected episodes in the aftermath of Columbus' first voyage in 1492. With the bull *Inter Caetera* of 14 May 1493, Pope Alexander VI donated to Spain all territories, discovered or to be discovered, west of an imaginary line drawn on the Atlantic Ocean from pole to pole at a distance of 100 leagues west of Cape Verde and the Azores, and to Portugal all such territories east of that line. A year later, on 7 June 1494, the two States concluded, at Tordesillas, a treaty repeating the terms of the 1493 donation, although shifting the line westward, to 370 leagues from Cape Verde and the Azores. While the Papal bull and the 1494 Treaty refer to territories, the separating line is drawn on the ocean, so that this may be seen as an early and most ambitious claim to sovereignty over the sea.

The Spanish and Portuguese claims (as well as similar, although more modest claims by Denmark) were not generally accepted and, in particular, were rejected by England and by the Dutch Republic. Of significance are the instructions given by Queen Elizabeth I in 1602 to envoys sent to meet in Bremen with Danish representatives.[2] The English envoys were to reject Danish claims of 'property' of the seas and, referring to English and Venetian practice, to stipulate that although 'property' of the sea 'at some small distance from the coast maie yield some Oversight and Jurisdiction', such oversight and jurisdiction did not include prohibition of fishing and much less passage of ships and merchandise, as such prohibition was excluded by the Law of Nations. We can see in this statement a very early (and possibly the first) formulation of the idea of the freedom of the seas, and of the existence of a jurisdictional right over a narrow band of waters adjacent to the coast, in which, however, passage and even fishing may not be prohibited to foreign vessels. These instructions thus contain also an early statement of the notions of the territorial sea and of innocent passage. The idea of freedom of fishing in coastal waters was not to last as England required foreign fishing vessels to obtain a licence (proclamations of King James I of 6 May 1609 and of King Charles I of 10 May 1636), even though the enforcement of these proclamations proved difficult.

---

[2] TW Fulton, *The Sovereignty of the Sea* (W Blackwood Edinburgh/London 1911) 110ff. See also Scovazzi, n 1, 58.

The seventeenth century was the century of the 'battle of the books'. The booklet anonymously published in 1609 by the Dutch jurist Huig de Groot (Hugo Grotius), *Mare Liberum* (in fact a chapter of a treatise entitled *De Jure Praedae*, never published by Grotius, and whose manuscript was discovered only in 1865), gave expression to the basic concept that the sea must be free because, by its nature, it is not susceptible of occupation. The book was occasioned by the defence of the Dutch East India Company, which had seized the Portuguese vessel *Catarina* in the strait of Singapore, against Portugal claiming sovereignty on that part of the seas. *Mare Liberum* acquired great fame, and the idea of the freedom of the seas, especially as far as navigation was concerned, found followers and opponents in books by scholars of many countries, including England, Scotland, Portugal, Venice, Genoa, and the Netherlands.

Among opponents one must recall the Englishman John Selden, who published in 1635 a treatise on the Closed Sea (*Mare Clausum, seu de dominio maris libri duo*), and the Scotsman William Wellwood, who published in 1613 an *Abridgment of All Sea-Lawes*, followed in 1615 by a treatise in Latin on the Domain of the Sea (*De Dominio Maris*, etc). Wellwood's *Abridgment* was the only book by his opponents to which Grotius wrote a reply, the unpublished manuscript of which was found in 1865 together with *De Jure Praedae*. The basic idea of the opponents of the freedom of the sea was not a defence of the Papal donation. In fact, the interests they were defending were mostly those of powers other than Portugal and Spain. Their idea was that the seas, similarly to land, could be subject to occupation and control by a State and that in fact, some States (as Selden argued for England), already in fact exercised such power as regards navigation and fishing in certain areas of the sea.

Grotius was not an absolute doctrinaire. He conceded that his main thesis did not apply to small enclosures of sea, where exclusive fishing rights could be claimed, and that the discussion in his book dealt with the vast ocean and not with bays, straits, and the part of the sea that can be seen from the shore. While he maintained that fishing was in principle to be as free as navigation, he conceded that there might be a difference between navigation and fishing, because in a sense (*quodadmodum*), it could be held that fishes may be exhausted. Consequently, while navigation could not in any case be forbidden, this was not completely ruled out for fishing. Moreover, in his treatise on 'The Law of War and Peace' (*De Jure Belli ac Pacis*, published in 1625), Grotius made more explicit some of the above points, and clearly held that occupation of small parts of the seas, such as in bays and straits, was possible for the coastal State through the presence of military fleets and by exercising coercion from the shore in the same way as on land.

In the eighteenth and nineteenth centuries the accepted regime of the sea was that described by Grotius, namely that of freedom, with the exception of a narrow band of waters adjacent to the coast. It was another Dutch author, Cornelius van Bynkershoeck, who although starting from premises close to those of the adversaries of the freedom of the seas, proposed a rational basis for this regime. In his *De Dominio Maris Dissertatio*, published in 1702, he admitted in principle that the seas could be subject of occupation, but stated that in the present 'no sea is possessed by anyone'.[3] He argued that coastal States' dominion of areas of the seas close to the coast depended on the exercise of sovereignty over the land and that its extension ended where the power of man's weapons ends: 'The control of the land [over the sea] extends as far as cannon will carry, as that is as far as we seem to have both command and possession.'[4] So the 'cannon shot rule' was proclaimed.

The cannon shot rule was relied upon in the practice of the eighteenth century and approved in scholarly works including in the authoritative treatise on the 'Law of Nations' by Emmerich de Vattel.[5] Yet the cannon shot rule, notwithstanding its logical basis, had the drawback of being uncertain and subject to change in response to changes in weapon technology. Moreover, was the rule to be applied when real artillery was present on the land, or a consequence of the mere possibility of such presence? In a book written in Italian and published in 1782, the Neapolitan illuminist Ferdinando Galiani proposed a fixed measure of 3 miles, as this was the maximum limit artillery as known at the time could reach.[6]

A fixed limit for the belt of coastal waters on which the sovereignty of the coastal State was recognized was adopted in State practice in the nineteenth and early twentieth centuries. Although the 3-mile limit was the most frequently adopted (in particular by maritime powers as Great Britain, the United States, and France), other States adopted a different fixed limit ranging from 4 (Demark, Norway, and Sweden) to 6 (Spain, Portugal, Italy, and others) to 12 miles (Russia and later the Soviet Union, Venezuela, and Guatemala). The basic idea of the freedom of the sea—which coincided with Asian practice followed for centuries[7]—corresponded to the interests of the great maritime powers of the time, principally Britain, but also France, the Netherlands, and the United States, which were keen to ensure unimpeded movement of their mercantile and military vessels for the building of empires and for the expansion of trade from far away territories. The recognition of innocent passage of foreign vessels in

---

[3] C van Bynkershoeck, 'De Dominio Maris Dissertatio' in *Opera Minora* (2nd edn Apud Joannem van Kerckhem Lugduni Batavorum 1744) ch VIII, 401, reproduced with an English translation in *Carnegie Classics of International Law* (Oxford University Press New York 1923) 111, 89.

[4] Ibid, ch II, 364 (44 of English trans).

[5] E de Vattel, *Le droit des gens ou principes de la loi naturelle, appliqués à la conduite et aux affaires des nations et des souverains* (London 1758), reproduction of books I and II of the 1758 edition (Carnegie Endowment for International Peace Washington 1916) 249 [289].

[6] F Galiani, *De' doveri dei principi neutrali verso i principi guerreggianti e di questi verso i Neutrali* (Napoli 1782) 422.

[7] C Alexandrovic, *An Introduction to the History of the Law of Nations in the East Indies* (Clarendon Press Oxford 1967) 42–9.

the territorial sea (already contained in the above mentioned 1602 instructions by Queen Elizabeth I) was consistent with the main objective of ensuring free movement of vessels.

Towards the end of the nineteenth century, a limited exception to the freedom of the high seas was recognized in order to fight smuggling. The British Hovering Act of 1736, last renewed in 1853, prescribed criminal penalties for smuggling activities offshore, even when conducted beyond a maritime league. Although the Act was repealed in 1876, signalling the British conviction that the coastal State's powers could not extend beyond the three-nautical-mile limit (nm) of the territorial sea, other States, in particular the United States,[8] had followed the British Hovering Act, so that it could be argued that a customary rule had emerged providing certain functional powers of the coastal State beyond the limits of the territorial sea, concerning, in particular, the repression of smuggling (the 'contiguous zone'). The so-called 'Liquor treaties' aimed at enforcing United States prohibition laws, concluded between the United States and Britain as well as other States between 1924 and 1930,[9] in which these States authorized the United States to board and search vessels flying their flags beyond the 3 nm limit of the United States' territorial sea to a distance of one hour sailing by the vessel suspected of endeavouring to commit the offence, may be seen as implicitly recognizing such an emerging rule. The very fact that they were concluded may, however, be an argument against this view.

The precise limits of this new zone were not clearly defined. This depended in part on the still controversial question of the maximum breadth of the territorial sea. In fact, the 'Liquor treaties' concluded with States supporting the 3 nm limit contained a clause declaring the intention of the contracting parties to uphold the principle that the 'proper limits of territorial waters' were 3 nm from the shore, while those concluded with States supporting a broader limit stated that the contracting parties retained 'their rights and claims'.[10]

---

[8] With the Act of 2 March 1799, providing for customs jurisdiction up to four leagues corresponding to 12 nm.

[9] The text of the conventions between the United States and the United Kingdom of 23 January 1924 (hereinafter 1924 USA–UK Convention) and between the United States and Norway of 24 May 1924 (hereinafter 1924 USA–Norway Convention) is, with references to the other conventions similar to one or the other, in *United Nations Legislative Series, Laws and Regulations on the Regime of the Territorial Sea* (United Nations New York 1957) 784.

[10] Respectively, 1924 USA–UK Convention, n 9, Art 1, and 1924 USA–Norway Convention, n 9, Art 1.

3 THE ATTEMPTS AT CODIFICATION BEFORE WORLD WAR II

At the beginning of the twentieth century, the law of the sea had attained a certain degree of stability. It was based on a few customary rules, providing for the recognition of two distinct maritime zones: the territorial sea and the high seas. Within the territorial sea, a narrow band of sea adjacent to the coast, coastal States exercised sovereignty, with some restrictions, consisting mainly in the obligation to recognize a right of innocent passage of foreign vessels. On the high seas, the principle was that of freedom of all States, exercised through vessels flying their flag. Certain functional rights beyond the limits of the territorial sea were nonetheless recognized to coastal States. These were the right of hot pursuit on the high seas and enforcement rights concerning, especially, customs matters within a narrow zone contiguous to the territorial sea.

After World War I, the changes in world power structures, and the beginnings of a multilateral institutionalized approach to international law and relations embraced by the League of Nations, were reflected in the need to introduce precision in the existing customary rules on the law of the sea, and to solve the main question on which there was a clear difference of opinion between States, that of the breadth of the territorial sea.

So the idea emerged of codifying the international rules on the law of the sea, or at least those dealing with certain aspects of the matter. Particularly important were the attempts made in the scholarly circles of the Harvard Research on International Law and of the Institut de Droit International and the more official one made in the framework of the League of Nations and culminating in the 1930 Hague Conference on the Codification of International Law.[11]

None of these attempts had the ambition to cover the whole of the law of the sea as we now conceive it. The Harvard Research produced two drafts, concerning the territorial sea (1929) and piracy (1932).[12] The Institut de Droit International produced, in 1928, a resolution on the territorial sea and a resolution on the regime of sea-going

---

[11] Hague Conference on the Codification of International Law (1930), *Acts of the Conference for the Codification of International Law, March 13–April 12, 1930*, 2 vols, League of Nations Doc Nos C.351.M.145.1930.V, 2 vols (1930); C.351(a).M.145(a).1930.V (1930), and Vol 1, Suppl., Doc No C.73.M.38.1929.V (1929); S Rosenne, *League of Nations Conference on the Codification of International Law (1930)* (Oceana Publications Dobbs Ferry NY 1975) (hereinafter Conference by the Preparatory Committee).

[12] Respectively, in 'Territorial Waters' (1929) 23 *American Journal of International Law Special Suppl* 243, and 'Part IV: Piracy' (1932) 26 *American Journal of International Law Special Suppl* 739.

vessels and their crews in foreign ports in time of peace.[13] Within the framework of the International Law Association (ILA), the Chilean jurist Alejandro Alvarez presented, in 1924, a pioneering proposal concerning the territorial sea of groups of islands, which may be seen as the first manifestation of the concept of archipelagic waters.[14] This proposal, although unsuccessful in the ILA, found some echo in the 1928 Resolution of the Institut.[15] The work under the aegis of the League of Nations began with studies on four law of the sea subjects, namely, territorial waters, the status of government ships, the suppression of piracy, and rules on the exploitation of the products of the sea. However, only territorial waters were discussed at the 1930 Hague Conference.

The unresolved problem of the breadth of the territorial sea was recognized in the Harvard Research and in the Institut's work. The drafts they produced endorsed the 3 nm limit, but acknowledged that 3 miles was just the breadth preferred by a majority of States and that other States strongly opposed it. Disagreement on the breadth of the territorial sea was the cause of the lack of success of the Hague Conference. The Conference worked on the basis of 28 'bases for discussion' (draft articles with commentaries based on the replies to a questionnaire by a number of States).[16] Base for discussion No 3 stated that the 'breadth of the territorial waters under the sovereignty of the coastal State is three nautical miles'.[17] Yet the 'Observations' accompanying the text state that while some States regarded 'the above formula as an accurate and sufficient statement of existing international law', others supported strongly 'the claim of sovereign rights over more than three miles'—a claim 'admitted by some and categorically rejected by other States'.[18] A 'Basis of Discussion', although noting divergences in views, accepted the idea that groups of islands not separated by more than double the territorial sea width from each other could have a territorial sea measured from the outermost islands of the group, while the waters 'included within the group' would be territorial waters.[19]

The Conference could not adopt a draft convention. It only adopted a recommendation containing, in an annex, a draft of 13 articles on the legal status of the territorial sea, as all the other provisions discussed were linked to the question of its breadth. In addition to the above-mentioned Resolution, the Conference adopted recommendations on inland waters and on the protection of fisheries. It furthermore recommended to the League that preparatory work for a new conference on the breadth of the territorial sea should be pursued and a conference convened when opportune.

---

[13] Institut de Droit International, Session de Stockholm, Resolution II, 'Règlement sur le régime des navires de mer et de leurs équipages dans les ports étrangers en temps de paix' (1928), available at <http://www.idi-iil.org/idiF/resolutionsF/1928_stock_02_fr.pdf> (hereinafter Resolution II of 1928 at Stockholm).
[14] International Law Association, *Report of the 33rd Conference 1924, Stockholm* (Sweet and Maxwell London 1924) 259.
[15] See Resolution II of 1928 at Stockholm, n 13, Art 5.
[16] Bases of discussion drawn up for the Conference by the Preparatory Committee, n 11, 10ff.
[17] Ibid, 26. [18] Ibid. [19] Ibid, 35.

The three attempts at codification were aimed at producing drafts for possible conventions, but the time was not ripe for reaching this objective. The modesty of the results of the Hague Conference notwithstanding, these three attempts in the post-World War I decades have provided the basis of further codification work pursued later in more favourable circumstances. Scholarly work conducted on the basis of these attempts, especially Gilbert Gidel's monumental work on 'Public International Law of the Sea'[20] and the involvement of Gidel and of the League of Nations Rapporteur on the territorial sea, the Dutch Professor JPA François, in work for the codification of the law of the sea conducted after World War II, emphasizes the connection of the apparently unsuccessful attempt under the aegis of the League with the much more successful codification work under the aegis of the United Nations.

The Hague Conference and the work conducted for its preparation (as well as the work of the Harvard Research and of the Institut) identified questions and indicated possible solutions that form part and parcel of today's international law of the sea. The most important of these comprise: the exercise of sovereignty in the territorial sea; the baseline for the determination of the breadth of the territorial sea including consideration of the presence of bays and islands; straits; the difference between inland and territorial waters; innocent passage of foreign vessels (including military ones) through the territorial sea; criminal and civil jurisdiction on vessels passing through the territorial sea and in port; and the right of hot pursuit from the territorial waters into the high seas. The materials collected, in particular the responses to the questionnaires submitted to States by the Committee of Experts of the League of Nations, as well as the debates at the Hague Conference, are an invaluable trove of materials on the views of States in that time. They show that while the generally accepted basis of the international law of the sea remained that expressed in the few simple rules of customary international law mentioned above, the development of maritime activities in the early twentieth century had led to the formation of more detailed rules, or required that States agree on such formation.

The Hague Conference also showed that States were aware of the main dilemma of all 'codification' work, namely, to use the contemporary terminology based on the UN Charter, the difference between 'codification' in the strict sense of the term and 'progressive development'. In the terminology of the League, in discussions on codification reference was made to the differences between mere 'registration' of existing rules and 'innovation' or 'adaptation to contemporary conditions of international life'. The League of Nations Resolution of 1927 recommended that codification 'should not confine itself to the mere registration of the existing rules, but should aim at adapting them as far as possible to contemporary conditions of international life'.[21]

---

[20] G Gidel, *Le droit international public de la mer: Le temps de paix* (Mellottée Chateauroux 1932).
[21] League of Nations Assembly Resolution of 24 September 1927, (1927) 53 *League of Nations Official Journal (Special Supplement)* 9, repr in (1947) 41 *American Journal of International Law Supplement* 105.

4 THE CLAIMS TO EXPAND THE COASTAL STATE'S JURISDICTION AFTER WORLD WAR II

Already in the 1930s, a number of States recognized that sovereignty over the territorial sea was not sufficient to ensure the proper conservation of fisheries in the areas adjacent to it. There was nonetheless widespread reluctance to entrust the subject to unilateral decision making by the coastal State. As Gidel remarked, 'the establishment of rules on fisheries applicable beyond the territorial sea to nationals and foreigners must not be left to be fixed autonomously by the coastal State' as, undoubtedly, 'extremist' and 'arbitrary' measures would result.[22] It was equally clear that contiguous zone rights could not apply to fisheries.[23]

The two Proclamations adopted by United States President Truman on 28 September 1945 (Truman Proclamations) marked a turning point towards the acceptance of coastal States' claims to exclusive rights beyond the limit of the territorial sea. They concerned respectively the 'Natural Resources of the Subsoil and the Seabed of the Continental Shelf' and 'the Policy of the United States with Respect to Coastal Fisheries in Certain Areas of the High Seas'.[24]

The Continental Shelf Proclamation is more radical than the Fisheries Proclamation. It was precipitated by the increased importance of oil resources, underscored by the necessities of World War II and by the development of exploration and exploitation technology. It was a claim that the natural resources of the subsoil and seabed of the continental shelf beneath the high seas but contiguous to the coasts of the United States 'appertain' to it under its jurisdiction and control. It went beyond what had hitherto been accepted in international law, with the exception of the immediate precedent of the 1942 Treaty between Great Britain and Venezuela Relating to the Submarine Areas of the Gulf of Paria.[25] In this treaty each of the two States recognized the 'rights

---

[22] Gidel, n 20, Vol III, 468.
[23] Ibid, Vol III, 473. In the French original:

Le droit international ne reconnait pas les intérêts de pêche comme susceptibles de servir de base à l'institution en cette matière d'une zone contiguë par la déclaration unilatérale de l'Etat riverain.

In 1959 the Cuban jurist and diplomat Garcia Amador, examining possible extensions of coastal States' fishery rights through the notion of the contiguous zone, stated that: 'the monopoly over or exclusive exploitation of the resources of the sea was entirely foreign to the purpose for which the establishment of this zone could be permitted'. See G Amador, *The Exploitation and Conservation of the Resources of the Sea* (2nd edn AW Sythoff Leydon 1959) 65.

[24] Proclamation No 2267 (1945) 12 *Federal Register* 12303; Proclamation No 2668 (1945) 12 *Federal Register* 12305; AV Lowe and SAG Talmon, *The Legal Order of the Oceans. Basic Documents on the Law of the Sea* (Hart Oxford/Portland 2009) 19, 20.

[25] 1942 Treaty between Great Britain and Northern Ireland and Venezuela Relating to the Submarine Areas of the Gulf of Paria; Lowe and Talmon, n 24, 16.

of sovereignty or control' of the other over an area delimited by an agreed line and extending beyond the 3 nm limit of the territorial sea of the two States.

The Truman Proclamation on fisheries, although trying to meet the 'pressing need' for conservation of fisheries resources in high seas waters contiguous to the coasts of the United States, remained much closer to traditional international law. The claim to exclusivity was limited to regulation and control. It did not apply to the resources as such. Moreover, it was put forward only in circumstances where it did not clash with other States' interests and for areas in which fisheries had been conducted by United States fishermen alone. Outside these areas, fisheries would have to be regulated through agreements between the United States and other States engaged in fishing therein.

Both Proclamations underline the 'character of high seas' of, respectively, the waters above the continental shelf and the areas in which the conservation zones were established and state that 'the right of free and unimpeded navigation' was 'in no way affected'.

Seen from Latin America, the two proclamations were welcome as an opening to the extension of the coastal States' control over resources beyond the limits of the territorial sea. It soon appeared, however, that the different regimes set out for the—primarily—mineral resources of the continental shelf and for the living resources of the waters adjacent to the coasts were tailored to the needs of the United States, a country with a sizable continental shelf and important fisheries interests off the coasts of other (especially Latin American) States.

Latin American States endowed with continental shelves, such as Argentina and Mexico, as well as some States in other areas of the world, were quick in following the United States in proclaiming sovereign rights on their continental shelves. They also proclaimed similar rights in the waters above the continental shelf. This was the notion of the 'epicontinental sea'. South American States with coasts on the Pacific had no extended continental shelves as the seabed adjacent to their coasts dropped abruptly towards the abyssal plains. They felt the injustice of the lack of the opportunity to exploit mineral resources and considered that they needed compensation.[26] Whaling by foreign vessels in the waters adjacent to their territorial seas was one of their main concerns. So, in 1947, Chile and Peru, invoking the Truman Proclamations and the Mexican and Argentinian proclamations, adopted enactments proclaiming their sovereignty and jurisdiction over the seabed as well as in the superjacent waters up to a limit of 200 nm from the coast. The right of free navigation (specified in the Chilean proclamation to be 'on the high seas') was not to be affected. On 18 August 1952, Chile and Peru, together with Ecuador, adopted at Santiago de Chile, a Declaration (Santiago Declaration)[27] which, after stating

---

[26] A de Ulloa, *Derecho internacional público* (4th edn Iberoamericanas Madrid 1957) 565ff.
[27] 1952 Declaration on the Maritime Zone (hereinafter Santiago Declaration).

that the former extensions of the territorial sea and of the contiguous zone were inadequate for the purpose of the conservation, development and exploitation of the natural resources of the maritime zones adjacent to their coasts, proclaimed 'as a norm of their international maritime policy that they each possess exclusive sovereignty and jurisdiction over the sea along the coasts of their respective countries to a minimum distance of 200 nautical miles from these coasts'. The Declaration specified that such sovereignty and jurisdiction included also the soil and subsoil corresponding to the 200 nm zone and that it was 'without prejudice to the necessary limitations to the exercise of sovereignty and jurisdiction established under international law to allow innocent and inoffensive passage through the area indicated for ships of all nations'.

The Declaration is formulated as a proclamation directed by the three participating parties to the rest of the world, and not as a treaty. This notwithstanding, it was registered as a treaty with the United Nations in 1976.[28]

The terminology and the very concepts utilized in the Santiago Declaration and in the proclamations of Latin American States are tentative and variable. They cannot be read with the precise meaning that the international law of the sea now gives them. The basic outlook adopted is that the rights claimed corresponded to those claimed by the United States for mineral resources of the continental shelf. This emerges clearly from the difference in the terminology (reproduced above) used in the Chilean and Peruvian Proclamations and in the Santiago Declaration to refer to the navigational and other rights of all States in the 200 nm zone, and to the clarifications given by representatives of the signatory countries as to the meaning of the terms 'sovereignty' and 'sovereign rights' as relating to exclusive functional rights for certain purposes.

When adopting their proclamations and the Santiago Declaration, Chile, Peru, and Ecuador were aware that their claims did not correspond to the international law of their time. The purpose was to start a process that, in the wishes of the three States, would eventually lead to the formation of new customary law. The strong protests in 1948 by the United Kingdom and the United States against the Chilean and Peruvian Proclamations, and later, against the Santiago Declaration, indicated that the main maritime powers of the time considered the claims as going beyond what was permitted by international law.

The 1950s saw another development towards the expansion of coastal States' rights. It consisted in the claims put forward in 1955 by the Philippines and in 1957 by Indonesia to draw straight lines joining the outermost islands of the archipelagos and considering the waters within such lines as internal waters. These were the seminal claims to the institution of archipelagic waters.

---

[28] UN Treaty Registration No 14758.

The claim set out in the Truman Proclamation on the continental shelf was to have a very quick impact on the evolution of the law. The more ambitious claims of the Latin American countries, as well as the archipelagic claims of the Philippines and Indonesia, took more time. Yet, about a quarter of a century after the Santiago Declaration they reached their purpose with the general acceptance of the notions of the exclusive economic zone and of archipelagic waters.

5 Codification in the Early Phase of the United Nations: The Geneva Conventions on the Law of the Sea

After World War II the United Nations assumed, under Article 13 of the Charter, the task of the progressive development and codification of international law, continuing, in a more institutionalized manner, the attempts made by the League of Nations. The International Law Commission (ILC), the body of experts entrusted with this task within the United Nations, identified, since the beginning of its work in 1949, the regime of the high seas and of the territorial sea among the topics ripe for codification, and started work on the subject in 1950. Continuity with the work conducted before World War II was stressed by the fact that the Rapporteur on the law of the sea of the Hague Conference of 1930, Professor François, was selected as Special Rapporteur. Up to the end of the Commission's work in 1956, the ILC, and the United Nations General Assembly (UNGA) that closely followed its work, proceeded through drafts concerning different aspects of the law of the sea. Only in the final report submitted to the General Assembly in 1956 were all provisions systematically ordered as one body of draft articles covering the whole of the law of the sea.

This final report was to be the main basis for the First United Nations Conference on the Law of the Sea (UNCLOS I), held in Geneva from 24 February to 27 April 1958 and convened by UNGA Resolution 1105(XI) of 21 February 1957. Attended by 86 States, the Conference followed rules of procedure similar to those of the UN General Assembly, so that, although provisions could be adopted in the Committees by simple majority, a two-thirds majority was required for adoption in Plenary. This procedural rule made it impossible to agree on the breadth of the territorial sea. While a 12 nm breadth could probably have secured approval in the competent Committee, it was clear that it could not do so in Plenary. Thus the question was left unresolved. However, the fact that one of the conventions adopted provided that the external limit of the contiguous zone could not exceed 12 nm from the baseline indicates that no breadth broader than 12 nm was acceptable for the great majority of participant States.

The UN General Assembly considered this key unresolved question, together with that of fishing limits, as worthy of further consideration, and made these the main items on the agenda of the Second United Nations Conference on the Law of the Sea (Geneva, 16 March–26 April 1960, UNCLOS II). This conference failed to achieve its objective. Among the various proposals, ranging from 3 to 200 nm maximum limits, a proposal for a 6 mile breadth of the territorial sea plus a 6 mile fishery zone adjoining it was accepted in the Committee of the Whole but failed to obtain the necessary two-thirds majority in Plenary.

UNCLOS I did not succeed in keeping the provisions on the law of the sea in one instrument. The unity of the law of the sea, reached at the final stages of the ILC's work, was lost. On 29 April 1958, as recorded in the Final Act,[29] UNCLOS I opened for signature four conventions and an optional protocol.

The adoption of four conventions and a protocol in lieu of one all-encompassing convention was conceived as a device to attract the acceptance of at least some of the Conventions by a broad number of States, thus avoiding radical reservations or the decision by certain States not to accept the all-encompassing convention because of disagreement concerning one or more of its main component parts. The fact that the CFCLR and the OPSD have attracted a number of ratifications and accessions substantially lower than the other conventions indicates that they were not acceptable to States that otherwise had no difficulty with the other conventions. Significant absences in the groups of States having ratified the TSC and the CSC indicate specific difficulties, for instance, as regards innocent passage through straits or the regime of the continental shelf.

The TSC sets out in detailed provisions the main rules on the territorial sea and the contiguous zone. Its rules consider, in particular: baselines, bays, delimitation between States whose coasts are adjacent or face each other, innocent passage, and the contiguous zone. The most controversial provisions were those of Article 16. Strong disagreements, having their roots in the Arab-Israeli conflict, were raised in respect of paragraph 4, which provided that innocent passage cannot be suspended in straits used for international navigation not only in straits connecting one part

---

[29] A/CONF.13/L.58 (29 April 1958), II *Official Records of the Third UN Conference on the Law of the Sea* 146. 1958 Convention on the Territorial Sea and the Contiguous Zone (TSC); the Convention on the High Seas (HSC); 1958 Convention on Fishing and Conservation of the Living Resources of the High Seas (CFCLR); 1958 Convention on the Continental Shelf (CSC); and 1958 Optional Protocol of Signature Concerning the Compulsory Settlement of Disputes (OPSD). The TSC entered into force on 10 September 1964; the CHS on 30 September 1962; the CFCLR on 20 March 1966; the CSC on 10 June 1964; and the OPSD on 30 September 1962. States bound by the conventions and protocol, are, as at 28 December 2013, for the TSC, 52; for the HSC, 63; for the CFCLR, 39; for the CSC, 58; for the OPSD, 38.

of the high seas to another part of the high seas, but also in straits connecting the high seas to the territorial sea of a foreign State, thus including the strait of Tiran. Second, a number of States were dissatisfied with the fact that Article 16 made innocent passage applicable to all ships without distinction as regards warships. Amendments to introduce such distinction in Article 16 did not reach the necessary majority. Such majority could have been reached had the States wishing to require the coastal State's consent agreed to vote together with the States favouring prior notification.

The CHS defines the high seas as comprising all parts of the sea not included in the territorial sea and internal waters. It deals especially with: the freedoms of the high seas, the right of a State to have ships flying its flag under conditions fixed by it, stating the controversial requirement of the existence of a 'genuine link' and the rights and obligations of the flag State, piracy, the right of visit, hot pursuit and the laying of submarine cables and pipelines. It also contains two pioneering provisions on pollution by the discharge of oil and radioactive wastes.

The CFCLR sets out principles and mechanisms for the rational management of fisheries in the high seas. It insists on cooperation between States engaged in the same fisheries, recognizes the special interest of the coastal State for fisheries in the high seas adjacent to its territorial sea, and provides for compulsory settlement of disputes concerning all the key rules. At the time of its adoption, the CFCLR was very controversial, as demonstrated by the low number of ratifications and accessions. For States keen on exclusive fishery rights beyond the territorial sea, a regime for fisheries on the high seas beyond the external limit of the territorial sea was not satisfactory. Moreover, most States at the time were not ready to accept the central role recognized by this Convention to compulsory settlement of disputes.

The CSC sets out rules on the notion, limits, and regime of the continental shelf. The basic concept of the sovereign rights of the coastal State as regards to resources of an area of the seabed beyond the external limit of the territorial sea had emerged in State practice only since 1945. It has been rightly said[30] that the CSC 'crystallizes' the result of a relatively quick process of formation of a customary rule emerging from practice just about a decade old (in particular the Truman Proclamation and the Treaty on the Gulf of Paria). This rule also includes the notion that the rights of the coastal State over the shelf do not require occupation or express proclamation. The provision on the external limit, based on the 200 meters isobath and on exploitability, was soon seen as obsolete in light of technological progress and was radically modified in the 1982 Convention.

---

[30] *North Sea Continental Shelf (Federal Republic of Germany v Denmark; Federal Republic of Germany v The Netherlands)* [1969] ICJ Rep 3, [63]. See also E Jiménez de Aréchaga, 'International Law in the Past Third of a Century' (1978) 159 *Recueil des Cours* 9, 12, 14, and 16–18.

The OPSD, of which only States parties to at least one of the Geneva Conventions can become parties, provides for compulsory jurisdiction of the ICJ for all disputes concerning the interpretation or application of the Conventions, unless the parties to the dispute agree to arbitration or conciliation. This Protocol has never been applied. The modest number of parties it has attracted shows that compulsory settlement of disputes in law of the sea matters, if it is to be practically relevant, must be an integral part of the instrument dealing with substance, a lesson learned by UNCLOS III in drafting the 1982 LOSC.

The importance of the Geneva Conventions is currently mostly historical, as an expression of the 'traditional law of the sea', namely of the law prevailing before the transformations in the international community and in the uses of the seas that brought about the UNCLOS III (1973–1982). They were influenced by the work conducted during the 1930s and by the Truman Proclamations. The trend already manifest especially in Latin America, for the extension of the coastal State's jurisdiction to a wide area beyond the territorial sea, already quantified in 200 miles, was rejected notwithstanding the strong support of Latin American representatives. Similarly, the claims for the recognition of the archipelagic waters concept did not find an echo in the Geneva Conventions.

The Geneva Conventions were adopted less than a decade before the famous speech by Arvid Pardo at the UN General Assembly in 1967 that started the process for the complete renewal of the law of the sea, and they entered into force just a few years before that event. This explains why they were soon seen by a majority of States as obsolete, as evidenced by the fact that ratifications and accessions deposited after entry into force were very few. Under Article 311(1) of the LOSC, the latter instrument 'shall prevail, as between States Parties, over the Geneva Conventions on the Law of the Sea of 29 April 1958'. As the 166 parties to the LOSC include most of the States bound by the Geneva Conventions, the latter conventions remain binding only as between, or in the relationships with, the few States that are parties to the relevant Geneva Convention and not to the 1982 Convention. These States include the United States, Colombia, Israel, and Venezuela.

Many provisions of the Geneva Conventions, at the time of their adoption, corresponded to customary international law. This seems particularly true as regards the HSC, most of which has been transposed into the 1982 Convention. The HSC preamble explicitly states that its purpose is 'to codify the rules of international law relating to the high sea'. This provision is not repeated in the other Conventions in which 'codification' was difficult to disentangle from 'progressive development'. Still, a number of provisions in the TSC, could, and still can, be seen as corresponding to customary law. Moreover, the basic provisions of the CSC, with the exception of those on the outer limit, have been indicated as contributing to the 'crystallization' of the customary notion of the continental shelf and still correspond to customary law.

6 The Contribution of International Courts and Tribunals to the Development of the Law of the Sea, from the End of the Nineteenth Century to the Aftermath of the Geneva Conventions

The development of the international law of the sea in the decades leading up to UNCLOS III cannot be fully understood without considering the impact of the decisions of international courts and tribunals in this area. This period is characterized by a growing reliance of States on international courts and tribunals including for disputes concerning law of the sea matters. In the early decades of this period, States relied on arbitral tribunals, while, with the establishment of the Permanent Court of International Justice after World War I, and of the International Court of Justice after World War II, permanent bodies played a pre-eminent role. The contribution of international courts and tribunals is, admittedly, unsystematic, as it arises from cases relating to specific situations and requiring the application of particular treaties. Still, specific situations stimulate exploration by both parties and judges of the scope of general rules as well as of their content. They may also throw light on the insufficiencies of existing customary law. Moreover, they have an impact on the codification process by focusing attention on new issues, proposing solutions sometimes followed, and sometimes contrasted by, codification conventions.

One early example of a statement of a customary rule is the *Muscat Dhows* arbitration between France and Great Britain. In the 1905 award, it is stated that 'it belongs to every Sovereign to decide to whom he will accord the right to fly his flag and to prescribe the rules governing such grants'.[31] This rule is the point of departure for that set out in the 1958 HSC (Articles 4 and 5) and later in the LOSC (Articles 91–92).

In the SS '*Lotus*' judgment of 1927, the Permanent Court of International Justice formulated the idea of the freedom of the high seas and its connection with the exclusive right of the flag State: 'vessels on the high seas are subject to no authority except that of the State whose flag they fly. In virtue of the principle of the freedom of the seas, that is to say, the absence of any territorial sovereignty upon the high seas, no State may exercise any kind of jurisdiction over foreign vessels upon them'.[32]

---

[31] *Muscat Dhows (France/Great Britain)* (PCA 1905) (1961) XI RIAA 83.
[32] *SS 'Lotus' (France v Turkey)* (Judgment) (1927) PCIJ Ser A, No 10, 25.

The Court specified however, that from this it 'by no means' followed 'that a State can never in its own territory exercise jurisdiction over acts which have occurred on board a foreign ship on the high seas'.[33] The further argument made by the Court, that there was no general international law rule prohibiting Turkey from exercising jurisdiction over the French officer of a French vessel involved in a collision on the high seas with a Turkish vessel and causing a number of victims of Turkish nationality, was controversial. The ILC underscored that the judgment had been adopted with the casting vote of the President, that it had been 'very strongly criticized and caused serious disquiet in international maritime circles', and that the International Convention for the Unification of Certain Rules relating to Penal Jurisdiction in matters of Collisions and Other Incidents of Navigation, signed at Brussels on 10 May 1952, supported the exclusive jurisdiction of the flag and of the national State of the accused. In view of the *SS 'Lotus'* judgment, the ILC 'felt obliged to take a decision'. 'With the object of protecting ships and their crews from the risk of penal proceedings before foreign courts', it concurred with the 1952 Convention.[34] Article 11 of the CHS and Article 97 of LOSC followed it adopting the view rejected by the PCIJ.

An example of the interaction between decisions of international courts and tribunals and the codification process is the *Corfu Channel* case between the United Kingdom and Albania.[35] In its 1949 judgment, the ICJ stated the rules concerning the duties of the coastal State as regards innocent passage through its territorial sea including the one according to which the coastal State has the duty to give appropriate publicity to dangers of navigation of which it has knowledge in the territorial sea. This rule was based 'on certain general and well-recognized principles, namely: elementary considerations of humanity, even more exacting in peace than in war; the principle of the freedom of maritime communication; and every State's obligation not to allow knowingly its territory to be used for acts contrary to the rights of other States'.[36] Stating these rules in the draft article that was to become Article 15 of the TSC, the ILC explicitly said that it confirmed the 'principles upheld' in the *Corfu Channel* judgment.[37]

In the same judgment, the Court had to deal with the (then and now) controversial issue of whether innocent passage through the territorial sea applies to warships. It did not find it necessary to take a stand on this question.[38] Having determined that the Corfu Channel was a strait used for international navigation, it considered sufficient to state that it was 'generally recognized and in accordance with international custom that States in time of peace have a right to send their warships

---

[33] Ibid.

[34] 'Report of the International Law Commission to the General Assembly: Commentary to the Articles Concerning the Law of the Sea' (1956) II *Yearbook of the International Law Commission* 253, 281 (hereinafter ILC Commentary).

[35] *Corfu Channel (United Kingdom v Albania)* [1949] ICJ Rep 4.   [36] Ibid, 22.

[37] ILC Commentary, n 34, 273.   [38] *Corfu Channel*, n 35, 30.

through straits used for international navigation between two parts of the high seas without the previous authorization of a coastal State, provided that the passage is innocent'.[39] This formulation was followed in the ILC's draft articles submitted to the Geneva Conference (Article 17(4)), while the corresponding rule of the TSC (Article 16(4)) added the controversial mention of straits connecting one portion of the high seas with a territorial sea.

A case in which a judicial formulation of the law was followed in codification conventions is the *Anglo-Norwegian Fisheries* case.[40] The 1951 ICJ judgment states that 'for the purpose of measuring the breadth of the territorial sea, it is the low-water mark as opposed to the high-water mark, or the mean between the two tides, which has generally been adopted in the practice of States'.[41] Confronted with the existence of deep indentations and the fringe of islands constituting the Norwegian *skjærgaard*, the court held that, as the latter 'constitutes a whole with the mainland, it is the outer line of the "skjærgaard" which must be taken into account in delimiting the belt of Norwegian territorial waters'. And specified that where 'a coast is deeply indented and cut into... or where it is bordered by an archipelago such as the "skjærgaard"... the base-line becomes independent of the low-water mark, and can only be determined by means of a geometrical construction'. Such method is that of straight baselines.[42] As 'the delimitation of sea areas has always an international aspect [and] it cannot be dependent merely upon the will of the coastal State as expressed in its municipal law',[43] the judgment states 'criteria' to guide courts in assessing the compatibility of straight baselines with international law. First, 'the drawing of base-lines must not depart to any appreciable extent from the general direction of the coast'. Second, the lines must be 'sufficiently closely linked to the land domain to be subject to the regime of internal waters'. Moreover, 'one consideration not to be overlooked' concerns the existence 'of certain economic interests peculiar to a region, the reality and importance of which are clearly evidenced by a long usage'.[44]

The impact of this judgment on the codification process and on the clarification of customary law is beyond doubt. The ILC stated that it 'interpreted the Court's judgement... as expressing the law in force' and that 'it accordingly drafted the article on the basis of this judgment'.[45] The language of the Court is repeated in Article 5 of the ILC draft and with some additions in Articles 4 of the TSC and 7 of LOSC.

There are cases in which international courts and tribunals found that customary law failed to regulate a question with sufficient precision and opened the way for the codification process to provide such precision. The criteria for defining the shape required for a bay to be enclosed in internal waters and the maximum length of the

---

[39] Ibid, 28.
[40] *Fisheries (United Kingdom v Norway)* (Judgment) [1951] ICJ Rep 116 (hereinafter *Anglo-Norwegian Fisheries*).
[41] Ibid, 128.   [42] Ibid, 128–9.   [43] Ibid, 132.   [44] Ibid, 133.
[45] ILC Commentary, n 34, 267.

closing line provide an example. The 1910 arbitral award in the *United States v United Kingdom* case regarding *North Atlantic Coast Fisheries*, while indicating in general terms the conditions for the control of a bay, stated that 'no principle of international law recognizes any specified relation between the concavity of the bay and the requirements for control by the territorial sovereignty'.[46] In the above-quoted *Anglo-Norwegian Fisheries* judgment of 1951, the ICJ stated that:

[A]lthough the ten-mile rule has been adopted by certain States both in their national law and in their treaties and conventions, and although certain arbitral decisions have applied it as between these States, other States have adopted a different limit. Consequently, the ten-mile rule has not acquired the authority of a general rule of international law.[47]

In Article 7 of its 1956 draft, the ILC proposed precise rules on both aspects and underlined that:

In adopting this provision, the Commission repaired the omission to which attention had already been drawn by The Hague Codification Conference of 1930 and which the International Court of Justice again pointed out in its judgement in the Fisheries Case.[48]

The Article was repeated with some additions in Article 7 of the TSC and in Article 10 of LOSC, both substituting 24 miles for the 15 proposed by the ILC. It is noteworthy that in its 1992 judgment in the *Land and Maritime Frontier* case, the ICJ stated that these provisions 'might be found to express general customary law'.[49]

The 1974 ICJ judgments on the *Fisheries Jurisdiction* cases, between the United Kingdom and the Federal Republic of Germany on the one hand and Iceland on the other, provide another example in which judicial decisions became intertwined with codification processes.[50] The ICJ went beyond what was decided at Geneva, but did not dare to take fully into account the contemporaneous developments brought in full view by the beginning of the UNCLOS III. While acknowledging that the Geneva Conferences of 1958 and of 1960 had failed to adopt a decision on the breadth of the territorial sea and on fishery zones, the Court observed that, after the 1960 Conference:

[T]he law evolved through the practice of States on the basis of the debates and near-agreements at the Conference. Two concepts have crystallized as customary law in recent years arising out of the general consensus revealed at that Conference. The first is the concept of the fishery zone, the area in which a State may claim exclusive fishery jurisdiction independently of its territorial sea; the extension of that fishery zone up to a 12-mile limit from the baselines appears now to be generally accepted. The second is the concept of

---

[46] *North Atlantic Coast Fisheries (Great Britain v United States of America)* (Award) (1910) XI RIAA 167, available at <http://www.pcacases.com/web/sendAttach/496> (see page 24).
[47] *Anglo-Norwegian Fisheries*, n 40, 131.   [48] ILC Commentary, n 34, 269.
[49] *Land, Islands and Maritime Frontier Dispute (El Salvador v Honduras: Nicaragua Intervening)* (Judgment) [1992] ICJ Rep 351, [383].
[50] *Fisheries Jurisdiction (United Kingdom of Britain and Northern Ireland v Iceland)* (Merits) [1974] ICJ Rep 3; *Fisheries Jurisdiction (Federal Republic of Germany v Iceland)* (Merits) [1974] ICJ Rep 175.

preferential rights of fishing in adjacent waters in favour of the coastal State in a situation of special dependence on its coastal fisheries, this preference operating in regard to other States concerned in the exploitation of the same fisheries.[51]

The Court decided the disputes brought against Iceland on the basis of these two concepts, in which it saw new rules of customary law. It acknowledged that at UNCLOS III (started during the ICJ proceedings) many proposals had been made for an extension of fishery limits beyond 12 miles. These were, however, in the view of the Court, mere aspirations 'not expressing principles of existing law'.[52] The Court could not rely on them as this would mean deciding *de lege ferenda* 'or anticipate the law before the legislator has laid it down'.[53] It seems difficult to deny that—as stated in a separate opinion of six judges—the numerous proposals put forward at UNCLOS III for the adoption of extended fisheries zones should have had an impact. The six judges stated in particular that:

The least that can be said ... is that such declarations and statements and the written proposals submitted by representatives of States are of significance to determine the views of those States as to the law on fisheries jurisdiction and their *opinio iuris* on a subject regulated by customary law.[54]

In assessing the role played by international courts and tribunals in the aftermath of the Geneva conventions, the 1969 ICJ judgments on the *North Sea Continental Shelf* cases are particularly relevant.[55] First, arguing from the fact that no reservations are allowed to Articles 1 to 3 of the CSC, the Court states that these articles were in 1958 'regarded as reflecting, or crystallizing, received or at least emergent rules of customary international law'.[56] The judgment lists the issues covered by these articles, including 'the seaward extent of the continental shelf': an issue on which the rule set out in the CSC was soon to appear as inadequate and was to be replaced by the different one of Article 76 of LOSC.

Second, and principally, the Court dealt with the question whether the 'equidistance-special circumstances' rule set out in Article 6 of the CSC for the delimitation of the continental shelf between States whose coasts are opposite or adjacent corresponded to customary law. The answer was in the negative. The Court stated that the 'delimitation has to be effected by agreement in accordance with equitable principles and taking into account all the relevant circumstances'.[57] This judgment was influential on the subsequent judgments of the Court, and on negotiations at the Third UN Conference on the Law of the Sea. Still, starting with the

---

[51] *Fisheries Jurisdiction (United Kingdom v Iceland)*, n 50, 23 [52].
[52] Ibid, 23 [53].   [53] Ibid, 23–4 [53].
[54] Ibid, 46 [13] (Joint separate opinion of Judges Foster, Bengzon, Jiménez de Aréchaga, Nagendra Singh, and Ruda).
[55] *North Sea Continental Shelf (Federal Republic of Germany v Denmark; Federal Republic of Germany v The Netherlands)* (Judgment) [1969] ICJ Rep 3.
[56] Ibid, 39 [63].   [57] Ibid, 53 [101, C.1].

1977 *Anglo-French Continental Shelf* arbitral award, courts came to recognize that the distance between Article 6 of the CSC and customary law was narrow. The 1977 award stated that:

[T]he role of the 'special circumstances' condition in Article 6 is to ensure an equitable delimitation; and the combined 'equidistance-special circumstances' rule, in effect, gives particular expression to a general norm that, failing agreement, the boundary between States abutting on the same continental shelf is to be determined on equitable principles.[58]

As is well known, the post-LOSC jurisprudence has come to recognize that the 'equitable principles-relevant circumstances' it now adopts is 'very similar' to the Geneva 'equidistance-special circumstances' rule.[59]

7 Conclusion

Through the centuries the law of the sea has been a battleground in which the interests of the main maritime powers have measured their strength and, at the same time, a laboratory for the development of international law rules. From the beginning of its evolution up to the mid-twentieth century, the international law of the sea, although applying to all the seas of the world, remained mostly Eurocentric, or Euro/North American-centric. The basic legal concepts and technique that made the essence of this branch of international law were, nonetheless, strong and resilient enough to adapt to the broadening to all States of the world of the community directly interested in the law of the sea and to the extension of maritime activities, and the changing priorities between them, beyond the traditional ones, which marked the post-colonial and post-Geneva era of the law of the sea.

Reliance on customary law in combination with a growing network of conventional rules and on the contribution made by codification efforts and international judgments and awards, developed in the traditional law of the sea provided the legal framework for the nuanced, and changing, degrees of coastal State exclusive rights on areas adjacent to the coasts, for the notions of the freedoms of the sea and of the exercise of such freedoms without prejudice to the corresponding freedoms of other States in the high seas, for the requirement of cooperation and the benefits of international adjudication. With necessary additions, such as the notion of the common

---

[58] *Arbitration between the United Kingdom of Great Britain and Northern Ireland and the French Republic on the Delimitation of the Continental Shelf* (1977) XVIII RIAA 3, 45 [70].

[59] *Land and Maritime Boundary between Cameroon and Nigeria (Cameroon v Nigeria: Equatorial Guinea Intervening)* (Judgment) [2002] ICJ Rep 303, [288].

heritage, the traditional legal framework and technique could adapt to encompass the coastal States' claims to exclusive rights over broad areas of the sea and combine these claims with the needs of international communication and with those of intensified and more institutionalized cooperation for the exploitation of common resources and the protection of the marine environment which characterize the law of the sea of the final decades of the twentieth century and of today.

2

THE 1982 UNITED NATIONS CONVENTION ON THE LAW OF THE SEA

ROBIN R CHURCHILL

1 Introduction

THE United Nations Convention on the Law of the Sea (LOSC)[1] is without doubt the most important source of the international law of the sea, although it is by no means the only source, as will become evident in later chapters of this book. The LOSC regulates, in greater or lesser detail, almost every possible activity on, in, under, and over the sea. No attempt will be made in this chapter to discuss the substantive provisions of the LOSC: that will be done in the following chapters. Instead, this chapter deals with the history and legal characteristics of the LOSC. Thus, it explains how the LOSC came into being; gives a brief overview of its provisions and considers their varying legal nature; explains which entities may and have become parties to the LOSC and considers the extent to which they are permitted to make reservations and declarations; outlines the relationship of the LOSC to other treaties and customary international law; explores the mechanisms for seeking to

---

[1] 1982 United Nations Convention on the Law of the Sea (hereinafter LOSC).

ensure compliance with the LOSC by its States parties; and finally discusses how the LOSC is kept under review and developed.

2 The Genesis, Adoption, and Entry into Force of the LOSC

As recounted at the end of the previous chapter, the UN General Assembly decided in 1970 to hold a Third United Nations Conference on the Law of the Sea (UNCLOS III) to 'deal with the establishment of an equitable international regime' for the resources of the seabed and subsoil beyond the limits of national jurisdiction and 'a broad range of related issues'.[2] By 1973, the mandate of the Conference had become to 'adopt a convention dealing with all matters relating to the law of the sea'.[3] The Conference met in 11 sessions, each (apart from the first) of several weeks' duration, between 1973 and 1982.[4] The Conference worked in a very different way from the First United Nations Conference on the Law of the Sea (UNCLOS I), held in 1958. First, it had before it no set of draft articles prepared by the International Law Commission. Instead, there was a mass of often conflicting proposals put forward both by States individually and by groups of States to promote their common interest. Such groups included not only those traditionally operating in international fora, such as the Group of 77, but also groups formed especially for the Conference, such as the Group of Landlocked and Geographically Disadvantaged States and the Group of Archipelagic States.[5] Many of the Conference negotiations, in fact, took place informally and off the record within and between such groups.[6] UNCLOS III was thus far more politicized than UNCLOS I. Over the course of the Third Conference, the numerous proposals made by States

---

[2] UNGA Res 2570C (XXV) (1970) [2]. UN General Assembly resolutions may be found at <http://www.un.org/en/ga/68/resolutions.shtml>.

[3] UNGA Res 3067 (XXVIII) (1973) [3].

[4] For detailed studies of the Conference negotiations, see the series of contemporaneous articles by JR Stevenson and BH Oxman in *American Journal of International Law* (1974) Vol 68, 1; (1975) Vol 69, 1 and 763; (1977) Vol 71, 247; (1978) Vol 72, 57; (1979) Vol 73, 1; (1980) Vol 74, 1; (1981) Vol 75, 211; and (1982) Vol 76, 1; JK Sebenius, *Negotiating the Law of the Sea* (Harvard University Press Cambridge MA 1984); *Virginia Commentaries*, Vol I, 29–152; and EL Miles, *Global Ocean Politics: The Decision Process at the Third United Nations Conference on the Law of the Sea 1973–82* (Martinus Nijhoff The Hague 1997). For a short serviceable account, see J Harrison, *Making the Law of the Sea* (Cambridge University Press Cambridge 2011) 37–48.

[5] See further B Buzan, '"United We Stand..."—Informal Negotiating Groups at UNCLOS III' (1980) 4 *Marine Policy* 183.

[6] This means that when it comes to interpreting LOSC, the official *travaux préparatoires* are quite limited.

were refined into a series of negotiating texts by the chairs of each of the three (eventually four) committees between which the subject matter of the Conference was divided.

A second way in which UNCLOS III differed from UNCLOS I was in relation to the process of decision-making. Whereas UNCLOS I had adopted all decisions by majority vote, UNCLOS III decided that it would work by consensus, resorting to a vote only if all attempts at consensus had failed.[7] UNCLOS III was the first UN lawmaking conference to use consensus decision-making and did so in order to try to obtain the greatest possible support, including from both developing and developed States, for the convention that would eventually be adopted.

A third significant difference between the two conferences was that UNCLOS III decided to utilize a 'package deal' approach. This meant that the product of the Conference should be a single convention, unlike UNCLOS I which had produced four conventions, which States could (and did) selectively ratify. The package deal approach thus implied, and required, a great deal of give and take by negotiating States. It also meant that there would inevitably be a certain amount of ambiguity and lack of precision in the convention in relation to matters where negotiating States could do no better than reach a weak compromise.[8]

UNCLOS III finally reached agreement on a new treaty, the UN Convention on the Law of the Sea, in 1982. Ultimately, the Convention could not be adopted by consensus. Instead a vote was taken at the request of the USA, which on the election of President Reagan in 1980 had markedly changed its attitude to the draft Convention. This resulted in 130 votes in favour of adopting the Convention, with four votes against (Israel, Turkey, USA, and Venezuela) and 17 abstentions (mainly developed States).

Article 308 of the LOSC provided for its entry into force 12 months after the deposit of the 60th ratification. Ratifications were initially slow to materialize, but in November 1993 the 60th ratification was deposited. Of those 60 ratifications, all but two—by Iceland and Yugoslavia (which by that time had ceased to exist de facto)—were by developing States. The reason why many developed States did not ratify was because of dissatisfaction with the regime for the mining of minerals in the seabed beyond national jurisdiction contained in Part XI of the LOSC, which in several important respects was in conflict with the neoliberal economic policy that had begun to dominate in the USA and a number of other Western States since the early 1980s. A law of the sea convention to which only developing States were parties was clearly undesirable, potentially divisive, and did not meet the UN General Assembly's aspirations for universal participation. The UN

---

[7] See further B Buzan, 'Negotiating by Consensus: Developments in Technique at the United Nations Conference on the Law of the Sea' (1981) 75 *American Journal of International Law* 324.

[8] Further on the package deal approach, see H Caminos and MR Molitor, 'Progressive Development of International Law and the Package Deal' (1985) 79 *American Journal of International Law* 871.

Secretary-General therefore began to explore whether there was a way of overcoming the objections of Western States to Part XI so as to encourage them to ratify the LOSC without alienating developing States. His diplomatic efforts were eventually successful and resulted in the Agreement relating to the Implementation of Part XI of the LOSC, which was adopted as an annex to UN General Assembly Resolution 48/263 in July 1994 (1994 Implementation Agreement).[9] While the Agreement is, for political reasons, an 'implementing' one in name, in reality it amends several key provisions of Part XI by baldly stating that they do not apply or that they apply with significant modifications. The changes made by the Agreement were sufficient to overcome the objections of developed States, most of which ratified the LOSC within a relatively short space of time after the adoption of the Agreement.

3 An Overview of the LOSC

The broad aim of the LOSC, according to its preamble, is to 'settle... all issues relating to the law of the sea',[10] and in particular to establish 'a legal order for the seas and oceans which will facilitate international communication, and will promote the peaceful uses of the seas and oceans, the equitable and efficient utilization of their resources, the conservation of their living resources, and the study, protection and preservation of the marine environment'.[11] The preamble goes on to state, in language that is a diminishing echo of that used by developing States when calling for the establishment of a New International Economic Order in the 1970s, that the achievement of such a legal order for the oceans 'will contribute to the realization of a just and equitable international economic order which takes into account the interests and needs of mankind as a whole and, in particular, the special interests and needs of developing countries, whether coastal or land-locked'.[12]

The LOSC seeks to achieve the above aims through 320 articles, arranged into 17 parts and supplemented by nine annexes. Part I, consisting only of Article 1, defines a number of the terms used in the LOSC: several other terms are defined in the substantive provisions. Parts II, V, and VI deal with the maritime zones that may be claimed by

---

[9] See further three articles by DH Anderson: 'Efforts to ensure Universal Participation in the UN Convention on the Law of the Sea' (1993) 42 *International and Comparative Law Quarterly* 654; 'Further Efforts to ensure Universal Participation in the United Nations Convention on the Law of the Sea' (1994) 43 *International and Comparative Law Quarterly* 886; and 'Legal Implications of the Entry into Force of the UN Convention on the Law of the Sea' (1995) 44 *International and Comparative Law Quarterly* 313. The Agreement is further discussed in Section 10 below.

[10] LOSC, n 1, Preamble, First Recital.   [11] Ibid, Fourth Recital.   [12] Ibid, Fifth Recital.

coastal States, namely the territorial sea and contiguous zone; exclusive economic zone (EEZ); and continental shelf. These Parts stipulate how such zones are to be delimited and set out the respective rights and obligations of coastal and other States therein.[13] They resolve previous uncertainties over the breadths and legal nature of coastal States' maritime zones and have put an end, at least for the foreseeable future, to the phenomenon of 'creeping jurisdiction', thereby achieving one of the main aims of UNCLOS III.[14] Part III of the LOSC is concerned with navigation through straits lying partly or wholly within the territorial sea.[15] Part VIII defines an island and stipulates how coastal State maritime zones are to be delimited from islands; while Part IV deals with that issue in relation to islands that comprise archipelagos.[16] Some provisions in Parts II, VI, and VIII are similar, or even identical, to provisions in the 1958 Territorial Sea and Continental Shelf Conventions,[17] but many others differ considerably or are concerned with matters (such as the EEZ and archipelagos) that are not addressed at all in the 1958 Conventions.

Part VII sets out the regime for the high seas, ie, the areas of sea beyond the maritime zones of coastal States.[18] Its provisions are largely identical, or similar, to the 1958 Convention on the High Seas and parts of the 1958 Convention on Fishing and Conservation of the Living Resources of the High Seas.[19] The remaining Parts of the LOSC, discussed below, are all quite new, having no equivalents in the 1958 Conventions.

Part IX of the LOSC calls for cooperation between States parties bordering enclosed or semi-enclosed seas. Part X deals with the access of landlocked States to the sea: there are also provisions elsewhere in the LOSC addressing other aspects relating to landlocked States and the sea.[20] Part XI, together with Annexes III and IV, as read with the 1994 Implementation Agreement, set out a detailed regime, based on the principle of the common heritage of mankind, governing the mining of the mineral resources found in 'the Area', ie the seabed and subsoil beyond the limits of national jurisdiction.[21] This regime is administered by a new international organization created by Part XI, the International Seabed Authority.[22]

Part XII of the LOSC is headed 'Protection and Preservation of the Marine Environment'. Considerably influenced by the Declaration and Action Plan adopted at the UN Conference on the Human Environment held at Stockholm in 1972,[23] which

---

[13] See further Chapters 4, 5, 8, and 9 in this volume.
[14] See further Chapter 1 in this volume.   [15] See further Chapter 6 in this volume.
[16] See further Chapter 7 in this volume.
[17] 1958 Convention on the Territorial Sea and the Contiguous Zone; 1958 Convention on the Continental Shelf.
[18] See further Chapter 10 in this volume.
[19] 1958 Convention on the High Seas; 1958 Convention on Fishing and Conservation of the Living Resources of the High Seas.
[20] See further Chapter 15 in this volume.   [21] See further Chapter 11 in this volume.
[22] See further Chapter 17 in this volume.
[23] Declaration and Action Plan adopted at the United Nations Conference on the Human Environment, UN Doc A/CONF.48/14/Rev 1 (1972).

for the first time placed the protection of the environment squarely on the agenda of the international community, Part XII begins by setting out some broad principles for the protection of the marine environment. The remainder of Part XII is concerned only with the prevention of marine pollution. These provisions require States parties to the LOSC to develop international norms and standards to prevent, reduce and control marine pollution from all sources, both at sea and on land, and to put in place and enforce national legislation that is no less strict than such norms and standards.[24] Part XIII is concerned with marine scientific research, stipulating the conditions under which such research may be carried out in different maritime zones and calling for cooperation in the carrying out of such research and the publication and dissemination of its results.[25] Part XIV calls on States to cooperate to promote the development and transfer of marine science and technology on fair and reasonable terms.

Unlike the Geneva Conventions, which dealt with the settlement of disputes in an optional protocol, the LOSC contains an ambitious set of provisions on dispute settlement in the body of the Convention. Part XV provides that disputes concerning the interpretation or application of the LOSC that cannot be settled by consensual means may, subject to some exceptions, be referred unilaterally by any party to the dispute to binding judicial settlement, utilizing either the International Court of Justice (ICJ); the International Tribunal for the Law of the Sea (ITLOS), a new international court established by Annex VI of the LOSC; arbitration in accordance with Annex VII; or, for certain kinds of dispute, arbitration in accordance with Annex VIII.[26] Disputes relating to Part XI are to be settled in accordance with the specialized dispute settlement provisions of that Part.

Part XVI consists of five articles dealing with a miscellaneous selection of general matters. The last Part of the LOSC, Part XVII, headed 'Final Provisions', deals with the usual kinds of matter found at the end of multilateral treaties, including signature and ratification/accession, conditions for entry into force, reservations, and amendment of the LOSC.[27]

4 The Legal Nature of the Provisions of the LOSC

The LOSC does not contain comprehensive and detailed rules regulating specific uses of the sea, such as navigation, fishing, the mining of minerals (including

---

[24] See further Chapter 23 in this volume. [25] See further Chapter 25 in this volume.
[26] See further Section 8 below and Chapters 17 and 18 in this volume.
[27] See further Sections 2, 5, 6, and 10 of this chapter.

hydrocarbons), scientific research, the laying of cables and pipelines, and so on. To have included such detailed rules (even supposing agreement could have been reached on them) would have made the LOSC completely unwieldy and liable to become quickly out of date. Instead, the LOSC sets out the legal framework within which detailed norms to regulate the various uses of the sea may be developed and applied. It does so by dividing up the sea into the various zones outlined in the preceding section. Within a coastal State's maritime zones (internal waters, archipelagic waters (in the case of archipelagic States), territorial sea, contiguous zone, EEZ, and continental shelf), the coastal State is primarily responsible for adopting and enforcing regulations governing uses of the sea, both by its nationals and the nationals of other States, subject to various obligations set out in the LOSC and other provisions of international law. On the high seas, States are to cooperate to develop regulatory norms and then apply them to ships having their nationality. In the Area, the LOSC itself provides for some detailed regulation of the mining of minerals. Further regulations are to be developed by the International Seabed Authority.[28]

The legal framework established by the LOSC is a mixture of codification and progressive development of the law, as is acknowledged in its preamble.[29] As regards codification, a number of provisions of the LOSC, as indicated above, are identical or similar to provisions of the four Geneva Conventions of 1958: some of those provisions in turn codify long-standing rules of customary international law. Most provisions of the LOSC, however, represent progressive development, either because they differ significantly from provisions of the Geneva Conventions dealing with the same issues, or because they address issues that had not been dealt with in the Geneva Conventions (or any other treaty), such as archipelagos, the EEZ, mining in the Area, marine scientific research, and the transfer of marine technology.

Whether codification or progressive development, the provisions of the LOSC are of varying normative strengths. Many are what Boyle and Chinkin call 'hard',[30] that is to say that they contain definite and specific norms, although not necessarily free of uncertainty as to their meaning, that confer rights or impose obligations on States parties. That is particularly the case with those parts of the LOSC dealing with maritime zones, the mining of minerals in the Area, and the settlement of disputes. Other provisions are, by contrast, what Boyle and Chinkin call 'soft'.[31] Thus, they call for certain forms of conduct without establishing any specific normative content, for example Articles 56(2), 58(3), and 87(2) which call on States, when exercising their rights in the EEZ and on the high seas, to have 'due regard' to the rights of other States. A particular kind of 'soft' provision is represented by the large number of LOSC articles

---

[28] See further Section 10 below and Chapter 11 in this volume.
[29] LOSC, n 1, Preamble, Seventh Recital.
[30] A Boyle and C Chinkin, *The Making of International Law* (Oxford University Press Oxford 2007) 220–2.
[31] Ibid.

calling on States to cooperate to develop norms either bilaterally (for example, the access of landlocked States to the sea[32]) or, more commonly, multilaterally (for example, in relation to fisheries conservation on the high seas, the prevention of pollution, and the transfer of marine technology[33]). It is the frequent presence of such provisions that has often led to the LOSC being described as being in part a framework treaty.

The LOSC is unusual, although not unique, in also containing what have been dubbed 'rules of reference'. These are provisions of the LOSC that require States parties to observe provisions contained in other treaties or standards adopted by international organizations, whether or not they are parties to those treaties or members of those organizations. Occasionally, such treaties and standards are identified by name: for example, ships exercising a right of transit passage through straits are required to comply with the International Regulations for Preventing Collisions at Sea.[34] More commonly, however, such treaties and standards are referred to in purely generic terms, such as 'generally accepted international regulations, procedures and practices',[35] 'internationally agreed rules, standards and recommended practices and procedures',[36] or 'generally accepted international rules and standards established through the competent international organization or general diplomatic conference'.[37] These and similar phrases, which are broad enough to cover both existing and future treaties and international standards, are found mainly in the provisions of the LOSC dealing with navigation in the territorial sea and straits, the safety and seaworthiness of ships, and the prevention of pollution. The LOSC does not define these terms or give any guidance as to which rules and standards are covered by them. The latter issue has been discussed quite widely by commentators, who have not infrequently reached differing conclusions as to what the quoted phrases embrace.[38] International courts have not yet had occasion to consider the matter.

5 Participation in the LOSC

Articles 305–307 provide that UNCLOS is open to signature and ratification/accession not only by all States, but also by three other kinds of entity. The first of

---

[32] LOSC, n 1, Art 125(2).   [33] Ibid, Arts 117–119, 207–212, and 271.
[34] Ibid, Art 39(2)(a).   [35] Eg ibid, Arts 94(5) and 212(1).   [36] Eg ibid, Art 207(1).
[37] Eg ibid, Art 211(2) and (5). '*The* competent international organization' (emphasis added) is understood as referring to the International Maritime Organization.
[38] For the most detailed study of this issue, and a survey of the existing literature up to the time of its publication, see International Law Association, 'Final Report of the Committee on Coastal State Jurisdiction relating to Marine Pollution' in *Report of the Sixty-Ninth Conference* (International Law Association London 2000) 443.

these is the UN Council for Namibia. The inclusion of the Council as a possible participant in the LOSC reflects the fact that UNCLOS was drafted and adopted at a time when the Council was administering Namibia, following the revocation by the UN of South Africa's mandate over South-West Africa (as Namibia was formerly known) in 1966 and before Namibia achieved independence in 1990. In practice, the Council both signed and ratified the LOSC. The second type of non-State entity that may become a party is a self-governing territory that is not independent but has competence over matters governed by the LOSC, including the competence to enter into treaties in respect of such matters.[39] It is not exactly clear which territories fall within that definition. In practice, two self-governing territories have become parties to the LOSC, the Cook Islands and Niue. The third kind of non-State entity that may become a party to the LOSC is an international organization to which its member States have transferred competence over matters governed by the LOSC, including the competence to enter into treaties in respect of such matters.[40] The inclusion of this provision in the LOSC is the result of heavy lobbying by the then Member States of the European Economic Community (EEC), as it then was, prompted by the fact that the early years of the negotiation of the LOSC coincided with a number of judgments of the European Court of Justice holding that the EEC had implied treaty-making powers, to the exclusion of its Member States, in relation to a number of matters that would be governed by the future LOSC.[41] In practice, only one international organization, the European Union (as the EEC has become) is currently a party to the LOSC and there seems little likelihood of any other organizations becoming parties in the near future.

One non-State entity that cannot become a party to the LOSC, as it does not meet any of the criteria in Article 305, is Taiwan, which is a significant actor in maritime affairs. At the time that the LOSC was drafted, the political climate did not favour the possibility of Taiwan becoming a party. More recently, relations between Taiwan and mainland China have become much less strained, and consequently Taiwan has been able to become a party (usually under the name 'Chinese Taipei') to a number of fisheries treaties that allow 'fishing entities' to become parties.[42]

---

[39] LOSC, n 1, Art 305, in fact, distinguishes between three different kinds of non-independent self-governing territory.

[40] The conditions under which an international organization may become a party to the LOSC are spelt out in detail in Annex IX.

[41] See T Treves, 'The EEC and the Law of the Sea: How Close to One Voice?' (1983) 12 *Ocean Development and International Law* 173. Further on participation of the EEC in the LOSC, see T Treves, 'The European Community and the Law of the Sea Convention: New Developments' in E Cannizzaro (ed), *The European Union as an Actor in International Relations* (Kluwer Law International The Hague 2002) 279.

[42] See further A Serdy, 'Bringing Taiwan into the International Fisheries Fold: The Legal Personality of a Fishing Entity' (2005) 75 *British Yearbook of International Law* 185; and the special issue of *Ocean Development and International Law*: see, in particular, N-TA Hu, 'Fishing Entities: Their Emergence,

By 2014, 163 States, all of them members of the United Nations, had become parties to the LOSC, as well as two self-governing territories (the Cook Islands and Niue) and one international organization (the European Union), making a total of 166 parties. That means that 30 Member States of the UN have not (yet) become parties to the LOSC. They comprise 14 coastal States (Cambodia, Colombia, El Salvador, Eritrea, Iran, Israel, Libya, North Korea, Peru, Syria, Turkey, the United Arab Emirates, the USA, and Venezuela) and 16 landlocked States. Even in recent years one or two States have ratified the LOSC each year, so that it may be that in the fullness of time the LOSC will attain the goal of universal participation called for by the UN General Assembly in its annual Oceans and Law of the Sea resolutions.[43]

6 Reservations and Declarations

Article 309 provides that 'no reservations or exceptions may be made to' the LOSC 'unless expressly permitted by other articles' of the LOSC.[44] The only 'reservation or exception' expressly permitted by other provisions of the LOSC appears to be in Article 298, which is headed 'Optional *exceptions* to applicability of section 2 [of Part XV]' (emphasis added) and permits States parties to exclude certain matters from the compulsory dispute settlement procedures of Section 2 of Part XV. The reason for the general prohibition on reservations in Article 309 is to preserve the 'package deal' nature of the LOSC, referred to in Section 2 above.[45]

While Article 309 in principle prohibits reservations to the LOSC, Article 310 permits a State, when signing, ratifying or acceding to the LOSC, to make a declaration or statement, 'with a view, *inter alia*, to the harmonization of its laws and regulations with the provisions of this Convention, provided that such declarations or statements do not purport to exclude or to modify the legal effect of the provisions of this Convention in their application to that State'. Declarations and statements made under Article 310 are to be distinguished from reservations, as the language

---

Evolution, and Practice from Taiwan's Perspective' (2006) 37(2) *Ocean Development and International Law* 149.

[43] See eg UNGA Res 68/70 (2013) [3].

[44] See further LDM Nelson, 'Declarations, Statements and "Disguised Reservations" with respect to the Convention on the Law of the Sea' (2001) 50 *International and Comparative Law Quarterly* 767.

[45] See the statement made by the President of the Third UN Conference on the Law of the Sea at the final session of the Conference, XVII *Official Records of UNCLOS III* (1984) 14.

of Article 310 makes clear: the quoted proviso at the end of the article echoes the definition of a reservation in the Vienna Convention on the Law of Treaties.[46]

Many States parties have availed themselves of the possibility given by Article 310 to make declarations.[47] A few declarations appear contrary to Article 310 because they do 'purport to exclude or to modify the legal effect' of certain provisions of the LOSC in their application to the State making the declaration.[48] Such declarations are in reality disguised reservations: they are therefore invalid and not opposable to other States, although they do not appear to prevent the State making the declaration from being treated as a party to the LOSC. Otherwise, it is not clear, certainly from the text of Article 310, what legal consequences, if any, attach to a valid declaration or statement. In general, they would not seem to have any legal consequences, certainly for States other than the State making the declaration. There is support for this view in the *Black Sea Case*, where the International Court of Justice stated that a declaration made by Romania relating to Articles 74 and 83 of the LOSC, concerning the delimitation of EEZ and continental shelf boundaries between opposite and adjacent States, had 'no bearing' on the Court's interpretation of those Articles.[49] The one situation where declarations made under Article 310 could have legal significance would be if there were a sufficiently large number of declarations expressing the same view of the meaning of a provision of the LOSC so that they constituted subsequent practice in the application of a treaty establishing the agreement of the parties regarding its interpretation, within the meaning of Article 31(3)(b) of the Vienna Convention on the Law of Treaties.

7 THE RELATIONSHIP OF THE LOSC TO OTHER TREATIES AND CUSTOMARY INTERNATIONAL LAW

There are a large number of treaties, both bilateral and multilateral, containing provisions that overlap with, or relate to, the subject matter of the LOSC.[50] The

---

[46] 1969 Vienna Convention on the Law of Treaties (hereinafter VCLT).
[47] The texts of such declarations are available at <http://www.un.org/depts/los/convention_agreements/convention_declarations.htm>.
[48] For examples, see Nelson, n 44.
[49] *Maritime Delimitation in the Black Sea (Romania v Ukraine)* [2009] ICJ Rep 61, 73 [42] (hereinafter *Black Sea Case*).
[50] See further Chapter 39 in this volume.

relationship between such treaties and the LOSC is dealt with by Article 311. The general effect of this provision is to claim for the LOSC a degree of superiority over other treaties, both those already existing and those that may be concluded in future. The one obvious exception to such a claim is the UN Charter. Article 103 of the latter provides that obligations under the Charter, including obligations arising from decisions of the Security Council,[51] prevail over conflicting obligations in other treaties, including therefore the LOSC.[52] In practice, there appears to be no conflict between the Charter and the LOSC; nor do there yet appear to have been any instances where decisions of the Security Council have conflicted with the LOSC. At first sight it might appear that the succession of resolutions adopted by the Security Council under Chapter VII of the Charter since 2008 authorizing other States to take enforcement action against suspected pirates in the territorial sea of Somalia[53] was incompatible with the LOSC, which provides that a State has sovereignty over its territorial sea. However, the resolutions are not incompatible as they make it clear that any enforcement action taken is with the consent of the Somali authorities.[54]

Treaties whose provisions overlap with, or relate to, the subject matter of the LOSC fall into a number of groups. A first group is the four 1958 Geneva Conventions on the law of the sea. Paragraph 1 of Article 311 provides that the LOSC prevails, as between its States parties, over those Conventions. There are still a handful of States, including the USA, that are parties to one or more of the Geneva Conventions but that are not parties to the LOSC. As between those States, the Geneva Conventions will continue to apply. That will also be the position in relations between those States and States parties to the LOSC that ratified the Geneva Conventions.[55] However, there is an important qualification to these two propositions. A treaty may be modified by the emergence of a subsequent rule of customary international law.[56] There are some provisions of the LOSC that have passed into customary international law that are inconsistent with provisions in the Geneva Conventions. Thus, the latter

---

[51] See B Simma (ed), *The Charter of the United Nations: A Commentary* (2nd edn Oxford University Press Oxford 2002) 1295–6, 1300. See also *Aerial Incident at Lockerbie case (Libyan Arab Jamahiriya v United Kingdom)* (Provisional Measures) [1992] ICJ Rep 3, 16 [39].

[52] Further on this issue, see R Churchill, 'Conflicts between UN Security Council Resolutions and the UN Convention on the Law of the Sea, and their Possible Resolution' (2008) 38 *Israel Yearbook on Human Rights* 185.

[53] UNSC Res 1816 (2008) [7]; UNSC Res 1846 (2008) [10]; UNSC Res 1897 (2009) [7]; UNSC Res 1950 (2010) [7]; UNSC Res 2020 (2011) [9]; UNSC Res 2077 (2012) [12]; and UNSC Res 2125 (2013) [12]. Security Council Resolutions may be found at <http://www.un.org/en/sc/documents/resolutions/>.

[54] See eg UNSC Res 2125 (2013) [13]. See further T Treves, 'Piracy and the International Law of the Sea' (2009) 20 *European Journal of International Law* 399, 406–8.

[55] VCLT, n 46, Art 30(4)(b).

[56] See *Fisheries Jurisdiction (United Kingdom v Iceland)* [1974] ICJ Rep 3, 24–5 [52], [54]. See also N Koutou, *The Termination and Revision of Treaties in the Light of New Customary International Law* (Clarendon Press Oxford 1994); ME Villiger, *Customary International Law and Treaties* (2nd edn Kluwer Law International The Hague 1997) ch 7.

have been modified to the extent that they are inconsistent with these new rules of customary international law. To give two examples: the ICJ has found that both the EEZ and the definition of the continental shelf in Article 76(1) of the LOSC have become part of customary international law.[57] That means that the definitions of the high seas in Article 1 of the 1958 HSC and of the continental shelf in Article 1 of the 1958 Convention on the Continental Shelf have been modified as they are inconsistent with these new rules of customary international law.

A second group of treaties are those that are expressly permitted or preserved by articles of the LOSC other than Article 311. An example of the first category can be found in Article 15 which provides that the rules for delimiting territorial sea boundaries found therein do not apply where there is a bilateral treaty between the States concerned to the contrary. An example of a treaty that is preserved by the LOSC may be found in Article 35(c), which provides that nothing in Part III (on passage through straits) affects 'the legal regime in straits in which passage is regulated in whole or in part by long-standing international conventions in force specifically relating to such straits'. Paragraph 5 of Article 311 confirms that this second group of treaties continue unaffected by the LOSC. In addition, specific provision is made elsewhere in the LOSC for treaties containing obligations on the protection and preservation of the marine environment. Article 237(1) provides that the provisions of Part XII of the LOSC 'are without prejudice to the specific obligations assumed by States under special conventions and agreements concluded previously which relate to the protection and preservation of the marine environment and to agreements which may be concluded in furtherance of the general principles set forth in [the LOSC]'. Nevertheless, paragraph 2 of Article 237 goes on to state that the obligations referred to in paragraph 1 'should be carried out in a manner consistent with the general principles and objectives' of the LOSC.

A third group of treaties whose provisions overlap with, or relate to, the subject matter of the LOSC are those that are compatible with the LOSC. In relation to such treaties, Article 311(2) provides that the LOSC shall not alter the rights and obligations of States Parties arising from such treaties that 'do not affect the enjoyment by other States Parties of their rights or the performance of their obligations under' the LOSC.

Paragraphs 3, 4, and 6 of Article 311 provide for the possibility for two or more parties to the LOSC to conclude between themselves treaties modifying or suspending the operation of provisions of the LOSC. However, this possibility is subject to strict conditions. Such *inter se* treaties must not relate to provisions derogation from which is incompatible with the effective execution of the object and purpose of the LOSC; must not affect the application of the basic principles embodied in the LOSC;

---

[57] See, respectively, *Continental Shelf (Libyan Arab Jamahiriya/Malta)* (Judgment) [1985] ICJ Rep 13, 33 [34]; *Territorial and Maritime Dispute (Nicaragua v Colombia)* (Judgment) [2012] ICJ Rep 624, [118].

must not amend the basic principle relating to the common heritage of mankind set out in Article 136; and must not affect the enjoyment by other States parties of their rights or the performance of their obligations under the LOSC. Furthermore, States parties intending to conclude such agreements must notify other States parties of that intention. In practice, no such agreements appear to have been so notified.[58]

As well as the LOSC providing for its relationship to other treaties whose provisions overlap with, or relate to, its subject matter, a number of such other treaties themselves have provisions that set out their relationship to the LOSC. Examples include four important environmental treaties adopted while the LOSC was being negotiated that provide that they are to be applied consistently with the LOSC;[59] and the later Convention on Biological Diversity, which provides that parties to that Convention are to implement it 'with respect to the marine environment consistently with the rights and obligations of States under the law of the sea'.[60] These treaties therefore reinforce the view that the LOSC is to be considered as superior to other treaties when it comes to marine matters.

Finally, the relationship between the LOSC and customary international law should be considered.[61] Some States and commentators, including the USA, take the view that the whole of the LOSC apart from Part XI represents customary international law. This seems an oversimplification. It is certainly true that many provisions of the LOSC have this character, either because they represent rules of customary international law of longstanding codified in the Geneva Conventions and repeated in the LOSC; or because they have passed into custom as a result of State practice during or subsequent to the negotiation of the LOSC, as has been recognized by international courts and tribunals.[62] However, some parts of the LOSC are simply not of a nature that can pass into customary international law: that is the case with those provisions concerning the three bodies that the LOSC establishes (the International Seabed Authority, the ITLOS, and the Commission on the Limits

---

[58] Further on such agreements, see D Freestone and AG Oude Elferink, 'Flexibility and Innovation in the Law of the Sea: Will the LOS Convention Amendment Procedures ever be used?' in AG Oude Elferink (ed), *Stability and Change in the Law of the Sea: The Role of the LOS Convention* (Martinus Nijhoff Leiden 2005) 169, 180–3.

[59] 1972 Convention on the Prevention of Marine Pollution by Dumping of Wastes and Other Matter, Art XIII; 1973 International Convention for the Prevention of Pollution from Ships, Art 9(2); 1973 Convention on International Trade in Endangered Species of Wild Fauna and Flora, Art XIV(6); 1979 Convention on the Conservation of Migratory Species of Wild Animals, Art XII(1).

[60] 1992 Convention on Biological Diversity, Art 22(2). Further on the relationship between the Convention and LOSC, see Boyle and Chinkin, n 30, 256–7.

[61] For fuller discussion of the relationship of the LOSC to customary international law, see R Bernhardt, 'Custom and Treaty in the Law of the Sea' (1987) 205 *Recueil des Cours* 251, 275–325; and T Treves, 'Codification du droit international et pratique des états dans le droit de la mer' (1990) 223 *Recueil des Cours* 9.

[62] For examples, see n 57.

of the Continental Shelf (CLCS)) and the provisions on the settlement of disputes. Furthermore, many of those provisions that were described earlier as being 'soft' would seem not to be of the 'fundamentally norm-creating character', which the International Court of Justice has said is necessary for a treaty provision to become part of customary international law.[63]

8 Compliance with the LOSC

It is a fundamental rule of international law, codified in Article 26 of the Vienna Convention on the Law of Treaties, that States are obliged to comply with treaties to which they are parties. In the case of the LOSC, there are good policy reasons why observance of this rule is particularly desirable. Any significant non-compliance will undermine the integrity and threaten the legitimacy of the LOSC as widespread non-compliance with a particular provision may suggest that the provision in question does not really apply and cause doubt as to its meaning, as well as encouraging non-compliance with that provision by other States. Furthermore, non-compliance may provoke disputes, deny States parties some of their rights under the LOSC, threaten good order at sea, and harm the marine environment.[64]

Certain kinds of treaties, notably multilateral environmental agreements, human rights treaties and arms control treaties, have their own, reasonably comprehensive, mechanisms to monitor compliance by States parties with their provisions and to address any non-compliance revealed by such monitoring.[65] Other treaties have no compliance mechanisms. The LOSC is somewhat between these two positions. It contains no general compliance mechanism, but it does provide three means by which alleged non-compliance may be addressed, albeit two of those means are limited to specific provisions of the LOSC.

The first such means is the International Seabed Authority. Its functions include seeking to ensure compliance with the rules governing the exploration and exploitation of mineral resources by all those undertaking activities in the Area.[66] To this end, the Authority has the power to request the provision of information and to

---

[63] *North Sea Continental Shelf (Federal Republic of Germany v Denmark; Federal Republic of Germany v The Netherlands)* (Judgment) [1969] ICJ Rep 3, 42–3 [72].

[64] See further R Churchill, 'The Persisting Problem of Non-Compliance with the Law of the Sea Convention: Disorder in the Oceans' (2012) 27 *International Journal of Marine and Coastal Law* 813.

[65] See further G Ulfstein, T Marauhn, and A Zimmerman (eds), *Making Treaties Work: Human Rights, Environment and Arms Control* (Cambridge University Press Cambridge 2007).

[66] LOSC, n 1, Arts 153(4) and (5), 162(2)(a) and (l), and 165(2)(c), (f), (k), and (m).

appoint inspectors to inspect installations and to see whether the terms of exploration and production contracts and the relevant rules and regulations are being complied with. Where they are not, the Authority may impose monetary penalties and/or suspend or terminate the contract.[67]

A second LOSC compliance mechanism is the Commission on the Limits of the Continental Shelf, a body of independent experts charged with examining States' submissions relating to the establishment of the outer limits of the continental shelf beyond 200 nautical miles (nm) in order to ensure that they comply with the complex geological and geomorphological criteria of Article 76 of the LOSC.[68] If the CLCS considers that a submission does so comply, it makes a recommendation to the coastal State concerned. Outer limits established on the basis of such recommendations are 'final and binding'.[69] The role of the CLCS is therefore designed to forestall possible non-compliance with Article 76.

A third means of seeking to ensure compliance with the LOSC is by utilizing its dispute settlement procedures, outlined in Section 3 above. Unlike the first two means just discussed, this means is dependent on individual States parties taking action, not on an institution whose functions specifically include ensuring compliance.[70] In practice, the dispute settlement procedures of the LOSC have so far been relatively little used to challenge alleged non-compliance. Excluding maritime boundary disputes (which cannot usually be characterized as instances of non-compliance), by the end of 2013, the total number of cases alleging non-compliance with the LOSC that had been referred for binding judicial settlement was 21. Of those, four were settled before a decision on the merits could be given, the settlement putting an end to the alleged non-compliance; in four cases, the tribunal found that it lacked jurisdiction; and five cases were pending. That means that a decision on the merits had been given in only eight cases, of which seven were cases where a flag State alleged that one of its vessels arrested for illegal fishing in the EEZ had not been released by the coastal State on payment of a bond or other security, as required by Article 73(2) of the LOSC. The one non-prompt release case was the *M/V 'Saiga' (No 2)* case, which concerned the arrest of an oil tanker registered in St Vincent that Guinea claimed had breached its customs laws by supplying fuel oil to vessels fishing in its EEZ. The ITLOS found that the arrest was in breach of the LOSC.[71]

Apart from the three means just discussed, a State party wishing to challenge alleged non-compliance with the LOSC by another State party may also make use of the individual compliance mechanisms of general international law: they include

---

[67] Ibid, Arts 153(5), 162(2)(z), and 165(2)(m); and Annex III, Art 18.
[68] See further Chapters 9 and 17 in this volume.   [69] LOSC, n 1, Art 76(8).
[70] On the distinction between individual and institutional (or collective) compliance mechanisms, and their respective merits, see R Churchill, 'Compliance Mechanisms in the Law of the Sea: From the Individual to the Collective' in H Hestermayer et al (eds), *Coexistence, Cooperation and Solidarity: Liber Amicorum Rüdiger Wolfrum* (Martinus Nijhoff Leiden 2012) Vol I, 777.
[71] *M/V 'Saiga' (No 2) (Saint Vincent and the Grenadines v Guinea)* (Judgment) [1999] ITLOS Rep 10.

retorsion, counter-measures, and dispute settlement outside the framework of the LOSC in relation to alleged non-compliance that falls within the matters excepted from the LOSC dispute settlement procedures under Articles 297 and 298. It would also be possible to use such compliance mechanisms as are found in other treaties that contain obligations that duplicate those of the LOSC, of which there are a number.[72]

The availability of compliance mechanisms is an important issue because various studies have revealed widespread non-compliance with the LOSC, suggesting that at least one third of all parties are in breach of one or more significant provisions.[73]

9 The Annual Cycle of Review of the LOSC

Article 319, which sets out the functions of the UN Secretary-General in relation to the LOSC, provides that he shall, *inter alia*, 'report to all States Parties, the Authority and competent international organizations on issues of a general nature that have arisen with respect to' the LOSC and 'convene necessary meetings of States Parties'. From these laconic provisions has developed an elaborate annual cycle of review of the LOSC and of the law of the sea generally. This cycle has four elements. In the order in which they occur during the year they are: the report(s) of the UN Secretary-General; the Meeting of States Parties; the meeting of the Open-Ended Informal Consultative Process on Oceans and Law of the Sea (ICP); and the debate and adoption of a resolution by the UN General Assembly.

The cycle begins with the publication, in the earlier part of the year, of a report by the Secretary-General which outlines developments not only in relation to the LOSC but also the law of the sea generally.[74] In more recent years the Secretary-General has also published reports on specific topics requested by the UN General Assembly: examples include reports on environmental impact assessment in areas beyond national jurisdiction (2011) and ocean acidification (2013). The

---

[72] See further Churchill, n 70.

[73] See Churchill, n 64; RR Churchill, 'The Impact of State Practice on the Jurisdictional Framework contained in the LOS Convention' in Oude Elferink (ed), n 58, 91; JRV Prescott and CH Schofield, *The Maritime Political Boundaries of the World* (2nd edn Martinus Nijhoff Leiden 2005); JA Roach and RW Smith, *Excessive Maritime Claims* (3rd edn Brill Leiden 2012).

[74] The reports of the Secretary-General are available at <http://www.un.org/depts/los/general_assembly/general_assembly_reports.htm>. Further on such reports, see Harrison, n 4, 247–9.

Secretary-General's reports form the basis for discussion at the General Assembly and often at the Meetings of States Parties and the ICP.

Meetings of States Parties are normally held in June. Their main function is to receive and consider reports from the three bodies established by the LOSC (the International Sea-Bed Authority, the ITLOS, and the CLCS) and periodically to elect members, and adopt the budgets, of the ITLOS and the CLCS. Some, mainly developing, States have argued for a more ambitious role for the Meetings of States Parties in developing the LOSC, but there is opposition to this from many developed States.[75] Nevertheless, the Meetings have occasionally gone beyond their largely administrative role and on a few occasions have de facto amended the LOSC, as explained in the following section.[76]

The ICP usually meets shortly after the Meeting of States Parties. It was established by the UN General Assembly in 1999 to facilitate the Assembly's review of developments in the law of the sea and ocean affairs.[77] The ICP usually focuses on a single topic (selected by the Assembly) at each of its sessions. Recent topics have included capacity building, marine renewable energy, and ocean acidification. The ICP is aided in its deliberations by presentations from experts on the topic at issue. Some time after the conclusion of a session the co-chairs publish a report summarizing discussion at the session.[78] Unlike the Meetings of States Parties, the ICP allows for some participation by civil society. Discussion at the ICP feeds into debate at the UN General Assembly and influences its actions. For example, a few months after the ICP had discussed the conservation and sustainable use of marine biodiversity in areas beyond national jurisdiction in 2004, the General Assembly established an Ad Hoc Open-Ended Informal Working Group to study the subject.[79]

The annual cycle of review ends with the adoption of a resolution on 'oceans and the law of the sea' by the General Assembly.[80] The resolutions, which are extremely

---

[75] See eg the debates at the thirteenth (2003) and fourteenth (2004) Meetings of the Parties: Report of the Thirteenth Meeting of States Parties, SPLOS/103, [94]–[102], and Report of the Fourteenth Meeting of States Parties, SPLOS/119, [78]–[89]. Reports and other documents of the Meetings are available at <http://www.un.org/depts/los/meeting_states_parties/SPLOS_documents.htm>.

[76] For more detailed discussion of the role of the Meetings of States Parties, see Harrison, n 4, 70–84; AG Oude Elferink, 'Reviewing the Implementation of the LOS Convention: the Role of the United Nations General Assembly and the Meeting of States Parties' in AG Oude Elferink and DR Rothwell (eds), *Oceans Management in the 21st Century: Institutional Frameworks and Responses* (Martinus Nijhoff Leiden 2004) 295; T Treves, 'The General Assembly and the Meeting of States Parties in the Implementation of the LOS Convention' in Oude Elferink (ed), n 58, 55.

[77] UNGA Res 54/33 (1999). Further on the ICP, see Harrison, n 4, 252–7 and 282–4; and United Nations Secretary-General, *Report of the UN Secretary-General Reviewing the Work of the ICP*, UN Doc A64/66 (2009), available at <http://www.un.org/depts/los/general_assembly/general_assembly_reports.htm>.

[78] Such reports are available at <http://www.un.org/depts/los/consultative_process/consultative_process.htm>.

[79] UNGA Res 59/24 (2004) [73].

[80] The resolutions, which have been adopted every year since the LOSC came into force in 1994, are conveniently gathered together at <http://www.un.org/depts/los/general_assembly/

lengthy, not only review the LOSC and call on Member States to take various kinds of action in relation thereto, but also do the same in respect of a large number of other normative instruments. The resolutions are not without a degree of normativity themselves. In some cases they may prompt practice, and indeed constitute practice, giving rise to a new rule of customary international law: this has happened in relation to the call for a ban on large-scale driftnet fishing on the high seas, for example.[81] On some occasions, the General Assembly's resolutions have indirectly given rise to a new treaty. This happened, for example, when the Assembly decided to call for a diplomatic conference to consider a new treaty to develop the provisions of the LOSC relating to straddling and highly migratory fish stocks, and may happen again as a result of the Ad Hoc Working Group that it has established on the conservation and sustainable use of marine biodiversity in areas beyond national jurisdiction, as explained below.

The annual review process has been important in several ways. It has kept the LOSC, and the law of the sea in general, continuously in the consciousness of the international community. It has helped to identify limitations in the LOSC and issues that the LOSC does not adequately address. To some degree, it has also helped to develop the LOSC, as intimated above and as explained in more detail in the section that follows.

10 Developing the LOSC

Treaties, like all laws, are liable to become outdated with the passing of time, as their provisions may no longer reflect the interests and values of the communities that they serve or be capable of addressing new issues and problems that have arisen since their adoption.[82] Some treaties anticipate this situation particularly well by having simplified amendment procedures that dispense with the need for ratification by their parties and thus allow for the treaty in question to be easily updated. The LOSC, however, is a treaty of a more traditional kind. Amendments to it, whether adopted by the simplified or more formal procedure, do not come into force unless and until

---

general_assembly_resolutions.htm>. Further on the resolutions, see Harrison, n 4, 250–2 and 280–1; Oude Elferink, n 76; and Treves, n 76.

[81] See further GJ Hewison, 'The Legally Binding Nature of the Moratorium on Large-scale High Seas Driftnet Fishing' (1994) 25 *Journal of Maritime Law and Commerce* 557.

[82] See further AE Boyle, 'Further Development of the 1982 Law of the Sea Convention: Mechanisms for Change' (2005) 54 *International and Comparative Law Quarterly* 563. See also Chapter 39 in this volume.

ratified by two-thirds of the parties (three-quarters in the case of amendments relating exclusively to activities in the Area or the ITLOS).[83] This entry into force requirement, it has been argued,[84] explains why no amendments to the LOSC have yet been adopted and means that it is unlikely that any will be adopted in the foreseeable future.

While the formal amendment procedures of the LOSC have not been used, there has nevertheless been some de facto amendment of its provisions. The Meetings of States Parties have adopted two decisions effectively amending the provisions of the LOSC governing the making of submissions to the CLCS on the outer limit of the continental shelf beyond 200 nm. The first decision extended the deadline for making submissions, while the second provided that within that deadline preliminary information could be given, rather than making a full submission.[85] The CLCS itself, through its Rules of Procedure[86] and its practice in responding to submissions, has arguably also de facto amended some of the provisions of Article 76 relating to the delineation of the continental shelf beyond 200 nm.[87]

The 1994 Implementation Agreement also de facto amends the LOSC, as explained in Section 2 above. A second implementation agreement, the so-called Fish Stocks Agreement (FSA), adopted in 1995, does not amend the LOSC but extensively develops its brief provisions on the conservation and management of straddling and highly migratory fish stocks.[88] The two implementation agreements have contrasting provisions on their relationship to the LOSC. The 1994 Agreement provides that it and the LOSC are to 'be interpreted and applied together as a single instrument'; however, in the event of any inconsistency, the Agreement prevails.[89] By contrast, the 1995 FSA is to be 'interpreted and applied in the context of and in a manner consistent with [the LOSC]', and 'does not prejudice the rights, jurisdiction or duties of States' under the LOSC.[90]

Since 1995, no further implementation agreements have been concluded. However, one of the options being considered arising out of the work of the Ad Hoc Working Group on the conservation and sustainable use of marine biodiversity

---

[83] LOSC, n 1, Arts 312–316.   [84] Freestone and Oude Elferink, n 58, 179–80.

[85] See, respectively, Report of the Eleventh Meeting of States Parties, SPLOS/73 (2001) [81], and decision of the Eighteenth Meeting of States Parties, SPLOS/183 (2008). For other de facto amendments made by the Meetings of States Parties, see Harrison, n 4, 77–80.

[86] Rules of Procedure of the Commission on the Limits of the Continental Shelf (17 April 2008), available at <http://www.un.org/depts/los/clcs_new/commission_rules.htm>.

[87] A Serdy, 'The Commission on the Limits of the Continental Shelf and its Disturbing Propensity to Legislate' (2011) 26 *International Journal of Marine and Coastal Law* 367.

[88] 1995 Agreement for the Implementation of the Provisions of the United Nations Convention on the Law of the Sea of 10 December 1982 relating to the Conservation and Management of Straddling Fish Stocks and Highly Migratory Fish Stocks (hereinafter FSA).

[89] 1994 Agreement Relating to the Implementation of Part XI of the United Nations Convention on the Law of the Sea of 10 December 1982, Art 2; see text accompanying n 9.

[90] FSA, n 88, Art 4.

in areas beyond national jurisdiction, and for which there appears to be considerable support from States, is the adoption of what would be a third implementation agreement.[91]

One form of development for which the LOSC does make explicit provision is in authorizing and requiring the International Seabed Authority to adopt regulations governing the mining of minerals in the Area.[92] So far, the Authority has adopted three sets of regulations, relating to the prospecting and exploration of various kinds of minerals, as explained in Chapter 101 in this volume.

Finally, some development of the LOSC has taken place through interpretation of its provisions by international courts and tribunals. Two examples may be given. First, tribunals have developed the laconic provisions of Articles 74(1) and 83(1), which provide simply that delimitation of EEZ and continental shelf boundaries between opposite and adjacent States shall be effected 'on the basis of international law... in order to achieve an equitable solution', by elaborating the equidistance/relevant circumstances method of delimitation.[93] Second, the ITLOS has read into the LOSC a requirement that force may only be used as a last resort when arresting a foreign vessel at sea and even then is limited to what is necessary and reasonable in the circumstances.[94]

11 Conclusions

The LOSC has frequently been described as a 'constitution for the oceans'.[95] Many of the features of the LOSC described in this chapter bear out that description—the

---

[91] See UNGA Res 68/70 (2013), [196]–[201]. See further E Druel, R Billé, and J Rochette, *Getting to Yes? Discussions towards an Implementing Agreement to UNCLOS on Biodiversity in ABNJ* (2013), available at <www.iddri.org>.

[92] LOSC, n 1, Arts 160(f)(ii) and 162(o)(ii).

[93] *Arbitration between Barbados and Trinidad and Tobago* (2006) XXVII RIAA 147, especially [220]–[245]; *Arbitration between Guyana and Suriname* (2007) XXX RIAA 1, especially [342]; *Black Sea Case*, n 49, [115]–[22]; *Delimitation of the Maritime Boundary in the Bay of Bengal (Bangladesh/Myanmar)* (Judgment) [2012] ITLOS Rep 4, especially [225]–[240] and [455], available at <http://www.itlos.org/fileadmin/itlos/documents/cases/case_no_16/C16_Judgment_14_03_2012_rev.pdf>.

[94] *M/V 'Saiga' (No 2)*, n 71, [155]–[156].

[95] This phrase is not one that is used in the LOSC itself. It appears to have been first used by the President of the Third UN Conference on the Law of the Sea at the closing session of the Conference: see United Nations, *The Law of the Sea: Official Text of the United Nations Convention on the Law of the Sea* (United Nations New York 1983) xxxiii. For a very useful discussion of the concept of the LOSC as a constitution, see S Scott, 'The LOS Convention as a Constitutional Regime for the Oceans' in Oude Elferink (ed), n 58, 9.

comprehensiveness of its scope (see Section 3 above); its framework nature in relation to many issues (see Section 4); its near universal application, with nearly 85 per cent of UN members being parties and those members that are not parties being bound by many of its provisions on the basis of customary international law (see Sections 5 and 7); its generally superior status to other sources of the law of the sea (see Section 7); the difficulty of its formal amendment (see Section 10); and, finally, its considerable flexibility that has permitted its development and adaptation to changing circumstances (see Section 10).

Describing the LOSC as a 'constitution for the oceans' is not just a matter of rhetoric. Arguably, some consequences of significance flow from such a designation. First, there is a presumption that any activity at sea, actual or potential, is regulated, at least to some degree, by the LOSC. Second, there is a presumption that other treaties regulating activities at sea are compatible with the LOSC. Third, the effect of the LOSC on third parties may extend beyond the traditional position in international law since even in relation to those parts of the LOSC that do not represent customary international law, such as most of Part XI, it would be politically difficult for non-parties to act contrary to the LOSC. Indeed, in the *Nicaragua/Colombia* case, the International Court of Justice appears to have come close to endowing the LOSC with the status of an objective regime with its observation that 'given the object and purpose of the LOSC, as stipulated in the Preamble, the fact that Colombia is not a party thereto does not relieve Nicaragua of its obligations under Article 76' of the LOSC.[96] A fourth consequence of considering the LOSC as a constitution is that one should not be too ready to conclude that the LOSC has been amended by informal means.

No treaties—and very few constitutions—last forever; they eventually become outdated. However, at the present time there appears to be no desire in the international community to replace the LOSC, or even radically to amend it. Its flexible and often framework nature, which has already allowed for some development of its provisions (as shown in Section 10), means that the LOSC should endure as the pre-eminent source of the law of the sea for many years to come.

---

[96] *Nicaragua v Colombia*, n 57, [126]. See also the *Peru v Chile* case where the ICJ 'took note' of a declaration by Peru, a non-party to the LOSC, during the proceedings that the 200 nm 'maritime domain' that it claimed was 'applied in a manner consistent with the maritime zones set out in' the LOSC. The ICJ considered that that declaration 'expresses a formal undertaking by Peru'. See *Maritime Dispute (Peru v Chile)*, Judgment of 27 January 2014 [178], available at <http://www.icj-cij.org/docket/index.php?p1=3&p2=3&k=88&case=137&code=pch&p3=4>.

3

BETWEEN STABILITY AND CHANGE IN THE LAW OF THE SEA CONVENTION

SUBSEQUENT PRACTICE, TREATY MODIFICATION, AND REGIME INTERACTION

IRINA BUGA

1 Introduction

TREATY provisions require adaptation to the changing international environment around them. Evolving norms and preferences, technological progress, the proliferation of new institutions and judicial bodies, all entail changes to the international regulatory framework—especially in a field as dynamic and extensive as the law of the sea. It is also crucial to be able to tackle shortcomings or unsatisfactory compromises made by the original drafters. The UN Convention on the Law of the Sea (LOSC) contains numerous explicit and implicit mechanisms to deal with change. One obvious example is that of the formal amendment procedures contained in Articles 312 and 313. The Convention is also developed through its dispute settlement system, including the International Tribunal for the Law of the Sea (ITLOS), and the activities of bodies such as, *inter alia*, the Meeting of States Parties (SPLOS), the Commission on the Limits of the Continental Shelf (CLCS), and the International Seabed Authority (ISA)—the strengths and weaknesses of which are discussed elsewhere in the present volume.[1]

There are, however, important limits to the extent to which these rules and institutions can ensure that the Convention is responsive to the changing needs of the international community. For instance, formal amendments can be cumbersome, if not altogether unworkable in practice.[2] As a result, the procedures in Articles 312 and 313 of the LOSC have yet to be utilized.[3] Thus, complex treaty regimes such as the LOSC tend to be amenable to subsequent development through a range of mechanisms that go beyond formal amendment. In fact, the more sophisticated the treaty, the more complex the range of mechanisms required for adaptation.[4] Treaties such as the LOSC can be modified and supplemented through general international law processes such as treaty interpretation and subsequent rules of customary law.

The informal character of subsequent practice can facilitate treaty adaptation, even if uncertainty remains as to certain aspects of the process.[5] Subsequent practice is legally relevant to the LOSC in a number of ways. First, it serves as a tool for treaty interpretation, pursuant to Article 31 of the Vienna Convention on the Law of Treaties (VCLT). Second, and crucially, it can constitute the parties' agreement to modify the treaty. This may be the case where subsequent practice diverges from the text to such an extent that it can no longer be said to constitute an act of treaty interpretation, but rather becomes, in effect, an act of modification.[6] Pressure

---

[1] See in particular Chapters 16–20 in this volume.

[2] See eg MJ Bowman, 'The Multilateral Treaty Amendment Process—A Case Study' (1995) 44 *International and Comparative Law Quarterly* 540; C McLachlan, 'The Evolution of Treaty Obligations in International Law' in G Nolte (ed), *Treaties and Subsequent Practice* (Oxford University Press Oxford 2013) 69, 71.

[3] OR Young, 'Commentary on Shirley V Scott, *The LOSC Convention as a Constitutional Regime for the Oceans*' in AG Oude Elferink (ed), *Stability and Change in the Law of the Sea: The Role of the LOS Convention* (Martinus Nijhoff Leiden 2005) 39, 44; DR Rothwell, 'The Impact of State Practice on the Jurisdictional Framework Contained in the LOS Convention: A Commentary' in Oude Elferink (ed), n 3, 145, 149; Y Tanaka, *The International Law of the Sea* (Cambridge University Press Cambridge 2012) 33. See also Chapter 2 in this volume.

[4] See eg Bowman, n 2, 542–3.

[5] See further I Buga, 'Subsequent Practice and Treaty Modification' in D Kritsiotis and MJ Bowman (eds), *Conceptual and Contextual Perspectives on the Modern Law of Treaties* (Cambridge University Press Cambridge forthcoming 2015) ch 13.

[6] The term 'modification' is used here to denote the variation of treaty provisions by means of the parties' implied consent—the counterpart to formal treaty amendment in the 1969 Vienna Convention on the Law of Treaties, Arts 39–41 (hereinafter VCLT). The ILC also preferred this term during the drafting of the VCLT in relation to the ultimately deleted article on 'modification of treaties by subsequent practice'. See Draft Articles on the Law of Treaties (1964) II *Yearbook of the International Law Commission* 198, Art 68, and (1966) II *Yearbook of the International Law Commission* 182, Art 38.

points on the Convention where change is desirable and already shows signs of occurring include many of its procedural provisions, and a number of key environmental notions in the Convention. This process of tacit modification by subsequent practice is not incompatible with the rigid mechanisms for formal amendment in the LOSC.[7] Third, subsequent practice can potentially generate new (regional or universal) customary norms that may, as *lex posterior*, impact LOSC obligations.[8]

Through its various legal effects, subsequent practice can also serve as a vehicle to regime interaction, adapting the Convention in line with developments in other fields such as environmental law. This bears upon the issue of fragmentation and treaty congestion in international law.[9] It is therefore submitted that subsequent practice has had a significant impact upon the development of the LOSC framework, and will continue to do so in the future.

An improved understanding of how tacit modification by subsequent practice impacts the Convention can contribute to more accurately defining States' expectations and aid judicial bodies in assessing obligations under the LOSC regime. Such insights can help strike a better balance between the stability of the LOSC regime and its ability to evolve—an issue of great significance, given the scope and subject matter covered by the Convention. The present chapter begins by describing the process of modification by subsequent practice in general (Section 2). It then explores examples of modification in the LOSC (Section 3). Section 4 looks at the role of subsequent practice in the process of regime interaction between the law of the sea and other regimes. It also explores alternative mechanisms that facilitate informal adaptation and regime interaction in the LOSC, therefore reducing the need for modification by subsequent practice. Section 5 brings the different sections together, exploring limitations and drawing conclusions as to the evolution of the Convention.

2 Subsequent Practice and Treaty Modification

The present section explores the parameters of the process of subsequent practice and the factors conducive to it, laying the groundwork for an analysis of its application in the law of the sea.

---

[7] RR Churchill, 'The Impact of State Practice on the Jurisdictional Framework Contained in the LOS Convention' in Oude Elferink (ed), n 3, 91, 97.

[8] See further eg M Akehurst, 'The Hierarchy of Sources of International Law' (1975) 47 *British Yearbook of International Law* 273, 275–6; N Kontou, *The Termination and Revision of Treaties in the Light of New Customary International Law* (Clarendon Oxford 1994) 132–3 and 145–7.

[9] See generally ILC, 'Report of the Study Group on Fragmentation of International Law', finalized by Martti Koskenniemi, UN Doc A/CN.4/L.682 (2006).

2.1 Defining 'relevant' subsequent practice

According to Article 31(3)(b) of the VCLT, there 'shall be taken into account... any subsequent practice in the application of the treaty which establishes the agreement of the parties regarding its interpretation'. There is debate as to what type and degree of practice can be considered relevant. The concept is taken here in a broad sense to include a large spectrum of acts, statements, and omissions relating to the application of a treaty and establishing the 'agreement of [*all*] the parties' to a certain interpretation, according to the requirements in Article 31(3)(b) of the VCLT.[10] Only some of the parties need actively to engage in the practice, as long as there is acceptance on the part of the rest ('qualified passive conduct').[11] The practice should be 'concordant, common and consistent'.[12] Also important is whether the most relevant States actively participate.[13] The duration of the practice, on the other hand, is not essential for it to be able to lead to modification or to crystallize into customary law, as long as other States have had enough time to become aware and react.[14] As for *whose* practice counts, the notion could arguably be taken to cover more than the practice of States. It may include, *inter alia*, the practice of *non*-State actors such as international organizations[15] or conferences of the parties.[16] An important example of the latter is the SPLOS, whose actions can have significant law-making effects.[17]

---

[10] Practice that does not satisfy these requirements can still be taken into account under VCLT, n 6, Art 32.

[11] See eg ME Villiger, *Commentary on the 1969 Vienna Convention on the Law of Treaties* (Martinus Nijhoff Leiden 2009) 432. See also Churchill, n 7, 101–3.

[12] I Sinclair, *The Vienna Convention on the Law of Treaties* (2nd edn Manchester University Press Manchester 1984) 137. See also *Japan—Taxes on Alcoholic Beverages—Report of the Appellate Body* WT/DS8/AB/R, WT/DS10/AB/R, WT/DS11/AB/R (1996) 13.

[13] *North Sea Continental Shelf (Federal Republic of Germany v Denmark; Federal Republic of Germany v The Netherlands)* [1969] ICJ Rep 3, [74]; AM Feldman, 'Evolving Treaty Obligations: A Proposal for Analyzing Subsequent Practice Derived from WTO Dispute Settlement' (2009) 41 *New York Journal of International Law and Politics* 655, 694, and 697–9.

[14] *North Sea Continental Shelf*, n 13, [74].

[15] See eg *Legality of the Use by a State of Nuclear Weapons in Armed Conflict* (Advisory Opinion) [1966] ICJ Rep 66, [19]; *Legal Consequences for States of the Continuing Presence of South Africa in Namibia* (Advisory Opinion) [1971] ICJ Rep 16, 22; *Legal Consequences of the Construction of a Wall in the Occupied Palestinian Territory* (Advisory Opinion) [2004] ICJ Rep 136, [27]–[28]; JE Alvarez, *International Organizations as Law-Makers* (Oxford University Press Oxford 2005) 88–9. Cf C Amerasinghe, *Principles of the Institutional Law of International Organizations* (2nd edn Cambridge University Press Cambridge 2005) 53.

[16] RR Churchill and G Ulfstein, 'Autonomous Institutional Arrangements in Multilateral Environmental Agreements: A Little-Noticed Phenomenon in International Law' (2000) 94 *American Journal of International Law* 623; MJ Bowman, '"Normalizing" the International Convention for the Regulation of Whaling' (2008) 29 *Michigan Journal of International Law* 293, 332; G Ulfstein, 'Treaty Bodies and Regimes' in DB Hollis (ed), *The Oxford Guide to Treaties* (Oxford University Press Oxford 2012) 428.

[17] See Section 3.2 below.

The distinction between subsequent practice and subsequent agreements is a fluid one.[18] Both constitute forms of authentic interpretation according to which the treaty parties are 'their own masters'.[19] Subsequent agreements show a higher degree of formality, posing less of a challenge to legal certainty. However, the scope of the term 'agreement' presumably also covers non-written agreements and, for instance, decisions by meetings of States parties.[20] This may cause some confusion as to the precise relationship between sub-paragraphs (a) and (b) of Article 31(3) of the VCLT: they fall along a spectrum ranging from the implicit to the explicit, with passive conduct on one end and treaties on the other. The case law indicates that the notion of subsequent practice can be taken to *comprise* subsequent agreements.[21] This approach will be adopted here, to avoid terminological complications and take full account of relevant subsequent practice going beyond the formal amendment procedures prescribed in the VCLT and the LOSC.

2.2 Treaty modification by subsequent practice

The process of tacit modification by subsequent practice has been acknowledged in the case law,[22] doctrine,[23] and in the work of the International Law Commission.[24] It has

---

[18] ILC, *Report of the International Law Commission*, 60th session, UN Doc A/63/10 (2008) Annex A, [24].

[19] Villiger, n 11, 429 and 432.

[20] MK Yasseen, 'L'interprétation des traités d'après la Convention de Vienne sur le droit des traités' (1976) 151 *Recueil des Cours* 1, [13]; A Aust, *Modern Treaty Law and Practice* (2nd edn Cambridge University Press Cambridge 2007) 191; Villiger, n 11, 430–1.

[21] See eg *Maritime Delimitation in the Area between Greenland and Jan Mayen (Denmark v Norway)* [1993] ICJ Rep 51, [28]; *Pulp Mills on the River Uruguay (Argentina v Uruguay)* (Provisional Measures) [2006] ICJ Rep 113, [53]. See also G Nolte, 'Jurisprudence of the International Court of Justice and Arbitral Tribunals of Ad Hoc Jurisdiction Relating to Subsequent Agreements and Subsequent Practice: Introductory Report for the ILC Study Group on Treaties over Time' in Nolte (ed), n 2, 169, 174 (referring collectively to 'subsequent conduct').

[22] See eg *Dispute regarding Navigational and Related Rights (Costa Rica v Nicaragua)* [2009] ICJ Rep 213, [64]; *Air Transport Services Agreement between the United States of America and France* (1969) 38 ILR 182, 249–59; *Taba Arbitration (Egypt/Israel)* (1988) 27 ILM 1421, [209]–[210], [235]; *Delimitation of the Border between Eritrea and Ethiopia* (2002) XXV RIAA 110, [3.6]–[3.10]; *Soering v UK* (1989) 11 EHRR 439, [103]–[104]; *Öcalan v Turkey* (2003) 37 EHRR 238, [196], [198], and *Öcalan v Turkey* [GC] (2005) 41 EHRR 985, [163]; *Al-Saadoon and Mufdhi v UK* (2010) 51 EHRR 9, [119]; *Islamic Republic of Iran and United States of America*, Interlocutory Award No ITL 83-B1-FT (9 September 2004) 2004 WL 2210709 (Iran–US CTR), [132].

[23] To name only a few, G Fitzmaurice, 'The Law and Procedure of the International Court of Justice 1951-4: Treaty Interpretation and Other Treaty Points' (1957) 33 *British Yearbook of International Law* 203, 225; Akehurst, n 8, 277; Yasseen, n 20, 51; Sinclair, n 12, 138; Rothwell, n 3, 148; Aust, n 20, 265; U Linderfalk, *On the Interpretation of Treaties* (Springer Dordrecht 2007) 168; R Gardiner, *Treaty Interpretation* (Oxford University Press Oxford 2008) 243–5; Feldman, n 13, 658; Villiger, n 11, 429; J Arato, 'Subsequent Practice and Evolutive Interpretation' (2010) 9 *Law and Practice of International Courts and Tribunals* 453, 464; J Harrison, *Making the Law of the Sea: A Study in the Development of International Law* (Cambridge University Press Cambridge 2011) 95.

[24] The ILC ultimately deleted a draft provision on 'modification by subsequent practice' from the final VCLT articles (see n 6) for practical reasons, but did not bring into doubt the underlying principle

recently been acknowledged in the context of discussions on treaties over time.[25] Some scholars have even gone so far as to consider it a rule of customary international law.[26]

'Modification' here refers both to the process of altering treaty provisions, and supplementing them with an important 'novel' element or direction.[27] One of the greatest challenges lies in distinguishing interpretation from modification, especially since States are reluctant to admit that their practice amounts to anything more than the former.[28] Ambiguous treaty provisions blur the line between interpretation and modification even further (granting parties more freedom to adopt a wider range of interpretations). However, this line is often indistinct even when dealing with relatively clear terms.[29] It nevertheless remains important to distinguish between the two.[30] For one thing, modifications become an integral part of the treaty, while agreed interpretations '*may* have legal effect, depending upon the possible conflicts with other means of interpretation ... [and] limited to the particular case at hand'.[31]

Tacit modification by subsequent practice cannot be identified by means of abstract criteria, but rather must be assessed on a case-by-case basis, with regard to a large array of factors. These include the nature of the treaty and obligations in question and the relevance of the contributing parties. For instance, older treaties are more susceptible to tacit modification.[32] Modification by subsequent practice is also easier to identify and less contentious with regard to bilateral treaties, as compared to multilateral treaties like the LOSC.[33] The same can be said of the effects of subsequent practice on procedural rather than substantive or 'essential' provisions.[34]

---

of modification—eg ILC, 'Third Report on the Law of Treaties', by Sir Humphrey Waldock (1964) II *Yearbook of the International Law Commission*, 61–2; ILC, 'Sixth Report on the Law of Treaties', by Sir Humphrey Waldock (1966) II *Yearbook of the International Law Commission*, 87–8; UN Conference on the Law of Treaties, 1st Session (1968), UN Doc A/CONF.39/C.1/SR.37, [57]–[59] and [66] [37th meeting of the Committee of the Whole], and A/CONF.39/C.1/SR.38, [28], [48], and [55] (hereinafter '37th meeting of the Committee of the Whole').

[25] See eg ILC, n 18, [31]; Nolte, n 21, 190, 200, 204, and 206.

[26] FG Jacobs, 'Varieties of Approach to Treaty Interpretation' (1969) 18 *International and Comparative Law Quarterly* 318, 332; W Karl, *Vertrag und Spätere Praxis im Völkerrecht* (Springer Berlin 1983) 292–3; J Pauwelyn, *Conflict of Norms in Public International Law* (Cambridge University Press Cambridge 2003) 50.

[27] I Venzke, *How Interpretation Makes International Law: On Semantic Change and Normative Twists* (Oxford University Press Oxford 2012) 236.

[28] See eg I Voicu, *De l'interprétation authentique des traités internationaux* (Pedone Paris 1968) 89; Akehurst, n 8, 204; A Orakhelashvili, *The Interpretation of Acts and Rules in Public International Law* (Oxford University Press Oxford 2008) 105.

[29] See further Nolte, n 21, 202.

[30] See eg T Treves, 'The General Assembly and the Meeting of States Parties in the Implementation of the LOS Convention' in Oude Elferink (ed), n 3, 55, 73–4.

[31] Linderfalk, n 23, 168 (original emphasis). See further Nolte, n 21, 207–8.

[32] ILC, n 18, 366; SD Murphy, 'The Relevance of Subsequent Agreement and Subsequent Practice for the Interpretation of Treaties' in Nolte (ed), n 2, 82, 94.

[33] See eg Murphy, n 32, 92.

[34] ILC, 'Summary record of the 866th meeting' (1966) I(2) *Yearbook of the International Law Commission* 163, [18] and [64]; 37th meeting of the Committee of the Whole, n 24, [69]; J Brunnée, 'Treaty Amendments' in Hollis (ed), n 16, 347, 351; Bowman, n 16, 333.

A treaty may impose significant limitations on the ability to derogate from its provisions through subsequent practice; such limitations in the LOSC context are discussed in detail in Section 5 below. Moreover, treaties may contain 'in-built' mechanisms that can facilitate adaptation, removing some of the appeal of subsequent practice. A good example is a specialized dispute settlement system. Another special mechanism is 'evolutionary interpretation', rooted in Articles 31(1) of the VCLT on 'ordinary meaning' and 'object and purpose', and Article 31(3)(c) on other 'relevant rules of international law'. Like subsequent practice, it can significantly alter the meaning of a provision.[35] However, evolutionary interpretation cannot amount to tacit modification; it relies on the parties' original intention to render the treaty evolutionary,[36] and never leaves the confines of the text.[37] The doctrine of implied powers, another form of 'dynamic' interpretation, has a similar effect with regard to treaties establishing international organizations: it permits terms to be 'read into' the text without technically modifying it.[38] Thus, the more room there is for evolutionary interpretation or an implicit conferral of powers under the treaty, the less room or need there is for modification by subsequent practice.[39]

3 Modification of the LOSC by Subsequent Practice

Modification by subsequent practice can play a significant role in a field as dynamic as the law of the sea, where there is greater need for responsiveness than some other areas of international law. The following examples illustrate the possible effects of subsequent practice.

3.1 The 1994 Implementation Agreement and 1995 Fish Stocks Agreement

A good starting point for the discussion is the 1994 Agreement relating to the Implementation of Part XI of the LOSC (1994 Implementation Agreement).[40]

---

[35] Its effects can be more drastic than those of subsequent practice—see *Costa Rica v Nicaragua*, n 22, 213, and ibid, Separate Opinion of Judge Skotnikov, [8]–[10]; Arato, n 23, 450.

[36] Arato, n 23, 453.   [37] See eg Gardiner, n 23, 243; Orakhelashvili, n 28, 291.

[38] K Skubiszewski, 'Implied Powers of International Organizations' in Y Dinstein (ed), *International Law at a Time of Perplexity: Essays in Honour of Shabtai Rosenne* (Martinus Nijhoff Dordrecht 1989) 855, 856–7.

[39] Nolte, n 21, 207.   [40] See further Chapter 2 in this volume.

According to Article 2(1) of the Agreement, coupled with its Annex, certain LOSC provisions are to be 'disapplied'[41] or replaced,[42] and a number of structural and institutional changes implemented.[43] Confusion stems from the fact that 'the provisions of the Agreement were carefully drafted to avoid any clear indication that what states were doing was amending Part XI of the Convention'.[44] Nevertheless, there can be no doubt that it represents a modification of the LOSC by subsequent agreement.[45]

Worthy of mention is that the 1994 Implementation Agreement does not as such modify the essential underlying purposes of the LOSC, including the principle of the common heritage of mankind, the purpose to benefit mankind as a whole, the prohibition on claiming sovereignty or sovereign rights in the Area, or the peaceful purposes requirement.[46]

The operation of the 1994 Implementation Agreement also illustrates the effects of tacit modification in a different way. According to Article 4(1) of the Agreement, States that ratify the LOSC *subsequent* to the adoption of the Agreement automatically become parties to the latter. This leaves unclear whether the Agreement also binds States that became parties to the LOSC *prior* to the Agreement's adoption, since many of them have not formally consented to such effect.[47] Nevertheless, 'members of the [International Seabed] Authority [pursuant to the LOSC] which are not parties to the 1994 Agreement necessarily participate in the work of the Authority under arrangements based on the Agreement'.[48] In other words, by participating in ISA activities, non-parties to the Agreement can be deemed to have consented to the Agreement as a result of their subsequent practice.[49]

The 1995 Agreement for the Implementation of the Provisions of the UN Convention on the Law of the Sea relating to the Conservation and Management of Straddling Fish Stocks and Highly Migratory Fish Stocks (Fish Stocks Agreement

---

[41] See eg 1994 Implementation Agreement, Annex, Sections 2(3), 3(8), 4, 6(7), and 8(2).

[42] See eg ibid, Annex, Section 5(2) and 6(1)(a).

[43] See eg ibid, Annex, Section 1(2) and (4); 2; 3(1), (2) and (5); and 4(1).

[44] Harrison, n 23, 92.

[45] See eg DH Anderson, 'Further Efforts to Ensure Universal Participation in the United Nations Convention on the Law of the Sea' (1994) 43 *International and Comparative Law Quarterly* 886, 889; LDM Nelson, 'The New Deep Sea-Bed Mining Regime' (1995) 10 *International Journal of Marine and Coastal Law* 189, 192–3; T Scovazzi, 'Evolution of International Law of the Sea' (2000) 286 *Recueil des Cours* 39, 125; Treves, n 30, 56; Churchill, n 7, 97; D Freestone and AG Oude Elferink, 'Flexibility and Innovation in the Law of the Sea—Will the LOS Convention Amendment Procedures Ever be Used?' in Oude Elferink (ed), n 3, 169, 184 and 187; AE Boyle, 'Further Development of the 1982 Law of the Sea Convention' in D Freestone, R Barnes, and D Ong (eds), *The Law of the Sea: Progress and Prospects* (Oxford University Press Oxford 2006) 40, 41 and 49; Tanaka, n 3, 33 and 178–84.

[46] Nelson, n 45, 203; Harrison, n 23, 93; Tanaka, n 3, 182–4.

[47] *Report of the Secretary-General of the International Seabed Authority*, Doc ISBA/6/A/9 (2000), [4]. See also Harrison, n 23, 93–4.

[48] *Report of the Secretary-General of the International Seabed Authority*, Doc ISBA/15/A/2 (2009) [5].

[49] Harrison, n 23, 95–6. This argument is separate from the question of whether the Part XI regime has not created an 'objective regime' applicable to all States in the international community.

or FSA) is a second example of adaptation by a subsequent agreement going beyond the formal amendment procedures of the LOSC. It introduces significant changes to the Convention, illustrating the difficulty of pinpointing the 'switch' from interpretation to tacit modification.[50]

Article 2 of the FSA declares the objective to 'ensure the long-term conservation and sustainable use of straddling fish stocks and highly migratory fish stocks'. It has been argued that the contemporary meaning of 'sustainable use' may amount to a modification of the term 'maximum sustainable yield' in Articles 61(3) and 119(1)(a) of the LOSC.[51] Moreover, the FSA, which admittedly only applies to certain species or stocks, adopts an 'ecosystem' approach (see Article 5(d)–(f)) that goes beyond the provisions of Part VII of the LOSC.[52] The FSA also introduces the precautionary principle, discussed further in the next section. This does not necessarily lead to incompatibility between the FSA and the LOSC. Wolfrum and Matz argue that the LOSC—as a framework convention—is sufficiently flexible to incorporate these approaches, as it lays down only minimum standards (see Articles 192 and 194(5) of the LOSC).[53] Moreover, Article 237 of the LOSC provides that Part XII is without prejudice to the specific obligations assumed by States under special conventions and agreements concerning the protection of the marine environment. The question of whether these examples constitute modification or 'dynamic' interpretation, is itself a matter of interpretation.

But the FSA also contains provisions such as Article 21, allowing members of regional management organizations to board and inspect vessels suspected of engaging in unauthorized fishing on the high seas—deemed a 'landmark' in fisheries management enforcement.[54] It is difficult to say whether this provision modifies or supplements the LOSC; in either case, it establishes concrete rights that the LOSC does not itself provide. Moreover, under Article 8(4) of the FSA, only States members of a regional fisheries management organization (RFMO), or which have agreed to the conservation measures established by an RFMO, 'shall have access to the fishery resources to which those measures apply'. Some commentators have questioned whether the practice of restricting access to fisheries is compatible with Article 116 of the LOSC (granting every State the right to fish on the high seas) and Article 119(3) of the LOSC ('conservation measures and their implementation ... [should] not discriminate against the fishermen of any State').[55] These provisions may point rather in the direction of a tacit modification.

---

[50] Anderson, n 45; Nelson, n 45; Scovazzi, n 45; Freestone and Oude Elferink, n 45, 184–5; Boyle, n 45, 40; Harrison, n 23, 86–92.

[51] Freestone and Oude Elferink, n 45, 193.

[52] Y Takei, *Filling Regulatory Gaps in High Seas Fisheries* (Brill Leiden 2013) 88–9.

[53] R Wolfrum and N Matz, *Conflicts in International Environmental Law* (Springer Berlin 2010) 30.

[54] Freestone and Oude Elferink, n 45, 201.

[55] See eg PGG Davies and C Redgwell, 'The International Legal Regulation of Straddling Fish Stocks' (1996) 67 *British Yearbook of International Law* 199, 265; Takei, n 52, 67.

Overall, there does not seem to be a strict incompatibility between the LOSC and FSA. The latter blurs the line between modification and interpretation much more than the 1994 Implementation Agreement. It also introduces 'novel' elements and objectives that can be said to constitute modifications of the LOSC by subsequent agreement,[56] as per the definition of modification discussed in Section 2.2. According to some commentators, the FSA may even come to undermine certain basic principles of the LOSC, such as the freedom of fishing on the high seas.[57] On the other hand, the differing membership of the FSA as compared to the LOSC may limit its effect upon the latter.[58] It may be interesting to note that this limitation would also apply to formal amendments, which do not bind States parties that have not accepted them.[59] This creates the risk of fragmentation within the law of the sea.

3.2 The Meeting of States Parties

Another source of modification of the LOSC by subsequent practice is the SPLOS. Its decisions have effectively altered the Convention in several ways—despite the fact that the LOSC appears to grant the SPLOS a merely informational and administrative role.[60] These decisions have been adopted by consensus, thus satisfying the requirement that subsequent practice must evidence the agreement of all parties to modify the LOSC.[61] However, if these decisions are regarded as being derived from implied powers (discussed in Section 2.2),[62] they no longer qualify as modifications, but as interpretations.

In 1994, the SPLOS decided, for policy reasons,[63] on a 'one-time deferment' of the first election of judges to ITLOS, beyond the date imposed by Article 4(3) of Annex VI of the LOSC.[64] It also provisionally varied Article 4(2) of Annex VI of the

---

[56] See eg Young, n 3, 44; Treves, n 30, 56; Freestone and Oude Elferink, n 45, 203, 209.

[57] See further Freestone and Oude Elferink, n 45, 203.

[58] If the provisions of the 1995 Agreement for the Implementation of the Provisions of the United Nations Convention on the Law of the Sea of 10 December 1982 Relating to the Conservation and Management of Straddling Fish Stocks and Highly Migratory Fish Stocks (hereinafter FSA) had been adopted by formal amendment under the 1982 United Nations Convention on the Law of the Sea (hereinafter LOSC), a much higher number of accessions would have been required than there are currently parties to the Agreement.

[59] LOSC, n 58, Art 316. See also VCLT, n 6, Art 40(4).

[60] See eg LOSC, n 58, Annex II, Art 2, and Annex VI, Arts 4, 6, 18, and 19. Article 319(2)(e) is admittedly vague.

[61] Theoretically, SPLOS Rules of Procedure, Doc SPLOS/2/Rev.4 (24 January 2005), Rule 52 provides for the possibility of voting if 'all efforts to achieving general agreement have been exhausted', but this 'would have the effect of altering the established treaty rights of those [dissenting] states against their will': Harrison, n 23, 82.

[62] Ibid, 84.   [63] See eg Treves, n 30, 69–70.

[64] *Report of the first Meeting of States Parties*, Doc SPLOS/3 (28 February 1995) [16(a)].

LOSC to allow States still in the process of *becoming* parties to the LOSC to nominate candidates for the Tribunal.[65] Similarly, in 1996, the SPLOS postponed the first election of the members of the Commission on the Limits of the Continental Shelf, thus deviating from Annex II, Article 2(2) of the LOSC.[66] What is more, at the first elections of the CLCS in 1997, the SPLOS agreed on a composition of the CLCS that departed from the geographical distribution requirement contained in Annex II, Article 2(3) of the LOSC.[67] Once again, it was emphasized that this was a one-off measure that should not be interpreted as, nor constitute a precedent for, derogation from the LOSC.[68] Nevertheless, the decision clearly (though temporarily) derogated from the Convention.[69] These four SPLOS decisions constitute modifications by subsequent practice, even if only with regard to relatively minor procedural provisions.[70]

More importantly, in 2001, the SPLOS extended the time limit prescribed by the Convention for coastal States' submissions concerning the outer limits of their continental shelf to the CLCS.[71] Article 76 of the LOSC requires coastal States, whose continental margin extends beyond 200 nautical miles, to submit information on those outer limits to the CLCS. Article 4 of Annex II of the LOSC requires submission 'as soon as possible but in any case within 10 years of the entry into force of this Convention for that State'. However, many developing coastal States faced difficulties in meeting this deadline,[72] and a formal amendment of the LOSC was not an option for various reasons.[73] In view of these difficulties, the SPLOS decided to calculate the 10-year submission period from the date of the adoption by the CLCS of its Scientific and Technical Guidelines,[74] allowing disadvantaged States more time to make their submissions.[75] The decision was presented in the form of an interpretation, but its terms undeniably diverge from the LOSC[76]—one of the likely reasons why calls for a second extension of the time limit have been denied.[77] This is clearly

---

[65] Ibid, [16(b)].
[66] *Report of the third Meeting of States Parties*, Doc SPLOS/5 (22 February 1996) [20].
[67] *Report of the sixth Meeting of States Parties*, Doc SPLOS/20 (29 March 1997) [12]–[13].
[68] Ibid, [13].   [69] Harrison, n 23, 79; Tanaka, n 3, 34.   [70] Harrison, n 23, 80.
[71] *Decision regarding the Date of Commencement of the Ten-Year Period for Making Submissions to the Commission on the Limits of the Continental Shelf Set out in Article 4 of Annex II to the United Nations Convention on the Law of the Sea*, Doc SPLOS/72 (29 May 2001).
[72] *Issues with respect to article 4 of Annex II to the United Nations Convention on the Law of the Sea; Background paper prepared by the Secretariat*, Doc SPLOS/64 (1 May 2001) [7].
[73] AG Oude Elferink, '"Openness" and Article 76 of the Law of the Sea Convention: The Process Does Not Need to Be Adjusted' (2009) 40 *Ocean Development and International Law* 36, 45.
[74] Doc SPLOS/72, n 71.
[75] *Report of the eleventh Meeting of States Parties*, Doc SPLOS/73 (14 June 2001) [70].
[76] See eg Freestone and Oude Elferink, n 45, 208–9; AG Oude Elferink, 'Current Legal Developments: Meeting of States Parties to the UN Law of the Sea Convention' (2008) 23 *International Journal of Marine and Coastal Law* 769, 770.
[77] See eg *Decision regarding the Workload of the Commission on the Limits of the Continental Shelf and the Ability of States, Particularly Developing States, to Fulfill the Requirements of Article 4 of Annex II*

to avoid the impression that the Convention can be modified by a decision of the SPLOS rather than by means of formal amendment.[78]

In fact, the SPLOS had previously considered four procedures for adopting the initial decision, in descending order of formality: the formal amendment procedures in Articles 312 and 313 of the LOSC, an implementation agreement, and, finally, a SPLOS decision.[79] In selecting the latter option, it relied on the precedents set by those decisions deferring the first elections of the CLCS and ITLOS[80]—despite the fact that these were not intended to be precedents.[81] Since formal amendment procedures were expressly considered, it is difficult to deny that the SPLOS decision is effectively a modification.[82] Also interesting is the fact that some participants considered the decision to be more than just procedural, pointing out that it carried direct relevance for States' rights and obligations under the Convention.[83]

Furthermore, in 2008, the SPLOS decided to grant developing States experiencing 'financial and technical difficulties' the option of submitting only 'preliminary information' in fulfilment of the CLCS submission deadline[84]—a possibility clearly not contained in the Convention. The CLCS is required by the Convention to consider the information submitted by coastal States under Article 4, Annex II, and then issue recommendations. By contrast, the 2008 SPLOS decision requires the Commission to *refrain* from doing so on the basis of the preliminary information submitted to it, pending final submissions by the coastal States concerned.

The 2001 and 2008 decisions could be regarded as procedural and not substantive, as they potentially improve the Commission's effectiveness, and the quality of States' submissions to it.[85] Either way, they institute more extensive changes than SPLOS decisions concerning the CLCS and ITLOS. Moreover, the more recent decisions had 'neither the same urgency nor the *de minimis* character as the previous instances'.[86] It is thus difficult to see them as anything other than modifications of the LOSC.

3.3 Article 105 LOSC

The current practice in relation to Article 105 of the LOSC, which grants universal jurisdiction in providing that 'every State may seize a pirate ship or aircraft',

---

to the United Nations Convention on the Law of the Sea, as well as the Decision Contained in SPLOS/72, Paragraph (a), Doc SPLOS/183 (20 June 2008) Preamble, [8].

[78] Oude Elferink, n 73, 45. This seems implied in the 2001 discussions—see Doc SPLOS/73, n 75.
[79] Doc SPLOS/73, n 75, [78].   [80] Ibid.   [81] See Doc SPLOS/20, n 67, [13].
[82] See eg Churchill, n 7, 97; Oude Elferink, n 73, 132; Harrison, n 23, 80–1; Tanaka, n 3, 34–5.
[83] Doc SPLOS/73, n 75, [79]. Cf Oude Elferink, n 73, 45.
[84] Doc SPLOS/183, n 77, [1]. See further *Report of the eighteenth Meeting of States Parties*, Doc SPLOS/184 (21 July 2008) [85]–[99].
[85] Oude Elferink, n 76, 774.   [86] Harrison, n 23, 82.

constitutes another potential instance of tacit modification. It specifies that prosecution of pirates is to be by 'the courts of the State which carried out the seizure'. It is unclear from the text—particularly given the use of the word 'may'—whether it is only the courts of the arresting State that have such jurisdiction. However, the *travaux préparatoires* strongly indicate that this is the case.[87]

There have been numerous instances of pirates arrested by one State and prosecuted by another. Memoranda of understanding were concluded by the United States, United Kingdom, and the European Union with Kenya in 2008 and 2009 to arrange such transfers of captured pirates for trial.[88] In fact, Kenya has taken custody of hundreds of pirates captured by other countries in recent years.[89] It should be noted that Kenya is party to the LOSC, while the United States is a (very influential) non-party. They are both, however, parties to the 1958 Geneva Convention on the High Seas, which contains near-identical piracy provisions that therefore apply between them.[90] Moreover, there is in principle no reason to ignore the practice of non-parties, even if it is not equal in (evidentiary) value to the practice of the States parties. Likewise, pirates captured by Denmark and Russia have been handed over to Yemen;[91] France has transferred pirates for trial in Somalia;[92] a Dutch court in Rotterdam asserted jurisdiction over pirates arrested by a Danish frigate;[93] and, in 2012, ten Somali pirates arrested by a Dutch frigate were handed over to Germany and prosecuted.[94] Some States 'catch and release' suspected pirates.[95] Overall, it seems to be the preferred practice of States involved in combating piracy to hand over arrested pirates to non-arresting States for prosecution.[96]

---

[87] ILC, *Report of the International Law Commission*, 18th Session, UN Doc A/3159 (1956) 283, Commentary to Art 43: 'This right cannot be exercised at a place under the jurisdiction of another State.' Cf JA Roach, 'Countering Piracy off Somalia: International Law and International Institutions' (2010) 104 *American Journal of International Law* 397, 404–5.

[88] Kenya has since withdrawn from some of these agreements, but continues to accept pirates for prosecution on a case-by-case basis—*Report of the Secretary-General on Specialized Anti-piracy Courts in Somalia and other States in the Region*, UN Doc S/2012/50 (2012) [78].

[89] E Kontorovich, '"A Guantanamo on the Sea": The Difficulties of Prosecuting Pirates and Terrorists' (2010) 98 *California Law Review* 243, 263.

[90] VCLT, n 6, Art 30(4)(b).   [91] Kontorovich, n 89, 255, 268.

[92] D Guilfoyle, 'Piracy Off Somalia: A Sketch of the Legal Framework', *EJIL:Talk!* (20 April 2009), available at <http://www.ejiltalk.org/piracy-off-somalia-a-sketch-of-the-legal-framework/>.

[93] *Somali Pirates* Case, District Court of Rotterdam, 17 June 2010, LJN: BM8116, 10/600012-09.

[94] C Ahlborn, 'Adjudicating Somali Piracy Cases—German Courts in a Double Bind', *CJICL Blog* (3 January 2013), available at <http://cjicl.org.uk/2013/01/03/adjudicating-somali-piracy-cases-german-courts-in-a-double-bind-2/>.

[95] Roach, n 87, 403 and 403 n 35.

[96] See eg *Report of the Secretary-General*, [124]; Roach, n 87, 404; E Papastavridis, 'Piracy off Somalia: The "Emperors and the Thieves of the Oceans" in the 21st Century' in A Abass (ed), *Protecting Human Security in Africa* (Oxford University Press Oxford 2010) 122, 140; A Middelburg, *Piracy in a Legal Context: Prosecution of Pirates Operating off the Somali Coast* (Wolf Legal Nijmegen 2011) 55; R Geiss and A Petrig, *Piracy and Armed Robbery at Sea* (Oxford University Press Oxford 2011) 21, 30–3, 168.

Some writers argue that this practice conflicts with Article 105 of the LOSC,[97] while others point out that the provision does not prohibit such transfers.[98] It has been argued that the stance that non-capturing States lack jurisdiction to prosecute pirates, though feasible, is not convincing given the customary norm regarding universal jurisdiction.[99] Moreover, a strict interpretation of Article 105 may not give full effect to the duty to cooperate in Article 100 of the LOSC, nor to calls by the Security Council for cooperation to combat piracy.[100] The LOSC drafters may have 'thought large-scale high seas piracy a thing of the past'.[101] If Article 105 is indeed undergoing a gradual modification by subsequent practice this represents more than a merely 'procedural' change, given that Article 105 derogates from flag State jurisdiction. Nevertheless, its effect is to enhance the performance of LOSC obligations in the light of present-day concerns, leaving the essential aims and purposes of the LOSC intact.

3.4 Other provisions impacted by State practice

The system of straight baselines reflected in Article 7 of the LOSC has attracted an extensive amount of State practice (although its effects may still be ambiguous). Article 7 allows the use of a system of straight baselines along deeply indented coastlines or where there is a fringe of islands in the immediate vicinity of the coast, setting out several conditions for this purpose. The ICJ has emphasized that straight baselines should only be used in cases involving exceptional geographical circumstances.[102] Nevertheless, a large proportion of States have done so, contrary to the requirements in Article 7.[103] Moreover, straight baselines are applied differently among the States participating in this practice. This has triggered objections from non-participating States. Thus, the practice in relation to Article 7 fails to qualify as 'concordant, common and consistent',[104] and cannot have modified the LOSC. It also cannot result in an *inter se* modification between the States that have taken a broad view of Article 7, since, aside from the inconsistency of practice, this would affect other States' rights and obligations under the LOSC. The practice has

---

[97] E Kontorovich, 'Case Report: *United States v Shi*' (2009) 103 *American Journal of International Law* 734, 739; Papastavridis, n 96, 142.

[98] Roach, n 87, 403; T Treves, 'Piracy and the International Law of the Sea' in D Guilfoyle (ed), *Modern Piracy: Legal Challenges and Responses* (Edward Elgar Cheltenham 2013) 117, 122.

[99] L Azubuike, 'International Law Regime Against Piracy' (2009) 15 *Annual Survey of International and Comparative Law* 43, 54–5.

[100] See eg UNSC Res 1897 (30 November 2009) [12]–[14].   [101] Kontorovich, n 89, 270.

[102] See eg *Maritime Delimitation and Territorial Questions between Qatar and Bahrain* (Merits) [2001] ICJ Rep 40, [212]–[215].

[103] See Churchill, n 7, 107.   [104] See Section 2.1 above.

nonetheless had a certain impact, in the sense that it has significantly 'weakened the authority' of Article 7.[105]

There are numerous other aspects of the LOSC that raise similar questions. For instance, a divisive issue is the question of whether warships passing through a coastal State's territorial sea require prior authorization (or notification). It is unclear from the *travaux* or the text of the LOSC whether such a right of passage exists, although it may be implied by some of its provisions.[106] A significant number of States currently require prior authorization, which would then seem to contradict the Convention. However, practice is not yet sufficiently widespread or consistent (especially in light of persistent objections from certain States) to draw any firm conclusions.[107]

One general lesson that can be drawn from these examples is that States have shown a preference for flexibility and expediency in relation to the LOSC, thereby granting subsequent agreements and practice a prominent role.

4 SUBSEQUENT PRACTICE AND REGIME INTERACTION IN THE LOSC

The law of the sea interacts with numerous other regimes, including international environmental law,[108] human rights,[109] trade law,[110] and security law.[111] Subsequent practice can serve as a vehicle for interaction between the different regimes, adapting

---

[105] Churchill, n 7, 108. See also JRV Prescott, 'Straight and Archipelagic Baselines' in G Blake (ed), *Maritime Boundaries and Ocean Resources* (Croom Helm London 1987) 38, 49 (referring to LOSC, n 58, Art 7 as 'effectively a dead letter').

[106] Churchill, n 7, 111–13, referring to LOSC, n 58, Arts 17, 19(2), and 20.

[107] For further examples, see eg Churchill, n 7; Rothwell, n 3.

[108] See eg T Stephens, *International Courts and Environmental Protection* (Cambridge University Press Cambridge 2009) ch 9; Wolfrum and Matz, n 53, 13–61.

[109] See eg BH Oxman, 'Human Rights and the United Nations Convention on the Law of the Sea' (1998) 36 *Columbia Journal of Transnational Law* 399; T Treves, 'Human Rights and the Law of the Sea' (2010) 28 *Berkeley Journal of International Law* 1.

[110] See eg the *Swordfish Cases* brought before the WTO and ITLOS: *Chile—Measures Affecting the Transit and Importing of Swordfish—Request for the Establishment of a Panel by the European Communities*, 7 November 2000, WT/DS193/2; *Conservation and Sustainable Exploitation of Swordfish Stocks in the South-Eastern Pacific Ocean (Chile/EC)* [2000] ITLOS Rep 148. See also MA Young, *Trading Fish, Saving Fish: The Interaction between Regimes in International Law* (Cambridge University Press Cambridge 2011).

[111] See eg 1998 Convention on the Suppression of Unlawful Acts against the Safety of Maritime Navigation.

the LOSC in line with external developments.[112] The following section explores how this process unfolds.

Fragmentation is endemic to international law. In the absence of clear hierarchies or of an overarching legislature or judiciary to enact new law and promote consistency—coupled with the constant expansion and diversification of international law—international legal 'regimes'[113] develop in parallel and often without regard to other regimes, producing 'specialized rules and rule-systems that have no clear relationship to each other'.[114] The ILC has concluded that the proliferation of specialized treaty regimes has increased the ability of the law to respond to the 'regulatory context' without seriously compromising legal certainty and predictability.[115] Nevertheless, fragmentation increases the likelihood of conflicting legal norms[116]—both *between* and *within* regimes—and with it the need for harmonization through interpretation and, increasingly, informal modification. In fact, regimes are shaped more by informal processes—as a result of an increased need for flexibility[117]—than through formal law-making.[118]

Potential conflicts can initially be addressed by means of 'harmonious interpretation'. According to Article 31(3)(c) of the VCLT, interpretation must take into account 'any other rules of international law' applicable between the parties—also known as the principle of 'systemic integration'.[119] This principle provides for recourse to the normative environment when there is 'an inconsistency, a conflict, an overlap between two or more norms—and no other interpretative means provides a resolution'.[120] Interpretation 'may resolve apparent conflicts; [but] it cannot resolve genuine conflicts'.[121] In the latter case, modification by subsequent practice can prove useful. Of course, there are also other strategies for resolving inter-regime conflicts. 'Collision-rules' such as *lex specialis* and *lex posterior* can be used on a case-by-case basis.[122] Also, when the same dispute is brought before multiple judicial bodies (including where one is within the law of the sea regime

---

[112] Wolfrum and Matz, n 53, 140.

[113] For a definition of the term 'regime', see ILC, n 9, [12]. See further MA Young (ed), *Regime Interaction in International Law: Facing Fragmentation* (Cambridge University Press Cambridge 2012).

[114] ILC, n 9, [483].   [115] Ibid, [491]–[492].

[116] 'Conflict' here is not only taken to include a strict incompatibility, implying that one obligation cannot be applied without violating the other, but also 'policy-conflicts' when one treaty frustrates the operation of another (ibid [24]). See further Pauwelyn, n 26.

[117] N Matz-Lück, 'Norm Interpretation across International Regimes: Competences and Legitimacy' in Young (ed), n 113, 201, 204–5.

[118] M Koskenniemi, 'Hegemonic Regimes' in Young (ed), n 113, 305, 317.

[119] ILC, n 9, [413]; C McLachlan, 'The Principle of Systemic Integration and Article 31(3)(c) of the Vienna Convention' (2005) 54 *International and Comparative Law Quarterly* 279.

[120] ILC, n 9, [420].

[121] CJ Borgen, 'Resolving Treaty Conflicts' (2005) 37 *George Washington International Law Review* 573, 640.

[122] ILC, n 9, [250].

and the other outside of it, such as in the *Swordfish*[123] and *MOX Plant*[124] cases), conflict can be avoided through strategies such as jurisdictional deference.[125] Thus, the Annex VII tribunal in the *MOX Plant Case* deferred to the European Court of Justice, *inter alia*, on the basis of the principle of 'mutual respect and comity which should prevail between judicial institutions'.[126]

Subsequent practice can also help reconcile norms *within* the law of the sea: 'accommodation is easiest between two instruments within a regime, especially between a framework agreement and a more specific (implementation) agreement'.[127] As discussed, subsequent practice seems to have led to the (tacit) adherence of all LOSC parties to the 1994 Implementation Agreement, promoting consistency between the two instruments.[128]

Subsequent practice—taken in its broadest sense to include subsequent agreements such as successive treaties—can impact LOSC provisions through treaties outside of the law of the sea domain. For instance, Article 3 of the 2001 UNESCO Convention on the Protection of the Underwater Cultural Heritage states that its provisions shall not prejudice the LOSC, yet concerns have been expressed that the rights it confers go far beyond coastal States' rights and jurisdiction under the LOSC.[129] Similarly, Article 22(1) of the 1992 Convention on Biological Diversity (CBD) declares that the LOSC shall prevail, *unless* it poses a serious threat or damage to biodiversity. It takes a protective, 'ecosystem' approach that goes beyond the LOSC's more management-oriented one.[130] To this extent, the CBD could modify the operation of LOSC Parts V and VII, while remaining compatible with the object and purpose of the LOSC.[131] This also shows how subsequent practice can constitute a *source* of regime conflict.

Normative conflict is only one aspect of regime interaction. 'Mainstreaming' is used to describe the technique by means of which one regime becomes part of another regime's 'daily routine and self-understanding', through cooperation and the pursuit of common goals.[132] One field that has heavily impacted upon the LOSC in this way is international environmental law. Vice-President Weeramantry of the ICJ pointed out the 'inter-temporal aspect' of treaties dealing with activities impacting the environment in the *Gabčíkovo-Nagymaros* case: '[t]he ethical and human

---

[123] *Chile—Measures Affecting the Transit and Importing of Swordfish; Conservation and Sustainable Exploitation of Swordfish Stocks in the South-Eastern Pacific Ocean.*

[124] *MOX Plant (Ireland v United Kingdom)* (Suspension of Proceedings on Jurisdiction and Merits and Request for Further Provisional Measures) (Procedural Order No 3) (2003) 42 ILM 1187.

[125] J Crawford and P Nevill, 'Relations between International Courts and Tribunals: The "Regime Problem"' in Young (ed), n 113, 235, 241–3.

[126] *MOX Plant*, n 124, [28].   [127] ILC, n 9, [278].

[128] See Section 3.1 above.

[129] See eg T Scovazzi, 'The Protection of Underwater Cultural Heritage' in Freestone et al (eds), n 45, 120, 134.

[130] See eg Wolfrum and Matz, n 53, 15–30.   [131] Boyle, n 45.

[132] Koskenniemi, n 118, 319.

rights related aspects of environmental law bring it within the category of law so essential to human welfare that we cannot apply to today's problems in this field the standards of yesterday.'[133]

The impact of the precautionary principle on the LOSC may be a good example of regime interaction through modification by subsequent practice in the environmental law context. The principle was first endorsed in Principle 15 of the 1992 Rio Declaration on Environment and Development. In its 2011 Advisory Opinion on *Responsibilities and Obligations of States Sponsoring Persons and Entities with Respect to Activities in the Area*, the ITLOS Seabed Disputes Chamber declared that the Nodules and Sulphides Regulations[134] have turned the 'precautionary approach'[135] in Principle 15 of the Rio Declaration into a binding obligation in relation to activities in the Area.[136] The precautionary approach was also introduced in the context of fisheries law by means of the FSA (admittedly, within the narrow scope of fish stocks covered by the Agreement), and other international fisheries instruments followed suit.[137] Indeed, in the *Southern Bluefin Tuna* case, ITLOS seemed to suggest that the precautionary approach might have modified LOSC fisheries provisions.[138] The precautionary approach is also linked to the ecosystem approach.[139]

More generally, these trends indicate that conservation measures are 'being gradually taken for the purposes of conservation as such, rather than conservation with a view to utilization'.[140] The concept of 'conservation of living resources' under the LOSC is thus undergoing modification by means of subsequent practice, mirroring developments in environmental law on the precautionary and ecosystem approaches, sustainable use, and biodiversity.[141]

---

[133] *Gabčíkovo-Nagymaros Project (Hungary/Slovakia)* (Sep Op Vice-President Weeramantry) [1997] ICJ Rep 88, 114.

[134] 2000 Regulations on Prospecting and Exploration for Polymetallic Nodules in the Area, Doc ISBA/6/A/18, Art 31(2); 2010 Regulations on Prospecting and Exploration for Polymetallic Sulphides in the Area, Doc ISBA/16/A/12/Rev1, Art 33(2).

[135] It is unclear whether the content of the 'precautionary approach' differs from the 'precautionary principle'.

[136] *Responsibilities and Obligations of States Sponsoring Persons and Entities with Respect to Activities in the Area* (Advisory Opinion) [2011] ITLOS Rep 10, [122], 125–35 (hereinafter *Deep Seabed Advisory Opinion*).

[137] See eg 1995 Food and Agriculture Organization Code of Conduct for Responsible Fisheries, Arts 6.5 and 7.5 (hereinafter FAO Code of Conduct); 2001 Reykjavik Declaration on Responsible Fisheries in the Marine Ecosystem, *Report of the Reykjavik Conference on Responsible Fisheries in the Marine Ecosystem*, Fisheries Report 658 (FAO Rome 2002) [5]; UNGA Res 67/79 (11 December 2012).

[138] *Southern Bluefin Tuna (Australia and New Zealand v Japan) (Nos 3 and 4)* (Provisional Measures) (1999) 117 ILR 148, [77]–[80]; Sep Op Judge Laing, [16]–[19]; Sep Op Judge Treves, [9]. See *Deep Seabed Advisory Opinion*, n 136, [132]; *Virginia Commentaries*, Vol III, 2888; Boyle, n 45, 51.

[139] FSA, n 58, Art 5(d)–(f); FAO Code of Conduct, n 138, Art 6.2; Reykjavik Declaration, n 137.

[140] Takei, n 52, 103.   [141] Ibid, 79–80, 103.

5 Implications for the Development of the LOSC

To determine the degree to which the LOSC is amenable to modification by subsequent practice, this section discusses the limits of such modification in the context of the Convention, as a result of the nature of the treaty regime, the type of treaty obligations, and the Convention's 'in-built' adaptation mechanisms.

First, as to the nature of the treaty regime, the LOSC may be a treaty 'creating an expectation of non-derogation',[142] given its nature as a 'package deal' and the character of certain of its core obligations. This implies that to safeguard the integrity of the Convention, a high degree of practice must be reached for tacit modification to occur.[143] A contributing factor is whether the practice is spread across the different geopolitical groupings of States parties.[144] However, total consistency of practice in relation to the LOSC is next to impossible to achieve, 'given the breadth, extent, and goals of the Convention and the vastly different expectations the Convention holds for many different States which have become parties'.[145]

Second, certain types of provisions in the LOSC limit the impact of subsequent practice. Some provisions explicitly rule out the possibility of modification: Article 311(6) of the LOSC expressly prohibits derogation from the cornerstone principle of the 'common heritage of mankind' laid down in Article 136. Article 311(3) highlights that the modifying potential of subsequent practice is also very limited with regard to other 'core' LOSC principles.[146] Generally, modification should not 'disrupt the balance established under the general treaty between the rights and obligations of States parties thereto',[147] as emphasized also in Article 311(3).

The impact of tacit modification is also limited with regard to obligations *erga omnes* (owed to the international community as a whole) or *erga omnes partes* (aimed at protecting the collective interests of all the treaty parties).[148] The same applies to obligations that are 'non-reciprocal' (a breach by one party amounts to a breach vis-à-vis all the other parties) or 'integral' in nature (the obligations they impose are 'independent of any expectation of reciprocity or performance on the part of other parties').[149] Examples in the Convention include the 'peaceful purposes' requirement and the invalidity of sovereignty claims over the high seas, enshrined in Articles 88 and 89 of the LOSC, respectively. Likewise, the general obligation in Article 192 to 'protect and preserve the marine environment'—albeit vague—can be

---

[142] ILC, n 9, [109].   [143] Churchill, n 7, 104.
[144] Ibid, 105.   [145] Rothwell, n 3, 147.   [146] See eg Section 3.1.
[147] SA Sadat-Akhavi, *Methods of Resolving Conflicts between Treaties* (Martinus Nijhoff Leiden 2003) 131, cited in ILC, n 9, [109].
[148] ILC, n 9, [390], and further ibid, eg [154].
[149] Ibid, [311]–[312], and further ibid, eg [154] and [385].

characterized as an integral obligation. As a core environmental provision, it may also be subject to the non-regression principle.[150]

Moreover, there is a general prohibition on derogation from obligations benefiting third parties.[151] One potential example is the right of innocent passage for 'ships of all States' or 'foreign ships'. This restricts the sovereignty of coastal States in favour of rights for (private) vessels, even presumably those of non-parties.[152]

Furthermore, the ambiguous nature or formulation of many provisions can grant States considerable 'leeway' in interpreting and implementing the LOSC. This reduces the need to achieve flexibility by means of modification by subsequent practice, and at the same time facilitates regime interaction, leaving room for manoeuvre to avoid normative conflict.

Third, treaties may contain 'in-built' adaptation mechanisms that provide (partial) alternatives to subsequent practice. In the case of the LOSC, these include institutions and processes such as the ISA, SPLOS, CLCS, dispute settlement, delegation to the International Maritime Organization, or other international standard-setting bodies, and incorporation by reference to external standards.

An example of the adaptation of the LOSC through dispute settlement, for instance, is the 'equidistance/relevant circumstances' method of delimitation, developed in the case law to supplement Articles 74(1) and 83(1) of the LOSC, which merely refer to achieving an 'equitable solution'.[153] The dispute settlement system also facilitates regime interaction. Pursuant to Article 293, tribunals under the LOSC shall apply 'other rules of international law' and can thus to some extent read external norms into the LOSC. Moreover, by means of Article 138 of its Rules of procedure, ITLOS introduced the possibility for an authorized 'body' to request an advisory opinion on a legal question based on an agreement related to the purposes of the Convention—a major innovation, with a basis in Article 21 of the ITLOS Statute, and a broad mandate, as compared for instance to the advisory procedure of the ICJ. Leaving aside the question of whether the Tribunal exceeded its powers under the Convention in constructing Article 138, this new competence may offer the Tribunal an additional means of facilitating regime interaction and adaptation in the LOSC.

Generally, the LOSC is developed through the activities of States parties and bodies like the SPLOS, CLCS, ISA, and the UN Informal Consultative Process on Oceans and the Law of the Sea, mostly in ways that do not exceed the realm of interpretation. For instance, the 2011 Advisory Opinion of the ITLOS Seabed Disputes

---

[150] M Prieur and G Sozzo, *La non-régression en droit de l'environnement* (Bruylant Brussels 2012).
[151] ILC, n 9, [154].
[152] See eg LOSC, n 58, Art 17. See further N St Skourtos, 'Legal Effects for Parties and Nonparties: The Impact of the Law of the Sea Convention' in MH Nordquist and JN Moore (eds), *Entry into Force of the Law of the Sea Convention* (Kluwer The Hague 1995) 187, 195ff.
[153] See eg *Delimitation of the Maritime Boundary in the Bay of Bengal (Bangladesh/Myanmar)* (Judgment) [2012] ITLOS Rep 4, [229]–[233] and [238].

Chamber demonstrates how certain parts of the LOSC, in that case those relating to the Area, are susceptible to development by subsequent practice through the ISA, most notably through the promulgation of the 'Mining Code'.[154] Similarly, the practice of the CLCS in relation to its Rules of Procedure and coastal States' submissions may have led to the tacit modification of certain parts of Article 76 of the LOSC.[155] Even *de facto* amendments by the SPLOS, if regarded as rooted in implied powers rather than as modifications by subsequent practice, could constitute a special adaptation mechanism.

Another key mechanism for adaptation and regime interaction in the LOSC is its system of 'rules of reference'.[156] For instance, many provisions in Part XII of the LOSC direct States to give effect to 'generally accepted international rules and standards' or look to 'competent international organizations' from other regimes. The 1973 International Convention for the Prevention of Pollution from Ships (MARPOL) and its Annexes, are the principal sources of the 'rules and standards' on pollution from vessels referred to in Articles 194, 211, 218, and 220 of the LOSC. Likewise, Article 237 of the LOSC is an umbrella provision for the protection of the marine environment, enhancing the function of the LOSC as a framework convention. This openness to external norms through 'rules of reference' is an adaptation mechanism that reduces the need for modification by subsequent practice.

Furthermore, the Convention contains 'evolutionary' provisions. These operate as implicit rules of reference, with the effect of importing general international law into the LOSC without the need for recourse to modification by subsequent practice. Terms that could be deemed evolutionary include 'pollution' and 'protection of the marine environment', 'conservation of living resources', 'natural resources', and 'generally accepted rules and standards' (also an express rule of reference). The more flexibility that can be achieved through evolutionary interpretation and Article 31(3)(c) of the VCLT as gateways to regime interaction,[157] the less of a need there is to formally or tacitly modify the Convention.

Nevertheless, where the 'in-built' mechanisms—bounded by the four corners of the text—fail to go far enough, modification by subsequent practice remains a strategic tool for parties to the LOSC.

The parts of the LOSC more susceptible to such modification include some of the more 'novel' issues codified in the Convention, such as the straight baselines system. These were not supported by longstanding practice prior to the Third United Nations Conference on the Law of the Sea (UNCLOS III), as compared to

---

[154] International Seabed Authority (ISA), Mining Code, available at <http://www.isa.org.jm/en/mcode>. See text accompanying nn 134 and 136 above.

[155] See eg A Serdy, 'The Commission on the Limits of the Continental Shelf and its Disturbing Propensity to Legislate' (2011) 26 *International Journal of Marine and Coastal Law* 367.

[156] See further B Oxman, 'Tools for Change: The Amendment Procedure' in *Proceedings of the Twentieth Anniversary Commemoration of the Opening for Signature of the UNCLOS* (United Nations 2003) 195.

[157] See Sections 2.2 and 4 above.

provisions such as those in Part II of the LOSC, which codify issues established well before UNCLOS III.[158] Moreover, provisions on subjects such as 'conservation' require frequent adaptation to maintain their relevance and also seem more amenable to tacit modification. In addition, procedural provisions—to the extent that the distinction between procedural and substantive provisions is practicable—are much more prone to modification by subsequent practice. By contrast, it is unlikely that practice could modify 'essential'[159] provisions such as the outer limits of the various maritime zones.[160] These provisions balance diverse State interests and sovereignty over resources, on the one hand, with the goal of multilateralism under the LOSC, on the other[161]—a balance reflective of the aims of the Convention as a 'package deal'. Likewise, as discussed, the modifying potential of subsequent practice is highly limited in relation to 'core' LOSC principles such as the common heritage of mankind or the peaceful purposes requirement. Many of these provisions also reflect customary law, implying that subsequent practice would have to modify both the treaty and the corresponding customary norm. With regard to provisions for which the high threshold required for a modification by subsequent practice is unattainable, States will have to resort to formal amendment procedures under the LOSC, or at least to more 'formalized' types of practice such as implementation agreements.[162]

6 Conclusion

The LOSC establishes an intricate regime, covering a wide range of substantive issues and objectives, setting up new institutional arrangements, and spanning an extensive membership with diverse interests. It is developed through numerous adaptation mechanisms, some more far-reaching than others. From among these, subsequent practice provides a maximum of flexibility, given the rigidity of the Convention's formal amendment procedures and the limitations of alternative adaptation mechanisms. This is significant in a rapidly developing field such as the law of the sea.

Moreover, the process of fragmentation of international law leads to occasional discord between the law of the sea and other regimes, as well as to fragmentation

---

[158] Rothwell, n 3, 145.   [159] See Section 2.2 above.   [160] Rothwell, n 3, 149.
[161] See further eg Y Tanaka, *A Dual Approach to Ocean Governance: The Cases of Zonal and Integrated Management in International Law of the Sea* (Ashgate Surrey 2008).
[162] See also Treves, n 30, 73.

within the law of the sea. Subsequent practice can help resolve the resulting normative inconsistencies by modifying and supplementing the LOSC, and clarifying its relationship to other instruments. Crosscutting issues such as the protection and conservation of the environment, which require a large degree of coordination between regimes, can be more effectively dealt with in this way.

A key challenge lies in distinguishing tacit modifications from mere interpretations. The process of subsequent practice also faces important limitations in the LOSC context, as a result of the flexibility of the LOSC as a 'framework' convention and its nature as a 'package deal', as well as the character of many of its key provisions. A number of important 'in-built' adaptation mechanisms in the LOSC also reduce the need for modification by subsequent practice. This sets a high threshold for such tacit modification of the Convention.

In most cases it is clear that modification by subsequent practice does not go so far as to undermine or detract from the object and purpose of the Convention, nor its fundamental provisions. Rather, it helps strike a balance between the core concepts of the LOSC and the contemporary norms that have emerged since its inception, in other treaty regimes and in the realm of custom. If approached with due caution—in line with safeguards such as the threshold of 'concordant, common and consistent' practice—subsequent practice can contribute to developing the Convention in accordance with the evolving needs of the international community, enabling it to fulfil its purpose as a 'Constitution for the Oceans'.[163]

---

[163] UN Division for Ocean Affairs and the Law of the Sea, *A Constitution for the Oceans—Remarks by T Koh* (1982), available at <www.un.org/depts/los/convention_agreements/texts/koh_english.pdf>.

4
BASELINES

COALTER G LATHROP[*]

1 THE FUNCTION AND SIGNIFICANCE OF BASELINES

In the seminal maritime delimitation case of the modern era, the International Court of Justice (ICJ) wrote 'the land dominates the sea'.[1] Two decades later Weil expanded the court's cryptic assertion writing that 'the land dominates the sea *and it dominates it by the intermediary the coastal front*'.[2] The ICJ further clarified the intermediate role of the coast: 'The juridical link between the State's territorial sovereignty and its rights to certain adjacent maritime expanses is established by means of its coast.'[3] As the legal expression of the coast,[4] baselines, in their many

---

[*] The author would like to thank Ariell Friedman, JD Duke Law, for her research and editorial assistance.

[1] *North Sea Continental Shelf (Federal Republic of Germany v Denmark; Federal Republic of Germany v Netherlands)* (Judgment) [1969] ICJ Rep 3, [96]. In French, 'le principe que la terre domine la mer'. As the International Court of Justice noted, '[t]he land is the legal source of the power which a State may exercise over territorial extensions to seaward.'

[2] P Weil, *The Law of Maritime Delimitation—Reflections* (Grotius Cambridge 1989) 50 (emphasis added).

[3] *Continental Shelf (Libyan Arab Jamahiriya/Malta)* (Judgment) [1985] ICJ Rep 13, [49].

[4] The term 'coast' is broader than the term 'baseline', but undoubtedly the low-water line is part of the coast. 'Coast' is defined as 'the edge or margin of land next to the sea'. GK Walker (ed), *Definitions for the Law of the Sea: Terms not Defined by the 1982 Convention* (Martinus Nijhoff Leiden 2012) 130. An earlier version of the International Hydrographic Organization glossary defines 'coast' as '[t]he sea-shore. The narrow strip of land in immediate contact with any body of water, including the area between high- and low-water lines' (at 131).

forms, are the features through which coastal States generate derivative title to maritime areas, and, as such, baselines are a foundational component of coastal State maritime jurisdiction.

Bederman, writing about the modern system of maritime jurisdictional zones emanating from the coast, notes that '[i]t very much matters "where" in the ocean a particular event takes place, because such a location determines the relevant set of rules for legal conduct.'[5] The answer to the question 'where?' hinges on the location of baselines. Baselines are the 'zero mark' for measuring the breadth of the territorial sea, contiguous zone, exclusive economic zone, and, in most circumstances, the continental shelf,[6] and are the starting point for delimitation between neighboring States claiming overlapping maritime areas. Baselines are 'a major ingredient' when used to delineate maritime zone outer limits and to delimit those zones between States.[7] Baselines are the only ingredient when used to designate the outer limits of internal waters separating areas in which States enjoy unimpeded sovereignty from the territorial sea beyond.[8] Maritime boundary delimitation and the functional and spatial aspects of archipelagic waters, the territorial sea, contiguous zone, exclusive economic zone, and continental shelf are addressed separately in this volume.[9] Internal waters, the jurisdictional zone limited by baselines, are addressed in the chapter covering port State jurisdiction but merit additional brief discussion here.[10]

Internal waters are subject to the legal regime of State sovereignty and are governed by the rules of the coastal State's municipal legal system. Coastal State sovereignty in internal waters is unencumbered by the rights of other States.[11] This is in contrast with the territorial sea lying just beyond the baselines, in which ships of all States enjoy the right of innocent passage.[12] As a consequence, the coastal State may deny foreign vessels, including warships, entry into its internal waters or may set conditions to that entry.[13] Foreign warships are insulated by the principle

---

[5] DJ Bederman, 'The Sea' in B Fassbender and A Peters (eds), *The Oxford Handbook of the History of International Law* (Oxford University Press Oxford 2012) 373.

[6] Where the outer edge of the continental margin extends beyond 200 nm the breadth of the continental shelf may be established by criteria other than distance measured from baselines. See 1982 United Nations Convention on the Law of the Sea, Art 76 (hereinafter LOSC).

[7] *Virginia Commentaries*, Vol II, 82.

[8] LOSC, n 6, Art 8(1) ('Except as provided in Part IV [Archipelagic States], waters on the landward side of the baseline of the territorial sea form part of the internal waters of the State.').

[9] See Chapter 5 on the territorial sea and contiguous zone, Chapter 7 on archipelagic waters, Chapter 8 on the exclusive economic zone, Chapter 9 on the continental shelf, and Chapter 12 on maritime delimitation in this volume.

[10] See Chapter 13 on coastal and port State jurisdiction in this volume.

[11] But see LOSC, n 6, Art 8(2), which recites an important exception to this rule for some internal waters created by Art 7 straight baselines.

[12] Ibid, Art 17.

[13] See eg 1987 Nuclear Free Zone, Disarmament, and Arms Control Act (NZ), § 9(2):

of sovereign immunity while in internal waters, but non-governmental vessels are not.[14] Private vessels entering internal waters may find themselves subjected to the full weight of coastal State jurisdiction with respect to criminal and environmental violations, for example, while just outside the baselines the same foreign vessel would enjoy significant protection from coastal State jurisdiction if engaged in innocent passage through the territorial sea. The location of baselines determines where this abrupt and consequential division occurs.

Any discussion of baselines must distinguish the unilateral delineation of zonal outer limits (including of internal waters) from the bilateral process of delimiting maritime boundaries between coastal States. It is important to make this distinction because most of the international decisions of any relevance to the law of baselines have been boundary delimitation cases, and such findings are not always applicable to baselines used for zonal limit delineation. Whether a State may lawfully use a feature, such as an island or jetty, for the purpose of measuring the breadth of the territorial sea and other zones in the unilateral context of establishing outer limits does not necessarily have bearing on whether a court or negotiating partner must or will accept that baseline feature in the bilateral context of boundary delimitation.[15] In fact, courts commonly disregard parties' official baseline claims when deciding a boundary. For example, the ICJ did not take issue with Romania and Ukraine using Sulina Dyke and Serpents' Island, respectively, to measure the breadth of their territorial seas, but ignored both of these features in the delimitation between the parties.[16] Negotiating States also may, and often do, discount otherwise legitimate baseline features in the process of boundary delimitation. Singapore may lawfully measure the breadth of its zones from the low-water line of reclaimed land, but Indonesia need not (and did not) accept that version of Singapore's baseline for the purpose of delimitation.[17]

> The Prime Minister may only grant approval for the entry into the internal waters of New Zealand by foreign warships if the Prime Minister is satisfied that the warships will not be carrying any nuclear explosive device upon their entry into the internal waters of New Zealand.

[14] See eg the ruling by the Supreme Court of Ghana that resolved the pending Annex VII *ARA Libertad Arbitration (Argentina v Ghana), Republic v High Court (Commercial Division) Accra, Ex parte Attorney General, NML Capital and the Republic of Argentina*, Civil Motion No J5/10/2013 (Supreme Court, Ghana, 2013) [24] ('There is no doubt that, under customary international law, warships are covered by sovereign immunity in foreign ports.').

[15] The Court observes that the issue of determining the baseline for the purpose of measuring the breadth of the continental shelf and the exclusive economic zone and the issue of identifying base points for drawing an equidistance/median line for the purpose of delimiting continental shelf and exclusive economic zone between adjacent/opposite States are two different issues.
Maritime Delimitation in the Black Sea (Romania v Ukraine) (Judgment) [2009] ICJ Rep 61, [108].

[16] Ibid, [138] and [149].

[17] C Schofield, TL McDorman, and IM Andi Arsana, 'Indonesia—Singapore' in CG Lathrop (ed), International Maritime Boundaries, Vol VII (Martinus Nijhoff Publishers, Leiden, forthcoming 2015). International Maritime Boundaries.

Baselines are a source of tension among States. Like many other aspects of the law of the sea, the historical development of rules and State practice with respect to baselines reveal the underlying tension between the interests of coastal States in expanding the scope of their authority on the one hand, and, on the other, the interests of maritime States in maintaining traditional freedoms of the seas in as much of the oceans as possible. Spatially excessive maritime claims begin with the baseline:[18] in all circumstances, the result of moving the legal coastline seaward 'is to increase the total area of water over which the coastal state possesses the most comprehensive authority and to decrease the total area within which coastal and noncoastal states share authority and use'.[19] One can easily observe through the baselines lens the tension between the *mare clausum* propensities of coastal States and the *mare liberum* leanings of maritime States. This is not a new phenomenon. Baselines have been contentious at least since they were addressed in the late 1920s by the Hague Codification Conference Preparatory Committee. Baselines continued to present challenging issues throughout subsequent codification efforts from the 1950s through to the adoption of the 1982 United Nations Convention on the Law of the Sea (LOSC). Even now, when the law is as clearly stated as it is ever likely to be, baseline rules carry unsettled questions related to their application by States and their adaptability to the realities of the physical environment.

This chapter sets out the international law of baselines as it stands today and identifies past, present, and possible future problematic issues in this area of the law of the sea. This chapter begins by considering the so-called 'normal baseline', consisting of the low-water line along the coast, and asks whether this baseline is fixed or ambulatory: a question of some consequence for low-lying, small-island States in an era of sea level rise.[20] Specific categories of coastal features that make up the normal baseline, including human-made coastal defences, harbour works, low tide elevations, and reefs, are addressed briefly before turning to the variety of baselines formed by straight line segments, including lines closing mouths of rivers, bay closing lines, port closing lines, straight baselines (*stricto sensu*), and archipelagic baselines. For convenience, the group of straight-line baselines is referred to as artificial baselines. Artificial baselines are, or should be, connected to the actual coast at their

---

[18] Spatially excessive claims should be distinguished from functionally excessive claims through which a coastal State might purport to exert more authority in a zone than is lawful. For example, denying innocent passage to foreign warships in the territorial sea without prior authorization.

[19] MS McDougal and W Burke, *The Public Order of the Oceans* (New Haven Press New Haven, CT 1987) 316. The Court captured this tension in this passage from the *Anglo-Norwegian Fisheries* case:

> The delimitation of sea areas has always an international aspect; it cannot be dependent merely upon the will of the coastal State as expressed in its municipal law. Although it is true that the act of delimitation is necessarily a unilateral act, because only the coastal State is competent to undertake it, the validity of the delimitation with regard to other States depends upon international law.

Fisheries (United Kingdom v Norway) (Judgment) [1951] ICJ Rep 116, 132 (hereinafter *Anglo-Norwegian Fisheries*). But see McNair's distinction between coastal State competence and coastal State discretion: ibid, Dissenting Opinion of Sir A McNair [1951] ICJ Rep 158, 160.

[20] See Chapter 34 on climate change in this volume.

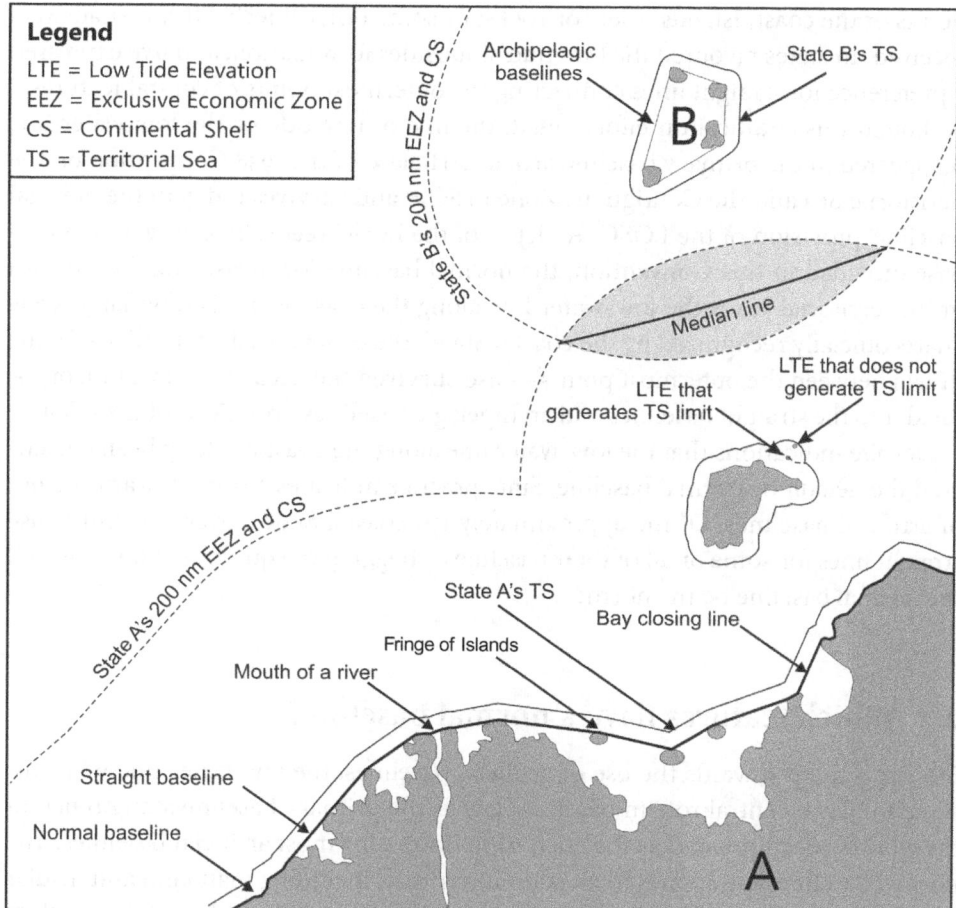

Figure 4.1 Maritime Limits and Boundaries

endpoints and are impacted by the 'fixed versus ambulatory' debate. But with artificial baselines the larger problem is the application of vague rules to complex and varied coastal configurations. Here, the coastal State/maritime State tension is at its most stark. Figure 4.1 illustrates some of the baselines and coastal features discussed in this chapter. Concluding remarks close the chapter.

2 Low-Water Line as Baseline

2.1 How normal is it?

During the preparatory work leading up to the 1930 Hague Codification Conference, States were asked the following question: 'Along the coasts. Is the line that of low tide following the sinuosities of the coast; or a line drawn between the outermost points of the coast, islands, islets or rocks; or some other line?'[21] Of the 21 answers received, 16 States favoured the low-tide/sinuosities formulation, and five expressed a preference for straight lines connecting the outermost points of coastal features.[22] Although this codification effort failed, the line of low-tide or the low-water line reappeared in the primary baseline article, Article 3, of the 1958 Convention on the Territorial Sea and the Contiguous Zone (TSC)[23] and survives today in the 'normal baseline' provision of the LOSC. Article 5 of the LOSC reads: 'Except where otherwise provided in this Convention, the normal baseline for measuring the breadth of the territorial sea is the low-water line along the coast as marked on large-scale charts officially recognized by the coastal State.' The disfavoured alternative—'a line drawn between the outermost points'—also survived the decades and was incorporated into the straight baselines and archipelagic baselines provisions of the LOSC.[24]

Despite indications that the low-water line along the coast has long been considered the default or normal baseline, State practice indicates a trend toward the use of artificial baselines. Of the approximately 150 coastal States, over two-thirds use straight lines for some or all of their baselines,[25] begging the question, how long will the normal baseline be the norm?

2.2 Which features have a normal baseline?

Despite a trend towards the use of artificial baselines, the low-water line will continue to play a central role in baselines law as the primary baseline along much of the world's coastlines and as the anchoring feature for most artificial baselines. The normal baseline rule applies to all coastal territory, including mainland and insular territory. The rule is augmented by several other provisions and norms regarding

---

[21] 'Second Report Submitted to the Council by the Preparatory Committee for the Codification Conference', League of Nations Doc No C.73.M.38.1929.V (1929), repr in (1930) 24(1) *American Journal of International Law Supplement* 3.

[22] The five-State minority consisted of Norway, Sweden, Poland, the USSR, and Latvia. WM Reisman and GS Westerman, *Straight Baselines in International Maritime Boundary Delimitation* (Macmillan Basingstoke 1992) 16.

[23] 1958 Geneva Convention on the Territorial Sea and Contiguous Zone.

[24] See primarily LOSC, n 6, Arts 7 and 47.

[25] States may choose more than one method for determining their baselines. See ibid, Art 14. Roach and Smith count over 85 States that have delimited straight baselines and several others that have enacted enabling legislation without publishing their straight baseline coordinates. JA Roach and RW Smith, *Excessive Maritime Claims* (3rd edn Martinus Nijhoff Leiden 2012) 20. Since their count, other States have delimited straight baselines, for example, Nicaragua in 2013. Over 20 States have claimed archipelagic status and are thus entitled to draw archipelagic baselines: Roach and Smith, *Excessive Maritime Claims*, 206. See also UN Division for Ocean Affairs and the Law of the Sea (DOALOS), *Table of Claims to Maritime Jurisdiction* (15 July 2011), available at <http://www.un.org/Depts/los/LEGISLATIONANDTREATIES/PDFFILES/table_summary_of_claims.pdf>. But see C Schofield, 'Departures from the Coast' (2012) 27 *International Journal of Marine and Coastal Law* 723, 724 ('The predominant type of baseline in use by coastal States is the "normal" baseline…').

specific categories of coastal features such as low-tide elevations, reefs, harbour works, and coastal protection works.[26]

The low-water line of a low-tide elevation—'a naturally formed area of land which is surrounded by and above water at low tide but submerged at high tide'[27]—may be included in the normal baseline if at least part of the low-tide elevation is situated within the territorial sea as measured from the low-water line of mainland or island territory. Low-tide elevations located outside the territorial sea do not contribute to the baseline, nor do low-tide elevations located within a part of the territorial sea generated solely by a qualifying low-tide elevation (thereby disallowing an extension of the territorial sea through a chain of low-tide elevations situated progressively further from shore).[28] The thin line separating islands (above water at high tide) from low-tide elevations (below water at high tide), and the respective treatment of these two categories, is of particular consequence in an era of sea level rise.

In certain situations, namely '[i]n the case of islands situated on atolls or of islands having fringing reefs',[29] reefs (a subcategory of low-tide elevation) are exempted from the distance limitation that applies to other low-tide elevations. Here, irrespective of distance from the associated island, 'the baseline for measuring the breadth of the territorial sea is the seaward low-water line of the reef'.[30] Early drafts of this article referred only to the 'seaward edge' of the reef, not to the low-water line.[31] The reference to the low-water line means that some part of the reef must be above water at low-tide in order for this exception to apply.

In addition to certain low-tide elevations and reefs, Article 11 specifies that 'the outermost permanent harbour works which form an integral part of the harbour system are regarded as forming part of the coast'.[32] As such, the low-water line along these human-made features contributes to the normal baseline. This rule expressly does not apply to offshore installations or artificial islands. Human-made objects situated beyond the harbour system and detached from naturally formed coast have no baseline and generate no maritime zones.[33] For clarity, Article 12, which addresses whether roadsteads are included within the territorial sea, is not a baselines provision although it does impact the outer limit of the territorial sea in cases where the roadstead is 'situated wholly or partly outside the outer limit of the territorial sea [as that limit would be drawn in the absence of the roadstead]'.[34]

---

[26] Note that 'rocks which cannot sustain human habitation or economic life of their own' may have a normal baseline for measuring the breadth of the territorial sea only: LOSC, n 6, Art 121.

[27] Ibid, Art 13.

[28] *Maritime Delimitation and Territorial Questions between Qatar and Bahrain (Qatar v Bahrain)* (Merits) [2001] ICJ Rep 40, [207] ('The law of the sea does not in these circumstances allow application of the so-called "leap-frogging" method.').

[29] LOSC, Art 6.

[30] Ibid.   [31] *Virginia Commentaries*, Vol II, 93.   [32] LOSC, n 6 Art 11.

[33] Ibid, Arts 11 and 60(8), but see eg ibid, Art 60(4) regarding the establishment of safety zones.

[34] Ibid, Art 12.

Non-harbour coastal works such as land reclamation projects and coastal protection works are not expressly addressed in the LOSC, but are often included within the appreciation of the 'coast' in the context of defining the normal baseline. Protecting existing coast with sea defences or expanding natural coastal territory through land reclamation projects should be differentiated from the creation of entirely human-made artificial islands noted above. State practice appears to confirm that such augmentations do contribute to the normal baseline, and publicists seem to agree.[35]

Lastly, permanently ice-covered coasts, like non-harbour coastal works, are not addressed explicitly in the LOSC. The question whether permanent year-round ice should be assimilated to land is complicated by the issue of detecting the non-ice, land/sea interface that, in the absence of ice, would constitute the normal baseline.[36]

2.3 The normal baseline: the big question

Once the status of a feature is determined (eg island, low-tide elevation, qualifying reef), the rules related to the normal baseline are relatively immune from subjective interpretation or misuse by self-interested actors.[37] Nonetheless, the normal baseline rules do raise one significant question: does the legal baseline move with the actual low-water line or may it be fixed by marking it on a chart? This question arises from the ambiguous text of Article 5 and from the chart-making process. The question is important because of the anticipated plight of low-lying States, especially small-island States, in an era of significant sea level rise.

In order to understand why the language of LOSC Article 5—'the low-water line along the coast as marked on large-scale charts officially recognized by the coastal State'—is subject to two different interpretations, one must have a basic understanding of the charting process. A nautical chart is merely a representation of a small portion of the maritime world, created, first and foremost, as a navigational

---

[35] See C Carleton, 'Problems Relating to Non-Natural and Man-Made Basepoints under UNCLOS' in CR Symmons (ed), *Selected Contemporary Issues in the Law of the Sea* (Martinus Nijhoff Leiden 2011) 31, 55 ('Provided the reclaimed land is an integral part of the mainland or an island, State practice would indicate that it is acceptable to consider it as part of the State's coast for the generation of maritime limits.'); McDougal and Burke, n 19, 422–3 ('There would seem to be no substantial objection to assimilating "coast protective works" to harbor installations even when they are isolated structures...').

[36] See DR Rothwell, 'Antarctic Baselines' in AG Oude Elferink and DR Rothwell (eds), *The Law of the Sea and Polar Maritime Delimitation and Jurisdiction* (Martinus Nijhoff The Hague 2001) 49; SB Kaye, 'Territorial Sea Baselines along Ice-Covered Coasts' (2004) 35 *Ocean Development and International Law* 75.

[37] The relative lack of abuse of the low-water line bears out findings from the 1953 Report of the Committee of Experts that governments would not be likely to be tempted 'unreasonably to extend their low-water lines on their charts'. ILC, 'Rapport du Comité d'experts sur certaines questions d'ordre technique concernant la mer territorial', UN Doc A/CN.4/SER.A/1953/Add.1 (1953), English translation repr in *Virginia Commentaries*, Vol II, 59.

aid meant to ensure safety at sea. Therefore, chart makers are mainly concerned with navigational hazards. The coast at low water is among those hazards. Because they depict the low-water line, nautical charts have long been recognized as the most readily available source of information about the shape and location of the low-water line along the coast. However, a chart is only as accurate as the data from which it was assembled. In many parts of the world, the coastal data used to depict the low-water line on nautical charts is several decades, if not more than a century, out of date. This may have little or no impact on navigational safety—ocean-going vessels rarely approach most coasts. However, out-of-date charts create the possibility of significant differences between the charted low-water line and the actual low-water line—differences great enough to impact the legal status of an island or low-tide elevation, for example.

The potential for consequential differences between the charted and actual low-water line has engendered a debate about whether the legal baseline is ambulatory—moving with natural changes in coastal configuration—or fixed by virtue of being depicted on an officially recognized nautical chart, and, if fixed, whether the coastal State is obligated to reassess its fixed baseline periodically to reflect geographic reality.[38] This is not an academic debate. The spectre of rapid sea level rise and the resulting wide-spread inundation of coastal areas, including of whole islands, and in the most extreme case the total submersion of a State's entire territory, raise serious legal questions. For example, does an island continue to have a legal baseline and the associated zones of maritime jurisdiction after the feature has, in fact, submerged below the high-tide line?

There are three approaches to this issue: (1) baselines ambulate automatically with geographic change; (2) baselines may be fixed permanently by the coastal State with no obligation to update baselines even in the event of significant geographic change; and (3) baselines may be fixed temporarily with an obligation to update in the event of significant geographic change. The first and third approaches take the view that the baseline provisions are applicable on a continuing basis: in order to remain lawful, baselines must remain in compliance with the rules as applied to the current coastal geography. The second approach takes the view that the baseline provisions are only to be applied at the time the baseline is claimed: if the baseline is lawful at the time of the claim, the coastal State has satisfied its obligations and need not ever revise its baselines, notwithstanding significant changes in coastal geography.

The automatic ambulation approach may be sustainable in theory but seems untenable in practice. Rigid adherence to this view might logically result in a coastal State's obligation to provide real-time notification of changing baselines and limits through continuous detection, depiction, and dissemination of the physical and legal geography. This impractical approach would undermine stability and certainty, and would

---

[38] Because artificial baselines 'anchor' to the low-water line, this debate has implications for those lines, too.

de-emphasize the authority of the coastal State to establish the location of its own baselines and limits for the purpose of exercising its rights and jurisdiction at sea.

At the other extreme, the permanently fixed approach divorces the legal baseline from geographic reality, relies heavily on the charted line as the manifestation of a State's claim to territory, and emphasizes the unfettered prerogative of the coastal State to declare its own physical make-up.[39] The permanently fixed baseline thesis has the strength of accounting for equitable considerations related to the developing States most heavily impacted by sea level rise, and carries significant policy advantages of stability, certainty, and public order. However, taken to its extreme, the permanently fixed view would flip the basis of maritime entitlement on its head: the land would no longer dominate the sea if maritime rights and jurisdiction could persist after the permanent disappearance or destruction of the territory from which that title was derived. In this extreme situation, moreover, a coastal State advocating the fixed baseline thesis in the teeth of geographic reality to the contrary would be making claims to the disadvantage of the broader community interest in non-exclusive ocean space.[40]

The temporarily fixed approach gives coastal States some limited discretion as to the timing of their chart updates, balances the use of the actual and charted low-water line by requiring periodic changes in the latter to reflect the former, but imbues the charted line with an official but not inviolable status for the period during which it is in effect. Deference to an officially recognized, large-scale, *reasonably up-to-date* chart acknowledges both clauses in the normal baseline definition while balancing practical concerns of notice, publicity, stability, and certainty with theoretical concerns about the source of title to maritime areas. Ambulatory purists and advocates of the permanently fixed baselines thesis would both be dissatisfied with this middle position, but aspects of the negotiating history indicate that this was the meaning understood by earlier drafters.[41] The few States that update their charts frequently in order to account for coastal change take this approach.[42]

The answer to the ambulatory-versus-fixed-baselines debate has major implications for the obligations of coastal States, the rights of mariners, and, in some cases, the very survival of coastal State sovereign rights and jurisdiction. Small-island States threatened with total submersion presumably favour the fixed approach. However, the majority of publicists currently believe that the baseline provisions are applicable on a continuing basis, either automatically or at the discretion of the

---

[39] For a proponent of the fixed approach, see K Purcell, 'Maritime Jurisdiction in a Changing Climate' in MB Gerrard and K Fischer Kuh (eds), *The Law of Adaptation to Climate Change* (American Bar Association Chicago 2012) 729.

[40] J Lisztwan, 'Stability of Maritime Boundary Agreements' (2012) 37 *Yale Journal of International Law* 153 (discussion regarding common heritage at 170).

[41] See eg the concerns raised in the ILC in 1952 about the charted line deviating appreciably from a scientific criterion, including because it was out of date. ILC, 'Summary Records of the Fourth Session' (4 June–8 August 1952) 1 *Yearbook of the International Law Commission*.

[42] For example, The Netherlands.

coastal State. Several publicists, while adopting the ambulatory perspective on the law as it stands today, recognize its weaknesses and have suggested fixes ranging from physical coastal protection to changing the law.[43]

Early assessments during the development of the normal baseline provisions predicted little room for abuse, and history has confirmed this assessment. Despite minor disagreements between delimiting neighbours about the status of particular features (eg an island, low tide elevation, or submerged feature)[44] or discrete stretches of coast,[45] there is no evidence low-water lines have been falsified to enlarge coastal State authority. Whether the normal baseline rules can accommodate the kind of physical coastal change anticipated in the coming decades is, however, of particular concern. Perhaps the next biggest concern is the increasing abandonment of normal baselines by coastal States in the move toward artificial baselines.

3 ARTIFICIAL STRAIGHT LINES AS BASELINES

Artificial straight-line baselines may be drawn across the mouths of rivers, bays, and ports, along coasts with certain geographic configurations, and to enclose the archipelagic waters of archipelagic States. These different forms of artificial baseline do not share historical origins, but in deciding which waters may be encompassed by artificial baselines, the three basic considerations the ICJ elucidated in the *Anglo-Norwegian Fisheries* case generally apply. Acknowledging that '[i]t is the land which confers upon the coastal State a right to the waters off its coasts', the court noted that 'the drawing of base-lines must not depart to any appreciable extent from the general direction of the coast'.[46] A second consideration, also flowing from the legal–geographic relationship between land and sea, was 'whether certain areas

---

[43] AHA Soons, 'The Effects of a Rising Sea Level on Maritime Limits and Boundaries' (1990) 37(2) *Netherlands International Law Review* 207; DD Caron, 'When the Law Makes Climate Change Worse: Rethinking the Law of Baselines in Light of a Rising Sea Level' (1990) 17 *Ecology Law Quarterly* 621; M Hayashi, 'Sea Level Rise and the Law of the Sea: Future Options' in D Vidas and PJ Shei (eds), *The World Ocean in Globalisation*, (Martinus Nijhoff Leiden 2011) 187; J Grote Stoutenburg, 'Implementing a New Regime of Stable Maritime Zones to Ensure the (Economic) Survival of Small Island States Threatened by Sea-Level Rise' (2011) 26 *International Journal of Marine and Coastal Law* 263.

[44] See *Qatar v Bahrain* (Merits) (disagreement about the status of Qit'at Jaradah).

[45] See Award of the Tribunal in the Matter of an Arbitration between Guyana and Suriname: *Arbitration between Guyana and Suriname* (2007) XXX RIAA 1 (disagreement about the location of the low-water line along the coast of Vissers Bank).

[46] *Anglo-Norwegian Fisheries*, n 19, 133.

lying within these lines are sufficiently closely linked to the land domain to be subject to the regime of internal waters'.[47] The third, non-geographic consideration was 'that of certain economic interests peculiar to a region, the reality and importance of which are clearly evidenced by a long usage'.[48]

The vivid phrase *inter fauces terrarum*, or 'in the jaws of the land', has been used to capture the physical characteristics that differentiate internal waters from waters beyond.[49] For rivers, bays, and ports, the 'jaws' are often readily apparent on charts. With respect to straight baselines and archipelagic baselines, the description often no longer applies. Nonetheless, the relationship between land and the water to be enclosed by baselines remains a fundamental consideration.[50]

Artificial baselines are just that: artifices for addressing concerns about coastal State authority in nearshore waters while providing a limit on the spatial extent of that authority. As such, they are prone to manipulation by coastal States for the purpose of self-aggrandizement.[51] The degree to which the artificial baseline provisions have been manipulated appears to be a function of the clarity with which they were drafted.[52] In some circumstances, the rules contain objective criteria; in others, the criteria are ill-defined and are subject to widely varying interpretations.

Unlike the normal baseline, for which no express notice is required,[53] notice must be provided for most artificial baselines by deposit of a chart or geographic coordinates with the United Nations Secretary-General. Notice serves to make ocean users aware of the existence of these imaginary lines where internal waters begin and from which maritime zones are measured. Article 16 of the LOSC requires due publicity of river and bay closing lines and straight baselines.[54] Article 47 sets forth the publicity requirements for archipelagic baselines.

When considering the suite of artificial baseline rules, one should recall that artificial baselines have long been regarded as the exception to the normal baseline rule.[55]

---

[47] Ibid.   [48] Ibid.
[49] Ibid, 130; ILC, 'Articles Concerning the Law of the Sea: Article 13' (1956) II *Yearbook of the International Law Commission* 258.
[50] See LOSC, n 6, Arts 7, 9, and 10.
[51] Reisman and Westerman posit that the purpose of straight baselines has always been to push zonal limits seaward. Reisman and Westerman, n 22, xiv–xv.
[52] See Schofield, n 25.
[53] The LOSC, n 6, Art 5 clause 'as marked on large-scale charts officially recognized by the coastal State' could be read as an implicit notice requirement.
[54] Symmons and Reed note a gap in the requirement that could allow coastal States to fulfill their publicity requirements without actually providing a mariner with all of the information he would need to understand the States' full baseline claim. CR Symmons and MW Reed, 'Baseline Publicity and Charting Requirements: An Overlooked Issue in the UN Convention on the Law of the Sea' (2010) 41 *Ocean Development and International Law* 77.
[55] Reisman and Westerman, n 22, 92 ('the normal regime applies automatically, whereas the coastal state seeking to avail itself of the straight baseline regime always has a burden of proof'); but see DP O'Connell, *The International Law of the Sea* (Clarendon Press Oxford 1982) Vol 1, 211 (commenting that LOSC, n 6, Art 14 'can only be construed as making the straight baseline system optional').

The ICJ noted in *Qatar v Bahrain* that 'the method of straight baselines, which is an exception to the normal rules for the delimitation of baselines, may only be applied if a number of conditions are met'. It added '[t]his method must be applied restrictively',[56] indicating that, where artificial baselines are concerned, the rules should be subject to strict interpretation: properly interpreted, the Convention prohibits drawing artificial baselines not expressly allowed.[57] Among other reasons for this approach, the international community should not be presumed to have allowed the appropriation of non-exclusive, international areas for exclusive coastal State use.[58] This leaves gaps in the conventional law,[59] some of which are filled with customary rules, but barring such rules it seems that States may not go beyond what has been prescribed. In practice, the artificial exceptions are beginning to overtake the use of normal baselines, and the application of these exceptions often stretches the legal language to the breaking point. What impact this will have on future development of the law is unclear.[60]

3.1 Artificial lines and rivers

Article 9 of the LOSC ('Mouths of rivers') reads: 'If a river flows directly into the sea, the baseline shall be a straight line across the mouth of the river between two points on the low-water line of its banks', and is a nearly verbatim adoption of Article 13 of the TSC. This article addresses the interface between rivers—long considered internal waters—and the sea beyond them. Several aspects of this short article deserve comment here. This article does not specify a maximum line length. Whatever the length of the line, it must be a single-segment line ('a straight line') connecting points on the low-water line of the river's banks. Therefore, river closing lines bring with them the interpretive problems of the normal baseline.

In the absence of a specified maximum closing line length, this article could be used to draw lines of considerable length encompassing vast amounts of water as internal waters, especially where a river widens as it approaches the sea. However, the phrase 'directly into the sea' limits the rivers to which this article may apply. The French 'sans former d'estuaire' (without forming an estuary)[61] and the drafting history

---

[56] *Qatar v Bahrain* (Merits), [212].

[57] Reisman and Westerman apply 'the presumption in favor of a strict rather than a permissive and extensive interpretation' to their interpretation of the straight baseline regime. Reisman and Westerman, n 22, 75.

[58] See ibid, 75–7.   [59] See eg multi-State bays.

[60] RR Churchill and AV Lowe, *The Law of the Sea* (3rd edn Juris Publishing Manchester 1999) 57 ('It may be that the widespread toleration of much of the practice… which clearly contravenes the relevant rules of international law (particularly as regards straight baselines) will in time lead to a modification of those rules themselves.').

[61] This phrase having been left in the French version was, apparently, a drafting error. O'Connell, n 55, Vol 1, 229.

of the TSC both help interpret this ambiguous phrase. In the 1956 International Law Commission (ILC) Draft Articles, this article included a second paragraph instructing that '[i]f the river flows into an estuary the coasts of which belong to a single State, article 7 [bays] shall apply.' This paragraph was dropped on adoption of the 1958 Convention, but lives on to some degree in the French version. Presumably, Article 9 does not apply to rivers that flow to the sea via an estuary. One possibility is that the estuary assimilates to a bay and would be subject, not to Article 9, but to the more restrictive rules for bays in Article 10.[62] In contrast, rivers flowing to the sea via a delta would be subject to the less restrictive rules for straight baselines to be drawn in the presence of a highly unstable deltaic coastline in Article 7(2).

If the dearth of protests is any indication, application of Article 9 has been unproblematic. The 135-mile line across the mouth of the Rio de la Plata, asserted by Argentina and Uruguay on the basis of Article 13 of the TSC, is the only example known to this author of a river mouth closing line subject to diplomatic protest.[63]

3.2 Bay closing lines

The article addressing bay closing lines has a more complex text and more involved drafting history than the article regarding river mouths. Article 10, which is largely identical to Article 7 of the TSC, contains the conventional rule set for juridical bays: so-called 'historic' bays are expressly excluded from these rules.[64] In order to draw a baseline enclosing all of the waters of a juridical bay, the bay must satisfy several clear criteria: it must pass the mathematical semi-circle test; 'the distance between the low-water marks of the natural entrance points' may not exceed 24 nautical miles (nm); and it must belong to a single State.

The first step in applying Article 10 is to differentiate indentations that qualify as bays from indentations that are 'a mere curvature of the coast'.[65] This concern, identified as early as the *North Atlantic Fisheries* case,[66] was often expressed in terms of an appropriate ratio of the width of the bay mouth to the depth of the indentation, ensuring bay waters were surrounded by coastal State territory on three sides, thus justifying their possible treatment as internal waters.[67] The Article 10 semi-circle test usually addresses that concern by requiring the area of the indentation to be 'as

---

[62] *Virginia Commentaries*, Vol II, 111.

[63] See US Department of State, 'Unclassified Airgram A-46, December 14, 1962' (1963) 57 *American Journal of International Law* 403. The Rio de la Plata closing line was also protested by France, the Netherlands, and the United Kingdom.

[64] LOSC, n 6, Art 10(6).   [65] Ibid, Art 10(2).

[66] *North Atlantic Coast Fisheries (Great Britain v United States of America)* (1910) XI RIAA 167.

[67] Boggs describes a version of a semi-circle test in his review of the proposal of the US delegation to the 1930 Hague Conference. See S Whittemore Boggs, 'Delimitation of the Territorial Sea' (1930) 24 *American Journal of International Law* 541, 550–2. See also the position of the United Kingdom in *Anglo-Norwegian Fisheries*, n 19,120.

large as, or larger than, that of the semi-circle whose diameter is a line drawn across the mouth of that indentation' in order to qualify as a bay.[68] Although a bay need not be perfectly semi-circular in shape in order to qualify, a shallow coastal concavity or 'mere curvature' would not satisfy this shape test. Article 10(3) provides specific rules for the application of the semi-circle test to indentations with more than one mouth or an indentation containing islands.

The size requirement of Article 10 is triggered only after the threshold shape requirement is satisfied. The maximum bay closing line length is 24 nm. Article 10(4) calls for this line to be drawn between the low-water marks of the natural entrance points of the bay. However, if that distance exceeds 24 nm, Article 10(5) provides for drawing a closing line not to exceed 24 nm 'within the bay in such a manner as to enclose the maximum area of water that is possible with a line of that length'. The application of this fallback option also is subject to the threshold shape requirement.

Finally, Article 10 only applies to 'bays the coasts of which belong to a single State'. An early proposal by the United States contained the language 'in the case of a bay or estuary the coasts of which belong to a single State, *or to two or more States which have agreed upon a division of the waters thereof*.'[69] It seems logical to include such multi-State bays under the same rules, but the record indicates that the ILC did not propose rules to cover multi-State bays because it did not have 'sufficient data at its disposal concerning the number of cases involved or the regulations at present applicable to them'.[70] This lacuna remains, yet multi-State bays do exist and the relevant States have drawn closing lines.[71] At least one multi-State bay, the Gulf of Fonseca, has been pronounced an historic bay.[72] The status of closing lines across other multi-State bays is less clear, but with respect to multi-State bays that would otherwise satisfy the Article 10 criteria, the absence of significant protest may indicate a customary rule is in operation.[73]

The rules regarding the juridical bay closing line requirements are very clear, containing two objective tests, both of which must be satisfied in order to claim as internal

---

[68] LOSC, n 6, Art 10(2). There are circumstances in which the semi-circle test alone is not sufficient to identify landlocked waters or waters *inter fauces terrarum*. In US practice, the '45-degree test' is applied, in addition to the semi-circle test, to identify appropriate bay headlands and to ensure that the waters of a juridical bay are in fact land-locked pursuant to Article 10(2). See US National Oceanic and Atmospheric Administration glossary for a definition of the 45-degree test, available at <http://www.gc.noaa.gov/gcil_glossary.html>.

[69] Boggs, 'Delimitation of the Territorial Sea', 551 (emphasis added).

[70] ILC, 'Articles Concerning the Law of the Sea: Commentary to Article 7' (1956) 2 YbILC 269.

[71] See T Scovazzi, 'Problems Relating to the Drawing of Baselines to Close Shared Maritime Waters' in Symmons (ed), *Selected Contemporary Issues in the Law of the Sea* 15.

[72] *El Salvador v Nicaragua*, repr in (1917) 11 *American Journal of International Law* 674.

[73] But see Westerman's concern that large water bodies which would otherwise qualify, including the Mediterranean and Baltic seas, might come under the bay closing line provisions if the single-State criterion were dropped. GS Westerman, *The Juridical Bay* (Clarendon Press Oxford 1987) 79.

waters all or some of the waters of a coastal indentation pursuant to Article 10. These clear rules may explain the low instance of disagreement about their application.[74] This author is unaware of any protests against States that have relied on Article 10 to close a juridical bay that violates the shape and size requirements of that article. But this apparent lack of controversy should also be attributed to coastal State reliance on the historic bays exception and the use of Article 7 straight baselines to close coastal indentations that would not have satisfied Article 10.

Claims to historic bays have created controversy. Historic bay claims are subject to customary rules of acquisitive prescription. In order for the waters of a coastal indentation to be deemed an historic bay, the coastal State must demonstrate its 'open, effective, long term, and continuous exercise of authority' over the waters of the bay,[75] and 'affirmative evidence of acquiescence' by other States.[76] There are no shape or size restrictions, and thus any coastal indentation could qualify irrespective of the depth of the bay-like formation if the coastal State can meet the high bar for establishing title. Some bays originally claimed on the basis of historic title now satisfy today's juridical bay shape and size requirements.[77] Not surprisingly, the historic bays which continue to cause concern fail the Article 10 tests.[78]

In addition to the historic bays exception, Article 10 contains an important reference to the straight baselines provisions of Article 7: 'The foregoing [bay] provisions do not apply... in any case where the system of straight baselines provided for in article 7 is applied.' With this exception, States have ignored the restrictive rules of Article 10 and instead applied the less specific language of Article 7 ('deeply indented and cut into') to enclose waters in indentations that would not have qualified as juridical bays. This practice has elicited protests and criticism.[79] Article 7 straight baselines, including their use to enclose bay-like indentations, are explored below.

---

[74] Schofield makes the connection between compliance and the 'laudably precise language' of Art 10. Schofield, 'Departures from the Coast', 729.

[75] Roach and Smith, n 25, 18.

[76] I Brownlie, *Principles of Public International Law* (6th edn Oxford University Press Oxford 2003) 157. Unlike acquisitive prescription of land territory usually involving only one other competitor, historic bay claims impact community interests. Therefore, widespread acquiescence by major maritime States may be required. (See ibid.) Roach and Smith note that the United States also take the position that 'a mere absence of opposition' is not enough to prove acquiescence. Roach and Smith, n 25, 19.

[77] For example, Guatemala's Gulf of Amatique, several bays of the Dominican Republic and the United States' Chesapeake Bay, and Delaware Bay. Roach and Smith, n 25, 54–5.

[78] For example, Italy's Gulf of Taranto, Russia's Peter the Great Bay, and Australia's Anxious, Encounter, Lacepede, and Rivioli Bays. Ibid, 39–40, 44–5, and 50–2.

[79] Ibid. Reisman and Westerman note that '[o]ne of the most problematic uses of the straight baseline option has been its use in circumventing other rules of international law', specifically rules on juridical bays and historic bays. Reisman and Westerman, n 22, 102.

3.3 Closing the waters of a port

The article addressing ports and harbour works (Article 11 LOSC) does not expressly allow enclosing the waters of a port with a straight line. However, this option may be inferred from Article 50 which allows archipelagic States to 'draw closing lines for the delimitation of internal waters, in accordance with articles 9 [mouths of rivers], 10 [bays] and 11 [ports].' There is no reason this rule would not apply to non-archipelagic coastal States. The closing lines would, in any event, be quite short, and the waters of a port are clearly regarded as having the character of internal waters. The Article 11 prohibition on using off-shore installations and artificial islands for drawing the normal baseline would apply equally to drawing a port closing line.

3.4 Straight baselines *stricto sensu*

The clear loser in the 1920s vote casting, straight baselines are now a favoured method to aggressively enclose ocean space. Early on, Norway led the straight baselines charge. Having drawn straight lines across several areas of coastal waters in the late 1800s, Norway answered the 1927 survey advocating for lines connecting the outermost points. By 1935, Norway had established a continuous system of straight lines along the northern portion of its coast. The United Kingdom challenged this system in the *Fisheries* case. The 1951 decision, endorsing Norway's straight baselines, contributed directly to the modern regime of straight baselines. With the exception of paragraph 2, the text of Article 7 is derived from Article 4 of the TSC, which in turn was derived from Article 5 of 1956 ILC Draft Articles, the language of which was borrowed, in many important instances, verbatim, from the closely related, contemporaneous judgment in *Fisheries*.

The direct lineage between the 1951 judgment and Article 7 of the LOSC combined with ambiguous language in Article 7 makes understanding the *Anglo-Norwegian Fisheries* case not only helpful, but necessary, in order to understand Article 7. While a full review of this 50-year-old case will not be attempted here, it is sufficient to note the 'peculiar geography' of the Norwegian coast with which the court was faced.[80] When considering the Article 7 phrase 'deeply indented', one should imagine the eastern section of Norway's coast which was 'broken by large and deeply indented fjords';[81] these fjords 'often penetrat[ed] for great distances inland'.[82] And the Article 7 phrase 'fringe of islands along the coast in its immediate vicinity' should conjure an image of the '"skjaergaard" (literally, rock rampart)', made up of an estimated 120,000 insular features.[83] In this geographic context, the court saw Norway's system as 'the

---

[80] *Anglo-Norwegian Fisheries*, n 19, 139.   [81] Ibid, 127.   [82] Ibid.   [83] Ibid.

application of general international law to a specific case'[84] and 'an adaptation rendered necessary by local conditions',[85] and asserted that the idea of a sufficiently close link between the land and the sea areas to be enclosed 'should be liberally applied in the case of a coast, the geographical configuration of which is as unusual as that of Norway'. Clearly, the court considered this section of the Norwegian coast to be exceptional. The British judge, Sir Arnold McNair, disagreed that the Norwegian coast was exceptional enough to merit application of a different method.[86] Presciently, he predicted that the effect of the 1935 Norwegian straight baselines decree 'will be to injure the principle of the freedom of the seas and to encourage further encroachments upon the high seas by coastal States'.[87] Today, approximately 90 coastal States apply Article 7 to some or all of their exceptional coasts.[88]

Article 7 sets out, in six paragraphs, the straight baseline provisions as they stand today.[89] This article establishes a two-option, threshold geographic test which must be satisfied before drawing straight baselines pursuant to the criteria, exceptions and limitations of the subsequent paragraphs. Coastal States may only draw straight baselines 'in localities where the coastline is *deeply indented and cut into*, or *if there is a fringe of islands along the coast in its immediate vicinity*'.[90] One of these tests must be met before straight baselines joining appropriate coastal points may be drawn, but the lines 'must not depart to any appreciable extent from the general direction of the coast, *and* the sea areas lying within the lines must be sufficiently closely linked to the land domain to be subject to the regime of internal waters'.[91] Although the text is not explicit, appropriate points are assumed to be points on the low-water line of mainland or island territory, that is, points on the normal baseline. However, appropriate points exclude low-tide elevations except those on which 'lighthouses or similar installations which are permanently above sea level have been built' or those for which the drawing of straight baselines has 'received general international recognition'.[92] Only if the threshold geographic test is met, may 'economic interests peculiar to the region concerned' be taken into account when drawing particular baselines; but this variance may only be enjoyed if 'the reality and the importance' of the economic interests 'are clearly evidenced by long usage'.[93] In any event, States may not draw straight baselines that 'cut off the territorial sea of another State from the high seas or an exclusive economic zone'.[94]

---

[84] Ibid, 131.   [85] Ibid, 133.

[86] *Anglo-Norwegian Fisheries*, Dissenting Opinion McNair, n 19.

[87] Ibid, 185. McNair further noted that 'the approbation of [the Norwegian system] would have a dangerous tendency in that it would encourage States to adopt a subjective appreciation of their rights instead of conforming to a common international standard'. Ibid, 169.

[88] Roach and Smith, n 25, 20, 74–82.

[89] Reisman and Westerman provide a detailed interpretation of the straight baseline regime; see Reisman and Westerman, n 22, ch 4.

[90] LOSC, n 6, Art 7(1) (emphasis added).   [91] Ibid, Art 7(3).   [92] Ibid, Art 7(4).

[93] Ibid, Art 7(5).   [94] Ibid, Art 7(6).

This formula repeats in large measure the formula of Article 4 of the TSC which adopted language and concepts from *Fisheries*. Unfortunately, throughout the decades following *Fisheries*, the international community was unable to make the straight baseline rules more precise, and coastal States are guided by language that the court itself admitted was 'devoid of any mathematical precision'.[95] Lack of precision does not equate to a lack of rules, but it does make arriving at a standard interpretation of those rules more difficult. The exorbitant straight baseline systems resulting from purported application of these rules are evidence of this difficulty.[96] The threshold test of 'deeply indented and cut into' has been applied to slightly undulating coastlines and to indentations that would not pass the bay shape test. The alternative threshold test of 'a fringe of islands along the coast in its immediate vicinity' has been used to justify straight baseline systems connecting a handful of dispersed insular features, often some distance from the mainland. Commentators note that the rules 'have been bent out of shape'[97] and that some applications 'are so far wide of the mark as to mock [the] language' of Article 7.[98]

The straight baseline regime contains two other important aspects. Article 7(2), which had no equivalent provision in the 1958 Convention, reads:

Where because of the presence of a delta and other natural conditions the coastline is highly unstable, the appropriate points may be selected along the furthest seaward extent of the low-water line and, notwithstanding subsequent regression of the low-water line, the straight baselines shall remain effective until changed by the coastal State in accordance with this Convention.

This exception for certain deltaic coastlines was introduced by Bangladesh during the Third United Nations Conference on the Laws of the Sea (UNCLOS III) negotiations and probably does not apply to many other coasts in the world. Note that the phrase 'notwithstanding subsequent regression of the low-water line'—a phrase otherwise absent in the baseline provisions—is used to argue that other baseline provisions, including the normal baseline, are applicable on a continuing basis thereby supporting the ambulatory approach discussed above.

With respect to enclosing internal waters with Article 7 straight baselines, Article 8 limits the effect on preexisting rights of innocent passage. Article 8(2) reads: 'Where the establishment of straight baselines...has the effect of enclosing as internal waters areas which had not previously been considered as such, a right of innocent passage...shall exist in those waters.' Practically speaking, the burden

---

[95] *Anglo-Norwegian Fisheries*, n 19, 142.
[96] For a list of protests made by the United States against excessive straight baseline claims, see Roach and Smith, n 25, 74–82.
[97] V Prescott and C Schofield, *The Maritime Political Boundaries of the World* (2nd edn Martinus Nijhoff Leiden 2005) 142.
[98] Reisman and Westerman, n 22, 190.

will be on the navigating State to exercise and maintain its residual right of innocent passage through nominally internal waters.

3.5 Archipelagic baselines: the latest artificial baseline

Baselines to be drawn around groups of islands were discussed as early as the 1920s, and by the ILC and delegates to the First United Nations Conference on the Law of the Sea (UNCLOS I) in the 1950s, but archipelagic baseline provisions were not adopted until UNCLOS III.[99] The articles related to archipelagic States, including archipelagic baselines, are found in Part IV of the LOSC. To date, 22 States have claimed archipelagic status.[100]

The rules for drawing archipelagic baselines, which separate maritime areas subject to the special regime of archipelagic waters from the territorial sea beyond, are defined in LOSC Article 47.[101] Only an archipelagic State—'a State constituted wholly by one or more archipelagos...'—may utilize archipelagic baselines.[102] Article 47 contains objective criteria for drawing baselines, including minimum and maximum water to land ratios (1:1 and 9:1, respectively) to be encompassed by the baselines[103] and maximum line length between turning points.[104] The article prohibits the use of low-tide elevations situated wholly outside the territorial sea 'unless lighthouses or similar installations which are permanently above sea level have been built on them'.[105] Archipelagic baselines 'shall not depart to any appreciable extent from the general configuration of the archipelago'[106] and certain interests of neighboring States must be accounted for when drawing archipelagic baselines.[107]

With clear rules on the water-to-land ratio and maximum line length, application of Article 47 has been less problematic than application of Article 7. However, some archipelagic States have claimed archipelagic baselines that violate the ratio restrictions,[108] and line length restrictions.[109] With such clear rules, protesting States easily point to violations, and, in some cases, the archipelagic State has rectified

---

[99] See *Virginia Commentaries*, Vol II, 399–404.   [100] Roach and Smith, n 25, 206–7.

[101] Note that archipelagic States may also have areas of internal waters landward of archipelagic waters, but only on the basis of LOSC, n 6, Arts 9, 10, and 11 (rivers, bays, and ports) and not on the basis of Art 7 (straight baselines).

[102] Ibid, Art 46. An archipelago is defined as 'a group of islands, including parts of islands, interconnecting waters and other natural features which are so closely interrelated that such islands, waters and other natural features form an intrinsic geographical, economic and political entity, or which historically have been regarded as such'.

[103] Ibid, Art 47(1).   [104] Ibid, Art 47 (2).
[105] Ibid, Art 47 (4).   [106] Ibid, Art 47 (3).   [107] Ibid, Art 47(5) and (6).

[108] See eg United States Department of State, 'Seychelles: Archipelagic and Other Maritime Claims and Boundaries' (14 February 2014) 132 (hereinafter 'Limits in the Seas: Seychelles').

[109] See eg United States Department of State, 'Maldives: Maritime Claims and Boundaries' (8 September 2005) 126.

its archipelagic baseline system to bring it into conformity with Article 47.[110] States have also chosen outermost turning points that fail the criteria of Article 47(4), using low-tide elevations situated wholly beyond the territorial sea[111] or submerged features.[112] Questions about the misapplication of these rules are relatively technical in nature. A more interesting question arises with respect to baselines and the dependent archipelagos of non-archipelagic States.[113]

Dependent archipelagos are groups of islands that are not, by themselves, a State and therefore the provisions of Article 47 do not apply.[114] Nonetheless, many continental States have drawn baselines around their dependent archipelagos.[115] On what legal basis these baselines have been drawn is a subject of some speculation. Clearly, Article 47 cannot provide the basis, and in any event several of these baselines systems were promulgated before the advent of LOSC Part IV.[116] Some coastal archipelagos, those near the coast or those formed by a large island fringed by smaller islands, might come under the language of Article 7 straight baselines. The remaining examples, however, appear to be 'motivated by the archipelagic concept'[117] in the absence of any conventional rule allowing such claims. In the view of one publicist, 'this practice is indicative of a considerable trend in international law towards the formation of a rule of customary law'.[118]

4 Conclusions

Baseline rules under the law of the sea face two major challenges to their legitimacy. First, are they able to accommodate the equitable considerations that arise when low-lying coastal States begin to lose large amounts of their territory to sea level rise, and, if not, is this a problem with the baseline rules or a problem to be addressed

---

[110] Roach and Smith, n 25, 209 (Cape Verde corrected its excessive water to land ratio and baselines length).

[111] See eg United States Department of State, 'Dominican Republic: Archipelagic and Other Maritime Claims and Boundaries' (31 January 2014) 130.

[112] See eg Limits in the Seas: Seychelles.

[113] See generally S Kopela, *Dependent Archipelagos in the Law of the Sea* (Martinus Nijhoff Leiden 2013).

[114] During UNCLOS III the question of baselines around archipelagos of non-archipelagic States was debated and ultimately resolved by excluding those archipelagos from LOSC, n 6, Art 47. See *Virginia Commentaries*, Vol II, 407–15.

[115] See Kopela, n 113, 112–40.

[116] See eg Supreme Decree No 959-A of 28 June 1971 (Ecuador); Decree No 598 of 21 December 1976 (Denmark).

[117] Kopela, n 113, 147.   [118] Ibid, 259.

elsewhere? This question arises when considering the impact of sea level rise on the normal baseline. Publicists tend to agree that normal baselines are ambulatory, but, when taken to a logical conclusion in conditions of extreme sea level rise, the normal baseline rules lead to an unsatisfactory result. A variety of solutions have therefore been suggested.

Second, do the baseline rules protect sufficiently the interests of all ocean users, or do they allow coastal States to expand their authority beyond what the drafters envisioned? The structural characteristic of the law of the sea that pits inclusive international community use against exclusive coastal State use of ocean areas incentivizes excessive baseline claims by coastal States. Each individual coastal State experiences a direct benefit from enclosing ocean area near its coast for its exclusive use, while the diffuse community of ocean users experiences only indirect and fractional costs from the loss of ocean area at the margins. This lopsided cost-benefit equation explains coastal State expansionism and the development of vague baseline rules. Concern about perverse incentives focuses primarily on artificial baseline provisions, and Article 7 straight baselines are the main offenders. The practice of drawing baselines around dependent archipelagos in the absence of any conventional basis demonstrates that new interpretations of existing rules or the development of entirely new customary rules is a real possibility in this field.

5

THE TERRITORIAL SEA AND CONTIGUOUS ZONE

JOHN E NOYES[*]

1 INTRODUCTION

The territorial sea is a narrow belt of water extending seaward from a coastal State's baselines or an archipelagic State's archipelagic baselines. Coastal States may regulate activities and take enforcement actions in the territorial sea because of their concerns respecting security, communications, the marine environment, resources, smuggling, immigration, health, safety of navigation, and other uses of the zone. International law, reflecting the pervasive nature of those economic, political, security, and environmental interests, accords the coastal State 'sovereignty' over the territorial sea, the air space above it, and the seabed and subsoil beneath it.[1]

Sovereignty does not, however, mean that the coastal State enjoys exclusive competence in the territorial sea. According to Article 2(3) of the 1982 UN Convention on the Law of the Sea (LOSC), a coastal State's exercise of rights in the territorial sea is 'subject to this Convention and other rules of international law'. In particular, navigational regimes recognize the rights of flag States and advance global values of trade, communication, and security.

---

[*] The author is grateful to the editors and Eric Jaap Molenaar for their comments on a draft of this chapter.

[1] 1982 United Nations Convention on the Law of the Sea, Art 2 (hereinafter LOSC).

States may also proclaim a contiguous zone, seaward of the territorial sea. There, the coastal State may enforce its customs, fiscal, immigration, and sanitary laws that apply within its territorial sea, and may regulate removal of historical and archaeological objects.[2] The coastal State's contiguous zone competence is much less extensive than its territorial sea competence.

Many aspects of the current territorial sea and contiguous zone regimes were codified in the 1958 Convention on the Territorial Sea and Contiguous Zone (CTSCZ),[3] although there was no agreement on the maximum breadth of the territorial sea until the Third United Nations Conference on the Law of the Sea (UNCLOS III) settled on a 12-nautical-mile maximum. The territorial sea and contiguous zone relate to many other issues in the law of the sea. Some of these issues, such as baselines and maritime boundary delimitation, reflect the traditional geographical orientation of the law of the sea; others, such as marine pollution and maritime security, require on-going international management. Other fields of international law, including human rights and the use of force, also affect rights and duties in the territorial sea and contiguous zone. Regional and global international organizations, notably the International Maritime Organization (IMO), develop standards that coastal States may apply in the territorial sea, and that flag States usually must implement.

Section 2 of this chapter discusses the breadth and location of the territorial sea, and Section 3 considers its juridical status. Section 4 briefly examines the navigational rights of foreign flag vessels in the territorial sea, while Section 5 highlights some 'other rules of international law' and actions of international organizations that apply there. Section 6 explores the contiguous zone.

2 Breadth and Location of the Territorial Sea

In 1610, the Dutch advanced the claim that a coastal State's authority was measured by a cannon's range, reflecting a concern with coastal State security.[4] Other early

---

[2] Ibid, Arts 33 and 303.
[3] 1958 Convention on the Territorial Sea and Contiguous Zone (hereinafter CTSCZ).
[4] See TW Fulton, *The Sovereignty of the Sea* (William Blackwood and Sons Edinburgh/London 1911; reprinted 1976) 156, 549–50; WL Walker, 'Territorial Waters: The Cannon Shot Rule' (1945) 22 *British Yearbook of International Law* 210, 222 (also noting cannon shot rule link to control of fisheries). France accepted the cannon shot rule 'as established law' in the seventeenth century: ibid.

claims depended on a flexible 'line of sight' doctrine.[5] By the late eighteenth century, States generally delimited their territorial seas according to exact distances from shore.[6] The preference for fixed distances over a conceptually variable 'cannon shot' or 'line of sight' rule did not always translate into a unitary territorial sea. Some coastal States claimed waters of different breadths for different purposes—a practice that still had a modicum of support in the mid-twentieth century.[7] State practice evolved, however, toward all coastal States having authority in one narrow belt of waters of determinate width. By the early twentieth century, States agreed that a three-nautical-mile territorial sea was consistent with international law. Several States asserted broader territorial sea claims, but the international legality of those claims was disputed.[8]

Neither the 1930 Hague Codification Conference nor the 1958 First United Nations Conference on the Law of the Sea (UNCLOS I) could reach agreement on the maximum breadth of the territorial sea, and hence on its boundary with the high seas. The 1958 CTSCZ was thus silent on the topic, and the 1960 Second United Nations Conference on the Law of the Sea (UNCLOS II) failed by one vote to settle the issue.[9] According to Oxman, this 'inability... to identify precisely where' the territorial sea ends and the high seas regime applies reflected 'the reemergence of the territorial temptation at sea'.[10]

Although three-nautical-mile claims predominated in the middle of the twentieth century, a trend of broader claims soon accelerated, with some States even claiming 200-nautical-mile territorial seas.[11] Maritime powers became concerned that the freedom of navigation and other high seas freedoms could be impaired. This concern provided one major impetus for convening UNCLOS III.

States reached widespread agreement on a maximum 12-nautical-mile territorial sea early in UNCLOS III. Article 3 of the LOSC enshrines the principle: '[e]very State has the right to establish the breadth of its territorial sea up to a limit not exceeding 12 nautical miles, measured from baselines determined

---

[5] See SA Swarztrauber, *The Three-Mile Limit of Territorial Seas* (Naval Institute Press Annapolis 1972) 36–41.

[6] See Y Tanaka, *The International Law of the Sea* (Cambridge University Press New York 2012) 21.

[7] For a survey of State practice in the early 1950s, see United Nations Special Rapporteur, *Regime of the Territorial Sea, Deuxième rapport de M. J. P. A. François, Rapporteur Spécial*, UN Doc A/CN.4/61 (1953), in (1953) II *Yearbook of the International Law Commission* 57, 60–3.

[8] See AV Lowe, 'The Development of the Concept of the Contiguous Zone' (1981) 52 *British Yearbook of International Law* 109, 123, 147.

[9] See AH Dean, 'The Second Geneva Conference on the Law of the Sea: The Fight for Freedom of the Seas' (1960) 54 *American Journal of International Law* 751.

[10] BH Oxman, 'The Territorial Temptation: A Siren Song at Sea' (2006) 100 *American Journal of International Law* 830, 833.

[11] See JA Roach and RW Smith, *Excessive Maritime Claims* (3rd edn Martinus Nijhoff Leiden/Boston 2012) 136, § 5.3.

in accordance with this Convention.' That agreement was, however, linked to assurances of navigational rights (notably the regime of transit passage through straits) and of coastal State control over resources and marine scientific research in the 200-nautical-mile exclusive economic zone (EEZ).[12]

The LOSC sets no minimum breadth of the territorial sea. The Convention suggests that a coastal State possesses a territorial sea even without proclaiming one: the State's sovereignty '*extends*, beyond its land territory and internal waters ... to an adjacent belt of sea, described as the territorial sea'.[13] Judge McNair argued that possession of a territorial sea 'is not optional, not dependent upon the will of the [coastal] State, but compulsory'.[14] States have duties in the territorial sea, for example, to publicize dangers, which ought not be avoidable by failing to proclaim a territorial sea.[15] The point is almost academic, however, since almost all coastal States have asserted territorial seas and set their breadth.[16]

Some territorial seas do not extend to 12 nautical miles (nm). This situation occurs when two opposite States less than 24 nm apart share a territorial sea boundary. Occasionally, a State will not claim a full 12 nm territorial sea in other situations. This restraint may retain a high seas corridor in straits[17] or may avoid antagonizing another State that has traditionally carried on activities outside a narrower territorial sea.[18]

State practice since 1982 has overwhelmingly supported the maximum 12 nm breadth of the territorial sea. As of December 2011, over 140 States claimed a territorial sea of up to 12 nm, and only seven States maintained broader claims.[19] In light of this consistent practice, the International Court of Justice and

---

[12] See JR Stevenson and BH Oxman, 'The Third United Nations Conference on the Law of the Sea: The 1974 Caracas Session' (1975) 69 *American Journal of International Law* 1, 13–14.

[13] LOSC, n 1, Art 2(1) (emphasis added). Cf ibid, Art 77(3).

[14] *Fisheries Case (United Kingdom v Norway)* [1951] ICJ Rep 116, 160 (dissenting opinion).

[15] See RR Churchill and AV Lowe, *The Law of the Sea* (3rd edn Juris Publishing Manchester 1999) 80–1.

[16] No data is available for the territorial sea of Bosnia and Herzegovina, perhaps due to its unsettled maritime boundary with Croatia. United Nations Division for Ocean Affairs and the Law of the Sea (DOALOS), *Table of Claims to Maritime Jurisdiction* (as at 15 July 2011), available at <http://www.un.org/Depts/los/LEGISLATIONANDTREATIES/PDFFILES/table_summary_of_claims.pdf> (hereinafter DOALOS, *Table of Claims*).

[17] See Roach and Smith, n 11, 269, § 11.2 n 4 (Finland, Germany, Japan, and South Korea).

[18] See DR Rothwell and T Stephens, *The International Law of the Sea* (Hart Publishing Oxford 2010) 73 (Greece and Turkey maintain 6 nm territorial seas for vessels in the Aegean).

[19] See Roach and Smith, n 11, § 5.3. The seven are: the Philippines (coordinates extending beyond 12 nm); Togo (30 nm); and Benin, Ecuador, El Salvador, Peru, and Somalia (each 200 nm). Of these seven States, only El Salvador and Peru have not become parties to the LOSC. Claims to territorial seas extending beyond 12 nm have been met with protests, see ibid, § 5.5, and over two dozen States rolled back excessive claims: ibid, § 5.4.

scholars have asserted that the 12-nautical-mile maximum is a rule of customary international law.[20]

Inside the baselines from which the territorial sea is measured lie land territory and internal waters (and, in the case of archipelagic States, archipelagic waters).[21] Various natural features may support a territorial sea. Archipelagic and coastal States, along with their territories and possessions, have territorial seas,[22] as do a few entities lacking statehood.[23] Every naturally formed island—a feature that must be above sea level at high tide—has a territorial sea. Even '[r]ocks which cannot sustain human habitation or economic life of their own' have one; however, unlike other islands, such rocks can have no EEZ or continental shelf extending beyond the territorial sea.[24]

In contrast, natural features below water at high tide do not have their own territorial seas. A partial exception to this rule is that the low-water line on a low-tide elevation 'may be used as the baseline for measuring the breadth of the territorial sea' if that elevation 'is situated wholly or partly at a distance not exceeding the breadth of the territorial sea from the mainland or an island'.[25] Man-made equipment and structures, including artificial islands and installations, 'do not possess the status of islands' and 'have no territorial sea of their own'.[26]

The limits of the territorial sea depend only in part on its breadth. Other determining factors include: (1) the location of baselines (see Chapter 4); (2) any territorial sea boundaries with adjacent or opposite States (see Chapter 12); and (3) the method used to draw the outer limit of the territorial sea. This outer limit marks the start of the coastal State's contiguous zone and EEZ (if they are proclaimed) and its continental shelf. The CTSCZ and LOSC both provide that '[t]he outer limit of the territorial sea is the line every point of which is at a distance from the nearest point of the baseline equal to the breadth of the territorial sea.'[27] This rule incorporates the 'arcs of circle' method, which yields an outer limit that smooths out indentations in normal baselines.[28]

---

[20] See *Territorial and Maritime Dispute (Nicaragua v Colombia)* (Judgment) [2012] ICJ Rep 624, [177]; Churchill and Lowe, n 15, 81; Rothwell and Stephens, n 18, 73; Tanaka, n 6, 84.

[21] LOSC, n 1, Art 2(1).

[22] For discussion of territorial sea claims off Antarctica, and complications arising from the status of territorial claims to that continent and from the baselines applicable in ice-covered regions, see Chapter 32.

[23] See LOSC, n 1, Arts 1(2) and 305.   [24] Ibid, Art 121.

[25] Ibid, Art 13; see also ibid, Art 47(4).

[26] Ibid, Arts 60(8), 259. Roadsteads 'normally used for the loading, unloading and anchoring of ships' and that 'would otherwise be situated wholly or partly outside the outer limit of the territorial sea', are included in it, although such roadsteads do not themselves support a territorial sea. Ibid, Art 12.

[27] Ibid, Art 4; CTSCZ, n 3 Art 6.   [28] *Virginia Commentaries*, Vol II, 84–5.

3 Juridical Character of the Territorial Sea

The juridical character of coastal State control in the territorial sea has historically generated controversy. Early theories linked control over the territorial sea to property rights in territory. Nineteenth-century German theorists developed concepts of jurisdiction not tied to territory to explain the nature of coastal State authority.[29] French legal scholar de La Pradelle argued that the coastal State possessed a 'bundle of servitudes' over a coastal belt, another route to explain how a coastal State could exercise jurisdiction concerning the territorial sea without 'owning' it.[30] Still another view, articulated in the early twentieth century, recognized that coastal, foreign, and community interests in the territorial sea may interact in changing ways; this realization contributed to 'a modern theory of maritime jurisdiction, which could detach itself from controversy over the juridical nature of the territorial sea'.[31] Indeed, current disputes concerning the coastal State's exercise of legislative or enforcement jurisdiction over foreign vessels or activities on board may be conceptualized as problems of resolving conflicts of jurisdiction.

The theory of coastal State 'sovereignty' over the territorial sea had been articulated in the Middle Ages,[32] but gained overwhelming support only in the twentieth century. Articles 1–2 of the CTSCZ and Article 2 of the LOSC adopt the sovereignty view. Sovereignty extends to the airspace above the territorial sea[33] and the seabed and subsoil beneath.[34] Sovereignty means that a coastal State need not expressly specify that its laws apply in the territorial sea; such an expression of intent is necessary only with respect to laws 'peculiar to the territorial sea', such as those relating to navigation.[35] Sovereignty also means that many enforcement measures are reserved to the coastal State, a view reflected in the ancillary rule that hot pursuit ceases once a pursued vessel enters the territorial sea of a country other than the pursuing State.[36]

---

[29] See DP O'Connell, 'The Juridical Nature of the Territorial Sea' (1971) 45 *British Yearbook of International Law* 303.

[30] See A de La Pradelle, 'Le droit de l'État sur la mer territoriale' (1898) 5 *Revue générale de droit international public* 309.

[31] DP O'Connell, *The International Law of the Sea* (Clarendon Press Oxford 1984) Vol II, 745.

[32] See DJ Bederman, 'The Sea' in B Fassbender et al (eds), *The Oxford Handbook of the History of International Law* (Oxford University Press Oxford 2013) 359, 363–5.

[33] See E Pépin, 'The Law of the Air and the Draft Articles Concerning the Law of the Sea Adopted by the International Law Commission at its Eighth Session', UN Doc A/CONF.13.4 (1957) [5]–[24].

[34] See G Marston, 'The Evolution of the Concept of Sovereignty over the Bed and Subsoil of the Territorial Sea' (1976) 48 *British Yearbook of International Law* 321–32.

[35] O'Connell, n 31, Vol II, 744.   [36] LOSC, n 1, Art 111(3).

In popular usage, 'sovereignty' connotes a completeness and exclusivity of authority that differentiates it from jurisdiction. However, sovereignty is limited in accordance with whatever rights and duties international law ascribes to independent States.[37] The International Law Commission (ILC), in its preparatory work for UNCLOS I, commented that although 'the rights of the coastal State over the territorial sea do not differ in nature from the rights of sovereignty which the State exercises over other parts of its territory[,] ... sovereignty over the territorial sea cannot be exercised otherwise than in conformity with the provisions of international law'.[38] Article 2(3) of the LOSC emphasizes the point: the coastal State's 'sovereignty over the territorial sea is exercised subject to this Convention and to other rules of international law'. As discussed in Section 4, the most notable qualifications of the coastal/archipelagic State's competence in the territorial sea relate to navigational rights. Even where coastal State rights concerning sensitive matters are explicitly deemed 'exclusive', as with respect to marine scientific research,[39] coastal State discretion is not absolute. If a coastal State authorizes marine scientific research in its territorial sea, that authorization could not unreasonably interfere with the rights of other States to, for example, engage in innocent passage; and such general international law precepts as good faith and abuse of rights apply.[40]

Sovereignty, in short, requires coastal States to observe duties and to balance their rights in the territorial sea with those of other States and the international community. This balance may most often be apparent with respect to enforcement jurisdiction. That is, a coastal State's competence to prescribe laws is in most respects plenary, but enforcement of those laws in the territorial sea will be limited if enforcement would impinge on certain rights of other States, for example, with respect to immunities accorded warships. Overall, Shearer's 1986 observation still rings true: we need not presumptively resolve assertions of coastal State jurisdiction in the territorial sea 'in favour of the rights of the coastal State'.[41] The balance of coastal and flag State rights and duties has been elaborated most fully with respect to navigation, to which this chapter now turns.

---

[37] See eg J Crawford, *The Creation of States in International Law* (2nd edn Oxford University Press Oxford 2006) 32.

[38] ILC, *Report of the International Law Commission to the General Assembly*, UN Doc A/3159 (1956), in (1956) II *Yearbook of the International Law Commission* 253, 265 (hereinafter 1956 ILC Report).

[39] See LOSC, n 1, Art 245.

[40] Ibid, Art 300. The same points apply to any number of other activities over which the coastal State exercises control in its territorial sea, for example, energy production, laying pipelines or cables, and constructing and operating artificial islands, installations, and structures.

[41] IA Shearer, 'Problems of Jurisdiction and Law Enforcement Against Delinquent Vessels' (1986) 35 *International and Comparative Law Quarterly* 320, 323.

4 Navigational Rights in the Territorial Sea

The most important limits on coastal State competence in the territorial sea relate to navigational rights of foreign flag vessels. Navigation furthers the values of trade, communication, and global mobility (a type of security interest)—values important to all. The scope accorded to navigational rights depends on: the type and condition of a foreign vessel; where it is heading; the activities of the vessel and those on board; and the coastal State's own activities and interests. Navigational rights are analysed in detail in Chapter 24, but some general points help to show how various rights and duties are accommodated in the territorial sea. These points relate to: (1) the geography of the territorial sea; (2) particular rights and obligations concerning warships and vessels carrying hazardous cargoes; and (3) other rights and obligations applicable to ordinary merchant vessels.

First, territorial sea navigational regimes differ based on certain geographical characteristics. The LOSC regime of transit passage through straits (see Chapter 6)—particularly important for maritime powers—provides more liberal navigational rights than does the right of innocent passage, which applies in some categories of straits and in non-strait territorial seas.[42] Transit passage allows ships to operate in their 'normal mode' (ie, submarines may pass submerged), provides a right of overflight, and is non-suspendable. By contrast, innocent passage requires that submarines navigate on the surface, denies a right of overflight, and may be temporarily suspended in limited circumstances. A coastal State may subject vessels in innocent passage to stricter regulations than vessels in transit passage.

Second, the question of innocent passage of warships through the territorial sea remains contentious. Maritime powers were concerned that the standard for non-innocence used in Article 14(4) of the CTSCZ—'prejudicial to the peace, good order or security of the coastal State'—was too subjective, according coastal States overbroad discretion. The LOSC made the right of innocent passage more determinate, specifying a list of 12 activities that render passage non-innocent.[43]

---

[42] Compare LOSC, n 1, Arts 37–44 with ibid, Arts 17–26 and 45.

[43] Ibid, Art 19(2). See also Joint Statement by the United States of America and the Union of Soviet Socialist Republics with Attached Uniform Interpretation of Rules of International Law Governing Innocent Passage, adopted 23 September 1989, (1989) 28 ILM 1445. Some provisions of LOSC, Art 19(2) may open the door to subjective evaluation, for example, the meaning of 'wilful' pollution in Art 19(2)(h). Some commentators also suggest that Art 19(1), which repeats the 'prejudicial to peace, good order or security' standard of the CTSCZ, continues to provide an independent basis for evaluating the innocence of passage. See LS Johnson, *Coastal State Regulation of International Shipping* (Oceana Publications Dobbs Ferry NY 2004) 64–6; EJ Molenaar, *Coastal State Jurisdiction over Vessel-Source Pollution* (Kluwer Law International The Hague 1998) 196–7; Tanaka, n 6, 87.

The innocent passage provisions apply to 'all ships' (not just merchant vessels) and refer to submarine navigation, the use of force, the launch of military devices, and weapons practice[44]—all activities associated with military vessels. However, the view that warships inherently threaten security still has adherents. Over 40 States have declared that a right of innocent passage for warships is subject to coastal State notice or permission—conditions 'generally considered' as incompatible with the LOSC[45]—or to other conditions; maritime powers have protested these restrictions.[46]

There has been controversy as well about other categories of vessels that may pose significant security or environmental threats, such as nuclear-powered ships or ships carrying hazardous cargoes. The LOSC recognizes their right to innocent passage, subject to safeguards established by international agreements.[47] Despite this provision, some coastal States, invoking progressive principles of international environmental law, have prohibited such passage or have insisted that such ships provide notice before entering the territorial sea (or even the EEZ).[48]

The coastal State's jurisdictional competence varies for merchant vessels and warships, particularly with respect to enforcement. A coastal State may exercise extensive legislative jurisdiction over merchant vessels in the territorial sea, even when they are in innocent passage,[49] as well as administrative jurisdiction (eg creating sea lanes and traffic separation schemes)[50] and enforcement jurisdiction.[51] A coastal State lacks enforcement jurisdiction over foreign warships and other government vessels operated for non-commercial purposes. Those ships are immune from boarding, arrest, detention, or the institution of proceedings,[52] although warships violating coastal State laws concerning passage through the territorial sea may be required to leave immediately, if they refuse a request to comply with such laws.[53]

Third, because overly aggressive coastal State regulation of foreign vessels in the territorial sea could curtail innocent passage, some limits exist on coastal State authority even with respect to ordinary merchant vessels. Coastal State regulations may not 'have the practical effect of denying or impairing the right of innocent passage', a right some authorities have recognized under customary international law

---

[44] See LOSC, n 1, Arts 19(2)(a), (b), and (h) and 20.

[45] United Nations Secretary General, *Oceans and the Law of the Sea: Report of the Secretary-General*, UN Doc A/59/62 (2004), [12].

[46] See Roach and Smith, n 11, § 10.3. See also T Stephens and DR Rothwell, 'The LOSC Framework for Maritime Jurisdiction and Enforcement 30 Years On' in D Freestone (ed), *The 1982 Law of the Sea Convention at 30: Successes, Challenges and New Agendas* (Martinus Nijhoff Leiden 2013) 27, 29–30.

[47] LOSC, n 1, Art 23.

[48] See Roach and Smith, n 11, § 10.4; M Miyoshi, 'Ocean Transport of Radioactive Fuel and Waste: A Japanese Perspective' in DD Caron and HS Scheiber (eds), *The Oceans in the Nuclear Age* (Martinus Nijhoff Leiden 2010) 197; JN Van Dyke, 'Ocean Transport of Radioactive Fuel and Waste' in DD Caron and HS Scheiber (eds), *The Oceans in the Nuclear Age* (Martinus Nijhoff Leiden 2010) 145.

[49] LOSC, n 1, Arts 21 and 211. [50] Ibid, Art 22.

[51] Ibid, Arts 25, 27–28, and 216(1). Other treaties also provide for coastal State enforcement, for example 1973 International Convention for the Prevention of Pollution from Ships (MARPOL).

[52] See LOSC, n 1, Art 32; Roach and Smith, n 11, § 19.1. [53] LOSC, n 1, Art 30.

as well as treaty law.[54] Although some serious violations of coastal State laws may deprive a ship of the right to innocent passage,[55] not all violations render innocent passage non-innocent.[56] Nor may a coastal State discriminate against ships based on their nationality or on the origin or destination of their cargoes, or by levying charges (which are permitted only for rendering specific services to a ship).[57] Coastal State regulations relating to innocent passage may not apply to a foreign vessel's construction, design, equipment, or manning (CDEM), unless those regulations implement generally accepted international standards.[58] Vessels complying with such standards thus need not modify their fundamental structure or their crew when they pass through the territorial seas of different States.[59] Coastal States must also publicize regulations and dangers—a requirement linked to a duty of information.[60] One particular step a coastal State may take to safeguard its security is suspending innocent passage. Such suspension is subject to restrictions: it is permitted only in specified areas of the territorial sea, only if temporary, only if imposed 'without discrimination in form or in fact among foreign ships', only if 'essential' to protect the coastal State's security, and only if duly publicized.[61] Overall, however, innocent passage entails only a limited incursion on coastal State authority.[62]

Articles 27 and 28 of the LOSC, concerning the exercise of criminal and civil jurisdiction on board merchant vessels in the territorial sea, leave the limits on coastal State enforcement jurisdiction imprecise. In many cases that State 'should not' arrest foreign flag vessels or those on board, or conduct investigations on board. This phrasing, while technically permitting a coastal State to enforce its laws, recognizes that coastal States' legal systems vary considerably, and that contextual application of jurisdictional competence is appropriate.[63] Article 27(4), providing that 'the local authorities shall have due regard to the interests of navigation' in considering arrests, is one expression of a general test of reasonableness for the exercise of enforcement jurisdiction.[64]

---

[54] Ibid, Art 24(1). On the right of innocent passage under customary international law, see *Maritime and Territorial Questions (Qatar v. Bahrain)* (Judgment) [2001] ICJ Rep 40, [253]. See also Churchill and Lowe n 15, 72, 87.

[55] '[W]hether a violation by a ship of the laws and regulations adopted by a coastal State in accordance with UNCLOS is sufficient to render passage non-innocent' is best answered 'by reference to the list of activities set forth in Article 19(2)'. Johnson, n 43, 66. See also LOSC, n 1, Arts 19(2)(i) and 21(1)(e).

[56] See Molenaar, n 43, 245, 250.   [57] LOSC, Arts 24(1)(b) and 26(1).

[58] Ibid, Art 21(2).

[59] States may still impose CDEM requirements as conditions of port entry; the limitation applies only to ships in lateral passage. See BH Oxman, 'The Third United Nations Conference on the Law of the Sea: The Seventh Session (1978)' (1979) 73 *American Journal of International Law* 1, 25–6.

[60] LOSC, n 1, Arts 16(2), 21(3), 22(4), 24(2), 25(3), and 42(3). See H Yang, *Jurisdiction of the Coastal State over Foreign Merchant Ships in Internal Waters and the Territorial Sea* (Springer Berlin 2006) 183–4.

[61] LOSC, n 1, Art 25(3). See also ibid, Art 45(2).   [62] Oxman, n 10, 839.

[63] O'Connell, n 31, Vol II, 961.

[64] Other 'reasonableness' provisions specify situations in which coastal State enforcement is clearly approved, and set out safeguards required when enforcing pollution violations. See nn 67–70 and accompanying text; LOSC, n 1, Arts 25(2), 27(1)–(2), 28(3), and 223–233; Molenaar, n 43, 245. The LOSC

One factor affecting whether a coastal State will exercise jurisdiction concerns where the effects of illegal acts are felt. If such acts have impacts only on board vessels, then coastal States may be reluctant to exercise jurisdiction.[65] Indeed, the scope of the coastal State's own criminal legislation may not reach shipboard disciplinary matters. If it does, the 'should not' formulation of Articles 27 and 28 in effect sanctions concurrent coastal State/flag State jurisdiction 'while inviting the coastal States not to exercise it'.[66] By contrast, when a vessel's operations affect the territorial sea or the coastal State itself, that State's interests may outweigh concerns with untrammelled navigation, and enforcement of coastal State laws is more likely.[67] For example, enforcement is reasonable if actions on board a vessel 'disturb the peace of' the coastal State,[68] a standard that varies in its application with the mores of each such State.

A coastal State has more extensive enforcement authority over ships heading to or from a coastal State port than it does over ships traversing the territorial sea. When a vessel is heading to port, the coastal State may take 'necessary steps to prevent any breach of the conditions' for port entry.[69] Similarly, ships in the territorial sea after leaving ports may be subject to broad coastal State rights of investigation or arrest.[70] Indeed, the provisions of Articles 27 and 28 of the LOSC specifying that the coastal State 'should' not or 'may' not exercise jurisdiction on board foreign ships formally apply to ships 'passing through' the territorial sea.

Coastal States may, in bilateral treaties concerning sensitive subject matters, grant other States enforcement authority in the territorial sea. Treaties directed at suppressing illicit drug trafficking and illegal immigration may authorize government vessels of one State to enter a second State's territorial sea for such law enforcement purposes as investigating suspicious activities or pursuing vessels suspected of violations. Such treaties may also allow shipriders from a coastal State to authorize foreign law enforcement actions in the territorial sea.[71]

---

prohibits a coastal State from exercising enforcement jurisdiction over vessels passing through the territorial sea only with respect to arrests for certain crimes 'committed before the ship entered the territorial sea', and for civil proceedings concerning obligations incurred by the ship outside coastal State waters. LOSC, n 1, Arts 27(5) and 28(2).

[65] The 'should not' phrasing of LOSC, Art 27 rejects the 'French doctrine', under which the flag State has exclusive jurisdiction over all criminal acts whose effects are confined to those on board a foreign flag vessel. See F Francioni, 'Criminal Jurisdiction over Foreign Merchant Vessels in Territorial Waters: A New Analysis' (1975) 1 *Italian Yearbook of International Law* 27. But the coastal State may nonetheless prefer—in the interest of comity or to encourage reciprocal treatment for its own vessels operating in another State's coastal waters—not to exercise jurisdiction, particularly with respect to incidents whose effects are felt only on board a vessel. See MS McDougal and WT Burke, *The Public Order of the Oceans* (Yale University Press New Haven 1962) 270, 291–4.

[66] LT Lee, 'Jurisdiction over Foreign Merchant Ships in the Territorial Sea: An Analysis of the Geneva Convention on the Law of the Sea' (1961) 55 *American Journal of International Law* 77, 86.

[67] See LOSC, n 1, Art 27(1).   [68] Ibid, Art 27(1)(b).   [69] Ibid, Art 25(2).

[70] Ibid, Arts 27(2) and 28(3); O'Connell, n 31, Vol II, 954–6, 958–9; Yang, n 60, 251–2, 259.

[71] See JE Kramek, 'Bilateral Maritime Counter-Drug and Immigrant Interdiction Agreements: Is This the World of the Future?' (2000) 31 *University of Miami Inter-American Law Review* 121.

How the LOSC balances international marine pollution standards, coastal State authority, and navigational rights in the territorial sea illustrates some of the complexity associated with managing environmental issues. Flag States must adopt laws to prevent their vessels from polluting the marine environment; those laws must 'at least have the same effect as' generally accepted international rules and standards.[72] The coastal State may also adopt vessel-source pollution laws applicable in the territorial sea, although such laws may 'not hamper innocent passage of foreign vessels'.[73] The coastal State 'shall' exercise prescriptive jurisdiction to prevent pollution by dumping, and national laws concerning dumping 'shall be no less effective' than any global rules.[74] As for enforcement, the Convention permits coastal State investigation when there are 'clear grounds for believing' a vessel navigating in the territorial sea has violated coastal State or international environmental measures, and authorizes proceedings against (including detention of) such vessels, subject to safeguards specified in Articles 223–233 of the LOSC.[75] There is no 'passing through' exemption for vessels committing environmental violations, as there is for other violations committed before a ship enters the territorial sea,[76] and the Convention contemplates coastal State enforcement measures (which often will occur in ports but may occur in the territorial sea or the EEZ) for vessel-source pollution occurring in the EEZ.[77] Other treaties also regulate marine pollution.

For merchant vessels not in innocent passage, the coastal State has full jurisdictional competence, even if it does not fully exercise it.[78] The traditional view is that such vessels are in status 'assimilated' to vessels in port.[79] Enforcement options in addition to boarding, arresting, detaining, or instituting proceedings are available against such vessels. The LOSC authorizes coastal States to take necessary steps in the territorial sea to prevent non-innocent passage,[80] and vessels not in innocent passage may be expelled from the territorial sea.[81] Even with respect to vessels not in innocent passage, however, coastal States remain subject to various duties.[82]

---

[72] LOSC, n 1, Art 211(2).
[73] Ibid, Art 211(4). Passage is, however, deemed not innocent in cases of 'wilful and serious pollution contrary to' the LOSC: Art 19(1)(h).
[74] Ibid, Art 210(1) and (6).   [75] Ibid, Art 220(2). See also ibid, Art 217 (dumping).
[76] Ibid, Arts 27(5) and 28(2). See n 64.   [77] See LOSC, n 1, Art 220(3)–(8).
[78] See ibid, Arts 27(2) and 28(3); Johnson, n 43, 62–3, 83; O'Connell, n 31, Vol II, 953; Yang, n 60, 151, 216.
[79] PC Jessup, *The Law of Territorial Waters and Maritime Jurisdiction* (GA Jennings Co. New York 1927; reprinted 1970) 123.
[80] LOSC, n 1, Art 25(1).   [81] Yang, n 60, 218.
[82] Eg LOSC, n 1, Arts 24(2) (requiring 'appropriate publicity to any danger to navigation') and 223–33 (safeguards for marine pollution violations).

5 'Other Rules of International Law' and International Organizations

The coastal State exercises sovereignty in its territorial sea subject to LOSC provisions and 'other rules of international law'.[83] The law of armed conflict contains 'other rules' that may supersede the law of the sea, which applies in peacetime.[84] There is, however, no reason to limit the scope of 'other rules' to the law of armed conflict. As the ILC put it in 1956, writing about the text that became Article 1 of the CTSCZ and, with slight modification, Article 2 of the LOSC: 'the limitations imposed by international law on the exercise of sovereignty in the territorial sea... set forth in the present articles... cannot... be regarded as exhaustive. Incidents in the territorial sea raising legal questions are also governed by the general rules of international law'. For this reason, "other rules of international law" are mentioned in addition to the provisions contained in the present articles'.[85]

Other rules of international law, including customary international law limits on the use of force, constrain coastal States in enforcing their laws and regulations. In the *M/V 'Saiga' (No 2)* case, the International Tribunal for the Law of the Sea (ITLOS) emphasized that:

Although the [LOSC] does not contain express provisions on the use of force in the arrest of ships, international law... requires that the use of force must be avoided as far as possible and, where force is unavoidable, it must not go beyond what is reasonable and necessary in the circumstances. Considerations of humanity must apply in the law of the sea, as they do in other areas of international law.[86]

Considerations of humanity also find expression in the obligations to assist and search for those in distress at sea, established in the LOSC and other treaties.[87] 'Passage' through the territorial sea, which normally 'shall be continuous and expeditious', includes stopping 'for the purpose of rendering assistance to persons, ships or aircraft in danger or distress'.[88] Warships may have a right of 'assistance entry' into the territorial sea without permission, to provide emergency help to those in

---

[83] Ibid, Arts 2(3), 19(1), 19(2)(a), 21(1), and 31(1).
[84] See GK Walker (ed), *Definitions for the Law of the Sea* (Martinus Nijhoff Leiden 2012) 269 n 798 (citing numerous authorities).
[85] 1956 ILC Report, n 38, 265. See JE Noyes, 'Interpreting the Law of the Sea Convention and Defining its Terms' in Walker (ed), n 84, 45, 62–9; M Wood, 'The International Tribunal for the Law of the Sea and General International Law' (2001) 22 *International Journal of Marine and Coastal Law* 351.
[86] *M/V 'Saiga' (No 2) (Saint Vincent and the Grenadines v Guinea)* (Judgment) [1999] ITLOS Rep 10, [155] (hereinafter *M/V 'Saiga' (No 2)*). See also LOSC, n 1, Art 225; Shearer, n 41, 341–2.
[87] Eg LOSC, n 1, Art 98; 1979 International Convention on Maritime Search and Rescue.
[88] LOSC, n 1, Art 18(2).

distress at sea, if the location of the distress is 'reasonably well known'.[89] In most cases, however, the coastal State will be responsible for search-and-rescue operations in its territorial sea. In situations of 'distress', the obligation to render assistance is clear, even if not always honoured in practice.

Once migrants or 'boat people' have been rescued, difficult questions arise concerning their treatment and resettlement. Under the Refugee Convention, obligations of non-refoulement and of providing facilities apply to individuals entering the 'territory' of States parties,[90] which includes the territorial sea.[91] However, some States have 'excised' their territorial sea and even particular islands from the scope of their national migration laws, or have prevented boat people from entering the territorial sea via actions in the contiguous zone.[92] Efforts by the UN High Commissioner on Refugees (UNHCR) and the IMO have not resolved problems facing those rescued at sea.[93] Ad hoc regional arrangements addressing resettlement challenges have been criticized for not meeting treaty and human rights obligations.[94]

More generally, international human rights law applies in the territorial sea. A coastal State could not escape its obligations via the argument, sometimes raised, that human rights treaties have no extraterritorial operation, since the coastal State has sovereignty over its territorial sea.[95] Furthermore, flag States, responsible for exercising effective control on their vessels, should respect the human rights of crew members.[96]

---

[89] *The Commander's Handbook on the Law of Naval Operations* (NWP [Navy Warfare Publication] 1-14M, July 2007), [2.5.2.6]; Roach and Smith, n 11, § 10.6; Tanaka, n 6, 91–2.

[90] 1951 Convention relating to the Status of Refugees, Arts 31 and 33. See also 1984 Convention against Torture and Other Cruel, Inhuman or Degrading Treatment or Punishment, Art 3 (non-refoulement obligation).

[91] See R Weinzierl and U Lisson (E Witte trans), *Border Management and Human Rights* (German Institute for Human Rights Berlin 2007) 13–14, 33–4, 43–4.

[92] See Rothwell and Stephens, n 18, 427–8; R Barnes, 'Refugee Law at Sea' (2004) 53 *International and Comparative Law Quarterly* 47, 65–71.

[93] See MSC Resolution 67(78) of 20 May 2004, *Guidelines on the Treatment of Persons Rescued at Sea*, MSC 78/26/Add.2, Annex 34 (2004); UNHCR, *Selected Reference Materials: Rescue at Sea, Maritime Interception and Stowaways* (November 2006), available at <http://www.unhcr.org/4d9486c39.pdf>.

[94] See Australian Government, *Report of the Expert Panel on Asylum Seekers* (13 August 2012); M Crock, 'Shadow Plays, Shifting Sands and International Refugee Law: Convergences in the Asia-Pacific' (2014) 63 *International and Comparative Law Quarterly* 247.

[95] See S Karagiannis, '1969 Vienna Convention: Article 29' in O Corten and P Klein (eds), *The Vienna Conventions on the Law of Treaties: A Commentary* (Oxford University Press Oxford 2011) Vol I, 731, 751–4. Some human rights obligations do apply extraterritorially, attaching wherever acts are carried out under a State's authority. See eg *Hirsi Jamaa et al v Italy*, Judgment of the European Court of Human Rights, Grand Chamber, Application No 27765/09 (23 February 2012).

[96] See LOSC, n 1, Art 94(3)(b) (flag State responsibility for labour conditions). See generally BH Oxman, 'Human Rights and the United Nations Convention on the Law of the Sea' (1997) 36 *Columbia Journal of Transnational Law* 399.

One particular obligation, applicable when a coastal State arrests people on board foreign flag vessels in the territorial sea, is the right of consular notification. This right is explicitly recognized in Article 27(3) of the LOSC, concerning the coastal State's exercise of criminal jurisdiction, but, 'incomprehensibl[y]', not in Article 28 on civil jurisdiction.[97] Still, a coastal State's consular rights treaties would apply in Article 28 situations.[98]

International organizations, both global and regional, develop treaties and standards applicable to coastal and flag States in the territorial sea. The IMO is particularly significant, since it is the source of many of the 'generally accepted' international rules or standards referred to in LOSC provisions concerning to the territorial sea.[99] As noted above, a coastal State's laws relating to innocent passage may not apply to CDEM matters unless those laws 'are giving effect to generally accepted international rules or standards'.[100] The IMO's tacit amendment procedures also facilitate technical amendments to treaties concerning vessel safety, vessel routeing, security, and marine pollution.[101]

In some respects, the roles of international organizations have exceeded what was anticipated under the LOSC. The LOSC addresses traffic separation, with respect to which the IMO has played a significant role as the 'competent international organization' referred to in the Convention,[102] and requires flag State compliance with 'generally accepted international regulations' on collision prevention.[103] However, the LOSC at most implicitly presages the IMO's significant role via the International Convention for the Safety of Life at Sea (SOLAS) in developing ship reporting and vessel tracking schemes that may apply in the territorial sea.[104] With respect to merchant vessels, SOLAS requirements to report or provide information are 'scarcely distinct in substance from prior notification'[105]—and notification was not adopted in UNCLOS III negotiations even for 'tankers, nuclear-powered ships and ships carrying nuclear or other inherently dangerous or noxious substances or materials'.[106] Although, as a general rule, 'States more readily accept international regulation of activities that relate exclusively or principally to areas that are not subject to territorial sovereignty than to

---

[97] Lee, n 66, 93.

[98] O'Connell, n 31, Vol II, 73. See generally LT Lee and J Quigley, *Consular Law and Practice* (3rd edn Oxford University Press Oxford 2008) 295–330.

[99] LOSC, n 1, Arts 21(2) and (4), 39(2), 41(3), and 211(2), (5), and (6)(c). See Committee on Coastal State Jurisdiction Relating to Marine Pollution, 'Final Report' in International Law Association, *Report of the Sixty-Ninth Conference* (2000) 443, 473–81.

[100] LOSC, n 1, Art 21(2). See nn 58–9 and accompanying text.

[101] Among the numerous IMO conventions are: International Convention for the Safety of Life at Sea (SOLAS), which now incorporates the 2002 International Ship and Port Facility Security Code; MARPOL; and the Collision Regulations (COLREGs).

[102] LOSC, n 1, Arts 22(3)(a) and 41(4) and (5). See DOALOS, '"Competent or relevant international organizations" under the United Nations Convention on the Law of the Sea' (1996) 31 *Law of the Sea Bulletin* 79, 81.

[103] LOSC, n 1, Art 21(4). [104] Ibid, Arts 21(1)(a) and (b). [105] Yang, n 60, 211.

[106] LOSC, n 1, Art 22(2). See *Virginia Commentaries*, Vol II, 206–13.

areas that are',[107] international organizations promote stable expectations by regulating a range of matters concerning the territorial sea.

Global and regional international organizations may also make rules applicable to individual countries' territorial seas. The IMO has adopted numerous traffic separation schemes for particular waters. The IMO's role in this regard is mandatory only for straits subject to the regime of transit passage.[108] However, some States, valuing the international recognition attending IMO approval of such schemes, have sought such approval for traffic separation schemes in territorial seas that are not part of straits.[109]

The IMO also has approved over a dozen particularly sensitive sea areas (PSSAs), one type of marine protected area.[110] Although the coastal State has sovereign authority to establish marine protected areas in its territorial sea,[111] subject to the duty not to hamper the right of innocent passage, some coastal States have received IMO approval of PSSAs that overlap at least in part their territorial seas. The IMO, relying on the International Convention for the Prevention of Pollution from Ships (MARPOL) or SOLAS as authority, has approved such protective measures for PSSAs as mandatory no anchoring areas, areas to be avoided, traffic separation schemes, and mandatory ship reporting requirements. Australia's compulsory pilotage requirement through the Torres Strait, an extended region of the Great Barrier Reef PSSA, has been controversial, because the IMO had merely 'recommend[ed]' compliance with Australia's pilotage system.[112]

Other global organizations may also affect rights and duties in the territorial sea. The UN Security Council, acting under Chapter VII of the UN Charter, may mandate measures in order to maintain international peace and security. These measures have authorized interdiction of vessels in the territorial sea. For example, during the break-up of the former Yugoslavia, Council Resolution 820 prohibited all commercial shipping from entering the Yugoslav territorial sea and exercising the right of innocent passage there, and authorized the interdiction of such shipping.[113] The Security Council has also authorized States to enter the territorial sea of Somalia

---

[107] Oxman, n 10, 845. [108] Compare LOSC, n 1, Art 22(3)(a) with ibid, Art 41.

[109] See IMO, *Ships' Routeing* (11th edn IMO Publishing London 2013), available at <http://www.imo.org/Publications/Documents/Newsletters%20and%20Mailers/Mailers/IE927E.pdf>; Molenaar, n 43, 228.

[110] IMO Resolution A.982(24) of 1 December 2005, *Revised Guidelines for the Identification and Designation of Particularly Sensitive Sea Areas (PSSAs)* (2005), available at <http://www.imo.org/ourwork/environment/pollutionprevention/pssas/Pages/Default.aspx>.

[111] Yang, n 60, 239.

[112] IMO Resolution MEPC.133(53) of 22 July 2005, *Designation of the Torres Strait as an Extension of the Great Barrier Reef Particularly Sensitive Area*, MEPC 53/24/Add.2, Annex 21 (2005), [4]. See Roach and Smith, n 11, § 11.8.17; Australian Government, Great Barrier Reef & Torres Strait Vessel Traffic Service (REEFVTS), *User Guide* (5th edn July 2011) 14–15.

[113] United Nations Security Council Resolution S/RES/820 of 17 April 1993, *Bosnia and Herzegovina* (1993) [28]–[29]. See R McLaughlin, 'United Nations Mandated Naval Interdiction Operations in the Territorial Sea?' (2002) 51 *International and Comparative Law Quarterly* 249, 264–7, 271.

and use 'all necessary means to repress acts of piracy and armed robbery' there; the Council emphasized that it had received the consent of the Transitional Federal Government of Somalia, which some governments had recognized.[114]

LOSC provisions and other international law rules limit or shape the exercise of coastal State sovereignty in the territorial sea. Many of the limitations pertain to navigational rights. Actions of international organizations concerning vessel safety and design, marine pollution, navigation, and international peace and security also affect how authority is exercised in the territorial sea.

6 Contiguous Zone

Within the contiguous zone, a narrow belt of water lying seaward of the territorial sea, a coastal State may enforce its customs, fiscal, immigration, and sanitary laws against foreign flag vessels. Historically, some States maintained 'hovering zones' to combat smuggling. In 1804, the US Supreme Court found coastal State control over vessels hovering off the coast to be consistent with international law. This control was not subject to 'any certain marked boundaries, which remain the same, at all times and in all situations'. Rather, there could be, '[i]n different seas, and on different coasts, a wider or more contracted range, in which to exercise the vigilance of the government'.[115]

Reliance on indeterminate hovering zones diminished by the mid-nineteenth century. Coastal States followed one of three approaches toward offshore activities that threatened their security or other interests.[116] First, some States declared different fixed zones for different purposes, in lieu of a territorial sea.[117] Second, some States maintained a territorial sea and, in addition, asserted control beyond and contiguous to it, in determinate zones established for customs or other specific purposes. This practice was common in Latin America.[118] Third, some States,

---

[114] See eg United Nations Security Council Resolution S/RES/1816 of 2 June 2008, *Somalia* (2008), [7]–[9].

[115] *Church v Hubbart*, 6 US (2 Cranch) 187, 235 (1804).

[116] See Lowe, n 8, 117, 121–2, 133–40.

[117] This approach fit the 'bundle of servitudes' theory of coastal State authority, see n 30 and accompanying text, for 'the extent of any one of those rights could quite easily exceed that of another'. Lowe, n 8, 140.

[118] The Central American Court of Justice recognized the legality of a zone contiguous to the territorial sea 'for defensive and fiscal purposes': *El Salvador v Nicaragua* (1917) 11 *American Journal of International Law* 674, 706. According to Lowe, the Court may have been articulating a rule of regional customary international law: Lowe, n 8, 138.

including the United Kingdom, maintained a narrow territorial sea and insisted that the waters beyond it were high seas, where foreign vessels were free from the application of coastal State laws and, in general, from coastal State enforcement.[119]

The modern contiguous zone emerged out of twentieth-century international law codification efforts. Both Article 24(1) of the CTSCZ and Article 33(1) of the LOSC provide that, in a zone contiguous to and beyond its territorial sea, a coastal State 'may exercise the control necessary to: (a) prevent infringement of its customs, fiscal, immigration or sanitary regulations within its territory or territorial sea; (b) punish infringement of the above regulations committed within its territory or territorial sea'. As Shearer has summarized, subsection (a) 'applies to inward-bound ships and is anticipatory or preventive in character', while subsection (b), 'applying to outward-bound ships, gives more extensive power, and is analogous to'—though not subject to all the constraints associated with—hot pursuit.[120] In short, the contiguous zone was recognized as a zone of limited coastal State control, conceptually linked to certain violations that had occurred or were anticipated in the territorial sea, rather than as a zone of sovereignty or legislative jurisdiction.

The 1958 CTSCZ maintains a distinction between the territorial sea, which is subject to coastal State sovereignty, and the high seas beyond. Indeed, Article 24(1) expressly characterizes the contiguous zone as 'a zone of the high seas'. This conception helps explain why a coastal State could not regulate activities taking place in the contiguous zone. The scope of coastal State competence was limited because of concerns about undue interference with the high seas freedom of navigation.[121]

The LOSC in one respect varies the rule that a coastal State only has enforcement jurisdiction in the contiguous zone by providing for coastal State jurisdiction to regulate the removal of archaeological and historical objects from the seabed of its contiguous zone.[122] The coastal State may exercise both legislative and enforcement jurisdiction with respect to such objects.

The contiguous zone, located beyond the territorial sea, may extend up to 12 nm from a coastal State's baselines under the 1958 CTSCZ, and up to 24 nm from its

---

[119] States following this third approach allowed a coastal State to enforce its laws outside its territorial sea only in narrow circumstances: if the coastal State began 'hot pursuit' of a vessel in the territorial sea and captured it beyond that zone; if the coastal State arrested a 'mother ship' that was outside the territorial sea, but was deemed 'constructively present' in it because the arrested vessel sent smaller boats into the territorial sea to transport contraband; or if a treaty authorized the coastal State to enforce specified laws outside its territorial sea. See eg 1924 Convention between the United States of America and Great Britain respecting the Regulation of the Liquor Traffic.

[120] Shearer, n 41, 330. See Rothwell and Stephens, n 18, 80.

[121] See eg Lowe, n 8, 148; Third United Nations Conference on the Law of the Sea, *Official Records* (UN Sales No E.76.V.4) vol II, 235 (views of Bahrain) (hereinafter 2 *UNCLOS III Official Records*).

[122] LOSC, n 1, Art 303. See MC Giorgi, 'Underwater Archaeological and Historical Objects' in R-J Dupuy and D Vignes (eds), *A Handbook on the New Law of the Sea* (Martinus Nijhoff Dordrecht 1991) vol I, 561, 568–70; Tanaka, n 6, 123; 2001 Convention on the Protection of the Underwater Cultural Heritage, Art 8.

baselines—ie, up to 12 nm beyond a 12 nm territorial sea—under the LOSC. A State must explicitly declare a contiguous zone, and if one is claimed, it need not extend to the maximum permissible breadth. Although some States prefer to concentrate their enforcement activities within the territorial sea, many have established contiguous zones. According to a 2011 study, 90 States have created contiguous zones, 83 of them extending to 24 nm from baselines, and six extending shorter distances.[123]

Since the contiguous zone is conceptually linked to the territorial sea, the same geographical features that may support a territorial sea also support a contiguous zone. Although rocks that cannot support human habitation or an economic life of their own are not entitled to EEZs or continental shelves, they are entitled to contiguous zones.[124]

The 1958 CTSCZ includes a provision on delimitation of contiguous zones,[125] which was not retained in Article 33 of the LOSC. According to one view, contiguous zone delimitations are unnecessary, because no resource allocation is involved; two or more States could exercise, over the same area, the preventive and punishment functions for which the contiguous zone was established.[126] However, some delimitation agreements determine the boundaries of the contiguous zone. Since that zone overlaps the EEZ, EEZ delimitations may affect the contiguous zone as well. Although the contiguous zone usually is not specifically mentioned in maritime boundary delimitations, a contiguous zone boundary may be established by agreements referring to 'maritime frontiers' or using other general formulations.[127]

The contiguous zone was developed before UNCLOS III, when most States had territorial seas of less than 12 nm. During UNCLOS III, delegates debated whether a contiguous zone was still needed, in light of the newly recognized EEZ and coastal State sovereignty over a 12 nm territorial sea. One view was that the contiguous zone was not necessary.[128] According to a second position, the contiguous zone should be maintained at 12 nm (the limit set in Article 24 CTSCZ), but could exist only where States chose not to proclaim a territorial sea to the 12 nm maximum breadth.[129] Other States suggested extending the contiguous zone to various breadths, with a maximum of 24 nm (12 beyond the territorial sea) being the standard eventually

---

[123] See DOALOS, *Table of Claims*, n 16; Roach and Smith, n 11, § 6.1.

[124] R Lavalle, 'Not Quite a Sure Thing: The Maritime Areas of Rocks and Low-Tide Elevations Under the UN Law of the Sea Convention' (2004) 19 *International Journal of Marine and Coastal Law* 43, 47 n 12, 67–8.

[125] CTSCZ, n 3, Art 24(3).

[126] See *Virginia Commentaries*, Vol II, § 33.8(b). However, disputes over regulation of underwater cultural heritage could arise absent delimitation of the contiguous zone. See n 122 and accompanying text.

[127] See D Colson, 'The Legal Regime of Maritime Boundary Agreements' in JI Charney and LM Alexander (eds), *International Maritime Boundaries* (Martinus Nijhoff Dordrecht 1993) Vol I, 42, 44–51.

[128] 2 *UNCLOS III Official Records*, n 121, 122 (views of Lebanon).

[129] Ibid, 234 (German Democratic Republic).

adopted.[130] The argument that the contiguous zone was unnecessary because it overlapped the EEZ was not ultimately persuasive. The EEZ concerns coastal State regulation of resources and economic uses of the zone itself, rather than customs, fiscal, immigration, and sanitary matters. In addition, 'the great advances in the speed and construction of modern ships' arguably made it sensible to extend coastal State enforcement jurisdiction to a contiguous zone broader than 12 nm.[131] Ultimately, extending the contiguous zone appears to be part of the compromise package that preserved navigational rights and various other high seas freedoms in the EEZ in exchange for considerable, but still limited, coastal State authority over the EEZ.

Notably absent from contiguous zone treaty provisions is any direct reference to security, although customs, fiscal, immigration, and sanitary laws may reflect security concerns. Historically, coastal States extended their jurisdiction and control for defence purposes.[132] The omission of 'security' from the list of subjects of coastal State control in the 1958 CTSCZ is probably explained by concerns that the 'extreme vagueness' of the term could unreasonably interfere with freedom of navigation and by the recognition that other avenues exist to safeguard coastal State security.[133]

Some have argued that the coastal State has authority to exercise limited legislative jurisdiction in the contiguous zone, with respect for example to transhipment operations affecting customs, fiscal, sanitary, or immigration matters.[134] It is, however, hard to find support for this position in the text or *travaux* of the CTSCZ and the LOSC.

The meaning of any treaty provision may change if subsequent practice reveals a new shared agreement about the provision's interpretation.[135] A few coastal States have not confined their contiguous zone authority concerning customs, fiscal, immigration, and sanitary matters to enforcing laws that apply only in the territorial sea or land territory. Instead, they have occasionally directly regulated such matters in the contiguous zone.[136] Other countries have claimed, inconsistently with the LOSC, that security matters fall within the scope of coastal State control in the

---

[130] Proposals included 30 nm from baselines (18 beyond territorial sea)—ibid, 121 (India), and 18 from baselines (6 beyond territorial sea)—ibid, 234 (Honduras).

[131] Ibid, 235 (Bahrain).   [132] See Lowe, n 8, 118.

[133] 1956 ILC Report, n 38, 295. See LB Sohn, JE Noyes, E Franckx, and KG Juras, *Cases and Materials on the Law of the Sea* (2nd edn Brill Nijhoff Leiden/Boston 2014) 427–8.

[134] See S Oda, 'The Concept of the Contiguous Zone' (1962) 11 *International and Comparative Law Quarterly* 131; Shearer, n 41, 330.

[135] 1969 Vienna Convention on the Law of Treaties, Art 31(3).

[136] Eg Maritime Drug Law Enforcement, 46 USC §§ 70502(c)(1)(F), 70503 (US narcotics legislation applicable to vessels in the contiguous zone). Much depends on how legislation is construed. For example, Maritime Zones Law No 22 of 1 September 1976 (Sri Lanka) § 12, available at <http://www.un.org/Depts/los/LEGISLATIONANDTREATIES/regionslist.htm> (hereinafter DOALOS National Legislation Compilation), provides that 'all written laws in force in Sri Lanka shall be read and construed as though the applicability of such laws, *wherever relevant*, extends to the limits of contiguous zone' (emphasis added).

contiguous zone.[137] Plausible treaty interpretation also might further the 'creeping jurisdiction' of coastal States. For example, broad interpretations of what constitutes the 'constructive presence' of a vessel in the contiguous zone could expand coastal State authority,[138] as could liberal views on what steps are 'necessary' to 'prevent' infringement of customs, fiscal, immigration, or sanitary regulations.[139]

Most instances of expanded coastal State control or jurisdiction in the contiguous zone have been met with protests, notably by the United States, on the grounds that broad assertions of jurisdiction would interfere with freedom of navigation in the EEZ.[140] The ITLOS has also reaffirmed the limited scope of coastal State customs authority under the LOSC, finding no support for Guinea's assertion of customs authority in part of its EEZ outside the contiguous zone. The Tribunal noted that a coastal State may apply customs laws in its territorial sea, take customs enforcement measures in its contiguous zone, and, in its EEZ, apply its customs laws on artificial islands, installations, and structures;[141] however, 'the Convention does not empower a coastal State to apply its customs laws in respect of any other parts of the exclusive economic zone not mentioned above'.[142] The fairest conclusion concerning State practice may still be that of Lowe, writing in 1981, who found 'no uniform practice establishing the agreement of parties' that would change the meaning of CTSCZ Article 24 and LOSC Article 33.[143]

7 Conclusion

In the territorial sea, the coastal State has significant interests relating to security, resources, pollution, marine scientific research, economic exploitation, immigration, communications, and a host of other matters related to the use of this zone. Yet coastal State sovereignty in the territorial sea is not without its limits. It is exercised subject to provisions in the LOSC—notably those concerning transit passage through straits and innocent passage, which reflect values associated with freedom

---

[137] Examples, with date of enactment, include legislation of Bangladesh (1974), Cambodia (1982), China (1992), Haiti (1977), India (1976), Myanmar (1977), Pakistan (1976), Saudi Arabia (1958 and 2011), Sri Lanka (1976), Syria (2003), United Arab Emirates (1993), and Yemen (1977). See DOALOS National Legislation Compilation, n 136. Most of this legislation was enacted before UNCLOS III concluded and before the countries accepted the LOSC. See also Roach and Smith, n 11, § 6.2.1.

[138] See n 119; WC Gilmore, 'Hot Pursuit: The Case of *R. v. Mills and Others*' (1995) 44 *International and Comparative Law Quarterly* 949.

[139] See Molenaar, n 43, 276.   [140] See Roach and Smith, n 11, § 6.2.1.

[141] *M/V 'Saiga' (No 2)*, n 87, [128]; see LOSC, n 1, Arts 2, 21(1)(h), 33(1), and 60(2).

[142] *M/V 'Saiga' (No 2)*, n 87, [128].   [143] Lowe, n 8, 168.

of navigation—and to other rules of international law. In the contiguous zone, the coastal State's control is even more limited. There, the coastal State has enforcement jurisdiction with respect to violations of its customs, fiscal, sanitary, and immigration laws occurring in its territory or territorial sea, and legislative and enforcement jurisdiction with respect to archaeological and historical objects. The basic contours of the territorial sea and contiguous zone regimes as set out in the LOSC appear stable, with almost all States exercising sovereignty or control only to the maximum geographical extent permissible—out to 12 and 24 nm, respectively.

The risk of instability through coastal State 'jurisdiction creep' nevertheless should be acknowledged. In the territorial sea and contiguous zone, this risk stems primarily from two sources. One is impermissible straight baselines, which push all coastal State zones farther seaward (see Chapter 4). The second is the possibility that coastal States, in these two zones, assert authority that exceeds permissible international law limits. Overly aggressive regulatory and enforcement actions directed at foreign flag vessels could effectively 'hamper' the right of innocent passage.[144] Jurisdiction creep in the contiguous zone is also possible if States assert excessive jurisdiction in the zone (in addition to the authority permissible in the EEZ and continental shelf, which the contiguous zone partially overlaps).[145] Appropriate protests against excessive coastal State claims, and efforts to manage legal change through international organizations or other multilateral processes, can minimize the possibility of destabilizing jurisdiction creep in the territorial sea and contiguous zone.

Although coastal States historically have expanded their authority in the territorial sea, some States have now refused to employ particular laws there. They have taken this step in order, for example, to avoid applying national migration or asylum standards and procedures to unauthorized migrants arriving by sea.[146] The issue then becomes whether such restrictions are permissible as a matter of international law. When human rights treaty and customary international law obligations apply in a State's 'territory', that term may well encompass the territorial sea; or such obligations may apply extraterritorially, wherever a State exercises its authority.[147] The application of human rights norms to migrants arriving by sea is but one illustration of how the law of the sea intersects with other realms of international law.

Disagreements among States over the right of innocent passage for warships and ships transporting hazardous cargoes are likely to remain sensitive. These disagreements concern whether innocence is to be determined only objectively by assessing flag State activities, and whether the coastal State may insist on prior notice or, even less plausibly, permission as a condition for innocent passage.[148] The world's leading maritime power, the United States, is in an awkward position to claim the advantage

---

[144] See Chapter 24 in this volume; Molenaar, n 43, 271–3; Yang, n 60, 268.
[145] See nn 136–9 and accompanying text.   [146] See n 92 and accompanying text.
[147] See nn 94–5 and accompanying text.   [148] See nn 43–6 and accompanying text.

of liberal LOSC navigational provisions developed at UNCLOS III, since the United States is not a party to the LOSC. Some authorities take the view that the United States remains bound by the CTSCZ and its more restrictive navigational provisions vis-à-vis other parties to the CTSCZ,[149] or that not all LOSC navigational rights exist as a matter of customary international law, given the package deal nature of the LOSC.[150] Regardless of whether the United States accedes to the LOSC, however, coastal States will remain sensitive to perceived environmental and security risks posed by certain ships operating near shore. It thus seems likely that disagreements over territorial sea navigational regimes will continue. It is an open question whether international organizations or international negotiations can successfully resolve some of these sensitive matters, for example by developing additional international rules and standards concerning shipments of radioactive waste or by fashioning ad hoc arrangements.

International cooperation does, in several respects, affect how activities in the territorial sea are governed. The work of international organizations helps shape coastal and flag State obligations in the territorial sea, with respect to such issues as vessel safety and routeing. Other opportunities for cooperation exist, including regional seas measures on environmental issues (see Chapters 27, 29, 30, and 32) and global, regional, and bilateral initiatives to combat, in the territorial sea, such criminal activity as drug trafficking and robbery at sea.[151] The contours of the 'coastal State sovereignty' that applies in the territorial sea depend on such cooperative measures, foreign flag navigational rights, and various other rules of international law.

---

[149] See eg Molenaar, n 43, 54.

[150] See eg JI Charney, 'International Agreements and the Development of Customary International Law' (1986) 61 *Washington Law Review* 971; United States Senate Committee on Foreign Relations, 108th Congress (2003), *Senate Executive Report 108-10 on the UN Convention on the Law of the Sea (Treaty Doc 103-39)*, Annex II (2004) 106 (statement of US Admiral M Mullen, Vice Chief of Naval Operations, noting that 'some coastal States contend that the navigational and overflight rights contained in the [LOSC] are available only to those States that also accept the responsibilities set forth in the Convention by becoming parties to it'). The United States relies on the provisions of the LOSC relating to navigational rights as customary international law. *United States Senate Committee on Foreign Relations (Treaty Doc. 103-39)* (2013) 14 (prepared statement of US Secretary of State Hillary Clinton).

[151] See eg nn 71 and 114 and accompanying text. See also Chapter 38.

6

INTERNATIONAL STRAITS

DONALD R ROTHWELL

1 Introduction

THE emergence of the modern law of the sea post World War II coincided with a global economic boom as new markets emerged and trade opportunities arose. In this setting, the law of the sea had an important role to play through the on-going realization of the Grotian vision of the freedom of the seas through the four 1958 Geneva Conventions on the Law of the Sea,[1] and subsequently the 1982 United Nations Convention on the Law of the Sea (LOSC).[2] Even allowing for the impact of new maritime zones,[3] and the gradual expansion in the breadth of the territorial sea,[4] a law of the sea constant during this period was the recognition of certain navigation rights within international straits. The importance of these rights was acknowledged in 1949 by the first decision of the International Court of Justice (ICJ) in the *Corfu Channel* case[5] where the court was prepared to accept the special status of straits used for international navigation.[6] The need

---

[1] The term 'Geneva Conventions on the Law of the Sea' include the four conventions concluded at the 1958 Geneva conference: 1958 Convention on the Territorial Sea and Contiguous Zone (hereinafter TSC); 1958 Convention on the High Sea; 1958 Convention on Fishing and Conservation of the Living Resources of the High Seas; 1958 Convention on the Continental Shelf.
[2] 1982 United Nations Convention on the Law of the Sea (hereinafter LOSC).
[3] Such as the exclusive economic zone (EEZ), ibid, Art 55. [4] Ibid, Art 3.
[5] *Corfu Channel (United Kingdom v Albania)* [1949] ICJ Rep 4.
[6] See discussion on the on-going significance of this decision of the International Court of Justice in K Bannelier, T Christakis, and S Heathcote (eds), *The ICJ and the Evolution of International Law: The Enduring Impact of the Corfu Channel Case* (Routledge New York 2012).

for a distinctive law of the sea regime dealing with straits arose because of the significance of international straits, or 'international maritime highways', to commerce. International maritime trade had historically developed using the shortest navigable route between ports and this naturally involved the use of straits connecting one area of high seas with another as a means of safe and expeditious passage. Throughout modern maritime history, the Straits of Gibraltar,[7] Straits of Dover,[8] the Danish Straits, and the Turkish Straits[9] acquired considerable strategic, political, and commercial significance because of the volume of maritime traffic passing through those waters.[10] Beyond Europe, other straits had similar strategic, political, and commercial importance, including the Straits of Malacca and Singapore,[11] Sunda Strait, Taiwan (Formosa) Strait, Torres Strait,[12] Bass Strait,[13] Strait of Juan de Fuca Strait, the Florida Strait, and the Straits of Magellan.[14]

First through the regime of innocent passage,[15] and then the transit passage regime,[16] the law of the sea sought to accommodate the special circumstances of straits and their pivotal role as part of a maritime highway that connected adjoining oceans and high seas areas. The special status of straits within archipelagic States has also been recognized in the law of the sea via the regime of archipelagic sea lanes navigation. This accommodation of the mutual rights and interests of littoral States and maritime States is on-going and continues to play out in State practice associated with the LOSC.

This chapter begins with a brief historical assessment of the regime of straits, before moving to consider some of the critical issues associated with Part III of the LOSC. Attention will then be given to a range of operational issues that exist for some straits, before a review of future issues facing the legal regime. The special position of straits located with IN archipelagic States is dealt with elsewhere in this volume.[17]

---

[7] SC Truver, *The Strait of Gibraltar and the Mediterranean* (Sijthoff & Noordhoff Alphen Aan Den Rijn 1980).
[8] L Cuyvers, *The Strait of Dover* (Martinus Nijhoff Dordrecht 1986).
[9] N Ünlü, *The Legal Regime of the Turkish Straits* (Martinus Nijhoff The Hague 2002).
[10] E Brüel, *International Straits* (Sweet & Maxwell London 1947) Vol II.
[11] M Leifer, *International Straits of the World: Malacca, Singapore and Indonesia* (Sijthoff & Noordhoff Alphen Aan Den Rijn 1978).
[12] SB Kaye, *The Torres Strait* (Martinus Nijhoff Boston 1997).
[13] DR Rothwell, 'International Straits and UNCLOS: An Australian Case Study' (1992) 23 *Journal of Maritime Law and Commerce* 461.
[14] MA Morris, *The Strait of Magellan* (Martinus Nijhoff Dordrecht 1989).
[15] TSC, n 1, Arts 14–23; LOSC, n 2, Arts 17–32.   [16] LOSC, n 2, Arts 37–44.
[17] See Chapter 7 in this volume.

2 Historical Development

While the focal point for the modern analysis of the international law with respect to straits is rightly the *Corfu Channel* case, various efforts were made in the late nineteenth and early twentieth centuries to consider the status of straits and whether a distinctive regime was necessary. A number of studies were made during this period by prominent associations of international lawyers, including the Institut de Droit International and the International Law Association, in order to reach agreement on a possible codification of aspects of the law of the sea in general and international straits in particular. Between 1924 and 1930 these initiatives resulted in a number of codification projects, including at the 1930 Hague Codification Conference; however, no significant breakthroughs occurred during this time in the development of the law.[18] In 1936, the Convention Regarding the Regime of Straits (Montreux Convention) was concluded, which sought to regulate transit and navigation in the Straits of the Dardanelles, the Sea of Marmora, and the Bosphorus so as to provide for Turkish security and those States bordering the Black Sea. While distinguishing between times of war and peace, the Montreux Convention recognized the important principle of the 'complete freedom of transit and navigation' by merchant vessels through the Straits. The Montreux Convention is also a prominent illustration of a pre-LOSC initiative to address questions of navigation through an international strait by warships, containing a range of measures which made distinctions between different types of naval vessels depending on their capacity and size, flag of origin, and overall maximum aggregate tonnage of a naval force exercising passage. A right of transit through the straits could be enjoyed with or without significant limitations and constraints, though any transit was to be preceded by notification to Turkey.[19]

Recognition of a distinctive customary international law with respect to straits came with the 1949 decision in the *Corfu Channel* case,[20] where the Court considered navigation rights of British warships through the Albanian territorial sea within the strait. The ICJ made clear that in a time of peace States had 'a right to send their warships through straits used for international navigation between two parts of the high seas', provided that the passage was innocent.[21] The Court went on to note that, unless otherwise prescribed by a convention, a coastal State could not prohibit innocent passage through a strait in peacetime.[22] In this respect, the Court's decision for the first time gave some legal definition to which straits may be subject

---

[18] DP O'Connell, *The International Law of the Sea* (ed IA Shearer) (Clarendon Press Oxford 1982) Vol 1, 301–6.
[19] Ibid, Art 13; see further discussion in Ünlü, n 9, 87–100.   [20] *Corfu Channel*, n 5.
[21] Ibid, [28].   [22] Ibid.

to this regime of innocent passage, while also suggesting that certain straits enjoyed a distinctive legal regime.

As to the characterization of the strait, the Court asked the question as to whether the volume of traffic passing through the strait or the importance of the strait for international navigation was significant, and responded:

> ... in the opinion of the Court the decisive criteria is rather its geographical situation as connecting two parts of the high seas and the fact of its being used for international navigation.[23]

To that end, the Court observed that it was not 'decisive' that the strait was not a necessary route between two parts of the high seas, but only an alternative route of passage between the Aegean and Adriatic Seas. However, it noted that the Corfu Channel had nevertheless 'been a useful route for international maritime traffic'.[24] Following consideration of the volume of international maritime traffic passing through the Corfu Channel, and noting that the North Corfu Channel was the frontier between Greece and Albania, the Court concluded:

> ... the North Corfu Channel should be considered as belonging to the class of international highways through which passage cannot be prohibited by a coastal State in time of peace.[25]

The ICJ also made observations as to the manner in which the passage right was exercised, which raised particular sensitivities when warships were involved. That the British warships were at action stations as they passed through the Corfu Channel did not render the passage non-innocent.[26]

The *Corfu Channel* case therefore provided considerable clarity to the then developing customary international law with respect to the innocent passage rights of warships through straits, and the types of straits through which innocent passage could be enjoyed, of which both geographic and functional criteria were emphasized. The case also proved influential when the International Law Commission (ILC) came to consider the regime of the territorial sea during the 1950s. While the ILC was unable to reach agreement as to the breadth of the territorial sea, there was a view expressed that it was not to extend beyond 12 nautical miles (nm).[27] This provided the Commission at a minimum with a clear sense as to the consequences for certain waters within which overlapping territorial sea claims of a certain breadth would mean that a foreign vessel would need to pass through the territorial sea of the littoral State so as to navigate its way through the strait. This in turn had implications for the innocent passage regime and the particular issues that arose within certain international straits. In that regard, section III of the ILC's Articles provided for the 'Right of Innocent Passage', and detailed its application within the territorial sea. Article 16 referred to the duties of the coastal State as being to not hamper the right of innocent passage, which the ILC identified as confirming principles upheld

---

[23] Ibid. [24] Ibid. [25] Ibid, [29]. [26] Ibid, [31].
[27] International Law Commission, 'Articles concerning the Law of the Sea with commentaries' (1956) II *Yearbook of the International Law Commission* 265, Art 3(2).

in *Corfu Channel*.[28] Draft Article 17(4) provided that there 'must be no suspension of innocent passage of foreign ships through straits normally used for international navigation between two parts of the high seas'.[29] The insertion of the word 'normally' was believed by the ILC to be in conformity with the ICJ's decision.[30] The ILC's debates on the status of straits had resolved upon two types of straits. The first were those straits that linked two high seas areas within which a vessel had to pass through the territorial sea to gain access from one high seas area to another. The second was that category of straits which led to inland waters.[31]

This remained a critical issue at the 1958 Geneva Conference, which adopted the Convention on the Territorial Sea and Contiguous Zone (TSC).[32] The proposed article dealing with international straits was modified so as to deal with the two types of straits that had been considered by the ILC, and appeared in the Article 16(4) of the TSC as follows:

There shall be no suspension of the right of innocent passage of foreign ships through straits which are used for international navigation between one part of the high seas and another part of the high seas or the territorial sea of a foreign State.

The result of this adjustment to the ILC's text was to include bodies of water such as the Gulf of Aqaba. Fitzmaurice, writing soon after the conclusion of the Convention, referred to the objective of not seeking to differentiate between two bodies of water:

[The] principle involved was almost exactly the same—namely, ships sail to reach a destination, and should be allowed access to it through the normal geographic approaches, even if this involves passage through the territorial sea of another country.[33]

3 THE PART III LAW OF THE SEA CONVENTION REGIME

Part III of the LOSC is titled 'Straits Used for International Navigation', and identifies the geographical attributes of the straits to which Part III applies and, in certain cases, creates for those straits detailed legal frameworks within which the rights of coastal States are acknowledged and the freedoms of navigation to be enjoyed by

---

[28] Ibid, 273, Art 16. [29] Ibid, 273. [30] Ibid. [31] O'Connell, n 18, Vol 1, 315.
[32] TSC, n 1, Arts 14–23.
[33] G Fitzmaurice, 'Some Results of the Geneva Conference on the Law of the Sea: Part 1—The Territorial Sea and Contiguous Zone and Related Topics' (1959) 8 *International and Comparative Law Quarterly* 89, 102.

maritime States are outlined. A threshold issue arising from the chapeau of Part III is how a strait used for international navigation is to be classified. The phrase suggests both a geographical and functional element. The geographical element relates to a strait being a body of water which lies between two areas of land, either continental landmasses,[34] a continent and an island,[35] or two islands.[36] Yet there is no guidance as to how proximate the bodies of land must be to one another, or at which point the width of the body of water which separates the two areas of land is no longer considered a strait but rather a sea or an ocean.[37] For practical purposes, this distinction may not be of great relevance as most bodies of water that separate sufficiently proximate areas of land are referred to as 'straits', or have equivalent titles.[38] Nevertheless, the recognition of a body of water as a strait is an important starting point in the application of the Part III legal regime. Accordingly, one of the initial issues that needed to be addressed in the LOSC was distinguishing between various navigational regimes that apply in the different bodies of water that may comprise a strait. One of those factors is clearly the width of the strait, and surveys have estimated that there are 52 international straits less than 6 nm in width, 153 international straits between 6 and 24 nm in width, and 60 other international straits in excess of 24 nm.[39]

The functional element is clearly drawn from *Corfu Channel* where the ICJ placed emphasis on the strait being one that was 'used for international navigation'.[40] While there was no analysis as to what volume of navigation through the strait would be required to meet the usage requirement, reference was made to the volume of navigation through the Strait between 1936 and 1937 which, in the view of the Court, assisted it in determining that the Corfu Channel had been 'a useful route for international maritime traffic'.[41] Therefore, while this functional element remains

---

[34] An example is the Bering Strait separating continental Asia and North America.
[35] The Dover Strait lies between the continent of Europe and an island comprising Great Britain.
[36] The Cook Strait separates the North and South Island of New Zealand.
[37] RR Baxter, *The Law of International Waterways* (Harvard University Press Cambridge, MA 1964) 3–4; GK Walker, 'Definitions for the 1982 Law of the Sea Convention—Part II: Analysis of the IHO Consolidated Glossary' (2003) 33 *California Western International Law Journal* 219, 298 observes that '[t]he geographic definition of a strait is a narrow passage of water between two land masses or islands, or groups of islands connecting two sea areas.' Some named straits can encompass very wide bodies of water such as is the case with the Fram Strait (253 nm (470 km) at its narrowest point), between the Arctic Ocean and the Greenland Sea with Denmark (Greenland) and Norway (Svalbard) as littoral States; and the Denmark Strait (approximately 161 nm (300 km) at its narrowest point) between the Atlantic Ocean and the Greenland Sea with Denmark (Greenland) and Iceland the littoral States.
[38] Of which the term 'channel' is often used as an alternate to 'strait', as in the Corfu Channel; an alternate term which is used is 'belt'. The terms 'mouth' and 'sound' are also associated with wide bodies of water adjacent to land within which navigation is permissible, though often these waters lead to an enclosed landmass or islands which front a landmass making complete transit impossible.
[39] AR Thomas and JC Duncan (eds), 'Annotated Supplement to The Commanders Handbook on the Law of Naval Operations' (1999) 73 *International Legal Studies* 1, 207–8, Table A2-5.
[40] *Corfu Channel*, n 5, [28].   [41] Ibid.

a feature of the LOSC, it is unclear as to what level of international navigation is required for a strait to be classified as an 'international strait'. This is a critical issue in the disagreement that has arisen between Canada and the United States over the status of the waters that make up the Northwest Passage given the relatively limited navigation that has taken place within those waters by way of complete transits.[42] Likewise, the strait must have been used by foreign flagged vessels; and not only by through or cross-strait local vessel traffic.

One matter on which the LOSC is silent is whether any distinction should be made between surface navigation and sub-surface navigation of a strait. This has some particular relevance in the Arctic due to evidence of submarine navigation throughout the region, especially during the Cold War.[43] However, as the LOSC does not seek to distinguish between various types of navigation there is nothing in principle that would bar sub-surface submarine navigation from also being taken into account in determining whether the strait was used for that purpose.

Straits used for international navigation between one part of the high seas and the exclusive economic zone (EEZ), and another part of the high seas or EEZ, are ones in which the transit passage regime applies, thereby seeking to ensure the ships engaged in international navigation are able to pass through a strait relatively unhindered.[44] Part III of the LOSC also makes reference to other categories of straits, including:

a) Straits which are regulated in whole or in part by longstanding international conventions;[45]

b) Straits where there exists a route through the high seas or EEZ of similar convenience;[46]

c) Straits which exist between the mainland and an island where there exists, seaward of the island, a route through the high seas or EEZ of similar convenience;[47]

d) Straits used for international navigation between one part of the high seas or EEZ and the territorial sea of a foreign State.[48]

---

[42] See discussion in D Pharand, *Canada's Arctic Waters in International Law* (Cambridge University Press Cambridge 1988); E Franckx, *Maritime Claims in the Arctic: Canadian and Russian Perspectives* (Martinus Nijhoff Dordrecht 1993); this issue is considered in more detail below.

[43] See K Zysk, 'Military Aspects of Russia's Arctic Policy: Hard Power and Natural Resources' in J Kraska (ed), *Arctic Security in an Age of Climate Change* (Cambridge University Press Cambridge 2011) 85, 91–4; DW Titley and CC John St, 'Arctic Security Considerations and the U.S. Navy's "Arctic Roadmap"' in Kraska (ed), *Arctic Security in an Age of Climate Change* (Cambridge University Press Cambridge 2011) 267, 274–5.

[44] LOSC, n 2, Art 37.   [45] Ibid, Art 35(c).   [46] Ibid, Art 36.   [47] Ibid, Art 38(1).

[48] Ibid, Art 45; this is the case of so-called 'dead end' straits where two bodies of adjoining land separated by a large body of water provide navigational access to land areas at the end of the strait. Examples include the Strait of Tiran, Gulf of Bahrain, and the Gulf of Honduras.

Within these straits, transit passage does not apply, and in its place alternate navigation regimes are recognized.[49] In that respect, it is doubtful whether those straits are properly classified as 'international straits' in the *Corfu Channel* sense. Navigation within those straits within which there exists an EEZ or high seas corridor is governed by the traditional freedoms of navigation found in Articles 58 and 87 of the LOSC.

Article 38(2) of the LOSC identifies the physical act of transit passage as including the freedom of navigation 'solely for the purpose of continuous and expeditious transit of the strait'. This reflects the objective of ensuring that the regime facilitates the movement of vessels physically through the strait from an entrance to an exit point and builds upon the ICJ's notion in *Corfu Channel* of a strait being an 'international highway'.[50] Allowance is also made in the case of where passage through the strait is undertaken for the purpose of 'entering, leaving or returning from a State bordering the strait',[51] thereby facilitating ships which are seeking to dock at a facility within a State adjoining a strait, of which Singapore is one of the most prominent examples.[52] Transit passage is therefore enjoyed by ships which seek to pass through the strait, or which are entering or exiting the strait after having stopped at or on their way to a State which borders the strait, and commences once a ship enters the territorial sea adjacent to the strait after having passed through the EEZ or high sea en route to the strait. This does, however, raise issues as to when transit passage commences, if a ship approaches a strait via the territorial sea of the coastal State which is not properly characterized as being encompassed within the waters of the strait, and at which point the exercise of innocent passage converts to transit passage.

Once engaged in transit passage, under Article 39 of the LOSC, ships have certain duties that are reflective of some of the elements of innocent passage, though these are by no means as extensive. They include the requirement to proceed without delay, to refrain from any use or threat of force against the sovereignty, territorial integrity, or political independence of the strait State, or in any other manner in violation of principles of international law found in the United Nations Charter, and to refrain from activities other than those which are incidental 'to their normal mode' of transit, unless rendered necessary by *force majeure* or distress. These duties of ships reflect an important balancing of rights and interests within the straits regime. On the one hand, transit passage was developed to permit the free

---

[49] See H Caminos, 'Categories of International Straits Excluded from the Transit Passage Regime under Part III of the United Nations Convention on the Law of the Sea' in T Malick Ndiaye and R Wolfrum (eds), *Law of the Sea, Environmental Law and Settlement of Disputes* (Martinus Nijhoff Leiden 2007) 583.

[50] *Corfu Channel*, n 5, [29].   [51] LOSC, n 2, Art 38(2).

[52] The only way in which Singapore can be approached by ship is via either the Straits of Malacca and Singapore or the Straits of Jahore; similarly for an aircraft making an approach by sea and not overflying the territory of adjoining States, these Straits provide the only means of air access.

and unimpeded passage of ships through international straits, thereby ensuring the continuation of important guarantees of the freedom of navigation recognized in *Corfu Channel*. On the other hand, strait States have legitimate security concerns relating to the presence of foreign ships within their territorial sea in what may be relatively confined waters as was highlighted by Albania's response to the passage of the British warships through its waters in 1946. Balancing those competing rights and objectives has at times proven to be a major challenge, and during the Cold War the United States and Soviet Union occasionally engaged in maritime clashes in incidents which arose from robust US attempts to exercise a right of navigation within Soviet-controlled waters.[53]

Article 44 of the LOSC makes clear that strait States are not to 'hamper' transit passage and are to give appropriate notification of any dangers to navigation within or over the strait of which they may be aware, which would extend to cases of shipwreck blocking parts of the strait or, as was also highlighted in *Corfu Channel*, mines that may be in the water. It is also made clear that strait States are not to suspend transit passage. Here one of the important distinctions that exists between the regime of transit passage in an international strait and innocent passage within the territorial sea is made clear—while transit passage cannot be suspended by the strait State, a coastal State may temporarily suspend innocent passage.[54] Therefore, even if a strait State has concerns regarding its national security because of the potential for transiting traffic to be caught up in internal disturbances, it may not suspend the right of transit passage.[55] However, it may seek to issue a warning to ships of the potential hazards that exist within its waters at any particular point in time.[56] This implies that even if certain waters are known to be favoured by pirates, or used by non-State actors such as terrorists, a coastal State remains under an obligation to continue to permit transit, though it would be under obligations to warn maritime traffic of the dangers.

The obligation upon the strait State not to 'hamper' transit passage suggests that no obligations or requirements may be imposed upon ships that create a burden for them. One traditional interpretation of this requirement is that the strait State

---

[53] The 12 February 1988 Black Sea 'bumping incident' involving the USS *Yorktown* and USS *Caron* and a Soviet frigate is a prominent example of such an incident: JA Roach and RW Smith, *Excessive Maritime Claims* (3rd edn Martinus Nijhoff The Hague 2012) 233–9.

[54] LOSC, n 2, Art 25(3).

[55] Nevertheless, a coastal State may be able to assert that in a state of necessity it had no option but to suspend innocent passage and in doing so rely upon UN General Assembly Resolution 56/83 (2001), *Articles on Responsibility of States for Internationally Wrongful Acts*, Art 25; see J Crawford, *The International Law Commission's Articles on State Responsibility: Introduction, Text and Commentaries* (Cambridge University Press Cambridge 2002) 178–86.

[56] Note that LOSC, n 2, Art 44 refers to 'any danger to navigation or overflight within or over the strait of which they have knowledge', which is a direct reference to the issues that arose in *Corfu Channel* regarding whether Albania did or did not have knowledge as to the existence of mines in the strait: see *Corfu Channel*, n 5, [22]–[23].

may not impose tolls or any other fees in return for a right of passage.[57] However, some strait States such as Indonesia have expressed concerns about the financial burdens they face in maintaining navigational aids and other safety and marine environmental protection measures within the waters of an international strait without receiving any recompense, and have argued there should be an entitlement to charge tolls or at least a fee-for-service that relates directly to the benefits they provide to international shipping that passes through the strait.[58]

Within the limits of the above obligations imposed upon strait States, the latter enjoy the capacity to enact laws and regulations relating to transit passage.[59] Yet the LOSC is unclear as to the level of enforcement action a strait State may undertake against a delinquent vessel engaged in transit passage. One scenario arises when a vessel is not complying with the requirements of transit passage and its actions are in breach of Article 39 such that it is posing a threat to the strait State or it is not engaging in 'normal mode' passage. A strait State retains its capacity of self-defence under international law and could rely upon that right in the face of a hostile act by a transiting ship. It also has the capacity, consistent with the LOSC, to prohibit passage to a ship that is not engaging in transit passage in conformity with Part III. Accordingly, even if the ship poses no threat to the national security of the strait State, a delinquent ship could be prevented from continuing its passage.

Another enforcement scenario arises when a ship undertaking transit consistent with Article 39 breaches the laws and regulations of the strait State. Part III is silent on the actual enforcement capacity of the strait State in such circumstances, which raises issues as to how a strait State may go about seeking to enforce its law in a manner that does not have the practical effect of hampering or impairing transit passage. Nevertheless, Article 34 makes clear that the Part III straits regime does not in other respects affect the legal status of the waters of a strait with regards to the coastal State's sovereignty and jurisdiction. This would extend to the coastal State's criminal and civil jurisdiction within the territorial sea of the strait. This view is supported by the text of Articles 27 and 28, which respectively deal with coastal State criminal and civil jurisdiction in the case of 'a foreign ship passing through the territorial sea'. These provisions make clear that, in the case of criminal jurisdiction, there is a limited right to board a ship and effect an arrest while that ship is within the territorial sea, which would also extend to a ship engaged in transit passage.

If the infraction by the transiting ship relates to a marine environmental measure, other provisions in the LOSC will also apply. Article 233 makes clear that ships that commit violations of certain environmental laws and regulations while undertaking transit passage, and which are 'causing or threatening major damage to the marine

---

[57] LOSC, n 2, Art 26; *Virginia Commentaries*, Vol II, 236.
[58] MJ Valencia and AB Jaafar, 'Environmental Management of the Malacca—Singapore Straits: Legal and Institutional Issues' (1985) 25 *Natural Resources Journal* 195.
[59] LOSC, n 2, Art 42.

environment of the straits', may be subject to 'appropriate enforcement measures' by the strait State.[60] The context of the provision suggests that law enforcement against delinquent foreign ships engaged in transit passage is permitted, which by implication would extend to stopping and barring further passage of a vessel to contain any threat to the marine environment. Spain indicated upon both its signature and ratification of the LOSC that it also interpreted Article 221 as providing a basis of intervention against international navigation following a maritime casualty,[61] a position apparently endorsed by the United States.[62] Given increased coastal State concern over the environmental impacts resulting from a major maritime incident such as the 2002 *Prestige* shipwreck off the Spanish coast, it would have to be anticipated the coastal States will take a more robust attitude to these interventions in the future.

It can be observed that the right of transit passage is also enjoyed by aircraft, and Article 38 makes clear that the right extends to the freedom of overflight. Aircraft exercising this right enjoy the same entitlements as do ships that are exercising the right through an international strait. Both ships and aircraft are subject to parallel and distinctive duties when exercising the right of transit passage.[63] Aircraft exercising transit passage shall observe rules of safe air navigation as provided for under the International Civil Aviation Organization (ICAO) for civil aircraft and those rules that normally apply to safety of air navigation for State aircraft, and also monitor radio frequencies by designated air traffic control authorities.[64]

4 Operational Issues

The transit passage regime has over time highlighted a number of matters where the LOSC is silent with respect to navigation through international straits; where the Convention has been subject to a range of interpretations; or where the intersection of the transit passage regime with other LOSC provisions has highlighted additional legal issues. Some of these issues were highlighted even prior to the formal conclusion of the LOSC when, in 1982, Malaysia, on behalf of itself, Indonesia, and Singapore, submitted a letter to the President of the Third United Nations Conference on the Law of the Sea (UNCLOS III) regarding the status of the Straits of Malacca and Singapore. The letter sought to indicate a 'common understanding'

---

[60] EJ Molenaar, *Coastal State Jurisdiction over Vessel-Source Pollution* (Kluwer Law International The Hague 1998) 295–8.
[61] Spain, 'Upon ratification' (15 January 1997), in DOALOS, *Declarations and Statements*, available at <www.un.org/Depts/los/convention_agreements/convention_declarations.htm>.
[62] Roach and Smith, n 53, 292–3.   [63] LOSC, n 2, Art 39(1).   [64] Ibid, Art 39(3).

as to the application of Article 233 with respect to the straits, especially as it related to the capacity of the coastal State to enact certain laws and regulations under Article 42 with respect to the safety of navigation, and threats posed to the marine environment. Particular reliance was placed upon an under-keel clearance requirement by ships passing through the strait of at least 3.5 metres, consistent with the 'peculiar geographic and traffic conditions of the Straits'.[65]

A further preliminary comment is the significance that can be attached to declarations and statements made by States under Article 310 as they relate to transit passage and international straits. A number of western States, in particular, sought to emphasize the importance attached to the new regime of transit passage, linking that to the newly confirmed outer limit of the territorial sea of 12 nm. The Federal Republic of Germany, for example, observed in its 1994 declaration upon accession that:

> A prerequisite for the recognition of the coastal State's right to extend the territorial sea is the regime of transit passage through straits used for international navigation. Article 38 limits the right of transit passage only in cases where a route of similar convenience exists in respect of navigational and hydrographical characteristics, which include the economic aspect of shipping.[66]

Some States also sought to make clear their opposition to interpretations of the LOSC they considered to be contrary to the enjoyment of rights associated with transit passage. The United Kingdom, for example, indicated that it would not consider certain declarations and statements to be in conformity with LOSC if they were 'incompatible with the provisions of the Convention relating to straits used for international navigation, including the right of transit passage'.[67] Through these measures, certain States attempted to make clear their particular positions on how the LOSC provisions with respect to international straits should be interpreted and their opposition to any interpretation which they viewed as contrary to the consensus position that was reached during the treaty's negotiations. Even the USA, though a non-party to the LOSC, has consistently sought to reaffirm the transit passage regime,[68] and in turn has sought to hold certain States to account when, in the view of the USA, their State practice is not in conformity with the Convention.[69]

---

[65] 'Letter dated 28 April from the representative of Malaysia to the President of the Conference', UN Doc A/CONF.62/L/145 (29 April 1982). This letter was confirmed by a number of other delegations, including the USA, Japan, Australia, and the Federal Republic of Germany: Roach and Smith, n 53, 306.

[66] Federal Republic of Germany, 'Upon Accession' (14 October 1994), in DOALOS, *Declarations and Statements*, n 62.

[67] Ibid.

[68] See Presidential Proclamation 5928, Territorial Sea of the United States of America, 17 December 1988, 54 Federal Register 777 (9 January 1989) where it is stated:

> In accordance with international law, as reflected in the applicable provisions of the 1982 United Nations Convention on the Law of the Sea...the ships and aircraft of all countries enjoy the right of innocent passage through international straits.

[69] See generally Roach and Smith, n 53, 271–5.

A critical issue associated with the operationalization of the transit passage regime has been the identification of those international straits within which the right applies, and those bodies of water properly characterized as straits within which alternate LOSC regimes may apply. At one level, the presumption that transit passage applies within an international strait is relatively straightforward if the strait is overlapped by the territorial sea of the adjoining coastal State or States. In this regard, the strait will still be subject to the regime of transit passage even if only a small portion of the strait is encompassed by territorial sea.[70] Transit passage may also be acknowledged as being applicable to a strait as a result of bilateral agreements or understandings reached between the littoral States,[71] of which the Straits of Malacca and Singapore are a prominent example. This in turn highlights the potential that, in straits that are bordered by two or more States, those States may take differing approaches as to their capacity under the LOSC to enact certain laws and regulations relating to transit passage under Article 42. While Article 43 does seek to promote cooperation between so-called 'user States' and the littoral States with respect to matters associated with the maintenance of navigational and other safety aids, and the control of pollution,[72] this does not directly address whether cooperation should also take place between the littoral States on other matters. There are certainly examples of where one of the littoral States has adopted very particular positions on the transit passage regime as it applies within the territorial sea of that State.[73]

Part III of the LOSC did not extend the regime of transit passage to certain categories of straits, which had the potential to raise issues as to which straits fell within these exceptions. A strait formed by an island of a State which borders the mainland where there exists, seaward of the island, a route of similar convenience through the EEZ or high sea is one of these exceptions.[74] A critical issue which arises in this instance is whether the alternate route is one 'of similar convenience with respect to navigational and hydrographical characteristics', suggesting that a range of possible

---

[70] This applies in the case of Bass Strait where only the eastern fringe of the strait is encompassed by territorial sea generated from islands located within the strait: Rothwell, n 13, 478–81.

[71] See eg 1978 Treaty between the Australia and the Independent State of Papua New Guinea concerning Sovereignty and Maritime Boundaries in the area of the two Countries, including the area known as Torres Strait, and Related Matters.

[72] An example is the cooperation that has developed between the three littoral States bordering the Straits of Malacca and Singapore—Indonesia, Malaysia, and Singapore—and certain user States, including Japan and more recently the International Maritime Organization: Roach and Smith, n 53, 283; B Oxman 'Observations on the Interpretation and Application of Article 43 of UNCLOS with Particular Reference to the Straits of Malacca and Singapore' (1998) 2 *Singapore Journal of International and Comparative Law* 408.

[73] See the position of Spain with respect to the Straits of Gibraltar, Roach and Smith, n 53, 290; DR Rothwell, 'Gibraltar, Strait of' in R Wolfrum (ed), *Max Planck Encyclopedia of Public International Law* (Oxford University Press Oxford 2012) Vol IV, 463.

[74] LOSC, n 2, Art 38(1).

factors can be taken into account including any additional distance that may need to be sailed by a ship navigating through the alternate EEZ or high seas route. The Strait of Messina, separating the Italian mainland from Sicily, is accepted as being an Article 38(1) strait, the consequence of which is that the right of innocent passage applies within the strait under Article 45.[75] However, one important distinction that arises in the application of the innocent passage regime within these straits is that it shall not be suspended.[76] In 1985, Italy temporarily suspended the right of innocent passage through the Strait of Messina to vessels in excess of 10,000 tons carrying oil, which prompted the USA to indicate to Italy its view that the regime of non-suspendable innocent passage applied within the strait.[77] The LOSC also contemplates the existence of so-called 'dead-end straits', that is those straits which, at one end, have no viable exit point into the EEZ or high sea but which may effectively terminate at the coast or an estuary or river where a port facility may be located. Notwithstanding that, in those instances, transit through the strait culminates in entry into a port, or internal waters, Article 45(1)(b) recognizes that, in these straits, innocent passage applies, which is non-suspendable.[78] Head Harbor Passage, which leads through the Canadian territorial sea to Passamaquoddy Bay in the USA, is an example of such a strait.[79]

The identification of straits governed by 'long-standing international conventions', within which transit passage also does not apply,[80] is a significant exception. At the time of the conclusion of the LOSC, the straits subject to such regimes were well known and understood to include the Turkish Straits (Turkey), Straits of Magellan (Argentina/Chile), the Great Belts (Denmark) and Sound (Denmark/Sweden), and the Aaland Strait (Finland/Sweden).[81] It is unclear whether this grouping is fixed, or whether there is the potential for other conventional regimes to gain similar status over time. The legal regime of these straits remains governed by pre-LOSC instruments, which in some instances reflect very particular historic circumstances associated with their development. The 1936 Montreux Convention Regarding the Regime of Straits which applies in the Turkish Straits is an example. The Convention extends to the Istanbul Strait, Çanakkale Strait, and the Marmara Sea, which are the waterways that link the Black Sea and the Mediterranean Sea. While the Convention recognizes the principle of the freedom of transit,[82] with distinctions made between merchant and naval vessels, Turkish sovereignty over the waters of the straits is maintained. This was reflected in one of the most

---

[75] Another such strait is the Pemba Channel off the coast of Tanzania: *Virginia Commentaries*, Vol II, 329. The United Kingdom also claims the regime of non-suspendable innocent passage applies in the Pentland Firth south of Orkney, and the passage between the Scilly Isles and the mainland: Roach and Smith, n 53, 276, and 344.

[76] LOSC, n 2, Art 45(2); cf ibid, Art 25(3).   [77] Roach and Smith, n 53, 308–11.

[78] LOSC, n 2, Art 45(2).

[79] TL McDorman, *Salt Water Neighbors* (Oxford University Press Oxford 2009) 254–69.

[80] LOSC, n 2, Art 35(c).   [81] *Virginia Commentaries*, Vol II, 308.

[82] Ibid, Arts 1 and 2.

significant modifications to the passage regime through the straits when the 1994 Maritime Regulations for the Turkish Straits was adopted by Turkey to establish a traffic separation scheme (TSS) within the straits. Turkey also sought International Maritime Organization (IMO) approval for the TSS as a means of gaining further international endorsement for these safety measures; and, following 1994 IMO endorsement of the proposal, Turkey reissued the Maritime Regulations in 1998.[83] This is an interesting example of how, notwithstanding the existence of a distinctive legal regime for a series of straits, the littoral State sought IMO approval for safety measures that reflected contemporary standards.

The safety and regulation of navigation through international straits is particularly dealt with by Article 41 of the LOSC, which allows the littoral State to declare sea lanes and implement TSS. The principal focus of this provision is the promotion of 'safe passage of ships' though the strait,[84] and to that end proposals must be referred to the IMO prior to their adoption. Appropriate publicity is also to be given to these sea lanes and TSS, and ships in transit are expected to respect these designations, which can also be regulated by the laws of the littoral State.[85] In practice, it is Rules 9 and 10 of the Collision Regulations (COLREGs)[86] that address the safety of navigation within narrow channels and a TSS.

A longstanding issue of sensitivity has been the ability of warships to exercise navigational rights through international straits. This is reflected by the demands of some States that consent be obtained prior to transit taking place.[87] The LOSC does not seek to differentiate between the rights of warships and the rights of merchant ships exercising transit passage, and Article 39 provides that warships engaged in transit passage are bound by the same constraints as merchant ships. Nevertheless, two particular constraints are applicable. The first is that warships are to refrain from any activity constituting a threat or use of force against the coastal State, and likewise refrain from any activities not incidental to their normal mode of operation. Of particular significance here is what constitutes 'normal mode' of operations for a warship and when would such operations be considered to cross the boundary so as to constitute a threat to the coastal State? In the *Virginia Commentary* it is observed that:

[I]t is clear from the context and from the negotiating history that the term was intended to refer to that mode which is normal or usual for navigation for the particular type of ship ... making the passage in given circumstances. In the case of surface ships, this means navigation on the surface in ordinary sailing conditions.[88]

---

[83] See discussion in Ünlü, n 9, 57–74.
[84] LOSC, n 2, Art 41(1).
[85] Ibid, Art 42(1)(a).
[86] 1972 Convention on the International Regulations for Preventing Collisions at Sea.
[87] See Declaration of Yemen (10 December 1982) in DOALOS, *Declarations and Statements*, n 61.
[88] *Virginia Commentaries*, Vol II, 342.

Some guidance on this point can be found in the *Corfu Channel* case where the ICJ was satisfied that, even when the British warships passed through the channel with crews at action stations and ready to retaliate if fired upon, this was consistent with the right of passage, given the tensions that then existed between Albania and the United Kingdom.[89] It is doubtful, however, whether this would be an acceptable mode of navigation on all occasions, as the court gave weight to the context of when the passage was being exercised and its manner.[90] For modern warships, the normal mode for surface vessels would extend to the launching and recovering of aircraft and the deployment of radar, sonar, and depth finding devices. For submarines, navigation through the strait could be submerged.[91] The conduct of weapons exercises, however, would not be consistent with normal mode, as such an activity would constitute a threat of the use of force against the coastal State. The second constraint is the expectation that all ships, including by implication warships, comply with legitimate coastal States laws and regulations relating to transit passage. Laws of particular relevance would be those relating to the safety to navigation, including passage through sea lanes and traffic separation schemes, and pollution control.[92] In recognition of the immunities enjoyed by warships and the difficulties therefore associated with the enforcement of any coastal State laws against warships, the LOSC makes clear that the flag State will bear international responsibility for any loss or damage that may arise as a result of the warship acting contrary to those laws and regulations.[93]

In the past decade, controversies have also arisen as to whether it is possible for littoral States to seek to impose a regime of compulsory pilotage upon non-government ships passing through an international strait. Such an initiative seeks to extend more traditional concepts of pilotage, more often associated with ports, harbours, and internal waters, into the territorial sea.[94] Under such a regime, a merchant ship would be required to take on board a pilot in order to undertake transit of the strait. Imposition of compulsory pilotage within an international strait runs up against the obligation that the coastal State shall 'not hamper transit passage',[95] which in the case of A legal obligation on the part of the ship may extend to the imposition of tolls or other fees in return for a right of passage. Just as there have been suggestions that a littoral State should be entitled to charge tolls and fees

---

[89] *Corfu Channel*, n 5, [31].

[90] At the other end of the spectrum, when British warships several weeks later conducted minesweeping operations in the strait the ICJ did not accept those actions as being legitimate under either the law of the sea or other general principles of international law: Ibid, [33]–[35].

[91] *Virginia Commentaries*, Vol II, 342–3; Roach and Smith, n 53, 270.

[92] LOSC, n 2, Art 42.   [93] Ibid, Art 42(5); see also ibid, Art 236.

[94] The 1923 Convention on the International Regime of Maritime Ports, Arts 2, 4, and 11 recognize the right of the contracting States to impose compulsory pilotage within the waters of a port and to impose dues.

[95] LOSC, n 2, Art 44.

to maintain a strait and ensure the safety of navigation,[96] a similar argument can be made in favour of compulsory pilotage, which has been introduced to ensure the safety of shipping passing through the strait. The issue then becomes whether the imposition of any fees arising from the service provided by a pilot is an imposition which amounts to the hampering or impairment of transit passage, or is instead a legitimate measure to reduce the risk of marine environmental damage and to ensure the safety of shipping.[97]

A further issue that arises is, even if a compulsory pilotage regime is permissible under the LOSC, what action can the strait State take to enforce the regime against a delinquent ship that may seek to exercise a right of transit passage without a pilot? In this instance, a ship that is otherwise legitimately engaging in transit passage in compliance with its Article 39 duties would be acting in violation of the laws and regulations of the strait State as a result of its failure to take on board a pilot. The LOSC is silent on the actual enforcement capacity of the strait State in such circumstances, which raises issues as to how a strait State may go about seeking to enforce its law in a manner that does not have the practical effect of hampering or impairing transit passage. If the infraction by the transiting ship relates to a marine environmental measure, other provisions in the LOSC will also apply. Article 233, dealing with the marine environment, makes clear that ships that commit violations of certain environmental laws and regulations while undertaking transit passage and that are 'causing or threatening major damage to the marine environment of the straits' may be subject to 'appropriate enforcement measures' by the strait State.[98] The context of the provision suggests that law enforcement against delinquent foreign ships engaged in transit passage is permitted, which by implication would extend to stopping and barring further passage of a vessel to contain any threat to the marine environment. Australia, in collaboration with Papua New Guinea, has sought to impose a compulsory pilotage regime within the Torres Strait. This initiative was taken following designation by the IMO of the Torres Strait as a 'particularly sensitive sea area' (PSSA) in 2005,[99] which was the basis for adjustments to Australian law providing for the imposition of the compulsory pilotage regime.[100] Both Singapore and the USA lodged protests over Australia's actions.[101]

---

[96] Valencia and Jaafar, n 58.

[97] See the differing views on this question in S Bateman and M White, 'Compulsory Pilotage in the Torres Strait: Overcoming Unacceptable Risks to a Sensitive Marine Environment' (2009) 40 *Ocean Development and International Law* 184; and RC Beckman, 'PSSAs and Transit Passage: Australia's Pilotage System in the Torres Strait Challenges the IMO and UNCLOS' (2007) 38 *Ocean Development and International Law* 325, 343–6.

[98] Molenaar, n 60, 295–8.   [99] IMO Resolution MEPC.133(53).

[100] Navigation Act 1912 (Australia) §§ 186I and 186L.

[101] Roach and Smith, n 53, 336–42 discuss the US response.

5 FUTURE ISSUES

Climate change has had a profound impact upon how the law of the sea is seen as being applicable in the Arctic and refocused interest on navigation throughout the Arctic Ocean and adjoining seas.[102] The combination of climate change and the potential for at least a partially ice-free Arctic Ocean, has generated considerable political interest, with accompanying legal and policy implications.[103] One particular dimension of this renewed interest in the Arctic has been the attention given to Arctic shipping in general, and navigational issues in particular.[104] A long-running Arctic navigational issue, which directly relates to the regime of international straits, is the status of the Northwest Passage and whether it is properly classified as a strait within which transit passage applies. While it is not contested that the Northwest Passage meets the geographic requirement of a strait or a series of straits,[105] the principal point of contention between Canada and the USA of its status is the functional requirement that the strait actually be used for international navigation. Pharand's view has been that, because of the low number of recorded transits of the strait, it would not be possible to classify the Northwest Passage as a 'strait used for international navigation'.[106] This clearly raises issues as to the actual recorded number of transits that have taken place, whether distinctions should be made between historical figures and more contemporary assessments, and the percentage of transits completed by non-Canadian flagged vessels.[107] Relying upon the actual use of the Northwest Passage since the first successful navigation, Pharand has maintained that the Passage is not an international strait.[108] He has argued that those who contend otherwise confuse potential use with actual use and that mere

---

[102] The 2009 *Arctic Marine Shipping Assessment (AMSA) Report* highlighted this increased level of interest: Arctic Council, *Arctic Marine Shipping Assessment 2009 Report* (Arctic Council Tromsø 2009).

[103] See eg J Kraska (ed), *Arctic Security in an Age of Climate Change* (Cambridge University Press Cambridge 2011); SG Borgerson, 'Arctic Meltdown: The Economic and Security Implications of Global Warming' (2008) 87 *Foreign Affairs* 63.

[104] See eg A Chircop, 'The Growth of International Shipping in the Arctic: Is a Regulatory Review Timely?' (2009) 24 *International Journal of Marine and Coastal Law* 355; EJ Molenaar, 'Arctic Marine Shipping: Overview of the International Legal Framework, Gaps, and Options' (2009) 18 *Journal of Transnational Law and Policy* 289.

[105] See Pharand, n 42, 223–4; and D Pharand 'Sovereignty in the Arctic: The International Legal Context' in EJ Dosman (ed), *Sovereignty and Security in the Arctic* (Routledge London 1989) 145, 153–4.

[106] Pharand, n 42, 202–14.

[107] From the time of the very first transit of the Passage in 1903–1906 by Amundsen until 2005, Pharand identified 69 foreign transits: D Pharand, 'The Arctic Waters and the Northwest Passage: A Final Revisit' (2007) 38 *Ocean Development and International Law* 3, 32–3.

[108] Pharand, n 42, 225; see also D Pharand 'Canada's Sovereignty over the Northwest Passage' (1989) 10 *Michigan Journal of International Law* 653, 669–70; D Pharand 'The Northwest Passage in International Law' (1979) 17 *Canadian Yearbook of International Law* 99, 112–13.

capacity is not what is required but rather actual use.[109] The USA, however, in May 2013 has reasserted its position that it enjoys the freedom of navigation through the Northwest Passage.[110] The position with respect to another significant Arctic strait, the Bering Strait, has not provoked any equivalent controversy, and there is an acceptance on the part of the Russian Federation and the USA that the regime of transit passage applies as a result of the gradual increase in international navigation through that strait by virtue of the effects of climate change and an increase in Arctic shipping.[111]

A reverse scenario to that of the Northwest Passage and Bering Strait arises in the case of those straits which may have previously been classified as 'international straits' as a result of the volume of navigation passing through the strait, but which are no longer actively used by international shipping. This may arise as a result of economic, environmental, or political factors. It raises for consideration whether the classification of a strait as an 'international strait' is one that remains on-going, or whether a strait could effectively be 'de-listed' as a result of lack of usage. The US position is that all straits that are capable of being used for international navigation to or from the EEZ or high seas are ones that fall within the Article 37 definition.[112] This is to be contrasted with the position adopted in *Corfu Channel* when the ICJ placed emphasis upon actual use. Nevertheless, it would most likely take some period of time before a strait, which previously had been considered one within which transit passage could be exercised, could lose that status as a result a lack of international shipping exercising that right.

Another dynamic which needs to be contemplated is that a strait can change its status as a result of significant political changes within the coastal State. The breakup of a State may result in the emergence of a new coastal State such that certain waters that were previously considered internal waters would become subject to the territorial sea regime and, accordingly, potentially be subject to the regime of transit passage. Alternatively, political developments may result in the emergence of a new archipelagic State with the consequence that a strait through which transit passage could previously be exercised may become a strait within which archipelagic sea lanes passage would apply. Likewise, the settlement of territorial and maritime claims in regions such as the South China may in the future result in the emergence of new international straits as shipping passes through those waters to reach new ports or related maritime facilities.

---

[109] Pharand, n 42, 225.

[110] President of the United States, *National Strategy for the Arctic Region* (White House Washington May 2013) 9.

[111] See DR Rothwell, 'International Straits and Trans-Arctic Navigation' (2012) 43 *Ocean Development and International Law* 267, 273–4.

[112] Roach and Smith, n 53, 278.

6 Concluding Remarks

The regime of international straits is one of the more important aspects of the modern law of the sea, reflecting the balance between the freedom of navigation and legitimate rights and interests of littoral States. That the decision in *Corfu Channel* still has significance for the regime demonstrates not only the longstanding nature of the issues considered by the ICJ but also how fundamental they are to the law of the sea. Part III of the LOSC substantially advanced and clarified the law in this area and has introduced significant stability into an area that has been contentious. That the USA has been a LOSC non-party and yet retained all of the rights of a flag State with respect to transit passage reflects how widely recognized this area of the law of the sea is.

While, in the short term, the regime of international straits appears settled, there have been occasional destabilizing incidents where littoral States have sought to close a strait to vessels carrying hazardous cargoes or when national security has been threatened. In the medium to longer term, ensuring a balance between national and international security and the freedom of navigation may prove to be one of the biggest challenges for the regime. Here the increasing reach of the United Nations Security Council on law of the sea matters is notable. There is the potential for an increasing number of straits to fall within the reach of a Security Council Resolution. In this exceptional case, regulation of navigation through the strait while not suspended may become subject to a UN-mandated interdiction regime as UN Member States seek to uphold the terms of the relevant Security Council Resolution in order to ensure the maintenance of international peace and security. Ensuring a balance between littoral State security, regional and international security as defined by security actors such as the UN, and the freedom of navigation will be one of the constant challenges for the law of the sea and international straits into the future.

7

THE ARCHIPELAGIC REGIME

TARA DAVENPORT

1 INTRODUCTION

THE archipelagic regime in Part IV of the 1982 United Nations Convention on the Law of the Sea (LOSC)[1] was a significant innovation in the law of the sea. It aimed to resolve an issue that had long challenged the international community, namely, whether a group of islands should be considered *a single entity*, and thus subject to a special regime distinct from the rules applicable to continental land masses and individual islands. The development of the regime was shaped by the exclusive interests of archipelagic States, which desired control over interconnecting waters surrounding their insular territory for historical, political, economic, and security reasons, and the inclusive interests of the maritime powers, which wanted to preserve maritime mobility through such waters.[2] Part IV of the LOSC purported to balance these competing interests by allowing the archipelagic State to draw straight baselines connecting the outermost islands, enclosing the interconnecting waters in which a special regime of *archipelagic waters* would apply, while recognizing certain rights of navigation of all States through these waters.

---

[1] 1982 United Nations Convention on the Law of the Sea (hereinafter LOSC).
[2] M Munavvar, *Ocean States: Archipelagic Regimes in the Law of the Sea* (Martinus Nijhoff Leiden 1995) 10.

Since the adoption of the LOSC, 22 States have claimed archipelagic status.[3] Compared to other aspects of the LOSC (for example, the Exclusive Economic Zone (EEZ), the deep seabed, the extended continental shelf, and the high seas), the application of the archipelagic regime has been uncontroversial and has, overall, enjoyed a relatively high level of compliance. That said, some issues have inevitably arisen with the implementation of the provisions in Part IV, which continue to challenge the effective operation of this regime. The objective of this chapter is to identify the critical issues with implementation of Part IV as well as any future issues that may arise. In this regard, Section 2 will discuss the development of the regime. Sections 3–5 will address the definition of an archipelago and an archipelagic State; archipelagic baselines; and archipelagic waters, respectively, and will examine issues in implementation. Section 6 will discuss the issue of 'dependent archipelagos' and whether there is a lacuna in LOSC in this regard. Section 7 will conclude with a discussion on future areas of focus for the archipelagic regime.

2 Development of the Archipelagic Regime

The physical characteristics of archipelagos vary widely. From a geographic perspective, there is a broad distinction between (1) continental or coastal archipelagos and (2) mid-ocean or outlying archipelagos. Coastal archipelagos consist of a group of islands 'which are situated so close to the mainland that they may reasonably be considered to be part and parcel thereof, forming more or less an outer coastline'.[4] Examples of coastal archipelagos include the Norwegian skjærgaard, the coasts of Finland, Greenland, Iceland, Sweden, Yugoslavia, and certain stretches of the coasts of Alaska and Canada.[5] Mid-ocean or outlying archipelagos are 'groups of islands situated at such a distance from the coasts of firm land as to be considered an independent whole rather than forming part or outer coastline of the mainland'.[6] For mid-ocean archipelagos, they are further sub-divided into (1) archipelagos forming the whole territory of States (for example, the Maldives, Fiji, Indonesia, and the

---

[3] International Law Association (ILA), *Draft Report on Baselines Under the International Law of the Sea* (ILA Biennial Conference, Washington DC, April 2014) 21, available at <http://www.ila-hq.org/en/committees/index.cfm/cid/1028> (hereinafter ILA Draft Report on Baselines).

[4] J Evensen, *Certain Legal Aspects Concerning the Delimitation of Territorial Waters of Archipelagos* (First United Nations Conference on the Law of the Sea, I Official Records) (Williams S Hein & Co Inc New York 1980) 290.

[5] Ibid.   [6] Ibid.

Philippines) and (2) dependent archipelagos belonging to continental States (for example, the Faeroe Islands, the Galapagos Islands, and the Andaman and Nicobar Islands under the respective sovereignty of Denmark, Ecuador, and India).[7]

Traditional law of the sea was designed to deal with continental masses and did not fit easily to groups of islands, either fringing the coast or situated in the middle of the ocean.[8] The issue of individual islands had been raised in several international forums since 1881, and rules had developed which dealt with maritime entitlement and delimitation of individual islands.[9] The issues confronting archipelagos were qualitatively different, and the challenge was devising a uniform regime, which would cater to a variety of geographical configurations, as well as balancing the competing interests of archipelagic States and maritime nations. The following sections briefly outline the historical evolution of the regime.

2.1 Early developments

In the late nineteenth century, several private international bodies, such as the Institut de Droit International, the International Law Association, and the American Law Institute,[10] acknowledged that groups of islands required some sort of special regime.[11] For example, in 1926, the American Institute of International Law proposed that the islands and keys comprising an archipelago should be treated as one unit with a territorial sea drawn around the islands rather than around each individual island.[12] However, subsequent codifications in both the 1929 Harvard Research in International Law Draft Convention on Territorial Waters and the 1930 Hague Codification Conference contained no provisions on archipelagos, due to failure to reach agreement on the requirements that needed to be met before a group of islands could be considered an archipelagic 'unit'.[13]

The next significant milestone occurred in 1951 in the *Anglo-Norwegian Fisheries* case.[14] The dispute stemmed from the unilateral delimitation by Norway of a fisheries zone reserved for Norwegian nationals to the exclusion of British fishermen who had traditionally fished there.[15] The area delimited had a distinctive configuration in that it is very broken by fjords and bays, dotted with countless islands and

---

[7] See Munavvar, n 2, 21–2. [8] Ibid, 2. [9] Ibid.
[10] For a description of the various formulations by these private international bodies, see Evensen, n 4, 290–4.
[11] CF Amerasinghe, 'The Problems of Archipelagos in the International Law of the Sea' (1974) 23 *International and Comparative Law Quarterly* 539, 540.
[12] 'American Institute of International Law: Project No 10 National Domain' (1926) 20 *American Journal of International Law, Special Supplement* 318–19.
[13] Evensen, n 4, 291–2.
[14] *Fisheries (United Kingdom v Norway)* (Judgment) [1951] ICJ Rep 116, 124–5 (hereinafter *Anglo-Norwegian Fisheries*).
[15] Ibid.

reefs, which form a continuous archipelago known as skjærgaard ('rock rampart').[16] The United Kingdom argued that Norway's baselines were contrary to the customary rule that baselines should follow the low-water mark along the coast. The International Court of Justice (ICJ) found that Norway's system of baselines, which followed the general direction of the coast, was not contrary to international law:

> Where a coast is deeply indented and cut into as is that of the Eastern Finmark, or where it is bordered by an archipelago such as the 'skjærgaard' along the western sector of the coast here in question the baseline becomes independent of the low-water mark and can only be determined by means of a geometric construction. In such circumstances, the line of the low-water mark can no longer be put forward as a rule requiring the coastline to be followed in all its sinuosities. Nor can one characterize as exceptions to the rule the very many derogations which could be necessitated by such a rugged coast: the rule would disappear under the exceptions. Such a coast viewed as a whole calls for the application of a different method: that is the method of baselines which within reasonable limits may depart from the physical line of the coast.[17]

The Court recognized that there were certain limitations in the drawing of straight baselines. First, 'the drawing of baselines must not depart to any appreciable extent from the general direction of the coast'.[18] Second, the areas lying within the baselines must be 'sufficiently closely linked to the land domain to be subject to the regime of internal waters'.[19] Further, the Court also emphasized the importance of 'certain economic interests peculiar to a region, the reality and importance of which are clearly evidenced by a long usage'.[20]

It warrants note that the decision dealt specifically with coastal archipelagos. It was unclear how far the above principles could be applied to mid-ocean archipelagos, which were 'totally out at sea' and 'not connected with a mainland coastline', and therefore posed a particular challenge to the freedom of navigation.[21]

2.2 International Law Commission

Article 5 of the 1956 International Law Commission (ILC) Draft Articles on the Law of the Sea, based on the *Fisheries Case*, recognized the drawing of straight baselines in the case of coastal archipelagos (although this term was not expressly mentioned).[22] However, the ILC faced considerable difficulty in obtaining agreement on the applicable rules for mid-ocean archipelagos. As noted by Dubner, 'widely scattered groups of islands with very extensive interior distance represent

---

[16] Ibid, 127. Summary of Judgment 1951/3, 21–2, available at <http://www.icj-cij.org/docket/files/5/1811.pdf>.
[17] *Anglo-Norwegian Fisheries*, n 14, 129.   [18] Ibid, 133.   [19] Ibid.   [20] Ibid.
[21] Amerasinghe, n 11, 546.
[22] ILC, 'Draft Articles Concerning the Law of the Sea with Commentaries' (1956) II *Yearbook of the International Law Commission* Art 5, Doc A/3159 (hereinafter ILC Draft Articles).

a very different situation from cases where islands are closely grouped, thus constituting more of a geographical and political unity'.[23] Thus, while the ILC Draft Articles recognized that every island is an area of land which is above water at high tide and is entitled to its own territorial sea,[24] it ultimately did not include any provision on groups of islands in the 1956 Draft Articles. Instead, it stated:

> The Commission had intended to follow up this article with a provision concerning groups of islands. Like The Hague Conference for the Codification of International Law of 1930, the Commission was unable to overcome the difficulties involved. The problem is singularly complicated by the different forms it takes in different archipelagos. The Commission was prevented from stating an opinion, not only by disagreement on the breadth of the territorial sea, but also by lack of technical information on the subject. It recognizes the importance of this question and hopes that if an international conference subsequently studies the proposed rules it will give attention to it.[25]

2.3 State practice

With regard to coastal archipelagos, there appeared to be a consistent body of practice which treated coastal archipelagos as a unit forming an outer coastline from which to measure the territorial sea.[26] States such as Norway, Iceland, Denmark Finland, Yugoslavia, Saudi Arabia, Egypt, and Cuba utilized straight baselines for territorial sea delimitation,[27] although some of them laid down a certain maximum length for such baselines.[28] They also treated the waters within these baselines as internal waters, which allowed them to prevent passage by foreign vessels unless the waters contained straits used for international navigation.[29] However, States such as the United Kingdom, Australia, and the United States did not apply straight baselines on the basis that archipelagos should not be treated differently from isolated islands with respect to territorial sea delimitation.[30]

In contrast to coastal archipelagos, there was a 'profusion of different views and approaches with regard to the delimitation of the territorial waters of outlying archipelagos'.[31] For example, there were a number of States such as Denmark (the Faeroes), Norway (the Svalbard Archipelago), Iceland, Bermuda, and Ecuador (the Galapagos) which viewed their mid-ocean archipelagos as a territorial unit and used straight baselines to delimit their territorial seas.[32]

The practice of the Philippines and Indonesia warrants a deeper examination, given that their claims were instrumental in the eventual recognition of a special

---

[23] BH Dubner, *The Law of Territorial Waters of Mid-Ocean Archipelagos and Archipelagic States* (Martinus Nijhoff The Hague 1976) 39.
[24] ILC Draft Articles, n 22, Art 10.   [25] Ibid, 270 (Commentary).
[26] Evensen, n 4, 297.   [27] Ibid, 295-7.   [28] Ibid, 296-7.   [29] Ibid, 297.
[30] Ibid.   [31] Ibid.   [32] Ibid, 297-9.

archipelagic regime. The Philippines consists of approximately 7,100 islands dispersed over a large expanse of water with a coastline length of about 18,000 km.[33] The Philippines had originally argued that the limits established by three treaties between Spain and the United States,[34] which form a rectangle around the main archipelago of the Philippines, provided its territorial borders and all waters from its baselines to the international treaty limits were considered the territorial sea of the Philippines. The first overt expression of this came in 1955 in response to the 1956 Draft Articles of the ILC (see Section 2.2 above) where the Philippines submitted a *Note Verbale* to the United Nations which claimed 'all waters around, between and connecting different islands belonging to the Philippine archipelago, irrespective of their width or dimension' to be 'necessary appurtenances of its land territory, forming an integral part of the national or inland water, subject to the exclusive sovereignty of the Philippines'.[35] The Philippines subsequently affirmed this in legislation.[36]

Indonesia consists of 18,108 islands which are scattered over a wide expanse of sea. As a Dutch Colony in 1939, the Netherlands' Territorial Sea and Maritime Districts Ordinance provided for a 3-mile territorial sea around each island of the Dutch East Indies, which 'effectively chopped Indonesia into pieces, as the high seas between the islands were not subject to Indonesian jurisdiction'.[37] However, in the 1950s, after its independence, Indonesia became increasingly concerned about the passage of Dutch warships in its waters.[38] Ultimately, the Indonesian Government issued the Djuanda Declaration of 13 December 1957.[39] After affirming the uniqueness of the Indonesian archipelago, it stated:

> ... [A]ll waters surrounding, between and connecting the islands constituting the Indonesian State, regardless of their extension and breadth, are integral parts of the territory of the Indonesian State and therefore parts of the internal or national waters which are under the exclusive sovereignty of the Indonesian State.

---

[33] MA Palma, 'The Philippines as an Archipelagic and Maritime Nation: Interests, Challenges and Perspectives', RSIS Working Paper No 182 (21 July 2009).

[34] 1898 Treaty of Paris between Spain and the United States; 1900 Treaty between Spain and the United States for the Cession of Outlying Islands for the Philippines; 1930 Convention between the United States and Great Britain Delimiting the Philippine Archipelago and the State of Borneo.

[35] 'Report of the International Law Commission Covering the Work of its Seventh Session 2 May–8 July 1955, Official Records of the General Assembly, Tenth Session, Supplement No. 9', UN Doc A/2934 (1955) 52–3.

[36] The Act to Define the Baselines of the Territorial Sea of the Philippines, Republic Act No 3048 (17 June 1961) (as amended by Republic Act No 5446 of 18 September 1968) (The Philippines).

[37] C Ku, 'The Archipelagic States Concept and Regional Stability in Southeast Asia' (1991) 23 *Case Western Reserve Journal of International Law* 463, 469.

[38] J Butcher, 'Becoming an Archipelagic State: The Juanda Declaration of 1957 and the "Struggle" to Gain International Recognition of the Archipelagic Principle' in R Cribb and M Ford (eds), *Indonesia Beyond the Water's Edge: Managing an Archipelagic State* (ISEAS Publishing Singapore 2009) 28, 36–7.

[39] Ibid, 39.

It went on to recognize that 'innocent passage for foreign ships in these internal waters is granted so long as it is not prejudicial to or violates the sovereignty and security of Indonesia'. While the Djuanda Declaration was based on some precedent such as the *Anglo-Norwegian Fisheries* case and the Philippines' *Note Verbale*, it went much further.

It applied baselines not to a group of islands that formed the fringe of a state, as the Norwegian government had done, nor to a small group of islands, as the Cuban government had to the Canarreos Archipelago, but to a massive archipelago. Moreover, the declaration defined far more clearly than the Philippines Note Verbale the principle by which the government would delimit the waters under its sovereignty. It marked, as Indonesian accounts assert, a radical development in the law of the sea. Most importantly, to look at the declaration within the context of Indonesia's history, it laid the basis of the archipelagic state.[40]

In February 1960, the President of Indonesia issued an Act Concerning Indonesian Waters (Act No 4) that confirmed his country's position as an archipelagic State and reaffirmed the Indonesian archipelagic principle.[41] The Indonesian government issued regulations setting out the conditions under which foreign vessels may sail through Indonesian waters, including a requirement that such vessels give notice of their intention to pass through Indonesian waters.[42]

Unsurprisingly, States such as Australia, the United Kingdom, the United States, Japan, and the Netherlands opposed the position of the Philippines and Indonesia, and argued that the normal regime of islands should apply to mid-ocean archipelagos leaving the territorial sea or high seas routes between most islands.[43] Further, neither the United Kingdom nor the United States considered their island possessions such as the Fiji Islands and Cook Islands or Hawaii as one integral unit as far as the delimitation of territorial waters was concerned. Instead, the practice of these States had been 'to draw a separate belt of territorial waters around each individual island of an archipelago, thus leaving stretches of high seas in between, provided that the distance between the various islands of the group is wider than twice the breadth of the marginal seas'.[44]

2.4 The First and Second United Nations Conferences on the Law of the Sea

The disagreement between archipelagic States and the maritime nations described above characterized the debate during the First United Nations Conference on the Law of the Sea (UNCLOS I), with the United States arguing that using straight

---

[40] Ibid, 40.   [41] Munavvar, n 2, 65.   [42] Butcher, n 38, 42.
[43] RR Churchill and AV Lowe, *The Law of the Sea* (3rd edn Manchester University Press Manchester 1990) 119.
[44] Evensen, n 4, 299.

baselines around the archipelago was a unilateral attempt 'to convert into territorial waters or possibly even internal waters vast areas of the high seas formerly freely used for centuries by the ships of all countries'.[45] Thus, mid-ocean archipelagos were a conspicuous gap in the 1958 Geneva Conventions, although coastal archipelagos were addressed in Article 4 of the Geneva Convention on the Territorial Sea and the Contiguous Zone, espousing the principles set forth in the 1951 *Anglo-Norwegian Fisheries* case. The Second United Nations Conference on the Law of the Sea (UNCLOS II), which met in Geneva from 17 March to 27 April 1960, failed to produce a Convention and the question of mid-ocean archipelagos was again unanswered.

2.5 The Third United Nations Conference on the Law of the Sea

In contrast to the First and Second Conferences on the Law of the Sea, time was ripe for the international community to seriously consider mid-ocean archipelagos at the Third Conference on the Law of the Sea (UNCLOS III). This was due to a slew of developments that occurred in the intervening years. First, the failure to obtain agreement on any special regime for mid-ocean archipelagos during UNCLOS I and UNCLOS II galvanized both the Philippines and Indonesia to make a concerted effort to gain international support for the archipelagic concept. Apart from the legislative measures described in Section 2.3, Indonesia began to negotiate a series of maritime boundary agreements with its neighbours such as Singapore, Malaysia, and Australia in the 1960s. Indonesia reportedly granted favourable terms to these States in exchange for implicit recognition of its archipelagic baselines and archipelagic waters regime.[46] In addition, Indonesian diplomats attended international conferences and used meetings of bodies such as the Asian African Legal Consultative Committee to gain support from newly independent States.[47] Second, the height of the Cold War and the consequent concern of Western States that Indonesia would turn into a communist State 'trumped their concern that their maritime rights were being impacted'.[48] Third, by the late 1960s, the great increase in the number of newly independent States, particularly in Africa and Asia, contributed to a general feeling that a new regime, which took into account the interests of these newly independent States, was necessary.

---

[45] US Delegation to the First United Nations Conference on the Law of the Sea, Press Release (3 March 1958).

[46] See eg Leo Bernard, 'Whose Side Is It On? The Boundaries Dispute in the North Malacca Strait' (2012) 9 *Indonesian Journal of International Law* 381, 388.

[47] Butcher, n 38, 43.   [48] Ibid.

This convergence of factors resulted in the recognition of the special nature of archipelagos and inclusion of this issue in the list of 'Subjects and Issues' by the Seabed Committee[49] which was engaged in preparatory work for UNCLOS III.[50] Ultimately, the Seabed Committee recognized that the unity of an archipelagic State and the protection of its security, the preservation of its political and economic unity as well as its marine environment, and the exploitation of its resources justified the archipelagic State's sovereignty over such waters.[51] However, the nature of this regime was still undecided, and there was a clear conflict of interest between the large maritime powers and the archipelagic States, which would shape negotiations during UNCLOS III. The ultimate result was Part IV of the LOSC on archipelagic States. The following sections will examine in detail key provisions of LOSC and issues, if any, in its implementation.

3 Definition of an Archipelago and an Archipelagic State

3.1 LOSC provisions

Article 46 (a) defines an archipelagic State as 'a State constituted wholly by one or more archipelagos and may include other islands'. An archipelago is defined in Article 46 (b) as:

A group of islands, including parts of islands, interconnecting waters and other natural features which are so closely inter-related that such islands, waters and other natural features form an intrinsic geographical, economic and political entity, or which historically have been treated as such.[52]

The first half of the definition sets out the different components that make up an archipelago. The primary factor in the definition of an archipelago is whether there exists a 'group of islands'. An island, under Article 121(1) of the LOSC is a naturally formed area of land, surrounded by water, which is above water at high tide. There were attempts to propose a minimum number of islands necessary to constitute

---

[49] Munavvar, n 2, 86–7. [50] Churchill and Lowe, n 43, 15–16.
[51] United Nations, *Report of the Committee on the Peaceful Uses of the Seabed and Ocean Floor Beyond the Limits of National Jurisdiction to the General Assembly*, UN GAOR, 28th Sess, Vol 1, Supp No 21, UN Doc 1/9021 (1973) 55.
[52] LOSC, n 1, Art 46(2).

a group[53] but archipelagic States rejected this.[54] The terminology 'parts of islands' was introduced to reflect the fact that parts of both Borneo and Papua New Guinea were under the sovereignty of Indonesia.[55] The words 'interconnecting waters' were added to 'emphasize the unifying function of the waters and relates to waters that connect and surround the waters'.[56] It affirmed for the first time the idea that waters and islands were considered an archipelago.[57] 'Other natural features' are not defined in the LOSC. It has been suggested that such natural features are distinguishable from 'islands' and that they refer to 'reefs', 'atolls', and 'low-tide elevations', all of which are mentioned in Article 47 on archipelagic baselines.[58] This reflects the actual geographic circumstances of archipelagic States which are often comprised not only of islands but a variety of other geographic features, as is the case of the Bahamas.[59]

The second half of the definition 'sets out the criteria for determining whether a group of islands can be considered an archipelago in the legal sense'.[60] It requires that the features be 'so closely interrelated so as to form an intrinsic geographical, economic and political entity'. The term 'geographic' implies a requisite closeness, and early proposals focused on what the distance between islands should be.[61] Ultimately, the question of distance between islands was addressed by specifying limitations to the length of straight baselines connecting the outermost islands of the archipelago. The notion of economic unity was borrowed from the *Anglo-Norwegian Fisheries* case, and it requires a 'close economic relationship between and among islands themselves as well as economic unity of the islands and interconnecting waters'.[62] With regard to the political criterion, early proposals had required that the archipelago belong to a single State, although there is no express limitation reflecting this in the definition of archipelago.[63] The historical element is an alternative requirement that is relevant when an entity does not constitute an intrinsic geographical, economic, and political unity but still may constitute an archipelago on a historical basis.[64]

A number of points can be made in relation to the definition of archipelagos and archipelagic States. First, it recognizes that an archipelagic State can consist of more than one archipelago (such as in the case of Papua New Guinea, which comprises a main island and two other archipelagos). It also recognizes that an archipelagic State may consist of a main archipelago and 'other islands' which are a further distance away such as Fiji and its islands of Cevi-i-Ra and Rotuma.[65] Second, it excludes continental States with mid-ocean archipelagos such as Denmark (the Faeroes), Ecuador (the Galapagos), and Portugal (the Azores) (this

---

[53] The United Kingdom had proposed that three or more islands were necessary to form an archipelago: see 'Draft Articles Relating to Passage through Territorial Sea', UN Doc A/AC138/SC.II/L.44 (2 August 1973).
[54] Munavvar, n 2, 110–11.   [55] Ibid.   [56] Ibid.   [57] Ibid.   [58] Ibid, 112.
[59] Ibid.   [60] Ibid, 113.   [61] Ibid.   [62] Ibid, 114.   [63] Ibid.   [64] Ibid.
[65] Ibid, 126–7.

will be dealt with in Section 6).[66] Third, the definition covers States that do not consider themselves to be archipelagic States such as Japan, New Zealand, and the United Kingdom.[67] However, these States are unable to meet the requirements necessary to draw archipelagic baselines (see Section 4), and indeed, have not declared themselves as archipelagic States (see discussion in Section 3.2), so the issue may be moot.[68]

3.2 Issues in implementation

As mentioned above, as of 2014, 22 States, all parties to the LOSC, have claimed archipelagic status.[69] These are Antigua and Barbuda, the Bahamas, Cape Verde, Comoros, Dominican Republic, Fiji, Grenada, Indonesia, Jamaica, Kiribati, Maldives, Marshall Islands Mauritius, Papua New Guinea, the Philippines, Saint Vincent and the Grenadines, Sao Tome and Principe, Seychelles, Solomon Islands, Trinidad and Tobago, Tuvalu, and Vanuatu.[70] In this regard, it warrants note that in *Qatar v Bahrain*, the ICJ has suggested that a State must *declare* itself as an archipelagic State before it can enjoy rights such as the drawing of archipelagic baselines under Part IV.[71]

The majority of the States referred to above meet the definition of an archipelagic State as set out in Article 46. One exception appears to be the Dominican Republic. Its 2007 legislation describes the archipelago as consisting of the island of Santo Domingo, an extensive group of 150 minor islands, a large number of reefs and low-tide elevations, a number of banks and straits, the Beata Ridge, other natural elements, and the connecting waters.[72] Both the United States and the United Kingdom have contended that the Dominican Republic does not fall within the definition of an archipelagic State.[73] Indeed, it has been observed that

---

[66] Churchill and Lowe, n 43, 120.   [67] Ibid, 121.   [68] Ibid.
[69] ILA Draft Report on Baselines, n 3, 21.
[70] JA Roach and RW Smith, *Excessive Maritime Claims* (3rd edn Martinus Nijhoff Leiden 2012) 206–7.
[71] In *Qatar v Bahrain*, Bahrain had argued that it was a de facto archipelago and was thus entitled to declare itself an archipelagic State under Part IV of the LOSC and draw archipelagic baselines. While the Court opined that it did not have to decide on the issue of Bahrain's status as an archipelagic State as it had not formally made an archipelagic claim, the Court observed that 'in such a situation the method of straight baselines is applicable only if the State has declared itself to be an archipelagic State under Part IV'. See *Maritime Delimitation and Territorial Questions between Qatar and Bahrain (Qatar v Bahrain)* (Merits, Judgment) [2001] ICJ Rep 40, [180]–[183].
[72] S Kopela, '2007 Archipelagic Legislation of the Dominican Republic: An Assessment' (2009) 24 *International Journal of Marine and Coastal Law* 501, 503.
[73] See United Nations Division of Ocean Affairs and the Law of the Sea (DOALOS), 'Joint Demarche undertaken by the United Kingdom of Great Britain and Northern Ireland, and the United States of America in relation to law of the Dominican Republic No 66-07 of 22 May 2007, done on 18 March 2007' (2008) 66 *Law of the Sea Bulletin* 98). For a contrary view, see generally Kopela, n 159.

the Dominican Republic is more akin to a mainland-type island fringed by coastal archipelagos.[74]

4 Archipelagic Baselines

4.1 LOSC provisions

Article 47(1) of the LOSC provides that 'an archipelagic State may draw straight archipelagic baselines joining the outermost points of the outermost islands and drying reefs of the archipelago'. All maritime zones of the archipelagic State are measured from archipelagic baselines.[75] The ability to draw archipelagic baselines in conformity with the conditions in Article 47 determines whether a State is an archipelagic State, even if it meets the definition of an archipelagic State in Article 46.

First, archipelagic baselines must be drawn so as to connect the outermost points of the outermost islands and drying reefs of the archipelago and include the main islands.[76] This requirement was intended to prevent 'attempts to enclose small separate clusters of islands that do not include one of the main islands of the archipelago'.[77] The meaning of main islands is not defined, and can be interpreted in a number of different ways; for example, it could mean 'the largest islands, the most populous islands, the most economically productive islands or the islands which are pre-eminent in an historical or cultural sense'.[78]

Second, archipelagic baselines must be drawn so that the ratio of land to water within the lines is not more than 1:1 and not less than 1:9.[79] This ensures that 'the archipelagic State is one in which there is a focus upon ocean spaces which connect the islands, rather than a State which is dominated by large island masses'.[80]

Third, the length of archipelagic baselines should not exceed 100 nautical miles (nm), except that up to 3 per cent of the total number of lines enclosing the archipelago may be between 100 and 125 nm in length.[81]

---

[74] C Narokobi, 'The Regime of Archipelagos in International Law' in J Van Dyke, LM Alexander, and JR Morgan (eds), *International Navigation: Rocks and Shoals Ahead?*, A Workshop of the Law of the Sea Institute, Honolulu Hawaii, 13–15 January 1986 (The Law of the Sea Institute Honolulu 1988) 232.
[75] LOSC, n 1, Art 48.   [76] Ibid, Art 47(1).   [77] ILA Draft Report on Baselines, n 3, 21.
[78] DOALOS, *The Law of the Sea: Baselines* (United Nations New York 1989) 35.
[79] LOSC, n 1, Art 47(1).
[80] ILA Draft Report on Baselines, n 3, 21. As noted by the ILA, Cuba would not qualify as an archipelagic State because of the size of its main islands compared to the size of its accompanying islands and the ramifications for the water to land ratio.
[81] LOSC, n 1, Art 47(2).

Fourth, Article 47(3) provides that the drawing of archipelagic baselines should not 'depart to any appreciable extent from the general configuration of the archipelago'.

Fifth, archipelagic baselines may be drawn to and from low-tide elevations only if lighthouses or similar installations which are permanently above sea level have been built on them where a low-tide elevation is situated wholly or partly at a distance not exceeding the breadth of the territorial sea from the nearest island.[82]

Sixth, archipelagic baselines may not be drawn in such a way as to cut off the territorial sea of another State from the high seas or from its EEZ.[83]

4.2 Issues in implementation

Out of the 22 States which have claimed archipelagic status, 19 have declared archipelagic baselines pursuant to Article 47 of the LOSC.[84] Generally speaking, the majority of archipelagic States appear to have complied with the requirements in Article 47 of LOSC.[85]

It is notable that two of the largest archipelagic States took a considerable amount of time to bring their baselines into conformity with the LOSC, despite their championing the regime during UNCLOS III. It was only in 2009 that Indonesia deposited with the United Nations a revised set of geographical coordinates of points.[86] This was the first time that Indonesia had publicized a complete, closed system of archipelagic baselines.[87] With regard to the Philippines, the Philippines had adopted straight baseline legislation in 1961 which provided that all waters within the baselines are considered inland or internal waters of the Philippines and that all waters from the baselines to the international treaty limits (described above) form part of the territorial sea of the Philippines.[88] This met with protests when

---

[82] Ibid, Art 47(4).   [83] Ibid, Art 47(5).

[84] ILA Draft Report on Baselines, n 3, 22. The three States which have not specified their archipelagic baselines are Kiribati, the Marshall Islands, and Saint Vincent and the Grenadines.

[85] See eg the comments of the US Department of State in their *Limits in the Seas* Series for: 'Antigua and Barbuda' (28 March 2014) *No 133 Limits in the Seas*; 'Bahamas' (31 January 2014) *No 128 Limits in the Seas*; 'Grenada' (28 March 2014) *No 135 Limits in the Seas*; 'Trinidad and Tobago' (31 January 2014) *No 131 Limits in the Seas*; 'Vanuatu' (28 March 2014) *No 137 Limits in the Seas*; 'Fiji' (30 November 1994) *No 101 Limits in the Seas*; 'Jamaica' (5 February 1994) *No 125 Limits in the Seas*, available at <http://www.state.gov/e/oes/ocns/opa/c16065.htm>.

[86] MZN67.2009 (Maritime Zones Notification) United Nations.

[87] DM Sodik, 'The Indonesian Legal Framework on Baselines, Archipelagic Passage and Innocent Passage' (2012) 43 *Ocean Development and International Law* 330, 332.

[88] The Republic Act No 3046 of 1961, an Act to Define the Baselines of the Territorial Sea of the Philippines (17 June 1961) (The Philippines).

enacted[89] and is generally considered to be contrary to Article 47.[90] After several unsuccessful attempts by Congress to enact archipelagic baselines legislation consistent with the LOSC,[91] new archipelagic baselines legislation was passed in 2009 that was deemed LOSC-compliant.[92] A constitutional challenge against the legislation was brought almost immediately thereafter on the basis that the archipelagic baselines law changed the territorial boundary of the Philippines enshrined in the constitution which could not be amended by a mere statute.[93] The Supreme Court held that the archipelagic baselines law was constitutional in 2011, but the petitioners filed for a Memorandum of Reconsideration which is still pending.[94]

There are also States that have not strictly complied with the requirements established in Article 47. For example, the archipelagic baseline system of Comoros does not appear to be consistent with the LOSC in that it uses a submerged feature as a basepoint (as opposed to an island or drying reef) and that its baselines appear to depart from the general configuration of the coast, contrary to Article 47(3).[95] Similarly, the Maldives archipelagic baselines legislation enacted in 1996 provided segment lengths for 37 baselines, three of which exceeded 100 nm but were less than 125 nm, contrary to Article 47(2),[96] and thus was objected to by the United States.[97] The United States and the United Kingdom have also argued that the archipelagic baselines used by the Dominican Republic[98] are contrary to the requirement that turning points of straight archipelagic baselines may only join the outermost islands and drying reefs of the archipelago and may not be drawn from low-tide elevations except in two enumerated circumstances.[99] Other instances of non-compliance with the requirements of Article 47 include the Seychelles (non-compliance with the water-to-land ratio in Article 47(1) and basepoints in open water contrary to Article 47(4))[100] and the Solomon Islands (one group of islands does not meet the water-to-land ratio in Article 47(1)).[101]

---

[89] Roach and Smith, n 70, 211.   [90] Ibid.

[91] H Bensurto, 'Archipelagic Philippines: A Question of Policy and Law' in MH Nordquist and JN Moore (eds), *Maritime Border Diplomacy* (Martinus Nijhoff The Netherlands 2012) 325, 333–5.

[92] Republic Act No 9522, An Act to Amend Certain Provisions of Republic Act No 3046, as Amended by Republic Act No 5446 to Define the Archipelagic Baselines of the Philippines and for other Purposes (10 March 2009) (The Philippines).

[93] Bensurto, n 91, 335.   [94] Ibid, 337.

[95] See United States Department of State, 'Comoros: Maritime Claims and Boundaries' (28 March 2014) *No 134 Limits in the Seas* 3, available at <http://www.state.gov/e/oes/ocns/opa/c16065.htm>.

[96] Roach and Smith, n 70, 216.   [97] Ibid.

[98] Law No 66-07 (22 May 2007) (Dominican Republic) (2007) 65 *Law of the Sea Bulletin* 18.

[99] Roach and Smith, n 70, 217.

[100] See United States Department of State, 'Seychelles: Maritime Claims and Boundaries' (14 February 2014) *No 132 Limits in the Seas* 2–3.

[101] See United States Department of State, 'Solomon Islands: Maritime Claims and Boundaries' (28 March 2014) *No 136 Limits in the Seas* 2–3.

5 Archipelagic Waters

5.1 LOSC provisions

5.1.1 Nature of archipelagic waters

The juridical nature of the waters within archipelagic baselines was a major issue during UNCLOS III. The debate centred on whether the waters enclosed within archipelagic baselines were more akin to internal waters as initially suggested by the Philippines and Indonesia, or whether they were similar to the territorial sea.[102] During the negotiations, a new term emerged, namely 'archipelagic waters', which would have the attributes of internal waters (complete sovereignty over the waters and their resources), as well as the territorial sea (which recognized the innocent passage of foreign vessels).[103]

Article 49 of the LOSC provides that 'the sovereignty of an archipelagic State extends to the waters enclosed by the archipelagic baselines drawn in accordance with article 47, described as archipelagic waters, regardless of their depth or distance from the coast'. This sovereignty extends to the air space above archipelagic waters as well as their bed and subsoil, and the resources contained therein.[104] An archipelagic State may also draw closing lines for the purpose of delimiting internal waters within archipelagic waters.[105]

In exchange for sovereignty over their waters, the LOSC provided for two categories of rights to other States, namely non-navigational rights to neighbouring States and navigational rights to all States.

5.1.2 Non-navigational rights

Article 51 (1) of LOSC obliges archipelagic States to respect existing agreements with other States and to recognize traditional fishing rights and other legitimate activities of immediately adjacent neighbouring States in certain areas in archipelagic waters and to conclude bilateral agreements in this respect.[106] Further, an archipelagic State must also respect existing submarine cables laid by other States and passing through its waters without making a landfall. It shall also permit the maintenance and replacement of such cables upon receiving due notice of their location and the intention to repair or replace them.[107]

This was to accommodate the concerns of Indonesia's neighbouring States such as Malaysia, Thailand, and Singapore that their traditional rights, such as rights of local access, rights to resources therein, rights pertaining to the laying and

---

[102] Munavvar, n 2, 153–6. [103] Ibid, 155. [104] LOSC, n 1, Art 49(2).
[105] Ibid, Art 50. [106] Ibid, Art 51 (1). [107] Ibid, Art 51 (2).

maintaining of submarine cables, may be impeded by the archipelagic regime.[108] In recognition of these rights, Malaysia and Indonesia signed the Jakarta Treaty in 1982 which covers traditional fishing rights, submarine cable and pipeline laying and repair activities, search and rescue, and marine scientific research.[109]

5.1.3 *Navigational rights through archipelagic waters*

There are two types of passage rights recognized under the archipelagic regime, the right of innocent passage and the right of archipelagic sea lanes passage (ASLP).

First, ships of all States enjoy the *right of innocent passage* through archipelagic waters that they enjoy in the territorial sea, as laid out in Part II, Section 3 of the LOSC.[110] Submarines are required to navigate on the surface and show their flag.[111] The archipelagic State can adopt certain specified laws and regulations relating to innocent passage through archipelagic waters[112] and may temporarily suspend innocent passage in specified areas of its archipelagic waters if such suspension is essential for the protection of its security, provided that the suspension has been duly published.[113]

The second type of passage right recognized in archipelagic waters is *archipelagic sea lanes passage*, which refers to the exercise of 'rights of navigation and overflight in the normal mode solely for the purpose of continuous, expeditious and unobstructed transit between one part of the high seas or an exclusive economic zone and another part of the high seas or an exclusive economic zone'.[114] In contrast to innocent passage, the reference to 'normal mode' has been interpreted to mean that:

> [S]ubmarines may transit submerged and military aircraft may overfly in combat formation and with normal equipment operation; surface warships may transit in a manner necessary for their security, including formation steaming and the launching and recovery of aircraft where consistent with sound navigational practices.[115]

Such sea lanes and air routes shall traverse archipelagic waters and the adjacent territorial sea and shall include all normal passage routes used as routes for international navigation or overflight through or over archipelagic waters.[116] Further, such

---

[108] Munavvar, n 2, 159.

[109] The full text of this is available in DOALOS, *The Law of the Sea: Practice of Archipelagic States* (United Nations New York 1992) 144–5.

[110] LOSC, n 1, Art 52. Please refer to Chapters 4 and 23 in this volume for a more detailed discussion of innocent passage.

[111] Ibid, Art 20.   [112] Ibid, Art 21.   [113] Ibid, Art 52(2).   [114] Ibid, Art 53(3).

[115] Commentary accompanying Message from the US President transmitting the United Nations Convention on the Law of the Sea and the Agreement relating to the Implementation of Part XI to the United States Senate for its advice and consent (7 October 1994) Sen Treaty Doc 103–139, reprinted in (1995) 34 ILM 1408. It has been said that the right of submarines to pass submerged through archipelagic sea lanes (ASL) is considered to be the biggest concession by the archipelagic States at UNCLOS III. See Narokobi, n 74, 232.

[116] LOSC, n 1, Art 53(4).

sea lanes and air routes shall be defined by a series of continuous axis lines from the entry points of passage routes to the exit points. Ships and aircraft in archipelagic sea lanes passage shall not deviate more than 25 nm to either side of such axis lines during passage, provided that such ships and aircraft shall not navigate closer to the coasts than 10 per cent of the distance between the nearest points on islands bordering the sea lane.[117]

An archipelagic State may designate sea lanes or air routes, prescribe traffic separation schemes through narrow channels in sea lanes, or substitute such sea lanes or traffic separation schemes, through or over its archipelagic waters and the adjacent territorial sea.[118] However, it does not have unfettered discretion to do this. First, as mentioned above, such sea lanes and air routes shall include *all normal passage routes* used as routes for international navigation or overflight or all *normal navigational channels*.[119] Second, such sea lanes and traffic separation schemes must conform to generally accepted international regulations.[120] Third, archipelagic States must refer proposals for designating or substituting sea lanes or prescribing or substituting traffic separation schemes to the competent international organization with a view to their adoption.[121] The organization may adopt only such sea lanes and traffic separation schemes as may be agreed with the archipelagic State, after which the archipelagic State may designate, prescribe, or substitute them.[122]

It should be noted that an archipelagic State is not obliged to designate archipelagic sea lanes passage. In the event that the archipelagic State does not designate sea lanes or air routes, 'the right of archipelagic sea lanes passage may be exercised through routes normally used for international navigation'.[123]

5.2 Issues in implementation

While the ASLP regime was detailed, its implementation was not as straightforward as initially envisaged, and several issues arose which have not as yet been resolved.

Indonesia's designation of its ASLP was a test case for the international community. Indonesia was reluctant to recognize the International Maritime Organization (IMO) as 'the competent international organization' for various reasons, including the fact that the United States, which was not a party to LOSC, 'was an influential member of the IMO'.[124] Nonetheless, after several phases of surveys, coordination meetings, and consultations with relevant stakeholders,[125] it submitted a designation of three routes running along a North–South axis in 1996.[126] However, several States,

---

[117] Ibid, Art 53(5).   [118] Ibid, Art 53(1).   [119] Ibid, Art 53(4).   [120] Ibid, Art 53(8).
[121] Ibid, Art 53(9).   [122] Ibid, Art 53(9).   [123] Ibid, Art 53(12).
[124] C Forward, 'Archipelagic Sea-Lanes in Indonesia—Their Legality in International Law' (2009) 23 *Australia and New Zealand Maritime Law Journal* 143, 152.
[125] H Djalal, 'Indonesia's Archipelagic Sea Lanes' in Cribb and Ford (eds), n 38, 59, 62–3.
[126] Ibid, 63.

including Australia and the United States, objected to the fact that Indonesia's submission had not included East–West sea lanes through the southern part of the archipelago,[127] despite the requirement for any submission to include 'all normal passage routes used as routes for international navigation'.[128] On the suggestion of the United States, the IMO accepted the concept of a 'partial proposal' and a 'partial designation', and included these concepts in its 'General Provisions for the Adoption, Designation and Substitution of Archipelagic Sea Lanes' (GPASL).[129] In 1998, the IMO subsequently accepted the partial designation of Indonesian archipelagic sea lanes passage. It has been argued that the IMO's actions went beyond what was envisaged in the LOSC.[130] As argued by one scholar:

> The idea that an ASL designation does not cover all routes through the archipelago is deemed a partial designation and does not prevent the exercise of the ASLP in other undesignated routes, renders the designation practically ineffective. No benefit is gained by the archipelagic State in making a partial proposal and designation since all routes not designated are still subject to ASLP anyway. A partial designation is like no designation at all.[131]

Notably, in 2002, Indonesia passed legislation that implied that foreign ships and aircraft may only exercise the right of ASLP through the three North–South routes.[132] The right of ASLP 'in other parts of Indonesian waters can be conducted after such a sea lane has been designated in those waters for the purpose of this transit',[133] which suggested that ships transiting through other routes would be limited to innocent passage. While it has publicly confirmed that its designation was only partial and has accepted that ASLP is available to transiting vessels that navigate through normal routes used for international navigation, this public position is at odds with its legislation.[134] This has led to some skirmishes between Indonesia and the USA, for example when the latter asserted its right to traverse the East–West passage when it sent an aircraft carrier, the *Carl Vinson* and five fighter aircrafts, on manoeuvres in the Java Sea.[135]

The other two issues that arose during the negotiations of Indonesia's ASLP regime was the axis line and the width of the ASLs and the 10 per cent rule. With regard to the axis line, the USA argued that it should be positioned so as to maximize the sea room available for the user State's vessel and aircraft, whereas

---

[127] Forward, n 124, 152. [128] Ibid.
[129] MSC Resolution MSC 71 (69), 19 May 1998, disseminated by Circular Sn/Circ 199. 59/22, [5.20] and Annex 8. The General Provisions came about as a result of a suggestion put forth by Australia that the IMO adopt a detailed process for the adoption of ASLs.
[130] See Forward, n 124, 153.
[131] JL Batongbacal, 'Barely Skimming the Surface: Archipelagic Sea Lanes Navigation and the IMO' in AG Oude Elferink and DR Rothwell (eds), *Oceans Management in the 21st Century: Institutional Frameworks and Responses* (Martinus Nijhoff Leiden 2004) 55.
[132] Government Regulation No 37 of 2002 (Indonesia), Art 15. [133] Ibid, Art 3(2).
[134] Sea Power Centre Australia, 'Indonesian Archipelagic Sea Lanes' (April 2005) Semaphore Issue 6.
[135] Djalal, n 125, 68.

Australia argued that the axis line should approximate the route normally used for international navigation that complied with maritime safety rules.[136] Indonesia argued that ASLs should only be designated over waters suitable for navigation regardless of room for manoeuvre or safety. The Indonesian proposal ultimately followed Australia's proposal of approximation but the GPASL does not contain any rule on the positioning of the axis line, meaning that different criteria could be used in subsequent designations.[137] With regard to the width of the ASL and the 10 per cent rule, issues were raised as to 'when an island should be considered as a bordering island, how the 10 per cent distance could be determined in cases where the bordering islands are not exactly opposite each other with the axis line directly between them and how to apply the rule to islands located on only one side of the ASL'.[138] This was a critical question, as 'it determined the breadth of a navigational buffer zone around archipelagic islands which vessels exercising ASLP should not cross'.[139] Both Indonesia and the United States had diametrically opposing positions, and it was eventually agreed that the issue should be left open for 'future determination by an international tribunal',[140] and until then, compliance with the outer limits of the ASL in cases where the 10 per cent rule applies will be based on national interpretation.[141]

Interestingly, Indonesia has not submitted any further designation to the IMO, and Dr Djalal has explained that, 'before any such lane is designated formally, thorough deliberation is required to ensure that navigational safety and the protection of the environment, as well as the security of Indonesia, would be safeguarded'.[142] As noted by Robin Warner, 'the adoption of Indonesia's ASL designation proposal in the IMO has elucidated some aspects of the UNCLOS archipelagic regime, but adoption of future ASL designation proposals may entail further adaptation of the articles to suit the particular circumstances of the archipelago in question'.[143]

Indeed, the Philippines has argued that the handling of the Indonesian ASLP designation should not represent a precedent for future ASLP designations considered by the IMO.[144] Two proposals on designating ASLs in the Philippines were made in 1997 and it was only in 2009 that Philippines' officials proposed a bill which sought to establish ASLs for the Philippines.[145] The Bill established three sea lanes: (1) an East–West passage along the Balintang Channel in the Northern

---

[136] Batongbacal, n 131, 56–7. [137] Ibid. [138] Ibid, 58. [139] Ibid. [140] Ibid.
[141] Ibid. [142] Ibid.
[143] R Warner, 'Implementing the Archipelagic Regime in the International Maritime Organization' in DR Rothwell and S Bateman (eds), *Navigational Rights and Freedoms and the New Law of the Sea* (Martinus Nijhoff Leiden 2000) 187.
[144] See [5.17], [5.30], and [16.8] proposed by the Philippines Delegation for the Draft Report of the MSC contained in IMO Doc MSC/WP/11, as reported to Assistant Secretary FM Ebdalin of the Department of Foreign Affairs of the Philippines, in a Memorandum submitted by Director TV Mariano.
[145] On 11 March 2011, Senator A Trillanes IV filed Senate Bill 2738 which sought to establish ASL for the Philippines.

tip of Luzon; (2) the North–South passage along Mindoro Strait in the North and the Basilan Strait in the South in Mindanao; and (3) another East–West passage along the Balabac Strait in the West and Surigao Strait in the East.[146] In January 2012, the Philippines' House of Representatives approved the bill that would establish ASLP and prescribe the rights and obligations of foreign ships and aircraft passing through identified sea lanes.[147] The Bill has been the subject of criticism. One scholar has argued that ASLP is only permissive and not mandatory, and therefore it is not necessary to designate ASLs, especially considering that it is going to be a burden on Philippines' security.[148] Further, it has also been argued that 'ASLs are really for the benefit of military vessels, its designation by Congress will necessarily and inevitably lure foreign military vessels including aircraft carriers to swamp Philippines waters'.[149] Environmental issues have also been raised by the Tubbataha Protected Area Management Board which has said that the sea lanes run through most of the country's significant marine habitats and may 'intensify the park's exposure to ship groundings, and therefore coral damage, and to the other devastating effects of escalated maritime activities in the Sulu Sea'.[150]

It warrants note that to date, the Philippines government has indicated that it intends to unilaterally designate the three sea lanes without waiting for the IMO's final approval.[151] The Philippines has argued that, due to the urgency of the threat posed to coral reefs and marine biodiversity by the unregulated and unrestricted passage of foreign vessels into the Philippines, that 'the Philippines need not wait procedurally for IMO's adoption before it takes action to protect its marine biodiversity'.[152] The 'substantive and inherent right of the Philippines to protect and preserve its resources for its people takes precedence over the procedural guideline in Article 53 (9)'.[153] That said, the Philippines has said that it will refer its legislated sea lanes to the IMO pursuant to the requirements of Article 53 and that such an interpretation is consistent with the letter and spirit of Article 53(9). It argues that Article 53(9) does not prohibit the archipelagic State from designating sea lanes even before these are referred to the IMO, because it provides that 'the organization may adopt only such sea lanes and traffic separation schemes as may be agreed with

---

[146] Bensurto, n 91, 339.

[147] B Rosario, 'House Okays Sea Lanes Bill', *Tempo Online* (26 January 2012) available at <http://www.tempo.com.ph/2012/01/house-okays-sea-lanes-bill/>.

[148] J Batongbacal, 'Premature Legislation on Archipelagic Sealanes to Benefit Foreign Not National Interest' (University of the Philippines College of Law Manila 2011).

[149] Bensurto, n 91, 340.

[150] A Calonzo, 'Tubbataha Board: Senate Sea Lanes Bill May Expose Coral Reefs to More Groundings', *GMA News Online* (13 September 2013) available at <http://www.gmanetwork.com/news/story/326326/news/regions/tubbataha-board-senate-sea-lanes-bill-may-expose-coral-reefs-to-more-groundings>.

[151] J Kraska and R Pedrozo, *International Maritime Security Law* (Martinus Nijhoff Leiden 2013) 274.

[152] Bensurto, n 91, 347.   [153] Ibid.

the archipelagic State, after which the archipelagic State may designate, prescribe or substitute them ... this is procedural and directory'.[154] Whether such arguments will pass muster with the international community remains to be seen.

6 A Lacuna in the LOSC: Dependent Archipelagos?

The archipelagic regime in Part IV was intended to apply only to archipelagic States and not to dependent archipelagos of continental States. During the negotiation of the LOSC, such continental States argued that their dependent archipelagos should be included in the archipelagic regime. At the second session of UNCLOS III in 1974, nine continental States drafted a working paper arguing that the archipelagic regime should be extended to mid-ocean archipelagos of continental States.[155] As argued by Portugal:

> [T]he arguments in favour of the establishment of a special regime for the archipelagic States were also valid for archipelagos forming part of the territory of a coastal State, particularly with regard to the security and economic interests of such States. Application of a different regime to the latter would mean that the archipelagic part of the territory of mixed States would be regarded as second class territory.[156]

These attempts to widen the applicability of the archipelagic regime were objected to by States that feared that a vague definition would lead to a slew of unfounded claims[157] and would undermine the freedom of navigation.[158] Ultimately, the suggestions of these continental States were not incorporated in the Informal Single Negotiating Text.

In this regard, there would appear to be a lacuna in LOSC in relation to dependent archipelagos. Arguably, Article 7 allowing coastal States to draw straight baselines where there is a fringe of islands around its coast, can be relied upon by

---

[154] Ibid, 349.
[155] Canada, Chile, Iceland, India, Indonesia, Mauritius, Mexico, New Zealand, and Norway: Working Paper, UN Doc A/CONF/62/L.4 (1973–74) III *Official Records of UNCLOS III* 81–3.
[156] UN Doc A/CONF.62/C.2/SR.37 (1974) II *Official Records of UNCLOS III* 266.
[157] See eg statements made by the representatives of Japan, Bulgaria, Thailand, Algeria, and Turkey at UNCLOS III (1982) XVII *Official Records of UNCLOS III* 90, 96.
[158] E Franckx and M Benetar, 'Straight Baselines around Insular Formations Not Constituting an Archipelagic State', Conference Paper, Third International Workshop on the South China Sea, organized by the Institute of East Sea Studies, Vietnam (November 2011) available at <http://nghiencuubiendong.vn/en/conferences-and-seminars-/the-third-international-workshop-on-south-china-sea/656-straight-baselines-around-insular-formations-not-constituting-an-archipelagic-state-by-erik-franckx-a-marco-benatar->.

continental States with dependent archipelagos. Kopela contends that, provided the general conditions of Article 7 are met, 'the continental state, in whose possession the archipelago lies, may apply a system of straight baselines around the whole archipelago or in parts of it for the delimitation of its territorial sea'.[159] According to her, archipelagos such as the Kerguelen Islands, Sjaelland, and the Furneaux Group could be classified in this category.[160] However, she acknowledges that the applicability of Article 7 for dependent outlying archipelagos may be limited particularly in cases concerning archipelagos with similarly sized islands or islands located in a random way.[161]

Given this gap in the LOSC, it has been argued that State practice may play an important role in the development of legal rules for dependent archipelagos.[162] Indeed, several continental States with offshore groups of islands which 'may be geographically described as archipelagos but which do not meet the juridical definition set out in Article 46 of the LOSC have sought to enclose these islands with straight baselines in a manner simulating an archipelago'.[163] For example, Portugal has drawn straight baselines around the Azores Islands, Denmark around the Faroe Islands, Ecuador around the Galapagos Islands, Canada around the Canadian Arctic Islands, the United Kingdom around the Falkland Islands and Turks and Caicos, and Spain around the Beleraic Islands of Majorca, Minorca, Ibiza, and Formentera in the Mediterranean.[164] However, it was not made clear whether these straight baselines are claimed pursuant to Article 7 of the LOSC or archipelagic baselines under Article 47—nonetheless, these claims have been described as 'excessive maritime claims' contrary to the LOSC.[165]

Another notable example which deserves mention is China's practice of drawing straight baselines around disputed insular territory. China has enacted legislation claiming straight baselines over both the Paracel Islands in the South China Sea (also claimed by Vietnam and Taiwan)[166] as well as the Senkaku/Diayou islands in the East China Sea (claimed by Japan and Taiwan).[167] It has not made clear whether these straight baselines are pursuant to Article 7 or archipelagic baselines under Article 47. In either case, it has been said that this would be contrary to the LOSC, as China does not meet the requirements in Article 7 or Article 47.[168] With regard to the disputed Spratly Islands in the South China Sea,

---

[159] S Kopela, *Dependent Archipelagos in the Law of the Sea* (Martinus Nijhoff Leiden 2013) 258.
[160] Ibid, 259. [161] Ibid. [162] Ibid. [163] Roach and Smith, n 70, 208.
[164] Ibid, 108–15. [165] Ibid.
[166] Declaration of the Government of the People's Republic of China on the Baselines of the Territorial Sea of the People's Republic of China, 15 May 1996.
[167] JA Roach, 'China's Straight Baseline Claim: Senkaku (Diaoyu) Islands' (13 February 2013) 17(7) *American Society of International Law Insights*.
[168] Ibid. See also, United States Department of State, 'China: Straight Baseline Claim' (7 September 1996) *No 117 Limits in the Seas*, with regard to the Paracel Islands.

also claimed by Vietnam, Malaysia, the Philippines, Taiwan, and Brunei, China's legislation provides that it will use straight baselines to draw the baselines of the territorial sea adjacent to the Spratly Islands[169] (it has not as yet). However, Chinese academics have recently argued that the archipelagic regime should be applied to the Spratly Islands.[170] They argue that, while only archipelagic States are entitled to draw archipelagic baselines, Part IV does not expressly exclude the option for continental States to apply straight baselines to their oceanic archipelagos.[171] Further, because oceanic archipelagos of continental States have the same geographic features as those of the archipelagos of archipelagic States, they should apply similar principles.[172]

Churchill and Lowe have argued that excluding continental States with dependent archipelagos from being able to draw archipelagic baselines 'seems an unnecessary and unreasonable restriction',[173] motivated by the fear that this would bring about a proliferation of claims. It was a 'political decision reflecting the objections raised by maritime powers to the proliferation of archipelagic wasters'.[174] It has been argued that, to the extent that such claims have been recognized by other States (straight baselines around Faroes Island, for example, have been recognized by other States), they must be regarded as being valid under customary international law.[175] Indeed, Kopela has examined the State practice of continental States with outlying archipelagos and argues that, while no firm principle of customary international law has been crystallized, there has been a trend in international law towards the formation of a rule of customary law in two situations. First, in small archipelagic formations where the islands composing the archipelago are located at close distances to each other and cover a small maritime space, straight baselines are used. Second, in cases of larger archipelagic formations which are spread in a broad maritime space and whose islands are located at considerable distances from each other, archipelagic baselines, as set out in Article 47, may be used.[176]

What is evident from the above discussion is that the status of dependent archipelagos is still mired in uncertainty, with divergent views as to whether there is indeed a customary international law principle that allows dependent archipelagos to draw straight baselines or archipelagic baselines around its islands. The question is whether the issue is important enough to draft another 'implementation

---

[169] Law on the Territorial Sea and Contiguous Zone (25 February 1992) (China), Arts 2 and 3.

[170] See eg H Nong, L Jianwei, and C Pingping, 'The Concept of Archipelagic State and the South China Sea: UNCLOS, State Practice and Implication' (2013) 1 *China Oceans Law Review* 209.

[171] Ibid, 221.   [172] Ibid, 222.   [173] Churchill and Lowe, n 43, 120.

[174] Kopela, n 159, 259.

[175] States such as the United States have also protested these claims of continental States with mid-ocean archipelagos undermining the status of these claims as customary international law. Churchill and Lowe, n 43, 121.

[176] Kopela, n 159, 261.

agreement' to the LOSC clarifying the status of such archipelagos, or whether it is acceptable that this issue is left to the vagaries of State practice. At this point in time, the latter option appears to be more likely.

7 Conclusion

Reisman notes that '[e]very legal arrangement is born out of political bargains and compromises. Each, reflecting the prevailing allocation of power as well as the calculus of fairness or justice, inevitably discriminates, in some degree, in favour of some and against others.' [177] Both archipelagic States and maritime States made certain compromises, but it would appear that archipelagic States got most of what they wanted, namely, the ability to draw straight baselines around their outermost islands and to assert sovereignty over the waters enclosed within these baselines. That said, 30 years after the adoption of the LOSC, Part IV is generally accepted and there has been minimal agitation from either the maritime States or archipelagic States for a radical overhaul of the regime. As mentioned above, it has enjoyed a relatively high degree of compliance, and arguably this is a sign of its effectiveness.

Notwithstanding this, problems in implementation have inevitably arisen. The major issue continues to be the right of ASLP, and both the Philippines and Indonesia have faced challenges in its implementation. Indonesia still has yet to make a full designation along the North–South axis despite pressure from the major maritime States to do so, and it remains to be seen whether it will actually do so or maintain the status quo. The Philippines is in the midst of designating ASLP but currently choosing to do so outside the auspices of the IMO and the ramifications of this are still unclear. Apart from these two countries, none of the other countries which have claimed archipelagic status have declared ASLs through their waters. The right to ASLP and the concomitant rights of the archipelagic State will continue to pose challenges to the effective operation of the regime. Hopefully, such issues can be resolved through dialogue, consultation, and cooperation between the relevant stakeholders.

The issue of dependent archipelagos was deliberately omitted from the LOSC, as the international community was not ready to address the issue. As mentioned

---

[177] WM Reisman, *The Quest for World Order and Human Dignity in the Twenty-First Century: Constitutive Process and Individual Commitment: General Course on Public International Law* (Martinus Nijhoff Leiden 2012) 90 and 441.

above, this apparent gap in the LOSC is likely to be filled by State practice, and there does not seem to be any serious push for more concrete rules on this issue at this point in time.

In conclusion, Part IV of the LOSC continues to be an important aspect of the LOSC. The inclusion of the regime facilitated the ultimate conclusion of the LOSC, settled years of debate over the status of groups of islands and established a legal regime for a vast expanse of maritime space. While some issues in its implementation have arisen, overall, it is an effective regime which has withstood the test of time.

8

THE EXCLUSIVE ECONOMIC ZONE

GEMMA ANDREONE

1 INTRODUCTION

THE role of the economic exclusive zone (EEZ) in the international law of the sea has been examined by many authors over the years.[1] Almost all the relevant aspects of this concept have been explored, including its legal, economic, political, and social implications.[2] Yet, 20 years after the entry into force of the 1982 United Nations Convention on the Law of the Sea (LOSC),[3] the EEZ continues to provoke a wide range of cases, discussion, and international disputes with regard to the related

---

[1] The legal literature on the EEZ is extensive. See JP Queneudec, 'La zone économique' (1975) *Revue Générale de Droit International Public* 321; WC Extavour, *The Exclusive Economic Zone: A Study of the Evolution and Progressive Development of the International Law of the Sea* (Martinus Nijhoff Leiden 1979); B Conforti (ed), *La zona economica esclusiva* (Giuffrè Milano 1983); DJ Attard, *The Exclusive Economic Zone in International Law* (Clarendon Press Oxford 1987); B Kwiatkowska, *The 200 Mile Exclusive Economic Zone in the New Law of the Sea* (Martinus Nijhoff Dordrecht 1989); F Orrego Vicuña, *The Exclusive Economic Zone* (Cambridge University Press Cambridge 1989); F Rigaldies, 'La zone économique exclusive dans la pratique des états' (1997) 35 *Canadian Yearbook of International Law* 3; RR Churchill and AV Lowe, *The Law of the Sea* (Manchester University Press Manchester 1999); DR Rothwell and T Stephens, *The International Law of the Sea* (Hart Oxford 2010).

[2] For an analysis of the economic implications of the EEZ, see EA Posner and AO Sykes, 'Economic foundations of the law of the sea' (2010) 104 *American Journal of International Law* 569, 584.

[3] 1982 United Nations Convention on the Law of the Sea (hereinafter LOSC).

provisions of the Convention, to the conformity of the latter to customary international law, and to the crucial issue of the gradual expansion of the jurisdiction of coastal States over new uses of the sea, leading to the risk of excessive restriction of freedom of navigation. This maritime zone, therefore, still constitutes a fundamental subject in the international law of the sea, owing to its wide extension and proximity to coasts, to the concentration within EEZs of the greater part of economically exploitable resources, and to the co-existence of several jurisdictional powers and economic and political interests, such as those of coastal States, of flag States, and of the international community as a whole. All these aspects generate, inevitably, a series of crucial ambiguities in the interpretation and application of existing rules, which are destined to increase in proportion to the growth of environmental concerns, to the improvement of new technologies and as a result of increased demand for the control of maritime spaces.

The main aim of this chapter is to illustrate the issues already emerging from recent State practice, which will influence future developments and trends in the international law of the sea. Thus, an analysis of the evolution of the concept and its juridical nature, and the legal regime applicable to the EEZ will be examined. Finally, the future development of the EEZ legal regime will be explored considering the principal controversial features that may influence its course.

2 The Evolution of the Concept and the Nature of the EEZ in Contemporary International Law

2.1 History and genesis of the concept

The origin of the concept of the EEZ can be traced to earlier claims by coastal States to exercise national jurisdiction and control over marine resources in zones adjacent to and beyond the territorial sea (TS), which were presented by some delegations participating in the 1930 Hague Conference for the Codification of International Law.[4] After the Hague Conference, these aspirations merged with the on-going debate on the concept and the extension of the TS. The turning point of this trend occurred only after World War II when a 'multiplication of unilateral

---

[4] *Virginia Commentaries*, Vol II, 493; D Vignes, G Cataldi, and R Casado Raigon, *Le droit international de la pêche* (Bruylant Bruxelles 2000) 18.

claims'[5] extending coastal State jurisdiction in the water column of the high seas beyond the TS began.[6]

The debate which took place within the First United Nations Conference on the Law of the Sea (UNCLOS I) led to the adoption of the concept of 'special interests' of coastal States regarding the management of the living resources of the high seas adjacent to the TS in Articles 6 and 7 of the 1958 Convention on Fishing and Conservation of the Living Resources of the High Sea.[7] Subsequently, a new maritime zone beyond the TS, corresponding to the Exclusive Fisheries Zone (EFZ), was gradually asserted by national and international[8] practice throughout the 1960s and 1970s, and, then, was widely debated at the Third United Nations Conference on the Law of the Sea (UNCLOS III).[9]

Thus, the EEZ regime, codified by the LOSC, was the result of the fusion of the EFZ concept with the notion of the 'patrimonial sea',[10] promoted during the 1970s by newly independent and developing States in order to re-appropriate their natural resources.[11] It was a revolutionary compromise between the interests of the coastal States and those of the flag States, as well as the general interests of the international community, unifying, in a multifunctional zone, the regime of the waters superjacent to the seabed and the one of the seabed and its subsoil.[12] Moreover, the solution agreed for the EEZ legal regime, as well as those concerning other zones, was facilitated by the consolidation of the theory of functional powers.[13]

---

[5] L Lucchini and M Voelckel, *Droit de la mer: Navigation et pêche* (Pedone Paris 1996) Vol 2, 412–21. The authors describe this 'multiplication des déclarations unilatérales' as a unilateralism not new in the international law of the sea.

[6] This movement, increasingly strong in the following twenty years, started with the US 'Truman Proclamations' of 1945 and continued with the claims of some Latin American States. Indeed, in 1952, the group of Chile, Ecuador, and Peru, adopted a 'Declaration on the Maritime Zone' (the so-called Santiago Declaration) claiming a sovereignty extension beyond the TS to a distance of 200 nm. See *Virginia Commentaries*, Vol II, 495; and RJ Dupuy and D Vignes, *A Handbook on the New Law of the Sea* (Martinus Nijhoff Dordrecht 1991) Vol 1, 39.

[7] 1958 Convention on Fishing and Conservation of the Living Resources of the High Seas. This convention proved to be largely a dead letter because many fishing States did not ratify it. See M Dahmani, *The Fisheries Regime of the Exclusive Economic Zone* (Martinus Nijhoff Dordrecht 1987).

[8] The reference is in particular to the *Fisheries Jurisdiction* cases: *Fisheries Jurisdiction (United Kingdom of Great Britain and Northern Ireland v Iceland)* (Merits) [1974] ICJ Rep 3; *Fisheries Jurisdiction (Federal Republic of Germany v Iceland)* (Merits) [1974] ICJ Rep 175.

[9] Different approaches were advanced by developed States, the groups of the Latin American States, of the Asian and African States, and the group of the landlocked and geographically disadvantaged States. The 'space approach' prevailed in the LOSC, but the 'species approach' was not completely excluded by it, as observed by Lucchini and Voelckel, n 5, 451.

[10] This notion appeared for the first time in the Declaration of Santo Domingo of June 1972 of Latin American States.

[11] See Rothwell and Stephens, n 1, 82.   [12] Lucchini and Voelckel, n 5, Vol 2, 449.

[13] On the functional powers theory, see B Conforti, *Il regime giuridico dei mari* (Jovene Napoli 1957) 1–308; Dupuy and Vignes, n 6; Lucchini and Voelckel, n 5, Vol 2, 451; ED Brown, *The International Law of the Sea* (Dartmouth Aldershot 1994) Vol 1, 220; and M Gavouneli, *Functional Jurisdiction in the Law of the Sea* (Martinus Nijhoff Leiden 2007) 59.

2.2 The legal status of the EEZ

The EEZ, envisaged by Part V and other provisions of the LOSC, thus emerges as a *sui generis* zone,[14] subject only to selected sovereign rights and powers of the coastal State in coexistence with some remaining freedoms of the high seas. Article 55 of the LOSC defines the EEZ as 'an area beyond and adjacent to the territorial sea', that is subject to the 'specific legal regime' applicable to the coastal State and to other States, and provided for by the relevant provisions of the convention.

Before the entry into force of the LOSC in 1994, the concept of the EEZ was already considered a part of customary international law,[15] as a result of a great number of unilateral claims and the recognition of its legal value by international jurisprudence.[16]

The maximum extension of 200 nautical miles (nm) was accepted, although it was the most extensive claim at that time and lacked any scientific or legally expressed rationale.[17] Thirty years after the conclusion of the LOSC, this maximum limit still stands, even though the process of extension of the outer continental shelf is likely to also affect the water column above.

At present, 166 States are parties to the LOSC[18] and almost[19] all the 143 coastal States claiming EEZs or EFZs are among them.[20] It can be asserted that the rights of the coastal States provided for by the LOSC within the EEZ have become part of customary international law, although there is still the possibility of a divergence with State practice on specific provisions.[21] Concerning the obligations of coastal

---

[14] In this sense, see Brown, n 13, Vol 1, 218; and Rothwell and Stephens, n 1, 84.

[15] The doctrine is almost unanimous on accepting the customary nature of the EEZ well before the entry into force of the LOSC. See Churchill and Lowe, n 1, 161.

[16] The ICJ stated expressly, for the first time, in the judgement of 1985 in the *Continental Shelf Case (Libyan Arab Jamahiriya v Malta)* [1985] ICJ Rep 13, 33 that 'the institution of the exclusive economic zone... is shown by the practice of States to have become a part of customary law'.

[17] AL Hollick, 'The Origins of 200 Mile Offshore Zones' (1977) 71(3) *American Journal of International Law* 71. On the breadth of the EEZ, see *Virginia Commentaries*, Vol II, 494.

[18] See the 'Table recapitulating the status of the Convention and of the related Agreements, as at 10 October 2014' (available at <www.un.org/Depts/los>).

[19] According to information from DOALOS, *Maritime Zones and Maritime Delimitation*, available at <www.un.org/Depts/los/LEGISLATIONANDTREATIES/index.htm>, only the following States have proclaimed EEZs or EFZs without ratifying the LOSC: Cambodia, Colombia, Democratic People's Republic of Korea, Eritrea, Georgia, Iran, Israel, Libya, Syria, Turkey, United Arab Emirates, USA, and Venezuela.

[20] While many States transformed their original EFZs to EEZs, some States still maintain EFZs. Excessive claims extending the territorial sea outside the limit of 12 nm are maintained by Benin, Ecuador, and Togo: see information from DOALOS, 'Maritime Space: Maritime Zones and Maritime Delimitation', available at <www.un.org/Depts/los/LEGISLATIONANDTREATIES/index.htm>.

[21] See Churchill and Lowe, n 1, 162.

States within the EEZ, it is much more difficult to ascertain whether, and if so to what extent, they acquired a customary nature.[22]

When geographical reasons do not allow the claim for the maximum EEZ extension, a delimitation of overlapping zones must be agreed on by States with opposite or adjacent coasts, according to Article 74. The envisaged delimitation method, aimed at the achievement of an equitable solution without fixing any prevailing criteria, was another important milestone achieved by the LOSC, but, at present, it can be considered a further element in the complexity of the EEZ legal regime.

2.3 *Minoris generis* zones

An analysis of State practice indicates that the persistence of *minoris generis* zones (also called *sui generis* zones)[23] claiming a reduced application of the EEZ legal regime is a result of particular political or geographical features of the particular seas.[24] These are the EFZ or Fishing Protection Zones (FPZ),[25] Ecological Protection Zones (EPZ) or mixed zones. The majority of authors consider these reduced zones legitimate, following the Latin adage *in maiore stat minus*.[26]

There is a widespread tendency to consider the relevant LOSC provisions applicable in such reduced EEZs, but it must be underlined that the legal regime applicable varies according to the type of powers claimed. In fact, exclusive or protected fishing zones, on one hand, and ecological protection zones, on the other, invoke different powers regulated by distinct chapters of the LOSC (Part V and Part XII, respectively). Nevertheless, it is often the case that the powers exercised by coastal States in such reduced zones do not correspond either to the claimed purpose for the zone, or to the powers asserted in the zone by means of a proclamation or legislation.[27]

---

[22] The relationship between the exclusive powers recognized to the coastal States and the obligations arising from the exercise of related rights cannot be underestimated. See on this point T Treves, *La Convenzione sul diritto del mare del 10 dicembre 1982* (Giuffré Milano 1983) 24.

[23] G Andreone and G Cataldi, '*Sui Generis* Zones' in D Attard, M Fitzmaurice, and N Martinez (eds), *The IMLI Manual on International Maritime Law: The Law of the Sea* (Oxford University Press Oxford 2014) Vol 1, 217.

[24] The United Kingdom proclamations of an ecological protection zone off the Falkland Islands' coasts and off the Chagos Archipelago are notable examples, since in these maritime areas more extensive claims to exclusive economic rights would complicate the highly controversial sovereignty disputed by the UK over those islands and maritime spaces.

[25] Since the difference between the EFZ and the FPZ is not substantial and depends only on the main purpose of the costal State proclamation, from now on both types of zones will be referred to as EFZ.

[26] A Del Vecchio Capotosti, 'In maiore stat minus: A Note on the EEZ and the Zones of Ecological Protection in the Mediterranean Sea' (2008) 39 *Ocean Development and International Law* 287.

[27] See G Andreone and G Cataldi, 'Regards sur les évolutions du droit de la mer en Méditerranée' (2010) 56 *Annuaire Français de Droit International* 3. As an example, in the Italian EPZ, established solely in the North Western Mediterranean sea, Liguria and Tyrrhenian sea, through Law No 61 (8 February 2006) and Decree No 209 (27 October 2011, entered into force 1 January 2012), the powers

The case of the UK has been particularly enlightening in this regard. Indeed, the UK provided for the designation of the EEZ by the 2009 Marine and Coastal Access Act,[28] but established it only by the Exclusive Economic Zone Order No 3161 of 2013.[29] Therefore, for a long period, the UK had a de facto EEZ, as it had exercised within its 200 nm EFZ and a conterminous renewable energy zone[30] exclusive powers on marine pollution prevention and marine scientific research.[31]

Similarly, a remarkable degree of uncertainty, regarding the types and the limits of coastal State claims beyond the TS, has characterized Mediterranean Sea practice. However, this tendency has recently been reversed, with many States deciding to proclaim EEZs or to transform their *minoris generis* zones to EEZs.[32]

In the light of this practice, it can be assumed that the names given to *minoris generis* zones are simply indicative,[33] and it can also be questioned whether the act of proclamation is a constitutive element of the EEZ.[34] Recently, this latter issue has been brought into focus in the case of the excessive proclamation by Somalia of a 200 nm TS. Indeed, the interpretation of the excessive Somali claim as an EEZ proclamation has been invoked as legitimate in order to assert the duty of third States to abstain from the looting of the living resources of the Somali people in that maritime zone.[35]

---

claimed are not strictly limited to protection of the marine environment, but are also extended to the protection of marine mammals and to the conservation marine biodiversity, as well as to archaeological heritage.

[28] Marine and Coastal Access Act 2009 (UK) c 23, part 2 — Exclusive Economic Zone, UK Marine Area, and Welsh Zone. See the official website of UK Legislation <http://www.legislation.gov.uk>.

[29] Exclusive Economic Zone Order 2013 No 3161 (11 December 2013, entered into force 31 March 2014) (UK). See the official website of UK Legislation <http://www.legislation.gov.uk>.

[30] The Energy Act 2004 (UK) which designated a Renewable Energy Zone beyond the TS.

[31] See Rothwell and Stephens, n 1, 85.

[32] Reference is made to the proclamation of EEZs by Tunisia in 2005 and to the transformation of the French EPZ to an EEZ in 2012, as well as the more recent proclamation made by Spain in April 2013. For a deeper analysis of Mediterranean State practice, see Andreone and Cataldi, n 27, 8; and M Grbec, *Extension of Coastal State Jurisdiction in Enclosed and Semi-enclosed Seas, A Mediterranean and Adriatic Perspective* (Routledge New York 2014) 88.

[33] On the 'fluctuating' terminology adopted by States proclaiming an EEZ or a *sui generis* zone, see Lucchini and Voelckel, n 5, Vol 2, 460. See also Andreone and Cataldi, n 27, 10.

[34] The necessity of an express proclamation of the EEZ has been considered by doctrine as an indispensable act according to an *a contrario* reading of pertinent LOSC provisions. For a possible reinterpretation of this assumption see G Andreone, 'Observations sur la "juridictionnalisation" de la mer Méditerranée' (2004) 8 *Annuaire du Droit de la Mer 7*.

[35] T Neumann and TR Salomon, 'Fishing in Troubled Waters: Somalia's Maritime Zones and the Case for Reinterpretation' (12 March 2012) 16(9) *American Society of International Law* Insights, available at <www.asil.org/insights/volume/16/issue/9/fishing-troubled-waters-somalia%E2%80%99s-maritime-zones-and-case>. On 30 June 2014, Somalia proclaimed an EZ; see UNDOALOS, Maritime Zones and Maritime Delimitation, available at <www.un.org/depts/los/LEGISLATIONANDTREATIES/PDFFILES/index.htm>.

3 THE APPLICABLE LEGAL REGIME

3.1 Coastal and third States' rights and obligations and the conflict over the attribution of rights

The preliminary issue for assessment concerns the rationale of the distinction, introduced by Article 56 of the LOSC, between 'sovereign rights' over living and non-living resources of the EEZ, as well as over other activities connected with the exploration and economic exploitation of the zone, and 'jurisdictional rights' over the establishment and use of artificial islands, installations and structures, scientific research, and the protection of the marine environment. The main question to ascertain is whether defining the resources-related rights of coastal States as 'sovereign rights', and thus as 'more than simply exclusive rights', corresponds to more extensive powers to prescribe, to enforce, and to adjudicate compared with the simple 'jurisdictional powers' attributed in the other domains.

This being so, for each area of coastal State competence, it is necessary to assess the exclusivity of the powers attributed to the State by the LOSC, their scope, nature, and the applicable regulatory regime, as well as the obligations related to such powers. Article 56(1)(b) expressly refers to the application of all relevant provisions of the convention in recognizing jurisdictional rights over non-resource related activities,[36] while the succeeding paragraph (c) recalls the existence in the LOSC of 'other rights and duties' of coastal States.[37] In any case, the rights, whether sovereign or jurisdictional, and the related duties of coastal States cannot be intended to be absolute, since due regard to the rights and duties of other States is expressly provided for by Articles 55, 56(2), and 58 of the LOSC.[38]

Article 58(1) specifically envisages the freedom of navigation and overflight, the laying of submarine cables and pipelines, and 'other internationally lawful uses of the sea' connected with the above-mentioned freedoms. Article 58(2) allows for the application of the provisions regarding the high seas and the pertinent rules of international law only if these are compatible with the EEZ regime. The controversial nature of the EEZ was well known to the drafters of the LOSC, who, by the introduction of Articles 56, 58, and 59, aimed to create a 'permanent legal arrangement' for balancing the diverse interests in the EEZ.

---

[36] R Beckman and T Davenport, 'The EEZ Regime: Reflections After Thirty Years' in HN Scheiber and MS Kwon (eds), *Securing the Ocean for the Next Generation: Papers from the Law of the Sea Institute-Korea Institute of Ocean Science and Technology Conference held in Seoul, Korea, May 2012* (2013) 9, available at <http://www.law.berkeley.edu/15589.htm>.

[37] This last reference is probably to the rights enjoyed in the Contiguous Zone and to the hot pursuit right. In this sense, see ibid, 10; and Churchill and Lowe, n 1, 169.

[38] On the due regard obligation, see Beckman and Davenport, n 36, 13.

As a final provision, Article 59, considered one of the most controversial of the convention,[39] seeks to resolve possible conflicts over the attribution of residual rights and jurisdiction within the EEZ not attributed or covered by the LOSC, with reference, at the same time, to equity and to all relevant circumstances.[40] Nevertheless, it does not offer a definite solution to possible conflicts between coastal and third States[41] and it does not call for a presumption in favour of one freedom or power over another. Therefore the interests of coastal States and other States must be constantly weighed and balanced, taking into account also the interests of the international community as a whole, and necessarily, also the applicability of any international obligation incumbent on all States.[42]

3.2 Powers over living resources

The provisions of Part V of the LOSC are primarily concerned with living resources. The coastal State enjoys exclusive sovereign rights over living resources, both on the regulatory level and on the enforcement and judicial level, but is also subject to a number of limitations in exercising these functional powers.[43]

3.2.1 Regulatory regime

According to Articles 61 and 62 of the LOSC, a coastal State that has proclaimed an EEZ, must first determine the total allowable catch (TAC) of living resources for any stock, then its capacity to harvest the living resources for every single stock, and, finally, the proper conservation and management measures necessary to promote the objective of optimum utilization of the living resources of its EEZ. The surplus fisheries can be allocated, through negotiations and agreements, to third

---

[39] See Rothwell and Stephens, n 1, 97; and I Shearer; 'Ocean Management Challenges for the Law of the Sea in the First Decade of the 21st Century' in AG Oude Elferink and DR Rothwell (eds), *Ocean Management in the 21st Century: Institutional Frameworks and Responses* (Martinus Nijhoff Leiden 2004) 10.

[40] See *Virginia Commentaries*, Vol II, 569.

[41] According to some authors, the reference to equity in Art 59 substantially indicates that, in case of a dispute, it is necessary to resort firstly to negotiations and to consensual means of settlement, before referring the dispute to judicial bodies. See Churchill and Lowe, n 1, 176; and Beckman and Davenport, n 36, 12.

[42] R Virzo, 'La convention des Nations Unies sur le droit de la mer et la pollution provenant d'activités militaires dans la zone économique exclusive' in G Andreone, A Caligiuri, and G Cataldi (eds), *Droit de la mer et émergences environnementales* (Editoriale Scientifica Napoli 2012) 255, 257; S Karagiannis, 'L'article 59 de la Convention des Nations Unies sur le droit de la mer' (2004) 37 *Revue Belge de Droit International* 392, 402.

[43] Brown, n 13, Vol 1, 219.

States selected by the coastal State, taking into account relevant factors indicated by the LOSC.[44]

The vagueness of the above-mentioned duties of conservation and of rational allocation of the surplus, in the light of all pertinent provisions of the LOSC and of State practice,[45] leads, however, to the conclusion that the power of management and conservation of EEZ living resources is highly discretionary.[46] This seems to be confirmed by the provisions of Article 297(3) of the LOSC concerning the settlement of disputes, as coastal States are not obliged to submit to settlement a dispute relating to their sovereign rights with respect to the living resources in the EEZ.[47]

Neither the reference to landlocked States (LLS) and geographically disadvantaged States (GDS) as favoured beneficiaries of the possible surplus[48] nor the allocation of the surplus itself to third States correspond to practice and customary law.[49] Coming to the specific legal regime for straddling stocks between one EEZ and another, as well as that regarding highly migratory species, marine mammals, anadromous, and catadromous stocks, Articles 63–67 of the LOSC provide for an ad hoc legal regime regulating rights and duties over those resources, which are by their nature shared by coastal States and maritime States fishing in the high seas. This regulatory system offers only general indications on the allocation of responsibility and on the need for cooperation among concerned States, leaving room for uncertain and conflicting interpretation. This led to the adoption, just one year after the entry into force of the LOSC, of the UN Agreement on Straddling Fish Stocks and Highly Migratory Fish Stocks (FSA), integrating and implementing the related provisions of the LOSC.[50]

The 1995 FSA recognizes a special role for competent regional fisheries management organizations (RFMOs) in respect of its main cooperative goals, thus integrating the LOSC provisions, and consequently partially modifying the possible

---

[44] LOSC, n 3, Art 62(3). The practice of the fisheries agreements concluded by the European Community (EC) in the 1980s and 1990s with both developed and developing States, and the reform of EC external fishing policy in 2000s is enlightening on this regards.

[45] Going through the legislative practice of States in this field, LOSC, Arts 61 and 62 are often considered as mere guidelines for the adoption of domestic laws on the EEZ.

[46] The largest part of the doctrine accepts this interpretation, also supported by the analysis of State practice. See Brown, n 13, Vol 1, 220 and Vignes et al, n 4, 20.

[47] LOSC, n 3, Art 297(3)(c). Moreover, under Annex V, Section 2 of the LOSC, a conciliation procedure is possible only in case of manifest violation of the duty of conservation or in the case of an arbitrary refusal to determine the TAC.

[48] Ibid, Arts 69 and 70; see the discussion in Chapter 15 in this volume.

[49] To date, no agreement admitting landlocked States and the geographically disadvantaged States to fish in the maritime zones of the coastal States has been signed, except few and not relevant cases. See Churchill and Lowe, n 1, 439.

[50] 1995 Agreement for the Implementation of the Provisions of the United Nations Convention on the Law of the Sea of 10 December 1982 relating to the Conservation and Management of Straddling Fish Stocks and Highly Migratory Fish Stocks (FSA).

allocation of rights and duties regarding these species in the high seas.[51] This agreement also favours a leading role of coastal States in the decision making process regarding the management of transboundary resources within RFMOs.[52] On the other hand, according to a combined reading of Articles 3, 6, and 7 of the FSA, the principles of sustainable development and the precautionary approach are to be applied also to the management of living resources within EEZs. To date, participation in the FSA is not as wide as participation in the LOSC, with only 81 ratifying parties (80 States and the EU).[53] Nonetheless, a large number of significant provisions have already been incorporated into many regional fisheries treaties.[54]

3.2.2 *Enforcement powers*

Coming to the enforcing and coercive powers of the coastal State, Article 73 of the LOSC provides for a broad range of measures, including boarding, inspection, arrest, and judicial proceedings, that can be adopted on foreign vessels in the exercise of the sovereign rights of the coastal State over living resources.

As a counterbalance to those wide enforcement powers, it is expressly provided that, when a foreign vessel is detained, its flag State must be notified immediately and the vessel and crew 'promptly released upon the posting of reasonable bond or other security'. Moreover, it is specified that the penalties, which the coastal State may impose in case of violation of its regulations, may not include 'imprisonment, in the absence of agreements to the contrary by the States concerned, or any other form of corporal punishment'.[55]

Within this context, it becomes crucial to define the activities that are associated with the exploitation of living resources, and thus those which are covered by the afore-described regulatory regime. Indeed, State practice shows a tendency to apply the coercive measures of Article 73 even to foreign vessels engaged in activities other than fishing, but apparently connected with it.

---

[51] On the distribution of fishing rights, see T Henriksen and A H Hoel, 'Determining allocation: from paper practice in the distribution of fishing rights between countries' (2011) 42 *Ocean Development and International Law* 66.

[52] On the role and the influence of coastal States on the management of transboundary living resources in the high seas, through the participation to RFMOs, see G Andreone, 'Fisheries in the Antarctic and in the Arctic' in G Tamburelli (ed), *The Antarctic Legal System: The Protection of the Environment of the Polar Regions* (Giuffrè Milano 2008) 71, 92; and C Cinelli, *El Ártico ante el derecho del mar contemporáneo* (Tirant lo Blanch Valencia 2012) 272.

[53] DOALOS, n 18.

[54] On the current status of the agreement and on the reasons of the slow ratifications process, see EJ Molenaar, 'Non-Participation in the Fish Stocks Agreement: Status and Reasons' (2011) 26 *International Journal of Marine and Coastal Law* 195.

[55] Notwithstanding this prohibition, many States, most of them having ratified the LOSC, provide in their legislation for imprisonment, even in the absence of agreements with other States. See Rothwell and Stephens, n 1, 429.

This debatable practice has been widely discussed before the International Tribunal for the Law of the Sea (ITLOS) in several cases, since the well-known *M/V 'Saiga'* case, relating to the prompt release of foreign tankers seized while refuelling vessels illegally fishing inside the EEZ of another State (so-called offshore bunkering).[56] Thus, in the *M/V 'Virginia G'* case, Panama called upon ITLOS to rule on a damages claim for the interception, arrest, and detention of the Panamanian flagged oil tanker M/V *'Virginia G'* and its crew by the Guinea Bissau authorities while the tanker was carrying out the supplying of fuel to four foreign vessels fishing illegally inside Guinea Bissau's EEZ.[57] The Tribunal, while finding lawful both the regulation of bunkering of foreign fishing vessels and the related enforcement measures, namely the boarding, the inspection, and the arrest, recognized the violation of Article 73(1) and (4) of the LOSC by Guinea Bissau for having confiscated the vessel and its cargo and for not having notified the flag State of its enforcement measures. Thus, in principle, ITLOS stated the lawfulness of the Guinea Bissau enforcement action, but it specified that, in applying coercive measures, due regard must be paid by the State to the particular circumstances of the case and the gravity of the violation, according to the principle of reasonableness.[58]

Looking at the interpretation of the Article 73(2) prompt-release procedures, ITLOS has adopted a restrictive attitude since *The 'Volga'* case [59] regarding the concept of 'reasonable bond and security' that must be posted by the flag State on the release of the seized vessel by the coastal State. Indeed, despite the broad interpretation of the concept of reasonable bond adopted by coastal States, ITLOS has always assumed a position in favour of flag State interests, even much more so than that taken by the European Court of Human Rights (ECtHR) in the *Mangouras v Spain* case in 2010.[60]

---

[56] The possible inclusion of bunkering among the domains on which the coastal State can lawfully legislate has been questioned for the first time before the ITLOS in the *M/V 'Saiga' (No 1) (Saint Vincent and the Grenadines v Guinea)* (Judgment) (Prompt Release) [1997] 110 ILR 736 and *M/V 'Saiga' (No 2) (Saint Vincent and the Grenadines v Guinea)* (Judgment) [1999] ITLOS Rep 10.

[57] *M/V 'Virginia G' (Panama v Guinea-Bissau)*, Judgment of the International Tribunal for the Law of the Sea, Case No 19 (14 April 2014), available at <http://www.itlos.org/fileadmin/itlos/documents/cases/case_no.19/judgment/C19-Judgment_14.04.14_corr.pdf>.

[58] Ibid, 270.

[59] *The 'Volga' (Russian Federation v Australia)* (Judgment) (Prompt Release) (2002) ITLOS Rep 10. See W Gullett, 'Prompt Release Procedures and the Challenge for Fisheries Law Enforcement: The Judgement of the International Tribunal for the Law of the Sea in the *Volga* Case (*Russian Federation v Australia*)' (2003) 31 *Federal Law Review* 395.

[60] In *Mangouras v Spain* (Application No 12050/04, [2010] ECHR 1364), the Grand Chamber of the ECtHR confirmed that no violation of Art 5(3) of the European Convention of Human Rights could be ascribed to Spanish courts for having fixed a bail of EUR 3,000,000 upon the release of Captain Mangouras, master of the ship Prestige. The court, with a cross reference to the ITLOS jurisprudence, affirmed that: In view of... the disastrous environmental and economic consequences of the oil spill, the [Spanish] courts were justified in taking into account the seriousness of the offences in question and the amount of the loss imputed to the applicant.

3.3 Powers over non-living resources and over all other economic resources

The power of the coastal State to exploit and conserve living and non-living resources of the seabed and subsoil, envisaged by Article 56(1)(a), overlaps with the power over the resources of the continental shelf and is regulated by the provisions of Part VI of the LOSC. Although the continental shelf regime is beyond the scope of this chapter, a number of interesting differences in the regulation of the seabed living resources (sedentary species) can be outlined.[61]

First of all, sedentary species are excluded from the application of the EEZ fisheries legal regime and are regulated under the continental shelf legal regime.[62] Secondly, the sovereign rights of the coastal State within 200 nm exist *ipso jure* and are expressly 'exclusive' and not limited by any duty of conservation and rational exploitation for the benefit of the international community.[63]

Lastly, notwithstanding the broad scope of the coastal States' sovereign rights, no specific enforcement powers are expressly envisaged, as in the case of those provided for fishing activities in Article 73.[64] Despite a tendency of coastal States to exercise full enforcement and judicial powers, the legitimate extent of such coastal State measures remains questionable.[65]

Similar perplexities arise in reading the pertinent provisions of the LOSC which recognize a coastal State 'sovereign rights... with regard to other activities for the economic exploitation and exploration of the zone, such as the production of

---

See T Treves, 'Cross-fertilization between Different International Courts and Tribunals: The *Mangouras* Case' in H Hestermeyer et al (eds), *Coexistence, Cooperation and Solidarity*: Liber Amicorum *Rüdiger Wolfrum* (Martinus Nijhoff Leiden 2012) Vol 2, 1787.

[61] LOSC, n 3, Art 77(4) specifies that the natural resources referred to in Part VI, devoted to continental shelf, are the mineral and other non-living resources of the seabed and subsoil together with living organisms belonging to sedentary species, organisms which are immobile on or under the seabed or are unable to move except in constant physical contact with the seabed or the subsoil; see discussion in Chapter 9 in this volume.

[62] LOSC, n 3, Art 68 provides explicitly that Part V, devoted to the EEZ, does not apply to sedentary species as defined in Art 77(4).

[63] See Rothwell and Stephens, n 1, 89; DM Ong, 'Towards and International Law for Conservation of Offshore Hydrocarbon Resources within the Continental Shelf' in D Freestone, R Barnes, and DM Ong (eds), *The Law of the Sea: Progress and Prospects* (Oxford University Press Oxford 2006) 93.

[64] Some doubts have arisen concerning the kind and limits of the coastal State coercive measure concerning extraction of minerals from the column of water. See Brown, n 13, Vol 1, 220.

[65] In this sense the attitude of Australian maritime officers in the case *Muslimin v The Queen* (2010) 240 CLR 470 is typical. The High Court excluded fisheries protection measures contained in the Fisheries Management Act 1991 (Cth) (FMA) from application to foreign vessels, navigating outside the Australian Fisheries Zone (but over its continental shelf), and equipped with nets, traps, or other equipment compatible with sedentary species fishing. Nevertheless, the case shows an extensive enforcement practice by the coastal State authorities. For a commentary of the decision, see G Andreone, 'Chronique de la jurisprudence' (2010) 15 *Annuaire du Droit de la Mer* 570.

energy from the water, currents and winds'.[66] This formulation seems to guarantee the coastal State full and exclusive rights over all economic resources, as well as over yet unknown activities that may develop as a result of technological advances. This general attribution of sovereign rights is not, however, followed by specific regulations and enforcement powers.

Activities related to the production of energy from the water, currents, and winds imply many different industrial sector activities that may be implemented at sea, which can therefore be regulated in a number of ways.[67] State practice concerning the exploitation of marine energy shows a lack of adequate knowledge about all the possible conflicts that may arise between the exercise of those activities and the freedoms enjoyed within the EEZ and even relating to the environmental impact of those activities.[68]

Diverse effects can arise from wave and tidal energy plants and offshore wind farms, particularly as the latter affect the surface of the water and the superjacent airspace, while the former involve only the water column or the seabed. Limitations to coastal State rights can be inferred from the general guarantee of the freedom of the high seas, and from the express regulation of connected activities, such as the construction of artificial islands and installations.

3.4 Construction of artificial islands and installations

Coastal State jurisdictional rights on the establishment and use of artificial islands, installations, and structures are regulated by Article 60. The legal regime envisaged by this provision is then applied, *mutatis mutandis*, to the continental shelf in accordance with the requirements of Article 80. The rights of the coastal State relating to islands and installations within the EEZ and the continental shelf are similar, with the sole difference that in this latter zone they are far more limited,[69] since within the EEZ such islands and structures can be legitimately constructed and used for many other purposes, such as the exploitation of renewable energy.

According to Article 60, an almost total exclusivity is accorded to the coastal State to authorize and regulate various kinds of offshore construction, their placement, and their use within the EEZ. The distinction between artificial islands, installations, and structures for all the authorized economic purposes expressly provided for in Article 56 and 'installations and structures which may interfere with the exercise of the rights of the coastal States in the zone' is rather vague and often not

---

[66] LOSC, n 3, Art 56(1)(a).

[67] KN Scott, 'Tilting at Offshore Windmills: Regulating Wind Farm Development within the Renewable Energy Zone' (2006) 18 *Journal of Environmental Law* 89.

[68] D Leary and M Esteban, 'Recent Developments in Offshore Renewable Energy in the Asia-Pacific Region' (2011) 42 *Ocean Development and International Law* 94, 111.

[69] See Churchill and Lowe, n 1, 168.

reproduced in national legislation,[70] but it seems to admit, in principle, the placement of such constructions by third States, as not interfering with coastal States rights.[71]

The legal regime provided by Article 60 is identical for all these types of construction, in relation both to rights and to duties. It is expressly provided that the coastal State can exercise on those constructions exclusive jurisdiction with respect to customs, tax, health, safety, and immigration.[72] Moreover, the coastal State has the right to establish safety zones around those constructions, with the aim of ensuring safer navigation or protection of the construction itself, to an extent fixed by the coastal State and not exceeding a radius of 500 metres around the construction.[73]

Coming to the duties, the coastal State is obliged to keep third States continuously informed about the placement of those constructions, as well as their falling into disuse, and also regarding all relevant technical aspects in order to ensure the safety of navigation. Towards this end, Article 60(3) specifically requires dismantlement according to general international standards established by international organizations, taking into account other possible implications concerning fisheries, protection of the marine environment, or other rights and duties of third States.

Inevitably, the exercise of exclusive jurisdiction over those spaces implies an assumption of responsibility of the coastal State over all the activities and the events occurring on them.[74] The features of artificial constructions at sea, as well as their legal implications, vary dramatically according to their characteristics and to the function to which they are destined. An interesting example regards the competence of coastal States regarding fish aggregating devices (FAD),[75] which are platforms of bamboo or other

---

[70] For national legislation not distinguishing among the different types of constructions, see Churchill and Lowe, n 1, 168; and S Kopela, 'The "Territorialisation" of the Exclusive Economic Zone: Implications for Maritime Jurisdiction', International Boundary Research Unit on 'The State of Sovereignty', 20th Anniversary Conference, Durham UK (1–3 April 2009) 6, available at <www.dur.ac.uk/resources/ibru/conferences/sos/s_kopela_paper.pdf>.

[71] On this point, see Brown, n 13, Vol 1, 243–4. The author argues that the construction of those installations by third States could be for military purposes.

[72] LOSC, n 3, Art 60(2).

[73] Ibid, Art 60(4) and (5). Article 60(5) also provides for an eventual extension of the safety zone breadth if authorized by generally accepted international standards or as recommended by the competent international organization. Nevertheless, to date, the IMO never accepted the proposals to agree on more extended safety zones. See A Harel, 'Preventing Terrorist Attacks on Offshore Platforms: Do States Have Sufficient Legal Tools?' (2012) 4 *Harvard National Security Journal* 131.

[74] In this context, the position of the Court of Justice of the European Union (CJEU) is worth noting. The Court stated that, according to LOSC, Arts 77, 60, and 80, an EU Member State has sovereignty (albeit functional and limited sovereignty) over the continental shelf adjacent to it and exclusive jurisdiction over the artificial islands and installations positioned on it. As a consequence, the 'work carried out on these fixed or floating installations ... is to be regarded as work carried out in the territory of that State for the purposes of applying EU law' and in particular EU law provisions designed to ensure the freedom of movement of persons: *A Salemink v Raad van bestuur van het Uitvoeringsinstituut werknemersverzekeringen* (C-347/10, CJEU, 17 January 2012) [33]–[35].

[75] They are used mainly in the Pacific and Indian Oceans. In the latter, the use of drifting fish aggregating devices is increasing and furthering calls for greater implementation of their management and

material anchored in the water to attract tuna, falls under Article 60 which regulates artificial installations.[76]

Looking, then, at oil, gas, or renewable energy platforms, the extent of the enforcement powers of coastal States over these items has recently caused concern and, in particular, the matters of their protection and of their environmental impact are likely to lead to significant developments in the EEZ legal regime. The major and irreparable damage to the environment, which occurred in the case of the 2010 explosion of the British Petroleum *Deepwater Horizon* platform in the Gulf of Mexico, drew attention to the particular vulnerability of such installations, including the possibility of terrorist attacks.[77]

Then, the 2013 seizure of the Greenpeace vessel *M/V Arctic Sunrise*, and of the activists protesting against Gazprom's oil platform in the Russian Arctic EEZ, raised a number of questions about the extent of coastal State enforcement powers to protect offshore platforms.[78] Indeed, upon the Netherlands request for provisional measures as the flag State of the *M/V Arctic Sunrise*, ITLOS ordered that the *Arctic Sunrise* and all detained persons be released,[79] but did not rule on the merits of the dispute between the Netherlands and Russia or on the lawfulness of the seizure and detention of the vessel and of the 30 volunteers, most of whom were arrested on board the *Arctic Sunrise* outside the 500-metre safety zone established by Russia around its platform.[80]

3.5 Marine scientific research

The jurisdictional rights of the coastal State for marine scientific research are established in Article 56 (b), but are set out in detail in Part XIII of the LOSC.[81] In the

---

sustainability. See T Davies, CC Mees, and EJ Milner-Gulland, 'The Past, Present and Future Use of Drifting Aggregating Devices (FADs) in the Indian Ocean' (2014) 45 *Marine Policy* 45.

[76] See Brown, n 13, Vol 1, 234. The author is in favour of defining them as installations or structures with the related attribution of duties to the coastal State.

[77] Harel, n 73, 131; S Kaye, 'Threats from the Global Commons: Problems of Jurisdiction and Enforcement' (2007) 8(1) *Melbourne Journal of International Law* 8.

[78] A Oude Elferink, 'The *Arctic Sunrise* Incident: A Multi-faceted Law of the Sea Case with a Human Rights Dimension' (2014) 29 *International Journal of Marine and Coastal Law* 250, 256.

[79] 'Artic Sunrise' Case (Netherlands v Russian Federation) Order of the International Tribunal for the Law of the Sea, Case No 22 (22 November 2013).

[80] According to Art 16 of the Federal Law on Continental Shelf, adopted on 25 October 1995, the Russian Federation established safety zones around its installations extended for not more than 500 metres. The English version of the Law text is available at <www.un.org/depts/los/LEGISLATIONANDTREATIES/PDFFILES/RUS_1995_Law.pdf>. It has to be recalled that the Russian Federation's Coast Guard communicated over the radio to the M/V Arctic Sunrise that it was not permitted to enter in a radius of 3 nm around the platform, but the Greenpeace vessel did it. On the irrelevance of the excessive Russian claim to a 3 nm zone, see Oude Elferink, n 78, 250, and 256.

[81] On the regime of marine scientific research, see A Soons, *Marine Scientific Research and the Law of the Sea* (Kluwer Law The Netherlands 1982).

absence of a definition of 'scientific research', the LOSC provides for the need of the explicit consent of the coastal State for research projects proposed by other States or international organizations within the EEZ independently of whether they are 'pure' or 'applied' research, the latter being destined to industrial and commercial purposes.[82]

Only general support for marine research aimed at peaceful purposes and at increasing scientific knowledge for the benefit of all mankind is included in Article 246, introducing a form of moral duty on the part of the coastal State to not unreasonably delay or deny its consent to this kind of research. Nevertheless, consent can be denied in a broad-spectrum of cases provided for by Article 246(5), according to the discretional evaluation of the coastal State,[83] thus producing controversial interpretations regarding research projects which involve commercialization of resources or installation and use of floating deployments or ocean upwelling pipes.

As an example, the activity of bioprospecting, which consists in gathering samples of resources for applied research purposes or for genetic manipulation, has increased dramatically in the high seas as well as within the EEZ or on the continental shelf of other States, thus giving rise to a number of unresolved legal disputes. Indeed, this technological exploitation of living resources, not foreseen by the LOSC, has no autonomous legal regime.[84] It cannot be considered solely as scientific research or a fishery activity, since it has characteristics of both. In either case, it remains doubtful whether the economic exploitation of these resources is connected principally with applied technological research, with all its related consequences regarding property rights, or whether it is more closely linked with, and a consequence of, the special value of the marine resource itself, taken as a single sample in a rare ecosystem.

A number of disagreements also arise from scientific research projects that imply the installation and use of equipment not fixed to the ocean floor or from research activities that can be connected to military interests, such as hydrographic surveying. The Argo Profiling Float Deployment, completed in 2007 under the auspices of several international organizations, is one significant example aimed at monitoring ocean signals related to climate change, thanks to the

---

[82] A lost occasion for defining 'scientific research' was the judgment of the ICJ in *Whaling in the Antarctic (Australia v Japan: New Zealand Intervening)* Judgment of the International Court of Justice, General List No 148 (31 March 2014), available at <http://www.icj-cij.org/docket/files/148/18136.pdf>. Indeed, the Court refrained from intervening on the meaning and the limits of marine scientific research. See JJP Smith, 'A Double-edged Harpoon: The Trial of Science in the Antarctic Whaling Case before the International Court of Justice' (2014) *Ocean Yearbook* 28; and E Doussis, 'Sauver les baleines contre les baleiniers: coup de projecteur sur l'arrêt de la CIJ du 31 mars 2014' (2013) 18 *Annuaire de Droit de la Mer* 175.

[83] See Rothwell and Stephens, n 1, 328.

[84] On the matter of access to marine genetic resources, see D Farrier and L Tucker, 'Access to Marine Bioresources: Hitching the Conservation Cart to the Bioprospecting Horse' (2001) 32 *Ocean Development and International Law* 213.

deployment in the high seas of more than 3,200 free-floating devices collecting a wide array of scientific data. However, those floating devices originally deployed in the high seas may drift into EEZs and thus also collect data related to this zone that could be useful to identify the position of fish stocks or other information concerning valuable natural resources.[85] Thus, a legal debate on whether the deployment of the floating devices should require the prior consent of the coastal State potentially affected by them led, in June 2008, to the adoption of the Guidelines for the Legal Regulation of the Argo Profiling Float Deployments on the High Seas.[86]

Similarly, ocean upwelling pipes, used for climate engineering through intervention in the global carbon cycle, can support both pure research and resource focused research and thus it can be difficult to foresee exactly and to control the use and the scope of this equipment.[87] In this context, it appears necessary to enhance multilateral cooperation in order to ensure a clearer interpretation and implementation of the pertinent LOSC provisions.[88]

State practice also shows a rise in the number of disputes relating to the classification of hydrographic surveying and intelligence gathering as pure or applied research, since they normally serve the goal of improving the safety of navigation, but can also be performed for military purposes.[89] Many national statutes do not distinguish between the different possible purposes of marine research and require coastal State consent for any kind of scientific project. The case of the interruption of the navigation of the US surveillance ship USNS *'Impeccable'* by the Chinese authorities in the South China Sea, highlights a major conflict between some coastal States, such as China and India, and maritime powers, such as the USA, on the interpretation of coastal State powers to restrict navigation and scientific research within the EEZ.[90]

---

[85] A Mateos and M Gorina-Ysern, 'Climate Change Guidelines for Argo Profiling Float Deployment on the High Seas' (8 April 2010) 14(8) *American Society of International Law* Insights, available at <http://www.asil.org/insights/volume/14/issue/8/climate-change-and-guidelines-argo-profiling-float-deployment-high-seas>.

[86] UNESCO Intergovernmental Oceanographic Commission, Executive Council Resolution EC-XLI.4 (30 June 2008).

[87] A Proelss and C Hong, 'Ocean Upwelling and International Law' (2012) 43 *Ocean Development and International Law* 371.

[88] Mateos and Gorina-Ysern, n 85.

[89] S Bateman, 'Hydrographic Surveying in the EEZ: Differences and Overlaps with MSR' (2005) 29 *Marine Policy* 171.

[90] The reference is to the Chinese-US dispute on US naval activities in the Chinese EEZ. See JR Crook, 'Contemporary Practice of the United States Relating to International Law: United States Protests Chinese Interference with U.S. Naval Vessel, Vows Continued Operations' (2009) 103 *American Journal of International Law* 349.

3.6 Environmental protection

As already mentioned, Article 56 recognizes the jurisdiction of coastal States with regard to the protection of the marine environment within the EEZ, but the provisions of Part XII of the LOSC do not grant coastal States exclusive and extensive rights in this field, but rather selected and specific powers, tailored according to the various types of pollutants under consideration: pollution from seabed activities, from installations and other devices, from dumping, or directly from vessels. For each of these types of pollution, except pollution from vessels, coastal States enjoy wide regulatory and enforcement powers, since the related activities are subject to their previous consent and are not limited by international standards.

By contrast, with respect to ship source pollution, coastal States cannot adopt domestic laws or regulations containing environmental protection measures that are less effective than generally accepted international laws or regulations, adopted by the competent international organizations, namely the International Maritime Organization (IMO)[91] and, for the most part, should not go beyond those international standards. The duty to respect the minimum international standards of environmental protection represents a form of limitation on the power of the coastal State to protect more strictly its EEZ environment.

Turning to the enforcement and judiciary powers of the coastal States, the provisions of Part XII, state a clear preference for the competence of the flag State to judge its vessel in cases of pollution violations within the EEZ of another State. Only in the case of clear proof of substantial discharge causing or threatening significant pollution, can the coastal State go beyond a simple request for information, and inspect the foreign vessel, with the *extrema ratio* of ordering the detention of the vessel and the institution of related judicial proceedings.[92] In this latter case, the flag State of the suspected polluting vessel can decide, within six months of the date on which proceedings were first instituted, to commence proceedings against the detaining ship in concomitance with the coastal State's judicial action. If this occurs, the coastal State has first to suspend and, then, if the 'proceedings instituted by the flag State have been brought to a conclusion', to terminate its judicial action against the vessel. The coastal State can continue its proceedings against the foreign vessel, only in the case of major damage or if the flag State in question has repeatedly disregarded its obligation to effectively enforce the applicable international standards.[93]

These limits of coastal State environmental powers came to light in the '*Fast Independence*' and '*Trans Arctic*' cases, decided by the French High Court in 2009. The Court, giving express application to Article 228, maintained that French criminal proceedings to prosecute illegal discharges within the French EEZ, carried out by two foreign vessels, had to be terminated since proceedings had been instituted by the flag States: Malta and Norway respectively. This was the case without it being

---

[91] LOSC, n 3, Art 211(5). [92] Ibid, Art 220(5) and (6). [93] Ibid, Art 228(1).

necessary to ascertain whether the polluting vessels had been found guilty or not, and independently of the amount of the fine, if any, imposed by each flag State.[94]

These decisions, on one hand, favour freedom of navigation and the predominance of flag State jurisdiction, but, on the other, highlight the weakness of the coastal State's enforcement action and its capacity to represent a deterrent to these pollution violations.[95]

4 Other States Rights and Obligations

There are two main freedoms still existing within the EEZ: navigation and overflight, on one hand, and the laying of submarine cables and pipelines, on the other. It is clear that freedom of navigation and overflight cannot have an identical spectrum of application within the EEZ as in the high seas, because of the several limitations inherent in the EEZ regime. Consequently, the degree of freedom of navigation and overflight[96] accorded to other States is inversely proportional to the intention of the coastal State to take an active part in the environmental protection of its EEZ, or to its engagement in intensive exploitation of living and/or non-living resources, and of all other resources which imply the placing of installations interfering with minor routes of international navigation.[97]

Having said this, it is also necessary to underline that all States are subject to a number of general obligations provided for by the LOSC, not directly connected to coastal State rights or to the exercise of jurisdiction of the latter. Mainly, those obligations refer to the generally recognized international standard of environmental protection such as those under Article 211(2), and imply the direct exercise of flag State jurisdiction over all kinds of vessels potentially involved in EEZ or high

---

[94] *'Fast Independence'* and *'Trans Arctic' Cases*, Cour de cassation [French Court of Cassation], 07-87362, 07-87931, 5 May 2009, reported in (2009) Bull Crim No 85. See G Andreone, 'Chronique de la jurisprudence' (2009) 14 *Annuaire du Droit de la Mer* 568; and JP Cot, 'International Decision' (2010) 104 *American Journal of International Law* 265.

[95] Nevertheless, this case represents only a part of the significant number of French courts decisions imposing high fines on pollutant foreign vessels. See the *Erika Case*, Cour de cassation [French Court of Cassation], No 3439, 25 September 2012. For a commentary, see G Andreone, 'Chronique de la jurisprudence' (2012) 17 *Annuaire du Droit de la Mer* 639.

[96] Also aircraft can be subject to restrictions regarding, as an example the dumping of wastes, which can be addressed in coastal State legislation or in binding treaties.

[97] LOSC, n 3, Art 60(7), indeed exclude that the placement of such construction can interfere 'with use of recognised sea lanes essential to international navigation'.

seas pollution. Also, restrictions upon the navigation of foreign vessels transporting ultra-hazardous cargoes have proved highly controversial, since a number of coastal States have introduced into their domestic laws the requirement of prior consent of the State for the navigation of this kind of vessel within their EEZs.[98]

As mentioned above, some normative and enforcement measures of coastal States, restricting the navigation of foreign warships and military manoeuvres in their EEZ, have raised a number of unsolved conflicts. Finally, a more specific limitation to the freedom to lay pipelines—but not cables—is envisaged in Article 79(3), which provides for the requirement of the consent of the coastal State in respect of the delineation of the course of the placement of the pipeline. Thus, it has been questioned whether the laying of submarine pipelines has been rightly classified among the freedoms enjoyed by other States within the EEZ,[99] since prior consent to the delineation of the course can be easily seen as a discretional power of the coastal State to concede this right to the third State.

5 The Future of the EEZ

As noted above, the likelihood of conflict in the attribution of rights and competences within the EEZ remains very high. There is no doubt, therefore, that the EEZ is to be seen as a concept in a state of permanent flux. In the multiform context of the LOSC and related State practice, different types of creeping jurisdiction can be found.[100]

Looking at creeping coastal State jurisdiction, the classic distinction is between the pressure toward spatial extension of national jurisdiction beyond 200 nm and claims for powers not foreseen by the LOSC, based on an extensive interpretation of implicit powers concerning fishing, the protection of the marine environment, and any resource-related functions of the EEZ.[101] Since the maximum limit of 200 nm has proved so far to be resistant to coastal State pressure, attention is being paid only to some individual attempts at creeping jurisdiction within the maximum spatial limit.

---

[98] JM Van Dyke, 'The Disappearing Right to Navigational Freedom in the EEZ' (2005) 29 *Marine Policy* 107.

[99] Churchill and Lowe, n 1, 174.

[100] The distinction between creeping coastal State jurisdiction and 'creeping common heritage' has been suggested by E Franckx, 'The 200-mile Limit: Between Creeping Jurisdiction and Creeping Common Heritage?' (2007) 39 *George Washington International Law Review* 467, 485.

[101] B Kwiatkowska, 'Creeping Jurisdiction beyond 200 Nautical Miles in the Light of the Law of the Sea Convention and State Practice' (1991) 22 *Ocean Development and International Law* 159.

As far as the fisheries legal regime of the EEZ is concerned, a number of controversial issues emerge from international practice. First, as has been remarked, there is a tendency on the part of coastal States to expand their powers or their influence over activities not strictly connected with fisheries. Second, the exact extent of the coastal State duty of conservation of its EEZ living resources is still uncertain. Finally, against this wide background of uncertainty, arising from the LOSC provisions, including Article 59, there is a general tendency on the part of both coastal and maritime States to refrain from referring to international tribunals doubtful and controversial interpretations of their LOSC obligations.[102] Accordingly, the 2013 request to ITLOS for an advisory opinion concerning the extent of the obligations of flag States and the rights and duties of coastal States with regard to illegal, unreported, and unregulated (IUU) fishing conducted within the EEZ, represents an important step forward in terms of utilizing the advisory competence of the Tribunal and of ascertaining contested issues related to IUU fishing within the EEZ.[103] In this respect, the 2014 ITLOS judgment in the *'Virginia G'* case is also to be welcomed for its contribution to the definition of activities related to fisheries.

Coming, then, to the freedom of navigation within the EEZ, many attempts to restrict this freedom for security or environmental reasons emerge from State practice.[104] Recently, the protection of the marine environment is one of the principal motives of the navigational restrictions upon foreign vessels.[105] Often, these claims, being originally unilateral, are, at a later stage, accepted and adopted by the IMO, thus becoming generally accepted.[106]

Some authors state that a new norm of customary international law is emerging from this State practice, allowing restrictions on navigation within the EEZ based on the nature of the ship and its cargo.[107] Nevertheless, until now, this coastal State

---

[102] In this sense the *Estai* dispute between Spain and Canada before the International Court of Justice and the dispute between Chile and European Union brought before the ITLOS and the OMC Dispute Settlement Body have been lost opportunities for clarifying several aspects of the transboundary stocks legal regime within the EEZ and in the High Sea.

[103] The advisory request was submitted by the Sub-regional Fisheries Commission (SFFC) on the 28 March 2013.

[104] The legislation of a number of coastal States contains restrictions, and sometimes interdictions, against the navigation or military manoeuvres of foreign warships in order to protect national security interests. See Churchill and Lowe, n 1, 171–2; Kopela, n 70, 4–5.

[105] EU policy on marine environmental protection has been frequently questioned as not being in compliance with the freedom of navigation. See B Oxman, 'The Territorial Temptation: A Siren Song at Sea' (2006) 100 *American Journal of International Law* 830, 839.

[106] A recent example is the amendment of the 1973 International Convention for the Prevention of Pollution from Ships (MARPOL) to including the designation of specific portions of US, Canadian, and French waters as an Emission Control Area in order to reduce air pollution from ships. The IMO adopted the amendments to Annex VI of the MARPOL on the proposal of the concerned coastal State: JR Crook, 'Contemporary Practice of the United States Relating to International Law: International Maritime Organization Approves US-Canadian Proposal for Strengthened Controls in Air Pollution from Ships in North American Waters' (2010) 104 *American Journal of International Law* 287.

[107] See, for all, Van Dyke, n 98, 121.

practice has been, in almost all cases, disputed by other maritime powers.[108] As a consequence, it cannot be considered sufficiently 'constant, uniform, and accepted as law' to warrant the formation of an international customary rule.

In this context, the majority of authors still have great confidence in the ability of the LOSC to cope with new challenges, to solve conflicts, and settle disputes in order to overcome tensions between opposing interests within the EEZ.[109]

Today, the emergence of collective environmental and security needs and the on-going changes in the structure of the international community inevitably call for fostering new forms of cooperative dialogue among States, non-State actors, and individuals regarding the rights and duties to be applied within the EEZ. In this context, it would not be considered contrary to the spirit of the LOSC to transform the 'freedoms of the sea' into a more specific regulatory regime of the rights of third States, through general or regional conventions implementing the LOSC provisions. The feared 'territorialization' of the EEZ has not yet happened, though it still remains a possible scenario for the future.[110]

---

[108] See, Kopela, n 70, 3.

[109] See T Stephens and DR Rothwell, 'The LOSC Framework for Maritime Jurisdiction and Enforcement 30 Years On' in D Freestone (ed), *The 1982 Law of the Sea Convention at 30: Successes, Challenges and New Agendas* (Martinus Nijhoff The Hague 2013) 35. As an example, the dispute settlement system, which is directly aimed at solving many disputes arising from the EEZ provisions, is evidently misused, and as a suggestion it is proposed to increase the recourse to the advisory function of the ITLOS. See Beckman and Davenport, n 36, 39–40.

[110] See, Oxman, n 105, 839; Kopela, n 70, 3.

9

THE CONTINENTAL SHELF

TED L MCDORMAN

1 INTRODUCTION

An interesting aspect of the international legal regime of the continental shelf is where, in a physical or geographic sense, does the legal regime apply?* This question makes the legal regime of the continental shelf different from the territorial sea regime, which applies to the water column and seafloor out to 12 nautical miles (nm) from a coastal State's baselines and the regime of the exclusive economic zone (EEZ), which applies to the marine resources within the water column and seafloor beyond the territorial sea out to 200 nm from a coastal State's baselines.

---

* Various sections of this chapter are drawn, with modification, from the following: TL McDorman, 'The Continental Shelf Regime in the 1982 Law of the Sea Convention: A Reflection on the First Thirty Years' (2012) 27 *International Journal of Marine and Coastal Law* 743; TL McDorman, 'The Continental Shelf beyond 200 nm: A First Look at the *Bay of Bengal (Bangladesh/Myanmar) Case*' in MH Nordquist, JN Moore, A Chircop, and R Long (eds), *The Regulation of Continental Shelf Development: Rethinking International Standards* (Martinus Nijhoff Leiden 2013) 89; TL McDorman, 'Rights and Jurisdiction over Resources in the South China Sea: UNCLOS and the "Seven Dashed Line"' in S Jayakumar, T Koh, and Beckman (eds), *The South China Dispute and Law of the Sea* (Edward Elgar Northampton 2014) 144; and TL McDorman, 'The Continental Shelf beyond 200 nm: Law and Politics in the Arctic Ocean' (2009) 18 *Journal of Transnational Law* 155.

For many States, the location of all or part of their adjacent continental shelf is certain as a result of bilateral agreements with neighbouring States or, as set out in Article 76(1) of the UN Convention on the Law of the Sea (LOSC), a State's legal continental shelf ends at the 200 nm limit.[1] For an ever-increasing number of States, however, it is apparent that all or part of their legal continental shelf extends well beyond 200 nm, with it not being immediately obvious where the outer limit of a State's legal shelf is located. At least 80 States were of the view that they had a legal continental shelf beyond 200 nm.[2] While this will be explained below, the difference between a coastal State whose legal shelf is confined to 200 nm and a State that has a legal shelf beyond 200 nm is based upon the physical attributes of the seafloor within and beyond 200 nm.

The 'legal' continental shelf has to be disconnected from the continental shelf that is a well-known physical feature of the seafloor. The continental margin is the physical extension of the landmass of the coastal State with the margin composed of the continental shelf (a platform at relatively shallow depths), the continental slope (the break of the platform towards the deep ocean floor), and the continental rise (the area beyond the slope which merges with the deep ocean floor).

Irrespective of the existence of a physical continental margin, a coastal State has rights to a continental shelf out to 200 nm and a State's legal continental shelf extends beyond 200 nm where the physical continental margin extends beyond 200 nm. The above is set out in Article 76(1) and (3) of the LOSC:

1. The continental shelf of a coastal State comprises the seabed and subsoil of the submarine areas that extend beyond its territorial sea throughout the natural prolongation of its land territory to the outer edge of the continental margin or to a distance of 200 nautical miles from the baselines from which the breadth of the territorial sea is measured where the outer edge of the continental margin does not extend up to that distance.

...

3. The continental margin comprises the submerged prolongation of the land mass of the coastal State, and consists of the seabed and subsoil of the shelf, the slope and the rise.

This chapter will proceed by providing a brief history of the legal regime of the continental shelf, a review of the core rights and obligations of the legal regime, a detailed explanation of the rules and procedures regarding the determination by a State of its continental shelf outer limit beyond 200 nm, and a few words on the relationship between the shelf regime and the 200 nm EEZ.

---

[1] 1982 United Nations Convention on the Law of the Sea (hereinafter LOSC).
[2] See Section 4.3.3 below.

2 History

The development of the legal regime of the continental shelf was directly tied to the potential for oil and gas in the seafloor area adjacent to States. The first international instrument dealing with the continental shelf, albeit using the phrase 'submarine areas' and 'sea-bed and sub-soil' outside territorial waters, was the 1942 Treaty between the United Kingdom and Venezuela respecting the Gulf of Paria.[3] At issue was the division of oil fields between Venezuela and Trinidad. The 1945 US Truman Proclamation on the Continental Shelf, more regularly associated with the commencement of the continental shelf legal regime, was explicitly tied to asserting exclusive US authority over hydrocarbon activity in the continental margin adjacent to the United States, most particularly in the Gulf of Mexico.[4]

Fisheries have also had a relationship with the continental shelf, though more as an afterthought. The continental shelf had been discussed prior to the 1940s in the context of fisheries.[5] Sedentary fisheries beyond territorial waters had been dealt with by treaty as early as 1839,[6] and it was lobster that were at stake in the 1909 Norway/Sweden *Grisbadarna Arbitration*.[7] In 1953, Australia's continental shelf claim was made 'with a view to exercising exclusive authority over sedentary fisheries',[8] rather than as regards concerns over offshore hydrocarbon resources. It was Australia that ensured that sedentary species were included in the natural resources of the continental shelf regime in the 1958 Geneva Convention on the Continental Shelf (CSC).[9]

Coastal States' exercise of continental shelf rights developed quickly.[10] Spurring these developments was the enhancement of the technology to search for and exploit offshore hydrocarbon resources wedded to the strategic knowledge of State's

---

[3] 1942 Treaty between the United Kingdom and Venezuela relating to the Submarine Areas of the Gulf of Paria. See generally DP O'Connell, *The International Law of the Sea* (ed IA Shearer) (Clarendon Press Oxford 1982) Vol I, 470.

[4] United States, Executive Order 9633 of 28 September 1945, *Reserving and Placing Certain Resources of the Continental Shelf Under the Control and Jurisdiction of the Secretary of the Interior*, 10 Federal Register 12303, and 59 US Stat 884. See O'Connell, n 3, Vol I, 470–2; and, more generally, Ann L Hollick, *U.S. Foreign Policy and the Law of the Sea* (Princeton University Press Princeton 1981) 18–61.

[5] O'Connell, n 3, Vol I, 469–70 and 498; MW Mouton, *The Continental Shelf* (Martinus Nijhoff The Hague 1952) 46.

[6] See O'Connell, n 3, Vol I, 450–6; Mouton, n 5, 138.

[7] *Maritime Boundary Dispute (Norway v Sweden)* (Award) (1909) XI RIAA 155, reprinted in (1909) 4 *American Journal of International Law* 226; and see DM Johnston, *The Theory and History of Ocean Boundary-Making* (McGill-Queen's University Press Kingston/Montreal 1988) 127.

[8] O'Connell, n 3, Vol I, 499.

[9] Ibid, Vol I, 499–500. 1958 Convention on the Continental Shelf, Art 2(4) (hereinafter CSC).

[10] See DR Rothwell and T Stephens, *The International Law of the Sea* (Hart Publishing Oxford 2010) 101.

that oil was critical to their economies and militaries. Another reason for the quick legal development of the continental shelf regime was that, unlike the water column, the continental shelf was not unduly encumbered by freedoms of the high seas pertaining to fisheries and navigation. In this regard, keeping the continental shelf legal regime distinct from that of the water column was critical.[11]

3 LEGAL REGIME

3.1 Inherent rights

An important feature of the legal regime of the continental shelf is set out in Article 2(3) of the CSC and repeated in Article 77(3) of the LOSC: 'The rights of the coastal State over the continental shelf do not depend on occupation, effective or notional, or any express proclamation.' The International Court of Justice (ICJ) in the *North Sea Continental Shelf Cases* commented 'that the rights of the coastal State in respect of the area of continental shelf ... exist *ipso facto* and *ab initio*, by virtue of its sovereignty over the land. In short, there is ... an inherent right'.[12] O'Connell has pointed out that:

The establishment of the continental shelf doctrine as an autonomous legal institution, independent of other methods of territorial acquisition, implied the automatic attribution of the continental shelf to the coastal State. One of the aims behind the propagation of the doctrine was to annul any priority of claim in time or nature over the rights of the coastal State, so that, for example, the doctrine of historic rights or acquisitive prescription would not be available.[13]

Recently, in the 2012 *Bangladesh/Myanmar Case*, the International Tribunal for the Law of the Sea (ITLOS) stated that: 'A coastal State's entitlement to the continental shelf exists by the sole fact that the basis of entitlement, namely sovereignty over the land territory, is present.'[14] This inherent-right aspect of the continental shelf legal

---

[11] The differing interests involved and regime development respecting the continental shelf and water column explains what appears to the uninitiated to be an illogical disconnect between coastal State rights over the continental shelf beyond 200 nm but exclusive national fisheries jurisdiction ending at the 200 nm limit.

[12] *North Sea Continental Shelf (Federal Republic of Germany v Denmark; Federal Republic of Germany v The Netherlands)* (Judgment) [1969] ICJ Rep 3, 23 [19].

[13] O'Connell, n 3, Vol I, 482.

[14] *Delimitation of the Maritime Boundary in the Bay of Bengal (Bangladesh/Myanmar)* (Judgment) [2012] ITLOS Rep 4, [409] (hereinafter *Bangladesh/Myanmar Case*).

regime can be contrasted with the EEZ regime which, while available to States, must be positively asserted by a State.

The inherent right of a State to a legal continental shelf raises squarely the issue of the legal definition of and title to the shelf. The ICJ in the 2012 *Nicaragua v Columbia* case indicated that Article 76(1) of the LOSC—the definition of the continental shelf—is part of customary international law.[15] Thus, without expressing a claim, a coastal State has an adjacent shelf out to 200 nm or to 'the outer edge of the continental margin'. Moreover, a State cannot be deprived of its legal continental shelf by the action of another State. A question raised and answered below is whether a State, by being a party to the LOSC, has agreed to limits on its inherent right to a shelf. The answer is yes, but only in a limited manner.

In the CSC, the legal basis for a State's inherent right to a continental shelf was adjacency.[16] The 1969 *North Sea Continental Shelf* cases introduced the concept of 'natural prolongation' in the context that a coastal State has rights over the area of the continental shelf 'that constitutes a natural prolongation of its land territory'.[17] The natural prolongation of the adjacent land territory was adopted in Article 76(1) of the LOSC. In the 2012 *Bangladesh/Myanmar Case* there was a sharp divide between Bangladesh and Myanmar on their understanding of natural prolongation. It was the view of Bangladesh that the wording meant that the State's ability to show geological and geomorphological continuity between the landmass and the seafloor of the Bay of Bengal (based largely on the sediments in the Bay of Bengal originating from Bangladesh) resulted in the continental shelf beyond 200 nm belonging to Bangladesh and not Myanmar.[18] The view of Myanmar was that the wording did not require 'any "test of natural geological prolongation"'.[19] The ITLOS commented that, while natural prolongation first arose in the *North Sea Continental Shelf* cases, 'it has never been defined'[20] and that it had been utilized at the Third United Nations Conference on the Law of the Sea (UNCLOS III) 'as a concept to lend support' to the trend of expansion of coastal State jurisdiction.[21] The Tribunal took the view that natural prolongation did not constitute 'a separate and independent criterion a coastal State must satisfy'.[22] For the State parties to the LOSC, what was to be applied

---

[15] *Territorial and Maritime Dispute (Nicaragua v Colombia)* (Judgment) [2012] ICJ Rep 624, 666 [118].
[16] CSC, n 9, Art 1.
[17] *North Sea Continental Shelf*, n 12, 2 [19], 31 [43]–[44], and 51 [95]–[96].
[18] *Bangladesh/Myanmar Case*, n 14, [415]–[417], [419], [424], and [426].
[19] Ibid, [420], [421], [425], and [427].   [20] Ibid, [432].   [21] Ibid, [433].
[22] Ibid, [435]. Judge Gao in his Separate Opinion strongly disagreed with the majority's view of natural prolongation. See ibid, [83]–[91] and, in particular, [87]:

> Furthermore, in paragraph 435 of the Judgment, 'the Tribunal ... finds it difficult to accept that natural prolongation referred to in article 76, paragraph 1, constitutes a separate and independent criterion a coastal State must satisfy in order to be entitled to a continental shelf beyond 200 mm.' And it goes on in paragraph 437 to conclude: 'Entitlement to a continental shelf beyond 200 nm should thus be determined by reference to the outer edge of the continental margin, to be ascertained in accordance with article 76, paragraph 4. To interpret otherwise is warranted neither by the text

in determining the outer limit of the shelf beyond 200 nm was not the abstract notion of natural prolongation but rather the wording of Article 76(3) which leads directly to the detailed criteria of Article 76(4).

3.2 Substantive rights

The key legal attributes of the continental shelf regime were set out in the 1958 Convention on the Continental Shelf and are largely repeated in the LOSC. The principal legal features reflect the economic and geopolitical importance for coastal States of controlling offshore hydrocarbon exploration and exploitation in their adjacent seafloor areas. Also important is that the rights of a coastal State over its adjacent continental shelf 'do not affect the legal status of the superjacent waters' or the airspace above those waters;[23] thus the navigational freedoms and other freedoms and rights of States both within the EEZ, where the continental shelf co-exists, and beyond 200 nm on the high seas, are to be balanced with a coastal State's shelf rights. It is worth noting that, where the continental shelf of a coastal State exists both within and beyond 200 nm, the balance that informs the exercise by a coastal State of its shelf rights may be different within and beyond 200 nm.[24]

A coastal State has exclusive sovereign rights for the purpose of exploring and exploiting the natural resources of its adjacent continental shelf.[25] These natural resources are mineral and other non-living resources of the shelf and sedentary species which are either 'immobile on or under the seabed or are unable to move except in constant contact with the seabed or subsoil'.[26] As noted above, the inclusion of sedentary species as part of the continental shelf regime has historic roots. What remains elusive is a definition of sedentary species, although it appears that over the last 30 years the only international disagreement has been between Canada and the United States respecting Iceland scallops, which, reportedly, the United States eventually agreed with Canada are a sedentary species.[27]

More explicitly, LOSC Article 81 provides that '[t]he coastal State shall have exclusive rights to authorize and regulate drilling on the continental shelf for all purposes.'

---

of article 76 nor by its object and purpose.' Not only are these bold interpretations of the relevant provisions of the Convention inaccurate in my view, but they are also stated more assertively than anything other courts and tribunals have said in previous cases.

[23] CSC, n 9, Art 3; LOSC, n 1, Art 78(1).

[24] See generally J Mossop, 'The Legal Framework for the Regulation of Safety and Environmental Issues on the Outer Continental Shelf' in MH Nordquist, JN Moore, A Chircop, and R Long (eds), *The Regulation of Continental Shelf Development: Rethinking International Standards* (Martinus Nijhoff Leiden 2013) 179; J Mossop, 'Protecting Marine Biodiversity on the Continental Shelf Beyond 200' (2007) 38 *Ocean Development and International Law* 283.

[25] CSC, n 9, Art 1; LOSC, n 1, Art 77(1).

[26] CSC, n 9, Art 2(4); LOSC, n 1, Art 77(1) and (4).

[27] Mossop, 'Protecting Marine Biodiversity', n 24, 291–2.

Moreover, the coastal State has the exclusive right to authorize and regulate the construction, placement, and operation of installations and structures involved in the exercise of its continental shelf mineral rights,[28] and this includes 'jurisdiction with regard to customs, fiscal, health, safety and immigration'.[29] Coastal States can establish safety zones around installations and structures of up to 500 metres, and greater if recommended by the competent international organization,[30] and within this zone, they 'may take appropriate measures to ensure the safety both of navigation and ... of the installations and structures'.[31]

As a result, it is the exclusive right of the coastal State to authorize through permits, leases, licences, or concessions the undertaking of any exploration or exploitation of the mineral resources or sedentary species that may exist on its adjacent continental shelf. In the case of mineral resources of the shelf, drilling rigs and other platforms utilized for oil and gas exploration and exploitation are under the exclusive jurisdiction of the adjacent coastal State. While each State has a different practice, many States have a combination of specific laws that apply to offshore oil and gas activities, including exploration and exploitation, and also extend general laws, such as criminal law, immigration, and labour standards to the platforms utilized. Canada, for example, has a complex domestic legal structure respecting offshore hydrocarbon activity primarily because of the role of provinces (sub-State units); but, of note are provisions in the Oceans Act that extend the application of all federal and provincial laws to 'any marine installation or structure from the time it is attached or anchored to the continental shelf of Canada in connection with the exploration of that shelf or the exploitation of its mineral or other non-living resources until the marine installation or structure is removed from the waters above the continental shelf of Canada in the regulation'.[32]

The 'Arctic Sunrise' Case, involving the Netherlands and the Russian Federation, raises questions about the balance between the authority of the coastal State to enforce its national laws related to offshore installations within its EEZ and the freedom of navigation that exists within the EEZ for foreign flag vessels, in particular where the clear intention of the foreign vessel is to engage directly or indirectly in protest against the offshore installation.[33] In the ITLOS decision on the request by the Netherlands for provisional measures, the above balance was noted but not commented upon.[34] The Joint Separate Opinion of Judge Wolfrum and Judge Kelly and the Dissenting Opinion of Judge Golitsyn took the view that, within a safety

---

[28] LOSC, n 1, Arts 80 and 60(1)(b).   [29] Ibid, Arts 80 and 60(2).
[30] Ibid, Art 60(4) and (5).   [31] Ibid, Art 60(6).
[32] Oceans Act, C 1996, c 31, §§ 20(1)(a) and 21 (Canada).
[33] See 'Arctic Sunrise' Arbitration (Netherlands v Russia), Permanent Court of Arbitration, Case No 2014-02 (pending), available at <http://www.pca-cpa.org/showpage.asp?pag_id=1556> (hereinafter 'Arctic Sunrise' Arbitration).
[34] 'Arctic Sunrise' Case (Netherlands v Russian Federation), Provisional Measures Order of the International Tribunal for the Law of the Sea, Case No 22 (22 November 2013) [60]-[68].

zone established pursuant to Article 60 of the LOSC, the coastal State has exclusive jurisdiction including for enforcement of its national laws.[35] The nuanced difference between the Joint Opinion and the Dissenting Opinion, at the heart of the dispute, is whether coastal State enforcement action can be taken against foreign flag vessels beyond the safety zone to prevent and/or deter illicit activities within the safety zone. On this point, the Joint Opinion appears to answer no,[36] whereas the Dissenting Opinion appears to answer yes.[37] However, both the Joint Opinion and the Dissenting Opinion note that, if applicable, the right of hot pursuit would allow for enforcement against foreign flag vessels beyond the safety zone.[38] The result in the *'Arctic Sunrise' Case*, given that the underlying facts involved a protest by foreign citizens of hydrocarbon exploration under the exclusive authority of the Russian Federation, may be read as a limitation on the rights exercisable by a coastal State over the exploration and exploitation of resources in its adjacent continental shelf. This may be further dealt with by the arbitral panel established pursuant to Annex VII to the LOSC.[39]

Pursuant to the LOSC, coastal States are under an obligation to enact and enforce laws and regulations 'to prevent, reduce and control pollution ... arising from or in connection with seabed activities subject to their jurisdiction ...'.[40] Coastal States are encouraged to develop global and regional rules, standards, practices, and procedures.[41] At present, beyond the LOSC, there are no legally binding global instruments that establish measures regarding the prevention of accidental pollution from offshore oil and gas activities.[42] Through the International Maritime Organization (IMO), States have accepted recommendations for the construction and operation of mobile offshore drilling units.[43] The establishment of global rules and standards for the prevention of marine pollution from offshore oil and gas activities has been called for, but thus far without response.[44]

---

[35] Ibid, Joint Separate Opinion of Judge Wolfrum and Judge Kelly, [11], and ibid, Dissenting Opinion of Judge Golitsyn, [25].

[36] Ibid, Joint Separate Opinion of Judge Wolfrum and Judge Kelly, [12]–[13].

[37] Ibid, Dissenting Opinion of Judge Golitsyn, [25].

[38] Ibid, Dissenting Opinion of Judge Golitsyn, [35]–[42]; ibid, Joint Separate Opinion of Judge Wolfrum and Judge Kelly, [12].

[39] See *'Arctic Sunrise' Arbitration*, n 33.

[40] LOSC, n 1, Arts 208(1) and 240; and see JA Roach, 'International Standards for Offshore Drilling' in Nordquist et al (eds), n 24, 106.

[41] LOSC, n 1, Art 208(5).

[42] S Vinogradov, 'The Impact of the Deepwater Horizon: The Evolving International Legal Regime for Offshore Accidental Pollution Prevention, Preparedness, and Response' (2013) 44 *Ocean Development and International Law* 335, 341.

[43] IMO Assembly Res A.649(16) of 19 October 1989, *Code for the Construction and Equipment of Mobile Offshore Drilling Units* (hereinafter MODU Code). See Vinogradov, n 42, 341; and Roach, n 40, 109–11.

[44] Roach, n 40, 121.

There has been global and regional success in reaching an agreement on enhancing the preparedness of and the cooperation among States to respond to marine pollution incidents from offshore oil and gas activities. In 1990, at the global level the International Convention on Oil Pollution Preparedness, Response and Cooperation (OPRC)[45] was adopted which has led to a number of regional arrangements,[46] including the 2013 Agreement on Cooperation on Oil Pollution, Preparedness and Response in the Arctic.[47]

LOSC Article 77 directs that a coastal State has jurisdiction over all cables and pipelines used in connection with the exploration or exploitation of the mineral resources of its shelf. However, subject to reasonable measures respecting exploration and exploitation of the mineral resources of the shelf resources and pollution prevention, all States are entitled to lay submarine cables and pipelines on another State's continental shelf.[48] Specifically respecting 'the delineation of the course for laying pipelines', coastal State consent is required.[49] Regarding both cables and pipelines, measures adopted by a coastal State are not to impede their laying and maintenance.[50] Questions have arisen whether coastal States that require permits for surveying cable routes and laying and repairing cables on their shelf are compliant with the LOSC and whether, in areas designated as marine protected areas (MPAs), coastal States can deny access for cables.[51]

4 THE OUTER LIMIT OF THE CONTINENTAL SHELF

4.1 Overview

Article 1 of the CSC provided criteria for the determination of the outer limit of a coastal State's adjacent continental shelf—the seabed and subsoil within the envelope of waters of a depth of 200 metres 'or, beyond that limit, to where the depth of the superjacent waters admits of the exploitation of the natural resources'. While

---

[45] 1990 International Convention on Oil Pollution, Preparedness, Response and Co-operation.
[46] See generally, Vinogradov, n 42, 343–9.
[47] Arctic Council Agreement on Cooperation on Oil Pollution, Preparedness and Response in the Arctic (adopted 15 May 2013), available at <http://www.arctic-council.org/eppr/agreement-on-cooperation-on-marine-oil-pollution-preparedness-and-response-in-the-arctic/>.
[48] CSC, n 9, Art 4; LOSC, n 1, Art 79.   [49] LOSC, n 1, Art 79(3).   [50] Ibid, Art 79(2).
[51] T Davenport, 'Submarine Communications Cables and Law of the Sea: Problems in Law and Practice' (2012) 43 *Ocean Development and International Law* 201, 212.

it was believed at the time that a definite limit was intended by the wording,[52] as a result of technological, political, and economic pressure primarily related to offshore hydrocarbon resource development, the exploitability criterion came to be seen as ambiguous and as effectively meaning that Article 1 did not provide a determinable outer limit of the legal continental shelf. Note needs to be made again of the 1969 *North Sea Continental Shelf Cases* where the Court introduced 'natural prolongation' and tied this to coastal fronts and geology,[53] thus substantially undermining the 200-metre depth as a delineator of the outer limit of the continental shelf.[54] For example, while in 1970 the United States proposed that coastal States should not make continental shelf claims beyond the 200-metre water depth,[55] Canada asserted shelf rights well beyond the 200-metre-depth line relying in part on the natural prolongation wording in the 1969 *North Sea Continental Shelf Cases*.[56]

Unlike in 1958, during the negotiation of the LOSC there was a necessity to provide for a definitive outer limit of the continental shelf regime where the shelf extended beyond 200 nm as a result of the Common Heritage of Mankind and the authority of the International Seabed Authority (ISA) that was to be apply to the mineral resources of the seafloor beyond national jurisdiction, in other words beyond the outer limits of coastal State's continental shelves.[57] With some States strongly of the view that customary law supported shelf rights beyond 200 nm and others arguing for 200 nm as the limit, a compromise emerged involving four components:

- A complex formula was adopted in Article 76 for the determination of the outer limit of a State's continental shelf beyond 200 nm.
- The Commission on the Limits of the Continental Shelf (CLCS, 'the Commission')[58] would be established to assist States in applying the complex formula and to which States are obligated to submit information respecting their proposed outer limits.

---

[52] See generally BH Oxman, 'The Preparation of Article 1 of the Convention on the Continental Shelf' (1972) 3 *Journal of Maritime Law and Commerce* 245, 445–72, and 683–723; ED Brown, *The Legal Regime of Hydrospace* (Stevens and Sons London 1971) 1–40.

[53] *North Sea Continental Shelf*, n 12, 51 [95].

[54] See RY Jennings, 'The Limits of Continental Shelf Jurisdiction: Some Possible Implications of the North Sea Case Judgment' (1969) 18 *International and Comparative Law Quarterly* 819, 826–30.

[55] President Nixon, 'Statement—United States Policy for the Seabed' (23 May 1970), reprinted in SH Lay, R Churchill, and M Nordquist (eds), *New Directions in the Law of the Sea* (Oceana Publications Dobbs Ferry NY 1973) Vol II, 751–2 [4].

[56] See *Act to amend the Oil and Gas Production and Conservation Act*, C 1969–1970, c 43, § 3 (Canada). The Minister of Energy, Mines and Resources claimed that the 1970 legislation amendments:

> ...will have the effect of confirming Canada's assertion of rights to offshore mineral resources in areas extending far beyond either our territorial limits or the 200-metre water depth.

House of Commons, *Debates*, 9 March 1970, 4570 (JJ Greene, Minister of Energy, Mines and Natural Resources).

[57] LOSC, n 1, Arts 1(1), 133, and 136.

[58] Ibid, Annex II, Commission on the Limits of the Continental Shelf (CLCS); and see the website of the CLCS at <http://www.un.org/depts/los/clcs_new/clcs_home.htm>.

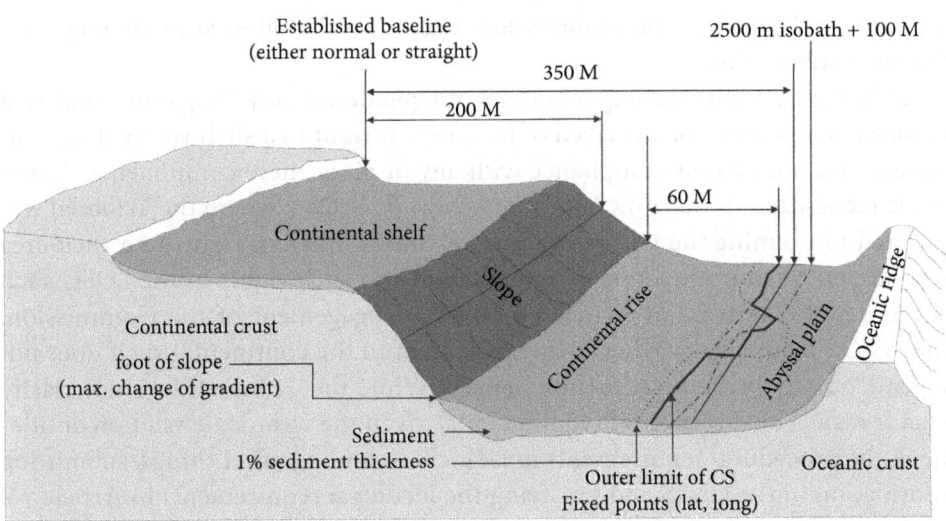

Figure 9.1 The Continental Shelf

- Where non-living resources are exploited from the shelf area beyond 200 nm, the adjacent coastal State is to provide payments or contributions to the international community as regards the exploited resources.[59]
- A coastal State's rights regarding its adjacent shelf, anchored in customary international law, was restated in, but not created by, Articles 76(1) and 77(3) of the LOSC.

The Article 76 criteria and the CLCS explicitly only deal with the outer limit of a State's continental shelf beyond 200 nm; thus States are not restricted by the Convention in unquestionably exercising jurisdiction over shelf areas within any reasonable calculation of the Article 76 criteria outer limits. Consistent with this, in the *Bangladesh/Myanmar Case*, the ITLOS stated that a coastal State's 'entitlement to the continental shelf ... does not require the establishment of outer limits'.[60] State practice supports this. Canada, for example, has long exercised national jurisdiction over hydrocarbon development and sedentary species beyond 200 nm including the prosecution of a US fishing vessel for illegally harvesting sedentary species beyond 200 nm.[61] There are also a number of bilateral maritime boundary agreements that deal with the shelf area beyond 200 nm entered into by States that had not made submissions to the Commission. For example, the 2004 Australia–New Zealand Treaty[62] divided large areas of shelf beyond 200 nm

---

[59] LOSC, n 1, Art 82.   [60] *Bangladesh/Myanmar Case*, n 14, [409].
[61] *R v Perry* (2003) 222 Newfoundland and Prince Edward Island Reports 313.
[62] 2004 Treaty between the Government of Australia and the Government of New Zealand Establishing Certain Exclusive Economic Zone Boundaries and Continental Shelf Boundaries. For an analysis, see N Fyfe and G French, 'Australia–New Zealand' in DA Colson and RW Smith (eds), *International Maritime Boundaries* (Martinus Nijhoff Leiden 2005) Vol V, 3759–77.

just prior to Australia's 2004 submission, subsequently followed in 2006 by New Zealand's submission.[63]

Further, the first three components are independent treaty obligations such that a coastal State cannot be deprived of its inherent right to a shelf where it extends beyond 200 nm by non-compliance with any or all of these components. Again, this is recognized in the 2012 *Bangladesh/Myanmar Case* where the Tribunal was required to examine the nature of a coastal State's inherent rights to a shelf area beyond 200 nm and the possible impediments on such rights in the LOSC such as the detailed criteria in Article 76 and the engagement of the Commission. The ITLOS judgment provides that entitlement to the continental shelf does not depend 'on any procedural requirements'.[64] While the Tribunal does not clarify what it means by 'procedural requirements', given the clear statement on entitlement, the procedural requirements must include, among other things, submitting information to the CLCS and satisfying the technical requirements in Article 76. At paragraph 407, the Judgment states that: 'It is clear from article 76, paragraph 8, … that the limits of the continental shelf beyond 200 nm can be established only by the coastal State' and that it is 'opposability with regard to other States' that is dependent on satisfying the requirements of Article 76, including the obligation to submit information to the CLCS.[65] Put a different way, a State has an inherent right to a shelf beyond 200 nm (where it physically exists), and the LOSC provides a procedural opportunity to establish the outer limits of that shelf that will enhance the opposability of those limits vis-à-vis other States or, as has been described elsewhere, the Commission process provides legitimacy to a coastal State's shelf outer limits.[66] Thus, a coastal State has and can exercise exclusive national authority over its adjacent legal continental shelf irrespective of the submission of information to the Commission and the receipt of recommendations from the Commission. As a corollary, a State not meeting the 10-year timeline for a submission of information to the CLCS, set out in Article 4 of Annex II to the Convention, noted below, cannot be deprived of its rights to a continental shelf beyond 200 nm.

None of the above undermines the importance of the Article 76 criteria, the role of the Commission, or the Article 82 revenue-sharing provision. As will be noted below, the State parties to the LOSC have been remarkably consistent in complying with the criteria and processes set out respecting the outer limit of the continental shelf.

---

[63] Australia, Executive Summary of Submission, 15 November 2004, and New Zealand, Executive Summary of Submission, 19 April 2006, are available on the CLCS website, n 58.

[64] *Bangladesh/Myanmar Case*, n 14, [408].   [65] Ibid, [407].

[66] See generally TL McDorman, 'The Role of the Commission on the Limits of the Continental Shelf: A Technical Body in a Political World' (2002) 17 *International Journal of Marine and Coastal Law* 301, 313–17.

4.2 The Article 76 criteria

One scholar has described the key paragraphs of Article 76 that establish the criteria for determining the outer limit of the continental shelf as combining the 'influences of geography, geology, geomorphology, and jurisprudence'.[67] Again, one must also acknowledge the importance that coastal States placed on obtaining or retaining exclusive control over any potential hydrocarbon resources in their adjacent seabed areas. This is evident from the negotiating history of Article 76.

The proposal that formed the basis of the negotiations of the outer limit criteria was the so-called 'Irish formula', which provided that the outer limit of the legal continental shelf should be determined on the basis of sediment thickness seaward of the foot of the slope or by a 60 nm limit from the foot of the continental slope. The foot of the slope was taken as the starting point since it was a recognizable geophysical characteristic in large parts of the ocean floor and thus was seen as providing some ease in locating the outer edge of the margin. Since the physical continental margin consists of the continental shelf, continental slope, and continental rise, the foot of the slope ensures that, at a minimum, a coastal State has legal authority over the key physical components of its adjacent offshore seafloor—which are most likely to contain hydrocarbon resources—plus at least part of the continental rise. The idea for the foot-of-the-slope-plus-zone, borrowed from American geologist Hollis D Hedberg,[68] was to provide a method of delineation that would not involve acquiring sediment thickness information which was seen at the time as being difficult to obtain. The rationale for the sediment thickness criteria, however, was to ensure that a coastal State secured jurisdiction over all the hydrocarbon resources that might possibly exist in the offshore areas adjacent to it.[69] Essentially, if the sediment was thick enough there might exist hydrocarbon resources, and, therefore, it should come under coastal State authority. Interestingly, the sediment thickness criterion was criticized by Hedberg as being:

---

[67] Johnston, n 7, 91.

[68] Professor HD Hedberg wrote about the foot of the slope-plus zone in numerous works. See HD Hedberg, *National-International Jurisdictional Boundary on the Ocean Floor* (Law of the Sea Institute Kingston, RI 1975) 19; HD Hedberg, 'The National-International Jurisdiction Boundary on the Ocean Floor' (1973) 1 *Ocean Management* 83; HD Hedberg, 'Limits of National Jurisdiction over Natural Resources of the Ocean Bottom' in LM Alexander (ed), *The Law of the Sea: National Policy Recommendations* (University of Rhode Island Kingston, RI 1970) 159; and HD Hedberg, 'Relation of Political Boundaries on the Ocean Floor to the Continental Margin' (1976) 17 *Virginia Journal of International Law* 57.

[69] FA Eustis III, 'Method and Basis of Seaward Delimitation of Continental Shelf Jurisdiction' (1976) 17 *Virginia Journal of International Law* 107, 125; and H Hedberg, 'Discussion' in E Miles and JK Gamble Jr (eds), *Law of the Sea: Conference Outcomes and Problems of Implementation* (Ballinger Publishing Co Cambridge, MA 1977) 215.

... based more on factors of economic advantage to certain coastal countries than on impartial considerations of where a boundary should most naturally, most logically and most rightfully be.[70]

The Soviet Union put forward a proposal to prevent coastal States from claiming jurisdiction on the basis of the Irish formula to areas beyond a 300 nm limit.[71] In the end, a compromise was reached that limited the extent of the Irish proposal to either 350 nm or 100 nm from the 2,500 metre isobath, whichever was further seaward.

A last issue concerning the criteria to be used for the establishment of the outer limit of the margin related to ridges. The concern was that underwater ridges might be used by some coastal States to extend their jurisdiction to the middle of the ocean. The compromise that was reached distinguishes between oceanic ridges, submarine ridges, and submarine elevations.

The criteria agreed upon in the LOSC to be applied by a coastal State in determining the outer limit of the continental margin beyond 200nm is succinctly set out below.

- Pursuant to Article 76(4), an envelope for the outer limit of the continental margin is first created by determining the foot of the continental slope[72] and then:
  - a line connecting the outermost points where 'the thickness of sedimentary rocks is at least 1 per cent of the shortest distance from such point to the foot of the continental slope',[73] or
  - a line connecting points 'not more than 60 nautical miles from the foot of the continental slope'.

- The envelope created by Article 76(4) is subject to two constraints. The lines created pursuant to Article 76(4) are not to extend beyond:
  - 350 nm from a State's baselines; or
  - 100 nm from the 2,500-metre isobath.[74]

- For submarine ridges, the 350 nm limit applies. However, for 'submarine elevations that are natural components of the continental margin, such as its plateaux,

---

[70] Hedberg, 'Discussion', n 69, 215.

[71] The Soviet proposal is discussed in BH Oxman, 'The Third United Nations Conference on the Law of the Sea: The Seventh Session (1978)' (1979) 73 *American Journal of International Law* 1, 19–21.

[72] LOSC, n 1, Art 76(4)(b) notes that:

In the absence of evidence to the contrary, the foot of the continental slope shall be determined as the point of maximum change in the gradient at its base.

[73] For example, if it is determined that the thickness of sedimentary rocks is 1 nm, then that point can be 100 nm seaward from the foot of the slope.

[74] The key point to note is that the 350 nm limit is not the only constraint line, as a result, a coastal State's continental margin can go well beyond 350 nm.

rises, caps, banks and spurs', the 100 nm from the 2,500-metre isobath criterion is the limitation.[75]
- There is a general limitation that the continental margin does not include the oceanic floor with its oceanic ridges.

The criteria are not easily applicable in any given situation because of the technical and definitional difficulties of determining the thickness of sedimentary rocks, the foot of the continental slope, the 2,500 metre isobath, and distinguishing among submarine ridges, oceanic ridges, and submarine elevations that are natural components of the continental margin.

4.3 Procedure: the Commission

4.3.1 *Overview*

Article 76(8) of the LOSC provides that a coastal State is to submit information supporting its proposed outer limit of its legal continental shelf to the Commission on the Limits of the Continental Shelf. The Commission is composed of 21 technical specialists elected by the State Parties to the LOSC (SPLOS).[76] Commission members are to be 'experts in the field of geology, geophysics or hydrography'[77] and are to act in their personal capacities. The State which nominates a member of the Commission is to 'defray the expenses' of that Commission member.[78]

The Commission is to consider the material submitted to it by a coastal State and make 'recommendations' to the submitting State regarding the information received and the relevant Article 76 criteria. Where differences exist, the State is to resubmit further information. What was envisaged was a process of 'ping-pong'—State submission, Commission recommendations, State resubmission, Commission recommendations, and so on—with the submitting State, acting in good faith, and the Commission eventually achieving accord.[79] Thus far, much of the to-and-fro between the Commission and submitting State has taken place during the consideration by the Commission of the submission, such that there have been few instances of the Commission recommending that a State either make a resubmission or that a recommendation by the Commission has resulted in a resubmission.[80]

---

[75] LOSC, n 1, Art 76(6).
[76] Ibid, Annex II, Art 2(1).   [77] Ibid, Annex II, Art 2(1).   [78] Ibid, Art 2(5).
[79] PRR Gardiner, 'The Limits of the Area beyond National Jurisdiction—Some Problems with Particular References to the Role of the Commission on the Limits of the Continental Shelf' in G Blake (ed), *Maritime Boundaries and Ocean Resources* (Croom Helm London 1987) 69.
[80] See Section 4.3.3 below.

The Commission is a *sui generis* body which has been described as being akin to an administrative institution.[81] Its role is to review the information provided and make recommendations to the submitting State. The CLCS does not have the legal authority to determine or impose its views respecting the location of the outer limit of the continental margin on a coastal State. It is the coastal State, and not the CLCS, that establishes the outer limit of its continental margin beyond 200 nm. This was duly acknowledged in the *Bangladesh/Myanmar Case*[82] and is consistent with the reality that the determination and delineation of a maritime boundary is a political act of a coastal State. Article 76(8) indicates that the 'limits of the shelf established by a coastal State on the basis of' the recommendations of the Commission 'shall be final and binding'. Note has already been made of the ITLOS views in the *Bangladesh/Myanmar Case* that what this wording is primarily about enhancing 'opposability with regard to other States'.[83]

4.3.2 Bilateral delimitation and disputes

Article 76(10) indicates that the provisions of the article 'are without prejudice to the question of delimitation of the continental shelf between States with opposite or adjacent coasts'. This is supplemented by Article 9 of Annex II where it states that the 'actions of the Commission' are also without prejudice to the shelf delimitation. These provisions do not inhibit or constrain States from explicitly acting, for example, through issuing *notes verbales*, to protect their rights, however a State defines these rights.

The manner in which the Commission procedurally deals with disputes is set out in Rule 46 of the Commission's Rules of Procedure and Annex I to the Rules of Procedure.[84] In particular, paragraph 5(a) of Annex I states: 'In cases where a land or maritime dispute exists, the Commission shall not consider and qualify a submission made by any of the States concerned in the dispute.' Reference should also be made to paragraph 1 of the Annex which indicates that 'the competence with respect to matters regarding disputes ... rests with States'. Paragraph 1 can and should be read as meaning that it is up to States to decide (rather than the Commission), amongst other things, whether or not a dispute exists.

The approach of the Commission has been not to deal with a submission (or those parts of a submission) which involve a land or maritime dispute without the consent of the engaged States. The political context of this is obvious. The CLCS has no authority

---

[81] O Jensen, 'The Commission on the Limits of the Continental Shelf: An Administrative, Scientific or Judicial Institution?' (2014) 45 *Ocean Development & International Law* 171.

[82] *Bangladesh/Myanmar Case*, n 14, [407]: 'It is clear from article 76, paragraph 8, ... that the limits of the continental shelf beyond 200 nm can be established only by the coastal State.'

[83] Ibid, [407].

[84] CLCS, Doc CLCS/40/Rev.1, *Rules of Procedure of the Commission* (17 April 2008), available at the CLCS website, n 58.

and is manifestly ill-equipped to evaluate whether or not a 'dispute' exists and/or to look behind or otherwise second-guess any communication made to it by a State that a 'land or maritime' dispute exists. Whether or not a dispute exists is a political determination by States.

4.3.3 The record

Annex II to the LOSC provides that a coastal State intending to establish outer limits of the continental shelf beyond 200 nm 'shall' submit information to the Commission 'within 10 years of entry into force' of the Convention for the State.[85] The ten-year mark for States that were parties to the LOSC when it came into effect in 1994 was adjusted by the State parties to the LOSC to commence as of 13 May 1999.[86] Further, in June 2008, the State Parties decided that the ten-year wording could be met by a coastal State submitting 'preliminary information indicative of the outer limits... and a description of the status of preparation and intended date for making a submission'. The preliminary information would not be acted upon by the Commission and would be without prejudice to a subsequent full submission.[87]

The first submission to the Commission was from Russia in 2001.[88] Since then, spurred by the above-noted ten-year time-frame, as of May 2014, the Commission had received 73 full, partial, joint, or revised submissions of information in respect of the outer limits of the continental shelf and 46 notices of Preliminary Information of intent to make future submissions. These numbers involve a degree of double-counting since some States have made two separate submissions, as in the case of Ireland, one for its proposed outer limit of shelf area adjacent to Ireland on the Porcupine Abyssal Plain and another as part of a Joint Submission with France, Spain, and the United Kingdom regarding the Celtic Sea and Bay of Biscay. Double-counting also arises, for example, regarding Cuba, which submitted a notice of Preliminary Information and shortly thereafter made its submission to the Commission, and Canada which on the same day submitted a partial submission in respect of the Atlantic Ocean and Preliminary Information regarding the

---

[85] LOSC, n 1, Annex II, Art 4.
[86] Eleventh Meeting of the State Parties, *Decision regarding the date of commencement of the ten-year period for making submissions to the Commission on the Limits of the Continental Shelf set out in article 4 of Annex II to the United Nations Convention on the Law of the Sea*, Doc SPLOS/72 (29 May 2001), available at <http://www.un.org/Depts/los/index.htm>.
[87] Eighteenth Meeting of the States Parties, *Decision regarding the Workload of the Commission and the Ability of States to fulfil the Requirements of Article 4 of Annex II*, Doc SPLOS/183 (20 June 2008) [1], available at the DOALOS website, n 86. See generally regarding the time limits and SPLOS decisions, AG Oude Elferink, 'Meeting of States Parties to the UN Law of the Sea Convention' (2008) 23 *International Journal of Marine and Coastal Law* 769.
[88] The executive summaries of the submissions referred to in this paragraph are available at the CLCS website, n 58.

Arctic Ocean. The number of States to have filed either a submission or a notice of Preliminary Information is approximately 80.

Thus far, the CLCS has provided 18 sets of recommendations which, in some cases like that of Russia, has been a recommendation for additional information. In February 2013, Russia made a revised submission to the Commission respecting the Okhotsk Sea. Four States, Australia, Ireland, Mexico, and the Philippines having received recommendations respecting their submissions have, pursuant to Article 76(9), submitted coordinates and maps respecting their outer limits of the continental shelf.

The number of States utilizing the Commission far surpasses what was projected when the LOSC continental shelf regime was being negotiated. At that time, it was surmised that only 30 or so States had adjacent continental margins beyond 200 nm that would result in the employment of the outer-limit criteria and procedures of Article 76.[89] The unexpected number of submissions and their arriving within a relative short period of time has put pressure on the CLCS, which has led to calls for measures to increase the pace of work of the Commission.[90] Part of this concern is based on the incorrect perception that, until a State completes the Commission process, it does not have exclusive jurisdiction over its adjacent legal continental shelf.

4.4 Revenue sharing: Article 82

Article 82 provides that, after a five-year commencement period, a coastal State not a developing country, which is a net importer of mineral resources produced from its continental shelf, is to make payments to developing States, 'through' the ISA, amounting to 1 per cent of the value or volume of the production from a site. This rate is to increase by 1 per cent annually for a period of seven years and remain at 7 per cent thereafter. To date, no mineral resource exploitation from the continental shelf beyond 200 nm has taken place, although some exploration activity has occurred.[91]

At least two States, the United States and Canada, have publicly notified potential holders of permits or leases for shelf areas beyond 200 nm of the Article 82 wording.[92] The Article 82 revenue obligation rests on the State party to the LOSC, and it is up to

---

[89] See DOALOS, *The Law of the Sea: Definition of the Continental Shelf* (United Nations New York 1993) 6.

[90] See CLCS, *Issues related to the workload of the Commission on the Limits of the Continental Shelf* (2012), available at the CLCS website, n 58.

[91] See generally International Seabed Authority, *ISA Technical Study No 12: Implementation of Article 82 of the United Nations Convention on the Law of the Sea: Report of an International Workshop convened 26–30 November 2012* (International Seabed Authority Kingston, RI 2013).

[92] See United States Bureau of Ocean Energy Management, *Leasing Activities Information: Lease Stipulations, Consolidated Central Gulf of Mexico Planning Area, Oil and Gas Lease Sale 216/222, Final*

the State to determine its own arrangements for collection and payment. Moreover, the understanding and application of Article 82, like any other provision of a treaty, is a matter for a State party taking into account the well-understood rules of treaty interpretation set out in the 1969 Vienna Convention of the Law of Treaties.[93]

The wording of Article 82 that the payment or contribution is to be made 'through' the ISA, which is to distribute the payment or contributions to State parties on the basis of equitable sharing criteria, indicates that the ISA is primarily in a recipient role with minimal engagement with the State making payments or contributions.

5 Continental Shelf and EEZ

The legal regime of the continental shelf predates the emergence of the EEZ and is separate from the EEZ in that, while a coastal State can have a continental shelf without an EEZ, it cannot have an EEZ without a continental shelf.[94] In the LOSC, the two regimes out to 200 nm were co-mingled.[95] Since the general acceptance of the EEZ, where maritime boundary delimitation involving the two regimes has taken place between States involving distances between coasts of less than 400 nm, State practice and adjudications have taken the view that the two regimes are harmonious in that the shelf regime and the EEZ are effectively conflated as evidenced by delimitations involving a 'single maritime boundary'[96] and a single line applying to both regimes.[97] In the 1985 *Libya v Malta* case, the ICJ, while careful to indicate that the continental shelf regime was not absorbed into that of the EEZ, nevertheless indicated the common element of distance in

---

Notice of Sale (2012) Stipulation 7, available at <http://www.boem.gov/Oil-and-Gas-Energy-Program/Leasing/Regional-Leasing/Gulf-of-Mexico-Region/Lease-Sales/216-222/fstips222-pdf.aspx>; and Canada—Newfoundland and Labrador Offshore Petroleum Board, *Call for Bids, N. NL13-01 (Area 'C'—Flemish Pass), Exploration Licence in the Newfoundland and Labrador Offshore Area*, § 3.1 [3], available at <http://www.cnlopb.ca/pdfs/nl1301.pdf>.

[93] 1969 Vienna Convention on the Law of the Treaties, Arts 31–32.

[94] *Continental Shelf (Libyan Arab Jamahiriya/Malta)* [1985] ICJ Rep 13, 33 [34] (hereinafter *Libya/Malta*).

[95] LOSC, n 1, Arts 56(1) and (3) and 68.

[96] See eg *Maritime Dispute (Peru v Chile)*, Judgment of the International Court of Justice, General List No 137 (27 January 2014) [198].

[97] See eg 2000 Agreement between China and Viet Nam on the Delimitation of the Territorial Seas, the Exclusive Economic Zones and Continental Shelves in Beibu Bay/Bac Bo Gulf (hereinafter 2000 China–Viet Nam Agreement).

the two regimes.[98] There are, however, bilateral agreements where this has not been accepted and where one delimitation line has been used for the shelf and another for the water column.[99] While the relationship between the regimes of the continental shelf and the EEZ is not usually a matter of great consequence, there are situations where a seafloor area is claimed by one State as being within 200 nm of its coasts (part of its EEZ) and by another State as being its continental shelf beyond 200 nm. This arose in the *Bangladesh/Myanmar Case* where, as a result of the delimitation method adopted by the Tribunal, a small area of shelf claimed by one State overlapped with an area of EEZ claimed by the other. The Tribunal resolved the matter in favour of the shelf rights, commenting that the LOSC 'embodies the concept of a single continental shelf... without any distinction being made between the shelf within 200 nm and the shelf beyond that limit',[100] and, at a further stage, that the existence of a shelf area beyond a State's EEZ does not limit the rights of another State within its EEZ, 'notably those with respect to the superjacent waters'.[101] The end result is a bifurcated area with one State having shelf rights and another having water column rights. The Tribunal noted that such bifurcated areas were not unknown to the law of the sea pointing to Article 78(1) of the LOSC where the high seas and continental shelf beyond 200 nm co-exists.[102]

6 Conclusion

There has been continuity throughout the last six decades of the core legal attributes of the continental shelf regime. Based on this, States have embraced their jurisdiction over the mineral resources (oil and gas) in their adjacent shelf areas within and beyond 200 nm. Nevertheless, there are challenges. While it can be anticipated that exploration for and exploitation of mineral resources in the continental shelf other than hydrocarbons may take place in the future, these activities clearly fall within the existing legal regime of the continental shelf. There is

---

[98] *Libya/Malta*, n 94, 33–4 [33]–[34].
[99] See eg 1997 Treaty between Australia and Indonesia establishing an Exclusive Economic Zone Boundary and Certain Seabed Boundaries. For discussion, see M Herriman and M Tsamneyi, 'The 1997 Australia—Indonesia Maritime Boundary Treaty: A Secure Legal Regime for Offshore Resource Development?' (1998) 29 *Ocean Development and International Law* 361.
[100] *Bangladesh/Myanmar Case*, n 14, [361].   [101] Ibid, [474] and [473].   [102] Ibid, [475].

less certainty about coastal State authority regarding marine genetic resources and bioprospecting on the shelf area beyond 200 nm.[103] States with, or hoping for, extractive activities on their adjacent shelves may feel the need to develop a global regime to enhance pollution prevention and safety for these activities in light of the Deepwater Horizon disaster and the concerns about offshore activity in the Arctic Ocean. Coastal States have taken important strides in global and regional cooperation regarding preparation and response to pollution incidents from shelf activities. The substantive continental shelf legal regime may have to adapt and better take into consideration the somewhat amorphous concern for biodiversity. Finally, the *'Arctic Sunrise' Case* has raised questions concerning the relationship between navigational freedoms and coastal State enforcement authority over shelf activities.

The continental shelf regime is different from the EEZ regime in that a coastal State has an inherent right to its shelf. This has been little altered or limited by the LOSC for those States with a shelf area beyond 200 nm. The principal limitation is the Convention obligation to submit information to the CLCS where an outer limit is proposed. A State establishing outer limits is to do so on the basis of a good-faith interpretation of the Article 76 criteria and the recommendations of the Commission. A further limitation is that, when a State finalizes its shelf outer limits and deposits the necessary maps and coordinates with the UN Secretary-General, the outer limits 'shall be final and binding' on it. Finally, while not a limitation per se, a coastal State exploiting mineral resources on its shelf beyond 200 nm is subject to the revenue-sharing obligation in Article 82.

One area where there has been an evolution of the continental shelf regime concerns the outer limit criteria. The history of the continental shelf legal regime is principally linked to hydrocarbon resources. The detailed Article 76 criteria were engineered to assure coastal States that, where offshore hydrocarbons were reasonably likely to exist, they would be subject to the exclusive authority of the adjacent State. The 'continental' in 'continental shelf' had some meaning since only if the seafloor adjacent to a State was continental in origin would there be a potential for oil and gas. However, the wording used in Article 76, base-of-the-slope and foot-of-the-slope, and the differences between submarine elevations, submarine ridges, and ocean ridges, point to geomorphology (the shape of the seafloor) rather than the geologic continuity between the adjacent land and seafloor. The geomorphological dominance inevitably ensures coastal State jurisdiction over adjacent offshore hydrocarbons but, nevertheless, can be seen as a change from what was the original motivation for the outer limit criteria.

The lure of mineral resources (real or imagined) has resulted in States spending untold millions to provide evidence that their adjacent continental shelf extends

---

[103] See Mossop, 'Protecting Marine Biodiversity', n 24, 295–6.

beyond 200 nm and to push proposed outer limits as far seaward as possible. Understandably, no coastal State wants to be in the position in 50 years of looking back and seeing that, because they were not aggressive in their assertion of the outer limit of the shelf, a valuable mineral resource is not within their sovereign control. The ethos of the 1970s when there was the international political will to accept the Common Heritage concept and a degree of global sharing increasingly appears to have been a blip on the historic law-of-the-sea radar.

10

THE HIGH SEAS

DOUGLAS GUILFOYLE

1 Introduction

The high seas form one of few areas over which no claim of sovereignty may be made, giving them a somewhat anomalous status in an international system based on territorial States. The idea that the high seas are inalienable and open to all States[1] is a deeply rooted reflection of *mare liberum*, expressed by Grotius as the principle that:

The sea is common to all, because it is so limitless it cannot become a possession of any one, and because it is adapted for the use of all, whether we consider [it] from the point of view of navigation or fisheries.[2]

Mare liberum reflects States' common interest in unhindered use of the high seas both as a route for trade and as a fishing ground, as well as naval powers' interest in a regime permitting 'unhindered passage' of their fleets.[3] However, the legal consequences that flow from this principle are not self-evident. Grotius noted that 'the sea is called indifferently the property of no one (*res nullius*), or a common possession (*res communis*), or public property (*res publica*)'.[4] These terms,

---

[1] 1982 United Nations Convention on the Law of the Sea, Arts 87 and 89 (hereinafter LOSC).
[2] H Grotius, *The Freedom of the Seas; Or, the Right which Belongs to the Dutch to Take Part in the East Indian Trade* (trans R Magoffin) (Oxford University Press Oxford 1916) 28.
[3] N Klein, *Maritime Security and the Law of the Sea* (Oxford University Press Oxford 2011) 14.
[4] Grotius, n 2, 20.

however, express less precise legal concepts than 'attitudes of mind'.[5] That is, one may view the freedom from sovereign claims positively (as a feature of world public order resulting in a common space inherently regulated by law) or negatively (creating a minimally regulated space where States may only act if 'authorised by international law').[6] Clearly, however, the high seas are not an unregulated legal vacuum.[7]

The present chapter first considers the law governing the high seas as a used space: its geographic extent and the core 'freedoms' all States enjoy there. It then turns to the legal structures underpinning or qualifying those considerations of space and usage: how the law of the sea allocates regulatory authority over high seas activities, the meaning of the high seas being reserved for 'peaceful purposes', and the interaction of the high seas with other maritime zones. This is followed by further consideration of the law of the high seas as regards shipping, including the duties of flag States, the law applicable to stateless vessels, and the vexed question of jurisdiction regarding collisions. The chapter concludes by examining questions of the 'policing' of the high seas (including the contemporary problems posed by maritime piracy, irregular migration, and weapons smuggling) and the current major challenges for the relevant legal regime.

2 Basic Features of the High Seas Regime: Extent and Freedoms

2.1 Introduction

The present chapter discusses the high seas legal regime as it presently stands: twentieth-century codification efforts, therefore, form the point of departure.[8] Among the first problems to confront the International Law Commission (ILC) and treaty negotiators in this task were the extent of the high seas (where are they?) and the freedoms of the high seas (what may States and their nationals do there?). These questions are explored in turn below.

---

[5] DP O'Connell, *The International Law of the Sea* (ed I Shearer) (Clarendon Press Oxford 1984) Vol 2, 792; compare L Lucchini and M Voelckel, *Droit de la mer* (Pedone Paris 1990) Vol 1, 275–6.

[6] O'Connell, n 5, Vol 2, 792.

[7] G Gidel, *Le droit international public de la mer: Le temps de paix* (Mellottée Chateauroux 1932) Vol 1, 225 and 229; compare O'Connell, n 5, Vol 2, 796.

[8] On the law's historical development, see Chapters 1 and 2 in this volume.

2.2 The spatial extent of the high seas

The high seas were negatively defined in early codification efforts. In 1956, the International Law Commission started from the proposition that: '[t]he waters of the sea belong either to the high seas or to the territorial sea or to internal waters.'[9] Similarly, the 1958 Convention on the High Seas (HSC) defined the high seas as: 'all parts of the sea not included in the territorial sea or in the internal waters of a State'.[10] The emergence, however, of the concepts of the exclusive economic zone (EEZ) and archipelagic waters (particularly the former) required a different approach.[11]

In particular, at the Third United Nations Conference on the Law of the Sea (UNCLOS III), it was not immediately clear in negotiations whether the EEZ should be treated as a high seas area 'with a special EEZ regime superimposed upon it (the "high seas minus" view)' or whether it was a new, sovereign coastal State zone in which 'high seas freedoms are the equivalent of the right of innocent passage in the territorial sea (the "EEZ minus" view)'.[12] The approach that emerged was that the EEZ is neither high seas nor an extension of the territorial sea but 'a zone *sui generis*'.[13] As such, it is a zone in which the high seas regime applies to the extent it is not displaced by rights specifically allocated to the coastal State.[14] This required the abandonment of the HSC's negative definition (which might have unduly restricted navigating States' rights in the EEZ) and instead simply specifying the scope of spatial application of the high seas regime.[15] Thus Article 86 of the LOSC stipulates that the provisions of the Convention relating to the high seas 'apply to all parts of the sea that are not included in' the EEZ, territorial sea, internal waters, or archipelagic waters of a State; but it also provides that this does not curtail the high seas 'freedoms enjoyed by all States in the exclusive economic zone in accordance with article 58'. The relationship between these high seas freedom(s) and the EEZ regime is discussed below.

---

[9] 'Commentary to the ILC Articles concerning the Law of the Sea', United Nations General Assembly Official Records (UNGAOR), 11th Sess, Supp No 9, UN Doc A/3159 (1956), (1956) II *Yearbook of the International Law Commission* 253, 277 (hereinafter ILC Commentary). See also *Virginia Commentaries*, Vol III, 61; O'Connell, n 5, Vol 2, 931.

[10] 1958 Convention on the High Seas, Art 1 (hereinafter HSC).

[11] See Chapters 2 and 7 of this volume.

[12] P Allott, 'Power Sharing in the Law of the Sea' (1983) 77 *American Journal of International Law* 1, 15.

[13] 'Introductory Note to the Revised Single Negotiating Text', UN Doc A/CONF.62/WP.8/Rev.1/Part II (1982) V *Official Records of UNCLOS III* 153 [17].

[14] LOSC, n 1, Art 58.

[15] R Platzöder, *Third United Nations Conference on the Law of the Sea: Documents* (Oceania Dobbs Ferry 1983) Vol 4, 328 and 426; *Virginia Commentaries*, Vol III, 67–9.

2.3 The freedom(s) of the high seas

The traditional freedoms of the high seas, as noted above, principally included navigation and fishing. Article 87 of the LOSC includes in a non-exhaustive list of all States' high-seas freedoms:

(a) freedom of navigation;
(b) freedom of overflight;
(c) freedom to lay submarine cables and pipelines, subject to Part VI;
(d) freedom to construct artificial islands and other installations ... subject to Part VI;
(e) freedom of fishing, subject to ... section 2;
(f) freedom of scientific research, subject to Parts VI and XIII.

Two preliminary observations can be made. The first four enumerated freedoms have their origins in the HSC[16] and the International Law Commission's 1956 Draft Articles on the law of the sea. The cross-references to other LOSC provisions underline that these freedoms are qualified by other rules of law. As the ILC put it:

Any freedom that is to be exercised in the interests of all entitled to enjoy it, must be regulated. Hence the law of the high seas contains certain rules ... designed not to limit or restrict the freedom of the high seas, but to safeguard its exercise in the interests of the entire international community.[17]

There is not enough space here for an exhaustive analysis of the enumerated freedoms, though certain points should be noted in relation to rights of navigation, fishing, marine scientific research, and laying cables and pipelines.[18]

Rights of navigation and overflight may be seen as a theme running through the LOSC.[19] As regards the high seas, their exercise is subject not only to other rules found in the high seas regime but elsewhere in the Convention.[20] In respect of the former, the high seas regime specifies the duties of flag States regarding such matters as the construction, equipment, seaworthiness, and manning of ships and the duty of flag States to ensure that masters render assistance to vessels in distress.[21] Other LOSC provisions which may affect the freedom of navigation include the obligations upon States to protect and preserve the marine environment and as regards vessel source pollution.[22]

---

[16] HSC, n 10, Art 2.
[17] ILC Commentary, n 9, 253, and 278. Compare *Virginia Commentaries*, Vol III, 80.
[18] See Chapters 19, 21, and 23–25 in this volume.   [19] See Chapter 23 in this volume.
[20] See eg LOSC, n 1, Art 192 and Part XII.   [21] Ibid, Arts 94 and 98.
[22] Ibid, Arts 192, 194(3)(b), and 211. See also ibid, Art 219 (limited port State control powers regarding vessel-source pollution).

In respect of fishing, the LOSC functions as a framework convention: it 'defer[s] much to subsequent agreement' among States as to how to manage fish stocks and consists 'largely of duties to negotiate, co-operate and take "necessary measures"'.[23] Nonetheless, the LOSC does set out a number of general principles. First, the right of all States to have 'their nationals engage in fishing on the high seas' is preserved subject to: (a) relevant treaty obligations; (b) the rights, duties and interests of coastal States provided for under the LOSC; and (c) the further provisions of Articles 117–120 of the LOSC on the conservation and management of marine living resources.[24] The overarching principle is found in Article 118, under which States have a broad duty to cooperate in the 'conservation and management of [high seas] living resources'. In particular, where their nationals are targeting the same living resources (or different resources in the same area) States must enter negotiations with a view to taking necessary conservation measures and 'shall as appropriate, cooperate to establish subregional or regional fisheries organizations to this end'. Article 118 thus contains a concrete duty not only to attempt to negotiate conservation measures, but to join or establish international fisheries organizations.[25] However, judging a breach of such duties to cooperate—other than in a case of manifest bad faith, such as an arbitrary rejection of negotiation—will be difficult.[26]

While all States have the right to conduct marine scientific research (MSR) on the high seas, one should note that this is qualified by reference to the general scientific research regime under Part XIII of the Convention. Thus, for example, activities by a vessel on the high seas involving research on a coastal State's legal continental shelf extending beyond the EEZ would be subject to coastal State consent.[27] All States however, have the right to conduct MSR in the water column beyond the EEZ and on seabed beyond national jurisdiction (the Area).[28] MSR in the Area is subject to further rules stipulated in Part XI. In particular, under Article 143 such research must be 'carried out exclusively for peaceful purposes and for the benefit of mankind as a whole' and the results of such research must be 'effectively disseminated'.

Turning to the laying of cables and pipelines, in 2010, the General Assembly recognized 'that fibre optic submarine cables transmit most of the world's data and communications and hence are vitally important to the global economy'

---

[23] D Guilfoyle, *Shipping Interdiction and the Law of the Sea* (Cambridge University Press Cambridge 2009) 100.

[24] LOSC, n 1, Art 116.

[25] Further duties are stipulated in ibid, Art 119. Regional fisheries management organizations are discussed in Chapter 19 in this volume.

[26] Y Tanaka, *The International Law of the Sea* (Cambridge University Press Cambridge 2012) 225–6.

[27] LOSC, n 1, Art 246(3) and (5).   [28] Ibid, Arts 256 and 257.

and all States' security.[29] The subject therefore merits some brief consideration. LOSC Article 112 confirms that '[a]ll States are entitled to lay submarine cables and pipelines on the bed of the high seas beyond the continental shelf.' As discussed below, the regimes of the territorial sea, archipelagic waters, the EEZ, and the continental shelf all have an impact on the right to lay cables.[30] The LOSC also contains provisions regarding both intentional interference with submarine cables and pipelines (in practice, relatively rare) and inadvertent damage to them, especially by anchors and fishing equipment (in practice, relatively common).[31] The wording of the relevant LOSC provisions draw heavily on earlier treaty law.[32] Curiously, a number of features of earlier treaties were not replicated in the LOSC, most notably: references to civil liability for cable or pipeline breakages; and provisions allowing the boarding and inspection at sea of vessels suspected of wilful or negligent damage to cables.[33]

3 The Legal Character of the High Seas: Allocation of Authority, Reservation for Peaceful Purposes, and its Relationship to Other Zones

3.1 The legal character of the high seas

As has already been noted, sovereign claims purportedly made in respect of the high seas are invalid. This, however, tells us relatively little about the legal character of the high seas. This section approaches that question through three particular issues. First, how authority is allocated over activities conducted on the high seas. This requires a discussion of the principle of flag State jurisdiction. Second, the impact of the idea, incorporated into the LOSC, that the high seas are reserved for peaceful purposes. Third, how the regime of the high seas interacts with other maritime zones of jurisdiction, and in particular the EEZ.

---

[29] 'Oceans and the Law of the Sea', UN Doc A/Res/65/37 A (7 December 2010) Preamble and [121] (adopted by 123 votes to 1, with 2 abstentions).
[30] LOSC, n 1, Arts 21(1)(c), 51(2), 58(1), and 79.   [31] Ibid, Arts 113–115.
[32] HSC, n 10, Arts 26–27; 1884 Convention for the Protection of Submarine Telegraph Cables (hereinafter Submarine Cables Convention).
[33] Submarine Cables Convention, Arts 2 and 10.

3.2 The role of flag States and the possibility of concurrent jurisdiction

While no State may extend its sovereignty over the high seas, '[t]he absence of any authority over ships' sailing there 'would lead to chaos'.[34] Public order, therefore, has been pursued through the principle of the nationality of ships and 'the jurisdiction of the flag State over the ship' on the high seas.[35] The rule is considered long-established[36] and is found in both treaty[37] and customary law.[38] Of this concept the International Tribunal for the Law of the Sea (ITLOS) said in *M/V 'Saiga' (No 2)*:

> [T]he [LOSC] considers a ship as a unit ... Thus the ship, everything on it, and every person involved or interested in its operations are treated as an entity linked to the flag State. The nationalities of these persons are not relevant.[39]

However, the phrase 'exclusive jurisdiction' may be misleading. Certainly, the most important aspect of so-called 'exclusive' flag State jurisdiction is that it confers immunity upon a ship from interference by foreign government vessels. The flag State thus has exclusive *enforcement* jurisdiction over its national vessels on the high seas (subject to exceptions based on consent, treaty law and custom). Nonetheless, it is clear in State practice that flag State jurisdiction does not prevent other States from attaching consequences to the conduct of their nationals on the high seas, even when aboard foreign vessels.[40] The high seas are a commons into which all States can, theoretically, project their authority to varying extents. There may thus be concurrent *prescriptive* jurisdiction over activities on the high seas.[41]

A simple example is the possibility in municipal law of punishing the ordinary crimes of nationals (such as assault) committed aboard a foreign flagged vessel while outside the territorial jurisdiction of the forum State.[42] A better example, perhaps, is the UN Food and Agriculture Organization's International Plan of Action on Illegal, Unreported and Unregulated Fishing 2001, which states that, under the LOSC:

---

[34] ILC Commentary, n 9, 279.

[35] MN Shaw, *International Law* (7th edn Cambridge University Press Cambridge 2014) 443; compare RR Churchill and AV Lowe, *The Law of the Sea* (3rd edn Manchester University Press Manchester 1999) 257.

[36] O'Connell, n 5, Vol 2, 799–801.   [37] HSC, n 10, Art 5; LOSC, n 1, Art 92.

[38] See eg *The 'Le Louis'* (1817) 2 Dods 210, 243.

[39] *M/V 'Saiga' (No 2) (Saint Vincent and the Grenadines v Guinea)* (Judgment) [1999] ITLOS Rep 10, [105].

[40] Guilfoyle, n 23, 101. See further *The Muscat Dhows (France/Great Britain)*, PCA 1905 (1961) XI RIAA 83, 96; compare LOSC, n 1, Art 117 (duty to cooperate in respect of nationals' high seas fishing) and Art 97(1) (flag State and State of nationality have jurisdiction over collisions incidents).

[41] Gidel, n 7, 261; *SS 'Lotus' (France v Turkey)* (Judgment) (1927) PCIJ (ser A) No 10, 4 (hereinafter *'Lotus' Case*).

[42] In UK law, this occurs only where the British national 'does not belong to the foreign ship' (ie as crew): Merchant Shipping Act 1995 (UK) c 21, § 281(a)(iii).

... and without prejudice to the primary responsibility of the flag State on the high seas, each State should, to the greatest extent possible, take measures or cooperate to ensure that nationals subject to their jurisdiction do not support or engage in IUU fishing.[43]

Indeed, the LOSC provides that '[a]ll States have the duty to take, or to cooperate... in taking, such measures *for their respective nationals* as may be necessary' to conserve high seas living resources.[44] Consistent with this understanding, the US Lacey Act makes it an offence for US nationals to violate any applicable fisheries regulations anywhere.[45]

As in general international law, there is no rule in the law of the sea that two national juridical orders cannot apply in the same space at the same time.[46] Indeed, the law of the sea only provides in limited cases for the exclusion of jurisdiction which might otherwise be available. The point is taken up below in relation to collisions at sea, where treaty law has come to restrict which States have jurisdiction regarding 'incidents of navigation'.[47] The necessary implication, however, of this approach is plain. Absent such treaty law restrictions, any State with an ordinary jurisdictional nexus to conduct on the high seas may assert jurisdiction. The only general prohibition is upon States exercising *enforcement* jurisdiction over foreign vessels on the high seas.[48] The interest preserved by such a rule is each State's interest in freedom of navigation.

3.3 The reservation of the high seas for peaceful purposes

Article 88 of the LOSC declares that the high seas are reserved for use for 'peaceful purposes'.[49] This language may appear 'to impose far-reaching limitations upon military activities at sea' and has proved controversial.[50] During the negotiation of the LOSC, many delegations appeared concerned with disarmament and preventing

---

[43] UN Food and Agriculture Organization, *International Plan of Action to Prevent, Deter and Eliminate Illegal, Unreported and Unregulated Fishing* (23 June 2001), available at <http://www.fao.org/docrep/003/y1224e/y1224e00.htm>.

[44] LOSC, n 1, Art 117 (emphasis added).

[45] 16 USC §§ 3371–3378 (1900). See further Guilfoyle, n 23, 101.

[46] Gidel, n 7, 261; see also L Savagado, 'Les navires battant pavillon d'une organisation internationale' (2007) 53 *Annuaire Français de Droit International* 640, 661.

[47] See text accompanying nn 108 ff.

[48] See further D Carson, 'Ships, Nationality and Status' in R Bernhardt (ed), *Encyclopedia of Public International Law* (North-Holland Publishing Amsterdam 2000) Vol 4, 404; compare Gidel, n 7, 229–33, and H Meyers, *The Nationality of Ships* (Martinus Nijhoff The Hague 1967) 318–21.

[49] For other references to peaceful purposes/uses, see the LOSC, n 1, Preamble and Arts 141, 143(1), 147(2)(d), 155(2), 240, 242(1), and 246(3).

[50] BA Boczek, 'Peaceful Purposes Provisions of the United Nations Convention on the Law of the Sea' (1989) 20 *Ocean Development & International Law* 359, 371.

the emplacement of nuclear weapons on the seabed, though few asserted that Article 88 as drafted had that effect.[51]

Nonetheless, the 'peaceful purposes' provision raises questions regarding the legality of high seas weapons testing and military manoeuvres. There are examples of treaties prior to the LOSC using similar language to proclaim that areas such as the Antarctic or outer space are reserved for 'peaceful purposes'.[52] However, in such treaties this language is accompanied by 'prohibitions on military fortifications, military manoeuvres' and weapons testing.[53] Similarly, in its preamble, the Seabed Treaty[54] recognizes the 'common interest' in using the seafloor for 'peaceful purposes', before prohibiting the emplacement of weapons of mass destruction on the seafloor.[55] If the intention had been to ban weapons testing and military manoeuvres under the LOSC, words could obviously have been included to that effect.[56] Further support for this conclusion can be drawn from Article 301 of the LOSC, which restates the general duty of States to 'refrain from any threat or use of force against the territorial integrity or political independence of any State' found in the UN Charter. On its face, this only bans such activities as would constitute acts of aggression or breaches of the non-intervention principle. It is also the only express prohibition on military activities in the Convention. Indeed, States parties have the option under Article 298(1)(b) of the LOSC to exclude disputes concerning military activities from the Convention's compulsory dispute settlement procedures. If such high seas activities were generally thought illegal this exclusion would be 'unjustifiable.'[57]

Thus it would appear some weapons testing and naval manoeuvres, at least, are permissible uses of the high seas.[58] That is, they may be considered an exercise of the freedom of navigation to be conducted with 'due regard' to other States' rights.[59] However, the legality of certain States'—principally France and the USA—historic practice of conducting nuclear atmospheric weapons tests and declaring large

---

[51] Other than Ecuador: 'Record of 67th plenary meeting' (1982) V *Official Records of UNCLOS III* 56.

[52] 1959 Antarctic Treaty, Art 1; 1967 Treaty on Principles Governing the Activities of States in the Exploration and Use of Outer Space, including the Moon and other Celestial Bodies, Preamble and Art 4. Compare UNGA Res 2749 (XXV) of 12 December 1970, *Declaration of Principles Governing the Sea-Bed and the Ocean Floor, and the Subsoil Thereof, Beyond the Limits of National Jurisdiction*, Preamble and Arts 5, 8, and 10.

[53] BH Oxman, 'The Regime of Warships under the United Nations Convention on the Law of the Sea' (1983–1984) 24 *Virginia Journal of International Law* 809, 830.

[54] 1971 Treaty on the Prohibition of the Emplacement of Nuclear Weapons and other Weapons of Mass Destruction on the Sea-Bed and the Ocean Floor and in the Subsoil Thereof.

[55] Ibid, Preamble and Art 1. Compare UNGA Res 2749 (XXV), n 52, Preamble and Arts 5, 8, and 10.

[56] Oxman, n 53, 831; similarly, see R Wolfrum, 'Restricting the Use of the Sea to Peaceful Purposes: Demilitarization in Being' (1981) 24 *German Yearbook of International Law* 200, 213.

[57] A Proelss, 'Peaceful Purposes' in R Wolfrum (ed), *Max Planck Encyclopedia of Public International Law* (Oxford University Press Oxford 2012) [15], available at <http://opil.ouplaw.com/home/EPIL>.

[58] Churchill and Lowe, n 35, 206.   [59] LOSC, n 1, Art 87(1)(a) and (2).

exclusion zones in surrounding high seas areas has certainly been questioned.[60] Such testing would now be prohibited under the Nuclear Test Ban Treaty[61] and be incompatible with obligations to protect the marine environment.[62] In any event, no State has conducted an atmospheric nuclear test since 1980. The question of military manoeuvres in the EEZ is discussed below.

3.4 The relationship of the high seas to the EEZ

While at first sight it appears to follow from Article 86 of the LOSC that the area of the high seas was diminished by the establishment of EEZs, it is not as simple as saying that at 200 nm from States' baselines 'the EEZ ends... and the high seas begin'.[63] The LOSC expressly provides for the continued application of certain high seas freedoms (navigation, overflight, and the laying of cables) in the EEZ along with 'other internationally lawful uses of the sea related to these freedoms'.[64] That is, freedoms of the high seas having application within the EEZ constitute only a narrow selection from what is otherwise a non-exhaustive list of high-seas freedoms.[65] Nonetheless, 'Articles 88 to 115 and other pertinent rules of international law' apply to the EEZ 'in so far as they are *not incompatible with*' the rights and jurisdiction granted to coastal States in the EEZ.[66] While the creation of the EEZ means that some rights 'formerly included within the concept of the freedom of the high seas, in particular those relating to natural resources, are [now] abridged or abrogated' in favour of the coastal State,[67] the legal regime of the high seas remains otherwise applicable in the EEZ.

The proposition that the high seas regime applies to the extent that it is 'not incompatible with' a coastal State's rights is less than a model of clarity and sets up a potential conflict of rights. The LOSC provides, on its face, no clear presumption in favour of either coastal State rights or navigating States' freedoms in the EEZ in the event of such conflict.[68] Instead, the Convention sets out a principle that, in exercising their respective rights (or performing their duties) under the LOSC within an EEZ, navigating and coastal States shall both 'have

---

[60] *Nuclear Tests (Australia v France)* (Merits) [1974] ICJ Rep 253; *Nuclear Tests (New Zealand v France)* (Merits) [1974] ICJ Rep 457; M McDougal, 'The Hydrogen Bomb Tests and the International Law of the Sea' (1995) 49 *American Journal of International Law* 356; E Margolis, 'The Hydrogen Bomb Experiments and International Law' (1958) 64 *Yale Law Journal* 629.
[61] 1963 Treaty Banning Nuclear Weapon Tests in the Atmosphere, in Outer Space and Under Water.
[62] LOSC, n 1, Art 192. On customary rules, see Proelss, n 57, [16].
[63] Allott, n 12, 15; contra, Lucchini and Voelckel, n 5, Vol 1, 267.
[64] LOSC, n 1, Arts 58 and 86.   [65] Ibid, Arts 58(2) and 87.
[66] Ibid, Art 58(2) (emphasis added).   [67] *Virginia Commentaries*, Vol III, 70.
[68] T Treves, 'High Seas' in R Wolfrum (ed). *Max Planck Encyclopedia of Public International Law* (Oxford University Press Oxford 2012) [6]; A Proelss, 'The Law on the Exclusive Economic Zone in Perspective: Legal Status and Resolution of User Conflicts Revisited' (2012) 26 *Ocean Yearbook* 87.

due regard to the rights and duties' of each other.⁶⁹ This leaves room for conflict even where navigating States' rights in the EEZ are expressly acknowledged, for example, in the laying of submarine cables. Laying a cable presupposes surveying a route to lay it, and conducting such a survey within an EEZ would therefore seem a lawful, incidental use of the ocean. However, in practice, 'the right to conduct cable route surveys in the EEZ appears to be a casualty of the long-standing debate on the permissibility of [EEZ] surveys' generally, and many coastal States consider EEZ surveys subject to their approval.⁷⁰ Further, while the LOSC makes it clear that a coastal State's consent is required for the delineation of *pipeline* routes on its continental shelf the text is silent on submarine *cable* delineation.⁷¹ The inference appears to be that coastal States cannot regulate the routing of a cable laid in their EEZ. Nonetheless, many coastal States adopt national laws regulating the issue.⁷²

Quite apart from conflicts as to the exercise by navigating States of expressly preserved freedoms of the high seas in a coastal State's EEZ, there is the issue of rights *not* expressly attributed either to the coastal State or navigating States. Questions of unattributed rights fall for resolution in accordance with Article 59 of the LOSC, which provides that such disputes 'should be resolved on the basis of equity and in the light of all the relevant circumstances' and taking into account the interests of both the parties and the international community. The Article 59 criteria have rightly been described as 'elusive'⁷³ and lacking 'normative content' in the absence of their application by a third-party dispute settlement mechanism.⁷⁴

Among the difficult questions left unresolved is the entitlement of foreign States to conduct military manoeuvres in a coastal State's EEZ. The plain text of the Convention suggests that what is permissible under Article 88 on the high seas (as discussed above) is permissible in the EEZ, to the extent it does not conflict with rights vested in the coastal State.⁷⁵ Nonetheless, States such as Bangladesh, Brazil, Cape Verde, India, Malaysia, Pakistan, and Uruguay have all asserted in declarations made upon signature or ratification of the LOSC that coastal State permission is required for such operations.⁷⁶ This is disputed by France, Germany, Italy, the

---

⁶⁹ LOSC, n 1, Arts 56(2) and 58(2).
⁷⁰ T Davenport, 'Submarine Communications Cables and Law of the Sea: Problems in Law and Practice' (2012) 43 *Ocean Development and International Law* 201, 210.
⁷¹ LOSC, n 1, Art 79(3).   ⁷² Davenport, n 70, 211–12.   ⁷³ Churchill and Lowe, n 35, 461.
⁷⁴ N Klein, *Dispute Settlement in the UN Convention on the Law of the Sea* (Cambridge University Press Cambridge 2005) 140. Note *Virginia Commentaries*, Vol II, 569.
⁷⁵ LOSC, n 1, Art 58(2).
⁷⁶ DR Rothwell and T Stephens, *The International Law of the Sea* (Hart Oxford 2010) 280; Boczek, n 50, 372. A list of declarations is available at <http://treaties.un.org/pages/ViewDetailsIII.aspx?&src=TREATY&mtdsg_no=XXI~6&chapter=21&Temp=mtdsg3&lang=en>.

Netherlands, the United Kingdom, and the United States.[77] What legal weight is to be given to this State practice? On one view, such statements by coastal States are simply attempts at impermissible reservations and therefore have no legal effect.[78] A fairer view is that the LOSC simply does not make it clear whether such exercises are 'included among the preserved EEZ freedoms' or are instead 'unattributed rights falling for decision under' Article 59.[79]

4 Shipping

4.1 Overview

As discussed, the key ordering principle of the high seas regime is that of the nationality of ships. The long-established rule is that any State may grant its nationality to a vessel, and thereafter shall exercise 'exclusive jurisdiction' over it on the high seas.[80] The US Supreme Court expressed it thus:

> Each State under international law may determine for itself the conditions on which it will grant its nationality to a merchant ship, thereby accepting responsibility for it and acquiring authority over it.[81]

This section therefore discusses: the nationality of ships; the law applicable to stateless vessels; and the question of jurisdiction in collisions.

4.2 The nationality of ships

The law and history of flag State regulation of shipping is notoriously vexed. For present purposes, every State has the right to confer its nationality upon a ship subject to several requirements: it must fix conditions for the grant of nationality and make provision for registering ships (unfortunately, there is no universal requirement that small vessels enjoying nationality be registered);[82] it must issue

---

[77] Rothwell and Stephens, n 76, 280; Churchill and Lowe, n 35, 427.

[78] LOSC, n 1, Arts 309 and 310. See eg R Pedrozo, 'Preserving Navigational Rights and Freedoms: The Right to Conduct Military Activities in China's Exclusive Economic Zone' (2010) 9 *Chinese Journal of International Law* 7, 10.

[79] Churchill and Lowe, n 35, 427. See further Wolfrum, n 56, 208; Pedrozo, n 78, 10.

[80] LOSC, n 1, Art 92; HSC, n 10, Art 6.

[81] *Lauritzen v Larsen*, 345 US 571, 571 (1953); compare *Muscat Dhows*, n 40, 93.

[82] See eg Merchant Shipping Act, n 42, § 1(1)(d) (exempting from registration vessels under 24 metres owned by nationals); Shipping Registration Act 1981 (Australia), § 13 (exempting vessels

documents of nationality to those ships it grants 'the right to fly its flag'; and, most problematically, there must exist a 'genuine link' between the flag State and a vessel granted its nationality.[83] The grant of nationality also brings with it certain duties.[84] The focus of discussion here will be on the question of genuine link and attribution of nationality.

The legal requirement of a 'genuine link' between a flag State and a vessel enjoying its nationality has been perennially controversial.[85] Treaty law is silent as to the consequences if such a link is lacking.[86] The underlying idea appears to be that a State's competence to confer its nationality upon ships is not unlimited. This follows the *Nottebohm* dictum that 'nationality is a legal bond having as its basis a social fact of attachment, a genuine connection'.[87] This, however, goes no further than saying that nationality as a legal status should reflect some 'factual link'.[88] Nonetheless, one might infer that absent such 'genuine connection' in matters of 'management, ownership, jurisdiction and control' other States need not recognize a grant of nationality.[89] This might be thought a useful approach, especially where ships apparently flying flags of convenience are engaged in undesirable activities.[90] ITLOS, however, held in *M/V 'Saiga' (No 2)* that the purpose of the genuine link requirement 'is to secure more effective implementation of the duties of the flag State [under Art 94], and not to establish criteria by reference to which the validity of the registration of ships in a flag State may be challenged by other States'.[91] ITLOS reiterated this position in *M/V 'Virginia G'*, but added that the existence of a 'genuine link' required that a flag State 'exercise effective jurisdiction and control over that ship in order to ensure

---

under 24 metres, government ships, pleasure craft; fishing vessels are registered under the Fisheries Management Act 1991); *Shipping*, 46 USC §§ 12102(b) and 12303(a) (exempting vessels under 5 tons; other exceptions by regulations); Shipping Act 2001 (Canada), § 47(a) (exempting pleasure craft).

[83] LOSC, n 1, Art, 91; HSC, n 10, Art 5.   [84] See further Chapter 13 in this volume.

[85] Historically, attempting to give the concept substance proved impractical. Any detailed proposals by codifiers were inevitably rejected by governments with laxer national standards. See M McDougal and W Burke, *The Public Order of the Oceans* (New Haven Press New Haven, CT 1987) 1013–15, 1026, and 1028–33; and Meyers, n 48, 205 and 208. See further VP Coglianti-Bantz, 'Disentangling the Genuine Link: Enquiries in Sea, Air and Space Law' (2010) 79 *Nordic Journal of International Law* 383, 390–8; and ILC Commentary, n 9, 280–1.

[86] Lucchini and Voelckel, n 5, Vol 1, 68–9.

[87] *Nottebohm (Liechtenstein v Guatemala)* (Judgment) [1955] ICJ Rep 4, 23.

[88] Churchill and Lowe, n 35, 258.

[89] *Barcelona Traction, Light and Power Company Ltd (Belgium v Spain)* (Judgment) [1970] ICJ Rep 161, 188 (Separate Opinion of Judge Jessup); compare McDougal and Burke, n 85, 1026 and 1028–33.

[90] R Rayfuse, 'The Anthropocene, Autopoiesis and the Disingenuousness of the Genuine Link: Addressing Enforcement Gaps in the Legal Regime for Areas Beyond National Jurisdiction' in AG Oude Elferink and EJ Molenaar (eds), *The Legal Regime of Areas beyond National Jurisdiction: Current Principles and Frameworks and Future Directions* (Martinus Nijhoff Leiden 2010) 165.

[91] *M/V 'Saiga' (No 2)*, n 39, [83].

that it operates in accordance with generally accepted international regulations, procedures and practices'.[92] The consequences of failing to discharge this duty went unspecified. It appears that, in practice, 'genuine link' either has no independent content outside each flag State's municipal law on nationality of vessels or is merely synonymous with a flag State fulfilling its duties regarding vessels granted its nationality.[93] While the concept of a 'genuine link' would appear on its face to require some higher standard than this, if so, it has 'not been widely observed in practice'.[94] The lack of substantive regulatory capacity (or interest in fulfilling their duties) on the part of some flag States can have egregious consequences. Not only are flag of convenience vessels over-represented in practices such as illegal, unreported, or unregulated (IUU) fishing, but failure to genuinely exercise control in social and technical matters is emerging as an area of significant concern. Increasingly, reports are documenting the extent to which forced labour is prevalent in parts of the fishing industry.[95] In the worst cases, unpaid fishermen may be held incommunicado at sea for years, given that a vessel transhipping its catch and resupplying at sea need seldom enter port.[96]

The idea that a vessel must be subjected to the national jurisdiction of a flag State has two further corollaries. The first is that a vessel, unlike a natural person, may not enjoy dual nationality. This would compromise the integrity of a flag State's regulatory responsibilities.[97] Thus, Article 92(2) of the LOSC provides that a 'ship which sails under the flags of two or more States' may not claim the benefit of any nationality in respect of third States. The second is that a vessel may be without nationality (a 'stateless vessel'), as discussed below.

4.3 Stateless vessels

The statelessness of a vessel may arise through failure to acquire any nationality, or a vessel may be treated as stateless where it 'sails under the flags of two or more States', according to convenience.[98] Neither the LOSC nor the HSC stipulates the consequences of statelessness, and scholarly views vary.[99]

---

[92] *M/V 'Virginia G' (Panama v Guinea-Bissau)*, Judgment of the International Tribunal for the Law of the Sea, Case No 19 (14 April 2014) [113].
[93] O'Connell, n 5, Vol 2, 752.
[94] Churchill and Lowe, n 35, 258.
[95] For a literature review, see E de Coning et al, *Caught at Sea: Forced Labour and Trafficking in Fisheries* (International Labour Organization 2013), available at <http://www.ilo.org/wcmsp5/groups/public/---ed_norm/---declaration/documents/publication/wcms_214472.pdf>.
[96] Environmental Justice Foundation, *All at Sea: The Abuse of Human Rights Aboard Illegal Fishing Vessels* (Environmental Justice Foundation London 2010) 8, available at <http://ejfoundation.org/sites/default/files/public/media/report-all%20at%20sea_0.pdf>.
[97] LOSC, n 1, Art 94.   [98] Ibid, Arts 91 and 92(2), as discussed above.
[99] Although see ibid, Art 110(1)(e).

While reference to stateless vessels is commonly found in the literature, the contours of the idea are less certain. It is certainly not enough for a vessel to be treated as stateless that it does not fly a flag, bear marks of registry, or carry documentation. As noted, there is no universal requirement that small vessels must be registered to enjoy nationality, and the LOSC provides disjunctively for the grant of nationality to vessels either by registration *or* the right to fly a flag.[100] Thus, many flag States have in municipal law a category of unregistered vessels nonetheless enjoying nationality.[101] In practice, it may thus be hard to determine whether a small craft on the high seas is in law stateless or not.

However, a vessel may become stateless by operation of law in one of two ways ('constructive statelessness').[102] First, as noted, if a vessel uses two nationalities at its convenience it loses the protection of both. Second, if hailed by a government vessel, a private vessel may declare a nationality ('the presumptive flag State'). If the presumptive flag State refutes that claim of nationality, the vessel is again rendered constructively stateless; if it attempted to claim an alternative nationality, it would fall foul of the rule against the dual nationality of ships.

The question of small vessels and statelessness is of more than academic interest. Small craft without registration documents or national markings are commonly used in irregular migration or the smuggling of migrants by sea. Such activities occur *inter alia* on maritime migration routes between North Africa and Europe, Indonesia and Australia, and across the Caribbean towards the United States.[103] However, any legal uncertainty as to the national status of such small craft does not in practice prevent their interdiction. First, as discussed below, any government vessel has a right to visit a vessel on the high seas suspected of being without nationality. This permits boarding and inspection. Second, interdicting governments can obtain control over persons aboard (their primary aim) through deeming the vessel dangerously overcrowded; this finding will then oblige them to rescue those aboard by removing them from the unsafe vessel.[104] This 'duty of compulsory rescue' has proved an important tool for maritime migrant interdiction and appears more generally relied upon than ship-boarding provisions in treaties such as the Migrant Smuggling Protocol.[105]

---

[100] Ibid, Art 91(1).   [101] See n 82.   [102] See further, Guilfoyle, n 23, 121, 124, and 249.

[103] Guilfoyle, n 23, ch 8; E Papastavridis, *The Interception of Vessels on the High Seas* (Hart Oxford 2013) ch 8.

[104] See generally V Moreno-Lax, 'Seeking, Asylum in the Mediterranean: Against a Fragmentary Reading of EU Member States' Obligations Accruing at Sea' (2011) 23 *International Journal of Refugee Law* 174.

[105] Ibid; Guilfoyle, n 23, 195; 2000 Protocol against the Smuggling of Migrants by Land, Sea and Air, Supplementing the United Nations Convention against Transnational Organized Crime, Art 8 (hereinafter Migrant Smuggling Protocol).

The consequences of statelessness, however, are unclear. Treaty law is silent on whether a vessel may be subjected to the national law of the interdicting State simply by virtue of being stateless. Indeed, it is sometimes deliberately ambiguous. A number of major multilateral treaties—including the Migrant Smuggling Protocol—provide that a State party may board a suspect vessel on reasonable suspicion of statelessness, and, if 'evidence confirming the suspicion is found', may 'take appropriate measures in accordance with relevant domestic and international law'.[106] Such phrasing covers divergent national (and academic) interpretations. The first view, taken by the United States and, historically, by the United Kingdom, is that a stateless vessel may be arrested by any State as it enjoys the protection of none.[107] The second view is that some further jurisdictional nexus between the acts of the vessel and the interdicting State (or a general permissive rule) is required to justify seizure.[108]

4.4 Jurisdiction in collisions

A further controversy has been the limits of jurisdiction over 'incidents of navigation' on the high seas, especially given the plurality of States which could assert jurisdiction over events such as collisions. The point is illustrated by the classic *'Lotus' Case*.[109] This concerned a high seas collision between the *Lotus*, a French mail steamer, and the *Boz-Kourt*, a Turkish colliers resulting in eight deaths aboard the latter. When the *Lotus* called at Constantinople, Turkey arrested the officer in charge at the time. The Permanent Court of International Justice (PCIJ) found, on the ordinary application of jurisdictional principles, that the offence of negligent navigation occasioning death (an offence commenced in French jurisdiction) could be treated as having occurred on *Boz-Korut* (where its effects were felt) and thus was subject to both flag States' jurisdiction.[110] The decision 'produced alarm among seafarers, and a long campaign against the rule',[111] which was thought to create the prospect of multiple prosecutions for the same offence. The ruling has

---

[106] Migrant Smuggling Protocol, n 105, Art 8; compare 1988 United Nations Convention against Illicit Traffic in Narcotic Drugs and Psychotropic Substances, Art 17(2) and 1995 United Nations Agreement for the Implementation of the Provisions of the United Nations Convention on the Law of the Sea of 10 December 1982 relating to the Conservation and Management of Straddling Fish Stocks and Highly Migratory Fish Stocks, Art 21(17).

[107] *Molvan v Attorney General for Palestine* [1948] AC 351, 369; (Privy Council) (1948) 15 ILR 115, 124; see discussion in Guilfoyle, n 23, 17.

[108] Churchill and Lowe, n 35, 214; Papastavridis, n 103, 266.   [109] *'Lotus' Case*, n 41.

[110] Churchill and Lowe, n 35, 208.

[111] P Malanczuk, *Akehurst's Modern Introduction to International Law* (Routledge New York 1997) 109.

since been limited by treaty law.[112] The LOSC now provides that, in cases of 'incidents of navigation', only the flag State of the vessel causing the injury or the State of nationality of the suspect offender may exercise jurisdiction. An exception is provided in relation to disciplinary proceedings which may be pursued by any State which issued 'a master's certificate or a certificate of competence or licence', irrespective of whether the licence-holder is a national.[113] A variety of occupations may require such certification including master, chief mate, and officer in charge of a navigational watch.[114] The concept of 'incidents of navigation' probably extends to cover a 'maritime casualty'[115] and may also include damage to submarine cables and pipelines.[116]

The scope of the rule became a live question in the 2012 *Enrica Lexie* incident in which two Italian marines placed aboard a private vessel to defend it from pirate attacks in the Indian Ocean mistakenly killed two Indian fishermen. Unsurprisingly, occasioning death by deliberate live fire from one vessel into another was not conceded by India to be an 'incident of navigation' falling within the LOSC rule.[117]

5 Policing the High Seas

Much of this chapter has focussed on the exclusive jurisdiction of flag States. The most notable exception to this principle is found in the general right of visit under customary and treaty law. Other exceptions are found in various law enforcement treaties which contemplate measures of visit, inspection, and arrest of vessels on the high seas in relation to particular subject matters. The right of visit is a tool for the suppression of various uses of the oceans perceived as contrary to the general interests of States—most notably piracy and the slave trade.[118]

---

[112] 1952 International Convention for the Unification of Certain Rules relating to Penal Jurisdiction in matters of Collisions and Other Incidents of Navigation, Arts 1 and 2; HSC, n 10, Art 11; LOSC, n 1, Art 97.

[113] LOSC, n 1, Art 97(2).

[114] See 1978 International Convention on Standards of Training, Certification and Watchkeeping, as amended.

[115] As defined in LOSC, n 1, Art 221(2); see *Virginia Commentaries*, Vol III, 168.

[116] ILC Commentary, n 9, 281. See LOSC, n 1, Arts 113–15.   [117] LOSC, n 1, Art 97(2).

[118] Guilfoyle, n 23, 23–5 and 28; and Rothwell and Stephens, n 76, 162–5; compare McDougal and Burke, n 85, 51–3 and 880–93.

Under the right of visit, a government vessel may send a boat under the command of an officer to visit and inspect a foreign private vessel.[119] This right clearly impinges on navigational freedoms and is, unsurprisingly, a limited one. Under Article 110 of the LOSC, it may be exercised only upon reasonable suspicion that the vessel in question is engaged in:

- piracy;[120]
- the slave trade;
- unauthorized broadcasting;

or the vessel is otherwise reasonably suspected of being either:

- without nationality (stateless); or
- of the same nationality as the warship (despite displaying either no flag or marks of registration or those of a different State).

This approach is narrowed still further by the fact that the LOSC codification of the right of visit only *expressly* provides for enforcement jurisdiction over piracy and unauthorized broadcasting.[121] In all other cases, presumably, one can inspect but not detain a vessel—and any authority to take enforcement action lies with the flag State unless a special customary or treaty right can be shown.[122] This produces notable discrepancies. While slavery is now considered contrary to *jus cogens*, it is uncertain that a right to arrest slave vessels on the high seas was ever generally accepted as customary law.[123] While it would be a brave flag State that objected to such an exercise of jurisdiction, there is nonetheless a jarring incoherence in allowing enforcement jurisdiction in respect of unauthorized broadcasting but not slave trading.[124] The peculiar collection of activities subject to a right of visit under the LOSC is explicable only as the result of a 'long accretive history of experiments in designing jurisdictional regimes' to address particular problems.[125] This piecemeal approach serves to highlight both the traditional jealousy with which States view any encroachment on flag State jurisdiction and the narrowness of the right of visit under the LOSC.[126] The emergence of new

---

[119] In the first instance, only papers should be inspected and a full search should only be initiated if suspicions remain: LOSC, n 1, Art 110(2). In practice a security sweep (ie search) may precede other action.

[120] See Chapter 37 in this volume.   [121] LOSC, n 1, Arts 105 and 109.

[122] Klein, n 3, 114–22; Churchill and Lowe, n 35, 212.

[123] McDougal and Burke, n 85, 881. Arguing a customary rule of enforcement jurisdiction has emerged: R Reuland, 'Interference with non-national ships on the high seas: peacetime exceptions to the exclusivity rule of flag state jurisdiction' (1989) 22 *Vanderbilt Journal of Transnational Law* 1161, 1195–6.

[124] Compare LOSC, n 1, Arts 109(4) and 110.   [125] Guilfoyle, n 23, 24.

[126] Reuland, n 123, 1170–1 n 22; N Klein, 'Legal limitations on ensuring Australia's maritime security' (2006) 7 *Melbourne Journal of International Law* 306, 335–6.

high-seas threats to public order has not been met with the creation (or even the unilateral assertion) of new general rights of interdiction.[127] Instead, bilateral and multilateral treaty arrangements—and occasionally Security Council resolutions—have had to fill the gap. Absent either such special arrangements or a flag State granting consent ad hoc, there may well be scenarios where a right of visit exercised on one ground reveals evidence of a different crime in respect of which nothing can be done under the LOSC. It is not uncommon, for example, for warships in the Gulf of Aden encountering suspect pirate vessels to discover the crew are 'merely' engaged in migrant smuggling (or even human trafficking).[128]

Among numerous crimes not attracting a right of visit under the LOSC, smuggling narcotics by sea at least gives rise to a duty for States to cooperate in its suppression.[129] Otherwise it forms a prime example of States having concluded treaties creating new rights of visit and even enforcement jurisdiction.[130] Under these treaties, a flag State may consent to boarding and inspection, and possibly even arrest, of one of its vessels suspected of being engaged in drug smuggling. One of the widely commented on (if little implemented) innovations created by these treaties are 'shipriders'. The essential idea of a shiprider is that a law enforcement official from State A might be embarked upon a government vessel belonging to State B, and could thus authorize interdiction of suspect vessels of A's nationality or even pursuit of a suspect vessel into A's territorial sea. While in many contexts a theoretically attractive proposition, in practice, embarking a foreign shiprider aboard a government vessel results in a number of logistical difficulties and requires the partner State to have both personnel to spare and legislation authorizing extraterritorial policing operations.[131]

Nonetheless, while there is a long international history of creating new multilateral and bilateral legal mechanisms to suppress narcotics smuggling by sea,[132] other maritime security threats have not necessarily attracted a similar response.

---

[127] Klein, n 3, 325; Guilfoyle, n 23, 24–5.
[128] On migrant smuggling in the Gulf of Aden, see eg UN High Commissioner for Refugees, 'More than 62,000 people, mostly Ethiopians, risk lives to cross Gulf of Aden this year' (8 November 2013), available at <http://www.unhcr.org/527cc7b66.html>.
[129] LOSC, n 1, Art 108(1).
[130] See eg ship-boarding provisions in 1988 United Nations Convention against Illicit Traffic in Narcotic Drugs and Psychotropic Substances; 2003 Agreement concerning Cooperation in Suppressing Illicit Maritime and Air Trafficking in Narcotic Drugs and Psychotropic Substances in the Caribbean Area; 1990 Treaty between the Kingdom of Spain and the Italian Republic to Combat Illicit Drug Trafficking at Sea; 1995 Council of Europe Agreement on Illicit Traffic by Sea, Implementing Article 17 of the United Nations Convention against Illicit Traffic in Narcotic Drugs and Psychotropic Substances. The extensive US bilateral treaty practice on point is discussed in Guilfoyle, n 23, ch 5; Papastavridis, n 103, ch 7; and Klein, n 3, 130–7.
[131] Guilfoyle, n 23, 91; D Guilfoyle, 'Combating Piracy: Executive Measures on the High Seas' (2010) 53 *Japanese Yearbook of International Law* 149, 171–2.
[132] See n 130.

Two subjects bear particular attention: the growth of irregular migration by sea and attempts to counter the proliferation of weapons of mass destruction (WMD) by sea. The first has resulted in bilateral treaty law practice and even a multilateral convention in the form of the Migrant Smuggling Protocol noted above.[133] However, there is little evidence that the at-sea boarding provisions in the Migrant Smuggling Protocol have been used in practice and some bilateral treaties have lapsed without renewal.[134] Efforts to suppress migration by sea now more commonly occur through unilateral action or under non-binding bilateral memoranda of understanding. One such example is Australia's recent, controversial 'turn back' or 'tow back' policy towards migrant boats under its 'Operation Sovereign Borders'. In one episode in 2014, 41 asylum seekers from Sir Lanka were intercepted by Australia at sea, 'screened' for asylum claims, and then transferred at sea to a Sri Lankan naval vessel.[135] In other incidents, Australia has either towed migrant boats back to the edge of Indonesian territorial waters or has transferred migrants at sea to life-craft before towing those to the edge of Indonesian territorial waters.[136] The compatibility of these practices with international law has been challenged.[137] Another major example is provided by the EU practice of conducting counter-migration patrols in Senegal, Mauritania, or Cape Verde's territorial waters with the coastal State's consent.[138]

Efforts to counter WMD proliferation by sea have also not resulted in any major innovations in the right of visit. There was certainly a hectic phase of treaty-making, lead by the USA, aimed at suppressing WMD proliferation by sea. This resulted, first, in bilateral US interdiction treaties with twelve significant flag States;[139] and, second, in efforts to conclude a multilateral WMD interdiction treaty under the auspices of the International Maritime Organization (IMO). Progress has, to some extent, stalled on both fronts. First, a number of major flag States clearly resisted entering such 'partnerships' with the USA

---

[133] See references at n 105.

[134] On terminated/lapsed agreements, see Guilfoyle, n 23, 189–91 (USA–Haiti) and 210 (Italy–Albania).

[135] P Farrell and N Evershed, 'Operation Sovereign Borders Timeline', *The Guardian* (7 July 2014), available at <http://www.theguardian.com/news/datablog/interactive/2014/jul/01/operation-sovereign-borders-timeline>.

[136] Ibid. See also Australian Government, Senate Standing Committees on Foreign Affairs Defence and Trade, *Report: Breach of Indonesian Territorial Waters* (27 March 2014), available at <http://www.aph.gov.au/Parliamentary_Business/Committees/>.

[137] B Doherty, '53 Australian lawyers condemn return of asylum seekers to Sri Lanka', *Sydney Morning Herald* (7 July 2014), available at <http://www.smh.com.au/federal-politics/political-news/53-australian-lawyers-condemn-return-of-asylum-seekers-to-sri-lanka-20140707-zsz13.html>; J Wardell, 'All at Sea: Is Australia's Fast-tracked Asylum Screening Policy Fair?', *Reuters* (Sydney) (9 July 2014), available at <http://uk.reuters.com/article/2014/07/09/uk-sri-lanka-australia-screening- idUKKBN0FD0TS20140709>.

[138] Moreno-Lax, n 104, 181; Papastavridis, n 103, 286–90.

[139] As discussed in Guilfoyle, n 23, ch 9, and Klein, n 3, ch 4, treaties were concluded with: Antigua and Barbuda, Bahamas, Belize, Croatia, Cyprus, Liberia, Malta, Marshall Islands, Mongolia, Panama,

(notably Greece and China), thus limiting the reach of hub-and-spoke bilateralism. In terms of multilateral treaty negotiation, the capstone treaty-making effort on maritime WMD counter-proliferation operations was the 2005 Protocol to the Convention for the Suppression of Unlawful Acts against the Safety of Maritime Navigation. This instrument, however, has languished. While it has entered into force among a small number of States these include few major flag States and—more critically for any treaty contemplating high seas interdiction operations—*no* major naval powers.[140] The situation has not been remedied by Security Council resolutions on point. For example, the Security Council sanctions regime targeting North Korea's weapons exports, including potential WMD materiel, provides only for high seas inspection of suspect shipments with the consent of the flag State—it creates no compulsory powers.[141] Instead, where consent is refused, the vessel may be directed into port for inspection.[142] The deference to flag State jurisdiction is striking. Overall, extensive efforts to broaden the legal basis for interdicting WMD shipments at sea have produced relatively little. They may also have been, from a certain perspective, misdirected. A greater threat to human security generally is posed by the proliferation of small arms by sea, especially through their shipment into Africa. This threat has, however, attracted no significant treaty-making attention (other than the Arms Trade Treaty which, in addition to its notable weaknesses, has no provisions for maritime interdiction).[143]

6 Challenges for the Law of the High Seas

The challenges facing the present legal regime of the high seas remain numerous. Most stem from questions of control, fragmentation of authority, the ad hoc nature of responses to new problems and interactions with other fields of international

---

St Vincent, and the Grenadines. For treaty texts see US Department of State, Proliferation Security Initiative Ship Boarding Agreements, available at <http://www.state.gov/t/isn/c27733.htm>.

[140] D Guilfoyle, 'Counter Proliferation Activities and Freedom of Navigation' in MH Nordquist et al (eds), *Freedom of Navigation and Globalization* (Brill/Nijhoff Leiden 2014) 69.
[141] UNSC Res 1874 (12 June 2009), [12] and [13]. [142] Ibid.
[143] See further Guilfoyle, n 140. See also 2013 Arms Trade Treaty, Art 2(3) (exemption for movement of arms owned by a State party) and Art 7(2) ('confidence-building measures' may mitigate export risks).

law. First, flag State jurisdiction presupposes a capacity for enforcement of international standards that is often clearly lacking in many States. As in other fields, however, the problem is usually less with the substantive law than with State capacity to implement it.

Second, enforcement jurisdiction under the law of the sea is fragmented into various small 'silos' and one cannot readily switch between them. A vessel suspected of being stateless might, on inspection, turn out to have a claim of nationality but present clear evidence of being engaged in human trafficking. Can a visiting warship intervene? Even if one asserts modern practises of trafficking people into conditions of exploitation constitute slavery, the law of the sea does not provide a clear-cut answer on whether slaving vessels may be arrested. The unsatisfactory division in the law of the sea between the power to inspect and arrest suspect vessels is not unique to the high seas regime, of course.[144]

Third, where innovative action is taken to try and counter new threats, it is not always clear that the mechanisms chosen are likely to succeed or are even targeting the right problem. As noted above, the attention paid to maritime counter-WMD proliferation looks like an extraordinary effort that has borne relatively little fruit. Worse, such efforts may be focused on the problems of the world's most developed States (the putative threat of terrorism) at the expense of the problems of the world's least developed States (the unchecked global proliferation of small arms).

Finally, the greatest challenge for the law of the high seas will likely come from human rights concerns. Lurid, though credible, suggestions that ships at sea have been used as interrogation centres in the course of the 'war on terror' are certainly alarming.[145] However, a more widespread problem may be the position of those interdicted by government vessels, especially when such interdictions occur in multinational operations as is increasingly common in counter-piracy and counter-migration operations. Moreno-Lax, in particular, has observed the risk of fragmentation of both State responsibility and applicable law in such cases.[146] By conceptualizing operations as 'rescue', or actions 'supporting the coastal State' or as occurring under the mandate of an international organization, governments may fudge or ignore *prima facie* applicable human by rights law claiming responsibility for such observance lies elsewhere. In fairness, some rules developed in a

---

[144] The management of high seas fisheries and vessel-source pollution provide examples. On the former, see Guilfoyle, n 23, ch 6; R Rayfuse, *Non-Flag State Enforcement in High Seas Fisheries* (Martinus Nijhoff Leiden 2004). On the latter, see Tanaka, n 26, 276–89; Churchill and Lowe, n 35, 344–53.

[145] D Campbell and R Norton-Taylor, 'US Accused of Holding Terror Suspects on Prison Ships', *The Guardian* (2 June 2008), available at <http://www.theguardian.com/world/2008/jun/02/usa.humanrights>.

[146] Moreno-Lax, n 104.

largely terrestrial setting are not always easily applied in maritime operations—or at least not without considerable effort. This has certainly been a concern for the European Naval Force, its contributing States all being bound by the European Convention on Human Rights (ECHR) in counter-piracy operations off Somalia. How to implement the ECHR right of an arrested person to be brought promptly before a judge in counter-piracy or counter-narcotics operations, where it might be weeks before a person is brought ashore, has proved a particularly difficult question.[147] In maritime interdiction operations generally, then, the stage is set for the interaction of human rights and the law of the sea to be a major concern in the coming decade.

---

[147] See *The 'Cygnus' Case (Somali Pirates)*, Rotterdam District Court, 17 June 2010, (2010) 145 ILR 491, 499–500; *Medvedyev and Others v France*, Judgment of the European Court of Human Rights, Grand Chamber, Application No 3394/03 (29 March 2010), [2010] ECHR 384, [67] and [132]–[134]; and *Vassis and Others v France*, Judgment of the European Court of Human Rights, Application No 62736/09 (27 June 2013) [52]–[62]. Compare: D Guilfoyle, 'Counter-Piracy Law Enforcement and Human Rights' (2010) 59 *International and Comparative Law Quarterly* 141; and SP Bodini, 'Fighting Maritime Piracy under the European Convention on Human Rights' (2011) 22 *European Journal of International Law* 829.

11

THE DEEP SEABED

MICHAEL W LODGE

1 INTRODUCTION

THIS chapter discusses the legal regime of the deep seabed; that is the part of the seabed that is beyond national jurisdiction and is referred to in the UN Convention on the Law of the Sea (LOSC)[1] as 'the Area'. The basic legal principles underpinning the regime are set out in Part XI (Articles 133 to 191) and Annex III of the Convention.

Ironically, given that, as of 2014, seabed mining is yet to take place on any commercial scale, Part XI is the longest part of the Convention, consisting of 58 out of its 320 Articles and an associated Annex, and it is also the most complex. It was born amidst controversy, in the face of opposition from most of the industrialized States, that for many years threatened to undermine the prospects for the success of the Convention as a whole. Thus, by November 1993, 11 years after the adoption of the Convention and on the eve of its entry into force, only one of the 60 States that had ratified or acceded to the Convention was not a developing country.[2]

Recognizing that it would be disastrous if the Convention were to enter into force without the participation of the industrialized States, which after all were

---

[1] 1982 United Nations Convention on the Law of the Sea (hereinafter LOSC).

[2] Iceland (ratified 21 June 1985). The 60 States together contributed less than 5 per cent of the United Nations budget in 1993. ED Brown, *The International Law of the Sea* (Dartmouth Publishing Aldershot 1994) Vol 1, 445.

'the major users of the sea, the heaviest polluters of the seas and ... important parties to disputes at sea',[3] the Secretary-General of the United Nations (UN), Javiér Perez de Cuéllar, had since 1999 convened a series of informal consultations as a way of resolving the problems with respect to Part XI prior to the inevitable entry into force of the Convention. Those consultations, under the guidance and leadership of the Secretary-General's Special Representative, Ambassador Satya N Nandan of Fiji,[4] culminated in the adoption by the UN General Assembly in July 1994 of the Agreement Relating to the Implementation of Part XI of the United Nations Convention of the Law of the Sea (1994 Implementation Agreement).[5] Although not expressly making any amendments to the Convention, the 1994 Implementation Agreement made radical changes to the legal regime set out in Part XI and Annex III.[6] It also paved the way to near-universal participation in the Convention. Most importantly, however, Article 2 of the 1994 Implementation Agreement provides that the provisions of the Agreement and Part XI of the Convention are to be interpreted and applied as a single instrument; in the event of any inconsistency between the Agreement and Part XI, the provisions of the Agreement prevail.[7] Moreover, the Agreement also provides that, after its adoption, any ratification of, or accession to, the Convention also represents consent to be bound by the Agreement, and that no State may establish its consent to be bound by the Agreement unless it has previously or at the same time become party to the Convention. As of 2014, the Convention has 166 parties, including all the major industrialized States, with the exception of the United States of America. There are 145 parties to the 1994 Implementation Agreement.[8]

---

[3] Introductory remarks by the Secretary-General at the Informal Consultations on outstanding issues relating to the deep seabed mining provisions of the United Nations Convention on the Law of the Sea, New York (16–17 June 1992), repr in International Seabed Authority, *Secretary-General's Informal Consultations on Outstanding Issues Relating to the Deep Seabed Mining Provisions of the United Nations Convention on the Law of the Sea: Collected Documents* (International Seabed Authority Jamaica 2002) 85, 86.

[4] Ambassador Nandan served as Special Representative of the Secretary-General and Under-Secretary-General for Oceans and the Law of the Sea from 1984 to 1993. In 1996, he was elected as the first Secretary-General of the International Seabed Authority, a position he occupied until 2007.

[5] 1994 Agreement Relating to the Implementation of Part XI of the United Nations Convention on the Law of the Sea of 10 December 1982 (hereinafter 1994 Implementation Agreement). The Agreement was provisionally applied from 16 November 1994 (the date of entry into force of the Convention) and itself entered into force on 28 July 1996.

[6] The 1994 Implementation Agreement sidesteps the question of whether it modifies or amends the Convention. In the view of Sir Michael Wood, as a matter of law, it modifies the application of the provisions of the Convention. MC Wood, 'The International Seabed Authority: The First Four Years' in JA Frowein and R Wolfrum (eds), *Max Planck Yearbook of United Nations Law* (Kluwer Law International The Hague 1999) Vol 3, 173.

[7] This formula has been repeated in most instruments adopted by the International Seabed Authority since 1994, including, for example, the Rules of Procedure of the Assembly and Council.

[8] Which means there are still 21 States that consented to be bound by the LOSC before the adoption of the 1994 Implementation Agreement and that have not yet ratified the Agreement. While this

It is true to say, therefore, that the legal regime of the deep seabed is set out in Part XI and Annex III of the Convention and the 1994 Implementation Agreement. Increasingly, this legal regime has been supplemented by rules, regulations and procedures drawn up by the International Seabed Authority (ISA), which is the international organization established under the Convention to administer the mineral resources of the Area.

2 Legal Status of the Area and its Resources

The Area is defined in Article 1(1)(1) of the LOSC as 'the seabed and the ocean floor and the subsoil thereof, beyond the limits of national jurisdiction'. The regime of the Area is therefore applicable to the seabed beyond the outer limits of the continental shelf established under Article 76 and Annex II.[9] It follows that the precise extent of the Area cannot be determined until all coastal States have fixed the outer limits of their continental shelves in accordance with the provisions of the Convention. Given the latest projections from the Commission for the Limits of the Continental Shelf (CLCS),[10] as well as the inability of that body to deal with submissions in relation to disputed areas of continental shelf,[11] it appears that fixing the limits of the continental shelf will take some considerable time. In some areas where disputes between opposite or adjacent States exist, the time period may be particularly prolonged.

Although this might well be seen as problematic, it has caused little difficulty in practice. Geologically, the main mineral resources of interest to the ISA (polymetallic nodules, polymetallic sulphides and cobalt-rich crusts) are found beyond areas of potential continental shelf, so the likelihood of the Authority having an interest

could in theory create a duality of regimes, in practice most of these States participate in the work of the International Seabed Authority under arrangements based on the single regime of the LOSC and the Part XI Agreement. Hayashi considers that, certainly in the case of those States that supported the General Assembly resolution adopting the 1994 Implementation Agreement, there is tacit acceptance of the modified regime. M Hayashi, 'The 1994 Agreement for the Universality of the Law of the Sea Convention' (1996) 27 *Ocean Development and International Law* 31.

[9] See the discussion in Chapter 9 in this volume.

[10] 'Progress of work in the Commission on the Limits of the Continental Shelf: Statement by the Chair', Doc No CLCS/83 (31 March 2014).

[11] Rules of Procedure of the Commission for the Limits of the Continental Shelf (CLCS/40/Rev.1) Rule 46 and Annex I, [5(a)].

in such an area is quite small. Furthermore, as will be seen in the discussion on Article 82 (Section 9 below), the Authority stands to benefit in any case from revenues derived from the exploitation of non-living resources on the continental shelf beyond 200 nautical miles (nm).

Under the LOSC, the Area and its resources are the 'common heritage of mankind'.[12] Whether the common heritage of mankind amounts to a principle or doctrine of international law has been the subject of much speculation.[13] As far as its application to the deep seabed is concerned, the 'common heritage' principle had been established as long ago as 1970 in the Declaration of Principles Governing the Sea-bed and Ocean Floor and the Subsoil Thereof, beyond the Limits of National Jurisdiction, adopted by the UN General Assembly.[14] Most of the principles outlined in the Declaration were simply repeated in Part XI of the Convention. It is worth noting that the 'common heritage' principle was regarded as so fundamental that Article 311(6) prohibits States parties to the LOSC from making any amendments to the basic principle relating to the common heritage or from becoming party to any agreement in derogation thereof.

Articles 137, 140, and 141 of the LOSC elaborate upon Article 136 and in so doing bring some degree of legal precision—certainly more than was contained in the Declaration of Principles—to the concept of the common heritage.[15] Article 137(1) provides that no State shall claim or exercise sovereignty or sovereign rights over any part of the Area or its resources, nor shall any State or natural or juridical

[12] LOSC, n 1, Art 136.
[13] For a discussion of the history of the common heritage principle, see H Tuerk, 'The Principle of the Common Heritage of Mankind' in H Tuerk, *Reflections on the Contemporary Law of the Sea* (Martinus Nijhoff Leiden 2012) ch 3; SN Nandan, M Lodge, and S Rosenne, *The Development of the Regime for Seabed Mining* (International Seabed Authority Jamaica 2002) 3; A Kiss, 'The Common Heritage of Mankind: Utopia or Reality' (1985) 40 *International Journal* 423.
[14] UNGA Res 2749 (XXV), *Declaration of Principles Governing the Sea-bed and Ocean Floor and the Subsoil Thereof, beyond the Limits of National Jurisdiction* (17 December 1970) (hereinafter Declaration of Principles). The Declaration stated, *inter alia*, that the seabed and ocean floor beyond the limits of national jurisdiction are the common heritage of mankind; that they shall not be subject to national appropriation; that no rights shall be exercised or claimed with respect to the resources of the seabed that may be incompatible with an international regime to be established; and that the seabed is to be reserved exclusively for peaceful purposes. By and large, these principles were retained throughout the Third United Nations Conference on the Law of the Sea (UNCLOS III), during which discussions focused mainly on the nature of the international machinery to be established for the purposes of managing the common heritage.
[15] For a detailed discussion of the principle of the common heritage of mankind, see MW Lodge, 'The Principle of the Common Heritage of Mankind' in HN Scheiber and MS Kwon (eds), *Securing the Ocean for the Next Generation: Papers from the Law of the Sea Institute of Ocean Science and Technology Conference held in Seoul, Korea, May 2012* (2013), available at <http://www.law.berkeley.edu/15589.htm>; and R Wolfrum, 'The Principle of the Common Heritage of Mankind' (1983) 43 *Zeitschrift für ausländisches öffentliches Recht under Völkerrecht* 312.

person appropriate any part thereof.[16] Article 137(2) of the LOSC vests all the rights in the resources of the Area in mankind as a whole and provides that these rights are to be exercised through the International Seabed Authority, on behalf of mankind as a whole.[17] Article 137(2) prohibits the alienation of the resources of the seabed other than in accordance with the provisions of the Convention. Article 137(3) further underlines the fact that no claim, acquisition, or exercise of rights with respect to minerals recovered from the seabed by any State (not just States parties) or any natural or juridical person shall be recognized other than in accordance with Part XI.

Clearly, Article 137 substantially qualifies the application of the common heritage principle set out in Article 136 by limiting its scope to the 'resources' of the Area. For the purposes of Part XI, 'resources' are defined as 'solid, liquid or gaseous mineral resources *in situ* in the Area at or beneath the seabed, including polymetallic nodules'.[18] This excludes living resources, including so-called marine genetic resources, from the scope of Article 137.

Article 140 provides that activities in the Area (essentially a term of art for deep seabed mining)[19] shall be carried out for the benefit of mankind as a whole, irrespective of the geographical location of States, whether coastal or landlocked, and taking into particular consideration the interests and needs of developing States and of people who have not yet attained full independence or other self-governing status. To give effect to this aspiration, the International Seabed Authority is tasked with the development of a mechanism to provide for the equitable sharing, on a non-discriminatory basis, of financial and other economic benefits derived from deep seabed mining.

Article 141 provides that the Area shall be open to use exclusively for peaceful purposes, by all States, whether coastal or landlocked. Article 141, as read with Article 301, is generally understood as prohibiting the use of the seabed for aggressive activities in the sense of Article 2 of the UN Charter rather than a complete prohibition on all military activities.[20]

---

[16] The rule relating to prohibition of sovereignty over the high seas was already stated in Art 2 of the 1958 Convention on the High Seas, as well as in paragraph 2 of the Declaration of Principles, n 14.

[17] As a counterpoint to this, Art 157(1) of the LOSC emphasizes that the ISA is 'the organization through which States Parties shall organize and control activities in the Area', suggesting that the participants with respect to the utilization of the common heritage are intended to be States, and not mankind itself as a subject of international law. See Wolfrum, n 15, 319.

[18] LOSC, n 1, Art 133(a).

[19] 'Activities in the Area' are defined in Art 1(3) of the LOSC as 'all activities of exploration for, and exploitation of, the resources of the Area'.

[20] Wolfrum, n 15, 320. The 1971 Treaty on the Prohibition of the Emplacement of Nuclear Weapons and other Weapons of Mass Destruction on the Sea-Bed and Ocean Floor and the Subsoil Thereof (hereinafter Sea-Bed Arms Control Treaty) prohibits the use of specified weapons in a specific environment.

3 The International Seabed Authority

The Authority is one of three international institutions established by the LOSC, the others being the International Tribunal for the Law of the Sea and the Commission for the Limits of the Continental Shelf. Article 157 provides that the ISA is 'the organization through which States Parties shall, in accordance with [Part XI] organize and control activities in the Area, particularly with a view to administering the resources of the Area'.

The ISA formally came into existence on 16 November 1994—the date of entry into force of the Convention—although it did not begin to function as an autonomous organization until 1996, when the first Secretary-General assumed office. The legal provisions relating to the powers and functions of the Authority, and its institutional structure, are contained in Section 4 of Part XI (Articles 156 to 185) and in relevant provisions of the 1994 Implementation Agreement.

As noted, the main function of the ISA is to regulate deep seabed mining. However, it also has a number of ancillary functions, including promoting and encouraging marine scientific research concerning the Area and its resources and potentially even carrying out such research;[21] promoting and encouraging the transfer to developing countries of technology and scientific knowledge relating to activities in the Area;[22] and promoting international cooperation regarding activities in the Area and the progressive development of international law relating thereto.[23] The Authority is also required to distribute certain revenues from the continental shelf beyond 200 nm—a topic which is discussed further below.[24]

All States parties to the Convention are *ipso facto* members of the ISA.[25] The main organs of the Authority are an Assembly composed of all the members; a Council with limited membership; a Secretariat, headed by a Secretary-General; and the Enterprise. The latter is discussed further in Section 3.5 below. There are also a number of important subsidiary bodies consisting of individual experts, including a Legal and Technical Commission and a Finance Committee.[26]

One of the primary characteristics that distinguish the ISA from other international organizations is the very careful balance that is struck between the

---

[21] LOSC, n 1, Art 143(2) and (3).   [22] Ibid, Art 144(1) and (2).   [23] Ibid, Art 160(2).
[24] Ibid, Art 82(4).
[25] Ibid, Art 156(2). This includes the European Union, which is a party to the Convention by virtue of Art 306 and Annex IX. The European Community deposited its formal confirmation for both the Convention and the 1994 Implementation Agreement in 1998. L Lijnzaad, 'Declarations of Competence in the Law of the Sea: A Very European Affair' in M Lodge and M Nordquist (eds), *Peaceful Order in the World's Oceans: Essays in Honour of Satya N. Nandan* (Brill Leiden 2014) 186, and R Long, 'Factors Influencing the Inexorable Rise of the United Nations Convention on the Law of the Sea within the European Legal Order' in Lodge and Nordquist (eds), *Peaceful Order in the World's Oceans*, 186.
[26] LOSC, n 1, Art 164 also provides for an Economic Planning Commission.

powers and functions of its various organs, largely as a result of composition and decision-making rules for the Council and Finance Committee introduced as part of the 1994 Implementation Agreement. This means that many matters require sequential action by the Finance Committee, Legal and Technical Commission, Council, and Assembly.

3.1 The Assembly

The Assembly, as the sole organ consisting of all the members of the Authority, is the supreme organ of the Authority.[27] It has power to establish general policies, as long as they are in conformity with the LOSC and the 1994 Implementation Agreement,[28] to elect the members of the Council and to elect the Secretary-General from among the candidates proposed by the Council.[29] In due time, the Assembly will also elect the Director-General and members of the Governing Board of the Enterprise.[30] The Assembly also approves the budget of the Authority, including the scale of assessment for contributions to the budget, as submitted by the Council[31] and approves the rules, regulations, and procedures relating to prospecting, exploration, and exploitation in the Area that have been provisionally adopted by the Council.[32]

Two important limitations on the powers of the Assembly were introduced by the 1994 Implementation Agreement. First, decisions of the Assembly on any matter for which the Council also has competence, or on any administrative, budgetary or financial matter shall be based on the recommendations of the Council. If the Assembly does not accept the recommendation of the Council on any matter, it shall return the matter to the Council for further consideration.[33] The Council is then bound to reconsider the matter in light of the views expressed by the Assembly. Second, decisions by either the Assembly or the Council having financial or budgetary implications shall be based on the recommendations of the Finance Committee.[34]

3.2 The Council

The Council is composed of 36 members, divided into five Groups (A, B, C, D, and E) that form four decision-making Chambers (Groups A, B, and C make up three voting chambers, and the developing States in Groups D and E make up the fourth voting chamber). Members are elected for terms of four years, with elections for one-half of the membership taking place every two years. The members are elected

---

[27] Ibid, Art 160(1). [28] Ibid. [29] Ibid, Art 160(2)(a) and (b).
[30] Ibid, Art 160(2)(c). [31] Ibid, Art 160(2)(e), (h). [32] Ibid, Art 160(2)(f).
[33] 1994 Implementation Agreement, n 5, Annex, Section 3 [4]. [34] Ibid.

by the Assembly, but in the case of Groups A, B, C, and D, the Assembly is required to elect the members nominated by each of those Groups.

Group A (largest consumers) comprises four members from among those States parties which have either consumed or imported more than 2 per cent in value terms of the total world consumption of the commodities produced from the categories of minerals to be derived from the Area,[35] provided that the four members shall include one State from the Eastern European region having the largest economy in that region in terms of gross domestic product and the State, on the date of entry into force of the Convention, having the largest economy in terms of gross domestic product.[36] Group B (major investors) comprises four members from among the eight States parties which have made the largest investments in deep seabed mining.[37] Group C (land-based producers) comprises four members from among States parties which are major net exporters of the categories of minerals to be derived from the Area, including at least two developing States.[38] Group D comprises six members from among developing States parties, representing special interests.[39] Group E comprises 18 members elected according to the principle of ensuring an equitable geographical distribution of seats in the Council as a whole, provided that each geographical region (Africa, Asia, Eastern Europe, Latin America and the Caribbean, and the Western Europe and Others) shall have at least one member elected under this subparagraph.[40]

The Council's role in the work of the Authority is extremely important. It is the executive organ of the Authority. Its primary function is to supervise and

[35] The minerals derived from the Area are copper, cobalt, manganese, and nickel.

[36] 1994 Implementation Agreement, n 5, Annex, Section 1 [15(a)]. The effect of this provision is to assure a permanent place on the Council for the United States of America (the State having the largest economy as at the date of entry into force of the Convention), thus meeting one of the key concerns of the United States during the negotiation of the 1994 Implementation Agreement. Since 1994, the State with the largest economy from the Eastern European region has been the Russian Federation, something that seems unlikely to change in the foreseeable future.

[37] 1994 Implementation Agreement, n 5, Annex, Section 1 [15(b)]. Since 1996, the following 17 States parties consider themselves eligible for election to Group B under Section 1 [15(b)]: Belgium, Bulgaria, Canada, China, Cuba, Czech Republic, France, Germany, India, Italy, Japan, Netherlands, Poland, Republic of Korea, Russian Federation, Slovakia, and the United Kingdom. There is no agreement as to which eight of these States parties have made the largest investments. See Indicative List of States members of the International Seabed Authority which would fulfill the criteria for membership in the various groups of States in the Council in accordance with paragraph 15 section 3 of the annex to the Agreement to the Implementation of part XI of the United Nations Convention on the Law of the Sea of 10 December 1982, Doc No ISBA/20/A/CRP.2 (29 May 2014) (hereinafter Indicative List of ISA member States).

[38] 1994 Implementation Agreement, n 5, Annex, Section 1 [15(c)].

[39] Ibid, Section 1 [15(d)]. The special interests to be represented include large populations, landlocked or geographically disadvantaged States, island States, least-developed States, major importers, and potential producers. This is a very broad category, potentially including almost 100 States. See Indicative List of ISA member States, n 37.

[40] In a further complication of this already complicated formula, during the election for the first members of the Council in 1996, it was agreed to allocate 10 seats on the Council to the African Group, nine seats to the Asian Group, eight seats to the Western European and Others Group, seven seats to the Latin American and Caribbean Group, and three seats to the Eastern European Group. However,

coordinate the implementation of Part XI on all matters within the competence of the Authority.[41] While it must act in accordance with the general policies established by the Assembly, the Council has extensive powers over a range of matters set out in Article 162 of the Convention that are not subject to further action by the Assembly. Among the most important of these are the power to propose to the Assembly a list of candidates for the election of the Secretary-General; to approve plans of work for exploration and exploitation; to adopt rules, regulations, and procedures relating to prospecting, exploration, and exploitation as well as the financial management and internal administration of the Authority; and to exercise control over activities in the Area in accordance with the Convention. These powers are not absolute, however, but in many cases must be exercised in accordance with the recommendations of the Legal and Technical Commission or, in financial and budgetary matters, the Finance Committee.

Decisions of substance in the Council require either consensus or a qualified majority vote. Consensus is required in the case of the matters specified in Article 161(8)(d) of the LOSC, including the adoption of rules, regulations, and procedures and amendments to Part XI. The 1994 Implementation Agreement also urges, as a general rule, that decision-making in all organs of the Authority 'should be by consensus'.[42] In the event that all efforts to reach consensus have been exhausted, decisions in the Council require a two-thirds majority of members present and voting, providing that such decisions are not opposed by a majority of any one of the four Chambers referred to above.[43] This means that a decision of substance can be blocked by three negative votes in any of Chambers A, B, or C, or a somewhat larger number of negative votes in Groups D and E combined, depending on how many developing countries are in those Groups.

A further variation of this decision-making procedure applies in connection with the approval of plans of work for exploration or exploitation upon the recommendation of the Legal and Technical Commission. In this case, the 1994 Implementation Agreement added an additional limitation on the decision-making power of the

---

since the total number of seats allocated according to that formula is 37, it was also agreed that each regional group, other than the Eastern European Group, would relinquish a seat in rotation. Although this arrangement was initially to be applied only in the first four years of the Council, it was also agreed that:

> [A]fter the first four years, the principle of burden-sharing, on an equal and equitable basis, shall continue to be respected involving the five regional groups and taking into account the situation at that time, in particular the effect of the termination of the provisional membership in the Assembly.

As a result, there has always been one additional seat on the Council. 'Composition of the first Council of the International Seabed Authority', Doc ISBA/A/L.8 (21 March 1996) and Corr.1 (2 April 1996).

[41] LOSC, n 1, Art 162(2)(a). [42] 1994 Implementation Agreement, n 5 Annex, Section 3 [2].
[43] Ibid, Annex, Section 3 [5].

Council. Thus, the Agreement states that the Council shall approve a recommendation for approval of a plan of work unless a two-thirds majority of members present and voting, including a majority of members present and voting in each Chamber, decides to disapprove the plan of work.[44] The effect of this provision is that as few as two members in any of Groups A, B, or C, could force approval of a plan of work even if an overall two-thirds majority of the Council were to oppose it.

As noted above, decisions by either the Assembly or the Council having financial or budgetary implications shall be based on the recommendations of the Finance Committee.[45]

3.3 Legal and Technical Commission

The Legal and Technical Commission is one of two organs of the Council that are established by Article 163 of the LOSC; the other is the Economic Planning Commission.[46] The Legal and Technical Commission plays a vital role in the functioning of the Authority as it is the body that reviews all proposed plans of work for activities in the Area and makes recommendations thereon to the Council.[47] The Commission is also the body that is responsible for formulating and submitting to the Council the rules, regulations, and procedures of the Authority relating to the conduct of activities in the Area.[48] In addition, the Commission has the general responsibility of supervising activities in the Area and reporting thereon to the Council. This includes making recommendations relating to environmental monitoring programmes and the protection of the marine environment;[49] recommending that emergency measures be taken to suspend operations to prevent serious harm to the marine environment;[50] and recommending the institution of legal proceedings before the Seabed Disputes Chamber.[51] It may fairly be said therefore that most of the substantive matters that come before the Council, except for financial and budgetary matters, require prior consideration by the Legal and Technical Commission. On a number of important matters, including, for example, the adoption of rules, regulations, and procedures relating to activities in the Area, the Council is required to 'take into account' the recommendations of the Commission.[52] And, as

---

[44] Ibid, Annex, Section 3 [11].   [45] Ibid, Annex, Section 3 [7].
[46] The purpose of the Economic Planning Commission is to review the trends of, and factors affecting, supply, demand, and prices of minerals and to recommend systems for compensation or economic adjustment assistance for developing States that suffer adverse economic effects from activities in the Area. With the realization that seabed mining is rather unlikely to have such adverse effects, the 1994 Implementation Agreement, n 5, Annex, Section 1 [4] provides that the functions of the Economic Planning Commission are, so far as necessary, to be performed by the Legal and Technical Commission.
[47] LOSC, n 1, Art 165(2)(b).   [48] Ibid, Art 165(2)(f) and (g).
[49] Ibid, Art 165(2)(e) and (h).   [50] Ibid, Art 165(2)(k).   [51] Ibid, Art 165(2)(i).
[52] Ibid, Art 162(2)(o)(ii).

noted above, in relation to the approval of plans of work for exploration or exploitation, the Council must follow the recommendation of the Commission, unless such a recommendation is disapproved by a negative resolution.

Members of the Legal and Technical Commission are elected in their personal capacity and are required to have appropriate qualifications in fields such as exploration for and exploitation and processing of minerals, oceanology, protection of the marine environment, or economic and legal matters. Although the Convention states that the Commission shall be composed of 15 members, it also states that the Council may decide to increase the size of the Commission, giving due regard to economy and efficiency. The Council has used this power to increase the size of the Commission to 22 (in 1996) and subsequently to 25 (in 2011).[53] Meetings of the Legal and Technical Commission are normally held in private, generally because the Commission deals with confidential matters, including commercially sensitive data and information.[54] There is, however, provision in the rules of procedure of the Commission for meetings to be opened to observers in certain specified cases and when issues of general interest to members of the Authority, which do not involve the discussion of confidential information, are being discussed.[55]

3.4 Finance Committee

The Convention did not provide for a Finance Committee, although it did include a provision requiring the Council to establish a subsidiary organ for the elaboration of draft financial rules.[56] The issue was, however, taken up in the negotiations for the 1994 Implementation Agreement, and it was considered necessary to provide in the Agreement itself for the establishment of a 15-member Finance Committee.[57] The Finance Committee is elected by the Assembly, which is required to take 'due account of the need for equitable geographic representation and the representation of special

---

[53] The initial decision in 1996 to increase the size of the Commission to 22 was taken at the proposal of the then President of the Council, Ambassador Ballah of Trinidad and Tobago. In light of the very difficult and protracted negotiations that had been necessary to enable the elections for the Council and Finance Committee to proceed, Ambassador Ballah proposed that all 22 candidates for 15 seats be elected. See Wood, n 6. Since no agreement has ever been reached on the distribution of seats on the Commission between the regional groups, this practice has continued, in each case 'without prejudice to future elections'.

[54] Commissioners are bound by obligations of confidentiality; see LOSC, n 1, Art 163(8).

[55] Rules of Procedure of the Legal and Technical Commission, Rules 6 and 53. See also Decision of the Council of the Authority concerning the Rules of Procedure of the Legal and Technical Commission, Doc No ISBA/6/C/9 (13 July 2000).

[56] LOSC, n 1, Art 162(2)(y).

[57] 1994 Implementation Agreement, n 5, Annex, Section 9. Ibid, Section 9 [9] notes that 'the requirement of Article 162(2)(y), of the Convention to establish a subsidiary organ to deal with financial matters shall be deemed to have been fulfilled by the establishment of the Finance Committee in accordance with this section'.

interests'.[58] However, it is also required that each of Groups A, B, C, and D of the Council are represented on the Committee.[59] Furthermore, until such time as the Authority has enough funds of its own to fund its activities other than assessed contributions of members, the Finance Committee must include one representative from each of the largest contributors to the budget.[60]

The responsibilities of the Finance Committee are set out in Section 9 of the Annex to the 1994 Implementation Agreement. As well as making recommendations on the proposed budget of the Authority and assessing the contributions of members to the budget, the Finance Committee is also required to prepare draft financial rules, regulations, and procedures, including those relating to internal financial administration, as well as the equitable sharing of financial and other economic benefits derived from deep seabed mining. It does not, however, have a role in establishing the financial terms and conditions under which mining is to be conducted, which is a responsibility of the Legal and Technical Commission. This is not surprising, given that the role and expertise of the Finance Committee is geared towards internal financial control and the management of expenditures rather than the determination of the financial terms of mining contracts.

3.5 The Enterprise

From the very beginning of discussions about how to realize the benefits of the common heritage of mankind there was a fundamental divergence of views as to whether deep seabed mining would be carried out by private sector or State entities under some kind of licensing system, with access controlled by a central licensing body or agency, or through an international entity specifically established to carry out mining on behalf of the international community. This fundamental difference of principle was to dominate negotiations in the Sea-Bed Committee from 1969 to 1973 and throughout the Third United Nations Conference on the Law of the Sea

---

[58] Ibid, Annex, Section 9 [3].   [59] Ibid, Annex, Section 9 [3].

[60] Ibid, Annex, Section 9 [3]. As at the 2011 election to the Finance Committee (for the period 2012–2016) the largest contributors were Japan, Germany, France, the United Kingdom, and Italy. The language of Section 9 [3]–[4] of the 1994 Implementation Agreement leaves ambiguity as to whether the Assembly may decide not to elect a candidate put forward by one of the five largest contributors. In 2006, France and Italy put forward candidates who had each already served two full terms of office as members of the Finance Committee. This was strongly opposed by the Group of Latin American and Caribbean States, which argued that a candidate could not be eligible for a third consecutive term if he had served for two consecutive terms in accordance with Section 9 [4]. Following a debate, the Assembly agreed to elect the nominees, on an exceptional basis, with the understanding that the decision to elect the French and Italian candidates was a one-time only decision that would not constitute a precedent for future elections: Statement of the President on the Work of the Assembly at the twelfth session, Doc No ISBA/12/A/13 (18 August 2006). The underlying question therefore remains unresolved.

(UNCLOS III) from 1974 to 1982.[61] At the heart of the issue were differences between two strongly held, but entirely different, perceptions of how the system for exploration and exploitation should work. The industrialized countries wanted a simple licensing system under which any State, person, or company might apply for a licence to an international agency on a first-come, first-served basis. The developing countries considered that the best way to implement the common heritage principle was through direct exploration and exploitation through an international organization in which they would be equal participants.[62] An uneasy truce was reached in 1976, when the US Secretary of State, Henry Kissinger, proposed a 'parallel system' of access, whereby some mine sites would be reserved for exclusive access by developing countries, through an international 'Enterprise', while others would be freely available to State and private operators.[63] Although this compromise quickly became accepted as the basis of the system for access to seabed minerals, and is embodied in Article 153 of the Convention, discussions over the operational details of the Enterprise, and, in particular, its financing and access to technology, were to remain controversial throughout UNCLOS III and the negotiations leading to the 1994 Implementation Agreement.

The 'Enterprise'[64] is established by Article 170 and Annex IV of the LOSC. It is described as the organ of the Authority which shall carry out activities in the Area directly, as well as the transporting, processing and marketing of minerals from the Area. It is autonomous in the conduct of its operations, which shall be directed by a Governing Board composed of 15 members elected by the Assembly. The Enterprise will also have a Director-General, elected by the Assembly on the recommendation of the Council and the nomination of the Governing Board, who shall be its Chief Executive Officer and legal representative.

The provisions of the LOSC relating to the Enterprise were radically affected by the 1994 Implementation Agreement. The industrialized countries had long

---

[61] Committee on the Peaceful Uses of the Seabed and the Ocean Floor beyond the Limits of National Jurisdiction, 1969–1973. For a complete legislative history of the Enterprise, see International Seabed Authority, *Legislative History of the Enterprise under the United Nations Convention on the Law of the Sea and the Agreement relating to the Implementation of Part XI of the Convention* (International Seabed Authority Jamaica 2002); and the *Virginia Commentaries*, Vol VI, 512–25 (on LOSC, Part XI, Art 170).

[62] See Roy S Lee, 'The Enterprise: Operational Aspects and Implications' (1980) 15(4) *Columbia Journal of World Business* 62.

[63] See *Virginia Commentaries*, Vol VI, 39–41.

[64] An 'International Seabed Enterprise' was first proposed in a working paper submitted to the Sea-Bed Committee by a group of Latin American States in 1971. Under this proposal, the Enterprise (*la Empresa*) would be the organ of the Authority empowered to 'undertake all technical, industrial and commercial activities relating to the exploration of the area and exploitation of its resources'. See 'Working Paper on the Regime for the Sea Bed and Ocean Floor and Its Subsoil Beyond the Limits of National Jurisdiction', UN Doc A/AC.138/49 (1971), reproduced in Committee on the Peaceful Uses of the Sea-Bed and the Ocean Floor beyond the Limits of National Jurisdiction, *Sea-Bed Committee Report* (1971) 93, 100.

regarded the provisions of the LOSC as unworkable and particularly objected to any suggestion that they would be responsible for financing the initial operations of the Enterprise. The 1994 Implementation Agreement therefore effectively puts the Enterprise 'on hold' for the foreseeable future. It does this by establishing a number of conditions that must be satisfied before the Enterprise may operate as an independent entity. First, it provides that the Enterprise shall conduct its initial deep seabed mining operations through joint ventures and removes the obligations of States parties to finance the operations of the Enterprise.[65] Second, it makes the decision to activate the Enterprise subject to a decision of the Council, which may only be taken contingent upon one of two possible 'trigger' events. These are: the approval of a plan of work for exploitation (by any qualified entity, for any mineral resource) or an application for a joint venture with the Enterprise.[66] If joint venture operations with the Enterprise accord with sound commercial principles, the Council shall issue a directive pursuant to Article 170(2) of the LOSC.[67] In the meantime, until such time as it begins to operate independently, certain limited functions of the Enterprise are to be performed by the Secretariat of the Authority.[68] These are mostly limited to monitoring of trends in metals markets and evaluation of information on potential mineral resources.

In 2013, to the surprise of many, the Authority received a proposal to develop a joint venture with the Enterprise, submitted by a private company incorporated in Canada.[69] After considering the proposal, the Council concluded that it was premature for the Enterprise to function independently, but requested the Secretary-General to carry out a further study of the legal, technical, and financial implications for the Authority and for States parties relating to the operation of the Enterprise.[70]

---

[65] 1994 Implementation Agreement, n 5, Annex, Section 2 [2] and [4].

[66] Ibid, Annex, Section 2 [2].

[67] The implication being that if they do not 'accord with sound commercial principles' the Council shall not issue such a directive.

[68] Ibid, Annex, Section 2 [1].

[69] Proposal for a Joint Venture Operation with the Enterprise. Report by the Interim Director-General of the Enterprise, Doc No ISBA/19/C/4 (20 March 2013).

[70] Statement of the President of the Council of the International Seabed Authority on the work of the Council during the 19th session, Doc No ISBA/19/C/18 (24 July 2013). Some of the legal and financial implications were discussed in a paper prepared by the Secretariat: Considerations relating to a proposal by Nautilus Minerals Inc. for a Joint Venture Operation with the Enterprise, Doc No ISBA/19/C/6 (4 April 2013).

4 Regulation of 'Activities in the Area'

As noted above, the primary function of the Authority is to regulate the way in which 'activities in the Area' may be carried out by qualified entities. 'Activities in the Area' are defined in Article 1(3) of the LOSC as 'all activities of exploration for, and exploitation of, the resources of the Area'. The term does not, therefore, include prospecting, which is considered briefly below, although prospecting is included in the regulations adopted by the Authority.

Activities in the Area shall be carried out by a qualified entity[71] in accordance with a formal written plan of work drawn up in accordance with Annex III and approved by the Council after review by the Legal and Technical Commission.[72] Such a plan of work shall be in the form of a contract,[73] which shall provide for security of tenure over the area covered by the contract.[74] The Authority shall exercise such control over activities in the Area as is necessary for the purpose of securing compliance with the relevant provisions of Part XI and the Agreement, Annex III, and the rules, regulations, and procedures of the Authority.[75] States parties are to assist the Authority by taking all measures necessary to ensure such compliance in accordance with Article 139.[76]

The basic conditions of prospecting, exploration, and exploitation are contained in Annex III of the LOSC, which elaborates upon the provisions of Article 153 by describing the procedures by which States, State enterprises, and other entities may apply for prospecting, exploration, and exploitation in the Area; the procedures for approval of plans of work for exploration and exploitation; and the basic legal and contractual conditions attached to such plans of work. The provisions of Annex III, as modified by the Agreement, are reflected in and in many instances further modified by the rules, regulations, and procedures adopted by the Council pursuant to Article 162 of the LOSC.

As of 2014, the Authority has adopted three sets of Regulations dealing with prospecting and exploration for mineral resources in the Area. The first set of Regulations was adopted in 2000 and dealt with prospecting and exploration for

---

[71] LOSC, n 1, Art 153(2).   [72] Ibid, Art 153(3).
[73] In the Convention, the requirement for a contract did not apply to the Enterprise (Art 153(3)). However, this provision was modified by the 1994 Implementation Agreement which provides that '[n]otwithstanding the provisions of Article 153(3) and Annex III Article 3(5) of the Convention, a plan of work for the Enterprise upon its approval shall be in the form of a contract concluded between the Authority and the Enterprise.' Annex, Section 2 [4].
[74] LOSC, n 1, Art 153(6).   [75] Ibid, Art 153(4).
[76] Ibid. The responsibility of States parties in this regard will be discharged by taking the measures set out in ibid, Annex III, Article 4(4), which requires sponsoring States to ensure, within their legal

polymetallic nodules.[77] Regulations on prospecting and exploration for polymetallic sulphides were adopted in 2010[78] and for cobalt-rich crusts in 2012.[79] In 2013, the Regulations on prospecting and exploration for polymetallic nodules were revised and updated to be consistent with the 2010 and 2012 regulations.[80] The three sets of regulations are broadly similar in format, scope, and content, with differences primarily to reflect the different spatial and geological characteristics of the mineral resources they deal with. Ultimately, it is intended that the Regulations would form part of a Mining Code, regulating all aspects of activities in the Area from prospecting through to exploitation.[81] For ease of reference, the 2010, 2012, and 2013 Regulations will be referred to and discussed collectively in this chapter as the 'ISA Regulations', with references to specific provisions highlighted where necessary.[82]

The Regulations are designed to implement the broad provisions of Part XI and Annex III of the LOSC and the 1994 Implementation Agreement. They thus cover all aspects of the prospecting and exploration phases of mineral development, including the process of applying for approval of a plan of work, the procedure for consideration of applications by the Legal and Technical Commission and the Council, and the form and content of the contract for exploration.

---

systems, that contractors carry out activities in the Area in conformity with the terms of the contract with the Authority and their obligations under the Convention.

[77] International Seabed Authority, Regulations on Prospecting and Exploration for Polymetallic Nodules in the Area (13 July 2000). The official text of the Regulations was published as Doc No ISBA/6/A/18 (13 July 2000) Annex, and reproduced in International Seabed Authority, *The Law of the Sea: Compendium of Basic Documents* (International Seabed Authority/The Caribbean Law Publishing Company Jamaica 2001) 226. For a general account of the process of negotiating the Regulations and their content, see MW Lodge, 'International Seabed Authority's Regulations on Prospecting and Exploration for Polymetallic Nodules in the Area' (2002) 20(3) *Journal of Energy and Natural Resources Law* 270.

[78] Regulations on Prospecting and Exploration for Polymetallic Sulphides in the Area, Doc No ISBA/16/A/12/Rev.1 (7 May 2010).

[79] Regulations on Prospecting and Exploration for Cobalt-rich Ferromanganese Crusts in the Area, Doc No ISBA/18/A/11 (27 July 2012).

[80] Regulations on Prospecting and Exploration for Polymetallic Nodules in the Area, Doc No ISBA/19/C/17 (22 July 2013) (hereinafter 2013 ISA Regulations).

[81] At present, there are no regulations relating to the exploitation of any mineral resources under the administration of the Authority.

[82] Although this chapter deals only with the latest version of the Regulations, it should be noted that earlier versions of the Regulations may still be applicable to contracts entered into prior to the entry into force of the revised Regulations in 2013. Although contract terms may be revised to 'facilitate the application of any rules, regulations and procedures adopted by the Authority subsequent to the entry into force of the contract' (2013 ISA Regulations, n 80, Annex 4, Section 24(2)), such modifications require the written consent of the contractor and ISA as evidenced by an appropriate instrument in writing.

Prospecting is defined in the ISA Regulations as the 'search for deposits [of minerals] including estimation of the sizes and distributions of [mineral] deposits and their economic values, without any exclusive rights'. This broad definition of prospecting refers to general searches for seabed mineral deposits rather than detailed pre-production surveys and is difficult to distinguish from marine scientific research.[83]

Exploration, for the purposes of the Regulations, is defined broadly as:

Searching for deposits of [minerals] in the Area with exclusive rights, the analysis of such deposits, the use and testing of recovery systems, and the carrying out of studies of the environmental, technical, economic, commercial and other appropriate factors that must be taken into account in exploitation.

The Regulations contain an important provision which enables the Legal and Technical Commission to issue from time to time recommendations of a technical or administrative nature for the guidance of contractors to assist them in the implementation of the rules, regulations and procedures.[84] Contractors are required to observe such recommendations as far as reasonably practicable.[85] In light of the *Advisory Opinion on Responsibilities and Obligations in the Area*, the contractual commitment to observe the recommendations has become an important element of the due diligence obligations of contractors, especially with regard to the need to collect environmental data and take measures for the protection of the marine environment.

The first set of recommendations was issued in 2001, one year after the adoption of the first set of Regulations, and dealt with the assessment of possible environmental impacts arising from exploration for polymetallic nodules.[86] The recommendations described the procedures to be followed in the acquisition of baseline data, and the monitoring to be performed during and after any activities in the exploration area with potential to cause serious harm to the environment. The 2001 recommendations were revised in 2010 in the light of increased understanding,[87] and in 2013 a

---

[83] See Lodge, n 77.

[84] Unlike the 'rules, regulations and procedures' referred to in LOSC, n 1, Art 162(2)(o), recommendations for guidance may be issued by the Legal and Technical Commission without further approval by the Council. Recommendations should be 'technical or administrative' in nature. The text of such recommendations must be reported to the Council which, if it finds that a recommendation is 'inconsistent with the intent and purpose of these Regulations', may request the Commission to modify or withdraw the recommendation.

[85] 2013 ISA Regulations, n 80, Annex 4, Section 13(2)(e). According to the first Secretary-General of the ISA, the recommendations 'form the basis of an acceptable code of conduct for contractors'. See SN Nandan, 'Administering the Mineral Resources of the Deep Seabed' in D Freestone, R Barnes, and DM Ong (eds), *The Law of the Sea: Progress and Prospects* (Oxford University Press Oxford 2006) 88.

[86] Recommendations for the guidance of the contractors for the assessment of possible environmental impacts arising from exploration for polymetallic nodules in the Area, Doc No ISBA/7/LTC/1/Rev.1, 2nd issue (13 February 2002).

[87] Recommendations for the guidance of contractors for the assessment of the possible environmental impacts arising from exploration for polymetallic nodules in the Area, Doc No ISBA/16/LTC/7 (2 November 2010).

comprehensive set of environmental guidelines dealing with all three types of marine minerals was released.[88] Other sets of recommendations cover matters such as the methodology for reporting of financial information and the implementation of training requirements.

Annex 4 to each set of Regulations contains standard clauses for exploration contracts which are automatically incorporated into each contract issued by ISA. These are identical for each category of resource. Exploration contracts have a fixed and limited duration of 15 years,[89] during which time the contractor is expected to undertake the necessary exploratory activities to prepare for exploitation. As can be seen from the definition of 'exploration', this may include testing of mining and recovery systems as well as geological analysis of mineral deposits and environmental, technical, and economic studies. Under standard clause 3.2, a contractor may, in limited circumstances, seek an extension of a plan of work for exploration for periods of five years each.

As at August 2014, 16 contracts for exploration were in force. These include 12 contracts for exploration for polymetallic nodules, two contracts for exploration for polymetallic sulphides, and two contracts for exploration for cobalt crusts.[90] A further nine plans of work for exploration had been approved by the Council and will enter into force during 2014 or 2015 once they have been converted into contracts.

---

[88] Recommendations for the guidance of the contractors for the assessment of possible environmental impacts arising from exploration for marine minerals in the Area, Doc No ISBA/19/LTC/8 (1 March 2013).

[89] The 15-year limitation was one of the important innovations introduced in the 1994 Implementation Agreement and is an important due diligence requirement. Until the 1994 Implementation Agreement there had been no explicit limit on the duration of exploration.

[90] The first group of contracts were issued in 2001 to the so-called registered pioneer investors, namely: Interoceanmetal Joint Organization (sponsored by Bulgaria, Cuba, Czech Republic, Poland, Russian Federation, and Slovakia), 29 March 2001; Yuzhmorgeologiya (Russian Federation) 29 March 2001; Government of the Republic of Korea, 27 April 2001; China Ocean Mineral Resources Research and Development Association (COMRA) (China), 22 May 2001; Deep Ocean Resources Development Ltd (Japan), 20 June 2001; Institut français de recherche pour l'exploitation de la mer (France), 20 June 2001; Government of India, 25 March 2002. Since then, contracts for exploration for polymetallic nodules have been granted to Federal Institute for Geosciences and Natural Resources (BGR) (Germany), 19 July 2006; Nauru Ocean Resources Inc (Nauru), 22 July 2011; Tonga Offshore Mining Ltd (Tonga), 11 January 2012; UK Seabed Resources Ltd (United Kingdom), 8 February 2013; Global Sea Mineral Resources NV (Belgium), 14 January 2013. Contracts for exploration for polymetallic sulphides have been granted to: COMRA (China), 18 November 2011; Government of the Russian Federation, 29 October 2012; Government of the Republic of Korea, 24 June 2014. Contracts for exploration for cobalt-rich crusts have been granted to: Japan Oil, Gas and Metals National Corporation (Japan), 27 January 2014; COMRA (China), 29 April 2014. Up-to-date details of the contracts in force, as well as new applications, can be found on the ISA website at <http://www.isa.org.jm>.

5 Commercial Exploitation

Exploitation is defined in the regulations as the:

... recovery for commercial purposes of [polymetallic nodules] in the Area and the extraction of minerals therefrom, including the construction and operation of mining, processing and transportation systems, for the production and marketing of metals ...[91]

Regulations governing the exploitation phase of seabed mining have yet to be developed. The 1982 Convention set out detailed and prescriptive policies for the conduct of commercial mining, including provisions relating to production authorizations and the financial terms of contracts. As a result of the 1994 Implementation Agreement, however, those provisions of the LOSC no longer apply. Instead, the Agreement sets out the principles intended to guide the ISA in the development of rules and regulations for commercial mining. These are contained in Sections 6, 7, and 8 of the Annex to the Agreement. Together, they provide broad guidance on the policy framework within which detailed regulations are to be developed.

Section 6, on production policy, emphasizes that the development of the resources of the Area shall take place in accordance with 'sound commercial principles' and that there shall be no subsidization of activities in the Area, nor shall there be any discrimination between minerals derived from the Area and from other sources.

Most importantly, Section 8(1), on financial terms of contracts, lays down general principles. These include the requirement that payments to the Authority shall be within the range prevailing in respect of land-based mining of the same or similar minerals in order to avoid giving deep seabed miners an artificial competitive advantage or imposing on them a competitive disadvantage. At the same time, the system should not be complicated and should not impose major administrative costs on the Authority or on a contractor.[92]

While these broad policy guidelines will no doubt help to inform and provide a basis for the work of the Legal and Technical Commission and the Council in developing a regulatory framework for exploitation, they will clearly require substantial further elaboration and technical input to discern what they mean in practice. While no precise timing can be given for the adoption of an exploitation code, the Authority has set itself an ambitious target date of 2016 to complete this work.[93]

---

[91] 2013 ISA Regulations, n 80, Annex, 1(3)(a).
[92] 1994 Implementation Agreement, n 5, Annex, Section 8.
[93] See eg the Statement of the President of the Council on the work of the Council during the twentieth session of the Authority, Doc No ISBA/20/C/32 (23 July 2014), in which it is noted that the development of exploitation regulations is a priority for the Authority.

6 Reserved Areas

It will be recalled that one of the core features of Kissinger's 'parallel system' of access, was the reservation of mine sites for exclusive access by developing countries through the 'Enterprise'. The way in which this would be achieved was to require applicants sponsored by developed countries to submit details of two sites, of 'equal estimated commercial value'.[94] One of these would be granted to the applicant, while the other would be held by the Authority in a 'site bank' for future development by the Enterprise, either by itself or in association with developing States. The money, and know-how, expended in evaluating the reserved area is considered as the 'contribution' of the developed State to the Enterprise and developing States.

While this basic concept was preserved in the 1994 Implementation Agreement and in the Authority's regulations, it has been substantially qualified in its implementation, largely because of the limitations placed on the operations of the Enterprise by virtue of the 1994 Implementation Agreement. The primary pathway through which a reserved area may be utilized is through an application by a developing State, or a natural or juridical entity sponsored by a developing State.[95] When this happens, the Enterprise is still to be given an opportunity to decide whether to carry out activities in the reserved area (thus retaining the spirit of the original notion of the parallel system) but, as we have seen, the provisions of the 1994 Implementation Agreement make this practically impossible.[96]

In recent years, developing countries have seized upon the available provisions to actively participate in activities in the Area. For the most part, this has been done in partnership with larger commercial entities through joint venture or similar business arrangements. At the time of writing, exploration contracts in reserved areas have been issued to entities sponsored by Nauru, Tonga, Kiribati, Singapore, and the Cook Islands. It can be argued that, while the implementation of the provisions of the LOSC has differed from what was originally envisaged, the spirit of the parallel system has been maintained by making it possible for developing States to participate in activities in the Area.

Two other important aspects should be mentioned. First, the 1994 Implementation Agreement included a new provision which gives the contractor that contributed a particular reserved area to the Authority the right of first refusal to enter into a joint

---

[94] LOSC, n 1, Annex III, Art 8.

[95] Ibid, Annex III, Art 9; and 2013 ISA Regulations, n 80, Regulation 17. Note that 'developing State' is not defined in the Convention and has thus received a broad interpretation based on United Nations practice.

[96] For the reason that the Enterprise is legally incapable of acting except through joint ventures and following a directive from the Council.

venture agreement with the Enterprise.[97] After 15 years (being the duration of an exploration contract) if the Enterprise has not made use of the area, the contractor that contributed the reserved area may itself utilize the area, providing it offers in good faith to include the Enterprise as a joint venture partner. With the expiration of a number of exploration contracts in 2016, it remains to be seen how this provision will be implemented in practice.

Second, in both the Sulphides and Cobalt-crust regulations, there was a move away from the implementation of the parallel system through the mechanism of reserved areas. Instead of requiring an applicant to provide a reserved area (which is costly), the newer regulations give the applicant the opportunity to elect either to provide a reserved area, or to offer the Enterprise a future equity interest (a minimum of 20 per cent and a maximum of 50 per cent) at the stage of exploitation. Unsurprisingly, most exploration contractors for sulphides and crusts have elected to offer an equity interest in a future joint venture, even though, or perhaps because, the precise terms on which such equity interest is to be given remain to be determined. It may be remarked that the commitments that have been made to the Enterprise through this avenue seem to be inconsistent with the attempts made through the 1994 Implementation Agreement to severely curtail, if not kill off entirely, the concept of the Enterprise.

7 Sponsorship by States Parties

For the international lawyer one of the most interesting features of the regime for the Area is the requirement that entities wishing to carry out activities in the Area must be sponsored by LOSC States parties. Under Annex III, Article 4(3), of the Convention, as read with Article 153 (2)(b), for natural and juridical persons to be eligible to carry out activities in the Area, they must satisfy two requirements. The first is that they must be either nationals of a State party or effectively controlled by it or its nationals. The second is that they must be sponsored by one or more States parties. If a State that is different to the State of nationality, or its nationals exercise effective control, or if the applicant has more than one nationality, the sponsorship of that State or States is also required.

---

[97] 1994 Implementation Agreement, n 5, Annex, Section 2 [15]. Presumably, in light of the qualifications on the operations of the Enterprise, this right could only be taken up if the Enterprise became operational (ie following one of the trigger events described in Section 2 of the Annex to the 1994 Implementation Agreement).

The decision to sponsor an entity that is otherwise qualified is left to the discretion of the State party. In the words of the Seabed Disputes Chamber, because:

… the Convention does not consider the links of nationality and effective control sufficient to obtain the result that the contractor conforms with the Convention and related instruments, it requires a specific act emanating from the will of the State or States of nationality and of effective control. Such act consists in the decision to sponsor.[98]

The act which evidences sponsorship is a certificate which shall contain 'a statement that the applicant for a plan of work for exploration is: (i) a national of the sponsoring State; or (ii) subject to the effective control of the sponsoring State or its nationals'.

The requirement of sponsorship by a State party is not differentiated between developing and developed States.

[E]quality of treatment between developing and developed sponsoring States is consistent with the need to prevent commercial enterprises based in developed States from setting up companies in developing States, acquiring their nationality and obtaining their sponsorship in the hope of being subjected to less burdensome regulations and controls. The spread of sponsoring States 'of convenience' would jeopardize uniform application of the highest standards of protection of the marine environment, the safe development of activities in the Area and the protection of the common heritage of mankind.[99]

The terms 'effective control' and 'effectively controlled' are not defined in any of the provisions quoted above. Nor are they defined in the *travaux préparatoires* of the LOSC, which give remarkably little guidance as to the background to this issue.[100] For the most part, discussions on Article 153 related to the question of the extent of control to be exercised by the Authority over activities in the Area. Issues relating to the qualification standards of the applicant were addressed only after 1977, after the 'mixed system' of access by States, natural or juridical persons and the Enterprise had been agreed upon. Once that had been agreed, it was clear that it would be necessary for the relevant applicant both to be sponsored by a State and to be in a position to provide the Authority with appropriate guarantees as to compliance.[101]

---

[98] *Responsibilities and Obligations of States Sponsoring Persons and Entities with Respect to Activities in the Area*, ITLOS Case No 17 (Advisory Opinion) [2011] ITLOS Rep 10, [77] (hereinafter *Area Advisory Opinion*).

[99] Ibid, [159]. [100] *Virginia Commentaries*, Vol VI, 293–312 (on LOSC, Art 153).

[101] The provision as it then appeared read as follows:

Sponsorship by the State Party of which the applicant is a national shall be sufficient unless the applicant has more than one nationality, as in the case of a partnership or consortium of entities from several States, in which event all States Parties involved shall sponsored the application, or unless the applicant is effectively controlled by another State Party or its nationals, in which event both States Parties shall sponsored the application.

Informal Composite Negotiating Text, Doc No A/CONF.62/WP.10/Rev.2 (ICNT/Rev.2, 1980) Annex III, Art 4(2).

Some guidance as to the meaning of effective control is provided by the material that an applicant which is a juridical person is required to include in the application. It must identify its place of registration and its principal place of business/domicile and attach a copy of its certificate of registration (Annex II of each set of ISA Regulations). However, it is the nature and scope of the obligations and liability of sponsoring States that provide us with essential insights as to the context and purpose of the effective control test. This was at the core of the advisory opinion rendered by the Seabed Disputes Chamber in 2011.[102]

The LOSC requires a sponsoring State to adopt laws and regulations and to take administrative measures which are, within the framework of its legal system, reasonably appropriate for securing compliance by persons under its jurisdiction and thence effective regulatory control, so that it may be exempted from liability for damage caused by any failure of a contractor under its sponsorship to comply with its obligations. In short, the purpose of sponsoring requirements is to ensure that obligations that are binding on States parties are fulfilled by entities that are subjects of domestic legal systems. The Seabed Disputes Chamber expressed it clearly:

> The sponsoring State may find it necessary, depending upon its legal system, to include in its domestic law provisions that are necessary for implementing its obligations under the Convention. These provisions may concern, inter alia, financial viability and technical capacity of sponsored contractors, conditions for issuing a certificate of sponsorship and penalties for non-compliance by such contractors.[103]

Of course, the expressions 'effective control' and 'effectively controlled' are also found elsewhere in the Convention in the context of nationality of ships flying the flag of the State whose nationality it has. Article 91 of the LOSC requires that there exists a 'genuine link' between a State and a vessel flying its flag. In terms of establishing a genuine link between a vessel and its flag State, it is the act of registration that conveys nationality to a ship and provides the basis for jurisdiction over the vessel, irrespective of ownership or financial interest in the vessel or its operations.[104] It is left to States to set in their domestic legal systems the conditions for the grant of its nationality to ships, for the registration of ships in its territory, and for the right to fly its flag. In this regard, the Part XI regime follows a consistent approach that emphasizes the fact of incorporation or registration and the grant of nationality (ie regulatory control) as the critical, or dominant, factor, notwithstanding the practical realities as to control over policy, capital, finance, and management.

---

[102] *Area Advisory Opinion*, n 98.

[103] Ibid, [234]. More details in ibid, [227]–[241] on the content of open-ended measures which are 'policy matters ... made by the sponsoring State' (ibid, [227]).

[104] See eg *M/V 'Saiga' (No 1) (Saint Vincent and the Grenadines v Guinea)* (Judgment) [1997] 110 ILR 736; *M/V 'Saiga' (No 2) (Saint Vincent and the Grenadines v Guinea)* (Judgment) [1999] ITLOS Rep 10; and *The Grand Prince (Belize v France)* (Prompt Release) [2001] ITLOS Rep 17.

8 Dispute Settlement

One of the distinguishing features of the law of the sea by the LOSC is the integration into the regime for deep seabed mining of a compulsory system for the settlement of disputes structured to match the particularities of the regime. While there is some overlap between the general provisions of the Convention relating to dispute settlement, found in Part XV, the specific provisions relevant to the deep seabed mining regime are located in Section 5 of Part XI, Articles 186 to 191.[105]

Article 186 establishes the Seabed Disputes Chamber as a special chamber of the International Tribunal for the Law of the Sea (ITLOS) established under Annex VI (Statute of the Tribunal). While proceedings before the Seabed Disputes Chamber are governed by the rules of the Tribunal, adopted under Annex VI, the jurisdiction of the Chamber is established under Part XI, Section 5. It is very important to note that the Seabed Disputes Chamber is not in any way an organ of the Authority but is part of an entirely independent body, namely the ITLOS.

Under Article 187, the Seabed Disputes Chamber has broad jurisdiction with respect to activities in the area including with respect to disputes between States parties; disputes between States parties and the Authority; disputes between parties to a contract, being States parties, the Authority or the Enterprise, State enterprises, and natural or juridical persons; and disputes between the Authority and a prospective contractor. In certain cases, disputes between States parties concerning the interpretation or application of Part XI and its related annexes may be submitted to a special chamber of the Tribunal or an ad hoc chamber of the Seabed Disputes Chamber.[106] Disputes concerning the interpretation or application of the contract may be submitted to binding commercial arbitration, which in default of any other agreement shall be conducted in accordance with the United Nations Commission on International Trade Law (UNCITRAL) arbitration rules.[107] Article 189 provides certain limitations on the jurisdiction of the Seabed Disputes Chamber with regard to decisions of the Authority. The chamber shall have no jurisdiction with regard to the exercise by the Authority of its discretionary powers and shall not substitute its discretion for that of the Authority.

Traditionally access to international courts and tribunals has been limited to States. The Seabed Disputes Chamber thus represents an unusual, albeit not

---

[105] Space does not permit a full discussion of the many complexities of the jurisdiction of the Seabed Disputes Chamber. A full treatise can be found in N-J Seeberg-Elverfeldt, *The Settlement of Disputes in Seabed Mining* (Nomos Baden-Baden 1998), which also contains an extensive bibliography of German publications relating to deep seabed mining and public international law.
[106] LOSC, n 1, Art 188.   [107] Ibid, Art 188(2).

unprecedented,[108] exception to the traditional principle by granting access to all the various categories of entities that may be involved in deep seabed mining, including States, State enterprises, natural or juridical persons, the Enterprise, and, of course, the Authority itself. In line with the requirement in Article 153 that natural and juridical persons must be sponsored by one or more States parties in order to carry out activities in the area, Article 190 of the LOSC provides that if a natural or juridical person becomes a party to a dispute referred to in Article 187, the sponsoring State must also be given notice thereof and shall have the right to participate in the proceedings.

Finally, the Seabed Disputes Chamber has jurisdiction to render advisory opinions at the request of the Assembly or the Council of the ISA on legal questions arising within the scope of their activities.[109] The jurisdiction of the Chamber in this respect is somewhat analogous to the jurisdiction of the International Court of Justice in relation to advisory opinions requested by the General Assembly of the United Nations. The first such advisory opinion was rendered in 2011 at the request of the Council.[110]

9 Responsibility of the International Seabed Authority under Article 82(4) of the LOSC

Although the regime of the Area as set out in Part XI and the 1994 Implementation Agreement is applicable only to the seabed beyond the outer limits of the continental shelf, the Authority has an additional and specific responsibility pursuant to Article 82(4) of the LOSC to distribute to States parties to the Convention payments or contributions in kind derived from exploitation of the resources of the continental shelf beyond 200 nm.

Article 82 stipulates an obligation on States parties to the Convention to make payments or contributions in kind with respect to the exploitation of the non-living

---

[108] Seeberg-Elverfeldt makes comparison with the rights of access granted to private persons in relation to the European Court of Justice within the framework of the Treaties of the European Communities.

[109] LOSC, n 1, Art 191.

[110] *Area Advisory Opinion*, n 98. See also D French, 'From the Depths: Rich Pickings of Principles of Sustainable Development and General International Law on the Ocean Floor—the Seabed Disputes Chamber's 2011 Advisory Opinion' (2011) 26(4) *International Journal of Marine & Coastal Law* 525.

resources of the continental shelf beyond 200 nm (often referred to as 'revenue-sharing'). These payments and contributions are made annually at a rate starting at 1 per cent of the value or volume of production and increasing progressively to 7 per cent. The payments or contributions are to be made through the Authority, which is then required to distribute such payments or contributions to States parties in accordance with equitable criteria, taking into account the interests and needs of developing States, and in particular the least developed and landlocked States, and peoples who have not yet achieved full independence or other self-governing status.

Article 82 has been described as a unique provision in international law. There are very few, if any, similar provisions in any other legal instrument which set out a legal obligation designed to address inequity in a practical way.[111] The negotiation of Article 82 was an integral part of the negotiations concerning coastal States' entitlement to a continental shelf extending beyond 200 nm. It was a *quid pro quo* for the re-definition of the continental shelf to encompass the continental margin, with the effect of reducing the size of the Area and potentially reducing the benefits to developing countries from the exploitation of the common heritage of mankind, particularly the land-locked and geographically disadvantaged States.[112] Unfortunately, Article 82 is also extremely short and lacking in precision both as to the way in which payments or contributions in kind are to be calculated and as to the mechanisms by which the ISA, as a conduit for those payments or contributions, is to collect and distribute such payments or contributions.[113]

So far, no coastal State has begun to exploit non-living resources beyond 200 nm—although it is predicted that this may happen soon—and as yet, Article 82 has not been implemented. The Authority has nevertheless conducted a number of technical studies and workshops on the implementation of Article 82 in recent years that have concluded, *inter alia*, that there will be a need to address textual ambiguities and process gaps within Article 82 in order to give effect to its intent.[114]

---

[111] International Seabed Authority, *ISA Technical Study No.4: Issues associated with Implementation of Article 82 of the United Nations Convention on the Law of the Sea* (International Seabed Authority Jamaica 2009) (hereinafter ISA Technical Study No 4).

[112] The detailed diplomatic history of Art 82 of the LOSC is recorded and commented upon in detail in the *Virginia Commentaries* and in literature cited in the ISA Technical Study No 4, n 111. See particularly *Virginia Commentaries*, Vol II, 930–47 (on Part VI Art 82); A Chircop, 'Energy Policy and International Royalty: A Dormant Servitude Relevant for Offshore Development' in MH Nordquist, JN Moore, and A Skaridov (eds), *International Energy Policy, the Arctic and the Law of the Sea* (Martinus Nijhoff Leiden 2005) 247.

[113] MW Lodge, 'The International Seabed Authority and Article 82 of the United Nations Convention on the Law of the Sea' (2006) 21(3) *International Journal of Marine and Coastal Law* 323.

[114] ISA Technical Study No 4, n 111; International Seabed Authority, *ISA Technical Study No. 5: Non-living Resources of the Continental Shelf Beyond 200 Nautical Miles: Speculations on the Implementation of Article 82 of the United Nations Convention on the Law of the Sea* (International Seabed Authority Jamaica 2010); International Seabed Authority, *ISA Technical Study No. 12: Implementation of Article 82 of the United Nations Convention on the Law of the Sea: Report of an International Workshop held*

Some of the suggestions that have been made include a formal treaty arrangement between the Authority and contributing coastal States, a collective memorandum of understanding between 'broad shelf' States and the Authority and a decision by the Meeting of States Parties to the Convention (thus taking the matter out of the hands of the Authority altogether, except to act as a passive recipient of funds). The conclusions of a 2013 workshop convened by the Authority[115] suggest that a workable approach might be to begin by reaching agreement on the definition of key terms used in Article 82, which could then lay the groundwork for a voluntary guidance document to be adopted by the Assembly of the Authority (or indeed, the Meeting of States Parties). Whichever solution is ultimately adopted, it seems clear that a 'do nothing' approach is not tenable.

10 Conclusion

The ISA has made commendable progress in developing a practical and stable legal regime under which deep seabed mining can be carried out with certainty and predictability. The inherently evolutionary design of Part XI and the 1994 Implementation Agreement has allowed the Authority to adapt to changing commercial, economic, and scientific realities as well as new developments in international law, particularly in the field of marine environmental law. In relation to the latter, the Authority has made an important contribution to the effective implementation of the broad environmental principles embodied in the modern law of the sea, including by specifying the details of the obligation to conduct prior environmental impact assessments. In addition, the Authority has taken a noteworthy first step towards regional scale, ecosystem-based management of activities in the Clarion–Clipperton Zone.

Nonetheless, there remain many unanswered questions for the Authority and many provisions contained in Part XI, the 1994 Implementation Agreement, and the ISA Regulations that will require further elaboration if they are to become operative in the future. Some of the more urgent matters that can be expected to be addressed in the coming years include the development of a commercially viable code for mineral exploitation; the development of rules and procedures for environmental impact assessment at the stages of test mining and commercial scale exploitation;

in Beijing, People's Republic of China, November 2012 (International Seabed Authority Jamaica 2013) (hereinafter ISA Technical Study No 12).

[115] ISA Technical Study No 12, n 113.

development of a mechanism for environmental guarantees, guidelines on monetary penalties that may be imposed by the Council for damage to the marine environment, and the development of a liability fund for uncompensated damage to the marine environment; implementation of an inspection regime; and the further development of guidelines for the implementation of Article 82 of the LOSC. The question of the Enterprise will also need to be addressed at some point in the future.

12

MARITIME BOUNDARY DELIMITATION

MALCOLM D EVANS

1 Setting the Scene

1.1 Introduction

It will often be impossible for States to extend their jurisdiction as far seawards as international law permits because of the claims of other States. The resulting problem of delimiting overlapping maritime zones[1] has long been a contentious issue, particularly as regards the extended zones of maritime jurisdiction—the continental shelf and the exclusive economic zone (EEZ). In addition to the focus on delimitation between 'opposite and adjacent' coastal States, the question of the outer limit of such zones has also become increasingly important, as the interests of the international community as a whole have begun to be defined through the submissions made to, and the work done by, the Commission on the Limits of the Continental Shelf (CLCS). As a result, the jurisprudence relating to maritime boundary delimitation is now moving away from being principally focused on the 'debate' between 'equidistance' and 'equitable

---

[1] The International Court of Justice has said that 'the task of delimitation consists in resolving the overlapping claims by drawing a line of separation between the maritime areas concerned': *Territorial and Maritime Dispute (Nicaragua v Colombia)* (Judgment) [2012] ICJ Rep 624, [141].

principles' which has for so long dominated the discussion.[2] Nevertheless, it remains impossible to understand the topic without appreciating the evolution of the law over time. This chapter will, then, present an overview of the subject, drawing on its history while focusing on points of contemporary relevance.

It is axiomatic that States are free to agree upon the course of the maritime boundaries between themselves in any way they wish. Yet, perhaps surprisingly, maritime boundary delimitation has given rise to more cases before the International Court of Justice (ICJ) than any other single subject. Ad hoc arbitral tribunals have also long been involved in such issues, and in the past few years there has also been an upsurge in decisions taken by arbitral tribunals within the framework of the Law of the Sea Convention's dispute settlement provisions. To this must now be added the work of the International Tribunal on the Law of the Sea (ITLOS) itself. This has a number of consequences. First, and despite the more general significance of State practice in the formation of customary law, it is the work of the judicial and arbitral bodies rather than State practice which has driven—and continues to drive—the subject in both theory and practice.[3] Second, the possibility of there being significant differences in approach between these various fora is an important question which those involved in the practice of maritime boundary delimitation increasingly need to take into account.

1.2 The delimitation of the territorial sea

The initial phase of any maritime boundary delimitation between adjacent States involves the delimitation of their overlapping territorial seas, and a delimitation between opposite States claiming a 12 nautical miles (nm) territorial sea whose coastlines are less than 24 nm apart will only ever involve a territorial sea delimitation. The rule to be applied is not in itself controversial and is set out in Article 15 of the 1982 United Nations Convention on the Law of the Sea (LOSC) which, in summary, provides that in the absence of agreement to the contrary, States may not extend their territorial seas beyond the median or equidistance line unless there are historic or other 'special' circumstances that dictate otherwise. Its origins lie in the proposals of the International Law Commission (ILC), which were reflected in Article 12 of the 1958 Geneva Convention on the Territorial Sea and Contiguous

---

[2] From the voluminous, though dated, literature taking this approach, see in particular P Weil, *The Law of Maritime Delimitation—Reflections* (Grotius Publications Cambridge 1989); M Evans, *Relevant Circumstances and Maritime Delimitation* (Oxford University Press Oxford 1989); GJ Tanja, *The Legal Determination of International Maritime Boundaries* (Kluwer Daventer 1990); NM Antunes, *Towards the Conceptualisation of Maritime Delimitation* (Martinus Nijhoff Leiden 2003); Y Tanaka, *Predictability and Flexibility in the Law of Maritime Boundary Delimitation* (Hart Publishing Oxford 2006).

[3] See H Thirlway, *The Sources of International Law* (Oxford University Press Oxford 2014) 72.

Zone, and the ICJ has accepted that this 'equidistance/special circumstances' rule represents customary international law.[4]

While it was understood from the outset that departures from the median or equidistant line were likely to be frequent, it is only in exceptional cases that such a line will not form the basis of the boundary between overlapping territorial seas. Nevertheless, there have been examples of such exceptions in recent practice. For example, in the *Territorial and Maritime Boundary Dispute between Nicaragua and Honduras in the Caribbean* the ICJ, while emphasizing that equidistance remained the general rule, thought that both the configuration and unstable nature of the relevant coastal area made it impossible to identify basepoints from which to construct a provisional equidistance line and that this 'special circumstance' justified the use of an alternative method, this being the use of a line bisecting two lines drawn along the coastal fronts of the States.[5] Also in that year, the Annex VII Arbitration Award in the *Guyana/Suriname* case concluded that historical and navigational issues amounted to special circumstances which justified a departure from the use of the equidistance line for the delimitation of the territorial sea.[6] As this suggests, no matter how clear the rule, the particular circumstances surrounding each delimitation are likely to be such as to render its outcome speculative. If this is so as regards the delimitation of the relatively narrow bands of a territorial sea, it is all the more so as regards the continental shelf and EEZ, stretching as they do for up to 200 nm or more from the coast. As far as the territorial sea is concerned, however, the point of departure, Article 15 of the LOSC, is at least clear. The same cannot be said of the continental shelf and EEZ.

1.3 The 'equidistance' or 'equitable principles' debate and the LOSC

As proposed by the ILC, Article 6 of the 1958 Geneva Convention on the Continental Shelf adopted an approach to the delimitation of overlapping continental shelves similar to that adopted for the territorial seas, and which provided that:

1. Where the same continental shelf is adjacent to the territories of two or more States whose coasts are opposite each other, the boundary of the continental shelf appertaining to such

---

[4] *Maritime Delimitation and Territorial Questions Between Qatar and Bahrain (Qatar v Bahrain)* (Merits) (Judgment) [2001] ICJ Rep 40, [175]–[176]. Cf ibid, Separate Opinion of Judge Oda, [13]–[21], who challenged the Court's views of customary law. The Court reaffirmed its view in *Territorial and Maritime Dispute between Nicaragua and Honduras in the Caribbean Sea (Nicaragua v Honduras)* (Judgment) [2007] ICJ Rep 659, [268] and [281].

[5] *Nicaragua v Honduras*, n 4, [268]–[281].

[6] *Arbitration between Guyana and Suriname* (2007) XXX RIAA 1, [323]–[325] (hereinafter *Guyana/Suriname*). See also the *Maritime Dispute (Peru v Chile)*, Judgment of the International Court of Justice,

States shall be determined by agreement between them. In the absence of agreement, and unless another boundary line is justified by special circumstances, the boundary is the median line, every point of which is equidistant from the nearest points of the baselines from which the breadth of the territorial sea of each State is measured.

2. Where the same continental shelf is adjacent to the territories of two adjacent States, the boundary of the continental shelf shall be determined by agreement between them. In the absence of agreement, and unless another boundary line is justified by special circumstances, the boundary shall be determined by application of the principle of equidistance from the nearest points of the baselines from which the breadth of the territorial sea of each State is measured.

The main difference between the two situations is that in the case of opposite coasts, and in the absence of agreement or special circumstances, 'the boundary is the median line', whereas as regards adjacent coasts the boundary 'shall be determined by the principle of equidistance'. Perhaps unwittingly, the drafters of Article 6 also ushered in the subtle distinction between a 'rule' and a 'principle' which has bedevilled the subject ever since.

The origins of the resulting problems stem from the seminal judgment of the ICJ in the *North Sea Continental Shelf* cases in which Denmark and the Netherlands argued that Article 6 of the CSC represented customary law and so bound Germany, even though it was not a State party to the Convention.[7] Applying this rule mechanically to the concave German coastline, which is sandwiched between that of Denmark and the Netherlands, restricted Germany to a modest triangle of continental shelf, to the substantial benefit of its neighbours. Rather than ameliorate this outcome by determining that the concave nature of the coast was a 'special circumstance' justifying the use of another line, the ICJ decided that Article 6 did not in fact reflect customary law at all, and that customary law in fact required that:

[D]elimitation is to be effected by agreement in accordance with equitable principles, and taking account of all the relevant circumstances, in such a way as to leave as much as possible to each Party all those parts of the continental shelf that constitute a natural prolongation of its land territory into and under the sea, without encroachment on the natural prolongation of the land territory of the other [8]

This opened up the prospect of there being two different approaches to delimitation, either that based on the more formulaic 'equidistance/special circumstances' rule found in Article 6 or the relatively more open-textured approach based

---

General List No 137 (27 January 2014) [91]–[92] where the ICJ found evidence of a tacit agreement between the parties concerning the use of a parallel as the maritime boundary, thus displacing the use of the equidistance line for the territorial sea boundary.

[7] *North Sea Continental Shelf (Federal Republic of Germany v Denmark; Federal Republic of Germany v Netherlands)* [1969] ICJ Rep 3. For the definitive account of the dispute, see AG Oude Elferink, *The Delimitation of the Continental Shelf between Denmark, Germany and the Netherlands: Arguing Law, Practicing Politics* (Cambridge University Press Cambridge 2013).

[8] *North Sea Continental Shelf*, n 7, [101(c)(1)].

around the application of 'equitable principles/relevant circumstances'—though it is doubtful whether there was ever much to choose between them in practice.[9] At the Third United Nations Conference on the Law of the Sea (UNCLOS III), groups of States championed the approach they considered best suited their interests and, as no consensus could be found, an anodyne formula, applicable to both continental shelf and EEZ delimitation, was adopted in the dying days of the conference. Thus Articles 74(1) and 83(1) of the LOSC both provide that such delimitations are to be 'effected by agreement on the basis of international law, as referred to in Article 38 of the Statute of the International Court of Justice, in order to achieve an equitable solution'. The chief virtue of this formulation is that it avoided any mention of the terms which at that time were a source of controversy—equidistance, equitable principles, special circumstances, or relevant circumstances—and is virtually devoid of substantive content,[10] as was intended. It is of next to no practical utility at all for those seeking to better understand how to delimit a boundary. As a result, it is to the work of the ICJ, ITLOS, and other arbitral bodies that one must look for the articulation and development of the principles applicable under both the LOSC and customary international law.[11]

Around the time that the LOSC was adopted, the ICJ delivered a trilogy of judgments, all of which emphasized the role of equity at the expense of equidistance, though in varying degrees.[12] Perhaps these cases were too close in time to UNCLOS III to shake off the ideological hostility to equidistance as a principle of delimitation. By 1993, however, the Court was prepared to declare in the *Jan Mayen* case that, '[p]rima facie, a median line delimitation between opposite coasts results in general in an equitable solution',[13] and in 2002 it confirmed, in the

---

[9] Thus the 1977 *Anglo-French Arbitration* generally considered to lean towards the equitable principles school of thought, proceeded on the basis that although 1958 Convention on the Continental Shelf, Art 6 (hereinafter CCS) and custom were different, the practical result of their application would be the same. *Arbitration between the United Kingdom of Great Britain and Northern Ireland and the French Republic on the Delimitation of the Continental Shelf* (1979) 18 ILM 397 (hereinafter *Anglo-French Continental Shelf Arbitration*).

[10] See eg RR Churchill and AV Lowe, *The Law of the Sea* (3rd edn Manchester University Press Manchester 1999) 191.

[11] CCS, n 9, Art 6 does however, remain a source of obligation for, and in relation to, the increasingly small number of States who are a party to it but not to the LOSC, these currently being Cambodia, Colombia, Israel, the USA, and Venezuela.

[12] *Continental Shelf (Tunisia/Libyan Arab Jamahiriya)* (Judgment) [1982] ICJ Rep 18; *Delimitation of the Maritime Boundary in the Gulf of Maine Area (Canada v United States of America)* (Judgment) [1984] ICJ Rep 246 (hereinafter *Gulf of Maine*); *Continental Shelf (Libyan Arab Jamahiriya/Malta)* (Judgment) [1985] ICJ Rep 13 (hereinafter *Libya/Malta*). Even in the latter two cases, in which the Court did apply an equidistance-based methodology, the Court went out of its way to deny the generally applicability of equidistance as a method, justifying its use on the basis its suitability to generate an equitable solution in light of relevant circumstances.

[13] *Maritime Delimitation in the Area between Greenland and Jan Mayen (Denmark v Norway)* (Judgment) [1993] ICJ Rep 38, [64] (hereinafter *Jan Mayen*), a position affirmed in *Eritrea v Yemen*, Award of the Arbitral Tribunal in the second stage of the proceedings between Eritrea and Yemen

Qatar v Bahrain case, that equidistance would provide the starting point in cases in adjacency too.[14] Thus after 35 years of hesitation, the ICJ finally accepted what it had rejected in the *North Sea Continental Shelf* cases, that the equidistance/special circumstances approach reflects customary international law.[15] It has subsequently confirmed that this is the case both for the delimitation of the territorial sea[16] and for the delimitation of the continental shelf, EEZ, or when drawing a single delimitation line.[17]

1.4 The 'three-stage test'

In the *Black Sea* case in 2009, the ICJ seemed to have gone even further when it systematized its previous practice into a delimitation methodology comprising a 'three-stage' approach with a seemingly high degree of specificity.[18] According to the Court, the first stage (a) is to draw a provisional line, which as between adjacent coasts 'will be' an equidistance line, 'unless there are compelling reasons that make this unfeasible in the particular case'.[19] As regards opposite coasts, the Court said—in unqualified terms—that the provisional line 'will be' the median line.[20] The second stage (b) is to 'consider whether there are factors calling for the adjustment or shifting of the provisional equidistance line in order to achieve an equitable result'.[21] Finally, the third stage (c) is to 'verify that the line (a provisional equidistance line which may or may not have been adjusted by taking into account the relevant circumstances) does not, as it stands, lead to an inequitable result by reason of any marked disproportion between the ratio of the respective coastal lengths and the ratio between the relevant maritime area of each State by reference to the delimitation line'.[22]

(Maritime Delimitation) (1999) XXII RIAA 335, [131]. See M Evans, 'Maritime Delimitation after Denmark v. Norway: Back to the Future?' in G Goodwin-Gill and S Talmon, *The Reality of International Law* (Clarendon Press Oxford 1999) 153.

[14] *Qatar v Bahrain*, n 4, [230]. See also *Land and Maritime Boundary between Cameroon and Nigeria (Cameroon v Nigeria: Equatorial Guinea Intervening)* (Merits) (Judgment) [2002] ICJ Rep 303, [288]; *Barbados/Trinidad and Tobago* (2006) XXVII RIAA 147, [242]–[244] and [306].

[15] See M Evans, 'Maritime Delimitation: Where Do We Go From Here?' in R Barnes, D Freestone, and D Ong, *The Law of the Sea Progress and Prospects* (Oxford University Press Oxford 2006) 137, 143–7.

[16] *Nicaragua v Honduras*, n 4, [262]–[298].

[17] *Guyana/Suriname*, n 6, [376]–[392]; *Maritime Delimitation in the Black Sea (Romania v Ukraine)* (Judgment) [2009] ICJ Rep 61, [116] (hereinafter *Black Sea*); *Nicaragua v Colombia*, n 1, [139]; *Peru v Chile*, n 6, [179].

[18] *Black Sea*, n 17, [116].   [19] Ibid.

[20] Ibid, where it also makes it clear that '[n]o legal consequences flow from the use of the terms "median line" and "equidistance line" since the method of delimitation is the same for both.'

[21] Ibid, [120].   [22] Ibid, [122].

This three-stage test was subsequently endorsed by the ITLOS in the *Bay of Bengal (Bangladesh/Myanmar)* case,[23] its first boundary delimitation case, and subsequently by the ICJ in both the *Nicaragua v Colombia* case in 2012[24] and *Maritime Dispute (Peru v Chile)* in 2014.[25] However, while endorsing this approach, both the ITLOS and the ICJ went on to apply it in a fashion which once again casts doubt upon the weight to be given to equidistance in practice. The ITLOS chose to emphasize the importance of the equitable solution[26] and set equidistance aside in favour of a bisector methodology.[27] In the *Nicaragua v Colombia* case, and while purporting to apply the three-stage approach,[28] the ICJ also produced an outcome which bears so little relationship to the 'provisional' equidistance line as to cast doubt on its real place within the delimitation process, other than being a potential point of departure.

This 'backtracking' from the high water mark of equidistance in the *Black Sea* case is further reflected in the way in which the ICJ has subtly but significantly rephrased the first stage of the three-stage test. In the *Peru v Chile* case it said that '[i]n the first [stage], it constructs a provisional equidistance line unless there are compelling reasons preventing that.'[29] This differs from the *Black Sea* case formulation in two significant ways. First, it now speaks of departures from equidistance if there are 'compelling' reasons, rather than the more stringent approach of doing so only if it were 'unfeasible' to draw such a line. Second, whereas in the *Black Sea* case this exception only applied to the case of adjacent coasts, the *Nicaragua v Colombia* case had already extended its applicability to opposite States,[30] something which the formulation used in the *Peru v Chile* case also confirms. This marks a significant dilution of the first stage of the test. Moreover, in both cases, the Court introduced the more general caveat that the 'three-stage test' is a methodology which will 'normally'[31] or 'usually'[32] be employed—whereas in the *Black Sea* case there was no such qualification.[33] Indeed, in the *Nicaragua v Colombia* case the Court went as far as to stress that 'the three stage process is not, of course to be applied in a mechanical fashion and ... it will not be appropriate in every case to begin with a provisional equidistance/median line'.[34] When set alongside the results of the delimitation exercises conducted in these recent cases, it is difficult to avoid concluding that, once again, 'equity' rather than 'equidistance' may

---

[23] *Delimitation of the Maritime Boundary in the Bay of Bengal (Bangladesh/Myanmar)* (Judgment) [2012] ITLOS Rep 12 [240] (hereinafter *Bangladesh/ Myanmar*).
[24] *Nicaragua v Colombia*, n 1, [190]–[194].   [25] *Peru v Chile*, n 6, [180].
[26] *Bangladesh/ Myanmar*, n 23, [235].   [27] Ibid, [334].
[28] *Nicaragua v Colombia*, n 1, [199].
[29] *Peru v Chile*, n 6, [180]; *Nicaragua v Colombia*, n 1, [180].
[30] *Nicaragua v Colombia*, n 1, [191].   [31] Ibid, [190].   [32] *Peru v Chile*, n 6, [180].
[33] *Black Sea*, n 19, [115].   [34] *Nicaragua v Colombia*, n 1, [194].

be re-emerging as the dominant approach, though couched in the language of equidistance.

2 THE PROCESS OF DELIMITATION

2.1 Establishing entitlement

Although the ICJ has said that 'the task of delimitation consists in resolving the overlapping claims by drawing a line of separation between the maritime areas concerned',[35] this is not entirely accurate. What is at issue is the generation of a line separating the overlapping *entitlements* of States, and so it is first necessary to establish whether the parties to a dispute do indeed have entitlements which overlap: just because a State claims that it has an entitlement does not mean that it does.[36] The starting point is, naturally, the coastline and it is clearly acknowledged that all States are entitled to exercise jurisdiction over a territorial sea to a distance of 12 nm from baselines constructed in accordance with the provisions of international law.[37]

It is also now accepted that all States are entitled to claim an EEZ of up to 200 nm from their baselines, and, in addition, that all States exercise jurisdiction *ipso facto* and *ab initio* over the continental shelf.[38] There is less certainty regarding the seawards extent of a State's entitlement to a continental shelf, however. In the *Nicaragua v Colombia* case,[39] the ICJ accepted that Article 76(1) of the LOSC represents customary law, so that all States, irrespective of whether they are a party to the LOSC, are entitled to a continental shelf comprising:

...the sea-bed and subsoil of the submarine area that extends beyond its territorial sea throughout the natural prolongation of its land territory to the outer edge of the continental margin, or to a distance of 200 nautical miles from the baselines from which the breadth of the

---

[35] Ibid, [141]. See also *Whaling in the Antarctic (Australia v Japan: New Zealand Intervening)*, Judgment of the International Court of Justice (31 March 2014) [39].

[36] Thus in the *Nicaragua v Colombia* case, the ICJ concluded it did not need to consider the delimitation of a boundary between Nicaragua and Colombia's 200 nm continental shelf generated from its mainland coast as 'Nicaragua...has not established that it has a continental margin the extends for enough to overlap...': n 1, [129].

[37] 1982 United Nations Convention on the Laws of the Sea, Art 3, referring to 'baselines determined in accordance with this Convention' (hereinafter LOSC).

[38] See DR Rothwell and T Stephens, *The International Law of the Sea* (Hart Publishing Oxford 2010) 109.

[39] *Nicaragua v Colombia*, n 1, [118].

territorial sea is measured where the outer edge of the continental margin does not extend up to that distance.

However, it reserved its position concerning whether the detailed formulae for determining the outer edge of the continental margin set out in Article 76(2)–(7) reflected customary international law.[40] As a result, there is still uncertainty over the extent of the entitlement which a State may have over the seabed and subsoil beyond 200 nm, and this remains a difficulty for the process of effecting a delimitation where coasts are more than 400 nm apart, or where the areas at issue are more than 200 nm seawards of the land boundary between adjacent States.

There may of course be contentious disputes concerning sovereignty over land territory or insular features, and where this is the case then these will usually need to be resolved before the entitlement to a maritime zone of any nature can be established, as has been the case in several disputes before the ICJ.[41] There may also be disagreements as to whether the course of the boundary has or has not been settled by virtue of some pre-existing agreement. If so, there is, by definition, no overlap of entitlements to be delimited.[42] There might also be disputes concerning the legitimacy of the baselines used for the generation of distance-based maritime zones. While it is arguable that these, too, ought to be determined upon prior to the delimitation exercise as a part of the more general task of determining the existence of overlapping entitlements, such disagreements tend to be 'rolled up' into the delimitation itself, and contentious baselines rarely influence the ultimate line. As the Court has put it,

[T]he issue of determining the baseline for the purpose of measuring the breadth of the continental shelf and the EEZ and the issue of identifying base points for drawing an equidistance/median line for the purpose of delimiting the continental shelf and the EEZ between adjacent/opposite States are two different issues.[43]

A further issue flows from Article 121 of the LOSC, concerning the legal regime of islands.[44] An island is 'a naturally formed area of land, surrounded by water, which is above water at high tide'. Islands are to be distinguished from 'low tide

---

[40] Ibid. These provisions do of course remain binding as between States parties to the LOSC. Both SV Suarez, *The Outer Limits of the Continental Shelf: Legal Aspects of their Establishment* (Springer Berlin 2008) 181, and Y Tanaka, *The International Law of the Sea* (Cambridge University Press Cambridge 2012) 141–2, express doubts as to the customary law status of LOSC, n 37, Art 76(2)–(7).

[41] See eg *Land, Island and Maritime Frontier Dispute (El Salvador v Honduras: Nicaragua Intervening)* (Judgment) [1992] ICJ Rep 351; *Cameroon v Nigeria*, n 14; *Qatar v Bahrain*, n 4; *Nicaragua v Colombia*, n 1.

[42] See eg *Jan Mayen*, n 13; *Peru v Chile*, n 6.

[43] *Black Sea*, n 17, [137]. The Court decided that, while a dyke stretching 7.5 km seawards might be used to generate a territorial sea entitlement, this did not mean that the end of that structure need be used as a basepoint for constructing the equidistance line.

[44] See generally HW Jayewadene, *The Regime of Islands in International Law* (Martinus Nijhoff Dordrecht 1990).

elevations' which, as their name suggests, are below water at high tide. Low-tide elevations are only entitled to be used as basepoints for the generation of a territorial sea—and hence also potentially for generating an entitlement to an EEZ or continental shelf—if they are situated within the territorial sea generated by an island or mainland.[45] Islands, so defined, are entitled to generate all forms of maritime zones, save that '[r]ocks which cannot sustain human habitation or economic life of their own shall have no exclusive economic zone or continental shelf.'[46] Both the status and meaning of this exception have been controversial, and while it is now settled that it reflects customary international law,[47] its practical application remains uncertain and can only be determined on a case by case basis, providing yet another element of indeterminacy at the threshold stage of the delimitation process.

2.2 Other preliminary issues

Once it has been established that there are overlapping entitlements, a series of further preliminary questions arise. The first—a largely overlooked issue in this context—concerns the nature of the relationship between the continental shelf and the EEZ, both of which grant exclusive jurisdiction over the resources of the seabed and subsoil.[48] It has long been understood that rights over the continental shelf do not have to be claimed: they exist by operation of law. An EEZ, on the other hand, has to be claimed. There is a certain oddity in this. If continental shelf rights are indeed pre-existing, then it is difficult to see how the pre-existing rights of State A can be encroached upon by the establishment of an EEZ by State B. On what basis can a State legitimately establish an entitlement to an area which already pertains to another? Of course, State B may also have an equally valid claim to the continental shelf area in question itself on the same basis, in which case there is the need to delimit the pre-existing entitlements of both. On the face of it, the relevance of the EEZ to the delimitation of pre-existing seabed and subsoil entitlements is difficult to discern. This may well be why there has long been something of a reluctance to draw on factors related to the water-column issues when determining maritime boundaries, although this reluctance is rarely explained on this basis.[49]

---

[45] LOSC, n 37, Art 13(1).   [46] Ibid, Art 121(3). See Section 3.2 below.

[47] *Nicaragua v Colombia*, n 1, [139]. But see Tanaka, n 40, 67–8, who, writing shortly before the judgment, felt there was insufficient evidence to justify such a conclusion.

[48] Rothwell and Stephens, n 38, 118–19. For older and fuller explorations of the relationship, see D Attard, *The Exclusive Economic Zone in International Law* (Oxford University Press Oxford 1987); F Orrego Vincuna, *The Exclusive Economic Zone* (Cambridge University Press Cambridge 1989).

[49] Cf the use of 'neutral factors' in the *Gulf of Maine*, n 12, [194]. See generally MD Evans, 'Delimitation and the Common Maritime Boundary' (1993) 64 *British Yearbook of International Law* 283. See also *Barbados/Trinidad and Tobago*, n 14, [228], noting that neutral criteria had come to prevail, with very few exceptions.

In the years immediately following the adoption of the LOSC, this question became bound up with that of whether delimitation should be conducted on the basis of 'equitable principles' or 'equidistance'.[50] Since the *North Sea Continental Shelf* cases had linked the idea of entitlement to the continental shelf on the basis of the 'natural prolongation' of the landmass into and under the sea with delimitation being conducted on the basis of 'equitable principles', it was understandable that those who supported the application of the 'equidistance/special circumstances' should find support for this in the emergence of a fixed 'distance' approach to entitlement. As the ICJ put it in the *Libya/ Malta* case:

> [T]he law applicable to the present dispute, that is, to claims relating to continental shelves located less than 200 miles from the coasts of the States in question, is based not on geological or geomorphological criteria, but on a criterion of distance from the Coast. … It therefore seems logical to the Court that the choice of the criterion and the method which it is to employ in the first place to arrive at a provisional result should be made in a manner consistent with the concepts underlying the attribution of legal title.[51]

That is to say, given that distance was the relevant basis of title, this suggested that equidistance ought to provide the relevant basis for delimitation. But what if distance was *not* the relevant basis of title?

This, then, raises a second, and related, preliminary issue. As has been seen, entitlement to the continental shelf under the LOSC is based on both distance and 'natural prolongation', in the sense of the coastal State being able to claim an entitlement to the outer limit of the continental margin as provided for in Article 76(2)–(7). This begs the question of whether entitlement based on 'distance' has priority over entitlement based on 'natural prolongation'.[52] To the extent that methods of delimitation are to reflect the basis of title to the area to be delimited, this raises the question of whether equidistance as a method ought to have a greater weight in delimitations where the basis of title of both parties is based on distance than would be the case in a delimitation where the entitlement of one State is based on distance while that of the other is based on natural prolongation.[53] In the *Libya/ Malta* case, this was irrelevant as the entitlement of each could be grounded in distance[54]—but what if this was not possible?

---

[50] The question of the relationship between the zone had previously also been raised directly by Trinidad in *Barbados/Trinidad and Tobago*, where it argued that its right to the continental shelf could not be 'trumped' by the claims of Barbados to an EEZ: n 14, [367]. The Tribunal concluded that it did not need to address this issue and so said it 'takes no position on the substance of the problem': ibid, [368].

[51] *Libya/ Malta*, n 12, [61].

[52] For further consideration of this see Chapter 9 in this volume.

[53] See also RR Churchill, 'The *Bangladesh/Myanmar* Case: Continuity and Novelty in the Law of Maritime Boundary Delimitation' (2012) 1 *Cambridge Journal of International and Comparative Law* 137, 149 who questions the use of the equidistance line as the starting point for the delimitation of the overlapping areas beyond 200 nm.

[54] *Libya/Malta*, n 12, [130].

What had previously been considered a largely theoretical debate has taken on a renewed practical dimension following the decision of the ICJ in the *Nicaragua v Colombia* case. Nicaragua argued that 'an entitlement to continental shelf based on the distance criterion does not take precedence over an entitlement based on the criterion of natural prolongation'.[55] The Court however, expressly reserved its position on this point, commenting that since Nicaragua had not satisfactorily established its entitlement to the continental margin beyond 200 nm it 'need not address any other arguments development by the Parties, including the argument as to whether a delimitation of overlapping entitlements which involves an extended continental shelf of one party can affect a 200-nautical miles entitlement to the continental shelf of another party'.[56] This longstanding and perplexing preliminary issue still, then, remains to be satisfactorily addressed.[57]

The implications of this for the first stage of the 'three-stage test' also remain to be addressed. It is, however, difficult to see how the role of equidistance could remain unaffected by a decision to prioritize entitlement founded upon distance over entitlement founded on 'natural' prolongation. It should also be noted that this question is now increasingly referred to as concerning the relationship between the 'inner' and the 'outer' continental shelf.[58] This language does not derive directly from the LOSC[59] and its usage tends towards the outcome that there is indeed a substantive difference in the 'quality'—or perhaps the 'intensity'—of entitlement, with the 'inner' shelf to be prioritized over the 'outer'.

A final preliminary issue concerns the nature of the line to be established. The distinction between the delimitation of a continental shelf and an EEZ has already

---

[55] *Nicaragua v Colombia*, n 1, [121].   [56] Ibid, [130].

[57] At the time of writing (December 2014), Nicaragua has brought a further case against Colombia which is focussed on this very issue. See *Alleged Violations of Sovereign Rights and Maritime Spaces in the Caribbean Sea (Nicaragua v Colombia)*, Order of the International Court of Justice (3 February 2014).

[58] In *Barbados/Trinidad and Tobago*, n 14, the Tribunal was hostile to distinguishing between an 'inner' and 'outer' shelf, noting that 'there is in law only a single "continental shelf" rather than an inner continental shelf and a separate extended or outer continental shelf' (ibid, [213]). The ITLOS quoted this with approval when deciding that it did have jurisdiction to determine the boundary beyond 200 nm (*Bangladesh/Myanmar*, n 23, [361]–[363]). Nevertheless, it seems that the mere act of rejecting this distinction has in fact helped to establish it. It remains to be seen if the approach of the ITLOS and ICJ on this point are mutually compatible. For an examination of State practice, see BM Magnusson, 'Outer Continental Shelf Boundary Agreements' (2013) 62 *International and Comparative Law Quarterly* 345.

[59] Article 82 does, however, provide for a system of payments or contributions in relation to exploitation in respect of the continental shelf beyond 200 nm. This however, hardly provides a basis for a general conceptual distinction between the 'inner' and 'outer' continental shelf, not least because this provision does not apply to 'a developing state which is a net importer of a mineral resource produced from its continental shelf in respect of that mineral resource': LOSC, n 37, Art 82(3). A provision which affects only some of the non-living resources produced by some of the States cannot justify a reconceptualization of the entitlement of all States over all non-living resources of the seabed and subsoil beyond 200 nm.

been noted. There are however, further possibilities, given that it seems to be accepted that parties to cases are free to agree upon how to characterize the task to be undertaken. Thus, in the *Gulf of Maine* case the Chamber of the Court was asked to determine the course of the 'single maritime boundary' separating the maritime zones of Canada and the USA. The Court took this to mean that it was undertaking a discrete exercise, which had consequences for the manner in which the delimitation was to be conducted, in particular that it ought to use methods and draw on factors which were common to both the EEZ[60] and the continental shelf regimes (which in practice meant excluding consideration of issues directly related to water column resources). This contrasts with the *Jan Mayen* case, in which the Court was in fact asked to determine by means of a single line the continental shelf and the Exclusive Fishing Zone between Norway and Denmark, an exercise which could have resulted in two separate lines but which the court thought might be addressed by producing two identical lines, using its 'equitable discretion' to bring this about. In doing so, it seems evident that considerations relating to the continental shelf dominated the proceedings and the reasoning. In the *Nicaragua v Colombia* case, the parties again asked the Court to determine a single maritime boundary between the areas of continental shelf and EEZ. It is, however, difficult to discern the impact of this characterization upon the outcome of the case. Perhaps most interestingly, the Court was also asked to determine the course of 'the boundary between the maritime zones of the two states' in the *Peru v Chile* case, the background to which concerned the establishment a 200 nm zone by Peru, Chile, and Ecuador in the 1950s with the avowed purpose of exercising jurisdiction over the water column. In considering the delimitation of the boundary, however, factors related to the water column played no role. In other words, it seems to be the case that it is the delimitation of the continental shelf which does in fact dominate the process, and the space for other considerations, though not excluded is exceedingly constrained.

2.3 The elements of the process

Once it is determined that there is an overlap of entitlements over which the parties are in dispute the 'process' of delimitation commences. While parties remain free to determine boundaries between themselves in whatever way they wish, the approach of international bodies entrusted with the task increasingly follows a clear pattern, which might be described as the elements of the process. Such an approach is to be preferred to the language of 'stages' since it permits a greater degree of flexibility and, as has been seen, the latest attempt in the *Black Sea* case to reduce the process to a series of fairly mechanical steps has already floundered. In what follows, a brief

---

[60] *Gulf of Maine*, n 12, [194].

outline will be given of the key elements of the process while in the following section some selected issues concerning their practical application will be explored in more detail.

The first element of the process concerns the identification of the 'relevant area' within which the delimitation is to be conducted. In earlier cases, this was particularly significant as it went to the question of whether the predominant relationship between the parties was one of 'oppositeness' or 'adjacency', which in turn affected the weight to be given to equidistance within the process.[61] As has been seen, later cases downplayed the importance of this distinction but the significance of determining the 'relevant area' remains, as this frames the context within which the dispute will be addressed. Increasingly, however, the idea of the 'relevant area' within which the delimitation is to be conducted has become secondary to, and largely a function of, the identification of the 'relevant coasts'. This is said to reflect the underlying idea that the coasts are the starting point for entitlement. Hence in the *Black Sea* case the Court focussed on identifying the 'relevant coasts' and observed that 'the relevant area may include certain maritime spaces and exclude others which are not germane to the case in hand'.[62] This probably was intended to justify its rather generalized approach to 'proportionality', which will be considered below.

Although the approach taken by the Court in the *Black Sea* case to 'the relevant area' was subsequently quoted by the Court in the *Nicaragua v Colombia* case, in that later case the question of the relevant area raised very different issues. The Court said that '[t]he relevant area comprises that part of the maritime space in which the potential entitlements of the parties overlap.' Colombia claimed that the 'relevant area' was limited to that lying between the Nicaraguan coastline and the Colombian islands which faced it, but the Court considered that this was not the case: it said that Nicaragua's potential entitlement 'extends from the Nicaraguan coast to a line in the east 200 nautical miles from the baselines from which the breadth of the territorial sea is measured'.[63] Thus the relevant area comprised all those areas to which Nicaragua might be entitled. This is a very different approach to that followed in the *Black Sea* case, where the Court excluded from the 'relevant area' areas to which Ukraine was clearly entitled but which it did not consider 'relevant'. As this suggests, not only is the relationship between the 'relevant area' and the 'relevant coasts' unclear, they are also quite malleable concepts.[64] Moreover, their role within the delimitation process is unclear and seems to vary from case to case. What does appear to be clear, however, is that the identification of relevant coasts and areas

---

[61] See eg *Tunisia/Libya*, n 12, [126] where the Court felt that as the coastal relationship changed from one which was predominantly adjacent to one in which it was predominantly opposite, the equitableness of equidistance as a method of delimitation increased. But cf *Black Sea*, n 17, [88], where this approach is still used to exclude the relevance of some areas of coast.
[62] *Black Sea*, n 17, [110].   [63] *Nicaragua v Colombia*, n 1, [159].   [64] See Section 3.1 below.

has become entrenched as a foundational element of the delimitation process, these uncertainties notwithstanding.

The second element of the delimitation process involves the identification of the primary method of delimitation. How this is done has varied over time. It may be that there is evidence of a prior agreement between the parties stipulating what that boundary is (though in such cases there is not really any overlapping entitlement and so this becomes a threshold issue, as described above) or evidence of an agreement concerning the nature of the boundary to be established. If this is not the case, it is for the court to determine the approach and, as the 'three stage test' suggests, the first step is to determine a provisional line. In the early cases, the provisional line was identified in the light of the 'relevant circumstances' identified by the court, and which might in principle indicate the applicability of any form of provisional line.[65] Over time, and as has been seen, equidistance emerged as the preferred—and in the *Black Sea* case the mandatory—starting point, although always with the possibility of this being set aside if other methods were considered more appropriate in the light of the circumstances. Thus in the *Nicaragua v Honduras* case, the Court concluded that it was not feasible to construct an equidistance line between these adjacent States because of their coastal configuration and in the *Bangladesh/Myanmar* case the ITLOS, having constructed a provisional equidistance line, ultimately set equidistance aside for 'a geodetic line starting at a particular azimuth'.[66] There is, then, still a decision to be made regarding the provisional delimitation line but it does seem safe to assume that equidistance will be used provisionally unless good reasons are advanced as to why it ought not. To that extent, it is fair to say that equidistance has become the point of departure at this stage of the delimitation process.

The third element of the process involves determining whether there are reasons to adjust the provisional line. This involves identifying what has previously been described as 'special' or 'relevant' circumstances. While there is no limit to the types of circumstances which might conceivably be relevant at this point, it has become increasingly clear over time that only a relatively small number of factors are likely to have a significant impact. Indeed, if there are significant reasons why the provisional line ought to be amended, then it is questionable whether the appropriate provisional line has been constructed. Of course, much will then depend on the rigidity of the approach taken at the previous stage of the process: if a rather doctrinal approach is taken to the application of equidistance, for example, it may well be that there remain significant reasons to adjust the provisional line, whereas if a more reflexive approach is taken to the identification of the relevant provisional method, then there is likely to be less need for dramatic adjustment. The types of circumstance which may affect the placement of the boundary at this stage tend to

---

[65] Evans, n 2, 80–3.   [66] *Bangladesh/Myanmar*, n 23, [334].

be either geographic or non-geographic in nature, and while the former are often accorded significant weight, the latter rarely have a significant influence, though they may play on the margins, or (more likely) have an unarticulated impact upon the manner in which the geographic factors are allowed to influence the outcome. Some examples of such factors will be considered in Section 3.3 below.

Over time, the forms of geographic factors which are perceived as having potential relevance have become fairly stylized and provide distinct (though non-exhaustive) 'categories' or 'issues' to be considered, three of which have become particularly important. The first is one of the most long established factors—described in the *North Sea Continental Shelf* cases as an 'equitable principle'—that delimitation must be conducted 'without encroachment on the natural prolongation of the land territory of the other',[67] subsequently understood in terms of there being no 'cut off'. This, however, raises more questions than it solves since it presupposes that there is knowledge of the extent of each State's natural prolongation within the area of overlapping entitlements, the very thing which the delimitation is meant to determine. Nevertheless, it does seem to offer some rough and ready guide, based on whether, in the case of adjacent coasts, the provisional line seems to stray too far into areas which intuitively appear to pertain to one State rather than another. As the Court put it in the *Peru v Chile* case, '[i]n this case, the equidistance line avoids any excessive amputation of either State's maritime projection.'[68] The second factor, which has come to carry great weight, is whether there is any significant disparity in the ratio between the lengths of the relevant coasts of the parties. Quite why this is so important is something of a mystery, though it probably rests on an assumption that the State with the longest coastal contact with the region in dispute has a more substantial presence within the area and that this ought to be reflected in the outcome. It needs to be recalled that the identification of the relevant coasts has also become critical to the identification of the relevant area within which the delimitation is to be conducted. As a result, this factor has an additional significance and so will be considered further shortly. The third issue concerns the presence of islands, an issue of such practical significance that it will be considered in more detail below in Section 3.2.

The final step in the delimitation process involves determining the equitability of the solution. This is, in fact, more a means of verifying that the previous elements of the process have yielded an appropriate outcome rather than an element of the delimitation process per se.[69] Over time, this has come to be indistinguishable from the question of

---

[67] *North Sea Continental Shelf*, n 7, [101 C (1)].

[68] *Peru v Chile*, n 6, [191]. It should be noted, however, that as the first 80 nm of the boundary followed a parallel of latitude, the full boundary is not really an equidistant line, and there is in fact significant 'cut off' of Peru's marine projection.

[69] *Black Sea*, n 17, [122]: 'a *confirmation* that no great disproportionality of maritime areas is evident by comparison to the ratio of coastal lengths' (emphasis added).

'proportionality'.[70] This is understandable, since in the *North Sea Continental Shelf* cases the Court pointed to '[t]he element of a reasonable degree of proportionality which a delimitation carried out in accordance with equitable principles ought to bring about between the extent of the continental shelf areas appertaining to the coastal state and the length of its coast measured in the direction of its coastline'.[71] In the *Black Sea* case, however, the Court made it clear that it was not so much a question of there being a degree of 'proportionality' that mattered at this stage, but whether there was 'significant disproportionality'.[72] Indeed, in the *Nicaragua v Colombia* case, the Court refers to the 'disproportionality test'.[73] Once again, this takes us back to the question of the 'relevant coasts', which have already been seen to be of interest at each of the previous elements of the process. Three points need to be made by way of conclusion. First, the Court seems to have set a surprisingly high threshold for determining that a relationship is 'significantly disproportionate'.[74] Second, if, and as has been seen, the 'relevant area' is itself identified with reference to the 'relevant coasts', then this relationship has already been factored into the process. Third, and most importantly, it might be asked whether it really is the case that there are no other issues which might reasonably be thought to have a bearing on the 'equitability' of the solution—which is what the process is meant to achieve—other than a ratio between highly contentious 'coastal lengths' and 'relevant areas'?

3 From Theory to Practice

3.1 Issues concerning the identification of the relevant area

While determining the relevant area for the purposes of delimitation is critical, it remains unclear and controversial. Given also the significance attached to the 'relevant coasts' for this purpose, and the relationships between them in terms both of

---

[70] See generally Y Tanaka, 'Reflections on the Concept of Proportionality in the Law of Maritime Boundary Delimitation' (2001) 16 *International Journal of Coastal and Maritime Law* 433.

[71] *North Sea Continental Shelf*, n 7, [101 (D)].

[72] *Black Sea*, n 17, [122]. The language of disproportionality was not new, having been used, for example in *Barbados/Trinidad and Tobago*, n 14, [238], where the Tribunal speaks of the outcome 'not being tainted by some form of gross disproportion'.

[73] *Nicaragua v Colombia*, n 1, [239]–[247]. See also *Bangladesh/Myanmar*, n 23, [499], where ITLOS speaks of checking for 'significant disproportion'.

[74] Cf *Nicaragua v Colombia*, n 1, where the relationship between the relevant coasts was 1:8.2 while that of the relevant area was 1:3.4—that is, a disparity of about 100 per cent.

geographical alignment and length, this too becomes a central question and this is reflected in their increasing prominence in recent cases. Yet even a cursory survey indicates the high degree of arbitrariness which attaches to these calculations.

For example, in the *Black Sea* case, Romania argued that its entire coastline was relevant and measured 270 km,[75] whereas Ukraine claimed it was only 204 km.[76] The Court, without explaining why, decided it was 248 km. Ukraine claimed that its relevant coast comprised its entire coastline from Romania to the southern tip of the Crimea, some 1,058 km, with an actual coastal façade of 684 km, or 664 km if measured along its baselines.[77] Romania argued that much of the Ukrainian coast abutting the Black Sea was irrelevant, and measured the relevant portions as 388 km, or 293 km along the baselines.[78] The Court agreed that only parts of the Ukrainian coast were relevant but measured them at 704 km, more or less splitting the difference between the parties' calculations.[79] This meant the ratio between the relevant coasts was 1:2.8.[80] It could easily have been considerably more—or considerably less.

Such indeterminacy is even more apparent in the *Nicaragua v Colombia* case. Nicaragua claimed its whole coastline was relevant and measured 701 km, whereas Colombia thought it 551 km. The Court excluded a small portion of the mainland coast and calculated it to be 531 km.[81] Colombia measured its relevant coasts, generated by a series of small islands and cays, at 75 km,[82] whereas Nicaragua, arguing that only those portions of the islands facing Nicaragua were relevant, thought it measured 21 km.[83] The Court ultimately concluded the figure to be 65 km, yielding a ratio of 1:8.2.[84]

While it would be wrong to suggest that almost any outcome is open to the Court, it is certainly correct to say that a broad range of outcomes are at its disposal. But in themselves such disparities are relatively meaningless. Their relevance lies in the extent to which they inform both the decision whether or not to amend a provisional line of delimitation and the assessment of whether there is any 'significant disproportionality' between this ratio and the ultimate result. It is obvious that in order to make this final assessment it is also necessary to have the ratio between the relevant areas accorded to each State as a result of the delimitation. At this point even greater problems emerge. For example, third parties might have potential claims within the area and thus affect the calculation.[85] It has long been understood

---

[75] *Black Sea*, n 17, [83]
[76] Ibid, [87]. It did, however, note that the Romanian straight baseline system was 204 km and, if measured along the sinuosities of the coast, was 258 km.
[77] Ibid, [97].   [78] Ibid, [93].   [79] Ibid, [103].   [80] Ibid, [104].
[81] *Nicaragua v Colombia*, n 1, [145].   [82] Ibid, [150].   [83] Ibid, [147].   [84] Ibid, [153].
[85] Thus when determining the relevant area in the *Nicaragua v Colombia* case, n 1, [165], the Court took account of a 'hypothetic equidistance line' between Nicaragua and Costa Rica in an area currently in dispute between them. Since this may not be the final line its use either understated or overstated the area accruing to the parties. In *Bangladesh/Myanmar*, n 23, [494], the ITLOS said that 'the fact that a third party may claim the same maritime area does not prevent its inclusion in the relevant maritime

that determining the 'relevant area' in the context of adjacent State delimitations projecting into open seas is particularly impressionistic[86] and in such cases it is just not really possible to calculate in any meaningful way the relationship between the area which the delimitation leaves to each party and the coastal lengths. No doubt this is why the 'proportionality' test has drifted into a 'significant disproportionality' test. It is noteworthy that in the *Peru v Chile* case, where the Court was faced with a situation in which because of the existence of a pre-existing agreement that the first 80 miles of the maritime boundary would follow a parallel of latitude and only after this point would the equidistance method kick-in, it concluded that it would be 'difficult, if not impossible, [to make] ... the usual calculation of the length of the relevant coasts and of the extent of the relevant area, were the usual mathematical calculation of the proportions to be undertaken'.[87] Noting that the final phase of the process 'does not purport to be precise and is approximate' and involves a 'broad assessment of disproportionality' the Court contented itself by observing that 'no significant disproportion is evident, such as would call into question the equitable nature of the provisional equidistance line'.[88] We are not told, however, what was not disproportionate with what.

3.2 Issues concerning islands and low-tide elevations

Issues concerning islands are some of the most contentious in the entire field of maritime boundary delimitation. As has already been explained, the definition of an island embraces any area of naturally formed land which is above water at high tide, and it is clear that any such feature is entitled to generate a territorial sea of up to 12 nm. In the *Nicaragua v Colombia* case, the Court affirmed that this entitlement will not be eroded merely because of the size of the feature, noting that 'the Court has never restricted the right of a State to establish a territorial sea of 12 nautical miles around an island on the basis of an overlap with the territorial sea and exclusive economic zone of another state'.[89] Thus even the smallest of features will generate a full territorial sea, unless constrained by an overlapping entitlement to a territorial sea of another State. At the same time, however, Article 121(3) of the LOSC provides that rocks which cannot sustain human habitation or economic life of their own do not generate a continental shelf or economic zone.

---

area for the purposes of the disproportionality test', prompting Churchill, n 53, 145–6, to observe that 'it is perhaps just as well that determining the size of the relevant area is not, according to the ITLOS, as exercise requiring "mathematical precision"'.

[86] For criticism of the use of this approach in the Tunisia/*Libya* case, see Tanaka, n 70, 444–53.
[87] *Peru v Chile*, n 6, [193].   [88] Ibid, [193] and [194].
[89] *Nicaragua v Colombi*a, n 1, [178].

The Court has so far been remarkably coy about shedding light on the meaning of this provision. In the *Nicaragua v Colombia* case it did accept, for the first time, that Article 121(3) reflected a rule of customary international law but, apart from noting that 'a comparatively small island may give an entitlement to a considerable maritime area'[90] (and thus hinting at its having a fairly restrictive meaning), it ultimately concluded that it was unnecessary to decide on whether a number of small features did have generative capacity since there were larger features which clearly did so as regards the relevant area.[91]

Turning now to the process of delimitation, a key question is whether the presence of islands may have an effect on the method of delimitation. This question arose in its most acute form in the 1977 *Anglo-French Continental Shelf Arbitration* concerning the Channel Islands, pertaining to the UK, which lay off the coast of France and 'on the wrong side' of a median line drawn between the mainland coasts.[92] It should be noted that the UK did not in fact claim that the Channel Islands represented the relevant 'opposite coast' to France, but that they had an entitlement to a full continental shelf which merged with that generated from the mainland of the UK. Perhaps unwittingly, this gave rise to the idea that islands belonging to mainland States had something less than a full generative entitlement when opposed to the mainland of another. The decision of the ICJ in the *Nicaragua v Colombia* case, stressing that islands and other land territory enjoy the same entitlement[93] might be thought to suggest otherwise. However, it is clear that this was a situation in which there was no clash of entitlements between 'mainlands' and, but for the presence of the Colombian islands being sufficiently proximate to the coasts of Nicaragua, there would be no delimitation dispute at all. In such situations, where the presence of islands is essential to the 'generation' of the dispute, it now seems clear that the presumption in favour of equidistance as the provisional methodology will remain. It seems equally clear, however, that where the presence of islands is not essential to the generation of the dispute it is less likely that equidistance between the island and the mainland will be the starting point, but the presence of the island will be factored in at the next stage of the process, that of considering whether there are any circumstances which justify the shifting of the provisional boundary.

In a sense, then, these two contrasting approaches appear to converge. However, it does seem that significant departures from the provisional equidistant line are considered appropriate where the presence of a 'distant' island is seen as being

---

[90] Ibid, [176].

[91] Ibid, [180]. The same approach had been taken in the *Black Sea* case as regards Serpent Island, reinforcing the view that the Court is likely to be reluctant to decide upon the generative capacity of small islands unless it is absolutely necessary to do so (and it can do much to ensure that that necessity does not arise). For academic discussion of Art 121(3), see eg J Charney, 'Rocks That Cannot Sustain Human Habitation' (1999) 93 *American Journal of International Law* 864; Tanaka, n 40, 64–7.

[92] *Anglo-French Continental Shelf Arbitration*, n 9, [199].

[93] *Nicaragua v Colombia*, n 1, [177].

responsible for the generation of the overlap of entitlements, as in the *Anglo-French Continental Shelf Arbitration*, the *St Pierre et Miquelon Arbitration*,[94] the *Jan Mayen* case, and the *Nicaragua v Colombia* case. On the other hand, there appears to be an increasing reluctance to allow the presence of an offshore island to have a significant effect on an equidistance line drawn from mainland coasts or generated by some other methodology without reference to it, as in the *Black Sea* case and the *Bangladesh/Myanmar* case. The overall result is that, despite their equal generative capacity, islands are rarely treated equally with mainland coasts within the delimitation process. Nowhere is this more evident than in the *Libya v Malta* case, in which the overlapping entitlement was between the mainland coasts of a large continental country—Libya—and a small island State—Malta. The Court saw no difficulty in letting the inevitable difference in coastal lengths of the two States justify a significant shift in a provisional equidistance line in favour of Libya.[95] The justification for not treating the generative capacities of the coastlines of island States as being on par with that of mainland coastlines remains unclear.

3.3 The relevance of economic and jurisdictional issues to the delimitation process

Few things appear more settled than that economic factors are routinely dismissed as having no relevance to the delimitation process, this being 'essentially.... determined in relation to what may properly be called the geographical features of the area'.[96] This is, to say the least, strange given that the entire point of the EEZ and continental shelf regimes is to facilitate the exploration and exploitation of a State's economic resources. Nevertheless, while the relative economic positions of the States concerned is not relevant,[97] issues relating to economic activity do play a role—though often at one stage removed—within the process.[98]

In the *North Sea Continental Shelf* case, the Court identified the 'unity of a deposit' as being a factor to consider. This has a long pedigree: the *Grisbadårna* arbitration sought to preserve the separation of existing fisheries interests.[99] Nevertheless, it was a factor for the *parties* to consider rather than the Court in the context of continental

---

[94] *St Pierre and Miquelon Arbitration* (1992) 95 ILR 645.
[95] *Libya/Malta*, n 12, [73] and [78].   [96] *Gulf of Maine*, n 12, [59].
[97] This might be contrasted with the approach of the ITLOS, which drew on the preambular paragraphs of the LOSC when interpreting the LOSC taking account of the desirability of encouraging developing States' participation in accessing oceanic resources. See *Responsibilities and Obligations of States Sponsoring Persons and Entitles with respect to Activities in the Area* (Advisory Opinion) [2011] ITLOS Rep 10 [163].
[98] For a helpful overview of practice, see Tanaka, n 2, 265–88.
[99] *Grisbadårna (Norway v Sweden)* (1909) XI RIAA 147.

shelf delimitation. There is much State practice on this point, including an increasing resort to complex joint development or other agreements in order to facilitate economic activity.[100] Yet it is only when such practice has had the effect of indicating a *modus vivendi* or tacit agreement that the Court seems willing to take formal note of such practice.[101] The key point here is the taking of 'formal' note: in the *Barbados/ Trinidad and Tobago* arbitration, the Tribunal observed that 'resource-related criteria have been treated much more cautiously by the decisions of international courts and tribunals, which have not generally applied this factor as a relevant circumstance'[102]—a comment endorsed by the ICJ in both the *Black Sea* and *Nicaragua v Colombia* cases.[103]

Despite all this, it may be safely assumed that *informal* notice is given to this factor, and if it is not formally recognized as a relevant circumstance in its own right it is likely to find an unarticulated reflection in the approach taken to other elements of the process. Indeed, the Court has in the past accepted that the equitability of the result of a delimitation can be tested by reference to whether it has any 'catastrophic repercussions for the livelihood and well being of the population of the countries concerned'[104] but, perhaps unsurprisingly, is yet to conclude that this has been the case.[105] This is, however, important since it indicates that when undertaking the delimitation process the Court is not blind to the consequences of what it is doing. Nevertheless, while there are some examples of the potential relevance of access to fisheries being recognized as an element within the earlier phases of the delimitation process, notably in the *Jan Mayen* case,[106] this is very much the exception, as was stressed by the Tribunal in the *Barbados/Trinidad and Tobago* case when it declined to take account of Barbados fishing interests when determining the location of the boundary.[107] It seems then, that the role of economic factors is destined to remain a 'hidden hand' for some while to come.

Despite what is said about the process being driven by geography and geographical factors this has never been entirely true, and economic factors are merely one example of broad range of issues the potential relevance of which is reflected in the practice of the parties, or which are recognized by the courts as either individually[108]

---

[100] See generally Rothwell and Stephens, n 38, 409–11; and Tanaka, n 40, 208–10.

[101] Thus *Cameroon v Nigeria*, n 14, [304], the Court concluded that the presence of oil wells was not a relevant circumstance, unless their presence amounted to evidence of an agreement between the parties.

[102] *Barbados/Trinidad and Tobago*, n 14, [241].

[103] *Black Sea*, n 17, [198]; *Nicaragua v Colombia*, n 1, [223].

[104] *Gulf of Maine*, n 12, [237].

[105] In *Barbados/Trinidad and Tobago*, n 14, [267], the Tribunal also rejected the claim that there were catastrophic repercussions as being unproven, but also noting that 'injury does not equate with catastrophe'.

[106] The Court took account of the need to ensure equitable access to Capelin stocks (albeit that it was, strictly speaking, determining the boundary of an EFZ at that point). *Jan Mayen*, n 13, [76].

[107] *Barbados/Trinidad and Tobago*, n 14, [269].

[108] See eg Tanaka, n 2, ch 8 for a consideration of a broad range of non-geographical factors.

or collectively indicating the predominant interest of a particular State over the area of overlapping entitlement.[109] One such factor, long acknowledged, has concerned navigational interests. From the very outset, the presence of navigable channels—though conceptually unrelated to the continental shelf—has been seen as a potentially relevant factor[110] in their delimitation, an approach confirmed in the *Anglo-French Continental Shelf Arbitration* which referred to the 'vital interests of the French Republic in the security and *defence* of its territory'.[111] This finds resonance in the *Nicaragua v Colombia* case, where the Court confirmed that 'legitimate security concerns might be a relevant consideration, if a maritime delimitation was effected particularly near to the coast of a State and the Court will bear this consideration in mind in determining what adjustment to make to the provisional median line or in what way that line should be shifted'.[112] This suggests that a rather broader range of factors bears upon the delimitation process—even if they are not always articulated within it—than might at first be thought.

4 THE 2014 *BAY OF BENGAL MARITIME BOUNDARY ARBITRATION*

The 2014 Award in the *Bay of Bengal Maritime Boundary Arbitration (Bangladesh/India)*, under Annex VII of the LOSC, was at the time of writing the most recent maritime boundary judgment of an international court or tribunal.[113] The decision is of sufficient interest to warrant separate observations highlighting a number of its key features and possible implications as regards the process of maritime boundary delimitation.

An important overarching point is the concern of the Award to uphold the stability of boundaries. The Award stresses that the possible impact over time of climate change on a coastline is not to be taken into account as a factor within the delimitation process, nor can climate change be subsequently appealed to in order to revisit an agreed boundary.[114] The primacy of the equidistance/special circumstances

---

[109] See Evans, n 2, ch 16.
[110] It had been identified as such by the ILC in its preparatory work for the CSC. See Evans, n 2, 179, though this was not without criticism at the time. See Tanaka, n 2, 314.
[111] *Anglo-French Arbitration*, n 9, [161], referring the navigational access to naval facilities.
[112] *Nicaragua v Colombia*, n 1, [222].
[113] *Bay of Bengal Maritime Boundary Arbitration (Bangladesh/India)*, Award of the LOSC Annex VII Tribunal (7 July 2014).
[114] Ibid, [216]–[218].

method for the delimitation of the territorial sea is again reaffirmed, despite the paucity and potential indeterminacy of relevant basepoints.[115] The Tribunal also took the view that not only was the concave nature of general coastal configuration insufficient to warrant a departure from the use of a provisional equidistant line, but that the coastal configuration was not relevant *at all* to the delimitation of 'the narrow belt of the territorial sea'.[116] Another very important element of the Award is its clear rejection of the use of basepoints located on low tide elevations for the purposes of delimitation (as opposed to the generation of maritime entitlements), the Tribunal insisting that such basepoints be located on the low-water line of coasts.[117]

Turing to the EEZ and continental shelf, the Award continued the trend of turning away from the rigidity of the 'three-stage test' as set out in the *Black Sea* case and, following the *Bangladesh/ Myanmar* case, it emphasizes the overriding importance of achieving an equitable solution.[118] Although a provisional equidistance line is used, this is largely because of the 'greater transparency' associated with the equidistance/special circumstances method rather than with its having any privileged status.[119] Moreover, once again, the provisional equidistance line is in fact largely abandoned in favour of a geodesic line in order to address the 'relevant circumstance' of its use resulting in India benefitting from a 'cut off' effect.[120] It is, in consequence, difficult to see why the provisional line was drawn at all, as it does not seem to have had any practical impact on the outcome.

Identification of the relevant coasts, and consequently the relevant area, had no real role to play in the process since the Award concluded that there was no significant disproportion between a coastal length ratio of 1:1.92 and a ratio of allocated areas of 1: 2.81 in favour of India.[121] This needs to be seen against the background of the Tribunal inflating the length of the relevant coastline of India by the inclusion of a part of the Andaman Islands in its assessment which even India did not request. Once again, all of the calculations made by the Tribunal appear to be both largely self-serving, yet ultimately pointless.

Attention needs to be drawn to a number of other interesting features. The Award stresses that there is only a single continental shelf and there is no distinction to be drawn between the 'inner' and 'outer' shelf.[122] This seems to be at odds with the approach of the ICJ in *Nicaragua v Colombia*.[123] Finally, the boundary of the

---

[115] Ibid, [246]–[247].

[116] Ibid, [248]. A small adjustment was, however, made to ensure that the starting point of the equidistance line commenced at the land terminus, another issue which it needed to address.

[117] Ibid, [260] and [353].   [118] Ibid, [339] and [397].

[119] Ibid, [343], though transparency is hardly the hallmark of this, and most other delimitation decisions.

[120] Ibid, [478].   [121] Ibid, [495]–[497].

[122] Ibid, [77] and [465]. However, this did not prevent it from determining the provisional method for the inner shelf and merely projecting that forward into the outer shelf (see ibid, [465] and [478]).

[123] *Nicaragua v Columbia*, n 1.

continental shelf results in an area which is within 200 nm of India but beyond 200 nm from Bangladesh being awarded to Bangladesh. This means that, since Bangladesh has no entitlement to an EEZ in this area, it remains within the EEZ of India. The Tribunal notes this, but observes that since the continental shelf pertains to Bangladesh, this 'does not otherwise limit India's sovereign rights to the EEZ in the superadjacent waters'.[124] It thus appears that within 200 nm, the continental shelf takes priority over the EEZ after all, and the EEZ is thus reduced to a residual right. The potential implication of this requires further attention.

5 Conclusion

While it is relatively easy to identify the relevant statements of treaty and customary law concerning maritime boundary delimitation, the application of that law remains complex and perplexing. The oscillation between predictability and flexibility seems set to remain a feature of the jurisprudence, with relatively 'easy' cases (such as the *Black Sea* case) being used to flagship the merits of the fairly formal application of objective criteria whereas the more complex (such as the *Nicaragua v Colombia* case) will continue to pull in the direction of a more results-oriented approach. The 'equidistance versus equitable principles' debate has never really gone away, nor is it ever likely to. We should continue to expect change, and whether such change is in the direction of increased certainty or of enhanced flexibility is secondary. The primary point is that this body of law is unlikely to remain conceptually static. But does this really matter? Some questions do not admit of an answer and, though it is important to chart these jurisprudential developments in order to understand where thinking currently lies along that spectrum, the real challenge is to look beyond these issues and focus on the essence of the process to be undertaken.

What does matter is that the almost inevitable fixation with the 'certainty versus flexibility', 'equidistance versus equitable principles' debates tends to obscure the debates which ought now to be taking place, concerning matters such as the relationships between the zones of extended maritime jurisdiction, the 'inner' and 'outer' continental shelf and the influence of the factors which, while playing a discernible role, are not formally accepted as being relevant and are hidden behind the language of 'equitable discretion'. At the same time, there is an ever greater willingness to consider in an increasingly stylized fashion a small number of factors which are generally accepted as being relevant—irrespective of whether they really are.

[124] *Bay of Bengal Maritime Boundary Arbitration*, n 113, [505].

Against this background, one of the most intriguing comments made by the ICJ in recent times was in the *Nicaragua v Colombia* case when, in the context of rejecting Nicaragua's argument that the Colombian islands ought to be enclaved, it observed that such a solution would have 'unfortunate consequences for the orderly management of maritime resources, policing and the public order of the oceans in general, all of which would be better served by a simpler and more coherent division of the relevant area'.[125] Almost every element of this statement is at odds with prevailing orthodoxies concerning continental shelf and EEZ delimitation, yet it probably far better encapsulates what an 'equitable solution' is meant to achieve.

---

[125] *Nicaragua v Colombia*, n 1, [230].

13

PORT AND COASTAL STATES

ERIK J MOLENAAR

1 Introduction

THE concepts 'port State' and 'coastal State' relate to different capacities in which a State can act to further or safeguard its own interests, or to comply with international obligations or commitments. Although the port State concept is more recent than the concepts of coastal and flag States,[1] the exercise of port State jurisdiction as such is likely to predate the exercise of coastal State jurisdiction. This nevertheless depends on the definitions for the concepts 'port State' and 'coastal State' that are employed. Neither term is defined in the 1982 United Nations Convention on the Law of the Sea (LOSC) or other global instrument with near-universal participation.[2]

Coastal States are universally understood to be States with a sea-coastline. Fresh-water lakes (eg the North American Great Lakes and Lake Victoria) and fully enclosed salt-water lakes or seas not connected to another sea or ocean (eg the Aral

---

[1] See chapter 1 in this volume. For an early discussion of port State jurisdiction, see British Branch Committee on the Law of the Sea, 'The Concept of Port State Jurisdiction' in International Law Association, *Report of the Fifth-Sixth Conference—New Delhi 1974* (International Law Association London 1976) 400.

[2] The 2009 Agreement on Port State Measures to Prevent, Deter and Eliminate Illegal, Unreported and Unregulated Fishing (hereinafter PSM Agreement) contains a definition of 'port' (in Art 1(g)) but not of 'port State'.

and Dead Seas) are generally accepted not to be subject to the international law of the sea.³ The prevailing view is that the same applies to the Caspian Sea.⁴

Entitlement to coastal State maritime zones is generally accepted to be based solely on sovereignty over land territory with a sea-coastline.⁵ A coastal State's jurisdiction is commonly regarded to relate to its own maritime zones, and encompasses the resources and activities therein as well as external impacts on them. In view of the agreement to disagree on the question of sovereignty over land territory in Antarctica (south of 60°S) enshrined in the 1959 Antarctic Treaty, States claiming title to such land territory are not generally recognized as coastal States⁶ and thereby also not recognized to be entitled to exercise coastal State jurisdiction over maritime zones adjacent to land territory in Antarctica. A collective exercise of jurisdiction by the Antarctic Treaty Consultative Parties (ATCPs) could be an alternative to coastal State jurisdiction, but the ATCPs have so far not pursued this.⁷ Outside of the Antarctic context, disputes relating to title to land territory concern competing claims by two or more States. While these competing claims may have implications for the exercise of coastal State jurisdiction (eg in terms of effectiveness), the ability to exercise such jurisdiction as well as the existence of a coastal State vis-à-vis the disputed territory is not questioned as such.

The spatial scope of a (sea)port includes the outermost permanent harbour works—but not offshore installations and artificial islands—as well as roadsteads that extend beyond the outer limit of the territorial sea, provided they are normally used for the loading, unloading, and anchoring of ships.⁸ Port State jurisdiction can be defined to relate to activities and standards occurring within, or applicable to:

(a) the port;
(b) the maritime zones of other coastal States;
(c) areas beyond national jurisdiction (ie the high seas and the 'Area'⁹); and
(d) the maritime zones of the coastal State in which the port is located. This component can also be defined as coastal State jurisdiction.¹⁰

---

³ See also 1982 United Nations Convention on the Law of the Sea, Art 122 (hereinafter LOSC).

⁴ The 'Table recapitulating the status of the Convention and of the related Agreements, as at 10 January 2014', available at <www.un.org/Depts/los>, lists Azerbaijan, Kazakhstan, and Turkmenistan as landlocked States despite the fact that they only border on the Caspian Sea. See also n 65.

⁵ See eg *Maritime Delimitation in the Area between Greenland and Jan Mayen (Denmark v Norway)* (Judgment) [1993] ICJ Rep 38, [80].

⁶ Apart from the mutual recognition that may exist between claimant States.

⁷ See R Lefeber, 'Marine Scientific Research in the Antarctic Treaty System' in EJ Molenaar, AG Oude Elferink, and DR Rothwell (eds), *The Law of the Sea and the Polar Regions: Interactions between Global and Regional Regimes* (Martinus Nijhoff Publishers Leiden/Boston 2013) 323, 329–31.

⁸ LOSC, n 3, Arts 11–12. See also, PSM Agreement, n 2, Art 1(g).

⁹ See LOSC, n 3, Art 1(1).

¹⁰ See EJ Molenaar, *Coastal State Jurisdiction over Vessel-Source Pollution* (Kluwer Law International The Hague/Boston/London 1998) 91–5.

The term 'port State jurisdiction' is broader than the term 'port State control'. The latter term is best understood in light of the rationale of the 1982 Paris Memorandum of Understanding (MOU)[11] and other regional merchant shipping port State control (PSC) arrangements modelled thereon. These regional PSC arrangements responded to inadequate performance by flag States as well as port States (ie 'flags of convenience' and 'ports of convenience') by, *inter alia*, harmonizing and coordinating PSC procedures and commitments to carry out inspections and taking predominantly corrective enforcement action (eg detention for the purpose of rectification). Even though regional PSC arrangements are non-legally binding, they nevertheless contain saving-clauses to ensure that nothing in them affects a port State's so-called 'residual' jurisdiction.[12] Such residual jurisdiction allows a port State to prescribe more stringent standards and take more onerous enforcement measures than those internationally agreed.

Within the sphere of international fisheries law, the term 'port State control' is often used together with the term 'port State measures'. The latter's consistent use in the 2009 Agreement on Port State Measures to Prevent, Deter and Eliminate Illegal, Unreported and Unregulated Fishing (PSM Agreement)[13] indicates that port State measures can relate to prescription as well as to enforcement, and that it is therefore more akin to port State jurisdiction than PSC.

The remainder of this chapter consists of three sections. The Sections 2 and 3 are devoted to 'Port States' and 'Coastal States' respectively, and Section 4 to 'Future Developments'.

2 Port States

2.1 Overview

Like land borders, seaports give access to the landmass of a State for persons and goods, and are therefore logical points of control for, *inter alia*, customs, immigration, sanitation, and national security purposes. Ports also offer an obvious opportunity for verifying whether visiting foreign ships comply with certain types of national or international standards and if they have engaged in certain illegal activities in the maritime zones of the coastal State in which the port is located, or beyond. The costs and difficulties of at-sea enforcement also mean that, despite its

---

[11] 1982 Paris Memorandum of Understanding on Port State Control (hereinafter Paris MOU). This chapter uses the version that includes the 36th amendment and came into effect on 20 August 2013.
[12] See eg ibid, §§ 1.7 and 9.1.   [13] See n 2.

shortcomings, in-port enforcement is often preferable or, in fact, the only enforcement option.

Port State jurisdiction may not just serve more immediate national interests but can also further the interests of the international community, for instance, in relation to maritime safety and security, marine environmental protection, sustainable use and conservation of marine living resources, and food security. The more immediate national interests and the interests of the international community can coincide as well. Illegal, unreported, and unregulated (IUU) fishing and illegal vessel-source pollution on the high seas, for example, can have transboundary effects on species or the broader marine environment in the maritime zones of the coastal State within which the port is located.

By complementing the flag State's responsibility over its ships, port States can make an important contribution to ensuring compliance with national and international regulatory efforts. Flag States, beneficial owners, and operators who benefit as flags of convenience or 'free riders' from the primacy of flag State jurisdiction on the high seas as well as the consensual nature of international law, can—through port State jurisdiction—be deprived of competitive advantages, for example, lower operating costs and avoidance of catch restrictions. The level playing field for maritime activities thereby promoted is an essential component of—or even a prerequisite for—safeguarding many of the aforementioned interests of the international community.

Where port State jurisdiction remains entirely optional, it inevitably leads to ports of convenience where less stringent levels and efforts of prescription and enforcement exist. Incentives for operating ports of convenience include port fees, use of port services (such as landing, transhipping, processing, refuelling, and resupplying), linkages with transport on land and associated socio-economic interests. These incentives may lead to situations where international standards, for instance those adopted within the International Maritime Organization (IMO), the International Labour Organization (ILO), or regional fisheries management organizations (RFMOs),[14] are poorly enforced or not at all.

2.2 Access to port

As ports lie wholly within a State's territory[15] and fall on that account under its territorial sovereignty, customary international law acknowledges that a port State has wide discretion in exercising jurisdiction over its ports. This was explicitly stated by the International Court of Justice (ICJ) in the *Nicaragua v USA* case, where it observed that it is 'by virtue of its sovereignty, that the coastal State may regulate

---

[14] For the purpose of this chapter, 'arrangements' are covered by this acronym.
[15] Apart from the exception provided in LOSC, n 3, Art 12. See n 8 and accompanying text.

access to its ports'.[16] While there may often be a presumption that access to port will be granted, customary international law gives foreign vessels no general right of access to ports.[17]

Articles 25(2), 38(2), 211(3), and 255 of the LOSC and Articles 4(1)(b) and 7–9 of the PSM Agreement as well as the many bilateral port access agreements in existence today, confirm the absence of a right of access for foreign vessels to ports under customary international law as well as a port State's wide discretion in exercising jurisdiction under customary international law. Article 2 of the Statute to the 1923 Convention on the International Regime of Maritime Ports (Maritime Ports Convention)—which provides for access to ports based on national treatment and reciprocity—does not affect this conclusion owing to the current limited participation in the Convention and the fact that the conditional right which it establishes is further qualified, for instance, in relation to fishing vessels and warships.[18]

These conclusions on the extensive nature of port State jurisdiction and the absence of a general right of access to ports under general international law are, *mutatis mutandis*, also applicable to airports and 'airport States' within the domain of international air law.[19]

A widely acknowledged exception to the above-mentioned discretion is a ship in distress or in a *force majeure* situation. Even in these cases, however, the specific circumstances may be such that the interests of the port or coastal State override those of the ship. This understanding is reflected in the neutral wording of Article 10 of the PSM Agreement. The 2003 IMO Guidelines on Places of Refuge for Ships in Need of Assistance[20]—adopted in the aftermath of the disaster with the *Prestige* in 2002—confirm the need to balance the various interests attached to the ship and its crew with those of the port and/or coastal State.[21] In January 2009, a majority within the IMO's Legal Committee did not see the need for a convention on places of refuge when discussing a draft instrument developed by the Comité Maritime International.[22]

---

[16] *Military and Paramilitary Activities In and Against Nicaragua (Nicaragua v United States of America)* (Judgment) [1986] ICJ Rep 14, [213].

[17] AV Lowe, 'The Right of Entry into Maritime Ports in International Law' (1977) 14 *San Diego Law Review* 597, 622.

[18] 1923 Statute on the International Regime of Maritime Ports, Arts 13 and 14. Cf LA De La Fayette, 'Access to Ports in International Law' (1996) 11 *International Journal of Marine and Coastal Law* 1, 4, and 17. At the time of writing, there are around 40 contracting parties, see <www.untreaty.un.org>.

[19] See eg *Air Transport Association of America and Others v Secretary of State for Energy and Climate Change* (C-366/10) [2011] ECR I-13755, [128].

[20] Assembly Resolution A.949(23), *Guidelines on Places of Refuge for Ships in Need of Assistance* (5 December 2003).

[21] Ibid, [3.12]–[3.14]. See also AE Chircop and O Lindén (eds), *Places of Refuge for Ships: Emerging Environmental Concerns of a Maritime Custom* (Nijhoff Leiden 2006).

[22] See 'Report of the Legal Committee on the Work of its Ninety-Fifth Session', IMO Doc LEG 95/10 (22 April 2009) 24–5.

Even though a right of access to ports does not exist in customary international law, it may be provided by an applicable treaty such as the Maritime Ports Convention or a bilateral port access agreement. Whether a right of access to ports could be covered by the freedom of transit laid down in Article XI of the 1994 General Agreement on Tariffs and Trade (GATT 1994) is discussed in the next subsection.

2.3 Conditions for entry into port

A port State's jurisdiction to prescribe conditions for entry into port is subject to a number of restrictions. These include the limitations arising from diplomatic immunities and sovereign immunities for foreign warships and other government ships operated for non-commercial purposes.[23] Moreover, port States commonly do not exercise jurisdiction with respect to affairs regarded to be internal to the ship and that do not affect the interests of the port State.

Other restrictions ensue from adherence to specific treaties. The principle of non-discrimination, for instance, is widely recognized in the international law of the sea[24] and in international trade law.[25] A State's adherence to IMO instruments such as MARPOL 73/78 may also affect its residual jurisdiction as a port State owing to specific provisions included in them.[26] At the same time, however, there are also provisions in IMO instruments that explicitly confirm a port State's residual jurisdiction.[27] The view that adherence to IMO instruments does not constrain a port State's residual jurisdiction per se, is supported by limited but significant State practice, including by the United States and the European Union (EU).[28]

A question that has so far not been resolved is whether or not the freedom of transit and the prohibition of quantitative restrictions laid down in Articles V(3) and XI of the GATT 1994 constrain a port State's residual jurisdiction. In 2000, these two provisions were invoked by the (then) European Community (EC) when it instituted a World Trade Organization (WTO) dispute settlement procedure against Chile for prohibiting Spanish fishing vessels to land swordfish in Chilean

---

[23] As, inter alia, confirmed in *ARA Libertad (Argentina v Ghana)* (Provisional Measures) [2012] ITLOS Rep 21, [95].

[24] See LOSC, n 3, Arts 24(1)(b), 25(3), 119(3), and 227.

[25] 1994 General Agreement on Tariffs and Trade, Art XX (GATT).

[26] See eg 1973 International Convention for the Prevention of Pollution, as modified by the Protocol of 1978, Annex VI, § 15(1) (hereinafter MARPOL).

[27] See eg 2001 International Convention on the Control of Harmful Anti-fouling Systems on Ships, Art 1(3). For other examples, see EJ Molenaar, 'Port State Jurisdiction: Toward Comprehensive, Mandatory and Global Coverage' (2007) 38 *Ocean Development & International Law* 225, 231.

[28] B Marten, *Port State Jurisdiction and the Regulation of International Merchant Shipping* (Springer Cham 2013), in particular chs 4–6; H Ringbom, *The EU Maritime Safety Policy and International Law* (Nijhoff Leiden 2008), in particular ch 5; and Molenaar, n 27, 231.

ports, even if just for the purpose of transhipment.[29] The large number of States that reserved their third-party rights in this procedure underlined the significance of the issues and the interests involved: Australia, Canada, Ecuador, Iceland, India, Norway, and the United States. Shortly thereafter, Chile instituted a dispute settlement procedure against the EC under the LOSC.[30] However, neither of these two swordfish cases culminated in a ruling as both procedures were suspended in 2001 and discontinued in 2009–2010.

Another opportunity for an international ruling on these issues could have arisen in the WTO dispute settlement procedure instituted in November 2013 by Denmark (in respect of the Faroe Islands) against the EU in relation to Atlanto-Scandian herring.[31] According to the Faroe Islands, certain coercive economic measures taken by the EU—including the closure of EU ports to Faroese vessels[32]—are inconsistent with Articles I(1), V(2), and XI of GATT 1994. An even larger number of States reserved their third-party rights than with regard to the WTO dispute settlement procedure on swordfish.[33] Interestingly, several months earlier—in August 2013—Denmark (in respect of the Faroe Islands) also instituted proceedings against the EU in relation to Atlanto-Scandian herring pursuant to the LOSC. In its Statement of Claim, the Faroe Islands holds that the (threats of) above-mentioned measures amount to a breach of the EU's obligation to cooperate in relation to shared fish stocks laid down in Article 63(1) of the LOSC.[34] By mid-2014, however, the Faroe Islands and the EU came to an agreement on the allocation of Atlanto-Scandian herring and both procedures were subsequently terminated.

2.4 Leaving port

As a corollary of the absence of a general right of access to ports under general international law and the port State's broad discretion in stipulating conditions for entry into port, there is in principle no objection to prescribe conditions for departure as conditions for entry. This so-called 'departure State jurisdiction' can,

---

[29] *Chile—Measures Affecting the Transit and Importation of Swordfish*, EC Request for consultations, WT/DS193 (19 April 2000).

[30] *Conservation and Sustainable Exploitation of Swordfish Stocks in the South-Eastern Pacific Ocean (Chile/European Community)* (Order) [2000] ITLOS Rep 148.

[31] *European Union—Measures on Atlanto-Scandian Herring*, Denmark Request for consultations, WT/DS469 (4 November 2013).

[32] Commission Regulation (EU) No 793/2013 (20 August 2013), Art 5(2).

[33] Australia, China, Guatemala, Honduras, Iceland, India, Japan, New Zealand, Panama, Russian Federation, Chinese Taipei, Turkey, United States, Argentina, Brazil, Mexico, Norway, Peru, and Thailand.

[34] *Kingdom of Denmark in respect of the Faroe Islands v European Union* (Coercive Economic Measures in respect of the Shared Stock of Atlanto-Scandian Herring). Statement of Claim, 16 August 2013 (on file with author).

for example, be used to require mandatory disposal of all types of waste in port to ensure that these will not be illegally discharged after departure.[35] The exercise of departure State jurisdiction may sometimes even be mandatory, for instance, in cases where 'applicable international rules and standards relating to seaworthiness of vessels' are violated and this 'threatens damage to the marine environment'.[36] As confirmed by the International Tribunal for the Law of the Sea (ITLOS) in its Judgment in the *M/V 'Louisa'* case, the freedom of navigation on the high seas laid down in Article 87 of the LOSC does not give a vessel 'a right to leave the port and gain access to the high seas notwithstanding its detention in the context of legal proceedings against it'.[37]

2.5 Legal bases for port State jurisdiction

2.5.1 *Territorial jurisdiction*

A general limitation on jurisdiction imposed by customary international law is the need for a sufficiently close or substantial connection with the person, fact, or event and the State exercising jurisdiction.[38] This aims at creating order by minimizing overlaps in jurisdiction. However, unless and until States are bound to more specific limitations on jurisdiction, for instance through their adherence to treaties containing such specifications, it will be up to an international court or tribunal to rule on the sufficiency of a jurisdictional link in a particular case.

Port State jurisdiction can either be territorial, quasi-territorial, or extraterritorial. The sufficiency of the territorial principle as a basis for jurisdiction can be presumed unless international law stipulates otherwise. Non-compliance with static standards or illegal behaviour occurring in port can be addressed through territorial jurisdiction. As regards behaviour prior to entry, port or coastal States can still rely on territorial jurisdiction in cases where the behaviour took place within maritime zones that are part of their territory, namely their internal waters, archipelagic waters, or territorial sea.[39]

Jurisdiction based on the territorial principle can sometimes still be used even though extraterritorial jurisdiction is not possible, for instance, with regard to unregulated high seas fishing. The focus of enforcement should then be not on illegal behaviour beyond the port but on illegal behaviour within the port. Obstruction

---

[35] See eg Directive 2000/59/EC *On port reception facilities for ship-generated waste and cargo residues* (consolidated version) (27 November 2000), Art 7.

[36] LOSC, n 3, Art 219.

[37] *M/V 'Louisa' (Saint Vincent and the Grenadines v Spain)*, Judgment of the International Tribunal for the Law of the Sea (28 May 2013), [109].

[38] A Mann, 'The Doctrine of Jurisdiction in International Law' (1964) 111 *Recueil des Cours de l'Académie de Droit International* 9, 83.

[39] See also the discussion below on areas in which the regime of transit passage applies.

of in-port inspection and investigation, or providing false or incomplete information to the inspection authorities (eg oil record books or declarations of not having engaged in, or supported, IUU fishing or fishing activities), could be options in that regard. The United States makes extensive use of this approach.[40]

Port State jurisdiction with regard to construction, design, equipment, and manning (CDEM) standards warrants separate discussion. Owing to their static nature, the level of non-compliance with CDEM standards is commonly uniform throughout a vessel's voyage. This is quite different from discharge standards and many types of fisheries conservation and management measures, where a vessel's non-compliance generally occurs only during part of the vessel's voyage. Unlike CDEM standards, these standards and measures essentially seek to regulate 'behaviour'. Irrespective of the question as to whether or not CDEM standards seek to regulate behaviour, however, it is conclusive for the jurisdictional basis that non-compliance continues to occur in port. Jurisdiction can therefore be safely based on the territorial principle.[41]

The use of port State jurisdiction in the context of the regime of transit passage in straits used for international navigation[42] led to heated debate following the 2003 joint Australia–Papua New Guinea proposals within the IMO to designate the Torres Strait as an extension of the Great Barrier Reef particularly sensitive sea area (PSSA), complemented with compulsory pilotage as an associated protective measure (APM). A 2005 IMO Marine Environment Protection Committee (MEPC) Resolution approved the PSSA extension but merely recommended that governments 'inform ships flying their flag that they should act in accordance with Australia's system of pilotage'.[43] Despite this non-mandatory wording, however, Australia issued Marine Notice 8/2006 (no longer current), which stipulated that non-compliance with its compulsory pilotage system by foreign vessels would lead to the imposition of non-custodial penalties in port or, for ships in transit, at the next port of call in Australia.[44] Australia thereby intended to circumvent the need for IMO approval by exercising port State jurisdiction. Mainly between 2006 and 2008, several States—including the United States and Singapore—repeatedly took the view within the IMO and the United Nations General Assembly (UNGA) that such sanctions would be inconsistent with the 2005 MEPC Resolution and the LOSC. Subsequently, Australia issued Marine Notice 07/2009, which stipulates that non-compliance triggers a 'risk' of prosecution. Classified United States embassy cables disclosed by WikiLeaks in 2011 suggest that these changes were the result of

---

[40] Cf Molenaar, n 27, 242–3.

[41] See also *Air Transport Association of America* (C-366/10), n 19, [125].

[42] Laid down in LOSC, n 3, Part III, Section 2.

[43] Resolution MEPC.133(53), *Designation of the Torres Strait as an extension of the Great Barrier Reef Particularly Sensitive Sea Area* (22 July 2005).

[44] Pursuant to §§ 186G–186L of its Navigation Act 1912 (Cth), since replaced by §§ 162–173 of the Navigation Act 2012 (Cth). This was softened somewhat by Marine Notice 16/2006 (no longer current), which notes that non-compliance 'may result' in prosecution.

diplomatic consultations between Australia and the United States.[45] In September 2013, Australian authorities advised that no instances of non-compliance had occurred since issuing Marine Notice 8/2006.[46] As Australia has therefore never actually denied access to port—either immediately or at a next call—or imposed non-custodial penalties for non-compliance with the pilotage requirements, its practice on port State enforcement jurisdiction is in line with State practice examined below in the scenario of unregulated fishing on the high seas.

2.5.2 *Quasi-territorial and extraterritorial jurisdiction*

Jurisdiction over behaviour that occurs beyond the port State's territory can either be quasi-territorial or extraterritorial. The former relates to jurisdiction over the port State's own exclusive economic zone (EEZ), another 200-nautical mile (nm) maritime zone 'derived from' the EEZ (such as a fishing zone), or continental shelf. Proceeding from this understanding of quasi-territorial jurisdiction, truly extraterritorial jurisdiction exercised by a port State relates to behaviour that occurs beyond its own maritime zones: on the high seas, in the Area, or in the maritime zones of other States.

The legality of extraterritorial port State jurisdiction under international law depends on two aspects, namely a sufficient jurisdictional basis and the type of enforcement measure taken.[47] A sufficient jurisdictional basis could, for instance, be provided by a treaty—whatever its underlying rationale—or by justifiable reliance on a jurisdictional principle, such as the universality principle or the security principle.

The relevance of the type of enforcement measures opted for is directly related to the absence of a general right of access to ports under general international law. Examples of port State enforcement measures include:

(a) denial of landing, transhipment, or processing of cargo;
(b) denial of use of other port services, such as refuelling, other forms of re-supplying (eg water, food, equipment, bait, and changing crew) and maintenance and drydocking;
(c) denial of access to ports (ad hoc or a priori);

---

[45] P Dorling, 'Reef Safeguard Sacrificed Secretly for US, Singapore' *Sydney Morning Herald* (12 September 2011). See also DK Anton, 'Does Australia Make or Break the International Law of Transit Passage? Meeting Environmental and Safety Challenges in the Torres Strait with Compulsory Pilotage' in DD Caron and N Oral (eds), *Navigating Straits: Challenges to International Law* (Brill Nijhoff 2014) 49; and RC Beckman, 'PSSAs and Transit Passage—Australia's Pilotage System in the Torres Strait Challenges the IMO and UNCLOS' (2007) 38 *Ocean Development and International Law* 325.

[46] Information provided by an Australian government official to the author by email on 13 September 2013.

[47] Marten, n 28, 108–11 and 234 takes the view that the type of enforcement measures is not relevant, even though this does not (yet) seem to be supported by State practice.

(d) boarding and inspection;

(e) detention until standards are complied with, (eg repairs to meet technical standards); and

(f) monetary or other penalties, including confiscation of ship or cargo, for violations of national legislation.

A distinction can be made between measures (a)–(c), on the one hand, and measures (e)–(f), on the other hand. The principal aim of the former three is to withhold benefits to which foreign vessels are not entitled under general international law. The latter two however, are punitive or at least have a punitive element. While the punitive character of detention for the purpose of making repairs appears at first sight less onerous than that of a monetary penalty, owners or operators of large merchant vessels may often prefer the latter. For such ships an extra day or even a couple of extra hours of idleness in port can be very costly.

There are two general rules on the relationship between prescriptive and enforcement jurisdiction. First, enforcement is only lawful if based on legislation that has been enacted in accordance with international law and which is applicable to the specific circumstances of the event calling for enforcement. Second, national legislation enacted in accordance with international law does not necessarily bring unlimited enforcement powers.[48]

The argument that the legality of extraterritorial port State jurisdiction depends above all on the two aspects mentioned above can be illustrated by comparing the scenario of illegal discharges on the high seas with so-called 'unregulated' fishing on the high seas. Unregulated high seas fishing essentially means fishing by flag States that are non-members of the relevant RFMO and fail to comply with the obligation to cooperate with respect to the fish stocks managed by that RFMO.[49]

In the former scenario, Article 218 of the LOSC grants port States the right to institute proceedings and impose monetary penalties for illegal discharges that have occurred beyond its own maritime zones. Conversely, no global treaty provides a similar right in relation to unregulated fishing on the high seas. Such a right is for instance not explicitly incorporated in Article 23(1) of the 1995 Fish Stocks Agreement (FSA), which merely stipulates that a port State 'has the right and the duty' to take certain measures in its ports. There also seem to be no States that either take the view that such a right is covered by the saving-clause in Article 23(4)— which reads: '[n]othing in this article affects the exercise by States of their sovereignty over ports in their territory in accordance with international law'—or that

---

[48] See eg LOSC, n 3, Art 220(5) and (6).

[49] This obligation is based on ibid, Arts 63(2), 64–67, and 116–119 and the 1995 Agreement for the Implementation of the Provisions of the United Nations Convention on the Law of the Sea of 10 December 1982 relating to the Conservation and Management of Straddling Fish Stocks and Highly Migratory Fish Stocks, Art 8(3) (hereinafter FSA).

have actually imposed such more onerous enforcement measures.[50] A few RFMOs nevertheless authorize or even require their members to confiscate catch of foreign vessels in their ports in certain very specific scenarios.[51] Article 4(1)(b) of the PSM Agreement acknowledges this practice and the right of port States to impose more onerous enforcement measures 'pursuant to a decision of' an RFMO.[52]

2.6 Port State cooperation through global and regional instruments and bodies

In 1991, the adoption of IMO Assembly Resolution A.682(17), entitled 'Regional co-operation in the Control of Ships and Discharges',[53] reflected broad recognition that—in most circumstances[54]—port State jurisdiction can only effectively address inadequate flag State performance if exercised collectively, thereby also addressing the problem of ports of convenience. The resolution implicitly acknowledged the added value of the 1982 Paris MOU and led to efforts to create a global network of regional merchant shipping PSC arrangements. The expansion in participation in the Paris MOU and the creation and expansion of eight new arrangements since then (ie Asia and the Pacific (Tokyo MOU); Latin America (Acuerdo de Viña del Mar); Caribbean (Caribbean MOU); West and Central Africa (Abuja MOU); the Black Sea region (Black Sea MOU); the Mediterranean (Mediterranean MOU); the Indian Ocean (Indian Ocean MOU); and the Arab States of the Gulf (Riyadh MOU)), means that almost complete global coverage has now been achieved.[55] While the Arctic Ocean/region and the Southern Ocean/Antarctic region constitute

---

[50] See EJ Molenaar, 'Non-Participation in the Fish Stocks Agreement. Status and Reasons' (2011) 26 *International Journal of Marine and Coastal Law* 195, 207–8.

[51] See eg Commission for the Conservation of Antarctic Marine Living Resources (CCAMLR), Conservation Measure 10-07 (2009), *Scheme to promote compliance by non-Contracting Party vessels with CCAMLR conservation measures*, [22(iv)(b)(i)]; North-East Atlantic Fisheries Commission (NEAFC), *Scheme of Control and Enforcement 2014* (version in effect from 5 March 2014), Art 23(3); and Northwest Atlantic Fisheries Organization (NAFO) *Conservation and Enforcement Measures*, NAFO/FC Doc 14/1, Art 43(7).

[52] Note that South East Atlantic Fisheries Organization (SEAFO), *System of Observation, Inspection, Compliance and Enforcement* (version in effect from 15 February 2014), Art 22(5) implements PSM Agreement, n 2, Art 9(5), without specifying a specific scenario (such as done by CCAMLR, NAFO, and NEAFC; see n 51).

[53] IMO Assembly Res A.682(17), *Regional co-operation in the Control of Ships and Discharges* (6 November 1991).

[54] Exceptions are States like the United States, which have relatively few ships that merely transit its maritime zones without calling at one of its ports. Also, many owners and operators of ships prefer to have the ability for their ships to call at United States ports.

[55] See the information at <http://www.imo.org/OurWork/Safety/Implementation/Pages/PortStateControl.aspx>.

gaps in global coverage, this does not necessarily mean that these gaps require the establishment of new PSC Arrangements.[56]

However, mere geographical coverage does not necessarily mean that the performance of the Paris and Tokyo MOUs is also achieved by the other regional PSC arrangements. Differences in performance are, among other things, caused by overdue updates of constitutive instruments owing to developments at the IMO and ILO, and by lack of adherence by the participating authorities with the underlying regulatory conventions. Efforts to address these and other challenges have been undertaken by the IMO—often together with ILO and the United Nations Food and Agriculture Organization (FAO)—including the establishment of international harmonized minimum standards[57] and the convening of (bi-annual) workshops for regional PSC arrangements Secretaries and Database Managers, which facilitate information exchange, harmonization, and policy recommendations.[58] Other forms of cooperation between regional PSC arrangements include joint inspection efforts and granting mutual observer status.[59]

In the sphere of marine capture fisheries, the entry into force of the 1995 FSA in 2001 meant that parties were required to exercise port State jurisdiction pursuant to its Article 23. In the same year, FAO Members committed to exercising port State jurisdiction through the International Plan of Action to Prevent, Deter and Eliminate Illegal, Unreported and Unregulated Fishing (IPOA-IUU);[60] both individually and collectively.[61] The inclusion of detailed provisions on port States in the IPOA-IUU was inspired by the practice of several RFMOs at the time, and constituted a first step in creating global minimum standards, even though those standards were not legally binding. This approach is essentially the same as that pursued in the IMO since 1991. The adoption within the FAO of the Model Scheme on PSM[62] in 2004 aimed to contribute to the creation of a global network of regional port State jurisdiction in the sphere of the regulation of marine capture fisheries, and offers guidance and opportunities for harmonization in this respect. The FAO's decision

---

[56] As regards the Arctic region, see EJ Molenaar, 'Options for Regional Regulation of Merchant Shipping Outside IMO, with Particular Reference to the Arctic Region' (2014) 45 *Ocean Development & International Law* 272, 284.

[57] See eg IMO Assembly Res A.1052(27), *Procedures for Port State Control* (30 November 2011).

[58] See eg IMO Doc PSCWS 6/11, *Record of Recommendations* (9 July 2013).

[59] See Paris MOU, *Annual Report* (2012) 11 and 16, available at <https://www.parismou.org/sites/default/files/Annual%20Report%202012%20%28final%29.pdf>.

[60] FAO, *International Plan of Action to Prevent, Deter and Eliminate Illegal, Unreported and Unregulated Fishing* (FAO Rome 2001), adopted by consensus by FAO's Committee on Fisheries on 2 March 2001 and endorsed by the FAO Council on 23 June 2001, available at <http://www.fao.org/docrep/003/y1224e/y1224e00.htm>.

[61] Ibid, [52]–[64].

[62] FAO, *Model Scheme on Port State Measures to Combat Illegal, Unreported and Unregulated Fishing*, implicitly endorsed by FAO's Committee on Fisheries in March 2005; FAO Fisheries Report No 759, *Report of the Technical Consultation to Review Port State Measures to Combat Illegal, Unreported and Unregulated Fishing* (2004), Annex E.

in 2007 to commence negotiations on the PSM Agreement nevertheless underscored that the Model Scheme on PSM was not regarded as an adequate solution for the aims it pursued.

The PSM Agreement lays down global minimum standards and thereby fosters a level playing field among regions. Articles 6 and 9(4)—in conjunction with Article 4(2)–(3)—of the PSM Agreement also link future parties, to some extent, to the conservation and management measures of RFMOs to which they would not otherwise be legally bound. These linkages could be regarded as a step towards the development of a duty under general international law for port States to cooperate with a relevant RFMO; quite similar to the flag and coastal States' obligation to do so under Article 8(3) of the 1995 FSA. Crucial for this development however, is the entry into force of the PSM Agreement. As of August 2014, only nine States and the EU had ratified, accepted, approved, or acceded to the Agreement—well short of the 25 required for entry into force.[63]

At the regional level, most RFMOs that deal with straddling, highly migratory, and discrete high seas fish stocks have developed port State practices. Some regions and some RFMOs have not, however, and some existing port State regimes lack transparency, are optional, insufficiently implemented, or apply exclusively to vessels flying the flag of non-members of the RFMO.[64]

3 Coastal States

3.1 Overview

At the time of writing, there are 152 coastal States and 43 landlocked States.[65] These numbers can change owing to processes such as secession, accession, and

---

[63] Information obtained from FAO, 'Treaties under Article XIV of the FAO Constitution', available at <www.fao.org/legal/treaties/treaties-under-article-xiv/en/>.

[64] See K von Kistowski et al, *Port State Performance: Putting Illegal, Unreported and Unregulated Fishing on the Radar* (PEW Environment Group Online 2010) available at <www.portstateperformance.org>.

[65] Based on United Nations Division for Ocean Affairs and the Law of the Sea (DOALOS), *Table of Claims to Maritime Jurisdiction* (as at 15 July 2011), and DOALOS, *Table Recapitulating the Status of the Convention and of the related Agreements* (as at 10 January 2014), both available at <www.un.org/Depts/los>; and the information on UN Membership at <www.un.org/en/members/index.shtml>. The Cook Islands and Niue are not UN Members at the time of writing. The following are landlocked States at the time of writing: Afghanistan, Andorra, Armenia, Austria, Azerbaijan, Belarus, Bhutan, Bolivia, Botswana, Burkina Faso, Burundi, Central African Republic, Chad, Czech Republic, Ethiopia, Hungary, Kazakhstan, Kyrgyzstan, Lao People's Democratic Republic, Lesotho, Liechtenstein, Luxembourg, Malawi, Mali, Moldova, Mongolia, Nepal, Niger, Paraguay, Rwanda, San Marino, Serbia, Slovakia,

dissolution. The implications of climate change induced sea-level rise on statehood are currently under examination.[66]

Post World War II, coastal States became more prominent in the law of the sea. This process—often called 'creeping coastal State jurisdiction'—involved a seaward expansion of coastal State maritime zones as well as an expansion of their substantive rights and jurisdiction within these zones. While coastal States initially focused on maximizing authority within a relatively narrow zone along their coasts, they subsequently claimed specific, exclusive resource-related rights in much larger adjacent areas. Some coastal States also advocated for jurisdiction to protect and preserve the marine environment within these areas. The LOSC eventually granted these, even though prescriptive jurisdiction over foreign vessels remains largely confined to applying international rules and standards.

In view of the considerable number of coastal State maritime zones as well as the significant differences between the rights and jurisdiction of coastal States and rights and freedoms of flag States in each zone, it is not possible to provide more than an overview here.[67]

3.2 Coastal State maritime zones

3.2.1 *Maritime zones under coastal State sovereignty*

The LOSC stipulates that a coastal State's sovereignty extends beyond its land territory to three maritime zones: internal waters, archipelagic waters (where applicable), and a territorial sea.[68]

The marine waters landward of the baseline (for measuring the breadth of the territorial sea) are part of the internal waters of a coastal State.[69] The normal baseline is the low-water line along the coast, but a coastal State can use straight baselines in certain scenarios, provided specific conditions are met.[70] These conditions are not applicable to 'historic bays' or 'historic waters', which are internal waters on account of longstanding effective administration and control by the coastal State and sufficient recognition or acquiescence by the international community.[71] So-called 'closing lines' are often used to delimit these bays and waters from the territorial sea.

As internal waters are part of the coastal State's territory and therefore subject to its sovereignty, it can be assumed that the coastal State has:

South Sudan, Swaziland, Switzerland, Tajikistan, The Former Yugoslav Republic of Macedonia, Turkmenistan, Uganda, Uzbekistan, Zambia, and Zimbabwe. See also n 4 and accompanying text.

[66] See eg the International Law Association (ILA) Committee on International Law and Sea Level Rise, information available at <www.ila-hq.org>.
[67] See in particular chapters 5 and 24 in this volume.   [68] LOSC, n 3, Arts 2(1) and 49 (1).
[69] Ibid, Art 8(1).   [70] Ibid, Arts 5, 7, and 9–10. See chapter 4 in this volume.
[71] See eg LOSC, n 3, Arts 10(6), 15, and 298(1)(a)(i).

(a) exclusive access to, and unlimited jurisdiction over, all living and non-living resources therein; and

(b) unlimited jurisdiction over all domestic and foreign persons, vessels and activities taking place therein.

These assumptions are rebuttable by restrictions imposed by international law, which in this case largely mirror those that apply to a port State in terms of its ability to deny access to internal waters and to prescribe conditions for entry or departure.[72] In addition, Article 8(2) of the LOSC stipulates that a right of innocent passage continues to exist in internal waters generated by a new use of straight baselines.

Only coastal States that also qualify as archipelagic States can have archipelagic waters. Article 46(a) of the LOSC defines an 'archipelagic State' as 'a State constituted wholly by one or more archipelagos and may include other islands'.[73] This definition is meant to confine archipelagic States to so-called 'mid-ocean archipelagic States' and thereby excludes coastal States whose land territory is in part continental (eg the Netherlands with regard to its islands in the Caribbean). Not all coastal States that qualify as archipelagic States also claim that status, and not all States claiming archipelagic status have chosen to designate archipelagic waters.[74]

As regards the regime of archipelagic waters, the rebuttable assumptions for internal waters identified above apply as well. The LOSC contains two relevant restrictions:

(a) the right of innocent passage in archipelagic waters *outside* routes normally used for international navigation or—if designated—archipelagic sea lanes; and

(b) the right of archipelagic sea lanes passage *within* routes normally used for international navigation or—if designated—archipelagic sea lanes.

The procedure for designating archipelagic sea lanes must be initiated by the archipelagic State and involves a need for approval by the IMO and the International Civil Aviation Organization (ICAO).[75] Only Indonesia has initiated this process so far, and this has led to a partial designation.[76] Controversial issues for the regime of innocent passage are whether or not coastal States have the right to request prior

---

[72] See Sections 2.2–2.4 above.

[73] The term 'archipelago' is defined in LOSC, n 3, Art 46(b).

[74] See chapter 7 in this volume.

[75] The procedure is laid down in LOSC, n 3, Art 53 of but has been operationalized in Annex 2 to the 'General Provisions on Ships' Routeing': IMO Resolution A.572(14) (20 November 1985), as amended; Annex 2 was added by means of IMO Resolution MSC.71(69), Adoption of Amendments to the General Provisions on Ships' Routeing (Resolution A.572(14) As Amended) (19 May 1998).

[76] IMO Resolution MSC.72(69), Adoption, Designation and Substitution of Archipelagic Sea Lanes (19 May 1998). The substantive scope of the rights and obligations of flag States and the jurisdiction of coastal States in waters where the regimes of innocent passage and archipelagic sea lanes passage apply are discussed in chapters 5 and 24 in this volume.

notification or authorization for warships, nuclear-powered vessels, and vessels carrying hazardous cargoes.

Article 3 of the LOSC stipulates that the territorial sea of a coastal State cannot be wider than 12 nm measured from the baselines. This resolved a long-lasting disagreement and uncertainty on the width of the territorial sea, which the first and second United Nations Conferences on the Law of the Sea were unable to resolve. Agreement on Article 3 was, *inter alia*, facilitated by agreement on a more liberal navigation regime—from a flag State perspective—in straits used for international navigation. While a large majority of coastal States have opted for the maximum width, some—including parties to the LOSC—have established outer limits (far) beyond this maximum, and a few have chosen widths less than 12 nm.[77] As regards the regime of the territorial sea, the rebuttable assumptions for internal waters identified above apply as well. The LOSC contains four relevant restrictions:[78]

(a) the (suspendable) right of innocent passage in 'normal' situations;

(b) the non-suspendable right of innocent passage for a special type of straits used for international navigation, namely those that connect the high seas or EEZ and the territorial sea of another State (eg the Strait of Tiran);[79]

(c) the right of transit passage in straits used for international navigation;[80] and

(d) navigational rights and freedoms laid down in long-standing conventions relating to straits (eg the 1936 Montreux Convention[81] regarding the straits of the Dardanelles, the Sea of Marmara, and the Bosphorus).[82]

3.2.2 *Maritime zones where coastal States have sovereign rights and/or jurisdiction*

In addition to maritime zones under coastal State sovereignty, the LOSC recognizes that coastal States can have three other maritime zones: a contiguous zone, an EEZ, and a continental shelf. This subsection provides an overview of the key aspects of these zones, including the main rights and obligations of coastal and flag States therein.[83]

As a coastal State's entitlement to a continental shelf is inherent (*ipso facto* and *ab initio*), it does not need to be proclaimed.[84] Conversely, contiguous zones and EEZs need to be proclaimed. The outer limits of the three zones are different but

---

[77] See chapter 5 in this volume.

[78] The substantive scope of the rights and obligations of flag States and the jurisdiction of coastal States in waters where these rights apply are discussed in chapters 5, 6, and 24 in this volume.

[79] LOSC, n 3, Art 45(1)(b).   [80] Ibid, Arts 37, 35(c), 36, and 45 contain exceptions.

[81] 1936 Convention Regarding the Regime of the Straits.   [82] LOSC, n 3, Art 35(c).

[83] Chapters 5, 8, and 9 in this volume, offer a more in-depth analysis of these three maritime zones.

[84] LOSC, n 3, Art 77(3).

their inner limits are all constituted by the outer limit of the territorial sea. All three zones have a *sui generis* character and serve specific purposes or functions; thus giving rise to functional jurisdiction. Within them, coastal States cannot assume to have (exclusive) access and (unlimited) jurisdiction over resources and domestic and foreign persons, vessels, and activities taking place therein, but only those (sovereign) rights and jurisdiction explicitly accorded by international law. This line of reasoning was, for instance, pursued by the ITLOS in the merits phase of the *M/V 'Saiga'* case, where it ruled that a coastal State does not have jurisdiction to regulate bunkering for the purpose of customs within its EEZ.[85]

The contiguous zone cannot extend further than 24 nm from the baselines.[86] Article 33(1) of the LOSC grants a coastal State enforcement jurisdiction for the purpose of preventing or punishing violations of its customs, fiscal, immigration, or sanitary laws and regulations within its territory (including internal waters and archipelagic waters) or territorial sea. Article 303(2) of the LOSC grants a coastal State both prescriptive and enforcement jurisdiction in the contiguous zone relating to the removal of archaeological and historical objects. While the LOSC does not give other States any rights or freedoms that apply specifically to the contiguous zone, as the contiguous zone overlaps with either the EEZ (if proclaimed) or the continental shelf/high seas, other States can exercise the rights and freedoms accorded within these maritime zones also in the contiguous zone.

The EEZ cannot extend further than 200 nm from the baselines.[87] Pursuant to Article 56 of the LOSC, a coastal State has in its EEZ sovereign rights and jurisdiction relating to the water column as well as the seabed and subsoil. The sovereign rights and jurisdiction with respect to the seabed and subsoil must be exercised in accordance with the LOSC's Part VI on the continental shelf (discussed below). The coastal State's sovereign rights—and associated jurisdiction—in its EEZ relate to all living and non-living natural resources as well as other activities for economic exploitation and exploration. As regards commercially exploitable species, Articles 61–67 constrain the coastal State's sovereign rights in various ways (eg to avoid over-exploitation, to strive for optimum utilization and to cooperate in relation to transboundary stocks). In addition to the specified sovereign rights and associated jurisdiction, the coastal State has jurisdiction relating to:

(a) artificial islands, installations and structures (see in particular Article 60);

(b) marine scientific research (see in particular Article 246); and

---

[85] *M/V 'Saiga' (No 2) (Saint Vincent and the Grenadines v Guinea)* [1999] ITLOS Rep 10, [127] and [136]. See also LOSC, n 3, Art 59.
[86] LOSC, n 3, Art 33(2).   [87] Ibid, Art 57.

(c) the protection and preservation of the marine environment (see in particular Part XII).

Within EEZs, other States have the freedoms of navigation, overflight, the laying of submarine cables and pipelines—subject to Article 79—and other internationally lawful uses of the sea related to these freedoms.[88]

Article 76 of the LOSC recognizes that in certain circumstances the juridical continental shelf extends beyond 200 nm from the baselines. This is the so-called 'outer continental shelf'. Coastal States with an outer continental shelf must submit information on its outer limits on the basis of the criteria in Article 76 to the Commission on the Limits of the Continental Shelf (CLCS). The limits of the outer continental shelf established by the coastal State 'on the basis of' the recommendations of the CLCS 'shall be final and binding'.[89] The sovereign rights—and associated jurisdiction—of a coastal State over its continental shelf relate to its natural resources, which include non-living resources and 'living organisms belonging to sedentary species'.[90] Other States have largely the same freedoms as in EEZs.[91]

A number of coastal States have not established EEZs so far. The majority have nevertheless proclaimed other types of 200 nm maritime zones, even though these are not explicitly recognized by the LOSC. The most common of these are Exclusive Fishery Zones (EFZs),[92] which were accepted to be part of customary international law before the EEZ reached that status. Some coastal States first established an EFZ and later also established an EEZ for the same waters, without revoking the EFZ (eg the Netherlands). While this approach can be preferred for domestic legislative reasons, from the perspective of international law, such a coastal State should be categorized as having established an EEZ as this is the more comprehensive zone. Coastal States may also decide to establish an EEZ adjacent to part of their territory and an EFZ to another part. Norway for instance, has established an economic zone off its mainland, a fishery zone off Jan Mayen, a fisheries protection zone (FPZ) off Svalbard, but no 200 nm maritime zones at all off its (claimed) territories in the Southern Ocean.[93] While Norway claims the right to establish an EEZ off Svalbard, it has established an FPZ as a consequence of the disagreement between Norway and other States parties to the 1920 Spitsbergen Treaty[94] as to whether or not the Treaty also applies seaward of the territorial sea.[95] Quite a few States have established EFZs or other types of

---

[88] Ibid, Art 58(1). [89] Ibid, Art 76(8). [90] Ibid, Art 77(4).
[91] Ibid, Art 78. But see eg ibid, Art 68.
[92] Or Exclusive Fisheries/Fishing Zone, Fishing/Fisheries Zone.
[93] These are Bouvet Island (north of 60°S), Peter I Island and Queen Maud Land (both south of 60°S).
[94] 1920 Treaty Concerning the Archipelago of Spitsbergen.
[95] For a discussion, see EJ Molenaar, 'Fisheries Regulation in the Maritime Zones of Svalbard' (2012) 27 *International Journal of Marine and Coastal Law* 3.

200 nm maritime zones off (part of) their coasts in the Mediterranean Sea, for instance an FPZ (Spain and Libya), an ecological protection zone (EPZ; Italy and Slovenia) or an ecological and fisheries protection zone (EFPZ; Croatia). In recent years, however, some of these maritime zones have been replaced by EEZs.[96]

These 200 nm maritime zones are in principle not inconsistent with the LOSC. As establishing an EEZ is a right and not an obligation, a coastal State can also choose to claim only some of the sovereign rights or jurisdiction to which it is entitled under general international law. Inconsistency with the LOSC could nevertheless occur if a coastal State only claims the rights but does not accept or comply with the associated obligations, including the duty to respect the freedoms of other States. Analysis of State practice may also highlight that a coastal State is in fact claiming more (sovereign) rights and jurisdiction than the LOSC allows.

Finally, there do not appear to be coastal States that have established or claimed maritime zones beyond 200 nm in clear non-conformity with general international law. Reference can be made here to the limited practice of coastal States that cede to other coastal States by means of a treaty their EEZ-derived sovereign rights and jurisdiction relating to a specific area within 200 nm of their baselines, even though the specific area is beyond 200 nm of the other coastal States.[97] It is also submitted that Chile's claim to a *mar presencial*, first included in its legislation in 1991,[98] is not necessarily inconsistent with international law as such. The *mar presencial* is defined as the area of high seas in a huge quadrangle between Chile's coast, Easter Island, and Antarctica.[99] Even though the concept has been included in Chilean legislation at several other instances since then, lastly in 2006,[100] no general clarification as to which rights or jurisdiction Chile claims in the *mar presencial* has yet been included in Chilean legislation.[101] Specific enactments nevertheless include a requirement for all vessels carrying nuclear substances or radioactive materials to obtain authorization prior to transit through the *mar presencial*.[102] Current international law offers no basis

---

[96] See chapter 8, subsection 2.3, in this volume.

[97] See eg 2010 Treaty between the Kingdom of Norway and the Russian Federation concerning Maritime Delimitation and Cooperation in the Barents Sea and the Arctic Ocean, Art 3.

[98] The concept of *mar presencial* was included in the *Ley N° 18.892 General de Pesca y Acuicultura* 1989 [General Law No 18.892 on Fisheries and Aquaculture] (Chile), by means of amendments included in Law No 19.080 (6 September 1991) (see Arts 2, 43, and 172). Both enactments are available at <www.leychile.cl>.

[99] General Law No 18.892 (Chile), n 98, Art 2.   [100] Ibid, Art 124(2).

[101] The description in the Chilean Ministry of Defense, *El Libro de la Defensa Nacional de Chile* (2010), Part 1 'El Estado De Chile', 39–40, merely emphasizes Chile's special interests and responsibilities in the *mar presencial*, rather than claiming rights or jurisdiction, available at <www.defensa.cl/libro-de-la-defensa-nacional-de-chile/libro-de-la-defensa-2010>.

[102] *Ley N° 18.302 de Seguridad Nuclear* [Law No 18.302 on Nuclear Security] of 16 April 1984 (Chile), Art 4(1), included by means of Law No 19.825, of 1 October 2002. See <www.leychile.cl>.

for such a right. It is nevertheless unclear if Chile has enforced non-compliance with the requirement by means of at-sea enforcement, port State jurisdiction or otherwise. Other Chilean enactments exert influence on fishing in the *mar presencial* by foreign vessels—in particular those targeting swordfish and jack mackerel—by exercising port State jurisdiction.[103] Chile does not seem to have imposed port State enforcement measures that are more onerous than denial of entry or use, however, and it was already concluded earlier that the consistency of such jurisdiction with in particular international trade law remains an unresolved question.

3.3 Regional coastal State cooperation

Regional cooperation is widespread, both in general and relating to the marine domain. Cooperation among regional States can be desirable for many reasons, for instance to enhance (bargaining) power in terms of international trade, collective defence, or common interests or values vis-à-vis extra-regional (groupings of) States, but also to address free riders or create harmonized regulation and thereby a level playing field among the regional States. As regards the law of the sea, regional cooperation may, for instance, be warranted owing to the spatial distribution of particular species or habitats, or the spatial reach of land-based and/or marine pollution. Enclosed or semi-enclosed seas, like the Black and Mediterranean Seas, are obvious candidates for regional cooperation, as is reflected in Article 123 of the LOSC.

The LOSC encourages or imposes (qualified) obligations to cooperate at the regional level.[104] A similar approach is pursued by various global organizations and their instruments that are part of the global framework of the law of the sea. As a consequence, regional cooperation exists, *inter alia*, in the following fields:[105]

(a) *Merchant shipping*. Regional cooperation occurs predominantly by States in their capacities as port States—mostly through regional PSC arrangements—and to a lesser extent as flag States, but only rarely as coastal States. This is due to the LOSC's objective of globally uniform minimum regulation, which is pursued by linking prescriptive jurisdiction by flag and coastal States through 'rules of

---

[103] See eg General Law No 18.892, n 98, Art 165 as implemented in part by Decree No 123, *Aprueba Política de uso de Puertos Nacionales por Naves Pesqueras de Bandera Extranjera que Pescan en Alta Mar Adyacente* (3 May 2004), as amended, and Chile's declaration of 28 August 2012 upon ratification of the PSM Agreement.

[104] Eg in LOSC, n 3, Part V (Arts 63–67) and Part XII (Arts 198–200).

[105] For a more comprehensive overview, see EJ Molenaar, 'Current and Prospective Roles of the Arctic Council System within the Context of the Law of the Sea' (2012) 27 *International Journal of Marine and Coastal Law* 553, 558–65.

reference' to the generally accepted international rules and standards adopted by competent international organizations like the IMO and ILO;[106]

(b) *Marine environmental protection*, in particular through Regional Seas programmes—the majority of which are supported or coordinated by the United Nations Environment Programme (UNEP)[107]—and large marine ecosystem (LME) mechanisms, many of which are supported by the Global Environment Facility (GEF);[108]

(c) *Conservation and management of marine living resources*, including through RFMOs, other types of regional fisheries bodies (RFBs; including those (also) dealing with marine mammals)[109] as well as regional bodies exclusively aimed at the conservation of species;

(d) *Marine scientific research*, for example the International Council for the Exploration of the Sea (ICES);

(e) *Search and rescue*, for instance the Arctic SAR Agreement[110] and its Meetings of the Parties; and

(f) *Pollution incidents*, whether by means of monitoring and surveillance, or contingency planning, preparedness and response (eg the 2013 Arctic MOPPR Agreement[111] and its Meetings of the Parties).

Owing to the considerable diversity and large number of these regional bodies and their instruments, it is not possible to provide even a concise overview of their key features and differences. One aspect is nevertheless worth singling out: as a general rule, the States participating as full members in these regional regimes do so in their capacity as coastal States. There are two exceptions to this general rule: the instruments of the Antarctic Treaty System and RFMOs whose regulatory areas consist partially or entirely of high seas. The former exception is a result of the agreement to disagree on the question of sovereignty over land territory in Antarctica (south of 60°S) and the latter a result of the freedom of high seas fishing.

---

[106] Eg LOSC, n 3, Art 211(1).
[107] See United Nations Environmental Programme (UNEP), Regional Seas Programme, available at <www.unep.org/regionalseas>.
[108] See eg Large Marine Ecosystems of the World, <www.lme.noaa.gov> and International Waters Learning Exchange & Resource Network, <www.iwlearn.net>.
[109] See the list of RFBs at FAO Fisheries and Aquaculture Department, Regional Fishery Bodies (RFB), available at <www.fao.org/fishery/rfb/en>; and chapter 20 in this Volume.
[110] 2011 Agreement on Cooperation in Aeronautical and Maritime Search and Rescue in the Arctic.
[111] 2013 Agreement on Cooperation on Marine Oil Pollution Preparedness and Response in the Arctic.

4 Future Developments

Port State jurisdiction is gradually moving from optional use in limited regulatory spheres towards comprehensive and mandatory use through regional and global instruments and bodies. Awareness that the interests of the international community are not only undermined by free riders in their capacity as flag States but also in their capacity as port States, is expected to spread due to current and future concerns on issues such as maritime safety and security, the marine environment, sustainable fisheries, and marine biodiversity.

It is submitted that the following four aspects of port State jurisdiction warrant special attention in the near future. First, will the residual prescriptive jurisdiction of port States be invoked more or less, and how will this affect the authority and effectiveness of competent international organizations like the IMO and ILO? Second, how does State practice develop with regard to treaty-based rights to exercise extraterritorial port State jurisdiction (eg Article 218 of the LOSC and Article 4(1)(b) of the PSM Agreement)? Third, will port States impose more onerous enforcement measures (eg monetary penalties or confiscation of catch or equipment) for extraterritorial behaviour without a treaty-based right to do so, for instance, by claiming that a foreign vessel's voluntary entry into port is sufficient?[112] Fourth, how will global and regional efforts to ensure that port States comply with their obligations—and thereby address ports of convenience—evolve? The answers to these questions will shed light on the popularity of (unilateral) port State jurisdiction, confidence in multilateral regulation and advances in flag and port State performance and the evolution of the notion of port State responsibility.[113]

As noted in Section 3.1 above, owing to the considerable number of coastal State maritime zones as well as the significant differences between the rights and jurisdiction of coastal States and the rights and freedoms of flag States in each zone, this chapter cannot provide more than an overview. Likewise, well-founded conclusions on current overall practice by coastal States in light of their rights and obligations under the international law of the sea—let alone future trends—are perhaps only feasible in the last chapter of this volume.

Having said this, it nevertheless seems safe to conclude that there is no evidence that creeping coastal State jurisdiction continued significantly after the adoption of the LOSC in 1982. While a considerable amount of State practice (eg on straight baselines, the width of territorial seas, rocks claimed as islands, requesting prior authorization for the passage of certain types of ships and cargoes, and regulating

---

[112] Marten, n 28, 234 takes the view that such practice is likely to emerge.
[113] See in this regard BH Oxman, 'The Territorial Temptation: A Siren Song at Sea' (2006) 100 *American Journal of International Law* 830, 851.

marine scientific research in the EEZ[114]) is inconsistent with the LOSC, such State practice has not become significantly more widespread since 1982. Fears for further creeping coastal State jurisdiction were above all prompted by Chilean and Canadian practice in the early 1990s. At the time of writing, however, Chile's *mar presencial* is not inconsistent with international law as such—even though the above-mentioned prior notification of transit requirement *is*—and Canada's claims to high seas enforcement jurisdiction over foreign vessels targeting straddling fish stocks—culminating in the arrest of the Spanish-flagged *Estai* in 1995—have largely—but not entirely[115]—been addressed by the inclusion of non-flag State enforcement powers in Articles 21 and 22 of the UN Fish Stocks Agreement. Finally, coastal States have so far acted in accordance with the rules and procedure for the establishment of the outer limits of the continental shelf. All this means that the balance laid down in the LOSC between the rights and interests of flag and coastal States—both geographically and substantively—remains essentially unchanged today.

---

[114] See eg JA Roach and RW Smith, *United States Responses to Excessive Maritime Claims* (2nd edn Martinus Nijhoff Publishers The Hague/Boston/London 1996) and the series *Limits in the Seas* issued by the United States Department of State, Office of Oceans and Polar Affairs, available at <http://www.state.gov/e/oes/ocns/opa/c16065.htm>.

[115] See Canada's Coastal Fisheries Protection Act, RSC 1985, c C-33, § 5.2, in conjunction with § 21(2)(b)(ii) and Table III of its Coastal Fisheries Regulations, CRC, c 413). Also, Canada has not withdrawn a relevant reservation to its acceptance of the compulsory jurisdiction of the ICJ so far, see Declaration of 10 May 1994, [(2)(d)]; available at <www.icj-cij.org>.

14
FLAG STATES

RICHARD A BARNES

1 INTRODUCTION

FLAG State jurisdiction provides one of the principal ways of maintaining legal order over activities at sea, although its significance has lessened as a consequence of extensions in coastal State jurisdiction over ocean spaces.[1] Any State may grant to a ship the right to sail under its flag.[2] The flag State then enjoys primary legislative and enforcement jurisdiction over its ships on the high seas, subject to some limited exceptions.[3] Ships located within coastal waters are subject to a more sophisticated combination of flag State and coastal State jurisdiction. The basic parameters of jurisdiction are set forth in the 1982 United Nations Convention on the Law of the Sea (LOSC), although other instruments develop how such jurisdiction is to be exercised in the context of specific activities such as navigation and fishing. One of the most fundamental concerns facing the law of the sea is the ability and willingness of

---

[1] On order, see A Watts, 'The Protection of Merchant Ships' (1957) XXXIII *British Yearbook of International Law* 52, 67; MS McDougal and WT Burke, *The Public Order of the Oceans: A Contemporary International Law of the Sea* (Yale University Press New Haven, CT 1962) 794. On expansionism, see B Oxman, 'The Territorial Temptation: A Siren Song at Sea' (2006) 100 *American Journal of International Law* 830.

[2] 1982 United Nations Convention on the Law of the Sea (hereinafter LOSC), Art 90. See further R Rienow, *The Test of Nationality of a Merchant Vessel* (Columbia University Press New York 1937) 214–9; MacDougal and Burke, n 1, 1057ff.

[3] LOSC, n 2, Arts 94–111.

flag States to exercise effective control over ships flying their flag.[4] This has resulted in attempts to secure better flag State compliance with their responsibilities, as well as provoking the development of alternative models of control, such as port State control. These factors pull towards more sophisticated models of regulation. Accordingly, a more careful and holistic view of jurisdiction is essential to understanding how order is maintained at sea.

2 THE DEVELOPMENT OF FLAG STATE JURISDICTION

Since ancient times, ships have been identified with particular communities through the use of flags and other insignia.[5] A ship's flag was a visible way of identifying the allegiance of a ship and determining how to treat those on board. Documentation and regulation of ship ownership can be traced to the practice of medieval Italian city States, and, possibly, even to Roman law as a means of facilitating private maritime claims.[6] The growth of international trade and expansion of activities at sea from the sixteenth century onwards generated pressure for a public system of law and order over the oceans. This was facilitated by the emergence of the modern political State after the peace of Westphalia. Within the emergent legal order, freedom of the high seas consolidated as a legal principle during the seventeenth century, along with its corollary, the exclusive jurisdiction of the flag State.[7] From this time, the concept of the nationality of ships evolved as a means of determining which States were responsible for and entitled to control the activities of ships at sea.[8] While the grant of nationality to a ship was a unilateral act, it was often recognized through bilateral treaties of friendship commerce and navigation.[9] By the twentieth century, the right of States to determine which

---

[4] See United Nations General Assembly (UNGA), *Oceans and the law of the sea. Consultative Group on Flag State Implementation. Report of the Secretary-General*, UN Doc A/59/63 (2005) 3.

[5] JNK Mansell, *Flag State Responsibility. Historical Development and Contemporary Issues* (Springer Dordrecht 2009) 13–15.

[6] R Coles and E Watt, *Ship Registration: Law and Practice* (2nd edn Informa Law London 2013) 3.

[7] See *The 'Le Louis'* (1817) 2 Dods 210, 243 per Sir W Scott; *The Marianna Flora* (1826) 24 US 1, 42–3.

[8] Illustrative of this were the British Navigation Acts of the seventeeth and eighteenth centuries, which were used to limit the benefits of protection and commercial trade to British ships. See D Konig, 'Flag of Ships' in R Wolfrum (ed), *Max Plank Encyclopedia of Public International Law* (June 2009) [2], available at <www.mpepil.com>.

[9] Eg 1946 Treaty of Friendship, Commerce and Navigation between the United States of America and the Republic of China, Art XXI(2).

ships could fly their flag was generally recognized.[10] However, the precise scope of this, as well as the international consequences of granting nationality to a ship, has continued to develop until the present day.

3 Registration and Nationality

Article 91(1) of the LOSC provides that 'ships have the nationality of the State whose flag they are entitled to fly'. States usually grant nationality to ships by way of registration. This is always a matter of domestic law, and its precise operation varies from State to State. However, given the importance of nationality, it is necessary to know the extent to which international law controls this.[11] Although it is generally accepted that States are entitled to determine the conditions for ship registration, the view that international law limits this authority has surfaced with some frequency and force.[12] For example, during the International Law Commission's (ILC) work on drafting the 1958 Convention on the High Seas (HSC), the view was advanced that State practice had established minimum requirements to be met if the nationality of a vessel was to be recognized.[13] This mainly concerned the requirement that the owner be a national or corporate domicile of the State.[14] However, given the ease with which ship-owning companies could move between countries and the growing objections to strong limits on the exercise of sovereignty, this approach faded. Instead, the concept of a genuine link emerged as a means of tackling the use of 'flags of convenience'.

In principle, there are three limits on the grant of nationality.[15] First, those accepted by the State when ratifying a treaty. Most shipping agreements assume the fact of registration as a prerequisite for the application of substantive law so such limits are uncommon in practice. One example is the right of establishment under

---

[10] This has been confirmed in the *Muscat Dhows (France/Great Britain)*, PCA 1905 (1961) XI RIAA 83 and *Lauritzen v Larsen* (1953) 345 US 571. See further CJ Colombos, *International Law of the Sea* (Longman London 1961) 250–1.

[11] At a minimum, international law requires documentation to be issued to ships evidencing registration. See LOSC, n 2, Art 91(2).

[12] See HW Wefers Bettink, 'Open Registry, the Genuine Link and the 1986 Convention on Registration Conditions for Ships' (1986) 18 *Netherlands Yearbook of International Law* 69, 81–7.

[13] 'Summary Records of the Third Session 16 May–27 July 1951' (1951) I *Yearbook of the International Law Commission* 330–4.

[14] DP O'Connell, *The International Law of the Sea* (Clarendon Press Oxford 1982–1984) Vol 2, 759.

[15] Boczek further suggests that a State cannot grant nationality to a ship if they reasonably suspect the ship will engage in illegal activities, although he provides no authority for this. BA Boczek, *Flags of Convenience. An International Study* (Harvard University Press Cambridge 1962) 106.

Article 49 of the Treaty on the Functioning of the European Union, which allows nationals from one Member State to pursue economic activities in other member States. This extends to the right to register ships in other Member States.[16] Konig suggests that the FAO Compliance Agreement is another such example.[17] However, it only limits State authorization of fishing activities, not the registration of ships.[18] A noteworthy attempt to regulate the grant of nationality was the 1986 United Nations Convention on Conditions for Registration of Ships (Registration Convention). Developed against concerns about the use of flags of convenience, the Convention sought to develop registration requirements in respect of national participation in ship-owning companies, manning of ships, and participation in the management of ship-owning companies.[19] However, these conditions were framed in discretionary and open-ended terms, so would not, even in the unlikely event the treaty enters into force, constrain States' rights to grant nationality.[20] The Registration Convention stands as a salutary lesson about States' resistance to limits on the exercise of sovereign powers. According to the LOSC, the right to grant nationality must be exercised in good faith.[21] Arguably, this means that States should refrain from registering vessels which will knowingly be used for acts contrary to international law. Given the ambiguities of this principle, such an argument is better articulated through specific treaty rules imposing limits on the right to grant nationality.[22] Of course, this faces the same challenge noted above.

Second, States cannot grant nationality to a ship already registered in another State.[23] Article 92 requires ships to sail under the flag of one State only. This serves to maintain order at sea by preventing overlapping and conflicting claims to jurisdiction. There is an exception to this in the case of ships chartered by demise. In such cases, it is common practice to permit the demise charterer to register the ship in a preferred jurisdiction, despite the existence of an original registration by the beneficial owner.[24]

---

[16] See *R v Secretary of State for Transport ex p Factortame* (Case 221/89) [1991] ECR I-3905, [20]–[22].

[17] 1993 Agreement to Promote Compliance with International Conservation and Management Measures by Fishing Vessels on the High Seas (hereinafter FAO Agreement). See Konig, n 8, [21].

[18] FAO Agreement, Art III(3).

[19] Articles 8, 9, and 10 respectively. See SG Sturmey, 'The United Nations Convention on Conditions for Registration of Ships' [1987] *Lloyd's Maritime and Commercial Law Quarterly* 97.

[20] ML McConnell, 'Business as Usual: an Evaluation of the 1986 United Nations Convention on Conditions for Registration of Ships' (1987) 18 *Journal of Maritime Law and Commerce* 435.

[21] See LOSC, n 2, Art 300, which provides that rights shall not be exercised in a manner which constitutes an abuse of right. See the Separate Opinion of Judge Anderson in *M/V 'Saiga' (No 2) (Saint Vincent and the Grenadines v Guinea)* (Merits) [1999] ITLOS Rep 4, 132. See generally M Byers, 'Abuse of Rights: An Old Principle, A New Age' (2002) 47 *McGill Law Journal* 389.

[22] See eg FAO, *International Plan of Action to Prevent, Deter and Eliminate Illegal, Unreported and Unregulated Fishing* (FAO Rome 2002) [35]–[36].

[23] Rienow, n 2, 10.

[24] A Odeke, *Bareboat Charter (Ship) Registration* (Kluwer Law International The Hague 1998) 23–31.

Third, international law requires there to be a genuine link between the ship and flag State.[25] This suggests that registration cannot be a mere administrative formality; otherwise, the act of registration would create a link and render meaningless the requirement of a genuine link.[26] However, beyond this, the meaning of genuine link is notoriously difficult to pin down.[27] Historically, maritime nations tended to require a link of ownership or nationality of the crew as a condition for registration.[28] However, this practice never consolidated into a clear rule of custom, and the emergence of open registries during the twentieth century confirms that ownership or crew nationality are not pre-requisites for registration. Some authors are strongly critical of the genuine link, seeking to limit its impact on liberal shipping regimes.[29] Others question the precise meaning of the concept, especially as regards the claims that effective control is a condition precedent to or consequence of registration.[30] Some are more sanguine, accepting that the existence of a genuine link is a consequence of registration.[31] Yet others argue more strongly for the existence of factual or legal elements that are a means of controlling flag ships.[32] Discussion of the genuine link frequently draws upon the concept of genuine connection as advanced in the *Nottebohm* case.[33] Here, the ICJ held, in respect of the grant of nationality to persons in the context of the law of diplomatic protection, that States cannot require other States to recognize municipal rules on nationality unless those are in accordance with the general aim of securing a genuine connection between an individual and the State. Although having obvious parallels with ship registration, this link between recognition and genuine link cannot now be sustained in light of the *M/V 'Saiga' (No 2)* and *M/V 'Virginia G'* cases in which the International Tribunal for the Law of the Sea (ITLOS) held that a genuine link is not a pre-requisite for the

---

[25] 1958 Convention on the High Seas, Art 5(1) (hereinafter HSC); LOSC, n 2, Art 91(1).

[26] International Law Commission, *Report of the International Law Commission*, ILC Art 29, Commentary [3(a)], reproduced in (1956) II *Yearbook of the International Law Commission* 253, 279.

[27] The ICJ side-stepped the issue in the *Constitution of the Maritime Safety Committee of the Inter-Governmental Maritime Consultative Organization* (Advisory Opinion) [1960] ICJ Rep 150, 171. For an excellent analysis of the genuine link, see RR Churchill, *The Meaning of the 'Genuine Link' Requirement in Relation to the Nationality of Ships* (Study prepared for the International Transport Workers Federation (ITF), 2000).

[28] See O'Connell, n 14.

[29] MS McDougal, WT Burke, and IA Vlasic, 'The Maintenance of Public Order at Sea and the Nationality of Ships' (1960) 54 *American Journal of International Law* 25.

[30] ML McConnell, '"...Darkening Confusion Mounted Upon Darkening Confusion": The Search for the Elusive Genuine Link' (1985) 16 *Journal of Maritime Law and Commerce* 365. Cf R Wolfrum, 'Reflagging and Escort Operation in the Persian Gulf: An International Law Perspective' (1989) 29 *Virginia Journal of International Law* 387, 392.

[31] HE Anderson, 'The Nationality of Ships and Flags of Convenience: Economics, Politics and Alternatives' (1996) 21 *Tulane Maritime Law Journal* 139, 149; NP Ready, *Ship Registration* (3rd edn Lloyds of London Press London 1998) 15.

[32] N Singh 'International Law Problems of Merchant Shipping' (1962) 107 *Recueil des Cours* 1, 55–64; H Meyers, *The Nationality of Ships* (Martinus Nijhoff The Hague 1967).

[33] *Nottebohm (second phase) (Liechtenstein v Guatemala)* (Judgment) [1955] ICJ Rep 4, 23.

grant of nationality to a ship.[34] The requirement of a genuine link is only intended to secure effective implementation of flag State duties.[35] Even if there is evidence of the absence of jurisdiction and control, States cannot refuse to recognize the right of a ship to fly the flag of the flag State.[36] Such an approach collapses the genuine link into the requirement that States exercise effective jurisdiction and control over flag ships. This seems logical since it is difficult to argue that a State which exercises actual control has no link to the vessel. ITLOS has also excised the ambiguities associated with genuine link from questions of jurisdiction; jurisdiction and control are thus questions of fact.[37]

It may be observed that the LOSC does not comprehensively deal with the consequences of an absence of a genuine link (or ineffective control).[38] During the drafting of the corresponding provision of the High Seas Convention, it was proposed that the absence of a genuine link would provide grounds for non-recognition.[39] This was removed from the final text since it undermined States' sovereignty and generated opposition from developing countries.[40] Regardless of this, some States have sought to dispute claims to the existence of a genuine link in particular cases.[41] However, no tribunal has yet upheld any such claim. Article 94 merely permits States to report to the flag State instances where proper jurisdiction and control have not been exercised. This is not the end of the matter, and it seems that the absence of a genuine link (effective jurisdiction) may entail the responsibility of a State under general international law (see further the discussion of due diligence in Section 6).

Notably, international law does not require the registration of small vessels, although the extent of this exception is unclear.[42] Such vessels remain in principle subject to flag State jurisdiction. However, this may generate problems in practice, particularly when such vessels engage in illegal, unreported, and unregulated (IUU) fishing[43] or people smuggling or irregular maritime migration.[44] Small or unflagged

---

[34] M/V 'Saiga' (No 2), n 21, [83]; M/V 'Virginia G' (Panama v Guinea-Bissau) Judgment of the International Tribunal for the Law of the Sea (14 April 2014), [110].

[35] M/V 'Saiga' (No 2), n 21, [83]; M/V 'Virginia G', n 34, [112–13].

[36] M/V 'Virginia G', n 34, [111].

[37] M/V 'Saiga' (No 2), n 21, [66]; Grand Prince (Belize v France) [2001] ITLOS Rep 17, [81].

[38] See M/V 'Virginia G', n 34, Dissenting Opinion of Judge Jesus [44].

[39] (1956) II Yearbook of the International Law Commission 15 and 278–9 (Draft Article 29, and Commentary).

[40] Discussed by Bettink, n 12, 86.

[41] See M/V 'Saiga' (No 2), n 21, [66]; Grand Prince, n 37, [81]. See also Magda Maria (Netherlands Court of Appeal), noted in (1989) 20 Netherlands Yearbook of International Law 351; Commission v Hellenic Republic (Case 62/96) [1997] ECR I-6725, Opinion of AG Tesauro [13].

[42] LOSC, n 2, Art 94(2)(a).

[43] TL McDorman, 'Stateless Fishing Vessels, International Law, and the UN High Seas Fisheries Conference' (2007) 25 The Journal of Maritime Law and Commerce 531.

[44] R Barnes, 'The International Law of the Sea and Migration Control' in B Ryan and V Mitsilegas, Extraterritorial Immigration Control. Legal Challenges (Martinus Nijhoff Leiden 2010) 102, 130–3; M den Heijer, Europe and Extraterritorial Asylum (Hart Oxford 2012) ch 6.

vessels are not beyond the law. Ships without nationality are susceptible to the jurisdiction of any State, subject to the right of relevant States to exercise diplomatic protection over nationals aboard the ship.[45] Unfortunately, this may pose problems in practice, when trying to identify the States entitled to exercise diplomatic protection and entrusting them to so with due regard to the human rights of those aboard interdicted vessels.[46]

4 The Operation of Flag State Jurisdiction

The principle that only *States* exercise jurisdiction over *ships* can be questioned in two respects. First, non-State actors may enjoy certain flag rights and duties.[47] Difficult questions arise about the position of Taiwan (Republic of China), which although not recognized as a State, operates a flag and has an important maritime presence, especially in respect of fisheries.[48] Its equivocal status means it has not ratified any international maritime treaties, although its participation is accommodated in some regional fisheries management agreements.[49] If one concedes that international personality is not limited to States, then it follows that other entities can be subject to rights and duties under international law.[50] Here, as in the case of

---

[45] RR Churchill and AV Lowe, *The Law of the Sea* (3rd edn Manchester University Press Manchester 1999) 214; D Guilfoyle, *Shipping Interdiction and the Law of the Sea* (Cambridge University Press Cambridge 2009) 18.

[46] Barnes, n 44, 103; Den Heijer, n 44, 252–66.

[47] For example, LOSC, n 2, Art 93 provides that ships employed by the UN, its specialized agencies or the International Atomic Energy Authority may fly the flag of that organization. Here, the flag is indicative of a particular status, rather than the law governing the operation of the vessel.

[48] Y-H Song, 'The Role of Taiwan in Global Ocean Governance' in HN Scheiber and J-H Paik (eds), *Regions, Institutions and Law of the Sea: Studies in Oceans Governance* (Martinus Nijhoff Leiden 2013) 293.

[49] See 1995 United Nations Agreement for the Implementation of the Provisions of the United Nations Convention on the Law of the Sea of 10 December 1982 relating to the Conservation and Management of Straddling Fish Stocks and Highly Migratory Fish Stocks (hereinafter FSA), Art 1(3); 2000 Convention on the Conservation and Management of Highly Migratory Fish Stocks in the Western and Central Pacific Ocean, Annex 1(1); 2003 Convention for the Strengthening of the Inter-American Tropical Tuna Commission Established Between The United States of America and The Republic of Costa Rica, Art XXVIII. See further A Serdy, 'Bringing Taiwan into the International Fisheries Fold. The Legal Personality of a Fishing Entity' (2004) 75 *British Yearbook of International Law* 183.

[50] M Tsamenyi, 'The Legal Status and Substance of Fishing Entities in International Law. A Note' (2006) 37 *Ocean Development and International Law* 123.

how the genuine link concept and the right to grant nationality operates, a pragmatic approach prevails.[51] This seeks to ensure that ships are brought within the purview of international law.

Second, the idea that only ships are subject to flag State jurisdiction may be questioned. Surprisingly, the LOSC does not define the term 'ship', so the precise object of flag State jurisdiction might be unclear. Some instruments define the term 'ship' as a vessel intended for use in navigation.[52] Thus navigation seems determinative of the scope of flag State control and would normally exclude devices permanently fixed to the seabed, such as oil and gas platforms. However, there is a range of floating and mobile devices, which can be used for offshore resource exploitation.[53] As a rule of thumb, such devices are subject to coastal State control while fixed to the seabed and flag State control when manoeuvring into position, although the position is not entirely clear-cut.[54] The status of a particular vessel, and hence the relevance of flag State jurisdiction, will ultimately depend upon its location, the nature of the activity it is engaged in, and how the relevant legal instruments define their scope of application.

The modalities of flag State control largely depend upon where the vessel is located.[55] Flag States enjoy prescriptive and enforcement jurisdiction over ships flying their flag wherever the vessel is located.[56] When a ship is within internal waters, port, or the territorial sea, jurisdiction is concurrent with the port/coastal State.[57] In the territorial sea, some States assert plenary jurisdiction whereas others assert only limited jurisdiction over certain activities.[58] In either case, coastal State jurisdiction must accord with the limits set forth in Part II, Section 3 of the LOSC. In the exclusive economic zone (EEZ), coastal States have exclusive jurisdiction over resource related activities, and other States shall have due regard to this. In practice, coastal States generally refrain from exercising criminal jurisdiction over foreign ships as regards matters that are purely internal to the ship (whether as a matter

---

[51] N-T Hu, 'Fishing Entities: Their Emergence, Evolution, and Practice from Taiwan's Perspective' (2006) 37 *Ocean Development and International Law* 149, 156.

[52] See eg 1954 International Convention for the Prevention of Pollution of the Sea by Oil (hereinafter OILPOL), Art 1; 1972 International Regulations for Preventing Collisions at Sea, Rule 3(a); 1973 International Convention for the Prevention of Pollution, as modified by the Protocol of 1978, Art 2(4) (hereinafter MARPOL); 2006 Maritime Labour Convention, Art 2.

[53] For example, the development of large floating liquefied natural gas vessels like Shell's 'Prelude' generates interesting questions as to vessel status.

[54] See AV Lowe, 'Ships' in N Boschiero et al (eds) *International Courts and the Development of International Law* (Springer Berlin 2013) 294.

[55] See generally J-A Witt, *Obligations and Control of Flag States: Developments and Perspectives in International and EU Law* (Lit Verlag Münster 2007).

[56] See further EJ Molenaar, *Coastal State Jurisdiction over Vessel Source Pollution* (Kluwer Law The Hague 1998) 95.

[57] See further Chapter 13 in this volume. [58] Churchill and Lowe, n 45, 92–100.

of comity or legal duty), leaving such matters to the flag State.[59] Flag States also remain responsible for the operational standards outlined in Article 94(5) within all of these zones.[60] However, it is important to note that flag States cannot exercise enforcement jurisdiction within the territory or territorial sea of third States, at least without their consent.[61] Coastal State jurisdiction over warships and State operated non-commercial vessels is limited because such vessels enjoy sovereign immunity.[62] However, the flag State is responsible for any loss or damage suffered by the coastal State resulting from the non-compliance of warships with the coastal State's laws and regulations concerning passage through the territorial sea or with other provisions of the LOSC or other rules of international law.[63]

On the high seas, the flag State enjoys exclusive jurisdiction subject to certain well-established exceptions.[64] First, the competent authorities of a coastal State may exercise the right of hot pursuit against a foreign ship.[65] Related to this is the doctrine of constructive presence, which allows the coastal State to take action against foreign vessels on the high seas that use their boats or work with other vessels to commit offenses within coastal waters.[66] Second, warships enjoy the right of visit in respect of vessels suspected of engaging in four types of activity: piracy, slave trade, unauthorized broadcasting, and vessels without nationality. These are longstanding exceptions and are considered in detail in other chapters.[67] The exceptions cover activities in which all States have an interest and, hence, authority to take action. They also reflect potential limitations in flag State jurisdiction, such as the lack of enforcement capacity or political will to deal with the offence. In recent years, concerns about maritime security have resulted in efforts to increase the role of non-flag States in enforcement activities on the high seas, for example by way of the Proliferation Security Initiative.[68] While these steps do not challenge the exclusive authority of flag States, they demonstrate a need for greater cooperation in addressing illegal activities on the high seas.

---

[59] *Wildenhus* (1887) 120 US 1, 12; *McCulloch* (1963) 372 US 10, 20–1. H Yang, *Coastal State Jurisdiction over Foreign Merchant Ships in Internal Waters and the Territorial Sea* (Springer Berlin 2006) 90ff.

[60] See also LOSC, n 2, Arts 211(2) and 217.   [61] Molenaar, n 56.

[62] LOSC, n 2, Art 32. This was reaffirmed in the *ARA Libertad (Argentina v Ghana)* (Provisional Measures) [2012] ITLOS Rep 21, [95]. On immunity of warships, see further TK Thommen, *Legal Status of Government Merchant Ships in International Law* (Martinus Nijhoff The Hague 1962) 3–8.

[63] LOSC, n 2, Art 31.   [64] See Chapter 10 in this volume.

[65] LOSC, n 2, Art 111 and HSC, n 25, Art 23. See O'Connell, n 14, Vol 2, 1075–93; NH Poulantzas, *The Right of Hot Pursuit in International Law* (Martinus Nijhoff The Hague 2002).

[66] Churchill and Lowe, n 45, 215–16; Y Tanaka, *The International Law of the Sea* (Cambridge University Press Cambridge 2012) 165–6; EJ Molenaar, 'Multilateral Hot Pursuit and Illegal Fishing in the Southern Ocean: The Pursuits of the *Viarsa 1* and the *South Tomi*' (2004) 19 *International Journal of Marine and Coastal Law* 19.

[67] For further discussion on the high seas and piracy, see Chapters 10 and 37 in this volume.

[68] See Chapter 26 in this volume.

5 Flag State Rights and Duties

5.1 Flag State rights

Flag State rights are mainly defined in terms of the right to exercise jurisdiction over flag ships. Absent any coastal State right to take action against ships in its coastal waters, flag States enjoy prescriptive and enforcement jurisdiction in respect of their ships. Flag States may permit third States to board and inspect flagged ships. Such permission constitutes a waiver of the right to exercise exclusive jurisdiction, and so is to be construed narrowly. Any authority to take further enforcement action, such as arrest or detention, must be expressly granted by the flag State.[69] Two important, related rights are the right to be notified of flag ship detentions and the right to apply for the prompt release of such ships.[70]

The right of navigation is the most important substantive right enjoyed by flag States. This is either freedom of navigation on the high seas and EEZ or rights of passage in the territorial sea, archipelagic waters and straits. The LOSC is somewhat inconsistent in the way it attributes such rights. Article 90 directly refers to the right of States, but Articles 17, 38, and 52 refer to the right of ships, although this may make little difference in practice, since navigation is mostly conducted by private persons. Other substantive rights include the right to fish on the high seas and to enjoy other freedoms of the high seas.[71]

Oxman and Bantz note that flag State rights and duties exist independently of each other.[72] This suggests that rights are not normally contingent on a duty to exercise them in a particular way. However, this seems to play down the relevance of the due regard principle in Article 87(2) of the Convention. It also runs counter to the way in which the genuine link concept has developed.[73] Moreover, as those authors accept, there are specific exceptions to the general rule, including Article 228(1), which denies a flag State the ability to suspend proceedings against its ships for pollution violations when the flag State has repeatedly disregarded its obligations to take enforcement action against its ships.[74] Also notable is Article 8(4) of the 1995 UN Fish Stocks Agreement, which makes fishing for certain stocks contingent upon participation in regional fisheries management mechanisms. This and other qualifications on flag State rights aim at strengthening the link between rights and duties.[75]

---

[69] Guilfoyle, n 45, 9–10.   [70] LOSC, n 2, Arts 73(4) and 292(2), respectively.
[71] LOSC, n 2, Art 87. See Chapter 10 in this volume.
[72] BH Oxman and V Bantz, 'MV Saiga (No 2) (Saint Vincent and the Grenadines v Guinea) Judgment (ITLOS Case No 2)' (2000) 94 *American Journal of International Law* 140, 149.
[73] See Section 3 above.   [74] See also FSA, n 49, Art 8(4).
[75] See the discussion in Section 6 below.

5.2 Flag State duties

Article 94 of the LOSC is the keystone provision on flag State obligations. It sets out a general and non-exhaustive range of duties. Although located in the part of the LOSC dealing with the high seas, its application is not limited spatially. It is subject to qualification in respect of the relevant rules permitting concurrent jurisdiction to be exercised by coastal/port States.[76] States are required to exercise effective jurisdiction and control over the somewhat ambiguously phrased 'administrative, technical and social matters'.[77] Since flag State jurisdiction is exclusive, this phrase must be construed broadly to include any matters affecting vessel operations in order to avoid regulatory lacunae. The term 'jurisdiction and control' indicates the full gamut of prescriptive, adjudicative, and enforcement jurisdiction.[78] This extends to assuming jurisdiction under domestic law over the ship and its crew as regards such matters.[79] More specifically, every State is to maintain a register of ships flying its flag, including details on the ship's name and particulars. The extent of particulars to be recorded is not defined and so left to domestic law.[80] Certain vessels may be excluded from the LOSC's registration requirements on account of their small size. The aim of this exception was to prevent burdensome and unworkable standards being applied to vessels, which because of their small size, would generally be used only within coastal waters. The range of excepted vessels is not defined in further detail, but it should be noted that the provision was not meant to exclude ocean-going vessels.[81] The range of ships falling within this framework is normally addressed within specific agreements constituting generally accepted international rules.[82] However, problems may arise in practice with regards to unflagged or stateless vessels, especially those engaged in IUU fishing[83] and people

---

[76] *Virginia Commentaries*, Vol. III, 136–43.
[77] LOSC, n 2, Art 94(1). For comments, see McDougall and Burke, n 1, 1015–16.
[78] Y Takei, 'Assessing Flag State Performance in Legal Terms: Clarifications of the Margin of Appreciation' (2013) 28 *International Journal of Marine and Coastal Law* 97, 101–2.
[79] LOSC, n 2, Art 94(2). It is not clear how far this extends to passengers and persons aboard illegally. On the one hand, in the *M/V 'Saiga' (No 2)*, n 21, [106], the ship was to be regarded as a unit for the purpose of the flag State exercising protective jurisdiction. On the other, the focus was on the master and other members of the crew, the owners or operators and other persons involved in the activities of the ship, although at points in the judgment it refers to persons generally, ibid, [105].
[80] 1986 United Nations Convention on Conditions for Registration of Ships, Art 11(1) might be regarded as illustrative of the kinds of detail to be included. More important is the present requirement of maintaining a Continuous Synopsis Record under 1974 International Convention for the Safety of Life at Sea, Art XI-1(5) (hereinafter SOLAS).
[81] *Virginia Commentaries*, Vol III, 146.
[82] This relates to the defined material scope of conventions. Thus the 1966 International Convention on Load Lines excludes warships, fishing vessels and pleasure craft from the scope of the rules (Arts 2 and 5). In contrast, the 1972 Convention on the International Regulations for Preventing Collisions at Sea (hereinafter COLREG) adopts a broad definition of ship in Rule 3(a).
[83] TL McDorman, 'Stateless Fishing Vessels, International Law, and the UN High Seas Fisheries Conference' (2007) 25 *Journal of Maritime Law and Commerce* 531.

smuggling or irregular maritime migration.[84] Such ships are not beyond the law, since ships without nationality are susceptible to the jurisdiction of any State, subject to the right of relevant States to exercise diplomatic protection over nationals aboard the ship.[85] However, this may pose problems in trying to identify the States entitled to exercise diplomatic protection and entrusting them to do so with due regard to the human rights of those aboard an interdicted vessel.[86]

5.3 Safety

Article 94(3) of the LOSC requires States to take measures to ensure safety, with regard to, *inter alia*, construction, equipment and seaworthiness, manning, labour conditions and training, and collisions regulation. This is reinforced by the requirement to take further measures to ensure vessels are periodically surveyed and equipped with suitable nautical charts and navigational equipment, and that masters and crew are appropriately qualified and conversant with the applicable international regulations.[87] Safety matters are addressed by a wide range of instruments which require flag States to transpose detailed technical standards into domestic law.[88] Day-to-day implementation will be carried out by ship owners/operators, with flag States' maritime agencies retaining responsibility for general authorizations and certification, monitoring and inspection, and enforcement measures. The problems of ineffective control by flag States over safety matters are well known, although this is compounded by easy movement of shipping between States and shortcomings within the private sector.[89] Appropriate responses are required not just from the flag State, but from across the maritime sector as a whole.[90]

---

[84] R Barnes, n 44, 130–3; M den Heijer, n 44, ch 6.
[85] Churchill and Lowe, n 45, 214; Guilfoyle, n 45, 18.
[86] Barnes, n 44, 103. Den Heijer, n 44, 252–66.   [87] LOSC, n 2, Art 94(4).
[88] 1966 International Convention on Load Lines; 1969 International Convention on Tonnage Measurement; COLREG, n 82; 1972 International Convention for Safe Containers; SOLAS, n 80, and 1988 Protocol; 1978 International Convention on Standards of Training, Certification and Watchkeeping for Seafarers (revised 1995); 1979 International Convention on Maritime Search and Rescue; 1989 International Convention on Salvage.
[89] Sir A Clarke, 'Port State Control or Substandard Ships: Who is to Blame? What is the Cure?' [1994] *Lloyds Maritime and Commercial Law Quarterly* 202; G Pambourides, *International Shipping Law: Legislation and Enforcement* (Kluwer Law International The Hague 1999); M Hayashi, 'Towards the Elimination of Substandard Shipping: The Report of the International Commission on Shipping' (2001) 16 *International Journal of Marine and Coastal Law* 501, 507. See also OECD, *Policy Statement on Sub-standard Shipping by the Maritime Transport Committee of OECD* (2002), available at <http://www.oecd.org/sti/transport/maritimetransport/2080990.pdf>.
[90] T Coghlin, 'Tightening the Screw on Substandard Shipping [2005] *Lloyds Maritime and Commercial Law Quarterly* 316.

5.4 Maritime casualties and assistance at sea

Article 98 of the LOSC obliges every State to require the master of a flagged ship to render assistance to persons and vessels in distress, unless this will place the ship in danger. It is also subject to a requirement of reasonableness. Assistance may be required upon receipt of a distress call or after a collision between the flag ship and another vessel.[91] Apart from rendering assistance, Article 94(7) concerns the duty of flag States to conduct enquiries into maritime casualties occurring on the high seas. This provision refers to harm occasioned upon vessels and installations of other States, and so requires cooperation between all concerned States. In general, it appears that there are significant variations in the investigation or reporting of casualties.[92]

5.5 Pollution

Some flag States have come in for sharp criticism of their lack of diligence in controlling substandard shipping and threats of pollution.[93] As in other areas, flag States do not have sole responsibility for poor shipping standards, but criticism tends to flow from the fact that they have primary legal responsibility for such matters. Article 211(2) of the LOSC extends flag State duties to include the adoption of laws and regulations to prevent, reduce and control pollution of the marine environment from ships. Article 212(1) provides the same for atmospheric pollution. Such laws and regulations shall have at least the same effect as generally accepted international rules and standards.[94] The corresponding enforcement jurisdiction is articulated in Article 217. This requires enforcement measures to be provided for regardless of where the violation occurs. Vessels should not be permitted to sail unless they comply with pollution control requirements. Furthermore, flagged ships shall be properly certificated.[95] In the event of a violation of pollution laws, the flag State shall investigate, and if appropriate, institute proceedings and impose penalties against the responsible parties.

---

[91] See generally R Barnes, 'Refugee Law at Sea' (2004) 53 *International and Comparative Law Quarterly* 44.

[92] Mansell, n 5, 156–60.

[93] 'Safer Ships, Cleaner Seas': *The Report of Lord Donaldson's Inquiry into the Prevention of Pollution from Merchant Shipping*, Cmd 2560 (17 May 1994). A K-J Tan, *Vessel Source Marine Pollution: The Law and Politics of International Regulation* (Cambridge University Press Cambridge 2006) ch 2.

[94] MARPOL, n 52, as modified by the 1978 Protocol, and, potentially, the 1994 International Convention for the Control and Management of Ships' Ballast Water and Sediments. See further the discussion of generally accepted international rules and standards below, Section 6.

[95] LOSC, n 2, Art 217(2).

5.6 Fisheries and mineral resources

As the Sub-Regional Fisheries Commission (SRFC) 2013 request to ITLOS for an advisory opinion indicates, there remain concerns within the international community regarding the effectiveness of flag State control over fishing activities.[96] There are well-documented concerns about weak ship registration mechanisms, gaps between fishing rights and responsibilities, and poor compliance with regulatory standards (by both States and individual vessels).[97] Although coastal States have exclusive authority for fisheries conservation and management within the territorial sea and EEZ, there is no reason why flag States should not also take steps to ensure fishing vessels flying their flag comply with such conservation and management requirements, especially when these are secured through international agreements.[98] On the high seas, flag States are subject to a general duty to take such measures, either individually or in cooperation, as are necessary for the conservation and management of living resources.[99] This cooperation extends to measures for straddling and highly migratory fish stocks.[100] The LOSC is notoriously vague as to the meaning of conservation and management, but has since been augmented by other instruments, principally the 1993 FAO Compliance Agreement[101] and the 1995 UN Fish Stocks Agreement 1995. Although not identical in scope, both these instruments require States to ensure vessels flying their flag do not engage in activities that undermine conservation and management.[102] They require flag States to authorize fishing only when they are able to exercise effectively their flag State responsibilities,[103] and to take enforcement measures, regardless of the place of violation, to investigate and initiate judicial proceedings, and impose sanctions.[104] Both agreements require flag

---

[96] *Request for an Advisory Opinion submitted by the Sub-Regional Fisheries Commission*, International Tribunal for the Law of the Sea Case No 21 (pending), available at <http://www.itlos.org/index.php?id=252> (hereinafter *SRFC Advisory Opinion*).

[97] There is a vast literature on the regulation of fisheries, especially IUU fishing. On flag States aspects of this, see FAO, *Report of and papers presented at the Expert Consultation on Illegal, Unreported and Unregulated Fishing. Sydney, Australia, 15–19 May 2000*. Fisheries Report No 666 (2001); R Rayfuse, *Non-Flag State Enforcement in High Seas Fisheries* (Martinus Nijhoff Leiden 2004) ch 1; High Seas Task Force, *Closing the Net. Stopping illegal fishing on the high seas* (High Seas Task Force London 2006); MA Palma, M Tsamenyi, and W Edeson, *Promoting Sustainable Fisheries. The International Legal and Policy Framework to Combat Illegal, Unreported and Unregulated Fishing* (Martinus Nijhoff Leiden 2010) ch 5.

[98] Although the LOSC contains no express provision on this, this seems to be implicit in Art 58(3) and, possibly, Art 62(4). Takei, n 78, 106.

[99] LOSC, n 2, Arts 117–18.   [100] Ibid, Arts 63(2) and 64.

[101] See also FAO Code of Conduct for Responsible Fisheries, Art 8.2, available at <http://www.fao.org/docrep/005/v9878e/v9878e00.htm>; and FAO Voluntary Guidelines for Flag State Performance (adopted 8 February 2013), available at <ftp://ftp.fao.org/FI/DOCUMENT/tc-fsp/2013/VolGuidelines_adopted.pdf>.

[102] FAO Agreement, n 17, Art III; FSA, n 49, Art 18(1).

[103] FAO Agreement, n 17, Art III(3); FSA, n 49, Art 18(2).

[104] FSA, n 49, Arts 18–19; FAO Agreement, n 17, Art III(8). Interestingly, the Fish Stocks Agreement also facilitates enforcement by non-flag States within regional arrangements (FSA, n 49, Art 21).

States to ensure that vessels can be identified[105] and that catch and landing information is recorded.[106] Flag States must also cooperate and engage in information sharing with regard to fishing activities.[107] Given its additional focus on prescriptive measures, the FSA provides more extensive duties, such as the use of the precautionary approach,[108] cooperation in scientific research,[109] and cooperation with coastal States and the development of compatible conservation and management measures.[110] Specific flag State duties are articulated within a range of regional fisheries management organizations.[111] These represent important steps in strengthening the responsibilities of (flag) States, but they do not allay all concerns, particularly in respect of compliance with such standards.

Many provisions of the LOSC seek to balance flag State rights and coastal State rights, a balance frequently reiterated by commentators.[112] This includes provisions on enforcement of fishing laws and prompt release under Articles 73 and 292. However, this balance may no longer be tenable, reflecting as it does an outdated view of how international fishing activities operate.[113] As noted by Judge Shearer in his Dissenting Opinion in *The 'Volga'* case, the fishing rights associated with flag States are frequently enjoyed by private companies that are readily able to manipulate the registry process and avoid control.[114] This requires a new balance to be struck between coastal States and private parties, a theme running through the SRFC request for an advisory opinion. The SRFC has requested an opinion on four points, three of which focus on flag States: (1) the obligations of flag States in cases of IUU fishing in third States' EEZs; (2) the extent of flag State liability for IUU fishing; and (3) the liability of a flag State or international agency for violations of coastal State fishing laws when fishing is conducted under a license issued under an agreement with the flag State or international agency. If ITLOS determines that it has jurisdiction to issue an advisory opinion, then it must answer some difficult questions concerning the extent of flag State responsibilities. In light of its earlier jurisprudence on the importance of effective flag State jurisdiction and control, it would be disappointing and problematic for the Tribunal to eschew strong flag State responsibility for such activities. What may be more challenging is the question of where to draw the threshold for the exercise of due diligence over flag ships.[115]

---

[105] FAO Agreement, n 17, Art III(6); FSA, n 49, Art 18(3)(c)–(d).
[106] FAO Agreement, n 17, Art III(7); FSA, n 49, Art 18(3)(e).
[107] FAO Agreement, n 17, Arts V–VI; FSA, n 49, Art 14.   [108] FSA, n 49, Art 6.
[109] Ibid, Art 14.   [110] Ibid, Arts 7–8.   [111] See further Chapter 20 in this volume.
[112] DR Rothwell and T Stephens, 'Illegal Southern Ocean Fishing and Prompt Release: Balancing Coastal and Flag State Rights and Interests' (2004) 53 *International and Comparative Law Quarterly* 171, 174.
[113] L Little and M Orellana, 'Can CITES Play a Role in Solving the problem of IUU Fishing?: The Trouble with Patagonian Toothfish' (2004) 15 *Colorado Journal of International Environmental Law and Policy* 22, 61.
[114] *The 'Volga' (Russian Federation v Australia)* (Prompt Release) [2002] ITLOS Rep 10 [19].
[115] See further Section 6 below.

The regulation of mineral resources beyond the limits of national jurisdiction is an issue which may require greater consideration in the future as regards the position of vessels used in support of mineral resource exploitation in the Area. Presently, such activities are governed under the Mining Code.[116] However, under the Code principal responsibility for the conduct of operations is placed upon the Contractor, and this appears to overlap with traditional flag State responsibilities in respect of safety, labour, and health standards.[117]

5.7 Crime and maritime security

Although many instruments stay faithful to the principle of flag State authority, a number of recent developments demonstrate the need for greater international cooperation to prevent crimes and security threats, especially on the high seas. Also, as the need for control over a wider range of illegal conduct at sea has grown, so too have the specific legal responsibilities of flag States.[118] The 1988 Convention for the Suppression of Unlawful Acts of Violence Against the Safety of Maritime Navigation (SUA Convention) establishes a range of offences involving the use of violence at sea and acts intended to intimidate populations or compel governments or international organizations to act, and measures for the extradition and prosecution of alleged offenders.[119] Although attributing a range of duties to States in different capacities, it stays faithful to the principle of exclusive flag State jurisdiction. Flag States are required to take measures to establish jurisdiction over offences committed against or on board flagged ships.[120] Flag States retain the right to permit and stipulate conditions in respect of boarding measures.[121] More specifically, flag States are required to consider requests for boarding of ships and further enforcement action.[122] When the master of a vessel seeks to deliver suspects to a receiving State, the flag State shall ensure, whenever practical and possible, that the authorities of the receiving State are notified and that the master furnishes the authorities with the relevant evidence in his possession.[123] The flag State may be requested to accept delivery of suspects from the receiving State, to consider such a request and, if the request is refused, to provide reasons for this.[124]

---

[116] International Seabed Authority (ISA), Mining Code, available at <http://www.isa.org.jm/en/mcode>.

[117] See ISA, Standard Clauses for Exploration Contracts, clauses 14–15, available at <http://www.isa.org.jm/files/documents/EN/Regs/Code-Annex4.pdf>.

[118] See generally N Klein, *Maritime Security and the Law of the Sea* (Oxford University Press Oxford 2011).

[119] 1988 Convention for the Suppression of Unlawful Acts of Violence Against the Safety of Maritime Navigation, amended by the 2005 Protocol, Arts 3 and 3(bis) (hereinafter SUA).

[120] Ibid, Art 6(a).   [121] Ibid, Art 8bis(8); Guilfoyle, n 45, 256–7.

[122] SUA, n 119, Art 8bis(5)(c).   [123] Ibid, Art 8(2).   [124] Ibid, Art 8(5).

The International Ship and Port Security (ISPS) Code was adopted within Chapter XI-2 of SOLAS.[125] Its mandatory provisions require, *inter alia*, flag States to approve ship security plans and to develop a Declaration of Security.[126] They are also responsible for assessing security threats and setting security levels for flagged ships.[127] Enforcement is left to flag States and the Code provides for flag States to issue guidance on measures to reduce security risks to ships.[128]

Flag States are obliged to take steps to ensure vessels flying their flag comply with Security Council resolutions adopted in order to maintain international peace and security.[129] The content of such resolutions has been characterized as legislative, and certainly impacts upon flag State authority.[130] In recent years, resolutions have implemented sanctions and controlled weapons proliferation, allowed for counter-piracy measures and facilitated counter-terrorism measures.[131] Security Council based sanctions typically impose embargoes, but may also require flag States to prevent the supply of goods on flagged ships.[132] Iran and the Democratic People's Republic of Korea (DPRK) have been subject to measures to counter the proliferation of weapons of mass destruction (WMD) and related material.[133] United Nations sanctions generally provide for boarding and inspection at sea, but flag State permission is still required for boarding and inspections at sea, although the flag State is expected to provide this. Notably, UNSC Resolution 1874 against the DPRK required flag States to direct vessels to port for inspection if consent to inspection on the high seas is refused.[134] While such resolutions allow flag States a degree of discretion as to how they implement the measures, they demonstrate the importance of coordinated and collective action. Outside the Security Council, the USA-led Proliferation Security Initiative has sought to coordinate existing efforts to control WMD proliferation.[135] Although it is designed to be consistent with the existing rights and duties of flag, port, and coastal States, it has resulted in supplementary steps by way of bilateral

---

[125] IMO Doc SOLAS/CONF.5/32 (12 December 2002) and IMO Doc SOLAS/CONF.5/34 (17 December 2002).

[126] Ibid, Part A, §§ 5 and 9.   [127] Ibid, Part A, § 4.   [128] Ibid, Part B, § 4.21.

[129] 1945 United Nations Charter, Art 25. See also *Questions of Interpretation and Application of the 1971 Montreal Convention arising from the Aerial Incident at Lockerbie (Libyan Arab Jamahiriya v United States of America)* [1992] ICJ Rep 16, [39].

[130] Guilfoyle, n 45, 238.   [131] See Takei, n 78, 113–14; Klein, n 118, 276–85.

[132] Congo: UNSC Res 1493 (2003) [20]; Liberia: UNSC Res 1521 (2003) [2(a)]; Sudan: UNSC Res 1556 (2004) [7]; Côte d'Ivoire: UNSC Res 1572 (2004); Eritrea: UNSC Res 1907 (2009) [5], [6], and [12]; Libya: UNSC Res 1970 (2011) [9].

[133] Iran: UNSC Res 1737 (2006) [3] and [7]; UNSC Res 1747 (2007), [5] and [6]; UNSC Res 1803 (2008) [8]; UNSC Res 1929 (2010) [8]; North Korea: UNSC Res 2094 (2013) [22].

[134] North Korea: UNSC Res 2094 (2013) [13].

[135] For details on the Statement of Interdiction Principles and related practice see United States Department of State, Bureau of Security and Non-Proliferation, *Proliferation Security Initiative*, available at <http://www.state.gov/t/isn/c10390.htm>. See generally M Byers, 'Policing the High Seas: The Proliferation Security Initiative' (2004) 98 American Journal of International Law 526; Klein, n 118, 193–210.

agreements that facilitate ship boarding and inspection by the participating States. To these collectively orientated efforts we should add recent initiatives in the field of maritime piracy.[136]

6 Key Issues

Flag State jurisdiction has not failed, but it is far from effective.[137] The consequences of ineffective flag State control are not to be tolerated, but the question remains how to reconcile new approaches with the principle of sovereign equality that underpins flag State jurisdiction. The multiplicity of actors and expanding range activities occurring at sea demands more sophisticated and flexible mechanisms for the exercise of jurisdiction by States. A binary approach relying upon the use of either flag or spatially based control is ill equipped to deal with contemporary issues of ocean use. In response to concerns about substandard shipping, illegal fishing, and security threats, more nuanced forms of jurisdiction and control are emerging in three ways: greater use of international minimum standards, improved enforcement and compliance mechanisms, and developing stronger links between rights and duties.

The principal means of setting international minimum standards is through the use of 'generally accepted international rules and standards' (GAIRS). Rules of reference in the LOSC allow for the development of more detailed standards of conduct within a coherent framework. This maintains the pre-eminence of international standards over domestic laws and regulations, thereby contributing to uniformity. GAIRS also help define the extent of discretion in the exercise of flag State jurisdiction.[138] The effectiveness of this mechanism depends on the existence of clear rules of reference and then being able to identify whether or not an instrument is 'generally accepted'. While clear rules of reference exist for shipping and pollution, the position of other activities, especially fisheries, is less certain.[139] Although not critical to the development of such international standards, the use of rules of reference has generated debate and uncertainty as to the precise relationship between

---

[136] See further Chapter 37 in this volume.

[137] Molenaar, n 56, 88ff; Rayfuse, n 97; M Gianni, *Real and Present Danger. Flag State Failure and Maritime Safety and Security* (International Transport Workers' Federation London 2008). See also the text and references at footnotes 89–90, 92, 93, and 96–97.

[138] J-P Cot, 'The Law of the Sea and the Margin of Appreciation' in TM Ndiaye and R Wolfrum (eds), *Law of the Sea, Environmental Law and Settlement of Disputes: Liber Amicorum Judge Thomas A Mensah* (Martinus Nijhoff Publishers Leiden 2007) 396; Takei, n 78, 115ff.

[139] LOSC, n 2, Art 119(1)(a) merely exhorts taking account of generally recommended international minimum standards.

different fisheries agreements and their impact upon non-States parties.[140] The means of identifying GAIRS has been considered at length elsewhere, but ultimately depends upon the practice of States.[141] Arguably the most important such test of this is the inclusion of an instrument within the various Memoranda of Understanding (MOUs) on port State control (PSC). Although non-binding, these MOUs establish common standards of conduct and seek to coordinate existing legal authority to act.[142] They provide clear evidence of State practice and create institutional support mechanisms. Furthermore, they provide scope for the inclusion of soft law non-binding instruments and so can accommodate non-treaty standards. In light of these advantages, it is suggested that this form of recognition, especially within a regional mechanism that gives effect to international standards through inspection and compliance mechanisms, provides the clearest indication of the international standards to which flag States must adhere. PSC mechanisms seem likely to expand to complement and reinforce, rather than replace flag State control.[143] Notably, this is extending to fisheries with the adoption of the FAO Port State Agreement in 2009.[144]

An interesting alternative to securing compliance through PSC regimes is the use of market-based controls. These are being developed in the context of IUU fishing and target the economic incentives for such activities by removing or limiting the market for IUU catch.[145] This supplements traditional legal controls and engages a wider range of private actors in regulation.

More generally, international efforts are focusing on holding States to account. In December 2013, the IMO Assembly adopted a mandatory members State audit scheme.[146] The IMO Instruments Implementation Code (III Code) will replace the Voluntary Member State Audit Scheme and become binding on member

---

[140] See E Franckx, '*Pacta Tertiis* and the Agreement for the Implementation of the provisions of the United Nations Convention on the Law of the Sea of 10 December Relating to the Conservation & Management of Straddling Fish Stocks & Highly Migratory Fish Stocks' (FAO Legal Papers Online 8 June 2008), available at <http://www.fao.org/fileadmin/user_upload/legal/docs/lpo8.pdf>.

[141] R Van Reenan, 'Rules of Reference in the new Convention on the Law of the Sea in particular connection with the pollution of the sea' (1981) 12 *Netherlands Yearbook of International Law* 3; B Oxman, 'The Duty to Respect Generally Accepted International Standards' (1991) 24 *New York University Journal of International Law and Politics* 109; G Kasoulides, *Port State Control and Jurisdiction: Evolution of the Port State Control Regime* (Martinus Nijhoff Leiden 1993) 38ff; ILA, *Final Report of the Committee on Coastal State Jurisdiction Relating to Marine Pollution* (2000) 31ff, available at <http://www.ila-hq.org/en/committees/index.cfm/cid/12>; J Harrison, *Making the Law of the Sea* (Cambridge University Press 2011) 171–9.

[142] See Chapter 13 in this volume.

[143] EJ Molenaar, 'Port State Jurisdiction: Towards Mandatory and Comprehensive Use' in D Freestone, R Barnes, and D Ong (eds), *Law of the Sea Progress and Prospects* (Oxford University Press Oxford 2006) 192.

[144] 2009 Agreement on Port State Measures to Prevent, Deter and Eliminate Illegal, Unreported and Unregulated Fishing.

[145] See DS Calley, *Market Denial and International Fisheries Regulation* (Martinus Nijhoff Leiden 2012).

[146] IMO Res A.1070(28), *IMO Instruments Implementation Code (III Code)* (4 December 2013).

States through amendments of the relevant IMO agreements. *Inter alia*, the III Code requires flag States to effectively implement international standards under domestic law,[147] prohibit flag ships sailing unless compliant with such standards,[148] and put in place evaluation and review procedures in order to assess its performance.[149] This will put pressure on States to improve compliance with international standards by developing clearer and more transparent standards of accountability.

The strengthening of the link between the rights and duties of the flag State is most apparent with regard to the development of the due diligence principle.[150] When primary obligations are framed in terms of result, including the duty to exercise effective control over flagged ships, the principle of due diligence requires States 'to deploy adequate means, to exercise best possible efforts, to do the utmost, to obtain this result'.[151] The principle is not new, having been articulated in the *Alabama Claims* and *Corfu Channel* cases.[152] It is an extension of the responsibility of States to ensure that activities within their jurisdiction or control do not cause harm to other States.[153] However, it has gained particular traction within the field of environmental law, as indicated in the *Pulp Mills Case* and the *Area Advisory Opinion*.[154] The principle can be used to reinforce flag State duties, for example, by drawing into the scope of due diligence those policy and guidance measures in soft law instruments that articulate how a State should give effect to its obligations of conduct.[155] While the acts of private ships cannot be attributed to the flag State, a failure to exercise effective control over flag ships may constitute an internationally wrongful act incurring the responsibility of that State.[156] A single breach by an individual vessel would probably be insufficient to incur responsibility, unless this State has clearly failed to comply with its own flag

---

[147] Ibid, [15]–[17].   [148] Ibid, [22].   [149] Ibid, [42]–[44].

[150] R Pisillo-Mazzeschi, 'The Due Diligence Rule and the Nature of the International Responsibility of States' (1992) 35 *German Yearbook of International Law* 9; D French, 'From the Depths: Rich Pickings of Principles of Sustainable Development and General International Law on the Ocean Floor—the Seabed Disputes Chamber's 2011 Advisory Opinion' (2011) 26 *International Journal of Marine and Coastal Law* 525, 537ff; Takei, n 78, 124ff.

[151] *Responsibilities and Obligations of States sponsoring persons and entities with respect to activities in the Area* (Advisory Opinion) [2011] ITLOS Rep 10 [109] (hereinafter *Area Advisory Opinion*).

[152] *Alabama Claims of the United States of America against Great Britain* (1872) XXIV RIAA 125; *Corfu Channel (United Kingdom v Albania)* [1949] ICJ Rep 4, 22. See also *United States Diplomatic and Consular Staff in Tehran (United States of America v Iran)* [1980] ICJ Rep 32, [63]; *Military and Paramilitary Activities in and against Nicaragua (Nicaragua v United States of America)* [1986] ICJ Rep 4, [157].

[153] *Legality of the Threat or Use of Nuclear Weapons (Advisory Opinion)* [1996] ICJ Rep 226, [29]; Also, the case concerning the *Gabčíkovo-Nagymaros Project (Hungary/Slovakia)* [1997] ICJ Rep 7, [53].

[154] *Pulp Mills on the River Uruguay (Argentina v Uruguay)* [2010] ICJ Rep 14 (hereafter, *Pulp Mills*); *Area Advisory Opinion*, n 151.

[155] See *SRFC Advisory Opinion*, n 96, Written Statements by the Federated States of Micronesia [23]–[24] and [33], and New Zealand [19]–[30].

[156] Ibid, Written Statement of the Federated States of Micronesia, [46]; Takei, n 78, 131–2.

State responsibilities. In this respect, a more general pattern of individual violations by flag ships might be enough to substantiate such a claim.[157]

The precise content of a due diligence obligation is difficult to ascertain, but it appears to have a number of key elements. First, it is to be construed in a contextual manner.[158] For example, riskier activities entail a higher degree of diligence than less risky activities. This means that due diligence may operate differently in the context of ship safety, fisheries or security. Thus, for example, IUU fishing may be regarded as both probable and serious, and so demanding of more vigilance than ship safety standards. Second, while States are left with a degree of discretion as to how they achieve certain outcomes, this discretion is not unfettered.[159] At a minimum, it entails some degree of positive vigilance over the conduct of private parties and positive steps of prevention.[160] This might include listing of vessels engaged in IUU fishing.[161] Third, it follows that States must have some degree of institutional capacity to control such activities.[162] This in turn, entails that States actually implement appropriate domestic laws, regulations and enforcement mechanisms in respect of their international obligations.[163] A failure to do so may give rise to a presumption that due diligence has not been exercised. Fourth, adherence to related direct obligations is relevant in meeting an obligation of due diligence.[164] In the context of flag State duties, this would mean ratifying relevant international agreements. Fifth, while due diligence is contextual and may be contingent on a States scientific knowledge and technical capacities, this does not provide a blanket excuse to release States from their obligations.[165] This point is crucial in the context of flagging since it is highly desirable to have a uniform regulatory regime.

Flag State jurisdiction provides just one component within an increasingly complex system of institutions and practices. These three areas of development do not depart from the principle of flag State jurisdiction; they seek to redefine the way in which it operates. The developments do not relieve flag States of their obligations; indeed they reinforce flag State responsibilities. However, they also require a more nuanced appreciation of the role and relationship of the flag State to other actors and institutions.

---

[157] R Rayfuse, 'Protecting the Marine Environment: Non-flag State Enforcement and IUU Fishing' in MH Nordquist, TB Koh, and JN Moore (eds), *Freedom of the Sea, Passage Rights and the 1982 Law of the Sea Convention* (Martinus Nijhoff Leiden 2009) 573, 584–8.

[158] *Area Advisory Opinion*, n 151, [117]; Takei, n 78, 125.

[159] *Area Advisory Opinion*, n 151, [230].

[160] *Pulp Mills*, n 154, [197]; *Area Advisory Opinion*, n 151, [119] and [218].

[161] *SRFC Advisory Opinion*, n 96, Written Statement of the EU [60]–[61].

[162] See the 2001 International Law Commission Draft Articles on Prevention of Transboundary Harm from Hazardous Activities, reproduced in (2001) II(2) *Yearbook of the International Law Commission* 155, Commentary on Art 3 [17].

[163] *Area Advisory Opinion*, n 151, [108] and [218].   [164] Ibid, [123].

[165] Ibid, [156]–[161], especially [159].

15

LANDLOCKED AND GEOGRAPHICALLY DISADVANTAGED STATES

HELMUT TUERK

1 INTRODUCTION

THE oceans and their marginal seas have played a significant role in the development of humanity, not only as a means of communication and trade, but also as an important source for satisfying nutritional needs.[1] In view of an ever-increasing world population, a growing necessity has arisen, particularly since the middle of the twentieth century, to intensify the exploitation of marine resources.[2] The growing realization of the enormous resources and the great economic potential of the seas was coupled with concern over the toll taken on coastal fish stocks by long-distance

---

[1] This chapter is essentially based on H Tuerk, *Reflections on the Contemporary Law of the Sea* (Martinus Nijhoff Publishers Leiden/Boston 2012) ch 4; H Tuerk, *The Landlocked States and the Law of the Sea* (2007) 40(1) *Revue Belge de Droit International* 91; and H Tuerk, 'Forgotten Rights—the Landlocked Countries and the Law of the Sea' in R Wolfrum, M Sersić, and T Sosić (eds), *Liber Amicorum Budislav Vukas* (Martinus Nijhoff Publishers Leiden/Boston forthcoming 2015). Opinions expressed in this chapter are strictly personal.

[2] See H Tuerk and G Hafner, 'The Landlocked Countries and the United Nations Convention on the Law of the Sea' in B Vukas (ed), *Essays on the New Law of the Sea* (Sveucilisna naklada Liber Zagreb 1985) 58.

fishing fleets and over the danger of pollution and waste from ships carrying noxious cargoes, threatening coastal communities and all forms of ocean life.[3]

A major shift thus occurred towards more national authority over maritime areas, leading to a diminution of the extent of the high seas and an attenuation of its freedoms,[4] which has been called a transition from a 'law of movement' to a 'law of territory and appropriation'.[5] This development directly affected the landlocked States as well as other States in a less favourable geographical position with respect to the seas and their resources, which would subsequently call themselves 'geographically disadvantaged States'.[6] These two groups of countries came to realize that they would have little or nothing to gain from an extension of sovereign rights and jurisdiction over vast, valuable maritime areas. On the contrary, this trend placed them in an increasingly disadvantageous position with respect to maritime uses,[7] as they were facing the loss of rights they had hitherto enjoyed either in practice or at least theoretically.

For landlocked countries, there could be no doubt that the disadvantages of their geographical situation would further increase in comparison with coastal States, as the lack of a sea-coast deprives them of claiming exclusive rights with respect to maritime areas.[8] They also need rights of transit, coupled with adequate physical infrastructure, across the territory of other countries in order to be able to enjoy the advantages of maritime communication and trade. As regards geographically disadvantaged States, many of which had important fishing fleets or were even long-distance fishing nations, it was obvious that an increasing 'nationalization' of oceanic resources would have substantial adverse effects on their economy.

It should be borne in mind that the geographical location of a State does not constitute an impediment to maritime uses and concerns,[9] which is true for both geographically disadvantaged and landlocked States. Quite a number of landlocked

---

[3] United Nations Division for Ocean Affairs and the Law of the Sea (DOALOS), *The United Nations Convention on the Law of the Sea—A Historical Perspective*, 1, available at <www.un.org/Depts/los/convention_agreements/convention_historical_perspective.htm>.

[4] D Anderson, 'The Development of the Modern Law of the Sea' in D Anderson, *Modern Law of the Sea: Selected Essays* (Martinus Nijhoff Publishers Leiden/Boston 2008) 1, 6.

[5] See RJ Dupuy, 'La mer sous compétence nationale' in RJ Dupuy and D Vignes (eds), *Traité du nouveau droit de la mer* (Economica Bruylant Paris/Bruxelles 1985) 219, 219–20. See also, RP Anand, 'Freedom of the Seas, Past, Present and Future' in H Caminos (ed), *Law of the Sea* (Ashgate/Dartmouth Aldershot/Burlington 2001) 261, 225.

[6] See G Hafner, 'Geographically Disadvantaged States' in R Wolfrum (ed), *Max Planck Encyclopedia of Public International Law* (Oxford University Press Oxford 2012) available at <http://opil.ouplaw.com/home/EPIL>.

[7] See also M Glassner, 'Developing Land-locked States and the Resources of the Seabed' (1973–1974) 11(3) *San Diego Law Review* 633, 636.

[8] See also Tuerk and Hafner, n 2, 61.

[9] See Tuerk, *Reflections in the Contemporary Law of the Sea*, n 1, 49; and Tuerk, *Landlocked States*, n 1, 92.

States thus have ocean-going vessels under their own flag[10] and also belong to the International Maritime Organization (IMO), which currently counts 18 landlocked members.[11] They participate in the work of the Intergovernmental Oceanographic Commission (IOComm),[12] have become parties to international maritime conventions, including those relating to the prevention of marine pollution[13] and, further, have conducted marine scientific research.[14] Several landlocked States have also adopted domestic legislation expressly criminalizing maritime piracy,[15] which many coastal States are still lacking.

This chapter analyses how landlocked and geographically disadvantaged States sought to safeguard their rights and interests in connection with the emergence of a new law of the sea, what rights were granted to them under the 1982 United Nations Convention on the Law of the Sea (LOSC), how these rights have been realized in practice and the role of these States in the further development of the law of the sea.

2 The Emergence of a New Law of the Sea

In view of the progressive extension of sovereign rights and jurisdiction over maritime areas by a rising number of coastal States, a thorough revision of the existing—and increasingly discarded—law of the sea had become inevitable if

---

[10] Azerbaijan, Belarus, Bolivia, Ethiopia, Kazakhstan, Laos, Luxembourg, Moldova, Mongolia, Paraguay, Slovakia, Switzerland, and Turkmenistan. See The World Merchant Fleet in 2012, Statistics from Equasis, Statistical Annex, Review of Maritime Transport 2013, Annex II (c), 167–72, available at <http://emsa.europa.eu/implementation-tasks/equasis-a-statistics/items/id/472.html?cid=95>.

[11] See IMO members States, available at <http://www.imo.org/About/Membership/Pages/MemberStates.aspx>.

[12] These States are: Afghanistan, Austria, Azerbaijan, Czech Republic, Ethiopia, Kazakhstan, Serbia, and Switzerland. See International Oceanographic Commission (of UNESCO), member States of the Commission as of 2 September 2013, available at <http://www.ioc-unesco.org/index.php?option=com_oe&task=viewDocumentRecord&docID=4017>.

[13] See the 1973 International Convention for the Prevention of Pollution from Ships as Modified by the Protocol of 1978 Relating Thereto (hereinafter MARPOL); 1972 London Convention on the Prevention of Marine Pollution by Dumping of Wasted and Other Matter and its 1996 Protocol; 1992 Convention for the Protection of the Marine Environment of the North-East Atlantic (OSPAR Convention).

[14] G Hafner, 'Austria and the Law of the Sea' in T Treves and L Pineschi (eds), *The Law of the Sea: The European Union and its Member States* (Martinus Nijhoff Publishers The Hague/London/Boston 1997) 27, 30.

[15] For instance Austria, Azerbaijan, Kazakhstan, Liechtenstein, Moldova, Czech Republic, and Serbia (on file with author).

this body of law was once again to be based on a consensus of the international community.[16] In the course of the negotiations leading to the convening of the Third United Nations Conference on the Law of the Sea in 1973 (UNCLOS III), landlocked States formed a single interest group with 'geographically disadvantaged States'.[17] The formation of the 'Group of Landlocked and Geographically Disadvantaged States'[18] was essentially prompted by the appearance during the negotiations, of the novel concept of a 200 nautical mile coastal State exclusive economic zone (EEZ), encompassing all living and non-living maritime resources.[19] A major concern of the members of the Group, apart from seeking to preserve some resource-related rights within such new maritime zones, was to safeguard, as far as possible, traditional high seas freedoms, in particular navigation rights in these areas, and to forestall attempts at their 'territorialization'.

It has been pointed out that the idea that some coastal States may be disadvantaged for the purposes of the law of the sea was also inspired by the Judgment of the International Court of Justice in the 1969 *North Sea Continental Shelf* cases,[20] where the Court underlined the importance of coastal configuration in continental shelf delimitation. The position, in particular advocated by the Netherlands, was therefore taken that 'shelf-locked States' should also be entitled to special consideration in a new law of the sea. This idea was later applied to countries with other geographical characteristics, such as short coastlines or narrow shelves, and to coastal States that would derive little economic benefit from or even be adversely affected by an extension of coastal State maritime jurisdiction.[21] At UNCLOS III, the Group of Coastal States, which promoted the right to establish an EEZ, initially completely refused to acknowledge the existence and legal relevance of geographical and other disadvantages.[22] During the course of negotiations, the Group then sought to confine the notion of geographically disadvantaged States to developing countries alone.[23]

---

[16] Tuerk, 'Forgotten Rights', n 1, 10.

[17] See also LC Caflisch, 'Land-locked States and their Access to and from the Sea' (1978) 49 *British Yearbook of International Law* 71, 71.

[18] The Group was originally called 'Group of land- and shelf-locked States'.

[19] Y Huang, 'Rights of Land-locked and Geographically Disadvantaged States in the Exclusive Economic Zone' in R Lagoni, P Ehlers, and M Paschke (eds), *Recent Developments in the Law of the Sea, Schriften zum See- und Hafenrecht* (Lit Verlag Berlin 2010) 87, 92.

[20] See *North Sea Continental Shelf (Federal Republic of Germany v The Netherlands; Federal Republic of Germany v Denmark)* (Judgment) [1969] ICJ Rep 3.

[21] SC Vasciannie, *Land-Locked and Geographically Disadvantaged Sates in the International Law of the Sea* (Clarendon Press Oxford 1990) 10.

[22] LC Caflisch, 'Fishing Rights of Land-Locked and Geographically Disadvantaged States in the Exclusive Economic Zone' in B Conforti (ed), *La zona economica esclusiva* (Giuffrè Milano 1983) 33.

[23] See also LC Caflisch, 'Land-locked and Geographically Disadvantaged States and the New Law of the Sea' in (1977) 7 *Thesaurus Acroasium* (Institute of Public International Law and International Relations Thessaloniki 1977) 347, 347–9.

This attitude was challenged by the Group of Landlocked and Geographically Disadvantaged States, which in 1976, proposed a comprehensive definition designed to cover all the members of the Group. This definition encompassed three categories of countries: (i) States which are prevented by their geographical situation from claiming any economic zone; (ii) States whose economic zone would amount to less than 30 per cent of the surface that they could have claimed had they been physically able to establish a full 200-mile zone; (iii) States which, for geographical, biological, or ecological reasons, would derive no substantial economic advantage from exploiting the living resources of their economic zones and whose rights of access to the living resources of the sea would be adversely affected by the establishment of such zones by other States.[24]

The proposed definition came under criticism for being arbitrary and lacking precision, as well as for going beyond geographical criteria by also including biological and economic elements.[25] In view of the intention of the Group of Landlocked and Geographically Disadvantaged States to ensure a 'blocking third' at UNCLOS III, such a wide definition, coupled with a liberal admission policy to the Group was, however, unavoidable.[26] At the same time, political criteria were nevertheless applied for not admitting certain States,[27] the question of admission being decided by consensus. A number of States to which that definition would also have applied chose, for whatever reasons, not to become members of the Group.[28] In the end, the Group of Landlocked and Geographically Disadvantaged States comprised 55 members including 29 landlocked and 26 geographically disadvantaged States of which 21 and 17, respectively, were developing countries.[29]

In this context, it should be borne in mind that, with certain exceptions—such as navigational rights—the basic interests pursued by the members of the Group with respect to a new law of the sea were quite divergent.[30] The primary concern of developing landlocked States was access to and from the sea and transit for that purpose. That issue was of much less importance for developed landlocked States,

---

[24] Caflisch, n 22, 33.   [25] See also Caflisch, n 22, 33–4.   [26] See also Vasciannie, n 21, 8.

[27] Iran and Israel were not admitted to the Group in light of determined resistance by Arab States. The Holy See left the Group as it did not want to be involved in political controversies.

[28] For instance Yugoslavia, Saudi-Arabia, Malaysia, Thailand, Tunisia, and Haiti. The non-participation of these States in the Group did not, however, in any way effect the outcome of UNCLOS III.

[29] For a list of the members of the Group of Landlocked and Geographically Disadvantaged States, see LM Alexander, 'The "Disadvantaged" States and the Law of the Sea' (1981) 5 *Marine Policy* 185, 187. Romania is missing on that list as it joined that Group only at a very late stage of the Conference. See also G Hafner, 'Die Gruppe der Binnen- und geographisch benachteiligten Staaten auf der Dritten Seerechtskonferenz der Vereinten Nationen' (1978) 38 *Zeitschrift für ausländisches öffentliches Recht und Völkerrecht* 568.

[30] See also JL Kateka, 'Landlocked Developing Countries and the Law of the Sea' in I Buffard et al (eds), *International Law between Universalism and Fragmentation, Festschrift in Honour of Gerhard Hafner* (Martinus Nijhoff Leiden/Boston 2008) 769, 771–2.

which were more interested in the exploitation of oceanic resources, in particular mineral resources, and marine scientific research. The landlocked States as a whole also realized that their claim to participation rights in the EEZ regarding living oceanic resources was largely theoretical in view of the increasing overexploitation of these resources in general. The creation of ocean-going fishing fleets would thus not have made much sense for them. For the geographically disadvantaged States, which already had such fleets, the question of a right to participate in the exploitation of the living resources of the EEZ was, however, a major issue in view of important economic interests involved. [31]

In spite of these different interests the Group of Landlocked and Geographically Disadvantaged States, chaired by Austria and co-chaired by Singapore, was marked by a true spirit of solidarity between its developing and developed members.[32] The Group showed great unity at UNCLOS III and endeavoured to forestall an exclusive partition among a majority of coastal States of maritime resources, which, under the traditional law of the sea, were common to all nations. While vigorously defending its interests,[33] that Group finally could not stand in the way of general agreement and had to accept political and economic realities. The LOSC, adopted as a 'package deal' in 1982, could by its very nature not wholly satisfy the aspirations of all the segments of the international community.[34]

3 THE LOSC AND THE LANDLOCKED AND GEOGRAPHICALLY DISADVANTAGED STATES

As of 1 January 2014, 165 States and the European Union were party to the LOSC. This number includes 28 landlocked States out of a total number of 44 such States with United Nations membership. Another seven landlocked States have signed the Convention but so far have not adhered to it.[35] It is to be noted that none of the Central Asian landlocked States have become a party to the LOSC. Of the 26 geographically disadvantaged States belonging to the respective Group at UNCLOS

---

[31] See also Tuerk, 'Forgotten Rights', n 1, 12.
[32] Tuerk, *Reflections on the Contemporary Law of the Sea*, n 1, 55.
[33] See also Vasciannie, n 21, 218.   [34] See also Tuerk, 'Forgotten Rights', n 1, 12.
[35] See landlocked States with UN membership, available at <www.un.org/en/members/>; and 'Chronological lists of ratifications of, accessions and successions to the Convention and the related Agreements as at 3 October 2014', available at <www.un.org/Depts/los/reference_files/chronological_lists_of_ratifications.htm>.

III, 21 have become parties to the Convention, and another three have signed it.[36] These figures clearly show that the acceptance of the provisions of the LOSC by landlocked and geographically disadvantaged States was essential for ensuring a universal agreement regarding the new law of the sea.

The LOSC contains definitions of both landlocked and of geographically disadvantaged States. Article 124(1)(a) of the Convention defines landlocked States as States which have no sea-coast, a definition based on Article 1(a) of the 1965 United Nations Convention on Transit Trade of Landlocked States (Transit Trade Convention).[37] The use of the term 'sea-coast' means that countries bordering a body of water that is in itself landlocked, even if called a 'sea', are also to be considered landlocked and not coastal States.[38]

The proposed definition of 'geographically disadvantaged States' was not accepted by the Group of Coastal States as a general term for the whole of the LOSC.[39] As a compromise, that term is used throughout the Convention, without being defined, except in Part V relating to the EEZ for 'the purposes' of that Part. These States are thus defined in Article 70(2) of the LOSC as:

> ...coastal States, including States bordering enclosed or semi-enclosed seas, whose geographical situation makes them dependent upon the exploitation of the living resources of the exclusive economic zones of coastal States of the same subregion or region for adequate supplies of fish for the nutritional purposes of their populations or parts thereof, and coastal States which can claim no exclusive economic zones of their own.

With respect to the question whether this rather restrictive definition can also be relied upon when considering the applicability of other rights of geographically disadvantaged States provided for by the LOSC, different views may be held.[40] It would, however, seem justifiable to consider that definition as, in principle, not only applying to Part V of the LOSC but also to other parts of the Convention.

The LOSC as a whole contains quite a number of references to landlocked States in contrast to geographically disadvantaged States. The Preamble recognizes the necessity to take into account the interests and needs of mankind as a whole and, in particular, the special interests and needs of developing countries, whether coastal or landlocked. Specific rights of landlocked States concern navigation, access to

---

[36] Ethiopia, which has since become a landlocked State, Syria, and the United Arab Emirates, have signed but not ratified the LOSC. The German Democratic Republic has since acceded to the Federal Republic of Germany.

[37] 1982 United Nations Convention on the Law of the Sea, Art 124(1)(a) (hereinafter LOSC), based on 1965 Convention on Transit Trade of Land-locked States, Art 1(a) (hereinafter Transit Trade Convention). The Transit Trade Convention has thus far been ratified by 42 States. Only 24 coastal States are party to the Transit Trade Convention, some of which do not border a landlocked country. See status of the Convention, available at <treaties.un.org/doc/publication/mtdsg/volume%20i/chapter%20x/x-3.en.pdf>.

[38] Huang, n 19, 88. These are the landlocked States bordering the Caspian Sea.

[39] See also Caflisch, n 22, 34.   [40] See eg Vasciannie, n 21, 64.

ports, and the living resources of the EEZ. An entire chapter of the LOSC—Part X[41]—is devoted to the right of access of landlocked States to and from the sea and freedom of transit.[42] Several provisions of the Convention dealing with scientific research and the international seabed 'Area'[43]—the common heritage of mankind—relate to both landlocked and geographically disadvantaged States.[44] A provision relating only to the latter group of States deals with their rights to living resources of the EEZ.[45]

When acceptance of the concept of the EEZ, which had at first been altogether rejected by the Group of Landlocked and Geographically Disadvantaged States, became unavoidable, these States demanded the right to participate, on an equal and non-discriminatory basis, in the exploration and exploitation of both the living and the non-living resources of the economic zones of 'neighbouring' coastal States or coastal States within the same region or sub-region.[46] In the end, a compromise was achieved with respect to the living resources of the EEZ, enshrined in Articles 69 and 70 of the LOSC. These articles, which apply to landlocked and geographically disadvantaged States respectively, are identical in substance. The determined resistance by the vast majority of coastal States did not, however, all for the provision of a right under the LOSC of participation by landlocked and geographically disadvantaged States in the exploration and exploitation of the non-living resources of the continental shelf.[47] At the time, the continental shelf doctrine, assuming the existence of sovereign rights of coastal States with respect to these resources, was already too firmly anchored in international law.[48]

Articles 69 and 70 of the LOSC grant landlocked and geographically disadvantaged States a right to participate 'on an equitable basis' in the exploration and exploitation of the living resources of EEZs of coastal States of the same subregion or region, taking into account the relevant economic and geographical circumstances of all the States concerned and in conformity with the provisions of these articles and of Articles 61 and 62.[49] It is important to note the term 'right' in these provisions, which had originally been firmly rejected by the majority of coastal States. The use of this term also implies that there is a corresponding obligation on coastal States to provide landlocked and geographically disadvantaged States with access to the living resources of the EEZ.[50]

---

[41] LOSC, n 37, Arts 123–132. [42] Tuerk and Hafner, n 2, 64.
[43] According to LOSC, Art 1(1)(1), 'Area' means the seabed and ocean floor and subsoil thereof, beyond the limits of national jurisdiction.
[44] Ibid, Arts 254, 148, 152, 158(4)(k), and 160(2)(k). [45] Ibid, Art 70.
[46] Tuerk and Hafner, n 2, 62. [47] See also *Virginia Commentaries*, Vol III, 371.
[48] See also SC Vasciannie, 'Landlocked and Geographically Disadvantaged States and the Question of the Outer Limit of the Continental Shelf' (1987) 58 *British Yearbook of International Law* 272.
[49] These articles grant the coastal State the right to determine the allowable catch of the living resources in its EEZ, respectively to determine its capacity to harvest these resources.
[50] See also M Dahmani, 'Access of Landlocked and Geographically-Disadvantaged States to the Fisheries Resources of the Economic Exclusive Zone (EEZ) under the New Convention on the Law of the Sea' (1983) 10(4) *Maritime Policy and Management* 269.

This right is, however, limited by additional requirements and conditions. Thus, it exists only in relation to an 'appropriate part of the surplus of the living resources' as determined by the coastal State, with a certain exception for developing landlocked States, which are entitled to an equitable share of the resources of the EEZ of the region or subregion regardless of the existence of a surplus.[51] In the subregion or region concerned, this right does not take precedence over other participation rights, but must compete with these, with the final decision being left to the coastal State.[52] This right also cannot be enjoyed in the EEZ of coastal States, which are overwhelmingly dependent on fisheries, or by developed landlocked and geographically disadvantaged States within the EEZs of developing States.

Furthermore, the exercise of this right relating to fisheries is made contingent upon additional agreements with the coastal States concerned, which must, *inter alia*, take into account the need to avoid effects detrimental to the fishing communities or industries of the coastal States, the extent to which other landlocked or geographically disadvantaged States are participating or are entitled to participate in the exploitation of the living resources of the EEZ, as well as the nutritional needs of the populations of the respective States. In addition, the direct or indirect transfer of these participation rights to third States or their nationals is not permitted, unless agreed to by the coastal State concerned.[53] Coastal States are not, however, precluded from granting landlocked and geographically disadvantaged States of the same sub-region or region equal or preferential rights for the exploitation of the living resources in their EEZs. This provision constitutes a faint echo of the demand, particularly by some African landlocked States, to create regional economic zones.[54]

It is obvious that several of the terms used and conditions contained in Articles 69 and 70 of the LOSC may lend themselves to divergent interpretations. Terms which may be subject to dispute include the 'appropriate part' of the surplus of the living resources of an EEZ, the 'effects detrimental' to fishing communities or industries of coastal States or the 'nutritional needs' of the respective States' populations.[55] The same holds true to some extent for the definition of the terms 'region' and 'subregion'. While the term 'region' may be understood as referring to the geographical areas covered by the regional economic commissions of the United Nations it is more difficult to define the term 'subregion',[56] as it may not always be clear in which sub-region a landlocked or geographically disadvantaged State is situated.[57] There are, in particular, landlocked States which may be considered as belonging to more than one subregion.[58] In connection with these questions of interpretation it should

---

[51] Caflisch, n 22, 41.   [52] Tuerk and Hafner, n 2, 65.   [53] LOSC, n 37, Art 72(1).
[54] Tuerk, 'Forgotten Rights', n 1, 17.   [55] Dahmani, n 50, 270. See also Huang, n 19, 97–8.
[56] See also Dahmani, n 50, 270; and Huang, n 19, 98.
[57] See RR Churchill and AV Lowe, *The Law of the Sea* (3rd edn Manchester University Press Manchester 1999) 437–9.
[58] Ibid, 434. Chad, for instance, borders four coastal States—Libya, Sudan, Cameroon, and Nigeria. Does it belong to the subregion of the Mediterranean, the Red Sea or the Gulf of Guinea?

be borne in mind that disputes relating to the sovereign rights of the coastal State with respect to the living resources within its EEZ or their exercise, including a State's discretionary powers for determining the allowable catch, harvesting capacity, the allocation of surpluses to other States, and the terms and conditions established in its conservation and management laws and regulations, are excluded from the compulsory dispute settlement procedures under the LOSC and are subject only to non-binding conciliation.[59]

The LOSC contains a number of provisions relating to the maritime rights of landlocked States. Article 17 of the Convention affirms that ships under the flag of landlocked States enjoy the right of innocent passage through the territorial sea of other States in the same manner as those of coastal States. Article 87 provides that the high seas are open to all States, whether coastal or landlocked—both kinds of States enjoying exactly the same rights regarding the freedom of the high seas. Article 90 reaffirms the right of landlocked States to sail ships flying their flag on the high seas.[60] This equality between landlocked States and all other States was already set forth in the 1958 Geneva Conventions on the Territorial Sea and the Contiguous Zone (TSC) and on the High Seas (HSC), respectively, and is undoubtedly also part of customary international law.[61]

Pursuant to Article 131 of the LOSC, ships of landlocked States are accorded treatment equal to that of other foreign ships in maritime ports, whereas Article 3 of the HSC provided for combined most-favoured-nation or national treatment, the more advantageous being applicable. Although Article 131 amounts to no more than a corollary of the right of landlocked States to sail ships under their own maritime flag[62] and thus may not be discriminated against in maritime ports, it is nevertheless more favourable than Article 3 of the HSC: it does not make access to ports and their use dependent on the prior conclusion of an agreement between the landlocked State and the port State and, furthermore, covers all maritime ports and not only those of coastal transit States.[63]

The right of access by landlocked States to and from the sea and freedom of transit through the territory of transit States by all means of transport is enshrined in Article 125 of the LOSC. Contrary to the 1965 Transit Trade Convention—which has had little practical value in view of the small number of Parties—the right of access is made contingent upon bilateral, sub-regional, or regional agreements between the landlocked States and transit States, laying down the terms and modalities for exercising freedom of transit. This right is, furthermore, restricted to the purpose

---

[59] LOSC, n 37, Art 297(3)(a) and (b).
[60] Tuerk, *Reflections on the Contemporary Law of the Sea*, n 1, 57.
[61] See also Vasciannie, n 21, 60. See further *Virginia Commentaries*, Vol II, 80.
[62] LOSC, n 37, Art 90. See also Caflisch, n 17, 97–8.
[63] J Monnier, 'Right of Access to the Sea and Freedom of Transit', in R-J Dupuy and D Vignes (eds), *A Handbook on the New Law of the Sea* (Martinus Nijhoff Publishers The Hague 1981) 507.

of exercising the rights provided for in the LOSC, including those relating to the freedom of the high seas and the common heritage of mankind.[64]

It is important to note that access to the sea is described as a 'right', while Article 3 of the HSC only stipulated that States having no sea-coast 'should have free access to the sea'. Moreover, the requirement of reciprocity was dropped, which undoubtedly represents an important improvement compared to the Transit Trade Convention and the High Seas Convention.[65] The LOSC as a whole also does not derogate from any greater transit facilities that landlocked States may enjoy, by agreement, with particular transit States nor is the grant of greater facilities in the future precluded by the Convention.[66] Part X of the LOSC has, in general, improved the legal situation of landlocked States in respect of access to and from the sea,[67] and further integrated the right of access into the framework of the law of the sea.[68] Part X of the Convention, by striking a certain balance between the interests of landlocked States on one hand and those of transit States on the other,[69] can be considered a significant achievement by the landlocked countries.

As regards the international seabed Area, dealt with in Part XI of the LOSC, the landlocked and geographically disadvantaged States sought to ensure that they would be able to fully take part in the international seabed regime and not be relegated to an inferior position because of their geographical location.[70] They succeeded in achieving this goal, as the basic principle enshrined in the Convention with respect to the Area is non-discrimination and equality of all States. Activities therein are to be carried out for the benefit of mankind as a whole, irrespective of the geographical location of States, whether coastal or landlocked.[71] The same principle applies to the use of the Area 'exclusively for peaceful purposes'.[72]

The LOSC contains a number of provisions specifically aimed at promoting the interests of landlocked and, to a lesser extent, geographically disadvantaged States.[73] Article 148 of the LOSC deals with the promotion of the effective participation of developing States in activities in the Area, with due regard, in particular, to the special need of the landlocked and geographically disadvantaged among them to overcome obstacles arising from their disadvantaged location, including remoteness from the Area and difficulty of access to and from it. In addition, Article 152 excludes special consideration for developing States, with particular consideration for the landlocked and geographically disadvantaged among them, from the

---

[64] Tuerk, *Reflections on the Contemporary Law of the Sea*, n 1, 58.
[65] Transit Trade Convention, n 37, Art 15. See also, Monnier, n 63, 519.
[66] LOSC, n 37, Art 132.   [67] See also Tuerk and Hafner, n 2, 64.
[68] Tuerk and Hafner, n 2, 67. See further *Virginia Commentaries*, Vol III, 382.
[69] Tuerk and Hafner, n 2, 64.   [70] See also Churchill and Lowe, n 57, 436.
[71] LOSC, n 37, Art 140(1).   [72] See ibid, Arts 140 and 141.
[73] Churchill and Lowe, n 57, 436.

non-discrimination rule to be applied by the International Seabed Authority (ISA) in the exercise of its powers and functions.

Within the ISA, landlocked and geographically disadvantaged States are also accorded some special, although limited rights.[74] The Assembly of the ISA is thus endowed with the competence to consider problems for States in connection with activities in the Area that are due to their geographical location, particularly for landlocked and geographically disadvantaged States.[75] The 1994 Implementation Agreement relating to Part XI of the LOSC provides that developing landlocked and geographically disadvantaged States are to have representation on the Council of the Authority[76]—in the same manner, however, as several other groups of States parties representing special interests. In electing the members of the Council, the Assembly of the ISA must ensure that landlocked and geographically disadvantaged States are represented to a degree which is reasonably proportionate to their representation in the Assembly.[77] In practice, that provision does not, however, seem to have had any particular effect on the composition of the Council, although a number of landlocked and geographically disadvantaged States have been elected to that organ of the ISA, actively participating in its work.

At UNCLOS III, landlocked and geographically disadvantaged States voiced their expectation to be compensated for the extension of coastal States' sovereign rights and jurisdiction and their own disadvantaged situation with respect to maritime uses, by being allotted a larger share of the benefits derived from the exploitation of the deep seabed,[78] at least for the developing countries among them. The system for the equitable sharing of financial and other economic benefits derived from activities in the Area[79] has, however, not yet been elaborated in view of the fact that—contrary to the original expectation that deep seabed mining would become an economic reality well before the end of the twentieth century—such exploitation has not so far not taken place nor does it seem to be imminent.

It is most probable that the first revenues for the international community to be derived from the exploitation of the seabed will accrue under the provisions of Article 82 of the LOSC from the exploitation of the continental shelf beyond 200

---

[74] Tuerk, *Reflections on the Contemporary Law of the Sea*, n 1, 61.

[75] LOSC, n 37, Art 16(2)(k).

[76] 1994 Agreement Relating to the Implementation of Part XI of the United Nations Convention on the Law of the Sea of 10 December 1982, Annex, Section 3(15)(d). See also *Virginia Commentaries*, Vol III, 383.

[77] LOSC, n 37, Art 161(2)(a). The issue of representation of the Group of Landlocked and Geographically Disadvantaged States in the organs of the ISA was also raised by the Chairman of that Group—at that time the author—in a letter addressed to the Chairman of the Preparatory Commission for the International Seabed Authority and for the International Tribunal for the Law of the Sea; see Doc No LOS/PCN/114 (28 August 1990).

[78] Tuerk and Hafner, n 2, 64.   [79] LOSC, n 37, Art 160(2)(f)(i).

nautical miles rather than from the Area. In determining equitable sharing criteria, the ISA is bound to take 'into account the interests and needs' of developing States, particularly the least developed and the landlocked among them.[80] It seems likely that those States parties that are both landlocked and least developed will be given the highest priority in receiving benefits through the ISA from the exploitation of the continental shelf by coastal States.[81]

The rights of landlocked and geographically disadvantaged States regarding marine scientific research are contained in Article 254 of the LOSC. Although such States are entitled to be informed of planned marine scientific research projects and to participate in such projects, this right depends on additional conditions and requirements. It permits them merely to participate in projects carried out by third States and competent international organizations in the EEZ of neighbouring coastal States and they must be given the 'opportunity' to participate in such research activities only 'whenever feasible'.[82] This right is thus quite limited and far from the original demand that these States be permitted to participate in research projects carried out in the economic zones of neighbouring coastal States.[83]

Although the LOSC tries to strike a careful balance between the rights of coastal States and the freedoms enjoyed by all States, whether coastal or landlocked, it is quite obvious that the pendulum has clearly swung from the principle of *mare liberum* to that of *mare clausum* by the recognition of expanded sovereign rights and jurisdiction of coastal States,[84] substantially limiting the rights to maritime resources of landlocked and geographically disadvantaged States. The LOSC has rightly been referred to as the greatest expansion of sovereign rights and jurisdiction in history.[85]

---

[80] Ibid, Art 82(4).

[81] At the International Workshop convened by the ISA in collaboration with the China Institute for Marine Affairs, Beijing, 26–30 November 2012, the implementation of LOSC, Art 82 was discussed.

> It was agreed that, based on the wording of 82(4), the eight States Parties that are both Land-Locked States (LLS) and Least Developed Countries (LDC) would have the highest priority and the highest ranking. The 37 States Parties that are either LLS or LDC would be next, and then other similar categories may be considered such as Small Island Developing States and Geographically Disadvantaged States. These would be followed by other developing States Parties, and then the remainder of the States Parties.

ISA, *Implementation of Article 82 of the United Nations Convention on the Law of the Sea. Technical Study: No. 12* (International Seabed Authority Kingston 2013), available at <http://www.isa.org.jm/files/documents/EN/Pubs/TS12-web.pdf>.

[82] The legislative history indicates that 'feasibility' must be determined according to the practicability of participation in light of available research facilities, and may be affected by the degree of anticipated participation by the coastal State; *Virginia Commentaries*, Vol IV, 596.

[83] Tuerk and Hafner, n 2, 62.

[84] See S Kaye, 'Freedom of Navigation in a Post 9/11 World: Security and Creeping Jurisdiction' in D Freestone, R Barnes, and DM Ong (eds), *The Law of the Sea—Progress and Prospects* (Oxford University Press Oxford 2006) 347, 347–8.

[85] See JN Moore, 'Conservatives and the Law of the Sea Time Warp', *The Wall Street Journal* (8 July 2012).

4 The Realization of the Rights of Landlocked and Geographically Disadvantaged States Under the LOSC

In considering the question of the realization of the rights of landlocked and geographically disadvantaged States recognized by the LOSC it should, first of all, be borne in mind that during the last few decades regional economic integration has made substantial progress in several parts of the world. This process has undoubtedly contributed to mitigating some of the difficulties faced by these States with respect to maritime uses. As far as the landlocked countries are concerned, the process of integration has also provided a new basis of access to and from the sea.

In respect of those developed landlocked States that have become members of the European Union it can rightly be said that a fundamental change has occurred and that they are landlocked in theory rather than in practice.[86] The developed geographically disadvantaged States that had been members of the respective Group at UNCLOS III have all joined the European Union.[87] Their situation has thus likewise undergone a major change, in particular with respect to the exploitation of the living resources within the EEZ. European Union Law applies to the entire area under the sovereignty of the member States and thus the four basic freedoms—freedom of movement of persons, goods, services and capital—are applicable,[88] any discrimination against nationals of member States being prohibited. If a member State extends its area of jurisdiction, the area of applicability of European Union Law is automatically extended, which also applies to the EEZ and to the continental shelf.[89]

When signing the LOSC, the then European Community[90] indicated that its member States had transferred competence to it with regard to the conservation and management of sea fishing resources, competences concerning rules and regulations for the protection and preservation of the marine environment as well as certain powers

---

[86] G Vitzthum, 'Die Europäische Gemeinschaft und das Internationale Seerecht' (1986) 111 *Archiv des Öffentlichen Rechts* 33, 62. See also, Hafner, n 14, 34. These EU member States are: Austria, Czech Republic, Hungary, Luxembourg, and Slovakia.

[87] These States are Bulgaria, Finland, Greece, Netherlands, Poland, Germany, Romania, and Sweden.

[88] See Treaty Establishing the European Community, Art 299(1).

[89] See 'Art 299, Rz 5' in J Schwarze (ed), *EU-Kommentar* (Nomos Baden-Baden 2000); and C Thun-Hohenstein et al (eds), *Europarecht* (Manz Wien 2008) 49.

[90] On 1 December 2009, the Treaty of Lisbon amending the Treaty on the European Union and the Treaty Establishing the European Community entered into force. As of that date, the European Union has replaced and succeeded the European Community and is exercising all its rights and assuming all its obligations.

with regard to the provisions of Part X of the Convention.[91] The Common European Fisheries Policy is of particular importance, providing for the allotment of quotas of the total allowable catch within European waters to individual member States.[92] As the criteria underlying the quota allocation are the traditional fishing patterns, the fishing rights of the geographically disadvantaged States have thus basically been safeguarded. There are, in principle, also no obstacles regarding fishing activities by the landlocked member States.[93] On the contrary, the coastal member States are prohibited from restricting the fishing activities of nationals of other member States undertaken from their territory.

The developing landlocked States, however, find themselves in a different situation, many of them facing severe challenges to growth and development.[94] Lack of territorial access to the sea, poor physical infrastructure, remoteness and isolation from world markets, as well as high transit costs continue to impose serious constraints on their overall socio-economic development.[95] In 2003, an international ministerial conference convened by the United Nations in Almaty, Kazakhstan, adopted a Declaration and Programme of Action to enhance transit transport cooperation between landlocked and transit developing countries.[96] The so-called São Paolo Consensus adopted by the United Nations Conference on Trade and Development (UNCTAD) in 2004, also deals with the special problems of landlocked developing countries as well as the related challenges faced by transit developing countries. The document outlines the goals of UNCTAD in addressing these problems within a new global framework for transit transport cooperation between the States concerned.[97]

---

[91] European Economic Community, 'Declaration Upon Signature' (7 December 1984), in DOALOS, *Declarations and Statements*, available at <www.un.org/Depts/los/convention_agreements/convention_declarations.htm>. See also Vitzthum, n 86, 36–7 n 15.

[92] The allocation is decided annually; see Council Regulations (EU) No 39/2013 and No 40/2013 (21 January 2013) fixing for 2013 the fishing opportunities available to EU vessels. The member States divide their quota among the ships of their fishing fleet; the ships must be under the flag of the member State or registered in that State. The freedom of establishment enables any citizen of the Union to register a ship in any member State. There must not be any limitations in this respect as underlined by the European Court of Justice (ECJ); see *R v Secretary of State for Transport, ex parte Factortame (No 3)* (C-221/89) [1991] ECR I-3905.

[93] G Hafner, 'The Rights of Landlocked States in the Baltic Area' in R Platzöder and P Verlaan (eds), *The Baltic Sea: New Developments in National Policies and International Cooperation* (Martinus Nijhoff Publishers The Hague/London/Boston 1996) 371, 385.

[94] See United Nations Conference on Trade and Development (UNCTAD), *UN Recognition of the Problems of Landlocked Developing Countries*, available at <www.unctad.org/Templates/Page.asp?intItemID=3619&lang=1>.

[95] UN Office of the High Representative for the Least Developed Countries, Landlocked Developing Countries and Small Island Developing States (UNOHRLLS), *Landlocked Developing Countries—About LLDCs*, available at <http://unohrlls.org/about-lldcs/>.

[96] See UNCTAD, n 94.

[97] See United Nations Secretary General, *Report of the Secretary-General on Oceans and the Law of the Sea*, UN Doc A/59/62/Add.1 (2004) [17]–[18].

The plight of many developing landlocked States and of some developing geographically disadvantaged States is nevertheless to a certain extent alleviated by the increasingly important role of regional economic integration. The Treaty Establishing the African Economic Community (AEC),[98] signed in 1991 by the member States of the Organization of African Unity (OAU), provides for the granting of special treatment to member States classified as least developed countries and the adoption of special measures in favour of landlocked, semi-landlocked, and island countries.[99] The existing and future regional economic communities are regarded as building blocks of the AEC.[100] The largest such economic community is the Common Market for Eastern and Southern Africa (COMESA), which comprises 19 States, including eight landlocked countries and one geographically disadvantaged State, the Democratic Republic of Congo.[101] The Economic Community of West African States (ECOWAS) consists of 15 States, including three landlocked ones.[102] The Southern African Development Community (SADC) has a membership of 15 States, including six landlocked countries and the DR Congo.[103] The Economic Community of Central African States (ECCAS) encompasses ten States, including three landlocked countries as well as two geographically disadvantaged States—Cameroon and the DR Congo.[104] The East African Community (EAC) comprises two coastal and three landlocked States.[105]

Beyond the African continent, it is to be noted that Bolivia has joined the Andean Community[106] and Paraguay has become a member of 'Mercosur'

[98] 1991 Treaty Establishing the African Economic Community.   [99] Ibid, Art 4(2)(k).
[100] See Africa's Regional Economic Communities Briefing to UN Member States (2010) 2, available at <http://www.un.org/africa/osaa/reports/new-reports/Background Note to the RECS briefings to Member States.pdf>.
[101] The member States are: Burundi, Comoros, Democratic Republic of Congo, Djibouti, Egypt, Eritrea, Ethiopia, Kenya, Libya, Madagascar, Malawi, Mauritius, Rwanda, Seychelles, Sudan, Swaziland, Uganda, Zambia, Zimbabwe. See 'COMESA Member States', available at <http://about.comesa.int/index.php?option=com_content&view=article&id=123&Itemid=121>.
[102] The member States are: Benin, Burkina Faso, Cape Verde, Côte d'Ivoire, Gambia, Ghana, Guinea, Guinea-Bissau, Liberia, Mali, Niger, Nigeria, Senegal, Sierra Leone, Togo; see 'ECOWAS in Brief', available at <www.comm.ecowas.int/sec/index.php?id=about_a&lang=en>.
[103] The member States are: Angola, Botswana, Democratic Republic of Congo, Lesotho, Madagascar, Malawi, Mauritius, Mozambique, Namibia, Seychelles, South Africa, Swaziland, United Republic of Tanzania, Zambia, and Zimbabwe, available at <www.sadc.int/about-sadc>.
[104] The member States are: Angola, Burundi, Cameroon, Central African Republic, Chad, Republic of the Congo, Democratic Republic of Congo, Equatorial Guinea, Gabon, and São Tomé and Príncipe; see United Nations Economic Commission for Africa, 'ECCAS—Economic Community of Central African States', available at <http://www.uneca.org/oria/pages/eccas-economic-community-central-african-states-0>.
[105] These States are: Kenya, Tanzania, Uganda, Rwanda, and Burundi; see East African Community, 'About EAC', available at <http://www.eac.int/index.php?option=com_content&view=article&id=1&Itemid=53>.
[106] The other members are Colombia, Ecuador, and Peru, see Communidad Andina, 'About us', available at <www.comunidadandina.org/ingles/who.htm>.

(Southern Common Market).[107] Bolivia has also become an accession member of Mercosur. The founding treaties of both organizations have established customs unions that are components of the continuing process of South American integration.[108] Nepal and Bhutan belong to the South Asian Free Trade Area (SAFTA)[109] and Laos has joined the Association of South-East Asian Nations (ASEAN), the aims of which include the acceleration of economic growth.[110] In Eastern Europe, Azerbaijan and Moldova as well as four landlocked central Asian States, are parties to a free-trade agreement, which provides for a stage-by-stage creation of an Economic Union.[111] Moldova, in 2013, also signed an Association Agreement with the European Union.[112]

The transit provisions of the LOSC seem to have had a positive effect on bilateral and regional agreements concluded between landlocked and transit States, which are nevertheless still based on reciprocity. These agreements generally also provide for most-favoured-nation treatment for merchant ships sailing under the flag of landlocked countries regarding navigation, entry into, and use of maritime ports and harbour facilities. They often complement the provisions of treaties on regional integration. The most far-reaching agreements have been concluded between Peru and Bolivia, whereby Bolivia was granted free use of port facilities and an industrial and special commercial free zone in the Peruvian port of Ilo, as well as the right of free transit to and from that zone.[113] In other notable agreements, Paraguay has been granted free access to and from the sea by Brazil,[114] and Argentina has accorded that country such access via the rivers Paraguay, Paraná, and de la Plata.[115]

---

[107] The other members are Brazil, Argentina, Uruguay, and Venezuela. See Mercosur, 'En pocas palabras', available at <http://www.mercosur.int/t_generic.jsp?contentid=3862&site=1&channel=secretaria>.

[108] See Communidad Andina, 'About us', n 106; see also Mercosur, n 107.

[109] 2004 Agreement on South Asian Free Trade Area (hereinafter SAFTA Agreement).

[110] The other member States are: Indonesia, Malaysia, the Philippines, Singapore, Thailand, Brunei, Myanmar, Cambodia, and Vietnam. See 'ASEAN Member States', available at <http://www.asean.org/asean/asean-member-states>.

[111] 1994 Free Trade Agreement. The State parties are: Azerbaijan, Armenia, Belarus, Georgia, Kazakhstan, Kyrgyzstan, Moldova, Tajikistan, and Uzbekistan. Available at: <http://www.wipo.int/wipolex/en/other_teaties/parties.jsp?treaty_id=423&group_id=24.

[112] 2014 Association Agreement between the European Union and the European Atomic Energy Community and their Member States, of the one part, and the Republic of Moldova, of the other part (hereinafter European Union–Republic of Moldova Association Agreement).

[113] 1992 Framework Agreement between the Government of Peru and the Government of Bolivia on the 'Grand Marshal Andrés de Santa Cruz' Binational Project for Friendship, Cooperation and Integration. This framework agreement provides for the conclusion of further agreements concerning free zones, transit, and fishing. See also 'Bolivia alcanza su acceso al mar por medio de Perú', *El Universo* (20 October 2010), available at <www.eluniverso.com/2010/10/20/1/1361/bolivia-alcanza-un-acceso-oceano-pacifico.html>.

[114] 1975 Treaty of Friendship and Co-operation between the Federative Republic of Brazil and the Republic of Paraguay.

[115] 1967 Treaty of Navigation, Buenos Aires.

Similarly, Djibouti has guaranteed Ethiopia a permanent right of access to the sea and to transit goods through its territory[116] as well as the right to use its port installations and equipment. The agreement concerning the Malawi–Tanzania corridor transport system recognizes that Malawi is a landlocked country dependent upon its neighbouring coastal States for access to the sea.[117] Uganda has concluded an agreement with Tanzania and Kenya on road transport,[118] and Burkina-Faso is a party to a similar agreement with Benin.[119] Burundi, Rwanda, Uganda, and the DR Congo are parties to the Northern Corridor Transit Agreement with Kenya, providing the most efficient route for the surface transport of goods to the sea.[120] In 2012, the African Union adopted an Integrated Strategy for the Seas and Oceans—Horizon 2050 which lists among its strategic objectives the protection of the right of access to the sea and of the freedom of transit for the landlocked countries.[121]

In Asia, Mongolia and China have concluded an agreement on access to and from the sea and transit transport by Mongolia through China's territory.[122] Nepal and Bhutan are parties to new agreements with India on trade and transit, replacing in part older treaties between the States.[123] Nepal has also signed a similar agreement with Bangladesh.[124] The Afghanistan Pakistan Transit Trade Agreement (APTTA) recognizes the right of Afghanistan to freedom of access to the sea as an essential principle for the expansion of its international trade and economic development.[125]

Regarding the navigational rights of landlocked States enshrined in the LOSC, it can be said that they are being fully respected and the same is true concerning

---

[116] 1993 Djibouti Port Utilization Agreement between the Transitional Government of Ethiopia and the Government of the Republic of Djibouti, and the 1993 Transit and Port Services Agreement between the Transitional Government of Ethiopia and the Government of the State of Eritrea.

[117] 1987 Agreement between the Government of the Republic of Malawi and the Government of the United Republic of Tanzania concerning the Malawi–Tanzania Transport System.

[118] 2001 East African Community, Tripartite Agreement on Road Transport between the Government of the United Republic of Tanzania, the Government of the Republic of Kenya and the Government of the Republic of Uganda.

[119] 1990 Accord de coopération en matière de transports et de transit entre le Burkina Faso et la République du Bénin, available at <http://www.toefrank.net/textes/acc1990.htm>.

[120] 1985 Northern Corridor Transit Agreement.

[121] Stratégie africaine intégrée pour les mers et les océans—horizon 2050 (16 December 2011) 13 (on file with author) (hereinafter Stratégie AIM 2050).

[122] 1991 Agreement between the Government of the Mongolian People's Republic and the Government of the People's Republic of China on the Access to and from the Sea and Transit Transport by Mongolia through China's Territory.

[123] 1991 Treaty of Trade between the Government of India and His Majesty's Government of Nepal; and 2006 Agreement on Trade, Commerce and Transit between the Government of the Republic of India and the Royal Government of Bhutan.

[124] 1976 Trade and Payments Agreements between His Majesty's Government of Nepal and the Government of the People's Republic of Bangladesh with Protocol.

[125] 2010 Agreement between the Governments of the Islamic Republic of Afghanistan and the Islamic Republic of Pakistan (Afghanistan–Pakistan Transit Trade Agreement, APTTA).

access to and use of ports. By contrast, with respect to marine scientific research, coastal States in their national legislation do not seem to have taken any account of the rights of landlocked or geographically disadvantaged States.[126] In relation to fishing rights, it likewise appears that coastal States in their legislation regarding the EEZ, have, in general, ignored the provisions of the LOSC in respect of sharing surplus living resources with landlocked and geographically disadvantaged States. In this context, the constantly diminishing yields owing to overexploitation of fish stocks as well as the rising demand for fish caused by population increase and the ensuing economic difficulties for many coastal States owning these resources certainly constitute an important factor. In any case, fishing rights granted by the LOSC to landlocked and geographically disadvantaged States, in particular as far as the landlocked States are concerned, essentially constitute a *nudum ius*.[127]

The situation is somewhat different regarding the fishing rights of certain developing landlocked States; the practical effects of these rights may, however, mostly seem doubtful. For example, Bolivia and Peru have concluded an agreement, which contemplates the possibility that Bolivia may enter into joint ventures with Peruvian companies to engage in fishing activities within the Peruvian EEZ.[128] Brazil has granted fishing rights to Paraguayan nationals or enterprises in its maritime zones under conditions to be established under bilateral agreements.[129] Morocco and Togo, in their relevant legislation referring to African solidarity, have indicated their readiness to allow neighbouring landlocked countries access to the living resources of their EEZs.[130] It is further important to note that the African States bordering the Atlantic Ocean have adopted a Regional Convention on Fisheries Cooperation, currently comprising 13 States parties, in which they also 'affirm their solidarity with the landlocked African States and with geographically disadvantaged States of the Region' with whom they actively cooperate.[131]

---

[126] See also Tuerk, *Landlocked States*, n 1, 110.

[127] See also Tuerk, *Reflections on the Contemporary Law of the Sea*, n 1, 62.

[128] Vasciannie, n 21, 65.

[129] See Treaty of Friendship and Cooperation between Brazil and Paraguay, n 114.

[130] Vasciannie, n 21, 65, n 6. See also Commonwealth Secretariat, 'Landlocked and Geographically Disadvantaged States under UNCLOS' (2004) 30 *Commonwealth Law Bulletin* 792.

[131] 1991 Convention régionale relative à la coopération halieutique entre les Etats africains riverains de l'océan Atlantique, Art 16. The States parties are: Angola, Benin, Cape Verde, Democratic Republic of Congo, Côte d'Ivoire, Gabon, Guinea, Guinea-Bissau, Equatorial Guinea, Morocco, Nigeria, Senegal, and Sierra Leone.

5 CONCLUSION

The provisions of the LOSC reflect the views of landlocked and geographically disadvantaged States only to a limited and, as far as access to resources is concerned, rather minimal degree. The Convention, however, constituted the only basis on which agreement with the majority of coastal States was possible and which nevertheless to some extent takes account of the demands of landlocked and geographically disadvantaged States.[132] Moreover, one of the major and lasting results of UNCLOS III was to heighten the awareness of the international community that the law of the sea is also of importance to landlocked States[133] and, that in this framework, the interests of geographically disadvantaged States likewise merit special consideration.

An overall assessment as to the realization of the rights of landlocked and geographically disadvantaged States recognized by the LOSC leads to a mixed conclusion. Important progress has undoubtedly been made in respect of transit to and from the sea, owing, at least in part, to increased cooperation and progressive economic integration in the respective geographical regions. Other rights granted to landlocked States, however, seem to have been largely, if not totally, forgotten.[134] This is equally true as regards geographically disadvantaged States, perhaps with the exception of the exploitation of living resources within the EEZ where intensified economic cooperation and integration with other coastal States has allowed them, in principle, to enjoy better access to these resources. As to the right to share in the benefits to be derived from the common heritage of mankind, landlocked and geographically disadvantaged States—like the remainder of the international community—find themselves in a waiting position that is most likely to continue for a still unforeseeable period of time.

It is a fact that the Group of landlocked and geographically disadvantaged States has practically ceased to exist after the entry of force of the LOSC in 1994. The active interest in the law of the sea in many of these countries, especially the landlocked States, has since similarly diminished, owing to the realization that genuine gains from most of the rights granted under the Convention are largely lacking. The current law relating to the oceans and seas, however, needs to be further developed in order to cope with new challenges facing the international community,[135] such as the

---

[132] Tuerk and Hafner, n 2, 67; Vasciannie, n 21, 60.
[133] Tuerk, *Reflections on the Contemporary Law of the Sea*, n 1, 67.
[134] See also Huang, n 19, 125–6.
[135] See EU Commission, *Green Paper: Towards a Future Maritime Policy for the Union: A European Vision for the Oceans and Seas*, EU Doc COM(2006) 275 Final (7 June 2006) Vol II, Annex, 43, available at <http://europa.eu/documents/comm/green_papers/pdf/com_2006_0275_en_part2.pdf>.

need for enhanced protection of the environment, a better conservation of natural resources, safeguarding biodiversity, and increased security from various threats of violence at sea.[136]

In this context, landlocked and geographically disadvantaged States have a cardinal role to play in contributing to responding to these challenges within the framework of a multilateral negotiating process and in watching over the safeguarding of the freedoms of the seas as enshrined in the LOSC. Although these States no longer form a coherent group as during the UNCLOS III negotiations, they are nevertheless bound together by common interests with respect to that important area of international law and its further development. In view of maintaining a universally acceptable order of the seas, the concurrence of the landlocked and geographically disadvantaged States continues to be indispensable, in particular, as an important goal of these States with respect to the development of the law of the sea has consistently been to safeguard the interests of humankind as a whole.

---

[136] See also Tuerk, *Reflections*, n 1, 185.

16

THE UNITED NATIONS

A PRACTITIONER'S PERSPECTIVE

HANS CORELL

1 Introduction

The adoption and opening for signature of the United Nations Convention on the Law of the Sea (LOSC) at Montego Bay, Jamaica, on 10 December 1982, and its entry into force on 16 November 1994, constitute a major contribution of the United Nations to the development of international law.[1] To a large extent, the Convention, presently (January 2015) ratified or acceded to by 167 parties, represents a codification of customary international law. However, it also contains important advances of the law of the sea.

The potential for disputes and conflicts relating to the law of the sea is great. However, because of the manner in which the Convention establishes the law and provides methods for resolving disputes, the Convention can actually be regarded as making a major contribution to the maintenance of international peace and security. This was noted by the General Assembly in its resolution recognizing the entry into force of the LOSC, where the Assembly recalled the historic significance of the Convention 'as an important contribution to the maintenance of peace, justice, and

---

[1] To maintain conformity in the present volume, the acronym LOSC is used in this chapter. It should be pointed out, however, that the acronym applied throughout the entire United Nations system is UNCLOS.

progress for all peoples of the world'.[2] The Convention has even been described as the most successful treaty adopted by the international community since the adoption of the 1945 Charter of the United Nations.[3]

The process leading up to the adoption of the LOSC, the institutions established by the Convention, and many of the features of the treaty, are described elsewhere in this volume. The present chapter addresses the contributions of the United Nations to the development of the law of the sea during the period following the adoption of the Convention in 1982. Particular attention is paid to the way in which the work of the UN is organized.

Consequently, the following sections focus on: preparing for the entry into force of the LOSC; informal consultations relating to the implementation of Part XI of the LOSC; establishing the Convention institutions after the entry into force of the LOSC; the Division for Ocean Affairs and the Law of the Sea (DOALOS); United Nations conferences on the human environment; the role of the General Assembly; the Meeting of States Parties to the LOSC (SPLOS); sustainable fisheries and straddling fish stocks and highly migratory fish stocks; the Oceans and Coastal Areas Network (UN-Oceans); the United Nations open-ended informal consultative process on oceans and the law of the sea; the so-called Regular Process; the conservation and sustainable use of marine biodiversity in areas beyond national jurisdiction; and piracy on the agenda of the Security Council. The final section contains some conclusions and reflections on the future, in particular, on the connection between the protection of the oceans and international peace and security.

2 Preparing for the Entry into Force of the LOSC

The Third United Nations Conference on the Law of the Sea (UNCLOS III) was serviced by the UN Office for Ocean Affairs and the Law of the Sea, headed by an Under-Secretary-General for Ocean Affairs and the Law of the Sea and Special Representative of the Secretary-General for the Law of the Sea. This position was

---

[2] UNGA Res A/49/28 (1994) [1]. Note that General Assembly resolutions are available at <http://www.un.org/documents/resga.htm>. Law of the sea resolutions can also be easily accessed at <http://www.un.org/Depts/los/general_assembly/general_assembly_resolutions.htm>.

[3] SN Nandan, 'UNCLOS Anniversary: What are the Challenges?' (2012) 106 *American Society of International Law Proceedings* 400, 402.

held by Bernardo Zuleta of Colombia from 1974 to 1983. He was succeeded by Satya Nandan of Fiji, who held the position until 1992, when his office was integrated into the United Nations Office of Legal Affairs and became the DOALOS. This Office is now the focal point for law of the sea matters within the UN system.

After the adoption of the LOSC, an important function of these offices was to be the secretariat servicing the Preparatory Commission for the International Seabed Authority and for the International Tribunal for the Law of the Sea (ITLOS), established by the Conference.[4] On 3 December 1982, the General Assembly, *inter alia*, approved the assumption by the Secretary-General of the responsibilities entrusted to him under the LOSC and related resolutions. It also approved the stationing of an adequate number of Secretariat staff in Kingston, Jamaica, for the purpose of servicing the Preparatory Commission as required by its functions and programme of work.[5]

3 Informal Consultations Relating to the Implementation of Part XI of the LOSC

In July 1990, Secretary-General Perez de Cuellar convened a series of informal consultations to address certain difficulties with the seabed mining provisions contained in Part XI of the LOSC. The purpose was to achieve universal participation in the Convention, a goal that by then had become formally set up by the General Assembly.[6] However, concerns had been raised, primarily by the industrialized countries, and the Secretary-General acknowledged that there were problems with some aspects of the deep seabed mining provisions of the Convention, which had prevented some States from ratifying or acceding to it. He noted that, in the eight years that had elapsed since the Convention was adopted, certain significant political and economic changes had occurred which had had a marked effect on the regime for deep seabed mining contained in the Convention.[7]

These informal consultations took place between 1990 and 1994. During this period, 15 meetings were convened, the two last held from 4 to 8 April 1994 and

---

[4] See Final Act of the Third United Nations Conference on the Law of the Seas, Annex I, available at <http://www.un.org/depts/los/convention_agreements/texts/final_act_eng.pdf> (hereinafter Final Act).

[5] UNGA Res A/37/66 (1982).   [6] UNGA Res A/44/26 (1989) [3].

[7] United Nations Secretary General, *Consultation of the Secretary-General on outstanding issues relating to the deep seabed mining provisions of the United Nations Convention on the law of the sea: Report of the Secretary General to the General Assembly,* UN Doc A/48/950 (1994) [2].

from 31 May to 3 June 1994. It was the privilege of the author of this chapter, who had joined the UN Secretariat on 6 March 1994, to conduct these last two consultations on behalf of the Secretary-General. A striking feature of these last rounds of consultations was the spirit of cooperation that was demonstrated by the delegates. The fact that the Convention would enter into force on 16 November the same year introduced a sense of urgency into the consultations. There were different informal groups that were active in the consultations. In particular, mention should be made of the contribution of the 'Boat Paper Group', chaired by Ambassador Satya Nandan of Fiji, who in his earlier capacity (see Section 2 of this chapter), had convinced the Secretary-General to initiate the informal consultations.

The consultations were successful and, on 28 July 1994, the General Assembly adopted the resulting Agreement Relating to the Implementation of Part XI of the United Nations Convention on the Law of the Sea of 10 December 1982 (1994 Implementation Agreement).[8] The Agreement entered into force on 28 July 1996.[9]

4 Establishing the Convention Institutions after the Entry into Force of the LOSC

4.1 The role of the United Nations Secretariat

According to Article 308(1) of the LOSC, the Convention would enter into force 12 months after the date of deposit of the sixtieth instrument of ratification or accession. When, on 16 November 1993, the LOSC received the sixtieth instrument of ratification or accession (Guyana), it was clear that the Convention would enter into force on 16 November 1994. This led to an intensification of the work in the UN Secretariat, focusing mainly on the establishment of the Convention institutions.

The three institutions established by the LOSC—the International Seabed Authority; the International Tribunal for the Law of the Sea; and the Commission on the Limits of the Continental Shelf—are examined in Chapter 17. However, it is important in this context to briefly describe the role of the United Nations

---

[8] UNGA Res A/48/263 (1993).
[9] A comprehensive description of this process is available on the website of DOALOS, at <http://www.un.org/Depts/los/index.htm>.

Secretariat in the establishment of these institutions. This was quite an undertaking from an administrative point of view.

4.2 The International Seabed Authority

As already mentioned, a Preparatory Commission for the International Seabed Authority and for the International Tribunal for the Law of the Sea was established by UNCLOS III. Its first meeting was held in Kingston, Jamaica, in March 1983 and, over the years, the Commission met on several occasions, reporting regularly to the General Assembly, which, in a consecutive number of resolutions, recognized the work of the Committee. Jose Lui Jesus, later Judge and President of ITLOS, chaired the Preparatory Commission from 1987 to 1994. This Commission was now serviced by DOALOS.

The International Seabed Authority was the first among the three institutions to be established. In preparation for this, the United Nations Office of Legal Affairs had established a local office in Kingston. The purposes of this local office were to support the Preparatory Commission and to prepare for a seamless handover to the International Seabed Authority the moment the LOSC entered into force. The Authority was therefore established on 16 November 1994 in the presence of UN Secretary-General Boutros Boutros-Ghali. In June 1996, the Authority took over the UN premises and facilities in Kingston and became fully operational as an autonomous international organization. Its first Secretary-General was Satya Nandan of Fiji.

The International Seabed Authority is an autonomous international organization through which States parties to the Convention shall, in accordance with the regime for the seabed and ocean floor and subsoil thereof beyond the limits of national jurisdiction (the Area) established in Part XI of the LOSC and the Agreement relating to Part XI, organize and control activities in the Area, in particular with a view to administering the resources of the Area.[10]

4.3 The International Tribunal for the Law of the Sea

As mentioned in Section 4.2 above, the first meeting of the Preparatory Commission took place in March 1983. During consecutive meetings, the Commission discussed all issues pertaining to the establishment and operation of the ITLOS.

---

[10] The website of the Authority contains detailed information on the organs of the Authority, including the Assembly, Council, Legal and Technical Commission, Finance Committee, and the Secretariat. The site also includes a full list of documents issued by the Authority at each of its sessions, and the full text of selected documents. See International Seabed Authority website, at <http://www.isa.org.jm/en/home>.

The General Assembly had also requested the Secretary-General to appoint an officer to prepare for the establishment of the Tribunal in the Free and Hanseatic City of Hamburg. This task was given to one of the officers of DOALOS, Mr Gritakumar Chitty.[11] Over the next couple of years, an intense interaction took place between the Secretariat and the German authorities and, in particular, the authorities of the host city. The very positive contribution by the First Mayor of Hamburg, Mr Henning Voscherau, should be particularly mentioned.

At the fifth Meeting of States Parties to the Convention, held on 1 August 1996, the first twenty-one Judges of the Tribunal were elected. The Tribunal held its first session from 1 to 31 October 1996 at its seat in Hamburg. The author of the present chapter had the privilege of presiding over the meeting until the election of the President. This occurred on 5 October 1996, when the Judges elected Thomas A. Mensah of Ghana the first President of the Tribunal and Rüdiger Wolfrum of Germany the first Vice-President.[12] On 21 October 1996, the Tribunal appointed Gritakumar Chitty of Sri Lanka as Registrar. The inauguration of the Tribunal took place in the town hall of the Free and Hanseatic City of Hamburg on 18 October 1996 in the presence of UN Secretary-General Boutros Boutros-Ghali and other dignitaries. On 3 July 2000, the official opening of the new building for the permanent headquarters of the Tribunal took place in the presence of UN Secretary-General Kofi Annan.

4.4 The Commission on the Limits of the Continental Shelf

In accordance with the provisions of Article 2 of Annex II to the Convention, 'the Commission shall consist of twenty-one members who shall be experts in the field of geology, geophysics or hydrography, elected by States Parties to the Convention from among their nationals, having due regard to the need to ensure equitable geographical representation, who shall serve in their personal capacities'. The members of the Commission were elected by the sixth Meeting of States parties in March 1997. The first meeting of the Commission was held from 16 to 20 June 1997.[13] At this meeting, serviced by DOALOS,[14] the Commission elected Yuri Borisovitch Kazmin of the Russian Federation as its first Chairman.

[11] UNGA Res A/49/28 (1994) [11].
[12] Reference is made to United Nations Convention on the Law of the Sea, Seventh Meeting of States Parties, Interim Report prepared by the Tribunal, Doc SPLOS/21 (9 May 1997), available at <http://www.itlos.org/fileadmin/itlos/documents/annual_reports/ar_interim_e.pdf>.
[13] *Statement by the Chairman of the Commission on the Limits of the Continental Shelf of the Progress on the Work in the Commission*, Doc CLCS/1 (30 June 1997), available at <http://www.un.org/depts/los/clcs_new/commission_documents.htm#Statements by the Chairman of the Commission>.
[14] 1982 United Nations Convention on the Law of the Sea, Annex II, Art 2(5) (hereinafter LOSC) states: '… The secretariat of the Commission shall be provided by the Secretary-General of the United Nations.'

The initial phase of the work of the Commission was a period when rules of procedure and other provisions were adopted. For the Secretariat, it was also a learning process since the Commission informed the Secretariat of the technical aspects of its work and its need for relevant technical equipment. Thus, a special meeting room was organized with computers and a screen on the wall that the members of the Commission needed for their work, in particular, for discussing among themselves details of submissions by coastal States.

Eventually, the substantive work started, triggered by the first communication that was submitted by the Russian Federation in 2001.[15] Since then, there has been tremendous development. The workload of the Commission and DOALOS has increased so dramatically that it has given cause for concern including within the General Assembly.[16]

The General Assembly is following the work of the Commission with great attention, noting the importance of the delineation of the outer limits of the continental shelf beyond 200 nautical miles and that it is in the broader interest of the international community that coastal States with such a shelf submit information on its outer limits. The Assembly has also welcomed the submissions to the Commission by a considerable number of States parties in this respect and that the Commission has continued to fulfil its role, including of making recommendations to coastal States, and that the summaries of recommendations be made publicly available.[17]

Currently, the list of submissions to the Commission contains 70 entries, of which a limited number have generated recommendations by the Commission. The status of submissions through the Secretary-General to the Commission pursuant to Article 76(8) of the LOSC appears on the website of DOALOS.[18]

At the request of the General Assembly, the Secretary-General has also established two trust funds. The first is for the purpose of defraying the cost associated with the participation of developing States Members of the Commission in the meetings of the Commission.[19] The purpose of the second fund is to assist developing States in the preparation of submissions to the Commission where their continental shelves extend beyond 200 nautical miles.[20]

---

[15] See DOALOS, 'Outer Limits of the Continental Shelf beyond 200 Nautical Miles from the Baselines: Submissions to the Commission: Submission by the Russian Federation' (20 December 2001), available at <http://www.un.org/Depts/los/clcs_new/submissions_files/submission_rus.htm>.

[16] See eg UNGA Res A/68/70 (2013) [69].   [17] Ibid, [63]–[67].

[18] See DOALOS, Submissions, through the Secretary-General of the United Nations, to the Commission on the Limits of the Continental Shelf, pursuant to article 76, paragraph 8, of the LOSC, available at <http://www.un.org/Depts/los/clcs_new/commission_submissions.htm>.

[19] UNGA Res A/55/7 (2000) [20].   [20] Ibid, [18].

5 The Division for Ocean Affairs and the Law of the Sea

In the present chapter, there are numerous references to the DOALOS of the United Nations Office of Legal Affairs. The simple reason for this is that this Division plays a key role in the law of the sea work within the United Nations system. This fact also explains why there are so many references in resolutions by the General Assembly and other bodies to DOALOS. For the sake of completeness, it is therefore appropriate to refer in this context to the provision that lays down the responsibilities of the Division, namely Section 9 of Secretary-General's Bulletin ST/SGB/2008/13, entitled 'Organization of the Office of Legal Affairs'.[21]

The following elements of the detailed provision on the responsibilities of DOALOS are of particular interest in this context:

- providing to States and intergovernmental organizations a range of legal and technical services, such as advice, studies, assistance, and research and information on the application of LOSC, the Agreement relating to the implementation of Part XI of the LOSC (see Section 3 above) and the Agreement for the implementation of LOSC relating to the conservation and management of straddling fish stocks and highly migratory fish stocks (see Section 9 below) with a view to promoting a better understanding of the LOSC and the implementing Agreements, their wider acceptance, uniform, and consistent application and effective implementation;

- providing substantive servicing to the General Assembly on the law of the sea and ocean affairs, including the United Nations open-ended informal consultative process (see Section 11 below); the meeting of States parties to the LOSC (see Section 8 below); and to the Commission on the Limits of the Continental Shelf (see Section 4.4 above);

- monitoring and reviewing developments in ocean affairs and the law of the sea and reporting thereon to the General Assembly through comprehensive annual reports on oceans and the law of the sea and fisheries-related issues, as well as special reports on specific topics of current interest;

- providing support to the organizations of the United Nations system to facilitate consistency with the LOSC of the instruments and programmes in their respective areas of competence;

---

[21] UN Secretary-General, 'Organization of the Office of Legal Affairs', *Secretary-General's bulletin*, Doc ST/SGB/1997/5 (1 August 2008), available at <http://legal.un.org/ola/media/st-sgb-2008-13.pdf>.

- discharging the responsibilities, other than depositary functions, of the Secretary-General under the LOSC and the UN Fish Stocks Agreement (see Section 9 below);
- conducting monitoring and research activities and maintaining a comprehensive information system and research library on the Convention and on the law of the sea and ocean affairs; and
- providing training, fellowships and technical assistance in the field of the law of the sea and ocean affairs.

Reference is here made specifically to the information on the website of DOALOS under the title 'Technical assistance provided by the Division for Ocean Affairs and the Law of the Sea'.[22]

All in all, it is fair to say that DOALOS is a key actor and a focal point in the work of the United Nations system relating to the law the sea. The interaction between the Division and the three organs established by the LOSC, with the Meeting of the States Parties, and with the UN General Assembly is intense. At the same time, the work is extremely interesting and rewarding. This also reflects on the work of the UN Legal Counsel who is charged with overseeing the Division. During ten years as the UN Legal Counsel the author of this chapter found the work relating to the law of the sea, and in particular the period during which the three institutions under the LOSC were established, very stimulating and challenging. It is important that DOALOS is provided with sufficient resources so that it can continue its work also in the future. After all, the seas represent some 70 per cent of the surface of the globe. It is extremely important that this area is administered effectively and competently by all those who are engaged in law the sea matters.

6 UNITED NATIONS CONFERENCES ON THE HUMAN ENVIRONMENT

It must be understood that the work performed by the United Nations in the field of the law of the sea has to be viewed against the background of the United Nations conferences on the human environment and the declarations and other documents adopted at these conferences. In this context, the following conferences

---

[22] See DOALOS, Technical Assistance provided by the Division for Ocean Affairs and the Law of the Sea, available at <http://www.un.org/Depts/los/TechAsst.htm>.

deserve to be mentioned specifically, namely the United Nations Conference on the Human Environment (Stockholm, 1972), the Conference on Environment and Development (Rio de Janeiro, 1992), the World Summit on Sustainable Development (Johannesburg, 2002), and the Rio+20 Conference on Sustainable Development (Rio de Janeiro, 2012).

From the declarations and other documents adopted at these conferences the following elements deserve particular attention.

6.1 Declaration of the United Nations Conference on the Human Environment

The Stockholm Conference adopted 25 principles to inspire and guide the peoples of the world in the preservation and enhancement of the human environment.[23]

Of particular importance in a law of the sea context is Principle 2 according to which the natural resources of the earth, including the air, water, land, flora and fauna, and especially representative samples of natural ecosystems, must be safeguarded for the benefit of present and future generations and that this must be done through careful planning or management, as appropriate.

The need to protect the seas from pollution is another example. According to Principle 7, States 'shall take all possible steps' to prevent such pollution by substances that are liable to create hazards to human health or to harm living resources and marine life or to damage amenities or to interfere with other legitimate uses of the sea.

The role of international organizations is also emphasized. Principle 25 requires that States shall ensure that such organizations play a coordinated, efficient, and dynamic role for the protection and improvement of the environment.

Principle 21 with its reference to the UN Charter and the principles of international law should also be mentioned here. The point of departure is that States have the sovereign right to exploit their own resources pursuant to their own environmental policies. However, in exercising this right, they also have a responsibility to ensure that activities within their jurisdiction or control do not cause damage to the environment of other States or of areas beyond the limits of national jurisdiction.

---

[23] *Report on the United Nations Conference on the Human Environment, Stockholm 5–16 June 1972*, UN Doc A/CONF/48/14/REV.1 (1972) ch 1.

6.2 The Rio Declaration on Environment and Development and Agenda 21

From the 27 principles adopted by the Rio Conference, the following elements are of particular interest in this context, namely that activities within the jurisdiction or control of States should not cause damage to the environment of other States or in areas beyond the limits of national jurisdiction (Principle 2); eradication of poverty as an indispensable requirement for sustainable development (Principle 5); the notion that States have 'common but differentiated responsibilities' (Principle 7); the idea that environmental measures addressing transboundary or global environmental problems should, as far as possible, be based on an international consensus (Principle 12); and the application of the precautionary approach to protect the environment, the 'polluter pays principle' and the importance of environmental impact assessment (Principles 15–17).[24]

The Conference also adopted an international programme of action for global sustainable development for the twenty-first century, commonly referred to as Agenda 21. Of particular importance here is Chapter 17 of the Agenda on protection of the oceans, all kinds of seas, including enclosed and semi-enclosed seas, coastal areas, and the protection, rational use, and development of their living resources.[25]

6.3 The Johannesburg Declaration on Sustainable Development and the Plan of Implementation of the World Summit on Sustainable Development

The conference in Johannesburg, often referred to the 'World Summit', adopted the Johannesburg Declaration on Sustainable Development.[26] This Declaration is also relevant in this context. Most importantly, it contains a commitment to the Plan of Implementation of the World Summit on Sustainable Development and to expediting the achievement of the targets in the Plan.[27] The actions necessary within the area of the law of the sea are addressed in paragraphs 30–36 of the Plan of Implementation.[28] In particular, States are invited to ratify or accede to and implement the LOSC and to promote the implementation of Chapter 17 of Agenda 21.

---

[24] *Report of the United Nations Conference on Environment and Development, Rio de Janeiro, 3–14 June 1992*, UN Doc A/CONF.151/26 (Vol I) (1992) Annex 1.

[25] United Nations Sustainable Development, Agenda 21, available at <http://sustainabledevelopment.un.org/content/documents/Agenda21.pdf>.

[26] *Report of the World Summit on Sustainable Development (Johannesburg, South Africa, 26 August– 2 September 2002)* UN Doc A/CONF.199/20, Res 1.

[27] Ibid, [6].   [28] Ibid.

6.4 The Rio+20 United Nations Conference on Sustainable Development and *The Future We Want*

The Outcome Document adopted by the Rio+20 Conference in 2012 is entitled *The future we want*. Of particular interest here is the part under the title 'Oceans and Seas' (paragraphs 158–77). Extensive references are made to this part by the General Assembly following its endorsement of the document.[29]

6.5 The relationship between the documents adopted by the United Nations Conferences on the Human Environment and the LOSC

As it appears, the documents adopted by the United Nations conferences on the human environment have a direct bearing on the LOSC and the work performed on the basis of the provisions of the Convention. The principles adopted are always borne in mind by the organs established by the Convention and also by other bodies dealing with law of the sea matters. The UN General Assembly should be mentioned in particular. A study of the resolutions adopted by the General Assembly through the years demonstrates that there are extensive references to the declarations and other documents adopted by the United Nations conferences on the human environment. The references to the Rio+20 Conference document *The future we want* just mentioned is a good example.[30]

7 THE ROLE OF THE GENERAL ASSEMBLY

From the very outset, the General Assembly became the central organ within the United Nations in dealing with law of the sea matters. At its first session in 1949, the International Law Commission (ILC) included in its provisional list of topics the regime of the high seas and the regime of the territorial sea, which caused the General Assembly to recommend that the ILC include the second of these topics in its list of priorities. After its eighth session in 1956, the ILC presented the result

---

[29] See *The future we want* endorsed by the General Assembly in UNGA Res A/66/288 (2012).
[30] See further Chapter 3 in this volume.

of its work in the form of a set of articles concerning the law of the sea dealing with both the territorial sea and the high seas.[31] The history of the development of the law of the sea is presented in Chapter 1 of the present volume. Suffice it to mention in this context that in 1972 the General Assembly decided to convene the Third United Nations Conference on the Law of the Sea.[32]

The actions of the General Assembly after the adoption of the LOSC in 1982 are dealt with in Section 2 of this chapter. After the entry into force of the Convention, the annual resolutions of the General Assembly under the item 'Law of the Sea' and later 'Oceans and the law of the sea' underwent a great change. The first of these resolutions was adopted on 19 December 1994.[33] In this resolution, the UN Secretary-General was asked to provide services required for the meetings of the States parties to the LOSC and for the Commission on the Limits of the Continental Shelf. Furthermore, the Secretary-General was requested to continue to carry out the responsibilities entrusted to him upon the adoption of the LOSC and to fulfil the functions consequent upon the entry into force of the Convention. In subsequent resolutions, which covered only a few pages, decisions were made in support of the institutions of the LOSC, in particular, the International Seabed Authority.

The mandate given to the UN Secretary-General on 19 December 1994 was refined by the General Assembly in a resolution on 26 November 1997 in which it requested the Secretary-General to continue to carry out the responsibilities entrusted to him in the LOSC and related resolutions of the Assembly.[34] These activities include, *inter alia*:[35]

- preparing annually a comprehensive report for the consideration of the General Assembly on developments relating to ocean affairs and the law of the sea;
- preparing periodically special reports on specific topics such as fisheries, transit problems of the landlocked developing States, or other topics of current interest, including those requested by intergovernmental conferences and bodies, taking into account the provisions of the LOSC;
- developing and maintaining the appropriate facilities for the deposit by States of charts and geographical coordinates concerning maritime zones, including lines of delimitation, and to give due publicity thereto, as required by Articles 16(2), 47(9), 75(2), 76(9), and 84(2) of the LOSC;
- strengthening the existing system for the collection, compilation, and dissemination of information on ocean affairs and the law of the sea and, in cooperation with

---

[31] See *Report of the International Law Commission on the Work of its Eight Session 23 4 July 1956*, UN Doc A/CN.4/104 (1956), available at <http://legal.un.org/ilc/documentation/english/a_cn4_104.pdf>.
[32] UNGA Res A/30/29 (XXVII) (1972). [33] UNGA Res A/49/28 (1994).
[34] UNGA Res A/52/26 (1997). [35] Ibid, [11(a)]–[11(i)].

the relevant international organizations, furthering the development of a centralized system for providing coordinated information and advice;
- undertaking efforts to promote better understanding of the LOSC and the 1994 Implementation Agreement in order to ensure their effective implementation;
- ensuring appropriate responses to requests from States, in particular developing States, for advice and assistance in implementing the provisions of the LOSC and the 1994 Implementation Agreement;
- preparing for and convening the meetings of States parties to the LOSC and providing the necessary services for such meetings, in accordance with the Convention;
- preparing for and convening the meetings of the Commission on the Limits of the Continental Shelf and providing it with the necessary services in accordance with the Convention; and
- strengthening training activities in ocean and coastal area management and development.

Subsequent resolutions by the General Assembly had a fairly limited scope, focusing to a large extent on the duties of the Secretary-General under the LOSC. However, in 2001, the General Assembly concluded that the substance of the item Oceans and the law of the sea had become very comprehensive. As it appears from resolution A/56/12 of 28 November 2001, the Assembly therefore deemed it necessary to structure the material in the resolutions under different headings. Thus, to give an idea of the development of the substance of the topic, the material in this resolution is organized under the following headings: implementation of the Convention; capacity-building; meeting of States parties; settlement of disputes; the Area; effective functioning of the Authority and the Tribunal; the continental shelf; marine science and technology; piracy and armed robbery; safety of navigation; marine environment, marine resources, and sustainable development; underwater cultural heritage; activities of DOALOS; international coordination and cooperation; and trust funds.

The latest resolution of the General Assembly adopted on 9 December 2013 demonstrates a dramatic development with respect to the substance dealt with by the Assembly.[36] In a 48-page document, the substance is organized under 17 titles. In addition to the ones already mentioned in relation to the resolution from 2001, the following topics now appear: the continental shelf and the work of the Commission; maritime safety and security and flag State implementation; marine environment and marine resources; marine biodiversity; 'Regular Process for Global Reporting and Assessment of the State of the Marine Environment, including Socioeconomic Aspects'; and the open-ended informal consultative process on oceans and the law of the sea.

---

[36] UNGA Res A/68/70 (2013).

8 The Meeting of States Parties to the LOSC

Article 319(2)(e) of the LOSC provides that the UN Secretary-General 'shall convene necessary meetings of States Parties in accordance with this Convention'. As previously mentioned, the General Assembly approved that the Secretary-General should assume the responsibilities entrusted to him under the LOSC and related resolutions,[37] and from Section 2 of this chapter it appears that the Secretary-General is obliged to continue preparing for and convening these meetings and providing the necessary services for them in accordance with the Convention.[38]

Among the obligations of these meetings are election of the members of the International Tribunal for the Law of the Sea and the members of the Commission on the Limits of the Continental Shelf. Every year, the meeting also considers the report of the Tribunal and deals with budgetary and administrative questions relating to the Tribunal. Furthermore, the meetings receive information provided by the Secretary-General of the International Seabed Authority and the Chairman of the Commission on the Limits of the Continental Shelf on the activities of these bodies. And, most importantly, the annual report on the law of the sea that the UN Secretary-General delivers to the General Assembly is also sent to the States parties in response to Article 319 of the LOSC.

The first meeting of States parties took place in New York on 21 and 22 November 1994, immediately following the entry into force of the Convention and the establishment of the International Seabed Authority. The meetings are serviced by DOALOS.[39]

9 Sustainable Fisheries and Straddling and Highly Migratory Fish Stocks

On 22 December 1992, the General Assembly decided to convene, in 1993, under the auspices of the United Nations, and in accordance with the mandate agreed upon at

---

[37] UNGA Res A/37/66 (1982) [7].
[38] UNGA Res A/49/28 (1994) [9]–[11]; and UNGA Res A/52/26 (1997) [11].
[39] Further information relating to the Meeting of States Parties appears in Chapter 17 in this volume.

the United Nations Conference on Environment and Development, an intergovernmental conference on straddling and highly migratory fish stocks.[40]

After successful negotiations, the conference was able to adopt the Agreement for the Implementation of the Provisions of the United Nations Convention on the Law of the Sea of 10 December 1982 relating to the Conservation and Management of Straddling Fish Stocks and Highly Migratory Fish Stocks (FSA).[41] The FSA was opened for signature on 4 December 1995. Presently (January 2015) 82 parties have ratified or acceded to the instrument.

Since the adoption of this agreement, the General Assembly has included straddling and highly migratory fish stocks in its agenda as a sub-item under the item relating to the law of the sea, nowadays framed as 'Oceans and the law of the sea'. The resolutions adopted by the General Assembly since then demonstrate a tremendous development, partly in response to the declarations and other documents adopted at the United Nations conferences in Johannesburg in 2002 and in Rio de Janeiro in 2012 (see Section 6 above). While the resolutions in the beginning dealt with fisheries matters in two to three pages, they have now developed into very substantive documents summarizing major yearly deliberations under the sub-item 'Sustainable fisheries, including through the 1995 Agreement for the Implementation of the Provisions of the United Nations Convention on the Law of the Sea of 10 December 1982 relating to the Conservation and Management of Straddling Fish Stocks and Highly Migratory Fish Stocks, and related instruments'.

By way of example, the latest resolution, adopted on 9 December 2013,[42] is a 32-page document addressing in a very comprehensive manner the following substantive elements: achieving sustainable fisheries; implementation of the FSA; related fisheries instruments; illegal, unreported, and unregulated fishing; monitoring, control and surveillance, and compliance and enforcement; fishing overcapacity, large-scale pelagic drift-net fishing, fisheries by-catch and discards; sub-regional and regional cooperation; responsible fisheries in the marine ecosystem; capacity-building; and cooperation within the United Nations system.

In this resolution, the General Assembly deplores the fact that fish stocks, including straddling and highly migratory fish stocks, in many parts of the world are overfished or subject to sparsely regulated and heavy fishing efforts, as a result of, *inter alia*, illegal, unreported, and unregulated fishing, inadequate flag State control and enforcement, including monitoring, control, and surveillance measures, inadequate regulatory measures, harmful fisheries subsidies and overcapacity, as well as inadequate port State control. The Assembly refers in this context to a report of the Food and Agriculture Organization of the United Nations (FAO).[43] The General Assembly

---

[40] UNGA Res A/47/192 (1992).   [41] UNGA Res A/50/24 (1995).
[42] UNGA Res A/68/71 (2013).
[43] United Nations Food and Agriculture Organization (FAO) Fisheries and Aquaculture Department, *The State of World Fisheries and Aquaculture 2012* (FAO Rome 2012).

also expresses particular concern that illegal, unreported, and unregulated fishing constitutes a serious threat to fish stocks and marine habitats and ecosystems, to the detriment of sustainable fisheries as well as the food security and the economies of many States, particularly developing States.

10 Oceans and Coastal Areas Network (UN-Oceans)

The Oceans and Coastal Areas Network (UN-Oceans) stems from the United Nations Conference on Environment and Development—'The Earth Summit'—held in Rio de Janeiro in 1992. As already mentioned, this Conference adopted an international programme of action for global sustainable development for the twenty-first century, commonly referred to as Agenda 21 (see Section 6 above). Chapter 17 of Agenda 21 deals with the protection of the oceans and the protection, rational use, and development of marine living resources. After extensive preparatory work by the UN agencies dealing with oceans and coastal issues, a proposal was made to form an Oceans and Coastal Areas Network. This proposal was endorsed by the United Nations System Chief Executives Board, the highest-level coordination forum of the United Nations system.[44] The result was that on 12 December 2002 the General Assembly invited the UN Secretary-General to establish an effective, transparent, and regular inter-agency coordination mechanism on oceans and coastal issues within the United Nations system.[45]

The objective of the UN-Oceans Network is to enhance cooperation and coordination among secretariats of the international organizations and bodies concerned with ocean related activities. The UN-Oceans has recognized the requirement for effective coordination and cooperation at the origin of the establishment of the Network and the strong connection with the open-ended informal consultative process on oceans and the law of the sea (see Section 11 below).

The terms of reference for the UN-Oceans are as follows:

- strengthening coordination and cooperation of the UN activities related to ocean and coastal areas;

---

[44] *Report of the High-level Committee on Programmes on its twenty-fourth session New York, 3 to 5 October 2012*, UN Doc CEB/2012/6 (2012).
[45] UNGA Res A/57/141 (2002).

- reviewing the relevant programmes and activities of the UN system, undertaken as part of their contribution to the implementation of the LOSC, Agenda 21, and the Johannesburg Plan of Implementation (see Section 6 above);
- identification of emerging issues, the definition of joint actions, and the establishment of specific task teams to deal with these, as appropriate;
- promoting the integrated management of ocean at the international level;
- facilitating as appropriate, the inputs to the annual report of the Secretary-General on oceans and the law of the sea; and
- promoting the coherence of the UN system activities on oceans and coastal areas with the mandates of the General Assembly, and the priorities contained in the Millennium Development Goals and the Johannesburg Plan of Implementation and of governing bodies of all UN-Oceans members.

UN-Oceans has agreed to operate as a flexible mechanism to review joint and overlapping on-going activities and to support related deliberations of the open-ended informal consultative process on oceans and the law of the sea, coordinating as far as possible its meetings with the sessions of this process (see Section 11 below). The participation in UN-Oceans appears on its website.[46] With respect to officers and secretariat it has been decided that there shall be a coordinator and a deputy coordinator and that the agency serving as coordinator will also serve as the secretariat for UN-Oceans for the period of the coordinator's term.

11 THE UNITED NATIONS OPEN-ENDED INFORMAL CONSULTATIVE PROCESS ON OCEANS AND THE LAW OF THE SEA

In 1999, an important development occurred when the General Assembly instituted the United Nations open-ended informal consultative process on oceans and the law of the sea.[47] The background was that the General Assembly had come to the conclusion that it was important to maintain the integrity of the LOSC through the annual consideration and review of ocean affairs and the law of the sea by the Assembly 'as the global institution having the competence to

---

[46] See UN-Oceans website, at <http://www.unoceans.org/>.
[47] UNGA Res A/54/33 (2000).

undertake such a review'. At the same time, the Assembly was convinced of the need, building on existing arrangements, for an integrated approach to all legal, economic, social, environmental, and other relevant aspects of oceans and seas, and the need to improve coordination and cooperation at both the intergovernmental and inter-agency levels. Therefore, the General Assembly endorsed recommendations made by the Commission on Sustainable Development through the Economic and Social Council under the sectoral theme of 'Oceans and seas' regarding international coordination and cooperation, and decided to establish an open-ended informal consultative process.[48] The purpose of this process should be to facilitate the annual review by the Assembly, in an effective and constructive manner, of developments in ocean affairs by considering the Secretary-General's report on oceans and the law of the sea and by suggesting particular issues to be considered by it. The emphasis should be on identifying areas where coordination and cooperation at the intergovernmental and inter-agency levels should be enhanced.

It was decided that the meetings would be open to all UN Member States and States Members of the specialized agencies, all parties to the LOSC, entities that had received a standing invitation to participate as observers in the work of the General Assembly pursuant to its relevant resolutions, and intergovernmental organizations with competence in ocean affairs.

It was also decided that the meetings would take place for one week each year and that the first meeting should be held from 30 May to 2 June 2000. The meetings

- would deliberate on the Secretary-General's report on oceans and the law of the sea, with due account given to any particular resolution or decision of the General Assembly, any relevant special reports of the Secretary-General and any relevant recommendations of the Commission on Sustainable Development;
- should, in identifying areas where coordination and cooperation are to be enhanced, bear in mind the differing characteristics and needs of the different regions of the world, and should not pursue legal or juridical coordination among the different legal instruments;
- would be coordinated by two co-chairpersons to be appointed by the President of the General Assembly in consultation with Member States and taking into account the need for representation from developed and developing countries.[49]

---

[48] See Commission on Sustainable Development, 'Report on the Seventh Session' (1999) *Official Records of the Economic and Social Council*, Suppl No 9 (E/1999/29) ch I, § C, Decision 7/1, [37]–[45], available at <http://www.un.org/documents/ecosoc/docs/1999/e1999-29.htm>.

[49] UNGA A/Res/54/33 (2000) [3].

An important element in the decision was that the format of the informal consultative process should ensure the opportunity to receive input from representatives of the major groups as identified in Agenda 21, in particular through the organization of discussion panels. The process would be supported by DOALOS in cooperation with other relevant parts of the Secretariat, including the Division for Sustainable Development of the Department of Economic and Social Affairs, as appropriate. The importance of the participation of developing countries, including least developed countries and small island developing States, in the consultative process was emphasized.

Since 1999, these informal consultations have provided extremely important input and ideas for the work of the General Assembly, bearing also on the activities of the other agencies involved. Over the years, the participants in the process have considered a number of specific items. Among these items are the following:

- marine science and the development and transfer of marine technology as mutually agreed, including capacity-building in this regard;
- coordination and cooperation in combating piracy and armed robbery at sea;
- protection and preservation of the marine environment;
- capacity-building, regional cooperation and coordination, and integrated ocean management, as important cross-cutting issues to address ocean affairs, such as marine science and transfer of technology, sustainable fisheries, the degradation of the marine environment, and the safety of navigation;
- protecting vulnerable marine ecosystems;
- the safety of navigation; for example, capacity-building for the production of nautical charts;
- new sustainable uses of the oceans, including the conservation and management of the biological diversity of the seabed in areas beyond national jurisdiction;
- fisheries and their contribution to sustainable development;
- marine debris;
- ecosystem approaches and oceans;
- marine genetic resources;
- maritime security and safety;
- capacity-building in ocean affairs and the law of the sea, including marine science;
- marine renewable energies; and
- impacts of ocean acidification on the marine environment.

The fifteenth meeting of this informal consultative process was held between 27 and 30 May 2014 and focused on the role of seafood in global food security.

12 The Regular Process

An important development occurred in 2002, when the General Assembly decided to establish the so-called Regular Process. The Process has its roots in the World Summit on Sustainable Development, held in Johannesburg in 2002 (see Section 6 above). In the Johannesburg Plan of Implementation, States agreed to 'establish by 2004 a regular process under the United Nations for global reporting and assessment of the state of the marine environment, including socio-economic aspects, both current and foreseeable, building on existing regional assessments' (the 'Regular Process'). On 12 December 2002, this agreement was endorsed by the General Assembly,[50] and the Secretary-General was requested to prepare proposals on modalities for a regular process for the global reporting and assessment of the state of the marine environment, drawing, *inter alia*, upon the work of the United Nations Environment Programme (UNEP) and taking into account a recently completed review by the Joint Group of Experts on the Scientific Aspects of Marine Environmental Protection (GESAMP), and to submit these proposals to the General Assembly.[51]

During the preparatory phase, the Secretary-General was requested to convene a group of experts to produce a draft document with details on various components of the process. In March 2004 the group of experts recommended that an 'Assessment of Assessments' be undertaken as part of the start-up phase of the Regular Process. International workshops were organized, and, on 29 November 2005, the General Assembly launched the start-up phase to the Regular Process, called the 'Assessment of Assessments'.[52] An Ad Hoc Steering Group to oversee the execution of the 'Assessment of Assessments' was established. UNEP and the Intergovernmental Oceanographic Commission of the United Nations Educational, Scientific and Cultural Organization (UNESCO) were asked to lead the process. A Group of Experts was appointed and charged with undertaking the actual work of assessing the various assessments. The result of the 'Assessment of Assessments' was presented in 2009.[53]

---

[50] UNGA Res A/57/141 (2002).

[51] An elaborate description of the Regular Process and its background is available on the website of DOALOS. See *A Regular Process for Global Reporting and Assessment of the State of the Marine Environment, including Socio-economic Aspects*, available at <http://www.un.org/Depts/los/global_reporting/global_reporting.htm>.

[52] UNGA Res A/60/30 (2005) [90]–[96].

[53] See *Regular process for global reporting and assessment of the state of the marine environment, including socio-economic aspects: the 'assessment of assessments'*, UN Doc A/64/88 (2009), available at <http://www.un.org/ga/search/view_doc.asp?symbol=A%2F64%2F88&Submit=Search&Lang=E>.

An Ad Hoc Working Group of the Whole had been established to recommend a course of action at the sixty-fourth session of the General Assembly based on the outcomes of the review by the Ad Hoc Steering Group of the completed 'Assessment of Assessments' report.[54] On 4 December 2009, the General Assembly endorsed the recommendations adopted by the Ad Hoc Working Group of the Whole.[55] Since then intense work has been put into the process, including with informal meetings and several workshops in different parts of the world.

The Regular Process is accountable to the General Assembly. It is an intergovernmental process guided by international law, including the LOSC and other applicable international instruments, and takes into account relevant General Assembly resolutions. In addition, it is overseen and guided by the Ad Hoc Working Group of the Whole of the General Assembly composed of member States. DOALOS provides secretariat support to the Process, including its established institutions. Technical and scientific support is provided by the Intergovernmental Oceanographic Commission of UNESCO, UNEP, the International Maritime Organization, FAO, and other competent United Nations specialized agencies. The Group of Experts is an integral part of the Process. Among other things, it provides guidelines for the experts who will contribute to the first global integrated marine assessment. The Group has estimated that a total of around 1,500–2,000 experts would be needed for the preparation of the first global integrated marine assessment due at the end of 2014.

On 10 December 2012, the General Assembly adopted the outline for the first global integrated marine assessment of the Regular Process and the terms of reference and working methods for the Group of Experts.[56] Furthermore, the General Assembly requested the secretariat of the Regular Process to send the first draft of the first global integrated marine assessment to member States for comments from June to August 2014. This assessment will be revised by the Group of Experts in the light of the comments received. Once revised, the draft will be presented to the Bureau of the Ad Hoc Working Group of the Whole together with the comments received. With the approval of the Bureau, the assessment will be transmitted for consideration by the Working Group and for final approval by the General Assembly in 2015.[57]

---

[54] Ibid.   [55] UNGA Res A/64/71 (2009) [174]–[177].
[56] UNGA Res A/67/78 (2012) [221]–[222].
[57] The Regular Process has established a website which contains general information on the Process as well as specific information on the development of the first global integrated marine assessment, or 'World Ocean Assessment', see <www.worldoceanassessment.org>.

13 Conservation and Sustainable Use of Marine Biodiversity in Areas beyond National Jurisdiction

One of the latest developments in the work of the United Nations in the field of the law of the sea is the question of the conservation and sustainable use of marine biodiversity in areas beyond national jurisdiction.[58] On 17 November 2004, the General Assembly decided to establish an ad hoc open-ended informal working group to study issues relating to this topic. The mandate given to the group was:

- to survey the past and present activities of the United Nations and other relevant international organizations with regard to the conservation and sustainable use of marine biological diversity beyond areas of national jurisdiction;
- to examine the scientific, technical, economic, legal, environmental, socio-economic, and other aspects of these issues;
- to identify key issues and questions where more detailed background studies would facilitate consideration by States of these issues; and
- to indicate, where appropriate, possible options and approaches to promote international cooperation and coordination for the conservation and sustainable use of marine biological diversity beyond areas of national jurisdiction.[59]

On 24 December 2011, the General Assembly decided to initiate, within the working group, a process with a view to ensuring that the legal framework for the conservation and sustainable use of marine biodiversity in areas beyond national jurisdiction effectively addresses those issues. This should be done by identifying gaps and ways forward, including through the implementation of existing instruments and the possible development of a multilateral agreement under the LOSC. Matters to be addressed in this process will include: the conservation and sustainable use of marine biodiversity in areas beyond national jurisdiction, in particular marine genetic resources, including questions on the sharing of benefits; measures such as area-based management tools, including marine protected areas; and environmental impact assessments, capacity-building, and the transfer of marine technology. The Assembly also decided that the process should take place within the existing working group and, in addition, in the format of inter-sessional workshops aimed at improving understanding of the issues and clarifying key questions as an input to the work of the working group.[60]

---

[58] See further Chapter 34 in this volume.
[59] UNGA Res A/59/24 (2004) [73].
[60] UNGA Res A/66/231 (2011) [167].

The latest development is reflected in the report of the working group from its meeting in August 2013 and the resolution by the General Assembly on 9 December 2013.[61] In this resolution, the General Assembly reaffirmed the commitment made by States in *The future we want* (see Section 6 above) to address, on an urgent basis, building on the work of the working group and, before the end of the sixty-ninth session of the Assembly, the issue of the conservation and sustainable use of marine biological diversity of areas beyond national jurisdiction, including by taking a decision on the development of an international instrument under the LOSC. The General Assembly thus charged the working group with preparing within its existing mandate for a decision to be taken at that session of the Assembly, and to make recommendations to the Assembly, on the scope, parameters, and feasibility of an international instrument under the LOSC.

14 Piracy on the Agenda of the Security Council

Unlike the General Assembly, the Security Council has not over the years addressed specifically matters relating to the law of the sea. The reason is the manner in which the UN Charter lays down the competence of the two organs; in contrast to the General Assembly, the Security Council's mandate focuses more narrowly on the maintenance of international peace and security. However, precisely because of this, the acts of piracy in recent years off the coast of Somalia have caused the Council to adopt a number of resolutions relating to that situation. Reference is made to the enumeration by the General Assembly in its law of the sea resolution of 9 December 2013.[62]

Maritime security and piracy are dealt with in Chapters 25 and 37 in this volume. However, the following brief presentation is of the essence in the present context.

In the several resolutions adopted by the Security Council since 2008 relating to piracy off the coast of Somalia, the Council has expressed grave concern over the threat that acts of piracy and armed robbery against vessels pose to the prompt, safe, and effective delivery of humanitarian aid to Somalia, to the safety of commercial maritime routes, and to international navigation. The Council has also affirmed that

---

[61] *Letter dated 23 September 2013 from the Co-Chairs of the Ad Hoc Open-ended Informal Working Group to the President of the General Assembly*, UN Doc A/68/399 (2013) and UNGA Res A/68/70 (2013) [194]–[201].

[62] UNGA Res A/68/70 (2013) [105].

international law, as reflected in the LOSC, sets out the legal framework applicable to combating piracy and armed robbery, as well as other ocean activities. In addition, the Council has affirmed that relevant provisions of international law provide guiding principles for cooperation to the fullest possible extent in the repression of piracy on the high seas or in any other place outside the jurisdiction of any State, 'including but not limited to boarding, searching, and seizing vessels engaged in or suspected of engaging in acts of piracy, and to apprehending persons engaged in such acts with a view to such persons being prosecuted'.[63]

Acting under Chapter VII of the UN Charter, the Council has also urged States whose naval vessels and military aircraft operate on the high seas and airspace off the coast of Somalia to be vigilant to acts of piracy and armed robbery and, in this context, encouraged States to increase and coordinate their efforts to deter acts of piracy and armed robbery at sea in cooperation with the Transitional Federal Government of Somalia.[64] Of particular interest in this context is that the Council has decided that States cooperating with the Transitional Federal Government in the fight against piracy and armed robbery at sea off the coast of Somalia, for which advance notification has been provided by the Transitional Government to the Secretary-General, may enter the territorial waters of Somalia for the purpose of repressing acts of piracy and armed robbery at sea, in a manner consistent with such action permitted on the high seas with respect to piracy under relevant international law.[65] On the same conditions, they are also authorized to use all necessary means to repress acts of piracy and armed robbery within the territorial waters of Somalia.[66]

At the same time, the Council has affirmed that the authorization in the resolutions that contain these provisions apply only to the situation in Somalia and do not affect the rights, obligations or responsibilities of member States under international law, including any rights or obligations under the LOSC, with respect to any other situation, and underscores, in particular, the fact these resolutions are not to be considered as establishing customary international law.[67]

The Council resolutions also contain provisions on information sharing, various forms of assistance, and cooperation in many fields, including in determining jurisdiction, and in the investigation and prosecution of persons responsible for acts of piracy and armed robbery off the coast of Somalia.

Finally in this context reference should be made to a letter dated 23 March 2012 from the UN Secretary-General to the President of the Security Council in response to a request from the Council in resolution 2015 (2011). The letter contains a compilation of information received from member States on measures they have taken to criminalize piracy under their domestic law and to support the prosecution of

---

[63] See eg UNSC Res 1816 (2008).   [64] Ibid.   [65] Ibid.   [66] Ibid.
[67] See eg UNSC Res 2125 (2013) [13].

individuals suspected of piracy off the coast of Somalia and imprisonment of convicted pirates.[68] The request by the Council should be seen against the background of the concern that the Council has expressed that the domestic law of a number of States lacks provisions criminalizing piracy and/or procedural provisions for effective criminal prosecution of suspected pirates.

15 Concluding Observations

As it appears from the foregoing discussion, the United Nations has been deeply involved in matters relating to the law of the sea almost since the Organization was established in 1945. Today, a wide-ranging number of components related to an area that covers 70 per cent of the surface of the globe are dealt with under the item Oceans and the law of the sea on the agenda of the General Assembly.

The traditional law of the sea issues, for example maritime zones and their delimitation are, of course, present in the discussions. However, the manner in which these questions are regulated in the LOSC means that any disputes are settled peacefully by negotiations or through proceedings before the International Court of Justice or the International Tribunal for the Law of the Sea. The existing disputes relating to the South China Sea and the Senkaku/Diaoyu Islands will also be resolved peacefully, provided that the main actors are able to demonstrate the necessary statesmanship.[69]

Interestingly, the law of the sea regime now also applies in areas where maritime activity was not possible in the past, notably in the Arctic. In the media there are often articles referring to the potential disputes over 'territory' in the Arctic where it is obvious that the authors do not understand that the Arctic Ocean is a sea and that the ordinary rules relating to the territorial sea, the exclusive economic zone and the continental shelf are applicable. Basically, the territorial disputes in the Arctic have been resolved with the exception of two cases where no doubt the parties will find solutions.[70] The issues that remain to be resolved relate to the delimitation

---

[68] See *Letter dated 23 March 2012 from the Secretary General to the President of the Security Council*, UN Doc S/2012/177 (2012).

[69] Disputes of this nature should be resolved through negotiations or other methods for peaceful settlement of disputes. To allow those disputes to develop in a manner that the parties resort to the use of force or other hostile acts is wholly irresponsible, not to say unacceptable in a modern world. Ultimately, the responsibility rests with the leaders of the States concerned.

[70] The cases concern Canada and the United States, and Canada and Denmark (Greenland), respectively.

of the exclusive economic zones and the continental shelves of the littoral States. However, since the rules that apply here are clear, there is good reason to conclude that also these issues will be peacefully resolved.[71]

Of greater concern are other aspects relating to the oceans, in particular, the effects generated by pollution, climate change and the overexploitation of marine resources. The outcome of the Regular Process (Section 12 above) will be of great importance here, most likely raising additional concerns. It is therefore to be expected that the work within the United Nations system relating to the law of the sea will be even more intense in the future.

As it appears from the foregoing, it is of crucial importance that the organs within the United Nations system that are responsible for this work are supported and provided with the necessary resources. Capacity building in developing countries is also an important element in this effort.

All this brings to the forefront the overarching issue of the human behaviour on the globe. The status of the oceans must be viewed in a very broad perspective, including through the dimension of international peace and security. It is important that determined efforts are made to protect the oceans in the future against the threats that they are exposed to through human behaviour. Additional efforts must be made to educate the general public and not least those who represent them at the political level about these matters and the need to address them effectively and with determination. If this is not done, there is great risk that the consequences for the future human habitat will be very serious.

---

[71] H Corell, 'The Arctic: An Opportunity to Cooperate and Demonstrate Statesmanship' (2009) 42 *Vanderbilt Journal of Transnational Law* 1065.

17

THE LAW OF THE SEA CONVENTION INSTITUTIONS

JAMES HARRISON

1 Introduction

THE 1982 United Nations Convention on the Law of the Sea (LOSC) is widely recognized as one of the most important treaties negotiated in the twentieth century. A recent intergovernmental meeting to celebrate the thirtieth anniversary of the opening for signature of the Convention recalled 'the historic significance of the Convention as an important contribution to the maintenance of peace, justice and progress for all peoples of the world'.[1] Today, the Convention is acknowledged by almost all States as 'the legal framework within which all activities in the oceans and seas must be carried out'.[2]

The drafters were keenly aware of the need to ensure the durability of the regime they were creating.[3] The sustainability of the Convention as 'the legal order of the

---

[1] States Parties to the UN Convention on the Law of the Sea (SPLOS), *Declaration on the thirtieth anniversary of the opening for signature of the 1982 United Nations Convention on the Law of the Sea*, Doc SPLOS/249 (12 June 2012) Preamble.

[2] See eg UNGA Res 67/78 (2012), Preamble.

[3] See eg Statement of Sri Lanka, 187th plenary meeting, (1984) XVII *Official Records of the Third United Nations Conference on the Law of the Sea* 48, 49–50 [161].

oceans'[4] depends upon its ability to adapt to changes in the legal, political, and technical environment in which it exists. There is little doubt that the work of various international institutions has played a vital role in ensuring the evolution of the Convention since its entry into force. It is largely through international institutions that States have responded to the major challenges of modern maritime affairs.[5] It follows that understanding the mandate and powers of these institutions is therefore a fundamental issue for the contemporary law of the sea.

The purpose of this chapter is to consider the institutional framework that is in place to oversee the implementation and development of the law of the sea regime. In particular, it will focus on the institutions established by the Convention, including the meeting of the States parties to the LOSC (SPLOS), the International Tribunal for the Law of the Sea (ITLOS), the Commission on the Limits of the Continental Shelf (CLCS), and the International Seabed Authority (ISA). The chapter will first consider the drafting history of the institutional framework established by the Convention. It will then explore some of the ambiguities surrounding the mandates of these institutions and how the subsequent practice of States has approached these issues. The institutional framework for overseeing the development of the Convention includes not only these institutions, but also a range of other autonomous institutions with a mandate related to maritime affairs. Therefore, the chapter will also explore the interrelationship between the Convention institutions and other international bodies, asking whether there is a coherent institutional framework in this field of law.

2 Drafting History of the Institutional Provisions in the Law of the Sea Convention

The need for an institutional framework to oversee the implementation and development of the United Nations Convention on the Law of the Sea was recognized at an early stage in the negotiation of the treaty. In the second session of the Third United Nations Conference on the Law of the Sea (UNCLOS III) in 1974, the UN Secretary-General noted in a speech to the plenary that 'the Conference might well consider whether some institutional means should be created whereby, within

---

[4] 1982 United Nations Convention on the Law of the Sea, Preamble (hereinafter LOSC).
[5] See generally J Harrison, *Making the Law of the Sea* (Cambridge University Press Cambridge 2011).

the framework of the new convention, common measures could be agreed upon and taken whenever necessary so as to avoid obsolescence under changing world conditions'.[6]

By referring to the need to avoid obsolescence, the UN Secretary-General probably had in mind the fate of the previous UN Conventions on the Law of the Sea concluded in 1958. Within a relatively short period of time, these treaties became the subject of significant criticism and they were swiftly put to one side in favour of negotiating a brand new legal regime that would accommodate the needs of all States.

At UNCLOS III, the question of the appropriate institutional framework was considered as part of the negotiations on the final provisions. Several proposals were put forward, including the creation of a permanent commission on the law of the sea,[7] a periodic conference on international ocean affairs,[8] and a review conference to take place after a particular period.[9] None of these proposals were, however, able to generate a consensus of delegates.[10] Ultimately, the need to create a mechanism to oversee the implementation and development of the 1982 Convention was accommodated in Article 319, which provides, *inter alia*, that 'the Secretary-General [of the United Nations] shall ... report to all States Parties, the Authority and competent international organizations on issues of a general nature that have arisen with respect to the Convention'.[11] Yet, perhaps because it is the product of compromise, Article 319 is incredibly vague. It neither lists precisely which organizations should receive reports from the UN Secretary-General, nor does it specify the role of these institutions or the division of competence between them. Indeed, a report prepared by the UN Secretary-General to analyse the scope of the reporting functions noted there were serious ambiguities in relation to the frequency, content, and purpose of the reports.[12]

Some clarification was achieved in 1994 when the Convention entered into force, at which time the UN General Assembly requested the UN Secretary-General to prepare 'a comprehensive annual report ... on developments relating to the law of

---

[6] Statement by the UN Secretary-General, 14th meeting (1973–1974) I *Official Records of the Third United Nations Conference on the Law of the Sea* 37, 38 [42].

[7] Peru, 'Proposal regarding an international commission on the law of the sea', Doc A/CONF.62/L.22 (1978) IX *Official Records of the Third United Nations Conference on the Law of the Sea* 180.

[8] Portugal, 'Proposal regarding periodic conferences on international ocean affairs', Doc A/CONF.62/L.23 (1978) IX *Official Records of the Third United Nations Conference on the Law of the Sea* 181.

[9] See Draft Articles prepared by the Chairman of the Group of Legal Experts on Final Clauses, in *Virginia Commentaries*, Vol V, 252–3.

[10] Ibid, 259–60.   [11] LOSC, n 4, Art 319(2)(a).

[12] UN Secretary-General, 'Study on the future functions of the Secretary-General under the draft convention and on the needs of countries, especially developing countries, for information, advice and assistance under the new legal regime', Doc A/Conf.62/L.76 (18 August 1981) XV *Official Records of the Third United Nations Conference on the Law of the Sea* 153, 157 [22]–[26].

the sea'.[13] This report was to be submitted not only to the UN General Assembly, but also to the meeting of States parties and other competent institutions.[14] The report is prepared upon the basis of information provided by States and international organizations, and the UN General Assembly regularly calls for competent international organizations to 'contribute to the preparation of the comprehensive report of the Secretary-General on oceans and the law of the sea'.[15]

While providing some answers on the frequency of reports, the General Assembly resolutions on this topic have not specified the role of the relevant institutions in relation to the report. Rather, this issue has been addressed through the practice of the institutions themselves. This chapter considers the issue from the perspective of the institutions created by the Convention itself and it analyses their relationship with each other, as well as their relationship with the wider network of institutions involved in law of the sea issues.

3 THE MEETING OF THE STATE PARTIES

The States parties are at the centre of the institutional framework created by the 1982 Convention. They are expressly listed in Article 319 as having a right to receive reports from the UN Secretary-General on developments relating to the law of the sea regime.

In this sense, the Convention follows a model utilized by many treaties which establish a body composed of the parties to the treaty as a 'supreme organ'[16] to oversee the future development of the treaty. For example, the 1992 United Nations Framework Convention on Climate Change is typical of many multilateral environmental agreements in establishing a 'Conference of the Parties, as the supreme body of this Convention, [which] shall keep under regular review the implementation of the Convention and any related legal instruments'.[17]

---

[13] See UNGA Res 49/28 (1994) [15(a)]. The resolution also foresees the UN Secretary-General 'preparing periodically special reports on specific topics of current interest'.
[14] Ibid, [15(a)].   [15] See eg UNGA Res 59/24 (2004) [96].
[16] G Ulfstein, 'Treaty Bodies', in D Bodansky, J Brunnée, and E Hey (eds), *Oxford Handbook of International Environmental Law* (Oxford University Press Oxford 2007) 879. See also J Brunnée, 'COPing with consent: Law-making under Multilateral Environmental Agreements' (2002) 15 *Leiden Journal of International Law* 1, 4 n 12.
[17] 1992 United Nations Framework Convention on Climate Change, Art 7(2). See also, eg, 1973 Convention on International Trade in Endangered Species, Art 11; 1992 Convention on Biological Diversity, Art 23 (hereinafter CBD).

Unlike many of these modern treaties, the LOSC does not expressly establish a Conference of the Parties as a supreme organ of the law of the sea regime. Rather, it simply provides that 'the UN Secretary-General shall ... convene necessary meetings of States Parties in accordance with this convention'.[18] Thus, the nature and functions of the States parties are ambiguous.

One ambiguity is how often meetings of the States parties shall take place. In practice, meetings of the States parties take place on an annual basis, usually at the headquarters of the United Nations in New York.[19] Each meeting of the States parties elects its own officers who serve until the next meeting[20] and the meetings are administered by the UN Secretariat.[21] From this perspective, the meeting of the States parties does resemble regular meetings of the parties of other treaties.[22] The more important question is whether it can and should exercise the same sorts of functions as those other treaty bodies.

There are a certain number of functions which are explicitly conferred upon the States parties by the Convention itself and these issues appear as fixed agenda items, dictated by the Rules of Procedure.[23] Such functions largely relate to the election and oversight of other Convention institutions. As will be seen below, the meeting of the States parties has taken an expansive view of its powers in this regard, which has allowed it to flexibly interpret the Convention in order to meet certain challenges that were not foreseen when the Convention was first drafted. On the other hand, it is unclear whether the States parties may play a wider role in overseeing the development of the Convention. This issue has been hotly contested since the Convention entered into force and the various arguments about the precise scope of its functions will be discussed in the sections below.

Another ambiguity in the Convention concerns how the States parties will take decisions when carrying out their functions. As a result, the States parties have been able to design their own decision-making procedures. As a general rule, the meeting of the States parties conducts its business on the basis

---

[18] LOSC, n 4, Art 319(2)(e).   [19] See Harrison, n 5, 71–2.

[20] SPLOS Rules of Procedure, Doc SPLOS/2/Rev.4 (24 January 2005) Rule 19. See also *Report of the Twenty-third Meeting of the States Parties*, Doc SPLOS/263 (10–12 June 2013) [101], at which it was decided that Meeting would be adjourned until the next Meeting takes place. The advantage of this practice is that it means that the Meeting can re-convene to deal with any urgent business without having to reassess the credentials of participants, which would remain valid from the previous meeting.

[21] SPLOS Rules of Procedure, n 20, Rules 25–26. See also UNGA Res 49/28 (1994) [15(g)], authorizing the UN Secretary-General to carry out the functions conferred upon him by the Convention, including 'preparing for and convening the meetings of States parties to the Convention and providing the necessary services for such meetings, in accordance with the Convention'.

[22] See T Treves, 'The Law of the Sea "System" of Institutions' (1998) 2 *Max Planck Yearbook of United Nations Law* 325, 331–2.

[23] SPLOS Rules of Procedure, n 20, Rule 6(c)–(f).

of 'general agreement'.[24] This should be understood as a reference to consensus decision-making, building upon the decision-making processes first developed at UNCLOS III.[25] It is only when all efforts to achieve consensus have been exhausted that the meeting of the States parties may proceed to a vote.[26] In that instance, votes on matters of substance shall be taken by a two-thirds majority of States parties present and voting, provided that such a majority includes a majority of States parties participating in the meeting.[27] These decision-making procedures are designed to ensure that, as far as possible, the development of the law of the sea regime has the support of the whole international community. To date, all decisions of the meeting of States parties have been adopted by consensus.[28] This reflects the success of the States parties to progressively developing the law of the sea regime in a manner that is generally acceptable to all States.[29] Indeed, the decision-making procedures are an important indication of the value that is attached by the States parties to ensuring continued consensual support for the Convention and its future development. This is a factor that is also prominent when analysing the practice of the States parties in exercising its functions under the Convention.

4 The International Tribunal for the Law of the Sea

The International Tribunal for the Law of the Sea is established as a judicial institution by Annex VI of the Convention.[30] However, the Tribunal does not operate completely autonomously from the other institutions established by the Convention. In particular, the States parties are responsible for a number of functions in relation to the Tribunal, including the election of judges and approval of the Tribunal's budget. Yet, the judicial nature of the Tribunal also has implications for the manner in which these two institutions interact.

---

[24] Ibid, Rule 52(1).
[25] See B Buzan, 'Negotiating by Consensus: Developments in technique at the United Nations Conference on the Law of the Sea' (1981) 75 *American Journal of International Law* 324.
[26] SPLOS Rules of Procedure, n 20, Rule 52(2).   [27] Ibid, Rule 53.
[28] The threat of a vote has been used in order to bring about consensus, however. See nn 38–9 and accompanying text.
[29] See the discussion in Sections 4 and 5 below.   [30] See also Chapter 18 of this volume.

4.1 Elections to the International Tribunal for the Law of the Sea

The States parties are responsible for electing members of the Tribunal.[31] Elections take place once every three years.[32] The Convention provides that '[e]lections shall be held at a meeting of the States Parties in the case of the first election and by a procedure to be agreed to by the States Parties in the case of subsequent elections.'[33] In theory, this provision allows some flexibility as to the manner in which elections are held. In practice, however, elections have always been held at meetings of the States parties.[34]

In exercising their function of electing members of the Tribunal, the States parties have also adopted an arrangement for the allocation of seats on the Tribunal.[35] This arrangement gives a substantive content to the requirement in the Convention that the Tribunal as a whole represents 'the principal legal systems of the world and equitable geographical representation'.[36] According to the arrangement adopted by the States parties, seats are divided between the five geographical regions of the United Nations. Originally, it was agreed that five judges would be elected from the African group, five judges from the Asian group, four judges from the Latin American and Caribbean group, four judges from the Western European and Other group, and three judges from the Eastern European group.[37] In 2009, the allocation was modified to reflect the growing number of States parties from Africa and Asia. The new allocation means that the Western European and Other group only has three judges, and the remaining seat is to be elected from amongst the African group, the Asian group, and the Western European and Other group.[38] This decision was achieved after a series of debates, as well as informal consultations led by the President of the meeting. Indeed, when it appeared at the eighteenth meeting of the States parties that consensus was elusive, the States parties adopted a decision that '[the meeting] will have exhausted all efforts to reach a general agreement by the

---

[31] LOSC, n 4, Annex VI, Art 4(4).

[32] Elections take place on a rolling basis so that seven judges are elected every three years; see ibid, Annex VI, Art 5.

[33] Ibid, Annex VI, Art 4(4).

[34] The States parties have also convened special meetings in order to fill vacancies on the Tribunal; see *Report of the Special Meeting of the States Parties*, Doc SPLOS/170 (30 January 2008) (convened to fill the seat vacated by the resignation of Judge Guangjian Xu in 2007); *Report of the Special Meeting of the States Parties*, Doc SPLOS/190 (6 March 2009) (convened to fill the seat vacated by the death of Judge Choon-Ho Park in 2008).

[35] *Arrangement for the Allocation of Seats on the International Tribunal for the Law of the Sea and the Commission on the Limits of the Continental Shelf*, Doc SPLOS/201 (26 June 2009) [1].

[36] LOSC, n 4, Annex VI, Arts 2(2) and 3(2).

[37] *Report of the Fifth Meeting of the States Parties*, Doc SPLOS/14 (24 July–2 August 1996) [15].

[38] *Arrangement for the Allocation of Seats on the International Tribunal for the Law of the Sea and the Commission on the Limits of the Continental Shelf*, Doc SPLOS/201 (26 June 2009) [1].

nineteenth meeting of the States Parties'.[39] Ultimately, consensus was reached at the nineteenth meeting, and no vote was necessary.[40] Thus, this decision demonstrates how the States parties have adapted the LOSC regime to reflect changing dynamics within the international community, while also maintaining the consensus that underpins the law of the sea.

As well as determining the composition of the Tribunal, the States parties have also used their decision-making powers to modify the timing of elections. According to the Convention, the first election to the Tribunal should have taken place within six months of its entry into force.[41] However, it was decided at the very first meeting of the States parties to postpone this election until August 1996.[42] The rationale for the decision was that many States had indicated their intention to ratify or accede to the LOSC and it was deemed to be desirable if they were able to participate in the first election for the Tribunal. Again, this decision provides an example of the States parties using their decision-making powers to ensure widespread support for the Convention and its institutions.

4.2 Financing of the International Tribunal for the Law of the Sea

The States parties are also principally responsible for bearing the expenses of the Tribunal.[43] More generally, the States parties have oversight of the budget of the Tribunal,[44] and this forms a regular item on the agenda of the meeting of the States parties.[45] In this regard, they are involved in determining the salaries, allowances, and compensation of the members of the Tribunal and the Registrar,[46] as well as the conditions of retirement pensions.[47] Decisions on financial and budgetary matters are first considered by an open-ended working group, which makes recommendations to the meeting.[48] In addition, the States parties must take into account a report from the Registrar on the financial and administrative implications of any proposal for the Tribunal.[49] This mechanism allows more detailed consideration to be given to financial decisions, although some States have suggested that the mechanism

---

[39] *Decision on the allocation of seats of the Commission on the Limits of the Continental Shelf and the International Tribunal for the Law of the Sea*, Doc SPLOS/182, [1]. See also *Report of the Eighteenth Meeting of the States Parties*, Doc SPLOS/184 (13–20 June 2008) [100]–[107].

[40] See *Report of the Nineteenth Meeting of the States Parties*, Doc SPLOS/203 (22–26 June 2009) [102].

[41] LOSC, n 4, Annex VI, Art 4(3).

[42] *Report of the First Meeting of the States Parties*, Doc SPLOS/3 (21–22 November 1994) [16].

[43] LOSC, n 4, Annex VI, Art 19(1). [44] Ibid, Annex VI, Art 19(1).

[45] SPLOS Rules of Procedure, n 20, Rule 6(3)(f). [46] LOSC, n 4, Annex VI, Art 18(5)–(6).

[47] Ibid, Annex VI, Art 18(7). [48] SPLOS Rules of Procedure, n 20, Rule 54.

[49] Ibid, Rule 50.

still does not permit sufficient scrutiny.[50] The role of the States parties in relation to the budget of the Tribunal clearly gives it some leverage over the practices of the Tribunal.[51]

Given the judicial nature of the Tribunal, there are also mechanisms in place to limit some of the powers of the States parties in order to uphold the principle of judicial independence. For instance, the Statute of the ITLOS expressly provides that payments to the members of the Tribunal 'may not be decreased during the term of office',[52] meaning that financial pressure cannot be put on judges by the meeting of the States parties.[53] In general, the States parties have sought to maintain parity between the payments for members of the Tribunal and members of the International Court of Justice (ICJ). To this end, the States parties took a decision in 2011 to ensure that adjustments were automatically made to the salaries of the Tribunal members when changes were made to the salaries of ICJ judges.[54] This decision can be seen as a positive development, as it means that decisions about adjusting salaries are removed from the political realm, respecting a key principle of judicial independence.[55] Nor can the States parties remove judges once they have been appointed, as this power belongs solely to the Tribunal itself.[56] This guarantees a certain security of tenure for members of the Tribunal, although this security is limited given that judges may wish to seek re-election after the expiry of their nine-year term.[57]

4.3 Oversight of the judicial work of the International Tribunal for the Law of the Sea

In addition to financial reports, the meeting of the States parties also receives an annual report on the judicial work of the Tribunal.[58] This is an innovation that is

---

[50] At the Twenty-third Meeting of the SPLOS in 2013, the United Kingdom proposed the establishment of a mechanism to scrutinize the budgets of the Tribunal in order to allow more detailed and effective scrutiny of the Tribunal's budgets. It draws upon the practice of other tribunals, which have similar mechanisms; see *Report of the Twenty-third Meeting of the States Parties*, n 20, [41].

[51] Treves, n 23, 331. He gives the example of the States parties only authorizing two meetings of the Tribunal in 1998, when the Tribunal had itself proposed three meetings.

[52] LOSC, n 4, Annex VI, Art 18(5).

[53] It has been argued elsewhere that 'any decision which was designed to decrease the salary or other payments to members of the Tribunal would arguably be ultra vires and without legal effect'; Harrison, n 5, 76.

[54] *Decision on the Adjustment Mechanism for Remuneration of Members of the International Tribunal for the Law of the Sea*, Doc SPLOS/230 (17 June 2011).

[55] See the Burgh House Principles on the Independence of the International Judiciary, [4.3], available at <http://www.ucl.ac.uk/laws/cict/docs/burgh_final_21204.pdf>.

[56] LOSC, n 4, Annex VI, Art 9. As this power must be exercised by unanimity, it is very difficult to remove a Member of the Tribunal.

[57] LOSC, n 4, Annex VI, Art 5.

[58] See *Report of the Fifth Meeting of the States Parties*, n 37, [36]. See also SPLOS Rules of Procedure, n 20, Rule 37.

not foreseen by the Convention. The presentation of a report by the President of the Tribunal provides an opportunity for the States parties to comment on and discuss decisions of the Tribunal, as well as other activities undertaken by the Tribunal, such as training and capacity-building. Yet, such interaction between the States parties and the Tribunal raises some interesting questions of the relationship between the two bodies. Political supervision of judicial organs is not completely unprecedented in the international sphere. In the Word Trade Organization for example, the Dispute Settlement Body is responsible for adopting reports of panels[59] and the Appellate Body,[60] before they become binding. The model adopted by the States parties does not go that far. Nevertheless, it provides the States parties with an opportunity to discuss and comment on the content of Tribunal decisions. This can give greater prominence to decisions of the Tribunal. It is also a means through which collective pressure for compliance could be placed upon the states involved in the dispute. In addition, according to some commentators, a clear link between international tribunals and States is to be welcomed because it helps to guarantee that international judges remain responsive to State interests, thus ensuring that States continue to trust these judicial institutions.[61] At the same time, in order to retain their impartiality, 'the court and judges shall exercise their judicial functions free from interference from other organs or authorities of [international] organizations'.[62] It would appear that there is a balance to be achieved in this regard. Luckily, to date, no tensions have arisen, as the reaction of the States parties has been positive to the jurisprudence of the Tribunal.[63] Nevertheless, it is important that the States parties consciously respect the principle of judicial independence when carrying out this role.

5 The Commission on the Limits of the Continental Shelf

The Commission on the Limits of the Continental Shelf is created by the Convention to oversee the delineation of the continental shelf beyond 200 nautical miles. The Commission is a technical organ composed of 'experts' in the fields of geology,

---

[59] WTO Dispute Settlement Understanding, Art 16(4) (hereinafter DSU).

[60] Ibid, Art 17(4).

[61] See eg EA Posner and JC Yoo, 'Judicial Independence in International Tribunals' (2005) 93 *California Law Review* 1.

[62] The Burgh House Principles, n 55, [1.2].

[63] See eg *Report of the Twenty-second Meeting of the States Parties*, Doc SPLOS/251 (4–11 June 2012) [24]–[28].

geophysics and hydrography, serving in their 'personal capacities'.[64] It makes recommendations to coastal States concerning the limits of their outer continental shelf on the basis of technical information submitted by States.[65] Although the Commission is an independent body, the States parties have a number of responsibilities in relation to the Commission.

The principal task of the States parties in relation to the Commission is the election of its members.[66] Elections take place every five years.[67] As in the case of the Tribunal, the meeting of the States parties has adopted an arrangement for the allocations of seats on the Commission, which seeks to secure an equitable geographical representation between the five regions recognized by the United Nations.[68]

Beyond this role, the precise relationship between the Commission and the States parties remains unclear. The States parties are not collectively responsible for financing members of the Commission, a function falling upon the State party which nominates a particular candidate.[69] Nevertheless, the States parties have discussed the financing of the Commission and they recommended the establishment of a Trust Fund for the purpose of facilitating the participation of Commission members from developing States parties.[70]

The States parties have also closely monitored the work of the Commission as it proceeds. The Commission is invited to participate as an observer at meetings of the States parties[71] and the Chair of the Commission regularly makes a statement to the meeting. This practice provides an opportunity for the States parties to discuss relevant issues arising in the work of the Commission. At the same time, the Rules of Procedure of the meeting of the States parties make clear that the independence of the Commission and its members must be respected.[72] Such independence is particularly important when it comes to the power of the Commission to make recommendations on individual submissions from coastal States. A more difficult issue arises as to whether the States parties are competent to provide more general

---

[64] LOSC, n 4, Annex II, Art 2(1).
[65] Ibid, Annex II, Art 3(1)(a). Coastal States shall establish the limits of the outer continental shelf 'on the basis of these recommendations'; ibid, Art 76(8).
[66] Ibid, Annex II, Art 2(3).   [67] Ibid, Annex II, Art 2(3).
[68] *Arrangement for the Allocation of Seats on the International Tribunal for the Law of the Sea and the Commission on the Limits of the Continental Shelf*, n 38, [1]. For the first election, the States parties authorized a deviation from the prescribed composition set out in the Convention, by providing that only two seats would be filled by representatives from the Eastern European region; see *Report of the Sixth Meeting of the States Parties*, Doc SPLOS/20 (10–14 March 1997) [13].
[69] LOSC, n 4, Annex II, Art 2(5).
[70] *Decision regarding the establishment of a voluntary trust fund for the purpose of the Commission on the Limits of the Continental Shelf*, Doc SPLOS/58 (6 June 2000). The trust fund was established by the UN General Assembly through UNGA Res 55/7 (30 October 2000) [20] and Annex II. For an explanation of why the trust fund was established by the UN General Assembly, see *Note by the Secretariat—Issues Submitted to the Meeting of the States Parties by the Commission on the Limits of the Continental Shelf*, Doc SPLOS/39 (21 May 1999).
[71] SPLOS Rules of Procedure n 20, Rule 4.   [72] Ibid.

guidance on the work of the Commission. Some commentators make the argument that the Commission should defer to the States parties on questions of interpretation of the Convention, as it does not have the expertise to address legal questions itself.[73] On the other hand, others have suggested that the Commission must be able to have the power to interpret at least those provisions of the Convention that are directly relevant to its own mandate.[74] Differing views continue to be expressed amongst delegates to meetings of the States parties.[75] The on-going controversy can be partly attributed to the broader disagreement about the role of the States parties in overseeing the development of the Convention regime, as discussed below.

It would seem to be agreed that the States parties have a role in relation to the practical issues concerning the workload of the Commission. There are currently 67 submissions before the Commission, which has issued only 18 recommendations to date.[76] Many States are concerned about how long it will take to process all of these outstanding submissions. In this context, the States parties have adopted a number of decisions addressing the procedures to be followed by States parties when making submissions to the Commission,[77] as well as decisions on the workload of the Commission.[78] There is no explicit basis in the Convention for such decisions, although they can be justified on the basis of the States parties' powers under general international law to interpret the Convention.[79]

This issue continues to appear on the agenda of the States parties and some more radical solutions are on the table, including the appointment of a full-time Commission.[80] It remains to be seen whether this proposal will gain the support of

---

[73] See eg International Law Association (ILA), *Legal Issues of the Outer Continental Shelf: ILA Report of the Seventy-First Conference* (International Law Association London 2004) 779–780.

[74] See eg B Kunoy, 'The Terms of Reference of the Commission on the Limits of the Continental Shelf: A Creeping Legal Mandate' (2012) 25 *Leiden Journal of International Law* 109.

[75] See eg *Report of the Eighth Meeting of the States Parties*, Doc SPLOS/31 (18–22 May 1998) [51]–[52]; *Report of the Nineteenth Meeting of the States Parties*, Doc SPLOS/203 (22–26 June 2009) [105]–[108]; *Report of the Twenty-first Meeting of the States Parties*, Doc SPLOS/231 (13–17 June 2011) [87]–[91]; *Report of the Twenty-second Meeting of the States Parties*, n 63, [72] and [79].

[76] See the Commission website, at <http://www.un.org/depts/los/clcs_new/commission_submissions.htm>.

[77] *Decision regarding the date of commencement of the ten-year period for making submissions to the Commission on the Limits of the Continental Shelf set out in Article 4 of Annex II to the United Nations Convention on the Law of the Sea*, Doc SPLOS/72 (29 May 2001); *Decision regarding the workload of the Commission on the Limits of the Continental Shelf and the ability of States, particularly developing States, to fulfill the requirements of Article 4 of Annex II of the United Nations Convention on the Law of the Sea, as well as decision contained in SPLOS/72, paragraph (a)*, Doc SPLOS/183 (20 June 2008).

[78] *Decision on issues related to proposals by the Commission on the Limits of the Continental Shelf*, Doc SPLOS/144 (23 June 2006); *Decision regarding the workload of the Commission on the Limits of the Continental Shelf*, Doc SPLOS/216 (23 June 2010); *Decision regarding the workload of the Commission on the Limits of the Continental Shelf*, Doc SPLOS/229 (16 June 2011).

[79] See 1969 Vienna Convention on the Law of Treaties, Art 31(3) (hereinafter VCLT).

[80] *Decision regarding the workload of the Commission on the Limits of the Continental Shelf*, n 78, [2]. See also *Report of the Twenty-first Meeting of the States Parties*, n 75, [100]–[104].

the States parties. It must also be asked whether this solution would require a formal amendment to the Convention. However, the past practice of the States parties suggests that they may be to willing to use more informal procedures to solve such technical problems, provided that decisions are supported by consensus.[81]

6 THE INTERNATIONAL SEABED AUTHORITY

Another institution established by the LOSC is the International Seabed Authority.[82] The Authority is responsible for overseeing the development and implementation of the deep seabed mining regime found in Part XI of the Convention.[83] It has a range of substantive powers to adopt rules and regulations to govern deep seabed mining, as well as the ability to enforce these rules and regulations against individual contractors. To date, the Authority has adopted rules and regulations relating to prospecting and exploration for polymetallic nodules, polymetallic sulphides, and cobalt-rich crusts.[84] There are currently 17 contractors exploring for seabed mineral resources in the Area,[85] and commercial exploitation for seabed mining is now on the horizon.[86]

The Authority is established as an autonomous institution, with international legal personality[87] and its own secretariat.[88] Indeed, the Authority also has its own very specialized decision-making processes, which differ significantly from the decision-making procedures employed by the meeting of the States parties.[89] Furthermore, a special amendment procedure applies to the adoption of amendments to Part XI of the Convention,[90] conferring this power on the organs of the

---

[81] See D Freestone and A Oude Elferink, 'Flexibility and Innovation in the Law of the Sea—Will the LOS Convention Amendment Procedures Ever Be Used?' in A Oude Elferink (ed), *Stability and Change in the Law of the Sea* (Martinus Nijhoff Leiden 2005) 218.

[82] LOSC, n 4, Art 158(1).   [83] Ibid, Art 157. See also Chapter 11 in this volume.

[84] These regulations are collectively referred to as 'the mining code'; see International Seabed Authority (ISA), Mining Code, available at <http://www.isa.org.jm/en/mcode>.

[85] See the ISA website, at <http://www.isa.org.jm/en/scientific/exploration/contractors>.

[86] The first exploration contracts are due to expire in 2016, at which stage, contractors will be expected to apply for an exploitation contract, unless they apply for an extension of the exploration contract.

[87] LOSC, n 4, Art 176.   [88] Ibid, Arts 158 and 166–168.

[89] Ibid, Art 161(8)(e) governs the adoption of rules and regulations. 1994 Agreement Relating to the Implementation of Part XI of the LOSC, s 3(11)(a) governs the adoption of contracts; s 3(5) governs the adoption of other decisions (hereinafter 1994 Implementation Agreement).

[90] LOSC, n 4, Art 314. Amendments to Part XI are explicitly excluded from Arts 311 and 312.

Authority, rather than the States parties.[91] The effect of the Convention is essentially to carve out responsibility for seabed mining issues from the role of the States parties, thereby creating a sort of 'self-contained regime'.[92]

Although the Convention establishes no formal link between the meeting of the States parties and the Authority, an informal link has been established in the practice. First, the Rules of Procedure of the meeting of the States parties provide that 'the International Seabed Authority may participate as an observer'.[93] However, the Authority is not an ordinary observer to the meeting. Rather, the Rules of Procedure provide that:

> [T]he Secretary-General of the International Seabed Authority shall be invited to meetings of the States Parties and may make written or oral statements concerning any question under consideration by the meeting and provide information on [the Authority], as appropriate.[94]

This differentiates the Authority from other intergovernmental organizations participating as observers at meetings of the States parties, which are only permitted to make oral statements and submit written statements on questions within the scope of their activities and upon invitation of the President of the meeting and with the approval of the States parties.[95] In practice, the Secretary-General is invited to give a statement to every meeting of the States parties and this is now a standing agenda item.[96]

As noted by other authors, this practice goes beyond the provisions of the Convention.[97] Indeed, it raises the question of the precise purpose of this reporting function. The title of the agenda item—'Information reported by the Secretary-General of the International Seabed Authority'—would seem to underline the fact that the report is for information purposes only. Given that all States parties are also members of the Authority, one could question the purpose of such a report. Yet, one explanation may be that many States do not attend meetings of the Authority,[98] often because of the high cost of sending a delegation to attend the annual sessions of the Authority at its headquarters in Jamaica, particularly for low-income countries.[99] In contrast, meetings of the States parties usually take place at the United Nations headquarters

---

[91] Amendments must first be approved by the Council and then approved by the Assembly. Amendments to Part XI enter into force for all States parties one year following the deposit of instruments of ratification or accession by three-fourths of the States parties; see LOSC, n 4, Art 316(5).

[92] This phrase is used in the same sense as when the Permanent Court of International Justice described the provisions on the Kiel Canal in the Versailles Treaty as 'self-contained'; see *SS Wimbledon* [1923] PCIJ Rep Series A No 1, 23–4.

[93] SPLOS Rules of Procedure, n 20, Rule 18(2).   [94] Ibid, Rule 37.   [95] Ibid, Rule 18(7).

[96] See eg *Agenda of the Twenty-third Meeting of the States Parties*, Doc SPLOS/261 (2013).

[97] T Treves, 'The General Assembly and the Meeting of the States Parties in the Implementation of the LOS Convention', in A Oude Elferink (ed), *Stability and Change in the Law of the Sea* (Martinus Nijhoff Leiden 2005), 69

[98] See eg UNGA Res 64/71 (2009) [36]; UNGA Res 66/231 (2011) [45].

[99] This is an issue that is regularly raised at meetings of the Authority. See eg *Statement of the President on the work of the Assembly at its nineteenth Session*, Doc ISBA/19/A/14 (31 July 2013) [17].

in New York and they are often attended by the diplomatic staff already based in that location. It follows that the presentation of the report by the Secretary-General of the Authority to the meeting of the States parties offers an alternative opportunity for States parties to inform themselves of the activities of the Authority.

There is usually a discussion of the information provided by the Secretary-General of the Authority, with various delegates expressing views on the work of the Authority and what they consider to be priorities. Ultimately, the meeting is limited to simply '[taking] note' of the information reported by the Secretary-General of the Authority.[100] Indeed, given the autonomous nature of the Authority, it would be inappropriate for the meeting of the States parties to adopt a decision seeking to direct the work of the Authority.

However, there is one area in which the Convention does confer a power on the States parties to adopt a decision that binds the Authority. According to the Convention, the States parties may agree any financial contribution to be made by the Authority to the International Tribunal for the Law of the Sea, if it is involved in any cases before the Tribunal.[101] This reflects the fact that it is the States parties which are responsible for the budget of the Tribunal. However, this decision-making power has not been exercised to date, despite the fact that the Seabed Disputes Chamber has delivered an advisory opinion at the request of the Authority.[102]

7 The Meeting of the States Parties as a Forum to Review General Developments in the Law of the Sea

It has already been observed that the scope of the powers attributed to the States parties has been a controversial issue since the Convention entered into force in 1994.[103] The issue was explicitly raised at the seventh meeting of the States parties in 1998 when 'the role of the meeting of the States Parties' was added to the agenda. At that meeting, it was suggested that a review of ocean affairs should be a regular

Similar concerns have been expressed at Meetings of the States parties, eg *Report of the Twenty-third Meeting of the States Parties*, n 20, [47].

[100] *Report of the Twenty-third Meeting of the States Parties*, n 20, [55].
[101] LOSC, n 4, Annex VI, Art 19.
[102] *Responsibilities and Obligations of States Sponsoring Persons and Entities with respect to Activities in the Area* (Advisory Opinion) [2011] ITLOS Rep 10.
[103] See also Chapter 3 in this volume.

item on the agenda of the meeting of the States parties.[104] However, this addition was short-lived, and the eighth meeting did not agree to retain the item on the agenda.[105] Indeed, it soon became clear that different viewpoints existed about the role of the States parties in relation to reviewing the law of the sea regime.[106] In a compromise solution, it was ultimately agreed that the agenda should include an item on the 'Report of the Secretary General under article 319 for the information of States Parties on issues of a general nature relevant to States Parties that have arisen with respect to the United Nations Convention on the Law of the Sea'.[107] Nevertheless, this agreement on wording has not solved the substantive disagreement as to what action the States parties may take in relation to this report.

On the one hand, many delegations are of the view that the role of the States parties should be solely budgetary and administrative in nature. This argument rests in part on the use in Article 319 of the Convention of the terms 'as necessary' and 'in accordance with the Convention' as qualifiers to the duty of the UN Secretary-General to convene meetings of the States parties. These delegations believe that this phrasing points towards a limited role for the States parties.[108] Furthermore, they argue that the Convention makes no explicit reference to a review role by the States parties[109] and that 'the Third United Nations Conference on the Law of the Sea had rejected proposals for a broader role for the meeting'.[110] Delegates holding this point of view emphasize that the compromise agenda item envisaged that the Secretary-General's report should be for information purposes only and limited to general issues.[111]

On the other hand, other delegations take the view that the mandate of the meeting of the States parties should not be interpreted restrictively. On this view, the States parties not only have a right to receive the report of the Secretary-General under Article 319, but they can also ask for further reports on specific issues of interest to the States parties.[112] Nor do delegates supporting this interpretation think that there is anything in the Convention that constrains the States parties from taking decisions on substantive issues relating to the implementation of the Convention.[113]

---

[104] *Report of the Seventh Meeting of the States Parties*, Doc SPLOS/24 (19–23 May 1997) [38].
[105] *Report of the Eighth Meeting of the States Parties*, n 75, [70].
[106] *Report of the Ninth Meeting of the States Parties*, Doc SPLOS/48 (19–28 May 1999) [50]–[53]. From the tenth Meeting to the fourteenth Meeting, the issue was discussed under the agenda item of 'Matters related to Article 319 of the United Nations Convention on the Law of the Sea'.
[107] *Report of the Fourteenth Meeting of the States Parties*, Doc SPLOS/119 (14–18 June 2004) [85]–[86].
[108] Ibid, [80].   [109] Ibid.
[110] *Report of the Twenty-third Meeting of the States Parties*, n 20, [93].
[111] *Report of the Fourteenth Meeting of the States Parties*, n 107, [87].
[112] Ibid, [82]. It has been noted on several occasions that the report submitted by the UN Secretary-General to the Meeting of the States parties is identical to the report submitted to the UN General Assembly in the autumn but that the report is no longer up-to-date when it was received by the States parties in the spring of the following year; see eg views expressed in the *Report of the Twenty-second Meeting of the States Parties*, n 63, [93].
[113] *Report of the Fourteenth Meeting of the States Parties*, n 107, [86]. However, there was a question as to whether such decisions should be taken by consensus or by a majority vote; ibid, [88].

This latter view finds some support in general international law, which recognizes that the parties to a treaty have the power to oversee its subsequent interpretation and development.[114] Indeed, this argument is further supported if one considers that it is the States parties which are responsible for adopting amendments to all aspects of the Convention, apart from Part XI.[115] Thus, it makes little sense from a legal perspective to argue that the powers of the meeting of States parties in relation to discussion of law of the sea issues are limited, with perhaps the exception of issues relating to Part XI, which, as noted above, can be considered a self-contained regime.

At the same time, this conclusion must be reconciled with the fact that 'this is not a purely legal dispute over the powers of the meetings of the States Parties, but also a political issue about which is the most appropriate forum for considering law of the sea issues'.[116] It must be recognized that the meeting of the States parties exists in a complex institutional environment that includes a number of other general and specialized organizations, many of which had been active in law of the sea affairs for many years before the Convention entered into force.[117] In particular, it has been noted that 'the General Assembly was the global forum with the mandate to undertake an annual substantive review and evaluation of the implementation of the Convention and other developments relating to ocean affairs and the law of the sea'.[118] The quasi-universal membership of the UN General Assembly is one reason why it is considered to be a more suitable organ in which to discuss law of the sea matters. As has been stated elsewhere:

[T]he fact that a number of important maritime states are not parties to the Convention is one reason why the meeting of the States Parties is not considered as an appropriate institution to oversee the implementation of the Convention as a whole. As most of the substantive rules found in the Convention are applicable to almost all states as a matter of customary international law, it is desirable that all states are able to participate in discussions concerning their development.[119]

Seen in this light, the arguments against the States parties having substantive discussions on the law of the sea regime are more political in nature.

In addition, there are also potential practical limitations on the ability of the States parties to carry out a broader oversight role. These limitations arise from the fact that it is the UN Secretariat which supports meetings of the States parties. Yet, this body is under the direct control of the UN General Assembly. According to

---

[114] See eg VCLT, n 79, Art 31(3). See also *Report of the Twelfth Meeting of the States Parties*, Doc SPLOS/91 (16–28 April 2002) [114].

[115] LOSC, n 4, Arts 312–313. As noted above, a different amendment procedure applies to Part XI of the Convention; see text accompanying nn 93–94 above.

[116] Harrison, n 5, 73.   [117] *Report of the Fourteenth Meeting of the States Parties*, n 107, [80].

[118] *Report of the Twenty-third Meeting of the States Parties*, n 20, [93].

[119] Harrison, n 5, 73. See also Treves, n 97, 66.

the UN Charter, the UN Secretary-General is subject to the authority of the United Nations and may not 'seek or receive instructions from any ... authority external to the Organization'.[120] Moreover, the secretariat is funded from the regular UN budget. This means that the States parties are limited as to what they can ask the Secretariat to do without the support of the UN General Assembly. For example, any solution to the problem of the workload of the Commission on the Limits of the Continental Shelf that requires additional support from the UN Secretariat potentially requires the support of the UN General Assembly in addition to the States parties. This reliance on the UN General Assembly has already been recognized by relevant decisions of the States parties, revealing an awareness of the interdependence of these institutions in addressing law of the sea issues.[121] Indeed, it is not without any significance that the General Assembly uses its annual resolution on the law of the sea to request the UN Secretary-General to convene meetings of the States parties.[122] This reminds us that the meeting of the States parties has an uncertain institutional status and it does not have complete autonomy from the wider UN system.

8 A System of Law of the Sea Institutions?

It is clear from the preceding analysis that the functions of the States parties have to be assessed against the background of a complex institutional framework that exists in relation to law of the sea issues. This complexity is recognized by the Convention itself, which makes reference to a variety of institutions throughout the text.[123] Alongside the institutions already mentioned in this chapter, there is also a range of other international organizations dealing with specific aspects of the law of the sea. They include UN specialized agencies, such as the International Maritime Organization in respect of shipping and the Food and Agriculture Organization in relation to fishing. There are also a large number of treaty bodies dealing with the protection of the marine environment. In many cases, the Convention is ambiguous about precisely which institutions are involved in its implementation, simply

---

[120] 1945 UN Charter, Art 100(1).
[121] Eg *Decision regarding the workload of the Commission on the Limits of the Continental Shelf*, Doc SPLOS/229 (16 June 2011) [2].
[122] See eg UNGA Res 64/71, 4 December 2009, [28].
[123] See United Nations Secretary General, *Impacts of the Entry into Force of the 1982 United Nations Convention on the Law of the Sea on related existing and proposed instruments and programs: Report of the Secretary General*, UN Doc A/52/491 (20 October 1997).

referring to the 'competent international organizations'.[124] This practice allows a flexible approach and decisions on which institutions are competent can be made on a case-by-case basis.

Such variety should not in itself be surprising. The idea of establishing a single forum to deal with all law of the sea issues had already been rejected in discussions concerning the draft articles on the law of the sea submitted to the First United Nations Conference on the Law of the Sea in 1958.[125] The International Law Commission considered the establishment of such a body to be impracticable on a number of counts. First, such an institution would have to deal with a wide range of different subjects, from fishing to navigation, and there was a danger that 'such an organization may tend to apply an excessively uniform standard to varying situations and fail to take adequate account of the different interests concerned'.[126] Second, it was considered that the establishment of a new body would be problematic given 'many organizations, each dealing with a specific sector, have already been created in this field'.[127]

These arguments were still relevant at UNCLOS III. Indeed, far from being problematic, the existence of a number of specialist institutions may bring some benefits. For instance, Hafner argues that 'specialization accommodates various needs and concerns of the states engaged in international law-making, and states perceive that their individual positions are better respected in these special regimes than in a global one'.[128]

If specialization and diversity in international law-making is to be embraced, the question becomes not how we can avoid fragmentation, but how we can manage it. The need for improved cooperation and coordination between international institutions involved in the law of the sea has been widely recognized in the literature.[129] Yet, coherence is a challenge in a decentralized legal system.

Cooperation and coordination is not an issue that is addressed by the Convention itself. This is hardly surprising, as it is a question that goes beyond the treaty regime to a broader question of cooperation between institutions that exist independently of the Convention. It is also for this reason that the

---

[124] For an early evaluation of this issue, see JD Kingham and DM McRae, 'Competent International Organizations and the Law of the Sea' (1979) 3 *Marine Policy* 106.

[125] 'Regime of the High Seas and Regime of the Territorial Sea' (1956) II *Yearbook of the International Law Commission* 1, [9].

[126] Ibid, [11].

[127] Ibid, [12]. The International Law Commission did, however, note the problems that also arise from having a large number of organizations; ibid, [16].

[128] G Hafner, 'Pros and Cons Ensuing from Fragmentation of International Law' (2004) 25 *Michigan Journal of International Law* 849, 858–9.

[129] See eg R Rayfuse and R Warner, 'Securing a Sustainable Future for the Oceans beyond National Jurisdiction: The Legal Basis for an Integrated Cross-Sectoral Regime for High Seas Governance for the 21st Century' (2008) 23 *International Journal of Marine and Coastal Law* 399, 413; G Ulfstein, 'The Marine Environment and International Environmental Governance', in MH Nordquist, JN Moore,

primary institution that has attempted to promote coordination of law of the sea institutions is the UN General Assembly.[130] One reason why the UN General Assembly is an appropriate forum is its universal membership, which means that all States have a say, on an equal basis, in the debate. The mandate of the UN General Assembly is also wide enough to encompass all law of the sea issues.[131] Furthermore, the UN is the only international organization with the ability to coordinate the activities of a wide range of international institutions. The UN Charter explicitly foresees that the United Nations shall, through the General Assembly and the Economic and Social Council, coordinate the policies and activities of various international institutions, including the specialized agencies.[132] To this end, the UN has concluded a variety of relationship agreements with various other international organizations, which allows it to share information and coordinate operational activities. This includes relationship agreements with some of the institutions created by the LOSC.[133] The UN General Assembly has also used its annual resolution on ocean affairs and law of the sea to call for improved cooperation and coordination at the international level.[134] It is the emergence of such mechanisms that perhaps allows us to talk about a 'system' of law of the sea institutions, even if it is only a loose system based more on consensus and common aims than legal authority.[135]

Ultimately, the position of the UN General Assembly at the apex of any system of law of the sea institutions would appear to be generally accepted by the international community. In debates on the role of the States parties, many States have recognized that 'the global forum having the mandate to undertake an annual substantive review and evaluation of the implementation of the Convention and other developments relating to ocean affairs and the law of the sea was the General Assembly'.[136] This allows the UN General Assembly to confidently play a role in promoting cooperation between the various parts of the system with a view to the coherent development of the law of the sea regime.

---

and S Mahmoudi (eds), *The Stockholm Declaration and the Law of the Marine Environment* (Kluwer International The Hague 2003) 104.

[130] See also Chapter 16 in this volume.

[131] 1945 Charter of the United Nations, Art 10 (hereinafter UN Charter).

[132] Ibid, Art 58. Inter-institutional cooperation is also a theme addressed by other UN bodies, such as the Informal Consultative Process; see UNGA Res 54/33 (24 November 1999) [2].

[133] UNGA Res 52/27, *Agreement concerning the Relationship between the United Nations and the International Seabed Authority* (1997), Annex; UNGA Res 52/251, *Agreement on Cooperation and Relationship between the United Nations and the International Tribunal for the Law of the Sea* (1998) Annex.

[134] See eg UNGA Res 66/231 (2011) [235].   [135] See further Treves, n 22, 339–40.

[136] *Report the Twenty-second Meeting of the States Parties*, n 63, [98]. See also *Report of the Ad-Hoc Open-Ended Informal Working Group to study issues relating to the conservation and sustainable use of marine biological diversity beyond areas of national jurisdiction*, UN Doc A/61/65 (20 March 2006) [7].

9 Conclusion

A variety of international institutions have played a vital role in the development of the law of the sea regime since the conclusion of the 1982 United Nations Convention on the Law of the Sea. They have provided the forum for developing treaties and other instruments which complement the legal framework in the Convention. It has been seen that the institutional provisions in the 1982 Convention are themselves vague in that they do not establish clear divisions of competence between the various institutions that are involved in this area of law. Rather, this has been an issue that has been left to progressive development in the practice of states and institutions themselves.

This chapter has traced some of the controversies surrounding the institutional framework created by the Convention. The States parties have undoubtedly contributed to the on-going vitality of the Convention and they have developed the relevant legal framework to meet challenges that were not foreseen at the time when the Convention was drafted. As has been seen throughout this chapter, they have played a particularly important role in supervising the other bodies created by the Convention. This work is on-going, particularly in relation to managing the workload of the Commission on the Limits of the Continental Shelf. This is a future issue that will continue to occupy the States parties in the coming years.

Having said that, the controversies surrounding the precise mandate of the States parties have not been conclusively resolved. This is particularly the case in relation to the role of the States parties in overseeing the future development of the law of the sea regime. This issue continues to elicit debate and contrasting opinions. Indeed, there seems to have been little movement in the positions of the protagonists, and the discussion has become rather formulaic. In reality, this state of affairs may conceal a preference amongst the States parties to simply leave the question open.

Indeed, as a practical matter, it would appear that there is general acceptance that the States parties cannot carry out all major functions in relation to the law of the sea regime. Rather, we have a complex system of institutions which interact in order to achieve a shared common aim: the implementation of the Convention and the maintenance of the consensus underpinning the modern law of the sea. It is a result of its broad composition and competence, as well as its position at the apex of the UN system, that the UN General Assembly is currently accepted as the body that is best placed to oversee the overall development of law of the sea issues. Indeed, given its unique characteristics, it is likely to continue to play this role, even if the Convention were to achieve universal participation.

COURTS AND TRIBUNALS: THE ICJ, ITLOS, AND ARBITRAL TRIBUNALS

BERNARD H OXMAN

1 INTRODUCTION

MOST disputes that arise between private parties, including nationals of different States, are subject to the jurisdiction of the courts of one or more States. Administrative and criminal proceedings against private persons for the enforcement of rules at sea, including international rules, ordinarily take place in municipal courts and tribunals.[1]

---

[1] The Law of the Sea Convention builds on that foundation. See 1982 United Nations Convention on the Law of the Sea, Arts 73, 94, and 292(3) (hereinafter LOSC). Section 6 of Part XII relies on municipal authorities and municipal courts of flag States, port States, and coastal States for enforcement of international environmental standards. Article 235(2) adds:

> States shall ensure that recourse is available in accordance with their legal systems for prompt and adequate compensation or other relief in respect of damage caused by pollution of the marine environment by natural or juridical persons under their jurisdiction.

The situation with respect to disputes between States is different. States are reluctant to submit such disputes to each other's courts. Subject to certain exceptions for commercial and other activities, States are immune from suit in foreign courts and sovereign property is immune from execution.[2] Also, the jurisdiction of a municipal court over its own government may be limited by the laws of that State.

Thus, unlike dispute settlement between private parties, settlement of disputes between States is generally not regulated by municipal law and municipal courts. Rather, it is a question of international law regulated by treaty. Because States are not subject to the jurisdiction of international tribunals absent express consent, an important function of dispute settlement clauses in treaties is to indicate whether such consent is granted and, if so, with respect to which disputes before which tribunals.[3] Similar considerations may apply to intergovernmental organizations.

2 THE OBLIGATION OF STATES TO SETTLE DISPUTES PEACEFULLY

Article 2(3) of the 1945 Charter of the United Nations provides that '[a]ll Members shall settle their international disputes by peaceful means in such a manner that international peace and security, and justice, are not endangered.' Article 33(1) of the Charter elaborates:

The parties to any dispute, the continuance of which is likely to endanger the maintenance of international peace and security, shall, first of all, seek a solution by negotiation, enquiry,

---

Even after an international tribunal has rendered judgment, there may be an enforcement role for municipal courts, especially in cases that involve private parties. Annex VI, Art 39, provides that decisions of the Sea-Bed Disputes Chamber of the International Tribunal for the Law of the Sea 'shall be enforceable in the territories of the States Parties in the same manner as judgments or orders of the highest court of the State Party in whose territory the enforcement is sought'.

[2] The provisional measures order of the International Tribunal for the Law of the Sea (ITLOS) in the *ARA Libertad* case emphasized the immunity of warships from the jurisdiction of foreign States and their courts. *ARA Libertad (Argentina v Ghana)* (Provisional Measures) [2012] ITLOS Rep 21 [97].

[3] But it should be borne in mind that the underlying dispute may involve one or more private parties, and at least some aspects of that dispute may well be within the civil, administrative, or criminal jurisdiction of a municipal court insofar as the private parties are concerned. A growing number of bilateral and multilateral treaties provide for arbitration of investment disputes between States and private foreign investors in order to minimize political risk and encourage investment.

mediation, conciliation, arbitration, judicial settlement, resort to regional agencies or arrangements, or other peaceful means of their own choice.

The key words are 'peaceful means of their own choice'. These provisions do not require States to use a specific means for settling disputes. Subject to the powers of the UN Security Council, they do not require a State to accept submission of a dispute to a third party, whether or not the outcome is a legally binding decision. Article 284 of the 1982 United Nations Convention on the Law of the Sea (LOSC) expressly affords States the option to submit a dispute to a conciliation commission in accordance with Section 1 of Annex V of the Convention, but only if they agree. This is so even though Annex V provides that '[t]he report of the commission, including its conclusions or recommendations, shall not be binding upon the parties.'[4] The jurisdiction of international tribunals to render legally binding decisions, be they standing courts and tribunals or ad hoc arbitral tribunals, depends on the consent of the States party to the dispute. This is true even of the International Court of Justice (ICJ), the principal judicial organ of the United Nations.

Thus dispute settlement clauses in treaties that merely repeat or refer back to Article 33 of the Charter add little, if anything. Even provisions for binding third-party settlement of disputes regarding the interpretation or application of a treaty may be optional:

- if they are contained in a separate instrument that must itself be accepted, as was the case with the dispute settlement protocol to the 1958 conventions on the law of the sea, or
- if they are subject to reservations, or
- if they require the subsequent consent or agreement of the parties to the dispute, which was the case, for example, with the dispute settlement provisions of the Convention for the Conservation of Southern Bluefin Tuna that were at issue in the *Southern Bluefin Tuna* arbitration brought under the dispute settlement provisions of the LOSC.[5]

One means of consenting to the jurisdiction of an international tribunal is for the parties to enter into a special agreement to submit to that tribunal a dispute that has already arisen. This, however, leaves it to each of the parties, including the State whose conduct is challenged, to decide whether to agree. It denies the aggrieved party something that municipal legal systems ordinarily take for granted, namely access to impartial tribunals empowered to render justice according to

---

[4] LOSC, n 1, Annex V, Art 7(2).
[5] *Southern Bluefin Tuna (Australia v Japan; New Zealand v Japan)* (Jurisdiction and Admissibility) (2000) XXIII RIAA 1, 43–4 [57]–[58].

law. Comparable access to an international tribunal can be assured only if there is advance consent to jurisdiction.

The notion of party autonomy operates on two different levels in this context. The first requires agreement on the type of dispute settlement means to be employed, including whether a dispute may be submitted to binding arbitration or adjudication. In the case of the LOSC, this is reflected in key clauses of Section 1 of Part XV. Article 279 refers back to Articles 2(3) and 33(1) of the UN Charter. Article 280 preserves 'the right of any States Parties to agree at any time to settle a dispute between them concerning the interpretation or application of this Convention by any peaceful means of their own choice'. Article 283 adds that when a dispute arises between States parties concerning the interpretation or application of the Convention, the parties 'shall proceed expeditiously to an exchange of views regarding its settlement by negotiation or other peaceful means'.[6]

Second, if the selected means entail resort to a third party, then there must also be agreement on the identity of that party, be it a mediator, a conciliator, an arbitrator, or a court or tribunal. A decision to resort to binding arbitration or adjudication in the abstract would not ordinarily be understood to confer jurisdiction on any particular tribunal. But, as Article 288(2) of the LOSC makes clear, the parties are free to confer jurisdiction by agreement even if they are not otherwise subject to the jurisdiction of a particular court or tribunal.

3 THE DUTY TO ARBITRATE OR ADJUDICATE DISPUTES UNDER THE LOSC

Section 2 of Part XV of the LOSC establishes advance consent to arbitration and adjudication of disputes and sets forth the relevant details. It begins with Article 286, which provides:

Subject to section 3, any dispute concerning the interpretation or application of this Convention shall, where no settlement has been reached by recourse to section 1, be

---

[6] While direct consultations between diplomatic or other government representatives would ordinarily be the means used, LOSC, n 1, Art 283 does not specify those or any other particular methods for exchanging views. This accommodates concerns expressed by certain Arab and other delegations about direct official contact that could arise, for example, in the absence of recognition or diplomatic relations.

submitted at the request of any party to the dispute to the court or tribunal having jurisdiction under this section.

The key words establishing advance consent to jurisdiction, and dispensing with any need for the consent of the respondent after the dispute arises, are 'at the request of any party to the dispute'.

This has three principal effects. First, the court or tribunal to which the dispute is submitted by one of the parties itself determines whether it has jurisdiction.[7] Second, that court or tribunal is also empowered to prescribe legally binding provisional measures 'to preserve the respective rights of the parties to the dispute or to prevent serious harm to the marine environment, pending the final decision'.[8] Because there may be an urgent need for such measures, (1) provisional measures may be prescribed before the court or tribunal makes a definitive decision on jurisdiction over the merits of the case,[9] and (2) where a dispute is submitted to an arbitral tribunal under Section 2 of Part XV, the International Tribunal for the Law of the Sea (ITLOS) is empowered to prescribe provisional measures pending the constitution of the arbitral tribunal 'if it considers that *prima facie* the tribunal which is to be constituted would have jurisdiction and that the urgency of the situation so requires'.[10] While the power of ITLOS to prescribe provisional measures in such circumstances terminates with the constitution of the arbitral tribunal, the measures remain in effect until modified or terminated by the arbitral tribunal,[11] and the determination of the urgency of the need for such measures is not limited to the time period prior to the constitution of the arbitral tribunal.[12]

Third, the court or tribunal having jurisdiction under Section 2 of Part XV of the LOSC is empowered to render a judgment or award that is legally binding on both parties.[13] This is so whether or not the respondent participates in the proceedings or in the constitution of an arbitral tribunal.[14] ITLOS stressed this point in the '*Arctic*

---

[7] 1945 Statute of the International Court of Justice, Art 36(6) (hereinafter ICJ Statute); LOSC, n 1, Art 288(4).

[8] LOSC, n 1, Art 290(1) and (6). Arts 7(5), 16(2), and 31(2) of the 1995 Agreement for the Implementation of the Provisions of the UN Convention on the Law of the Sea relating to the Conservation and Management of Straddling Fish Stocks and Highly Migratory Fish Stocks, (hereinafter FSA) include conservation of these stocks within the functions of provisional measures under Art 290 of the LOSC.

[9] The jurisdictional standard for doing so is that there is a basis upon which jurisdiction over the merits might be founded. *Fisheries Jurisdiction (UK v Iceland)* (Interim Protection Order) [1972] ICJ Rep 12, [17]; *M/V 'Saiga' (No 2) (St Vincent and the Grenadines v Guinea)* (Provisional Measures) [1998] ITLOS Rep 24, [29]; *Southern Bluefin Tuna (New Zealand v Japan; Australia v Japan)* (Provisional Measures) [1999] ITLOS Rep 280, [52].

[10] LOSC, n 1, Art 290(5).   [11] Ibid.

[12] *Land Reclamation (Malaysia v Singapore)* (Provisional Measures) [2003] ITLOS Rep 10, [65]–[69].

[13] LOSC, n 1, Art 296; Annex VI, Art 33; Annex VII, Art 11; Annex VIII, Art 4.

[14] LOSC, n 1, Annex VI, Art 28; Annex VII, Arts 3 and 9; Annex VIII, Arts 3 and 4.

Sunrise' case, and applied it in proceedings regarding provisional measures pending the constitution of an arbitral tribunal.[15]

4 Choice of Forum for Compulsory Settlement of LOSC Disputes

For purposes of compulsory jurisdiction under Section 2 of Part XV of the LOSC, Article 287 permits States parties to make declarations accepting the ICJ,[16] ITLOS, arbitration under Annex VII, or for certain types of disputes arbitration under Annex VIII. A State that makes no relevant declaration is deemed to have accepted arbitration under Annex VII. If the applicant and respondent have made (or are deemed to have made) the same choice, then the dispute may be submitted only to that forum. If they have made different choices, then the dispute may be submitted only to arbitration under Annex VII unless they agree otherwise.

The result is that unless both parties have chosen the same forum by parallel declarations or agreement, the procedure for compulsory settlement under Section 2 of Part XV is arbitration under Annex VII. There are, however, three exceptions:

- disputes under Part XI of the LOSC and the 1994 Implementation Agreement are subject to the jurisdiction of the Seabed Disputes Chamber of ITLOS or commercial arbitration;[17]
- requests for provisional measures may be submitted to ITLOS pending the constitution of an arbitral tribunal to which the dispute is being submitted under Section 2 of Part XV;[18]

---

[15] *'Arctic Sunrise' (Netherlands v Russia)* Provisional Measures Order of the International Tribunal for the Law of the Sea (22 November 2013) [46]–[57]. The fact that the text of the LOSC expressly addresses the effect of non-participation may be understood to imply that a State is not obliged to participate, but a different view was expressed by two judges in the *'Arctic Sunrise'* case. Ibid, Joint Separate Opinion of Judges Wolfrum and Kelly [5]–[6].

[16] The reference to the ICJ is presumably subject to the requirements of the Court's Statute. For example, the States parties to the LOSC, as defined in Art 1(2)(2) of that Convention, include entities that may not be States within the meaning of Art 34 of the Court's Statute to which the Court is open under Art 35 of its Statute.

[17] LOSC, n 1, Arts 188, 288(3). The 1994 Agreement Relating to the Implementation of Part XI of the LOSC provides in Art 2 that it applies together with Part XI as a single instrument, and also contains specific references to the dispute settlement provisions of the LOSC (hereinafter 1994 Implementation Agreement).

[18] LOSC, n 1, Art 290(5).

- applications for prompt release of a detained vessel and crew under Article 292 may be submitted either to ITLOS or to any court or tribunal accepted by the detaining State under Article 287.

5 Nature of the Dispute

Part XV applies to disputes concerning the interpretation or application of the LOSC. What about so-called 'mixed' disputes that involve law of the sea issues addressed by the Convention as well as other issues? A typical example is a dispute concerning a maritime boundary that also involves a sovereignty dispute over an island from which coastal State rights may be generated in the disputed area.[19]

Three different situations should be distinguished in respect of 'mixed' disputes. First, States may submit a 'mixed' dispute to the ICJ, arbitration or some other forum without regard to the dispute settlement provisions of the LOSC. Many have done so.[20] While such disputes may involve the interpretation or application of the substantive provisions of the LOSC, the jurisdiction of the court or tribunal is based on some other instrument.

Second, there would appear to be nothing to preclude States from agreeing to submit a 'mixed' dispute to ITLOS or an Annex VII arbitral tribunal. That agreement would be the source of jurisdiction.[21]

Third, the submission by only one party of a 'mixed' dispute to a court or tribunal under Section 2 of Part XV of the LOSC poses the question of whether Article 286 and related provisions of Section 2 constitute the requisite consent to jurisdiction by the other party. Is it a dispute concerning the interpretation or application of the LOSC? A negative response would appear to follow from the fact that land sovereignty questions are not addressed by the LOSC and that there is no indication that becoming party to the LOSC entails consent to adjudicate disputes regarding sovereignty over land territory. However, some contend that there might be jurisdiction where the land sovereignty question is incidental or ancillary to the main subject of the dispute.[22]

---

[19] Where a party to the dispute has elected to exclude maritime boundary disputes from jurisdiction under Art 298(1)(a), either party may submit the dispute to conciliation, provided that 'any dispute that necessarily involves the concurrent consideration of any unsettled dispute concerning sovereignty or other rights over continental or insular land territory shall be excluded from such submission'.

[20] A recent example between parties to the LOSC is *Land and Maritime Boundary Between Cameroon and Nigeria (Cameroon v Nigeria: Equatorial Guinea Intervening)* (Judgment) [2002] ICJ Rep 303.

[21] LOSC, n 1, Art 288(2); Annex VI, Arts 20–22.

[22] Statement by ITLOS President Wolfrum before the UN General Assembly (8 December 2006) [7], available at <http://www.itlos.org/fileadmin/itlos/documents/statements_of_president/wolfrum/

6 Procedural Limitations on Jurisdiction under Section 2 of Part XV

Article 286 applies only 'where no settlement has been reached by recourse to section 1 of Part XV'. Section 1 itself imposes procedural requirements that reflect the principle of the right of the parties to agree on the means for settling the dispute.

Article 281 provides that if the parties 'have agreed to seek settlement of the dispute by a peaceful means of their own choice, the procedures provided for in this Part [XV] apply only where no settlement has been reached by recourse to such means and the agreement between the parties does not exclude any further procedure'. Article 282 provides that if the parties to the dispute 'have agreed, through a general, regional or bilateral agreement or otherwise, that such dispute shall, at the request of any party to the dispute, be submitted to a procedure that entails a binding decision, that procedure shall apply in lieu of the procedures provided for in this Part'.

The distinction between the two is that Article 282 of the LOSC applies only to a procedure that entails a binding decision to which the dispute may be submitted at the request of the aggrieved party alone. Article 282 therefore does not derogate from the principle of compulsory jurisdiction reflected in Section 2 of Part XV; it merely defers to other agreements that afford the aggrieved party the right to submit the dispute to binding arbitration or adjudication. In this connection it is not clear how much specificity might be required to exclude jurisdiction under the LOSC. For example, does Article 282 apply where both parties have not made declarations accepting the jurisdiction of the ICJ under Article 287 of the LOSC but have made general declarations under Article 36(2) of the ICJ Statute that would cover the dispute regarding the interpretation or application of the LOSC, but that do not refer specifically to such disputes or to the LOSC? In this regard, it should be borne in mind that the question is not whether the aggrieved party may submit the dispute to the ICJ, but whether that party is precluded by Article 282 from submitting the dispute to the otherwise applicable procedure under Section 2 of Part XV of the LOSC. Construing Article 282 strictly so as to afford the aggrieved party a choice of forum may entail some tactical

---

ga_081206_eng.pdf>. The statement was made before ITLOS received its first maritime delimitation case. The question of jurisdiction to determine sovereignty over land territory has been raised in a pending arbitration. See *The Republic of Mauritius v The United Kingdom of Great Britain and Northern Ireland*, LOSC Annex VII Tribunal (pending), available at <http://www.pca-cpa.org/show page.asp?pag_id=1429>. Such a question also arose in the *Guyana/Suriname* maritime boundary arbitration with respect to the terminus of the land frontier, but the tribunal did not find it necessary to address the issue in its award. *Arbitration between Guyana and Suriname* (2007) XXX RIAA 1, [174]–[185] and [280] (hereinafter *Guyana/Suriname*). The question of *prima facie* jurisdiction with respect to the immunity from detention of a visiting warship in port was addressed in the ITLOS provisional measures order in the *ARA Libertad* case, n 2, [60]–[67].

advantage, but it ought not be considered a calamity. The ICJ is not wanting for cases. Private international law provides useful guidance to ITLOS and Annex VII tribunals regarding comity in such situations, including practice regarding *lis pendens*.[23]

Article 282 is primarily a matter of choice of forum. Article 281 poses more serious issues regarding compulsory jurisdiction in principle. It applies to agreements regarding means for settlement of the dispute that do not necessarily entail a binding decision and to which the dispute may not necessarily be submitted only by one party. The deference to such agreements is therefore more limited. The requirement that no settlement has been reached by recourse to such means may entail delay, but does not preclude ultimate resort to binding arbitration or adjudication by the aggrieved party under Section 2 of Part XV. However, Article 281 also requires that the agreement does not exclude any further procedure. Since the agreement need not itself provide the aggrieved party with the right to submit the dispute to binding arbitration or adjudication without the specific consent of the respondent, this provision does derogate from the principle of compulsory jurisdiction reflected in Section 2 of Part XV. Given the large number of agreements regarding maritime matters that contain dispute settlement provisions that do not establish compulsory jurisdiction, the interpretation and application of this provision can have a significant impact in practice on the effect of Section 2 of Part XV. This may explain the reluctance of other tribunals to rely on the finding in the *Southern Bluefin Tuna* arbitration that the dispute settlement clauses of the Southern Bluefin Tuna Conservation Convention, which do not provide for compulsory jurisdiction, impliedly preclude resort to the compulsory jurisdiction provisions of Section 2 of Part XV of the LOSC.[24] Prior to reaching this conclusion, the award quoted the applicants' argument that this position renders the compulsory jurisdiction provisions of the LOSC 'a paper umbrella which dissolves in the rain'.[25]

While the same question of scope may arise under both Articles 281 and 282, the context and consequences are different, and so may be the answers. For example, is it necessary that the other agreement apply to the dispute arising under the LOSC as such, or is it sufficient that it be the same dispute in substance even if it arises under another treaty? ITLOS seemed to adhere to the former position in its provisional measures decisions in *Southern Bluefin Tuna* and *MOX Plant*, while the arbitral tribunal in *Southern Bluefin Tuna* took the latter position.[26]

---

[23] See Y Shany, 'Contract Claims vs. Treaty Claims: Mapping Conflicts Between ICSID Decisions on Multisourced Investment Claims' (2005) 99 *American Journal of International Law* 835, 849–51.

[24] The author of this chapter analysed the award and its implications in BH Oxman, 'Complementary Agreements and Compulsory Jurisdiction' (2001) 95 *American Journal of International Law* 277.

[25] *Southern Bluefin Tuna* (Jurisdiction and Admissibility), n 5, [41(k)].

[26] *Southern Bluefin Tuna* (Provisional Measures), n 9 [55]; *MOX Plant (Ireland v United Kingdom)* (Provisional Measures) [2001] ITLOS Rep 95 [48]–[53]; *Southern Bluefin Tuna* (Jurisdiction and Admissibility), n 5, [56]–[64]. It is unclear whether Ireland's withdrawal on 15 February 2007 of its claim in the *MOX Plant* arbitration under LOSC Annex VII is properly regarded as entailing the application of Art 282, or the separate and independent application by Ireland of its obligations under a binding judgment of the European Court of Justice (ECJ) holding that the constitutive

Article 283 provides that when a dispute arises, the parties to the dispute shall proceed expeditiously to an exchange of views regarding its settlement by negotiation or other peaceful means.[27] This may entail some good faith efforts to explore the possibilities for agreement before a party may institute proceedings under Section 2 of Part XV. It has not, however, been interpreted to require a State to wait indefinitely.[28]

Article 295 incorporates the international law rule of exhaustion of local remedies. That rule typically applies in situations of diplomatic protection where the claim relates to an injury to a national of a State rather than to the State itself. ITLOS has ruled that interference with navigation in contravention of the Convention constitutes a wrong to the flag State in its own right.[29] In that context, the flag State may claim damages for injury to crew members and losses sustained by the owners of the ship and its cargo, without regard to the nationality of those persons.[30]

7 Substantive Limitations on Jurisdiction under Section 2 of Part XV

Article 286, the first article in Section 2 of Part XV, begins with the words, '[s]ubject to section 3'. Section 3 of Part XV sets forth limitations (in Article 297) and exceptions (in Article 298) to applicability of Section 2, that is, to the scope of compulsory jurisdiction under Section 2 of Part XV of the Convention. Section 3 does not apply in cases in which jurisdiction is based on another agreement, unless that agreement itself incorporates the relevant provisions of Part XV by reference.[31]

---

instruments of the European Union prohibited Ireland from submitting the MOX Plant dispute with the United Kingdom to arbitration under the LOSC. *Commission v Ireland* (Case C-459/03) [2006] ECR I-4635.

[27] See n 6.   [28] See *MOX Plant* (Provisional Measures), n 26, [60].

[29] *M/V 'Saiga' (No 2) (St Vincent and the Grenadines v Guinea)* (Judgment) [1999] ITLOS Rep 10, [97] and [98]; *M/V 'Virginia G' (Panama v Guinea-Bissau)* Judgment of the International Tribunal for the Law of the Sea, Case No 19 (14 April 2014) [157]. The latter judgment also held that failure to comply with the requirements of Art 73 regarding enforcement of fisheries regulations in the EEZ constitutes a violation of the rights of the flag State in its own right. Ibid.

[30] *M/V 'Saiga' (No 2)* (Judgment), n 29, [103]–[109]; *M/V 'Virginia G'*, n 29, [125]–[129].

[31] For such an incorporation by reference, see FSA, n 8, Art 30(1). An agreement to transfer a dispute to ITLOS that had been submitted to arbitration under Section 2 of Part XV does not necessarily waiver objections to jurisdiction or admissibility. See *M/V 'Saiga' (No 2)* (Provisional Measures), n 9, [14] and [27]–[30]; *M/V 'Virginia G'*, n 29, [2]–[5] and [98]–[101].

7.1 Article 297

Article 297 addresses the question of the extent to which the exercise of coastal State sovereign rights or jurisdiction can be challenged by resort to arbitration or adjudication under Section 2 of Part XV of the Convention. The first paragraph establishes the basic rule generally limiting such challenges to the three situations enumerated in that paragraph, of which the first and third are the most important.

The first enumerated situation in which compulsory jurisdiction is preserved applies where it is alleged that the coastal State has contravened the provisions of the Convention regarding navigation, overflight, submarine cables, and pipelines and related activities. This includes, among other things, interference with navigation resulting from regulatory or enforcement measures with respect to pollution from ships that exceed the authority of the coastal State under the LOSC or otherwise contravene the Convention.[32]

The third enumerated situation in which compulsory jurisdiction is preserved applies where it is alleged that the coastal State has contravened specified international environmental rules and standards that are applicable to the coastal State. The reference is to rules and standards that are determinate and specific.[33] Such rules and standards are typically found in IMO conventions and their technical annexes. The duty of the coastal State to implement such rules and standards in the exercise of its rights with respect to seabed activities, offshore installations, and dumping can be found in Articles 208(3), 210(6), 214, and 216.

There is no express reference to particular zones of coastal State jurisdiction in paragraph 1 of Article 297. While the term 'sovereign rights' is used by the Convention in connection with the EEZ and the continental shelf, the word 'jurisdiction' is used more generally, and both terms embrace rights that are subsumed within the broader term 'sovereignty' that is used in connection with internal waters, archipelagic waters, and the territorial sea.[34] It may not make much difference whether the limitation on compulsory jurisdiction set forth in paragraph 1 of Article 297 is understood to apply to internal waters, archipelagic waters, and the territorial sea (including straits), since rights of navigation and overflight may be the principal issues subject to compulsory jurisdiction whether or not the paragraph applies.

---

[32] Such measures are not excluded from compulsory jurisdiction under the subsequent paragraphs of Art 297; those provisions specifically refer to coastal State jurisdiction with respect to marine scientific research and with respect to marine living resources.

[33] The French text refers to 'règles ou normes internationales déterminées', the Russian text to 'конкретные международные нормы и стандарты', and the Spanish text to 'reglas y estándares internacionales específicos'.

[34] The word 'jurisdiction' is used in Arts 27 and 28 regarding the territorial sea and in Art 34 regarding straits used for international navigation.

Paragraphs 2 and 3 of Article 297 impose significant limitations on the jurisdiction of a court or tribunal under Section 2 of Part XV with respect to the exercise of coastal State rights regarding scientific research in the EEZ and on the continental shelf (Art 297(2)) and regarding fishing in the EEZ (Art 297(3)).[35] The absence of a specific reference to the territorial sea in paragraphs 2 and 3, and to the continental shelf in paragraph 3, presumably reflects the absence of relevant duties in the Convention regarding coastal State regulation of such matters in those areas. In procedural terms, therefore, the appropriate objection might be to admissibility of the claim rather than to jurisdiction, but the expected outcome ordinarily would be the same.

Paragraphs 2 and 3 of Article 297 afford either party the right to submit to conciliation, pursuant to Section 2 of Annex V, certain disputes excluded from compulsory arbitration or adjudication by those paragraphs. The respondent is 'obliged to submit to such proceedings', which may continue in its absence. As in the case of conciliation by agreement, the report of the conciliation commission is not binding on the parties.[36] No State has thus far instituted conciliation proceedings under this provision.

7.2 Article 298

Article 309 of the LOSC provides '[n]o reservations or exceptions may be made to this Convention unless expressly permitted by other articles of this Convention.' Article 298 enumerates specific optional exceptions to compulsory jurisdiction under Section 2 of Part XV. A State may invoke one or more of those exceptions by declaration at the time it becomes party to the Convention or at any time thereafter. The declaration remains effective until modified or withdrawn, and applies to cases brought against or by the declarant under Section 2 of Part XV. Declarations under Article 298 have been made by a significant minority of parties to the Convention.

---

[35] Unlike paragraph 1 of Article 297, which directly addresses which disputes are subject to settlement under Section 2 of Part XV, paragraph 2 and 3 provide that 'the coastal State shall not be obliged to accept the submission to such settlement' of the disputes to which they refer. This wording might suggest the need for express objection during the proceedings. The *Barbados/Trinidad and Tobago* award concluded that ruling upon the rights and duties of the Parties in relation to fisheries within [a Party's exclusive economic zone is] outside the jurisdiction of this Tribunal because Article 297(3)(a) stipulates that a coastal State is not obliged to submit to the jurisdiction of an Annex VII Tribunal "any dispute relating to [the coastal State's] sovereign rights with respect to the living resources in the exclusive economic zone", *and* Trinidad and Tobago has made plain that it does not consent to the decision of such a dispute by this Tribunal.
See *Barbados/Trinidad and Tobago* (2006) XXVII RIAA 147, [276] (emphasis added).

[36] See LOSC, n 1, Annex V, Art 7(2).

Paragraph 1(a) of Article 298 permits a State to exclude from compulsory jurisdiction under Section 2 of Part XV 'disputes concerning the interpretation or application of articles 15, 74 and 83 relating to sea boundary delimitations, or those involving historic bays or titles'. The final text of paragraph 1 emerged from a negotiating group whose mandate was maritime boundaries between States with opposite or adjacent coasts, substance as well as dispute settlement.[37]

Like paragraphs 2 and 3 of Article 297, paragraph 1(a) of Article 298 provides for compulsory conciliation of excluded disputes, subject to an exclusion for a dispute that necessarily involves concurrent consideration of a land sovereignty dispute.[38] However, paragraph 1(a) goes on to provide that after the conciliation commission has presented its report, 'the parties shall negotiate an agreement on the basis of that report; if these negotiations do not result in an agreement, the parties shall, by mutual consent, submit the question to one of the procedures provided for in section 2, unless the parties otherwise agree'. No State has thus far instituted conciliation proceedings under this provision. Were a State to do so, and were those proceedings to fail to result in agreement, an issue might arise regarding the meaning of the clause requiring the parties to submit the question to arbitration or adjudication under Section 2 of Part XV 'by mutual consent'. It seems reasonably clear that a court or tribunal would not have jurisdiction under this clause absent such consent. But what of a court or tribunal that would otherwise have jurisdiction under Section 2 of Part XV? Are we to suppose that the delegations that insisted on the right to exclude maritime boundary disputes between States with opposite or adjacent coasts from arbitration or adjudication, often as a condition of their acceptance of Section 2 of Part XV or Article 309, and the governments and parliaments that approved the Convention on that understanding, nevertheless consented to the binding jurisdiction of a court or tribunal on the question of a duty to agree to submit the excluded dispute to arbitration or adjudication?

Paragraph 1(b) of Article 298 permits a State to exclude from compulsory jurisdiction under Section 2 of Part XV 'disputes concerning military activities, including military activities by government vessels and aircraft engaged in non-commercial service, and disputes concerning law enforcement activities in regard to the exercise of sovereign rights or jurisdiction excluded from the jurisdiction of a court or

---

[37] Virtually all discussion of this exclusion at the Third United Nations Conference on the Law of the Sea (UNCLOS III) and thereafter relates to delimitation of maritime boundaries between States with opposite or adjacent coasts. There has been very little discussion of the reference to historic bays or titles, its association with the exclusion for maritime boundaries, or its relation to the two substantive provisions that use those terms, Arts 10(6) and 15. The dispute between El Salvador and Honduras regarding the Gulf of Fonseca looms large in the history of the inclusion of the reference to historic bays or title in this context; Ambassador Reynaldo Galindo Pohl of El Salvador was co-chair of the influential informal negotiations on dispute settlement and presented the first set of drafts with bracketed options to the Conference, almost all of which contained the reference. It remains to be seen what a court or tribunal faced with the issue may make of this.

[38] See n 19.

tribunal under article 297, paragraph 2 or 3'. The text focuses on the nature of the activity. Depending on the laws and practices of the flag State, a warship, military aircraft, or other government vessel or aircraft may be engaged in only one type of activity or may be engaged in either military activities or law enforcement activities at different times. The distinction is important. The exception for law enforcement activities is limited to the exercise of sovereign rights or jurisdiction excluded from Section 2 of Part XV by Article 297, paragraph 2 or 3, namely, enumerated coastal State rights concerning marine scientific research in the EEZ and on the continental shelf or concerning fishing in the EEZ.[39] The exclusion for military activities is not so limited.[40] No State has thus far invoked the military activities exception.[41] Nor has it been contended that the exception for enforcement of coastal State fisheries laws in its EEZ is a bar as such to proceedings under Article 292 for prompt release on bond of fishing vessels arrested in the EEZ where the detaining State has made a declaration under Article 298(1)(b).[42]

Article 298(1)(c) permits a State to exclude from compulsory jurisdiction under Section 2 of Part XV 'disputes in respect of which the Security Council of the United Nations is exercising the functions assigned to it by the Charter of the United Nations, unless the Security Council decides to remove the matter from its agenda or calls upon the parties to settle it by the means provided for in this Convention'. This text presumably encompasses all the functions of the Council under the Charter, including those provided for in Chapters VI and VII. The provision does not authorize the Council to confer jurisdiction; rather it permits the Council to remove an obstacle to jurisdiction posed by its own agenda. In this regard it should be noted that issues of institutional authority and coordination pertinent to the relationship between the exercise of the functions of the Council under the Charter and those of a court or tribunal under the Convention may arise independently of any declaration under Article 298,

---

[39] The Russian declaration under Art 298 tracks the wording of the article, but omits the qualifying words 'excluded under article 297, paragraph 2 or 3'. ITLOS limited the declaration by those qualifying words. 'Arctic Sunrise', n 15, [41]–[45]. This interpretation of A similar approach to the Russian declaration was also adopted by the LOSC Annex VII Tribunal. 'Arctic Sunrise' Arbitration (Kingdom of the Netherlands v Russian Federation) (Award on Jurisdiction) (26 November 2014) [69], available at <http://www.pca-cpa.org/showpage.asp?pag_id=1556>.

[40] In either case, the question is whether the flag State is subject to jurisdiction. There is no question of jurisdiction over the vessel or aircraft.

[41] Argentina withdrew its declaration regarding military activities prior to instituting proceedings in its dispute with Ghana regarding detention of the naval training ship *ARA Libertad*. See Argentina, 'After ratification' (26 October 2012) in Division for Ocean Affairs and the Law of the Sea (DOALOS), *Declarations and Statements*, available at <http://www.un.org/Depts/los/convention_agreements/convention_declarations.htm#Argentina after ratification>.

[42] The law enforcement exception was invoked by France in Art 292 proceedings in connection with the applicant's challenge to the confiscation of the detained fishing vessel ordered by a French court. *Grand Prince (Belize v France)* (Prompt Release) [2001] ITLOS Rep 17, [60].

although Council action where there is a declaration may have the effect of clarifying the Council's position.

8 Institutional Constraints on the Exercise of Jurisdiction

A court or tribunal to which a dispute is submitted does not exist in an institutional vacuum. Other institutions, including other courts and tribunals, may have actual or potential functions that are, in some measure, related to the dispute in question. Some of the potential problems of overlapping functions are averted by express jurisdictional limitations.[43] But these do not exhaust the full range of possibilities.

Where the dispute concerns provisions of another instrument that are incorporated by reference, and that instrument contains its own dispute settlement procedures, should the parties to such an instrument be required to use those procedures, at least as an initial matter? Section 6(1)(b) of the 1994 Implementation Agreement regarding Part XI incorporates by reference 'the General Agreement on Tariffs and Trade, its relevant codes and successor or superseding agreements'. In that connection, paragraph 1(f)(i) specifies that parties to those agreements shall have recourse to the dispute settlement procedures of such agreements with respect to disputes concerning their provisions.

A number of issues may be relevant in deciding whether similar deference is appropriate in connection with other instruments whose provisions are incorporated by reference into the LOSC, be it as a jurisdictional matter under Articles 281 and 282 or as a question of whether the exercise of jurisdiction should be deferred or declined. These include the risk of inconsistent rulings; whether the incorporated rules are closely linked to specialized dispute settlement organs with unique competence to interpret and apply those rules; whether the meaning of the incorporated rules is the central legal issue in the case; whether the issue posed is one of first impression; and whether the rules are incorporated as such or only by virtue of a reference to generally accepted international rules or the like.[44]

Another difficulty involves the question of which court or tribunal should decide related issues pending before more than one court or tribunal in proceedings affecting the same parties. After arbitral proceedings under LOSC Annex VII had

---

[43] The limitations set forth in the LOSC, n 1, Arts 281, 282, 292, and 298 were previously discussed.
[44] The question of references to international law is discussed in Section 10 below.

commenced in the *MOX Plant* case brought by Ireland against the United Kingdom, the Commission of the European Communities informed the European Parliament that it was considering whether to institute proceedings in the European Court of Justice against Ireland under relevant Community instruments. The Annex VII Tribunal observed that:

In these circumstances, there is a real possibility that the European Court of Justice may be seised of the question whether the provisions of the Convention on which Ireland relies are matters in relation to which competence has been transferred to the European Community and, indeed, whether the exclusive jurisdiction of the European Court of Justice, with regard to Ireland and the United Kingdom as Member States of the European Community, extends to the interpretation and application of the Convention as such.[45]

While the interpretation and application of Article 282 of the LOSC was of course within the jurisdiction of the Annex VII Tribunal, the underlying questions 'essentially concern the internal operation of a separate legal order (namely the legal order of the European Communities)' and 'are to be determined within the institutional framework of the European Communities'.[46] Whatever their positions on the jurisdictional issues, Ireland and the United Kingdom were not themselves competent to definitively determine their obligations under European Community law. Accordingly, the arbitral Tribunal, while remaining seized of the dispute, decided to suspend further proceedings on jurisdiction and the merits 'bearing in mind considerations of mutual respect and comity which should prevail between judicial institutions both of which may be called upon to determine rights and obligations as between two States'.[47]

---

[45] *MOX Plant Arbitration (Ireland v United Kingdom)*, Procedural Order No 3 of the Arbitral Tribunal (24 June 2003) 7 [21], available at <http://www.pca-cpa.org/showpage.asp?pag_id=1148>.
[46] Ibid, [24].
[47] Ibid, [29]. The ECJ ultimately decided that Ireland's institution of the proceedings under LOSC Annex VII violated its obligations under European law, and Ireland thereafter withdrew the case submitted to arbitration. See n 26.
Different aspects of the swordfish dispute between Chile and the European Union were submitted by the former to arbitration under the LOSC (and subsequently, by mutual agreement, transferred to a special chamber of ITLOS), and by the latter to a panel under the World Trade Organization (WTO) Dispute Settlement Understanding. The former case basically posed the question of EU compliance with the conservation requirements of the LOSC, while the latter basically posed the question of whether Chile's exclusion of EU fishing vessels from Chilean ports violated the 1994 General Agreement on Tariffs and Trade (GATT). While the dispute was ultimately settled and the cases withdrawn, had that not occurred, it is possible that certain issues might have been relevant to both proceedings. If, for example, the issue of the EU's compliance with its conservation obligations under the LOSC were also considered relevant to the WTO proceedings, then the question might have arisen as to whether one forum should await decision on that issue by the other. In this connection, it would seem that the ITLOS chamber might have greater familiarity with that particular issue.
The dispute with respect to Atlanto-Scandia herring might have posed similar issues. See *Atlanto-Scandian Herring Arbitration (Denmark in respect of the Faroe Islands v EU)* Submitted to a LOSC Annex VII Tribunal (16 August 2013), available at <http://www.pca-cpa.org/showpage.

Another such difficulty involves the question of the relationship between a court or tribunal, on the one hand, and a political or administrative body, on the other hand. The Convention addresses this issue in connection with the relationship between the Sea-Bed Disputes Chamber of ITLOS and the International Seabed Authority (ISA). Article 189 of the LOSC expressly confirms the Chamber's power, among other things, to entertain 'claims concerning excess of jurisdiction or misuse of power', but prohibits the Chamber from substituting its discretion for that of the Authority.

Similar issues could arise with respect to regional and other fisheries management organizations. Such organizations have important conservation and management functions on the high seas under Articles 63, 64, and Part VII of the LOSC as well as the 1995 Implementation Agreement on Straddling Fish Stocks and Highly Migratory Fish Stocks (FSA). The ability of these organizations to command the level of agreement among their members necessary to fulfil their functions varies considerably. Often the issue is more likely to be non-performance or under-performance rather than over-reaching. For this reason, the 1995 FSA places special emphasis on the power of courts and tribunals to prescribe binding provisional measures, expressly including conservation as one of the objectives of such measures.[48] Among other things, this looming power conferred on courts and tribunals to impose urgently needed conservation measures that may endure for at least the remainder of a fishing season may stimulate more constructive behaviour in the organizations themselves.[49]

Both the ICJ and ITLOS have had the occasion to consider whether to exercise their power to delimit the continental shelf beyond 200 nautical miles (nm) in light of the provisions of Article 76(8) and Annex II of the LOSC and the role of the Commission on the Limits of the Continental Shelf (CLCS). Both before and after ITLOS delimited the continental shelf beyond 200 nm,[50] the ICJ declined to do so pending review of the status of the areas by the CLCS.[51] In neither of the ICJ cases had the parties made full submissions to the CLCS (and one of the parties in the

asp?pag_id=1554>; *European Union—Measures on Atlanto-Scandian Herring*, Denmark Request for consultations 4 November 2013 (WT/DS469). The parties withdrew both cases by agreement on 21 August 2014.

[48] See n 8.

[49] The humourist HL Mencken observed: 'Conscience is the inner voice that warns us somebody may be looking.' See HL Mencken, *A Mencken Chrestomathy* (Alfred A Knopf New York 1956) 617.

[50] *Delimitation of the Maritime Boundary in the Bay of Bengal (Bangladesh/Myanmar)* [2012] ITLOS Rep 4, [342]–[476] (hereinafter *Bangladesh/Myanmar*). An Annex VII arbitral tribunal thereafter delimited the continental shelf beyond 200 nm between Bangladesh and India in the Bay of Bengal. *Bay of Bengal Maritime Boundary Arbitration (Bangladesh/India)*, Award of the LOSC Annex VII Tribunal (7 July 2014) [438]–[480], available at <http://www.pca-cpa.org/showpage.asp?pag_id=1376>. Three of the five arbitrators had participated in the prior ITLOS judgment.

[51] *Territorial and Maritime Dispute between Nicaragua and Honduras in the Caribbean Sea (Nicaragua v Honduras)* (Judgment) [2007] ICJ Rep 659, [319]; *Territorial and Maritime Dispute (Nicaragua v Colombia)* (Judgment) [2012] ICJ Rep 624, [125]–[131]. Nicaragua subsequently brought a new action

second case was not even party to the LOSC). Nor was the status of the relevant areas beyond 200 nm as continental margin clearly and uncontrovertibly established. This difference between the ITLOS and ICJ cases is a particularly important consideration given the fact that neighbouring coastal States both may have expansive views of the extent of their entitlements in the area off their coasts, and less than optimum concern for the direct or indirect impact of their positions on the limits of the international seabed area and the common heritage of mankind. Such considerations prompted both the detailed criteria and constraints in Article 76 regarding the limits of the continental shelf beyond 200 nm and the creation of the CLCS under Article 76(8) and Annex II of the Convention.[52]

In the case between Bangladesh and Myanmar, ITLOS observed:

> The Convention sets up an institutional framework with a number of bodies to implement its provisions, including the Commission, the International Seabed Authority and this Tribunal. Activities of these bodies are complementary to each other so as to ensure coherent and efficient implementation of the Convention.[53]

In this regard ITLOS distinguished between determination of the seaward limits of the continental shelf under Article 76, a matter with respect to which the CLCS makes recommendations that become 'final and binding' if implemented by the coastal State, and delimitation of overlapping entitlements to the continental shelf under Article 83, with respect to which the 'function of settling disputes... is entrusted to dispute settlement procedures under article 83 and Part XV of the Convention, which include international courts and tribunals'.[54] In considering 'whether it can and should in the present case determine the entitlements of the Parties to the continental shelf beyond 200 nm' under Article 76,[55] ITLOS distinguished between issues that are 'predominantly legal in nature',[56] on the one hand, and 'scientific and technical issues arising in the implementation of article 76 on the basis of submissions [to the CLCS] by coastal States',[57] on the other hand. In

---

against Colombia with respect to delimitation of the continental shelf. *Delimitation of the Continental Shelf (Nicaragua v Colombia)*, Application Instituting Proceedings filed in the International Court of Justice (16 September 2013), available at <http://www.icj-cij.org/docket/files/154/17532.pdf>.

[52] Those concerned with protecting the common heritage may have breathed a sigh of relief when the ICJ declined to consider Colombia's audacious contention that its status as a non-party not only relieves it of the duty to comply with the institutional provisions of the LOSC but confers upon it the exceptional benefit of a continental shelf that is not limited by the detailed substantive criteria and constraints set forth in Art 76. See *Territorial and Maritime Dispute (Nicaragua v Colombia)*, n 51, [117]–[118]. In light of the fact that the ICJ did find paragraph 1 of Art 76 to be declaratory of customary international law, it may be noted that ITLOS concluded that 'the notion of natural prolongation and that of continental margin under article 76, paragraphs 1 and 4, ... refer to the same area' and that 'the reference to natural prolongation in article 76, paragraph 1, of the Convention, should be understood in light of the subsequent provisions of the article defining the continental shelf and the continental margin'. *Bangladesh/ Myanmar*, n 50, [434]–[437].

[53] *Bangladesh/Mynanmar*, n 50, [373].   [54] Ibid, [376].   [55] Ibid, [402].
[56] Ibid, [413].   [57] Ibid, [411].

light of these and other considerations, including the unique characteristics of the continental margin in the Bay of Bengal and the fact that the persistence of the delimitation dispute precluded the CLCS, under its rules, from performing its recommendatory functions with respect to the parties' submissions,[58] ITLOS determined that the parties had overlapping entitlements to the continental shelf beyond 200 nm under Article 76, and delimited those entitlements without prejudice to the question of their seaward limits or the rights of third States.

9 Entities other than States

Because the definition of States parties to the Convention includes certain entities other than States, those entities are also subject to the dispute settlement provisions of the Convention.[59] This includes an international organization such as the European Union, which is a party to the Convention in its own right with respect to 'matters governed by this Convention in respect of which competence has been transferred to the organization by its members States which are Parties to this Convention'.[60] Article 305 also refers to certain self-governing territories and associated States.

Article 187 of the LOSC includes within the jurisdiction of the ITLOS Sea-Bed Disputes Chamber not only disputes involving States parties but those involving the International Seabed Authority[61] and private individuals or companies sponsored by States parties that have or seek a contract from the ISA for exploration or exploitation of the non-living resources of the international seabed Area. Under Article 188(2), a dispute concerning the interpretation or application of a contract with respect to such exploration or exploitation 'shall be submitted, at the request of any party to the dispute, to binding commercial arbitration, unless the parties

---

[58] Ibid, [385]–[392].

[59] LOSC, n 1, Art 1(2)(2). See n 16. In what has been understood to be a reference to Taiwan, FSA, n 8, Art 1(3) provides that the Agreement 'applies mutatis mutandis to other fishing entities whose vessels fish on the high seas'. But the Agreement's provisions on settlement of disputes refer only to States or States parties, and paragraph 3 does not incorporate these fishing entities into the definition of States parties. On the other hand, the 2000 Convention on the Conservation and Management of Highly Migratory Fish Stocks in the Western and Central Pacific Ocean, which was negotiated in light of the LOSC and the FSA, provides in Annex I, paragraph 3, for arbitration of disputes involving a fishing entity. More generally, it may be noted that LOSC, n 1, Annex VI, Art 20, provides that ITLOS 'shall be open to entities other than States Parties… in any case submitted pursuant to any other agreement conferring jurisdiction on the Tribunal which is accepted by all the parties to that case'.

[60] LOSC, n 1, Art 305 and Annex IX.   [61] Including the Enterprise.

otherwise agree'.[62] However, when the dispute 'also involves a question of the interpretation of Part XI and the Annexes relating thereto', the arbitral tribunal must refer that question to the Sea-Bed Disputes Chamber for a ruling. It would accordingly appear that judicial review functions with respect to the Authority are focused on the Chamber.[63]

Article 292 of the Convention provides that an application for prompt release may be made 'by or on behalf of the flag State of the vessel'. This formulation was intended as a compromise with those who advocated direct access in prompt release proceedings for the owner or operator of the detained ship.[64] But the ITLOS Rules reflect a traditional State-centric position in which the intended compromise all but vanishes. Essentially, all that remains in practice is the ability of the owner or operator to hire counsel if the State agrees; this does not of course require any distinction between applications made 'by' or 'on behalf of' the State. Be that as it may, the Convention text would appear to allow a flag State to implement the intended compromise if it wishes, for example by enacting a general statute designating the class of persons (such as a vessel owner or operator) authorized to file an application for prompt release on its behalf with notice to the flag State but without the need for specific authorization in each case.

10 Applicable Law

The LOSC does not exist in isolation. It forms part of the corpus of international law. Thus Article 293 provides that a court or tribunal with jurisdiction under Section 2 of Part XV 'shall apply this Convention and other rules of international law not incompatible with this Convention'.[65]

At the same time, it should be borne in mind that the LOSC is a comprehensive convention. The preamble begins with a reference to 'all issues relating to the law of the sea' and ends by specifically limiting the application of other rules of international law to 'matters not regulated by this Convention'. This is best understood as referring to rules other than those arising under the law of the sea, such as rules concerning the law of treaties or the law of State responsibility.

---

[62] LOSC, n 1, Annex III, Art 13(15) contains a similar provision regarding the financial terms of such a contract.

[63] The Chamber is also the only dispute settlement body to which requests for advisory opinions may be submitted by the Assembly or the Council of the Authority under Art 191.

[64] And perhaps a labour union that represents detained crew members.

[65] With respect to the Seabed Disputes Chamber, Annex VI, Art 38, adds the rules and regulations adopted by the Seabed Authority and mining contracts with the Authority.

Of course, the text of the Convention may itself specifically incorporate certain rules of international law, including law of the sea rules. Perhaps the best-known example is the reference to international law in Articles 74(1) and 83(1) regarding delimitation of the EEZ and the continental shelf. But even in that context, ITLOS took care to make clear that the reference is to be understood and applied in light of the provisions of the Convention.[66]

To be sure, the meaning of the text of the Convention may itself be clarified by reference to rules found in other instruments or customary international law, such as those that help explain the provenance, wording, or function of the text. This does not, however, entail the application of rules external to the Convention.

In addition, care should be taken to avoid conflating the question of applicable law with the question of jurisdiction.[67] Under Section 2 of Part XV of the LOSC, jurisdiction is limited to disputes concerning the interpretation and application of the Convention. Other rules of international law may be applied as such in that context, only if they relate to matters not regulated by the Convention, and only if they are not incompatible with the Convention.

11 Advisory Opinions

The only references to advisory opinions in the Convention are to those of the ITLOS Sea-Bed Disputes Chamber in response to a request from the Assembly or Council of the International Seabed Authority.[68] There is no mention of advisory opinions in the provisions of the Convention regarding jurisdiction under other agreements.[69] However, Article 138(1) of the Rules adopted by the Tribunal provides

---

[66] LOSC, n 1, Arts 74(1) and 83(1) 'state that delimitation must be effected on the basis of international law, as referred to in article 38 of the Statute of the International Court of Justice, in order to achieve an equitable solution. ... Accordingly, the law applicable under the Convention with regard to delimitation of the exclusive economic zone and the continental shelf includes rules of customary international law. It follows that the application of such rules in the context of articles 74 and 83 of the Convention requires the achievement of an equitable solution, as this is the goal of delimitation prescribed by these articles.' *Bangladesh/Myanmar*, n 50, [183].

[67] See *MOX Plant* (Procedural Order No 3), n 45, [19].

[68] LOSC, n 1, Arts 159(10), 191; Annex VI, Art 40(2). Such an opinion was rendered by the Chamber in *Responsibilities and Obligations of States Sponsoring Persons and Entities with Respect to Activities in the Area*, [2011] ITLOS Rep 10.

[69] LOSC, n 1, Art 288(2) refers to jurisdiction over a 'dispute' concerning the interpretation or application of an international agreement related to the purposes of the Convention. LOSC, n 1, Annex VI, Art 21, the ITLOS Statute, refers to jurisdiction over all 'matters' specifically provided for in any other agreement which confers jurisdiction on the Tribunal, although the articles that precede and follow

that '[t]he Tribunal may give an advisory opinion on a legal question if an international agreement related to the purposes of the Convention specifically provides for the submission to the Tribunal of a request for such an opinion.' The question of the basis for this rule may be addressed in connection with a pending request for an advisory opinion.[70]

12 CONCLUSION

The award in the *Southern Bluefin Tuna* arbitration gave rise to a debate as to whether the dispute settlement regime of the LOSC is comprehensive. That is the wrong question. The LOSC itself is comprehensive, and Part XV applies to all disputes concerning the interpretation or application of the Convention.

Under Part XV and related provisions of the LOSC, not all of these disputes are subject to arbitration or adjudication under Section 2 of Part XV. Some are subject to the dispute settlement procedures of other treaties, at least as a first step, or perhaps definitively, especially where those procedures entail a binding decision. In many, if not most, cases, this is a matter of pre-requisites to jurisdiction or choice of forum, neither of which in the end excludes arbitration or adjudication.

Other disputes are excluded by Section 3 from arbitration or adjudication under Section 2 of Part XV. If these excluded disputes are not subject to the jurisdiction of a court or tribunal under some other treaty, they can still be submitted by special agreement. In this respect the problem, if problem there be, arises not from the Convention but from the fact that, under international law, a State is not subject to the jurisdiction of an international court or tribunal absent express consent.

In that light the significance of the LOSC is clear. As of this writing, it has attracted 166 parties. The fact that all States that become party to the Convention thereby consent to arbitration or adjudication of most disputes concerning its interpretation and application represents a remarkable, and abidingly important, step forward in furthering the rule of law in international affairs.

---

this provision refer in the context of submissions under other agreements to 'case', 'all parties to that case', and 'disputes'. The 1995 FSA, n 8, also makes no mention of advisory opinions; Art 30 incorporates the provisions of Part XV of the LOSC with respect to 'any dispute between States Parties' concerning the interpretation or application of the Agreement or of a sub-regional, regional, or global fisheries agreement relating to straddling fish stocks or highly migratory fish stocks to which they are parties.

[70] *Request for an Advisory Opinion Submitted by the Sub-Regional Fisheries Commission (SRFC)* (2013), available at <http://www.itlos.org/index.php?id=252#c1276>.

19
THE INTERNATIONAL MARITIME ORGANIZATION

ALDO CHIRCOP

1 INTRODUCTION

THE 1982 United Nations Convention on the Law of the Sea (LOSC) sets out duties to cooperate for States at the global and regional level in several areas. The duties are often to be performed directly or through international organizations generally or, more specifically, through competent international organizations. As an agency of the United Nations (UN), the International Maritime Organization (IMO) is an intergovernmental organization having special competence in matters relating to navigation and shipping. The LOSC rarely mentions specific organizations by name and the IMO is expressly mentioned only once.[1] In addition to the IMO, there are other international organizations that are considered competent in some respect in maritime matters and through which States cooperate, including the United Nations Conference on Trade and Development (UNCTAD), United Nations Commission on International Trade Law (UNCITRAL) and the International Labour Organization (ILO). However, the IMO is widely regarded as the principal

---

[1] 1982 United Nations Convention on the Law of the Sea, Annex VIII, Art 2 (hereinafter LOSC).

competent international organization with regards to the regulation of international shipping and navigation for safety, vessel-source pollution, and maritime security purposes in the LOSC.[2] While its work has been preponderantly in the public law area, the IMO has also addressed trade facilitation and private maritime law aspects, especially with regard to civil liability regimes. The IMO has over 170 Member States, and its headquarters are located in London, United Kingdom.

The idea of an intergovernmental organization dedicated to shipping was first mooted at the International Maritime Conference convened by the United States of America in Washington in 1889, but was not considered feasible.[3] The first organization to be established was the non-governmental Comité Maritime International (CMI) in 1897 and whose efforts focused on the development of a suite of maritime conventions.[4] The League of Nations took steps to establish an Organization for Communications and Transit with the purpose to secure and maintain freedom of communications and transit, convening a series of conferences and providing initial secretariat support for the proposed organization, but only to be interrupted by World War II.[5] The genesis of the IMO can be traced to World War II when a United Maritime Authority was established by the allied powers to consider and advise on shipping matters. The Authority went through various institutional mutations until the convening of the United Nations Maritime Conference in 1948[6] where the decision to establish a permanent international organization dedicated to maritime matters was taken. The conference adopted the 1948 Convention on the Inter-Governmental Maritime Consultative Organization, now known as the Convention on the International Maritime Organization (IMO Convention), establishing the IMO under its original name of Intergovernmental Maritime Consultative Organization (IMCO). The 1948 Convention is the IMO's constitutive instrument and has been amended several times by the Organization's Assembly, most importantly to modify the size of Council, establish new Committees, clarify its purposes and change its name.[7] The change of name from IMCO to IMO came into effect in 1982.[8]

---

[2] United Nations Division for Ocean Affairs and the Law of the Sea (DOALOS), '"Competent or Relevant International Organizations" under the United Nations Convention on the Law of the Sea' (1996) 31 *Law of the Sea Bulletin* 79–95, available at <http://www.un.org/depts/los/doalos_publications/LOSBulletins/bulletinpdf/bulletinE31.pdf>.

[3] *Protocols of the Proceedings of the International Maritime Conference, Washington DC, 16 October–31 December 1889* (Government Printing Office Washington DC 1890) Vol 2, 984ff.

[4] E McDonald, 'Toward a World Maritime Organization: A Half-Century of Developments in Ocean Shipping' (25 January–1 February 1948) *Department of State Bulletin* 1, 1ff.

[5] Ibid, 3–5. The International Law Association also considered the idea at that time. See CJ Colombos, *The International Law of the Sea* (6th edn Longmans Green London 1967) 439–42; KR Simmonds, *The International Maritime Organization* (Simmonds & Hill Publishing Ltd London 1994) 1.

[6] McDonald, n 4, 5ff.

[7] IMO, *List of Resolutions Adopted by the Assembly, Council, FAL, LC, LEG, LP, MEPC, MSC, and TC Committee* (12 August 2013) 5, available at <http://www.imo.org/KnowledgeCentre/IndexofIMOResolutions/Documents/Subject%20list%20with%20resolutions.pdf>.

[8] IMO Assembly Res A.358(IX), *Amendments to the IMCO Convention* (14 November 1975); IMO Assembly Res A.371(X), *Correction of Assembly Resolution A.358(IX)* (9 November 1977).

The IMO plays a critical role in the international law of the sea. The various international navigation rights in the LOSC were collectively one of the most contentious issues negotiated at the Third United Nations Conference on the Law of the Sea, 1973–1982 (UNCLOS III). The Convention crafted a delicate balance between, on the one hand, the rights and jurisdictions that may be exercised by coastal States in their maritime zones and, on the other hand, the traditional freedom of navigation enjoyed by all flag States and its mutations in the various zones. As discussed elsewhere in this *Handbook*,[9] the LOSC reaffirms a flag State's primary right and duty to exercise effective jurisdiction and control over its ships. The Convention largely sets out the legislative and enforcement jurisdiction of coastal States with regards to international navigation through their maritime zones; producing regimes for innocent passage in the territorial sea; transit passage through straits used for international navigation; archipelagic sea lanes passage through archipelagic waters; and freedom of navigation in the exclusive economic zone (EEZ) and over the continental shelf.[10] In this conventional scheme, the IMO plays a central role in facilitating international cooperation and maintaining the balance between the pursuit of flag and coastal State interests. Through the navigation regimes and other areas, the Convention provides the IMO with a mandate to exercise specified responsibilities and pursue the purposes of its constitutive instrument. The Organization has performed these tasks by facilitating the adoption and overseeing of over 50 international conventions on diverse maritime matters and numerous codes, guidelines and resolutions.[11] Through this opus, the Organization has provided substantive content to the jurisdictional schemes and prescriptions for cooperation on navigation and shipping matters in the LOSC. In doing so, the IMO has enabled State parties to perform important duties stipulated in the Convention.

2 Purposes, Functions, and Governance Structure

2.1 Purposes and functions

Set out in its constitutive instrument, the quintessential purpose of the IMO is:

To provide machinery for co-operation among Governments in the field of governmental regulation and practices relating to technical matters of all kinds affecting shipping engaged in

---

[9] See Chapter 14 in this volume. [10] See Chapter 13 in this volume.
[11] See IMO, *List of the Conventions, Other Multilateral Instruments and Amendments in respect of which the Organization Performs Depositary and other Functions* (as at 18 November 2013), available

international trade; to encourage and facilitate the general adoption of the highest practicable standards in matters concerning the maritime safety, efficiency of navigation and prevention and control of marine pollution from ships; and to deal with administrative and legal matters related to the purposes set out in this Article.[12]

The key aspect to observe is that the mission of the IMO is global in scope, taking into account the global nature of maritime trade. During the negotiation of the IMO Convention, several States, in particular the Scandinavian States, felt that the Organization should essentially perform only technical and operational functions and that matters concerning shipping economics were better addressed by other organizations.[13] Their view did not prevail, and the opening technical purpose would eventually be followed by 'the removal of discriminatory action and unnecessary restrictions by Governments affecting shipping engaged in international trade so as to promote the availability of shipping services to the commerce of the world without discrimination',[14] and 'consideration of unfair restrictive practices by shipping concerns'.[15] The inclusion of these purposes explains in part why the IMO Convention took 10 years to come into force.[16] A fourth purpose concerning shipping and its impact on the marine environment was added in the wake of *Torrey Canyon*.[17] The *Torrey Canyon* was a major maritime casualty involving the loss of vessel and oil cargo off the coast of the United Kingdom that highlighted major gaps in the international law of the sea and maritime law concerning the vessel-source pollution regulation, rights of State intervention, and civil liability. As will be explained below, the casualty led to major structural changes in the IMO and the initiation of a suite of international marine environmental conventions. The last purpose of the IMO is to enable the exchange of information among Members.[18]

---

at <http://www.imo.org/About/Conventions/StatusOfConventions/Documents/List%20of%20instruments%20%20as%20at%2027%20November%202014.pdf>.

[12] 1948 Convention on the International Maritime Organization, Art 1(a) (hereinafter IMO Convention). This provision is the basis for the mission in its strategic plan:

> ...to promote safe, secure, environmentally sound, efficient and sustainable shipping through cooperation. This will be accomplished by adopting the highest practicable standards of maritime safety and security, efficiency of navigation and prevention and control of pollution from ships, as well as through consideration of the related legal matters and effective implementation of IMO's instruments, with a view to their universal and uniform application.

IMO Assembly Res A.1037(27), *Strategic Plan for the Organization (2013-2017)* (22 November 2011) 3.

[13] JM Cates Jr, 'U.N. Maritime Conference: Geneva, 1948' (18 April 1948) *Department of State Bulletin* 17, 18.

[14] IMO Convention, n 12, Art 1(b). This purpose includes the following proviso:

> [A]ssistance and encouragement given by a Government for the development of its national shipping and for purposes of security does not in itself constitute discrimination, provided that such assistance and encouragement is not based on measures designed to restrict the freedom of shipping of all flags to take part in international trade.

[15] Ibid, Arts 1(c) and (d).   [16] Simmonds, n 5, 10.

[17] Other UN organs and specialized agencies may refer issues concerning the effect of shipping on the marine environment. IMO Convention, n 12, Art 1(d).

[18] Ibid, Art 1(e).

The original conception of the IMO was an organization that was essentially consultative and technical, without binding standard-setting powers similar to the International Civil Aviation Organization (ICAO).[19] Throughout most of its early years, traditional maritime States preferred to limit its powers and to protect their maritime interests from undue interference.[20] Since those early days, and most especially after the *Torrey Canyon* incident, the reluctance of Member States to confer anything beyond minimal consultative power diminished to some extent, and although Members remained cautious in allocating more power than absolutely necessary, the Organization's functions evolved considerably. Technological developments and shifts in national interests were important triggers of change.[21] The IMO has powers to consider and make recommendations to fulfil its purposes and machinery for consultation, development of maritime instruments, and facilitation of technical cooperation.[22] A key function relates to international maritime law-making, primarily consisting of rules, regulations, standards, and procedures. The IMO's powers in this regard stem from three main sources, namely (a) the general mandate set out in its constitutive instrument, (b) international maritime conventions which delegate a function to the Organization in the maintenance of those and subsidiary instruments, and (c) specific provisions in the LOSC that task the IMO as a competent international organization.

With regard to (a), the IMO is specifically allocated the function of 'drafting of conventions, agreements, or other suitable instruments, and recommend these to Governments and to intergovernmental organizations, and convene such conferences as may be necessary'.[23] At face value, this suggests a legislative function, but as Kirgis points out, '[f]ew knowledgeable observers contend that the international community is yet ready for a true world legislature.'[24] The negotiation of those formal instruments and the decision to be bound by the adopted instruments remain prerogatives of Member States using the governance structures of the Organization. Kirgis further notes that in addition to treaty-making, the IMO is an organization that finds 'ways how to channel members' conduct in discrete areas',[25] for example through codes and guidelines which, while not always mandatory, may have a similar effect to formal rules.

---

[19] A Popp, 'The Treaty-Making Work of the Legal Committee of the International Maritime Organization' in A Chircop et al (eds), *The Regulation of International Shipping: International and Comparative Perspectives* (Nijhoff Leiden 2012) 209, 209.

[20] H Silverstein, *Superships and Nation-States: The Transnational Politics of the Intergovernmental Maritime Consultative Organization* (Westview Press Boulder, CO 1976) 183.

[21] Ibid, 184–5.   [22] IMO Convention, n 12, Art 2.   [23] Ibid, Art 2(b).

[24] FL Kirgis, 'Specialized Law-Making Processes' in O Schacter and CC Joyner (eds), *United Nations Legal Order* (Cambridge University Press Cambridge 1995) Vol 1, 161.

[25] Ibid. See also FL Kirgis 'Shipping' in Schacter and Joyner (eds), n 24, Vol 2, 715.

Insofar as (b) is concerned, the IMO Convention[26] and several international maritime law conventions endow the IMO with the responsibility to maintain the instrument, including its technical amendment through a tacit acceptance procedure.[27] This power has led Wolfrum and Allen to observe that the IMO is an organization with quasi-prescriptive jurisdiction or a quasi-legislative power, respectively.[28] The 'tacit acceptance procedure' is possible where the main instrument delegates the amendment procedure to an IMO Committee. The procedure is a major innovation to treaty-amendment, in particular for technical annexes that may require frequent change to ensure they remain current. Having the necessary technical expertise, the IMO Committee concerned (generally the Maritime Safety Committee (MSC) and Marine Environment Protection Committee (MEPC)) develops and adopts the amendment through a specified majority (eg two-thirds) of voting States in the Committee and enters into force after the expiry of a specified period thereafter unless a specified minority (eg one-third) of parties to the instrument object within that period.[29] States that object may opt out of the amendment. This procedure is in lieu of the otherwise cumbersome and time-consuming diplomatic conference for changes that may be purely technical and need to be undertaken fairly frequently. Naturally, amendments to basic treaty provisions, principles, and administrative matters would still require the traditional procedure for treaty amendment under the law of treaties.[30] The open membership of the MSC and MEPC, enabling all Member States to participate in the technical amendment process, further facilitates this procedure.

2.2 Governance structure

The IMO's governance structure consists of an Assembly, a Council and five main committees, namely the Maritime Safety Committee, Marine Environment

---

[26] 'Perform functions arising in connexion with paragraphs (a), (b) and (c) of the Article, in particular those assigned to it by or under international instruments relating to maritime matters and the effect of shipping on the marine environment.' IMO Convention, n 12, Art 2(d).

[27] This procedure is explained by Adede. The procedure was studied jointly by the LEG and MSC and the recommendations of the joint report were adopted by the Assembly. AO Adede, 'Amendment Procedures for Conventions with Technical Annexes: The IMCO Experience' (1976–1977) 17 *Virginia Journal of International Law* 201. Adede further explains how law of treaties concerns with tacit acceptance were addressed. For examples in IMO conventions see: 1974 International Convention for the Safety of Life at Sea, as amended, Art 8 (hereinafter SOLAS); 1966 International Convention on Load Lines, as amended by Protocol of 1988, Art 29.

[28] R Wolfrum, 'IMO Interface with the Law of the Sea Convention' in MH Nordquist and JN Moore (eds), *Current Maritime Issues and the International Maritime Organization* (Nijhoff The Hague 1999) 223, 225; CH Allen, 'Revisiting the Thames Formula: The Evolving Role of the International Maritime Organization and its Member States in Implementing the 1982 Law of the Sea Convention' (2009) 10 *San Diego International Law Journal* 265, 271.

[29] Adede, n 27, 206.   [30] Ibid, 210.

Protection Committee, Legal Committee (LEG), Facilitation Committee (FAL), and Technical Cooperation Committee (TCC). This scheme includes an extensive system of specialized technical sub-committees. The Assembly and Council are composed of Member States, and the Committees primarily comprise Member Delegations as the key actors. Although the Secretariat fulfils various roles assigned to the Organization by the constitutive treaty and other international instruments, it is Member States that are the principal drivers of key IMO work, in particular the legislative activity, frequently in pursuit of specific international legal duties stipulated by international conventions or in response to customary law developments.

The Assembly is the plenary forum for all members and the senior decision-making level of the Organization. Three functions are of particular interest from a law of the sea perspective.[31] The first consists of making recommendations to members regarding the adoption of regulations and guidelines concerning maritime safety, vessel-source pollution, and the effects of shipping on the marine environment referred to the IMO by international instruments. The second concerns the promotion of technical cooperation taking into account the special needs of developing countries. The third enables the IMO to convene international conferences or to use any other procedure for the adoption of new international conventions or of amendments to any international conventions developed by the Committees or other organs of the Organization, unless the tacit approval procedure applies.

The Council is the executive organ and, with the exception of the power to make recommendations to Members, performs the Assembly's functions when the latter is not in session.[32] It also coordinates the work of the various committees and organs and considers matters within the scope of the committees in consultation with the committees. The composition of the Council (as eventually also in the case of the MSC), was a sensitive matter dating back to the negotiation of the IMO Convention. Traditional maritime States exerted efforts to maintain influence in an increasingly diverse international community and a balance between 'ship-providing nations and ship-using nations'.[33] An early symptom of future composition issues in the IMO governance structure was Panama's formal withdrawal from the 1948 Geneva Conference because it felt its interests were being systematically overlooked.[34] This was followed by China's voting against and Egypt's abstention during the vote on the final text because of objections to provisions concerning the Council.[35] The problem of fair representation became more difficult with decolonization and emergence of numerous new States, the vast majority of which were developing States.[36] Many of these States would eventually follow the models of Liberia and Panama

---

[31] IMO Convention, n 12, Art 15(j), (k), and (l). The other functions are listed in this provision.
[32] Ibid, Arts 21 and 26.   [33] Cates, n 13, 20.   [34] Ibid, 20.   [35] Ibid, 22.
[36] A Ademun-Odeke, 'From the "Constitution of the Maritime Safety Committee" to the "Constitution of the Council": Will the IMCO Repeat itself at the IMO Nearly Fifty Years On? The Juridical Politics of an International Organization' (2007) 43 *Texas International Law Journal* 55, 91–2.

in establishing open registries and lure away even more tonnage from traditional maritime States, fundamentally altering the dynamics within the Organization. Under constant pressure, the IMO responded through successive enlargements of the Council, elected by the Assembly, to ensure more equitable representation of all interests, in particular between States with the largest interest in providing international shipping services, States with the largest interest in international seaborne trade, and States which have special interests in maritime transport or navigation representing all major geographic areas of the world.[37] The effect has been to enable traditional maritime States to retain seats in the Council while increasing the number of seats to ensure broader geographical representation. These measures per se may not have fully dispelled concerns over composition.[38] An interesting observation is that the regular annual dues payable to the Organization by Member States are determined by a formula based in large measure on registered tonnage, effectively placing open registry States in an influential position as major contributors and to voice their concerns.[39]

Historically, the MSC was the first and perhaps the most important subsidiary body. The core of the MSC's mandate is:

---

[37] The latest enlargement has increased Council membership to 40 Members as follows:

(a) Eight shall be States with the largest interest in providing international shipping services;
(b) Eight shall be other States with the largest interest in international seaborne trade;
(c) Sixteen shall be States not elected under (a) or (b) above which have special interests in maritime transport or navigation, and whose election to the Council will ensure the representation of all major geographic areas of the world.

IMO Convention, n 12, Art 17.

[38] Ademun-Odeke, n 36, 95–7. Ademun-Odeke points critically to the non-election of Liberia to Council in the 2005 elections. In the elections at the Assembly's 28th Session (26 November–4 December 2013) Liberia was elected under category (c) consisting of States with a special interest in maritime transport or navigation, but notably, not under category (a) consisting of States with the largest interest in providing shipping services. 'IMO Assembly elects new 40-Member Council' (29 November 2013), available at <http://www.imo.org/MediaCentre/PressBriefings/Pages/53-A28-council.aspx>. In 2012, Liberia had the world's largest registered tonnage. United Nations Conference on Trade and Development (UNCTAD), *Review of Maritime Transport 2012* (UNCTAD Geneva 2012) 47.

[39] The dues are based on three principles: (1) a minimum assessment of 2.94 per cent of the total budget divided equally among Member States; (2) a basic assessment according to the UN scale of contributions; and (3) an additional assessment based on gross registered tonnage as shown in the latest edition of Lloyd's Register of Shipping. IMO Assembly Res A.726(17), *Apportionment of Expenses among Member States and Amendments to the Rules of Procedure of the Assembly* (7 November 1991). Principle (3) produces the largest assessed contributors to the IMO budget. At the end of 2012, the five largest assessed contributors in pounds were: Panama (5,404,125); Liberia (2,940,450); Marshall Islands (1,776,527); United Kingdom (1,366,318); and Bahamas (1,325,700). Panama and Liberia respectively accounted for 18.63 per cent and 10.14 per cent of all assessed contributions. The IMO also receives voluntary contributions from international organizations and Member States. The largest contributor in 2012 was the European Commission (2,211,431). IMO, *International Maritime Organization Financial Statements Year Ended 31.12.2012* (2012) 54–5, available at <http://www.imo.org/Documents/IMO_Financial_Statements_for_the_year-ended_31_12_2012.pdf>.

... to consider any matter within the scope of the Organization concerned with aids to navigation, construction and equipment of vessels, manning from a safety standpoint, rules for the prevention of collisions, handling of dangerous cargoes, maritime safety procedures and requirements, hydrographic information, log-books and navigational records, marine casualty investigation, salvage and rescue, and any other matters directly affecting maritime safety.[40]

This function is accompanied by the mandate to propose safety regulations, amendments to regulations, recommendations, and guidelines to Council.[41] With the entry into force of the IMO Convention in 1958, the composition of the MSC quickly became a controversial matter, reflecting tensions in other organs, pitting traditional maritime States against emergent maritime States competing for registration tonnage through open registries. Open registries were also dubbed 'flags of convenience' because the registering flag State included vessels in its register which had no 'genuine' or 'beneficial' link to it. Neither Liberia nor Panama was elected even though their registered tonnage clearly placed them in the top ten ship-owning States. Instead, the Members that were elected primarily comprised traditional maritime States. This helped reinforce the impression that, as long as these States retained such a hold on composition and activities, the Organization would be perceived as a 'club'.[42]

The MSC composition controversy served to reinforce that impression. The Assembly resolved to refer the matter of MSC composition to the International Court of Justice (ICJ) for an Advisory Opinion.[43] The heart of the question referred to the ICJ required the Court to determine whether the Committee's composition in accordance with the IMO Convention was to be determined on the basis of simple registered tonnage or on the volume of tonnage based on a beneficial link between the vessel and the State. The Court decided with a large majority in favour of registered tonnage as the most logical and natural meaning to be given to the rule on composition in the IMO Convention.[44] This interpretation was consistent with the usage of the term in other international maritime conventions. The issue of Committee composition was subsequently resolved by enabling all Member States to be members of all the committees.

The other Committees did not share similarly controversial origins, although the LEG and MEPC were established in the wake of the *Torrey Canyon* casualty. This casualty highlighted the need for the Organization to develop a structure to deal with issues of maritime jurisdiction and emerging international maritime legal issues, hence the establishment of the LEG in 1967.[45] Prior to the establishment of the LEG, and since

---

[40] IMO Convention, n 12, Art 28(a).   [41] Ibid, Art 29(a) and (b).

[42] E Gold, *Maritime Transport: The Evolution of International Marine Policy and Shipping Law* (Lexington Books Toronto 1981) 260.

[43] Ademun-Odeke, n 36, 63–90. This author provides an in-depth critical analysis of the controversy.

[44] *Constitution of the Maritime Safety Committee of the Inter-Governmental Maritime Consultative Organization* (Advisory Opinion) [1960] ICJ Rep 150.

[45] Simmonds, n 5, 34; Popp, n 19, 209–11; N Gaskell, 'Decision-Making and the Legal Committee of the International Maritime Organization' (2003) 18 *International Journal of Marine & Coastal Law* 155,

1897, the development of international maritime law conventions was primarily a function undertaken by the CMI.[46] The mandate of the LEG is to consider any legal matters within the scope of the Organization[47] and prepare drafts of international conventions and amendments to conventions developed by the Committee.[48] Established in 1973, the rationale for the MEPC was that international shipping was clearly raising fundamental questions regarding the environmental impacts of ships which needed to be addressed by the Organization on a regular basis. The MEPC has a more elaborate mandate than LEG, possibly reflecting the general lack of understanding of the impacts produced by shipping on the marine environment at the time of its establishment and the need for a broad mandate. This Committee considers any matters within the IMO mandate concerning vessel source-pollution and performs such functions conferred by international conventions on the subject, particularly with regard to the adoption and amendment of regulations or other provisions as provided for in such conventions, including measures to facilitate the enforcement of conventions.[49] Its functions include the development of marine pollution regulations, recommendations, and guidelines for consideration by the Council.[50]

The TCC was established in 1977 and given the principal responsibility for the IMO's technical cooperation activities and the implementation of technical cooperation projects funded by UN and voluntary trust fund programmes.[51] The FAL Committee is the most recent. Initially established in 1991 by an Assembly amending resolution,[52] the required number of instruments of acceptance was not received within the time frame stipulated in the IMO Convention to bring it into effect until 2008.[53] FAL's functions[54] are primarily with reference to maritime documentation and amendments to the 1965 Convention on Facilitation of International Maritime Traffic,[55] expected to be adopted in 2014.[56]

A major strength of the IMO is that its committees and sub-committees include numerous accredited observers consisting of non-governmental organizations representing all aspects of the marine transportation industry, cargo interests, maritime labour and environment protection interests. The advantage of this inclusive approach is that the Organization has access to the broadest range of technical and other expertise

---

155–6. Although dated, Mankabady's major work is valuable for historical perspectives: S Mankabady, *The International Maritime Organisation* 2 Vols (Croom Helm London 1984).

[46] Popp, n 19, 210–11.   [47] IMO Convention, n 12, Art 33(a).   [48] Ibid, Art 34.

[49] Ibid, Art 38(a) and (b); Simmonds, n 5, 32.

[50] IMO Convention, n 12, Art 39(a) and (b).   [51] Ibid, Art 43(a); Simmonds, n 5, 34.

[52] IMO Assembly Res A.724(17), *Amendments to the Convention on the International Maritime Organization* (institutionalization of the Facilitation Committee) (7 November 1991).

[53] The amendment required instruments of acceptance from at least two-thirds of the membership within 12 months of the Resolution. IMO Convention, n 12, Art 66.

[54] Ibid, Art 48; Simmonds, n 5, 32–3.

[55] 1965 Convention on Facilitation of International Maritime Traffic.

[56] IMO Facilitation Committee (FAL), *38th session, 8–12 April 2013* (12 April 2013), available at <http://www.imo.org/MediaCentre/MeetingSummaries/FAL/Pages/FAL-38th-session-.aspx>.

as well as representation of major affected interests. Observers regularly submit documents for consideration in all committees and subsidiary organs. As a former LEG chairperson writes:

Active industry participation in the work of the Committee is evidenced by the presence of a large number of observer delegations representing every sector of the maritime industry at sessions of the Legal Committee. These delegations are given wide latitude to intervene and contribute to the work of the Committee.[57]

The process of IMO treaty-making and amendment raises interesting questions as to what constitutes *travaux préparatoires*, as a supplementary source of treaty interpretation,[58] since the process of development of a particular instrument may include key inputs from non-State actors.[59] With regard to technical regulations it is often the case that there is a close interplay between industry practices and IMO technical standards. For example, the International Maritime Dangerous Goods Code essentially consists of industry practices that have been formalized as regulations by the IMO under the 1974 International Convention for the Safety of Life at Sea (SOLAS).[60] In another example, the current development of a mandatory polar code draws on the Requirements Concerning Polar Class (also known as Unified Requirements) adopted by the International Association of Classification Societies (IACS).[61] The CMI, composed of national maritime law associations with members having close links to industry, has played an important role in helping to develop liability and salvage conventions, among others.[62] Environmental non-governmental organizations have also played useful roles in better informing the Organization in particular discourses, such as proposals for particularly sensitive sea areas (PSSAs). However, the dominance of the shipping industry should be underscored, and one author notes that non-State actors representing 'the shipping sector have been shown to be more

---

[57] Popp, n 19, 224.
[58] 1969 Vienna Convention on the Law of Treaties, Art 32; see Gaskell, n 45, 168 and 176–7 on particular issues with understanding *travaux* of the IMO's work.
[59] A Chircop and S Shiels, 'The Continuum of International Maritime Law and Canadian Maritime Law: Explaining a Complex Relationship' (2012) 35 *Dalhousie Law Journal* 295, 301–2.
[60] The International Maritime Dangerous Goods Code (IMDG) was originally adopted by IMO Assembly Res A.81(IV) (1965) and again in 1991, by IMO Assembly Res A.716(17) (1991). It has had numerous amendments. Amendments occur as a result of changes introduced within the IMO and as a result of changes introduced by the United Nations Recommendations on the Transport of Dangerous Goods, the UN body responsible establishing the basic requirements for all the transport modes.
[61] International Association of Classification Societies (IACS), *Requirements Concerning Polar Class* (IACS Req 2011), available at <http://www.iacs.org.uk/document/public/Publications/Unified_requirements/PDF/UR_I_pdf410.pdf>. The IACS polar class requirements are a key component of the current draft of the mandatory polar code. Report of Correspondence Group of Sub-Committee on Ship Design and Equipment, *Development of a Mandatory Code for Ships Operating in Polar Waters*, IMO Doc DE 57/11/6 (14 December 2012).
[62] Popp, n 19, 210–11; Gaskell, n 44, 177–8; A Lilar and C van den Bosch, *International Maritime Committee 1897–1972* (1973), available at <http://www.comitemaritime.org/Uploads/History/LILAR-VAN%20DEN%20BOSCH-Le%20Comit%C3%A9%20Maritime%20International.pdf>.

influential in affecting the views of decision-making State delegations than those representing environmental interests'.[63]

Inputs from such non-State actors should not be surprising as the substantive expertise required for the development of international rules and standards for shipping frequently reside in such organizations. Thus, to the extent that industry and other non-State actors contribute to the development of international maritime law, and the role of the IMO in providing 'legal substance' to generally applicable international rules and standards on maritime safety and marine pollution,[64] such non-State actors play, through the medium of the IMO, an indirect role with regard to aspects of the international law of the sea. It is likely that no other international organization provides non-State actors opportunities of similar scope and indirect influence on the law of the sea.

4 Functions of the IMO in the LOSC

4.1 The IMO within the framework of the LOSC

While it is widely regarded as a constitution for the world's oceans, the LOSC probably has more provisions that address some aspect of international navigation and shipping than for any other ocean use, with the possible exception of mining in the international seabed area. This is not surprising because, as noted earlier, international navigation rights through zones of national jurisdiction and beyond were a sensitive matter during UNCLOS III. Further, there is virtually no ocean use that does not require shipping support in some form, and in turn, issues relating to appropriate safety and environmental standards arise with regard to all classes of vessels. Thus the IMO has developed safety rules and standards that apply not only to commercial cargo ships, but also to fishing vessels, cruise ships, and offshore installations among other vessels.

The IMO Convention and many international maritime conventions were adopted prior to the adoption of the LOSC, but the operations of the IMO are conducted within the framework of the latter. At the same time, the LOSC provides that it

---

[63] MN Tsimplis, 'Shipping and the Marine Environment in the 21st Century' in M Clarke (ed), *Maritime Law Evolving: Thirty Years at Southampton* (Hart Publishing Oxford/Portland, OR 2013) 95, 107.
[64] Wolfrum, n 28, 229.

... shall not alter the rights and obligations of States Parties which arise from other agreements compatible with this Convention and which do not affect the enjoyment by other States Parties of their rights or the performance of their obligations under this Convention.[65]

Effectively, IMO treaties, while clearly establishing relationships among parties to them, cannot have the effect of undermining the rights of other States under the LOSC. In particular, and given the large number of IMO environmental instruments adopted before, during and following UNCLOS III, the LOSC states that Part XII provisions

... are without prejudice to the specific obligations assumed by States under special conventions and agreements concluded previously which relate to the protection and preservation of the marine environment and to agreements which may be concluded in furtherance of the general principles set forth in this Convention.[66]

States will always be bound by particular instruments to which they are parties. Their obligations under environmental agreements 'should be carried out in a manner consistent with the general principles and objectives of this Convention'.[67] Although this latter provision is couched in non-mandatory terms, it is clear that the intention behind treaty interpretation and the performance of obligations is to produce harmony between the LOSC as a framework agreement and specialized instruments, such as the IMO conventions.

The IMO Convention places parameters for the work of its committees, that 'when exercising the functions conferred upon it by or under any international convention or other instrument, [they] shall conform to the relevant provisions of the convention or instrument in question'.[68] As early as during UNCLOS III, the IMO adopted the practice of including non-prejudice provisions in instruments to ensure that the instrument concerned is without prejudice to 'the codification and development of the law of the sea in UNCLOS or any present or future claims and legal views of any State concerning the law of the sea and the nature and extent of coastal and flag State jurisdiction'.[69] In adopting rules and standards in new or amended conventions, codes, and guidelines, the IMO has at times had to address new issues that may not have been foreseen by the LOSC or which juxtaposed competing principles of international law.[70]

---

[65] LOSC, n 1, Art 311(2).   [66] Ibid, Art 237(1).   [67] Ibid, Art 237(2).
[68] IMO Convention, n 12, Arts 31 (MSC), 36 (LEG), 41 (MEPC), 46 (TCC), and 51 (FAL).
[69] *Implications of the United Nations Convention on the Law of the Sea for the International Maritime Organization: Study by the Secretariat of the IMO*, IMO Doc LEG/MISC.7 (19 January 2012) 7 (hereinafter LOSC Implications).
[70] For example with regard to places of refuge for ships. While the LOSC recognizes aspects of the custom of granting refuge to ships in distress as exceptions to 'continuous and expeditious' innocent passage (Art 18(2)) and 'normal modes of continuous and expeditious transit' in straits used for international navigation (Art 39(1)(c)), the content of the custom is not codified. In the wake of the *Erika*,

4.2 A 'Competent international organization'

The IMO's functional competence lies in the areas of work of its five major committees. In some areas the IMO has exclusive competence, such as with regards to maritime safety and operational vessel-source pollution. The use of the definite article in reference to 'the competent international organization' in various provisions concerning maritime safety and vessel-source pollution refers to the IMO. However, the IMO does not have exclusive competence with regard to all shipping matters, or where matters normally within its core jurisdiction overlap with responsibilities of other international organizations. In these instances, the IMO, in agreement with other concerned competent organizations, has exercised leadership or undertaken joint initiatives. For example, the IMO initiative leading to the adoption of the 2009 Hong Kong International Convention for the Safe and Environmentally Sound Recycling of Ships (Hong Kong Convention) was undertaken in consultation with the ILO and the Secretariat of the 1989 Basel Convention on the Control of Transboundary Movements of Hazardous Wastes and their Disposal, because the mandates of these organizations concerning the protection of maritime labourers and transboundary movement of hazardous wastes respectively were also affected.[71] There are also numerous instances where the IMO, together with other intergovernmental organizations, is tasked with general responsibilities to give effect to particular provisions of the Convention. The Part XIII provisions assigning tasks to international organizations regarding marine scientific research are a case in point (see Section 4.7). In these instances various international organizations may have some competence with reference to the purposes of a particular provision, and hence, may be tasked collectively as competent international organizations.

4.3 Quasi-legislative functions

Perhaps the most important LOSC function of the IMO is that of a quasi-legislative body, in particular with regard to maritime safety and environmental impacts from ships. Wherever it addresses international navigation and shipping matters, the LOSC makes frequent reference to generally accepted or internationally agreed or applicable international regulations, rules, standards, procedures,

---

Castor, and *Prestige* incidents, which raised questions on the state of the custom, the IMO developed guidelines to assist decision-making by coastal State authorities, masters of the vessel and salvors on the basis of a risk assessment framework. IMO Assembly Res A.949(23), *Guidelines on Places of Refuge for Ships in Need of Assistance* (5 December 2003).

[71] 2009 Hong Kong International Convention for the Safe and Environmentally Sound Recycling of Ships.

recommendations, and practices.[72] As Judge Wolfrum writes, the LOSC '... does not specify the content of the rules and standards for the protection of safety at sea or against marine pollution. The respective clauses are open which are to be filled by legal substance'.[73] The LOSC assigns the task of developing these rules to State parties through the IMO. State parties may discharge that task through traditional diplomatic conferences or through the IMO. The IMO itself may facilitate the convening of diplomatic conferences, but its quasi-legislative function may also be exercised by using its own governance structure referred to earlier. Using this structure, the IMO has successfully facilitated the negotiation, adoption, and regular amendment of numerous international instruments.

The explicit duty of States to act through the competent international organization necessarily invokes the quasi-legislative jurisdiction of the IMO. For example, State parties have a duty to act through the IMO or general diplomatic conference to establish international rules and standards for the prevention, reduction and control of vessel-source pollution, and to promote the adoption of routeing measures to minimize threats of accidents, as appropriate.[74] This jurisdiction is further buttressed by specific duties for flag and coastal States. Flag States have a duty to adopt laws and regulations for vessel-source pollution which at least have the same effect as generally accepted rules and standards adopted through the IMO or general diplomatic conference.[75]

The prescriptive competence of the IMO is again referred to with regards to the exercise of enforcement jurisdiction by States. In exercising their right to enforcement jurisdiction over vessel-source pollution in their EEZs, coastal States are to give effect to generally accepted international rules and standards adopted through the IMO or diplomatic conference.[76] The IMO appears to have a mandate also to develop procedures to facilitate enforcement by coastal States.[77] The LOSC sets out wide-ranging duties for flag States in exercising enforcement jurisdiction to ensure compliance with IMO rules and standards for vessel-source pollution,[78] maritime safety,[79] and maritime documents.[80] Infringements of IMO rules and standards are

---

[72] LOSC, n 1, Arts 21(2), 21(4), 22(3)(a), 23, 39(2)(a), 41(4), 53(9), 60, 80, 94(3) and (4)(c), 210(4) and (6), 211, 217(2), 218, 219, 220(3), and 226(1)(c).

[73] Wolfrum, n 28, 229.

[74] LOSC, n 1, Art 211(1). The IMO and other competent organizations have similar roles regarding land-based sources of pollution (Art 207(4)), seabed activities subject to national jurisdiction (Art 208(5)), dumping (Art 210(4)), and pollution from or through the atmosphere (Art 212(3)).

[75] Ibid, Art 211(2).   [76] Ibid, Art 211(5).

[77] This is with regard to a coastal State's duty to allow a vessel to proceed when it complies with procedures for securing a bond or other financial security. Ibid, Art 220(7).

[78] Ibid, Art 217(1).

[79] These duties permit port States to prohibit vessels from sailing until compliance with rules relating to ship design, construction, equipment and manning is assured. Ibid, Art 217(2).

[80] Ibid, Art 217(3).

to be investigated and enforced.[81] Port State enforcement action is similarly guided by IMO rules and standards.[82]

In other provisions, the LOSC makes implicit reference to the IMO's competence in a specific subject matter when stipulating duties for State parties. In these provisions the LOSC does not establish a direct duty for States to develop such rules through the IMO, but implies that the IMO develops such rules. For example, in Part V on the EEZ, the LOSC stipulates a duty for coastal States to remove abandoned or disused installations or structures, taking into account any generally accepted international standards established by the IMO.[83] In a related provision, the breadth of safety zones around artificial islands, installations, and structures has a limit of 500 metres, except as authorized by generally accepted international standards or as recommended by the IMO.[84] In these instances, the IMO draws direct authority to adopt such standards from its constitutive instrument and particular maritime conventions, such as SOLAS.

However, not all IMO instruments, even those of a same class (eg conventions) are equal and to be considered as generally accepted or applicable without qualification and without specific reference to the prescription in the pertinent LOSC provision. The general applicability of an instrument needs to be determined on an instrument-by-instrument basis. While numerous conventions can be so characterized without doubt because of the large number of States that are parties (such as MARPOL (see Section 4.4) and SOLAS), there are also instruments which have not received the same level of general subscription and others which have achieved few ratifications so as not to enter into force, such as the 2009 Hong Kong Convention and the 2007 Nairobi International Convention on the Removal of Wrecks. Other instruments cannot be held to be generally accepted when the benefits of the instruments are clearly intended for State parties only, such as the civil liability conventions.[85] A further complicating factor is determining general applicability when the degree of implementation of a particular instrument varies among State parties.[86] It is conceivable that the status of an instrument changes as a result of growth of support or perhaps because of disuse. Resolutions are a different category. They are usually adopted by consensus among the IMO membership, but even when they are adopted by a majority vote, they may still potentially be characterized as generally applicable.

---

[81] Ibid, Art 217(4).　　[82] Ibid, Art 218(1).　　[83] Ibid, Art 60(3).　　[84] Ibid, Art 60(5).

[85] 1969 International Convention on Civil Liability for Oil Pollution Damage as replaced by 1992 Protocol; 1971 International Convention on the Establishment of an International Fund for Compensation for Oil Pollution Damage as superseded by 1992 Protocol.

[86] A helpful initiative by the IMO to assist implementation is the Code for the Implementation of Mandatory IMO Instruments, IMO Assembly Res A.1054(27), *Code for the Implementation of Mandatory IMO Instruments, 2011* (20 December 2011).

4.4 Overseeing and approving requests for routeing measures

The IMO performs a unique function in considering particular requests from coastal States for routeing measures which, while intended to enhance maritime safety or promote an environmental objective, might otherwise be perceived as infringing on rights of international navigation within zones of national jurisdiction if not approved by the IMO.[87] Individual and collective State requests for PSSAs,[88] including associated protective measures, and special area designation for entire marine regions under particular annexes of the 1973/78 International Convention for the Prevention of Pollution from Ships (MARPOL)[89] have also been considered and approved. The IMO's deliberation and approval of such requests, possibly with conditions, have the effect of legitimizing such State requests and subsequent implementation of the approved designation and related measures.

The LOSC anticipates instances where existing international rules and standards are not sufficient to address the threat of vessel-source pollution in clearly defined areas of EEZs. In such instances, special mandatory measures may be requested by the coastal State concerned where such measures are required for recognized technical reasons with regards to oceanographic and ecological conditions, the utilization or protection of natural resources, and particular maritime traffic characteristics in the area of the EEZ in question. The coastal State can advance its case for special mandatory measures through the IMO. The IMO enjoys a deliberative function in determining 'whether the conditions in that area correspond to the requirements set out above', and if the IMO so determines, the coastal State may adopt laws and regulations for that area by implementing international rules and standards or navigational practices 'as are made applicable through the organization, for special areas'.[90] In order for the IMO to discharge this task, this provision seems to implicitly suggest that the IMO also has prescriptive jurisdiction for marine areas requiring special mandatory measures.

There are instances where a coastal State's initiative to impose requirements for the exercise of international navigation rights within maritime zones subject to its sovereignty also require resort to the IMO. In exercising its right to adopt laws and regulations regarding the exercise of innocent passage through the territorial sea in conformity with the LOSC,[91] the coastal State may establish sea lanes and traffic separation

---

[87] SOLAS, n 27, in particular Chapter V (Navigation). See also IMO Assembly Res A.572(14), *General Provisions on Ships' Routeing* (20 November 1985); IMO, *Ships' Routeing* (9th edn IMO London 2008).

[88] IMO Assembly Res A.982(24), *Guidelines for the Identification and Designation of Particularly Sensitive Sea Areas* (1 December 2005) (hereinafter PSSA Guidelines).

[89] See also *Guidelines for the Designation of Special Areas under MARPOL 73/78*, IMO Doc MEPC 63/9 (25 November 2011), containing an amended version of the guidelines and which were adopted by the Assembly at its 28th session in December 2013 (hereinafter Special Area Guidelines).

[90] LOSC, n 1, Art 211(6)(a).   [91] Ibid, Art 21.

schemes, taking into account IMO recommendations.[92] With regard to transit passage, coastal States have a duty to refer proposals concerning designation, prescription, or substitution of sea lanes and traffic separation schemes to the IMO with a view to their adoption.[93] There is a similar requirement for archipelagic States with regard to archipelagic sea lanes passage.[94] These are further examples of how the LOSC empowers the IMO to balance coastal State interests and international navigation rights.

4.5 Clearing house for information and receiver of notification requirements

There are several situations where States are required to notify or report to the IMO and other competent international organizations. In these instances, the IMO acts as a depositary of such information. States that are aware of actual or imminent danger of a threat to the marine environment have a duty to notify other States likely to be affected and the IMO.[95] States are required to publish reports concerning monitoring of risks and effects of pollution and to provide them to the IMO.[96] States undertaking activities within their jurisdiction are expected, in certain cases, to assess the potential effects of such activities and to report results to the IMO.[97] States have a duty to communicate their particular requirements for prevention, reduction, and control of marine pollution as a condition of entry into their ports, internal waters, or offshore terminals.[98] Coastal States which request special mandatory measures for particular areas in their EEZs are required to notify the IMO of additional laws and regulations for special areas on pollution from vessels in accordance with generally accepted international rules and standards.[99] The flag State has a duty to promptly inform a requesting State and the IMO of action taken in enforcement and its outcome.[100] These duties accompany rights that States may have and in that regard reflect a measure of transparency towards other State parties. To the extent that the IMO is a recipient of the required reports, it acts as a medium to facilitate accountability.

4.6 Capacity-building and technology transfer

Like other international organizations, the IMO is tasked by the LOSC with capacity-building functions. The Convention sets out this task in two ways. First,

---

[92] Ibid, Art 22(3)(a).
[93] Ibid, Art 41(4). Further, strait-bordering States are to cooperate in formulating proposals for sea lanes or traffic separation schemes in consultation with the IMO. Ibid, Art 41(5).
[94] Ibid, Art 53(9).   [95] Ibid, Art 198.   [96] Ibid, Art 205.   [97] Ibid, Art 206.
[98] Ibid, Art 211(3).   [99] Ibid, Art 211(6)(c).   [100] Ibid, Art 217(7).

the IMO is to provide a medium through which States may choose to fulfil their duty to provide scientific and technical assistance to developing States.[101] Second, and more directly, the IMO is required to grant preferential treatment to developing States in the allocation of funds, technical assistance, and utilization of specialized services in its fields of competence.[102] In practice the IMO has performed such services through the technical assistance programme administered by the TCC and perhaps more significantly through the education and technical programmes of the World Maritime University[103] and International Maritime Law Institute[104] which operate autonomously within the IMO framework to deliver higher degree and professional programmes in maritime affairs.

4.7 Facilitation and contribution to international cooperation

Like other global international organizations, the IMO plays an important role in facilitating the duty of States to cooperate on a global and regional basis to develop rules, standards, and recommended practices and procedures to protect and preserve the marine environment.[105] This function is reiterated with regard to pollution from land-based activities, seabed activities within national jurisdiction, dumping and atmospheric sources, as well as related enforcement.[106] In addition to facilitating cooperation in international maritime law-making, the IMO serves as a medium for cooperation in other respects. For example, States have a duty to cooperate directly or through the IMO, among other organizations, to promote studies, research, and exchange of information and data about pollution of the marine environment.[107] Similarly, States have a duty to cooperate directly or through the IMO and other organizations in establishing appropriate scientific criteria for the formulation and elaboration of rules, standards, and recommended practices and procedures for marine pollution.[108] Again, they have a duty to monitor the risks and effects of marine pollution through the IMO and other competent organizations.[109]

In other instances, the IMO is a potential partner for State parties, as in the case of enclosed and semi-enclosed seas where it may be invited to cooperate with bordering States.[110] Similarly, the IMO and other competent international organizations have a duty to cooperate with affected States with regard to pollution contingency plans to eliminate the effects of pollution and prevent or minimize the damage.[111]

---

[101] Ibid, Art 202.   [102] Ibid, Art 203.
[103] World Maritime University (Malmö Sweden), available at <http://wmu.se>.
[104] International Maritime Law Institute (Malta), available at <http://www.imli.org/>.
[105] LOSC, n 1, Art 197.   [106] Ibid, Arts 207(4), 208(5), 210(4), 212(3), 213, 214, and 216(1).
[107] Ibid, Art 200.   [108] Ibid, Art 201.   [109] Ibid, Art 204.   [110] Ibid, Art 123(d).
[111] Ibid, Art 199.

Although, at first blush, the IMO's relevance to the regime of marine scientific research might seem remote, there are several provisions in this part of the LOSC where the IMO is jointly tasked with other competent international organizations. The mandate in its constitutive instrument does not specifically provide the IMO with the planning or conduct of marine scientific research. However, the IMO benefits from such research and its work has at times depended on the state of scientific knowledge on a particular matter. For example, the designation of special areas under MARPOL and PSSAs requires scientific evidence to demonstrate vulnerability of the candidate areas to shipping activity.[112] Accordingly, together with other competent international organizations, the IMO is called upon to play a role in marine scientific research,[113] and in the event that it conducts research its responsibility and liability are potentially engaged.[114] The IMO's maritime safety rules and standards are also applicable to the conduct of marine scientific research.[115]

4.8 Interaction with and assistance to other intergovernmental organizations

The IMO retains cooperative arrangements with numerous intergovernmental organizations.[116] The IMO Convention anticipates that it might be called upon to consider 'any matters concerning shipping and the effect of shipping on the marine environment that may be referred to it by any organ or specialized agency of the United Nations'.[117] In addition, the LOSC anticipates the possibility of entertaining requests from other organizations. The Economic Planning Commission and Legal and Technical Commission of the International Seabed Authority (ISA) may consult the IMO, where appropriate, in its area of competence.[118] In this regard, the Secretary-General of the ISA is tasked with making suitable arrangements for consultation and cooperation with the IMO, among other organizations.[119]

4.9 Support for dispute settlement

To date, the opportunity for the IMO to support dispute settlement has not yet arisen. The LOSC provides for the constitution of special arbitral tribunals, including for disputes concerning navigation, vessel-source pollution, and dumping.[120]

---

[112] Special Area Guidelines, n 89; PSSA Guidelines, n 88.
[113] LOSC, n 1, Arts 238, 239, 243, 244(1) and (2), 246(3) and (5), 247, 248, 249(1), 251, 252, 253, 254(1) and (2), 254(3) and (4), 256, 257, and 262.
[114] Ibid, Art 263.   [115] Ibid, Art 262.   [116] Allen, n 28, 272.
[117] IMO Convention, n 12, Art 2(d).   [118] LOSC, n 1, Art 163(3).
[119] Ibid, Art 169(1) and (2).   [120] Ibid, Annex VIII, Art 1.

The IMO's services may also be called upon 'to carry out an inquiry and establish the facts giving rise to the dispute'.[121] The IMO is designated the organization responsible for maintaining a list of experts for special arbitration purposes in its areas of competence.[122]

5 Conclusion: Achievements and Issues

Over its history, the IMO has received criticism and praise probably in equal doses. Arguably it has operated in a reactive manner, frequently in response to maritime casualties. This is true of the development of international maritime law generally at least since the adoption of the first SOLAS convention in 1914 in the wake of the sinking of the *Titanic*. Earlier, this chapter referred to the *Torrey Canyon* and how that casualty triggered structural change in the IMO and the development of a suite of new maritime law conventions. Several other casualties, such as *Amoco Cadiz, Exxon Valdez, Herald of Free Enterprise, Erika, Prestige*, and, more recently, *Costa Concordia*, among others, triggered law reform in various safety, pollution, and civil liability fields. Ideally, international maritime law reform should be proactive and anticipate rather than respond to problems. However, this criticism should be moderated by the on-going and low-profile technical work of the various committees and sub-committees, which regularly respond to technological change to enhance safety and environment protection that does not make headlines like casualties. Regulatory reviews by the IMO Committees tend to lead to the incremental raising of standards, resulting in frequent amendments to SOLAS and other rules, and therefore cannot simply be characterized as reactive.

As is the case in all international diplomatic arenas, IMO conventions (as well as other instruments) frequently aim for the lowest common denominator to secure consensus or a wide measure of agreement, and eventually enter into force or become effective at a slow pace. An example of a convention not yet in force, years after adoption, is the 2009 Hong Kong Convention. In other instances, a rule may be in force but not necessarily in effect because of a particular procedural failure by affected States. For example, the 'effectivity' of special area designations under MARPOL is frequently protracted because the provision of reception facilities by regional States, a condition for bringing the special area for the marine region

---

[121] Ibid, Annex VIII, Art 5.   [122] Ibid, Annex VIII, Art 2(2).

concerned into effect, has tended to lag.[123] However, the choice of low common denominator and slow pace in bringing instruments into force or effectiveness are driven by national interests.

Despite the criticisms, in a contemporary setting, the IMO is so instrumental to maritime trade and occupies such an important place in the international law of the sea that should it not have existed by now, it would have had to be created. Coastal and flag States rely on the IMO to give substance to the LOSC framework through the development of common rules and standards in an independent and yet inclusive forum. Within the framework of the LOSC, the IMO has been able to broaden the application of its instruments, even its resolutions, as generally acceptable rules, standards, and practices.[124] The effect is to universalize its rules, standards, and practices among LOSC parties, possibly even with regard to particular States that may not be party to a specific IMO convention.[125] As a result, there is likely no other ocean use that has the scope and depth of regulation as international shipping. This work appears to have made a difference. At its last session, the UN General Assembly noted that

> ...international shipping rules and standards adopted by the International Maritime Organization in respect of maritime safety, efficiency of navigation and the prevention and control of marine pollution, complemented by best practices of the shipping industry, have led to a significant reduction in maritime accidents and pollution incidents.[126]

However, universalization has not always been accompanied by uniformity, a key concern in the IMO mission. A former IMO Secretary-General notes that 'we do not need more treaties and more regulations, and that our focus should be placed on achieving uniform implementation of IMO global standards that are already on the books'.[127] While the Organization makes every attempt to broaden the scope of application of its instruments and facilitate implementation, the Achilles' heel of global shipping governance is flag State implementation and compliance. While the IMO is at the centre of global shipping governance, the effectiveness of international rules and standards is largely dependent on flag State implementation and compliance. While ship registration is a national prerogative and competitive business, it should also be accompanied by the exercise of effective jurisdiction and control by

---

[123] A Chircop, 'The Designation of Particularly Sensitive Sea Areas: A New Layer in the Regime for Marine Environmental Protection from International Shipping' in A Chircop et al (eds), *The Future of Ocean Regime-Building: Essays in Tribute to Douglas M Johnston* (Nihoff Leiden 2009) 573, 583.

[124] Kirgis, n 24, 73–4; Allen, n 28, 289. This author notes that IMO resolutions may be a source of generally accepted international rules and standards. The IMO is of the view that 'national legislation implementing IMO recommendations can be applied with binding effect to foreign ships.' LOSC Implications, n 69, at 10.

[125] Allen, n 28, 292.   [126] UNGA Res/68/70 (2013) [147].

[127] W O'Neil, 'Welcoming Remarks' in MH Nordquist and JN Moore (eds), *Current Maritime Issues and the International Maritime Organization* (Nijhoff The Hague 1999) 3, 4.

the flag State.[128] There is increasing concern about the inability or unwillingness of many flag States to discharge this basic duty and, as a result, there is a growing chorus of voices demanding that unless a State is able to undertake effective maritime administration and address substandard ship issues, it should not establish a ship registry, or should decline registration for certain ships, or suspend the existing ship registry altogether.[129] The IMO response to this on-going problem is the gradual introduction of a mandatory flag State audit system by 2016, currently operated on a voluntary basis, which includes amendments to several key conventions to institutionalize the audit scheme.[130]

One writer suggests that the problem with flag State compliance is potentially linked to the IMO's own success as a quasi-legislative body. He states that the IMO 'has largely supplanted the flag State as the primary source of prescriptive maritime law, thereby diminishing the flag State's significance and stature and providing a convenient excuse for flag States to take a more passive role'. He goes on to write that the breadth and detail of IMO regulation has 'effectively reduced the flag State's role to one of implementing rules established in London'.[131] However, those States' ability to reap financial benefit from ship registration should occur without externalizing the risk of substandard shipping and effectively generate business at an international subsidy. The lack of implementation and enforcement of international rules and standards is not an IMO failure, but failures of Member States or State parties to a convention. Non-compliant States are in violation of their duty to enforce or comply with generally accepted standards.[132] This issue continues to create tension and should the new IMO mandatory flag State audit system not succeed, it may well force further development of the law of the sea to reconsider the rights of flag States and redraw the balance between exclusively national and inclusively international interests.

---

[128] LOSC, n 1, Art 94(1).

[129] Most recently the UN General Assembly urged

> ... flag States without an effective maritime administration and appropriate legal frameworks to establish or enhance the necessary infrastructure, legislative and enforcement capabilities to ensure effective compliance with and implementation and enforcement of their responsibilities under international law, in particular the Convention, and, until such action is taken, to consider declining the granting of the right to fly their flag to new vessels, suspending their registry or not opening a registry, and calls upon flag and port States to take all measures consistent with international law necessary to prevent the operation of substandard vessels.

See UNGA Res/68/70 (2013) [147].

[130] 'IMO Assembly Adopts Mandatory Audit Scheme', IMO Briefing 54 (4 December 2013), available at <www.imo.org/MediaCentre/PressBriefings/Pages/53-A28-council.aspx>.

[131] Allen, n 28, 322.   [132] LOSC, n 1, Art 94.

REGIONAL FISHERIES MANAGEMENT ORGANIZATIONS

ROSEMARY RAYFUSE

1 Introduction

FISH are a quintessential common resource. Recognized as such as long ago as the *Codex Justinianus*, their status as a common resource was immortalized by Grotius who, in his famous treatise *Mare Liberum*, reiterated that, like the sea, their apparently limitless character rendered them capable of possession by no one and available for exploitation by all.[1] It is axiomatic that, as a biologically renewable resource, the supply of fish is potentially unlimited. However, to achieve this potential and to avoid the 'tragedy of the commons',[2] appropriate management of exploitation of the resource is necessary. The 1982 United Nations Convention on the Law of the Sea (LOSC) allocates

---

[1] H Grotius, *Mare Liberum sive de ivre qvod Batavis competit an Indicana commercia, dissertatio* (1608). H Grotius, *The Freedom of the Seas of The Right Which Belongs to the Dutch to Take Part in the East Indian Trade* (trans R Van Deman Magoffin) (Carnegie Endowment for International Peace/ Oxford University Press New York 1916) 27–32.

[2] G Hardin, 'The Tragedy of the Commons' (1968) 162(3859) *Science* 1243, 1244. According to Hardin, '[r]uin is the destination toward which all men rush, each pursuing his own best interest in a society that believes in the freedom of the commons. Freedom in a commons brings ruin to all.' He later reworded this idea to: '[u]nder conditions of over-population, freedom in an unmanaged

responsibility for the conservation and management of fisheries within the exclusive economic zone (EEZ) to coastal States.[3] On the high seas, this responsibility is shared by all States, each of which is under both an individual and a collective duty to cooperate in the conservation of the living marine resources of the high seas.[4] The recognized *modus operandi* for this cooperation is through the establishment of sub-regional or regional fisheries organizations. Of central importance are those organizations that have a management, as opposed to an advisory, function: regional fisheries management organizations (RFMOs).

Since the extension of coastal State jurisdiction and the enclosure of vast ocean areas within the EEZs of States, RFMOs have become the management mechanism of choice through which the principles of conservation and cooperation, articulated in the LOSC, are to be achieved. Yet despite the establishment of an increasing number of RFMOs, the status of global marine capture fish stocks has declined markedly. According to the United Nations Food and Agriculture Organization (FAO),[5] a staggering 87 per cent of global fish stocks are now either overexploited or fully exploited and in need of effective management either to rebuild stocks or to avoid further decline. Further broken down, the report reveals that 57 per cent of stocks are fully exploited and 30 per cent are overexploited; figures which represent an increase over past years.[6] The situation is said to be 'more critical for some highly migratory, straddling and other fishery resources that are exploited solely or partially in the high seas'.[7] This continuing decline in the status of high seas fisheries resources rather begs the question as to the efficacy of the measures adopted by RFMOs to ensure the long-term conservation and sustainable use of the fish stocks under their management. This in turns raises the question as to the legitimacy of RFMOs as stewards for the international community of the world's high seas fisheries resources. Taken together, these questions represent the most fundamental and most critical challenges for contemporary international fisheries law and for the law of the sea as it relates to the conservation and management of marine living resources.

---

commons brings ruin to all': G Hardin, 'An Ecolate View of the Human Predicament' (1985), available at <http://www.garretthardinsociety.org/articles/art_ecolate_view_human_predicament.html>.

[3] 1982 United Nations Convention on the Law of the Sea, Art 56 (hereinafter LOSC).

[4] Ibid, Arts 116–119.

[5] UN Food and Agriculture Organization (FAO), *The State of World Fisheries and Aquaculture: 2012* (FAO Rome 2012).

[6] In 2006, the FAO identified 75 per cent of the world's fish stocks as either fully exploited or overexploited or depleted and recovering from depletion. In 2010, the number had risen to 85 per cent, representing 53 per cent of global fish stocks as fully exploited and 32 per cent as either overexploited (28 per cent), depleted (3 per cent), or recovering from depletion (1 per cent). See FAO, *The State of World Fisheries and Aquaculture: 2006* (FAO Rome 2006); FAO, *The State of World Fisheries and Aquaculture: 2008* (FAO Rome 2008); and FAO, *The State of World Fisheries and Aquaculture: 2010* (FAO Rome 2010).

[7] FAO, n 5, 59.

This chapter assesses the contribution of RFMOs to the achievement of the principles of conservation and cooperation articulated in the LOSC. It begins with a brief historical introduction to the institutionalization of cooperation through RFMOs and an examination of their structural limitations. It then examines the role and contribution of RFMOs in developing the specific content of the obligation to conserve including the implications for RFMOs of the increasing recognition of the need to protect, conserve and manage marine biodiversity in general. Finally, the chapter examines the challenges to RFMOs posed by climate change.

2 RFMOs and the Institutionalization of Cooperation

The duty to cooperate is a natural corollary of the duty to conserve a shared natural resource and arises from the duty to have due regard to the interests of other States. It has its origins in the general principles of international law that have evolved governing the exploitation of transboundary resources, both living and non-living.[8] As applied to high seas fisheries, the duty's lineage can be traced at least as far back as the *Bering Fur Seals Arbitration*,[9] where it was decided that conservation measures relating to high seas resources could be taken only on the basis of agreement between States.

The duty to cooperate is now codified in Article 117 of the LOSC, which requires all States to take or cooperate with other States in taking necessary conservation measures for their respective nationals. Article 118 specifies the modalities for this cooperation as being through the establishment of sub-regional or regional fisheries organizations. This is further strengthened by the 1995 United Nations Fish Stocks Agreement (FSA),[10] Article 8 of which 'institutionalizes' the duty to cooperate in respect of straddling fish stocks and highly migratory fish stocks by requiring its exercise through regional or sub-regional fisheries organizations or arrangements. Importantly, only those States which are members of such an organization or arrangement are entitled to have access to the fishery resources managed by that

---

[8] E Hey, *The Regime for the Exploitation of Transboundary Marine Fisheries Resources* (Springer Heidelberg 1989) 28–41.

[9] *Bering Fur Seals* (*Great Britain v United States*) (1893) 1 Moore Digest 755.

[10] 1995 Agreement for the Implementation of the Provisions of the UN Convention on the Law of the Sea relating to the Conservation and Management of Straddling Fish Stocks and Highly Migratory Fish Stock (hereinafter Fish Stocks Agreement or FSA). For a detailed discussion of the FSA, see Chapter 22 in this volume.

organization or arrangement. Where no organization or arrangement exists, States are obliged to cooperate to establish one. Where organizations or arrangements already exist, coastal and fishing States are obliged either to become members or to agree to apply their conservation and management measures. All States having a 'real interest' in the fisheries concerned are expected to join the relevant arrangement and to fully participate in its work. Where a formal organizational structure is unnecessary the objectives of conservation and management may be achieved through bilateral or other arrangements. However, where more than two States are interested in a fishery, establishment of some form of regional fisheries body or arrangement will be necessary.

While some regional fisheries organizations have an advisory function only, the obligation to cooperate in respect of high seas fisheries has predominantly manifested itself in the establishment of RFMOs. These organizations seek to regulate exploitation either of particular species throughout their area of distribution or of various species distributed throughout a particular geographic area. Management is conducted through the adoption of regulatory measures relating, *inter alia*, to data acquisition, fishing practices and technologies, fishing effort and capacity, and control and enforcement. It is RFMOs that have a management function that are the focus of this chapter.

In terms of species specific RFMOs, there are currently five RFMOs that manage highly migratory species (mostly tuna):

- the International Commission for the Conservation of Atlantic Tunas (ICCAT);
- the Indian Ocean Tuna Commission (IOTC);
- the Western and Central Pacific Fisheries Commission (WCPFC);
- the Inter-American Tropical Tuna Commission (IATTC) and its related Agreement on the International Dolphin Conservation Programme (AIDCP); and
- the Commission for the Conservation of Southern Bluefin Tuna (CCSBT).

Given their commonality of object and purpose, since 2007 these five tuna RFMOs have worked together through the 'Kobe Process' to ensure a harmonized approach to scientific research and the acquisition of data, the adoption of management measures and the adoption of control and enforcement measures.[11]

RFMOs that manage non-tuna stocks within particular geographical areas include:

- the North-East Atlantic Fisheries Commission (NEAFC);
- the Northwest Atlantic Fisheries Organization (NAFO);
- the North Atlantic Salmon Conservation Organization (NASCO);

---

[11] Three joint meetings have been held to date, in 2007, 2009, and 2011. Reports of the meetings of the Kobe Process are available at <http://www.tuna-org.org>.

- the South-East Atlantic Fisheries Organization (SEAFO);
- the South Pacific Regional Fisheries Management Organization (SPRFMO);
- the Commission on the Conservation of Antarctic Marine Living Resources (CCAMLR);
- the General Fisheries Commission for the Mediterranean (GFCM);
- the South Indian Ocean Fisheries Agreement (SIOFA); and
- the Convention on the Conservation and Management of Pollock Resources in the Central Bering Sea (CCBSP).

The latter two, the SIOFA and the CCBSP, are not self-standing organizations but, rather, 'arrangements' with decisions to be taken by meetings of the parties. The North Pacific Anadromous Fish Commission (NPAFC) is often included in lists of RFMOs, however, it has no management mandate. The 1992 Convention for the Conservation of Anadromous Stocks in the North Pacific Ocean (NPAFC Convention) area is confined to the high seas area of the North Pacific where fishing for anadromous species is prohibited by virtue of Article 66 of the LOSC. The NPAFC does, however, have a significant enforcement mandate in the North Pacific area pursuant to its Convention, which it implements with alacrity in support of the United Nations General Assembly global moratorium on large-scale high seas driftnet fishing.[12] The CCBSP similarly currently has no management role as the moratorium it establishes on fishing for pollock in the Central Bering Sea remains in place. No formal process exists for the institutionalization of cooperation between all RFMOs; however, consistent approaches to common conservation, management, compliance, and enforcement issues are sought through cooperation at the inter-organizational level via observer representation at each other's meetings.

3 RFMOs AND THE LIMITS OF COOPERATION

Although RFMOs are the international community's mechanism of choice through which the duty to cooperate in the conservation and management of high seas fisheries resources is to be implemented, they face a number of 'structural' challenges

---

[12] UNGA Res 46/215 (1991). For discussion see R Rayfuse, *Non-Flag State Enforcement in High Seas Fisheries* (Martinus Nijhoff The Hague 2004) 79–82 and 117–36.

in fulfilling their obligations. These challenges result from the inherent structure of international law with its emphasis on the sovereign equality of States and the particular emphasis in the law of the sea on high seas freedoms and flag State jurisdiction. The nature of this legal framework is such that it places considerable limitations on the potential efficacy of RFMOs.

The most basic challenge to RFMOs arises as a result of the application of the *pacta tertiis* rule. Treaties are only binding on their parties.[13] All States have the right for their vessels to fish on the high seas subject only to treaty obligations which these States have assumed.[14] However, international law does not compel treaty adherence. In other words, States are free to choose whether to become party to a treaty. Thus, States whose vessels fish in areas of the high seas may not be members of RFMOs or parties to the FSA. Their vessels are therefore not obliged to comply with the various conservation and management measures adopted by those RFMOs. These 'free riders' can undermine conservation and management measures and any incentive for member State nationals to comply. Free riders are likewise under no obligation to supply data to RFMOs, so stock assessments may be unreliable rendering the adoption of meaningful conservation and management measures impossible. Free riders also reap the economic benefit associated with not having to fund the operations of RFMOs and the implementation of their measures.

The non-State entity of Taiwan, which flags a significant distant water fishing fleet, poses particular difficulties in that traditional international law provides no mechanism by which it can become bound by treaty obligations. To overcome this difficulty, Article 1(3) of the Fish Stocks Agreement extends the application of the FSA to all 'fishing entities' whose vessels fish on the high seas. RFMOs have variously secured Taiwan's participation as a 'fishing entity' through a number of mechanisms.[15] The CCSBT, for example, adopted a resolution for the establishment of an Extended Commission and an Extended Scientific Committee which provided for Taiwan's participation in these bodies. The IATTC took the opportunity presented by a revision of its constitutive treaty to include provisions on the admission of fishing entities as members. The WCPFC similarly provides for membership of fishing entities. Other organizations, such as ICCAT, have granted Taiwan observer status pursuant to resolutions on

---

[13] 1969 Vienna Convention on the Law of Treaties, Art 34 (hereinafter VCLT).

[14] LOSC, n 3, Art 116.

[15] See generally W Edeson, 'Some Future Directions for Fishing Entities in Certain Regional Fisheries Management Bodies' (2006) 37(2) *Ocean Development and International Law* 245; PSC Ho, 'The Impacts of the UN Fish Stocks Agreement on Taiwan's Participation in International Fisheries Fora' (2006) 37(2) *Ocean Development and International Law* 133; N-TA Hu, 'Fishing Entities: Their Emergence, Evolution and Practice from Taiwan's Perspective' (2006) 37(2) *Ocean Development and International Law* 149; and Y-H Song, 'The Regional Fisheries Management Organisation and Ocean Law: A Perspective from Taiwan' in DD Caron and HN Scheiber (eds), *Bringing New Law to Ocean Waters* (Brill Leiden 2004) 145.

non-contracting parties and entities either in its own name or, not entirely uncontroversially, as 'Chinese Taipei'.[16]

Another manifestation of the challenge posed by the *pacta tertiis* rule is seen in the decision-making structures in RFMOs, many of which provide for 'opt-out' or objection procedures whereby member States can escape the application of otherwise binding measures that have been adopted by a RFMO. A perennial problem in RFMOs, the use and effect of objections and opt-outs has lain at the heart of major disputes including the Southern Bluefin Tuna dispute between Australia and New Zealand on the one hand and Japan on the other.[17] Recently, RFMOs have begun to adopt institutionalized procedures for the settlement of disputes relating to the use of opt-out powers. Such a procedure was used for the first time in 2013 in the SPRFMO after Russia objected to a quota allocation measure and adopted its own unilateral allocation.[18] The issue also lies at the heart of the EU—Faroe Islands herring stock dispute in the World Trade Organization which involves the GATT compatibility of measures taken by the EU in retaliation for the Faroe Islands opting out of a NEAFC negotiated total allowable catch (TAC) allocation for Atlanto-Scandian herring.[19]

A particularly troublesome manifestation of the *free rider* phenomenon has been the use of 'flags of convenience' or flagging/reflagging of fishing vessels for practical expediency. This has not always involved the use of an open registry State. Any State not bound by a particular regional fisheries agreement can be considered a 'flag of convenience' or 'flag of non-compliance' State. The flag of convenience phenomenon has been especially problematic for RFMOs, as vessels can be—and have been—deliberately deregistered from member States and reregistered in

---

[16] See ICCAT Recommendation 03-20 on criteria for attaining the status of Cooperating non-Contracting Party, Entity or Fishing Entity in ICCAT (2003).

[17] *Southern Bluefin Tuna (New Zealand v Japan; Australia v Japan)* (Provisional Measures) [1999] 117 ILR 148; (Jurisdiction and Admissibility) [2000] 119 ILR 508.

[18] The 2009 Convention on the Conservation and Management of the High Seas Fishery Resources of the South Pacific Ocean establishes a formal procedure for resolving disputes over objections: Art 17 and Annex II (hereinafter SPRFMO Convention). For the texts of the objections, the submissions to the Review Panel and the Review Panel findings, see South Pacific Regional Fisheries Management Organization, Review Panel Findings, available at <http://www.southpacificrfmo.org/objections> (hereinafter Review Panel Findings).

[19] Since 2007, the EU and the other members of the NEAFC, including the Faroe Islands, have negotiated annual TAC limits for the Atlanto-Scandian herring stock. In 2013, the Faroe Islands refused to accept these limits, withdrew from the negotiations, and unilaterally set its own catch limits. In May 2013, the European Commission notified the Faroe Islands that it was considered a 'country allowing unsustainable fishing practices' and, after having received what it considered to be an inadequate response, in August 2013 the European Commission adopted trade restrictions against the Faroe Islands, closing it ports to Faroese herring vessels. This has prompted a challenge by the Faroe Islands under the General Agreement on Tariffs and Trade 1994. For discussion, see Y Ishikawa, 'The EU–Faroe Islands Herring Stock Dispute at the WTO: the Environmental Justification' (14 February 2014) 18(4) *ASIL Insights*, available at <http://www.asil.org/insights/volume/18/issue/4/eu-faroe-islands-herring-stock-dispute-wto-environmental-justification>.

non-member States in order to avoid application of conservation and management measures adopted by those organizations. In the past decades, attempts to more fully articulate the responsibilities incumbent on all flag States have resulted in the adoption of the 1993 Agreement to Promote Compliance with International Conservation and Management Measures by Fishing Vessels on the High Seas (FAO Compliance Agreement), the FSA, and the FAO's Guidelines for Assessing Flag State Performance.[20] These responsibilities include, for example, the requirement to maintain schemes for vessel licensing and fishing authorizations, national registers of authorized fishing vessels, vessel reporting and recording systems, and compliance and enforcement systems capable of ensuring their vessels do not engage in activities that undermine the effectiveness of RFMO measures. Importantly, Article 18 of the FSA makes clear that States shall only authorize their vessels to fish on the high seas where they can exercise these flag States responsibilities effectively. However, there remains no globally applicable sanction that would see access denied for a breach of these responsibilities.

One way to deal with non-member and flag-of-convenience States is to invite them to become members of the relevant RFMO, and, in many cases, RFMOs have done so. However, States have not always wished to take on the financial and other obligations associated with membership, particularly where their flag was granted in the absence of any other connection with the owners, operators, crew, home port, or ultimate customers of the vessel. In some cases, joining an RFMO would have disadvantaged a State's vessels because no quota allocation was provided when the pre-existing members took the position that the fishery concerned was already fully exploited or that the new member lacked any historical participation and thus did not have any 'real interest'[21] in the fishery. The preferable solution in such cases (at least to the flag State) appears to have been for flag States to remain outside the RFMO and allow their vessels to fish pursuant to the traditional open access regime of high seas fishing. While attempts have been made to lure free riders with cooperating non-member status, that status does not necessarily bring with it the right to participate in decision making or quota allocation. Its efficacy has therefore, in some cases, been limited.

One of the most significant challenges for RFMOs, however, arises as a consequence of the rule of flag State jurisdiction. Traditional law of the sea posits that in relation to activities on the high seas only the flag State has jurisdiction over its vessels and can take action in respect of them. The ineffective exercise of flag State jurisdiction through inadequate enforcement can thus undermine

---

[20] FAO Voluntary Guidelines for Assessing Flag State Performance (8 February 2013), available at <ftp://ftp.fao.org/FI/DOCUMENT/tc-fsp/2013/VolGuidelines_adopted.pdf>.

[21] FSA, n 10, Art 8. See EJ Molenaar, 'The Concept of "Real Interest" and other Aspects of Cooperation through Regional Fisheries Management Mechanisms' (2000) 15(4) *International Journal of Marine and Coastal Law* 475.

RFMO measures. The 1993 Compliance Agreement seeks to address this by requiring parties to make its contravention an offence under national law and to ensure the imposition of sanctions of sufficient gravity to effect compliance and deprive offenders of the benefits accruing from their unlawful activities.[22] The FSA seeks to ensure compliance not only with its provisions but with measures adopted by RFMOs, requiring States to take enforcement action against their vessels for non-compliance with RFMO measures, irrespective of where the violation occurs.[23] Moreover, it requires international cooperation between members of RFMOs to assist flag States—whether members or non-members of RFMOs—to meet their obligations to ensure compliance by their vessels with RFMO measures.[24] It then goes even further to provide for a right of non-flag State jurisdiction where the flag State is unwilling or unable to act. RFMO members are thus able, in certain situations, to take action, both at sea and in port, against non-member vessels where the flag State of those vessels is also a party to the FSA.[25] The application of these provisions remains, however, limited by the *pacta tertiis* rule and by the willingness of non-flag States to exercise this jurisdiction. Thus, while progress has been made on developing the content of flag State responsibilities,[26] in the absence of sanctions for a flag State's failure to meet those responsibilities, the effective exercise of flag State jurisdiction cannot be guaranteed.[27]

Moreover, even assuming fishing States are members of RFMOs and/or parties to the FSA, this is no guarantee of their willingness or ability to ensure compliance with conservation and management measures by their vessels and nationals. In many cases it is nationals of member States who own and/or operate flag of convenience fishing vessels. Member States may also fail to adopt legislation to implement measures that have been agreed upon within the RFMO. Even where implementing legislation exists, member States are often hampered from controlling the activities of their vessels and nationals by the sheer tyranny of geography and the inability to pierce the corporate—and the flag State—veil. In many cases, flag States simply fail

---

[22] 1993 Agreement to Promote Compliance with International Conservation and Management Measures by Fishing Vessels on the High Seas, Art II (hereinafter FAO Compliance Agreement).

[23] FSA, n 10, Arts 18–21.   [24] Ibid, Arts 17(4) and 26.

[25] Ibid, Arts 20–22. See generally, R Rayfuse, *Non-Flag State Enforcement in High Seas Fisheries* (Martinus Nijhoff The Hague 2004).

[26] In addition to the general duties set out in LOSC, n 3, Arts 92 and 94 for its parties, detailed responsibilities are clearly articulated in FSA, n 10, Art 18. See Chapter 22 in this volume. The FAO Guidelines on Assessing Flag State Performance, n 20, provide further content. However, their status as 'voluntary guidelines' undermines their general normative effect.

[27] R Rayfuse, 'Non-Flag State Enforcement and Protection of the Marine Environment: Responding to IUU Fishing' in MH Nordquist, TB Koh, and J Norton-Moore (eds), *Freedom of Seas, Passage Rights and the 1982 Law of the Sea Convention* (Martinus Nijhoff Leiden/Boston 2009) 573; and R Rayfuse, 'To Our Children's Children's Children: Achieving Compliance in High Seas Fisheries' (2005) 20(3–4) *The International Journal of Marine and Coastal Law* 509.

to prosecute violations either because of lack of interest, lack of legally acceptable evidence or lack of resources.

Since the 1990s, the collective effects of all of these challenges has been summed up in the terminology of illegal, unreported and unregulated (IUU) fishing. Briefly put, IUU fishing is fishing that 'occurs in violation of—or at least with disregard for—applicable fisheries rules, [whether those rules have been] adopted at the national or international level'.[28] Thus, while IUU fishing also relates to fishing activities carried out within the EEZ of coastal States, the focus here is on high seas IUU fishing where the term is used to encompass a wide range of fishing activities that undermine the regulatory activities of, and conservation and management measures adopted by, RFMOs.

The whole point of the objection to IUU fishing is that it directly threatens effective conservation and management of fish stocks thereby adversely affecting both fisheries and the people who depend on them. Of course, if States were effectively exercising their jurisdiction over their vessels and nationals in support of accepted conservation and management measures then IUU fishing would not have become a significant problem. However, the open access regime of high seas fisheries, coupled with the lack of flag State control, have been identified, along with the problem of overcapacity in the fishing area, as the primary causes of the IUU fishing phenomenon. The practice of reflagging to avoid application of internationally agreed conservation and management measures has further compounded the problem.[29]

4 RFMOs and the Requirements of Conservation

Despite the 'structural' limitations inherent in international law, RFMOs are established for the express purpose of conserving and managing high seas fish stocks. The duty to conserve and to take conservation measures arises, in the context of the marine living resources of the high seas, because of the exhaustible nature of

---

[28] FAO, *Implementation of the International Plan of Action to Prevent, Deter and Eliminate Illegal, Unreported and Unregulated Fishing*, Technical Guidelines for Responsible Fisheries No 9 (FAO Rome 2002) 6.

[29] R Rayfuse, 'The Anthropocene, Autopoiesis and the Disingenuousness of the Genuine Link: Addressing Enforcement Gaps in the Legal Regime for Areas Beyond National Jurisdiction' in AG Oude Elferink and EJ Molenaar (eds), *The International Legal Regime of Areas beyond National Jurisdiction: Current and Future Developments* (Martinus Nijhoff Leiden/Boston 2010) 165.

this common property resource. No definition or articulation of conservation or conservation measures is included in the LOSC. Article 117 refers only to 'necessary' measures. Article 118 similarly (merely) requires States to 'enter into negotiations with a view to taking the measures necessary for the conservation of the living resources concerned'. Article 119, however, provides some guidance as to what conservation requires. In particular, in recognition of the various competing non-biological interests, Article 119(1)(a) adopts what is known as the 'qualified maximum sustainable yield' ('qualified MSY') approach.

MSY refers to the maximum catch that can be taken from a species or stock over an indefinite period. It is designed to ensure that stocks are exploited at the level of 'maximum physical output and natural rate of increase, preserving their highest resilience'.[30] As a single species management tool, MSY does not take account of interrelations between targeted species or other species in the ecosystem. Nor does it take account of other factors impacting on sustainable resource exploitation such as the economic value of the catch, the cost of catching and the natural instability of some stocks.[31] The qualified MSY approach called for in Article 119(1)(a) of the LOSC therefore requires States to take conservation measures 'on the basis of the best scientific evidence available' in order to:

...maintain or restore populations of harvested species at levels which can produce the maximum sustainable yield, as qualified by relevant environmental and economic factors, including the special requirements of developing States, and taking into account fishing patterns, the interdependence of stocks and any generally recommended international minimum standards, whether subregional, regional or global.

Article 119(1)(b) further requires conservation measures to take into consideration the effects on associated and dependent species to ensure they are maintained or restored to levels at which their reproduction is not seriously threatened.

By requiring consideration of both the qualified MSY and dependent and associated species, the LOSC goes beyond the earlier conception of conservation as being directed solely at ensuring the sustainability of stocks for exploitation as a food source to include both social and ecosystem considerations. This broader interpretation of the meaning of conservation was adopted by the International Tribunal for the Law of the Sea in the *Southern Bluefin Tuna* cases, where it noted that 'conservation of the living resources of the sea is an element in the protection and preservation of the marine environment'.[32] With the emergence of the concept of sustainable development the concept of conservation has further evolved to mean the sustainable use of living resources to ensure their continuing availability to meet the needs of both present and future generations. To that end, Article 5 of the FSA requires

---

[30] FAO, *High Seas Management: New Concepts and Techniques*, Doc FI/HSF/TC/92/5 (FAO Rome 1992) [15].
[31] Ibid. [32] *Southern Bluefin Tuna* (Provisional Measures), n 17, [70].

States, through the medium of RFMOs, to adopt conservation measures to ensure the long-term sustainability and promote the optimum utilization of the resource.

Measures adopted by RFMOs (generally referred to as conservation and management measures) can roughly be divided into five broad categories: measures relating to stock assessment; management of fishing effort; allocation of fishing opportunities; compliance and enforcement; and protection of the wider marine environment. Across these broad categories, RFMOs have adopted an increasingly dizzying array of measures. By way of illustration, the Conservation and Management Measures adopted by NAFO for 2014 extend to 113 pages,[33] while CCAMLR's Conservation Measures fill 280 pages,[34] and those adopted by the IOTC fill 227 pages.[35] While predominantly concerned with the management of target species, increasingly, RFMO measures also deal with management issues related to associated or dependent species and broader ecosystem concerns.

4.1 Stock assessment

Measures relating to stock assessment are aimed at providing RFMOs with the knowledge necessary to set total allowable catches and determine participatory rights. Data reporting requirements exist across all RFMOs and include requirements for data on effort and on catches and discards in both established and exploratory fisheries. These requirements have become increasingly complex and detailed over the years, requiring ever finer scale and more comprehensive data, as RFMO scientific committees and independent scientific bodies such as the International Council for the Exploration of the Sea (ICES) and the North Pacific Marine Science

---

[33] See Northwest Atlantic Fisheries Organization, 'Conservation and Enforcement Measures, 2014', NAFO FC Doc 14/1, available at <http://www.nafo.int/>.

[34] See Commission for the Conservation of Antarctic Marine Living Resources, 'Schedule of conservation measures in Force 2013/14', available at <http://www.ccamlr.org/en/document/publications/schedule-conservation-measures-force-2013/14>. Admittedly, CCAMLR is not a 'normal' RFMO. Pursuant to 1980 Convention on Conservation of Antarctic Marine Living Resources, Art II (hereinafter CAMLR Convention), its mandate is the sustainable conservation, including rational use, of all Antarctic marine living resources, with the exception of whales and seals, and the control of harvesting activities to ensure, among other things, the maintenance of ecological relationships between harvested and dependent and related species. This specific requirement of an ecosystem approach means that CCAMLR conservation and management measures must deal with more than just fisheries. However, while CCAMLR may be something *more* than a normal RFMO, it functions as *at least* a normal RFMO, as all but 10 pages of its Conservation Measures attest. Indeed, CCAMLR's ecosystem mandate is now required of all RFMOs by virtue of FSA, n 10, Art 10(d) which calls upon RFMOs to 'obtain and evaluate scientific advice, review the status of the stocks and assess the impact of fishing on non-target and associated or dependent species'.

[35] See Indian Ocean Tuna Commission, Compendium of Active Conservation and Management Measures for the Indian Ocean Tuna Commission (last updated 8 October 2014), available at <http://www.iotc.org/cmms>.

Organization (PICES) which provide scientific advice to some RFMOs, struggle to deal with the scientific uncertainty resulting either from the absence of data, or from non-reporting of data by members, or from the problem of non-reporting by non-members. Unfortunately, both under reporting and mis-reporting remain common occurrences, with RFMO annual reports evidencing a litany of calls for better compliance by members with data reporting requirements. CCAMLR and other RFMOs have therefore instituted scientific observer programs for the independent at-sea acquisition, recording, and verification of catch data and have adopted measures stipulating actions to be taken in cases of non-report.[36] In addition, a number of RFMOs have moved specifically to implement a precautionary approach to management that allows scientific committees to develop formula for the inclusion of estimates of unreported catch, or the effects of climate change or other environmental stressors, into their stock assessments.[37] Several RFMOs have begun adopting measures relating to the definition and use of the 'best available scientific evidence',[38] the requirement for and use of which is intended to ensure that their management decisions are both scientifically and politically, as well as legally, justified. Nevertheless, discrepancies remain between official catch figures and scientific estimates. To that end, NAFO, for example, has engaged in an independent peer review of the way catches are estimated in stock assessment to see if they can identify the reasons for these discrepancies.[39]

4.2 Management of fishing effort

RFMOs have adopted a vast array of measures aimed at managing fishing effort including closed seasons and closed areas (including in some cases total moratoria), restrictions on types of gear, the manner, time, and season of setting and use of gear, and other catch and effort restrictions all designed to control where, when and in what manner fishing activity takes place. Thus, measures are often adopted to prohibit or control the taking of juvenile fish, or fishing in spawning areas or during spawning times. In addition, catch limits, or overall TACs for target species are standard fare across all RFMOs. Once limits have been reached, fishing is to stop. As more and more fisheries have become depleted and new species and

---

[36] See eg CCAMLR Scheme of International Scientific Observation, as adopted at CCAMLR-XI ([6.11]) and amended at CCAMLR-XVI ([8.21]) and CCAMLR-XXVII ([13.68]). CCAMLR, *Schedule of Conservation Measures in Force 2013* (2013) 231.

[37] See eg the NAFO Precautionary Approach Framework, NAFO/FC Doc 04/18 (2004).

[38] See eg CCAMLR Res 31/XXVIII on Best Available Science.

[39] See 'Report of external experts on Peer Review of the method of catch estimation on NAFO Stocks' in *NAFO Report of the General Council and its Subsidiary Body (STACFAD)*, 34th Annual Meeting St Petersburg, Russian Federation (17–21 September 2012) 38.

stocks have been sought out, RFMOs have also moved to adopt measures to manage exploratory fisheries, a primary objective being to ensure the capture of relevant data for future stock management and TAC/quota allocation purposes.[40] However, perhaps the greatest challenge to management of fishing effort, global over-capacity, remains. The IATTC has sought to address the issue through the introduction of fleet capacity limitations to restrict fishing effort to only those vessels listed on the Vessel Register.[41] Within the WCPFC a Record of Fishing Vessels[42] and a Vessel Day Scheme (VDS) implemented by the parties to the Nauru Agreement[43] are used to restrict levels of fishing effort. ICCAT, the IOTC, and others similarly attempt to restrict capacity by limiting authorizations to fish to listed vessels or to vessels that have previously fished in the area. Capacity, however, continues to outstrip supply with the inevitable consequence of continued overfishing.

4.3 Allocation of fishing opportunity

Management of capacity and effort are also related to the issue of the allocation of fishing opportunities.[44] Many RFMOs divide the TAC for a stock into national quotas[45] while others, like CCAMLR, provide for an 'Olympic style' fishery where the race for the fish is open to all but ends with the closure of the fishing season as soon as the TAC is reached. As between members, quota allocations are generally based on historic catch and capacity taking into account scientific advice regarding stock status. Nevertheless, negotiation and allocation of national quotas can be a fraught exercise.

With respect to new entrants, some RFMOs, such as NEAFC, take the position that they can expect no quota allocation in already fully allocated fisheries. Others, such as ICCAT, have adopted measures setting out criteria for allocating

---

[40] See eg CCAMLR Conservation Measure 21-02 (2013) *on Exploratory Fisheries*.

[41] IATTC Resolution C-14-01 (as amended 2014) *on a Regional Vessel Register*.

[42] WCPFC Conservation and Management Measure 2013-10 *for WCPFC Record of Fishing Vessels and Authorizations to Fish*.

[43] The eight Parties to the Nauru Agreement (PNA), the Federated States of Micronesia, Kiribati, Republic of Marshal Islands, Nauru, Papua New Guinea, Palau, Solomon Islands, and Tuvalu, established the VDS in 2007. The Scheme limits the total number of fishing days available in areas under the jurisdiction of the PNA.

[44] EJ Molenaar, 'Participation, Allocation and Unregulated Fishing: The Practice of Regional Fisheries Management Organizations' (2003) 51 *The International Journal of Marine and Coastal Law* 457.

[45] See eg the table of NAFO quota allocations for 2013, available at <http://www.nafo.int/fisheries/frames/fishery.html>. See also the information on the total catch and its allocation, including recognition of uncertainty in relation to unaccounted catch mortality and planned Quality Assurance Reviews in the *Report of the Twentieth Annual Meeting of the CCSBT* (14-17 October 2013) [59]-[78], available at <http://www.ccsbt.org/site/reports_past_meetings.php>.

new fishing opportunities. As between existing members, the 2013 dispute between Russia and the other members of the SPRFMO over quota allocation clearly demonstrates that allocation of fishing opportunities remains one of the most contentious issues confronting RFMOs. In that case, Russia was denied a quota allocation for jack mackerel on the basis that information it had supplied to the Commission did not evidence any verifiable historic catch record. The Review Panel established to consider Russia's objection considered that the refusal unjustifiably discriminated against Russia which, as a member of the Commission, was fully entitled to an allocation. Russia was therefore entitled to authorize its vessels to fish, albeit only once it was clear that the other members were not going to fill their quota and only until the overall TAC set by the Commission had been reached.[46]

4.4 Compliance and enforcement

Perhaps the most difficult challenge for RFMOs relates to compliance and enforcement. As stocks have dwindled and the efficacy of management measures has increasingly come under pressure, RFMOs have adopted a plethora of measures aimed at persuading flag States to ensure their vessels comply with international rules and to address the enforcement challenges posed by flag States which are unwilling or unable to do so. As a matter of basic treaty law, these measures are only binding on members of the relevant RFMO. However, given Article 18 of the FSA, which requires States to refrain from authorizing their vessels to fish on the high seas unless they can effectively exercise their flag State jurisdiction, these measures are intended to, and often do, influence and affect the behaviour of non-member States as well. In that respect, they demonstrate the resolve of RFMOs to develop creative legal responses to overcome the structural challenges referred to above.

A comprehensive discussion of RFMO compliance and enforcement measures is beyond the scope of this chapter. Suffice to say that, in general, such measures include 'positive' and/or 'negative' lists of vessels which are either authorized, or not authorized, to fish in the regulatory area, transhipment bans, the use of observers, port State controls, catch documentation schemes, and at-sea measures.

Negative lists of IUU vessels are now routinely shared amongst RFMOs and member States are required to take action against listed vessels including, for example: refusing to grant their flag to listed vessels; refusing to issue licences to fish in waters under national jurisdiction; refusing authorization to land catch or to tranship in port; ensuring that fishing support vessels, cargo vessels, and mother-ships flying their flag do not participate in any transhipment operations with listed vessels; and prohibiting chartering of listed vessels. Beyond this, States are to encourage their importers, transporters and other sectors to refrain from any transactions with, or transhipments from, listed

[46] See Review Panel Findings, n 18.

vessels. Members, themselves, may be subject to trade-related measures, and possibly even loss of quota. However, as the EU–Faroe Islands dispute demonstrates, such trade measures are controversial in many RFMOs and thus rarely resorted to. In addition, while negative lists are useful in identifying individual offending vessels and in revealing patterns of flag State behaviour, they are subject to limitations. Evidentiary burdens are high, and mechanisms for the provision of evidence from national authorities to RFMOs may be complex or non-existent. Even assuming the availability of cogent and legally acceptable evidence, the tyranny of consensus decision-making in many RFMOs may allow members to block the listing of their own vessels. Procedural rules have been adopted in some RFMOs aimed at ensuring that member States cannot block consensus vis-à-vis their vessels. However, given the annual cycle of RFMO meetings, these procedures are somewhat cumbersome and maintaining up to date lists is problematic, particularly given that listed vessels, once identified, can simply move into another RFMO area or change their name and register to avoid detection. RFMOs have therefore adopted the practice of making their lists publicly available and transmitting them to other RFMOs. In 2007, the five tuna RFMOs agreed to establish a common IUU list,[47] while other RFMOs, such as NAFO, NEAFC, SEAFO, and CCAMLR, have agreed to reciprocal recognition of each other's IUU lists.

RFMOs have also moved to adopt 'positive lists', or registers of fishing vessels authorized to fish in a regulatory area. Unauthorized vessels are deemed to be IUU vessels. However, authorizations are not necessarily linked to quotas, so States are free to authorize vessels with capacity far in excess of that needed to take allocated quota. This does nothing to reduce the likelihood of over-fishing. Moreover, as with negative lists, problems of consistency and application can arise as between the different lists adopted by different organizations. It is hoped that the development of the FAO 'Global Record of Fishing Vessels, Refrigerated Transport Vessels and Supply Vessels',[48] which is intended to serve as a single record of all fishing, refrigerated transport, and supply vessels, will ameliorate this situation.

Controls, and in some cases bans, on transhipments, either as between vessels of members or between vessels of members and non-members, are also increasingly frequent. Controls may include the requirement to establish a record of carrier vessels and conditions for at-sea transhipment such as flag State authorization, notification procedures, and the use of on-board observers. However, monitoring and controlling at-sea transhipments is notoriously difficult and even the presence of third-party observers may be an insufficient deterrent to IUU fishing if the observer's role is limited to catch-data recording for scientific purposes only or if transhipment occurs beyond the jurisdictional area of the observer. For these reasons,

---

[47] *Report of the Joint Meeting of Tuna RFMOs*, Tuna RFMOs, Kobe (22–26 January 2007), available at <www.tuna-org.org/meetingspast.htm>.

[48] FAO, *Global Record of Fishing Vessels, Refrigerated Transport Vessels and Supply Vessels*, available at <http://www.fao.org/fishery/global-record/en>.

NEAFC, for example, requires transhipment to take place only within designated member ports after advance notification to the port State of the precise details of the catch to be transhipped, including total weight to be landed and the port and time of landing.[49]

Nevertheless, vessels may tranship at sea or off-load in ports of States not party to the relevant RFMO scheme. Under customary international law, port States are entitled to control access to their ports and persons and activities within their territory, subject only to exception in the case of *force majeure* or in cases specifically agreed to in treaties.[50] However, a natural corollary of the right to control is the right not to control. The existence of 'ports of convenience' therefore poses a real threat to the efficacy of RFMO measures. The banning of at-sea transhipment and the imposition of conditions on landing goes some way to alleviating this. However, measures requiring more significant aspects of port State control have increasingly been called for in RFMOs with some schemes, such as those adopted by NEAFC and NAFO, showing particular success in exerting strong influence on the conduct of non-party flag States and their vessels by imposing *de facto*, even if not *de jure*, adherence to RFMO standards as a condition of port entry. Vessels are required to provide prior notification of landing, including a declaration that the vessel has not been engaged in IUU fishing, which must also be confirmed by the flag State. Failure to make the appropriate declaration will result in denial of port access and if there is evidence that the catch was taken in contravention of RFMO measures then the port State must not allow it to be landed or transhipped.[51] Nevertheless, the proliferation of inconsistent, un-harmonized RFMO port State control schemes remains problematic. Indeed, despite—or perhaps because of—the adoption of the FAO Agreement on Port State Measures, a number of RFMOs have been unable to agree on their introduction.[52]

Increasingly intertwined with port State measures, the use of trade-related measures, such as catch documentation and certification schemes, as well as export and import controls or prohibitions, is becoming more widespread. The purpose of certification schemes is to create negative incentives to deter non-compliance with measures adopted by RFMOs by removing competitive advantage, thereby creating positive incentives to comply. Importantly, they also provide information on

---

[49] NEAFC Scheme of Control and Enforcement, Arts 20–25, available at <http://neafc.org/mcs/scheme/2014>.

[50] On port State control more generally, see Chapter 13 in this volume.

[51] See eg NAFO Port State Control Measures in NAFO Conservation and Enforcement Measures (2014), n 33, ch VII, Arts 42–47; NEAFC Port State Control of Foreign Fishing Vessels in NEAFC Scheme of Control and Enforcement (2014), n 49, ch V, Arts 20–27.

[52] This is perhaps not surprising given that a number of States who are members of RFMOs are not yet party to the FAO Agreement and therefore consider adoption by an RFMO of port State measures to be merely a veiled attempt to bring the FAO Agreement in through the back door. Many of the same States are similarly responsible for the impasses in some RFMOs relating to at-sea inspection programs as called for in the FSA to which they are also not party.

the amount of fish in trade and which countries are involved in that trade thereby enabling more effective management and enforcement decisions to be taken. Catch certifications are issued at the point of harvesting and cover all fish to be landed or transhipped. They thus enable landings and trade flows to be monitored and make it possible to restrict access to markets for fish taken in contravention of RFMO measures.[53] However, the efficacy of these certification schemes is somewhat limited by their *inter partes* application, by their circumvention by landing in non-member ports, and by a number of technical shortcomings including double counting of catch, inadequate application to all catch and all species, and the ever-present practice of fraudulent reporting. Technological hurdles aside, the introduction of electronic documentation has reduced the potential for fraud, improved the speed at which information can be exchanged, and reduced the compliance burden on legitimate operators and regulatory authorities. Nevertheless, there remains a need to harmonize the various RFMO schemes to make their application by port States more streamlined and therefore both more attractive and more effective.

A range of at-sea measures have also been adopted by RFMOs to enhance compliance and enforcement. Increasingly, requirements for the use of Vessel Monitoring Systems (VMS) are becoming the norm and are being further supplemented by a move to satellite monitoring. At-sea observer programs, already used for scientific data gathering purposes, are increasingly being introduced for compliance purposes. In general, RFMO measures seek to maintain a strict separation between the science and compliance functions, both to ensure the safety of observers and to ensure the integrity of either the scientific data or the compliance related information they obtain.

Measures reflective of those in Article 19 of the FSA are increasingly found in most RFMOs. Such measures positively require flag States to board, inspect and enforce against their vessels wherever and whenever a violation occurs, conduct immediate and full investigations of alleged violations, refer the matter to investigating and judicial authorities as necessary, and ensure that sanctions imposed are adequate in severity to be effective in securing compliance and discouraging violations and that sanctions imposed deprive offenders of the benefits accruing from their illegal activities and include the possibility of loss of authorizations either to fish or to operate vessels, or both.

Measures reflective of FSA Articles 21 and 22 providing for non-flag State boarding and inspection also exist in a number of RFMOs, including CCAMLR, NAFO, NEAFC, SEAFO, the WCPFC, and the NPAFC. Admittedly,

---

[53] See eg CCAMLR Conservation Measure 10-05 Catch Documentation Scheme for *Dissostichus spp*; CCSBT Resolution on the Implementation of a Catch Documentation Scheme (2010), replacing the CCSBT Statistical Document Programme (Trade Information Scheme) adopted in 2000. On the development and operation of these schemes, see generally R Rayfuse, 'Building Sustainable High Seas Fisheries through Certification Processes: Issues and Perspectives' (2009) 35 (1–2) *Revue Océanis* 93.

these latter schemes only operate *inter partes* or as against stateless vessels. However, consent to boarding, inspection, and arrest can be, and sometimes is, given by a flag State on an ad hoc basis. Where these boarding and inspection schemes exist, they seem to have been reasonably successful in ensuring compliance, although issues of cost and availability mean that inspection rates are generally limited to a small percentage of the fleet, and, of course, enforcement still needs to be backed up by adequate flag State engagement in the investigation and prosecution stages.

4.5 Protection of the broader marine environment

Despite the increasing recognition of the requirements of precautionary and ecosystem management, RFMOs and other arrangements generally manage stocks either on a species-specific or geographic basis. However, even in managing targeted fish stocks, RFMOs must be alive to the problem of by-catch of non-targeted species. Indeed, some RFMOS, such as CCAMLR, are specifically mandated to take into account effects on dependant and associated species.[54] The implementation of a broader ecosystem approach as called for by Article 5 of the FSA now requires all RFMOs to consider the effects of fishing activities on dependent and related species and on the broader marine ecosystem. To that end a number of RFMOs, including NAFO, NEAFC, and the IATTC, have moved to update their management mandates, in some cases even adopting amended conventions[55] which include the requirements of the precautionary and ecosystem approaches.

Traditionally, the most basic measures adopted relate to by-catch of other fish species. In some RFMOs fisheries for targeted fish stocks are to stop where pre-set levels of by-catch are reached. Measures also regulate whether by-catch is to be retained or discarded with a general preference being for retention to enable more holistic management of stocks. Beyond non-targeted fish stocks the effects of fishing on other species have increasingly occupied RFMOs which have adopted measures aimed at preventing or reducing by-catch of species like sharks, dolphins, turtles, and sea birds. For example, measures adopted in the CAMLR Convention area,

---

[54] CAMLR Convention, n 34, Art II.
[55] For example, in 1997 the GFCM adopted a revised convention which entered into force on 29 April 2004. On 28 September 2007, NAFO adopted a document entitled 'Amendment to the Convention on Future Multilateral Cooperation in the Northwest Atlantic Fisheries', constituting the first formal step towards a reformed Convention for NAFO. As of 2013, five parties have ratified the amended Convention which has yet to enter into force. In 2007, NEAFC adopted a revised Convention which the parties have agreed to apply on a provisional basis pending its ratification. In 2003, the IATTC adopted a new Convention for the Strengthening of the Inter-American Tropical Tuna Commission (the Antigua Convention), which came into force on 27 August 2010.

like requirements for the use of tori poles or weighted hooks,[56] appear to have been particularly successful in reducing seabird mortality. Similarly, concerns over high levels of dolphin mortality in the Eastern Pacific Ocean led to the adoption of the IATTC's AIDCP. The agreement establishes a system of dolphin mortality limits for vessels which, when reached, require the vessel to stop fishing. Compliance is monitored by on-board observers, which has helped ensure the success of the program in reducing dolphin mortality to near zero.[57]

More recently the international community has broadened its concerns to include the effects of fishing on vulnerable marine ecosystems (VMEs) and RFMOs have begun to implement the various UNGA resolutions on bottom fisheries[58] and international guidelines on deep-sea fisheries[59] by adopting measures to control destructive fishing practices like bottom trawling and to establish marine protected areas. NEAFC, for example, has closed a number of areas to bottom trawling and has adopted what have come to be called 'move-on' rules. These rules require vessels to stop fishing and move off a certain pre-determined distance if they bring up more than prescribed quantities of listed indicator species, such as deep-water corals, that indicate they are fishing on a VME. Since 2010, NEAFC has adopted measures requiring prior impact assessments of bottom fisheries in 'new' fishing areas to complement the 'move on' rules in existing fishing areas.[60]

Similar types of measures have been adopted in NAFO, CCAMLR, and SEAFO. However, both the implementation and the efficacy of these measures have been seriously questioned by non-governmental organizations (NGOs) which point to the extreme complexity of the regulations, the need for enhanced mapping of VMEs, the need for new requirements for exploratory fisheries, the need to ensure that any closures triggered by the move on rules/encounter protocol in existing fishing areas are applicable to all vessels fishing in that area and not just the vessel reporting the encounter, and the need to ensure mechanisms are in place to monitor closed areas to ensure no fishing takes place there.[61] In 2012, several

---

[56] CCAMLR Conservation Measure 25-02 (2012), *Minimisation of the incidental mortality of seabirds in the course of longline fishing or longline fishing research in the Convention Area*.

[57] According to the IATTC, during 2013, 95.4 per cent of all sets made on tuna associated with dolphins were accomplished with no mortality or serious injury to the dolphins and the total mortality of dolphins in the fishery has been reduced from about 132,000 in 1986 to about 800 in 2013. See information on Total Mortalities and Mortalities per Set, available at <http://www.iattc.org/DolphinSafeENG.htm>.

[58] UNGA Res 61/105 (2007) and UNGA Res 64/72 (2009).

[59] International Guidelines for The Management of Deep-Sea Fisheries in the High Seas (FAO Rome 2009).

[60] Consolidated text of all NEAFC recommendations on regulating bottom fishing as amended by Recommendation 12: 2013, available at <http://neafc.org/rec/2011/na>.

[61] Deep Sea Conservation Coalition, *Unfinished Business: A Review of the Implementation of the Provisions of United Nations General Assembly Resolutions 61/105 and 64/72, Related to the Management of Bottom Fisheries in Areas Beyond National Jurisdiction* (September 2011), available at <http://www.savethehighseas.org/publicdocs/DSCC_review11.pdf>.

NGOs pointed out that no reports of VME encounters had yet been communicated to NEAFC, prompting them to ask whether this was because none had actually occurred or whether it was merely that the Commission's reporting requirements had not been met.[62]

With the exception of the apparent success of NEAFC in closing certain areas to bottom trawling, thereby effectively designating them marine protected areas (MPAs), establishment of high seas MPAs seems to be proving extremely difficult. In CCAMLR, where the parties have specifically agreed to establish MPAs, they have so far failed to do so. In 2012, the Commission was forced to hold only its second-ever extraordinary meeting precisely to finalize the establishment of a number of MPAs. However, rather than reaching agreement, certain members actually raised new objections contesting the legality of CCAMLR taking such measures—despite the apparently clear mandate to do so in its Convention. At the time of writing, CCAMLR has still yet to adopt any MPA proposals.[63]

5 RFMOs AND CLIMATE CHANGE

A significant emerging challenge for RFMOs relates to their ability to manage fisheries under conditions of climatic uncertainty. In 2006, scientists predicted that at current catch rates and levels of habitat destruction global fish stocks would be commercially extinct by 2100.[64] These classical threats are now compounded by climate change. In its Fifth Assessment Report, released in 2014, the Intergovernmental Panel on Climate Change unequivocally confirmed that the oceans are warming and becoming more acidic.[65] These changes are leading to increasingly rapid biological responses and ecological shifts including species depletion, migration, and range shifts and the increasing prevalence of disease-causing agents, exotic and potentially invasive alien species, and other threats to fisheries and marine biodiversity in general.[66] The transformation of ocean ecosystems as a result of climate change and

---

[62] Statement by Deep Sea Conservation Coalition, Iceland Nature Conservation Association, Pew Environment Group, Seas at Risk, WWF, *Report of the 31st Annual Meeting of the North-East Atlantic Fisheries Commission* (12–16 November 2012) Vol II, Annex.

[63] See CCAMLR, *Report of the Thirty-Second Meeting of the Commission* (Hobart 23 October–1 November 2013) [7.32]. See further Chapter 32 in this volume.

[64] B Worm et al, 'Impacts of Biodiversity Loss on Ocean Ecosystem Services' (2006) 314 *Science* 787.

[65] H-O Pörtner et al, 'Ocean Systems' in *Climate Change 2014: Impacts, Adaptation, and Vulnerability. Contribution of Working Group II to the Fifth Assessment Report of the Intergovernmental Panel on Climate Change* (2013) ch 6, available at <http://ipcc-wg2.gov/AR5/report/final-drafts/>.

[66] Ibid, ch 6, 58–9.

ocean acidification[67] and the difficulty of grafting climate change impacts such as changes in species distribution and productivity onto the range of factors already to be considered in implementing the precautionary and ecosystem approaches pose significant challenges for RFMOs.[68]

Stock or species management boundaries often do not align with ecological boundaries. In addition, there is a tendency in many RFMOs to ignore both precaution and the best scientific evidence available and to adopt measures, instead, on the basis of political, rather than biological, considerations. Moreover, many areas remain unregulated, and many stocks and species remain unmanaged. The problems that climate change induced species migration pose here are threefold. First, the efficacy of RFMO management measures will be significantly impacted by changes in species abundance. Second, where species or stocks migrate outside the area of competence of an RFMO they may move into an area regulated by another RFMO, leading to conflict between the two RFMOs as to the proper locus of managerial competence. The issue has already arisen in the context of Southern Bluefin Tuna (SBT) migrating southwards into the CAMLR Convention area with the Commission claiming managerial and enforcement competence over vessels fishing for SBT within the CAMLR Convention area and the CCSBT contesting this competence. Third, the species or stock may migrate into a wholly unregulated area of ocean, rendering the existing management regime obsolete and leaving the species or stock vulnerable to unregulated and unstoppable overexploitation. It is precisely this concern that is driving calls for a moratorium on fishing in the Arctic Ocean pending the establishment of appropriate fisheries regimes in both areas under national jurisdiction (AUNJ) and areas beyond national jurisdiction (ABNJ).

Even where regulation exists, the difficulties of managing migratory species and stocks which cross biologically arbitrary geo-political and legal jurisdictional lines will only increase as species distributions change. In the case of transboundary or shared stocks (those shared between two States), climate-induced stock migration may affect the share of a stock in each State. As both States seek to maintain their share of the catch, this will have adverse implications for stock management and for stock status. If the State with the diminishing percentage of the stock fails to reduce its catch, this will undermine conservatory efforts and catch limits in the other country. In a worst-case scenario, continued take by the State losing the stocks coupled with increased take by the State acquiring more of the stock will lead to the stock being fished possibly to extinction.

Similarly, in high seas fisheries, Article 7 of the FSA requires coastal States and RFMOs to adopt 'compatible' conservation and management measures in respect of straddling and highly migratory fish stocks. A range shift away from the coastal State

---

[67] On the issue of ocean acidification, see Chapter 34 in this volume.
[68] For fuller discussion, see R Rayfuse, 'Climate Change and the Law of the Sea' in R Rayfuse and S Scott (eds), *International Law in the Era of Climate Change* (Edward Elgar Cheltenham 2012) 147.

will weaken its conservation incentives and aggravate management as between that State and the relevant RFMO. A range shift to a coastal State will similarly aggravate management and conservation status if it leads to increased fishing pressure within the areas under national jurisdiction and no corresponding reduction in the high seas, RFMO, area. Dramatic shifts in migration will be particularly problematic in the case of highly migratory species, such as tuna, in areas where pockets of high seas are interspersed with areas under national jurisdiction such as in the Western and Central Pacific.[69] According to Axelrod, States most vulnerable to these anticipated changes are more likely to push for greater control over the resources which straddle their EEZs through more stringent RFMO measures including a reduction of quota to distant water fishing fleets. The latter, however, are more likely to insist on maintaining their quota and less restrictive measures while shifting the organizational goals away from catch limits to enable them to maintain their presence in the fishery even in the face of increasing catches in AUNJ.[70]

It will be immediately apparent that climate change and ocean acidification threaten not only fish stocks, but also both the robustness and the institutional resilience of the very RFMOs that manage them. Nevertheless, to date only six RFMOs have taken 'action' related to climate change either by 'deciding to undertake climate adaptation or mitigation activities or to allocate funds towards climate change research'.[71] Clearly, there is a growing imperative for RFMOs to take seriously the need to directly address climate change in their activities and decisions.

6 Conclusion

RFMOs hold the privileged position of stewards of the world's high seas fisheries resources. The ultimate goal of all RFMOs is the achievement of the long-term conservation and sustainable use of the fish stocks under their management. To that end, they are charged with a wide range of functions encompassing everything from data acquisition and dissemination, to the development and implementation of precautionary and ecosystem based management systems, to ensuring compliance and enforcement. Particularly in the decades since the adoption of the FSA, RFMOs have moved with varying degrees of alacrity to take seriously their mandates and fulfil their stewardship role through the adoption of an increasing range

---

[69] O Hoegh-Guldberg et al, 'The Ocean' in *Climate Change 2014*, n 65, ch 30.
[70] M Axelrod, 'Climate Change and Global Fisheries Management: Linking Issues to Protect Ecosystems or to Save Political Interests?' (2011) 11(3) *Global Environmental Politics* 64, 73.
[71] The six are CCAMLR, IOTC, NAFO, NASCO, NPAFC, and WCPFC.

of measures aimed at controlling the activities of both members and non-members alike. RFMOs have also begun to work together to address the common concern of IUU fishing through the sharing of information and the development of harmonized approaches and measures. In this respect they can be seen to be fulfilling, or at least attempting to fulfil, the obligations of cooperation and conservation.

However, as international organizations, RFMOs remain hamstrung by the limits of cooperation inherent in the very structures of international law. Moreover, RFMOs are creatures of a world viewed through essentially biologically stable conditions. In this respect they are generally considered to be deficient in the essential capacities for adaptive, integrated governance and management that will be required to effectively support the resilience of marine ecosystems in an increasingly dynamic, climate-change challenged environment.[72] Lockwood et al have identified a number of regime requirements for the governance and management of marine biodiversity conservation in a climate change challenged world. Key requirements include: institutional flexibility; effective leadership and adaptive capacity; inclusive, effective, and meaningful participation and decision making; strategic connectivity, coordination, and cohesion through alignment of purpose, strategy, and action; and legitimacy, transparency, and accountability.[73] Independent performance reviews of RFMOs indicate that some progress has been made towards achieving at least some of these requirements. Nevertheless, the continuing prevalence of IUU fishing and the continuing decline in high seas fish stocks attest to the on-going inadequacy of RFMO measures and the need to resist complacency.

Clearly, there remains a need for RFMOs to develop more robust traditional measures for the conservation and management of the fish stocks under their mandate. In addition, decision-making processes within RFMOs will need to be strengthened to enable them to respond expeditiously and effectively to the challenges posed by climate change to the stocks they manage. Mechanisms for cooperation between existing RFMOs will need to be strengthened, and wholly new regulatory regimes may need to be developed to ensure the sustainable conservation and use of fisheries resources in a climate changed ocean. The challenge for the future for RFMOs will be in ensuring both their continuing relevance and their *raison d'être*.

---

[72] C Folke, 'Social-ecological Systems and Adaptive Governance of the Commons' (2007) 22 *Ecological Research* 14.

[73] M Lockwood et al, 'Marine Biodiversity Conservation Governance and Management: Regime Requirements for Global Environmental Change' (2012) 69 *Ocean and Coastal Management* 160.

21

INTEGRATED OCEANS MANAGEMENT

A NEW FRONTIER IN MARINE ENVIRONMENTAL PROTECTION

KAREN N SCOTT

1 INTRODUCTION

THE conservation of living resources and the protection and preservation of the marine environment are key objectives of the 1982 United Nations Convention on the Law of the Sea (LOSC). Despite this, and that many treaties relating to the marine environment have been in place for half a century or more, the health of the oceans globally continues to be significantly degraded by human activities.[1] Threats range from coastal development, over-fishing, habitat degradation, exploitation of hydrocarbons, the introduction of invasive species, climate change, and

---

[1] See generally BS Halpern et al, 'A Index to Assess the Health and Benefits of the Global Ocean' (2012) 488 *Nature* 615.

ocean acidification.[2] The Census of Marine Life, a project carried out over a decade and which reported its findings in 2010, concluded that 'ocean life is richer than imagined...more connected and more impacted than previously thought'.[3] And it is the second element in this conclusion—that the oceans are more connected than previously thought—that explains the impetus for integrated oceans management (IOM), the dominant contemporary approach to oceans governance, and the topic of this chapter.

Traditionally, marine environmental protection and the management of ocean-based activities more generally have been undertaken on the basis of a zonal and/or sectoral approach with little regard for the cumulative impact of multiple activities or the ecological constraints imposed by individual ecosystems. Despite a cursory acknowledgement of the close interrelationship of the oceans and the need to consider them as a whole within the preamble of the LOSC, the zonal/sectoral approach to oceans governance underpins and guides the implementation of the Convention. Increasingly, however, it is apparent that this inherently fragmented approach to oceans governance is contributing to the degradation of the marine environment.[4]

Integrated oceans management is an attempt to respond to the deficiencies of a zonal/sectoral, fragmented approach to oceans governance and has been widely endorsed—in theory if not in practice—at national, regional, and global levels. This chapter will explore IOM as a concept and attempt to assess the extent to which it has been implemented at all levels of oceans governance. In analysing it as a governance tool, this chapter will attempt to deconstruct IOM in order to identify its key components, their relationship to one-another and their role in supporting an integrated approach to oceans management. The importance of IOM deconstructed becomes apparent in Section 5 of this chapter, where the applicability of IOM—both actual and potential—to areas beyond national jurisdiction (ABNJ) is assessed. The chapter will conclude with observations as to the future development of IOM and its role in driving forward a new frontier in marine environmental protection and oceans governance more generally.

---

[2] Ibid. See also United Nations Environment Programme (UNEP), *Marine and Coastal Ecosystems and Human Well-being. A Synthesis report based on the findings of the Millennium Ecosystem Assessment* (UNEP 2006).

[3] Census of Marine Life, *Scientific Results to Support the Sustainable Use and Conservation of Marine Life. A Summary of the Census of Marine Life for Decision Makers* (2010) 4, available at <http://www.coml.org/policy-report>.

[4] JA Ekstrom et al, 'A Tool to Navigate Overlaps in Fragmented Ocean Governance' (2009) 33 *Marine Policy* 532, 532.

2 Integrated Oceans Management as a Tool for Marine Environmental Protection

Integrated oceans management describes an approach to oceans governance that is holistic, and which aims to integrate the management of activities that impact upon or affect the oceans across sectors, space and time under a unified over-arching vision.[5] Over 30 States have developed or are in the process of developing integrated oceans strategies in respect of waters under their jurisdiction.[6] Moreover, integrated approaches with an emphasis on marine and coastal planning have been adopted at a regional level within European waters—in particular the Mediterranean, Baltic and North Seas and the North-East Atlantic—as well as, to a more limited extent, the Western Indian Ocean and Caribbean Sea.[7] Globally, IOM was identified as a key tool for promoting the sustainable development of the oceans and the protection of the marine environment in Chapter 17 of Agenda 21, adopted at the UN Conference on Environment and Development in 1992.[8] Integrated, multidisciplinary, and multi-sectoral ocean management was subsequently endorsed at the 2002 World Summit on Sustainable Development[9] and at the 2012 Rio + 20 UN Conference on Sustainable Development.[10] The integration of oceans management has become a regular and, increasingly, a prominent theme within both the annual UN General Assembly resolutions on the law of the sea[11] and the accompanying Secretary General reports[12] as well as in the work of the UN Open-ended Informal Consultative Process on the Law of the Sea.[13] Moreover, whereas IOM within the

---

[5] See R Barnes, 'The Law of the Sea Convention and Integrated Regulation of the Oceans' (2012) 27 *International Journal of Marine and Coastal Law* 859, 860; A Underdal, 'Integrated Marine Policy. What? Why? How?' (1980) 4 *Marine Policy* 159, 159.

[6] Information on these developments at a national level, with a particular emphasis on marine spatial planning can be found at <http://www.unesco-ioc-marinesp.be/msp_around_the_world>.

[7] See the discussion in Section 4 below.

[8] UNEP, Agenda 21 (1992), ch 17 [17.1], [17.5], [17.6], and [17.22(c)], available at <http://sustainabledevelopment.un.org/content/documents/Agenda21.pdf> (hereinafter Agenda 21).

[9] *Plan of Implementation of the World Summit on Sustainable Development (WSSD)* (2002) [30], [31(g)], and [32(c)] reproduced in *Report of the World Summit on Sustainable Development (Johannesburg South Africa, 26 August–2 September 2002)*, UN Doc A/CONF.199/20 (2002) 1 (hereinafter *WSSD Implementation Plan*).

[10] Endorsed by the General Assembly in UNGA Res A/66/288 (2012) [158].

[11] See eg UNGA Res A/67/68 (2012) 2.

[12] See eg United Nations Secretary General, *Oceans and the Law of the Sea: Report of the Secretary General to the General Assembly*, UN Doc A/68/71/Add.1 (2013) [80], [103]–[104].

[13] See the *Report on the work of the United Nations Open-ended Informal Consultative Process on Oceans and the Law of the Sea at its Twelfth Meeting*, UN Doc A/66/186 (2011) [22].

context of the UN conferences in 1992, 2002, and 2012 was articulated in the context of coastal areas and waters under the jurisdiction of States,[14] the UN Secretary General has recognized its more general application, including to areas beyond national jurisdiction.[15] Integrated management of oceans activities beyond national jurisdiction has also been advocated[16] by States party to the 1992 Convention on Biological Diversity (CBD) and by members of the Ad Hoc Open-ended Informal Working Group to study issues relating to the conservation and sustainable use of marine biological diversity beyond areas of national jurisdiction (BBNJ Working Group).[17]

Despite the endorsement and, in many cases, adoption and application of IOM by national, regional, and global institutions a definitive definition of the concept remains elusive. Typically, an 'integrated' oceans policy is multi-sectoral in that it is designed to manage conflicts between, and cumulative impacts of, a wide range of activities taking place within or proximate to a marine and coastal environment. It is spatially focused in that activities are managed according to location and, increasingly, in the context of an ecosystem. It also has a strong temporal dimension, and long-term, forward planning, is an important feature of an integrated oceans policy. Finally, IOM requires a relatively high level of political, legal, and institutional coordination at all levels of implementation including meaningful stakeholder participation.

Nevertheless, the application of IOM varies significantly between regions and States.[18] For example, in the Mediterranean, IOM is primarily focused on the interface between the coastal and the marine environment, and is commonly referred to as integrated coastal (zone) management (ICM/ICZM).[19] In Northern Europe, by contrast, IOM emphasizes marine spatial planning (MSP) and the development of oceans policy has largely been driven by the need to manage multiple activities offshore, such as renewable energy generation and oil and gas exploitation.[20] In Australia, IOM is

---

[14] See Agenda 21, n 8; *WSSD Implementation Plan*, n 9; UNGA Res A/66/288 (2012).

[15] For example, in 2012, the UN Secretary General noted that '[i]ntegrated management and ecosystem approaches are essential to mitigate the cumulative impacts of sectoral activities taking place beyond areas of national jurisdiction.' United Nations Secretary General, *Oceans and the Law of the Sea: Report of the Secretary General to the General Assembly*, UN Doc A/67/79 (2012) [115].

[16] CBD Decision X/29 (2010), *Marine and coastal biodiversity* [15].

[17] See the *Letter dated 8 June 2012 from the Co-Chairs of the Ad Hoc Open-ended Informal Working Group to the President of the General Assembly*, UN Doc A/67/95 (2012) [13].

[18] See generally NA Hu, 'Integrated Oceans Policy-making: An Ongoing Process or a forgotten Concept?' (2012) 118 *Coastal Management* 107; Y Tanaka, *A Dual Approach to Ocean Governance. The Cases of Zonal and Integrated Management in the Law of the Sea* (Ashgate Farnham Surrey 2008).

[19] See B Cicin-Sain et al, 'Education and Training in Integrated Coastal Management: Lessons from the International Arena' (2000) 43 *Ocean & Coastal Management* 29; MF Frost, 'The Convergence of Integrated Coastal Zone Management and the Ecosystems Approach' (2009) 52 *Ocean and Coastal Management* 294.

[20] F Douvere, 'The Importance of Marine Spatial Planning in Advancing Ecosystem-based Sea Use Management' (2008) 32 *Marine Policy* 762, 767.

similarly implemented through a process of MSP, but is principally motivated by principles of conservation rather than by competitive-use planning.[21] Implementation of IOM also significantly diverges in terms of the scope and extent of policy integration. Typically, fisheries management is excluded from oceans policy at both the national and regional level, although it is noteworthy that the Commission for the conservation of the North-East Atlantic (the OSPAR Commission) has recently begun to coordinate its activities with regional fisheries organizations in order to develop fully integrated management of the OSPAR area. Similarly, while IOM is increasingly ecosystem-based, often with an emphasis on the interface between the marine and coastal environment, it seldom, if ever, fully addresses land-based activities such as agriculture and industrial development that impact on the oceans through river and other land-based runoff. The institutional, political, and indeed financial challenges of developing IOM with both scope and depth—at all levels—are significant, and some commentators have expressed scepticism as to whether IOM is actually a rational and realistic goal.[22]

Despite the challenges associated with defining the concept, it is possible to deconstruct IOM into its principal components, which are common to integrated oceans policy at both the national and the regional level. These components, which constitute principles and concepts in their own right comprise: ecosystem-based management; the precautionary approach; environmental impact assessment (EIA); and spatial planning, which may include a focus on the coastal/marine interface and will commonly provide for a system of marine protected areas (MPAs). Finally, IOM necessarily requires a level of institutional coordination to manage multi-sectoral activities and to provide leadership in developing an overarching oceans policy. The components identified in this chapter are by no means exclusive to the application of IOM and might be characterized as contributing to what has more generally been described as 'oceans governance'.[23] However, applied in aggregate, these principles and concepts as a *collective* perform a function arguably more ambitious in depth and scope than that which could be achieved by isolated or partial application. Nevertheless, pulling IOM apart and identifying its core components serves a valuable function, in that it enables an assessment to be made as to the extent to which IOM has global application, and more significantly, the potential to be meaningfully applied in areas beyond national jurisdiction.

---

[21] S Jay, G Ellis, and S Kidd, 'Marine Spatial Planning: A New Frontier?' (2012) 14 *Journal of Environmental Policy and Planning* 1, 2.

[22] See J Lévy, 'A National Ocean Policy: An Elusive Quest' (1993) 17 *Marine Policy* 75; DC Watt, 'An Integrated Marine Policy. A Meaningful Concept?' (1990) 14 *Marine Policy* 299.

[23] See D Freestone, 'Modern Principles of High Seas Governance: The Legal Underpinnings' (2009) 39 *International Environmental Policy and Law* 44; DR Rothwell and T Stephens, *The International Law of the Sea* (Hart Publishing Oxford 2010) ch 19.

3 NATIONAL IMPLEMENTATION OF INTEGRATED OCEANS MANAGEMENT

Probably the earliest IOM initiative was adopted in Australia in 1975, with the passage of the Great Barrier Reef Marine Park Act.[24] The Act goes beyond establishing the Great Barrier Reef as an MPA, and introduces a system of multiple use zoning designed to regulate and manage activities within the Park—such as fishing, tourism, shipping, and extractive industries—according to their impact on the multiple ecosystems found within the Park.[25] More generally, Australia's Oceans Policy was released in 1998[26] and comprises seven goals including the establishment of integrated oceans planning. Precaution, ecosystem-based management, environmental impact assessment, and spatial planning, including the creation of a network of MPAs, comprise key components of Australia's oceans policy.[27] Australia has eschewed the adoption of overarching legislation for the implementation of its oceans policy in favour of relying on existing legislation to implement its various components.[28] Similarly, the dedicated infrastructure originally established to implement the Oceans Policy was dissolved in 2004, with the merger of the National Oceans Office into the marine division of the Department of the Environment.[29] The transfer of the Oceans Policy from a trans-departmental organization to a single-sector department with an environmental focus, combined with provision for regional marine planning being made under the 1999 Environmental Protection and Biodiversity Act (EPBC),[30] has undoubtedly contributed to a conservation-driven approach to IOM.[31] Moreover, the scope of IOM in Australia is limited by the focus of the Oceans Policy on federal government initiatives and by the tension between the national government and the individual states and Northern Territory in respect of bioregional planning.[32]

---

[24] Great Barrier Reef Marine Park Act 1975 (Cth), as amended.

[25] See JC Day, 'Zoning—Lessons from the Great Barrier Reef Marine Park' (2002) 45 *Ocean and Coastal Management* 139.

[26] Australia's Oceans Policy (Vols 1 and 2), in Australian Government Department of the Environment, *Publications Archive*, available at <http://www.environment.gov.au/about-us/publications/archive>.

[27] For an overview of Australian oceans policy see M Tsamenyi and R Kenchington, 'Australian Oceans Policymaking' (2012) 40 *Coastal Management* 119.

[28] Ibid, 123.   [29] Ibid, 127.

[30] Environmental Protection and Biodiversity Act 1999 (Cth) as amended, § 176.

[31] Tsamenyi and Kenchington, n 27, 129.

[32] E Foster, M Haward, and S Coffen-Smout, 'Implementing Integrated Oceans Management: Australia's South East Regional Marine Plan (SERMP) and Canada's Eastern Scotian Shelf Integrated Management (ESSIM) Initiative' (2005) 29 *Marine Policy* 391, 392–3; G Wescott, 'Stimulating Vertical Integration in Coastal Management in a Federated Nation: The Case of Australian Policy Reform' (2009) 37 *Coastal Management* 501, 511.

The challenges of implementing an oceans policy in a federal State have also characterized the Canadian experience of IOM, which was initiated in 1996 with the adoption of the Oceans Act,[33] and which has been more recently developed with the creation of an Oceans Strategy in 2002[34] and a National Oceans Action Plan in 2005.[35] In contrast to Australia, IOM in Canada is founded in dedicated overarching legislation. However, while the Department of Fisheries and Oceans (DFO) has the principal role of coordinating the implementation of the Oceans Policy, individual responsibility for marine activities is divided among 27 Federal departments and agencies in addition to multiple organizations at the State and territory level.[36] Integrated ocean management in Canada is primarily implemented through strategic or spatial planning within five 'large ocean management areas' (LOMAs).[37] Spatial and integrated planning is most advanced thus far in the Eastern Scotian Shelf area with a comprehensive and complex Eastern Scotian Shelf Integrated Ocean Management Plan being adopted in 2007.[38] Overall, however, progress on implementing the Canadian Oceans Policy has been relatively slow, impeded at times by constitutional and sectoral jurisdictional disputes.[39]

The most ambitious example of IOM implementation to date has been developed to apply within United Kingdom (UK) waters. In 2009, following an extensive trial period in the Irish Sea, the Marine and Coastal Access Act was adopted in England and Wales.[40] The Act provides for the development of a Marine Policy Statement (MPS) designed to establish general policies for achieving sustainable development in the UK marine area and to provide a framework for preparing marine plans for eight large planning regions.[41] The planning regions are divided into smaller planning areas and the 2009 Act requires marine plans to be developed in respect of

---

[33] Oceans Act, SC 1996, c 31 (Canada).

[34] *Canada's Oceans Strategy: Policy and Operational Framework for Integrated Management of Estuarine, Coastal and Marine Environments in Canada* (2002), available at <http://www.dfo-mpo.gc.ca/oceans/publications/cosframework-cadresoc/pdf/im-gi-eng.pdf>.

[35] *Canada's Oceans Action Plan* (2005), available at <http://www.dfo-mpo.gc.ca/oceans/publications/oap-pao/pdf/oap-eng.pdf>.

[36] T McDorman and A Chircop, 'Canada's Oceans Policy Framework: An Overview' (2012) 40 *Coastal Management* 133, 129.

[37] Ibid, 142–3.

[38] See W Flannery and M Ó Cinnéide, 'Deriving Lessons Relating to Marine Spatial Planning from Canada's Eastern Scotian Shelf Integrated Management Initiative' (2012) 14 *Journal of Environmental Policy and Planning* 97.

[39] For a discussion of some of these disputes which have arisen in the context of the Eastern Scotian Shelf Integrated Management Initiative, see ibid, 100.

[40] Marine and Coastal Access Act 2009, c 23 (UK). See also the Marine (Scotland) Act 2010 asp 5 (Scot) and the Marine Act (Northern Ireland) 2013 c 10 (NI).

[41] Marine and Coastal Access Act, n 40, §§ 44 and 49. The MPS was formally adopted in 2011 and is available at <https://www.gov.uk/government/publications/uk-marine-policy-statement>.

each of these areas. To date, in England, planning has begun in the East Inshore and Offshore areas[42] and in the South Inshore and Offshore areas.[43] The 2009 Act also established the Marine Management Organisation (MMO), a non-departmental public body, and transferred to it decision-making powers from existing government departments and agencies in respect of a range of maritime activities including, *inter alia*, fishing, extractive industries, laying of cables and pipelines, dumping at sea, and scientific research.[44] In contrast to both Canada and Australia, oceans policy in the UK is relatively well integrated with a designated agency responsible for implementing marine planning, managing a wide range of maritime activities including inshore fishing, and supporting marine conservation through the development of a network of MPAs.[45] However, even this ambitious example of IOM is not entirely complete in scope: the management of fisheries beyond 12 nautical miles, for example, is managed largely externally to the UK under the EU Common Fisheries Policy, and decisions in respect of large infrastructure projects such as new offshore wind farms are managed by the Department of Energy and Climate Change rather than by the MMO.

Elsewhere in Europe, prompted by developments at the regional level,[46] a number of States are in the process of implementing IOM primarily through the mechanism of MSP.[47] For example, in 2004, Germany amended the 1996 German Federal Spatial Planning Act in order to extend the application of the Act to its exclusive economic zone (EEZ). It adopted a National Strategy for Integrated Coastal Zone Management in 2006 and drafted multiple-use marine spatial plans for areas of the North[48] and Baltic Seas[49] under its jurisdiction, which came into effect in 2009. The plans adopt a system of zoning designed to manage multiple activities and to provide for MPAs within which human impacts are

---

[42] For details on progress, see UK Government, East Inshore and East Offshore Marine Plan Areas (2004), available at <http://www.marinemanagement.org.uk/marineplanning/areas/east.htm>.

[43] For details on progress, see UK Government, South Inshore and South Offshore Marine Plan Areas (2014), available at <http://www.marinemanagement.org.uk/marineplanning/areas/south.htm>.

[44] Marine and Coastal Access Act, n 40, ch 2.

[45] See generally S Kidd, 'Rising to the Integration Ambitions of Marine Spatial Planning: Reflections from the Irish Sea' (2013) 39 *Marine Policy* 273.

[46] Discussed in Section 4 below.

[47] For an overview of European initiatives, see P Drankier, 'Embedding Maritime Spatial Planning in National Legal Frameworks' (2012) 14 *Journal of Environmental Policy & Planning* 7.

[48] Ordinance on Spatial Planning in the German EEZ in the North Sea, BGBl I, 2009, 3107 (21 September 2009) (Germany), available at <http://www.bsh.de/en/Marine_uses/Spatial_Planning_in_the_German_EEZ/documents2/ordinance_north_sea.pdf>; *Spatial Plan for the German Exclusive Economic Zone in the North Sea*, available at <http://www.bsh.de/en/Marine_uses/Spatial_Planning_in_the_German_EEZ/documents2/Spatial_Plan_North_Sea.pdf>.

[49] Ordinance on Spatial Planning in the German EEZ in the Baltic Sea, BGBl I, 2009, 3861 (10 December 2009) (Germany), available at <http://www.bsh.de/en/Marine_uses/Spatial_Planning_in_the_German_EEZ/documents2/ordinance_baltic_sea.pdf>; *Spatial Plan for the German Exclusive Economic Zone in the Baltic Sea*, available at <http://www.bsh.de/en/Marine_uses/Spatial_Planning_in_the_German_EEZ/documents2/Spatial_Plan_Baltic_Sea.pdf>.

reduced. Marine spatial planning and other measures have also been adopted by Belgium, the Netherlands, and Norway. Unusually, the integrated management plans adopted by Norway for the Barents Sea—Lofoten area and the Norwegian Sea, in 2006 and 2009 respectively, include *all* economic sectors including fisheries management.

In Asia, IOM is significantly less-well developed, although a number of States, including Indonesia[50] and the Philippines,[51] are involved in initiatives focusing on integrated coastal zone management and planning, with a particular emphasis on mitigating and adapting to the impact of sea-level rise and other consequences of climate change. Nevertheless, ecosystem-based planning and IOM is undoubtedly in the early stages of development in South Korea[52] and China.[53]

The final development worthy of note in the context of IOM has taken place recently in respect of United States' waters. Marine planning or spatial management has a relatively long lineage in certain states in the USA such as Massachusetts. However, in 2010, the Interagency Ocean Policy Task Force recommended the implementation of 'comprehensive, integrated, ecosystem-based coastal and marine spatial planning and management in the United States' and the establishment of a National Ocean Council (NOC) to implement the National Oceans Policy.[54] The Recommendations of the Task Force were adopted by Executive Order in July 2010,[55] which also established the NOC and charged it with implementing the National Oceans Policy, overseeing the development of marine spatial plans for the nine planning regions set out in the Recommendations, and coordinating activities among the 27 US Federal agencies with responsibility for maritime affairs.[56] Notably, the Recommendations suggest that regional plans should address a diverse range of issues including management of resources, fisheries, security, transportation, and health.[57] Good progress is being made with

---

[50] AR Farham and S Lim, 'Integrated Coastal Zone Management Towards Indonesia Global Ocean Observing System (INA-GOOS): Review and Recommendation' (2010) 53 *Ocean and Coastal Management* 421.

[51] RK Larsen, JM Acebes, and A Belan, *Philippines Integrated Coastal Management: Diverging Stakeholder Agendas and Elite Co-option in the Babuyan Islands*, Stockholm Environment Institute Working Paper (2010).

[52] See SG Kim and H Choi, 'The Evaluation of the 2nd Ocean Plan in Korea: Focused on the Implementing Power of the Plan' (2013) 41 *Coastal Management* 470.

[53] See K Zou, 'China's Ocean Policymaking: Practice and Lessons' (2010) 40 *Coastal Management* 145.

[54] White House Council on Environmental Quality, *Final Recommendations of the Interagency Ocean Policy Task Force* (19 July 2010) 4, 6, 19–27, 32, and 41–69, available at <http://www.whitehouse.gov/files/documents/OPTF_FinalRecs.pdf>.

[55] Executive Order 13547 (19 July 2010), available at <http://www.whitehouse.gov/files/documents/2010stewardship-eo.pdf>.

[56] Ibid. See also National Oceans Council website, at <http://www.whitehouse.gov/administration/eop/oceans>.

[57] *Final Recommendations of the Interagency Ocean Policy Task Force*, n 54, 52.

respect to developing IOM in the USA with the release of the National Ocean Policy Implementation Plan[58] and the Regional Marine Planning Handbook in April 2013.[59]

Principles and environmental management concepts such as precaution, EIA and MPAs are integral to most regimes at the national level developed to protect the oceans environment and to manage maritime activities. However, a growing minority of States are going beyond the deployment of these governance tools, and developing overarching oceans policies and managing and planning activities on the basis of an integrated and ecosystem approach. The above non-exhaustive and necessarily brief survey demonstrates that while all examples of IOM comprise five core elements—the precautionary approach, EIA, ecosystem-based management, spatial planning, and designation of MPAs—its implementation diverges significantly among States. A minority, including the UK, is in the process of developing an ambitious integrated strategy that attempts to unify the process of regional ecosystem-based spatial planning with the management of most maritime activities under a unified legislative and administrative structure. Others, as illustrated by Australia, Canada, and the USA, are implementing IOM primarily through a sophisticated system of regional MSP guided by a national overarching policy. In some cases, States have chosen to adopt dedicated legislation for the purpose of implementing IOM and in others, such as Germany, terrestrial planning legislation has simply been extended to apply to the marine environment. Some States, such as Australia and the Netherlands, have opted not to adopt any legislative base for their oceans policy. All States have attempted to create or deploy administrative and political support for implementing IOM but that support varies from a dedicated organization with overall control for maritime activities (in the UK) to a body with a the principal function of coordinating the activities of multiple agencies with maritime functions (in Canada and the USA) to management within a non-dedicated existing government department (Australia). Nevertheless, despite the divergence in the practice of implementing IOM, there is little doubt that over the last decade oceans governance at the national level is increasingly—although not ubiquitously—integrated, ecosystem-based, and developed according to a long-term, overarching oceans policy.

---

[58] National Oceans Council, *National Oceans Policy Implementation Plan* (April 2013), available at <http://www.whitehouse.gov//sites/default/files/national_ocean_policy_implementation_plan.pdf>.

[59] National Oceans Council, *Marine Planning Handbook* (July 2013), available at <http://www.whitehouse.gov//sites/default/files/final_marine_planning_handbook.pdf>.

4 REGIONAL IMPLEMENTATION OF INTEGRATED OCEANS MANAGEMENT

At the regional level, the implementation of IOM unsurprisingly mirrors developments at the national level, with progress being most advanced within European waters.[60] Three of the four regional seas regimes within Europe—the Mediterranean, Baltic, and North East Atlantic—have been particularly active over the last decade in developing ecosystem-based integrated management approaches, with a particular emphasis on spatial and/or coastal planning. Furthermore, the European Union has also taken significant steps in developing an overarching integrated maritime policy of application to all 28 Member States.

The EU Integrated Maritime Policy (IMP) was released in 2007, accompanied by an Action Plan adopted later that year.[61] The IMP was designed to identify policy synergies and to overcome sectoral divisions within the EU, and placed strong emphasis on MSP both offshore and the coastal/marine interface.[62] In 2008, the European Parliament and Council adopted the Marine Strategy Framework Directive,[63] which adopts an explicitly ecosystem approach to oceans governance by dividing European waters into a series of European Marine Regions on the basis of environmental and geographical criteria, and requires the littoral States to cooperate in developing strategies for the management of these regions. The IMP was reviewed in 2009,[64] and its principal recommendation, to fund a work programme implementing the core components of the Policy, was adopted in 2011.[65] The most recent review of the IMP noted its contribution to supporting economic

---

[60] For a general introduction to IOM in European waters, see J Reis, T Stojanovic, and H Smith, 'Relevance of systems approaches for implementing Integrated Coastal Zone Management principles in Europe' (2014) 43 *Marine Policy* 3.

[61] 'Communication from the European Commission to the European Parliament, the Council, the European Economic and Social Committee and the Committee of the Regions', *An Integrated Maritime Policy for the European Union*, Doc COM(2007) 575 Final (10 October 2007).

[62] T Koivurova, 'Integrated Maritime Policy of the European Union: Challenges, Successes, and Lessons to Learn' (2012) 40 *Coastal Management* 161, 164–6. See also W Qiu and PJS Jones, 'The Emerging Policy Landscape for Marine Spatial Planning in Europe' (2013) 39 *Marine Policy* 182.

[63] Directive 2008/56/EC of the European Parliament and of the Council of 17 June 2008 establishing a framework for community action in the field of marine environmental policy, OJ L 164/19 (hereinafter Marine Strategy Framework Directive).

[64] 'Report from the Commission to the Council, the European Parliament, the European Economic and Social Committee and the Committee of the Regions', *Progress Report on the EU's Integrated Maritime Policy*, Doc COM(2009) 540 Final (15 October 2009).

[65] Regulation No 1255/2011 of the European Parliament and of the Council of 30 November 2011 establishing a Programme to support the further development of an Integrated Maritime Policy, OJ L/321/1. The 2011–2012 Programme of Work had a budget of 40 million Euros.

development and recovery within the EU as well as its impact on improving environmental management within the region.[66] This is an ambitious initiative that involves the coordination of policies within 28 States and extends from the Arctic to the Mediterranean and from the Black Sea to the Atlantic, and even beyond, to the extent that it is applied to dependent territories of European States in the Caribbean and the Pacific.[67] The greatest challenge to the success of the IMP lies in its implementation. Although the IMP relies heavily on MSP as the means to implement IOM within European waters, it currently lacks a mechanism to mandate the application of MSP within Member States, and it has been questioned as to whether MSP is even an EU competence.[68] More pragmatically, the implementation of MSP, particularly within Northern waters, has been criticized as permitting the strategic development of certain activities—notably the establishment of offshore wind farms—at the expense of other activities in a so-called 'race for space'.[69] More generally, the scope of integration between policies within the EU is far from complete with, in particular, a failure to fully coordinate environmental and fisheries policies being subject to criticism.[70] Nevertheless, the IMP and other EU initiatives have undoubtedly proven influential in the development and implementation of IOM at both the national level and within the context of the four principal regional seas regimes that operate within Europe.

Sub-regionally, IOM is most advanced in the Baltic Sea.[71] The 1992 Convention on the Protection of the Marine Environment of the Baltic Sea Area (Helsinki Convention) provided early and robust endorsement of both the precautionary principle and EIA as tools for the protection of the Baltic marine environment.[72] In 1994, the States party to the Helsinki Convention initiated the process of establishing

---

[66] 'Report from the Commission to the Council, the European Parliament, the European Economic and Social Committee and the Committee of the Regions', *Progress Report on the EU's Integrated Maritime Policy*, Doc COM(2012) 491 Final.

[67] R Churchill, 'The European Union and the Challenges of Marine Governance: From Sectoral Response to Integrated Policy' in D Vidas and PJ Schei (eds), *The World Ocean in Globalisation. Climate Change, Sustainable Fisheries, Biodiversity, Shipping, Regional Issues* (Martinus Nijhoff Leiden 2011) 395, 395.

[68] Qiu and Jones, n 62, 188–9. Nevertheless, the European Commission issued guidance for States on MSP in 2008 and, in 2013, proposed the adoption of a framework directive on MSP and integrated coastal management. For the 2008 guidance, see: 'Communication from the Commission', *Roadmap for Maritime Spatial Planning: Achieving Common Principles in the EU*, Doc COM(2008) 791 Final (25 November 2008). For the 2013 draft Directive see 'Proposal for a Directive of the European Parliament and of the Council', *Establishing a framework for maritime spatial planning and integrated coastal management*, Doc COM(2013) 133 Final (12 March 2013).

[69] Qiu and Jones, n 62, 187. [70] Ibid.

[71] See generally H Backer, 'Transboundary Maritime Spatial Planning: A Baltic Sea Perspective' (2011) 15 *Journal of Coast Conservation* 279.

[72] 1992 Convention on the Protection of the Marine Environment of the Baltic Sea Area, Arts 3(2) and 7 (hereinafter Helsinki Convention).

a network of MPAs,[73] and, by 2014, 163 Baltic Sea Protected Areas (BSPAs) covering 11.7 per cent of the Baltic marine and coastal area had been established.[74] Ecosystem-based and integrated spatial management provided for the foundation of the 2007 Helsinki Commission (HELCOM) Baltic Sea Action Plan,[75] and, in 2010, a Working Group on MSP was launched by the Helsinki Commission and the Vision and Strategies around the Baltic Sea (VASB) Committee on Spatial Planning and Development of the Baltic Sea Region.[76] That year HELCOM and VASAB adopted the Baltic Sea Broad-scale Maritime Spatial Planning Principles,[77] which set out 10 principles designed to provide guidance for achieving better coherence in developing MSP in the Baltic Sea region. The principles include the ecosystem approach; the precautionary principle; the need to adopt a long-term perspective and overall environmental and economic goals; coherent terrestrial and maritime spatial planning; and effective transnational coordination and consultation. These general principles alongside more detailed guidance and management frameworks were endorsed in the Regional Baltic MSP Roadmap 2013–2020, which was adopted as part of the 2013 HELCOM Ministerial Declaration.[78] The Regional Baltic MSP Roadmap also set out short- and medium-term goals for the implementation of MSP in the Baltic, including the drafting of guidelines relating to the application of ecosystem-based management and public participation in MSP by 2015, and the application of those guidelines by 2018.[79] Thus far, planning is most advanced in respect of the Bothnian Sea, which has benefited from the implementation of a MSP pilot project carried out jointly by the two littoral States concerned, Sweden and Finland.[80]

[73] Helsinki Commission (HELCOM) Recommendation 15/5, *System of coastal and marine Baltic Sea protected areas* (1994).
[74] For an overview of BSPAs, see HELCOM, *HELCOM Protect—Overview of the status of the network of Baltic Sea marine protected areas* (HELCOM 2013).
[75] HELCOM Baltic Sea Action Plan (15 November 2008), available at <http://helcom.fi/Documents/Baltic sea action plan/BSAP_Final.pdf>. The ecosystem approach had also been previously endorsed by a joint HELCOM/OSPAR Commission statement in 2003 at the first joint meeting of the OSPAR and the HELCOM Commissions. See the *Record of the First Joint Ministerial Meeting of the Helsinki and the OSPAR Commissions* (25–26 June 2003) Annex 5.
[76] For information on this process, see Joint HELCOM-VASAB Maritime Spatial Planning Working Group, available at <http://helcom.fi/helcom-at-work/groups/helcom-vasab-maritime-spatial-planning-working-group/>.
[77] Baltic Sea Broad-Scale Maritime Spatial Planning (MSP) Principles, available at <http://helcom.fi/Documents/HELCOM%20at%20work/Groups/MSP/HELCOM-VASAB%20MSP%20Principles.pdf>.
[78] HELCOM, Regional Baltic Maritime Spatial Planning Roadmap 2013–2020, available at <http://helcom.fi/Documents/Ministerial2013/Ministerial%20declaration/Adopted_endorsed%20documents/Regional%20Baltic%20MSP%20Roadmap.pdf>.
[79] Ibid.
[80] See *Planning the Bothnian Sea. Outcome of Plan Bothnia—A Transboundary Maritime Spatial Planning pilot in the Bothnian Sea* (2013), available at <http://helcom.fi/Documents/Action%20areas/Maritime%20spatial%20planning/Planning%20The%20Bothnian%20Sea%20(digital%20edition%202013).pdf>.

In the North Sea and North-east Atlantic, ecosystem-based integrated management has an equally dynamic recent history.[81] The precautionary approach was arguably conceived as an environmental principle of international application in the crucible of the North Sea conferences and it, alongside the ecosystem-based approach provide much of the foundation for environmental management under the 1992 Convention for the Protection of the Marine Environment of the North-east Atlantic (OSPAR Convention).[82] Ecosystem-based management has since been endorsed in numerous declarations and decisions under the OSPAR Convention, most recently in the 2010–2020 North-East Atlantic Strategy,[83] where it was described as the 'overarching principle' in the OSPAR Commission's work.[84] Integrated ecosystem-based management also provides the basis for oceans governance as articulated within several North Sea declarations,[85] in particular, the 2006 Gothenburg Declaration.[86] The creation of a network of representative MPAs within the OSPAR area has been a key component of the OSPAR maritime strategy since 2003[87] and, significantly, in 2010, the OSPAR Commission established the first global network of six MPAs on the high seas.[88] As of 1 January 2013, 333 MPAs had been designated, comprising 5.17 per cent of the OSPAR maritime area.[89] The 2010–2020 North-East Atlantic Environment Strategy notes that the OSPAR Convention is the principal platform through which Member States should implement the EU Maritime Framework Directive[90] and stipulates that the OSPAR Commission will 'develop, and encourage application of, regionally coordinated tools for the implementation of integrated management of human

---

[81] For a discussion of the North East Atlantic more generally, see Chapter 29 in this volume.

[82] 1992 Convention for the Protection of the Marine Environment of the North-east Atlantic, Art 2(1) and (2) and Annex 5 (hereinafter OSPAR Convention).

[83] The North-East Atlantic Environment Strategy, Strategy of the OSPAR Commission for the Protection of the Marine Environment of the North-East Atlantic 2010–2020 (hereinafter OSPAR Agreement 2010–2020), available at <http://www.ospar.org/html_documents/ospar/html/10-03e_nea_environment_strategy.pdf#BDC>.

[84] Ibid, Preamble [2].

[85] E Hey, 'The International Regime for the Protection of the North Sea: From Functional Approaches to a More Integrated Approach' (2002) 17 *International Journal of Marine and Coastal Law* 325.

[86] Declaration, North Sea Ministerial Meeting on the Environmental Impact of Shipping and Fisheries (Göteborg, Sweden 4–5 May 2006), available at <http://qsr2010.ospar.org/media/assessments/Basic_documents/Gothenburg_Declaration.pdf>.

[87] OSPAR Recommendation 2003/3 *on a network of marine protected areas*, as amended by OSPAR Recommendation 2010/2.

[88] See OSPAR Decisions 2010/1–2010/6 and OSPAR Recommendations 2010/12–2010/17 adopted by the OSPAR Commission at its meeting in Bergen, Norway (20–24 September 2010). The initial network of six MPAs was increased to seven in 2010 with the designation of the Charlie-Gibbs North High Seas MPA in 2010 (see OSPAR Decision 2012/1).

[89] OSPAR Commission, *2012 Status Report on the OSPAR Network of Marine Protected Areas* (2013) 4, available at <http://www.ospar.org/documents/dbase/publications/p00618/p00618_2012_mpa_status%20report.pdf>.

[90] The North-East Atlantic Environment Strategy, n 83, Part I [1.3].

activities and ecosystems. This includes tools such as marine spatial planning, ICZM and cumulative impact assessment.'[91] Like the Helsinki Commission, the OSPAR Commission has responsibility for the management of all maritime activities within the region with the exception of fishing. Moreover, both Commissions are active in their cooperation with other regional bodies that have regional marine-related responsibilities, and the OSPAR Commission, in particular, is charged with cooperating with fisheries organizations in respect of mutually relevant matters.[92]

In contrast to the seas of Northern Europe, where IOM is principally driven by the need to manage competing offshore activities and implemented through MSP, in the Mediterranean, IOM is much more focused on the coastal/marine interface, responding directly to the particular vulnerability of the Mediterranean basin to pollution and development.[93] The core components of IOM including the precautionary principle, EIA and ecosystem-based management also provide the foundation for oceans governance as set out in the 1976 Convention for the Protection of the Marine Environment and the Coastal Region of the Mediterranean (amended and renamed in 1995) (Barcelona Convention).[94] The implementation of ecosystem-based management, in particular, has benefited from detailed consideration within several decisions adopted by the meeting of parties to the Barcelona Convention,[95] and features prominently within the revised Mediterranean Action Plan adopted in 1995.[96]

The 1995 Protocol Concerning Specially Protected Areas and Biological Diversity in the Mediterranean (SPA Protocol) provides for the creation of a network of specially protected areas both within the jurisdiction of States and on the high seas.[97] There are currently 32 sites of Specially Protected Areas of Mediterranean

---

[91] Ibid, Part I [4.4.d]. See also ibid, Part II [3.1.c].

[92] OSPAR Convention, n 82, Annex 5, Art 4. See KN Scott, 'Conservation on the High Seas: Developing the Concept of the High Seas Marine Protected Areas' (2012) 27 *International Journal of Marine and Coastal Law* 849, 853.

[93] For a discussion of the Mediterranean Sea more generally, see Chapter 27 in this volume.

[94] 1976 Convention for the Protection of the Marine Environment and the Coastal Region of the Mediterranean (amended and renamed in 1995), Art 4(3)(a), (c), and (d) (hereinafter Barcelona Convention).

[95] In particular, see Decision IG 17/6, *Implementation of the ecosystem approach to the management of human activities that may affect the Mediterranean marine and coastal environment* (2008), and Decision IG 20/4, *Implementing MAP ecosystem approach roadmap: Mediterranean Ecological and Operational Objectives, Indicators and Timetable for implementing the ecosystem approach roadmap* (2012).

[96] The revised 1995 Mediterranean Action Plan is available at <http://195.97.36.231/dbases/webdocs/BCP/MAPPhaseII_eng.pdf>.

[97] 1995 Protocol Concerning Specially Protected Areas and Biological Diversity in the Mediterranean, Arts 4–9 (hereinafter 1995 SPA Protocol). See also Decision IG 20/7 *Conservation of sites of particular ecological interest in the Mediterranean* (2012).

Importance (SPAMI), and one site incorporates an area of high seas within its parameters.[98] Integrated management, particularly in respect of the coastal/marine interface, is identified as a key management tool under both the 1995 Barcelona Convention[99] and the revised Mediterranean Action Plan.[100]

Significantly, in 2008, the States party to the Barcelona Convention adopted a Protocol to the Convention on Integrated Coastal Zone Management in the Mediterranean (ICZM Protocol), which entered into force in 2011. Under the Protocol, ICZM is defined as:

> ...a dynamic process for the sustainable management and use of coastal zones, taking into account at the same time the fragility of coastal ecosystems and landscapes, the diversity of activities and uses, their interactions, the maritime orientation of certain activities and uses and their impact on both the marine and land parts.[101]

The implementation of ICZM under the Protocol is underpinned by the ecosystem approach with a strong emphasis on EIA and strategic planning. Moreover, the Protocol recognizes the importance of coordination and cooperation among terrestrial and marine agencies in the implementation of ICZM. However, although the Protocol can be regarded as providing the most prominent legal commitment to the process of ICZM and the implementation of IOM more generally at the regional level, its scope is not entirely comprehensive. For example, it applies (unless the parties express otherwise) to the seaward limit of the territorial sea and to the land area under the jurisdiction of competent coastal units as defined by the parties.[102] While this focus on the coastal/marine interface reflects the overall objectives of the Protocol, the arbitrary parameters of its application are not necessarily coterminous with appropriate ecological boundaries. Moreover, although the Barcelona Convention and its Protocols are committed to IOM in the Mediterranean more generally, in contrast to the seas of Northern Europe, there has been negligible development in respect of MSP beyond the territorial sea within the region. Finally, there is minimal recognition of the interaction between fisheries management and environmental protection more generally in the Mediterranean. Nevertheless, at the most recent meeting of the States party to the Barcelona Convention in 2012, the parties committed to strengthening the implementation of integrated governance and establishing a network of representative MPAs,[103] and adopted an Action Plan for the implementation of the ICZM Protocol in the Mediterranean.[104]

---

[98] The Pelagos Sanctuary for Marine Mammals. For further information on SPAMI sites see <http://www.rac-spa.org/spami>.

[99] Barcelona Convention, Art 4(3)(e).   [100] 1995 Mediterranean Action Plan, [1.4].

[101] 2008 ICZM Protocol, Art 2(f).   [102] Ibid, Art 3(1).

[103] See the Paris Declaration adopted at the 17th Meeting of the Contracting Parties to the Convention for the Protection of the Marine Environment and the Coastal Region of the Mediterranean Region and its Protocols (Paris 8–10 February 2012) Annex I, available at <http://www.pap-thecoastcentre.org/razno/PART%20I_Report.pdf>.

[104] Decision IG 20/2 (2012), *Adoption of the Action Plan for the implementation of the ICZM Protocol for the Mediterranean (2012–2019)*.

Outside of European waters, regional commitment to IOM is much weaker. Although most, if not all, regional seas regimes endorse a precautionary approach to environmental decision-making and utilize tools such as EIA, the designation of MPAs, and, to a lesser extent, the application of ecosystem-based management, few have made meaningful progress in actually integrating maritime policies across multiple sectors to date. Nevertheless, there are signs that this may be changing. For example, the 2010 Amended Nairobi Convention for the Protection, Management and Development of the Marine and Coastal Environment of the Western Indian Ocean,[105] which is not yet in force, requires parties to promote ICZM in addition to applying ecosystem-based management, EIA, the precautionary approach, and the designation of MPAs in their environmental management of the region.[106] Moreover, although a recent feasibility assessment indicated that the time is not yet right for the adoption of an ICZM protocol to the Convention,[107] the 2008–2012 Work Programme for the Nairobi Convention promotes an ecosystem-based, multi-sector approach to policy and management, taking into consideration whole systems rather than individual components of those systems and focusing on ecosystem integrity as the primary goal of oceans governance.[108] Similarly, within the Caribbean,[109] the emphasis thus far has been on oceans governance through precaution, EIA, and the designation of MPAs.[110] However, the 1983 Cartagena Convention and the 1990 Cartagena SPA Protocol both emphasize the importance of an ecosystem-based approach to managing environmental impacts in the region,[111] and the 1999 Protocol Concerning Pollution from Land-Based Activities, which entered into force in 2010, promotes 'integrated coastal area management' as a key tool to address land-based sources of pollution.[112] Nevertheless, despite the endorsement

---

[105] The 2010 Amended Convention will replace the 1985 Nairobi Convention for the Protection, Management and Development of the Marine and Coastal Environment of the Eastern African Region once it enters into force. For a discussion of the Indian Ocean region more generally, see Chapter 31 in this volume.

[106] 2010 Amended Nairobi Convention, n 105, Arts 4, 11, and 14. The 1985 Protocol Concerning Protected Areas and Wild Fauna and Flora in the East African Region, Arts 8–11, also provides for the designation of MPAs.

[107] R Billé and J Rochette, *Feasibility Assessment of an ICZM Protocol to the Nairobi Convention* (UNEP 2010), available at <http://www.unep.org/NairobiConvention/docs/UNEP(DEPI)_EAF_CP_6_INF_20_Feasibility%20Assessment%20of%20an%20ICZM%20Protocol%20to%20the%20Nairobi%20Convention.pdf>.

[108] The Work Programme for the Nairobi Convention 2008–2012 is available at <http://www.unep.org/NairobiConvention/docs/COP5_WORK_PROGRAMME.pdf>.

[109] For a discussion on the Caribbean region more generally, see Chapter 30 in this volume.

[110] 1983 Convention for the Protection and Development of the Marine Environment of the Wider Caribbean Region (Cartagena Convention), Arts 10 and 12; 1990 Protocol Concerning Specially Protected Areas and Wildlife to the Convention for the Protection and Development of the Marine Environment of the Wider Caribbean Region (Cartagena SPA Protocol), Arts 4–9 and 13.

[111] Cartagena Convention, n 110, Preamble; 1990 Cartagena SPA Protocol, n 110 Preamble.

[112] 1999 Protocol Concerning Pollution from Land-Based Sources and Activities to the Convention for the Protection and Development of the Marine Environment of the Wider Caribbean Region, Art III.2.

of an integrated management approach to the Caribbean Sea by the UN General Assembly over a decade ago,[113] IOM in this region is to date characterized more by promise than by progress.

Finally, it is worth noting that within a number of regions littoral States are cooperating and collaborating outside of the formal framework of a regional seas regime in the designation of MPAs in waters under their jurisdiction with a view to establishing an ecologically coherent network across the region. Examples include: the Micronesia Challenge, which aims to protect 30 per cent of near-shore marine resources by 2020 in waters under the jurisdiction of the Marshall Islands, Guam, Palau, and the Commonwealth of the Northern Marianas Islands;[114] the Eastern Tropical Pacific Seascape, which is designed to establish a network of MPAs within national waters off the coasts of Columbia, Costa Rica, Panama, and Ecuador;[115] the Caribbean Challenge, under which 10 Caribbean nations have committed to protecting 20 per cent of their nearshore and marine environments by 2020;[116] and the Coral Triangle Initiative, under which Indonesia, Malaysia, Papua New Guinea, the Philippines, the Solomon Islands, and Timor Lesté are cooperating to create a network of MPAs.[117] All four initiatives were praised by the UN General Assembly in 2013, which noted their mutually supportive aims 'to create and link domestic marine protected areas to better facilitate ecosystem approaches' and affirmed 'the need for further international cooperation, coordination and collaboration in support of such initiatives'.[118]

5 Implementation of Integrated Oceans Management in ABNJ: Progress and Prospects

As noted in Section 1 of this chapter, the concept of IOM has been endorsed and recommended across a range of institutions and in respect of all areas of the oceans. However, oceans governance in ABNJ today remains divided between maritime zones—most notably based on the distinction between the water column and the

---

[113] UNGA Res A/57/261 (2002).
[114] See further the Micronesia Challenge website, at <www.micronesiachallenge.org>.
[115] See further Conservation International, at <http://www.conservation.org/global/marine/initiatives/seascapes/etps/pages/etps.aspx>.
[116] See further The Nature Conservancy, 'The Caribbean Challenge Initiative' available at <http://www.nature.org/ourinitiatives/regions/caribbean/caribbean-challenge.xml>.
[117] See further Coral Triangle Initiative, at <http://www.coraltriangleinitiative.org>.
[118] UNGA Res A/68/70 (2013) [214].

seabed—and among sectors. In no sense can it be described as 'integrated'. However, progress is being made in respect of each of the components of IOM, which as identified above, are integral to its effective implementation at both the national and regional level: ecosystem-based management; the precautionary approach; EIA; MPAs; MSP; and institutional integration and coordination. This section will provide an abbreviated analysis of the implementation of each principle or concept in ABNJ[119] with a view to assessing the overall prospects of for IOM across jurisdictional boundaries and in *all* parts of the oceans.

5.1 Ecosystem-based management

Although the LOSC acknowledges the oceans as an 'integrated whole' in its preamble, the Convention contains few references to the concept of the ecosystem,[120] and primarily conceives oceans governance as being largely zonal and sectoral in both principle and application. Nevertheless, ecosystem approaches to oceans governance have been subsequently endorsed at the UN conferences on environment and development in 1992, 2002, and 2012, as well as by all UN General Assembly Resolutions on oceans and the law of the sea over the last decade.[121] The ecosystem approach has also provided the primary focus for two reports of the UN Open-ended Informal Consultative Process—in 2003[122] and 2006[123]—and underpins the approaches of other instruments with mandates associated with oceans governance such as the 1992 CBD.[124] The application of the ecosystem approach in ABNJ is particularly advanced in the context of fisheries management[125] and is promoted as best practice by the 1995 UN Fish Stocks Agreement (FSA),[126] as

---

[119] For a more general discussion of oceans governance in ABNJ, see Chapter 33 in this volume.

[120] 1982 United Nations Convention on the Law of the Sea, Art 194(5) (hereinafter LOSC) does require parties to protect rare or fragile ecosystems and Art 145(a) calls upon states to prevent interference with the 'ecological balance of the marine effects of fishing on dependent or associated species' (ibid, Arts 61(4) and 119(1)(b)).

[121] For example, the UNGA Res A/68/70 (2013) advocates the application of ecosystem approaches to ocean management, which 'should be focused on managing activities in order to maintain and, where needed, restore ecosystem health to sustain goods and environmental services...' [184(b)].

[122] *Report on the work of the United Nations Open-ended Informal Consultative Process on Oceans and the Law of the Sea at its Fourth Meeting*, UN Doc A/58/95 (2003).

[123] *Report on the work of the United Nations Open-ended Informal Consultative Process on Oceans and the Law of the Sea at its Seventh Meeting*, UN Doc A/61/156 (2006).

[124] 1992 Convention on Biological Diversity, Art 8(d) (hereinafter CBD).

[125] The earliest instrument to endorse an ecosystem approach to fisheries management in ABNJ is the 1980 Convention for the Conservation of Antarctic Marine Living Resources (CAMLR Convention).

[126] 1995 Agreement for the Implementation of the Provisions of the UN Convention on the Law of the Sea relating to the Conservation and Management of Straddling Fish Stocks and Highly Migratory Fish Stock Art 5(d)–(g) (hereinafter FSA).

well as by the 1995 FAO Code of Conduct for Responsible Fisheries[127] and the FAO International Guidelines for the Management of Deep-Sea Fisheries in the High Seas, adopted in 2008.[128] However, there is a significant difference between the ecosystem approach, which increasingly characterizes fisheries management[129] and ecosystem-based management,[130] which 'is fundamentally a place-based approach, where the ecosystem represents the place'.[131] It is ecosystem-based management that is integral to the implementation of IOM, and which is increasingly providing a foundation for the development of national and regional oceans policy. Globally, particularly in ABNJ, ecosystem-based management—in contrast to the ecosystem approach—is under-developed and, thus far, principally confined to the context of designating MPAs in ABNJ.[132]

5.2 Precautionary approach

The precautionary approach, like the ecosystem approach, is also absent within the text of the LOSC. Despite this, however, the 'language of precaution has entered the lexicon of the law of the sea'[133] and the precautionary approach is now an integral component of oceans governance and widely applied across jurisdictions and sectors.[134] Furthermore, the International Tribunal for the Law of the Sea (ITLOS) has recently confirmed its application to activities taking place in the Area[135] and provided support for its status as a principle of customary international law of general and universal application.[136] There can be no doubt that the precautionary approach,

---

[127] 1995 FAO Code of Conduct for Responsible Fisheries, Art 6(2) (hereinafter FAO Code of Conduct).

[128] FAO International Guidelines for the Management of Deep-Sea Fisheries in the High Seas (2008), available at <http://www.fao.org/docrep/011/i0816t/i0816t00.HTM> (hereinafter 2008 FAO Deep-Sea Fisheries Guidelines).

[129] J Morishita, 'What is the Ecosystem Approach for Fisheries Management?' (2008) 32 *Marine Policy* 19; S Parsons 'Ecosystem Considerations in Fisheries Management: Theory and Practice' (2005) 20 *International Journal of Marine and Coastal Law* 381.

[130] H Wang, 'Ecosystem Management and its Application to Large Marine Ecosystems: Science, Law, and Politics' (2004) 35 *Ocean Development and International Law* 41, 43.

[131] UNEP, *Taking Steps towards Marine and Coastal Ecosystem-Based Management—An Introductory Guide* (2011) 10.

[132] Discussed in Section 5.4 below.

[133] R Rayfuse, 'Precaution and the Protection of Marine Biodiversity in Areas beyond National Jurisdiction' (2012) 27 *International Journal of Marine and Coastal Law* 773, 774.

[134] See generally S Marr, *The Precautionary Principle and the Law of the Sea. Modern Decision-Making in International Law* (Martinus Nijhoff Leiden 2003).

[135] *Responsibilities and Obligations of States Sponsoring Persons and Entities with Respect to Activities in the Area* (Advisory Opinion) [2011] ITLOS Rep 10 (hereinafter *Area Advisory Opinion*).

[136] Ibid, [135]. See also *Pulp Mills on the River Uruguay (Argentina v Uruguay)* (Judgment) [2010] ICJ Rep 14, [164] (hereinafter *Pulp Mills Case*).

an integral component of IOM at the national and regional level, is of general application globally, and applies within ABNJ.

5.3 Environmental impact assessment

The prior assessment of the environmental impacts of activities likely to have a detrimental effect on the oceans is, like the precautionary approach, an integral tool of oceans governance. The basic obligation to carry out an EIA provided for in Article 206 of the LOSC has since been broadened in both scope and depth within numerous other global and regional instruments such as the CBD.[137] The principle has been endorsed as a tool for marine environmental management by the UN conferences held in 1992, 2002, and 2012, as well as in UN General Assembly resolutions on the oceans and the law of the sea over the last decade.[138] In ABNJ,[139] EIA is required in respect of activities such as dumping at sea[140] and the exploitation of minerals in the Area[141] and, increasingly, measures analogous to EIA have been applied in the context of fisheries management, particularly in relation to new and exploratory fisheries.[142] More generally, the CBD has recently developed guidelines to support the application of EIA[143] in ABNJ,[144] and it has been identified as a key component of oceans environmental governance by the UN BBNJ Working Group.[145] In fact, EIA is now so widely applied that it has been recognized as a general principle of international environmental law where the impacts of an activity have transboundary or commons implications.[146] Nevertheless, the

---

[137] CBD, n 124, Art 14.   [138] See eg UNGA Res A/68/70 (2013) [160].

[139] On the application of EIA in ABNJ generally, see AG Oude Elferink, 'Environmental Impact Assessment in Areas beyond National Jurisdiction' (2012) 27 *International Journal of Marine and Coastal Law* 449; R Warner, 'Oceans beyond Boundaries: Environmental Assessment Frameworks' (2012) 27 *International Journal of Marine and Coastal Law* 481.

[140] 1996 Protocol to the 1972 Convention on the Prevention of Marine Pollution by Dumping of Wastes and other Matter, Annex 2.

[141] Legal and Technical Commission of the International Seabed Authority, *Recommendations for the guidance of contractors for the assessment of the possible environmental impacts arising from exploration for marine minerals in the Area*, ISBA/19/LTC/8 (2013).

[142] See eg the 2010 Convention for the Conservation and Management of High Seas Fishery Resources in the South Pacific Ocean, Art 22. See also the 2008 FAO Deep-Sea Fisheries Guidelines, n 128.

[143] CBD Decision VIII/28 (2006), *Impact Assessment: Voluntary guidelines on biodiversity-inclusive impact assessment*.

[144] The guidelines developed in CBD Decision VIII/28 were annotated with a view to their application in ABNJ at a workshop held in 2009 and formally adopted in 2012. See CBD, *Report of the Expert Workshop on Scientific and Technical Aspects Relevant to Environmental Impact Assessment in Marine Areas Beyond National Jurisdiction*, UNEP/CBD/EW-EIAM/2 (2 November 2009), and CBD Decision XI/18 (2012), *Marine and coastal biodiversity: sustainable fisheries and addressing adverse impacts of human activities, voluntary guidelines for environmental assessment and marine spatial planning*, Part B.

[145] See the *Letter dated 23 September 2013 from the Co-Chairs of the Ad Hoc Open-ended Informal Working Group to the President of the General Assembly*, UN Doc A/68/399 (2013) (BBNJ) [34].

[146] *Pulp Mills Case*, n 136, [204]; *Area Advisory Opinion*, n 135, [145] and [148].

procedural and substantive components of EIA vary significantly between sectors and, as yet, there is no overarching regime for the application of EIA in ABNJ.

5.4 Marine protected areas

The designation of MPAs at the national and regional level is an integral component of IOM and a principal means of implementing ecosystem-based management.[147] The designation of MPAs in ABNJ, however, is not uncontroversial owing to the absence of a clear legal mandate permitting such designation under the LOSC, and the complex range of jurisdictional issues arising from the separation of the seabed and the water column into distinct regulatory zones.[148] Moreover, a relative lack of information on the ecological processes within, and environmental state of, ABNJ represents a more pragmatic challenge to the designation of MPAs beyond State jurisdiction.[149] Nevertheless, high seas MPAs have been created under a number of regimes including the 1946 International Convention for the Regulation of Whaling,[150] the 1980 Convention on the Conservation of Antarctic Marine Living Resources (CAMLR Convention),[151] and the 1973/78 International Convention for the Prevention of Pollution (MARPOL).[152] However, with the exception of the regional network of seven areas established recently in the OSPAR high seas area noted above,[153] high seas MPAs thus far are largely focused on a single or a narrow range of issues such as shipping or fishing rather than being multifunctional.[154] A broader notion of the MPA, as part of a more integrated approach to oceans management, has nevertheless been endorsed by the UN General Assembly—most

---

[147] See B Cicin-Sain and S Belfiore, 'Linking Marine Protected Areas to Integrated Coastal and Ocean Management: A Review of Theory and Practice' (2005) 48 *Ocean & Coastal Management* 847.

[148] A detailed discussion of these issues is beyond the scope of this chapter. See Scott, n 92.

[149] A 'Regular Process' for reporting on the global marine environment was launched by the UN General Assembly and the first draft of the first global marine assessment is due to be released in 2015. It is envisaged that this process will begin to fill the many knowledge gaps. For further information, see DOALOS, 'A Regular Process for Global Reporting and Assessment of the State of the Marine Environment, including Socio-economic Aspects (Regular Process)', available at <http://www.un.org/depts/los/global_reporting/global_reporting.htm>.

[150] Whale sanctuaries in the Indian and Southern Oceans currently encompasses approximately 20 per cent of ocean space.

[151] The first formal MPA was established under CAMLR Convention in respect of the South Orkney Islands Southern Shelf in 2009. See CCAMLR Conservation Measure (CM) 91-03 (2009), *Protection of the South Orkney Islands Southern Shelf*.

[152] Special Areas have been designated under 1973 International Convention for the Prevention of Pollution, as modified by the Protocol of 1978, Annexes I, II, and IV–VI (hereinafter MARPOL) within which stricter discharge regulations are applicable.

[153] See the text accompanying nn 82–4.

[154] For an overview of existing high seas MPAs, see P Drankier, 'Marine Protected Areas in Areas beyond National Jurisdiction' (2012) 27 *International Journal of Marine and Coastal Law* 291.

recently in the 2012 *The Future We Want* Resolution,[155]—and by the CBD.[156] Multifunctional high seas MPAs are also under active consideration as part of the mandate of the UN BBNJ Working Group.[157] Designating MPAs in ABNJ, however, represents only part of the challenge. In order to support the implementation of IOM, such MPAs need to be properly integrated into oceans management more generally and actively managed alongside other spatial policies.[158]

5.5 Marine spatial planning

Marine spatial planning has, in less than a decade, 'become one of the most widely endorsed tools for integrated management of coastal and marine environments'.[159] It is seen as key to implementing ecosystem-based management[160] and can be defined as 'a public process of analyzing and allocating the spatial and temporal distribution of human activities in marine areas to achieve ecological, economic, and social objectives that are usually specified through a political process'.[161] The challenge of implementing MSP within ABNJ is formidable, but even within areas under the jurisdiction of States, the ocean is a dynamic environment that changes rapidly with the tides and seasons, and which is three dimensional and, consequently, potentially permits multiple activities to take place simultaneously on the surface, in the water column and on or under the seabed.[162] Some commentators have abandoned the notion of physical space within the oceans altogether. Stephen Jay, for example, argues that 'the emphasis is less upon space as a pre-existing plane upon which things can be located, arranged and mapped, and more upon space as generated by inter-relationships, both within and beyond discrete areas and time periods'.[163]

---

[155] UNGA Res A/66/288 (2013) [177].

[156] CBD Decision IX/20 (2008), *Marine and Coastal Biodiversity*, [14], [19], and Annexes I and II; CBD Decision XI/17 (2012), *Marine and coastal biodiversity: ecologically or biologically significant marine areas*. In 2010, the parties to the CBD extended the deadline originally agreed at the World Summit on Sustainable Development to protect 10 per cent of the oceans by 2012 to 2020 as part of the Aichi Biodiversity Targets. See CBD Decision X/2 (2010), *The Strategic plan for biodiversity 2011–2020 and the Aichi Biodiversity Targets*, Target 11. This was subsequently endorsed in UNGA Res A/66/288 (2012), [177].

[157] *Letter dated 23 September 2013 from the Co-Chairs of the Ad Hoc Open-ended Informal Working Group to the President of the General Assembly*, UN Doc A/68/399 (2013) (BBNJ), [31].

[158] Cicin-Sain and Belfiore, n 147, 848–850.

[159] G Carneiro, 'Evaluation of marine spatial planning' (2013) 37 *Marine Policy* 214.

[160] See Douvere, n 20.

[161] C Ehler and F Douvere, *Marine Spatial Planning: A Step-by-Step Approach Toward Ecosystem-Based Management*, IOC Manual and Guides No 53, ICAM Dossier No 6 (Paris 2009) 19.

[162] RW Duck, 'Marine Spatial Planning: Managing a Dynamic Environment' (2012) 14 *Journal of Environmental Policy and Planning* 67, 69–70.

[163] S Jay, 'Marine Space: Manoeuvring Towards a Relational Understanding' (2012) 14 *Journal of Environmental Policy and Planning* 81.

Within the LOSC the strongest implicit reference to MSP can be found in Article 123, which encourages States to cooperate and coordinate their policies in respect of the management of enclosed or semi-enclosed seas. More generally, the LOSC relies on the principle of 'due regard' as the predominant tool for arbitrating between activities competing for space on the high seas.[164] In the absence of an overarching global oceans organization, however, it is difficult to see how MSP can be effectively applied in ABNJ. Nevertheless, the competition for ocean space between activities and—potentially conflicting—interests is as existent in ABNJ as it is within coastal areas, and this competition is likely to intensify as novel activities such as geo-engineering and bioprospecting emerge and new threats, such as ocean acidification, are identified. The importance of developing tools and processes for arbitrating between competing use of ocean space was recognized by the General Assembly in 2012 *The Future We Want* Resolution, which called for not only the creation of ecologically representative and well-connected MPAs but also the adoption of 'other area-based conservation measures'.[165] The broader language of 'area-based conservation' was also adopted by the CBD in Aichi Biodiversity Target 11, and the parties to the Convention have recently recommended the development of MSP in areas both within and beyond national jurisdiction.[166] More specifically, MSP has been implicitly endorsed by the 1995 FAO Code of Conduct for Responsible Fisheries,[167] and there is increasing academic support for its adoption to support effective ecosystem-based fisheries management.[168] This notwithstanding, however, the most prodigious challenge to realizing MSP in ABNJ lies not in the implementation of ecologically focused principles but, rather, in creating the appropriate institutional infrastructure to manage and coordinate the process of spatial planning and associated management.

---

[164] For example, LOSC, n 120, Art 87(2) provides that high seas freedoms 'shall be exercised by all States with due regard for the interests of other States in their exercise of the freedom of the high seas, and also with due regard for the rights under this Convention with respect to activities in the Area'. Although the International Seabed Authority undoubtedly has functions permitting it to engage in a level of MSP with respect to the seabed beyond national jurisdiction under Part XI of the LOSC, those functions are limited to activities associated with minerals exploitation.

[165] UNGA Res A/66/288 (2012) [177].

[166] CBD Decision XI/18 (2012), *Marine and coastal biodiversity: sustainable fisheries and addressing adverse impacts of human activities, voluntary guidelines for environmental assessment and marine spatial planning*. See also, *Synthesis Document on the Experience and Use of Marine Spatial Planning*, UNEP/CBD/SBSTTA/16/INF/18 (2 April 2012).

[167] FAO Code of Conduct, n 127, Art 10.1.1.

[168] See E Norse, 'Ecosystem-based Spatial Planning and Management of marine Fisheries: Why and How?' (2010) 86 *Bulletin of Marine Science* 179; A Rassweiler, C Costello, and D A Siegel, 'Marine Protected Areas and the Value of Spatially Optimized Fishery Management' (2012) 109 *Proceedings of the National Academy of Sciences* 11884.

5.6 Institutional integration of oceans management

The creation of overarching, integrated institutional infrastructure is integral to the success of implementing IOM at both the national and the regional level. Effective IOM relies on political coordination in the identification of ecological, sociological, and economic goals as well as administrative implementation, oversight or, at the very least, coordination in the management of oceans activities. At the global level, while the LOSC provides the overall, constitutional framework for the regulation of all maritime activities there is no overarching oceans body with a mandate to implement the Convention in its entirety. Instead, there are numerous institutions with designated mandates to manage activities such as (but by no means limited to) shipping (the IMO), fishing (regional fishery management organizations and the FAO), scientific research (Intergovernmental Oceanographic Commission (UNESCO)), and environmental protection (UNEP). There is little formal coordination among these institutions and even where an organization has multiple mandates, such as the IMO, internal institutional divisions often separate the management of maritime activities. Moreover, many other bodies and regimes with environmental, transport, and even commercial mandates have responsibility for activities and issues that impact directly or indirectly upon the oceans. Without institutional integration between, or coordination among, global oceans bodies it is unlikely that IOM can be implemented in a manner which is both effective and meaningful.

Institutional integration and the coordination of agencies and regimes with overlapping or at least mutually supportive mandates has dominated the development of international environmental law over the last decade, particularly within the fields of biodiversity conservation and the management of chemicals and hazardous wastes.[169] Less progress has been made by institutions with responsibilities for oceans governance[170] although two developments in this context are worthy of note. First, the UN-Oceans, which was established in 1993[171] and which constitutes an inter-agency coordination network on oceans issues under the auspices of the UN. Its objective is to enhance cooperation among oceans institutions and, in the past, has focused on issues such as biodiversity in ABNJ, climate change, fisheries, and MPAs. In 2013, its mandate was renewed and revised by the UN General Assembly, and UN-Oceans is explicitly tasked with strengthening the coherence of UN oceans-related activities through planning, information exchange and the

---

[169] See KN Scott, 'International Environmental Governance: Managing Fragmentation through Institutional Connection' (2011) 12 *Melbourne Journal of International Law* 177.

[170] See more generally Chapter 3 in this volume.

[171] Created in order to support the implementation of Agenda 21, n 8, ch 17, UN-Oceans was originally named the Sub-committee on Oceans and Coastal Areas of the Administrative Committee on Coordination before being renamed in 2003 as the Oceans and Coastal Areas Network (and subsequently renamed again as UN-Oceans). See further UN Oceans website, at <http://www.unoceans.org>.

identification of areas suited to collaboration and the creation of synergies.[172] The second initiative comprises The Oceans Compact, which was instituted by the UN Secretary General in 2012 in order to respond to the challenges set out in *The Future We Want* UN General Assembly Resolution.[173] Its mandate is to adopt pragmatic strategies to increase cross-sectoral coordination and cooperation at national, regional, and global levels as well as within the UN system in order to address the cumulative impacts of sectoral activities on the marine environment.[174] The relationship between these two initiatives with parallel, if not indistinguishable, mandates is unclear and it must be noted that progress in improving collaboration and developing synergies among oceans institutions has been negligible thus far despite the ostensible operation of UN-Oceans for over 20 years.

Nevertheless, some promise of a coordinated institutional approach lies in the prospect of an instrument dedicated to managing oceans activities in ABNJ, most likely in the form of an Agreement to the LOSC. The UN BBNJ Working Group, which has been charged with exploring the feasibility of such an instrument, has emphasized the necessity of an integrated approach 'to the conservation and sustainable use of marine biodiversity beyond areas of national jurisdiction' and expressed support for 'existing and enhanced cooperation among relevant States, institutions, organizations and sectors to achieve better management of, and planning for, sustainable multiple uses of marine biodiversity in areas beyond national jurisdiction'.[175] Nevertheless, even in the event that such an instrument is adopted, it remains to be seen whether it can facilitate meaningful coordination among a broad range of institutions including those responsible for shipping and fishing in ABNJ.

6 Concluding Remarks

Until recently, the history of the law of the sea and oceans governance was defined by division: division in respect of maritime zones, sectoral competence and jurisdictional mandates. However, at all levels of oceans governance—national, regional, and global—it is now recognized that fragmented and sector-based

---

[172] UNGA Res A/68/70 (2013) [279] and Annex.

[173] See further DOALOS, Ocean Compact, available at <http://www.un.org/depts/los/ocean_compact/oceans_compact.htm>.

[174] Ibid.

[175] *Letter dated 8 June 2012 from the Co-Chairs of the Ad Hoc Open-ended Informal Working Group to the President of the General Assembly*, UN Doc A/67/95 (2012) [13].

management 'is a major contributor to deteriorating ocean health'.[176] Consequently, the last 15 years have witnessed a remarkable sea change in approaches to oceans governance with the development of strategies that seek to integrate policies across sectors, and proactively manage multiple activities within ecological boundaries with a view to preserving and enhancing valuable ecosystem services. Integrated oceans management is most advanced at the national level to date although rapid developments to support the implementation of IOM are taking place within European waters and as well as within a number of other regions. Practice in the implementation of IOM varies significantly between States and regions but variation in of itself is by no means problematic. Deconstructing IOM reveals six core components—ecosystem-based management, the precautionary approach, EIA, the designation of MPAs, MSP, and the integration of institutional infrastructure—and it is the collective implementation of these core components that results in an integrated approach to oceans management. Nevertheless, no one solution fits all, and managing the interaction between the core components of IOM permits a sufficiently flexible tool capable of facilitating the development of measures designed to address the coastal/marine interface, the management of competing activities in the offshore area, or which focus on the vulnerability of a particular ecosystem. The challenge facing States and regions in the future is how to expand both the scope and depth of IOM in order to achieve comprehensive ecosystem-based management of waters under their jurisdiction, including the incorporation of fisheries management and ecologically relevant terrestrial activities into oceans policies.

In ABNJ, the challenge is rather different. Three of the six components of IOM are generally applied or are close to being of general application within ABNJ. Progress is less advanced with respect to spatial or place-based management tools including the designation of MPAs. Similarly, integration or even coordination among oceans institutions is also underdeveloped. In contrast to the national and regional level where MSP and/or ICZM are essential to the effective implementation of IOM, at the global level, it is institutional integration/coordination that is likely to prove critical. Without an overarching oceans body—which is neither feasible nor, arguably, desirable—proactive spatial planning (outside of the parameters of MPAs) is simply quixotic. However, a level of integration can be achieved through much greater coordination and cooperation between international institutions mandated to manage ocean-based activities or with responsibility for the health of the marine environment. The zonal approach to oceans environmental management, which underpins the LOSC, is unlikely to be abandoned within ABNJ but, as Tanaka suggests, 'the contemporary law of the sea should be considered as a dialectic legal system between the

---

[176] Ekstrom et al, n 4, 532.

zonal and integrated management approaches'.[177] Moreover, the time for developing IOM within ABNJ is now: the on-going negotiations for an instrument or agreement under the LOSC for the protection and management of biodiversity beyond national jurisdiction providing the best opportunity to develop a more integrated approach to oceans management in ABNJ.

---

[177] Y Tanaka, 'Zonal and Integrated Management Approaches to Oceans Governance: Reflections on a Dual Approach in International Law of the Sea' (2004) 19 *International Journal of Marine and Coastal Law* 483, 514.

22

MARINE LIVING RESOURCES

NELE MATZ-LÜCK AND JOHANNES FUCHS

1 INTRODUCTION

THE exploitation and conservation of marine living resources (MLR) is a question of utmost relevance for global society, given the importance of MLR as a source of protein for human consumption and the dependence of many local communities upon fishing. While the regulation of MLR has been an issue of international law for decades, early codifications rather reflected sovereignty over maritime dominions and exploitation interests than conservation. Historic disputes such as the *Bering Fur Seals* arbitration[1] demonstrated the desire of coastal States to project sovereignty from their land towards the sea, a process that gained further momentum in the twentieth century as exemplified in the *Anglo-Norwegian Fisheries* case.[2] While rudimentary ideas of sustainability were expressed in agreements concluded during the late first half of the twentieth century, they focused on economic exploitation, not ecological sustainability.[3] The prime example of this approach is the objective of 'proper conservation of whale stocks' to 'make possible the orderly development of

---

[1] *Bering Sea Fur Seals (Great Britain v United States)* (1898) 1 Moore 755.
[2] *Fisheries (United Kingdom v Norway) (Judgment)* [1951] ICJ Rep 116.
[3] VM Kaczynski and DL Fluharty, 'European Policies in West Africa' (2002) 26 *Marine Policy* 75, 82.

the whaling industry' in the Preamble to the 1946 International Convention for the Regulation of Whaling (ICRW).

Rising awareness of the threat that overfishing poses to marine life did not become a focal point before the 1970s. Growing concerns regarding the loss of biological diversity, including in the marine environment, resulted, *inter alia*, in the adoption of the 1992 Convention on Biological Diversity (CBD). At the same time, the concept of sustainability was increasingly featured in environmental law and policy. These developments helped shift the focus of fisheries management from a purely exploitation-oriented approach to one which included considerations of ecologically sustainable development.

This chapter discusses the international legal framework of contemporary management and conservation of MLR, and its shortcomings, challenges, and possible future progress. Following the introduction, the chapter seeks to define the notion and explain the relevance of MLR (Section 2) before the applicable general principles to their management are discussed (Section 3). The legal frameworks of the 1982 UN Convention on the Law on the Sea (LOSC) and the 1995 Fish Stocks Agreement (FSA) are analysed in Sections 4 and 5 respectively. The subsequent parts deal with specific challenges such as the regulation of fishing methods (Section 6), compliance, and enforcement of legal rules (Section 7) and the management of marine mammals (Section 8). After the discussion of two emerging approaches to MLR conservation (Section 9), the chapter closes with a conclusion and an outlook on the potential development for sustainably managing MLR.

2 Marine Living Resources: Relevance and Notion

The term MLR refers to the living organisms of the oceans, and is used alongside the term non-living resources of the sea or seabed (such as oil, gas or minerals). MLR are vital as a source of protein for human consumption. For numerous States fishing is an important economic sector. In addition to fisheries products for consumers, industrial fishing enterprises also harvest MLR to produce fishmeal and oil to be used, *inter alia*, as fertilizer or animal feed (eg in aquaculture). The growing pressure upon MLR from human activities has led to the overexploitation and depletion of many economically relevant fish stocks.[4] Taking into account the state of the

---

[4] B Worm et al, 'Rebuilding Global Fisheries' (2009) 325 *Science* 578; United Nations Food and Agriculture Organization (FAO), *The State of World Fisheries and Aquaculture 2014* (FAO Rome 2014) 7.

world's fisheries and the dependence of large parts of humankind on MLR, their conservation and sustainable use is a common interest of the international community.[5]

There are different approaches taken as to which species are included in the term MLR. A broad definition refers to 'bony fish, sharks and rays, cephalopods, crustaceans, and other invertebrates, such as corals' as well as 'birds, turtles, and marine mammals'.[6] A narrower notion emphasizes the denomination as 'resources', stressing economic exploitation and monetary value. This perspective excludes many birds and other species which depend upon marine ecosystems, but are not of commercial interest (eg polar bears). Most commonly, the notion of MLR is understood to comprise fish, cephalopods, crustaceans and marine mammals.

The LOSC does not provide for a definition of living resources, although the term is frequently used. Even an explicit definition of 'fish' is not contained in the LOSC (although note that a definition is included in Article 1(1)(c) of the FSA). In addressing MLR the LOSC focuses on fishing for commercial purposes, and this chapter likewise follows this approach.

3 General Principles

A number of general principles for the management and exploitation of MLR have been gaining relevance as the underlying legal basis, such as the principle of sovereign rights over natural resources; as guiding concepts for management objectives, such as sustainability; or, more specifically, as guidance for management criteria, such as the precautionary approach.

3.1 Sovereign rights over natural resources

The principle of permanent sovereignty over natural resources under national jurisdiction evolved in the post-war period and has been frequently acknowledged by international law and policy, most prominently in United Nations General Assembly (UNGA) Resolution 1803(XVII) (1962), Principle 21 of the Stockholm

---

[5] Y Tanaka, *The International Law of the Sea* (Cambridge University Press Cambridge 2012) 219ff.
[6] P Sands and J Peel (eds), *Principles of International Environmental Law* (Cambridge University Press Cambridge 2012) 396. Another broad definition is provided by 1980 Convention on the Conservation of Antarctic Marine Living Resources, Art 1(2).

Declaration,[7] Principle 2 of the Rio Declaration,[8] the preamble to the CBD, and the International Court of Justice (ICJ) in *Armed Activities on the Territory of the Congo*.[9] This principle embodies the right of States and peoples to dispose freely over their resources.[10] Its scope has been extended to include MLR although, in contrast to resources such as oil or minerals, there is often no fixed stock of MLR over which States permanently exercise sovereign rights due to the migratory nature of many marine species.[11] Instead, rights are exercised over all resources within areas of national jurisdiction at a given time.

The 1970s marked a gradual shift from a rights-based approach to natural resources to one encompassing certain duties of States concerning environmental protection and conservation.[12] A balance between the exercise of sovereign rights over natural resources and environmental conservation follows in particular from the second half of Principle 21 of the Stockholm Declaration. The principle is furthermore exemplified by Article 193 of the LOSC in that it adds the caveat that the 'sovereign right to exploit their natural resources' must be exercised 'in accordance with [the] duty to protect and preserve the marine environment'. This balancing reflects a compromise with regard to the expansion of coastal State jurisdiction.

Sovereignty over MLR, specifically fish stocks, in waters adjacent to coasts was one of the central issues during the Third United Nations Conference on the Law of the Sea (UNCLOS III).[13] Expanding coastal State jurisdiction reflected, in particular, the aspiration of developing States for control over resources off their coasts as part of their economic development. The principle of sovereignty over natural resources still functions as the legal basis for sovereign rights over MLR in areas under national jurisdiction, but it is no longer disconnected from environmental considerations and allows reference, *inter alia*, to the sustainable use of resources.

---

[7] States have, in accordance with the Charter of the United Nations and the principles of international law, the sovereign right to exploit their own resources pursuant to their own environmental policies, and the responsibility to ensure that activities within their jurisdiction or control do not cause damage to the environment of other States or of areas beyond the limits of national jurisdiction.
Declaration of the United Nations Conference on the Human Environment, UN Doc A/Conf.48/14/Rev. 1 (1972) (hereinafter Stockholm Declaration).

[8] Rio Declaration on Environment and Development, UN Doc A/Conf.151/26/Rev.1 (1992).

[9] *Armed Activities on the Territory of the Congo (Democratic Republic of the Congo v Uganda)* (Judgment) [2005] ICJ Rep 168, 182.

[10] JL Jacobson, 'Managing Marine Living Resources in the Twenty-First Century' in MH Nordquist and JN Moore (eds), *Entry into Force of the Law of the Sea Convention* (Martinus Nijhoff The Hague 1994) 311.

[11] The same applies to migratory species on land as far as they are considered natural resources.

[12] N Schrijver, *Sovereignty over Natural Resources* (Cambridge University Press Cambridge 1997) 127–33.

[13] UNGA Res 2750 C (XXV) (1970); UNGA Res 3067 (XXVIII) (1973).

3.2 Sustainable development and sustainable use

Sustainable development is a concept that has been frequently invoked in international law and policy since the early 1990s (eg in the conventions concluded at the 1992 Rio Earth Summit and in Agenda 21).[14] While many different notions of sustainability exist, the Brundtland Commission described it as 'development that meets the needs of the present without compromising the ability of future generations to meet their own needs'.[15] To this end, Article 4 of the Rio Declaration requires that 'environmental protection shall constitute an integral part of the development process and cannot be considered in isolation of it'.[16] Although the exact meaning is far from clear, the interdependence between economic and social development and environmental protection with the long-term perspective to safeguard inter-generational equity seems agreed.[17] Sub-facets of the concept such as sustainable use, utilization, and yield of resources follow from the same idea. The sustainable use of natural resources calls upon resource-rich States, and any State seeking access to such resources to use them in a manner ensuring their maintenance.[18] All States should act as equal members of a community working towards the preservation of natural resources as a common welfare goal.[19]

In a strict sense, putting sustainable use into practice should mean that over a certain period of time only as much of a renewable resource is taken for human purposes as can be naturally replenished. The sustainable use of MLR would therefore oblige States to allow for catches of a target species only to the extent to which the relevant stock reproduces. Limiting fisheries at a sustainable level requires collecting and processing considerable amounts of reliable scientific data on the target stock. It also depends upon States overcoming short-term economic and social interests. The concept of sustainability as an inherent restriction on the exploitation of resources is no longer a new idea. Yet, despite obvious necessity, the international legal framework in place and on-going efforts towards its implementation,[20] it seems doubtful that management of MLR at sustainable levels will be fully achieved in the near future.

---

[14] *Report of the United Nations Conference on Environment and Development, Rio de Janeiro, 3–14 June 1992*, UN Doc A/CONF.151/26 (1992) Annex II.

[15] World Commission on Environment and Development, *Our Common Future* (Oxford University Press Oxford 1987) 43.

[16] Rio Declaration, n 8.

[17] U Beyerlin, 'Sustainable Development' in R Wolfrum (ed), *The Max Planck Encyclopedia of Public International Law* (Oxford University Press Oxford 2012) Vol IX, 716, 718 [8]–[9].

[18] F Bosselman, 'Adaptive Resource Management through Customary Law' in P Ørebech et al (eds), *The Role of Customary Law in Sustainable Development* (Cambridge University Press Cambridge 2005) 245.

[19] E Brown-Weiss, 'What Obligation Does Our Generation Owe to the Next?' (1990) 84 *American Journal of International Law* 198, 201.

[20] Cf eg the revised EU Common Fisheries Policy: Council and Parliament Regulation (EU) No 1380/2013 (11 December 2013).

The LOSC supports the sustainable use of resources by limiting exclusive economic zone (EEZ) and high seas fisheries to the maximum sustainable yield (MSY).[21] The 1958 Geneva Convention on Fishing and the Conservation of Marine Living Resources of the High Seas (CFCLR), similarly tied conservation objectives to achieving and maintaining the 'optimum sustainable yield' in order to secure the supply of fish as food for human consumption.[22] Both agreements therefore envisage restricting the exploitation of what had previously been considered an open access resource. Identifying the MSY is particularly difficult in the light of scientific uncertainty. To prevent unsustainable practices due to a lack of scientific data, the precautionary approach should be linked to sustainable management.

3.3 Precautionary approach

The precautionary approach or principle[23] intends to improve the conservation and sustainable management of MLR by guiding State behaviour towards preservation in the face of scientific uncertainty. Particularly, the determination of total allowable catch (TAC) within safe biological limits to obtain the MSY should follow a precautionary approach to prevent overexploitation.[24]

Originating from domestic policy and legislation in the 1970s, the precautionary approach was first internationally featured in the World Charter for Nature in 1982[25] and in Principle 15 of the Rio Declaration. In its essence, it requires States to abate possible environmental damage despite scientific uncertainties as to whether the potential damage will eventuate.[26]

With regard to the approach's potential characteristic as customary law or a general principle, the jurisprudence of international courts, so far, appears undetermined. With regard to MLR, the ICJ in the *Whaling in the Antarctic* case briefly noted that New Zealand had invoked the precautionary approach in its intervening submission.[27] While two judges made more detailed remarks on the precautionary

---

[21] 1982 United Nations Convention on the Laws of the Sea, Arts 61(3) and 119(1) (hereinafter LOSC).

[22] 1958 Geneva Convention on Fishing and Conservation of the Living Resources of the High Seas, Art 2 (hereinafter CFCLR).

[23] On these two notions, see A Trouwborst, *Status and Evolution of the Precautionary Principle in International Law* (Kluwer The Hague 2002) 3–6.

[24] D Freestone, 'International Fisheries Law Since Rio' in A Boyle and D Freestone (eds), *International Law and Sustainable Development* (Oxford University Press Oxford 1999) 135, 141.

[25] UNGA Res 37/7 (1982).

[26] On different variations of the approach see JB Wiener, 'Precaution' in D Bodansky, J Brunnée, and E Hey (eds), *The Oxford Handbook of International Environmental Law* (Oxford University Press Oxford 2007) 595, 604–7.

[27] *Whaling in the Antarctic (Australia v Japan; New Zealand intervening)*, Judgment of the International Court of Justice, General List No 148 (31 March 2014), 81.

principle in their separate opinions,[28] the majority followed the findings in the *Pulp Mills on the River Uruguay* case, where the Court stated that a precautionary approach 'may be relevant' in treaty interpretation without elaborating on the principle's legal status.[29] The International Tribunal for the Law of the Sea (ITLOS) applied the approach implicitly in its Order on provisional measures in the *Southern Bluefin Tuna* case.[30] The most explicit reference so far stems from ITLOS's Seabed Dispute Chamber's Advisory Opinion regarding activities in the Area, recognizing *obiter dictum* 'a trend towards making this approach part of customary international law'.[31]

While the LOSC does not mention the precautionary approach, it is enshrined in Article 6 of the FSA and incorporated in Article 7.5 of the non-binding 1995 FAO Code of Conduct for responsible fisheries.[32] Both the FAO Code and the FSA stipulate that the absence of adequate scientific information shall not be used as a reason to postpone or fail to enact conservation measures. Yet, the FAO Code of Conduct goes further in specifically requesting States to consider elements such as stock productivity and effects on non-target species when implementing the precautionary approach.[33] These and other elements are further specified in the 1996 FAO Technical Guidelines on the Precautionary Approach to Capture Fisheries.[34] They underline how voluntary and non-binding instruments can complement the general legal framework on MLR management.

4 THE FRAMEWORK OF THE LAW OF THE SEA CONVENTION

The LOSC's objective to provide the legal framework for all relevant issues of marine affairs naturally includes regulations for the exploitation and management of MLR. Historically, the development of the legal framework for MLR falls into two distinct

---

[28] Ibid, Separate Opinion of Judge Cançado Trindade, [70]; ibid, Separate Opinion of Judge ad-hoc Charlesworth, [9].

[29] *Pulp Mills on the River Uruguay (Argentina v Uruguay)* (Judgment) [2010] ICJ Rep 14, [164].

[30] *Southern Bluefin Tuna (New Zealand v Japan; Australia v Japan)* (Provisional Measures) [1999] ITLOS Rep 280, [77], [79].

[31] *Responsibilities and Obligations of States Sponsoring Persons and Entities with Respect to Activities in the Area* (Advisory Opinion) [2011] ITLOS Rep 10, [135] (hereinafter *Area Advisory Opinion*).

[32] 1995 Food and Agriculture Organization Code of Conduct for Responsible Fisheries, available at <ftp://ftp.fao.org/docrep/fao/005/v9878e/v9878e00.pdf> (hereinfter FAO Code of Conduct).

[33] Ibid, Arts 7.5.1 and 7.5.2.

[34] FAO, *Precautionary Approach to Capture Fisheries and Species Introductions* (FAO Rome 1996).

phases. The first phase, until the 1970s, was characterized by narrow zones under national jurisdiction, while the second, since the mid-1970s, is marked by the extension of national jurisdiction over MLR.[35] Since the degree of jurisdiction to regulate and to enforce is tied to the maritime zone in which exploitation activities are conducted, their designation and extent is of crucial importance.

4.1 Internal waters, territorial sea, and archipelagic waters

States enjoy full sovereignty over their territorial sea and internal waters. The same applies to archipelagic waters.[36] Yet, it follows from the sovereignty of the coastal State that it exercises exclusive jurisdiction over MLR. Hence, their exploitation is primarily subject to national regulation. As a minimum standard, States are bound by Part XII of the LOSC, that is, the general obligation to protect and preserve the marine environment and to exploit their natural resources accordingly.[37]

4.2 Living resources in the exclusive economic zone

Fish stocks in EEZs embrace the majority of economically exploitable MLR.[38] Article 56 of the LOSC provides that the coastal State enjoys 'sovereign rights for the purpose of exploring and exploiting, conserving and managing the natural resources'.[39]

Article 61 of the LOSC not only grants rights to coastal States with regard to the exploitation of MLR but adds duties to ensure the maintenance of those resources by proper conservation and management measures. This duty has been said to be 'a natural corollary to conserving the living resources of the high seas'.[40] Crucial issues of proper management centre around the identification of the MSY, access by third States, and the conservation of migratory fish stocks.

4.2.1 *Identifying the maximum sustainable yield*

The LOSC envisages the management of MLR in the EEZ and the high seas by setting limits for TAC based upon the MSY for each species.[41] The most common definition of MSY refers to 'the largest average catch...that can continuously be

---

[35] RR Churchill and AV Lowe, *The Law of the Sea* (Juris Publishing Yonkers 1999) 283.
[36] LOSC, n 21, Art 49(1).   [37] Ibid, Art 193.
[38] R Barnes, 'The Convention on the Law of the Sea' in D Freestone, R Barnes, and DM Ong (eds), *The Law of the Sea* (Oxford University Press Oxford 2006) 233, 233.
[39] On sedentary species, see Section 4.3 below.   [40] *Virginia Commentaries*, Vol II, 597.
[41] LOSC, n 21, Arts 61(3), 119(1).

taken from a stock under existing environmental conditions'.[42] Several factors, such as natural mortality, the relationship to other species and their abundance, as well as the age and size of the fish caught, play a crucial role in setting and implementing TAC limits based upon MSY. As reliable data and the sound and precautionary interpretation of that data are pre-requisites for sustainable management, the identification and implementation of fisheries at the MSY can pose significant difficulties.[43]

The MSY concept has continued to face criticism. One reproach is that the concept is too exploitation-oriented and does not follow a conservationist approach. As a consequence, some critics suggest replacing it altogether with different approaches.[44] But while MSY is indeed focused on maximum utilization, it is primarily its implementation that is problematic such as the setting of unsustainable TACs by coastal States. A properly implemented MSY concept taking into account the precautionary approach in defining safe biological limits and effects on non-target species as required by Article 61(4) of the LOSC seems, in principle, suitable to contribute to the goal of sustainable fisheries, particularly if MSY is not considered a goal for catch-levels to reach but rather their (utmost) limit.[45]

4.2.2 *Access to fish stocks by third States*

Article 62(2) of the LOSC is often cited to illustrate the Convention's focus on utilization instead of conservation. The provision obliges the coastal State to grant access to other States to the living resources of its EEZ if it cannot harvest the entire TAC itself. While the coastal State is given broad discretion in granting or preventing access to the surplus, the recovery of fish stocks to a conservation status beyond MSY levels or ecological considerations is not explicitly mentioned as a reason to withhold permission. Nevertheless, the coastal State maintains the authority to implement a conservation-friendly approach. Even if access is granted, the coastal State can prescribe the conditions for fishing and thus implement conservation measures.[46]

4.2.3 *Shared and highly migratory stocks*

Fish stocks frequently occur within the EEZs of adjacent States (shared or joint stocks) or within the EEZ and the adjacent high seas (straddling stocks). Some

---

[42] WE Ricker, 'Computation and Interpretation of Biological Statistics of Fish Populations' (1975) 191 *Bulletin of the Fisheries Research Board of Canada* 1, 3.

[43] Y Tanaka, *A Dual Approach to Ocean Governance* (Ashgate Farnham 2008) 53–6.

[44] E Hey, 'The Persistence of a Concept' (2012) 27 *International Journal of Marine and Coastal Law* 763.

[45] Cf R Froese and A Proelss, 'Rebuilding Fish Stocks No Later Than 2015' (2010) 11 *Fish and Fisheries* 194, 199.

[46] DR Rothwell and T Stephens, *The International Law of the Sea* (Hart Oxford 2010) 88.

species, such as tuna and cetaceans, are highly migratory and travel long distances crossing a variety of different zones in annual cycles.[47] Shared, straddling, and highly migratory fish stocks require cooperation to prevent overexploitation because they are fished under the authority of more than one State.

The LOSC recognizes the necessity for inter-State cooperation and coordination concerning shared stocks and highly migratory species.[48] Well before the adoption of the FSA, the duty to cooperate and coordinate resulted in different forms of formal cooperation. Yet, many stocks remained unregulated and the conservation effectiveness of management regimes differed considerably. The most common forms of cooperation consist of framework treaties with periodic settings of TACs for participating States, bilateral fisheries commissions such as the Iceland–Norway Fisheries Commission or regional fisheries organizations.[49] With regard to highly migratory species, Article 64 of the LOSC refers the conservation and optimum utilization to regional approaches either by direct cooperation between States or by an international organization.[50]

4.3 Living resources of the continental shelf

The regime of the continental shelf is primarily concerned with the exploration and exploitation of mineral and other non-living resources of the seabed and subsoil. Yet, Article 77(4) of the LOSC refers to 'living organisms belonging to sedentary species' as natural resources for the purposes of Part VI of the LOSC. The provision defines these organisms as those 'which, at the harvestable stage, either are immobile on or under the seabed or are unable to move except in constant physical contact with the seabed or the subsoil'. These include, *inter alia*, mussels, oysters, and some crustaceans. In accordance with Articles 77(1) and 68 of the LOSC, the coastal State may regulate the exploitation including the conservation of sedentary species based upon its rights over the shelf.

4.4 Living resources and the freedom of the high seas

Due to the absence of coastal State jurisdiction, MLR management on the high seas differs considerably from EEZ fisheries, although the LOSC refers to the MSY for both zones.[51] The relevance of high seas fisheries has been diminished considerably by the EEZ in which most stocks are harvested. Nonetheless, there is increasing interest in fishing on the high seas, where all States enjoy the long-recognized

---

[47] LOSC, n 21, Annex I. [48] Ibid, Arts 63, 64. [49] Churchill and Lowe, n 35, 295–9.
[50] See also Chapter 20 in this volume. [51] LOSC, n 21, Arts 61(3), 119(1)(a).

freedom to fish[52] (although, in contrast to Grotius' rationale for the freedom,[53] fish can no longer be treated as an inexhaustible resource).

Despite the LOSC's focus on utilization of high seas living resources, the freedom to fish is not unlimited but made subject to the 'conditions laid down in section 2' of Part VII and has been further regulated under the FSA. Article 118 of the LOSC imposes a duty on all States to cooperate with a view to exercise their right to fish on the high seas within the framework of existing fisheries management organizations. This can be considered the primary duty, while Article 119 of the LOSC provides the means and modalities for compliance with this obligation.[54]

5 THE UNITED NATIONS STRADDLING AND HIGHLY MIGRATORY FISH STOCKS AGREEMENT

In relation to straddling and highly migratory stocks the LOSC only codifies a general framework of rules and calls for further multilateral and regional cooperation to give these practical effect.[55] The FSA not only supplements the LOSC with regard to such stocks, but it also is an example of the incorporation of new regulatory approaches such as precaution and ecosystem-based management.

5.1 Development and membership

While several regional fisheries management organizations (RFMOs)[56] and arrangements were already in place during UNCLOS III, gaps in the international framework governing straddling and migratory fish stocks were of increasing concern, in particular with changes in fishing gear technology and the poor conservation status of many stocks.[57] The FSA was adopted in 1995 by a diplomatic conference

---

[52] Ibid, Art 87(1)(e).
[53] H Grotius, *The Free Sea [Mare Liberum]* (trans R Hakluyt) (Elsevier Amsterdam 1609) (repr Liberty Fund Indianapolis 2004).
[54] Freestone, n 24, 147.
[55] N Matz-Lück, 'Framework Agreements' in Wolfrum (ed), n 17, Vol IV, 220 [4].
[56] See Chapter 20 in this volume.
[57] R Barston, 'The Law of the Sea and Regional Fisheries Organisations' (1999) 14 *International Journal of Marine and Coastal Law* 333, 334.

convened by the UNGA.[58] Although labelled an implementation agreement to the LOSC, membership is open to LOSC non-parties, thereby allowing, inter alia, the United States to accede. With 81 parties (as of 2014), FSA membership is well below the almost universal acceptance of the LOSC. Yet, important fishing nations have ratified the agreement, such as the Japan in 2006, Korea in 2008, and the EU in 2003. With Belize ratifying the FSA in 2005 and Panama in 2008, two important 'open register' countries have also joined.

5.2 Management approach

In addition to its focus on cooperation between parties to ensure the compatibility of conservation measures,[59] the FSA has been praised for incorporating principles of environmental law and biodiversity-related elements into international fisheries law.[60] Where the LOSC's text focuses on the exploitation and management of living resources, the FSA's objectives refer to 'long term conservation' even before mentioning 'sustainable use'.[61] In addition to the overall goal of long-term sustainability of fisheries-related measures and the duty to apply best scientific practices and procedures, the FSA obliges States parties to apply the precautionary approach and engage in ecosystem-based management.[62]

Another merit of the FSA is that it intends to achieve a more effective management regime for fisheries via regional fisheries bodies (RFBs), namely RFMOs and regional fisheries management arrangements (RFMAs).[63] In its core, the Agreement states that fisheries under RFB management are open to members of said RFMO or participants in the RFMA only,[64] while non-members shall not issue licences for such fisheries.[65] This is reinforced by the duty of all flag States under the FSA to comply with RFB measures, irrespective of their member- or participant-status.[66] As a result, the Agreement significantly constrains the 'freedom' of high seas fisheries for its parties.

Given the FSA's *de facto* expansion of RFB measures to all FSA State parties, accession to the FSA does not seem necessarily beneficial to long distance fishing nations. Yet, FSA non-member status may come at a price, since the FSA explicitly

---

[58] UNGA Res 47/192 (1992).

[59] 1995 Agreement for the Implementation of the Provisions of the United Nations Convention on the Law of the Sea of 10 December 1982 Relating to the Conservation and Management of Straddling Fish Stocks and Highly Migratory Fish Stocks, Art 7 (hereinafter FSA).

[60] F Orrego Vicuña, 'International Law of High Seas Fisheries' in O Schram Stokke (ed), *Governing High Seas Fisheries* (Oxford University Press Oxford 2001) 23, 33; DH Anderson, 'The Straddling Stocks Agreement of 1995' (1996) 45 *International and Comparative Law Quarterly* 463–75, 469.

[61] FSA, n 59, Art 2.   [62] Ibid, Arts 2(a)(b), 5(d)(e), and 6(2).

[63] On the notion of RFMAs, see ibid, Art 1(1)(d). See further E Meltzer, *The Quest for Sustainable International Fisheries* (NRC Research Press Ottawa 2009) 56–7.

[64] FSA, n 59, Art 8(4).   [65] Ibid, Arts 8(1) and 17.   [66] Ibid, Art 18(1).

calls upon parties to take measures to deter the activities of non-party vessels if they undermine the effective implementation of the FSA.[67]

6 INTERNATIONAL REGULATION OF FISHING METHODS

A second tier of MLR regulation apart from limits on access to fisheries is a focus on fishing methods and gear. These rules focus on technical efforts by the fishing industry to catch more of the remaining fish and their adverse effects on marine biodiversity, such as large quantities of discarded by-catch resulting from increased net sizes,[68] or habitat destruction by bottom trawling.[69] Relevant restrictions differ as to their scope and legal basis.

International efforts to abandon driftnet fishing focus on the use of large-scale pelagic nets with a length of 2.5 kilometres or more.[70] Several regional organizations either prohibit the use of large driftnets or at least call for their prohibition, such as the 1989 Tarawa Declaration of the Pacific Forum.[71] The 1989 Convention for the Prohibition of Fishing with Long Drift Nets in the South Pacific goes as far as to restrict port access for driftnet fishing vessels.[72] The UNGA supported and strengthened this development calling for moratoria on all large-scale pelagic driftnet fishing in Resolutions 44/225 and 46/215.[73] Following implementation on the national level, Resolution 46/225 is often quoted as a rare example of a provision of an UNGA resolution evolving into binding customary law.[74]

This effort has not been repeated for other damaging fishing practices, such as bottom trawling. This refers to scraping large, weighted nets across the seabed (benthos), which can be particularly harmful to coral reefs, seamounts and sponges where most target fish aggregate.[75] Despite some regional efforts to prohibit bottom

---

[67] Ibid, Art 33(2).
[68] FAO, *The Regulation of Driftnet Fishing on the High Seas* (FAO Rome 1991) 57–8.
[69] FAO, *Options to Mitigate Bottom Habitat Impact of Dragged Gears* (FAO Rome 2007) 3.
[70] UNGA Res 44/225 (1989).
[71] 1989 Tarawa Declaration on Driftnet Fishing (1989) *Law of the Sea Bulletin* 14, 29.
[72] See 1989 Convention for the Prohibition of Fishing with Long Drift Nets in the South Pacific, Art 3(2) (hereinafter Wellington Convention).
[73] UNGA Res 46/215 (1991).
[74] GJ Hewison, 'The Legally Binding Nature of the Moratorium on Large-Scale High Seas Driftnet Fishing' (1994) 25 *Journal of Maritime Law and Commerce* 557.
[75] *Report of the Secretary-General: Impacts of fishing on vulnerable marine ecosystems: actions taken by States and regional fisheries management organizations and arrangements to give effect to paragraphs*

trawling in the EU[76] and the Mediterranean,[77] no consensus has been reached on the international level, apart from voluntary instruments, for example those adopted by the FAO.[78] The UNGA has not addressed the issue in a specific resolution, but instead referred the issue to RFMOs.[79] However, only some RFMOS have responded, for example the South Pacific RFMO[80] which required parties to reduce bottom trawling to the annual average levels between 2002 and 2006 (ie their 'bottom fishing footprint').[81]

These examples demonstrate how the UNGA can become an important forum in the further development of the law of the sea relating to MLR. Beyond the declaratory annual resolutions on Oceans and the Law of the Sea[82] and on Sustainable Fisheries,[83] the example of driftnet fishing shows how the UNGA can amplify and channel efforts to towards sustainable fisheries.

7 Compliance and Enforcement

The effectiveness of international law is determined by the degree to which States comply with it. Implementation and compliance can be either induced by incentives and assistance or enforced by the threat with and the application of sanctions.[84] Confrontational means of enforcement relating to MLR conservation standards can include trade restrictions as well as the arrest of fishing vessels and their crew or the confiscation of illegally caught fish.

7.1 Illegal, unreported, and unregulated Fishing

Illegal, unreported, and unregulated (IUU) fishing is one of the gravest threats to the sustainable exploitation of MLR. The term refers to the failure to comply with

66 to 69 of General Assembly resolution 59/25 on sustainable fisheries, regarding the impacts of fishing on vulnerable marine ecosystems, UN Doc A/61/154 (2006) [50]–[56].

[76] Council Regulation (EC) for the Conservation of Fishery Resources, No 850/98 (30 March 1998).

[77] 1949 Agreement for the Establishment of the General Fisheries Commission for the Mediterranean. See GFCM Res 2005/1 (2005) and 2006/3, available at <http://www.gfcm.org/gfcm/topic/16100/en>.

[78] FAO, *Guidelines for the Management of Deep-Sea Fisheries in the High Seas* (FAO Rome 2009).

[79] UNGA Res 61/105 (2006) [80]–[91].

[80] 2009 Convention on the Conservation and Management of High Seas Fishery Resources in the South Pacific Ocean.

[81] Conservation and Management Measure for the Management of Bottom Fishing in the South Pacific Regional Fisheries Management Organization Convention Area, CMM 2.03 (binding as of 4 May 2014).

[82] UNGA Res 68/70 (2013) [135]. [83] UNGA Res 68/71 (2013) [6].

[84] See R Wolfrum, 'Means of Ensuring Compliance with and Enforcement of International Environmental Law' (1998) 272 *Recueil des Cours* 9.

existing standards and also the gaps in the coverage and implementation of fisheries regulations. IUU fishing is attracting increasing attention, including in international courts and tribunals. The obligations of flag States to control IUU fishing is a major component of the request by the Sub-Regional Fisheries Commission (comprising seven West African States) for an advisory opinion from ITLOS.[85] Whether the opinion—which also raises difficult questions with regard to jurisdiction—will contribute to comprehensively clarify rights and duties of coastal States is doubtful and remains to be seen.[86]

Illegal fishing includes fishing without a licence or in excess of assigned quotas, catching different species than the licence provides, and any breaches of applicable flag State regulations on high seas fisheries or standards set by an RFMO. Unreported fishing likewise implies a breach of obligations, namely those to report catches (eg under a licence with a quota) to the relevant authority. If fisheries are unregulated, the resulting open access approach has the effect of fishers competing for the greatest short-term profit by catching as much as they can.[87]

The LOSC and the FSA deal with some of the issues related to IUU fishing. Examples include allowing the arrest of ships and crews for breaches of national conservation and management standards in the EEZ (Article 73(1) of the LOSC). The 2001 FAO Plan of Action on Illegal, Unreported and Unregulated Fishing[88] serves as an example of a non-binding instrument that gives guidance on the implementation of LOSC and FSA provisions. The ITLOS advisory opinion requested by the Sub-Regional Fisheries Commission bears further potential for clarifying flag State obligations in the context of IUU fishing.

7.2 Flag State responsibility

7.2.1 *General obligations*

The principle of flag State responsibility combines the State's exclusive jurisdiction over ships flying its flag when on the high seas with the expectation that jurisdictional control is actually exercised.[89] Effective control of compliance with international and national legislation requires the flag State to monitor vessel activities as

---

[85] Resolution of the Conference of Ministers of the Sub-Regional Fisheries Commission (SRFC) on authorizing the Permanent Secretary of the Sub-Regional Fisheries Commission, Request for Advisory Opinion to the International Tribunal for the Law of the Sea (27 March 2013), available at <http://www.itlos.org/fileadmin/itlos/documents/cases/case_no.21/Request_eng.pdf>

[86] On the Tribunal's competence to give advisory opinions and respective scientific debate, see R Wolfrum, 'Advisory Opinions: Are they a Suitable Alternative for the settlement of International Disputes' in R Wolfrum and I Gätzschmann (eds), *International Dispute Settlement: Room for Innovations?* (Springer The Hague 2012) 35, 53–5.

[87] Churchill and Lowe, n 35, 281.

[88] FAO, *International Plan of Action to Prevent, Deter and Eliminate IUU Fishing* (Rome 2001).

[89] RG Rayfuse, *Non-Flag State Enforcement in High Sea Fisheries* (Nijhoff Leiden 2004) 38–48.

well as sanctioning violations. However, reliance on flag State control has proven to be an obstacle to effective enforcement of conservation standards because of so-called 'flags of convenience' (States with open registers). Flags of convenience are associated with low national standards concerning labour and environmental law and/or not enforcing international standards.[90] In response to such failures to comply with international obligations (eg with regard to sustainable fisheries) other LOSC States parties can potentially initiate compulsory dispute settlement procedures under Part XV of the LOSC.[91]

7.2.2 *Under the LOSC*

The LOSC focuses exclusively on flag State jurisdiction for the monitoring and enforcement of conservation measures for MLR on the high seas.[92] In principle, no State may control compliance with or enforce international standards against a foreign ship on the high seas. Inspections of ships suspected of breaching international obligations are restricted to those enumerated in Article 110(1) of the LOSC, and a violation of international fishing standards is not among them. In response to this gap in compliance control, port-State measures such as inspections of ships voluntarily entering the port of a coastal State are potentially viable mechanisms that can better serve the community interest in the context of illegal fishing.[93] The LOSC does not explicitly provide for such mechanisms as far as high seas fisheries are concerned. However, the right of port State control can be exercised in accordance with general international law.

7.2.3 *Under the Fish Stocks Agreement*

The FSA seeks to enhance flag State compliance by obliging parties to *inter alia* maintain records on fishing vessels' activities on the high seas and vessel monitoring schemes. Furthermore, the FSA departs from the LOSC's focus on exclusive flag State jurisdiction and allows for at-sea boarding and inspections of documents, catches and fishing gear by members of the competent RFB.[94] Regarding port State measures, the FSA requires port States to take enforcement measures.[95] These measures can also be enforced against non-members/non-participants of an RFB.

---

[90] The 1976 ILO Convention (No 147) Concerning Minimum Standards in Merchant Ships mentions flags of convenience in its Preamble without any further definition.
[91] Y Takei, 'International Legal Responses to the Flag State in Breach of its Duties' (2013) 82 *Nordic Journal of International Law* 283, 286.
[92] LOSC, n 21, Art 117.
[93] D Nelson, 'Maritime Jurisdiction' in Wolfrum (ed), n 17, Vol VI, 1117, 1126.
[94] FSA, n 59, Arts 21 and 22.   [95] Ibid, Art 23(1).

7.2.4 *Under FAO instruments*

The principle of flag State responsibility is further refined in Article III of the 1993 Agreement to Promote Compliance with International Conservation and Management Measures by Fishing Vessels on the High Seas (FAO Compliance Agreement). The Agreement prohibits a flag State from authorizing high seas fisheries unless it is able to effectively exercise its responsibilities under the agreement.[96] Furthermore, the Compliance Agreement prohibits the registration of vessels that have been engaged in IUU fishing in the past. This 'black listing' approach is promising if coastal States, port States, and existing and potential new flag States cooperate with each other and exchange data on offences. In 2013, the FAO adopted further Voluntary Guidelines for Flag State Performance.[97] Notable elements of these guidelines include performance assessment criteria and cooperative actions to promote compliance.[98]

7.3 Port State measures

Reliance upon the port States is often seen as a means to overcome shortcomings of compliance control and enforcement by flag States and, hence, a remedy for the practices of reflagging and flags of convenience.[99] As the exclusivity of flag State jurisdiction is unlikely to be entirely abandoned, the regulatory focus has increasingly shifted towards the port State.[100] To date, port States have often restricted their enforcement of national legislation on foreign merchant ships as a matter of comity or through bilateral or multilateral treaties, with fishing vessels in most cases being explicitly excluded.[101] Two examples of a shift towards port State control in fisheries comprise the measures envisaged by Article 23 of the FSA and the 2009 Agreement on Port State Measures to Prevent, Deter and Eliminate Illegal, Unreported and Unregulated Fishing, negotiated under the auspices of the FAO.

---

[96] 1993 Agreement to Promote Compliance with International Conservation and Management Measures by Fishing Vessels on the High Seas, Art III(2) (hereinafter FAO Compliance Agreement).

[97] FAO, *Voluntary Guidelines on Flag State Performance* (adopted on 8 February 2013), available at <ftp://ftp.fao.org/FI/DOCUMENT/tc-fsp/2013/VolGuidelines_adopted.pdf>.

[98] Ibid, [4.1.1].   [99] On port State measures, see Chapter 13 in this volume.

[100] See eg D König, 'Port State Control' in PN Ehlers, E Mann-Borgese, and R Wolfrum (eds), *Marine Issues* (Springer The Hague 2002) 37, 38.

[101] K Bangert, 'Fisheries Agreements' in Wolfrum (ed), n 17, Vol IV, 40, 48–9.

8 Marine Mammals

While many species are included in a definition of MLR based upon economic value, the management of marine mammals—of which the regulation of whaling is only one element—follows distinct approaches compared to other fisheries. Marine mammals have increasingly been regulated not for reasons of commercial exploitation, but rather in the service of conservation objectives as demonstrated by the 1972 Convention on the Conservation of Antarctic Seals, which refers in its Preamble to 'the vulnerability of Antarctic seals to commercial exploitation', and by the ICRW. In addition to controlling catches of commercially relevant species, other challenges for marine mammal management include by-catch of marine mammals, the destruction of habitat, pollution including underwater noise, and challenges associated with the migratory nature of many species.

8.1 Marine mammals and the LOSC

The LOSC specifically refers to marine mammals in Article 65 (as regards the EEZ) and in Article 120 (as regards the high seas) but the Convention itself does not provide comprehensive regulation. Nor indeed does it prohibit the taking of marine mammals. Management standards—which may be stricter than those for EEZ fisheries—can be adopted either by the coastal State or by an international organization. To fill in the legal framework, several regional agreements on the conservation and management of marine mammals have been adopted,[102] while globally the whaling for large species is addressed by the ICRW.

8.2 Legal regulation of migratory marine mammals

Many marine mammals are migratory species. The particular challenges faced by migratory species including marine mammals are acknowledged *inter alia* by the 1979 Convention on the Conservation of Migratory Species of Wild Animals (CMS). The CMS is designed as a framework convention with general obligations, while conservation needs of specific species are regulated in additional binding agreements or non-binding memoranda of understanding (MoUs). The approach

---

[102] For an overview on agreements on cetaceans, see J Braig, 'Whaling' in Wolfrum (ed), n 17, Vol X, 881, 883–4; on regional approaches, see A Proelß, 'Marine Mammals' in Wolfrum (ed), n 17, Vol VI, 1036, 1041.

of the CMS reflects its character as a conservation-oriented environmental treaty in contrast to fisheries instruments.

Relevant agreements on marine mammals adopted in accordance with Article IV(3) of the CMS currently consist of the 1996 Agreement on the Conservation of Cetaceans of the Black Sea, Mediterranean Sea and Contiguous Atlantic Area (ACCOBAMS), the 1992 Agreement on the Conservation of Small Cetaceans of the Baltic and North Seas (ASCOBANS), and the 1990 Agreement on the Conservation of Seals in the Wadden Sea. In accordance with Article IV(4) of the CMS, MoUs have been reached for Conservation Measures for the Eastern Atlantic Populations of the Mediterranean Monk Seal,[103] and for the Conservation of Cetaceans and their Habitats in the Pacific Islands Region.[104]

With regard to conservation approaches, the participation of the so-called 'range States' is crucial for effectiveness.[105] In the case of marine mammals, range States are those exercising jurisdiction over the waters through which marine mammals cross more or less predictably during their annual migration cycles. With regard to substance, the agreements and MoUs, while necessarily all focusing on cooperation of the range States, differ with regard to the envisaged duties of the parties, including, inter alia, the establishment of conservation plans[106] or the prohibition of deliberate taking and the establishment of protected areas.[107]

8.3 Whaling

The whaling agreements of 1931 and 1937 failed to introduce overall catch limits for whales despite the decline of many stocks. In 1946, States agreed upon limitations to allow for the recovery of stocks for continued exploitation as a means to protect the whaling industry. The main operative part of the ICRW is contained in an annex, the 'Schedule'. It is an integral and legally binding part of the ICRW[108] and contains regulations on the conservation and utilization of whales, for example protected species and seasons. It also provides catch quotas which should be established subject to scientific findings and a balancing of utilization and conservation objectives. The amendment of the Schedule (by a three-quarter-majority

---

[103] 2007 Memorandum of Understanding (MoU) Concerning the Conservation Measures for the Eastern Atlantic Populations of the Mediterranean Monk Seal.
[104] 2006 MoU for the Conservation of Cetaceans and their Habitats in the Pacific Islands Region.
[105] N Matz, 'Chaos or Coherence?—Implementing and Enforcing the Conservation of Migratory Species By Different Legal Instruments' (2005) 65 Heidelberg Journal of International Law 179, 198.
[106] 1992 Agreement on the Conservation of Small Cetaceans of the Baltic and North Seas ASCOBANS, Art 2.2 (hereinafter ASCOBANS).
[107] 1996 Agreement on the Conservation of Cetaceans of the Black Sea, Mediterranean Sea and Contiguous Atlantic Area, Art II(1) (hereinafter ACCOBAMS).
[108] 1946 International Convention for the Regulation of Whaling, Art 1 (hereinafter ICRW).

vote) is the task of the International Whaling Commission (IWC)—the ICRW's main organ.

In 1982, the IWC amended the Schedule to prohibit commercial whaling as of the whaling season 1985/86.[109] Due to the influence of non-whaling parties, the IWC's contemporary 'conservational' management approach fundamentally differs from the framework's initial approach of utilization.[110] The moratorium is legally binding for all Member States with the exception of Norway and the Russian Federation. As a response to the moratorium, Greenland, the Faroe Islands, Iceland, and Norway concluded the 1992 Agreement on Cooperation in Research, Conservation and Management of Marine Mammals in the North Atlantic (NAMMCO Agreement). The NAMMCO Agreement is generally perceived as symbolic of the dissatisfaction with the ICRW, despite the fact that the NAMMCO Commission has not yet challenged the IWC's authority concerning the conservation and management of large whales.[111]

In addition to catch limits the establishment of whale sanctuaries in which commercial whaling is prohibited is another conservation tool. The necessity of sanctuaries has been questioned due to the current moratorium. Yet, as proponents of commercial whaling perceive the moratorium as only temporary—until stocks have recovered—the sanctuaries would regain relevance should the ban be lifted. The IWC has established two sanctuaries in accordance with paragraph 7(b) and (c) of the Schedule: the Indian Ocean Sanctuary (1979) and the Southern Ocean Sanctuary (1994). Proposals for further sanctuaries in the South Pacific and the South Atlantic have failed to achieve the necessary majority.

Exemptions to the moratorium under the ICRW apply to so called 'aboriginal subsistence whaling' by assigning specific catch limits for certain species to indigenous communities.[112] The distribution and use of whale products are restricted to local consumption and use and are, hence, not of international commercial relevance.

Another exception which is more relevant than aboriginal whaling with regard to the quantity of animals that are taken applies to so called 'scientific whaling'. Non-whaling nations consider scientific whaling in accordance with Article VIII of the ICRW the main 'loophole' to the moratorium on commercial whaling. The provision exempts the taking of whales for scientific purposes from the ICRW's scope and, effectively, from international control. Scientific whaling is regulated by national governments, which grant licences according to domestic standards and procedures. Whales killed for scientific purposes may be processed in accordance with Article VIII(2) of the ICRW and enter the commercial market. Since 2003,

---

[109] Ibid, Schedule, [10(e)].
[110] U Beyerlin and T Marauhn, *International Environmental Law* (Hart Oxford 2011) 139.
[111] Proelß, n 102, 1041.
[112] ICRW, n 108, Schedule, [13(b)]. On aboriginal whaling, see M Fitzmaurice, 'Indigenous Whaling and Environmental Protection' (2012) 55 *German Yearbook of International Law* 419, 427–37.

Iceland—after rejoining the ICRW—has relied upon scientific whaling for the authorization of its catches. The extensive scientific whaling programmes of Japan has led to the *Whaling in the Antarctic* case in the ICJ.

On the application of Australia, the ICJ reviewed the compatibility of Japan's Second Phase of the Whale Research Program under Special Permit in the Antarctic (JAPRA II) with the obligations under the ICRW. Australia alleged that Japan did not observe in good faith the zero catch limits for commercial purposes. The Judgment basically supported this submission, albeit with a different reasoning, and decided that the JAPRA II programme was not implemented 'for the purposes of scientific research' in terms of Article VIII(1) of the ICRW, thus violating Japan's compliance with the moratorium.

With regard to the scope and application of the 'loophole' provision in Article VIII of the ICRW the Court assessed if the program as such constituted scientific research, and whether measures taken were reasonable in relation to achieve the stated objectives.[113] The Court concluded that while JARPA II can 'broadly be characterized' as scientific research, the programme's design and implementation were not reasonable in relation to achieving the stated objectives.[114] With regard to the question whether the Japanese programme qualified as commercial whaling contrary to the Schedule, the Court argued that if whaling activities were neither for scientific purposes nor aboriginal subsistence whaling, they must be in violation of the zero catch limit.[115]

8.4 Protection of marine mammals by trade restrictions

In addition to international treaties focusing on restricting or prohibiting the taking of marine mammals, trade restrictions may be used to implement conservation criteria. On the global level, the 1973 Convention on International Trade in Endangered Species of Wild Fauna and Flora provides for restrictions on international trade in those marine mammals which are listed in its appendices. Prohibitions of imports apply to all species which are considered the most endangered (Appendix I) and include, *inter alia*, certain species of sea otters, fur seals, sea lions, manatees, walrus, most large whales, and dolphins. The whole family of cetaceans, if not listed on Appendix I, is included in Appendix II, which provides for strict trade controls.

On the level of regional trade measures the EU has effectively banned all seal products from entering the EU market for conservation purposes.[116] This import ban, which has some exceptions (eg for products derived from indigenous seal

---

[113] *Whaling in the Antarctic*, n 27, [67].   [114] Ibid, [227].   [115] Ibid, [229]–[230].
[116] Regulation of the Parliament and Council (EC) No 1007/2009 (16 September 2009); Commission Regulation (EC) No 737/2010 (10 August 2010).

hunting) was challenged through World Trade Organization (WTO) dispute settlement procedures. The Appellate Body in May 2014 concluded that the EU had failed to justify the restrictions by not meeting the requirements of the chapeau language to Article XX of the 1994 General Agreement on Tariffs and Trade (GATT).[117]

9 Emerging Concepts Relevant to the Management of MLR

The obvious need to further develop the existing regulations on the exploitation of MLR has led to discussions on more integrated approaches and a balancing of interests including conservation and sustainability. The following discussion assesses whether the ecosystem approach and marine spatial planning are viable tools for promoting sustainable fisheries management.[118]

9.1 Ecosystem approach

To a certain degree the LOSC's zonal approach runs counter to the reality that the oceans and the resources within it represent, ultimately, one ecological unit.[119] An approach to fisheries management that focuses not only on exploited stocks but the ecosystem of which it is part has the potential to ensure long-term sustainability, although the content and criteria of such a regime may be difficult to define from a management perspective. Article 2 of the CBD provides a definition of an ecosystem as 'a dynamic complex of plant, animal and micro-organism communities and their non-living environment interacting as a functional unit'. The origins of the so-called ecosystem approach can be traced to Principle 7 of the Rio Declaration, calling upon States to cooperate 'to conserve, protect and restore the health and integrity of the Earth's ecosystem'. According to the FAO, the ecosystem approach 'strives to balance diverse societal objectives, by taking account of the knowledge and uncertainties of biotic, abiotic and human components of ecosystems and their

---

[117] *European Communities—Measures Prohibiting the Importation and Marketing of Seal Products* (Report of the Appellate Body) WT/DS400/AB/R, WT/DS401/AB/R (2014).

[118] See also Chapter 21 in this volume.

[119] EA Kirk, 'Maritime Zones and the Ecosystem Approach' (1999) 8 *Review of European, Comparative and International Environmental Law* 67, 69.

interactions' and therefore represents 'an integrated approach to fisheries in ecologically meaningful boundaries'.[120]

Core characteristics of the approach include recognition of multi-species interactions, the inclusion of the non-living environment, and the awareness of dynamic biological processes. This surpasses traditional management schemes and incorporates wider socio-ecologic considerations as a factor of the decision-making process on management measures. It also implies recognition of the intrinsic value of nature and biodiversity as opposed to an anthropocentric focus on commercially valuable resources. Moreover, the focus on ecosystems allows for consideration of the relevant land–sea interface since ecosystem units can extend over both maritime zones and coastal areas.

One major problem of the ecosystem approach is that it requires understanding of biological processes that often surpassing the current state of knowledge. In its core, it reflects not only a policy approach, but also a call for the gathering of scientific data on ecosystem components, interactions and, notably, positive or adverse effects of management measures, in addition to standards for scientific modelling.[121] While implementation of this knowledge may refer to the precautionary approach, protected areas and habitats or the rebuilding of fish stocks, a more suitable device for integrated MLR management is marine spatial planning (MSP).

9.2 Marine spatial planning

Spatial approaches to ocean governance provide a framework that takes into consideration the various, often conflicting, aspects of ocean uses and may also address the interests involved with and influences of the use of coastal areas at the land–sea interface. While the LOSC takes account of spatial balancing of various activities under the jurisdiction of a coastal State, it does not do so in a structured or comprehensive manner. Increasing occupation of ocean spaces by traditional uses (shipping, coastal fisheries, exploration of continental shelf resources, and communication) and the emergence of new activities (aquaculture, renewable energy production, and tourism) coincide with increasing awareness for the protection of biodiversity 'hot spots' and fragile habitats. The concept of MSP tries to address these challenges.

First attempts at MSP date back to Australian planning activities in the Great Barrier Reef in the 1990s.[122] Over the last decade, the concept has gained increasing attention (eg in EU policy making).[123] While a uniform definition is still lacking, a

---

[120] FAO, *The Ecosystem Approach to Fisheries* (FAO Rome 2003) 14.
[121] FAO, *Models for an Ecosystem Approach to Fisheries* (FAO Rome 2007).
[122] E Franckx and C van Assche, 'Contemporary High Seas Fisheries Law' in E Franckx (ed), *Contemporary Regulation of Marine Living Resources Regulation* (Maklu Antwerp 2007) 29, 45.
[123] Commission Communication, 'Maritime Spatial Planning in the EU', COM/2010/0771 (2010).

study carried out in response to Decision X/29 at the tenth Conference of the Parties (COP10) of the CBD describes MSP as a 'spatial (place-based) management process, no matter at what scale and in what social context or biome' which can be characterized as 'temporal, utilizing forecasting methods' and built on integrated coastal zone management and the ecosystem approach.[124] In essence, MSP represents a comprehensive theoretical model for the structured balancing of marine and coastal uses with conservation interests.[125] As such it serves as an umbrella-term offering a planning framework instead of any distinct obligations under international law.

MSP is not to be equated with the establishment of marine protected areas, although they constitute one possible consequence of the MSP process. Relevant steps in the planning process start with the collection of data and the identification of interests including conservation objectives. In a second step, these findings should be forged into a legal instrument which balances the respective interests. Third, this plan should provide for periodic review and adaptation opportunities, and the constant exchange on ecological data and socio-economic needs.

A full implementation of an integrated MSP programme that allows for stakeholder, non-governmental organization (NGO), and local community participation is resource-intensive.[126] Yet, MSP demonstrates a structured way for implementing the coastal State duties of balancing exploitation interests, conservation needs, and third-State rights in maritime and coastal spaces. Putting MSP into practice in future MLR regulation therefore seems a worthwhile objective.

10 Conclusion and Outlook

The utilization and conservation of MLR has been a focus of international law and policy for decades. Concepts such as sustainability, precaution, best practice, and even an integrated ecosystem approach for fisheries can no longer be considered 'new' management criteria. Yet, the state of the world fisheries demonstrates that past and current approaches have not limited catches to sustainable levels. This is either because legal regulation is inadequate for pursuing these objectives, or because of a lack of implementation of and compliance with otherwise suitable legal

---

[124] Secretariat of the Convention on Biological Diversity (CBD Secretariat), *Marine Spatial Planning in the Context of the Convention on Biological Diversity*, CBD Technical Series No 68 (2012) 6.

[125] F Douvere, 'The Importance of Marine Spatial Planning in Advancing Ecosystem-Based Sea Use Management' (2008) 32 *Marine Policy* 762.

[126] JF Caddy, 'A Minority View on Ecosystem-Based Management and Ecosystem-Based Fisheries Management' (2010) 24 *Ocean Yearbook* 171, 172.

standards. Although inadequate or absent regulation is an issue, a mere increase in international treaties is unlikely to solve the problem of unsustainable fisheries. In essence, one of the main problems today—in addition to a lack of resources and capacity in many developing countries—seems to be a lack of political will to implement integrated approaches and to cooperate where local capacities alone cannot meet respective challenges.

Whether new legal initiatives at the global or regional level will prove successful depends upon the implementation of sustainable management approaches, compliance control, and enforcement. Piecemeal regulation of destructive fishing practice such as bottom trawling can supplement an improved framework for sustainable fisheries. Whether discussions concerning a new implementing agreement to the LOSC give a new dynamic to the process of sustainable fisheries regulation is doubtful as fisheries are unlikely to be covered by the prospective instrument. While new soft-law approaches should not be disregarded in initiating more sustainable fishing practices, their non-binding nature will lead to the exclusion of decisive issues such as compliance control and enforcement.

Bearing in mind the often lengthy negotiations and the even longer period of time it may take for multilateral agreements to enter into force, close cooperation and implementation of existing regulations and voluntary instruments will be vital for MLR regulation in the short and long term. Rather than discussing whether implementation of existing law or negotiations of a new instrument is preferable, international efforts need to pursue both approaches in order to halt the on-going decline in marine biodiversity.

SCIENCE AND THE INTERNATIONAL REGULATION OF MARINE POLLUTION

ELIZABETH A KIRK[*]

1 INTRODUCTION

THE definition of marine pollution found in Article 1 of the 1982 UN Convention on the Law of the Sea (LOSC) originated in the work of the Joint Group of Experts on the Scientific Aspects of Marine Pollution (GESAMP).[1] It is, in that respect, firmly rooted in received scientific understandings of pollution. One might anticipate then that scientific understanding would underpin the development

---

[*] With thanks to Robin Churchill and to the Editors of the Handbook for their insightful comments on an earlier draft.

[1] Though GESAMP itself drew on the work of other organizations in arriving at it. See Joint Intergovernmental Maritime Consultative Organization (IMCO)/ Food and Agriculture Organization (FAO)/ United Nations Educational, Scientific and Cultural Organization (UNESCO)/World Meteorological Organization (WMO) Group of Experts on the Scientific Aspects of Marine Pollution, 'Report of the First Session', GESAMP I/11 (1969).

of the law. For science to play such a key role, however, the decision-making processes must allow for policies or laws to be revised in light of new scientific information. One might also anticipate that the decision-making processes used will be rooted in adaptive management.[2] Adaptive management involves consciously following an iterative approach to regulation. The approach is based upon an acknowledgement that information within the system is imperfect and that decisions must be made on the basis of that imperfect information. In adaptive management processes a range of possible responses to a given issue are reviewed and a choice is made as to which response to test in one or more pilot projects. The pilot projects are monitored and reviewed after a period of time to determine whether the law or policy reflected in them should be developed in a particular direction or whether further adaptation in policy or regulatory response is required. In the environmental context reviews are based upon, *inter alia*, data on the state of the environment and changes to it as a result of the implementation of policies and as a result of the effects of other drivers. As such, scientific information sits at the heart of the process, though other information such as on economic or social pressures may also be relevant.

This chapter considers the approaches taken by international regimes addressing marine pollution, drawing out similarities and differences in approach across time and different sources of pollution, the degree to which they follow an adaptive management approach and the role of science in particular within decision-making. It begins with an overview of the historical development of the law, though aspects of that development are returned to throughout the chapter to illustrate the factors that have influenced the shape of the current regime. Section 2 on historical development is followed by a discussion of the current regime (Section 3), which is split into a discussion of general obligations and certain source-specific obligations. The final Section 4 contains conclusions and a discussion of current and future issues.[3]

---

[2] For a discussion of types of adaptive management, see BC Karkkainen, 'Adaptive Ecosystem Management and Regulatory Penalty Defaults: Toward a Bounded Pragmatism' (2002–2003) 87 *Minnesota Law Review* 57; BC Karkkainen, 'Toward Ecologically Sustainable Democracy?' in A Fung and EO Wright (eds), *Deepening Democracy: Institutional Innovations in Empowered Participatory Governance* (Verso London 2003); KN Lee and J Lawrence, 'Adaptive Management: Learning from the Columbia River Basin Fish and Wildlife Program' (1986) 16 *Environmental Law* 431; JB Ruhl, 'Taking Adaptive Management Seriously: A Case Study of the Endangered Species Act' (2004) 52 *University of Kansas Law Review* 1249; C Walters and CS Holling, 'Large-Scale Management Experiments and Learning by Doing' (1990) 71 *Ecology* 2060.

[3] The discussion throughout the chapter is illustrated with appropriate examples. While every effort has been made to draw examples from across the globe, the clearest illustrations of problems with pollution often times come from the northern hemisphere and in particular from around Europe where seas have been the most heavily polluted.

2 HISTORICAL DEVELOPMENT OF THE LEGAL REGIME IN RELATION TO MARINE POLLUTION

While a relative latecomer to the law of the sea, the law on marine pollution was, paradoxically, at the vanguard of the development of international environmental law. It shares a common root with many aspects of that area of law, in the concept of State responsibility. This root may help explain why the laws relating to marine pollution have developed in the way they have.

The first attempt to develop laws on marine pollution arose as a result of concerns from coastal States about the deleterious effects of oil pollution.[4] At the 1926 Preliminary Conference on Oil Pollution of Navigable Water the parties focussed their attention on shipping, their assumption being that the impacts of land-based sources of oil pollution were felt only by the coastal State from which they emanated and that these sources were in any event subject to sufficient control by coastal States. While the conference did result in a draft convention it never entered into force. In all likelihood, the failure of the draft convention to enter into force can be linked to the comment made during the conference—that the problem of oil pollution was much diminished and that efforts were being made by both coastal States and ship owners to address it. Thus while the potential harm to fisheries and to the high seas in general were discussed at the conference no agreement could be reached on their significance. Instead, both in drafting the convention and in (the failed) implementation of it, the key issue for States was the question of whether harm to State interests was likely to occur, and the perceived lack of harm to such interests undermined the convention. A second, and more successful, attempt to regulate pollution from oil resulted in the 1954 International Convention for the Prevention of Pollution of the Sea by Oil (OILPOL).

Interest in the control of marine pollution did not really become a live issue, however, until there had been a number of significant incidents. The 1958 Geneva Conventions, for example, contain few provisions on marine pollution. The disposal of offshore installations is addressed in the 1958 Convention on the Continental Shelf (CSC), and the 1958 Convention on the High Seas (HSC) addresses oil pollution from ships or pipelines and the dumping of radioactive waste in Articles 24 and 25. The most famous of the early pollution incidents were the Minamata mercury poisoning which became evident in the 1950s, and the grounding of the *Torrey Canyon* off Land's End in 1967, but the responses of the international community

---

[4] 'Final Act and Draft Convention of the Preliminary Conference on Oil Pollution of Navigable Water' (1926) 1 *Foreign Relations of the United States* 238.

to the problems of land-based and vessel-source pollution flagged up by these events differed. The *Torrey Canyon* disaster prompted the development of the 1969 International Convention on Civil Liability for Oil Pollution Damage (CLC), the 1969 International Convention Relating to Intervention on the High Seas in Cases of Oil Pollution Casualties (Intervention Convention), and the 1971 International Convention on the Establishment of an International Fund for Compensation for Oil Pollution Damage (Fund Convention),[5] whereas no treaties were adopted in direct response to the Minamata poisoning. The first treaties in this area were the 1974 Convention on the Protection of the Marine Environment of the Baltic Sea Area (1974 Helsinki Convention), and the 1974 Convention on the Prevention of Marine Pollution from Land-based Sources (Paris Convention), but these are regional conventions focused on the north-east Atlantic area, not the seas around Japan where the Minamata poisoning occurred.

In part, the general lack of attention to land-based activities was because States still assumed that any impacts would be local and controllable by the State from which the pollutants emanated.[6] That the Baltic and North-Sea areas were the first to see regional agreements tackling marine pollution from land-based sources again was unsurprising given that these were the areas where the impacts of land-based sources were first noticed. The Baltic Sea in particular suffered greatly, in part as a result of its geography and in part as a result of a significant pollutant load. As a result, the transboundary effects of marine pollution from land-based sources were more obvious in these areas than in others. Pollution from shipping on the other hand did, more obviously, raise problems akin to transboundary issues. While many of the effects of that pollution were felt within coastal areas and thus the coastal State might wish to legislate, the ships causing the pollution could of course be registered in another State, and that State might have less insight into the needs for particular forms of regulation in particular areas, or be less willing to address it than coastal States would be. There was, therefore, a more obvious need to establish global rules for the regulation of shipping to prevent harm to State interests.

Another source of pollution that was an early recipient of attention from the international community is pollution from dumping. Again the international community's attention was focussed on this form of pollution as a result of certain significant pollution events. For example, the discovery of very high levels of arsenic in Baltic waters was traced to the dumping of about 7,000 tons of arsenic in the 1930s.[7] Staying in the Baltic, Danish fishermen were burned by fish contaminated by

---

[5] See A Khee-Jin Tan, *Vessel-Source Marine Pollution: The Law and Politics of International Regulation* (Cambridge University Press Cambridge 2006), particularly ch 6.

[6] As late as 1970, it was still assumed that impacts would be local. See eg Joint IMCO/FAO/UNESCO/WMO Group of Experts on the Scientific Aspects of Marine Pollution, *Report of the Second Session*, GESAMP II/11 (1970).

[7] O Shachter and D Serwer, 'Marine Pollution Problems and Remedies' (1971) 65 *American Journal of International Law* 65.

mustard gas dumped following World War II. Again these types of incidents raised questions of State responsibility for harm to others whether through transboundary impacts or through harm to shared interests or through injury to nationals as in the case of the Danish fishermen. The response of the international community was to develop international regulation in the form of the 1972 Convention on the Prevention of Marine Pollution by Dumping of Wastes and Other Matter (London Convention) and the regional 1972 Convention for the Prevention of Marine Pollution by Dumping from Ships and Aircraft (Oslo Convention).

This brief review of the historical development of the law indicates that scientific understanding played a role in the development of these treaties, but that other interests have also proved influential. In particular, it appears that the regimes developed primarily in response to perceived harm to State interests rather than in response to harm to the environment per se.

3 Current Legal Regime

In relation to marine pollution, as in the law of the sea generally, the LOSC provides the framework that holds together the current regulatory regime and the provisions of Part XII are largely accepted as reflecting customary international law and in effect provide content to the requirement to act with due diligence.[8] The LOSC contains the general obligations that apply to the control of marine pollution across all areas and sources as well as elaborating on those obligations through measures tailored to individual sources and zones. As in other areas, the LOSC does not provide a great deal of detail; rather, it establishes the basic obligations and jurisdictional framework for coastal, flag, and port States. This approach was adopted for a number of reasons: the third United Nations conference on the law of the sea was not ideally suited to the elaboration, or the necessarily regular updating of the technical rules that marine pollution demands. Moreover, it was possible for the LOSC to draw upon existing treaties aimed at the control of many sources of marine pollution, and to draw in specialized bodies with the ability to update rules on a regular basis. Thus the LOSC has the potential to unify disparate pollution control regimes,

---

[8] The ITLOS Seabed Disputes Chamber recognized the need for due diligence in protecting the environment as a rule of customary international law: *Responsibilities and Obligations of States Sponsoring Persons and Entities with Respect to Activities in the Area* (Advisory Opinion) [2011] ITLOS Rep 10, [131] (hereinafter *Area Advisory Opinion*). Given that the majority of the provisions of LOSC are accepted as customary international law, custom is not discussed further in this section.

but it also leaves open the possibility of fragmentation within the law on marine pollution.

3.1 General Obligations

The primary obligation placed on States by Part XII of the LOSC is 'to protect and preserve the marine environment'.[9] This provision is balanced by the right of States to exploit their resources,[10] and by the obligation not to unduly interfere with other States' activities when regulating polluting activities,[11] but, in the context of Part XII of the LOSC, these latter obligations are designed to be subordinate provisions.

The general obligation of Article 192 is elaborated upon in subsequent Articles beginning with Article 194(1), which provides that:

States shall take, individually or jointly as appropriate, all measures consistent with this Convention that are necessary to prevent, reduce and control pollution of the marine environment from any source, using for this purpose the best practicable means at their disposal and in accordance with their capabilities, and they shall endeavour to harmonize their policies in this connection.

Article 194(2) goes on to reiterate the general obligation not to cause harm by pollution to areas beyond the control of the individual State concerned. Article 192 is also supported by the obligation not to transfer damage or harm from one area to another or to transform pollution from one type to another.[12]

These provisions raise some points that are worth noting. The first is that the standard that States are to meet in controlling pollution is not a fixed standard but a relative one. It takes account both of best practice and of the differential abilities of States to tackle marine pollution. This simple device allows the standard of control required of States to develop across time. By referring to best practicable means it takes account of developments in techniques and mechanisms to control, reduce, or eliminate pollution and by taking account of the variation in capacities of States to address pollution it ensures that progress in the development of controls, and so on, is not delayed by the requirement to advance at the pace of the slowest while at the same time avoiding placing impossible burdens upon States that have more limited capacity to address pollution. This type of obligation is also found in other treaties that address marine pollution. For example, the 1992 Convention on the Protection of the Marine Environment of the Baltic Sea Area (1992 Helsinki Convention) (which brings together developed States and States with economies in transition) requires parties 'to prevent and eliminate pollution of the Baltic Sea

---

[9] 1982 United Nations Convention on the Law of the Sea, Art 192 (LOSC).
[10] Ibid, Art 193.   [11] Ibid, Art 194(4).   [12] Ibid, Art 195.

Area from land-based sources by using, *inter alia*, Best Environmental Practice for all sources and Best Available Technology for point sources'.[13]

Second, the obligations found in Article 194 of the LOSC relate to conduct rather than result. That is, it appears that the final decision on how to meet these obligations is left to individual States, or more particularly, to the regulatory agencies charged with implementing the LOSC.[14] In this way these obligations give 'priority to the source state's right to authorize an activity, and, as a result, the rights of States that are possibly affected by the activity are set to the background'.[15] It would, however, be inappropriate to characterize these obligations as completely open-ended. Article 194 and the subsequent provisions in Part XII add more detail to the general provisions, in particular, they aim at ensuring consistency in the control of pollution through requiring States to try to harmonize their policies (Article 194) and to cooperate at the regional and global levels (as appropriate) to develop international rules, standards, practices, and procedures to address marine pollution (Article 197). The obligation to cooperate, which has been described by ITLOS in the *MOX Plant* case as 'a fundamental principle in the prevention of pollution of the marine environment',[16] is further developed through obligations to cooperate in the production and implementation of contingency plans (Article 199) and in scientific research in relation to marine pollution (Article 200). This latter obligation is particularly significant in that the LOSC also provides that the data acquired through the research conducted under Article 200 should be used to form the basis of the rules and standards, and so on, to be adopted under Part XII (Article 201 of the LOSC). In this way the LOSC not only sets out the primary obligations for addressing marine pollution, but it also puts in place a process for developing the law, which follows the principles of adaptive management and which indicates that scientific understanding is to provide the primary basis for that development. These adaptive management processes are given further shape through the obligation to conduct environmental impact assessments (Article 206 of the LOSC) where it is thought that activities may be harmful to the environment and through the obligation to monitor and report on existing activities (Articles 204 and 205 of the LOSC).

The adoption of these adaptive management techniques in the LOSC originally passed without much comment. It has only been with the general trend towards proceduralization in international environmental law that the import of these provisions is beginning to be fully realized. The *MOX Plant* and *Paper Mills*[17] cases, combined with the adoption of the 1991 Convention on Environmental Impact

---

[13] 1992 Convention on the Protection of the Marine Environment of the Baltic Sea Area, Art 6.

[14] EA Kirk, K Sherlock, and AD Reeves, 'SUDS Law: Non-state Actors and the Haphazard Route to Implementation of International Obligations' (2004) 4 *Non-State Actors and International Law* 87.

[15] I Plakokefalos, 'Prevention Obligations in International Environmental Law' (2012) 23 *Yearbook of International Environmental Law* 3, 36.

[16] *MOX Plant (Ireland v United Kingdom) (Request for Provisional Measures)* (2002) 41 ILM 415, [82].

[17] *Pulp Mills on the River Uruguay (Argentina v Uruguay)* (Judgment) [2010] ICJ Rep 14.

Assessment in a Transboundary Context (Espoo Convention) played significant roles in changing perceptions of the importance of these provisions, but the change is also reflected in the growing number of instruments incorporating these types of obligations. A requirement to conduct an Environmental Impact Assessment (EIA) is found particularly in regional treaties and protocols addressing land-based sources of marine pollution.[18]

These sorts of procedural obligations help address shortcomings in understanding or in regulations by providing an opportunity to ensure that the data upon which decisions are based is as accurate and complete as possible. The conduct of an EIA, for example, helps demonstrate that a State has done all that is required to meet the test of due diligence in endeavouring to avoid harm to other States or to areas beyond national jurisdiction and that it has or will apply best available techniques or processes to control pollution. It also enables States to meet the requirement to cooperate with others through the sharing of information as part of the EIA process. These provisions thus enabled the States negotiating the LOSC to sidestep the need for detailed provisions while ensuring that the standards adopted in the LOSC had meaningful content and that environmental considerations are taken into account in the appropriate contexts. The focus on process is also in keeping with customary international law: the law on State responsibility also imposes obligations of conduct rather than result.

In addition to the procedural obligations outlined above, more specific obligations and powers are provided in Sections 5 and 6 of Part XII. These are examined in more detail in the following source specific sections, but one aspect germane to all is discussed here first. States are required to take the internationally agreed rules, and so on, adopted in line with Section 5 of Part XII as the starting point for their own regulation (Articles 207–212). This requirement has as an effect the creation of a network of treaty obligations drawing together treaties adopted prior to the LOSC entering into force and those agreed subsequent to it. This, at the time, rather innovative approach to law-making made it easier for States to accept the general principles in relation to marine pollution while leaving room for the development of the detailed regulations and standards as States become aware of new forms of pollution or new ways of reducing, controlling, or preventing it, or simply become more willing to accept the adoption of more detailed regulations. There are, however, two key issues with this approach.

In certain areas, in particular the control of marine pollution from land-based activities, the internationally agreed rules are somewhat lacking. All that exists at the global level are soft law instruments. In these areas then it appears that States retain considerable discretion unless globally applicable international rules can be

---

[18] See eg 1982 Regional Convention for the Conservation of the Red Sea and Gulf of Aden, Art XI; 2010 Nairobi Convention for the Protection, Management and Development of the Marine and Coastal Environment of the Western Indian Ocean (not yet in force).

gleaned from elsewhere. One possibility is that they are to be found in common terms in other treaties, such as the regional seas conventions. A second option is that the global soft law provisions can be treated as internationally agreed rules or standards for the purposes of Part XII of the LOSC. The LOSC does not make it clear which internationally agreed rules are to be applied in this area, or in other areas of marine pollution, nor does it make clear when it can be said that international rules have been agreed. For example, if a global treaty is agreed in relation to the control of pollution from shipping, one must decide whether the very fact of concluding the treaty means that rules have been agreed, or whether agreement comes on entry into force of the treaty, or if it can be said to arise when a certain percentage of the world's shipping States have joined the agreement, or a certain percentage of the world's shipping tonnage is represented through membership of the treaty, or if indeed the rules must be accepted as customary international law. While these issues may be (and in some areas have been) resolved in practice in relation to the laws on particular sources,[19] the potential of disputes as to the precise international rules to apply always remains,[20] and so too does the potential for fragmentation.

The use of the phrase 'internationally agreed rules' as part of the LOSC provisions also leaves new activities and forms of pollution unregulated at the international level until specific agreements are entered into to address them, meaning States retain discretion as to how to address these sources of pollution until rules are agreed. This (retrospective) approach to regulation is not surprising given that the precautionary approach was only really introduced in international law in the 1990s.[21] At the time the LOSC was being negotiated, it was almost inevitable that any form of wording used in the Convention would leave gaps that would have to be addressed by subsequent agreements. It is, however, worth noting that the discretion left to States is limited by the general obligations upon States to take all necessary measures to control, reduce, and prevent pollution. Their freedom of action is therefore somewhat curtailed compared to the position prior to the adoption of the LOSC when rights to control pollution were accompanied by only limited, or vague, obligations to take preventive measures. The provisions of Part XII of the LOSC do therefore change the tenor of the law from permissive to restrictive, but the problem of gaps in the law does remain a real one.

---

[19] In shipping, for example, the IMO Conventions are generally accepted as providing the relevant rules, see eg Tan, n 5, in relation to dumping the London Convention and its 1996 Protocol are generally accepted as providing the global rules. See eg R Rayfuse, MG Lawrence, and KM Gjerde, 'Ocean Fertilisation and Climate Change: The Need to Regulate Emerging High Seas Uses' (2008) 23 *International Journal of Marine and Coastal Law* 297.

[20] See eg *MOX Plant*, n 16.

[21] N de Sadeleer, *Environmental Principles From Political Slogans to Legal Rules* (Oxford University Press Oxford 2005).

The mechanism of linking the LOSC to other treaties while contributing to the problem of unregulated issues also contains a potential solution to it, which is additional to the solution of creating new treaty regimes or rules to deal with specific problems. The links the LOSC creates with different treaties have allowed the import of new approaches and principles into the LOSC regime as a whole. For example, the precautionary approach was introduced to the regulation of dumping at sea through the 1992 Convention for the Protection of the Marine Environment of the North-East Atlantic (OSPAR Convention) and the 1996 Protocol to the London Convention. It is now also reflected in certain provisions addressing vessel source pollution, for example, the 2001 International Convention on the Control of Harmful Anti-Fouling Systems on Ships, which addresses the use of tributyl tin as an anti-fouling agent, and the 2004 International Convention for the Control and Management of Ships' Ballast Water and Sediments (Ballast Water Convention). It may then become possible to conclude that the precautionary approach is an internationally agreed rule applicable to both dumping and vessel-source pollution. It may also be or become possible to conclude that the approach is applicable across the regulation of marine pollution as a whole. The mechanism of linking the LOSC to other treaties may also allow other principles and approaches to be diffused through the LOSC framework.

There is, however, a further point that arises from the reliance on a raft of external treaties to provide the detailed legal regime. While provisions such as those providing for EIA point to a potentially significant role for scientific understanding in the development of the law, its role is not guaranteed. The role science plays is, instead, dependent upon the approach taken in the specific treaty regimes addressing different sources of pollution. Thus the role of science may vary across different areas of marine pollution law.

3.2 Source-specific obligations

Before getting to the discussion of source-specific obligation it should be noted that the focus of this section is largely on three of the six sources named in the LOSC. Pollution from seabed activities and activities in the Area are not addressed as there are limited international rules in these areas which makes drawing clear conclusions on the role of science difficult. Atmospheric pollution is included to some degree in the discussion of land-based sources and activities, though the discussion is by no means comprehensive. Many of the treaties on atmospheric pollution have a wider remit than simply preventing pollution of the marine environment. It is therefore much harder on the whole to tie their development to events or to scientific developments relating specifically to the seas and for that reason they are not discussed here.

3.2.1 *Land-based sources and activities*

The provisions in the LOSC represent the first real step in regulating marine pollution from land-based sources and activities (MPLBS/A). Despite the fact that this source has been recognized as the most significant source of marine pollution for several decades,[22] in that around 70 per cent of marine pollution emanates, directly or indirectly, from land-based activities, it has received the least attention in terms of international regulation. Prior to the LOSC, it was addressed as a form of marine pollution only at the regional level and then only by two treaties: the 1974 Helsinki Convention and the 1974 Paris Convention. Atmospheric pollution was addressed only in 1979 through the Convention on Long-range Transboundary Air Pollution. The LOSC in itself does not appear, however, to significantly develop the law. It simply requires coastal States to adopt legislation and regulations and take all necessary measures to reduce, control, and prevent MPLBS/A taking account of international rules and standards (Article 207). States are also called upon to harmonize their national measures at regional level and to 'endeavour' to agree regional and global standards, rules, and recommended practices and procedures. Coastal States are also given enforcement jurisdiction over this form of marine pollution under Article 213. There is no further detail provided as to the content of the global or regional rules to be adopted, nor as to the content of the national law. The fact that coastal States are required only to *take account* of international rules and standards leaves a great deal of discretion to adopt stricter, or indeed weaker, national or regional provisions.

These measures are, however, supported by certain global 'rules' found in the 1995 Washington Declaration on Protection of the Marine Environment from Land-Based Activities (Washington Declaration) and the Global Programme of Action on Protection of the Marine Environment from Land-Based Activities (GPA). The GPA Declaration establishes a significant role for science at the heart of three levels of adaptive management regimes. Operative paragraph 77 of the GPA provides for review of implementation and ensures an exchange of information and data from research both on pollutant sources and impacts and on regulatory techniques to address this source of marine pollution at the global level. At the regional and national levels States are encouraged to adopt appropriate measures, plans, or programmes of action and to review these through processes involving monitoring, review, and revision of the measures. And at each level these processes are being used.

For example, at the global level, the GPA identifies priority issues for attention by drawing upon scientific understanding. Of these priority areas two have been addressed through global treaties: persistent organic pollutants (POPs) addressed in the 2001 Stockholm Convention on Persistent Organic Pollutants

---

[22] See eg GESAMP, *Report on the State of the Marine Environment*, Report No 39 (1990).

(POPS Convention) and mercury addressed in the 2013 Minamata Convention on Mercury. Though neither of these conventions is focused solely on pollution of the marine environment, they do both control these forms of pollution from land-based activities. Other sources have also received attention at the global level with wastewater discussed in the Millennium Declaration[23] and the Johannesburg Plan of Implementation[24] and litter now receiving attention,[25] but discussions in these areas have yet to give rise to conventions.

At the regional level the impact of the GPA can be seen in the fact that, of the 18 regional seas, only the Antarctic and Pacific Region do not have programmes that address this form of marine pollution. All others contain measures that reflect the priorities of the GPA. For example, all of the programmes and plans addressing MPLBS/A contain and, indeed, start from the premise that monitoring is essential. It is used as a first step to developing plans or programmes (such as the Black Sea, Caspian Sea, and Southeast Pacific)[26] and as a means of monitoring or strengthening the implementation of existing plans or programmes. The monitoring that has taken place under the programmes of action has informed the development of revised programmes and plans of action across time. For example, the 2000 East Asian Regional Sea's Vision and Plan of Action[27] ties monitoring to a database network to be established under the action plan. This network was first suggested in the 1994 action plan.[28]

What we see then in relation to the MPLBS/A is both the development of norms through an adaptive management process and the apparent acceptance of those soft law 'rules' adopted under the GPA, together with the provisions of the POPs and Mercury Conventions as the international rules and standards to be applied under

---

[23] UNGA Res 55/2 (18 September 2000).

[24] World Sustainable Development Summit, Plan of Implementation, UN Doc A/CONF.1999/20 (4 September 2002) Res 2.

[25] See Manila Declaration on Furthering the Implementation of the Global Programme of Action for the Protection of the Marine Environment from Land-based Activities, UNEP/GPA/IGR.3/CRP.1/Rev.1 (26 January 2012); the Honolulu Commitment (20–25 March 2011), available at <http://5imdc.files.wordpress.com/2011/03/honolulucommitment.pdf>; and the UN Environment Programme, *Honolulu Strategy: A Global Framework for Prevention and Management of Marine Debris* (20–25 March 2011), available at <http://5imdc.wordpress.com/about/commitment/> (hereinafter Honolulu Strategy).

[26] In relation to the Black Sea, see the Commission on the Protection of the Black Sea Against Pollution, *Plan for the Environmental Protection and Rehabilitation of the Black Sea* (17 April 2009), available at <www.blacksea-commission.org/_bssap2009.asp>; in relation to the Caspian, see 2003 Framework Convention for the Protection of the Marine Environment of the Caspian Sea (hereinafter Tehran Convention); in relation to the Southeast Pacific see the website of the Comisión Permanente del Pacífico Sud, available at <www.cpps-int.org>.

[27] United Nations Environment Programme (UNEP), *Regional Programme of Action for the Protection of the Marine Environment of the East Asian Seas from the Effects of Land-based Activities: '2000 Vision and Plan of Action'* (2000), available at <www.cobsea.org/documents/report_landbased/RegionalPAfor_Protection_of_the_EAS_from_LBA_Activities2000.pdf>.

[28] UNEP, *Action Plan for the Protection And Sustainable Development of the Marine and Coastal Areas of the East Asian Region*, UNEP(OCA)/EAS IG5/6 (1994) Annex IV, 3.

Part XII of the LOSC. These developments in the law also signify a move away from the traditional prompts for development in the law. Whereas the early history of the law on marine pollution has been one of response to significant incidents, it is much harder to link single incidents to the development of the POPs Convention and the Minamata Convention on Mercury. What has prompted the development of these conventions, however, is an understanding of how dangerous POPs and mercury are for both human health and the environment. The current focus on litter and wastewater again indicates that priorities are being set based on the impact on the environment and human health, rather than as a result of single, high profile events.

3.2.2 *Dumping*

The regulation of dumping presents an unusual story in terms of the role of science. Article 210(6) of the LOSC provides quite simply that States are to adopt laws and measures 'to prevent, reduce and control pollution of the marine environment by dumping' (Article 210(1) and (2)) and that these laws and measures are to be 'no less effective' than global rules and standards. The content of the regime then depends upon those global rules and standards. They are to be found in the London Convention as amended by its 1996 Protocol, which is supported by regional seas agreements, such as the OSPAR Convention, the protocol to the 1976 Convention for the Protection of the Marine Environment and the Coastal Region of the Mediterranean (Barcelona Convention), and the 1992 Convention on the Protection of the Black Sea against Pollution (Black Sea Convention), which contain similar provisions. For the purposes of this discussion the 1996 Protocol to the London Convention is focused upon. The Protocol introduces an adaptive management approach to dumping by providing for monitoring of the state of the sea by States that issue permits. It also provides for review and updating of the Protocol by the Meeting of Parties following reports by States of the data acquired on the state of the marine environment and data from reviews of the effectiveness of measures taken to implement it. The importance of basing regulation upon sound science is also reflected in the requirements to prioritize scientific research and the sharing of data from such research under Article 14. In addition, the Protocol requires States to follow a particular decision-making process which is akin to carrying out an EIA and in which prescribed factors are to be taken into account. Similar provisions are found in some of the regional seas agreements addressing dumping, such as the 1995 amendments to the 1976 Dumping Protocol to the Barcelona Convention.[29] All of this suggests that scientific understanding should play a key role in the development of the law. The history of development of the law in this area points, however, to a different conclusion, which is that scientific understanding on the impacts of

---

[29] See UNEP, *Mediterranean Action Plan for the Barcelona Convention* (2014), available at <www.unepmap.org>.

dumping of material at sea is sometimes overshadowed by other considerations. This conclusion is also supported by some recent developments in this area, which have taken place under the 1996 Protocol to the London Convention regime.

The international rules in operation at the time that the LOSC was introduced were contained in the London Convention which largely permitted dumping. Some key steps in tightening those rules came about not directly as a result of scientific evidence, but rather as a result of campaigns by non-governmental organizations (NGOs) in the 1980s and 1990s. First, the actions of the International Transport Federation and the UK National Union of Seamen in 1983 preventing dumping of radioactive wastes at sea paved the way for a ban on such activity.[30] Second, the actions of Greenpeace influenced the adoption of the 1996 Protocol to the London Convention. The key change in the law introduced by the 1996 Protocol was a move from a largely permissive approach to dumping under which States were free to dump all materials that were not expressly prohibited (under the London Convention), to a largely restrictive approach with dumping prohibited for all materials save those that are expressly permitted (under the 1996 Protocol). This move did to some degree reflect growing scientific understanding of the dangers posed by the dumping of materials at sea, but the provisions went further than some sections of the scientific community believed necessary at the time they were adopted.[31] The motivation for adopting more stringent requirements was largely political with NGOs and the public placing pressure on governments following proposals to dump the Brent Spar oil rig at sea. The argument presented by NGOs and others was that decisions on this type of issue ought to take account of a range of values, not just scientific evidence.[32]

Recent developments under the auspices of the 1996 Protocol also show decisions being influenced by issues other than scientific understanding. For example, scientific understanding has indicated that permitting sequestration of carbon dioxide in the water column or seabed should not be permitted until clear regulations are in place.[33] However, in 2006, the parties to the London Convention permitted sequestration in the seabed (though not in the water column), prior to ensuring that adequate regulation existed.[34] In this instance, the decision appears to have

---

[30] S Charnovitz, 'Two Centuries of Participation: NGOs and International Governance' (1997) 18 *Michigan Journal of International Law* 183, 264.

[31] A Sielen, 'The New International Rules on Ocean Dumping: Promise and Performance' (2008–2009) 21 *Geo International Environmental Law Review* 295.

[32] EA Kirk, 'Marine Governance, Adaptation and Legitimacy' (2011) 22 *Yearbook of International Environmental Law* 110.

[33] See International Panel on Climate Change, *Special Report on Carbon Dioxide Capture and Storage* (Cambridge University Press Cambridge 2005), [5.7.3], which points to the need for concrete standards to ensure the safe storage of carbon dioxide. See also the 'Summary for Policy Makers', [25].

[34] Resolution LP.1(1) (2 November 2006). In the 1992 Convention for the Protection of the Marine Environment of the North-East Atlantic (hereinafter OSPAR Convention) a subtly different approach to disposal of carbon dioxide in the seabed is taken. Parties may not authorize the storage of carbon

been influenced by the objectives of the climate change regime, rather than being based upon the advice of the scientific community.[35] There are, of course, examples of other decisions adopted by the parties to the 1996 Protocol, which do more closely reflect scientific understanding[36] and the examples given here should not undermine that fact. They are designed instead to highlight the point that although the regime provides for an adaptive management process, which should provide a significant role for science, that role is (and always has been) at times overshadowed by other considerations.

3.2.3 *Vessel source pollution*

As with MPLBS/A and dumping, the law on vessel source pollution is grounded in the regime established by Part XII of the LOSC. This draws together the obligations found in the various other treaties addressing vessel source pollution. In this role the LOSC is supported by (or perhaps supports) the International Maritime Organization (IMO), which oversees around 50 treaties. The IMO is not only involved in the development of new treaties and revision of existing ones, but it also adopts recommendations, codes, and guidelines on their implementation. In this sense, one could say that an adaptive management approach is followed by the IMO through the regular review and updating of treaties such as the 1973 International Convention for the Prevention of Pollution, as modified by the Protocol of 1978 (MARPOL).[37]

A review of the development of treaties and soft law instruments within the IMO indicates, however, that the role of science is not in practice always as significant as one might hope. Instead, development is oftentimes influenced by the views of particular States and interest groups as well as being prompted by high profile shipping incidents. For example, environmental groups and States such as Australia (which was particularly affected by invasive species from ballast water) have successfully persuaded others to follow the precautionary approach in adopting the Ballast Water Convention. While the Convention may chime with scientific understanding, the key to its adoption lies in politics not science and this example is not unique. Throughout the history of the law on vessel source pollution, science has played, at best, an accompanying role to the role of special interests, be they State interests or the interests of non-State actors.

---

dioxide in the seabed unless authorizations follow OSPAR standards. See OSPAR Decision 2007/2 (25–29 June 2007).

[35] See the discussion in Kirk, n 32.   [36] See eg Resolution LC-LP.1 (31 October 2008).
[37] 1973 International Convention for the Prevention of Pollution by Ships, as amended by the Protocol of 1978 and Amendments to the Annex of the Protocol of 1978 relating to the International Convention for the Prevention of Pollution from Ships (hereinafter MARPOL). MARPOL is kept under constant review by the Marine Environment Protection Committee.

Beginning with the earliest regulation a significant focus of the law on vessel source pollution appeared to be the protection of coastal State interests rather than the protection of the marine environment per se. Thus, for example, the 1969 CLC and the 1971 Fund Convention were adopted.[38] In part this focus reflects the fact that much of the development of the law took place following significant pollution events, such as the *Torrey Canyon, Amoco Cadiz,* and *Exxon Valdez* disasters. These all had an obvious impact on the interests of particular coastal States. And indeed the development has continued to follow incidents such as the *Erika* and *Prestige* disasters.[39] Of course, other conventions, which had a broader role in protecting the environment, were also adopted at an early stage, such as OILPOL, addressing operational pollution, which was superseded by MARPOL.[40] But even these did not always reflect best scientific understanding on how to address marine pollution. For example, although some States recognized the need for ocean wide standards to address vessel source pollution in the 1950s, such standards were not adopted in OILPOL. Instead, the provisions focused on protecting coastal areas from oil pollution.[41]

The relative influence of other special interest groups, besides States, can also be seen in the adoption of some new standards, for example, when crude oil washing (COW) was initially accepted as an alternative to segregated ballast tanks, its adoption reflected the impact of the oil industry in moderating the standards to be adopted and the adoption of the double hull standard was largely as a result of lobbying by the USA which reflected domestic concerns. The influence of special interests has also been seen in other areas such as in the regulation of anti-fouling systems and control of air pollution from ships.[42] Similarly, the impact of competing interest groups can be seen in debates over whether or not to adopt more stringent measures in particularly sensitive sea areas under MARPOL.[43]

---

[38] See also the 1996 International Convention on Liability and Compensation for Damage in Connection with the Carriage of Hazardous and Noxious Substances by Sea; and for a detailed discussion of the treaties on nuclear damage, see P Birnie, A Boyle, and C Redgwell, *International Law and the Environment* (Oxford University Press Oxford 2009) 520ff.

[39] Eg 1969 International Convention on Civil Liability for Oil Pollution Damage (hereinafter CLC) and 1971 International Convention on the Establishment of an International Fund for Compensation for Oil Pollution Damage (hereinafter Fund Convention) were each amended by the 1984 Protocol to Amend the CLC and the 1984 Protocol to Amend the Fund Convention. These were replaced by two further Protocols in 1992 which replaced 1969 CLC and 1971 Fund Convention with new 1992 Conventions. See also N Liu and F Maes, 'The European Union and International Maritime Organization: EU's External Influence on the Prevention of Vessel-Source Pollution' (2010) 41 *Journal of Maritime Law and Commerce* 581.

[40] MARPOL, n 37, also contains provisions to prevent or minimize disasters (introducing the double hull standard for tankers, for example).

[41] Tan, n 5, ch 3.   [42] Ibid.

[43] See C Purvis, 'Coastal State Jurisdiction under UNCLOS: The *Shen Neng 1* Grounding on the Great Barrier Reef Comment' (2011) 36 *Yale Journal of International Law* 207.

Even within the LOSC the provisions of Part XII to a degree could be described as reflecting the interests of particular groups. The LOSC allocates jurisdiction to each of the three groups of States that may have an interest in shipping—flag, coastal, and port States—but the rights of each vary. Thus flag States are to ensure that their laws 'at least have the same effect as that of generally accepted international rules and standards' (Article 211(2)). Port States have no such requirement; nor indeed does there appear to be a limitation on the measures that they may adopt. Coastal States, however, must ensure that any measures they adopt do not impede innocent, or transit passage, or freedom of navigation and that measures relating to the design, construction, manning, or equipment of foreign vessels may only be adopted if 'they are giving effect to generally accepted international regulations' (Articles 21) and 'giving effect to applicable international regulations' (Article 42). This formulation of the rights of coastal States is inevitable, given that any alternative approach might hamper global trade through shipping, but it also privileges the interests of shipping rather than of the marine environment save to the extent that coastal States are also port States.

The role played by special interests and significant events in the development of the laws on vessel source pollution points then to less emphasis being placed upon scientific understanding in the development of this area of law than might be anticipated. While it clearly plays a role, it appears to be often times outweighed by other considerations.

4 Conclusions

A key objective of this chapter was to establish the role that science played and plays in the regulation of marine pollution. What has become clear is that a singular conclusion on that role cannot be given. While it does appear that as a whole the marine pollution regimes are moving towards affording scientific understanding a more significant role, variations exist between the different regimes. The move towards affording science a more significant role is evident in the adoption of an adaptive management approach within the Part XII of the LOSC and within the relatively new regime to address MPLBS/A. It is also seen in the regime on dumping, and is present to a degree in relation to vessel source pollution. In both dumping and vessel-source pollution, the role of science appears, however, to be less significant than in relation to MPLBS/A and, instead, the influence of special interest groups or the effects of politics appear to be key to the development of the law. Nevertheless, in these areas too we have witnessed a move in the direction of affording scientific understanding more significance with, for example, the adoption of some treaties and measures following a precautionary approach. It seems likely therefore that the role of science will continue to grow in the regulation of marine pollution. There are, however, certain key challenges that are still present and likely to be faced in the future.

The first challenge is to provide greater clarity in relation to certain approaches and obligations. The variations in approach to adaptive management point to the need to develop a clear understanding of what is meant by adaptive management in the context of marine pollution. The regime as a whole would also benefit from further clarification of some obligations. Within the specific regime on MPLBS/A there is a need to clarify the nature of obligations at the international level. For example, consideration is needed of the degree to which the regional treaty regimes combine to establish a clear interpretation of the provisions of Part XII, or to provide customary international law. Similarly, it would be beneficial to have a greater understanding of the degree to which principles and approaches apply across all sources of marine pollution. For example, it is not clear that the precautionary approach is applicable to the law on MPLBS/A, though it quite clearly applies in other areas, such as dumping.

Such clarification may help us address current problem sources such as pollution from plastics. In part the problem that plastics give rise to is one of scale: ever more plastic is finding its way into the ocean whether from land-based sources or from disposal at sea. In part, the problem is one that we have seen with other forms of pollution: plastics generally take a long time to break down and cannot be neutralized by the oceans. The inability of the oceans to neutralize plastics leads them to accumulate in, for example, large mid-ocean rubbish patches. The results of the pollution include fish being caught in ghost fishing nets[44] and whales killed by eating plastic sheeting from agriculture.[45] As well as raising issues of coordination and integration across regimes, the increasing pollution from plastics raises the question of who will provide a solution to the problem. While the general obligation to prevent, reduce, and control pollution requires all States to address pollution from plastics through regulations and enforcement action, and while some measures already exist which give more shape to this obligation,[46] it still leaves the question of how to address pollution that is already in the marine environment. Where plastics accumulate within the exclusive economic zone (EEZ) or territorial sea of a State that State may have an incentive to remove the plastic. Where they

---

[44] UNGA Res 44/225 (22 December 1989).

[45] G Tremlett, 'Spanish Sperm Whale Death Linked to UK Supermarket Supplier's plastic: Sperm Whale on Spanish Southern Coast had Swallowed 17 kg of Plastic Waste Dumped by Greenhouses Supplying Produce to UK', *Guardian* (8 March 2013), available at <www.theguardian.com/world/2013/mar/08/spain-sperm-whale-death-swallowed-plastic>.

[46] See MARPOL, n 37, Annex V.

accumulate on the high seas the incentives for single State action are weaker and so a coordination problem arises. On-going efforts to address these issues can be seen in the Honolulu Strategy and the Honolulu Commitment and in the work being done to establish the Global Partnership on Marine Litter. There is, however, still a need for considerable development in the regulation of this type of pollution and in particular in the mechanisms to address it. One option might be to adopt a fund approach similar to that operating in relation to vessel source pollution. The resulting fund could then commission companies to remove and recycle any plastics or other materials. In addition, pollution from plastics highlights the problems that a responsive approach to pollution gives rise to which include significant accumulation of pollutants in the environment and significant harm to the environment and to State interests before measures are taken to address the problem. Clarifying the measures necessary to implement approaches such as the precautionary approach and adaptive management may help ensure prompter attention to such pollutants before they become particularly problematic.

Second, if the current marine pollution regime(s) are to be truly effective in tackling certain current issues then they must be fully integrated with related regimes, such as the climate change regime, the biodiversity regime, and fisheries regimes. For example, various measures have been proposed to help mitigate human impact on the climate.[47] Some of these, such as fertilizing the oceans with iron to increase the growth of plankton and so ensure more carbon dioxide is removed from the atmosphere, or sequestering carbon dioxide in the water column or in or on the seabed, are regarded in the marine context as polluting activities. As discussed earlier, these two examples fall under the London Convention regime and both have been discussed by the parties to the Convention. The parties decided in Resolution LC-LP.1 (2008) to treat ocean fertilization as a prohibited dumping activity until scientific research proves its safety following the advice of its scientific group. But ocean fertilization has also been considered by the parties to the Convention on Biological Diversity (CBD)[48] and could equally be considered by the parties to the UN Convention on Climate Change. As it happens, the Parties to the CBD took a similar approach to that taken by the parties to the London Convention, though there are some differences between the two. This example illustrates the possibility of fragmentation in the law. The second example, points to the potentially 'undue' influence of one regime upon another. Although the London Convention adopts a precautionary approach to dumping, it permitted sequestration in the seabed (though not in the water column) prior to ensuring that an adequate regulatory system was in place contrary to scientific advice. And as noted earlier, the decision

---

[47] For a fuller discussion, see Chapter 34 in this volume.
[48] See UNEP, *Report of the Conference of the Parties to the Convention on Biological Diversity on the Work of Its Ninth Meeting*, UNEP Doc UNEP/CBD/COP/9/29 (2008) 154.

appears to have been influenced by the objectives of the climate change regime, rather than being based upon the principles of the London Convention itself.

Similar challenges are raised by other new technologies and activities. For example, the installation of offshore wind farms may cause disruption to marine life both during the construction phase and through the noise pollution that results from their operation. Tidal power installations may also create noise pollution and cause disruption to species through changing the water flow where they are placed. The need for an integrated approach to decision-making is evident here too. In this sense integration may mean both ensuring that decision-making operates in a complementary way across regimes, but also that scientific and other data is shared between regimes. These forms of integration may not on their own, however, be sufficient to ensure the best outcome in managing these potential sources of pollution. It may also be necessary to draw upon tools such as the ecosystem approach in decision-making. Several treaties relating to the marine environment already adopt elements of the ecosystem approach.[49] For example, the LOSC and London Convention note the need to control pollution to prevent interference with other uses of the seas and to prevent harm to marine life.[50] The LOSC also notes the need to prevent the transfer of pollution from one medium to another[51] and the London Convention and its 1996 Protocol are designed to address precisely this problem. Similarly the POPs Convention is based on the premise that account should be taken of both the immediate and the long-term environmental impacts of chemicals such as pesticides when deciding on their use. None of the conventions embrace all elements of this approach, however, and so further work is needed to address the question of how best to implement this approach or others designed to ensure integrated decision-making.

It is difficult, when faced with the challenges outlined above, to draw a clear conclusion as to the future of the LOSC. While integrated decision-making will be key to managing our oceans, and while the LOSC provides a strong framework to support such decision-making, the influence of the wider regulatory context may significantly impact upon the role that the LOSC is able to play. The examples given suggest that steps are being taken to try to prevent fragmentation, by ensuring that decision-making is integrated both within and across regimes. They also point to the possibility that, at times, the interests and issues governed by the LOSC will be overshadowed by other interests or issues and that where that happens the principles and provisions of the LOSC will become less important in their regulation.

---

[49] See UNGA, *Report of the UN Open Ended Informal Consultative Process*, 7th Meeting, UN Doc GA 61/63 (2006).
[50] LOSC, n 9, Art 194; London Convention, Art I.
[51] LOSC, n 9, Art 195.

24

NAVIGATIONAL RIGHTS AND FREEDOMS

YOSHIFUMI TANAKA

1 INTRODUCTION

NAVIGATIONAL rights and freedom of navigation are of particular importance in international relations for economic and strategic reasons, which are mutually intertwined.

First, the freedom of navigation has been, and remains, a pre-requisite for international trade and commerce. In this regard, it may be relevant to recall that Hugo Grotius' *Mare Liberum*, which advocated the freedom of the seas, was written at the request of the Dutch East India Company to vindicate the right of that Company to trade in the Far East against the exclusive claim of Portugal upon the Bull of Pope Alexander VI.[1] Indeed, the subtitle of the book was 'A Disputation Concerning the Right Which the Dutch Ought to Have to the Indian Merchandise for Trading'. This episode demonstrates that the freedom of navigation was essentially characterized by the economic interests of maritime States. In fact, maritime shipping has never

---

[1] D Armitage, 'Introduction' in H Grotius, *The Free Sea* (trans R Hakluyt, ed D Armitage) (Library Fund Indianapolis 2004) xii; F Ito, 'The Thought of Hugo Grotius in the *Mare Liberum*' (1974) 18 *Japanese Annual of International Law* 1, 12; RP Anand, *Origin and Development of the Law of the Sea: History of International Law Revisited* (Nijhoff The Hague 1983) 79. Generally on this history of the law of the sea, see Chapter 1 in this volume. See also DJ Bederman, 'The Sea' in B Fassbender et al (eds), *Oxford Handbook of the History of International Law* (Oxford University Press Oxford 2012) 359ff.

lost its importance and currently around 90 per cent of world trade is carried by the international shipping industry.[2] One can thus safely argue that navigational rights have always been crucial to the development of seaborne trade and the world economy.

Second, historically the freedom of navigation was essential for maritime powers to expand their political or military influence over their overseas colonies and secure their maritime networks. It cannot pass unnoticed that the freedom of navigation contributed to European overseas expansion.[3] Even in the age of decolonization, navigational rights and the freedom of navigation remain essential for military powers to deploy their navies and air force and secure their strategic interests at sea. Hence the navigational rights of warships and military airplanes are considered as an important element in the strategy of military powers.

However, navigation of foreign vessels in maritime zones of coastal States creates particular sensitivities associated with protection of their interests. For instance, the passage of foreign warships through the territorial sea may be a serious threat to the security of coastal States. Given that the size of vessels continues to increase and that certain cargoes may be highly dangerous to the marine environment in the event of an accident, marine environmental protection from vessel-source hazards becomes a more pressing concern for coastal States. A crucial issue thus arises as to how to reconcile the navigational interests of shipping States and interests of coastal States. In this regard, the 1982 UN Nations Convention on the Law of the Sea (LOSC) provides multiple navigational rights according to each jurisdictional zone: the right of innocent passage, the right of non-suspendable innocent passage, the right of transit passage, the right of archipelagic sea lane passage, and the freedom of navigation (see Table 24.1 below).

Before examining those navigational rights, it is necessary to specify the scope of this chapter. Navigational rights of third States normally do not exist in internal waters since, under customary international law and Article 2(1) of the LOSC, every coastal State enjoys full sovereignty over its internal waters and the right of innocent passage does not apply to them.[4] A notable exception in this regard concerns waters newly enclosed as internal waters by a straight baseline under Article 8(2) of the LOSC. In the contiguous zone, apart from the coastal State's control over the items set out in Article 33(1) of the LOSC, navigational rights of States are governed by the same rules applicable to the exclusive economic zone (EEZ) or the high seas.[5]

---

[2] International Chamber of Shipping (ICS), *Sustainable Development: IMO World Maritime Day* (2013) 3, available at <http://www.ics-shipping.org/docs/default-source/resources/policy-tools/sustainable-development-imo-world-maritime-day-2013.pdf>.

[3] QD Nguyen et al, *Droit International Public* (8th edn LGDJ Paris 2009) 1334; A Hoffmann, 'Navigation, Freedom of' in R Wolfrum (ed), *Max Planck Encyclopaedia of Public International Law* (Oxford University Press Oxford 2008–2011) [3].

[4] Concerning access to foreign ports, see Chapter 13 in this volume.

[5] See Chapter 5 in this volume.

Table 24.1 **Navigational Rights in the LOSC**

Marine spaces under territorial sovereignty

Internal waters	No navigational rights (exception: Art 8(2) of the LOSC)
Territorial Sea	Right of innocent passage
International straits	Right of transit passage/the right of non-suspendable innocent passage
Archipelagic waters	Right of archipelagic sea lane passage/the right of innocent passage

Marine spaces under the sovereign rights

Exclusive Economic Zone	Freedom of navigation
Continental shelf	Freedom of navigation in the superjacent waters of the continental shelf

Marine spaces beyond national jurisdiction

High seas	Freedom of navigation
The Area	Freedom of navigation in the superjacent waters of the Area

Rules governing the continental shelf concern the exploration and exploitation of mineral resources on the seabed and its subsoil. Under Article 78(1) of the LOSC, the rights of the coastal State over the continental shelf do not affect the legal status of the superjacent waters or of the airspace above those waters. It follows that, where the coastal State has not claimed an EEZ, the superjacent waters above the continental shelf are the high seas and that the superjacent waters above the continental shelf beyond 200 nautical miles (nm) are always the high seas. Hence all States enjoy the freedom of navigation there. Under Article 78(2) of the LOSC, the exercise of the coastal State's rights over the continental shelf must not infringe or result in any unjustifiable interference with navigation. Yet the language of this provision seems to imply that the coastal State may interfere in a justifiable manner with navigation in the exercise of its sovereign rights over the continental shelf.[6]

---

[6] T Treves, 'Navigation' in R-J Dupuy and D Vignes (eds), *A Handbook on the New Law of the Sea* (Nijhoff Dordrecht 1991) Vol 2, 891. See also S Oda, 'Proposals for Revising the Convention on the Continental Shelf' in S Oda (ed), *Fifty Years of the Law of the Sea: With a Special Section on the International Court of Justice* (Nijhoff The Hague 2003) 275; Y Takei, *Filling Regulatory Gaps in High Seas Fisheries: Discrete High Seas Fish Stocks, Deep-sea Fisheries and Vulnerable Marine Ecosystems* (Leiden Nijhoff 2013) 45.

Conversely, certain uses of the sea related to the freedom of navigation, including anchoring, may affect uses of the continental shelf, such as laying submarine cables and pipelines there.[7] The superjacent waters to the Area (ie the seabed and ocean floor and subsoil thereof, beyond the limits of national jurisdiction) remain the high seas, and freedom of navigation applies there. However, freedom of navigation in the superjacent waters of the Area may be affected by the deep seabed activities and, conversely, navigation may affect activities in the Area.[8] Hence some issues can arise with regard to the freedom of navigation in the superjacent waters of the continental shelf and the Area. Apart from these issues, however, navigational rights are primary at issue in the territorial sea, international straits, archipelagic waters, the EEZ, and the high seas. Thus this chapter will seek to examine navigational regimes applicable to these zones.

2 The Right of Innocent Passage through the Territorial Sea

2.1 General considerations

The right of innocent passage through the territorial sea becomes an important mechanism for reconciling territorial sovereignty of the coastal State and the navigational right of other States. The concept of innocent passage was developed in Emer de Vattel's, *Le droit des gens* published in 1758. Vattel presented the modern concept of the territorial sea, which was distinguished from the high seas, and the concept of innocent passage. In his words:

> These parts of the sea, thus subject to a nation, are comprehended in her territory; nor must any one navigate them without her consent. But, to vessels that are not liable to suspicion, she cannot, without a breach of duty, refuse permission to approach for harmless purposes, since it is a duty incumbent on every proprietor to allow to strangers a free passage, even by land, when it may be done without damage or danger.[9]

---

[7] R Lagoni, 'Pipelines' in Wolfrum (ed), n 3, [18].

[8] Indeed, activities in the Area include those in its superjacent waters. In this regard, see *Responsibilities and Obligations of States Sponsoring Persons and Entities with Respect to Activities in the Area* (Advisory Opinion) [2011] ITLOS Rep 10, [87]–[88]. See also Chapter 11 in this volume.

[9] E de Vattel, *The Law of Nations; or Principles of the Law of Nature, Applied to the Conduct and Affairs of Nations and Sovereigns* (trans J Chitty) (T and JW Johnson and Co Law Booksellers Philadelphia 1853) § 288. For the original French text, see E de Vattel, *Le droit des gens ou principes de la loi naturelle, Appliqués à la conduite et aux affaires des Nations et des Souverains* (The Classics of International Law Washington 1916).

In Vattel's view, permission was still required to exercise the right of innocent passage. Later, the right of innocent passage was more clearly advocated by Lord Stowell in the *Twee Gebroeders* case of 1801:

> The passage of ships over territorial portions of the sea, or external water, is a thing less guarded, than the passage of armies over land ... the act of inoffensively passing over such portions of water, without any violence committed there, is not considered as any violation of territory belonging to a neutral state—permission is not usually required.[10]

It may be considered that the right of innocent passage became established in the middle of the nineteenth century.[11]

While the right of innocent passage was recognized at the 1930 Hague Conference for the Codification of International Law, the Conference did not adopt a treaty governing the territorial sea.[12] The right of innocent passage was, for the first time, codified in Article 14(1) of the 1958 Geneva Convention on the Territorial Sea and the Contiguous Zone (TSC). This provision was followed by Article 17 of the LOSC. As provided in Article 18(1) of the LOSC, innocent passage comprises lateral passage and inward/outward-bound passage. Lateral passage is the passage traversing the territorial sea without entering internal waters or calling at a roadstead or port facility outside internal waters. Inward/outward-bound passage concerns the passage proceeding to or from internal waters or a call at such roadstead or port facility. The direction of the passage is relevant in relation to the criminal jurisdiction of coastal States over vessels of foreign States in the territorial sea.[13] It is important to note that the right of innocent passage does not comprise the freedom of overflight.

The coastal State is obliged not to hamper the innocent passage of foreign ships.[14] No charge may be levied upon foreign ships by reason only of their passage through the territorial sea.[15] Further, the coastal State is required to give appropriate publicity to any danger to navigation under Article 24(2) of the LOSC. This obligation was mentioned in the *dictum* of the *Corfu Channel* judgment.[16]

---

[10] KR Simmonds, *Cases on the Law of the Sea* (Oceana Publications New York 1976) Vol I, 23–4.

[11] DP O'Connell, *The International Law of the Sea*, (ed IA Shearer) (Clarendon Press Oxford 1982) Vol I, 19, 275. See also Chapter 1 in this volume.

[12] S Rosenne (ed), *League of Nations Conference for the Codification of International Law [1930]* (Oceana New York 1975) Vol 4, 1412.

[13] See also Chapter 5 in this volume.

[14] 1982 United Nations Convention on the Law of the Sea, Art 24(1) (hereinafter LOSC).

[15] Ibid, Art 26.

[16] *Corfu Channel (United Kingdom v Albania)* (Judgment) [1949] ICJ Rep 4, 22; *Virginia Commentaries*, Vol II, 226.

2.2 Exercise of the right of innocent passage

Two principal issues arise with regard to the exercise of the right of innocent passage. The first issue concerns the *manner* of passage through the territorial sea and the second issue relates to non-innocent activities.

Concerning the manner of innocent passage, the LOSC provides several rules on this matter.

First, passage shall be continuous and expeditious. Hence, ships must proceed with due speed, having regard to safety and other relevant factors. Under Article 18(2) of the LOSC, passage includes stopping and anchoring only in so far as the same are incidental to ordinary navigation or are rendered necessary by *force majeure* or distress or for the purpose of providing assistance to persons, ships, or aircraft in danger or distress. Accordingly, normally the act of hovering by a foreign vessel is not considered as innocent passage.

Second, in the territorial sea, submarines and other underwater vehicles must navigate on the surface and show their flag.[17] In this connection, an issue is whether or not a breach of the requirement to navigate on the surface can lead to the loss of the right of innocent passage. While submerged passage in the territorial sea is not considered as innocent passage, such passage will not instantly justify the use of force against the submarine. Instead, every measure short of armed force to require the submarine to leave may be taken.[18]

Third, foreign ships exercising the right of innocent passage through the territorial sea must comply with all such laws and regulations and all generally accepted international regulations relating to the prevention of collisions at sea pursuant to Article 21(4) of the LOSC. In this regard, the most important regulations are those in the 1972 Convention on the International Regulations for Preventing Collisions at Sea (COLREG).

The second issue to be examined is when passage becomes prejudicial to the peace, good order or security of the coastal State and hence non-innocent. In this regard, Article 19(1) of the LOSC provides that '[p]assage is innocent so long as it is not prejudicial to the peace, good order or security of the coastal State'. Article 19(2) then contains a catalogue of prejudicial *activities* which are: (a) any threat or use of force; (b) any exercise with weapons of any kind; (c) spying; (d) any act of propaganda; (e) the launching, landing, or taking on board of any aircraft; (f) the launching, landing, or taking on board of any military device; (g) the loading or unloading of any commodity, currency, or person contrary to the customs, fiscal, immigration, or sanitary laws of the coastal State; (h) any act of wilful and serious pollution; (i) fishing activities; (j) research or survey activities; (k) interference with coastal communications or any other facilities; and (l) any

---

[17] LOSC, n 14, Art 20.   [18] O'Connell, n 11, Vol I, 297.

other activity not having a direct bearing on passage. The last item in the list, (l), indicates that the list is non-exhaustive. The term 'activities' in Article 19(2) appears to suggest that the prejudicial nature of innocent passage is judged on the basis of the *manner* in which the passage is carried out, not the type of a ship. This approach is echoed by the International Court of Justice (ICJ) in the 1949 *Corfu Channel* case. In that case, the Court relied essentially on the criterion of 'whether the *manner* in which the passage was carried out was consistent with the principle of innocent passage'.[19]

Several elements of Article 19(2), such as Article 19(2)(a), (c), and (j), are widely drafted and, as a consequence, there is a risk that international disputes may arise concerning their interpretation. In this regard, it is to be noted that paragraph 4 of the 1989 Uniform Interpretation between the United States and the USSR stated that: 'A coastal State which questions whether the particular passage of a ship through its territorial sea is innocent shall inform the ship of the reason why it questions the innocent passage, and provide the ship an opportunity to clarify its intentions or correct its conduct in a reasonable short period of time'.[20]

A contentious issue concerning Article 19 is whether its paragraph 2 is meant to be an illustrative list of paragraph 1 of the same provision, or whether the coastal State may evaluate innocence solely on the basis of paragraph 1, without having recourse to paragraph 2. Unlike the second paragraph, the first paragraph makes no explicit reference to 'activities'. Hence there appears to be some scope for arguing that the criterion for judging innocence under Article 19(1) is not limited to the *manner* of the passage of ships. Indeed, if paragraph 2 is an illustrative list of paragraph 1, paragraph 1 would seem to be superfluous. Hence the coastal State can regard a certain passage of a ship as non-innocent on the basis of Article 19(1), even if activities engaged in during the passage do not fall within the list of Article 19(2). On the basis of this interpretation, the Japanese government, for instance, takes the view that the passage of foreign warships carrying nuclear weapons through its territorial sea is not innocent, while Japan generally admits the right of innocent passage of foreign warships.[21]

---

[19] *Corfu Channel*, n 16, 30 (emphasis in original).

[20] 'Joint Statement with attached Uniform Interpretation of the Rules of International Law Governing Innocent Passage of 23 September 1989' (1989) 14 *Law of the Sea Bulletin* 12–13.

[21] A Kanehara, 'The Japanese Legal System Concerning Innocent Passage of Foreign Vessels 1990-1998' (1999) 42 *The Japanese Annual of International Law* 105. The Japanese policy is based on 'Three Non-Nuclear Principles', which means 'not possess, not produce, not permit introducing into Japan nuclear weapons'.

2.3 The regulation of the right of innocent passage by the coastal State

The right of innocent passage is not free from regulation by the coastal State. In this regard, the LOSC empowers the coastal State to exercise legislative and enforcement jurisdiction over ships in innocent passage in order to safeguard its interests in the territorial sea.[22]

First, under Article 21(1) of the LOSC, the coastal State possesses legislative jurisdiction relating to innocent passage through the territorial sea, with respect to all or any of the following: (a) the safety of navigation and the regulation of maritime traffic; (b) the protection of navigational aids and facilities and other facilities or installations; (c) the protection of cables and pipelines; (d) the conservation of the living resources of the sea; (e) the prevention of infringement of the fisheries laws and regulations of the coastal State; (f) the preservation of the environment of the coastal State and the prevention, reduction and control of pollution thereof; (g) marine scientific research and hydrographic surveys; or (h) the prevention of infringement of the customs, fiscal, immigration, or sanitary laws and regulations of the coastal State. However, such laws and regulations shall not apply to the design, construction, equipment, or manning of foreign ships unless they are giving effect to generally accepted international rules or standards.[23]

In this regard, the question arises as to whether a violation of a coastal State's laws or legislation would *ipso facto* make passage non-innocent. When drafting Article 14(4) of the TSC, the members of the International Law Commission were divided on this matter. The literal interpretation of this provision appears to suggest that the violation of the coastal State's laws or regulations does not *ipso facto* make passage non-innocent, unless such violation is prejudicial to the coastal State's interests.[24] The only one exception concerns illegal fishing provided in Article 14(5) of the TSC. This provision was inserted in order to introduce an additional criterion of innocence. It suggests that apart from the violation of fishing legislation, the breach of the laws or regulations of the coastal State *ipso facto* does not deprive a passage of its innocence in the TSC. Likewise, it can be argued that, under the LOSC, the violation of the laws or regulations of the coastal State does not *ipso facto* deprive a passage of its innocent character, unless such violation falls within the scope of Article 19.[25]

---

[22] On this issue, see also Chapter 5 in this volume.   [23] LOSC, Art 21(2).
[24] RR Churchill and AV Lowe, *The Law of the Sea* (Manchester University Press Manchester 1999) 84.
[25] C Espaliú Berdud, *Le passage inoffensif des navires de guerre étrangers dans la mer territoriale: portée du régime contenu dans la Convention des Nations Unies sur le droit de la mer* (Bruylant Brussels 2006) 54; P Birnie, A Boyle and C Redgwell, *International Law and the Environment* (3rd edn Oxford University Press Oxford 2008) 417.

Second, the coastal State is empowered to take regulatory measures concerning innocent passage of foreign vessels in its territorial sea. In this regard, it is particularly important to note that the innocent passage of foreign vessels may be suspended by the coastal State in accordance with Article 25(3) of the LOSC. This provision sets out five conditions:

(i) Suspension must be essential for the protection of its security;

(ii) Suspension must be temporal;

(iii) Suspension must be limited in specific areas of its territorial sea;

(iv) Suspension must be without discrimination; and

(v) Suspension shall take effect only after having been duly published.

The coastal State may require foreign ships exercising the right of innocent passage through its territorial sea to use such sea lanes and traffic separation schemes as it may designate or prescribe for the regulation of the passage of ships.[26] At the same time, the coastal State is under the obligation to clearly indicate such sea lanes and traffic separation schemes on charts to which due publicity shall be given.[27]

Further, the coastal State may take the necessary steps in its territorial sea to prevent passage which is not innocent.[28] While this provision does not specify the necessary steps, they could include requesting an offending ship to stop certain conduct, requesting a ship to leave the territorial sea, and the intervention of State authorities to board and exclude the ship from its territorial sea, and so on.[29] In the case of ships proceeding to internal waters or a call at a port facility outside internal waters, the coastal State has the right to take the necessary steps to prevent any breach of the conditions to which admission of those ships to internal waters or such a call is subject.[30] Concerning the preservation of the environment of the coastal State, in particular, Article 220(2) of the LOSC clearly provides that where there are clear grounds for believing that a vessel navigating in the territorial sea of a State has violated laws and regulations of that State during its passage therein, the coastal State may undertake physical inspection of the vessel relating to the violation, and may, where the evidence so warrants, institute proceedings, including detention of the vessel.

Article 27 of the LOSC provides for the criminal jurisdiction of the coastal State in its territorial sea. Where a crime had been committed before the ship entered the territorial sea and the ship is only passing through the territorial sea without entering internal waters, however, the coastal State may not exercise criminal jurisdiction over the ship.[31] This is a mandatory prohibition on the exercise of the criminal jurisdiction of the coastal State in the territorial sea.

---

[26] LOSC, n 14, Art 22 (1).   [27] Ibid, Art 22(4).   [28] Ibid, Art 25(1).
[29] DR Rothwell and T Stephens, *The International Law of the Sea* (Hart Publishing Oxford 2010) 218.
[30] LOSC, n 14, Art 25(2).   [31] Ibid, Art 27(5).

Under Article 28(1) of the LOSC, 'the coastal State should not stop or divert a foreign ship passing through the territorial sea for the purpose of exercising civil jurisdiction in relation to a person on board the ship'. The term 'should not' seems to suggest that the restriction of the civil jurisdiction is a matter of comity.[32] Under Article 28(2), the coastal State may not levy execution against or arrest the ship for the purpose of any civil proceedings, save only in respect of obligations or liabilities assumed or incurred by the ship itself in the course or for the purpose of its voyage through the waters of the coastal State. However, Article 28(2) is not applicable to inward/outward-bound navigation.[33]

2.4 The right of innocent passage of foreign warships

The right of innocent passage of foreign warships is one of the most contentious issues concerning navigational rights. On the one hand, this right is of paramount importance for major naval powers in order to secure global naval mobility. On the other hand, the passage of foreign warships through the territorial sea may be a threat to the security of the coastal State. These two groups of States thus have different views as to whether or not foreign warships have the right of innocent passage in international law.

The right of innocent passage of foreign warships was at issue in the 1949 *Corfu Channel* case. Albania asserted that it could regulate the passage of foreign warships in its territorial waters. In contrast, the United Kingdom maintained that warships possess a right of innocent passage through the territorial sea of another State. While the ICJ accepted the right of innocent passage of foreign warships in straits used for international navigation, it did not directly address the question whether foreign warships have the same right of innocent passage in the territorial sea.[34] It may have to be accepted that customary international law is obscure on this subject.

The Territorial Sea Convention contains no provision relating to the right of innocent passage of foreign warships.[35] Likewise the LOSC contains no explicit provision on this particular issue. Nonetheless, three points must be noted. First, Article 17 of the LOSC, which provides the right of innocent passage, is under the rubric 'Rules Applicable to All Ships'. It can be presumed, therefore, that Article 17 is

---

[32] O'Connell, n 11, Vol II, 874; G Fitzmaurice, 'Some Results of the Geneva Conference on the Law of the Sea: Part I—The Territorial Sea and Contiguous Zone and Related Topics' (1959) 8 *International and Comparative Law Quarterly* 107.

[33] LOSC, n 14, Art 28(3).

[34] *Corfu Channel*, n 16, 27–8. However, several members of the Court addressed this question. See ibid, Dissenting Opinion of Judge Azevedo, 99; ibid, Dissenting Opinion of Judge Krylov, 74; and ibid, Separate Opinion of Judge Alvares, 46–7.

[35] These points mentioned in relation to the LOSC are also relevant to the 1958 Convention on the Territorial Sea and Contiguous Zone.

applicable to all ships, including warships. Second, Article 20 requires submarines and other underwater vehicles to navigate on the surface and to show their flag in the territorial sea. Third, Article 19(2) sets out a catalogue of activities which render passage non-innocent. Some of these activities, such as any exercise or practice with weapons, the take-off or landing of aircraft, and the launching or receiving of any military device, relate specifically, if not exclusively, to warships. All in all, those provisions suggest that warships have the right of innocent passage.[36]

On the other hand, State practice is sharply divided on this subject. Some 40 States, mainly developing States, require prior notification or prior authorization of the passage of warships through their territorial sea.[37] By way of example, upon ratification of the LOSC in 1996, the People's Republic of China declared as follows:

The People's Republic of China reaffirms that the provisions of the United Nations Convention on the Law of the Sea concerning innocent passage through the territorial sea shall not prejudice the right of a coastal State to request, in accordance with its laws and regulations, a foreign State to obtain advance approval from or give prior notification to the coastal State for the passage of its warships through the territorial sea of the coastal State.

Article 6 of Chinese Law on the Territorial Sea and the Contiguous Zone of 25 February 1992 stipulates that: 'To enter the territorial sea of the People's Republic of China, foreign military ships must obtain permission from the Government of the People's Republic of China.'[38]

Some other States, such as Germany, Italy, the Netherlands and the United Kingdom, expressed the view that claims to prior authorization and prior notification are at variance with the LOSC. The United States has also protested against the claims to both prior authorization and prior notification.[39] In this regard, it is of particular interest to note that paragraph 2 of the 1989 Uniform Interpretation of

---

[36] This interpretation is supported by writers, including ED Brown, *The International Law of the Sea Introductory Manual* (Dartmouth Aldershot 1994) Vol I, 66; Berdud, n 25, 14–15; RR Churchill, 'The Impact of State Practice on the Jurisdictional Framework contained in the LOS Convention' in AG Oude Elferink (ed), *Stability and Change in the Law of the Sea: The Role of the LOS Convention* (Nijhoff Leiden 2005) 91, 111–12; R-J Dupuy, 'The Sea under National Competence' in Dupuy and Vignes (eds), n 6, Vol 1, 259; DHN Johnson, 'Innocent Passage, Transit Passage' in R Bernhardt (ed), *Encyclopaedia of Public International Law* (North-Holland Amsterdam 1989) Vol 11, 152; Z Keyuan, 'Innocent Passage for Warships: The Chinese Doctrine and Practice' (1998) 29 *Ocean Development and International Law* 211; L Lucchini and M Voelckel, *Droit de la mer*. Vol 2: *Navigation et Pêche* (Pedone Paris 1996) 250–5; Rothwell and Stephens, n 29, 268; T Treves, 'Codification du droit international et pratique des Etats dans le droit de la mer' (1990) 223 *Recueil des Cours* 3, 116–17; P Vincent, *Droit de la mer* (Larcier Bruxelles 2008) 51–2.

[37] For a list of States restricting innocent passage of foreign warships, see JA Roach and RW Smith, *Excessive Maritime Claims* (3rd edn Nijhoff Leiden 2012) 50–1; Churchill, n 36, 112–13; WK Agyebeng, 'Theory in Search of Practice: The Right of Innocent Passage in the Territorial Sea' (2006) 39 *Cornell International Law Journal* 371, 396–8.

[38] Chinese Law on the Territorial Sea and the Contiguous Zone (25 February 1992) (1992) 21 *Law of the Sea Bulletin* 25.

[39] Roach and Smith, n 37, 243–51; Churchill, n 36, 114.

the Rules of International Law Governing Innocent Passage between the USA and the USSR states that:

All ships, including warships, regardless of cargo, armament or means of propulsion, enjoy the right of innocent passage through the territorial sea in accordance with international law, for which neither prior notification nor authorisation is required.

While the Uniform Interpretation applies only to these two States, the influence of these two naval powers cannot be neglected politically.

In approaching the question as to whether prior notification or prior authorization is compatible with the LOSC, a distinction must be drawn between the requirement of prior notification and that of prior authorization. There may be some scope to argue that the requirement of prior notification could fall within the scope of Article 21(1)(a) of the LOSC which allows the coastal State to adopt laws and regulations in respect of the safety of navigation and the regulation of maritime traffic.[40] If this is the case, the right of innocent passage of foreign warships and the requirement of prior notification by the coastal State could be compatible. However, the legality of prior authorization seems to be questionable.[41]

In any case, coastal State action against foreign warships is qualified by the sovereign immunity afforded to warships. However, the coastal State may require any warship to leave its territorial sea if the warship does not comply with its laws and regulations.[42] Under Article 31 of the LOSC, the flag State is also obliged to bear international responsibility for any loss or damage to the coastal State resulting from the non-compliance by a warship or other governmental ship operated for non-commercial purposes with the laws and regulations of the costal State concerning passage through the territorial sea or with the provisions of the LOSC or other rules of international law.

2.5 The right of innocent passage of foreign nuclear-powered ships and ships carrying inherently dangerous or noxious substances

The right of innocent passage of foreign nuclear-powered ships and ships carrying inherently dangerous materials, such as long-lived highly radioactive and radiotoxic nuclear materials, creates particular sensitivity associated with environmental protection of coastal States. These materials could cause very serious contamination of the marine environment and endanger coastal populations in the event of an accident. This raises the issue as to how to reconcile navigational

---

[40] See also Churchill, n 36, 114.   [41] Ibid, 113–14; Rothwell and Stephens, n 29, 223.
[42] LOSC, n 14, Art 30.

interests of user States and the environmental interests of coastal States.[43] When the *Akatsuki Maru*, a Japanese vessel carrying around 1,000 kg of plutonium, was in transit in 1992 from France to Japan, travelling around the Cape of Good Hope, then going eastward south of Australia and New Zealand, and finally turning north through the Pacific Islands to Japan, South Africa, and Portugal requested that the vessel stay out of their EEZs. When the *Pacific Pintail* carrying 28 logs of high-level vitrified nuclear wastes in glass blocks was in transit in 1995, States along the route (Brazil, Argentina, Chile, South Africa, Nauru, and Kiribati) purported to ban the vessel from their EEZs.[44]

The key provision on this subject is Article 23 of the LOSC.[45] As is apparent from the expression 'when exercising the right of innocent passage', foreign nuclear-powered ships and ships carrying hazardous cargoes enjoy the right of innocent passage through the territorial sea. The coastal State may require 'tankers, nuclear-powered ships and ships carrying nuclear or other inherently dangerous or noxious substances or materials' to confine their passage to such sea lanes and traffic separation schemes as it may designate or prescribe for the regulation of the passage of ships.[46] In this regard, the question arises whether coastal States may require prior notification or prior authorization of the passage of foreign nuclear-powered ships and ships carrying hazardous cargoes through their territorial sea. This issue became a matter of extensive debate when drafting the 1989 Basel Convention on the Control of Transboundary Movements of Hazardous Wastes and Their Disposal (Basel Convention).[47] Article 6(1) of the Basel Convention obliges the State of export to notify the competent authority of the States concerned of any proposed transboundary movement of hazardous wastes or other wastes. Under Article 6(4), the State of export shall not allow the transboundary movement to commence until it has received the written consent of the State of transit.[48] Some States considered that under the Basel Convention, the coastal State is not entitled to require prior notification or the consent for the innocent passage of a vessel carrying hazardous

---

[43] See generally JM Van Dyke, 'The Legal Regime Governing Sea Transport of Ultrahazardous Radioactive Materials' (2002) 33 *Ocean Development and International Law* 77. See also M Roscini, 'The Navigational Rights of Nuclear Ships' (2002) 15 *Leiden Journal of International Law* 251.

[44] JM Van Dyke, 'Applying the Precautionary Principle to Ocean Shipments of Radioactive Materials' (1996) 27 *Ocean Development and International Law* 379, 380, and 386.

[45] LOSC, n 14, Art 23 refers to 'international agreements'. Examples of international agreements regulating the passage of nuclear-powered ships or ships carrying hazardous substances include the 1962 Convention on the Liability of Operators of Nuclear Ships, the 1973 International Convention for the Prevention of Pollution from Ships as modified by the 1978 Protocol (hereinafter MARPOL), and the 1974 International Convention for the Safety of Life at Sea (SOLAS).

[46] LOSC, n 14, Art 22(1) and (2).

[47] See also T Mizukami, *The Law of the Sea* (Yushindo Tokyo 2005) 70–1 (in Japanese).

[48] See also 1989 Basel Convention on the Control of Transboundary Movements of Hazardous Wastes and Their Disposal, Art 4(12) (hereinafter Basel Convention).

wastes.[49] Other States took a more nuanced view, however. When ratifying the Basel Convention in 1991, for instance, Mexico confirmed that the Convention duly protects its rights as a coastal State in the areas subject to its national jurisdiction, including the territorial sea, the EEZ, and the continental shelf and, in so far as it is relevant, its airspace, and the exercise in those areas of its legislative and administrative competence in relation to the protection and preservation of the environment, as recognized by international law and, in particular, the law of the sea.[50] Similar declarations were made by Colombia, Ecuador, Uruguay, and Venezuela.[51]

In practice, some States require prior notification or authorization of the passage of foreign nuclear-powered ships and ships carrying hazardous cargoes through their territorial sea.[52] A question analogous to that of foreign warships has been raised with regard to the navigation of foreign nuclear-powered ships and ships carrying hazardous cargoes. If the coastal State is not entitled to know about the passage of those ships, arguably that State cannot exercise its right set out in Articles 22(1) and (2) of the LOSC. One can thus argue that a requirement of prior notification would not be contrary to the LOSC.[53] However, the compatibility of a requirement of prior authorization with the LOSC is questionable since such a requirement amounts to denial of the right of innocent passage of foreign nuclear-powered ships and ships carrying hazardous cargoes.[54]

3 Navigational Rights through International Straits

3.1 The right of transit passage

The LOSC provides for two types of navigational rights in international straits: the right of transit passage and the right of non-suspendable innocent passage.

The right of transit passage is defined in Article 38(2). As shown in the second sentence of this provision, transit passage includes lateral and inward/

---

[49] See eg the declarations of the United Kingdom, Italy, Japan, and Germany. The declarations to the Basel Convention are available at <https://treaties.un.org/pages/ViewDetails.aspx?src=TREATY&mtdsg_no=XXVII-3&chapter=27&lang=en#9>.

[50] Ibid.   [51] Ibid.

[52] Churchill, n 36, 115–16. See also T Scovazzi, 'The Evolution of International Law of the Sea: New Issues, New Challenges' (2000) 286 *Recueil des Cours* 39, 157–8; Roach and Smith, n 37, 259–62.

[53] Van Dyke, n 43, 87; M Roscini, 'The Navigational Rights of Nuclear Ships' (2002) 15 *Leiden Journal of International Law* 251, 253.

[54] Churchill, n 36, 115; K Hakapää and EJ Molenaar, 'Innocent Passage: Past and Present' (1999) 23 *Marine Policy* 131, 144.

outward-bound passage. The right of transit passage in international straits differs from the right of innocent passage in the territorial sea in four respects. First, Article 38(1) makes it clear that all ships and aircraft enjoy the right of transit passage. It is clear, therefore that warships enjoy the right of transit passage. Second, the right of transit passage includes overflight by all aircraft, including military aircraft. Third, unlike the right of innocent passage through the territorial sea in general, there shall be no suspension of transit passage.[55] Fourth, the LOSC provides no explicit obligation for submarines to navigate on the surface and to show their flag. Article 39(1)(c) provides that ships and aircraft, while exercising the right of transit passage, shall 'refrain from any activities other than those incident to their normal modes of continuous and expeditious transit unless rendered necessary by *force majeure* or by distress'. Arguably, the normal mode for submarines to transit is submerged navigation.[56] Article 38(2) further stipulates that transit passage means the exercise 'in accordance with this Part [III]' of the freedom of navigation and overflight. It follows that transit passage is to be subject only to provisions in Part III. There is no cross-reference to the specific provision on innocent passage which requires on-surface navigation. This interpretation is consistent with the *travaux préparatoires* of the LOSC.[57] Accordingly, it can be argued that submarines and other underwater vehicles in transit passage are not required to navigate on the surface and to show their flag.

The regime of transit passage includes a number of duties for ships and aircraft. First, ships and aircraft are obliged to comply with four duties enunciated in Article 39(1) of the LOSC:

(a) proceed without delay through or over the strait;
(b) refrain from any threat or use of force against the sovereignty, territorial integrity or political independence of States bordering the strait, or in any other manner in violation of the principles of international law embodied in the Charter of the United Nations;
(c) refrain from any activities other than those incident to their normal modes of continuous and expeditious transit unless rendered necessary by *force majeure* or by distress; and
(d) comply with other relevant provisions of this Part.

Second, ships in transit passage are under the duties to:

---

[55] LOSC, n 14, Art 44. [56] *Virginia Commentaries*, Vol II, 342.
[57] H Caminos, 'The Legal Regime of Straits in the 1982 United Nations Convention on the Law of the Sea' (1987) 205 *Recueil des Cours* 9, 155-8.

(i) comply with generally accepted international regulations, procedures, and practice for safety at sea, including the International Regulations for Preventing Collisions at Sea;[58]

(ii) comply with generally accepted international regulations, procedures and practices for the prevention, reduction, and control of pollution from ships;[59]

(iii) refrain from carrying out any research or survey activities without the prior authorization of the States bordering straits;[60]

(iv) respect applicable sea lanes and traffic separation schemes;[61] and

(v) comply with law and regulations adopted by States bordering a strait under Article 42 (1) of the LOSC.[62]

Third, in accordance with Article 39(3)(a) and (b), aircraft in transit passage shall (a) observe the Rules of the Air established by the International Civil Aviation Organization as they apply to civil aircraft; and (b) at all times monitor the radio frequency assigned by the competent internationally designated air traffic control authority or the appropriate international distress radio frequency.

3.2 The regulation of the right of transit passage by States bordering straits

The right of transit passage is not free from the regulation of States bordering straits. A State bordering a strait has a right to adopt laws and regulations relating to transit passage in accordance with Article 42(1) of the LOSC. At the same time, States bordering straits are required to give due publicity to all such laws and regulations in accordance with Article 41(3) of the LOSC. However, the legislative jurisdiction of the State bordering a strait is qualified by Article 42(2) in two respects. First, the laws and regulations of a State bordering an international strait 'shall not discriminate in form or in fact among foreign ships'. Second, the application of the laws and regulations shall not 'have the practical effect of denying, hampering or impairing the right of transit passage'. In addition, a State bordering a strait may designate sea lanes and prescribe traffic separation schemes for navigation in straits where necessary to promote the safe passage of ships pursuant to Article 41(1). However, further consideration must be given to the question as to whether, under Part III of

---

[58] LOSC, n 14, Art 39(2)(a). SOLAS, n 45, and its 1988 Protocol would fall within 'generally accepted international regulations'.

[59] LOSC, n 14, Art 39(2)(b). MARPOL, n 45, would be included in international regulations referred to in this provision.

[60] LOSC, n 14, Art 40.   [61] Ibid, Art 41(7).   [62] Ibid, Art 42(4). See also ibid, Art 42(5).

the LOSC, a State bordering a strait has a right to introduce a compulsory pilotage system in an international strait.[63]

Foreign ships exercising the right of transit passage shall comply with laws and regulations of the coastal State.[64] An issue in this connection is whether, in the case the violation of the municipal law of the State bordering a strait, that State could terminate the right of transit passage unilaterally. The language of Article 42(2) of the LOSC suggests that a States bordering a strait may not directly deny the right of transit passage merely on grounds of breach of its municipal law.[65] In the case of a violation of the laws and regulations referred to in Article 42(1)(a) and (b), however, Article 233 explicitly allows the State bordering a strait to exercise its enforcement jurisdiction.

3.3 Non-suspendable innocent passage

The right of innocent passage applies to straits used for international navigation which are excluded from the application of Article 38(1) of the LOSC; or between a part of the high seas or an EEZ and the territorial sea of a foreign State.[66] Unlike the right of innocent passage through the territorial sea, there shall be no suspension of innocent passage through international straits.[67] As with innocent passage through the territorial sea, aircraft do not enjoy the freedom of overflight. Further, submarines and other underwater vehicles are required to navigate on surface and to show their flag in the exercise of the right of non-suspendable innocent passage.

4 Navigational Rights in the Archipelagic Waters

4.1 The right of innocent passage

In archipelagic waters, States enjoy the right of innocent passage and that of archipelagic sea lanes passage. The right of innocent passage in archipelagic waters is essentially identical to the right of innocent passage in the territorial sea.[68] Accordingly, the archipelagic State may temporarily suspend the right of innocent passage in

---

[63] See also Chapter 6 in this volume. [64] LOSC, n 14, Art 42(4).
[65] *Virginia Commentaries*, Vol II, 377; JN Moore, 'The Regime of Straits and the Third United Nations Conference on the Law of the Sea' (1980) 74 *American Journal of International Law* 77, 103.
[66] LOSC, n 14, Art 45(1).   [67] Ibid, Art 45(2).   [68] Ibid, Art 52.

archipelagic waters if such suspension is essential for the protection of its security.[69] Although Part IV of the LOSC contains no provision concerning submarines and other underwater vehicles, submarines, and other underwater vehicles will arguably be required to navigate on the surface and to show their flag in archipelagic waters. There is no right of overflight in archipelagic waters.

4.2 The right of archipelagic sea lanes passage

In addition to the right of innocent passage, all ships and aircraft can enjoy the more extensive right of archipelagic sea lanes passage through archipelagic waters. This right is defined in Article 53(3) of the LOSC. The principal elements of the right of archipelagic sea lines passage can be summarized as follows. First, as with the right of transit passage, the right of archipelagic sea lanes passage applies between one part of the high seas or an EEZ and another part of the high seas or an EEZ. Second, all ships and aircraft enjoy the right of archipelagic sea lanes passage in such sea lanes and air routes.[70] In this regard, the archipelagic State may designate archipelagic sea lanes and air routes in accordance with the relevant provisions of LOSC Article 53.[71] The right of archipelagic sea lanes passage contains the rights of overflight by aircraft. In common with the right of transit passage, foreign warships and military aircraft have the right of archipelagic sea lanes passage. Third, like the right of transit passage, archipelagic sea lanes passage is defined as the exercise of the rights of navigation and overflight solely for the purpose of continuous, expeditious, and unobstructed transit.

Since Articles 39, 40, 42, and 44 of the LOSC apply *mutatis mutandis* to archipelagic sea lanes passage,[72] ships and aircraft during their passage are under the duties contained in those provisions. Article 53(5) of the LOSC further requires that ships and aircraft in archipelagic sea lanes passage shall not deviate more than 25 nm to either side of the axis line (ie the centre line of a sea lane) during passage. This provision also provides that such ships and aircraft shall not navigate closer to the coast than 10 per cent of the distance between the nearest points on islands bordering the sea lane. In this regard, two different interpretations can be identified.

According to one interpretation, the phrase 'the 10 per cent of the distance between the nearest points on islands' means the whole width of the channel between the bordering islands.[73] If the channel is 40 nm, for example, the two prohibited zones would each measure 4 nm. As a consequence, the sea lane would be 32 nm wide, and the maximum deviation from the sea lane's axis line would be 16 nm. According

---

[69] Ibid, Art 52(2).   [70] Ibid, Art 53(2).   [71] See also Chapter 7 in this volume.
[72] LOSC, n 14, Art 54.
[73] V Prescott and C Schofield, *The Maritime Political Boundaries of the World* (2nd edn Nijhoff Leiden 2005) 179.

to this interpretation, only if the channel between islands is at least 62.5 nm wide, will the full deviation of 25 nm on either side of the axis line be permissible.

On a second interpretation, the formula embodied in LOSC Article 53(5) means 10 per cent of the distance from the axis line to the nearest island. In this case, the narrowest channel, which allows ships and aircraft to deviate by 25 nm from the axis of the sea lane, is 55.6 nm wide. In 1996, Indonesia applied the 10 per cent rule in this way in designating its archipelagic sea lanes, and in 1998 the Maritime Safety Committee of the IMO accepted Indonesia's submission. Thus this interpretation has been supported by the IMO.[74]

5 Navigational Rights in the EEZ

In the EEZ, all States enjoy the freedom of navigation. This is clear from Article 58(1) of the LOSC. At the same time, Article 58(3) provides that States must 'have due regard to the rights and duties of the coastal State and shall comply with the laws and regulations adopted by the coastal State in accordance with the provisions of this Convention and other rules of international law in so far as they are not incompatible with this Part [V]'. Consequently, unlike in the high seas, the freedom of navigation may be qualified by the coastal State's jurisdiction in the EEZ. For instance, overflight in the EEZ for the purposes of the exploration and exploitation is subject to the permission of the coastal State. Navigation of foreign vessels through an EEZ is also subject to regulation of the coastal State with respect to marine pollution. In addition to this, shipping in the contiguous zone, which overlaps with the first 12 nm of the EEZ, will be subject to coastal State jurisdiction under Article 33. In this sense, the freedom of navigation enjoyed by foreign States in the EEZ is not the exactly same as in the high seas.

A further issue to be considered is whether vessels providing bunkering services to fishing vessels in the EEZ can be considered to be exercising the freedom of navigation.[75] This issue was discussed in the 1999 *M/V 'Saiga' (No 2)*

---

[74] Ibid, 180. See also R Warner, 'Implementing the Archipelagic Regime in the International Maritime Organisation' in DR Rothwell and S Bateman (eds), *Navigational Rights and Freedoms and the New Law of the Sea* (Nijhoff The Hague 2000) 170, 179–84.

[75] See generally D Anderson, 'The Regulation of Fishing and Related Activities in Exclusive Economic Zones' in E Franckx and P Gautier (eds), *The Exclusive Economic Zone and the United Nations Convention on the Law of the Sea, 1982-2000: A Preliminary Assessment of State Practice* (Bruylant Brussels 2003) 31, 31–49.

case between Saint Vincent and Grenadines and Guinea.[76] Saint Vincent and the Grenadines contended that bunkering in the EEZ by ships flying its flag constituted the exercise of the freedom of navigation and other internationally lawful uses of the sea related to the freedom of navigation, as provided for in Articles 56 and 58 of the LOSC. In contrast, Guinea maintained that bunkering was not an exercise of the freedom of navigation or any of the internationally lawful uses of the sea related to freedom of navigation, as provided for in the Convention, but a commercial activity.[77] In this case, the International Tribunal for the Law of the Sea (ITLOS) did not make any finding on this issue since it already found that in applying its customs laws in the EEZ, Guinea acted in a manner contrary to the LOSC.[78] In the 2014 M/V 'Virginia G' case between Panama and Guinea-Bissau, however, the ITLOS ruled that the regulation by a coastal State of bunkering of foreign vessels fishing in its EEZ is among those measures which the coastal State may take in its EEZ to conserve and manage its living resources under Article 56 of the LSOC read together with Article 62(4) of the Convention.[79] At the same time, ITLOS added that the coastal State does not have such competence with regard to other bunkering activities, unless otherwise determined in accordance with the LOSC.[80]

State practice with regard to bunkering is not uniform.[81] For example, the Act on the Protection of the Marine Environment and Ocean Space under Belgian Jurisdiction of 20 January 1999 stipulates that industrial and commercial activities in the Belgium ocean space, including its EEZ, require a permit or authorization from the Minister.[82] In United Kingdom legislation, however, the transfer of oil between two ships is regulated by the Merchant Shipping Act 1995 for environmental purposes, but it covers transfers only within internal waters and the territorial sea.[83] Thus it seems to follow that fishing vessels remain free to supply and to receive bunkers in the EEZ.[84] On this issue, a commentator argues that when bunkering serves navigation, the rules on navigation apply, but when it serves fishing in the EEZ, rules on fishing apply.[85] This view is in line with the M/V 'Virginia G' judgment.

---

[76] M/V 'Saiga' (No 2) (Saint Vincent and the Grenadines v Guinea) (Judgment) [1999] ITLOS Rep 10.
[77] Ibid, [137].   [78] Ibid, [136].
[79] M/V 'Virginia G' (Panama v Guinea-Bissau), Judgment of the International Tribunal for the Law of the Sea (14 April 2014) [208]–[217].
[80] Ibid, [223].   [81] Anderson, n 75, 39–42.
[82] 1999 Act on the Protection of the Marine Environment and Ocean Space under Belgian Jurisdiction (Belgium) Art 25(1)(v) and (vi). 'The Minister' means the Minister or Secretary of State whose portfolio includes protection of the marine environment under Art 2(20) of the Act.
[83] Merchant Shipping Act 1995 (UK) § 130, available at <http://www.legislation.gov.uk/ukpga/1995/21/section/130>.
[84] Anderson, n 75, 42.   [85] Ibid, 49.

6 Navigational Rights on the High Seas

As the high seas are open to all, all States, whether coastal or landlocked, enjoy the freedom of navigation.[86] Concerning landlocked States, LOSC Article 125 explicitly provides that: 'Land-locked States shall have the right of access to and from the sea for the purpose of exercising the rights provided for in this Convention including those relating to the freedom of the high seas' which include the freedom of navigation. A key element of the freedom of navigation is that ships shall sail under the flag of one State only and they are under the exclusive jurisdiction of the flag State. The principle of the exclusive jurisdiction of the flag State is a corollary of the freedom of the high seas and the requirement of the submission of the high seas to law.[87] The principle of exclusive jurisdiction of the flag State ensures the freedom of activities of vessels, including the freedom of navigation, by preventing any interference by other States with vessels flying its flag on the high seas. At the same time, the flag State has the responsibility to ensure compliance with national and international law of vessels flying its flags on the high seas.

The freedom of navigation in the high seas is not without any limitations. Article 87(2) of the LOSC provides that freedoms of the high seas 'shall be exercised by all States with due regard for the interests of other States in their exercise of the freedom of the high seas, and also with due regard for the rights under this Convention with respect to activities in the Area'. In appropriate circumstances, the freedom of navigation on the high seas can be restricted by the right of hot pursuit[88] and the right of visit.[89] Further, the freedom of navigation may be qualified by specific treaties, such as 1988 UN Convention against Illicit Traffic in Narcotic Drugs and Psychotropic Substances and the 2005 Protocol to the Convention for the Suppression of Unlawful Acts (2005 SUA Protocol) against the Safety of Maritime Navigation. However, no interference under any circumstances is permitted with regard to warships and governmental-vessels used only for non-commercial purposes.

---

[86] LOSC, n 14, Art 87(1). See also Chapter 10 in this volume.
[87] For a discussion of the role of the flag State, see Chapter 14 in this volume.
[88] LOSC, n 14, Art 111.
[89] Ibid, Art 110. For an examination of physical interference with the navigation of foreign vessels see Chapters 14 and 10 in this volume.

7 Further Developments

Multiple navigational regimes exist under the LOSC, that is, the right of innocent passage, the right of non-suspendable innocent passage, the right of transit passage, the right of archipelagic sea lane passage, and the freedom of navigation and that the contents of navigational rights differ according to each jurisdictional zone. These regimes are a product of history and their scope may change over time. Indeed, the right of transit passage and the right of archipelagic sea lane passage are newly created rights under the LOSC. The navigational rights rest on a careful balance of navigational interests of shipping States and interests of coastal States.[90] The balance may need reconsideration in the future since international relations surrounding the oceans are always changing. In this regard, two issues merit highlighting.

The first issue concerns the balance of navigational interests and marine environmental protection. Owing to the growing environmental awareness, coastal States may claim further regulation of the passage of foreign vessels through the territorial sea, international straits, and the archipelagic waters to protect their offshore environment. The compulsory pilotage system adopted by Australia in the Torres Strait and Great North East Channel is a case in point.[91] As shown in the protests of coastal States against passage of foreign vessels carrying inherently dangerous substances through their territorial seas and EEZs, conflicts may arise with regard to navigational interests and marine environmental protection. In order to address this issue, cooperation between shipping States and coastal States is important.

The second issue relates to the reconciliation between navigational interests and security interests. In order to suppress unlawful activities at sea and to prevent the proliferation of weapons of mass destruction, the freedom of navigation is increasingly compromised via special treaties, including the 2005 SUA Protocol, political initiatives, such as the Proliferation Security Initiative (PSI), and United Nations Security Council (UNSC) Resolutions. By way of example, UNSC Resolution 1874 (2009) called upon all Member States to inspect vessels, with the consent of the flag State, on the high seas, if they have information that provides reasonable grounds to believe that the cargo of such vessels contains items the supply, sale, transfer, or export of which is prohibited by Resolution 1718 (2006) or by paragraph 9 or 10 of this resolution.[92] If the flag State does not consent to inspection on the high seas,

---

[90] It must be noted that most shipping States are also coastal States and that they have interests of shipping States and those of coastal States at the same time.

[91] See Chapter 5 in this volume.

[92] UNSC Res S/RES/1874 (12 June 2009) [12]. UNSC Res 1718 (2006) (14 October 2006) decided that all Member States shall prevent supply to the Democratic People's Republic of Korea certain arms and materials.

it shall direct the vessel to proceed to an appropriate and convenient port for the required inspection by the local authorities.[93]

Overall, attaining the right balance between navigational rights, marine environmental protection and international security should be an important issue when considering the future development of navigational rights in the international law of the sea.

---

[93] UNSC Res S/RES/1874 (12 June 2009) [13].

25
MARINE SCIENTIFIC RESEARCH

TIM STEPHENS AND DONALD R ROTHWELL

1 INTRODUCTION

It is often said that humankind knows less about the oceans than the heavens.[*] While it is certainly the case that much remains unknown, progress in marine scientific research (MSR), especially in recent decades, has greatly enhanced our understanding of the oceanic environment. This is well demonstrated by advances in climate science that have provided insights into the role of the oceans in the global climate system. Beyond the study of ocean circulation, a staple oceanographic concern, scientific research in ocean space is directed to a multitude of topics. These include seabed topography (ie bathymetry, which is critical for drawing nautical charts), the geology and geomorphology of the seabed (for locating hydrocarbon resources, and to understand tectonic processes), and fisheries and marine ecosystems (for improving fisheries management and for biological prospecting ('bioprospecting') for genetic resources, both for pure research and

---

[*] This is a revised and updated version of chapter 14 extracted from DR Rothwell and T Stephens, *The International Law of the Sea* (Hart Oxford 2010) 320. The comments provided by Alex G Oude Elferink and Karen N Scott on an earlier version of this chapter are acknowledged.

for commercial purposes[1]). Improved scientific understanding of human impacts on many aspects of the oceanic environment has been a particularly important impetus for giving the law of the sea an increasingly environmental focus. In this regard, Chapter 17 of Agenda 21,[2] emphasizes throughout its plan for integrated management and sustainable development of the oceans that scientific capacity should be enhanced, particularly in developing States, and that sound science should be at the centre of assessments of environmental risks, and the making of management decisions.

The subjects of marine scientific inquiry are seldom discrete, in that research on one phenomenon (such as the distribution of a fishery) often sheds important light on another (such as the biological effects of pollutants). Likewise, the purposes to which scientific research may be put often overlap. For instance, knowledge of the geomorphology of continental margins is of interest not only because it is relevant to the study of the seismic activity responsible for catastrophes such as the 2004 Indian Ocean tsunami,[3] or to assist in the Indian Ocean search for Malaysian Airlines Flight 370 in 2014,[4] but also because physical oceanographic data must be gathered in order for a coastal State to establish the outer limits of its continental shelf beyond 200 nautical miles (nm), pursuant to Article 76 of the 1982 United Nations Convention on the Law of the Sea (LOSC).[5] This latter point highlights the difficulty in drawing a distinction between 'pure' or 'fundamental' research on the one hand, and 'applied' research on the other. In this context the military dimensions of oceans research should not be ignored, especially when it is recalled that the LOSC was negotiated against the backdrop of the Cold War. The reality is that there is considerable cross-over between pure and applied research, with pure science often forming the basis for practical oceans management decisions, and for further, commercially oriented, research. One consequence of this has been increasing regulation of MSR by coastal States within their exclusive economic zones (EEZs) and continental shelves, which has in turn raised sensitivities over the conduct of MSR within those maritime areas.

---

[1] See generally D Leary et al, 'Marine Genetic Resources: A Review of Scientific and Commercial Interest' (2009) 33 *Marine Policy* 183.

[2] United Nations Conference on Environment and Development, *Protection of the Oceans, all Kinds of Seas, Including Enclosed and Semi-Enclosed Seas, and Coastal Areas and the Protection, Rational Use and Development of their Living Resources*, UN Doc A/CONF.151/26 (Vol II) (13 August 1992), available at <http://www.un.org/depts/los/consultative_process/documents/A21-Ch17.htm>.

[3] The Indian Ocean tsunami resulted in the death of a quarter of a million people in landmasses surrounding the Indian Ocean, and was caused by an exceptionally large undersea earthquake that struck off the west coast of Sumatra on 26 December 2004.

[4] WHF Smith and KM Marks, 'Seafloor in the Malaysian Airlines Flight MH370 Search Area' (2014) 95 *Eos, Transactions, American Geophysical Union* 173.

[5] 1982 United Nations Convention on the Law of the Sea (hereinafter LOSC).

Compared to the regime of the 1958 Conventions,[6] the LOSC is a major advance in the promotion and regulation of MSR. The Preamble to the LOSC makes clear that one of its key purposes is to promote the '*study*, protection and preservation of the marine environment',[7] a formulation that highlights the critical linkages between MSR and the sustainable development of ocean space. Part XIII of the Convention sets out an 'exceptionally comprehensive'[8] body of rules to facilitate and regulate MSR. This chapter commences with consideration of the definition of MSR, followed by a brief assessment of the development of the regime dealing with MSR. Detailed consideration will be given to the MSR regime contained within the LOSC from a zonal and operational perspective, after which there will be an analysis of how MSR is dealt with in complementary legal regimes. A brief review will be undertaken of current coastal State legislative frameworks regulating MSR, before concluding comments on future issues confronting the regime.

2 Defining Marine Scientific Research

The term MSR is not defined in the LOSC; however, international law has in recent years begun to consider in more detail the parameters of 'scientific research', and accordingly the interaction between science and international law. In 2014, the International Court of Justice (ICJ) for the first time considered the meaning of the term in the context of the 1946 International Convention for the Regulation of Whaling. In *Whaling in the Antarctic*,[9] the Court declined to give a definition of scientific research,[10] preferring to focus on the elements comprising 'for the purposes of scientific research' in order to adjudge whether Japan's conduct of its Southern Ocean 'special permit' whaling program was consistent with Article VIII of the Convention.[11]

---

[6] The term 'Geneva Conventions on the Law of the Sea' include the four conventions concluded at the 1958 Geneva conference.

[7] LOSC, n 5, Preamble, Fourth Recital (emphasis added).

[8] P Birnie, 'Law of the Sea and Ocean Resources: Implications for Marine Scientific Research' (1995) 10 *International Journal of Marine and Coastal Law* 229.

[9] *Whaling in the Antarctic (Australia v Japan; New Zealand intervening)*, Judgment of the International Court of Justice, General List No 148 (31 March 2014).

[10] Ibid, [86].

[11] Ibid, [87]–[97] and [223]–[227]; see also discussion in Section 7 below. Some members of the ICJ cast doubt over whether the Court could properly define 'scientific research', observing the differences

The findings of the Court provide some guidance to an appreciation of the interpretation of the term MSR under the LOSC.

During the Third United Nations Conference on the Law of the Sea (UNCLOS III), various possible definitions of MSR were mooted, some which sought to restrict the term only to pure research, and others which encompassed all scientific studies in the oceans, including research connected with the exploitation of natural resources.[12] No definition was ultimately included in the LOSC because it was considered that the provisions in Part XIII adequately gave meaning to the concept.[13] In its ordinary sense, and the one adopted in this chapter, MSR means 'any form of scientific investigation, fundamental or applied, concerned with the marine environment, i.e. that has the marine environment as its object'[14] which is carried out in the oceans. As such, MSR will include physical oceanography, marine chemistry and biology, scientific ocean drilling and coring, geological and geophysical research, and other activities that have a scientific purpose.[15] So defined, MSR must be distinguished from research conducted at sea that has as its object non-marine environments, such as atmospheric or astronomical observation. Such research is not subject to the LOSC regime for MSR. Also not encompassed by the LOSC is MSR undertaken outside of the surface, water column, subsoil or seabed in the marine environment.[16] Despite the extensive use of *ex situ* research techniques, such as remote sensing from satellites that are increasingly displacing *in situ* ship-based methods for obtaining data on the marine environment, these are not addressed by Part XIII of the Convention nor do they fall within the reach of coastal State jurisdiction. Similar considerations apply to remote sensing from satellites over internal waters, the territorial sea, and archipelagic waters.

---

of opinion that existed over the term within the scientific community: see *Whaling in the Antarctic*, n 9, Dissenting Opinion of Judge Owada, [25]; and ibid, Separate Opinion of Judge Cançado Trindade, [74] who observed that '"Scientific research" is surrounded by uncertainties; it is undertaken on the basis of uncertainties'.

[12] *Virginia Commentaries*, Vol IV, 444–9.

[13] AHA Soons, 'Marine Scientific Research Provisions in the Convention on the Law of the Sea: Issues of Interpretation' in ED Brown and RR Churchill (eds), *The UN Convention on the Law of the Sea: Impact and Implementation* (Law of the Sea Institute Honolulu 1989) 365, 366.

[14] Birnie, n 8, 242.

[15] JA Roach and RW Smith, *Excessive Maritime Claims* (3rd edn Martinus Nijhoff Leiden 2012) 414.

[16] For a United States position on activities that are encompassed by MSR, see ibid, 415.

3 Development of the Regime for Marine Scientific Research

The 1958 Geneva Conventions provided the first opportunity for the international community to develop a comprehensive regime for MSR, but there was little substantive development in the law other than the provision of a broad legal framework. The 1958 Convention on the Territorial Sea and the Contiguous Zone does not deal with MSR, but it necessarily follows from the definition of the territorial sea as a zone in which the coastal State enjoys sovereignty in the seabed, subsoil, water column, and airspace,[17] that MSR could only be conducted by foreign States with coastal State consent. By contrast, the 1958 Convention on the High Seas effectively preserved the freedom of scientific research to the fullest extent. Although the Convention made no reference to MSR, it did broadly define high seas freedoms in Article 2 in a way that implicitly protected the freedom of scientific research beyond the limits of coastal State jurisdiction, which at the time meant ocean space beyond the territorial sea.[18] In relation to living resources, the 1958 Convention on Fishing and Conservation of the Living Resources of the High Seas encouraged greater levels of research, in emphasizing the importance of MSR to fisheries management. It referred to the importance of 'scientific findings' in devising and implementing measures to achieve optimum sustainable yield.[19]

More detailed provisions are to be found in the 1958 Convention on the Continental Shelf which sought, on the one hand, to safeguard the interests of coastal States by requiring that 'the consent of the coastal State shall be obtained in respect of any research concerning the continental shelf and undertaken there'.[20] On the other hand, it promoted fundamental research in providing that 'the coastal State shall not normally withhold its consent if the request is submitted by a qualified institution with a view to purely scientific research into the physical or biological characteristics of the continental shelf', subject to the right of the coastal State, 'if it so desires, to participate or to be represented in the research'.[21] Moreover, it was made clear to coastal States that activities directed at exploring or exploiting resources on the continental shelf should not result 'in any interference with fundamental oceanographic or other scientific research carried out with the intention of open publication'.[22] While the

---

[17] 1958 Convention on the Territorial Sea and the Contiguous Zone, Art 2.
[18] In its commentary on the draft article that was to become this provision, the ILC observed that MSR was an accepted freedom of the high seas even though not specifically referred to in the text: (1956) II *Yearbook of the International Law Commission* 278.
[19] 1958 Convention on Fishing and Conservation of the Living Resources of the High Seas, Art 7(2).
[20] 1958 Convention on the Continental Shelf, Art 5(8).   [21] Ibid.
[22] Ibid, Art 5(1).

Geneva Conventions sought to protect high seas scientific research, in practice this was limited over time because of the emergence of claims to exclusive fishing zones (EFZs), most of which post-dated these treaties. A necessary incident of EFZs was an assertion of sovereign rights over fisheries, and jurisdiction to regulate their taking, whether for economic or for research purposes.[23]

4 The LOSC Regime for Marine Scientific Research

The LOSC made a number of significant changes to the existing customary and conventional regime relating to MSR. These resulted in an expansion in the geographical extent, scope, and the content of coastal State jurisdiction over MSR.

4.1 The 'right' to conduct MSR

Part XIII of the LOSC begins by providing that all States (and not only parties to the LOSC), regardless of their geographical circumstances, and also competent international organizations, have the right to conduct MSR subject to the rights and duties of other States under the LOSC.[24] This is an important general statement of the right to conduct MSR not found in the Geneva Conventions. It is significant also in recognizing the right of intergovernmental organizations with particular competence in marine science, such as the Intergovernmental Oceanographic Commission (IOComm) of the United Nations Educational, Scientific and Cultural Organization (UNESCO), to undertake and to promote MSR.[25]

4.2 General provisions

The right to engage in MSR is supplemented by general principles set out in Article 240 and Article 241 of the LOSC that apply to oceanic research in all maritime

---

[23] Coastal State fisheries legislation applicable in the EEZ often requires foreign fishers to obtain licenses for the taking of any fish, whether for commercial or research purposes. See eg Fisheries Act 1996 (New Zealand) §§ 83, 89, and 97.

[24] LOSC, n 5, Art 238.   [25] See also ibid, Art 239.

zones. Article 240 requires that MSR shall (a) be conducted exclusively for peaceful purposes; (b) be conducted with appropriate scientific methods;[26] (c) not unjustifiably interfere with other legitimate uses of the sea and shall be duly respected in the course of such uses; and (d) be conducted in compliance with all relevant regulations adopted consistent with the LOSC, including those for the protection and preservation of the marine environment.

The LOSC is silent with respect to MSR conducted for military objectives. Although the requirement that research be conducted for peaceful purposes suggests that research serving military objectives is prohibited, Article 240(a) adds no additional disciplines to other similar provisions of the Convention, such as Article 88 which provides that the high seas 'shall be reserved for peaceful purposes'. Rather than imposing a blanket ban on the use of the oceans for military purposes, the effect of these provisions is to apply the general prohibition on the use of force except in self-defence, or where authorized by the United Nations Security Council under its Chapter VII powers.

The other three general principles referred to in Article 240 serve to reaffirm that the right to undertake MSR for legitimate scientific ends must be balanced against other lawful ocean activities, and must respect coastal State laws adopted consistently with the Convention, especially, but not only, those dealing with environmental protection. Also somewhat otiose is Article 241, which provides that MSR cannot be the legal basis for any claim to the marine environment or its resources. This reaffirms not only that areas beyond the limits of national jurisdiction (the high seas and the sea bed) cannot be subject to appropriation on the basis of MSR conducted there,[27] but is also protective of the sovereign rights of coastal States in the resources of the continental shelf and EEZ.[28]

The remaining provisions that round out the opening general principles for the conduct of MSR (Articles 242 to 244) are directed primarily to promoting international cooperation, especially in enhancing the flow of scientific knowledge gained from research to developing States where there is less capacity to fund and administer oceanographic programs. One of the key purposes of international cooperation in MSR is outlined in Article 242(2), which provides that States should allow other States a reasonable opportunity to obtain information necessary to prevent and control damage to the health and safety of persons and to the marine environment. As was noted by the United States during UNCLOS III, cooperation which allows States to understand ocean-driven processes such as the South Asian Monsoon can be vital not only to economic development, but to the very survival of societies dependent upon them.[29] This observation has added resonance today in the context

---

[26] This was a matter considered in the *Whaling in the Antarctic* case in considerable detail, albeit in the context of the International Convention for the Regulation of Whaling: *Whaling in the Antarctic*, n 9, [127]–[227].

[27] See also LOSC, n 5, Arts 89 and 137(1).   [28] *Virginia Commentaries*, Vol IV, 464.

[29] Ibid, 469.

of human-induced climate change which is having a variety of effects on the oceans, and has the potential to shift ocean circulation systems, leading to major changes in regional climate and weather patterns.[30]

Further articles of a general character are found towards the conclusion of Part XIII. These include a provision addressing the issue of liability, which makes researching States or international organizations liable for damage caused by measures contrary to the LOSC,[31] and for pollution of the marine environment arising out of MSR.[32] There is also a provision that highlights the special arrangements applicable to the settlement of disputes concerning MSR.[33] Whereas most disputes concerning the LOSC are subject to compulsory arbitration or judicial settlement, coastal States are not obliged to accept submission to dispute settlement in relation to any dispute arising out of its exercise of a right or discretion to grant or withhold consent to conduct MSR in its continental shelf or EEZ,[34] or a decision to order suspension or cessation of a research project.[35] The only possibility for compulsory dispute settlement in such circumstances is reserved by Article 297(2)(b) which allows a researching State to invoke compulsory conciliation of a dispute with a coastal State if it alleges that the latter is not complying with the LOSC in relation to a request to carry out research, unless that research is of direct significance for the exploration and exploitation of natural resources.

Against the backdrop of these general provisions, the LOSC addresses MSR more specifically in relation to all LOSC maritime zones.

4.3 Internal waters, archipelagic waters, and the territorial sea

In the territorial sea, the coastal State has complete control over MSR.[36] Research may only be conducted with the express consent of the coastal State, and subject to any conditions it imposes. The same position applies by necessary implication in internal waters and archipelagic waters.[37] However, while Article 245 recognizes coastal State sovereignty over MSR in these waters, this does not imply that research within those waters will be only be conducted by nationals of the coastal State. If the coastal State so chooses, it may elect by way of licence to permit nationals of a foreign State to conduct MSR within these waters. Such activities could also be undertaken in conjunction with local scientists.

---

[30] See D Herr and GR Galland, *The Ocean and Climate Change: Tools and Guidelines for Action* (International Union for Conservation of Nature Gland 2009) 12.
[31] LOSC, n 5, Art 263(2).   [32] Ibid, Art 263(3).   [33] Ibid, Art 264.
[34] Ibid, Art 297(2)(i).   [35] Ibid, Art 297(2)(ii).   [36] Ibid, Art 245.
[37] Ibid, Art 2(1). For further details see Chapters 5 and 7 in this volume.

Coastal State control over research in the territorial sea is further reinforced by Article 19(2)(j), which provides that passage will be prejudicial to the peace, good order, and security of the coastal State, and will therefore become non-innocent, if it involves any research or survey activities. Article 21(g) further stipulates that coastal States may adopt laws and regulations relating to innocent passage in respect of MSR. While this would allow the coastal State to prevent the conduct of any MSR during the exercise of innocent passage in both the territorial sea (and archipelagic waters[38]), it would not affect the use of sonar for depth sounding, the use of radar, or the monitoring of ocean and wind currents, where necessary for the safe navigation of a vessel.[39] Similarly, the gathering of such data would also be a permissible exception to the prohibition on research and surveying undertaken during the exercise of transit passage through international straits,[40] or while exercising the similar right of archipelagic sea lanes passage.[41] These conclusions would apply not only to research and survey vessels, but also to military vessels, the passage of which would be rendered neither non-innocent in the territorial sea, nor outside the 'normal mode' of navigation in straits or archipelagic sea lanes,[42] by the gathering of such information, even though it could potentially be used for tactical purposes.

4.4 Continental shelf and exclusive economic zone

The EEZ regime makes reference in Article 56(1)(b)(ii) to the exclusive jurisdiction of coastal States with regard to MSR, but this provision must be read in light of Article 246 in Part XIII. The LOSC addresses MSR in the EEZ and continental shelf in a combined set of provisions in Article 246. Coastal States are accorded a general right to regulate, authorize, and conduct MSR in both of these zones in accordance with relevant provisions of the Convention. The overriding rule is that MSR in the EEZ and on the continental shelf is only to be conducted with the consent of the coastal State.[43] However, the LOSC limits the impact of this broad-based consent

---

[38] LOSC, n 5, Art 52(1).
[39] AHA Soons, *Marine Scientific Research and the Law of the Sea* (Kluwer Deventer 1982) 149.
[40] LOSC, n 5, Art 40.   [41] Ibid, Art 54.   [42] Ibid, Arts 39 and 53.
[43] Ibid, Art 246(2). See generally Chapters 8 and 9 in this volume. Upon its accession to the LOSC in 1994, Germany lodged a Statement that made precise reference to the MSR regime in which it stated:

> ...the exclusive economic zone and the continental shelf, which are of particular interest to marine scientific research, will be subject to a consent regime, a basic element of which is the obligation of the coastal State under article 246, paragraph 3, to grant its consent in normal circumstances. In this regard, promotion and creation of favourable conditions for scientific research, as postulated in the Convention, are general principles governing the application and interpretation of all relevant provisions in the Convention.

Germany, 'Upon accession' (14 October 1994) in United Nations Division for Ocean Affairs and the Law of the Sea (DOALOS), *Declarations and Statements* (29 October 2013), available at <www.un.org/Depts/los/convention_agreements/convention_declarations.htm>.

regime by stipulating in Article 246(3) that coastal States shall 'in normal circumstances' grant consent for research carried out 'exclusively for peaceful purposes and in order to increase scientific knowledge of the marine environment for the benefit of all mankind'. In addition, it mandates that coastal States must 'establish rules and procedures ensuring that such consent will not be delayed or denied unreasonably'. In this way, the LOSC promotes MSR projects conducted by the scientific community in the public interest. By contrast, under Article 246(5)(a), coastal States are given absolute discretion to withhold consent for MSR which is 'of direct significance for the exploration and exploitation of natural resources, whether living or non-living'. Consent may also be withheld in the discretion of coastal States in relation to research, whether pure or applied, if it involves drilling into the continental shelf, the use of explosives, the introduction of harmful substances into the marine environment, or involves the construction, operation, or use of artificial islands and structures.[44]

The triggers for enlivening the qualified consent regime in the LOSC provide a much clearer basis for determining when consent may be withheld than those set out in the 1958 Convention on the Continental Shelf which drew a distinction between pure and applied research in a way that left much room for subjective interpretation.[45] However, there are areas where further clarification is needed. The 'direct significance' test in Article 246(5)(a) may have functioned satisfactorily at the time the LOSC was negotiated in relation to the natural resources then of interest, but today the reach of the provision is not as clear when one considers advances in biotechnology which allows organisms recovered as part of a 'pure' research program to be the subject of commercial development well after they have been located in, and collected from, the marine environment.[46] Bioprospecting in the marine environment involves a wide range of activities including the search for valuable compounds and genetic materials, their extraction and analysis, and research and commercial development.[47] In terms of process surrounding the actual collection of samples, bioprospecting does not differ from pure MSR, and it might therefore be argued that it should normally be consented to by coastal States. However, later steps in the bioprospecting process which involve the commercialization of

---

[44] LOSC, n 5, Art 246(5)(b), (c).

[45] The value of the Convention on the Continental Shelf as a legal framework within which to regulate MSR was further constrained because the definition of the continental margin was imprecise, which in most instances limited the breadth of the continental shelf to a relatively narrow band of seabed adjacent to the coast.

[46] D Leary, *International Law and the Genetic Resources of the Deep Sea* (Martinus Nijhoff Leiden 2007) 49. Note that the 1992 Convention on Biological Diversity, and the 2010 Nagoya Protocol on Access to Genetic Resources and the Fair and Equitable Sharing of Benefits Arising from their Utilization have sought to resolve this 'gap' within the LOSC.

[47] A Hemmings and M Rogan-Finnemore, 'Access, Obligations and Benefits' in MI Jeffery, J Firestone, and K Bubna-Litic (eds), *Biodiversity Conservation, Law + Livelihoods: Bridging the North-South Divide* (Cambridge University Press Cambridge 2008) 539, 537.

a discovery has the practical effect of transforming the activity into one that is of direct significance to the exploitation of a natural resource. Hence sampling that is conducted within the continental shelf or the EEZ for the express purpose of later commercialization should only proceed where the advance consent of the coastal State has been sought and granted.[48]

Special provision is made in Part XIII for the outer continental shelf, that is those parts of the seabed where the continental shelf extends beyond 200 nm within the limits laid down in Article 76. In these areas the water column is high seas but seabed resources come within the sovereign rights of the coastal State. Article 246(6) provides that coastal States may not withhold consent to other States to undertake MSR except in relation to specific areas publicly designated by coastal States as areas in which exploration or exploitation is occurring, or is about to occur.

Several other provisions place important limits on the capacity of coastal States to withhold consent for research within the EEZ or on continental shelf within 200 nm. Coastal State consent will be implied where the research is being undertaken by an international organization of which the coastal State is a member, and where it has not expressed an objection to the project within four months of notification.[49] There will also be implied consent where a coastal State fails to inform a researching State or international organization of its decision to grant or withhold consent within six months of a valid request containing all of the required information.[50]

The duty of researchers to provide information to the coastal State is contained in Article 248. States or international organizations intending to conduct MSR in the EEZ or on the continental shelf must provide, at least six months in advance of the expected starting date of a project, full details relating to (a) the nature and objectives of the project, (b) the method and means to be used, (c) the area where it will be conducted, (d) the time period during which the research will take place, (e) details as to the body sponsoring the project, and the person in charge and, in the spirit of scientific cooperation, (f) the extent to which the coastal State could potentially participate in the project. Compliance with this duty to provide information is critical for any research project, as it is the very basis for coastal States assessing whether consent should be given to the proposed project, and the consequences for providing inaccurate information may be significant. Under Article 246(5)(d), one of the grounds upon which a coastal State may withhold or withdraw consent is where the nature or objectives of a marine science project has been inaccurately documented in the information dossier provided. Consent may also be

---

[48] S Arico and C Salpin, *Bioprospecting of Genetic Resources in the Deep Seabed: Scientific, Legal and Policy Aspects* (UN University Institute for Advanced Studies Report Tokyo 2005) 33–4. For further analysis, see J Mossop, 'Protecting Marine Biodiversity on the Continental Shelf Beyond 200 Nautical Miles' (2007) 38 *Ocean Development and International Law* 283, 292–4; D Leary, *Bioprospecting in the Arctic* (UN University Institute for Advanced Studies Report Tokyo 2008) 25–6.
[49] LOSC, n 5, Art 247.   [50] Ibid, Art 252.

refused or revoked if the researching State or competent international organization has outstanding obligations to the coastal State from a prior research project.

If a coastal State grants consent to MSR, the permission need not be on a *carte blanche* basis. Researchers must respect the right of coastal States to participate or be represented in the project,[51] and be provided with both preliminary and final reports and conclusions arising from the research.[52] Researching States are also under a duty to make the results internationally available as soon as practicable,[53] and to remove scientific research installations or equipment once the research project is complete, unless the coastal State agrees otherwise.[54] For pure research, it is only these specified conditions that may be laid down by the coastal State, in conformity with the intent of Part XIII to promote free scientific inquiry as far as possible. As such, coastal States could not require payment for granting consent to a marine scientific project, although a fee for assessing an application to conduct research could be levied.

When it comes to research of direct significance for the exploration and exploitation of natural resources a different situation pertains. Coastal States may impose conditions by its laws and regulations in relation to the granting or withholding of research.[55] Although such conditions that may be laid down are not limited, only one receives specific mention: a coastal State may insist that its agreement be obtained before the results of any resource-related research is made internationally available.[56]

A significant disagreement has arisen between some maritime powers and coastal States over whether Part XIII extends to all forms of data collection in the EEZ.[57] Among others, the United States and the United Kingdom argue that surveying of a hydrographic[58] and military[59] nature is a freedom that may be exercised in the EEZ, free from coastal State regulation, just as is the case on the high seas. The legal basis for this contention is that the LOSC refers to MSR and surveying (including hydrographic surveying) in separate provisions. Both MSR and surveying of any kind are clearly referred to as activities not permitted in the territorial sea during the exercise of innocent passage, transit passage, and archipelagic sea lanes passage.[60] However, surveying is not mentioned at all in Part XIII, which prompts the conclusion that hydrographic and military surveying would be neither pure nor applied

---

[51] Ibid, Art 249(1)(a). [52] Ibid, Art 249(1)(b). [53] Ibid, Art 249(1)(e).
[54] Ibid, Art 249(1)(g). [55] Ibid, Art 249(2). [56] Ibid.

[57] S Bateman, 'Hydrographic Surveying in the EEZ: Differences and Overlaps with Marine Scientific Research' (2005) 29 *Marine Policy* 163.

[58] Hydrography is the science of surveying and charting bodies of water and is concerned with properties including depth, configuration of the bottom, direction and force of currents, and heights and times of tides.

[59] Military surveys involve not only the gathering of hydrographic data but also a range of other oceanographic information including chemical, biological, and acoustic data: Bateman, n 57, 167.

[60] See LOSC, n 5, Arts 19(j), 21(1)(g), 40, and 54.

research subject to the coastal State consent regime. The United States has taken the view that, in addition to hydrographic and military surveys, activities not regulated by Part XIII include environmental monitoring and assessment of marine pollution (carried out pursuant to Part XII), activities related to submerged wrecks or objects of an archaeological character,[61] and operational oceanography.[62]

Several coastal States disagree with this interpretation of Part XIII, most notably India and China, both of which have lodged a series of protests over the survey activities of United States and United Kingdom vessels in their EEZs. China enacted legislation in 2002 requiring authority from the Chinese government for all surveying and mapping carried out within China's EEZ.[63] The maritime security dimension of the issue was highlighted in March 2009 by the encounter involving the USNS *Impeccable*. While undertaking ocean surveillance activities within China's EEZ 75 nm to the south of Hainan Island, five Chinese vessels surrounded the *Impeccable* and sought to block its path.[64] The event highlighted how China's active interpretation of its EEZ rights such as to limit navigation, and the conduct of surveillance, could flare into a major international incident.[65]

One argument that may be made in support of China's assumption of jurisdiction is that hydrographic and military surveying is essentially MSR, concerned as it is with much the same type of phenomena as oceanographers have always been interested in. The only real difference stems from the motivation for the activity, with hydrographic and military surveying tending to serve different purposes from either pure or applied research. Hydrographic surveying is carried out primarily to improve the safety of navigation for all maritime users, including navies, while military surveying is relevant for a range of non-classified and classified military purposes from tactical and strategic planning in relation to potential theatres of conflict, through to the testing and development of military equipment such as underwater acoustic sensor systems. In relation to hydrographic surveys an appropriate response to the apparent lacuna in Part XIII would be to allow foreign States to conduct these with the permission of the coastal State, with the caveat that consent should normally be granted given the high value of accurate hydrography for the safety of navigation.[66] The situation for military information gathering is potentially different, because most of the data gathered by navies in the EEZs is not

---

[61] On this see S Dromgoole, 'Revisiting the Relationship between Marine Scientific Research and the Underwater Cultural Heritage' (2010) 25 *International Journal of Marine and Coastal Law* 33, 44–54.

[62] Roach and Smith, n 15, 415 noting the US Senate Reports on the Law of the Sea Convention.

[63] Surveying and Mapping Law (People's Republic of China) Order No 75 (29 August 2002), available at <http://english1.english.gov.cn/laws/2005-10/09/content_75314.htm>.

[64] D Sevastopulo, 'White House Protests to Beijing over Naval Incident', *Financial Times* (10 March 2009), 3.

[65] F Ching, 'China will Avoid Military Showdown with the US', *Business Times Singapore* (18 March 2009).

[66] Bateman, n 57, 172.

publicly released and therefore has less value as a tradable commodity in the same sense as mapping data obtained through hydrographic surveying.[67] In both cases, the capacity of the coastal State to regulate these activities must be balanced against the rights of other States within the EEZ to exercise 'other internationally lawful uses of the sea' as recognised in Article 58.

4.5 High seas

The LOSC expressly provides in Article 257 that all States, irrespective of their geographic circumstances, and competent international organizations may conduct MSR in the water column beyond the EEZ. This by implication extends to the high seas, including that part of the water column of the high seas above the continental shelf beyond 200 nm. However, there are some potential limitations on this freedom stemming from the need to accommodate other high seas uses. Hence, if research installations or equipment is deployed on the high seas, then they must not interfere with established international shipping routes.[68] Additionally, the infrastructure is to bear identification markings and adequate warning signals to ensure safety at sea.[69]

While coastal States exercise oversight over MSR conducted within the EEZ and on the continental shelf, MSR on the high seas is largely left to self-regulation, although it would be possible for the dispute settlement provisions of Part XV to be invoked if there was a breach of the general principles of Part XIII set out in Article 240. At UNCLOS III, Malta submitted a proposal for the establishment of an International Ocean Space Institution, which would have been competent to regulate MSR in areas beyond national jurisdiction, and would have been responsible for issuing permits for conducting MSR.[70] However, there were strenuous objections by the United Kingdom, the United States, and other States which maintained that MSR should be as free from regulation as possible, consistent with the objective of increasing scientific knowledge.[71]

4.6 Area

Research on the deep seabed has given rise to some of the most significant scientific findings of the last century. These include the discovery of chemosynthetic-based ecosystems at hydrothermal vents, which are found at ocean ridges where

[67] Ibid, 170 and 173.   [68] LOSC, n 5, Art 261.   [69] Ibid, Art 262.
[70] Leary, n 46, 190–6.
[71] Ibid, 194; however, as noted in Section 4.6, part of this role has been assumed by the International Seabed Authority.

superheated and mineral-rich water streams are driven by sub-surface volcanism. They sustain a multitude of species, some of which are endemic to specific vents, and these organisms are notable for producing energy from chemical compounds (chemosynthesis) rather than sunlight and for being able to tolerate extreme water temperatures. Heavy concentrations of sulphides found around hydrothermal vents also contain valuable minerals, including precious metals, and are the subject of growing interest from the mining industry.

All States and competent international organizations are entitled to conduct MSR on the deep seabed, that is the area beyond the continental shelf ('the Area'). However, this research must be conducted in conformity with the provisions of the LOSC relating to the Area set out in Part XI.[72] The primary provision of relevance is Article 143, which emphasises that MSR in the Area must be carried out for peaceful purposes and for the benefit of humankind as a whole. States parties may carry out such research,[73] as may the International Seabed Authority (ISA). The ISA has no general competence to regulate MSR conducted in the Area. For instance, although 'pure' MSR at hydrothermal vent sites poses the most immediate and significant risk to the environment of these areas it does not come under the oversight of the ISA, unless conducted by the body itself.[74] Research involving the actual prospecting or exploring for mineral resources would be applied research that could only occur with the approval of the ISA, as MSR of this character would constitute 'activities in the Area'.[75] However, pure MSR, which may extend to identification of the mineral resources of the seabed, and MSR for non-mineral resources such as genetic materials are not matters subject to ISA control.[76]

4.7 Intergovernmental Oceanographic Commission and marine scientific research

The IOComm was established in 1960 to promote international cooperation and to coordinate programmes in MSR in order to improve knowledge of the nature and resources of the oceans and coastal areas, and to provide a sound basis for oceans management, sustainable development of marine resources and marine environmental protection.[77] UNESCO, through the IOComm, is the recognized competent international organization for the purposes of Parts XIII and XIV of the LOSC. In 2014 it had a total of 147 member States. Programmes being undertaken by IOComm in the past decade have included assessing climate change, ocean

---

[72] See further Chapter 11 in this volume.   [73] LOSC, n 5, Art 143(3).
[74] L Glowka, 'Putting Marine Scientific Research on a Sustainable Footing at Hydrothermal Vents' (2003) 27 *Marine Policy* 303, 305.
[75] LOSC, n 5, Art 1(3).   [76] Leary, n 46, 50.
[77] See the website of the Intergovernmental Oceanographic Commission, at <ioc-unesco.org>.

health, coastal research and management, improving scientific capacity, the Global Ocean Observing System, to develop an observation capacity for all of the world's oceans, the International Oceanographic Data and Information Exchange, which is designed to enhance MSR by facilitating the exchange of data between members, the International Ocean Carbon Coordination Project, which is examining the role of the oceans in the carbon cycle, including the acidification effects of increased absorption of carbon dioxide from the atmosphere, and maintaining tsunami warning systems for the Pacific and Indian Oceans. The IOComm has also sought to assist members in implementing three elements of the LOSC concerning MSR: Part XIII, Part XIV, and Article 76. To this end, the IOComm has, among other things, generated criteria and guidelines for the transfer of marine technology, a procedure for the operation of Article 247 relating to MSR undertaken by international organizations and, most importantly, continues to work on an 'IOComm Legal Framework for the Collection of Oceanographic Data' within the context of LOSC which, among other things, seeks to clarify the meaning of MSR for the purposes of the LOSC.

4.8 Scientific research installations and equipment

Specific provisions in Part XIII apply to the deployment and use of any type of scientific research installations or equipment, in any area of the marine environment. The basic principle, set out in Article 258, is that this activity is governed by the same rules as are prescribed in Part XIII for the conduct of MSR in any area in which such installations or equipment are deployed or used. However, a distinction can be drawn between equipment that is not fixed to the ocean floor (such as floating buoys) and 'artificial islands, installations and structures' that are. Coastal States should not normally withhold consent for the deployment and use of floating devices for the purposes of pure research.[78] Conversely, the use of such technologies for resource-focussed research can only proceed with coastal State consent.[79] In addition, if the research involves the construction, operation or use of artificial islands, installations and structures then the coastal State may withhold consent regardless of the purpose or character of the research being proposed.[80]

A number of unresolved questions surround the use of floating objects, vehicles and other devices for MSR, and these are attracting increasing scrutiny because of the growing use of these technologies for monitoring marine conditions.[81] Many thousands of floats have been deployed across the world's oceans to measure a

---

[78] LOSC, n 5, Art 246(3).　　[79] Ibid, Art 246(5)(a).　　[80] Ibid, Art 246(5)(c).
[81] K Bork et al, 'The Legal Regulation of Floats and Gliders—In Quest of a New Regime?' (2008) 39 *Ocean Development and International Law* 298.

range of variables including wave height, ocean temperature, salinity, and currents. These include the more than 3,300 Argo floats launched from ships or aircraft that periodically sink to, and rise from, determined depths to collect data which is transmitted via satellite to shore where it is used by the Argo Project to understand better the role of the oceans in the climate system.[82] More recently, use has been made of autonomous submersible vehicles known as gliders, which can be pre-programmed or controlled from shore to navigate to designated waypoints in order to collect data not only at various depths but over a wide geographical area.

One difficulty that arises in a legal framework focused upon activities occurring within certain maritime zones is that once these devices are set loose in the marine environment it is impossible to maintain complete control over them, as they may be carried by currents a considerable distance from their original place of deployment, into the EEZs and territorial seas of foreign States. The strict application of Part XIII would mean that the deploying State must seek coastal State consent before this occurs, yet this is impractical as researching States would need to obtain approval from a potentially large number of States.[83] In so doing, researching States would need to provide information on the matters listed in Article 248 including the precise geographical area in which the equipment will be used at least six months in advance, which is a difficult if not impossible task given the uncertainties involved.

Another question that arises is which State or States may exercise jurisdiction over floating objects. The position in the territorial sea (where the coastal State would have complete jurisdiction) and the high seas (where the deploying, flag State, would have complete jurisdiction) is clear enough. However for the EEZ and the continental shelf the matter is not resolved by Part XIII. The placement of research infrastructure on or connected to the seabed would clearly be covered by Article 60 and Article 80 which gives coastal States exclusive jurisdiction over the construction and use of installations and structures. For floats and gliders there is no guidance in the LOSC precisely on point as to how they would be characterized. If utilized for applied research, then Article 249(2), which allows the coastal State to impose a wide range of conditions, probably means that the coastal State would have jurisdiction.

Novel law of the sea issues surrounding the use of floats and gliders were anticipated to some extent in a convention drafted in 1972 at the instigation of the

---

[82] Deployment of Argo floats (named after the ship in Greek mythology captained by Jason) began in 2000 and the array was completed in 2007 (although deployments continue to be made to maintain the total array at around 3,000 floats). This array permits real-time and continuous monitoring temperature, salinity and currents in the upper 2000 m of the oceans. See Argo website, at <www-argo.ucsd.edu>; Bork et al, n 81, 305–6; Roach and Smith, n 15, 446–7.

[83] Bork et al, n 81, 311–12.

IOComm and the International Maritime Organization (IMO) to deal with 'ocean data acquisition systems'.[84] However, the treaty has never been completed, as negotiations were placed on hold during UNCLOS III, and work that was restarted on the project in 1982 was ultimately brought to an end in 1993 without agreement on a finished text. The last iteration of the text dealt more comprehensively with ocean data acquisition systems than does the LOSC, including issues concerning jurisdiction over, and the recovery and return, of floating research devices.[85] It would have required deploying States to take steps to monitor the position of devices to prevent unauthorized entry into coastal State jurisdictional zones, would have required coastal States to notify the deploying State of a device found in its jurisdiction and facilitate its return, and would have given the deploying State the same rights in, and jurisdiction over, devices as it has over vessels flying its flag. In the absence of a concluded text, the IOComm has sought to fill the gap in regulation through the adoption of non-legally binding guidelines as part of its work on a 'Legal Framework Within the Context of [the LOSC] for the Collection of Oceanographic Data'.[86]

5 Marine Scientific Research under Other Regimes

Although the LOSC is the principal global regime for MSR, there are other instruments at a regional and global level that are of relevance to the conduct of scientific research in ocean space as they relate to research being conducted in the context of a particular activity. Examples include fisheries treaties which commonly speak of the need for using the 'best scientific evidence available' when taking measures to ensure the long-term sustainability of fish stocks,[87] and which may establish

---

[84] Preliminary Draft Convention on Ocean Data Acquisition Systems, UN Doc SC-72/CONF.85/3, Annex III (1972).

[85] Draft Convention on the Legal Status of Ocean Data Acquisition Systems, Aids and Devices, UN Doc IOC-XVII/Inf. 1 (1993).

[86] For discussion, see PA Verlaan, 'Current Developments: Intergovernmental Oceanographic Commission of the United Nations Educational, Scientific and Cultural Organization (IOC/UNESCO)' (2009) 24 *International Journal of Marine and Coastal Law* 173.

[87] See eg 1995 Agreement for the Implementation of the Provisions of the United Nations Convention on the Law of the Sea Relating to the Conservation and Management of Straddling Fish Stocks and Highly Migratory Fish Stocks, Arts 5(b), 6(3) and (7), 10(f), and 16(1). These provisions are generally consistent with the provisions of the LOSC that contemplate reliance upon scientific information in fisheries management: LOSC, n 5, Arts 61 and 119.

scientific committees for the purpose of advising fisheries commissions on the status and trends of stocks, to coordinate on-going research, and make recommendations on matters relating to conservation, management, and optimum utilization.[88] Marine living resources conventions may also include provisions privileging scientific research, as is the case with Article VIII of the 1946 International Convention on the Regulation of Whaling which allows parties to issue special permits in relation to the taking of whales for research purposes. Article VIII became contested following the moratorium on commercial whaling that commenced in 1985/1986, after which Japan began issuing special permits to conduct whaling for research purposes in the Southern Ocean. In 2014, the ICJ ruled in favour of Australia that Japan was not undertaking whaling activities 'for the purposes of scientific research' via its special permit whaling program but rather was undertaking commercial whaling and in doing so assessed the meaning of that term in the context of Article VIII.[89]

In the context of marine pollution, the parties to relevant IMO conventions have been particularly active in promoting scientific research and monitoring new forms of research that may be damaging to the marine environment. A watching brief, for example, has been maintained on scientific research involving iron fertilization of the oceans, a technique to stimulate plankton blooms and thereby result in greater ocean absorption of carbon dioxide from the atmosphere. The parties to the 1972 Convention on the Prevention of Marine Pollution by Dumping of Wastes and Other Matter[90] and its 1996 London Protocol[91] adopted a resolution in 2010 adopting an 'Assessment Framework for Scientific Research Involving Ocean Fertilization' to be used to assist in determinations as to whether 'proposed ocean fertilization activity constitutes legitimate scientific research' not contrary to the London Protocol.[92] This interim measure will eventually be replaced by two new Annexes and associated amendments to the London Protocol adopted in 2013.[93] Annex 4 introduces a definition for Marine Geoengineering Activities in the context of ocean fertilization, while Annex 5 establishes a legally binding assessment framework for such activities. The effect of these London Protocol amendments is that ocean fertilization is prohibited unless it is 'assessed as constituting legitimate scientific research taking into account any specific placement assessment framework'.[94] Considerations that will be assessed in determining the MSR activity include whether it will answer

---

[88] See eg 1993 Convention for the Conservation of Southern Bluefin Tuna, Art 9.
[89] *Whaling in the Antarctic*, n 9.
[90] 1972 Convention on the Prevention of Marine Pollution by Dumping of Wastes and Other Matter; status of treaty details available at <http://www.imo.org/About/Conventions/StatusOfConventions/Pages/Default.aspx>.
[91] 1996 Protocol to the Convention on the Prevention of Marine Pollution by Dumping of Wastes and Other Matter.
[92] Res LC-LP.2 (2010).   [93] Res LP.4 (8) (2013).   [94] Ibid, Annex 4 (1.3).

questions that will add to scientific knowledge, if the research methodology is appropriate and based on best available scientific knowledge and technology, whether the activity is subject to scientific peer review, and whether economic interests have influenced the design of the proposed activity.[95] At the time of writing, the new 2013 Annexes had yet to enter into force.

An ocean area where there is substantial overlap between the regime for MSR supplied by the LOSC and another system for regulating MSR is the Southern Ocean, which lies within the purview of the Antarctic Treaty System built upon the 1959 Antarctic Treaty, a fundamental objective of which is to promote scientific investigation within Antarctica.[96] The 1959 Antarctic Treaty itself imposes few controls on the conduct of research, other than to promote international cooperation in scientific investigation in Antarctica through the transfer of plans for scientific research, the exchange of personnel, and the exchange and publication of scientific observations and results.[97] By contrast, the 1991 Environmental Protocol to the Antarctic Treaty has broad application to activities within the Antarctic Treaty Area, that is the land and sea areas south of 60°S, that may have effects on the Antarctic environment, including scientific research. As regards other activities, the Environmental Protocol requires scientific research to be planned to minimise adverse environmental impacts,[98] and to establish a system for the granting of permits involving interference with wildlife.[99] However, because of the unique status of territorial claims in Antarctica, and the constraints placed upon the active assertion of coastal State jurisdiction by the provisions of the Antarctic Treaty,[100] an unusual dynamic exists in the Southern Ocean with respect to the limited capacity of coastal States to regulate MSR within the maritime zones adjoining their Antarctic claims, the freedoms to conduct MSR under the LOSC, and the active promotion of the freedom of scientific research under the Antarctic Treaty. This gap in the regulatory regime could be overcome if the Antarctic Treaty parties exercised a form of 'collective jurisdiction' over MSR, but to date state practice indicates a reluctance on the parties to do so.[101]

---

[95] Ibid, Annex 5 (8). [96] See Chapter 32 in this volume. [97] 1959 Antarctic Treaty, Art 3.
[98] 1991 Protocol on Environmental Protection to the Antarctic Treaty, Arts 3 and 8.
[99] Ibid, Art 3 and Annex II. [100] See discussion in Chapter 32 in this volume.
[101] R Lefeber, 'Marine Scientific Research in the Antarctic Treaty System' in EJ Molenaar, AG Oude Elferink, and DR Rothwell (eds), *The Law of the Sea and the Polar Regions: Interactions between Global and Regional Regimes* (Martinus Nijhoff Leiden 2013) 323, 327–31.

6 Coastal State Legislation Concerning Marine Scientific Research

State practice when it comes to coastal State regulation of MSR has been far from uniform.[102] A compilation of the relevant municipal laws of coastal States in 1989 indicated that most had not enacted detailed legislation specifically applicable to MSR, and that the most common approach was simply to assert jurisdiction over research in quite general terms.[103] A 2003 survey of coastal States legislation on MSR conducted by the IOComm at the request of the United Nations General Assembly[104] drew responses from 31 coastal States, 21 of which reported having some type of regulation. These differ substantially in their specificity. Some legislation such as that of Canada[105] and Australia[106] is quite general in nature and does not seek to mirror the relevant provisions of the LOSC, whereas other regimes are more detailed and largely replicate Part XIII, as is the case for the Polish legislation concerning its maritime zones and maritime administration.[107] Recognizing these variations in state practice, the United Nations Division on Ocean Affairs and the Law of the Sea in 2010 published a guide to the implementation to the relevant LOSC MSR provisions.[108] The guide, which revised an earlier 1991 publication, takes into account trends in MSR including marine data acquisition, marine data dissemination, and large-scale international collaborative research programs.[109] The guide highlights increasing engagement by coastal States with the MSR regime and development of legislative frameworks and policy regimes to give effect to the relevant provisions of Part XIII of the LOSC.[110] Nevertheless, the guide contains a general statement that 'States are strongly encouraged to harmonize their national legislation

---

[102] See further M Gorina-Ysern, *An International Regime for Marine Scientific Research* (Transnational Publishers Ardsley 2003) pt I.

[103] United Nations, *The Law of the Sea: National Legislation, Regulations and Supporting Documents on Marine Scientific Research in Areas Under National Jurisdiction* (United Nations New York 1989).

[104] UNGA Res A/RES/56/12 (2001).

[105] See the Oceans Act 1996, RSC 1996, c 31 (Canada) §§ 14 and 42ff.

[106] See the Fisheries Management Act 1991 (Australia) § 3; Offshore Petroleum and Greenhouse Gas Storage Act 2006 (Australia) pt 2.6; Offshore Minerals Act 1994 (Australia) § 315. See also the Australian Foreign Research Vessel Guidelines.

[107] See the Act Concerning the Maritime Areas of the Polish Republic and Marine Administration (1991), Arts 28–32, reprinted in United Nations, *The Law of the Sea: National Legislation on the Exclusive Economic Zone* (United Nations New York 1993) 270

[108] DOALOS, *Marine Scientific Research: A revised guide to the implementation of the relevant provisions of the United Nations Convention on the Law of the Sea* (2010), available at <www.un.org/Depts/los/doalos_publications/publicationstexts/msr_guide%202010_final.pdf>.

[109] Ibid, v.   [110] Ibid, 29–35.

with the provisions of the Convention, and where applicable, relevant agreements and instruments, to ensure the consistent application of those provisions'.[111] Several States have expressed no intention to regulate MSR, such as the Netherlands and the United States. The Proclamation issued by United States President Ronald Reagan in 1983 in relation to the EEZ did not assert jurisdiction over MSR, as the Reagan administration took the view that this would be contrary to the encouragement of MSR both within the United States EEZ and in the EEZs of other States. The United States Department of State requires researching States to apply for advance consent only if (a) the research is conducted within its territorial sea, (b) is conducted within a national marine sanctuary or other marine protected area, (c) involves the study of cetaceans or endangered species, (d) involves the taking of commercial quantities of marine resources, or (e) involves contact with its continental shelf.[112]

7 Future Developments

There has been a significant intensification in MSR across all maritime zones and in places (such as the deep ocean and polar seas) that were previously explored to only a limited extent, if at all. During this time the focus of MSR has also broadened, and the fruits of MSR have significantly improved an understanding of an ever-growing list of ocean phenomena and the pressure that humanity is placing upon the oceans. The UN World Ocean Assessment provides an example of the way in which the marine science community is seeking to understand in a holistic way the overall state of the world's oceans and seas, and the extent to which their health is declining. But further comprehensive scientific understanding of the global oceans remains perhaps the greatest single challenge for MSR. This should not be seen as a future challenge, but is instead one requiring urgent attention in order to assess whether the oceans will continue to provide the ecological services and resources upon which humanity depends.

A distinctive feature of contemporary MSR is the way in which it is being pursued by three main protagonists: independent marine scientists engaged in pure research (eg in respect of ocean acidification), commercially-backed scientific programs (eg fisheries researchers and marine 'bioprospectors'; ocean fertilization projects), and governments and their navies (eg geoscience expeditions identifying continental shelf limits, or naval hydrographers surveying seafloor features to inform naval tacticians). An immediate challenge for the MSR regime is bringing clarity to the

---

[111] Ibid, 37 [129].   [112] Roach and Smith, n 15, 425–7.

application or not of Part XIII of the LOSC to military surveying, and the extent to which coastal States have an entitlement to exclude such activities from their EEZs. However, this is part and parcel of a broader debate about the legitimacy of military activities within coastal State maritime zones and is best resolved in the context of that debate rather than the narrower topic of MSR.

A less expansive challenge for MSR concerns the manner in which it is conducted, and whether it can be effectively regulated by the international community to minimize any environmental and other risks. As noted above, MSR is referred to in a range of provisions within the LOSC, including Part XIII which is concerned mainly with regulating MSR within EEZs. Yet while the LOSC places significant emphasis on the desirability of MSR, for the most part the LOSC has played a relatively low-key role in facilitating scientific research or in regulating its conduct. Instead, many of the most significant developments in recent decades have been outside the LOSC, and, in some contexts, this has involved major international disputes over the meaning and purpose of marine science. The *Whaling in the Antarctic* case is the most prominent example of this phenomenon, with the ICJ being invited by the parties to define marine science. Australia contended that meaningful science must involve the articulation of a hypothesis that seeks to make sense of the world, while Japan argued that simply collecting raw data could be considered good science. As a result, the Court did not enter into this difficult philosophical territory, instead finding that while Japan was engaged in an activity that 'can broadly be characterized as "scientific research"'[113] the methods it was using to explore its scientific aims were not reasonable.[114] In this way, the decision provides significant general guidance on how contemporary MSR can and should be conducted.

A major implication of the *Whaling in the Antarctic* case and developments in other regimes, such as the 1996 London Protocol and the deep seabed mining system administered by the ISA, is that in the law of the sea MSR is an activity that should be subjected to increasing oversight. As such, MSR can no longer be pursued by States or other actors entirely unilaterally, particularly if (as in the case of ocean fertilization, or lethal research on marine species) it involves risks to the marine environment or ecosystems. Enhancing processes for MSR oversight is an on-going challenge for the LOSC, but one for which there are positive signs that the international community is up to the task of addressing.

---

[113] *Whaling in the Antarctic*, n 9, [172].   [114] Ibid, [227].

26

MARITIME SECURITY

NATALIE KLEIN

1 INTRODUCTION

SECURITY has always been an influential dimension in the law of the sea. The earliest articulations of maritime law included the view that a State's territory extended into the sea as far as its terrestrial-based military force could reach.[1] The long-ago voyages of navies as part of military campaigns and the conquest of new territory further reflected the realization of State policies designed to promote the power and influence of that State. Throughout the nineteenth and twentieth centuries, the movement of warships remained of critical importance for a State in promoting and securing its national interests. In the twenty-first century, the concept of maritime security continues to embrace the military interests of States, as well as extending to a range of maritime crimes that may threaten a State's economic, political, social, and cultural values.

Maritime security is best understood as encompassing two key dimensions: (1) traditional security concerns and (2) responses to perceived maritime security threats. By traditional security concerns, this dimension primarily refers to border protection, to prevent incursions into areas considered as the sovereign domain of a State, as well as power projections, which entail a State exercising military power in its

---

[1] This is commonly known as the 'cannon-shot' rule. The jurist Bynkershoek, who is credited with the theory, claimed that 'territorial sovereign ends where the power of arms ends'. See AH Dean, 'The Second Geneva Conference on the Law of the Sea: The Fight for the Freedom of the Sea' (1960) 54 *American Journal of International Law* 751, 759–60.

relationship with other States in respect of particular maritime areas. Responses to perceived maritime security threats then reflect the steps taken by States to reduce the risk of certain crimes or activities that would prejudice or injure their interests and society. This chapter addresses both dimensions of maritime security, particularly as the latter dimension has come to influence increasingly the law of the sea.

For the purposes of this chapter, the term 'maritime security' will be understood as 'the protection of a state's land and maritime territory, infrastructure, economy, environment, and society from certain harmful acts occurring at sea'.[2] The threats to maritime security encompass piracy and armed robbery; terrorist acts; illicit trafficking in arms and weapons of mass destruction; drug trafficking; people smuggling and human trafficking; illegal, unreported, and unregulated fishing.[3] In casting the definition of maritime security broadly, the intention is to encompass both traditional and more recent security concerns.

The law related to maritime security is largely addressed within the existing law of the sea framework, but it has gathered force as a justification for elaborating new legal arrangements. These are addressed in the first part of the chapter. Second, there is discussion of the critical issues in contemporary maritime security, highlighting ongoing boundary disputes, transnational crime, and intelligence gathering. Third, in light of the legal framework and the current efforts to improve maritime security, the question then considered is what the future may hold for maritime security. It will be seen that maritime security will likely remain of fundamental concern and continue to influence legal developments, but perhaps only to the extent that national interests can be asserted and accepted as shared interests.

2 MARITIME SECURITY AND THE LAW OF THE SEA

Many facets of the law of the sea reflect maritime security interests, even if in conjunction with other concerns, such as economic interests or environmental

---

[2] N Klein, J Mossop, and DR Rothwell, 'Australia, New Zealand and Maritime Security' in N Klein, J Mossop, and DR Rothwell (eds), *Maritime Security: International Law and Policy Perspectives from Australia and New Zealand* (Routledge Oxford 2010). For further definitional discussions, see KG Hawkes, *Maritime Security* (Cornell Maritime Press Centreville 1989); MQ Mejia Jr, 'Maritime Gerrymandering: Dilemmas in Defining Piracy, Terrorism and Other Acts of Maritime Violence' (2003) 2 *Journal of International Criminal Law* 153, 155.

[3] UN Secretary General, *Oceans and the Law of the Sea: Report of the Secretary-General to the General Assembly*, UN Doc A/63/63 (10 March 2008) [39].

protection. The increasing claims of coastal States over maritime areas closest to land territory reflect defensive interests in keeping foreign warships at a safe distance.[4] These claims to exclusive use were countered by other States seeking to ensure the ongoing freedom of movement of warships and other military vessels across as broad an expanse of ocean space as possible.[5] In asserting rights over a growing range of maritime zones, States have taken steps to reduce criminal activity that could threaten the security of the State and have increasingly elaborated on the rights and duties exercised in the different maritime zones to prevent crime and improve the security of shipping. These different ways that maritime security features in the law of the sea are discussed in this part.

2.1 Traditional maritime security concerns

Protection from attack or invasion by another State is a key security interest for any government. Certainty of borders and the protection of those borders and the areas within are fundamental to the defence of a State. The oceans have served as theatres of war and specific rules were developed governing the use of force at sea, particularly in protecting the neutrality of vessels from States not engaged in hostilities.[6] The most recent iteration of these rules takes account of the current maritime zones under the 1982 United Nations Convention on the Law of the Sea (LOSC), including the ongoing freedoms of navigation that are maintained by vessels flagged to neutral States.[7]

In times of peace, the movement of naval vessels remains of critical importance. States are keen to ensure that their naval vessels are able to reach without restriction any part of the globe that is of importance in the State's international relations.

---

[4] For example, the claims of extending the territorial sea to 12 nm were sometimes premised on the idea that States would be safer if warships were not allowed to come too close to a State. See eg *Official Records of the Second UN Conference on the Law of the Sea, Summary Records of Plenary Meetings and of Meetings of the Committee of the Whole*, Annexes and Final Act, 101, [14] (Albania). The reality, even at the time these arguments were made, was that modern weaponry could still reach a State even across the distances being claimed as under the sovereignty of the State. See eg (1958) III *Official Records of the UN Conference on the Law of the Sea* 167, [3] (Mr Drew, Canada), available at <http://legal.un.org/diplomaticconferences/lawofthesea-1958/docs/english/vol_III/16_51ST_TO_55TH_MEETINGS_1st_Cttee_vol_III_e.pdf>.

[5] This debate being seen most clearly in the establishment of the EEZ under the 1982 United Nations Convention on the Law of the Sea (hereinafter LOSC) and the balance of interests established in Arts 56 and 58 of that Convention.

[6] A series of conventions were adopted in The Hague in 1907. N Ronzitti (ed), *The Law of Naval Warfare: A Collection of Agreements and Documents with Commentaries* (Martinus Nijhoff Dordrecht 1988).

[7] See L Doswald-Beck (ed), *San Remo Manual on International Law Applicable to Armed Conflicts at Sea* (Cambridge University Press Cambridge 1995) [20], [23], [26], [27], [31], and [32].

The International Court of Justice (ICJ) in the *Corfu Channel* case recognized the central interest of navies in accessing straits. There, the Court stated:

It is, in the opinion of the Court, generally recognized and in accordance with international custom that States in time of peace have a right to send their warships through straits used for international navigation between two parts of the high seas without the previous authorization of a coastal State, provided that the passage is *innocent*. Unless otherwise prescribed in an international convention, there is no right for a coastal State to prohibit such passage through straits in time of peace.[8]

This key security interest in the movement of naval vessels is reflected in the protection afforded to navigation under the modern law of the sea, even when there are no explicit references to military activities or the specific rights of naval vessels.[9] Thus, the creation of transit passage under the LOSC ensured protection of the rights of warships and other naval vessels to traverse straits in 'their normal modes' that would otherwise be territorial sea and require restricted operations.[10] The freedom of navigation 'and other internationally lawful uses of the sea related to' this freedom have also been protected in the large swathes of ocean space now designated as exclusive economic zones (EEZ).[11] Whether and what military activities are permissible in the EEZ of another State continue to be controversial questions in the practice of States.[12]

Protecting access to resources has also been an important security concern that has traditionally been protected under the law of the sea. One of the rationales for expanding the breadth of the territorial sea was to safeguard the supply of marine living resources for the nourishment of the local population, as well as fostering profitable export markets.[13] Maintaining exclusive control over these resources was an impetus to the subsequent establishment of the EEZ. The legal recognition of the continental shelf provided States with economic certainty for their rights over the

---

[8] *Corfu Channel (United Kingdom v Albania)* (Judgment) [1949] ICJ Rep 4, 28.

[9] See further discussion in Chapter 24 in this volume.

[10] LOSC, n 5, Art 39(1). For discussion of this view, see WM Reisman, 'The Regime of Straits and National Security: An Appraisal of International Lawmaking' (1980) 74 *American Journal of International Law* 48; BH Oxman, 'The Regime of Warships under the United Nations Convention on the Law of the Sea' (1984) 24 *Virginia Journal of International Law* 809.

[11] LOSC, n 5, Art 58(1).

[12] For discussion, see R Pedrozo, 'Military Activities in and Over the Exclusive Economic Zone' in MH Nordquist et al (eds), *Freedom of Seas, Passage Rights and the 1982 Law of the Sea Convention* (Martinus Nijhoff Leiden/Boston 2009) 235; R Ziafeng and CX Cheng, 'A Chinese Perspective' (2005) 29 *Marine Policy* 139. See further Chapter 38 in this volume.

[13] As noted in International Law Commission debates—see (1955) 1 *Yearbook of the International Law Commission*, UN Doc A/CN.4/SR.295, 72, [51]—as well as at the First United Nations Conference on the Law of the Sea (UNCLOS I). See eg (1958) III *Official Records of the UN Conference on the Law of The Sea*, First Committee (Territorial Sea and Contiguous Zone), UN Doc A/CONF.13/C.1/SR.1–5 (1958) 7, [11] (Peru).

seabed resources.[14] Ensuring that States' economic interests are protected is clearly part of the security of a State because it reduces the likelihood of dependence on other States for these important resources.

In the current governance framework for the oceans, the LOSC sought to give greater certainty to entitlement to resources through the definition of the different maritime zones. While there is no strict formula to be applied for the delimitation of overlapping maritime zones, the LOSC does provide general parameters, as well as a mechanism for provisional arrangements.[15] In addition, States may resort to compulsory dispute settlement procedures entailing binding decisions for the resolution of maritime boundary disputes.[16] However, as will be discussed further below, many maritime boundaries remain to be delimited and are highly contested precisely because access to resources remains an important security issue for coastal States.

2.2 Responding to maritime security threats

Within each maritime zone, States are accorded rights and duties permitting responses to a range of maritime crimes or other unlawful acts. Beginning closest to the coast, a State's national criminal law would normally apply to the territorial sea and internal waters in accordance with the sovereignty that the coastal State exercises over these waters. This sovereignty permits the coastal State to take action against vessels engaged in terrorism, transnational crimes (such as drug trafficking and people smuggling), intentional pollution, illegal fishing, and intelligence gathering. Criminal activity would fall within Article 27 of the LOSC and the actions in question would otherwise be in violation of the right of innocent passage accorded to foreign-flagged vessels in the territorial sea.[17] The coastal State is only limited in taking action against warships and other government vessels operating on non-commercial service as these vessels are subject to sovereign immunity.[18]

In the contiguous zone, the coastal State may act under particular circumstances to prevent and punish offences related to fiscal, immigration, sanitary, and customs matters.[19] These powers allow a coastal State to respond to some maritime security threats, such as drug or arms trafficking as violations of customs law and to people smuggling as a violation of immigration laws. Coastal State action against

---

[14] Especially as these rights were recognized as belonging *ipso facto* and *ab initio* to the coastal State. *North Sea Continental Shelf (Federal Republic of Germany v Denmark; Federal Republic of Germany v The Netherlands)* [1969] ICJ Rep 3, [18]–[20].

[15] LOSC, n 5, Arts 74(3) and 83(3).

[16] Ibid, Part XV. States do, however, have the option of excluding maritime boundary disputes from these mandatory proceedings. See ibid, Art 298(1)(a).

[17] N Klein, *Maritime Security and the Law of the Sea* (Oxford University Press Oxford 2011) 75–7.

[18] LOSC, n 5, Art 32.   [19] Ibid, Art 33.

other maritime security threats in the contiguous zone would otherwise be governed according to the rights and duties adhering to States within the EEZ and the high seas.

The enforcement powers of the coastal State significantly diminish in the EEZ, as authority is explicitly granted to the coastal State to enforce its laws in relation to fishing and pollution.[20] On the high seas, States may normally only interfere with vessels bearing their flag,[21] which limits the actions States may take to protect against maritime security threats. Piracy has been one of the few crimes whereby any State is granted authority to arrest and prosecute pirates whenever caught outside the territorial sea of a State.[22]

An increasing number of treaties have instead been adopted that create processes and mechanisms that allow warships to visit foreign-flagged vessels and potentially take action against suspected offenders as a matter of international law.[23] These treaties cover drug trafficking,[24] people smuggling,[25] illegal fishing,[26] terrorist activity,[27] and unlawful transportation of weapons of mass destruction.[28] In this regard, it may be seen that States have sought modifications to the existing law of the sea in response to common concerns in preventing and responding to particular maritime crimes that are considered as a threat to the security of the State.[29]

States have also taken action to improve ship security. Given that over 90 per cent of the world's international trade is carried by sea, ensuring the free and safe movement of this cargo is vital for the economic interests of States. Significant economic harm through the shut down of international shipping reflects a key security

---

[20] Ibid, Arts 73 and 220. It is also argued that there is implicit authorization to exercise enforcement jurisdiction in relation to artificial islands and the exploitation of non-living resources. See eg Y Tanaka, *The International Law of the Sea* (Cambridge University Press Cambridge 2012) 129, 143.

[21] The two main exceptions relate to the right of visit and the right of hot pursuit. LOSC, Arts 110 and 111, respectively.

[22] LOSC, Art 105. See further Chapter 37 in this volume on piracy.

[23] In implementing these treaties, States need to consider whether their warships have powers to exercise criminal enforcement jurisdiction.

[24] 1990 UN Convention against Illicit Traffic in Narcotic Drugs and Psychotropic Substances (hereinafter Drugs Convention).

[25] 2000 Protocol against the Smuggling of Migrants by Land, Sea and Air Supplementing the Convention against Transnational Organized Crime (hereinafter Migrant Smuggling Protocol).

[26] 1995 UN Agreement for the Implementation of the Provisions of the UN Convention on the Law of the Sea of 10 December 1982 relating to the Conservation and Management of Straddling Fish Stocks and Highly Migratory Fish Stocks (hereinafter FSA). This agreement allows for visits and inspections.

[27] 2005 Convention for the Suppression of Unlawful Acts against the Safety of Maritime Navigation (encompassing the 1988 Convention for the Suppression of Unlawful Acts against the Safety of Maritime Navigation, amended by the Protocol of 2005 to the Convention for the Suppression of Unlawful Acts against the Safety of Maritime Navigation) (hereinafter SUA Convention).

[28] Ibid. The United States has also entered into a series of bilateral agreements to this effect. See discussion in D Guilfoyle, *Maritime Interdiction and the Law of the Sea* (Cambridge University Press Cambridge 2009) 246–54.

[29] Such modifications are envisaged under LOSC, n 5, Art 311(3).

interest. To avoid this situation, States have sought to identify and minimize risks that may be posed to international shipping through collective action, primarily under the auspices of the International Maritime Organization (IMO), and in some instances, on a unilateral basis.[30]

Following the September 11 attacks on the United States, in 2004 the IMO took steps to amend the 1974 International Convention on the Safety of Life at Sea (SOLAS) with the introduction of an International Ship and Port Facility Security Code (ISPS Code), which was included as part of a new chapter to that treaty.[31] The ISPS Code sets out both mandatory steps as well as recommendations to identify potential threats to ships and to ports, provides for specific roles and procedures to be performed on ships and at port, and sets out what steps are to be taken in the event a risk is identified.[32]

The IMO also adopted regulations under the SOLAS Convention to enable the long-range identification and tracking (LRIT) of ships so that States will have better information as to what ships are navigating where, and particularly what ships are voyaging towards that State's territory.[33] The LRIT Regulations are part of broader efforts to improve information gathering and monitoring of maritime areas to detect threats to maritime security.[34]

The responses to maritime security threats reflect steps taken by States to address particular activities that may prove detrimental to the State individually. In addition, there has been a shared interest in recognizing the rights and duties of States under the law of the sea to reduce the impact that any one act may have on the community of States. So, for example, an oil tanker being rammed by a small vessel and exploding in a mega-port not only affects the flag State of the vessel concerned, and those States interested in the oil being carried, but all other States that have cargo delayed because of the damage to or closure of the port in question. The current analysis indicates that security concerns are most commonly protected under the law of the sea when States have recognized that there is a shared interest at stake.

---

[30] Such unilateral action has particularly been taken by the United States to improve information and security regarding what cargo is moving into the United States. See GW Bowman, 'Thinking Outside the Border: Homeland Security and the Forward Deployment of the US Border' (2007) 44 *Houston Law Review* 189.

[31] 1974 International Convention for the Safety of Life at Sea (SOLAS), 1983 Amendments to the Annex, contained in Resolutions 1, 2, 6, and 7 of the 2004 Conference of Contracting Governments and including the International Ship and Port Facility Security (ISPS) Code.

[32] For further discussion, see Klein, n 17, 158–62; HG Hesse, 'Maritime Security in a Multilateral Context: IMO Activities to Enhance Maritime Security' (2003) 18 *International Journal of Maritime and Coastal Law* 327, 331.

[33] For further discussion on the LRIT Regulations, see Klein, n 17, 229–34.

[34] This initiative is part of broader policies of maritime domain awareness. See C Rahman, 'Maritime Domain Awareness in Australia and New Zealand' in Klein et al (eds), n 2, 202, 202–7.

3 CRITICAL ISSUES IN CONTEMPORARY MARITIME SECURITY

The discussion thus far has indicated how the varied maritime security interests of States have been accommodated within the law of the sea, either in the LOSC or in the adoption of additional agreements or regulations as the need has arisen. As previously indicated, the evolution of the law has been possible in situations where a shared common interest in articulating the necessary rights and duties existed. However, where the exclusive interests of States clash with those of another State, or with the inclusive interests of all States, there remain difficult issues to determine as to how the law is to be interpreted and applied. Questions also arise as to whether gaps or ambiguities in existing law need to be resolved. This part considers some of the main sources of current concern for maritime security: boundary disputes, transnational crime, and intelligence gathering.

3.1 Ongoing boundary disputes

Protection of borders and the assertion of authority over maritime space remain critical maritime security concerns. The most controversial maritime boundary disputes most typically concern areas where there are significant seabed resources to be exploited so the neighbouring States have an interest in gaining access to these resources and the financial benefits accruing from their exploitation. In the absence of certainty of title, the oil or gas companies that would undertake the necessary exploration and extraction usually refrain from entering into agreements with States.[35]

Two of the most significant flashpoints in this regard are the South China Sea and the East China Sea. In the South China Sea, there are contested maritime boundaries and sovereignty disputes between seven States.[36] Japan and China are in dispute over their maritime boundaries and certain insular features in the East China Sea. These States have great interest in these areas as they seek to benefit from not only the natural resources but also the strategic importance of shipping lanes through the region.

Boundary disputes also arise in relation to the drawing of baselines from which maritime zones are then measured. There has been considerable controversy in the

---

[35] L Brilmayer and N Klein, 'Land and Sea: Two Sovereignty Regimes in Search of a Common Denominator' (2001) 33 *New York University Journal of International Law and Politics* 703, 732–6.
[36] Brunei, China, Indonesia, Malaysia, the Philippines, Taiwan (albeit not a State in the view of China and some other States), and Viet Nam.

past about how States have interpreted Article 7 of the LOSC, which sets out the criteria for the drawing of straight baselines. States will protest against the questionable drawing of straight baselines, or closing lines across bays, that have the effect of reducing areas subject to the freedom of navigation. The United States has undertaken military action in this regard, with a notable example being the Freedom of Navigation Program applied, *inter alia*, against Libya's closure of the Gulf of Sirte. Tensions are also currently arising in relation to the North West Passages and the increasing movement of vessels through Arctic waters. These ongoing disputes underline a core interest in maritime security in terms of ensuring free movement of naval vessels.

3.2 Transnational crime

Piracy and the illegal trafficking of people, weapons, and drugs remain critical policing concerns for coastal States. Piracy, which is examined in detail in Chapter 37, has posed a significant threat to international shipping, jeopardizing international trade, and has exacted a human toll with hostage taking and violence against masters, crews, and passengers on diverse vessels. States have clear authority under the LOSC to stop and exercise jurisdiction over pirates,[37] and these powers have been augmented by the Security Council in relation to piracy off the coast of Somalia.[38] Ongoing difficulties in responding to piracy include whether the naval vessels involved in piracy operations have authority to exercise criminal jurisdiction over an individual in arresting them at sea, and whether obligations exist in prosecuting a pirate once arrested.[39] Practical difficulties in prosecuting pirates include the sufficient collection of evidence, and the timely transport of a pirate to the arresting vessel's home country.[40] The domestic laws of the prosecuting State must also allow for jurisdiction to be asserted over a foreign national charged with piracy and have appropriate penalties in place.[41]

People smuggling has prompted strong policy responses from destination States seeking to deter the arrival of illegal migrants and asylum seekers. The United States, the European Union and Australia have all undertaken operations intended to prevent the passage of vessels carrying illegal migrants and thereby stop arrival

---

[37] See LOSC, n 5, Arts 105 and 110.

[38] See United Nations Security Council (UNSC) Res 1816 (2 June 2008); UNSC Res 1851 (16 December 2008). These resolutions were subsequently renewed for longer time periods.

[39] MS Karim, 'Is there an International Obligation to Prosecute Pirates?' (2011) 58 *Netherlands International Law Review* 387.

[40] See eg H Fouche and J Meyer, 'Investigating Sea Piracy: Crime Scene Challenges' (2012) 11 *World Maritime University Journal of Maritime Affairs* 33.

[41] See eg Ashley Roach, 'Agora: Piracy Prosecutions Countering Piracy off Somalia: International Law and International Institutions' (2010) 104 *American Journal of International Law* 397.

into their territory.⁴² Under the 2000 Protocol Against the Smuggling of Migrants by Land, Sea and Air Supplementing the United Nations Convention against Transnational Organized Crime (Migrant Smuggling Protocol), a procedure has been laid out whereby States may exercise the right of visit and arrest those suspected of engaging in people smuggling or human trafficking enterprises.⁴³ There are a number of conditions imposed on the exercise of the right of visit against a foreign flagged vessel in these circumstances.⁴⁴

The actions of destination States in responding to threats to their border security highlight a critical aspect of law enforcement: the alignment of domestic law with international law. In relation to deterring the arrival of illegal migrants, concerns may rightly be raised that the policies and laws put in place at the national level do not properly account for the international law obligations of States.⁴⁵ For piracy and other crimes at sea, the concern may be that national laws have not been implemented to reflect the international obligations imposed under treaties to which a State becomes party addressing transnational crimes and terrorist offences. An example of the latter may be the failure of States to assert jurisdiction over alleged offenders as required under the 2005 SUA Convention.⁴⁶ Maritime security will only be improved when there is proper alignment between national and international laws addressing those threats.

3.3 Intelligence gathering

As discussed previously, coastal States have a keen interest in being aware of what activities are occurring in their maritime zones. At the same time, other States may seek to learn more about the maritime domain of a particular coastal State, as well as gaining information and data about the coastal defences of a State.⁴⁷ The conduct of foreign-flagged military activities in the EEZ of a coastal State remains a

---

⁴² See discussion in E Papastavridis, 'Interception of Human Beings on the High Seas: A Contemporary Analysis under International Law' (2009) 36 *Syracuse Journal of International Law and Commerce* 145; Guilfoyle, n 28, 187–221.

⁴³ Migrant Smuggling Protocol, n 25, Arts 8 and 9.

⁴⁴ Some of these conditions include ensuring the safety and humane treatment of people on board and not prejudicing the legal interests of the flag State: ibid, Art 9.

⁴⁵ Particularly in relation to the protection of asylum seekers, as established in the Refugee Convention: 1951 United Nations Convention Relating to the Status of Refugees and 1967 Protocol Relating to the Status of Refugees. The importance of these and human rights obligations in maritime interceptions were highlighted in *Hirsi Jamaa and Others v Italy*, Judgment of the European Court of Human Rights, App No 27765/09 (23 February 2012).

⁴⁶ SUA Convention, n 27, Art 6.

⁴⁷ See discussion in D Ball, 'Intelligence Collection Operations and EEZs: the Implications of New Technology, (2008) 28 *Marine Policy* 67.

source of controversy, particularly because of differing interpretations of the LOSC on this issue.

Coastal States will protest the presence of foreign naval vessels in their maritime zones when those vessels are suspected of spying. For example, Japan has protested against Chinese research vessels believed to be gathering intelligence and also attacked and sunk a North Korean vessel in 2001.[48] China has actively sought to restrain the presence of US surveillance vessels in as well as US aircraft over its EEZ.[49] Such events not only jeopardize the lives of those on board the vessels, but also escalate tensions between States and within regions.

The United States and commentators closely involved in negotiating the LOSC have maintained that the protection of the freedom of navigation and other related uses anticipated that States would be able to conduct military activities in the EEZ of another State, subject only to due regard requirements.[50] China, among other States, has instead declared that such conduct is not permissible in the EEZ.[51] Indeed, several States expressly declared at the time they became parties to the LOSC that military activities by other States were not considered permissible in their EEZ.[52] A set of guidelines negotiated by senior officials and analysts in the Asia-Pacific region with the intention to reach agreement on this controversy support the view that military activities in the EEZ of another State are part of the freedom of navigation,[53] but have not yet garnered widespread agreement among States.

Overall, it may be argued that these current controversies have arisen because States are constantly seeking to promote their own national security interests, and these may not be shared with other States but instead may well come at the expense of other common interests that may exist. James Kraska has argued forcefully that the increasing number of claims against the freedom of navigation will ultimately prove detrimental to maritime security.[54] Each of the critical issues discussed in this

---

[48] See MJ Valencia, *The Proliferation Security Initiative: Making Waves in Asia* (Routledge Oxford 2005) 20–2.

[49] Klein, above n 17, 218–19.

[50] JM Van Dyke, 'Military Ships and Planes Operating in the Exclusive Economic Zone of Another Country' (2004) 28 *Marine Policy* 29, 31 (citing statement of Ambassador Tommy Koh from the negotiations of the LOSC). See also R Pedrozo, 'Preserving Navigational Rights and Freedoms: The Right to Conduct Military Activities in China's Exclusive Economic Zone' (2010) 9 *Chinese Journal of International Law* 9.

[51] See eg S Yee, 'Sketching the Debate on Military Activities in the EEZ: An Editorial Comment' (2010) 9 *Chinese Journal of International Law* 1; Ziafeng and Cheng, above n 12.

[52] Eg Brazil, India, Iran, and Malaysia. See discussion in GA Galdorisi and AV Kaufman, 'Military Activities in the Exclusive Economic Zone: Preventing Uncertainty and Defusing Conflict' (2002) 32 *California Western International Law Journal* 253.

[53] S Bateman, 'Prospective Guidelines for Navigation and Overflight in the Exclusive Economic Zone' (2005) 144 *Maritime Studies* 17, 23.

[54] See J Kraska, *Maritime Power and the Law of the Sea: Expeditionary Operations in World Politics* (Oxford University Press Oxford 2011) 221–90.

section reflect situations where States are seeking to gain greater exclusive control at the expense of inclusive interests in maintaining high seas freedoms.

4 Future Challenges in Maritime Security

What will be perceived as maritime security threats in the years ahead will obviously change over time. In this regard, it may be worth recalling Edwin D Dickinson authored an article entitled 'Is the Crime of Piracy Obsolete' in 1925.[55] Nonetheless, piracy remains an ongoing issue for international shipping and it could be predicted that as pirates access improved technology, their threat may become greater than it is at present. While accurate predictions may be elusive, there are some indications of issues that may emerge as greater maritime security concerns in the years ahead. This part discusses the evolving threats that may arise as a result of technological development, new uses of the oceans, and changes in the environment. The examination then shifts to the under-analysed aspect of human dimensions and the many jurisdictional issues that arise and are yet to be fully resolved.

4.1 Evolving maritime security threats

Technological advances will inevitably impact on how States conceive of their maritime security. One dimension is that States may take the view that their defences are weakened by the use of technology deployed from the sea to gain greater information about their coastal border security operations, forces, and equipment. Greater efforts are also being undertaken to gather communications and signal intelligence, which may potentially be used for electronic or information warfare.[56] Rules relating to the freedom of overflight may be reassessed with the use of unmanned aerial vehicles (drones) for military surveillance activities.

A second dimension is that States will be able to benefit from technological developments to improve their policing of maritime areas and be in a better position to detect and respond to crimes and other illegal activities within their waters. The Pacific Island nation of Palau, for example, has been the subject of a pilot project involving the use of unmanned aerial vehicles as a potential means to improve

---

[55] ED Dickinson, 'Is the Crime of Piracy Obsolete?' (1925) 38 *Harvard Law Review* 334.
[56] See Ball, n 47.

surveillance in monitoring its vast EEZ against illegal fishing.[57] Laws relating to hot pursuit, the right of visit, and the exercise of enforcement jurisdiction may need to be reviewed to align with information obtained and shared through advancing technology.

A further impact on maritime security by technology could be the increased sophistication of criminal activities as perpetrators are able to access new means and methods to conduct their activities and avoid detection. In the development of tracking devices, such as those envisaged for the LRIT Regulations as well as the Automatic Identification System, security measures are necessary to ensure that only State authorities are able to access information and not criminal organizations.[58]

Transnational criminal organizations are also turning to new forms of transportation for trafficking at sea, as submarines have now been detected for drug trafficking operations in Central America and the Caribbean.[59] Submarines have more typically been used by State authorities as part of their naval forces and rules regulating the passage of submarines, especially in maritime areas close to the coast, have been predicated on the understanding that submarines are not privately owned and operated. While submarines must navigate on the surface for the purposes of innocent passage in the territorial sea,[60] it is generally understood that no such requirement exists in relation to transit passage.[61] Will this need to be reconsidered in the context of submarines that are not subject to sovereign immunity?

What constitutes maritime security threats may further expand as States perceive of situations or other circumstances that jeopardize the safety and well-being of their communities. At present, wilful and intentional damage to the environment is considered a maritime security threat,[62] but it could be the case that other environmental harm will similarly be viewed within the context of maritime security. Anthropogenic harm to the marine environment may become increasingly problematic and have an increased impact on the security of the State. The changes to the marine environment resulting from climate change may further prompt action by States to protect their maritime and terrestrial interests.[63]

Ultimately, while technological and environmental changes influence the uses of the oceans, these challenges will continue to be met within the existing framework of

---

[57] 'Pacific's Palau Mulls Drone Patrols to Monitor Waters', *Global Post* (4 October 2013), available at <http://www.globalpost.com/dispatch/news/afp/131004/pacifics-palau-mulls-drone-patrols-monitor-waters>.

[58] See IMO Doc MSC80/5/5 (2 March 2005) 3–4 (submitted by the International Mobile Satellite Organization (IMSO)).

[59] MS Schmit and T Shanker, 'To Smuggle More Drugs, Traffickers Go Under the Sea', *New York Times* (9 September 2012), available at <http://www.nytimes.com/2012/09/10/world/americas/drug-smugglers-pose-underwater-challenge-in-caribbean.html>.

[60] LOSC, n 5, Art 20.   [61] See further discussion in Chapter 24 in this volume.

[62] See UN Secretary General, n 3, [39].

[63] See eg A McIlgorm et al, 'How will Climate Change Alter Fishery Governance? Insights from Seven International Case Studies' (2010) 34 *Marine Policy* 170.

rights and duties for each maritime zone as established under the LOSC. Where certain activities were not contemplated in this treaty, there may be need for additional rules or guidelines. Depending on the urgency of the threat, the Security Council may step in to determine State action on a more immediate basis. Otherwise, treaties or non-binding agreements may be needed to expand on the existing framework in response to widely recognized threats and challenges that arise.

4.2 Human dimension

In looking ahead, maritime security will need to address ways to improve control over non-State actors (such as pirates, illegal fishers, people smugglers, terrorists, crews on vessels) in an area that is not readily controlled. There are a range of laws that address the particular activities and interests of humans at sea. These include rights and duties for seafarers, for those rescued at sea, stowaways, as well as alleged criminal offenders. While a framework of laws and guidelines therefore exists, there is scope for further study as to the regulation of these individuals.

There are considerable jurisdictional complexities when dealing with the perpetrators of maritime crimes and other acts that threaten maritime security. The location of any act determines if a coastal State has authority and what authority it may have depending on what has occurred. As a vessel will typically be involved, the flag State of that vessel may have a jurisdictional interest. The nationality of the perpetrators and potentially of any victims may further be relevant. On one vessel, the master and crew members may be of different nationalities. While international law focuses on the nationality of the vessel (or its State of registration), the legal and beneficial owners, as well as the insurers, may be from different States. The financial interests at stake may prompt these actors to influence events, including through their own State of nationality. The interests of these many different States may all be put in play depending on any given factual scenario.

The *Achille Lauro* reflects a classic example of these jurisdictional clashes. The *Achille Lauro* was a cruise ship flagged to Italy and was 30 miles off the coast of Egypt when members of the Palestinian Liberation Front took control of the vessel. Holding all crew and passengers as hostages, a demand was made to Israel to release certain prisoners. When the demand was not met, a US national was pushed overboard and killed. An agreement was subsequently reached where passage to Tunisia was to be granted to the hostage-takers for the release of the *Achille Lauro*. The United States then forced the aircraft to land in Italy, where Italian authorities arrested the hostage-takers. A number of States could have potentially prosecuted the hostage-takers in light of the varied bases of jurisdiction available as a matter of international law.[64] The 1988 SUA Convention ultimately sought to resolve some of

---

[64] For discussion, see CC Joyner, 'Suppression of Terrorism on the High Seas: the 1988 IMO Convention on the Safety of Maritime Navigation' (1989) 19 *Israel Yearbook on Human Rights* 341;

these jurisdictional difficulties,[65] although there is still no priority accorded to any particular basis of jurisdiction.

Other jurisdictional controversies may arise in search and rescue scenarios, where a vessel performing obligations in its Search and Rescue Region retrieves illegal migrants. The Search and Rescue Region does not necessarily overlap with a State's maritime zones and a vessel of another nationality may be requested to assist. Questions may arise as to where the vessel that has taken illegal migrants on board may deliver them and what obligations arise in prosecuting those responsible for the people smuggling activity.[66] In this situation, it is not only the law of the sea that is at play but also obligations in relation to the treatment of asylum seekers. There is undoubtedly more analysis needed on how these legal regimes should interact and how gaps and ambiguities within existing legal regimes should be resolved.

5 The Influence of Maritime Security on the Development of the Law of the Sea

Maritime security is largely not a distinct body of law in its own right, as may be the case with maritime boundary delimitations or fisheries regulations. Instead, the concept of maritime security encompasses the regulation of armed force and peacetime military activities as well as law enforcement operations and shipping safety regimes. Maritime security further sits within the general body of the law of the sea when assessing the rights and duties of States within different maritime zones. Hence, in considering the influence of maritime security on the development of the law of the sea, it is more a matter of how security concerns have influenced the articulation, interpretation, and application of the law in this area. Moreover, regard may be had to the growing network of treaties, guidelines, and other agreements that are intended to respond to and prevent particular maritime security threats. These two dimensions are examined in the discussion below.

M Halberstam, 'Terrorism on the High Seas: The *Achille Lauro*, Piracy and the IMO Convention on Maritime Safety' (1988) 82 *American Journal of International Law* 269.

[65] See SUA Convention, n 27, Art 6.

[66] These questions were starkly demonstrated in relation to the Norwegian vessel, the *MV Tampa*, and its rescue of asylum seekers who had left Indonesia and were bound for Australia. For discussion, see DR Rothwell, 'The Law of the Sea and the *MV Tampa* Incident: Reconciling Maritime Principles with Coastal State Sovereignty' (2002) 13 *Public Law Review* 118.

5.1 Maintain the ambiguities?

A hallmark of the law of the sea has been the preference to treat security concerns implicitly rather than explicitly. There are many examples in this regard within the LOSC. As mentioned earlier, the regime of transit passage allows for passage 'in normal mode'.[67] This term has then typically been interpreted as allowing launching and recovery of aircraft and helicopters, as well as putting up air patrols and formation steaming.[68] Although this interpretation of the clause has not been without debate,[69] it did resolve an issue of significant controversy within the law of the sea (namely, the breadth of the territorial sea) and reflected a compromise between the competing interests of littoral States and the superpowers of the time.

Similarly, deliberate ambiguity was employed in relation to the rights accruing to States in foreign EEZs, as these include the freedom of navigation and 'other internationally lawful uses of the sea related to these freedoms'.[70] As discussed, States have adopted differing interpretations as to whether this term is broad enough to allow military activities in a foreign EEZ. The ambiguity within the express terms of the LOSC allows for States to argue their position either way and while a clearer prescription may be optimal, the existing phrase allowed for States to reach agreement on the treaty text and has largely maintained minimal order on this issue.

The LOSC only explicitly references security in a few specific instances. What constitutes the 'peace, good order or security' of a State is an essential element in determining whether passage through the territorial sea of a State is innocent or not.[71] A series of activities that render passage non-innocent provides some indication of what conduct threatens the security of the coastal State.[72] The LOSC also references security in the context of permitting States to withhold evidence the disclosure of which is 'contrary to the essential interests of its security'.[73] Such an exclusion holds particular importance when it is recalled that the LOSC entails a compulsory dispute settlement system,[74] whereby States may be subjected to arbitration or adjudication once becoming parties to the LOSC.[75] These compulsory procedures prompted further explicit protection of security in the LOSC, as States may opt to exclude disputes concerning military activities or those concerning the

---

[67] LOSC, n 5, Art 39(1).
[68] See WF Doran, 'An Operational Commander's Perspective on the 1982 LOS Convention' (1995) 10 *International Journal of Marine and Coastal Law* 335, 340.
[69] See eg V Lowe, 'The Commander's Handbook on the Law of Naval Operations and the Contemporary Law of the Sea' (1991) 64 *International Law Studies: The Law of Naval Operations* 109, 111 and 122.
[70] LOSC, n 5, Art 58.   [71] Ibid, Art 19.
[72] S Kaye, 'Freedom of Navigation in a Post 9/11 World: Security and Creeping Jurisdiction' in D Freestone, R Barnes, and DM Ong (eds), *The Law of the Sea: Progress and Prospects* (Oxford University Press Oxford 2006) 347, 348–9.
[73] LOSC, n 5, Art 302.   [74] See further Chapter 18 in this volume.   [75] LOSC, n 5, Part XV.

functions of the UN Security Council from the scope of mandatory arbitration or adjudication.[76]

In light of the existing ambiguities in the LOSC, States have otherwise been left to negotiate separate agreements, which are discussed in the next section, or the expectation is that other avenues will be pursued,[77] including the development of customary international law, to govern maritime security matters. The Proliferation Security Initiative (PSI) is an example of States seeking to test the bounds of the LOSC language and potentially develop customary international law for the purposes of detecting the shipment of weapons of mass destruction and related material to non-State actors. The PSI was spearheaded by the United States and attracted support from approximately 60 States.[78] The Statement of Interdiction Principles adopted by the participants intended them to take action 'to the extent their national legal authorities permit[ted] and consistent with their obligations under international law and frameworks'.[79] There has been considerable debate as to whether the PSI was intended or has had the effect of shaping customary international law,[80] and it could not be said that there is yet a definitive answer to this question.

To the extent that customary international law may influence the interpretation and application of the LOSC, there is a concern that such development will upset the delicate compromise achieved in the LOSC at the time of its drafting and should be avoided.[81] With technological advances and shifting perceptions of what constitutes threats to maritime security, it would seem that this position will become increasingly difficult to maintain.

5.2 An increasing labyrinth

Beyond the general rights and obligations accruing to States in the different maritime zones that implicate responses to maritime security threats, States have also sought to conclude agreements to deal with specific concerns. In this regard, there are an increasing number of agreements, concluded on bilateral, regional, and multilateral bases, to address diverse aspects of maritime security.[82] An exceptional

---

[76] See ibid, Art 298(1)(c).

[77] The other means and fora available to develop the law of the sea, or potentially amend the LOSC, include through the meetings of States Parties (known as SPLOS) or under the auspices of the UN General Assembly. See discussion in Tanaka, above n 20, 32–7.

[78] Klein, above n 17, 195–6.

[79] US Department of State, *Proliferation Security Initiative: Statement of Interdiction Principles: Fact Sheet* (2003) Principle 4, available at <http://www.state.gov/t/isn/c27726.htm>.

[80] See eg Valenica, above n 48, 47–8; TC Perry, 'Blurring the Ocean Zones: The Effect of the Proliferation Security Initiative on the Customary International Law of the Sea' (2006) 37 *Ocean Development and International Law* 33.

[81] See Kraska, above n 54, 224.

[82] These have been surveyed in J Kraska and R Pedrozo, *International Maritime Security Law* (Brill Leiden 2013).

example of a broad maritime security agreement was adopted by States members of the Caribbean Community.[83] It is readily seen that there has been considerable law-making activity at different levels of governance.

Within the IMO, the primary work has been in relation to maritime safety and other standards for international shipping. The IMO first became engaged in matters of maritime security when the UN General Assembly requested the IMO to draft what became the 1988 SUA Convention.[84] Following the September 11 attacks on the United States, the IMO has become increasingly engaged in issues of maritime security. In its global governance role, the IMO has overseen the adoption of the ISPS Code,[85] the LRIT Regulations,[86] guidelines for rescues at sea,[87] seafarers identification agreement,[88] and ship routing measures along with spatial planning.[89] Against this expanding body of law, it must be recalled that the IMO does not typically deal with enforcement powers in relation to its agreements. At most, there are reporting mechanisms to the institution, but the more common situation is to anticipate enforcement consistently with existing rules relating to enforcement under the law of the sea.

For the augmentation of enforcement powers, States have instead devised regimes addressing particular maritime security threats and set out jurisdictional bases for the prevention and suppression of the relevant activities. Additional powers for exercising the right of visit have been granted under multilateral treaties such as the 1988 Drugs Convention,[90] the 1995 Fish Stocks Agreement,[91] the 2000 Migrant Smuggling Protocol,[92] and the 2005 SUA Convention.[93] These treaties have all attracted wide participation across all regions of the world.[94]

Regional agreements have also been pursued to address specific threats, such as the Council of Europe agreement on drug-trafficking,[95] the 2004 Regional Cooperation Agreement on Combating Piracy and Armed Robbery Against Ships in Asia (ReCAAP),[96] and in the broader context, the 2008 CARICOM Maritime

---

[83] 2008 CARICOM Maritime and Airspace Security Co-operation Agreement.
[84] UNGA Resolution 40/61, UN Doc A/RES/40/61 (9 December 1985).
[85] See SOLAS, 1983 Amendments to the Annex, n 31.   [86] See n 33 and accompanying text.
[87] IMO, Guidelines on the Treatment of Persons Rescued at Sea, IMO Res MSC.167(78), IMO Doc 78/26/Add.2 (10 May 2004) Annex 34.
[88] 1958 ILO Convention (No 108) Concerning Seafarers' Identity Documents (revised 2003).
[89] Safety zones and security zones may be established to protect, for example, submarine cables, offshore installations, offshore platforms.
[90] Drugs Convention, n 24.   [91] FSA, n 26.   [92] Migrant Smuggling Protocol, n 25.
[93] 2005 Protocol to Convention for the Suppression of Unlawful Acts Against the Safety of Maritime Navigation (hereinafter 2005 SUA Protocol).
[94] The 1998 Drugs Convention, n 24, has 188 States Parties, the 1995 FSA, n 26, has 81, the 2000 Migrant Smuggling Protocol, n 25, has 138. The 1988 SUA Convention, n 27, has 164 whereas its 2005 Protocol, n 93, has attracted 29 States parties thus far.
[95] 1995 Agreement on Illicit Traffic by Sea, Implementing Article 17 of the Drugs Convention, n 24.
[96] 2004 Regional Cooperation Agreement on Combating Piracy and Armed Robbery Against Ships in Asia.

and Airspace Security Co-operation Agreement. Regional fisheries management organizations are also active in taking steps to reduce illegal, unregulated, and unreported fishing activities.[97] These sorts of regional responses have been preferred where there is a shared concern to address a specific geographic area, or where neighbouring States have a common interest in responding to specific maritime security threats. In some instances, the regional response is intended to implement a multilateral commitment, as was the case with the European drug-trafficking convention as an implementation of Article 17 of the 1988 UN convention on drug trafficking.

The United States has also been very active in concluding bilateral treaties with neighbouring States to respond to the illicit trade in narcotics,[98] and also to prevent the transport of weapons of mass destruction in violation of international law.[99] Bilateral treaties have also been pursued between European and North-African States in response to people smuggling concerns.[100] At the bilateral level, States have been able to improve their law enforcement capabilities by cooperative arrangements, such as allowing for officials from one State to accompany officials of another State on the latter's vessels for the purposes of granting authority to act in the first State's maritime zones or against its vessels.[101] The possibility of multilateral hot pursuit has been set out in a bilateral agreement between Australia and France to improve responses to illegal fishing in remote Antarctic waters.[102]

Formal agreements may be supplemented with non-binding guidelines, or codes of conduct or memoranda of understanding. The PSI and its Statement of Interdiction Principles may be seen as a broad political agreement that has provided a basis for cooperation among participants, and has extended to facilitating joint exercises and training. While it has been reported that the

---

[97] For further discussion, see Chapter 20 in this volume.

[98] See discussion in MJ Williams, 'Bilateral Maritime Agreements Enhancing International Cooperation in the Suppression of Illicit Maritime Narcotics Trafficking' in MH Nordquist and JN Moore (eds), *Oceans Policy: New Institutions, Challenges and Opportunities* (Martinus Nijhoff Leiden 1999) 179; see also J Gonzalez-Pinto, 'Interdiction of Narcotics in International Waters' (2008) 15 *University of Miami International and Comparative Law Review* 443.

[99] AJ Roach, 'Proliferation Security Initiative (PSI): Countering Proliferation by Sea' in MH Nordquist, JN Moore, and K Fu (eds), *Recent Developments in the Law of the Sea and China* (Martinus Nijhoff Leiden 2006) 351.

[100] See V Moreno-Lax, 'Seeking Asylum in the Mediterranean: Against a Fragmentary Reading of EU Member States' Obligations Accruing at Sea' (2011) 23 *International Journal of Refugee Law* 174, 178–85.

[101] These are commonly referred to as ship rider agreements.

[102] See W Gullett and C Schofield, 'Pushing the Limits of the Law of the Sea Convention: Australian and French Cooperative Surveillance and Enforcement in the Southern Ocean' (2007) 22 *International Journal of Marine and Coastal Law* 545. See further EJ Molenaar, 'Multilateral Hot Pursuit and Illegal Fishing in the Southern Ocean: The Pursuits of the *Viarsa I* and the *South Tomi*' (2004) 19 *International Journal of Marine and Coastal Law* 19.

PSI has provided the basis for several interdictions, full details have not been made public.[103] Other non-binding agreements designed to enhance cooperation within the existing confines of international law include the Bali Process on people smuggling,[104] and the Djibouti Code of Conduct to address piracy among eastern African States.[105]

The Security Council could potentially influence the development of the law relating to maritime security through its mandatory resolutions adopted under Chapter VII. The weight of these resolutions may rightly be questioned as a source of law, given that they commonly target particular States or specific situations. Hence resolutions that permit States to conduct a right of visit for the purposes of enforcing sanctions imposed under Article 41 of the UN Charter do not grant authority more broadly and otherwise upset the exclusive jurisdiction of the flag State.[106] More typically, Security Council resolutions will reflect the existing law of the sea. For example, the resolutions relating to enforcement of sanctions against North Korea still deferred to the authority of flag States in consenting to actions against their vessels.[107] Equally, the resolutions addressing piracy off the coast of Somalia were intended to sit within existing law rather than potentially influence the law of piracy or allow for the possibility that other situations of piracy could constitute a threat to peace and security warranting action under Chapter VII of the UN Charter.[108] The potential of the Security Council to influence the development of the law relating to maritime security will only be realized if the Council opts to exercise its powers under Chapter VII. The engagement of the Security Council in this regard may provide a considerable scope of authority for legal developments if it decides that certain maritime security threats are threats to international peace and security and then authorizes a wide range of actions in response to that threat.[109]

---

[103] A Prosser and H Scoville Jr, *The Proliferation Security Initiative in Perspective* (2004), available at <http://www.docstoc.com/docs/22652143/The-Proliferation-Security-Initiative-in-Perspective>.

[104] The Bali Process on People Smuggling, Trafficking in Persons and Related Transnational Crime, available at <http://www.baliprocess.net/>.

[105] Code of Conduct Concerning the Repression of Piracy and Armed Robbery Against Ships in the Western Indian Ocean and the Gulf of Aden (29 January 2009), IMO Doc C 120/14 (3 April 2009).

[106] For discussion, see R McLaughlin, 'United Nations Mandated Naval Interdiction Operations in the Territorial Sea' (2002) 51 *International and Comparative Law Quarterly* 249.

[107] See UNSC Res 1872 (12 June 2009) [11], [12].

[108] See interventions by Indonesia and South Africa: UN Doc S/PV.5902 (2 June 2008).

[109] The 'legislative' activity of the Security Council has been seen in response to terrorism more generally. See discussion in E Rosand, 'Security Council Resolution 1373, the Counterterrorism Committee, and the Fight Against Terrorism' (2003) 97 *American Journal of International Law* 333.

6 Conclusion

Maritime security is a very dynamic area of the law of the sea. As discussed in this chapter, it encompasses traditional security concerns, which may engage the law of armed conflict, as well as law enforcement and shipping safety issues. Critical problems presently confronting States include unresolved boundary disputes, increasingly sophisticated and menacing criminal enterprises, and the collection of data and information at sea that threatens the interests of a State. Looking ahead, States will need to consider the positive and negative impacts of advancing technology in their regulation of maritime activities. Laws will need to develop apace to the extent possible, and will not only need to consider what is happening but also who is engaged in those activities and how authority may be asserted over them. Responding to these challenges will no doubt influence the development of laws relating to maritime security in the future.

Maritime security has already clearly influenced the development of the law of the sea, as evidenced by the increasing number of agreements and arrangements concluded by States. While the international law framework is becoming increasingly complex and comprehensive, there are gaps remaining. Most notably, the gaps arise because not all States are participating in the myriad of agreements. Obviously not every State will share the same level of concern and interest in responding to maritime security threats as may be the case for other States. Some regimes may work effectively without universal participation, provided the States most interested and most affected are part of the relevant regime.

Moreover, those States that do become parties to the different international treaties or engage in other arrangements do not necessarily take all of the required steps to implement their international obligations. Implementation may be a particularly difficult question for countries that do not bestow policing powers on naval forces and in federal States where criminal prosecution happens on the state or provincial level rather than on the national level. In the former situations, States will need to give careful consideration to the deployment of their vessels in international policing operations. In the latter, States will potentially need to undertake legislative reform or make other internal arrangements to ensure international obligations can be fulfilled.

It may further be the case that States lack the resources to operationalize fully the requirements for improving maritime security or for enforcing prescribed standards to reduce risks. Such concerns were already manifested in the implementation of the ISPS Code and in changes to seafarer identification requirements.[110] In

---

[110] See Klein, n 17, 162, 237–9.

each instance, developed States undertook regional and bilateral initiatives to assist developing States. However, not all coastal States will be agreeable to the intervention of third States in improving maritime security regimes within their waters. So much was evident in the responses of Indonesia and Malaysia to US proposals to undertake greater surveillance and other security measures within the Malacca Straits.[111] Nonetheless, greater cooperation and capacity building will be necessary tools to strengthen the overall international law framework for maritime security.

---

[111] TM Sittnick, 'State Responsibility and Maritime Terrorism in the Strait of Malacca: Persuading Indonesia and Malaysia to take Additional Steps to Secure the Strait' (2005) 14 *Pacific Rim Law and Policy Journal* 743, 755.

THE MEDITERRANEAN SEA

IRINI PAPANICOLOPULU

1 INTRODUCTION

A sea of legends and harsh realities, the Mediterranean Sea provides a unique combination of complex geographical, political, cultural, and economic factors that have shaped regional solutions and have prompted developments in the general law of the sea.

Before turning to its legal regime, it is therefore useful to provide a brief overview of its main features to the reader. The Mediterranean Sea covers 2.51 million km² and borders three continents. The Strait of Gibraltar connects it to the Atlantic Ocean, of which the Mediterranean Sea is a part, and the Suez Canal connects it to the Red Sea and the Indian Ocean. The Mediterranean is generally considered as distinct from the Black Sea, to which it is connected via the Dardanelles and Bosporus, although some regional treaties apply to both seas. From a hydrographic point of view, the Mediterranean Sea is usually split into an eastern basin and western basin, each possessing its own marine and biological characteristics.[1] It can be further divided into a number of sub-seas, such as the Adriatic Sea, the Aegean

---

[1] International Hydrographic Organization (IHO), *Limits of Oceans and Seas* (IHO Bremerhaven 1953) 15.

Sea, the Sea of Alboran, the Balearic Sea, the Ionian Sea, the Ligurian Sea, and the Tyrrhenian Sea.[2]

The Mediterranean Sea is bordered by 21 States: Albania, Algeria, Bosnia-Herzegovina, Croatia, Cyprus, Egypt, France, Greece, Israel, Italy, Lebanon, Libya, Malta, Monaco, Montenegro, Morocco, Slovenia, Spain, Syria, Tunisia, and Turkey (Mediterranean coastal States). The United Kingdom has also a territorial presence, exercising its sovereignty over three territories: the sovereign bases of Akrotiri and Dekhelia, on the island of Cyprus, and Gibraltar. Palestine also borders the Mediterranean, through the coastal front of the Gaza Strip. Mediterranean States fall into different political and economic groupings: the States on its northwestern shore are generally developed countries while those on its eastern and southern shores are mostly developing States. Nine of them are members of the European Union,[3] eight of the Arab League,[4] and four of the African Union.[5] Most European Mediterranean States are also members of the North Atlantic Treaty Organization.[6]

The position of the Mediterranean Sea, which links three continents, Africa, Asia, and Europe, has been at the heart of the development of the region since ancient times. The Egyptian, Phoenician, Greek, Persian, and Roman civilizations have all developed along its shores and with mutual exchanges have constituted the basis of the Mediterranean culture. In the centuries that followed the Mediterranean shores witnessed the rise and fall of the Byzantines and the arrival of the Arabs and the Normans. The nineteenth century saw the colonization of North Africa by European States. During the twentieth century, the collapse of the Ottoman Empire after World War I, the creation of the State of Israel, and the decolonization process taking place along the eastern and southern shores of the Mediterranean transformed the political configuration of the Mediterranean Sea. This picture has again been altered following the more recent conflicts in the former Yugoslavia and as a result of the 'Arab Spring'.

Today, the Mediterranean Sea supports intense human activity by both riparian and non-riparian States. Activities include navigation, the exploitation of marine living resources, transportation of people and of goods, energy production and transportation, and tourism.[7] Illegal activities, such as drug trafficking, illegal,

---

[2] Ibid, 16–18.

[3] Croatia, Cyprus, France, Greece, Italy, Malta, Slovenia, Spain, and the United Kingdom.

[4] Algeria, Egypt, Lebanon, Libya, Morocco, Syria, and Tunisia. Palestine is also a member State of the Arab League.

[5] Algeria, Egypt, Libya, and Tunisia.

[6] Albania, Croatia, France, Greece, Italy, Spain, Turkey, and the United Kingdom.

[7] See generally International Union for the Conservation of Nature (IUCN), *Towards a Better Governance of the Mediterranean* (2010), available at <http://cmsdata.iucn.org/downloads/medgov_final_aveccouv_opt.pdf>; and with respect to the impact of shipping, A Abdulla and O Linden (eds), *Maritime Traffic Effects on Biodiversity in the Mediterranean Sea, Volume 1—Review of Impacts, Priority Areas and Mitigation Measures* (2008), available at <http://cmsdata.iucn.org/downloads/maritime_v1_lr.pdf>.

unreported, and unregulated (IUU) fishing, illegal operations targeting the underwater cultural heritage, migrant smuggling, and human trafficking pose significant problems.

All people who have lived along its shores have shown a keen interest in securing their dominion over the Mediterranean, including by regulating maritime activities therein. The island of Rhodes gave its name to the *lex Rhodia*, possibly the world's oldest maritime law.[8] The *Llibre del Consolat de Mar*, a collection of Mediterranean maritime customs and ordinances in the Catalan language, first published in 1494, constituted the basis for further codifications of maritime customs in other Mediterranean countries.[9] The maritime interests of Venice were the basis of the book by Paolo Sarpi on the *dominium* of the sea that forebode future developments in the law of the sea.[10] In modern times, Mediterranean States have actively contributed to the development of the law of the sea during the First and Third United Nations Conferences on the Law of the Sea (UNCLOS I and III) and have promoted further developments following the entry into force of the 1982 United Nations Convention on the Law of the Sea (LOSC).

This chapter focuses on the Mediterranean Sea legal regime, in order to critically examine past achievements and present challenges.[11] The legal regime of any given ocean or sea is a composite product, which includes the unilateral acts of States by which they establish maritime zones and regulate the exercise of their power therein, the bilateral agreements for the delimitation of maritime boundaries, and the multilateral legal instruments, which provide uniform substantial regulation and institutionalize cooperation.[12] The legal regime of the Mediterranean is examined on the basis of this division, looking first at the jurisdictional framework (Section 2), then at the delimitation of maritime boundaries (Section 3), and finally at the multilateral instruments adopted by coastal States in order to regulate a number of activities (Section 4). The chapter closes with the identification of successes and ongoing challenges (Section 5).

---

[8] W Ashburner, *The Rhodian Sea Law* (Clarendon Press Oxford 1909).

[9] S Corrieri and T Scovazzi (eds), *La Formazione del Diritto Marittimo nella Prospettiva Storica* (Giuffrè Editore Milan 2010).

[10] G Acquaviva and T Scovazzi (eds), *Il Dominio di Venezia sul mare Adriatico nelle Opere di Paolo Sarpi e Giulio Pace* (Giuffrè Editore Milan 2007).

[11] This chapter focuses on law of the sea issues and will not discuss political aspects, except as they directly relate to the application of law of the sea rules, or the relationship between Mediterranean States in other areas, such as the Euro-Mediterranean Partnership (launched during the Euro-Mediterranean Ministerial Conference held in Barcelona in November 1995) and the EU European Neighbourhood Policy.

[12] In the case of semi-enclosed seas, cooperation among coastal States is further promoted by 1982 United Nations Convenion on the Law of the Sea, Art 123 (hereinafter LOSC).

2 THE JURISDICTIONAL FRAMEWORK

A unique characteristic of the Mediterranean, setting it apart from all other seas, is the number and variety of maritime zones claimed by its coastal States. On the one hand, Mediterranean States have advanced claims of *sui generis* jurisdictional zones. Alongside the traditional maritime zones endorsed by the LOSC (internal waters, territorial sea, contiguous zone, exclusive economic zone, and continental shelf) there are archaeological zones, fisheries zones, ecological protection zones, and even an ecological and fisheries protection zone. On the other, coastal States have manifested a reluctance to claim maritime areas or to extend them to the maximum limit allowed under the law of the sea. This has resulted in a patchwork of jurisdictional rights and duties of States and the enduring presence of high seas areas that are within 200 nautical miles (nm) of the coasts. This section will first briefly discuss the existence and extent of LOSC zones, as well as the baselines from which they are measured, and will then turn to non-LOSC zones before concluding with some comments on the Mediterranean high seas.

2.1 Baselines and Maritime Zones under the LOSC

Many Mediterranean States have drawn straight baselines along parts of their coasts, from which they measure their maritime zones.[13] While not always following the criteria set by Article 7 of the LOSC, straight baselines do not significantly depart from the general practice of States worldwide. Furthermore, two States have drawn straight baselines enclosing gulfs, which are claimed as historic bays and are considered as internal waters: Italy (Gulf of Taranto) and Libya (Gulf of Sidra). Both claims have met with protests by some States.[14] In both cases, the 'historical' nature of the claim was hard to substantiate at the time of the adoption of the baseline and in the case of the closing line of the Gulf of Sidra, measuring 300 miles, its length puts to the test the absence of a maximum length for the closing lines of historical bays.

All Mediterranean States have a territorial sea, generally extending 12 nm from the baselines, except for three States: the United Kingdom has a 3 nm limit off Gibraltar

---

[13] Straight baselines have been drawn by Albania, Algeria, Croatia, Cyprus, France, Italy, Libya, Malta, Morocco, Montenegro, Spain, Tunisia, and Turkey. English translations of relevant national legislation can be found in the database maintained by the United Nations Division on Ocean Affairs and the Law of the Sea (DOALOS), *Maritime Space: Maritime Zones and Maritime Delimitation*, available at <http://www.un.org/Depts/los/LEGISLATIONANDTREATIES/index.htm>. Normative references will be given only for acts that are not to be found in this database.

[14] JA Roach and RW Smith, *Excessive Maritime Claims* (3rd edn Martinus Nijhoff Leiden 2012) 44–5 and 47.

and the sovereign bases of Akrotiri and Dekhelia in Cyprus; Greece has a general 6 nm limit; and Turkey a 6 nm limit off its Aegean Sea coast and a 12 nm limit off the remaining coasts. The extension of territorial waters of Greece and Turkey, which is permitted under international law, is hindered by political issues between the two States. Due to its geographical position, the territorial sea of Bosnia-Herzegovina is enclaved by the internal waters of Croatia and extends for less than 12 nm.

Beyond the territorial sea a distinction has to be made between the seabed and subsoil, on one hand, and the water column, on the other. Due to the geography of the Mediterranean Sea, the maximum distance between opposite coasts being less than 400 nm, all the seabed and subsoil falls under the regime of the continental shelf. In other words, there are no parts of the international seabed area in the Mediterranean Sea.

As to the waters above the continental shelf, different regimes apply. Algeria, Cyprus, Egypt, France, Malta, Morocco, Spain, and Syria have enacted legislation proclaiming a contiguous zone adjacent to their territorial sea, for the enforcement of customs, fiscal, immigration, and sanitary laws and regulations.[15] Exclusive economic zones have been claimed by Morocco (1980), Syria (2003), Cyprus (2004), Tunisia (2005), Libya (2009), Lebanon (2011), and France (2012).[16] Two further States should be considered as having claimed exclusive economic zones.[17] Egypt on ratifying the LOSC in 1983 declared that it would exercise, as from that day, the rights attributed by the LOSC in its exclusive economic zone.[18] While no legislation is known to have been passed concerning this zone, it can be considered that Egypt has an exclusive economic zone, in particular since its delimitation with Cyprus in 2003. The second is Israel, which, following the 2010 boundary treaty with Cyprus, deposited a list of coordinates delimiting the outer limits of its exclusive economic zone with the UN Secretary General in 2011.[19] The delimitation of the outer limit of the exclusive economic zone provides strong evidence of the existence of such a zone. However, it does not necessarily follow that the coastal State actually exercises its rights within that zone.

---

[15] It is debatable whether Italy has a contiguous zone for purposes other than the protection of the underwater cultural heritage.

[16] Eg Decree No 2012-1148 (France) (12 October 2012).

[17] One more State might soon extend its jurisdiction in the Mediterranean Sea. In 2005 Malta adopted legislation enabling the Prime Minister to extend the jurisdiction of Malta beyond the actual 25 nm limit of its fisheries zone. Law No 10 of 26 July 2005 [26 July 2005] 17795 *The Malta Law Gazette*, Supp.

[18] Egypt, 'Declaration Upon Ratification' (26 August 1983) in DOALOS, *Declarations and Statements*, available at <http://www.un.org/depts/los/convention_agreements/convention_declarations.htm>.

[19] Permanent Mission of Israel to the United Nations, 'List of Geographical Coordinates For the Delimitation of the Northern Limit of the Territorial Sea and Exclusive Economic Zone of the State of Israel in WGS84' (12 July 2011), available at <http://www.un.org/Depts/los/LEGISLATIONANDTREATIES/PDFFILES/isr_eez_northernlimit2011.pdf>.

2.2 *Sui generis* zones

Mediterranean States have played a major role in the promotion of initiatives to protect the exceptional underwater cultural heritage present in Mediterranean waters from destruction and looting.[20] In addition to an active role in the negotiation of dedicated legal instruments, such as the 2001 UNESCO Convention on the Protection of the Underwater Cultural Heritage (CPUCH), more and more States have established an archaeological zone adjacent to the territorial sea and measuring 24 nm from the baseline. Following an action by Tunisia in 1986—probably the first State worldwide to extend its jurisdiction beyond the territorial sea in this matter—such zones were created by France (1989), Algeria, Cyprus, and Italy (all in 2004). This action is based on Article 303(2) of the LOSC and, more recently, on Article 8 of the CPUCH. The creation of these 24 nm archaeological zones constitutes an interesting precedent and has contributed to raising awareness of the threats menacing this heritage, leading to the adoption of similar zones beyond Mediterranean waters.[21]

Five States have proclaimed fisheries zones, where they exercise exclusive rights and jurisdiction with regard to fisheries. The width of these zones differs and their extension is sometimes limited so as to avoid delimitation issues with neighbouring States; their names also vary. The Algerian fisheries zone extends for 52 nm along the eastern part of its coast and for 32 nm along the western part, so as not to reach the equidistance line with Italy and Spain. The Libyan fisheries protection zone extends for 62 nm beyond the outer limit of its territorial sea, which is short of the equidistance line with opposite States. The Tunisian fisheries zone, which has been preserved by the law establishing the exclusive economic zone, is measured according to the bathymetric criterion of 50 m depth. The Spanish fisheries protection zone, which extends up to the equidistance line with neighbouring States, has not been proclaimed in the Sea of Alboran, where complex issues of sovereignty and delimitation exist. Malta claims a 25 nm fisheries zone. Finally, under the 1995 Israeli-Palestinian Interim Agreement, Palestine was granted a fishing zone extending up to 20 nm off the coast of the Gaza Strip. However, its present extent is uncertain, as Israel has often unilaterally reduced the actual area open to fishing by Palestinian fishers.[22]

---

[20] Mediterranean States have been among the proponents and chief supporters of the adoption of legal rules to protect underwater cultural heritage, both during the Third United Nations Conference on the Law of the Sea (UNCLOS III) and the negotiations for the adoption of the CPUCH. See A Strati, *The Protection of the Underwater Cultural Heritage: An Emerging Objective of the Contemporary Law of the Sea* (Martinus Nijhoff Leiden 1995); R Garabello and T Scovazzi, *The Protection of the Underwater Cultural Heritage: Before and After the 2001 UNESCO Convention* (Martinus Nijhoff Leiden 2003).

[21] MJ Aznar, 'The Contiguous Zone as an Archaeological Maritime Zone' (2014) 29 *International Journal of Marine and Coastal Law* 1.

[22] It is not clear whether this action has affected the extent of the zone as such.

In 2003, France proclaimed an ecological protection zone, where it claimed exclusive jurisdiction with respect to the protection of the marine environment, marine scientific research, and the establishment and use of artificial islands, installations, and structures. The French ecological zone, which partially overlapped with the Spanish fisheries protection zone, has now been replaced by an exclusive economic zone. In 2005, Slovenia also proclaimed an ecological zone beyond its territorial sea. In 2006, Italy enacted framework legislation allowing for the creation of ecological protection zones and, in 2011, instituted the first of its 'ecological protection zones'[23] comprising areas of the north-western Mediterranean Sea, the Ligurian Sea, and the Tyrrhenian Sea. Within this zone, Italy has claimed jurisdiction concerning the protection of the marine environment and of underwater cultural heritage.

Environmental protection and the conservation of living resources have been combined by Croatia, which in 2005 declared an ecological and fisheries protection zone, which merges the two zones mentioned earlier and comes, in fact, very close to the concept of the exclusive economic zone. The desire to avoid unwelcome effects on its relationship with the European Union and the process towards membership seem to have been at the basis of this unusual solution.[24]

The adoption of *sui generis* zones can be seen as an ingenious way of ensuring protection of common interests, in particular the protection of the environment, in circumstances in which a State may be unwilling to fully extend its jurisdiction or sovereign rights beyond the outer limits of its territorial sea.[25] At the same time, this practice certainly introduces an element of uncertainty, as these zones do not squarely fall into the LOSC categories, and their legal regime needs to be reconstructed each time from national legislation—possibly not an easy task for nationals of other States. Furthermore, the adoption of *sui generis* zones has been perceived by some as frustrating the purpose of the exclusive economic zone, in which the coastal State is attributed duties, as well as rights, to further communitarian interests. This argument does not seem persuasive if one considers the actual nature of the ecological zones, in which coastal States have unilaterally taken upon themselves duties, without at the same time benefiting from rights. As far as fisheries zones are concerned, the actual legal regime adopted again points towards their legitimacy, since the coastal State exercises both its sovereign rights over living resources and its duties concerning protection and sustainable management of these resources.

In conclusion, while not an ideal solution, the establishment of *sui generis* zones can be accepted as a practical, temporary step towards the adoption of

---

[23] Presidential Decree No 209 of 27 October 2011, adopted on the basis of Law No 61 of 8 February 2006, (2006) 147/52 *Gazzetta Ufficiale della Repubblica Italiana* 5.

[24] D Vidas, 'The UN Convention on the Law of the Sea, the European Union and the Rule of Law: What is going on in the Adriatic Sea?' (2009) 24 *International Journal of Marine and Coastal Law* 1.

[25] G Andreone, G Cataldi, 'Regards sur les évolutions du droit de la mer en Méditerranée (2010) 56 *Annuaire français de droit international* 1; A Del Vecchio Capotosti, 'In Maiore Stat Minus: A Note on the EEZ and the Zones of Ecological Protection in the Mediterranean Sea' (2008) 39 *Ocean Development and International Law* 287.

fully fledged exclusive economic zones in the longer term. Meanwhile, they should not be seen as contrary to the law of the sea or as frustrating its purposes and aims. In the case of sensitive political relationships between neighbouring States, step-by-step extension of jurisdiction may serve the interest of friendly relationships and may be instrumental in avoiding disputes and conflict. To the extent that it allows States to balance political considerations and the achievement of some societal aims, without violating their obligations under the law of the sea, this practice deserves consideration and might serve as an example for other contested areas.

2.3 The high seas

Putting together the different claims discussed above, it emerges that there are still significant pockets of high seas in the Mediterranean. While the regime of Part VII of the LOSC applies to them, these high seas areas present two characteristics that set them apart from similar areas in other regions.[26] First, the seabed and subsoil beneath these areas of high seas is part of the continental shelf of States, rather than of the Area.[27] This means that coastal States retain sovereign rights with respect to sedentary species and non-living resources as well as their rights concerning artificial islands, platforms, and installations. The latter may have a significant, albeit confined, impact on the utilization of the waters above. Second, since all high seas areas are within 200 nm from the coasts of Mediterranean States, they could be claimed at any moment by one or other of the coastal States. While this does not affect their current status, it may play a role in the evaluation of the lawfulness of measures that purport to regulate activities vis-à-vis third States.

Claiming jurisdictional zones, or extending them up to the outer limit permitted under international law, is a right of the State. As a consequence, not doing so cannot be considered as contrary to an existing rule. At the same time, the presence of high seas pockets in the Mediterranean renders more difficult, and sometimes frustrates, the adoption of measures to protect common goods, including the environment and marine living resources. Refusal to claim jurisdiction on the part of the coastal States, resulting in the exclusive jurisdiction of the flag State in such matters, leaves parts of the Mediterranean Sea open to illegal or unregulated activities.

---

[26] T Treves, 'The High Seas as Potential Exclusive Economic Zones in the Mediterranean' in M Kohen, R Kolb, and DL Tehindrazanarivelo (eds), *Perspectives of International Law in the 21st Century: Liber Amicorum Professor Christian Dominicé* (Martinus Nijhoff Leiden 2012).

[27] Also, the conditions posed by LOSC, n 12, Art 82 do not apply to these portions of continental shelf, since they are not beyond 200 nm. This circumstance sets the Mediterranean apart from other seas, such as the Barents Sea and the Sea of Okhotsk, where portions of continental shelf exceeding 200 nm lie under the high seas.

3 Delimitation of Maritime Boundaries

3.1 Settled boundaries

The dimensions of the Mediterranean Sea—no point being beyond 200 nm from the nearest land—result in numerous overlaps of maritime entitlements and require maritime delimitation.[28] Most settled maritime boundaries have been agreed upon by treaty. In two instances the States involved have addressed their claim to the ICJ (*Tunisia v Libya* and *Libya v Malta*) and in another a maritime delimitation dispute has been referred to arbitration (*Croatia v Slovenia*).

Delimitation in the Mediterranean has followed patterns common to other regions of the world. Early treaties have dealt with the delimitation of either the continental shelf or the territorial sea.[29] Recent delimitation agreements tend to adopt either an all-purpose boundary that delimits all maritime areas or a boundary that delimits the exclusive economic zone, which includes both the seabed and subsoil and the water column.[30] With the exception of the France/Monaco and Libya/Tunisia boundaries, agreements reached so far are based on an equidistance line, often modified to take into account geographical circumstances. The presence of islands, coastal length and the desire to avoid a cutting off effect have played a role in drawing the final line.

---

[28] On delimitation of boundaries in the Mediterranean, see T Scovazzi, 'Maritime Delimitations in the Mediterranean Sea' in JC Llorens (ed), *Bancaja Euromediterranean courses of International Law* (Aranzadi Pamplona 2009) Vol 8, 349; I Papanicolopulu, 'A Note on Maritime Delimitation in a Multizonal Context: The Case of the Mediterranean' (2007) 38 *Ocean Development and International Law* 381.

[29] The territorial sea has been delimited between Cyprus and the United Kingdom (1960, delimitation of the territorial sea of the sovereign British bases of Akrotiri and Dhekelia); Italy and the former Yugoslavia (1975; Croatia and Slovenia have succeeded in the agreement); France and Italy (1986); and Bosnia-Herzegovina and Croatia (1999, for the delimitation of Croatian internal waters and Bosnian territorial sea; ratification of the agreement is still pending). Continental shelf delimitation agreements have been concluded between Italy and Tunisia (1971), Italy and Spain (1974), Greece and Italy (1977), Libya and Malta (1986, following *Continental Shelf (Libyan Arab Jamahiriya v Malta)* (Judgment) [1985] ICJ Rep 13 (hereinafter *Libya v Malta*)), Libya and Tunisia (1988, following *Continental Shelf (Tunisia v Libyan Arab Jamahiriya)* (Judgment) [1982] ICJ Rep 18 (hereinafter *Tunisia v Libya*)), and Albania and Italy (1992).

[30] The first solution was adopted by France and Monaco (1984), Algeria and Tunisia (2002, temporary boundary), and Albania and Greece (2009; ratification of the agreement is still pending also following a decision by the Constitutional Court of Albania stating that the agreement was in violation of the Albanian Constitution). The delimitation of the exclusive economic zone forms the content of the agreements between Cyprus and Egypt (2003), Cyprus and Lebanon (2007; ratification of the agreement is still pending), and Cyprus and Israel (2010).

The institution of exclusive economic zones and *sui generis* zones, subsequent to the delimitation of continental shelf boundaries, has raised the issue of the possible extension of the seabed boundary to the delimitation of the water column.[31] Unlike States in other regions, Mediterranean States have generally abstained from extending the seabed boundary to delimit the water column, but have instead sought to negotiate new boundaries.

3.2 Pending delimitations

Apart from Monaco, which has settled all its maritime boundaries, Mediterranean States still face pending delimitations. In a few cases, States have negotiated boundary lines, but the treaties concerned have not entered into force as they are yet to be ratified by at least one of the parties. This is the case of the all-purpose maritime boundary between Albania and Greece; the boundary delimiting the maritime area of Bosnia Herzegovina and the internal waters of Croatia; and the exclusive economic zone boundary between Cyprus and Lebanon. The remaining bilateral boundaries, as well as all tripoints, still need to be delimited and, in many cases, involve complex problems of a legal, geographical, or political nature. Factors that prevent a final settlement are not dissimilar from those relevant in other regions: territorial disputes, complex geographical circumstances, and conflicting economic and security interest are all factors that, often in combination, prevent the final settlement of maritime boundaries.

A number of maritime delimitations are complicated by the existence of unsettled territorial claims and illegal occupation of territory. Delimitation between Morocco and Spain is rendered more complicated by the presence of the Spanish enclaves in Morocco. In the Eastern Mediterranean, the delimitations involving Cyprus are rendered more complex by the military occupation of the northern part of the island, as well as by Turkish claims extending beyond the median line with Cyprus. The uncertain status of Palestine and the effective control exercised by Israel over the coastline and the waters off the Gaza Strip not only create political tensions but also legal uncertainties as to the rights over resources and the potential delimitation of maritime zones.

Complex geographical factors relevant to delimitation include the configuration of coasts and the presence of islands. The configuration of the coast influences the delimitation between France and Spain and between France and Italy.[32] The

---

[31] I Papanicolopulu, 'Some Thoughts on the Extension of Existing Boundaries for the Delimitation of New Maritime Zones' in R Lagoni and D Vignes (eds), *Maritime Delimitation* (Martinus Nijhoff Leiden 2006).

[32] The delimitation between France and Spain in the Mediterranean is affected by the concavity of the Gulf of Lyon and the presence of Cap Creus on the Spanish side of the boundary, which pushes the equidistance line towards the French side. The delimitation between France and Italy in the Tyrrhenian

delimitations in the central Mediterranean between Greece, Italy, Libya, Malta, and Tunisia influence one another and are conditioned by the objections of the other States to Libya's closing line for the Gulf of Sidra.

The presence of the Spanish island of Alboran halfway between Morocco and Spain could play a role in determining the boundary between the two States. The delimitation between Greece and Turkey involves considering the geographical configuration of the Aegean Sea and the presence of numerous Greek islands spreading its whole extension, from the Greek mainland to the Turkish coasts, but is also influenced by the tides in bilateral relations between the two States.[33] Efforts to settle the dispute have so far been unsuccessful. In 1976, Greece applied to the ICJ for the delimitation of the continental shelf in the Aegean Sea, asking, at the same time, for the adoption of interim measures to prevent Turkish seismic surveys in parts of the Aegean Sea. By its order of 11 September 1976[34] the Court found that the circumstances of the case did not require the adoption of provisional measures, while in its decision of 19 December 1978, the Court found that it did not have jurisdiction to examine the case. Lack of ratification of the LOSC by Turkey closes the door to a judicial settlement which is not agreed upon by both parties.[35]

The significance of access to resources for the delimitation of maritime boundaries is illustrated by the recent efforts at delimitating maritime zones in the eastern Mediterranean Sea. The discovery of gas fields has prompted a series of delimitation agreements between Cyprus and some of its neighbours. However, the desire to ensure access to seabed resources has also increased tensions, preventing the entry into force of the Cyprus/Lebanon treaty and contributing to the so far unsuccessful negotiations between Cyprus and Syria and between Lebanon and Israel.[36]

Sea needs to take into account the convexity of the Gulf of Genoa and the marked prominence of Cape Corse.

[33] Among the rich bibliography on the Aegean Sea and the disputes between Greece and Turkey, see TC Kariotis (ed), *Greece and the Law of the Sea* (Kluwer Law International The Hague 1997); Y Acer, *The Aegean Maritime Disputes and International Law* (Ashgate Aldershot 2003); JM Van Dyke, 'An Analysis of the Aegean Disputes under International Law' (2005) 36 *Ocean Development and International Law* 63.

[34] *Aegean Sea Continental Shelf (Greece v Turkey)* (Provisional Measures) [1976] ICJ Rep 6.

[35] Ratification of the LOSC by Turkey could be accompanied by an Art 298 declaration, which would significantly limit access to judicial settlement.

[36] See Lebanon: A letter dated 20 June 2011 from the Minister for Foreign Affairs and Emigrants of Lebanon addressed to the Secretary-General of the United Nations concerning the Agreement between the Government of the State of Israel and the Government of the Republic of Cyprus on the Delimitation of the Exclusive Economic Zone, signed in Nicosia on 17 December 2010 and Lebanon: A letter dated 3 September 2011 from the Minister for Foreign Affairs and Emigrants of Lebanon addressed to the Secretary-General of the United Nations concerning the geographical coordinates of the northern limit of the territorial sea and the exclusive economic zone transmitted by Israel , available at <http://www.un.org/Depts/los/LEGISLATIONANDTREATIES/STATEFILES/LBN.htm>.

3.3 The management of disputes

In all these cases, factors that prevent a final settlement are similar to those that can be found in other parts of the world, where narrow areas, characterized by complex geographical configurations and uncertain legal status, are the scene of political tensions and threats of armed conflict. In the Mediterranean Sea, the successful management of disputes over contested waters has traditionally taken the path of individual (albeit sometimes mutual) self-restraint, rather than joint action. When a dispute concerning the delimitation of areas of potential overlap arises, and in order to avoid the escalation of the conflict, States have more than once abstained from the proclamation of maritime zones or the full extension of their jurisdiction. The Sea of Alboran and the Aegean Sea constitute examples of such exercise of self-restraint.

Another similarity with other regions concerns the few instances of joint provisional arrangements, which have been adopted in just two cases. In the 1960s and 1970s, and in order to allow for exploitation of oil resources in the area between Malta and Sicily, Italy and Malta had adopted an informal *modus vivendi* concerning areas licensed for oil exploration and exploitation.[37] More recently, Algeria and Tunisia adopted a treaty establishing a provisional all-purpose boundary between the two States for a six-year period.[38] The latter case provides an interesting example for States willing to test a boundary line before adopting it definitively.

After the two ICJ decisions in the first half of the 1980s,[39] it appeared that Mediterranean States preferred to settle their boundaries through bilateral negotiations, rather than by third-party intervention. It was only in 2009 that Croatia and Slovenia agreed to submit their dispute to third party settlement. The delimitation of the maritime area between the two States involves not only a complex geographical configuration but also legal issues.[40] In addition, this is the first instance in which a court or tribunal charged with the delimitation of maritime boundaries was asked to apply, in addition to international law rules, 'equity and the principle of good neighbourly relations'. While this formulation falls short of a decision *ex aequo et bono*, it allows wider room for the application of principles and methods which depart from the 'three step approach' developed by international courts during the past decades.[41] This is certainly a novel approach to the delimitation of maritime

---

[37] GP Francalanci and P Presciuttini, *Storia dei Trattati e dei Negoziati per la Delimitazione della Piattaforma Continentale e del Mare Territoriale* (Istituto Idrografico della Marina Genova 2000).

[38] L Savadogo, 'Le paragraphe 3 des articles 74 et 83 de la CMB: une contribution à l'accord sur les arrangements provisoires relatifs à la délimitation des frontières maritimes entre la République Tunisienne et la République Algérienne Démocratique et Populaire' (2002) 7 *Annuaire du Droit de la Mer* 239.

[39] *Tunisia v Libya*, n 29; *Libya v Malta*, n 29.

[40] M Grbec, *The Extension of Coastal State Jurisdiction in Enclosed or Semi-Enclosed Seas. A Mediterranean and Adriatic Perspective* (Routledge Oxford 2014).

[41] *Maritime Dispute (Peru v Chile)*, Judgment of the International Court of Justice (27 January 2014) [180].

boundaries and a good illustration of the ingenious approach of Mediterranean States to the settlement of complex disputes. It is however, hard to determine whether a similar precedent will be followed by other States, in the Mediterranean Sea or other regions, as it clearly requires strong political will to settle the dispute.[42]

4 Institutionalized Cooperation

The Mediterranean Sea has had a pioneering role in the development of cooperative agreements and the establishment of institutions to pursue common aims, shared by its coastal States. This has been achieved despite the disagreements and conflicts, occasionally involving the use of armed force, between some Mediterranean States. Cooperation is being pursued in a number of fields, including environmental protection, management of living resources, protection of the underwater cultural heritage, and migration by sea. However, it is only in two areas—the protection of the environment and the management of living resources—that Mediterranean States have been able to adopt binding legal instruments.

4.1 Protection of the marine environment: the Barcelona Convention system

The complex geopolitical conditions of the Mediterranean were one of the main reasons for the choice of this sea to launch the first United Nations Environment Programme (UNEP) regional seas programme, with the adoption of the Mediterranean Action Plan (MAP) in 1975 aiming at combating environmental degradation of the sea.[43] The following year, Mediterranean States adopted the Convention for the Protection of the Mediterranean Sea Against Pollution, one of the first regional treaties for the protection of the marine environment. Initially focusing on the protection of the marine environment from pollution, the MAP and the 1976 Convention were thoroughly revised and renamed in 1995, the latter becoming the Convention for the Protection of the Marine Environment and the Coastal Region of the Mediterranean (Barcelona Convention), to take into account

---

[42] The dispute and the decision to settle it by means of an arbitral award have been greatly influenced by the EU, also due to the status of Croatia as a candidate country. It is, however, doubtful whether the EU could play a significant role in other delimitation disputes, unless they involve candidate countries.

[43] Intergovernmental Meeting on the Protection of the Mediterranean, 'MAP Phase 1 (Unofficial), UN Doc UNEP/WG.2/5 (11 February 1975) Annex.

the developments in the law of the sea subsequent to the adoption and entry into force of the LOSC, and of environmental law, in particular following the 1992 Rio Conference.[44] All Mediterranean States, with the exception of the United Kingdom, are party to the 1976 Barcelona Convention, while only two still have to ratify the 1995 amendments.

The Barcelona Convention is a framework treaty and is implemented by protocols dealing with specific types of pollution and issues, as well as other legal instruments. Seven protocols have been so far adopted, dealing with: dumping (1976, amended in 1995); prevention of marine pollution from ships and management of emergencies (1976, replaced by a new version in 2002); land-based pollution (1980, amended in 1996); specially protected areas and biodiversity (1982, replaced by a new version in 1995); offshore activities (1994); hazardous wastes (1996); and integrated coastal zone management (ICZM) (2008). The ICZM Protocol is the first and, for the time being, only international legal instrument dedicated to an integrated protection of the coastal zone, and has formed the basis for recent EU legislation.[45] Participation of coastal States in the Protocols varies and, in some cases, not all members of the 'old' version have also ratified the 'new' one.[46]

Alongside substantial obligations, the Barcelona Convention and its Protocols have created institutional structures intended to provide a stable framework for the implementation of States' duties. The main bodies are the Meeting of States Parties (MOP), which decides on MAP strategies, budget, and programme, the Bureau, the Co-ordination Unit, the Mediterranean Commission on Sustainable Development, and 6 Regional Activities Centres (RACs). The Regional Marine Pollution Emergency Response Centre for the Mediterranean Sea (REMPEC) plays an important role in providing technical assistance and is a centre for the coordination of efforts to tackle environmental emergencies.[47] This structure, which looks familiar today to the eye

---

[44] E Raftopoulos, 'The Mediterrean Response to Global Challenges: Environmental Governance and the Barcelona Convention System' in D Vidas and PJ Schei (eds), *The World Ocean in Globalisation: Climate Change, Sustainable Fisheries, Biodiversity, Shipping, Regional Issues* (Martinus Nijhoff Leiden 2011). Other environmental protection treaties adopted at the regional and sub-regional level include the 1996 Agreement on the Conservation of Cetaceans in the Black Sea, Mediterranean Sea and Contiguous Atlantic Area (hereinafter ACCOBAMS), which aims at the protection of cetaceans and has been ratified by most Mediterranean States and the 1997 Mediterranean Memorandum of Understanding on Port State Control in the Mediterranean Region, which applies to ports of the southern and eastern Mediterranean sea, and the 1982 Paris Memorandum of Understanding on Port State Control, which applies to ports of the northern Mediterranean (and other sea regions as well).

[45] European Parliament, Committee on Transport and Tourism, *Proposal for a Directive of the European Parliament and of the Council Establishing a Framework for Maritime Spatial Planning and Integrated Coastal Management*, Doc 2013/0074 (COD) (2013).

[46] Updated tables of ratification are provided in the UNEP MAP website (2014) available at <http://195.97.36.231/dbases/webdocs/BCP/StatusOfSignaturesAndRatifications.doc>.

[47] While the mandate of REMPEC concerns mostly pollution from vessels, it has played a significant role in coordinating efforts to target marine pollution during the 2006 Israel–Lebanon war. See UNEP, *Lebanon. Post-Conflict Environmental Assessment* (2007) 136–7, available at <http://postconflict.unep.ch/publications/UNEP_Lebanon.pdf>.

of anyone involved with environmental law, was innovative at the time it was first developed, and has provided the paradigm whereupon most subsequent framework treaties for the protection of the marine environment were moulded.

The Barcelona system presents many features of interest. Four will be addressed in this section: its scope of application; the compliance mechanism; the adoption of guidelines to address liability and compensation; and the Offshore Protocol.

The scope of the Barcelona Convention and its Protocols is particularly wide. Its geographical reach embraces the entire Mediterranean Sea, irrespective of the legal status of its waters, including high seas portions.[48] High seas management is addressed in Article 3(4), according to which State parties 'shall take individual or joint initiatives compatible with international law through the relevant international organizations to encourage the implementation of the provisions of this Convention and its Protocols by all the non-party States'. Mediterranean States have complied with this provision by bringing outstanding issues to the attention of international organizations, as in the case of the action by France and Italy that led to the designation of the Strait of Bonifacio as a Particularly Sensitive Sea Area (PSSA) by the IMO Marine Environment Protection Committee.[49]

The one instance in which parties to the Barcelona Convention have regulated areas not subject to their jurisdiction is the Protocol concerning Specially Protected Areas and Biological Diversity in the Mediterranean, which has established a List of Specially Protected Areas of Mediterranean Importance (SPAMIs). SPAMIs can also be established on the high seas; in this case, the decision is taken by consensus by the parties to the Protocol (Article 9(4)(c)).[50] This measure has raised the interest of numerous States, scholars, and other entities and has been hailed as the first attempt to establish marine protected areas beyond national jurisdiction.[51]

Furthermore, the Barcelona Convention provides for a comprehensive protection against pollution by vessels enjoying sovereign immunity, which goes beyond that in the LOSC and other regional treaties. First, such vessels are included within the scope of the Convention, even though their immunity from the jurisdiction of States other than the flag State is preserved.[52] Second, Article 3(5) of the Barcelona

---

[48] 1995 Convention for the Protection of the Marine Environment and the Coastal Region of the Mediterranean., Art 1(1) (hereinafter Barcelona Convention). Parties may extend its application to the coastal areas (ibid, Art 1(2)) and each Protocol may extend its geographical coverage (ibid, Art 1(3)).

[49] IMO Res MEPC.204(62), *Designation of the Strait of Bonifacio as a Particularly Sensitive Sea Area* (15 July 2011).

[50] This is the Pelagus Sanctuary, created by the 1999 Agreement concerning the Creation of a Marine Mammal Sanctuary in the Mediterranean, concluded between France, Italy, and Monaco and inscribed in the SPAMI list in 2001. Following the adoption of ecological protection zones by France and by Italy, the waters of the Pelagus Sanctuary are not high seas any more.

[51] Y Tanaka, 'Reflections on High Seas Marine Protected Areas: A Comparative Analysis of the Mediterranean and the North-East Atlantic Models' (2012) 81 *Nordic Journal of International Law* 295.

[52] Compare eg LOSC, n 12, Art 236, according to which '[t]he provisions of this Convention regarding the protection and preservation of the marine environment do not apply to any warship, naval

Convention does not include any of the qualifications to the flag States' duties provided by Article 236 of the LOSC.[53] In conclusion, by reserving the exercise of jurisdiction over State vessels to the flag State, while upholding the obligation of the latter to respect its commitments, this provision carefully balances the sovereignty of the State over its vessels, on one hand, and its duties concerning protection of the marine environment, on the other. Nor can it be said that this is an empty provision, since non-compliance with this obligation will result in State responsibility and the triggering of the non-compliance mechanism. It thus provides a good example and an exportable solution that may find application in other regional contexts and in global instruments.

From the point of view of the topics addressed by the Barcelona Convention system, the 1994 Protocol for the Protection of the Mediterranean Sea against Pollution Resulting from Exploration and Exploitation of the Continental Shelf and the Seabed and its Subsoil (Offshore Protocol) deserves particular attention. This was one of the first legal instruments to be adopted in this field and the first treaty to address pollution deriving from offshore activities in a comprehensive way.[54] The Protocol applies to a broad range of activities that include both exploratory activities and exploitation, and regulates issues such as authorizations and environmental impact assessments (EIAs), treatment of waste and other harmful substances, contingency planning, removal of installations, and cooperation.[55] The Protocol also contains a provision addressing liability and compensation for damage, which mandates the adoption of laws and regulations concerning the liability of operators and adequate insurance (Article 27). The broad scope, which includes internal waters up to the freshwater limit, and its comprehensive normative content, including detailed obligations for both States and industry, make it the most advanced instrument of its kind.[56]

---

auxiliary, other vessels or aircraft owned or operated by a State and used, for the time being, only on government non-commercial service.'

[53] Ibid, Art 236 refers to 'appropriate measures not impairing operations or operational capabilities of such vessels' and requires States to try and comply with their environmental obligations only 'so far as is reasonable and practicable'. Barcelona Convention, n 48, Art 3(4) requires that 'each Contracting Party shall ensure that its vessels and aircraft, entitled to sovereign immunity under international law, act in a manner consistent with this Convention'.

[54] Due to an insufficient number of ratifications, the Offshore Protocol was not in force for many years but gained attention following the *Deepwater Horizon* disaster and came into force in 2011.

[55] The development of the law of the sea and environmental law in the 20 years since the adoption of the Protocol require some adjustments to take into account recent knowledge and current practices. The Offshore Working Group meeting recommended that this needs to be done through interpretation and application of the Protocol, rather than by formal amendment; UNEP(DEPI)/MED, Report of the 1st Offshore Protocol Working Group Meeting, WG.384/4 (4 July 2013) [54].

[56] S Vinogradov, 'The Impact of the Deepwater Horizon: The Evolving International Legal Regime for Offshore Accidental Pollution Prevention, Preparedness, and Response' (2013) 44 *Ocean Development and International Law* 335, 346. Of course, there are still aspects not regulated by it, in particular concerning safety: Decision IG.20/12, UNEP(DEPI)/MED WG.384/INF.2 (6 June 2013).

A further field in which Mediterranean States have shown some initiative concerns liability for environmental damage. Article 12 of the 1976 Barcelona Convention already contained an obligation for the parties to cooperate to address liability and compensation, but it was only in 2007 that the Parties to the Barcelona Convention adopted Guidelines for the Determination of Liability and Compensation for Damage resulting from Pollution of the Marine Environment in the Mediterranean Sea Area, consisting of the first step towards the adoption of a binding instrument in this field.[57] The guidelines reflect the state of the art in the field and have been drafted so as to take stock and not interfere with other international treaties dealing with compensation from particular sources. An innovative feature is that they provide for the compensation not only of 'traditional damage', but also of 'environmental damage' (Guideline D, [8]). Contained in a soft law instrument, their success will very much depend on their incorporation into domestic legal systems and the degree of effectiveness that such measures will have vis-à-vis operators and third States.

A major challenge faced by the Barcelona Convention system concerns compliance. The Barcelona Convention and Protocols contain some of the more advanced regulations concerning prevention of pollution, response to emergencies, and the preservation of the marine ecosystem. These provisions, however, risk remaining a dead letter. While the provisions of the Barcelona Convention and Protocols have generally been incorporated into national legislation, they are not always applied in practice for various reasons, which include lack of financial or technical capacity, but also of political will. In order to ameliorate this situation, a non-compliance mechanism, including a newly created Compliance Committee and a binding reporting system, was established in 2008.[58] Although the Decision is binding upon all States parties to the Barcelona Convention, it was intended from the beginning as 'non confrontational, non judicial, transparent, cost effective and preventive in nature, simple, flexible, and oriented in the direction of helping parties to comply with and implement the provisions' of the Convention, the protocols, and the MOP decisions. This approach and the fact that the Compliance Committee cannot act *proprio motu*, and may be triggered only by States and, under specific conditions,

---

[57] Draft Decision 17/4, UN Doc UNEP(DEPI)/MED IG.17/10 (18 January 2008) Annex V. On the negotiating history of the Guidelines, see T Scovazzi, 'The Mediterranean Guidelines for the Determination of Environmental Liability and Compensation: The Negotiations for the Instrument and the Question of the Damage that Can Be Compensated' (2009) 13 *Max Planck Yearbook of United Nations Law* 183.

[58] Draft Decisions 17/2 and 17/3, UN Doc UNEP (DEPI)/MED IG.17/10 (18 January 2008) Annex V; I Papanicolopulu, 'Procedures and Mechanisms on Compliance under the 1976/1995 Barcelona Convention on the Protection of the Mediterranean Sea and its Protocols' in T Treves et al (eds), *Non-Compliance Procedures and Mechanisms and the Effectiveness of International Environmental Agreements* (TMC Asser Press The Hague 2009) 155.

the Secretariat, have raised doubts about its effectiveness and have led to amendments of the procedure.[59]

4.2 Management of living resources

The decline in Mediterranean fisheries, and the almost total depletion of some fish stocks, has precipitated the adoption of measures designed to ensure the recovery of fish stocks.[60] Mediterranean States have thus accepted that the unilateral creation of exclusive fisheries zones should be accompanied by joint efforts to foster regional co-operation to ensure compliance with management measures and to prevent IUU fishing.[61]

Two regional fisheries organizations have competence over Mediterranean fisheries, the General Fisheries Commission for the Mediterranean (GFCM) and the International Commission for the Conservation of Atlantic Tunas (ICCAT).[62] The oldest and more relevant one is the GFCM, created in 1949 and revised in 1997 to promote the development, conservation, rational management, and best utilization of marine living resources, as well as the sustainable development of aquaculture in the Mediterranean, Black Sea and connecting waters.[63] Subject to an opt-out clause, the GFCM can now adopt binding measures concerning fishing methods and fishing gear, minimum size for individuals of specified species, open and closed fishing seasons and areas, and the regulation of the amount of total catch and fishing effort, and their allocation among members.

Following its revision, the GFCM now constitutes the central forum for the discussion and adoption of binding measures for the protection of fish stocks in the

---

[59] Another aspect that gave rise to concerns related to the role of non-governmental organizations: Papanicolopulu, n 58, 164.

[60] A biodiversity 'hot spot', the Mediterranean Sea is home to more than 500 fish species and subspecies. Of these, roughly 8 per cent are classified as threatened in IUCN Red List; however, numbers may be much higher as almost a third is classified as 'data deficient'; IUCN, D Abdul Malak et al, *Overview of the Conservation Status of the Marine Fishes of the Mediterranean Sea* (2011) available at <https://portals.iucn.org/library/efiles/documents/RL-262-001.pdf>.

[61] 2003 Declaration of the Ministerial Conference for the Sustainable Development of Fisheries in the Mediterranean, adopted by the Ministers of the Mediterranean States and the European Commission.

[62] ICCAT, created by the 1966 Convention for the Conservation of Atlantic Tunas for the conservation and management of tuna and tuna-like species, also has competence in the Mediterranean Sea, particularly over bluefin tuna, fished for millennia but now seriously overexploited. ICCAT recommendations specifically applying to the Mediterranean are regularly endorsed by the GFCM; compliance with them however is still far from satisfactory.

[63] After decades of relative inaction, the 1997 amendments to revitalize the Commission were adopted, including a change of name and important modifications in the powers and working methods of the GFCM as well as to the obligations of contracting parties; Amendment to the Agreement for the Establishment of a General Fisheries Council for the Mediterranean. Among Mediterranean coastal States, only Bosnia-Herzegovina is not a member.

Mediterranean. Though the main threat for Mediterranean fisheries is overfishing, the GFCM does not determine quotas due to the wide variety of species present and fished in Mediterranean waters. It has, however, taken a number of measures on fishing gear and methods, minimum size, and closed areas.

As with other regional fisheries bodies, the GFCM is hampered by the incomplete data provided by those involved in fisheries activities and by the fact that, in some cases, binding measures cannot be adopted due to the lack of political will or financial and technical capacity. Compliance with measures still remains an issue of particular concern. Unlike some other regions, much IUU fishing in the Mediterranean is conducted by vessels from the coastal States, rather than by distant-fishing vessels. The conflicting interests of coastal States—preserving living resources and at the same time avoiding the social impact of highly restrictive measures on their fishing communities—has been a factor that has delayed the adoption of measures to ensure compliance. However, in recent times, Mediterranean States have taken significant steps to tackle this issue and have developed innovative solutions that may constitute an example for similar instances.

Recent initiatives of the GFCM includes steps to combat IUU fishing with the creation of a Compliance Committee in 2006[64] and the adoption in 2008 of a binding recommendation on a regional scheme on port State measures to combat IUU fishing.[65] The latter measure presents evident limitations. It applies, for the time being, only to Mediterranean waters and only to vessels flying the flag of non-members and raises questions as to its effectiveness, since IUU fishing in the Mediterranean is carried out mainly by vessels flying the flag of its coastal States. Nonetheless, it constitutes the first of its kind and preceded the adoption of the United Nations Food and Agriculture Organization (FAO) Port State Agreement.[66]

4.3 Ongoing efforts at cooperation

States bordering the Mediterranean have been at the forefront of normative developments and could be once again in the near future, in particular by furthering regional cooperative arrangements in fields that traditionally have not been the object of concerted action by States bordering regional seas. Two cases are of particular interest due to their significance in the Mediterranean and global context: protection of the underwater cultural heritage and regulation of forced migration by sea.[67]

---

[64] Recommendation GFCM/2006/6, *Terms of Reference for the GFCM Compliance Committee* (2006).

[65] Recommendation GFCM/2008/1, *Regional Scheme on Port State Measures to Combat Illegal, Unreported and Unregulated Fishing in the GFCM Area* (2008).

[66] 2009 Agreement on Port State Measures to Prevent, Deter and Eliminate Illegal, Unreported and Unregulated Fishing.

[67] Another area in which cooperation could be strengthened concerns the fight against trafficking of arms and drugs. The significance of the Mediterranean Sea as a major transport route and the fact

The rich cultural heritage found on the seafloor in Mediterranean waters has often attracted plunderers,[68] and may be best protected by a combination of unilateral and multilateral actions by coastal States. Regional instruments are expressly provided for in Article 6 of the CPUCH and Article 303(4) of the LOSC and a first step in this direction was the adoption, in 2001, of the Syracuse Declaration on the Submarine Cultural Heritage of the Mediterranean Sea, by a meeting of experts of Mediterranean States.[69] While no binding legal instrument has yet been adopted, the establishment of archaeological zones by a number of Mediterranean States and the widespread ratification of the CPUCH seem to point towards the political will to ensure a better protection for this heritage.

The use of the Mediterranean Sea as a route for migration has brought to the forefront the issue of cooperation in order both to prevent illegal activities and to safeguard human life at sea. The tragic fate faced by many people, who are left alone to cope with the sea while private and State vessels sail nearby, and the disputes following salvage operations concerning the disembarkation of migrants and refugees highlight the gaps in the current legal regime and the practical difficulties of cooperation.[70] The acute situation following the Arab Spring and the conflicts in Libya and in Syria have fuelled discussions on this issue, and the IMO is currently considering the adoption of a regional code on search and rescue and disembarkation. If such an instrument were to be adopted, Mediterranean States would again set the example for other regions.[71]

---

that many States bordering this sea are the destination of drugs or arms trafficking, demand action against trafficking and cooperation between coastal States. There exist some bilateral treaties, but there is no regional instrument to address these activities. In this area, Mediterranean States could follow the example of Caribbean States, which adopted the 2003 Agreement Concerning Co-Operation in Suppressing Illicit Maritime and Air Trafficking in Narcotic Drugs and Psychotropic Substances in the Caribbean Area.

[68] Efforts to plunder cultural heritage off the coast of Spain were at the background of the recent M/V 'Louisa' (*Saint Vincent and the Grenadines v Kingdom of Spain*), Judgment of the International Tribunal for the Law of the Sea (28 May 2013).

[69] 2001 Syracuse Declaration on the Submarine Cultural Heritage of the Mediterranean Sea, English version in T Scovazzi and G Camarda (eds), *La Protezione del Patrimonio Culturale Sottomarino nel Mare Mediterraneo* (Giuffrè Editore Milan 2004) 353.

[70] On this issue, see E Papastavridis, 'Enforcement Jurisdiction in the Mediterranean Sea: Illicit Activities and the Rule of Law on the High Seas' (2010) 25 *International Journal of Marine and Coastal Law* 569.

[71] The problems faced by Mediterranean States are not unique to the region, but are similar to those existing in other areas, such as the Caribbean Sea, where migrants from other countries attempt to reach the United States, and the Pacific Ocean, where Australia is the main destination. Their cause is a fragmented legal regime and the lack of will of States to face their responsibilities.

5 Conclusion

After decades of normative development, the Mediterranean Sea presents some unique features and, while it has achieved some notable successes, still faces a number of challenges.

On the side of success, Mediterranean States have one of the most developed and comprehensive regimes for the protection of the marine environment, the Barcelona system, which combines substantial regulation covering almost all fields of environmental concern with an institutional structure designed to address not only the legal but also the political and economic issues that hinder the realization of an effective protection of the marine environment.[72] Furthermore, this system, as well as that set up to address management of living resources, have achieved participation of all Mediterranean coastal States and provide good examples of the capacity of States to overcome political divides and discuss common concerns.

Mediterranean States have often been at the forefront of legal development furthering cooperation in regional seas. The Barcelona Convention was the first UNEP regional treaty adopted and the model for those that followed. The creation of the Pelagus Sanctuary and its inscription in the SPAMI list was the first step towards the development of marine protected areas in the high seas. The ICZM Protocol is the first of its kind and has introduced the concept of integrated coastal management, now endorsed by the EU. The adoption of port State measures to address the depletion of fish stocks by the GFCM has foreshadowed the 2009 FAO Port State Agreement.

Turning to challenges, in addition to new ones such as the protection of underwater cultural heritage, the prevention of loss of life during migration by sea and the sustainable development of coastal regions, a number of issues remain unsettled. First, a significant number of maritime boundaries are still to be drawn. Second, Mediterranean States share in the global failure to ensure sustainable fisheries and the conservation of marine living resources. In common with other regions, the development of more stringent measures and mechanisms has so far not been successful in preventing the depletion of stocks and impoverishment of the sea. Efforts are, however, ongoing, and it is hoped that the tide on these matters will change.[73] Third, environmental treaties are also not always complied with, and ensuring their full implementation probably constitutes one of the great challenges for the future. Fourth, and finally, the fragmented legal framework poses challenges

---

[72] In particular through the work of the Mediterranean Commission on Sustainable Development and the programmes and expertise offered by the Regional Activity Centres.

[73] M Gavouneli, 'Mediterranean Challenges: Between Old Problems and New Solutions' (2008) 23 *International Journal of Marine and Coastal Law* 477, 494–7.

for a closer cooperation and for the protection of communitarian interests. The Barcelona Convention is the only treaty ratified by all coastal States and while most Mediterranean States are parties to the LOSC and bound by its provisions, Israel, Libya, and Turkey are not and they have forcefully contested the customary nature of some of its provisions.[74]

Such a complex picture is seen in many seas, but what is perhaps unique to the Mediterranean is the fragmented extension of coastal State jurisdiction. The extension of territorial seas ranges from 3 to 6 or to 12 nm, while the jurisdictional zones often do not reach the maximum permissible extent, as in the case of the Algerian fishing zone. Contiguous zones are claimed by some States only but not by others, and *sui generis* jurisdictional zones have been declared alongside more straightforward claims of exclusive economic zones. The result is a complex patchwork of claims and zones that is proper to the Mediterranean Sea and is not witnessed, to the same extent, in any other sea.

In conclusion, the Mediterranean provides an intriguing example of merging of opposites. Innovation and forward-thinking in some fields are still counteracted by resistance to change and attachment to old concepts in others.[75] But this is nothing new in the law of the sea, which has always fluctuated between the heritage of the past and the achievements of the future.[76]

---

[74] Israel and Turkey were among the four States that voted against the adoption of the text of the LOSC. The position of Turkey has not changed much since; see N Oral, 'Non-Ratification of the 1982 Law of the Sea Convention: An Aegean Dilemma of Environmental and Global Consequence' (2009) 1 *Publicist* 53.

[75] The struggle to fully endorse and apply the concept of the exclusive economic zone, more the 30 years after the adoption of LOSC, is a prominent instance of resistance to modern developments.

[76] This fluctuation being at the basis of its 'intellectual attraction and intrinsic elegance' as pointed out by T Scovazzi, 'The Evolution of International Law of the Sea: New Issues, New Challenges' (2000) 286 *Collected Courses of the Hague Academy of International Law* 39, 53.

28

THE SOUTH CHINA SEA

KEYUAN ZOU

1 INTRODUCTION

DISPUTES in the South China Sea have recently generated serious concerns in the world community in relation to regional peace and security. The South China Sea is located in Southeast Asia, with an area of 648,000 square nautical miles (nm^2), twice the area of the Sea of Japan.[1] It can be defined as a semi-enclosed sea under the 1982 UN Convention on the Law of the Sea (LOSC). Article 122 of the Convention defines a 'enclosed or semi-enclosed sea' as 'a gulf, basin, or sea surrounded by two or more States and connected to another sea or the ocean by a narrow outlet or consisting entirely or primarily of the territorial seas and exclusive economic zones of two or more coastal States'. The South China Sea is surrounded by six States: Brunei, People's Republic of China (PRC), Indonesia, Malaysia, the Philippines, and Vietnam.[2] While the Gulf of Thailand is occasionally considered part of the South China Sea (eg for the purpose of marine environmental protection), for the purpose of this chapter the Gulf of Thailand is excluded.

There are hundreds of small islands in the South China Sea, including uninhabited islets, shoals, reefs, banks, sands, cays, and rocks.[3] There are four main groups

---

[1] JRV Prescott, *The Maritime Political Boundaries of the World* (Methuen London 1985) 209.

[2] In one sense Singapore can be also regarded as a coastal State in the South China Sea as one of its islands, Pedra Branca, is situated in the South China Sea just beyond the Singapore Strait.

[3] According to Hungdah Chiu, there are 127 islands in the South China Sea based upon a survey conducted during 1946–1947 sponsored by the then Chinese Ministry of Internal Affairs: H Chiu, 'South China Sea Islands: Implications for Delimiting the Seabed and Future Shipping Routes' (1977) 72 *China Quarterly* 756.

of islands and underwater features, namely the Pratas Islands (Dongsha Qundao in Chinese), the Paracel Islands (Xisha Qundao in Chinese and Quan Dao Hoang Sa in Vietnamese), the Macclesfield Bank (Zhongsha Qundao in Chinese),[4] and the Spratly Islands (Nansha Qundao in Chinese and Quan Dao Truong Sa in Vietnamese). It is interesting to note that in Chinese and Vietnamese these groups of small islands have an expansive name 'qundao', meaning archipelago. Such a nomenclature may be questionable in both legal and geographical terms,[5] particularly in respect of the Macclesfield Bank where most of the features are permanently submerged under water (except for the Scarborough Reef).[6]

Geo-strategically, the South China Sea connects the Indian Ocean and the Pacific Ocean through international straits including the Straits of Malacca, Bashi Channel, and the Taiwan Strait. These are important sea lanes which are vital for the adjacent countries in East Asia and also for the rest of the world. More than half of the world's merchant fleet capacity sails through the straits of Malacca, Sunda, and Lombok and the South China Sea.[7] More than 10,000 vessels of greater than 10,000 deadweight tonnage (dwt) move southward through the South China Sea annually, with well over 8,000 proceeding in the opposite direction.[8] In addition, with the rise of China and the fast growth of the economy in East Asia, the recent trend towards greater intra-Asian trade (relative to trade with Europe and North America) has resulted in more shipping in the littoral waters of Southeast Asia and the South China Sea.[9] Thus the sea routes in the region are usually regarded as economic lifelines for East Asian countries, particularly Japan. For this reason, it is perceived that control over the Spratly Islands in the South China Sea brings with it control, direct or indirect, over maritime transit from the Straits of Malacca to Japan, from Singapore to Hong Kong and from Guangzhou to Manila.[10]

The South China Sea has rich reserves of marine living and non-living resources and biodiversity. For instance, in comparison with the Great Barrier Reef and Caribbean regions, the Southeast Asia region, including the South China Sea, has

---

[4] The Chinese term 'Zhongsha Qundao' not only comprises the Macclesfield Bank, but also other banks such as Truro Shoal, Helen Shoal, Dreyer Shoal, and even Scarborough Reef.

[5] According to 1982 United Nations Convention on the Law of the Sea, Art 46 (b) (hereinafter LOSC), 'archipelago' means a group of islands, including parts of islands, interconnecting waters, and other natural features which are so closely interrelated that such islands, waters, and other natural features form an intrinsic geographical, economic, and political entity, or which historically have been regarded as such. Clearly, the term 'archipelago' ('qundao' in Chinese or 'quan dao' in Vietnamese) used in the South China Sea does not fit the above definition.

[6] For details on this reef and the dispute over it, see K Zou, 'Scarborough Reef: A New Flashpoint in Sino-Philippine Relations?' (1999) 7 *IBRU Boundary and Security Bulletin* 71, 71–81.

[7] See SB Weeks, 'Sea Lines of Communications (SLOC) Security and Access' in M Stankiewicz (ed), *Maritime Shipping in Northeast Asia: Law of the Sea, Sea Lanes, and Security*, IGCC Policy Paper No 33 (Institute on Global Conflict and Co-operation University of California 1998) 55.

[8] H Olson, 'Marine Traffic in the South China Sea' (1996) 12 *Ocean Yearbook* 137.

[9] See SJ Meyrick, 'Development in Asian Maritime Trade', in Stankiewicz (ed), n 7, 21.

[10] See MS Samuels, *Contest for the South China Sea* (Methuen New York 1982) 4.

the greatest biodiversity in marine fish species and hard coral species.[11] The South China Sea is in the central ecosystem of the United Nations Food and Agriculture Organization's (FAO) Pacific West Central Region, the most diverse and extensive shallow-water marine region in the world.[12] In 2000, over 11 million metric tons of fish and invertebrates were harvested from this region.[13] However, with the increase of human population and economic development, the rich resources in the South China Sea have become depleted over time. According to one study, '[m]ost of the small pelagic species comprising the South China Sea capture fisheries, which could be shared or straddling stocks, are already fully exploited'.[14]

In addition to marine living resources, mineral reserves, including oil and gas, have enormous potential. It is estimated that there are five sedimentary basins in the northern part of the South China Sea with an area of 420,000 km^2. As of 1997, 56 oilfields or structures had been discovered, containing 700 million tons of oil and 310 billion m^3 of gas.[15] In the Spratly area, there are eight sedimentary basins with an area of 410,000 km^2, and 260,000 km^2 are within China's unilaterally declared U-shaped line.[16] An incomplete figure from China shows that these eight sedimentary basins contain 34.97 billion tons of petroleum reserves, including the discovered 1.182 billion tons of oil and 8,000 billion m^3 of gas.[17] Thus the South China Sea is sometimes called a second 'Persian Gulf'. In contrast with the Chinese estimation, the general view outside China of hydrocarbon potential in the South China Sea is less optimistic. The US Geological Survey has estimated the sum total of discovered oil reserves and undiscovered resources in the offshore basins of the South China Sea at 28 billion barrels.[18] However, if reserves of natural gas which, according to the US Geological Survey, account for 60 to 70 per cent of the total potential hydrocarbon resources in this region are added to this figure,[19] the overall picture of petroleum exploration and development is still very encouraging.

---

[11] See Global Environment Facility (GEF)/ United Nations Development Programme (UNDP)/ International Maritime Organization (IMO) Regional Programme on Partnership in Environmental Management for the Seas of East Asia (PEMSEA), Sustainable Development Strategy for the Seas of East Asia: Regional Implementation of the World Summit on Sustainable Development Requirements for the Coasts and Oceans (PEMSEA Quezon City 2003) 52 (hereinafter PEMSEA).

[12] See D Rosenberg, 'Fisheries Management in the South China Sea', in S Bateman and R Emmers (eds), *Security and International Politics in the South China Sea: Towards a Cooperative Management Regime* (Routledge Abingdon 2009) 62.

[13] Ibid.   [14] PEMSEA, n 11, 30.

[15] See H Zhao et al, *Geomorphology and Environment of the South China Coast and the South China Sea Islands* (Science Press Beijing 1999) 484 (in Chinese).

[16] For details of this line and its legal implications, see K Zou, 'The Chinese Traditional Maritime Boundary Line in the South China Sea and Its Legal Consequences for the Resolution of the Dispute over the Spratly Islands' (1999) 14 *International Journal of Marine and Coastal Law* 27.

[17] Zhao et al, n 15, 484.

[18] See US Energy Information Agency, *Country Analysis Briefs: South China Sea* (2013), available at <http://www.eia.gov/countries/regions-topics.cfm?fips=scs>.

[19] Ibid.

Rich resources often become a trigger for international disputes, and the South China Sea is no exception. The complicated political landscape of the South China Sea contains potential conflicts with various different national interests. For the status of the four groups of islands, because of their different geographical locations, their political statuses are accordingly different from each other. The Pratas Islands are under the full control of the Taiwanese authorities. No competing claims exist there under the current 'one China' policy across the Taiwan Strait.[20] For the Macclesfield Bank, the only claimant is China (including mainland China and Taiwan).[21] Nevertheless, as the Scarborough Reef is considered part of the Macclesfield Group, recent developments indicate that the Philippines have also lodged a territorial claim over the Reef, and over the Macclesfield Group accordingly. The Paracel Islands are under the control of China, though contested by the Vietnamese. Because of the firm control by the Chinese, the political situation around the Paracel Islands is relatively calm and stable in comparison with that around the Spratly Islands. The dispute over the Spratly Islands is most complicated since it has been lingering for a long time and involves as many as five States and six parties (China, Chinese Taipei, Malaysia, Vietnam, the Philippines, and Brunei). It is not usual in the history of international relations that so many countries make claims over such small islets such as the Spratly Islands and their surrounding water areas (see Figure 28.1). Many predict that, if the issue of the Spratly Islands is not handled well, it could endanger peace and security in the East Asian region and even beyond.

Generally speaking, there are three layers of disputes in the South China Sea. The first and most fundamental is the overlapping claims of sovereignty to the geographic features between or among littoral States; the second is the overlapping claims to the maritime zones generated either from the islands or from the surrounding coasts of the littoral States which are basically in terms of sovereign rights and jurisdiction as stipulated under the LOSC; and the third is the disputes in relation to the use of the oceans including conflicting uses of marine resources and development by littoral States, the use of sea lanes, and the conduct of military activities, as a purported exercise of the freedom of navigation, between littoral States and user States. These disputes are entangled, thus making the South China Sea the most complicated and disputed of all territorial and maritime regions in the world.

This chapter first discusses legal issues concerning the South China Sea such as sovereignty and territorial disputes, maritime disputes, the controversy on China's

---

[20] This policy has been held by Beijing and Taipei based on the so-called '92 Consensus' which supports one China but with different interpretations. For Beijing, 'one China' is the People's Republic of China, while for Taipei, it refers to the Republic of China on Taiwan.

[21] A main reason that there is no other claimant for the Macclesfield Bank is that this Bank is permanently submerged under the water. Otherwise, Vietnam or the Philippines might have claimed it as well. However, the Vietnamese government recently extended continental shelf claims so as to intrude into the area of 'Zhongsha Qundao' claimed by the Chinese.

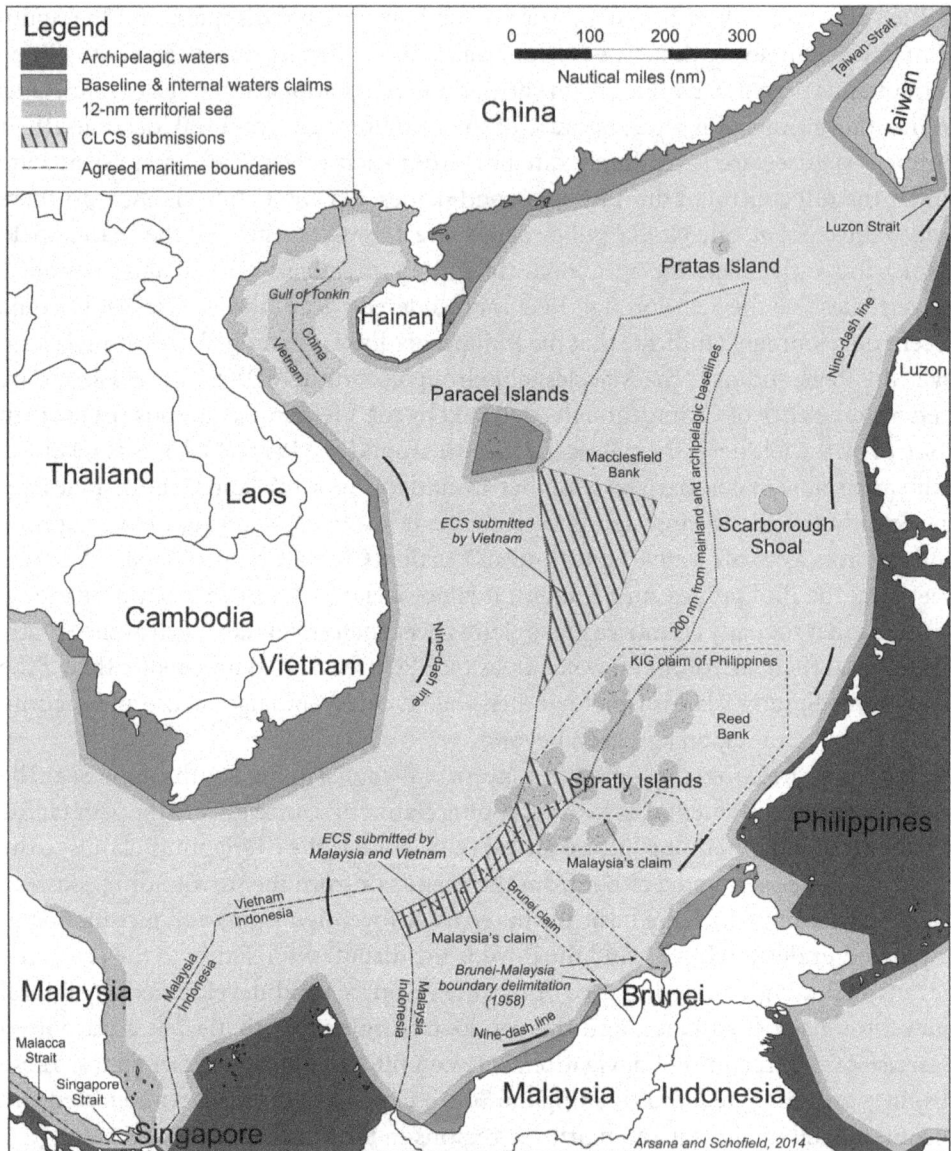

Figure 28.1 The South China Sea. This map is based on an earlier version that appeared in the January 2013 issue (Vol. 107, No. 1) of the *American Journal of International Law*.

'U-shaped' line, and the relation between conventional rights deriving from the LOSC and historic rights embodied in international customary law. It then considers the applicable international law in the South China Sea, including the LOSC and regional arrangements such as the 2002 Declaration on the Conduct of Parties in the South China Sea. The final section of the chapter looks at the latest developments in the South China Sea including the *Philippines v China* case, and discusses the possibility of cooperation in the region between or among claimants as well as between Association of Southeast Asian Nations (ASEAN) and China through feasible means such as joint development, joint management of fishery resources, common responsibilities for the protection of the marine environment, and cooperation in non-traditional security issues.

2 Territorial Disputes and Legal Issues

The most fundamental question concerning the South China Sea is which State or States possess sovereignty over its islands and other geographic features. In this respect, international law is indispensable to justifying a State's claim to sovereignty and jurisdiction over disputed areas.

Traditional international law allows States to acquire territorial sovereignty through one of the five defined methods—'accretion', 'occupation', 'prescription', 'conquest', and 'cession'. However, the UN Charter prohibits the use of force except in self-defence or under Security Council authorization, thus forced cession and conquest are no longer valid methods of acquiring territorial sovereignty. Legal scholars usually refer to three important cases concerning the acquisition of territory in international law[22]—the *Island of Palmas* case[23] (between the United States and the Netherlands), the *Clipperton Island* case[24] (between France and Mexico) in 1931, and the *Eastern Greenland* case.[25] These cases, in the eyes of Chinese scholars, are significant in international law and also meaningful in the context of the territorial sovereignty over South China Sea islands. China claims to have discovered the South China Sea islands as early as in the Han Dynasty (206 BC–220 AD). Such discovery is decisive for China in acquiring sovereignty, since according to modern international law, only discovery can satisfy the conditions of territorial acquisition.[26] On the other hand, Chinese scholars have realized that it is not sufficient for China's sovereignty over the South China Sea islands to rest upon discovery, as under modern international law effective occupation is much more crucial and forceful to justifying and/or defending territorial sovereignty. China seeks to establish effective occupation of the South China Sea islands by identifying a host of Chinese activities in

---

[22] For details see L Wang, 'International Legal Norms Applicable to the Sovereignty Issue of the South China Sea Islands' in China Institute for Marine Development Strategy (ed), *Selected Papers of the Workshop on the South China Sea Islands* (1992) 9 (in Chinese).
[23] *Island of Palmas* (1928) II RIAA 829.
[24] *Clipperton Island* (1932) 26 *American Journal of International Law* 390.
[25] *Eastern Greenland* (1933) PCIJ Rep Ser A/B No 53.   [26] Wang, n 22, 24.

the sea, including economic development and operations, such as fishing, planting, residential development, and so on; administrative jurisdiction; navy patrols; and astronomical surveys.[27] However, modern international law tends to recognize more recent practice of effective occupation rather than earlier or ancient State practice.

In addition, a legal argument Chinese scholars like to use is the concept of inter-temporal law in international law. Inter-temporal law refers to the response of international law to disputes with an historical dimension. Its rules and principles come from subsystems of international law such as the law of treaties and customary international law.[28] In the *Island of Palmas* case, Judge Huber considered that 'the act creative of a right' has to be judged by the 'law in force at the time the right arises'.[29] In 1975, the Institut de Droit International adopted a resolution on 'the Intertemporal Problem in Public International Law' which calls on States to apply the principle that:

... the temporal sphere of application of any norm of public international law shall be determined in accordance with the general principle of law by which any fact, action or situation must be assessed in the light of the rules of law that are contemporaneous with it.[30]

In the context of the South China Sea islands, any applicable rules in international law must be those valid at that time when the rights of a State were created. This argument is favourable for China since it is the earliest country to discover these islands and to conduct relevant human activities in the South China Sea.

Another argument which may not be purely legal concerns Vietnam's early recognition of China's sovereignty over the South China Sea islands. As recorded, in the 1950s and 1960s, Vietnam expressly rendered its recognition to China several times.[31] However, after 1975, Vietnam reversed its position and itself claimed the Paracel and Spratly Islands. As pointed out by Chinese scholars, such behaviour is in violation of the principle of 'estoppel' or preclusion. Since Vietnam has already recognized China's sovereignty over these two islands groups, it is now precluded from questioning China's possession of these islands.[32] However, according to Vietnam, it has inherited the territorial claims to the South China Sea from South Vietnam after the reunification of the country.

Vietnam's claim to the South China Sea is based on its self-asserted effective and continuous sovereignty over the Spratly and Paracel islands since the seventeenth century

---

[27] Ibid, 24–6. For details, see S Wu, *Solving Disputes for Regional Cooperation and Development in the South China Sea: A Chinese Perspective* (Chandos Oxford 2013) chs 2–3.

[28] See TO Elias, 'The Doctrine of Intertemporal Law' (1980) 74 *American Journal of International Law* 285.

[29] *Island of Palmas*, n 23, 833.

[30] 'The Intertemporal Problem in Public International Law', Session of Wiesbaden (11 August 1975), available at <http://www.idi-iil.org/idiE/resolutionsE/1975_wies_01_en.pdf>.

[31] See Wu, n 27, ch 4 for details.

[32] See L Zhao, *Studies on the Law of the Sea Issues* (Peking University Press Beijing 1996) 14–15 (in Chinese).

and on succession to the rights of its former colonial ruler France that claimed to have taken possession of Spratly Island in the 1930s.[33] The Philippines' claim to the Kalayaan Islands (part of the Spratly Islands) is based on the so-called discovery by Tomas Cloma in 1956. As for Brunei and Malaysia, their claims are mainly based on the fact that the features are located within their respective exclusive economic zones (EEZs).

In order to consolidate their claims in the South China Sea, all the claimants have conducted unilateral activities such as legislation, construction, and military reinforcement. Even the official description of the South China Sea is different in different countries. In China, it is called South Sea while in Vietnam it is known as the East Sea. Recently, the Philippines renamed the South China Sea as the West Philippine Sea. With the passage of time, historical facts as to who was first on the islands have faded from memory, and the claims made by all countries adjacent to the South China Sea are acknowledged by the international community.

Among all the claims, China's claim seems unique in the sense that it is accompanied by a U-shaped line in the South China Sea. In China, the U-shaped line is known as the 'Chinese traditional maritime boundary line', and refers to the line with nine segments off the Chinese coast on the South China Sea. The line first appeared on a Chinese map in December 1914, which was compiled by Hu Jinjie, a Chinese cartographer.[34] The maps published during the 1920s and 1930s followed Hu's map.[35] The line at that time only included the Pratas and the Paracel Islands. It began from the Sino-Vietnamese land boundary next to the Gulf of Tonkin, extending southeastwards along the offshore of the Vietnamese coast, then running eastwards to the west side of the Island of Luzon, then northeastwards along the east side of the Pratas Islands, through the Taiwan Strait, and finally meeting the Chinese boundary line in the East China Sea. The southernmost end of this demarcation was located at about 15° and 16° north latitude.[36]

1933 was an important year for the modification and emphasis of the line in Chinese maps. In July 1933, France, the colonial power in Vietnam, occupied nine of the Spratly Islands. This action was strongly protested by China, and afterwards the line in the maps relating to the South China Sea was extended further south to

---

[33] See DJ Dzurek, 'The Spratly Islands Dispute: Who's On First?' (1996) 2 *International Boundaries Research Unit Maritime Briefing* 47.

[34] The map was named as 'the Chinese territorial map before the Qianglong-Jiaqing period' (AD 1736–1820) of the Qing Dynasty in his compilation *New Geographical Atlas of the Republic of China*. See Z Han (ed), *A Compilation of Historical Materials on China's South China Sea Islands* (Oriental Press Beijing 1988) 355 (in Chinese).

[35] See eg 'The Chinese Map of Boundary Changes' in S Tu (ed), *The New Chinese Situation Atlas* (Geographical Association Shanghai 1927); and 'The Chinese Map of Territorial Changes' in D Chen (ed), *China's Model Atlas* (Geographical Association Shanghai 1933); Han, n 34, 355–6.

[36] See H Zhang, *The Legal System Applicable to the Islands in the South China Sea*, PhD dissertation (Peking University Beijing 1995) 43 (on file with the author) (in Chinese).

7°–9° north latitude.[37] The intention behind this step was clear: indicating that the Spratly Islands belonged to China. However, the James Shoal (Zengmu Ansha) was not included. While the line at that time on most of the maps was drawn between 7° and 9° north latitude, there was at least one atlas collection which included the James Shoal (ie the line extended to 4° north latitude). This is the *New China's Construction Atlas* edited by Bai Meichu and published in 1936. In fact in 1935, the Committee of Examining the Water and Land Maps of the Republic of China published the names of 132 islets and reefs of the four South China Sea 'archipelagos'. The publication had an annexed map which marked the James Shoal at the location of about 4° north latitude, 112° east longitude, though the line was not shown on the map. It indicated that the then Chinese Government considered the southernmost territory of China at 4° north latitude.[38] It is therefore clear that Bai took the above publication as the basis for the line in his compilation.

It should be noted that all the collections of the above atlases including the U-shaped line were compiled by individuals. They may, suffice to say, constitute indirect evidence to show the official position of the Government. Only in 1947, after World War II, was the line officially confirmed by the Chinese Government. On 1 December 1947, the Chinese Ministry of Interior renamed the islands in the South China Sea and formally allocated them to the Hainan Special District.[39] Meanwhile, the same ministry prepared a location map of the islands in the South China Sea, which was first released for internal use. In February 1948, the *Atlas of Administrative Areas of the Republic of China*, which included the above map, was officially published. This is the first official map with the line for the South China Sea and it has had a substantial influence on subsequent maps published by both mainland China and Taiwan. It has two general characteristics: the southernmost end of the line is set at 4° north latitude including the James Shoal; and the line consists of 11 segments instead of the previous continuous line.[40] According to the then official explanation, the basis for drawing the line was that:

The southernmost limit of the South China Sea territory should be at the James Shoal. This limit was followed by our governmental departments, schools and publishers before the

---

[37] For example, D Chen (ed), *Newly-Made Chinese Atlas* (Shanghai Geographical Association 1934); L Tan and K Chen (eds), *Civilised Geography of China* (Shanghai: Commercial Press 1936); and S Ge (ed), *Newly-Made Large Hanging Atlas* (Shanghai: Commercial Press 1939). See Han, n 34, 356–359.

[38] See Zhang, n 36, 46.

[39] See Ministry of Interior, *An Outline of the Geography of the South China Sea Islands* (1947) *National Territory Series* 861 fig 11, as cited in JKT Chao, 'South China Sea: Boundary Problems Relating to the Nansha and Hsisha Islands' in RD Hill, O Norman, and EV Roberts (eds), *Fishing in Troubled Waters: Proceedings of the Academic Conference on Territorial Claims in the South China Sea* (Hong Kong Centre for Asian Studies University of Hong Kong 1991) 88.

[40] Two segments in the Gulf of Tonkin were removed by the People's Republic of China in the 1950s without an official explanation to the public, though it is believed that the removal was linked to the transfer of ownership over the Bai Long Vi Island from China to Vietnam.

anti-Japanese war, and it was also recorded on file in the Ministry of Interior. Accordingly it should remain unchanged.[41]

Chinese scholars face a dilemma of how to define this line in a legal and political context so as to defend China's rights and interests in the South China Sea. The crucial question concerns the legal status of the line: is it a maritime boundary line like a territorial border, or a line only indicating that the islands, not the waters, within the line belong to China? Though still debated, the majority of Chinese scholars tend to recognize that the line is used to identify the islands and other territories within the line as Chinese territory.[42] While there is no official clarification from the Chinese Government, the President of the National Institute for South China Sea Studies, a Chinese think tank specifically focusing on South China Sea issues, during a recent interview with the Observer Research Foundation, expressed the view that the U-shaped line

> ... is based on the theory of 'sovereignty + UNCLOS + historic rights'. According to this theory, China enjoys sovereignty over all the features within this line, and enjoys sovereign right and jurisdiction, defined by the LOS Convention, for instance, EEZ and continental shelf when the certain features fulfill the legal definition of Island Regime under Article 121 of the LOS Convention. In addition to that, China enjoys certain historic rights within this line, such as fishing rights, navigation rights and priority rights of resource development.[43]

Historic rights have been asserted by China in its 1998 Law on the Exclusive Economic Zone and the Continental Shelf, Article 14 of which provides that 'the provisions of this Law shall not affect the historic rights enjoyed by the People's Republic of China'.[44]

Despite its existence on Chinese maps for more than six decades, the U-shaped line has never received wide recognition in the international community, much less from other claimants in the South China Sea. The U-shaped line remains a legal conundrum not only for China but also for other States, particularly after the map with the U-shaped line, together with China's *note verbale* against the claims to outer continental shelves made by Malaysia and Vietnam in the South China Sea, was submitted to the Commission on the Limits of Continental Shelf in May 2009.[45] The Philippines has officially challenged the U-shaped line in an arbitration against China and requested the Arbitral Tribunal to declare that China's maritime

---

[41] See Han, n 34, 181–4.

[42] For example, see Zhao, n 32, 37–8. For further reference, see J Li and D Li, 'The Dotted Line on the Chinese Map of the South China Sea: A Note' (2003) 43 *Ocean Development and International Law* 287.

[43] Observer Research Foundation, 'ORF South China Sea Interview' (2013) 2 *South China Sea Monitor* 9. Chinese approaches are also reflected in Z Gao and B Jia, 'The Nine-Dash Line in the South China Sea: History, Status, and Implications' (2013) 107 *American Journal of International Law* 98.

[44] See *People's Daily* (30 June 1998) (in Chinese). An unofficial English version of the law is appended to K Zou, *China's Marine Legal System and the Law of the Sea* (Martinus Nijhoff Leiden/Boston 2005) 342.

[45] For details on the line and its legal implications, see Zou, n 16.

claims based on the U-shaped line are contrary to the LOSC and invalid.[46] However, despite the challenge, there is no sign that China is retreating from its original position on the U-shaped line. On the contrary, recent practice demonstrates that China has attempted to further consolidate claims based on the line by various activities including undertaking regular and intensified law enforcement patrols within the line in the South China Sea.[47]

3 Applicable Law and Institutional Arrangements

International law requires States to resolve their disputes through peaceful means. There are a number of mechanisms for the settlement of territorial and maritime disputes, including political means such as negotiation and consultation between the parties concerned, mediation, good offices, conciliation and investigation involving third parties, and judicial means such as arbitration and international adjudication.[48] Since China and all the Member States of the ASEAN are UN members, they are obliged to comply with the requirements imposed by the UN Charter in terms of the settlement of their disputes. Apart from the above means, international organizations, whether universal or regional, can also play an active role in dispute settlement, as is seen through the ASEAN itself which has played a role in diffusing tension in the South China Sea and exerted efforts in solving this thorny issue.

Under the pressure of some of its members with South China Sea interests, ASEAN adopted the 1992 ASEAN Declaration on the South China Sea, which was a first concerted statement of ASEAN members regarding their position on the South China Sea issue. The Declaration urges 'all parties concerned to exercise restraint with the view to creating a positive climate for the eventual resolution of all disputes', 'to explore the possibility of cooperation in the South China Sea relating to the safety of maritime navigation and communication, protection against pollution of the marine environment, coordination of search and rescue operations, efforts towards combating piracy and armed robbery as well as collaboration in the campaign against illicit trafficking in drugs', and 'to apply the principles contained

---

[46] The diplomatic note and the Philippines' 'Notification and Statement of Claim' are available at <http://www.gov.ph/downloads/2013/01jan/20130122-Notification-and-Statement-of-Claim-on-West-Philippine-Sea.pdf>.

[47] For recent developments on the line, see K Zou, 'China's U-shaped Line in the South China Sea Revisited' (2012) 43 *Ocean Development and International Law* 18.

[48] 1945 Charter of the United Nations, Art 33(1).

in the Treaty of Amity and Cooperation in Southeast Asia as the basis for establishing a code of international conduct over the South China Sea'.[49] Although it was adopted by the original six ASEAN members, it has since been endorsed by the newer ASEAN members. Some of the content of the Declaration was later reflected in the 2002 Declaration on the Conduct of Parties in the South China Sea (DOC) adopted by China and all 10 ASEAN Member States. This was the first regional document to mention the adoption of a code of conduct for the South China Sea.

Following the Mischief Reef incident in 1995, ASEAN Foreign Ministers issued a statement urging the claimants to refrain from exacerbating the South China Sea situation, and to undertake cooperative activities which increase trust and confidence and promote stability in the area.[50] In the same year, China agreed to discuss the dispute over the Spratly Islands with ASEAN countries, and China and the Philippines adopted a bilateral code of conduct for the South China Sea.[51] Later, the ASEAN requested the Philippines and Vietnam prepare a Regional Code of Conduct for the South China Sea, which was based on ASEAN–China documents such as the five principles of peaceful coexistence; the 1976 Treaty of Amity and Cooperation in South East Asia; the 1992 ASEAN Declaration on the South China Sea; the 1997 ASEAN–China Joint Statement; the 1995 Joint Statement between the Philippines and the PRC on the South China Sea and Other Areas of Cooperation; the 1995 code of conduct agreed between Vietnam and the Philippines; and the 1998 Hanoi Plan of Action at the Sixth ASEAN Summit.[52]

Initially China rejected the ASEAN initiative for a regional code of conduct, since China regarded the South China Sea issue as a bilateral issue between itself and individual Southeast Asian countries. However, China subsequently modified its original position and agreed to consider the possibility of a regional code of conduct. According to some scholars, 'China's interest in the code was motivated by the need to prevent further American involvement in the area and to head off military exercises between ASEAN with the United States'.[53] In March 2000, the first ASEAN–China Consultations on the code of conduct in the South China Sea were held in Thailand. In November 2002 the two sides reached the agreement on the DOC.

Under the DOC the parties undertake to resolve their disputes in the South China Sea by peaceful means in accordance with universally recognized principles

---

[49] See the Association of South-East Asian Nations (ASEAN) Declaration on the South China Sea, available at <http://www.aseansec.org/3634.htm>.

[50] See Recent Developments in the South China Sea (18 March 1995), cited in Rodolfo C. Severino, 'ASEAN and the South China Sea' (2010), 6 *Security Dialogue* 43.

[51] Text appended to HT Nguyen, 'Vietnam and the Code of Conduct for the South China Sea' (2001) 32 *Ocean Development and International Law* 125.

[52] See ibid, 114. The draft appended to ibid, 127–9.

[53] L Buszynski and I Sazlan, 'Maritime Claims and Energy Cooperation in the South China Sea' (2007) 29 *Contemporary Southeast Asia* 154.

of international law. Pending the settlement of the disputes, the parties have agreed to exercise self-restraint in the conduct of activities and to undertake cooperative activities, particularly in the non-traditional security field.[54] The document is significant in the sense that it has transformed the South China Sea issue from being a bilateral issue into a regional one to be solved under the framework of the China–ASEAN cooperation. After the signing of the DOC, in 2005, the ASEAN and China established two mechanisms for the purpose of implementing the Declaration: the 'ASEAN–China Senior Officials Meeting on the Implementation of the Declaration on the Conduct of Parties in the South China Sea (DOC)' and the 'ASEAN–China Joint Working Group on the Implementation of the DOC'. While the former, which is ad hoc, will review the progress of the implementation of the DOC and discuss principles and methods thereof,[55] the latter, which meets twice a year, will function under the direction of the ASEAN–China Senior Officials Meeting.

The DOC clearly endorses a number of principles and documents of international law and specifically refers to the LOSC. China and most of the ASEAN States (except for Cambodia) have ratified and acceded to the LOSC. As the South China Sea is a semi-enclosed sea, the States bordering it are required to cooperate under the LOSC. According to Article 123 of the LOSC, the States adjacent to a semi-enclosed such as the South China Sea have the obligation of cooperation in the management, conservation, exploration, and exploitation of the living resources of the sea; the protection and preservation of the marine environment; marine scientific research; and cooperation with other interested States or international organizations.[56] The LOSC also contains a chapter on dispute settlement through peaceful means as in accordance with the UN Charter. The LOSC provisions on maritime delimitation can provide legal guidelines for the States concerned to delimit their overlapping maritime zones in the South China Sea. It is worthwhile noting that China and Vietnam successfully reached an agreement on the delimitation of the maritime boundary in the Gulf of Tonkin in 2000,[57] which set a good example for maritime boundary delimitation in the South China Sea.

Nevertheless, the LOSC has its limitations in the settlement of disputes since it only governs disputes over maritime zones and maritime activities and not disputes over the sovereignty of islands. That is why the DOC, while specifying the LOSC,

---

[54] 2002 Declaration on the Conduct of Parties in the South China Sea, available at <http://www.asean.org/asean/external-relations/china/item/declaration-on-the-conduct-of-parties-in-the-south-china-sea> (hereinafter DOC).

[55] See Database on the Cooperation Progressing in the ASEAN Plus Three and ASEAN Plus One Cooperation Frameworks (as of 17 October 2006) 81, available at <http://www.asean.org/archive/DATABASE_Consolidated ASN+3_DB as of 17 Oct 06.pdf>.

[56] See LOSC, n 5, Art 123.

[57] For details, see K Zou, 'The Sino-Vietnamese Agreement on Maritime Boundary Delimitation in the Gulf of Tonkin' (2005) 36 *Ocean Development and International Law* 13.

mentions the whole body of general international law including customary international law in connection with dispute settlement in the South China Sea. Secondly, the emergence and the entry into force of the LOSC itself has complicated the South China Sea situation as a number of claimant States such as Brunei and Malaysia have used the provisions of the LOSC relating to the EEZ in making their claims over reefs in the South China Sea.[58]

4 Prospects and Trends

While tensions remain high in the South China Sea, regional cooperation and promotion of regional peace and security between ASEAN and China through feasible means such as joint development, joint management of fishery resources, common responsibilities for the protection of the marine environment, and cooperation in non-traditional security issues remain an option. The DOC could become a basis for such cooperation.

In 2011, the ASEAN and China signed the Guidelines for the Implementation of the DOC in regard to possible joint cooperative activities, measures, and projects.[59] Following this, the two sides held a workshop on the tenth Anniversary of the DOC in Phnom Penh in 2012 and stressed

> ...the significance of the strategic partnership to continue their constructive engagement, to keep the momentum of the progress of dialogue and consultation with the view to further promoting the ASEAN–China Strategic Partnership in the implementation of and moving forward towards eventual adoption of a legally binding Code of Conduct in the South China Sea (COC) based on consensus.[60]

This is a positive development.

While the ASEAN members are anxious to adopt the COC as early as possible, China takes a more cautious approach towards the process. While China supports the DOC, it has clearly expressed the view that the DOC is only a mechanism for

---

[58] The effect of the LOSC on conflict management is examined by a recent article: Y Song and S Tønnesson, 'The Impact of the Law of the Sea Convention on Conflict and Conflict Management in the South China Sea' (2013) 44 *Ocean Development and International Law* 235.

[59] Guidelines for the Implementation of the DOC (2 August 2011), available at <http://id.china-embassy.org/eng/sgdt/t844905.htm>.

[60] Association of Southeast Asian Nations, *Workshop on 10th Anniversary of the Declaration on the Conduct of Parties in the South China Sea (DOC)* (2 November 2012), available at <http://www.asean.org/news/asean-secretariat-news/item/workshop-on-10th-anniversary-of-the-declaration-on-the-conduct-of-parties-in-the-south-china-sea-doc>.

functional cooperation and crisis management, not a mechanism for the resolution of the sovereignty and maritime disputes. In 2013, Wang Yi, the Chinese Minister of Foreign Affairs raised four points in Hanoi (during his visit to Vietnam) regarding the adoption of the COC:

- 'First, reasonable expectations. Some countries are talking about 'quick fix', like reaching consensus on COC within one day. It is an attitude neither realistic nor serious. COC involves multilateral interests from different parties, and its formulation is a process of sophisticated and complex coordination.'
- 'Second, consensus through negotiations. We should refer to the experience of reaching DOC to move forward COC. To seek consensus as broadly as possible and to keep the comfort of all parties in mind. Wills of individual country or of a few countries should not be imposed on other countries, as an old Chinese saying, nothing forcibly done is going to be agreeable.'
- 'Third, elimination of interference. China and ASEAN countries tried several times to discuss on COC before, but got stuck due to some interferences. All parties concerned should do more to help moving forward the process of COC, and create the necessary conditions and atmosphere, not going the opposite way.'
- 'Fourth, step-by-step approach. The formulation of COC is stipulated in DOC. COC is not to replace DOC, much less to ignore DOC and go its own way. The top priority now is to continue to implement DOC, especially promoting maritime cooperation. In this process, we should formulate the road map for COC through consultations, and push it forward in a step-by-step approach.'[61]

In September 2013, the ASEAN and China held the Sixth Senior Officials' Meeting and the Ninth Joint Working Group's Meeting on the DOC in Suzhou, China. This was the first official meeting on the consultation for a legally binding COC in the South China Sea. According to Chinese mass media, the meeting received positive feedback from participating countries.[62] However, China's reluctant position may delay the process of adopting the COC as is expected by the ASEAN members.

Another recent significant development is the *Philippines v China* case.[63] In January 2013, the Philippine Government officially notified the Chinese Government that it had commenced arbitral proceedings under Article 287 and Annex VII of the LOSC concerning the sovereign rights and jurisdiction of the Philippines over its

---

[61] Foreign Minister Wang Yi, *Code of Conduct in the South China Sea* (5 August 2013), available at <http://www.fmprc.gov.cn/ce/cena/eng/zgxw/t1064869.htm>.

[62] See '6th Senior Officials' Meeting on Implementation of DOC held in Suzhou', *CNTV* (15 September 2013), available at <http://english.cntv.cn/program/newsupdate/20130915/103210.shtml>.

[63] The case has been registered with the Permanent Court of Arbitration in The Hague. For relevant information, see <http://www.pca-cpa.org/showpage.asp?pag_id=1529>.

maritime entitlement in the West Philippine Sea (South China Sea) against China.[64] However, China stated that it would not participate in the arbitration and accused the Philippines of complicating the issue.[65] China accused the Philippines of distorting 'the basic facts underlying the disputes between China and the Philippines. In so doing, the Philippines attempts to deny China's territorial sovereignty and clothes its illegal occupation of China's islands and reefs with a cloak of "legality".[66] China asked the Philippines to return to negotiation and consultation to settle the disputes so as to avoid further damage to the bilateral relations between the two countries.[67]

Except for the World Trade Organization disputes settlement mechanisms and investment arbitration, China has not accepted the compulsory jurisdiction of other international forums. China has not accepted the compulsory jurisdiction of the International Court of Justice (ICJ), nor has China accepted the compulsory settlement mechanisms under the LOSC for disputes concerning maritime boundary delimitation, historic bays and titles, or military activities.[68] As most of the relief sought by the Philippines is in fact closely related to the territorial sovereignty to the disputed islands and islets, maritime boundary delimitation, and even historic title and historic rights, China had a compelling reason to raise preliminary objections as such disputes are excluded by China in accordance with Article 298 of the LOSC. For these reasons, it is extremely unlikely that the Arbitral Tribunal will establish its jurisdiction over the case.[69] But on the other hand, China's reluctance to participate in international dispute settlement mechanisms such as Annex VII Arbitration could have a negative impact on China's image in the world. It is suggested that China should participate in the arbitral proceedings to defend itself no matter how the case is disguised.[70] As the case is highly politicized with strong support from the

---

[64] See Republic of the Philippines, Department of Foreign Affairs, 'Diplomatic Note No 13-0211' and 'Notification and Statement of Claim', available at <http://www.gov.ph/downloads/2013/01jan/20130122-Notification-and-Statement-of-Claim-on-West-Philippine-Sea.pdf>.

[65] See 'China: No to UN Arbitration on Sea Row', *ABS CBN News* (1 February 2013), available at <http://www.abs-cbnnews.com/nation/02/01/13/china-no-un-arbitration-sea-row>.

[66] 'Foreign Ministry Spokesperson Hua Chunying's Remarks on the Philippines' Efforts in Pushing for the Establishment of the Arbitral Tribunal in Relation to the Disputes between China and the Philippines in the South China Sea', *Ministry of Foreign Affairs of the People's Republic of China* (26 April 2013), available at <http://www.fmprc.gov.cn/eng/xwfw/s2510/2535/t1035577.shtml>.

[67] 'Answers from the Foreign Ministry to the Questions at a Press Conference on the Search for the Disappearing Passenger Airplane of the Malaysian Airlines and the issue of the South China Sea', *People's Daily* (26 March 2014), available at <http://world.people.com.cn/n/2014/0326/c1002-24745397.html>.

[68] In August 2006, China made a declaration to exclude the categories of disputes set forth in LOSC, n 5, Art 298. China's declaration is available at <http://www.un.org/Depts/los/convention_agreements/convention_declarations.htm#China after ratification>.

[69] For relevant literature, see S Talmon, 'The South China Sea Arbitration: Is There a Case to Answer?' in S Talmon and J Bing Bing (eds), *The South China Sea Arbitration: A Chinese Perspective* (Hart Oxford 2014) 15.

[70] See M Yu, 'China's Response to the Compulsory Arbitration on the South China Sea Dispute: Legal Effects and Policy Options' (2014) 45 *Ocean Development and International Law* 1.

US Government,[71] there is a suspicion that this politically backed case is part of the overall rebalancing strategy of the United States in order to contain a rising China. Even if the Arbitral Tribunal were to grant all the contested reefs to the Philippines, such an award would in reality only exacerbate the tensions in the South China Sea, rather than assist in settling the disputes. Nevertheless, while it is acknowledged that the Annex VII of the LOSC mechanism is not a proper forum for the settlement of sovereignty disputes, it is suggested that China and the Philippines could learn from their neighbours, such as Indonesia, Malaysia, and Singapore, to bring their disputes to the ICJ for settlement when they could not reach agreement through bilateral talks.

For the purpose of defusing tensions and promoting regional cooperation in the South China Sea, some positive experiences could be learned from other regions. As some commentators have suggested 'the Spratly Islands area could be a regional analogue to Antarctica—a demilitarised zone designed to evolve into a zone of genuine peace and cooperative development'.[72] While it is certainly not intended to suggest that the regime established for Antarctica based on the Antarctic Treaty System (ATS) is applicable to the South China Sea wholesale, some elements of the ATS are useful, and to some extent necessary, for a regional order to be established for the South China Sea.[73] First, the principle of peaceful purposes is not only embodied in the 1959 Antarctic Treaty, but also in general international law. In a similar vein, the LOSC provides that oceans and seas should be used for peaceful purposes, and any threat or use of force against the territorial integrity or political independence of any State, or in any other manner inconsistent with the principles of international law embodied in the 1945 Charter of the United Nations shall be prohibited.[74] No country adjacent to the South China Sea would object to this principle.

---

[71] For example, the Assistant Secretary of State Daniel Russell recently gave testimony to the US Congress:

> I want to reinforce the point that under international law, maritime claims in the South China Sea must be derived from land features. Any use of the 'nine dash line' by China to claim maritime rights not based on claimed land features would be inconsistent with international law.... [And] we fully support the right of claimants to exercise rights they may have to avail themselves of peaceful dispute settlement mechanisms. The Philippines chose to exercise such a right last year with the filing of an arbitration case under the Law of the Sea Convention.

See DR Russell, Assistant Secretary, Bureau of East Asian and Pacific Affairs, *Maritime Disputes in East Asia*, Testimony, House Committee on Foreign Affairs Subcommittee on Asia and the Pacific Washington, DC (5 February 2014), available at <http://www.state.gov/p/eap/rls/rm/2014/02/221293.htm>.

[72] DM Johnston and MJ Valencia, *Pacific Ocean Boundary Problems: Status and Solutions* (Martinus Nijhoff Dordrecht 1991) 124.

[73] For details, see K Zou, 'Bringing the South Pole to the South China Sea: Towards the Establishment of an International Regime for Peace and Security' in Y Song and K Zou (eds), *Major Law and Policy Issues in the South China Sea: European and American Perspectives* (Ashgate Farnham 2014) 137.

[74] See LOSC, n 5, Art 301.

Based on this principle, it is useful to consider whether the South China Sea should be declared as a nuclear weapons free zone. The ASEAN members signed the 1995 Treaty on the Southeast Asia Nuclear Weapon-Free Zone declaring a Southeast Asia Nuclear Weapon-Free Zone (SEANWFZ).[75] At the annual meeting of ASEAN foreign ministers held in July 2011, a working group on the SEANWFZ called for a meeting between ASEAN arms control specialists and representatives of the permanent members of the United Nations Security Council (P-5 countries).[76]

In 2009, then Chinese President Hu Jintao made a statement titled 'Work Together to Build a Safer World for All' at the UN Security Council Summit on Nuclear Non-Proliferation and Nuclear Disarmament. According to President Hu, China has adhered to the policy of no-first-use of nuclear weapons at any time and under any circumstances and made the unequivocal commitment that China will unconditionally not use or threaten to use nuclear weapons against non-nuclear-weapon States or nuclear-weapon-free zones.[77] China has signed and ratified Protocol II to the 1967 Treaty for the Prohibition of Nuclear Weapons in Latin America and the Caribbean, Protocols II and III to the 1985 South Pacific Nuclear-Free Zone Treaty, and Protocols I and II to the 1996 African Nuclear-Weapon-Free Zone Treaty.[78] As China has already expressed its support of the establishment of the ASEAN nuclear-weapon free zone and its readiness to sign relevant protocols as early as possible,[79] there should be little problem in extending SEANWFZ to cover the South China Sea in future.

It is to be noted that the 1971 Treaty on the Prohibition of the Emplacement of Nuclear Weapons and other Weapons of Mass Destruction on the Sea-bed and the Ocean Floor is also relevant as it provides that the non-nuclear zone extends seaward from the 12-nm territorial sea of its parties.[80]

The countries adjacent to the South China Sea could also consider whether they should reach a consensus on the regulation of foreign military activities including intelligence collection and surveillance, military exercises, ordnance testing and firing, and hydrographic and military surveys conducting within the sea areas under

---

[75] Under Art 1, the 'Southeast Asia Nuclear Weapon-Free Zone' is defined as the area comprising the territories of all States in Southeast Asia, namely, Brunei Darussalam, Cambodia, Indonesia, Laos, Malaysia, Myanmar, the Philippines, Singapore, Thailand and Vietnam, and their respective continental shelves and exclusive economic zones (EEZ). For discussion, see R Mütsenich, 'Nuclear Weapon-Free Zone in Southeast Asia' (1997) 48 *Aussen Politik* 391.

[76] See 1995 Southeast Asia Nuclear-Weapon-Free Zone Treaty (Treaty of Bangkok).

[77] See President Hu Jintao, *Statement at the United Nations Security Council Summit on Nuclear Non-Proliferation and Nuclear Disarmament* (24 September 2009), available at <http://www.china-un.org/eng/hyyfy/t606550.htm>.

[78] See generally United Nations Office for Disarmament Affairs (UNODA), Nuclear-Weapon-Free Zone, available at <http://www.un.org/disarmament/WMD/Nuclear/NWFZ.shtml>.

[79] See ibid.

[80] ASEAN countries including Cambodia, Laos, Malaysia, Myanmar, the Philippines, Singapore and Vietnam and China are parties to this treaty. See also M Rosen, 'Nuclear-Weapon-Free Zones' (1996) 48 *Naval War College Review* 46.

national jurisdiction in the South China Sea in accordance with international law including the LOSC.

As we know, freedom of scientific research is fully guaranteed in the Antarctic region. It should be encouraged in the South China Sea. Like the Antarctic, the South China Sea is an important medium to study climate change and sea level rise, and their impact on human societies. The First Assessment Report of the Intergovernmental Panel on Climate Change (IPCC) anticipated that the South China Sea would experience significant climate and ecological change to the detriment of the region's coastal inhabitants, ecosystems, and economies.[81]

Marine scientific research has been undertaken under the Track II Informal Workshop on Managing Potential Conflicts in the South China Sea, which established several technical working groups and one of them is intended to promote marine scientific research in the South China Sea.[82] There is also some Track I cooperation, but this is mainly limited to a few countries, such as the Philippine-Vietnam Joint Oceanographic and Marine Scientific Research Expedition (JOMSRE-SCS I to IV) between 1996 and 2007. There is much room for regional cooperation in marine scientific research. Natural science is also the basis for resource conservation and environmental protection.

Third, as for marine resources conservation, the main principle contained in the ATS is the ecosystem approach. This approach has in fact been endorsed by the countries around the South China Sea. For example, China began to pay attention to the ecosystem approach in the late 1980s and adopted the ecosystem approach in the *China Ocean Agenda 21*, attached to which is a project proposal on the sustainability and protection of the Yellow Sea large marine ecosystem for the purpose of restoring the degrading Yellow Sea ecosystem, promoting sustainable development of natural resources, and mitigating and preventing environmental threats.[83] The real question is how to implement this approach in the management of the marine resources in the South China Sea. In that sense, taking the whole ecosystem into the consideration, integrated ocean management is required. Regional fishery management schemes in other regions such as the Regional Fisheries Committee for the Gulf of Guinea and the International Baltic Sea Fishery Commission are also good examples for the South China Sea fishery management.[84]

---

[81] IPCC, *First Assessment Report* (1990), available at <http://www.ipcc.ch/publications_and_data/publications_ipcc_first_assessment_1990_wg1.shtml>.

[82] For details, see Y Song, 'A Marine Biodiversity Project in the South China Sea: Joint Efforts Made in the SCS Workshop Process' (2011) 26 *International Journal of Marine and Coastal Law* 119.

[83] Appendix 6: 'Sustainability and Protection of the Yellow Sea Large Marine Ecosystem' in State Oceanic Administration (SOA) (ed), *China Ocean Agenda 21* (Ocean Press Beijing 1996) 163.

[84] For relevant account, see K-H Wang, 'Resolution to High Seas Fisheries Issue: A View from the South China Sea and an Expectation on National Ocean Policy' in S Lee and HE Lee (eds), *Northeast Asian Perspectives on International Law: Contemporary Issues and Challenges* (Martinus Nijhoff Leiden 2013) 63.

In terms of sustainable management of non-living resources, a moratorium has to be seriously considered by the littoral States. Joint development for oil and gas resources in the South China Sea has been proposed,[85] and the State-owned oil companies of China, the Philippines and Vietnam (China National Offshore Oil Corporation (CNOOC), PetroVietnam, and Philippine National Oil Company) did sign an agreement on joint seismic exploration in a designated area (143,000 km²) of the South China Sea in March 2005.[86] However, after the first stage of joint seismic survey in 2008, there has been no follow-up activity sponsored by the above three countries. Apparently, this preliminary joint development scheme has encountered a political stalemate resulting from distrust and conflicting maritime interests.

While joint development, as a temporary measure, can be still used as a means of diffusing tensions and enhancing regional cooperation, it is obviously not an optimal solution to accommodate the interests of all the countries bordering the South China Sea. The most optimal option for the South China Sea countries to consider is a moratorium such as the arrangement made in the ATS in relation to seabed mining.

For marine environmental protection, there exist several regional cooperative mechanisms such as the East Asian Seas Programme (EAP) as part of UN Environmental Programme's (UNEP) Regional Seas Programme. The Coordinating Body of the Seas of East Asia (COBSEA) recently adopted the New Strategic Direction for COBSEA (2008–2012) and the Strategic Action Programme (SAP) for the South China Sea.[87] The other regional marine environmental program involving both ASEAN members and China is the Regional Programme on Partnerships in Environmental Management for the Seas of East Asia (PEMSEA), jointly sponsored by the International Maritime Organization (IMO), the United Nations Development Programme (UNDP), the Global Environmental Facility (GEF), and the World Bank, with the mission 'to build interagency, intersectoral, and intergovernmental partnerships for achieving the sustainable development of the Seas of East Asia'.[88] China–ASEAN cooperation in marine environmental protection is mainly undertaken under the abovementioned regional programs. Since these programs have a wider coverage than specifically for the area of the South China Sea, they may not serve the special purpose of focusing on marine environmental protection in the South China Sea only. Some calls have thus been put forward for

---

[85] For details, see K Zou, 'Joint Development in the South China Sea: A New Approach' (2006) 21 *International Journal of Marine and Coastal Law* 83.

[86] See 'China, Philippines and Vietnam sign agreement to explore oil in the South China Sea', *Lianhe Zaobao* (15 March 2005) (in Chinese), available at <http://www.zaobao.com/gj/yx501_150305.html>.

[87] For details, see COBSEA, 'Strategic and Emerging Issues', available at <http://www.cobsea.org/activities/activities_strategic.html>.

[88] See 'PEMSEA at a Glance', available at <http://www.pemsea.org/about-pemsea/pemsea-at-a-glance/>.

the introduction of ecosystem-based management into the South China Sea. A call for the establishment of a Spratly Islands International Marine Peace Park has also been voiced.[89]

As the South China Sea contains important sea lanes, freedom of navigation should be maintained. Though the territorial and maritime disputes so far have not affected the normal shipping activities in the South China Sea, there is a concern that escalating tensions could hamper free and safe navigation. In that sense, the management and control of the disputes pending their settlement is necessary to safeguard the safety of navigation in the South China Sea.

5 Conclusion

With the entry into force of the LOSC, the maritime enclosure movement around the world has been further intensified. The disputes in the South China Sea exactly reflect the intensified claims of the littoral States to maritime spaces and marine resources. In considering the fact that all the countries adjacent to the South China Sea are developing countries and pursuing rapid economic development, their energy thirst for marine resources will inevitably be stronger. Due to overlapping maritime claims in the South China Sea, tensions and even conflicts between China and its neighbouring countries concerning marine resource exploration and development do exist.[90] It is predicted that the South China Sea will not be quiet in the years to come as the disputes there are entangled with various national interests of the coastal States and involved with external powers that attempt to influence the discourse of the dispute settlement. But we still hold the belief that the political leadership of the countries adjacent to the South China Sea has sufficient wisdom and willingness to find feasible and peaceful ways and means to solve the disputes in future. A regional order based on general international law and the DOC could be thus gradually developed so as to maintain long-lasting peace and cooperation in the South China Sea.

---

[89] For details, see JW McManus, K-T Shao, and S-Y Lin, 'Toward Establishing a Spratly Islands Marine Peace Park: Ecological and Supportive Collaborative Activities with an Emphasis on the Role of Taiwan' (2011) 41 *Ocean Development and International Law* 270.

[90] K Zou, 'China's Ocean Policymaking: Practice and Lessons' (2012) 40 *Coastal Management* 147.

29

NORTH-EAST ATLANTIC AND THE NORTH SEA

RONÁN LONG

1 INTRODUCTION

THE development of the law of the sea in a number of discrete fields such as fisheries and maritime boundaries is often associated with regional practice in the North-East Atlantic and the North Sea.[1] The former region is a constituent part of the Atlantic Ocean and the latter is an immensely important sub-regional sea on its eastern periphery, separating the United Kingdom and Ireland from the continental landmass of Europe.

The chapter opens by mentioning some of the geographical, economic, environmental, strategic, and geopolitical factors that are shaping the very distinctive regional regimes that give effect to the basic principles, as well as to many of the substantive provisions embodied in the 1982 United Nations Convention on the Law of the Sea (LOSC) and related agreements. There is a summary of the various maritime jurisdictional zones and boundaries claimed by the 12 coastal States that make-up the region, namely: Belgium, Denmark, France, Germany, Iceland,

---

[1] DJ Bederman, 'The Sea' in B Fassbender, AP Peters, and D Högger (eds), *Oxford Handbook of the History of International Law* (Oxford University Press Oxford 2012) 359.

Ireland, the Netherlands, Norway, Portugal, Spain, Sweden, and the UK, all but two of which (Norway and Iceland) are European Union (EU) Member States. This is followed by a description of some of the principal regional bodies that are responsible for formulating and implementing various aspects of the law of the sea, most notably: the regional seas environmental body, the EU, and several fisheries management organizations.

From the outset, it should be noted that regional State practice is increasingly informed by greater political and public awareness of the strategic importance of the ocean and adjacent seas for the economic prosperity and sustainable development of the Atlantic and North Sea maritime regions. Thus it is unsurprising to see that the EU and its constituent Member States, together with the neighbouring coastal States of Norway and Iceland, are making considerable efforts to improve the effectiveness and coherence of regional law on fisheries, offshore energy, maritime transport, marine scientific research, and the protection of the marine environment. In the EU, much impetus is derived from the Integrated Maritime Policy,[2] its associated Maritime Strategy for the Atlantic Ocean area,[3] along with the so-called Blue Growth Strategy,[4] which all aim to make the region one of the most dynamic and resilient maritime economies in the world. At the same time, the EU is striving to implement a uniform approach to maritime spatial planning and coastal management,[5] as well as making great efforts to apply new normative principles to the tasks associated with ocean governance including the precautionary principle and the ecosystem approach.[6] As will be seen below, all of these initiatives are shaping regional trends and influencing the progressive development of the law of the sea.

---

[2] European Commission, 'Conclusions from the Consultation on a European Maritime Policy', COM(2007) 574 (10 October 2007); European Commission, 'Progress of the EU's Integrated Maritime Policy', COM(2012) 491 (11 September 2012).

[3] European Commission, 'Action Plan for a Maritime Strategy in the Atlantic area: Delivering smart, sustainable and inclusive growth', COM(2013) 279 (13 May 2013); European Commission, 'Developing a Maritime Strategy for the Atlantic Ocean Area', COM(2011) 782 (21 November 2011).

[4] European Commission, 'Blue Growth: Opportunities for marine and maritime sustainable growth' COM(2012) 494 (13 September 2012).

[5] Directive 2014/89/EU *Establishing a framework for maritime spatial planning*, OJ L 257/135 (28 August 2014).

[6] R Long, 'Principles and Normative Trends in European Union Ocean Governance' in C Schofield, S Lee, and M Kwon (eds), *The Limits Of Maritime Jurisdiction* (Brill/Nijhoff Leiden 2014) 629.

2 The Context: General Description of the North-East Atlantic and the North Sea

2.1 Defining the region

The precise spatial extent of the North-East Atlantic is open to discussion. From a purely geographical standpoint, for instance, it could be argued that the region includes all sea areas, both within and beyond national jurisdiction, extending across the Atlantic from Greenland in the west, as far as the European continental landmass in the east. Adjacent oceans and seas include the Arctic Ocean, the Norwegian and Greenland Seas, the Denmark Strait, as well as the broader Atlantic to the south and west. From a legal perspective, however, the precise geographical extent of the region varies considerably for different legislative purposes. Notably, the 1992 Convention for the Protection of the Marine Environment of the North-East Atlantic (OSPAR Convention) defines the OSPAR 'maritime area' by reference to the various maritime spaces under contracting party jurisdiction, as well as by reference to a specific area of high seas and seabed beyond national jurisdiction in the Atlantic and Arctic Oceans, which are delineated by lines of longitude running south from the North Pole and that intersect a parallel latitude (36° N) touching the southern tip of Spain.[7] The North Sea comes within the scope of this definition but it excludes the Baltic Sea and the Mediterranean Sea.[8] For the purpose of EU law, the Marine Strategy Framework Directive (MSFD) further divides the North-East Atlantic into four marine sub-regions, namely: the Greater North Sea, including the Kattegat and the English Channel; the Celtic Seas; the Bay of Biscay and the Iberian Coast; and in the Atlantic Ocean, the Macaronesian biogeographic region, being the waters surrounding the Azores, Madeira, and the Canary Islands.[9] Considerable care needs to be taken with this approach, as there is considerable divergence between international and EU law regarding the extent of many of the regional seas within this subdivision. A case in point relates to the Greater North Sea and its Wider Approaches, which are defined by a regional pollution agreement

---

[7] 1992 Convention for the Protection of the Marine Environment of the North-East Atlantic, Art 1(a)(i) and (ii) (hereinafter OSPAR Convention). Ratified by Belgium, Denmark, France, Germany, Iceland, Ireland, the Netherlands, Norway, Portugal, Spain, and Sweden, the EU (formal instrument of confirmation), Finland (a Baltic State with rivers flowing into the Barents Sea), as well as by two landlocked States, Luxembourg and Switzerland, that are linked with North Sea by means of the River Rhine and its tributaries.

[8] Ibid, Art 1(a)(i) (1), (2).

[9] Directive 2008/56/EC *establishing a framework for community action in the field of marine environmental policy*, OJ L 164/19 (25 May 2008) Art 4.

(1983 Agreement for Cooperation in Dealing with Pollution of the North Sea by Oil and other Harmful Substances (Bonn Agreement)) to include the North Sea proper, the Skagerrak, the English Channel and its approaches, and other waters, comprising the Irish Sea, the Celtic Sea, the Malin Sea, the Great Minch, the Little Minch, part of the Norwegian Sea, and parts of the North East Atlantic.[10] This may be contrasted with some early EU marine environmental measures, which are less extensive in geographical scope but nonetheless include both the Skagerrak and the Kattegat as part of the North Sea.[11] Other EU legislation, such as the law applicable to the pilotage of deep-sea vessels, avoids the problems associated with the legal definition of regional maritime space by simply referring to countries that have coasts bordering on the North Sea and the English Channel.[12] Prudently, EU fisheries law avoids ambiguity by using the International Council for the Exploration of the Seas (ICES) statistical area maps for the purpose of fisheries management under the Common Fisheries Policy (CFP).[13]

In light of these definitional difficulties, the scope of this chapter is limited to the geographical area that corresponds to OSPAR Regions II, III, IV and V but excludes the Arctic (OSPAR Region I), as the latter is comprehensively reviewed elsewhere in this volume.[14]

2.2 Ocean, coastal, and political geography

Amounting to 15 per cent of the world's oceans in terms of size, the North-East Atlantic has many distinctive geographical and geomorphological features including the mid-Atlantic ridge, which runs south from Iceland through the Azores and onwards towards Antarctica.[15] The east coast of Greenland forms a natural border to the region, and the Greenland-Scotland Ridge divides the Atlantic from the Nordic Seas. Oceanographic features include the North Atlantic Drift, which sweeps diagonally from the Sargasso Sea towards northern Europe, influencing the climate and marine biodiversity in the shallower coastal waters of the littoral States on the Atlantic margin. There are many hotspots of biodiversity associated with

---

[10] 1983 Agreement for Cooperation in Dealing with Pollution of the North Sea by Oil and other Harmful Substances, Art 2 (hereinafter Bonn Agreement), as amended by the Decision of 21 September 2001 by the Contracting Parties to enable the Accession of Ireland to the Agreement.

[11] Resolution of 28 June 1988, OJ C 209/3 (9 August 1988).

[12] Directive 79/115/EEC *Concerning pilotage of vessels by deep-sea pilots in the North Sea and English Channel*, OJ L 33/32 (8 February 1979), Art 1; Council Regulation 3908/91/EEC *On Community action to protect the environment in the coastal areas and coastal waters of the Irish Sea, North Sea, English Channel, Baltic Sea and NorthEast Atlantic Ocean*, OJ L 370/28 (31 December 1991).

[13] Regulation 218/2009 *On the submission of nominal catch statistics by Member States fishing in the North-East Atlantic*, OJ L 87/70 (31 March 2009).

[14] See Chapter 32 in this volume.

[15] OSPAR Commission, *Quality Status Report 2010* (OSPAR London 2010) 11.

deep-water corals, fragile marine ecosystems, hydrothermal vents, as well as submarine canyons and seamounts.[16]

Apart from the Norwegian Trough, the North Sea is relatively shallow with an average depth of 200 metres and is enclosed by the English Chanel in the south and the Norwegian Sea in the north. As a regional sea, it separates the UK in the west from Belgium, the Netherlands, Germany, Sweden, and Norway in the east. The coastal geography varies considerably from the deeply indented fjords and islands in Norway to the relatively featureless west coast of Denmark, the low-lying German Bight bordered by the Danish Islands and Frisian Islands. In the Atlantic, three of the coastal States (Iceland, Ireland, and the UK) are insular and have coastlines that are characterized by striking cliffs, deep bays, numerous offshore islands and rocks, along with meandering rivers and broad estuaries. Further south on the European mainland, the concave Bay of Biscay gives way to the relative linear coastlines of northern Spain and Portugal. Offshore in the wider Atlantic, oceanographic features include a number of mid-ocean archipelagos and islands, which are constituent territories of their parent European States, namely: Denmark (the Faroe Islands), Portugal (the Azores and Madeira), and Spain (the Canary Islands).

The peaceful settlement of law of the sea disputes including maritime boundary disputes is greatly facilitated by the relative contemporary political stability of the region.[17] In some instances, this stability is enhanced by the systems of devolved government that are in place in the UK, Spain, Portugal and Denmark. Such arrangements pose few problems from a maritime governance perspective with some notable exceptions such as the management of fisheries in relation to Greenland and the Faroe Islands, which are self-governing parts of the Kingdom of Denmark, but remain outside of the scope of the EU's CFP.[18]

2.3 Economic significance

For obvious practical reasons, the economic significance of national maritime interests informs the positions adopted by coastal States concerning regional law of the sea issues. On the macro scale, much commercial strength is derived from the industrial powerhouses of Germany, France, and the UK, all of whom have strategic interests in shipping, foreign trade, and energy security. Similarly, several smaller coastal States, such as Norway, Denmark, and the Netherlands, are global leaders in sectors such as offshore oil and gas, aquaculture, wind energy, and coastal engineering services. The fishing industry and aquaculture are significant in the Atlantic regions of Spain and France, and for the national economies of Norway, Scotland, Iceland, and Ireland.[19] Taking all the sectors

---

[16] Ibid, 10–11 and 13–16.   [17] See Sections 3.2 and 3.3 below.   [18] See Section 5.1 below.
[19] European Commission, *Agriculture, Forestry and Fisheries Statistics* (Eurostat Luxembourg 2013) 213–28.

together, however, the overall economic impact of maritime industries is relatively modest in that it makes up no more than a meagre 2.5 per cent of OSPAR Contracting Parties Gross Domestic Product.[20] This figure belies, nonetheless, the strategic importance of industries, such as shipping, to the economic prosperity and stability of all States within the region, with close to 90 per cent of Europe's foreign trade in terms of volume going by sea, much of it through ports located around the North Sea.[21] Indeed, one-third of the total economic value of the entire maritime sector within the region is derived from two industries: shipping and coastal tourism.[22] The pace and direction of regional initiatives on the law of the sea may be increasingly influenced by the EU, which is seeking to establish a socially inclusive and sustainable model of economic development in relation to offshore industries as part of its general maritime policy.[23]

2.4 Environmental threats

Regional law does not evolve in a vacuum and many regulatory measures are aimed at addressing anthropogenic threats posed to the marine environment including those associated with the highly urbanized and industrialized coastal settlements around the North Sea, unsustainable fishing, pollution from shipping, the eutrophication of coastal waters from agriculture, as well as unacceptable levels of marine litter.[24] Impacts from shipping include illegal discharges of toxic substances, air pollution, the introduction of non-indigenous invasive species into the marine environment along with acoustic pollution.[25] In the wider Atlantic, the most pressing challenge is the continued depletion of fisheries, with some scientific estimates suggesting that EU catches have declined at an average of 2 per cent per year since 1993.[26] The difficulties encountered in the sustainable management of marine resources are compounded by the warming of the ocean in OSPAR Region II by 1° to 2°C since 1985.[27] Ominously, the Fifth Assessment Report of the Intergovernmental Panel on Climate Change concluded that the North Atlantic will continue to warm in the twenty-first century, and that this in turn will affect ocean circulation and sea level-rise.[28]

---

[20] OSPAR Commission, n 15, 10.

[21] European Environmental Agency (EEA), *Balancing the Future of Europe's Coasts—The Knowledge Base for Integrated Management* (EEA Copenhagen 2013) 12.

[22] Ecorys, *Blue Growth, Scenarios and Drivers for Sustainable Growth from the Oceans, Seas and Coasts, Third Interim Report* (13 March 2012) 65, available at <http://ec.europa.eu/maritimeaffairs/documentation/studies/documents/blue_growth_third_interim_report_en.pdf>.

[23] European Commission, 'Action Plan for a Maritime Strategy in the Atlantic area Delivering smart, sustainable and inclusive growth', COM(2013) 279 (13 May 2013) 4.

[24] European Environmental Agency, n 21, 66.   [25] OSPAR Commission, n 15, 92–3.

[26] European Commission, 'Impact assessment concerning the Commission's proposal for the 2012 reform of the Common Fisheries Policy', SEC(2011) 891 (13 July 2011) 8.

[27] OSPAR Commission, n 15, 17–26.

[28] Intergovernmental Panel on Climate Change (IPCC), *Climate Change 2013: The Physical Science Basis* (Cambridge University Press Cambridge 2013) 23, 25.

3 LAW OF THE SEA: NORTH-EAST ATLANTIC AND THE NORTH SEA

3.1 Regional influences and participation in the law of the sea

The claiming of authority over the sea by the great European maritime powers has shaped the law of the sea since the Age of Discovery and is a quintessential feature of the region's heritage.[29] When viewed with the benefit of hindsight, however, the deployment of regional naval power often lacked benevolence and was sometimes aimed solely at enhancing royal prerogatives, as well as at advancing European hegemony globally. History also teaches us that regional interests in maritime matters were closely aligned with the spread of imperialism, colonization, trade, and religion, as well as with the quest for new scientific discoveries and navigational routes. Indeed, much of the early law evolved in disputes between European powers over their maritime interests in the North Sea and adjacent waters, as well as over sovereignty and freedom of the seas further afield, as evidenced by the great classical and canonical writings of the era including those vindicating the mercantile entitlements of the Dutch East India Company.[30] Similarly, the gradual creep of coastal State jurisdiction over a narrow band of water close to shore for security and fisheries purposes is usually attributed to the practice of north European countries since the 1600s, again supported by erudite scholarship on the normative rules applicable to territorial waters.[31]

In more recent times, economic uses of the region for fisheries and petroleum development had a major bearing on disputes concerning the use of straight baselines,[32] the establishment of continental shelf boundaries, as well as the unilateral extension of fisheries zones.[33] This in turn had a profound influence on shaping the rules of customary law as it pertains to the ocean, as well as on the momentous inter-governmental efforts to codify and develop the law of the sea in the latter part of the twentieth century, culminating at the Third United Nations Conference on the Law of the Sea. At the latter, the Member States of the European Economic Community (EEC), including seven Atlantic and North Sea States,[34] had too many

---

[29] DP O'Connell, *The International Law of the Sea* (Clarendon Press Oxford 1982) Vol 1, 1–28.

[30] Bederman, n 1, 359–378.

[31] C Bynkershoek, *De Dominio Maris Dissertatio* in JB Scott (ed), *Classics of International Law* (2nd edn Oxford University Press New York 1923) 1744.

[32] *Fisheries (United Kingdom v Norway)* (Judgment) [1951] ICJ Rep 116.

[33] *Fisheries Jurisdiction (United Kingdom v Iceland)* (Jurisdiction) [1973] ICJ Rep 3; (Merits) [1974] ICJ Rep 3; *(Federal Republic of Germany v Iceland)* (Jurisdiction) [1973] ICJ Rep 49; (Merits) [1974] ICJ Rep 175.

[34] Belgium, Denmark, the Netherlands, France, Germany, Ireland, and the UK. Luxembourg, Greece, and Italy were the other EEC Member States.

divergent interests to forge a strong regional identity on the substantive and procedural matters under negotiation. In particular, they held conflicting positions on many fundamental matters, including: coastal State jurisdiction in the EEZ, particularly in relation to fishing; the extent of the extended continental shelf beyond 200 nautical miles (nm), explained by the fact that several of the States were 'margineers' and members of the Group of Broad-Shelf States; navigation rights in international straits; the rules applicable to maritime delimitation; and how well the draft Convention ought to address the interests of the great maritime powers, which included the UK and France.[35] As a result, EEC countries played only a minor role as a regional interest group, other than ensuring that the EEC was eligible to become party to the LOSC in its own right.[36] Sometimes forgotten, five EEC member States abstained when the draft Convention was finally put to a vote in 1982, primarily because of the proposed regime on seabed mining.[37]

According to this narrative, the regional history of the law of the sea appears to be inextricably linked with the struggle by States bordering the Atlantic for control of the sea and with the difficulties that they encountered in reconciling the principle of freedom of the seas with the principle of coastal State sovereignty and jurisdiction over maritime space and resources.[38] More recently, this dichotomy is increasingly resolved by recourse to regional solutions that reflect mutual restraint on the part of States. As a result, coastal States within the region have set new international benchmarks for working together in the fields of environmental protection and fisheries management.[39]

Today, there is universal regional acceptance of the international legal framework as it applies to the ocean and all regional States are parties to the LOSC, the 1994 Agreement Relating to the Implementation of Part XI of the United Nations Convention on the Law of the Sea of 10 December 1982 (1994 Implementation Agreement)[40] and the 1995 Agreement for the Implementation of the Provisions of the United Nations Convention on the Law of the Sea of 10 December 1982 Relating to the Conservation and Management of Straddling Fish Stocks and Highly Migratory Fish Stocks (Fish Stocks Agreement, FSA).[41] In addition, the EU is party in its own right to the LOSC, the Fish Stocks Agreement, and

---

[35] *Virginia Commentaries*, Vol I, 68–86, especially 84.
[36] M Hayes, *The Law of the Sea Convention: The Role of the Irish Delegation at the Third UN Conference* (Royal Irish Academy Dublin 2011) 166, 261.
[37] Member States abstaining included Belgium, the Federal Republic of Germany, Luxembourg, the Netherlands, and the UK. Spain also abstained and later became a member of the EEC.
[38] Y Tanaka, *The International Law of the Sea* (Cambridge University Press Cambridge 2012) 16–19.
[39] See Sections 3–5.
[40] 1994 Agreement Relating to the Implementation of Part XI of the United Nations Convention on the Law of the Sea of 10 December 1982 (hereinafter 1994 Implementation Agreement).
[41] 1995 UN Agreement for the Implementation of the Provisions of the United Nations Convention on the Law of the Sea of 10 December 1982 relating to the Conservation and Management of Straddling Fish Stocks and Highly Migratory Fish Stocks (hereinafter FSA).

the 1993 Agreement to Promote Compliance with International Conservation and Management Measures by Fishing Vessels on the High Seas (FAO Compliance Agreement).[42] As will be seen further below, there are many other global, regional, and sub-regional instruments, which are binding on the States within the region and that contribute to the protection of the marine environment, as well as the management and utilization of marine resources.[43]

3.2 Maritime jurisdictional zones

Regional State practice on the establishment of maritime zones is relatively well settled, from an international law perspective, with all of the coastal States, apart from Belgium, applying straight baselines to all or parts of their coasts. The drawing of baselines lacks uniformity, however, with several examples of non-compliance with the LOSC, including the baseline system adopted by Portugal along its mainland coast.[44] In contrast, the straight baselines of Norway, Ireland, France, and the Netherlands are considered by one authority to be in 'substantial conformity with international law', even if not applied restrictively in all instances.[45] Contrary to the express provisions of the LOSC, however, Denmark and Portugal apply a system of baselines similar to archipelagic baselines around the Faroe Islands and the Azores, respectively, even though they do not qualify as archipelagic States under the LOSC for this purpose.[46] Importantly, the tendency of States, such as the UK and Ireland that have enclosed large segments of their coastlines by using straight baselines, is to allow for innocent passage on the landward side of the baselines. A case in point is the navigation regime that applies in the Minches Strait within the UK's internal waters.[47] Several States claim historic bays or titles including Iceland with respect to Breidafjordhur and Faxafloi Bays.[48]

All 12 coastal States have established a 12 nm territorial sea where legally and geographically possible, with the exception of a 3-nm territorial sea that applies around Greenland. Significantly, Germany rolled back its territorial sea limits to 12 nm in 1995

---

[42] Decision 98/392/EC *Concerning the conclusion by the European Community of the LOSC and the 1994 Implementation Agreement*, OJ L 179 (23 June 1998); Decision 98/414/EC *On the ratification by the European Community of the FSA*, OJ L 189/14 (3 July 1998); Decision 96/428/EC, OJ L 177/24 (16 July 1996).

[43] See Sections 4 and 5 below.

[44] JA Roach and RW Smith, *Excessive Maritime Claims* (3rd edn Martinus Nijhoff Leiden/Boston 2012) 89.

[45] M Reisman and G Westerman, *Straight Baselines in International Maritime Boundary Delimitation* (St Martin's Press New York 1992) 107.

[46] 1982 United Nations Convention on the Law of the Sea, Art 46(a).

[47] Ibid, Art 8(2); Territorial Waters Order in Council, SI, 1965, Part III, 6452A.

[48] LOSC, n 46, Art 10(6). See further CR Symmons, *Historic Waters in the Law of the Sea: A Modern Re-Appraisal* (Martinus Nijhoff Leiden/Boston 2008).

and withdrew a claim to a deep-water roadstead as part of its territorial sea.[49] In 2004, Norway extended its territorial sea limits from 4 to 12 nm around the mainland, Jan Mayen, and Svalbard. Apart from Germany, Iceland, and the UK, all coastal States have established a 24-nm contiguous zone for the purpose of preventing or punishing violations of customs, fiscal, immigration, or sanitary laws and regulations within their territory or territorial seas.[50] The rolling-out of territorial sea limits beyond 3 nm has made three of the European coastal States (France, Spain, and the UK) strait States, and brings the strategically important Straits of Dover and the Strait of Gibraltar within coastal State jurisdiction. Apart from concerns voiced by Spain in relation to the Strait of Gibraltar,[51] the general regional trend is to uphold the regime of transit passage in international straits in accordance with Part III of the LOSC.[52]

In a concerted move, EEC member States pushed their respective fishery limits out to 200 nm from their North Atlantic and North Sea coasts from 1977.[53] Since then, all coastal States have established 200-mile exclusive economic zones (EEZs) where possible, with some such as Ireland and the UK, turning fisheries zones into full-scale EEZs.[54] Spain has established an EEZ in the Atlantic and around the Canary Islands but has not done so in the Mediterranean Sea.[55] Portugal has a 200-mile EEZ projected from its mainland and around the Azores and Madeira, which makes it one of the largest EEZs in the world. In general, coastal State practice within the region appears to uphold the *sui generis* legal status of the EEZ and thereby reflects the functional balance of the rights and duties set down by the LOSC.[56]

Although it is well settled that the rights of a coastal State over the continental shelf do not depend on occupation, effective or notional, or on any express proclamation,[57] all of the coastal States have confirmed their entitlements to the

---

[49] Germany, (1995) 27 *Law of the Sea Bulletin* 55–61.

[50] LOSC, n 46, Art 33.

[51] JA de Yturriaga, *Straits Used for International Navigation: A Spanish Perspective* (Martinus Nijhoff Leiden 1991) *passim*.

[52] T Treves and L Pineschi (eds), *The Law of the Sea: The European Union and its Member States* (Martinus Nijhoff The Hague 1997) *passim*.

[53] Council Resolution of 3 November 1976 on certain external aspects of the creation of a 200-mile fishing zone in the Community with effect from 1 January 1977, OJ C 105/1 (7 May 1981); R Long, 'Stepping over Maritime Boundaries to Apply New Normative Tools in EU Law and Policy' in M Nordquist et al (eds), *Maritime Border Diplomacy* (Martinus Nijhoff Leiden/Boston 2012) 213.

[54] Sea Fisheries and Maritime Jurisdiction Act 2006 (Ireland); Exclusive Economic Zone Order 2013 (UK).

[55] See Chapter 27 in this volume.

[56] E Franckx and P Gautier (eds), *The Exclusive Economic Zone and the United Nations Convention on the Law of the Sea, 1982–2000: A Preliminary Assessment of State Practice* (Bruylant Brussels 2003) *passim*.

[57] LOSC, n 46, Art 77(3); *North Sea Continental Shelf (Federal Republic of Germany v Denmark; Federal Republic of Germany v The Netherlands)* (Judgment) [1969] ICJ Rep 31.

continental shelf by means of national legislation.[58] Furthermore, Denmark, France, Portugal, Iceland, Ireland, Norway, Spain, and the UK have made submissions to the Commission on the Limits of the Continental Shelf (CLCS) concerning the outer limits of continental shelf beyond 200 nm.[59] The Commission in turn has made recommendations with respect to Ireland's partial submission,[60] along with Norway's submissions of 2006,[61] the partial submission made by Denmark together with the Government of the Faroes in respect of the continental shelf north of the Faroe Islands,[62] as well as the joint submission made by Ireland, France, Spain, and the UK in the area of the Celtic Sea and the Bay of Biscay.[63] The latter submission was the first example of a joint submission to the CLCS and thus established an important international precedent since followed by States in other ocean regions. By virtue of the LOSC and its own Rules of Procedure,[64] the CLCS is unable to consider the submissions made by Ireland, the UK and Denmark in relation to the disputed continental shelf in the Hatton Rockall Area/Faroe-Rockall Plateau Region[65] and, as a result, the three States, along with Iceland, are committed to further quadrilateral negotiations to resolve these boundaries.[66]

In separate developments, Nordic States within the region have concluded two diplomatic agreements on the provisional delimitation of the shelf in areas beyond national jurisdiction in the southern part of the Norwegian Sea and in the vicinity of the Reykjanes Ridge respectively.[67]

3.3 Maritime boundaries

Maritime boundary delimitation is a matter of common concern for all coastal States in the region, and over 20 bilateral maritime boundary agreements have

---

[58] See United Nations Division for Ocean Affairs and the Law of the Sea (DOALOS), *Maritime Space: Maritime Zones and Maritime Delimitation* (2011), available at <http://www.un.org/Depts/los/LEGISLATIONANDTREATIES/index.htm>.

[59] See DOALOS, *Submissions, Through the Secretary-General of the United Nations, to the Commission on the Limits of the Continental Shelf, Pursuant to Article 76, Paragraph 8, of the United Nations Convention on the Law of the Sea of 10 December 1982* (2014), available at <www.un.org/depts/los/clcs_new/commission_submissions.htm>.

[60] CLCS 54 (5 April 2007). [61] CLCS 62 (27 March 2009).
[62] CLCS 83 (31 March 2014). [63] CLCS 62 (24 March 2009).
[64] LOSC, n 46, Art 9, Annex II; CLCS, *Rules of Procedure of the Commission*, Doc CLCS/40/Rev.1 (17 April 2008), Rule 46, Annex I.
[65] CLCS 64 (31 March 2009); Denmark, CLCS 70 (2 December 2010).
[66] CLCS 64 [41]–[52]; Denmark, CLCS 70, n 65, [31]–[34].
[67] T Heidar, 'Delimitation of the Continental Shelf: The Nordic Model' in M Lodge and MH Nordquist (eds), *Peaceful Order In The World's Oceans: Essays in Honor of Satya N. Nandan* (Martinus Nijhoff Leiden/Boston 2014) 146–56.

been concluded.[68] The majority of the settlements pertain to continental shelf delimitation, most notably in the North Sea, the Denmark Strait, the English Channel and, to a lesser extent, to the west of mainland Europe along the Atlantic margin. Many of the early agreements pertaining to the North Sea were concluded on the basis of the equidistance principle, taking into account special circumstances, under Article 6 of the 1958 Convention on the Continental Shelf,[69] and more recently on the basis of just and equitable principles in accordance with the judgment of the International Court of Justice (ICJ) in the *North Sea Continental Shelf* cases.[70] Settlements are usually achieved by negotiation, with some notable exceptions that required recourse to third party dispute settlement in the ICJ and by means of international arbitration, as well as to a Conciliation Commission in one unique instance.[71] In some cases, settlement has been achieved by a combination of these methods, including by negotiation following judgments of the ICJ.[72] Notably, three of the settlements have resulted in the establishment of cooperative arrangements for the exploitation of natural resources including the agreement between France and Spain that provides for an equal distribution of continental shelf resources in a zone that straddles both jurisdictions in the Bay of Biscay.[73] Other examples of a pragmatic approach to regional cooperative arrangements include the bilateral agreements between the UK and Norway for the joint exploitation of cross-boundary hydrocarbon fields in the North Sea.[74]

Traditionally, the equidistant principle was used as the starting basis for negotiation but it is now common for States within the region to apply many methods and diverse practices to achieve a settlement. As a result, many factors have influenced negotiated settlements, as well as curial and arbitral determinations, including geographical, economic, and political considerations. In particular, the location of offshore natural resources continues to influence the political division of the ocean. Cases in point include the location of hydrocarbons in the North

---

[68] DH Anderson, 'Region IX. Northern and Western European Maritime Boundaries' in DA Colson and RW Smith (eds), *International Maritime Boundaries* (American Society of International Law/ Martinus Nijhoff Leiden/Boston 2011).

[69] Norway and the UK (supplemented by 1978 Protocol); Denmark (Faroe Islands) and Norway (supplemented by 1979 Protocol); Norway and Sweden; Denmark and the UK; and the Netherlands and the UK.

[70] *North Sea Continental Shelf*, n 57; *Maritime Delimitation in the Area between Greenland and Jan Mayen (Denmark v Norway)* (Judgment) [1993] ICJ Rep 38 (hereinafter *Jan Mayen*).

[71] *Report and Recommendation of the Conciliation Commission on the Continental Shelf Area between Iceland and Jan Mayen* (1981) 20 ILM 787.

[72] See *North Sea Continental Shelf*, n 57; *Jan Mayen*, n 70.

[73] 1974 Convention between France and Spain on the Delimitation of the Continental Shelves of the Two States in the Bay of Biscay (Golfe de Gascogne/Golfo de Vizcaya), Art 3 and Annex 2. The other examples pertain to Iceland and Norway in relation to Jan Mayen, and between the UK and Denmark (Faroe Islands).

[74] 2005 Framework Agreement between the UK and Norway Concerning Cross-Boundary Petroleum Cooperation.

Sea, which had a bearing on the commencement of negotiations concerning the delimitation of maritime boundaries in the North Sea, as well the geographical location of a fish stock (capelin), which influenced the maritime delimitation of an area between Greenland and Jan Mayen.[75] Since the early 1980s, there is not the same pressing requirement on EU Member States to agree fisheries boundaries between opposite or adjacent States, as all fisheries under national jurisdiction are treated as a common pool resource under the CFP.[76] As a consequence, one of the general trends in the North Sea is the use of continental shelf boundaries for other purposes including fisheries law enforcement and offshore wind energy development, resulting *de facto* in a single boundary. An illustrative example of contemporary trends in this regard is the single maritime boundary concluded between the UK and Ireland, which delimits the EEZs of the two countries and parts of their continental shelves.[77]

Similar to other ocean regions, there are a number of on-going disputes in the region concerning the legal status attributed to low-tide elevations, islands, and rocks, as well as their use as basepoints for the purpose of maritime boundary delineation and delimitation.[78] The use of low-tide elevations in the delimitation of the territorial sea is particularly problematic in the southern part of the North Sea because of the extraordinary range of tides and the dynamic nature of the coastal environment.[79] Other difficulties that have arisen stem from the legal status of islands and rocks including the projection of 200-nm fishery limits from the renowned rock, Rockall, which were retracted by the UK in 1995.[80] There is inordinate delay in the formal conclusion of a boundary agreement between Iceland and Denmark with respect to the maritime zones adjacent to the Faroe Islands, which is sometimes linked to the projection of maritime limits from Hvalbakur by Iceland.[81]

---

[75] *Jan Mayen*, n 70, [75]–[76]. In relation to the North Sea, see A Oude Elferink, *The Delimitation of the Continental Shelf between Denmark, Germany and the Netherlands; Arguing Law, Practicing Politics?* (Cambridge University Press Cambridge 2013).

[76] See Section 5.1 below.

[77] 2014 Agreement between the Government of Ireland and the Government of the United Kingdom of Great Britain and Northern Ireland establishing a Single Maritime Boundary between the Exclusive Economic Zones of the two Countries and parts of their Continental Shelves.

[78] LOSC, n 46, Art 121.

[79] C Carleton and CH Schofield, 'Developments in the Technical Determination of Maritime Space: Delimitation, Dispute Resolution, Geographical Information, Systems and the Role of the Technical Expert' (2002) 3 *International Boundaries Research Unit Maritime Briefing*, 1, 38–9 and 59–62.

[80] UK statements reprinted in (1997) 68 *British Year Book of International Law* 599; and in (2000) 71 *British Year Book of International Law* 601.

[81] JI Charney and LM Alexander (eds), *International Maritime Boundaries* (Martinus Nijhoff Leiden/Boston 1998) Vol III, 2528.

4 Marine Environmental Regional and Sub-Regional Cooperation

4.1 OSPAR Convention

The region sets a global example in the establishment of collaborative maritime governance structures to protect and preserve the marine environment.[82] The approach has evolved steadily from instruments that were aimed initially at addressing land-based pollution and dumping at sea but have since developed into a broad suite of treaties and EU legislation in conformity with the LOSC.[83] Chief among these is the OSPAR Convention, which provides a comprehensive and unified framework for regional action to prevent and eliminate pollution of the sea, safeguard human health, as well to conserve and restore marine ecosystems.[84] The OSPAR Commission is tasked with supervisory, review, and oversight functions including making recommendations on the best course of action on how to address transboundary pollution.[85] Although largely consensus-based, there is nonetheless provision for decision-making by a three-quarters majority vote of the Commission.[86] The scheme of protection afforded by the Convention entails the application of new normative principles and approaches pertaining to precaution, pollution control and the ecosystem approach.[87] Much of the technical detail of the regulatory scheme is set out in five annexes and three appendices to the Convention addressing specific topics, namely: pollution from land-based and offshore sources, dumping and incineration, environmental assessment, as well as the protection and conservation of the ecosystems and biological diversity.[88] In line with this framework, OSPAR Contracting Parties have adopted a broad range of programmes and measures in the form of six thematic strategies addressing: biodiversity and ecosystems, eutrophication, hazardous substances, offshore industry, radioactive substances, and the joint assessment and monitoring of the marine environment. As a matter of regular practice, OSPAR works closely with regional fisheries management organizations, the EU and the International Maritime Organization (IMO).[89]

---

[82] V Frank, *The European Community and Marine Environmental Protection in the International Law of the Sea. Implementing Global Obligations at the Regional Level* (Brill/Nijhoff Leiden/Boston 2006) passim.

[83] LOSC, n 46, Art 197.   [84] OSPAR Convention, n 7, Art 2.   [85] Ibid, Art 10.

[86] Ibid, Art 13 (1).

[87] Ibid, Art 2(2). Strategy of the OSPAR Commission for the Protection of the Marine Environment of the North-East Atlantic 2010–2020, adopted Bergen, September 2010.

[88] OSPAR Convention, n 7, Annexes 1–5.   [89] Ibid, Art 4(1), (2), and Annex V.

The efficacy of the OSPAR regime is dependent upon contracting parties implementing regional obligations by means of national and EU law including the harmonization of national environmental policies and strategies.[90] Certainly, OSPAR contracting parties are industrious with close to 150 decisions and recommendations adopted over the past two decades, and these measures have contributed in no small way to the reduction of pollution from land-based and offshore sources, the abatement of dumping and incineration at sea, reduction of discharges from nuclear power plants to close to zero, and setting down higher regulatory standards applicable to the offshore hydrocarbon industry.[91] The principal environmental challenges faced by OSPAR are biodiversity loss, ocean acidification, marine litter and addressing the impacts of climate change.[92]

4.2 Role of the EU in fostering regional cooperation

The EU plays a vital role in fostering regional cooperation through two mechanisms: first, by adopting legislation within its fields of competence that is legally binding on all EU Member States;[93] and second, by entering into agreements with third countries, as well as with regional and multilateral bodies that have a mandate in maritime affairs.[94] To this end, it needs to be emphasized that the LOSC is an integral part of the European legal order and the EU treaties contain extensive provisions on subject matters that are directly relevant to the regional implementation of the law of the sea including provisions on fisheries, maritime transport, industrial competitiveness, the coordination of economic policies of the member States, research and technological development, climate change, as well as on environmental protection and the prudent use of natural resources.[95] The importance of EU law became clearly evident in the *Mox Plant* case when the European Court of Justice censured Ireland for initiating dispute-settlement procedures under the LOSC on matters that fell within shared European competence, the protection of the marine environment, and which were regulated by the European Community to a large extent.[96]

---

[90] Ibid, Art 2(1).
[91] OSPAR Commission, *Decisions, Recommendations and Other Agreements* (2013), available at <http://www.ospar.org/html_documents/ospar/html/list_of_decs_and_recs_2013.doc>.
[92] OSPAR Commission, n 7, n 15.
[93] On EU competences, see L Lijnzaad, 'Declarations of Competence in the Law of the Sea, A Very European Affair' in M Lodge and MH Nordquist (eds), *Peaceful Order In The World's Oceans: Essays in Honor of Satya N. Nandan* (Nijhoff Leiden/Boston 2014) 186.
[94] 1992 Treaty on European Union, Art 21 (hereinafter TEU).
[95] *Commission v Ireland* (C-459/03) [2006] ECR I-4635, [82] citing, inter alia, IATA and ELFAA (C-344/04) [2006] ECR I-403, [36]; 2008 Treaty on the Functioning of the European Union, Arts 43(2), 91(1), 100(2),173(3), 175, 188, 192(1), 194(2), and 195(2) (hereinafter TFEU).
[96] *Commission v Ireland* (C-459/03) [2006] ECR I-4635.

An excellent and illustrative example of the regional approach can be seen in the EU's MSFD, which requires EU Member States to apply an ecosystems-based approach to the management of human activities with a view to achieving good environmental status of all marine waters in the North East Atlantic by 2020.[97] This instrument requires each member State to undertake a detailed assessment of the status of the environment, agree on a definition marine of good environmental status on the basis of 11 descriptors,[98] establish environmental targets and scientific monitoring programmes, and implement appropriate management measures.[99] Most importantly, the MSFD compels EU member States to coordinate their conservation and management measures and to work with third countries through the regional seas agreements, and with land-locked countries through the cooperative structures and procedures established under the EU's Water Framework Directive.[100]

4.3 Regional network of marine protected areas

Coastal States have established a regional network of protected areas, both within and beyond national jurisdiction, through regional, EU, and national designations. As a result, 324 marine protected areas (MPAs) are established under the OSPAR Convention in sea areas that are under the sovereignty and jurisdiction of North East Atlantic coastal States, with nine others designated in Areas Beyond National Jurisdiction (ABNJ).[101] The vast majority of MPAs have been established within territorial waters and the spatial extent of this coverage amounts to approximately 5 per cent of the entire OSPAR Maritime Area.[102]

Four brief comments can be made about the regional approach to MPAs. First, designations pursuant to the OSPAR Convention are made on the basis of scientific merit and in order to achieve conservation objectives including mitigating the potential threat of damage from human activities.[103] Second, the establishment of MPAs conforms to multilateral initiatives taken in conformity with the

---

[97] Marine Strategy Directive, n 9. R Long, 'The EU Marine Strategy Framework Directive: A New European Approach to the Regulation of the Marine Environment, Marine Natural Resources and Marine Ecological Services' (2011) 29 *Journal of Energy and Natural Resources Law* 1.

[98] Commission Decision 2010/477/EU *On criteria and methodological standards on good environmental status of marine waters*, OJ L 232/14 (2 September 2010).

[99] Marine Strategy Directive, n 9, Arts 8–13.

[100] Ibid; Directive 2000/60/EC *Establishing a framework for Community action in the field of water policy* (22 December 2000), Art 6.

[101] OSPAR, *2012 Status Report on the OSPAR Network of Marine Protected Areas* (OSPAR London 2013) 9.

[102] Ibid, 46.

[103] OSPAR Recommendation 2003/3 adopted by OSPAR 2003 (OSPAR 03/17/1, Annex 9), amended by OSPAR Recommendation 2010/2 (OSPAR 10/23/1, Annex 7).

Convention of Biological Diversity 1992.[104] The practical aspects of MPA management nevertheless require a strong collaborative approach at a regional level with bodies such as the North East Atlantic Fisheries Commission (NEAFC), which has adopted area-based management measures restricting fishing activity in OSPAR's MPAs in ABNJ.[105] Third, the network complements the EU's MSFD and should therefore not be viewed in isolation from the overall scheme of regional environmental protection.[106] Finally, the success of MPAs is very much contingent upon the quality and effectiveness of the management measures. In 2012, the OSPAR Commission reported that the network of MPAs lacked sufficient ecological coherence, and that, in the absence of specific information from contracting parties, it was impossible to conclude on the extent to which OSPAR MPAs are well managed.[107]

4.4 Regional measures on vessel-source pollution

The Atlantic coast of Europe has witnessed its fair share of maritime disasters including those associated with the loss of the *Torrey Cannon* (1967), the *Urquiola* (1976), the *Amoco Cadiz* (1978), the *Braer* (1993), the *Sea Impress* (1996), the *Erika* (1999), the *Prestige* (2002), and the *MSC Flaminia* (2012). All of these incidents have shaped regional agreements on marine pollution and State practice on places of refuge,[108] as well as cajoled coastal States within the region into assuming a leadership role at the IMO by pressing for the adoption of more rigorous multilateral standards to address vessel source pollution.[109] The regional approach is very much embedded in the 1983 Bonn Agreement, which provides a solid framework for coordination and cooperation between North Sea and Irish Sea States in dealing with pollution by oil and other harmful substances from ships and offshore installations. The Agreement requires contracting parties to

---

[104] Conference of Parties (COP) to the Convention on Biological Diversity, Decision VII/28, UNEP/CBD/COP/DEC/VII/28 (13 April 2004), Art 8(a)–(e).

[105] See Section 5 below.   [106] See Section 4.2 above.   [107] OSPAR, n 101.

[108] Regional treaties include, *inter alia*, the 1971 Agreement on Cooperation in Taking Measures Against Pollution of the Sea by Oil, superseded by the Agreement between Denmark, Finland, Island, Norway and Sweden concerning Cooperation in taking Measures against Pollution of the Sea by Oil or Other Harmful Substances; 1990 Agreement for Cooperation in Protecting the Shores and Coastal Waters of the North East Atlantic Ocean from Accidental Pollution by Oil and Other Harmful Substances (not in force); OSPAR Convention, n 7.

[109] Frank, n 82; H Ringbom and M Nesterowicz, 'Place of Refuge and Environmental Liability and Compensation in the EU: an Update' in H Rak and P Wetterstein (eds), *Environmental Liabilities in Ports and Coastal areas. Focus on Public Authorities and Other Actors* (Akademi Universitys Åbo 2011) 79.

exchange information on national pollution contingency plans; undertake oil spill surveillance and notification; develop common operational training and response procedures; and to support each other when dealing with emergencies including the sharing of expertise, equipment and other resources.[110] The Agreement is supplemented by an Action Plan, which is updated periodically to strengthen regional cooperation on prevention, preparedness and response.[111] These arrangements are further bolstered by novel enforcement and compliance mechanisms.[112]

Regional measures are enhanced by the application of IMO special mandatory methods in areas that have been designated as special areas in North-West European Waters to prevent pollution,[113] and in the North Sea to prevent garbage and air pollution by shipping.[114] In parallel, associative protection measures are in place to reduce the pollution risk from shipping in areas that are designated as IMO Particularly Sensitive Sea Areas in the Wadden Sea,[115] Western European Waters,[116] and the Canary Islands.[117] The North Sea is designated as a Sulphur Emission Control Area to minimize exhaust emissions from ships.[118] Moreover, although clearly applicable beyond the region, the 1982 Paris Memorandum of Understanding on Port State Control has helped considerably in establishing a comprehensive system of port-State control aimed at eliminating the operation of sub-standard ships. Although not unique to the region, the EU has also taken many law and policy initiatives applicable to the safety of navigation and to reducing the environmental impact of shipping.[119]

---

[110] 1983 Bonn Agreement, n 10, Arts 4–7.

[111] Bonn Agreement Action Plan (BAAP) 2010–2013; First Ministerial Meeting of the Bonn Agreement Dublin Ireland (24 November 2010).

[112] OSPAR Commission, *North Sea Manual on Maritime Oil Pollution Offences* (OSPAR London 2010).

[113] IMO Res MEPC.75(40) (25 September 1997) Annex 5; IMO Res MEPC.77(41) (1 August 1999).

[114] IMO Res MEPC.36(28) (17 October 1989); IMO Res MEPC.37(28) 25 (18 February 1991; 25 September 1997).

[115] Belgium, the Netherlands, and Germany: IMO Res MEPC.101(48) (October 2002).

[116] Belgium, France, Ireland, Portugal, Spain, and the UK: IMO Res MEPC.121(52) (October 2004).

[117] Spain: IMO Res MEPC.134(53) (March 2004).

[118] IMO Res MEPC.132(53) (22 July 2005).

[119] V Power, 'The Historical Evolution of European Union Shipping Law' (2014) 38 *Tulane Maritime Law Journal* 311.

5 Regional Cooperation in the Conservation and Utilization of Living Resources

The regulation and utilization of marine living resources is undertaken on the basis of coastal State law, bilateral, and regional agreements, and on foot of EU law and policy.

5.1 European Common Fisheries Policy

The conservation and management of marine biological resources is an exclusive EU competence and the European institutions have adopted a large corpus of secondary legislation in the form of the CFP.[120] This legislation has extensive geographical, material, and personal scope, and applies to all third-country vessels operating in Union waters, as well as to the vessels and nationals of EU member States, irrespective of where they operate.[121] By virtue of EU law, fisheries are a common pool resource within the region, and all EU fishing vessels enjoy, in theory, equal access to the waters under the sovereignty and jurisdiction of EU member States.[122] In practice, however, access is curtailed by the principle of relative stability, which stipulates that the allocation of fishing opportunities is based upon a predictable share of the stocks for each member State, as well as the protection of the entitlements of local populations dependent upon fisheries.[123] Moreover, access arrangements to the coastal waters up to 12 nm from the baselines is restricted to those vessels that have traditionally operated from ports on the adjacent coasts.[124] The practical aspects of fisheries management is undertaken by national authorities in the member States, and in some instances by producers organizations, who operate within the agreed framework set down by the EU institutions, and allocate fishing opportunities to vessels on the basis of environmental, social, and economic criteria such as historic catch levels. Regional fisheries law amounts to a highly technical legislative code addressing many matters including fishing licences and permits, management plans, technical conservation measures, fleet size limitations, economic incentives, as well as detailed quota and fishing effort restrictions.[125]

---

[120] TFEU, n 95, Art 3(1)(d).
[121] Regulation (EU) 1380/2013 *On Common Fisheries Policy*, OJ L 354/22 (28 December 2013) Art 1.
[122] Ibid, Art 5.   [123] Ibid, Art 16.   [124] Ibid, Art 5(2), Annex 1.
[125] RR Churchill and D Owen, *The EC Common Fisheries Policy* (Oxford University Press Oxford 2010) 150–1, 153.

The problems besetting the CFP extend to unsustainable fisheries, fleet overcapacity, non-compliance, short-term management practices, government and EU subsidies, environmentally destructive fishing practices, and the failure of the EU to follow scientific advice when adopting conservation measures.[126] In line with major reform of the policy in 2013, however, the EU has sought to introduce a policy with a distinctive regional focus in the North Sea, the Celtic seas, the Bay of Biscay, and the wider Atlantic, with the overall objective of achieving greater sustainability, together with enhanced economic, social, and employment benefits for the sector.[127] Significantly, the new regulation prohibits the practice of discarding fish back into the marine environment (a long-term weakness in the CFP) and provides for the use of multi-annual plans for the management of selected fisheries, as well as the application of the ecosystem and precautionary approaches to the various tasks undertaken in fisheries management.[128] Under the revised policy, there is scope for EU member States to adopt implementation measures to give effect to the policy at a regional level, as well as an advisory role in management for regional stakeholder consultative bodies.[129] National authorities in member States are obliged to apply common EU rules on enforcement and to ensure compliance with the regulatory scheme pertaining to illegal, unreported, and unregulated (IUU) fishing.[130] The EU also has longstanding bilateral fisheries agreements with Norway and Iceland, as well the Faeroes, which are updated periodically.[131]

5.2 Straddling and highly migratory fish stocks

The regional arrangements governing the management and conservation of straddling and highly migratory fish stocks conform to the scheme advanced by the Fish Stocks Agreement. More specifically, the 1980 Convention on Future Multilateral Co-Operation in North-East Atlantic provides for regional coordination and cooperation in the conservation and optimum utilization of fishery resources and

---

[126] European Commission, 'Green Paper: Reform of the Common Fisheries Policy', COM(2009)163 (22 April 2009).
[127] Regulation 1380/2013, n 121.   [128] Ibid, Arts 2, 9, 10, and 14.   [129] Ibid, Annex III.
[130] Ibid. See also Regulation 1005/2008 *Establishing a Community system to prevent, deter and eliminate illegal, unreported and unregulated fishing*, OJ L 286/1 (29 October 2008) Arts 36–39.
[131] Regulation 2214/80 *On the conclusion of the Agreement on fisheries between the European Economic Community and the Kingdom of Norway*, OJ L 226 (29 August 1980); Regulation 1737/93 *On the conclusion of the Agreement on fisheries and the marine environment between the European Economic Community and the Republic of Iceland*, OJ L 161 (2 July 1993); Regulation 2211/80 *On the conclusion of the Agreement on fisheries between the European Economic Community and the Government of Denmark and the Home Government of the Faroe Islands*, OJ L 226 (29 August 1980).

marine ecosystems in the Convention Area.[132] The latter is predominantly under coastal State jurisdiction but also has four large areas (including an area extending to the North Pole), which are high seas and constitute the Regulatory Area.[133] The Commission established under the Convention, the NEAFC, is empowered to make management recommendations for straddling fish stocks and deep-sea species (namely, Norwegian spring spawning herring, blue whiting, mackerel, haddock, redfish, and 50 different deep-water species) in waters both within and beyond the national jurisdiction of Contracting Parties.[134] This approach allows fishery resources to be managed as a single biological unit and as part of the same ecosystem.[135] The NEAFC, however, can only make recommendations concerning fisheries conducted within an area under national jurisdiction at the behest and with the approval of the relevant contracting party.[136] All of the stocks subject to NEAFC management measures are fully allocated between existing contracting parties, and fishing opportunities for new contracting parties are thus extremely limited.[137] NEAFC has adopted a Scheme of Control and Enforcement, along with an extensive scheme of measures applicable to IUU fishing.[138] The principal challenges facing NEAFC relate to the management of deep-water species and to restrict the impacts of fishing activities on fragile marine ecosystems in the Regulatory Area.

The conservation and management of tunas and tuna-like fishes found in the wider Atlantic Ocean and adjacent seas continues to be problematic under the 1966 International Convention for the Conservation of Atlantic Tunas (ICCAT Convention), which is oceanic in scope and thus has much broader geographical application than the North-East Atlantic region.[139] ICCAT recommendations are binding on all Contracting Parties unless subject to the objection procedure. Although much of ICCAT's work is undertaken on a consensual basis, considerable difficulties have been encountered over the past decade in adhering to scientific advice and in taking affirmative action, with this contributing to the overfishing of Bluefin tuna and several other regulated species under the Convention. The effectiveness and transparency of ICCAT management measures has been questioned, and the United States and Norway have sought to amend the ICCAT Convention to eliminate unnecessary delays in the entry into force of management recommendations, and

---

[132] Contracting Parties: Denmark in respect of the Faroe Islands and Greenland, the EU, Iceland, Norway, and the Russian Federation. Cooperating non-contracting parties: Canada, St Kitts and Nevis, and New Zealand.

[133] New NEAFC Convention, Art 1(a).   [134] Ibid, Arts 5 and 6.   [135] Ibid, Art 5(e).

[136] Ibid, Art 6(1).

[137] Guidelines for the expectation of future new Contracting Parties with regard to fishing opportunities in the NEAFC Regulatory Area, 22nd Annual Meeting of NEAFC (November 2003).

[138] NEAFC, *Control and Enforcement Scheme* (2013), available at <www.neafc.org/scheme>.

[139] DA Russell and DL VanderZwaag, *Recasting Transboundary Fisheries Management Arrangements in Light of Sustainability Principles* (Nijhoff Leiden 2010) 279–305.

with a view to improving the decision-making and dispute settlement procedures.[140] ICCAT observer, enforcement and compliance schemes operate within the region.[141]

5.3 Anadromous stocks

The management of anadromous stocks is undertaken primarily in the States of origin and on a trans-boundary basis on foot of regional agreement.[142] Specifically, the North Atlantic Salmon Conservation Organization (NASCO) provides for the management, restoration, and conservation of salmon within the region pursuant to the 1982 Convention for the Conservation of Salmon in the North Atlantic Ocean (NASCO Convention). The latter applies to salmon stocks which migrate beyond the fisheries jurisdiction of coastal States of the Atlantic Ocean north of 36°N latitude throughout their migratory range.[143] The North-East Atlantic Commission is one of three constituent commissions, and can propose regulatory measures for the region, including those that apply in areas beyond national jurisdiction.[144] Over the past decades, the iconic species of Atlantic salmon has suffered nothing short of catastrophic collapse in its abundance, leading to the closure of commercial sea-fisheries in Ireland, Scotland, England, Norway, as well in the Faroe Islands and Greenland. Although Iceland withdrew from NASCO in 2009, the Icelandic Salmon Management System has contributed to the preservation of salmon stocks and entails a complete prohibition on coastal fisheries. Norway has also adopted comprehensive regulatory and management measures,[145] which among other matters give effect to the NASCO Plan of Action for the Protection and Restoration of Atlantic Salmon Habitat, and help minimize the impacts of aquaculture on wild salmon stocks. Apart from the legal moratorium on commercial sea fisheries, the principal challenges faced by NASCO relate to habitat destruction, the effects of climate change, and the expansion of fish farming in coastal waters.

5.4 Catadromous species

States in whose waters catadromous species spend most of their life cycle undertake management tasks in relation to migrating fish.[146] In the EU, such species come within the scope of the CFP, and measures have been adopted to facilitate the

---

[140] ICCAT Working Group, *Report on the Future of ICCAT* (2012) available at <http://www.iccat.int/Documents/Meetings/Docs/2012_FIWG_REP_ENG.pdf>.
[141] Russell and VanderZwaag, n 139, 295–303.   [142] LOSC, n 46, Art 66.
[143] 1982 Convention for the Conservation of Salmon in the North Atlantic Ocean, Art 1(1) (hereinafter NASCO Convention).
[144] Commission members: Denmark (in respect of the Faroe Islands and Greenland), the EU, Norway, and the Russian Federation, with some voting rights for USA and Canada.
[145] Act Relating to Salmonids and Fresh-Water Fish, No 47 (May 1992).
[146] LOSC, n 46, Art 67.

recovery of the European eel species *Anguilla anguilla*, whose abundance is estimated to have depleted by 95 per cent since the 1980s, with few signs of recovery.[147] Conservation measures apply in EU waters, coastal lagoons, estuaries, rivers, and the inland waters of member States.[148] In addition, EU law prohibits trade in European eel and the species is listed for protection under Annex II of the 1973 Convention on International Trade in Endangered Species of Wild Fauna and Flora. Only two coastal States within the region, Norway and Ireland, have adopted legislation prohibiting fishing for European eel in all coastal and inland waters. Scientific experts have called for the management of the species as a single unit and greater coordination of international conservation efforts including the implementation of scientific monitoring programmes in the Saragasso Sea.[149]

5.5 Marine mammals

The regional approach to the protection of marine mammals varies considerably with a clear north/south divide between the EU and its member States on the one hand, and Norway, Iceland, and Denmark (Faroe Islands and Greenland), on the other hand, most particularly in relation to the conservation of whales and small cetaceans. The former States have strongly supported the global moratorium on commercial whaling and sought to strengthen the international regulatory framework for the conservation and management of whales. In response to developments at the International Whaling Commission (IWC), all EU member States bordering the Atlantic and the North Sea have adopted legislation that provides for the protection and conservation of marine mammals and national laws are complemented by EU trade measures.[150] In addition, the Habitats Directive protects all cetaceans by prohibiting their deliberate disturbance, capture or killing, as well as by placing an affirmative obligation on all member States to maintain or restore species populations and habitats at a favourable conservation status.[151] The directive prohibits the resumption of commercial whaling by any EU member State, or indeed the

---

[147] Regulation 1100/2007 *Establishing measures for the recovery of the stock of European eel*, OJ L 248/17 (22 September 2007). On the status of European eel, see International Council for the Exploration of the Seas (ICES), *Joint EIFAAC/ICES WGEEL Report* (2012), available at <http://www.ices.dk/sites/pub/Publication%20Reports/Expert%20Group%20Report/acom/2012/WGEEL/wgeel_2012_FAO.pdf>.

[148] Regulation 1100/2007, n 148, Art 1(1). Reference is made to ICES areas III, IV, VI, VII, VIII, and IX.

[149] T Als et al, 'All Roads Lead to Home: Panmixia of European Eel in the Sargasso Sea' (2011) 20 *Molecular Ecology* 1333.

[150] Regulation 338/1997 *On the protection of species of wild fauna and flora by regulating trade therein*, OJ L 61 (9 December 1996); Regulation 348/81 *On common rules for imports of whales or other cetacean products*, OJ L 39 (20 January 1981).

[151] Directive 92/43/EEC *On the conservation of natural habitats and of wild fauna and flora*, OJ L 206 (21 May 1992), Arts 2, 12, 16 (hereinafter Habitats Directive).

deliberate taking of any marine mammal listed for protection therein. In parallel, several EU member States, including Germany, France, the UK, and Ireland, have designated special areas of conservation (SACs) in the Atlantic and the North Sea to protect marine mammals such as dolphins, porpoises (toothed whale), and seals. The EU has not, however, implemented an absolute blanket prohibition worldwide on all aspects of commercial activity associated with the hunting of marine mammals in so far as it has specific trade rules applicable to the hunting activities of indigenous communities.[152] There are also regional agreements for the protection of small cetaceans including the 1992 Agreement on the Conservation of Small Cetaceans of the Baltic and North Seas (ASCOBANS), and the 1990 Agreement on the Conservation of Seals in the Wadden Sea.

In marked contrast to the EU member States, the hunting of marine mammals is permitted by Norway and Iceland, as well as by Denmark in relation to the Faroe Islands and Greenland. These three States are parties to the 1992 Agreement on Cooperation in Research, Conservation and Management of Marine Mammals in the North Atlantic. Although the continuation of subsistence whaling is undoubtedly controversial and opposed vociferously by many environmental groups, the OSPAR Commission has noted there was 'no evidence of major environmental problems, if these activities are properly carried out within the relevant management plans'.[153]

6 Conclusions

The North-East Atlantic region has a well-defined body of international, EU, and national law applicable to an ever-increasing array of maritime activities. The regional approach to the formulation and the implementation of the law of the sea is very much focused on overcoming many of the juridical and inter-jurisdictional difficulties encountered in the use of ocean space for economic and spatial purposes such as shipping, fishing, offshore mineral extraction, renewable energy production, and the protection of biodiversity. What is more, all of the coastal States appear committed to promoting shared objectives including regional cooperation and stability, economic integration, combating the effects of climate change, and ensuring a high level of protection of the marine environment and the resources that it supports. As a result, greater levels of inter-State cooperation and coordination

---

[152] Regulation 1007/2009 *On trade in seal products*, OJ 2009 L 286 (16 September 2009) 36; *Inuit Tapiriit Kanatami and Others* [2013] All ER (D) 246.

[153] OSPAR Commission, n 15, 89.

are evident on difficult law of the sea issues than has perhaps been achieved elsewhere.[154] Similarly, the establishment of maritime zones by coastal States is relatively well settled and not marred by the difficulties encountered in other ocean regions.[155] That said, there is little doubt that the plurality of flag, coastal, and port State interests that are at play makes it exceedingly difficult, at times, for all concerned to agree a common regional position in relation to contentious issues concerning the law of the sea, particularly when there is a close interrelationship between the various economic and resource-related interests that are at stake. On the other hand, it can be concluded that regional State practice has influenced the development of international treaty and customary law in a number of specialist fields, including navigation rights and freedoms, the delineation and delimitation of maritime boundaries, along with the creation of new regional institutional structures and procedures for the management of transboundary ocean resources and the protection of the marine environment. In this respect, the EU is a major facilitator of regional action and has in some instances adopted more rigorous rules and standards than those taken by international bodies such as the regional fisheries management organizations and the IMO.[156]

When viewed together, these trends strongly suggest that the principle of interdependence, the advancement of the rule of law, the fostering of good ocean governance and the sustainable use of natural resources, together with the forging of strong collaborative relationships with international bodies, are the principal *leitmotivs* of contemporary regional practice on the law of the sea.

---

[154] See Chapters 27, 28, 30, 31, and 32 in this volume; DR Rothwell and T Stephens, *The International Law of the Sea* (Hart Publishing Oxford/Portland 2010) 483–4.

[155] See Chapter 27 in this volume.

[156] Churchill and Owen, n 126; Power, n 120.

CHAPTER 30

THE CARIBBEAN SEA AND GULF OF MEXICO

DAVID FREESTONE AND CLIVE SCHOFIELD

1 INTRODUCTION

THE Caribbean Sea region has a longstanding association with the development of the international law of the sea. The first seabed boundary delimitation took place between the United Kingdom (on behalf of Trinidad and Tobago) and Venezuela with respect to the Gulf of Paria in 1942. Early sessions of the Third United Nations Conference on the Law of the Sea (UNCLOS III) took place within the region[1] and the United Nations Convention on the Law of the Sea (LOSC) resulting from those negotiations was finalized and opened for signature in Montego Bay, Jamaica in 1982. The region's continuing connection to the law of the sea is also provided by the presence of a key institution created through the LOSC, the International Seabed Authority (ISA), headquartered in Kingston, Jamaica.[2]

After providing a contextual backdrop, this chapter examines regional maritime claims before reviewing marine activities, environment and resources within the Caribbean. The current status of the delimitation of maritime boundaries in the

---

[1] The Second Session of the Third United Nations Conference on the Law of the Sea (UNCLOS III) took place in Caracas, Venezuela from 20 June to 29 August 1974.

[2] See International Seabed Authority (ISA) website, available at <http://www.isa.org.jm/en/home>.

Caribbean Sea, through agreements as well as judicial settlement is then addressed, and remaining problems are highlighted before concluding observations are offered.

2 Background

The Caribbean Sea, and the Gulf of Mexico to the north, are semi-enclosed seas largely surrounded by continental coasts and sub-divided by islands (see Figure 30.1).[3] Although the exact geographical scope of the Caribbean Sea is not generally agreed, the International Hydrographic Organization (IHO) draws a distinction between the Caribbean Sea and the Gulf of Mexico.[4] The Caribbean Sea is the largest of the world's regional seas, with an area of some 2,640,000 square km. The combined area of the Caribbean Sea 'proper' together with the Gulf of Mexico has been estimated at 4,391,000 square km.[5] It stretches from the mainland coast of Central America in the west to the islands of the Lesser Antilles in the east and, from the southern coast of the North American mainland to the northern coasts of South America.

The Caribbean Sea takes its name from the warlike *Caribs*, the dominant indigenous native American occupants of the main islands at the time of Christopher Columbus' first voyage in 1492. After 1492, the area was quickly settled by Europeans, first the Spanish and then the Portuguese, English, French, the Dutch, and Danes. The initial industrialization of the Caribbean islands was through sugar growing, but nowadays tourism has become the mainstay of many of these economies. Old colonial legacies persist in the fact that the region has distinct Hispanic, Anglophone, and Francophone areas and the fact that the region has a relatively large number of States, including a number of micro-States, as well as areas that are still possessions of, or parts of, European countries—known in the region as the metropolitan countries.

The region is geographically and geopolitically diverse, featuring large continental and small-island States, developed and developing States, States with long coastlines and those with restricted coastal fronts, as well as States with broad and narrow continental shelves. An overarching geopolitical reality in the region is the dominant presence of the United States to the north—something which has had

---

[3] The authors are indebted to Dr I Made Andi Arsana of the Department of Geodetic and Geomatic Engineering, Faculty of Engineering, Gadjah Mada University, Indonesia for his assistance in the preparation of the illustrations accompanying this chapter.

[4] International Hydrographic Organization, *Limits of Oceans and Seas, Special Publication No 23* (3rd edn IHO Monte Carlo 1953) 14–15.

[5] KG Nweihed, 'Middle American and Caribbean Maritime Boundaries' in JI Charney and LM Alexander (eds), *International Maritime Boundaries* (Martinus Nijhoff Dordrecht 1993) Vol I, 271, 271–84.

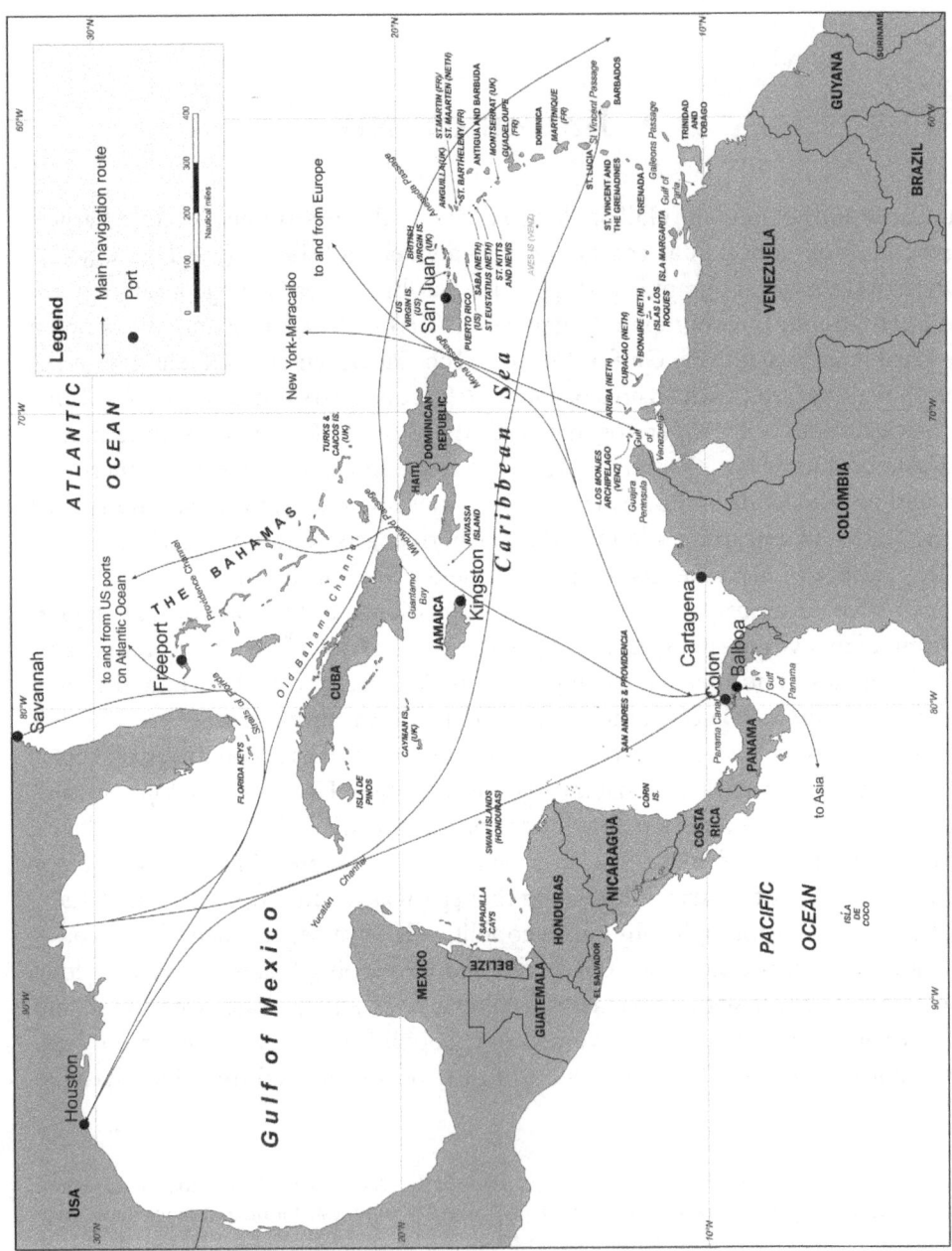

Figure 30.1 Main Navigation Routes in the Caribbean Region

implications for oceans governance and maritime security in the wider Caribbean, for instance in relation to efforts to counter drug trafficking via Caribbean routes.

As Figure 30.1 illustrates, a clear distinction can be drawn between the Caribbean Sea 'proper' and the Gulf of Mexico to the north. The latter maritime space is bordered by only three coastal States while the former boasts 24 littoral States.[6] Fringing the Caribbean Sea there are currently nine continental countries,[7] 12 independent islands States,[8] seven of which claim archipelagic status,[9] as well as 16 islands with links to the metropolitan countries of the United Kingdom, the United States, the Netherlands, and France.[10] The countries and islands of the Caribbean Sea are positioned in such a way so that there are no high seas areas within the Caribbean Sea itself and only two restricted areas or 'polygons' in the Gulf of Mexico. This has resulted in a particularly complex web of maritime boundary issues.

3 Claims to Maritime Jurisdiction in the Caribbean Region

The majority of the coastal States bordering the Caribbean Sea and Gulf of Mexico are parties to the LOSC.[11] Additionally, the extra-regional, 'metropolitan' powers with territories within the Caribbean region—France, the Netherlands, and the United Kingdom—are all parties to the Convention, although the United Kingdom has yet to comprehensively apply the terms of the LOSC to its dependent territories in the Caribbean.[12]

---

[6] See Table 30.1, at 677 below. It should be noted that Cuba and Mexico have coastlines on both the Gulf of Mexico and Caribbean Sea and so are counted twice in these figures.

[7] Mexico, Belize, Guatemala, Honduras, Nicaragua, Costa Rica, Panama, Colombia, and Venezuela. The United States is to the north in the Gulf of Mexico.

[8] Antigua and Barbuda, Barbados, Cuba, Dominica, Dominican Republic, Grenada, Haiti, Jamaica, St Kitts and Nevis, St Vincent and Grenadines, St Lucia, and Trinidad and Tobago.

[9] Antigua and Barbuda, Dominican Republic, Grenada, St Kitts and Nevis, St Vincent and Grenadines, and Trinidad and Tobago

[10] United States Virgin Islands (USVI), Puerto Rico (United States); Aruba, Bonaire, Curaçao, Saba, St Eustatius, and St Maarten (The Netherlands); Guadeloupe, Martinique, St Martin, and St Barthélemy (France); Anguilla and British Virgin Islands (BVI), Cayman Islands, Montserrat, and Turks and Caicos Islands (United Kingdom). The French Islands of Guadeloupe and Martinique are Overseas Departments, St Barthélemy and the northern part of the French/Dutch island of St-Martin/Sint Maarten are French overseas *collectivités*. The island was divided in 1648 between France and the Netherlands, and the southern part of the island, Sint Maarten, together with Aruba, Curaçao, and the Netherlands, is one of the four constituent countries that form the Kingdom of the Netherlands. Bonaire, St Eustatius, and Saba are special municipalities of the Netherlands. Puerto Rico and the USVI (formerly the Danish West Indies) are organized, unincorporated United States territories. The United Kingdom islands are United Kingdom overseas territories.

[11] See Table 30.1 at 677 below.   [12] Ibid.

There are, however, three countries in the region that are not a party to the LOSC: Colombia, Venezuela, and the United States. Opposition to the Convention on the part of Colombia and Venezuela related to issues concerning the regime of islands and potential implications for the role of islands in the delimitation of maritime boundaries,[13] while United States concerns centred on the regime for seabed mining in areas beyond national jurisdiction. This has not, however, prevented these States from acting in accordance with the terms of the LOSC and claiming the maritime zones set out therein.[14]

The location of baselines along coasts of the Caribbean Sea, from which maritime zones are measured, have proved to be problematic on occasion. Normal baselines consistent with the low-water line along the coast as specified in Article 5 of the LOSC generally apply in the Caribbean. Concerns have arisen over the potential for sea level rise in the region[15]—a phenomenon that carries with it the potential for impacts on the location of normal baselines and thus the outer limits and geographic scope of claims to maritime jurisdiction.[16] Further, as illustrated in Table 30.1, a number of Caribbean States have opted to draw straight baselines, some of which are questionable according to the LOSC criteria. This is particularly the case with regard to Cuba's straight baselines which enclose the entirety of its coastline[17] and with respect to Venezuela's straight baselines which, as a result of its territorial dispute with neighbouring Guyana concerning sovereignty over areas located to the west of the Essequibo River, are anchored on the latter State's coastline.[18]

---

[13] For example, Venezuela was anxious to ensure that small insular features retained their ability to generate extended maritime zones in order to preserve its claims related to Aves Island in the eastern Caribbean Sea and with respect to the Los Monjes archipelago, strategically positioned in the mouth of the Gulf of Venezuela, and therefore relevant to maritime delimitation with both Colombia to the west and Aruba (Netherlands) to the east (see Figure 30.3). See eg JI Charney and LM Alexander, 'The Netherlands (Antilles)–Venezuela', in JI Charney and LM Alexander (eds), *International Maritime Boundaries* (Martinus Nijhoff Dordrecht 1993) Vol I, 615.

[14] With the exception of Part XI of the 1982 United Nations Convention on the Law of the Sea (hereinafter LOSC), the USA generally regards the Convention as being reflective of customary international law and pursues its oceans policy accordingly.

[15] United States National Intelligence Council, CENTRA Technology Inc and Scitor Corporation, *Mexico, The Caribbean and Central America: The Impact of Climate Change to 2030: Geopolitical Implications* (2010), available at <http://www.offnews.info/downloads/cr201003_MexicoCaribCentralAm_climate_change.pdf>.

[16] See eg D Freestone and C Schofield, 'Options to Protect Coastlines and Secure Maritime Jurisdictional Claims in the Face of Global Sea Level Rise' in M Gerrard and G Wannier (eds), *Threatened Island Nations: Legal Implications of Rising Seas and a Changing Climate* (Cambridge University Press Cambridge 2013) 141.

[17] For analysis of Cuba's claim to straight baselines, see US Department of State, 'Straight Baselines: Cuba' (28 October 1977) No 76 *Limits in the Seas*, available at <http://www.state.gov/e/oes/ocns/opa/c16065.htm>. See also JA Roach and RW Smith, *Excessive Maritime Claims* (3rd edn Martinus Nijhoff The Hague 2012) 102–3.

[18] See US Department of State, 'Straight Baselines: Venezuela' (11 June 1970) No 21 *Limits in the Seas*, available at <http://www.state.gov/e/oes/ocns/opa/c16065.htm>. See also, Roach and Smith, n 17, 122–3.

Table 30.1 Maritime claims in the Caribbean Sea and Gulf of Mexico

Country	Party to LOSC	Archipelagic State	Straight baselines	Territorial sea	Contiguous zone	EEZ	Fishing zone	Extended continental shelf submission
Independent States								
Antigua & Barbuda	2 February 1989	✓	-	12	24	200	-	-
Bahamas	29 July 1983	✓	-	12	-	200	-	✓
Barbados	12 October 1993	-	-	12	-	200	-	✓
Belize	13 August 1983	-	✓	12[a]	-	200	-	-
Colombia	X	-	✓	12	-	200	-	-
Costa Rica	21 September 92	-	✓	12	-	200	-	✓
Cuba	15 August 84	-	-	12	24	200	-	-
Dominica	24 October 91	-	-	12	24	200	-	-
Dominican Republic	10 July 09	✓	-	12	24	200	-	-
Grenada	25 April 1991	✓	-	12	-	200	-	-
Guatemala	11 February 97	-	-	12	-	200	-	-
Guyana	16 November 93	-	-	12	24	200	-	✓
Haiti	31 July 1996	-	✓	12	24	200	-	-
Honduras	5 October 1993	-	✓	12	24	200	-	-
Jamaica	21 March 1983	✓	-	12	24	200	-	-
Mexico	18 March 1983	-	✓	12	24	200	-	✓[b]

(Continued)

Table 30.1 Continued

Country	Party to LOSC	Archipelagic State	Straight baselines	Territorial sea	Contiguous zone	EEZ	Fishing zone	Extended continental shelf submission
Nicaragua	3 May 2000	-	-	12	24	200	-	✓
Panama	1 July 1996	-	-	12	24	200	-	-
St. Kitts & Nevis	7 January 1993	-	-	12	24	200	-	-
St. Lucia	27 March 1985	-	-	12	24	200	-	-
St. Vincent & Grenadines	1 October 1993	✓	-	12	24	200	-	-
Suriname	9 July 1998	-	-	12	-	200	-	✓
Trinidad and Tobago	25 April 1986	✓	-	12	24	200	-	✓
USA[c]	X	-	-	12	24	200	-	-
Venezuela	X	-	✓	12	15	200	-	-
Territories and Possessions of Metropolitan States								
France[d]	11 April 1996							
French Guiana		-	-	12	24	200	-	✓
Guadeloupe		-	-	12	24	200	-	-
Martinique		-	-	12	24	200	-	-
St Barthélemy		-	-	12	24	200	-	-
St Martin		-	-	12	24	200	-	-

THE CARIBBEAN SEA AND GULF OF MEXICO

The Netherlands[e]	28 June 1996				
Aruba		–	12	24	200
Curaçao		–	12	24	200
St Maarten		–	12	24	200
Bonaire		–	12	24	200
St Eustatius		–	12	24	200
Saba		–	12	24	200
UK	25 July 1997				
Anguilla		–	12	–	200
British Virgin Islands		–	12	–	200
Cayman Islands		–	12	–	200
Montserrat		–	3	–	200
Turks and Caicos Islands		✓	12	–	200

[a] Belize claims a reduced, 3 nm breadth, territorial sea in the Gulf of Honduras.
[b] Submission made concerning the eastern and western polygons in the Gulf of Mexico.
[c] Including Puerto Rico and the US Virgin Islands.
[d] The French Islands of Guadeloupe and Martinique are Overseas Departments, St Barthélemy and Saint Martin are French overseas *collectivités*. Saint Martin constitutes the northern part of the island of the same name with the southern part being Sint Maarten under the sovereignty of the Kingdom of the Netherlands.
[e] Aruba, Curaçao and Sint Maarten are constituent countries of the Kingdom of the Netherlands. The islands of Bonaire, Sint Eustatius and Saba are special municipalities of the Netherlands.

Haiti has also promulgated a problematic system of straight baselines, the basis of which has been termed 'obscure' and which includes an 89-nautical-mile (nm) closing line for the Golfe de la Gonave.[19] Colombia has applied straight baselines to almost the entirety of its coastline, despite the relatively smooth configuration of that coastline and absence of all but a few islands off its coast,[20] while Honduras has also defined questionable straight baselines along its northern coastline.[21]

The Caribbean is also host to a number of archipelagic States. Antigua and Barbuda,[22] the Bahamas,[23] Grenada,[24] Jamaica,[25] St Vincent and the Grenadines,[26] and Trinidad and Tobago[27] have all defined systems of archipelagic baselines consistent with Article 47 of the LOSC but have yet to designate archipelagic sea lanes through their claimed archipelagic waters.[28] The Dominican Republic has defined archipelagic waters, but it has done so in a manner arguably contrary to Article 47[29] and has not designated archipelagic sea lanes. The relevant legislation of the Dominican Republic

---

[19] US Department of State, 'Straight Baselines: Haiti' (25 May 1973) *No 51 Limits in the Seas* 5, available at <http://www.state.gov/e/oes/ocns/opa/c16065.htm>.

[20] US Department of State, 'Straight Baselines: Colombia' (30 April 1985) *No 103 Limits in the Seas* 8, available at <http://www.state.gov/e/oes/ocns/opa/c16065.htm>. See also, Roach and Smith, n 17, 83.

[21] US Department of State, 'Straight Baselines: Honduras' (28 June 2001) *No 124 Limits in the Seas*, available at <http://www.state.gov/e/oes/ocns/opa/c16065.htm>.

[22] See US Department of State, 'Antigua and Barbuda: Archipelagic and other Maritime Claims and Boundaries' (28 March 2014) *No 133 Limits in the Seas*, available at <http://www.state.gov/e/oes/ocns/opa/c16065.htm>.

[23] See US Department of State, 'The Bahamas: Archipelagic and other Maritime Claims and Boundaries' (3 February 2014) *No 128 Limits in the Seas*, available at <http://www.state.gov/e/oes/ocns/opa/c16065.htm>.

[24] See US Department of State, 'Grenada: Archipelagic and other Maritime Claims and Boundaries' (28 March 2014) *No 135 Limits in the Seas*, available at <http://www.state.gov/e/oes/ocns/opa/c16065.htm>.

[25] See US Department of State, 'Jamaica's Maritime Claims and Boundaries' (5 February 2004) *No 125 Limits in the Seas* 4, available at <http://www.state.gov/e/oes/ocns/opa/c16065.htm>.

[26] See UN, 'Notice of deposit by St Vincent and the Grenadines of a list of geographical coordinates and points pursuant to Article 16, paragraph 2, and Article 47, paragraph 9, of the Convection', MZN 108.2014.LOS (Maritime Zone Notification) (22 September 2014), available at <http://www.un.org/Depts/los/LEGISLATIONANDTREATIES/PDFFILES/mzn_s/mzn108ef.pdf>. Coordinates and points are published in 'Notice 60' (1 April 2014) 147(18) *St Vincent and the Grenadines Government Gazette* 253–8, available at <http://www.un.org/Depts/los/LEGISLATIONANDTREATIES/PDFFILES/DEPOSIT/VCT_2014_147_Gazette.pdf>.

[27] See US Department of State, 'Trinidad and Tobago's Maritime Claims and Boundaries' (3 February 2014) *No 131 Limits in the Seas*, available at <http://www.state.gov/e/oes/ocns/opa/c16065.htm>.

[28] MB Tsamenyi, CH Schofield, and B Milligan, 'Navigation through Archipelagos: Current State Practice' in MH Nordquist, TB Koh, and JN Moore (eds), *Freedom of the Seas, Passage Rights and the 1982 Law of the Sea Convention* (Martinus Nijhoff Leiden 2009) 413, 431–6.

[29] The US Department of State analysis of the baseline claims of the Dominican Republic highlights the construction of eight baseline segments utilizing low-tide elevations lacking lighthouses or similar installations, contrary to the terms of LOSC, n 14, Art 47(4). See US Department of State, 'Dominican Republic: Archipelagic and other Maritime Claims and Boundaries' (3 February 2014) *No 130 Limits in the Seas* 3, available at <http://www.state.gov/e/oes/ocns/opa/c16065.htm>. See, however, the conclusions of S Kopela, '2007 Archipelagic Legislation of the Dominican Republic' (2009) 24 *International Journal of Marine and Coastal Law* 501, 532.

also claims certain bodies of water as internal waters as well as historic bays—claims which have led to international protests.[30] The claims to maritime jurisdiction of the littoral States of the Caribbean Sea and Gulf of Mexico that have been advanced from their baselines are predominantly compliant with the framework of maritime zones laid out under the LOSC, at least in spatial terms.[31] Indeed, the Caribbean region boasts a near-complete set of claims to 12 nm territorial sea[32] and 200 nm exclusive economic zone (EEZ) limits measured from baselines along the coast.[33] Additionally, the majority of the Caribbean coastal States (17 of 25 considered here) have claimed contiguous zones out to 24 nm from baselines.[34] Previously excessive maritime claims have been 'rolled back', including Haiti's claim to a 100 nm territorial sea, and claims on the part of Nicaragua and Panama to 200 nm territorial seas.[35]

A number of Caribbean States have made submissions to the Commission on the Limits of the Continental Shelf (CLCS), predominantly relating to seabed areas on the fringes of the Caribbean Sea, projecting beyond the 200-nm EEZ limits in the Atlantic Ocean (see Table 30.1). Additionally, Nicaragua has made a submission relating to areas within the Caribbean 'proper'. Submissions have been made by the Bahamas, Barbados, France (on behalf of the French Antilles and French Guiana), Nicaragua, Suriname and Trinidad and Tobago.[36] Further, with respect to the Gulf of Mexico, Mexico has made a submission with respect to both the western and eastern 'polygons' or gaps between pre-existing agreed continental shelf boundaries.[37] Cuba has made a submission covering part of the eastern polygon.[38] A number of these submissions overlap with one another, giving rise not only to potential extended continental shelf boundaries to delimit but also to disputes concerning extended continental shelf rights.

Within these claimed maritime spaces there exists a large and complex marine ecosystem which supports significant marine fisheries. Additionally, these semi-enclosed maritime spaces host seabed hydrocarbon resources of increasing scale and importance as well as marine activities vital to the coastal States concerned, most notably with respect to shipping.

---

[30] US Department of State, 'Dominican Republic', n 29, 5.

[31] A number of the territorial sea claims of the Caribbean States, include requirements for prior notification or permission for the entry of foreign warships (Antigua and Barbuda, Barbados, Grenada, Guyana, and St Vincent and the Grenadines)—something that has drawn international protests from maritime powers such as the United States: see Roach and Smith, n 17, 244–51.

[32] LOSC, n 14, Arts 3 and 4. Belize claims a 3 nm territorial sea in the Gulf of Honduras with a view to facilitating settlement of territorial and maritime disputes with Guatemala: Roach and Smith, n 17, 137–8.

[33] LOSC, n 14, Art 57. For details see Table 30.1 at 677 above.

[34] LOSC, n 14, Art 33. Venezuela has claimed a contiguous zone to the 15-nm limit, 3 nm seaward of its 12 nm territorial sea limit.

[35] See Roach and Smith, n 17, 141–2.

[36] Submission documents available from United Nations Division for Ocean Affairs and the Law of the Sea (DOALOS), *Submissions, through the Secretary-General of the United Nations, to the Commission on the Limits of the Continental Shelf* (2014), available at <http://www.un.org/Depts/los/clcs_new/commission_submissions.htm>.

[37] Ibid. See also Figure 30.3.   [38] Ibid.

4 Marine Activities, Environment, and Resources

4.1 Navigation

The Caribbean Sea is an important route for international navigation, especially for ships on their way to and from the Panama Canal. Caribbean sea lanes are particularly important for the United States which is the top country of origin and destination for all commodities carried by over 14,000 vessels that traverse the Panama Canal annually—60 per cent of which are engaged in US coast-to-coast trade.[39] Current work to double the capacity of the canal,[40] coupled with proposals for the construction of an additional canal through Nicaragua will serve to enhance still further the importance of navigation through Caribbean waters.[41]

The main deep-water entry points to the Caribbean basin are through the Anegada Passage—between the Virgin Islands and the Lesser Antilles, where water depths are in the order of 2,000 m—and the Windward Passage between Cuba and the island of Hispaniola (which is divided between the States of Haiti and the Dominican Republic) (see Figure 30.1).

4.1.1 *Shipping in the Caribbean and role of the IMO*

A number of Caribbean countries run 'open registries' for shipping. Three of them—Panama, the Bahamas, and Antigua and Barbuda—are listed in the top 20 merchant fleets in the world.[42] By contrast, other countries, such as Belize and St Vincent

---

[39] US Energy Information Administration, *World Oil Transit Chokepoints* (2012), available at <http://www.eia.gov/countries/analysisbriefs/World_Oil_Transit_Chokepoints/wotc.pdf>.

[40] The expansion project involves building a third set of locks and deepening the channel. It will double the capacity of the Panama Canal by 2015. See Canal de Panamá, Panama Canal Expansion Project, *Project Progress Report* (October 2012), available at <http://www.pancanal.com/eng/expansion/rpts/informes-de-avance/expansion-report-201210.pdf>; and Canal de Panamá, *Expansion Program*, available at <http://www.pancanal.com/eng/expansion/>.

[41] The Nicaragua canal which will be routed through Lake Nicaragua is to be financed by China. Nicaragua was an early favoured site for the original transoceanic canal in the nineteenth century.

[42] Panama has the world's largest merchant fleet in registered gross tonnes (201,264,453). The Bahamas is number five with 50,369,836 tonnes. Antigua and Barbuda is number 20 at 10,737,659 tonnes. Data based on IHS Fairplay, 'World Fleet Statistics 2010' data in IMO, Maritime Knowledge Centre, *International Shipping Facts and Figures—Information Resources on Trade, Safety, Security, Environment* (2012), available at <http://www.imo.org/KnowledgeCentre/ShipsAndShippingFactsAndFigures/TheRoleandImportanceofInternationalShipping/Documents/International%20Shipping%20-%20Facts%20and%20Figures.pdf>.

and the Grenadines, have had their registries associated with vessels involved in alleged illegal activities.[43]

The Caribbean is also one of the top destinations for cruise ships, with consequent concerns about negative impacts on the marine environment. Indeed, in 1991, responding to concerns about the amount of sea traffic within the region and the fragility of many of its ecosystems, the Marine Environmental Protection Committee of the International Maritime Organization (IMO) declared the Wider Caribbean and the Gulf of Mexico as a Special Area for the purposes of Annex V (regarding discharges of garbage) of the 1973 International Convention for the Prevention of Pollution, as modified by the Protocol of 1978 (MARPOL). In 1994, the Global Environment Facility (GEF) provided a USD $5.5 million grant for a Wider Caribbean Initiative on Ship-generated Waste to establish a regional strategy for the ratification of Annexes I, II, and V of MARPOL by the 22 developing countries of the region, which included development of national reception facilities and increased ratification of MARPOL.[44]

4.2 Marine environment and fisheries

Situated largely in the tropics—the Tropic of Cancer runs at 23.5°N through Mexico and the Bahamas, north of Cuba—the Caribbean region hosts about nine per cent of the world's coral reefs, mostly around the coasts of the Central American countries and the Antillean islands. The oceanography of the Caribbean Sea is highly diverse. As Fanning, et al have pointed out, the most productive areas are the shallow coastal shelves off South America that are influenced by heavy nutrient inputs from the Orinoco and Amazon Rivers.[45] To the north, the nutrient-poor north equatorial current flows into the Caribbean Sea though the Antilles islands, carrying with it seasonally mats and windrows of *Sargassum*

---

[43] Fish products from Belize were blacklisted by an EU Council decision in March 2014: Decision 2014/170/EU (24 March 2014). Vessels registered in St Vincent and the Grenadines have been involved in ITLOS proceedings after being arrested for alleged illegal activities: *M/V 'Saiga' (Saint Vincent and the Grenadines v Guinea)* (Judgment) [1997] ITLOS Rep 16; *M/V 'Saiga' (No 2)* (Judgment) [1999] ITLOS Rep 10 (concerning alleged smuggling); *M/V 'Louisa' (Saint Vincent and The Grenadines v Spain)*, Judgment of the International Tribunal for the Law of the Sea (28 May 2013) (concerning alleged illegal marine scientific research).

[44] Implemented by the World Bank using the IMO as an executing agency, the project was closed early for unsatisfactory progress: The World Bank, *Implementation Completion Report. Developing Countries Of The Wider Caribbean Region. The Wider Caribbean Initiative on Ship-Generated Waste (WCISW) Project* (1999), available at <http://iwlearn.net/iw-projects/585/project_doc/caribbean-ship-waste-project-document-58p-2-6mb.pdf>.

[45] L Fanning et al, 'The Symposium on Marine Ecosystem Based Management in the Wider Caribbean Region' in L Fanning, R Mahon, and P McConney (eds), *Towards Marine Ecosystem Based Management in the Wider Caribbean* (Amsterdam University Press Amsterdam 2011) 13.

weed with accompanying species.[46] The coastal ecosystems of the islands including sea grass beds, mangroves, and coral reefs provide oases of productivity, but the regional interrelationships between these island systems and between the larval stages of their most exploited species are not well studied. Like elsewhere in the world, land-based pollution and heavy use has degraded many of the finest Caribbean reefs.[47]

Most fishing activity is artisanal. Such fishermen, often using potentially destructive gear like homemade chicken-wire fish pots, take most of the inshore species such as spiny lobster, queen conch, and the demersal stocks, both coastal and on the shelf, slopes, and banks. There are many reports of inter-island poaching of these stocks that are generally reported as heavily overexploited. [48]

The majority of the commercial exploitation of large pelagic species, such as tunas and swordfish, is conducted by distant water fishing vessels, managed by the International Commission for the Conservation of Atlantic Tunas (ICCAT).[49] A number of Caribbean island States are parties to ICCAT,[50] but there is little participation by them in commercial pelagic exploitation. ICCAT tends to concentrate its attention on high-value tunas, and a number of other commercially important species, although technically 'tuna-like species' for the purpose of ICCAT, are not managed by it at all. There is 'urgent need' for information and regional level management of these species, which include dorado (dolphin fish), wahoo, kingfish, and smaller tunas.[51]

---

[46] For more details of the Sargasso Sea and efforts to conserve it, see Sargasso Sea Commission website, at <www.sargassoalliance.org>. See also D Freestone and KK Morrison, 'The Sargasso Sea Alliance: Seeking to Protect the Sargasso Sea.' (2012) 27 *International Journal of Marine and Coastal Law* 647; D Freestone and KK Morrison, 'The Signing of the Hamilton Declaration on Collaboration for the Conservation of the Sargasso Sea: A New Paradigm for High Seas Conservation?' (2014) 28 *International Journal of Marine and Coastal Law* 345.

[47] See Global Coral Reef Monitoring Network, JBC Jackson et al (eds), *Status and Trends of Caribbean Coral Reefs: 1970–2012* (2014), available at <http://cmsdata.iucn.org/downloads/caribbean_coral_reefs___status_report_1970_2012.pdf> which identifies the key driver for reef degradation in the Caribbean as poor fishing practices—particularly loss of parrotfish and spiny sea urchins—rather than climate change.

[48] United Nations Food and Agriculture Organization (FAO), Western Central Atlantic Fishery Commission, *Report of the Seventh Session of the Working Party on the Assessment of Marine Fishery Resources*, FAO Fisheries Report No 576 (1998), available at <http://www.fao.org/docrep/007/w9881b/w9881b00.htm>.

[49] Established by the 1966 International Convention for the Conservation of Atlantic Tunas.

[50] Caribbean members are Barbados, Belize, Guatemala, Honduras, Mexico, Nicaragua, St Vincent and the Grenadines, Trinidad and Tobago, United Kingdom (for its Overseas Territories), and Venezuela. The United States is also a member. Curaçao, Suriname, and El Salvador are 'co-operators.'

[51] FAO, Centre for Resource Management and Environment Studies, R Mahon, and PA McConney (eds), *Management of Large Pelagic Fisheries in CARICOM. FAO Fisheries Technical Paper No 464* (2004), available at <http://www.fao.org/docrep/007/y5308e/y5308e00.htm>.

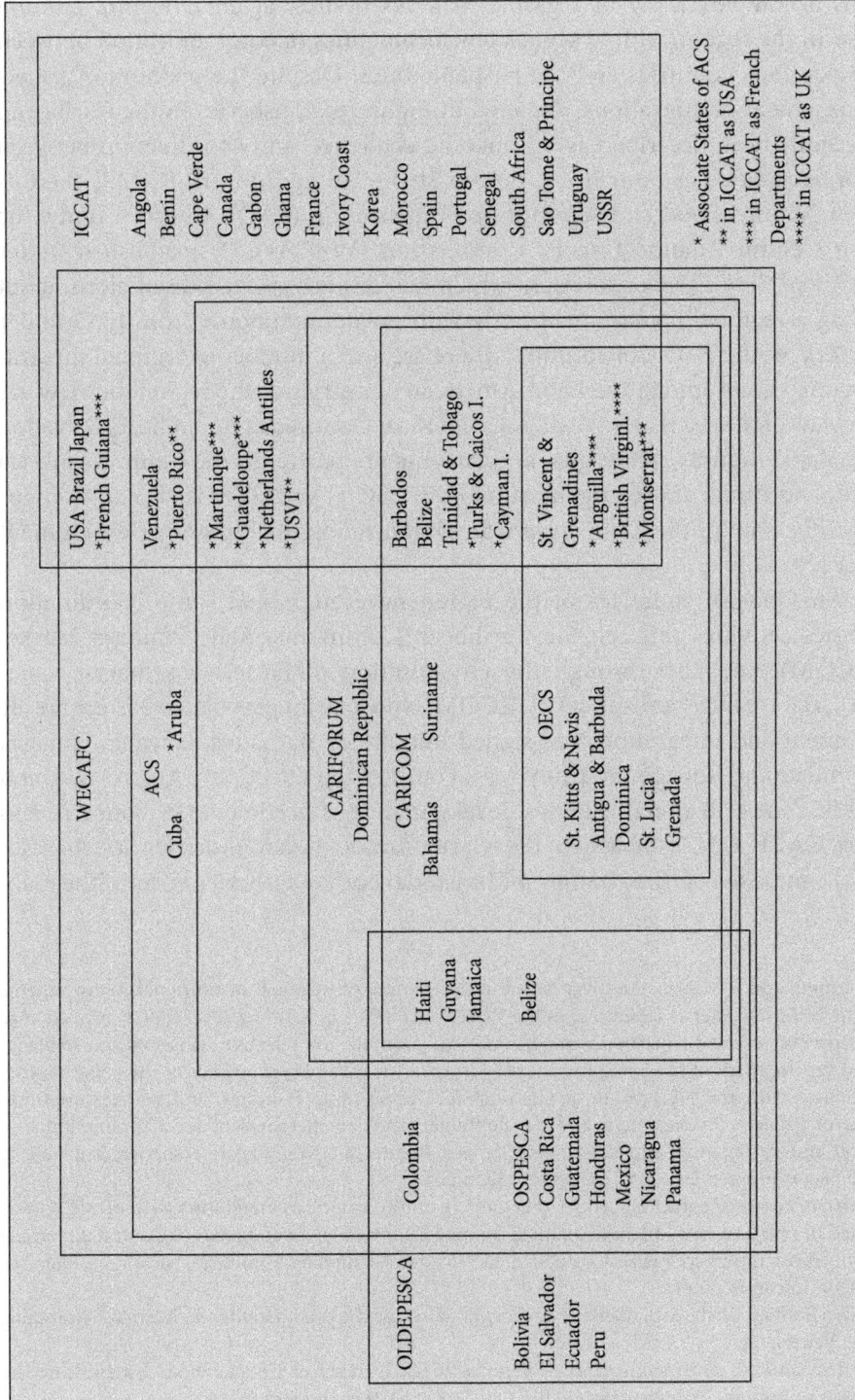

Figure 30.2 Fisheries Organisations in the Caribbean Region. Diagram is based on Chakalall, B, Mahon, R, and McConney, P 1998. 'Current issues in fisheries governance in the Caribbean Community (CARICOM)'. (1988) 22 Marine Policy 2, at 34.

4.2.1 Relevant regional organizations

There is a complex array of regional fisheries bodies, again reflecting cultural affinities in the region, with, it seems, few formal lines of communication between the Anglophone countries and the Hispanic ones. Despite the plethora of fisheries management organizations, depicted in Figure 30.2, fisheries in the Caribbean have recently been described as 'an ongoing challenge' and coordination between these organizations as poor if not non-existent.[52] In addition to ICCAT, there is a United Nations Food and Agriculture Organization (FAO) Advisory Body, the Western Central Atlantic Fishery Commission (WECAFC),[53] established under Article VI of the FAO Constitution, which has recently started discussions about becoming a regional management body with greater autonomy from FAO under Article XIV of the FAO Constitution. There are also a number of regional integration organizations among the Latin American countries of the region, but few are active in law of the sea issues.[54] Belize, Costa Rica, Dominican Republic, El Salvador, Guatemala, Honduras, Nicaragua, and Panama are parties to the Central America Fisheries and Aquaculture Organization (OSPESCA) and there is also an overlapping membership of the Latin American Organization for Fisheries Development (OLDEPESCA).[55]

The Anglophone countries of the region have attempted some coordination of fisheries activities through the Caribbean Community and Common Market (CARICOM), and also through the Organisation of Eastern Caribbean States (OECS). The treaty establishing CARICOM, whose primary objective is economic development and integration, was signed initially by Barbados, Guyana, Jamaica, and Trinidad and Tobago on 4 July 1973, coming into effect on 1 August 1973 and revised in 2001.[56] Regional fisheries development has become a key concern, and in 2003 CARICOM established the Caribbean Regional Fisheries Mechanism (CRFM) composed of three bodies: a Ministerial body, a Fisheries Forum (the main

---

[52] L Fanning and R Mahon, 'An Overview and Assessment of Regional Institutional Arrangements for Marine EBM of Fisheries Resources in the Wider Caribbean' in Fanning et al (eds), n 46, 259, 264.

[53] The general objective of the Commission is to promote the effective conservation, management and development of the living marine resources of the area of competence of the Commission, in accordance with the FAO Code of Conduct for Responsible Fisheries, and address common problems of fisheries management and development faced by members of the Commission. See 1995 Food and Agriculture Organization Code of Conduct for Responsible Fisheries, available at <ftp://ftp.fao.org/docrep/fao/005/v9878e/v9878e00.pdf>.

[54] El Sistema de la Integración Centroamericana (Central American Integration System: SICA) was established in 1991 as a new juridical-political framework for all levels and areas of Central American integration. Its members are Belize, Costa Rica, El Salvador, Guatemala, Honduras, Nicaragua, Panama, and the Dominican Republic.

[55] Belize, Bolivia, Costa Rica, Cuba, Ecuador, El Salvador, Guyana, Honduras, Mexico, Nicaragua, Peru, and Venezuela.

[56] For text and current members, see the 2001 Revised Treaty of Chaguaramas Establishing the Caribbean Community Including the CARICOM Single Market and Economy.

technical and scientific decision-making body), and a Fisheries Technical Unit and Secretariat.[57] One of its key projects has been the development of a Caribbean Common Fisheries Policy loosely modelled on the EU Common Fisheries Policy.[58] A draft agreement was finalized in 2011 in a project supported by the EU[59] and approved by the Ministerial Meeting—but has been slow to progress further.

The OECS, created on 18 June 1981, by the Treaty of Basseterre, is headquartered in Castries, St Lucia, with a fisheries unit in Kingstown, St Vincent. The members of the OECS are the Anglophone countries of the Eastern Caribbean.[60] The OECS has been active in promoting capacity-building for marine resource management and maritime boundary delimitation among its members.[61]

The most recent newcomer to the framework is the Association of Caribbean States (ACS), established on 24 July 1994.[62] It is the only regional body that unites the Anglophone, Dutch speaking, Francophone and Hispanic countries. Its 28 contracting States, countries, and territories in the Greater Caribbean seek to enhance cooperation within the region. The ACS Membership has identified five areas of concern for the attention of the Association, of which the first is '[t]he preservation and conservation of the Caribbean Sea as a very tangible shared birthright.'[63] In 2008, the ACS established the Caribbean Sea Commission to promote and oversee the sustainable use of the Caribbean Sea. While an active funded work plan has been slow to eventuate, the Commission seeks to have the Caribbean Sea declared Special Area for Sustainable Development.'[64]

4.2.2 *The Caribbean Environment Programme*

The Wider Caribbean region hosts a United Nations Environment Programme (UNEP) administered Regional Seas Action Plan and Convention. The 1981

---

[57] The objective of the CRFM is to promote the sustainable use of fisheries and aquaculture resources in and among Member States. CRFM membership includes all CARICOM countries as full members. Other countries and territories in the Caribbean may join the Mechanism as Associate Members.

[58] See also the 2002 Agreement Establishing the Caribbean Regional Fisheries Mechanism. For an assessment, see MO Houghton, 'International Environmental Instruments and the Ecosystem Approach to Fisheries in CARICOM States' in Fanning (eds), n 46, 271, 290.

[59] See IBF International Consulting, ACP Fish II, *Finalizing the Caribbean Common Fisheries Policy, Final Technical Report* (2011), available at <http://www.crfm.int/index.php/projects/crfm-projects.html>.

[60] Members are Antigua/Barbuda, Dominica, Grenada, Montserrat, St Kitts and Nevis, St Lucia, and St Vincent and the Grenadines. Anguilla and the British Virgin Islands are Associate Members.

[61] See Organisation of Eastern Caribbean States (OECS) website, at <www.oecs.org>.

[62] The ACS has 25 members and four associate members. See further Association of Caribbean States (ACS) website, at <http://www.acs-aec.org/>.

[63] The others are Sustainable Tourism, Trade and Economic External Relations, Natural Disasters, and Transport.

[64] For documents of the 12th meeting of the Commission in 2013, see Association of Caribbean States, *12th CSC Meeting Documents* (2013), available at <http://www.acs-aec.org/index.php?q=events/2013/12th-meeting-of-the-caribbean-sea-commission>.

Caribbean Action Plan was adopted by representatives from 22 States of the region at an Intergovernmental Meeting in Montego Bay, Jamaica in April 1981.[65] As well as allocating priorities for the programme, the Action Plan envisaged a Regional Coordinating Unit (CAR/RCU)—subsequently established in Kingston, Jamaica in 1986—and that the plan would be supported by a 'flexible and general Regional Agreement'.[66]

Two years later, the Convention for the Protection and Development of the Marine Environment in the Wider Caribbean Region (Cartagena Convention) was concluded on 23 March 1983, together with a Protocol Concerning Co-operation in Combating Oil Spills.[67] Like many of the UNEP Regional Seas agreements from the early 1980s, both instruments are showing their age. Virtually every marine environment protection agreement finalized after the 1992 United Nations Conference on Environment and Development (UNCED), includes reference to the precautionary principle, the polluter pays principle, and the ecosystem approach, and makes at least some reference to public participation, all missing from the 1983 Cartagena Convention.[68] As long ago as 1997, it was pointed out that the Oil Spill Protocol is 'largely devoid of technical and operation details, and restrictive in areas such as the range of pollutants covered, and therefore requires supplementation'.[69] This remains the case.

Two subsequent protocols address specially protected areas and wildlife (SPAW)[70] and marine pollution from land-based sources and activities.[71] The 1990 Kingston SPAW Protocol, which came into force in 2000, was seen as ahead of its time when it was adopted. Although it does not expressly endorse the precautionary approach, it does espouse a precautionary approach in that it requires in Article 3(3) that:

Each Party, to the extent possible, consistent with each Party's legal system, shall manage species of fauna and flora with the objective of preventing species from becoming endangered or threatened.

---

[65] United Nations Environment Programme (UNEP), *Action Plan for the Caribbean Environment Programme*. UNEP Regional Seas Reports and Studies No 26 (1983), available at <http://iwlearn.net/publications/regional-seas-reports/unep-regional-seas-reports-and-studies-no-26>.

[66] Ibid, 12 [76].

[67] 1983 Protocol Concerning Co-operation in Combating Oil Spills in the Wider Caribbean Region.

[68] Although note that Convention for the Protection and Development of the Marine Environment of the Wider Caribbean Region, Art 12 does make provisions for Environmental Impact Assessments (EIAs).

[69] W Anderson, *The Law of Caribbean Marine Pollution* (Kluwer Law International London 1997) 255.

[70] 1990 Protocol Concerning Specially Protected Areas and Wildlife in the Wider Caribbean Region (1990 Kingston SPAW Protocol). See further D Freestone, 'Specially Protected Areas and Wildlife in the Caribbean: the 1990 Kingston Protocol to the Cartagena Convention' (1990) 5 *International Journal of Estuarine and Coastal Law* 396; D Freestone, 'Protection of Wildlife and Ecosystems in the Wider Caribbean—The New Protocol on Protected Areas and Wildlife' (1991) 22 *Marine Pollution Bulletin* 579.

[71] 1999 Protocol Concerning Pollution from Land-Based Sources and Activities.

The Protocol established Annexes listing protected flora (Annex I) and fauna (Annex II), but it also lists in Annex III species of either flora or fauna from which harvesting is permitted but only on a 'rational and sustainable basis'.[72] Listing species such as turtle grass, mangrove forests, and coral reefs in this Annex was felt to be 'an appropriate measure to ensure protection and recovery'.[73] Protection was to be focused on the system rather than individual species. This is effectively the ecosystem approach.

The Protocol concerning Pollution from Land-Based Sources and Activities (LBS Protocol) was adopted in 1999, coming into force 11 years later, in 2010. The provisions on land-based sources of the Cartagena Convention itself are weak, Anderson suggests, even by the standards of an umbrella agreement.[74] By contrast, the Protocol—negotiations for which started in 1992—contains regional effluent limitations for domestic wastewater (sewage) and requires specific plans to address agricultural non-point sources. Specific schedules for implementation have also been included. The slow process of ratification is perhaps understandably, given the cost of some of the required measures. In 2010 it reached the nine ratifications necessary to come into force (as required by Article 28(2) of the Cartagena Convention). The Protocol currently has ten parties.[75]

4.2.3 *Caribbean Large Marine Ecosystem Project*

In 2009, after nearly a decade of preparation, the GEF Council approved a grant for the Caribbean Large Marine Ecosystem Project. This is one of a series of such projects financed by the International Waters Programme of the GEF.[76] The objective of this project is the sustainable management of the shared living resources of the Caribbean large marine ecosystem and adjacent areas.[77] The shared methodological approach of these LME projects is to first develop a Transboundary Diagnostic Analysis (TDA), identifying key problems issues. Then the project develops a Strategic Action Plan (SAP) for endorsement by all the countries of the region participating in the project.

The preliminary TDA for the Caribbean project identified three priority transboundary problems that affect the Caribbean Large Marine Ecosystem (CLME) and Adjacent Regions. These were: unsustainable exploitation of marine living resources;

---

[72] 1990 Kingston SPAW Protocol, n 71, Art 11(1)(c).

[73] Freestone, 'Protection of Wildlife and Ecosystems in the Wider Caribbean', n 71.

[74] 1999 Protocol Concerning Pollution from Land-Based Sources and Activities, Art 7; Anderson, n 70, 260.

[75] UNEP, The Caribbean Environment Programme, *Ratification of the LBS Protocol* (2014), available at <http://cep.unep.org/cartagena-convention/ratification-lbs.png/view>.

[76] D Freestone, 'The Role of the World Bank and the Global Environment Facility in the Implementation of the Regime of the Law of the Sea Convention' in D Freestone, R Barnes, and D Ong (eds), *The Law of the Sea: Progress and Prospects* (Oxford University Press Oxford 2006) 308.

[77] See further UNDP and Global Environment Facility, *Caribbean Large Marine Ecosystem Project*, available at <http://clmeproject.org/> (hereinafter CLME Project).

habitat degradation; and pollution. Drilling down in the unsustainable fisheries area, three distinct fisheries ecosystems were identified: reef ecosystems (including mangroves and sea-grasses), pelagic ecosystems, and continental shelf ecosystems. Causal Chain Analyses (CCAs) were then conducted for each, designed to visualize the linkage between problems and their direct, intermediate and root causes.[78]

The final TDAs prepared under the full-sized CLME Project then served as the scientific basis for the development of the Strategic Action Plan—which sets out a series of actions ('an agreed program of interventions' in GEF jargon) including policy, legal and institutional reforms, conservation measures, and pollution control.[79] On 6 March 2013, the 22 countries participating in the CLME approved the Strategic Action Plan, which it is planned will be implemented with another GEF grant.[80] The CLME Project has accomplished much in developing a regional governance framework which can pull together all the disparate organizations and processes in the region although substantial additional awareness raising and capacity-building is still necessary.[81]

4.3 Seabed resources

The Caribbean Sea and Gulf of Mexico is one of the world's leading oil and gas producing regions with the main producers, being the USA and Mexico in the Gulf of Mexico, as well as Colombia, Trinidad and Tobago, and, particularly, Venezuela in the southern part of the region.[82]

In the Gulf of Mexico, oil and gas development in shallow waters is well-established, but more recently there have been significant advances in offshore exploration technologies[83] which, in combination with high oil prices, has allowed for drilling for hydrocarbon resources in deeper waters (up to and beyond 3,000 m depth) further offshore.[84]

---

[78] These are available on the CLME Project website, at <http://clmeproject.org/documentscenter.html>.
[79] The objectives of the Project and the approaches it adopts to a range of issue are well set out in Fanning et al (eds), n 46.
[80] See CLME Project, n 78.
[81] R Mahan, L Fanning, and P McConney, 'Assessing and Facilitating Emerging Regional Ocean Governance Arrangements in the Wider Caribbean Region' (2014) 28 *Ocean Yearbook* 631.
[82] See eg BP, *BP Statistical Review of World Energy 2013* (2013), available at <www.bp.com/statisticalreview>, 6–10, 20–25.
[83] See PL Kelly, 'Deepwater Oil Resources: The Expanding Frontier' in MH Nordquist, JH Moore, and TH Heidar (eds), *Legal and Scientific Aspects of Continental Shelf Limits* (Martinus Nijhoff Publishers Leiden 2004) 414.
[84] See eg GRID Arendal, 'Worldwide Progression Of Water Depth Capabilities For Offshore Drilling And Production' (2014), available at <http://www.grida.no/graphicslib/detail/worldwide-progression-of-water-depth-capabilities-for-offshore-drilling-and-production_a460>.

The *Deepwater Horizon* accident led to the venting of over four million barrels of oil into the Gulf of Mexico in 2010[85] and resulted in moratoriums on offshore drilling in deep waters and deep and ultra-deep water drilling for seabed energy resources,[86] in the Gulf of Mexico and elsewhere in the Caribbean region. However drilling is likely to increase markedly in the future with significant projected increases in capital investments in deep water oil and gas exploration efforts.[87] The Caribbean Environment Programme has voiced concerns about the potential impacts on the marine environment of these seabed energy resource exploitation activities and the shipments of oil and gas associated with them.[88]

4.4 Illegal maritime activities and enforcement concerns

The Caribbean Sea and Gulf of Mexico together form what was known as 'the Spanish main', an area synonymous with the 'golden age of piracy' in the latter part of the seventeenth and early part of the eighteenth centuries. While pirates have long been the figure of romance in the popular imagination, piracy was largely eradicated thanks to the actions of navies, especially the Royal Navy. This experience did, however, help to establish piracy as one of the select number of crimes subject to universal jurisdiction which is punishable by any State regardless of the nationality of the victim or perpetrators.[89]

While piracy is no longer a major threat in Caribbean waters, the region does feature other types of illegal activities at sea. Of note in this context is illegal, unreported, and unregulated (IUU) fishing activities. While the precise scale of IUU fishing in the Caribbean is unknown, the Caribbean States, through the CRFM, have treated this threat seriously and have taken action by adopting the 2010

---

[85] See National Commission on the BP Deepwater Horizon Oil Spill and Offshore Drilling, *Deep Water: The Gulf Oil Disaster and the Future of Offshore Drilling: Report to the President* (2011), available at <http://www.gpo.gov/fdsys/pkg/GPO-OILCOMMISSION/pdf/GPO-OILCOMMISSION.pdf>.

[86] There is no consensus on definitions of the terms 'deep water' and 'ultra-deep water'. However, 1,000 ft (305 m) and 5,000 ft (1,524 m) are used for deep water and ultra-deep water respectively by the United States government. See eg R McLaughlin, 'Hydrocarbon Development in the Ultra-Deepwater Boundary Region of the Gulf of Mexico: Time to Re-examine a Comprehensive US–Mexico Cooperation Agreement' (2008) 39 *Ocean Development and International Law* 1, 1.

[87] Projected to increase 'by 130%, compared to the preceding five-year period, totaling $260 billion': see Douglas Westwood Ltd, Douglas Westwood: Energy Business Advisors, *World Deepwater Market Forecast 2014–2018*, available at <http://www.douglas-westwood.com/shop/shop-infopage.php?longref=1266>. It should be noted that these projections pre-date the decline in oil prices experienced from mid-2014, something which suggests that investments in deep water exploration are likely to be moderated. The longer-term trend is, nonetheless, towards significant increases in deep water exploration efforts.

[88] Especially via the Yucatán Channel, the Bahamas Channel, and the Florida Straits. See UNEP, The Caribbean Environment Programme (CEP), 'Oils (hydrocarbons)' (2014), available at <http://www.cep.unep.org/publications-and-resources/marine-and-coastal-issues-links/oils-hydrocarbons>.

[89] DP O'Connell, *The International Law of the Sea* (ed IA Shearer) (Clarendon Press Oxford 1984) Vol II, 966. See also Chapter 37 in this volume.

Castries (St Lucia) Declaration on Illegal, Unreported and Unregulated Fishing.[90] The Declaration outlines a range of legislative, operational, market-related, information sharing, technical, and conservation measures in the pursuit of a 'comprehensive and integrated approach to prevent, deter and eliminate IUU fishing'.[91]

A further prominent type of illegal activity at sea in the Caribbean region is drug smuggling.[92] Thanks to the US 'war on drugs', from the 1970s, shipments of illicit drugs by air became more difficult, meaning that maritime routes became more important. In this context, the establishment of cooperative enforcement mechanisms through agreements concerning cooperation in suppressing illicit maritime drug trafficking, otherwise known as 'shiprider agreements', which afford the United States Coast Guard the opportunity to operate in the waters of other Caribbean States have proven to be crucial tools.[93] They have not, however, been without controversy.[94]

4.5 The delimitation of maritime boundaries in the Caribbean Sea and the Gulf of Mexico

The Caribbean witnessed the world's first continental shelf boundary delimitation, between the United Kingdom (on behalf of Trinidad and Tobago) and Venezuela in 1942 concerning the Gulf of Paria.[95] The division of the relatively shallow Gulf of Paria area was driven by the desire to access potential offshore oil and gas resources.[96]

Considerable progress has been achieved in the delimitation of maritime boundaries, whether through negotiation or by means of international judicial settlement.[97]

---

[90] 2010 Castries (St Lucia) Declaration on Illegal, Unreported and Unregulated Fishing, available at <http://www.caricom-fisheries.com/LinkClick.aspx?fileticket=eeRVRXUBWGA%3d&tabid=37>.

[91] Ibid.

[92] Predominantly cocaine, heroin, and ganja (marijuana). See generally United Nations Office on Drugs and Crime (UNODC), *Drug Trafficking*, 'Mexico, Central America and the Caribbean' (2014), available at <https://www.unodc.org/unodc/en/drug-trafficking/mexico-central-america-and-the-caribbean.html>.

[93] TA Bethel, 'Caribbean Narcotics Trafficking: What is to be Done?' (Fall/Winter 2002–2003) *The DISAM Journal* 80.

[94] The negotiation of such arrangements has encountered difficulties with respect to sensitivities over national sovereignty on the part of small Caribbean States, in particular in the context of inevitably asymmetrical relations with the United States. See eg I Allen, 'The Shiprider Agreement: No Smooth Sailing', *Jamaica Gleaner* (8 February 2004), available at <http://jamaica-gleaner.com/gleaner/20040208/cleisure/cleisure2.html>.

[95] See the 1942 Treaty Between His Majesty in Respect of the United Kingdom and the President of the United States of Venezuela Relating to the Submarine Areas of the Gulf of Paria, Art 1, reproduced in JI Charney and LM Alexander (eds), *International Maritime Boundaries* (Martinus Nijhoff Dordrecht 1993) 1,651–4.

[96] JI Charney and LM Alexander (eds), *International Maritime Boundaries* (Martinus Nijhoff Dordrecht 1993) 1,641.

[97] KG Nweihed, 'Middle American and Caribbean Maritime Boundaries' in RW Smith and D Colson (eds), *International Maritime Boundaries* (Martinus Nijhoff The Hague 1993) Vol I; CW

Agreed maritime boundaries and theoretical equidistance lines, where boundaries have yet to be delimited, are illustrated in Figure 30.3. Equidistance represents the predominant concept in the delimited maritime boundaries in the Caribbean.[98] However, an element of equity has also been infused in a number of the boundary agreements achieved.[99] The Caribbean also hosts two innovative cooperative arrangements—the Joint Scientific Research and Common Fishing Exploitation Zone between Colombia and the Dominican Republic[100] and a 'Joint Regime Area' (JRA) defined by Colombia and Jamaica.[101]

The delimitation picture in the Gulf of Mexico is near complete thanks to multiple agreements concluded between Cuba, Mexico, and the USA.[102] The absence of islands isolated far offshore has helped to facilitate the swift resolution of maritime boundaries in the Gulf of Mexico, but the fact that a major resource in terms of proven seabed hydrocarbon reserves, and thus revenues are at stake has also, no doubt, been a key driver, coupled with the desire of the states concerned to avoid disputes.[103]

The experience of the Caribbean States, especially through a series of international judicial cases has made a significant contribution to ocean law in this area.

4.5.1 *Barbados/Trinidad and Tobago Arbitration*

Both Barbados and Trinidad and Tobago are States composed of islands, with the latter, as noted above, being an archipelagic State. The Award in the Arbitration between Barbados and Trinidad and Tobago[104] emphasized the role of geographic factors in the delimitation of maritime boundaries.[105] It used a two-stage approach to delimitation[106] and delimited a single, equidistance-based, but adjusted, boundary line. The relevant circumstance that led to an adjustment in the provisional equidistance line essentially related to a disparity in the lengths of the relevant frontages,[107] with regard to which the

---

Dundas, 'Middle American and Caribbean Maritime Boundaries' in RW Smith and D Colson (eds), *International Maritime Boundaries* (Martinus Nijhoff The Hague 2005) Vol V, 3405–13 and 3423. See also JRV Prescott and CH Schofield, *The Maritime Political Boundaries of the World* (Martinus Nijhoff Leiden/Boston 2005) 347–63.

[98] Prescott and Schofield, n 98, 347.

[99] For instance, the 'corridor'-type arrangement allowing Dominica's claims out to 200 nm east into the Atlantic Ocean between the French islands of Guadeloupe and Martinique. See ibid, 347–8.

[100] See the 1978 Agreement on the Delimitation of the Marine and Submarine Areas and Maritime Cooperation between the Dominican Republic and the Republic of Colombia; see also Charney and Alexander, n 5, 477.

[101] Within this area, two 12-nm-radius areas around the Colombian Seranilla Bank and Bajo Nuevo Cays were excluded. See the 1993 Maritime Delimitation Treaty between Colombia and Jamaica; see also JI Charney and LM Alexander (eds), *International Maritime Boundaries* (Martinus Nijhoff Dordrecht 1998) Vol III, 2179–204.

[102] See Figure 30.3.   [103] See eg McLaughlin, n 86, 4–5.
[104] *Barbados/Trinidad and Tobago* (Award) (2006) XXVII RIAA 147.
[105] Ibid, [230]–[234].   [106] Ibid, [236]–[240].   [107] Ibid, [372].

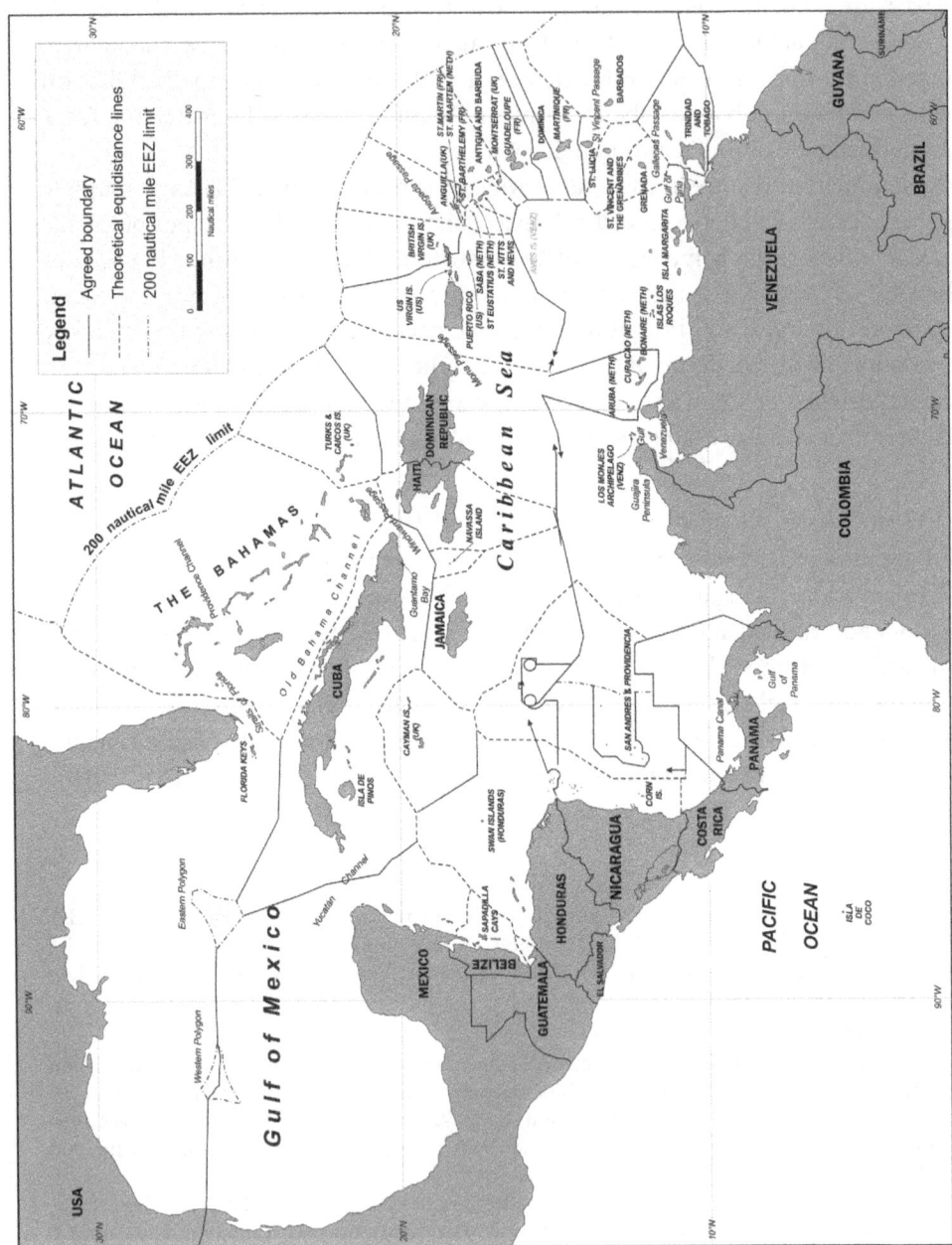

Figure 30.3 Maritime Delimitation in the Caribbean Sea and Gulf of Mexico

Tribunal noted there were 'no magic formulas' as to precisely what adjustments should be made,[108] rather than an issue related to the treatment of islands per se.[109]

4.5.2 *Guyana/Suriname arbitration*

While strictly speaking this case related to waters outside Caribbean Sea 'proper', the *Guyana/Suriname* arbitration[110] represents a noteworthy decision not only because it resulted in the delimitation of the single maritime boundary between the parties,[111] but also because it offers insights concerning the scope or limits to unilateral activities by one of the parties to a dispute in maritime areas subject to overlapping and competing claims to jurisdiction. In particular, the Tribunal found that the actions of Suriname in evicting a Guyana-licensed oil rig and drill ship belonging to Canadian company CGX Resources Inc. from disputed waters to have constituted a threat of the use of force in breach of the LOSC, the 1945 Charter of the United Nations, and general international law.[112] The Tribunal also found that both parties had not met their obligations to make every effort to enter into provisional arrangements of a practical nature and to make every effort so as not to jeopardise or hamper the reaching of a final delimitation agreement in accordance with Articles 74(3) and 83(3) of the LOSC.[113]

4.5.3 *Nicaragua v Honduras*

The ICJ's 2007 Judgment in the *Nicaragua v Honduras* case dealt with interrelated questions of sovereignty over a number of islands and cays and the delimitation of the maritime boundary between the parties.[114] The Court concluded that the islands and cays in question[115] were under the sovereignty of Honduras.[116] Concerning delimitation between mainland coasts, the case provides an exception to the rule in terms of the trend toward the use of equidistance lines in the

---

[108] Ibid, [373].

[109] See eg B Kwiatkowska, 'The 2006 Barbados/Trinidad and Tobago Award: A Landmark in Compulsory Jurisdiction and Equitable Maritime Boundary Delimitation' (2007) 22 *International Journal of Marine and Coastal Law* 7.

[110] The case was heard by an arbitral tribunal constituted in accordance with Annex VII of the LOSC. See *Arbitration between Guyana and Suriname* (2007) XXX RIAA 1.

[111] Featuring a notable departure from a median line on the basis of special circumstances relating to navigation out to the three nm limit but on the basis of equidistance with respect to the delimitation of the continental shelf and EEZ a median line with a straight line linking the two sections of boundary between 3 and 12 nm offshore. See ibid, [306]–[307], [323]–[325], [392], and [400].

[112] Ibid, [445]–[446].   [113] Ibid, [476]–[477] and [479]–[484].

[114] *Territorial and Maritime Dispute in the Caribbean Sea (Nicaragua v Honduras)* (Judgment) [2007] ICJ Rep 659, [72]–[74].

[115] Specifically Bobel Cay, Savanna Cay, Port Royal Cay, South Cay, and a number of associated smaller islets, cays, and reefs: ibid, [136].

[116] Ibid, [227].

delimitation of maritime boundaries, at least at the initial stage.[117] In this case, while the Court noted the 'certain intrinsic value' of this method of delimitation on account of its 'scientific character',[118] it reached the conclusion that 'the equidistance method does *not* automatically have priority over other methods of delimitation'.[119] The Court found it inappropriate to apply equidistance in this case in large part because of the fact that the land boundary terminated at the coast at the Rio Coco, acknowledged by the parties to be highly unstable,[120] something which made it 'impossible' for the Court to identify basepoints suitable for constructing a provisional equidistance line.[121] The Court, instead, approximated the coastal fronts of the two States and defined a bisector line between these two coastal direction lines as the basis for delimitation proceeding offshore.[122] Concerning delimitation with respect to the above-mentioned cays, as these were determined to be under Honduran sovereignty but are located to the south, that is on the Nicaraguan side, of the bisector line, they were semi-enclaved with 12 nm territorial sea arcs and equidistance lines with the nearest Nicaraguan offshore feature.[123]

4.5.4 *Nicaragua v Colombia*

The *Territorial and Maritime Dispute* case between Nicaragua and Colombia, on which the ICJ rendered its Judgment on the merits in November 2012,[124] featured an important reaffirmation of the 'three-stage approach' to maritime delimitation that was first overtly articulated in the *Black Sea* case[125] and was subsequently employed by the International Tribunal on the Law of the Sea (ITLOS) in the *Bay of Bengal* Case.[126] This approach involves first the construction of a provisional delimitation line on the basis of equidistance. In the second stage consideration is given as to whether any factors exist that should lead to an adjustment of the

---

[117] While the Court did conclude that it was faced with an exception as provided for in Article 15 of the LOSC, it nonetheless maintained that 'equidistance remains the general rule' for delimitation of the territorial sea; ibid, [281].

[118] Ibid, [272].   [119] Ibid (emphasis added).

[120] In this context it is notable that in light of 'the changing conditions of the area' the Court made no finding concerning conflicting claims to sovereignty over islands in the mouth of the River Coco. Ibid, [14].

[121] Ibid, [280].

[122] Ibid, [294]–[297]. The resulting bisector line was determined as having an azimuth of 70° 14' 41.25': ibid, [298].

[123] This being Edinburgh Cay: ibid, [305].

[124] *Territorial and Maritime Dispute (Nicaragua v Colombia)* (Judgment) [2012] ICJ Rep 624, 695–7 [191]–[193].

[125] Albeit on the basis of 'its settled jurisprudence on maritime delimitation': see *Maritime Delimitation in the Black Sea (Romania v Ukraine)* (Judgment) [2009] ICJ Rep 61, 101–3 [118] and [115]–[122].

[126] *Dispute Concerning Delimitation of the Maritime Boundary in the Bay of Bengal (Bangladesh v Myanmar)* (Judgment) [2012] ITLOS Rep 4.

provisional line in the interests of achieving an equitable result; a disproportionality test or checking procedure constitutes the third stage. This approach was used by the ICJ in the *Nicaragua v Colombia* case in spite of the geographical complexities of the case,[127] that is, where numerous Colombian islands, notably San Andrés, Providencia, and Santa Catalina and associated features, face the Nicaraguan mainland coastal front at a distance of approximately 105–125 nm (while simultaneously being of the order of 380 nm from the mainland of Colombia).[128] The Court did, at the second stage of the delimitation process, adjust the equidistance line in Nicaragua's favour.[129]

The case is also of note regarding its treatment of aspects of the regime of islands, especially with respect to its treatment of the feature, Quitasueño. The Court indicated that what an insular feature was composed of and its size was irrelevant to whether the feature in question qualified as being subject to the regime of islands.[130] The ruling was, however, less helpful regarding the longstanding conundrum of distinguishing between islands capable of generating EEZ and continental shelf rights and 'rocks' which cannot.[131]

Further judicial settlement of maritime delimitation issues among the Caribbean States is on the horizon. In February 2014, Costa Rica instituted proceedings before the ICJ concerning a dispute with Nicaragua over maritime delimitation and requested the Court to determine the course of a single maritime boundary between the two States in both the Caribbean Sea and Pacific Ocean.[132] Additionally, Nicaragua and Colombia are set to return to the Court with respect to the division of their extended continental shelf entitlements.

---

[127] *Nicaragua v Colombia*, n 125, [18]–[24] and [195]. [128] Ibid, [22].

[129] The central part of the provisional equidistance line was adjusted in a ratio of 3:1 in Nicaragua's favour, in light of the disparity in the lengths of the relevant coasts in play: ibid, [234]. To the north and south of the 'weighted line', Nicaragua was awarded maritime areas out to 200 nm by restricting certain Colombian insular features, Quitasueño, Roncador and Serrana in the north and Albuquerque Cays and East-Southeast Cays in the south, to 12 nm territorial seas: ibid, [236]–[237].

[130] Nicaragua had argued that because a particular feature, identified as 'QS32' located on a large bank called Quitasueño did not fall under the definition of an island/rock entitled to generate maritime claims on account of it being composed of coral debris and, further, that it was very small. The Court dismissed both arguments stating that QS32 is 'composed of solid material attached to the substrate', that the fact that the feature 'is composed of coral is irrelevant' and further that '[t]he fact that QS 32 is very small does not make any difference': *Nicaragua v Colombia*, n 125, [37].

[131] As neither party to the dispute had characterized QS32 as 'anything other than a rock which is incapable of human habitation or an economic life of its own, under Article 121, paragraph 3, of UNCLOS', this issue did not need to be addressed: *Nicaragua v Colombia*, n 125, [183].

[132] See *Maritime Delimitation in the Caribbean Sea and Pacific Ocean (Costa Rica v Nicaragua)*, Application Instituting Proceedings in the International Court of Justice (25 February 2014).

5 Outstanding Delimitation Issues in the Caribbean

Some overlapping maritime claims and maritime boundary disputes in the Caribbean region arise as a consequence of major territorial disputes. Notable among these are the dispute between Guyana and Venezuela relating to the latter's sovereignty claim over all of the territory west of the Essequibo River—an area of around 140,000 km² or about two-thirds of the territory of Guyana. Guatemala's longstanding, and apparently dormant but occasionally resurrected, territorial ambitions concerning the entirety of Belize arguably falls into the same category.

Many of the remaining maritime jurisdictional uncertainties in the Caribbean Sea relate to disputes concerning islands, both with respect to sovereignty and their capacity to generate extensive maritime claims and thus their potential role in the delimitation of maritime boundaries. Notable island-related disputes in the Caribbean region include the sovereignty dispute between Belize and Honduras over the Sapodilla Cayes,[133] Haiti's claims to sovereignty over USA-administered Navassa Island, and, in the eastern Caribbean, the role of Venezuela's Los Monjes archipelago in the delimitation of a maritime boundary with Colombia and the contentious issue of the role of Aves Island in the generation of claims to maritime jurisdiction and thus the delimitation of maritime boundaries in the eastern Caribbean.[134]

In addition to issues concerning islands, overlapping extended continental shelf submissions are likely to be problematic in the Caribbean, as they are elsewhere around the world. A key area of overlap towards the periphery of the region is that between Barbados, Trinidad and Tobago, Guyana, Suriname and France (on behalf of French Guiana) which it is estimated covers an area of 30,788 km². Within the Caribbean proper, the most controversial dispute of this sort is between Colombia and Nicaragua. While the *Territorial and Maritime Dispute* case between these States resolved delimitation issues within 200 nm of the coast, it did not address delimitation of extended continental shelf areas seawards of the 200-nm limit measured from the baselines of the parties.[135] Consequently, and subsequent to its

---

[133] Namely, Frank's, Nicholas, Lime, Tom Owen's, Northeast Sapodilla, Hunting, Ragged, and Seal.

[134] See D Freestone, 'Maritime Boundary Delimitation in the Eastern Caribbean' in C Grundy-Warr (ed), *International Boundaries and Boundary Conflict Resolution: Proceedings of the 1989 Conference* (International Boundaries Research Unit Durham University 1990) 195, 199–200; Prescott and Schofield, n 98, 348; see also Charney and Alexander, n 97, 603–38, and 691–704.

[135] Although Nicaragua had requested that the Court to indicate that it's continental shelf entitlement was divided from Colombia's 'by a delimitation line which has a defined course', the Court concluded that it was not in a position to do so since Nicaragua, which at that time had made only a submission of preliminary information rather than a full submission to the CLCS, 'had not established that it has

full submission being lodged with the CLCS,[136] on 17 September 2013 Nicaragua instituted proceedings against Colombia before the ICJ requesting the Court to 'definitively determine the question of the delimitation of the continental shelf between Nicaragua and Colombia in the area beyond 200 nm from the Nicaraguan coast'.[137]

6 Conclusions

The broad semi-enclosed seas of the Caribbean Sea and Gulf of Mexico are geographically and geopolitically complex, featuring long continental coasts and numerous islands. Despite progress with the delimitation of maritime boundaries, including a number of cases before international tribunals, these factors mean that the maritime jurisdictional picture remains complex and incomplete. The region hosts a rich marine ecosystem and valuable marine resources, both living and non-living, vital to the littoral States, but also under increasing pressure. For example, projected increases in maritime traffic through the region, in part as a result of on-going oil and gas developments, raise further threats to the marine environment. The impacts of climate change are also likely to add further pressures, notably through the impacts of ocean acidification and sea-level rise.[138]

These pressures will demand enhanced efforts in managing, preserving, and protecting the Caribbean region's marine environment and associated biodiversity. However, the region's cultural and linguistic diversity has clearly complicated the development of comprehensive regional ocean governance mechanisms, particularly in respect of fisheries management. Two initiatives are very promising in addressing these concerns, however. First, the evolution of the inclusive

---

a continental margin that extends far enough to overlap with Colombia's continental shelf entitlement measured from its mainland coast': *Nicaragua v Colombia*, n 125, [113]–[131], especially [127]ff.

[136] Nicaragua made its submission regarding the outer limits of its continental shelf to the CLCS on 24 June 2013: see DOALOS, *Submissions, through the Secretary-General of the United Nations, to the Commission on the Limits of the Continental Shelf* (2014), available at <http://www.un.org/Depts/los/clcs_new/commission_submissions.htm>.

[137] International Court of Justice, 'Nicaragua institutes proceedings against Colombia', Press Release No 2013/21 (17 September 2013), available at <http://www.icj-cij.org/docket/files/154/17530.pdf>.

[138] Acceptance by the Intergovernmental Panel on Climate Change (IPCC) of approximately one metre by 2100 can now be taken as a conservative estimate with 'a strong regional pattern, with some places experiencing significant deviations of local and regional sea level change from the global mean change': see JA Church et al, '2013: Sea Level Change' in IPCC, TF Stocker et al (eds), *Climate Change 2013: The Physical Science Basis. Contribution of Working Group I to the Fifth Assessment Report of the Intergovernmental Panel on Climate Change* (Cambridge University Press Cambridge 2013) ch 13, 1140.

Association of Caribbean States and secondly the new perspectives on regional governance of marine resources brought about by the innovative CLME Project.[139]

The Caribbean experience with respect to the law of the sea and ocean affairs can perhaps be best characterized as mixed. The Caribbean littoral States have been major beneficiaries of the significant extension of maritime claims codified, in particular, by the LOSC, though these have been implemented in an uneven manner, in keeping with the complex coastal and political geography of the region. The huge economic disparities between the wealthiest and the poorest countries of the region have made the development of strong regional governance institutions problematic. Similarly, a number of unfinished agendas remain between and among many of the countries of the region, including disputes over jurisdictional claims, and undelimited maritime boundaries.

---

[139] See Fanning and Mahon, n 53, 264.

31

THE INDIAN OCEAN AND THE LAW OF THE SEA: A WORK IN PROGRESS

ALEX G OUDE ELFERINK*

1 Introduction

The Indian Ocean in the past decades undoubtedly has acquired an increased geostrategic significance. The economic rise of India has led to a growing power projection into the Indian Ocean. The simultaneous rise of China as a global player with a major interest in the region and its energy resources has given the Chinese-Indian rivalry a pronounced maritime dimension. The United States also has a major presence in the Indian Ocean.[1] Due to the significance of the Indian Ocean

---

* I would like thank Rudolf Hermes, Youna Lyons, Erik Molenaar, and Don Rothwell for their comments on a draft of this chapter. Any mistakes or omissions remain the sole responsibility of the author.

[1] For recent literature discussing the strategic significance of the Indian Ocean, see eg C Bouchard and W Crumplin, 'Neglected No Longer: the Indian Ocean at the Forefront of World Geopolitics and Global Geostrategy' (2010) 6 *Journal of the Indian Ocean Region* 26; RD Kaplan, *Monsoon: the Indian Ocean and the Future of American Power* (Random House New York 2010); M Kearney, *The Indian Ocean in World History* (Routledge New York 2004); J Kraska, 'I.O. 2.0: Indian Ocean Security and the

for maritime transport, coupled with the maritime security threats posed by among others Somali piracy, other extra-regional States also have an increased presence in the Indian Ocean. Some of those States have also been heavily involved in high seas fisheries.

Notwithstanding the significance of outside actors, the coastal States of the Indian Ocean are critical to shaping the implementation of the law of the sea in the region.[2] Coastal States have the primary responsibility for defining its legal regime by establishing the geographical extent of coastal State jurisdiction and are key actors in most regional regimes which have been developed to further the implementation of the law of the sea and to pursue the effective management of the Indian Ocean and its resources.

The present chapter is intended to give an overview of the current status of the implementation of the law of the sea in the Indian Ocean. Due to the Indian Ocean's size, number of coastal States and the manifold relevant regimes, the chapter is not intended to present an exhaustive picture in this respect, but focuses on general trends and identifying interesting recent developments. The chapter starts by providing a definition and general description of the Indian Ocean. This is followed by sections on maritime zones and boundaries and on regional and sub-regional cooperation and conclusions.

2 Definition and General Description of the Indian Ocean

The Indian Ocean borders on the continents of Africa, Asia, and Australia to respectively the west, north, and east. South of the continents of Africa and Australia, the Indian Ocean borders on the Atlantic, Pacific, and Southern Oceans.[3] The boundary

---

Law of the Sea' (2011–2012) 43 *Georgetown Journal of International Law* 433; D Michel and R Sticklor (eds), *Indian Ocean Rising: Maritime Security and Policy Challenges* (Stimson Washington DC 2012).

[2] In view of the definition of the Indian Ocean employed in this chapter (see text accompanying nn 3ff) this concerns the following States: Australia, Bahrain, Bangladesh, Comoros, Djibouti, Egypt, Eritrea, France, India, Indonesia, Iran, Iraq, Israel, Jordan, Kenya, Kuwait, Madagascar, Malaysia, Maldives, Mauritius, Mozambique, Myanmar, Oman, Pakistan, Qatar, Saudi Arabia, Seychelles, Singapore, Somalia, South Africa, Sri Lanka, Sudan, Tanzania, Thailand, Timor-Leste, United Arab Emirates, United Kingdom, and Yemen.

[3] The current edition of *Limits of Oceans and Seas: Special Publication No 23* (3rd edn International Hydrographic Bureau Monaco 1953) 22, puts the limit between the Indian and Atlantic Oceans at the meridian passing through Cape Agulhas in South Africa and the limit between the Indian and Pacific Oceans at the meridian passing through South East Cape in Tasmania. The third edition of *Limits of Oceans and Seas* does not clearly define the limits between the Indian and Pacific Oceans in the

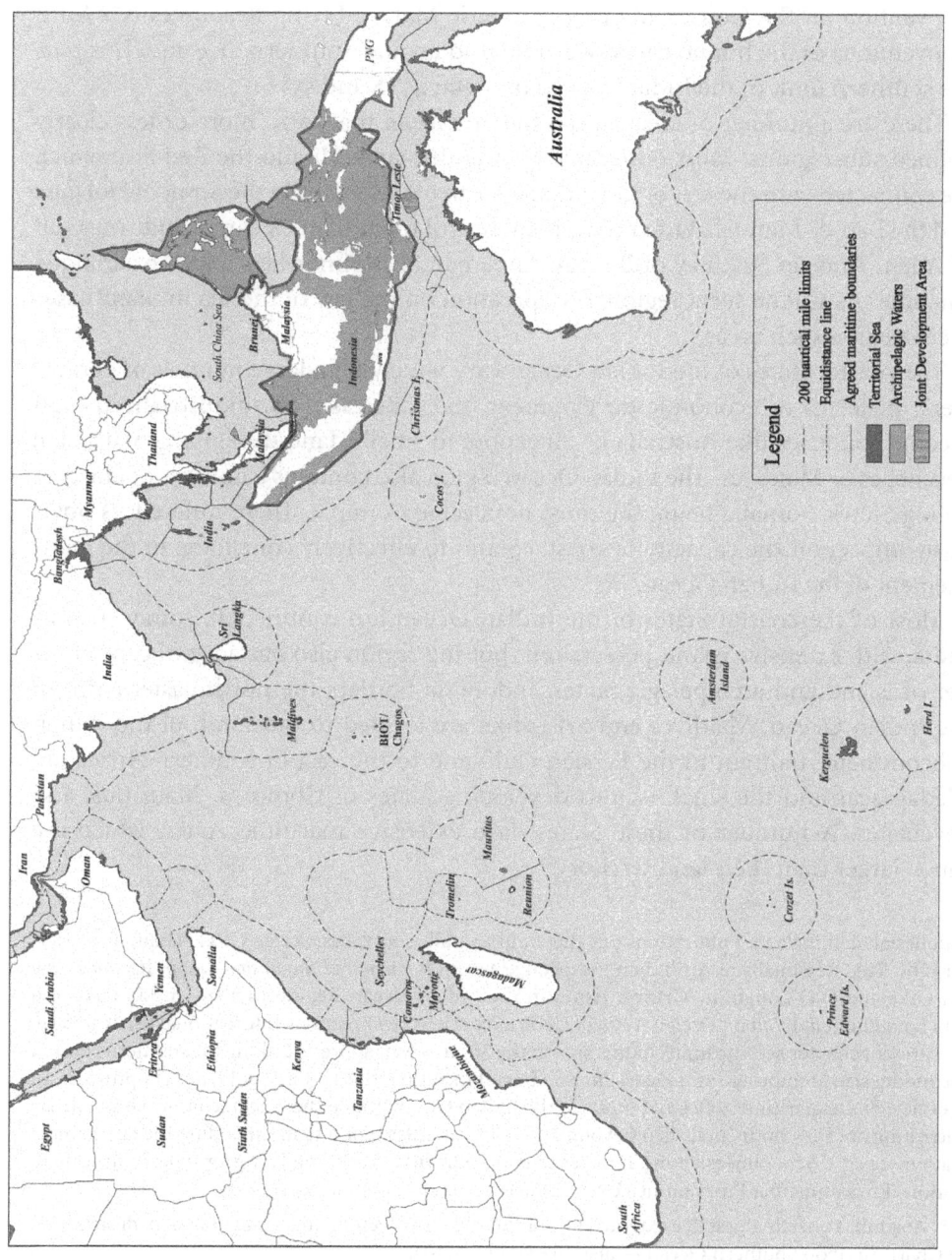

Figure 31.1 The Indian Ocean—Maritime Zones and Limits

between the Indian and Southern Oceans has been defined differently. Both the parallel of 60° S and the Antarctic convergence have been used in this connection.[4] The present chapter employs the Antarctic convergence as defined in the 1980 Convention on the Conservation of Antarctic Marine Living Resources (CAMLR Convention) as the boundary between the Indian and Southern Oceans.[5] This puts the southern limit of the Indian Ocean between 45° S and 55° S.

There are a number of areas in the Indian Ocean that form more or less clearly defined sub-regions. Most noticeable are the Persian Gulf and the Red Sea, which are connected with the rest of the Indian Ocean by respectively the Strait of Hormuz and the Bab-el-Mandeb. Other peripheral seas of the Indian Ocean include the Gulf of Aden, Arabian Sea, Bay of Bengal, Andaman Sea, Timor Sea, and Mozambique Channel. As will be seen, regional cooperation on the law of the sea in many cases is centred on such areas.

The coastal States of the Indian Ocean vary widely on a large number of parameters. In terms of economic development, the range is from industrialized high income countries like Australia or Singapore to small island developing States like Seychelles or Maldives. The Indian Ocean region also contains a number of failed or failing States, Somalia being the most noticeable example. These differences obviously impact on the capacity of coastal States to effectively contribute to the management of the Indian Ocean.

Most of the coastal States of the Indian Ocean are continental, some, such as India, with extensive island possessions, but the region also has a significant number of island and archipelagic States. Indonesia borders the north-eastern rim of the Indian Ocean, Maldives and Sri Lanka are located to the south of the Indian subcontinent, Bahrain in the Persian Gulf, and to the east of southern Africa are Madagascar and the small islands developing States of Comoros, Mauritius, and Seychelles. A number of these States have extensive maritime zones, which are much larger than their land territory.[6]

Indonesian archipelago. Publications put this limit in different places: see eg GVC Naidu, 'Prospects for IOR-ARC Regionalism: An Indian Perspective' (2012) 8 *Journal of the Indian Ocean Region* 21, 23; LG Luke and C O'Loughlin, 'Critical Issues in the Indian Ocean Region to 2020' in LG Luke and C O'Loughlin (eds), *Indian Ocean: A Sea of Uncertainty* (Future Directions International Perth 2012) 9. The present chapter sets the limits in this area in the Strait of Singapore and along the southern coast of the Indonesian archipelago and East Timor up to and including the Timor Sea. Figure 31.1 provides an overview of the maritime zones and limits in the Indian Ocean. It does not include information on the outer limits of the continental shelf beyond 200 nautical miles. For a figure incuding the latter information see eg T Schoolmeester and E Baker (eds), *Continental Shelf; The Last Maritime Zone* (United Nations Environmental Programme (UNEP)/GRID-Arendal Arendal 2011) 14–15.

[4] Australia's charting practice extends the Southern Ocean even up to the Australian continent (see eg Chart Aus4709 Southern Ocean—Australia South Coast).

[5] 1980 Convention on the Conservation of Antarctic Marine Living Resources, Art I(4) (hereinafter CAMLR Convention) defines the Antarctic convergence by parallels and meridians between the points 50°S, 0°; 50°S, 30°E; 45°S, 30°E; 45°S, 80°E; 55°S, 80°E; 55°S, 150°E; 60°S, 150°E; 60°S, 50°W; 50°S, 50°W; 50°S, 0°.

[6] See Figure 31.1.

Prior to decolonization most of the Indian Ocean littoral was controlled by colonial powers. Today, only a number of islands are part of States from beyond the region. The islands of Reunion and Mayotte are overseas departments of France and the islands of St Paul and Amsterdam and the Îles Éparses—a number of islands in the Mozambique Channel and Tromelin to the east of Madagascar—are French overseas territories. The only remaining British possession in the Indian Ocean is the British Indian Ocean Territory, also known as the Chagos Archipelago, which is the home of a major United States naval base. The title to a number of these islands is disputed. Tromelin is also claimed by Mauritius, which also has a dispute with the United Kingdom over the Chagos Archipelago. Mayotte is also claimed by Comoros, of which it formed a part before the latter's independence, and the Îles Éparses in the Mozambique Channel are also claimed by Madagascar. These disputes also extend to the maritime zones generated by these islands.[7] The most noticeable dispute in this respect at present concerns the Chagos Archipelago. Following the establishment of a marine protected area extending up to the 200-nautical-mile limit of the Chagos Archipelago by the United Kingdom in 2010 Mauritius instituted arbitral proceedings under the 1982 United Nations Convention on the Law of the Sea (LOSC), alleging that the United Kingdom was not a coastal State within the meaning of the Convention and not competent to establish this area.[8] Another territorial dispute concerns Abu Musa and Greater and Lesser Tunb. These islands, which are strategically located in the Persian Gulf at the entrance to the Strait of Hormuz are administered by Iran, but are also claimed by the United Arab Emirates. Apart from these disputes over islands, disputes over a number of land boundaries affect the starting point of maritime boundaries. In the case of India, this affects its maritime boundary with both Bangladesh and Pakistan. Other land boundary disputes with an impact on maritime boundaries concern Djibouti and Eritrea, Egypt and Soudan, and Saudi Arabia and Yemen.

A 2010 agreement between France and Mauritius concerning the island of Tromelin provides an interesting approach to managing the maritime zones of disputed territory.[9] The agreement provides for co-management in relation to the

---

[7] See eg the protest of France against the inclusion of Mayotte in the archipelagic baselines of Seychelles: Permanent Mission of France to the United Nations, Note No 378 to the UN Secretary-General (30 July 2009), available at <http://www.un.org/Depts/los/LEGISLATIONANDTREATIES/PDFFILES/DEPOSIT/communicationsredeposit/mzn63_2008_fra_en.pdf>.

[8] For some additional information, see I Papanicolopulu, 'Mauritius v United Kingdom: Submission of the Dispute on the Marine Protected Area around the Chagos Archipelago to Arbitration', EJIL Talk! (11 February 2011), available at <http://www.ejiltalk.org/mauritius-v-united-kingdom-submission-of-the-dispute-on-the-marine-protected-area-around-the-chagos-archipelago-to-arbitration/>.

[9] Accord-cadre entre le Gouvernement de la République française et le Gouvernement de la République de Maurice sur la Cogestion Économique, Scientifique et Environnementale Relative à l'Île de Tromelin et à ses Espaces Maritimes (7 June 2010), available at <http://www.senat.fr/leg/pjl11-299.html>.

island, its territorial sea and exclusive economic zone (EEZ) and specifies that it is without prejudice to the issue of sovereignty over Tromelin.[10] The French Minister of Foreign Affairs has pointed out that the agreement could serve as a model to deal with the situation of the Îles Éparses in the Mozambique Channel, without addressing the issue of sovereignty.[11] The hydrocarbon potential of this latter area may make that solution more difficult to attain in that case.

3 Maritime Zones and Boundaries

All coastal States of the Indian Ocean except for Eritrea, Iran, Israel, and the United Arab Emirates presently are parties to the LOSC. Indian Ocean coastal States generally adhere to the maximum breadth of maritime zones provided for in the Convention. Almost all of them have established a 12-nm territorial sea.[12] The only State that currently claims a larger breadth—200 nm—is Somalia. Two States—Jordan and the United Kingdom in relation to the British Indian Ocean Territory—still claim a 3-nm territorial sea. In 1972, on the eve of the Third United Nations Conference on the Law of the Sea (UNCLOS III), practice was more diverse: over 20 States claimed a territorial sea of 12 nm and 17 States and territories had a territorial sea of under 12 nm. In most cases, this concerned a breadth of 3 nm. Only Maldives claimed a territorial sea of more than 12 nm in 1972. Few Indian Ocean coastal States claimed jurisdiction over fisheries or other economic uses of the oceans beyond the territorial sea—safe for the rights of coastal States under the continental shelf regime—in 1972. A couple of States and territories had a 12 nm fishing zone beyond their territorial sea (Australia, Mozambique, and South Africa) or a fishing zone extending 100 nm beyond their territorial sea (Pakistan and Sri Lanka).[13] Maldives had established a fishing zone of varying distance extending up to 150 nm from its coast. Asian and African States at the time already supported

---

[10] Ibid, Arts 1 and 2.

[11] See the explanatory memorandum to the agreement, *Exposé des Motifs* (25 January 2012), available at <http://www.senat.fr/leg/pjl11-299.html>.

[12] All information on regional practice on the extent of maritime zones is based on US Department of State, 'National Claims to Maritime Jurisdiction' (1972) in No 36 *Limits in the Seas*, available at <http://www.state.gov/e/oes/ocns/opa/c16065.htm>; DOALOS, 'Table of Claims to Maritime Jurisdiction (as at 15 July 2011)', available at <http://www.un.org/Depts/los/LEGISLATIONANDTREATIES/PDFFILES/table_summary_of_claims.pdf>; and information on the website of the Commission on the Limits of the Continental Shelf (CLCS), available at <http://www.un.org/Depts/los/clcs_new/clcs_home.htm>, unless indicated otherwise.

[13] India reserved the right to establish such a zone.

the extension of coastal State resource jurisdiction to 200 nm.[14] Currently, only Bahrain, Iraq, Jordan, Kuwait, Saudi Arabia, and Sudan are listed in the DOALOS *Table of Claims to Maritime Jurisdiction* as not claiming resource jurisdiction on the basis of Part V of the LOSC.

In the early 1970s, the coastal States of the Indian Ocean largely relied on the 1958 Convention on the Continental Shelf (CSC) to define the extent of their continental shelf. Article 1 of the CSC defines the continental shelf by reference to the 200 m isobath and the so-called exploitability criterion. National legislation at the time in no instance referred to the concept of natural prolongation that is central to the 1969 judgment of the International Court of Justice in the *North Sea Continental Shelf* cases and the definition of the continental shelf in Article 76 of the LOSC. Coastal States of the Indian Ocean at this time held different views on the future definition of the continental shelf. A number of them were part of the group of broad margin States (Australia, India, Madagascar, and Sri Lanka), which supported extension of the continental shelf to the outer edge of the continental margin.[15] On the other hand, landlocked and geographically disadvantaged States opposed extension of coastal State jurisdiction beyond 200 nm. This group included Kenya, Kuwait, Oman, Pakistan, and Singapore.[16]

Article 76 of the LOSC requires States parties to the LOSC to submit information on the outer limits of their continental shelf beyond 200 nm to the CLCS. Nearly all Indian Ocean coastal States have complied with this obligation. Australia, Bangladesh, France, India, Indonesia, Kenya, Madagascar, Maldives, Mauritius, Mozambique, Myanmar, Pakistan, Seychelles, South Africa, and Yemen have submitted information to the CLCS, while Comoros, Oman, Somalia, and Tanzania have submitted preliminary information.[17] The only State for which no information is available on the website of the CLCS is the United Kingdom in relation to the British Indian Ocean Territory.[18] The information that is available does not allow establishing whether or not the United Kingdom intends to make a submission in the future.

This short review of the outer limits of maritime zones in the Indian Ocean indicates a nearly universal adherence to the LOSC regime. A much more chequered pattern exists in relation to the baselines from which the breadth of the

---

[14] See *Virginia Commentaries*, Vol II, 497.

[15] Other Indian Ocean coastal States, such as Bangladesh also supported this position: *Official Records of the Third UN Conference on the Law of the Sea, Official Records* (Office of Legal Affairs New York 1975) Vol 1, 102 [56] (hereinafter *UNCLOS III Official Records*).

[16] Ibid, Vol 1, 152 [49]–[50] and 156 [33]; ibid, Vol II, 151 [32], 154 [74], and 162 [19].

[17] On these two modalities for complying with the time limit for submitting information on the outer limits of the continental shelf, see further Chapter 8 in this volume.

[18] Mauritius submitted preliminary information on the outer limits of the continental shelf of the Chagos Archipelago on 6 May 2009.

territorial sea and other maritime zones is measured.[19] A number of Indian Ocean coastal States has drawn straight baselines that are not in accordance with Article 7 of the LOSC. This concerns coasts that are neither deeply indented and cut into nor have a fringe of island in front of them. This is, for instance, the case for the straight baselines established by Iran and Pakistan. Other straight baselines do not meet the requirement that they must not depart to an appreciable extent from the general direction of the coast. An example in this respect is the straight baseline of Myanmar across the Gulf of Martaban. This baseline in part deviates about 60° from the general direction of the coast.[20] Bangladesh's straight baselines are not linked to points on the low-water line, as is required by Article 7 of the LOSC.

Five coastal States of the Indian Ocean—Comoros, Indonesia, Maldives, Mauritius, and Seychelles—claim the status of archipelagic States.[21] Four Indian Ocean island States—Madagascar, Bahrain, Timor-Leste, Singapore, and Sri Lanka—do not claim such status. Although these latter States possibly could be argued to fall under the definition of an archipelagic State, apart from Bahrain none of them would be able to draw archipelagic baselines in accordance with Article 47 of the LOSC. All five proclaimed archipelagic States have established archipelagic baselines. In contrast to the practice on straight baselines under Article 7 of the LOSC, this practice is generally in conformity with the requirements set out in Article 47 of the Convention.[22]

The legislation of coastal States of the Indian Ocean that is applicable to their maritime zones also shows departures from the regime contained in the LOSC. This mostly concerns limitations on the navigational rights of third States in the territorial sea, straits used for international navigation and the EEZ.[23] Controversy concerning the extent of navigational rights also extends to a number of the straits in the Indian Ocean that are of vital importance to merchant shipping and warships. Iran, one of the States bordering the Strait of Hormuz, has argued that the regime of transit passage contained in the LOSC does not reflect customary international law. This position would first of all affect the United States which is not a party to the Convention. Oman has only recognized the right of innocent passage through its territorial sea in the Strait of Hormuz.[24] In relation to the Bab el Mandeb, linking the Indian Ocean to the Red Sea and the Suez Canal, Yemen, in signing the

---

[19] See eg Kraska, n 1; JA Roach and RW Smith, *Excessive Maritime Claims* 3rd edn (Martinus Nijhoff Publishers Leiden 2012).

[20] Roach and Smith, n 19, 116.   [21] *Table of Claims to Maritime Jurisdiction*, n 12.

[22] The *Limits in the Sea Series* issued by the Office of Ocean and Polar Affairs, Bureau of Oceans and International Environmental and Scientific Affairs in the US State Department indicates minor divergences of the archipelagic straight baselines established by Comoros, Maldives, and Seychelles assessed against the requirements of LOSC, Art 47 (see respectively (2014) 134 *Limits in the Seas* 2–3; (2005) 126 *Limits in the Sea* 3; (2014) 132 *Limits in the Sea* 4). In all these cases, it would seem possible to comply with the requirements of Art 47 by minor adjustments in the existing baselines.

[23] See eg Kraska, n 1, 450, 456–7, and 459.   [24] Ibid, 467; Roach and Smith, n 19, 293–6.

LOSC, declared that warships and military aircraft must obtain prior authorization for passage.[25]

A count of potential maritime boundaries based on the equidistance method results in 69 maritime boundaries between Indian Ocean coastal States.[26] Most of these boundaries delimit areas within 200 nm, but there also exist some 14 continental shelf boundaries beyond 200 nm.[27]

The practice of Indian Ocean coastal States in respect of maritime boundary delimitation is similar to that of States in other regions. The first continental shelf delimitation agreements between States in the Persian Gulf in the 1960s were mainly triggered by the presence of hydrocarbon resources. The genesis of the 200 nm zone led to a proliferation of maritime boundary agreements. The majority of settled maritime boundaries has been delimited through agreements and has employed the equidistance method. In a number of cases islands have been given limited weight. Methods other than equidistance have been used in some instances. A limited number of maritime boundaries have been determined through adjudication. On all these points, the Indian Ocean is similar to other regions.

Notwithstanding the extension of coastal State jurisdiction in the second half of the 20th century, large parts of the Indian Ocean remain part of the high seas and the Area. This mostly concerns the central Indian Ocean. Some peripheral seas are completely covered by 200-nm zones. In other cases, such as the Bay of Bengal, there remains an area of high seas, but most, or all, of the seabed is part of the continental shelf beyond 200 nm. There currently are a number of exploration areas for polymetallic nodules (India) and polymetallic sulphides (Republic of Korea and China Ocean Mineral Resources Research and Development Association (COMRA) (sponsored by China)) in the Area under contract or approved by the International Seabed Authority (ISA). China's interest in mining sites in the Indian Ocean, for which a licence was granted in 2011, has led to concern on the part of India.[28]

---

[25] For the Yemeni declaration, see Yemen, 'Upon ratification' (21 July 1987) in United Nations Division for Ocean Affairs and Law of the Sea (DOALOS), *Declarations and Statements*, available at <http://www.un.org/Depts/los/convention_agreements/convention_declarations.htm>; and Roach and Smith, n 19, 284–6.

[26] List on file with the author. This concerns pairs of States. Some of these pairs of States share more than one maritime boundary. Four bilateral boundaries are affected by the existence of sovereignty disputes over islands. Depending on the outcome of these disputes these maritime boundary relations might no longer exist.

[27] Based on the equidistance method and information on the website of the CLCS. The actual number of such boundaries may differ because, in some cases, the equidistance method has not been applied.

[28] See Kraska, n 1, 459 and 461–2.

4 Regional and Sub-regional Cooperation

The effective implementation of the law of the sea generally requires cooperation between coastal States and in certain cases will also need to involve other States. The present section will focus on regional and sub-regional cooperation in the Indian Ocean. Within the confines of this chapter it is not feasible to pay separate attention to bilateral cooperation between the many coastal States of the region. This section will first briefly look at a number of institutions that have been dealing with a wide range of law of the sea issues or have the potential to do so. After that, cooperation in relation to a number of specific issue areas is discussed.

4.1 Institutions with a broad mandate

The Indian Ocean Marine Affairs Co-operation (IOMAC) was set up in the wake of the negotiation of the LOSC. IOMAC was intended to provide an awareness of the (resource) potential of the Indian Ocean and furthering cooperation between the Indian Ocean coastal States, taking into account the new oceans regime of the LOSC. In addition, IOMAC aimed to develop a strategy that would allow Indian Ocean coastal States to integrate ocean-related activities in their development strategy and assist them in developing a framework for integrated ocean management.[29] Participation in IOMAC has never even come close to including all Indian Ocean coastal States. A 1990 Agreement on the Organization for Indian Ocean Marine Affairs Cooperation, which was intended to provide a formal basis for IOMAC, was signed or ratified by only nine Indian Ocean coastal States: Indonesia, Iran, Kenya, Mozambique, Mauritius, Nepal, Pakistan, Sri Lanka, and Tanzania. Due to the limited number of ratifications, the agreement has not entered into force.[30] The limited success of IOMAC has been attributed to the non-participation of Australia and India, two of the region's major powers.[31]

The Indian Ocean Rim-Association for Regional Co-operation (IOR-ARC) provides another example of the challenges of region-wide cooperation in the Indian Ocean. The initiative for the IOR-ARC was taken in the middle of the 1990s and

---

[29] Ibid, 116–17; HW Jayewardene, 'The Indian Ocean: Lessons Learned' in MJ Valencia (ed), *Maritime Regime Building* (Kluwer Law International The Hague 2001) 105, 113–14.

[30] Kraska, n 1, 117; Luke and O'Loughlin, n 3, 22.

[31] Jayewardene, n 29, 124–125; Luke and O'Loughlin, n 3, 22. The latter publication doubts that IOMAC would have fared much better with the participation of Australia and India.

it presently has 20 Member States, including important regional States such as Australia, India, Indonesia, and South Africa.[32] The IOR-ARC has a broad range of objectives, including ocean activities, but its basic focus has been on trade-related issues.[33] The IOR-ARC is far from a success story. Assessments of its achievements have used qualifications like 'at best modest', 'largely moribund', 'little of substance has been achieved', and 'lacklustre performance'.[34] A number of recent studies and articles have argued for a reinvigoration of the IOR-ARC.[35] In this connection it has been suggested that there could be a larger focus on ocean activities.[36] At the same time, these analyses indicate that the role of a region-wide organization like the IOR-ARC in the management of ocean activities is likely to remain limited. Naidu, in taking issue with the criticism that the Indian Ocean region is too vast and diverse to successfully cooperate, points out that 'one needs to keep in mind that regions are primarily subjective constructs and most often politically driven'.[37] However, as Naidu also points out, regionalism requires a sense of 'Indian-Oceanness', which 'can be realised only if strongly backed by political will, which is something sorely missing in the case of the IOR-ARC'.[38] On certain issue areas initiatives by the IOR-ARC would be competing with existing institutions, raising the question to what extent the IOR-ARC would offer added value.[39] Wagner suggests that the function of IOR-ARC could primarily concern the exchange of information between its member States and between other regional organizations.[40]

The adoption of the Perth Principles in November of 2013 signals an attempt to revitalize the IOR-ARC, which at the same time was renamed Indian Ocean Rim Association (IORA).[41] The Perth Principles reiterate that 'IORA is the apex pan-regional organisation for the Indian Ocean'. The focus of the Principles is on the productive and sustainable use of the Indian Ocean and its resources, with particular

---

[32] For information on the history and current membership of the IOR-ARC, see Indian Ocean Rim Association website, at <http://iorarc.org/>; see also Naidu, n 3, 21–36; C Wagner, 'The Indian Ocean Rim-Association for Regional Co-operation (IOR-ARC): the Futile Quest for Regionalism?' (2013) 9 *Journal of the Indian Ocean Region* 6; S Bateman and A Bergin, *Our Western Front; Australia and the Indian Ocean* (Australian Strategic Policy Institute Barton 2010); S Bateman and A Bergin, 'New Challenges for Maritime Security in the Indian Ocean—an Australian Perspective' (2013) 9 *Journal of the Indian Ocean Region* 18.

[33] See Naidu, n 3, 26.

[34] Wagner, n 32, 13; Luke and O'Loughlin, n 3, 19 and 20; Naidu, n 3, 24–5; see also Bateman and Bergin, 'New Challenges', n 32, 122.

[35] Bateman and Bergin, *Our Western Front*, n 32, 47; Naidu, n 3, 32–4.

[36] See eg Wagner, n 32, 6; Bateman and Bergin, *Our Western Front*, n 32, 47; see also text accompanying nn 42ff.

[37] Naidu, n 3, 27. [38] Ibid; see also Wagner, n 32, 7.

[39] Wagner, n 32. [40] Ibid, 14.

[41] Declaration of the Indian Ocean Rim Association on the Principles for Peaceful, Productive and Sustainable Use of the Indian Ocean and its Resources (1 November 2013), available at <http://www.dfat.gov.au/geo/indian-ocean/perth-principles-2013.html>.

attention for sustainable fisheries management.[42] The Perth ministerial meeting also stressed that IORA should look to enhance maritime security and safety.[43]

In contrast to region-wide initiatives, sub-regional organizations dealing with a range of ocean issues seem to have been more successful.[44] The limited success of the IOR-ARC has been attributed to the fact that its member States have shown a greater interest in such cooperation.[45] Naidu in this connection refers to the Gulf Cooperation Council, the South Asian Association for Regional Cooperation (SAARC), the Association of South-East Asian Nations (ASEAN), and the Southern Africa Development Community (SADC).[46] However, the focus of these organizations in general is on economic cooperation and ocean affairs are not central to their activities. The Indian Ocean Commission (IOC) provides an example of the potential of such sub-regional organizations to take on ocean issues. The IOC got started in the first half of the 1980s and currently has Comoros, France (for Reunion), Madagascar, Mauritius, and Seychelles as Member States.[47] The IOC has been concerned with such varying issues as piracy, fisheries, oil spill contingency planning, and regional coral reef monitoring.[48]

4.2 Sectoral cooperation

4.2.1 *Marine capture fisheries*

The Indian Ocean has witnessed similar increases in fisheries catches as other ocean areas. Between 1950 and 2010, catches increased from 861,000 tonnes to 11.3 million tons.[49] Comparing the trends in marine capture fisheries between 1970 and 2012, a notable difference emerges between the Indian Ocean and almost all other major fisheries areas that are used by the United Nations Food and Agriculture Organization (FAO) in compiling statistical information. Of these 19 areas, only the Western and Eastern Indian Ocean (respectively Major Fishing

---

[42] Ibid.
[43] Perth Communiqué, 13th Meeting of the Council of Ministers of the Indian Ocean Rim Association, Perth, Australia (1 November 2013) [6], available at <http://www.dfat.gov.au/geo/indian-ocean/perth-communique-2013.html>.
[44] Naidu, n 3, 24.
[45] Ibid, 25, referring to S Kelegama 'Indian Ocean Regionalism: is There a Future?' (2002) 37(25) *Economic and Political Weekly* 2422, 2423.
[46] Naidu, n 3, 24.
[47] For information on the history and activities of the IOC, see Wikipedia, 'Indian Ocean Commission', available at <http://en.wikipedia.org/wiki/Indian_Ocean_Commission>.
[48] Ibid; A Tahindro, 'The Implementation of UNCLOS in the Indian Ocean Region: The Case of Madagascar' (2006) 12 *African Yearbook of International Law* 349, 390–4.
[49] LO Hayward, 'China in the Indian Ocean: A Case of Uncharted Waters' in Luke and O'Loughlin (eds), n 3, 101, 103.

Areas 51 and 57) and the Western Central Pacific have shown sustained growth throughout most of this period.[50] The Eastern Indian Ocean is still experiencing significant growth in catches. Between 2007 and 2010 catches increased by 17 per cent and are now totalling 7 million tonnes.[51] Catches in the Western Indian Ocean peaked at 4.5 million tonnes in 2006; 4.3 million tonnes were reported in 2010.[52] The FAO estimates that globally about 90 per cent of catches are taken in the EEZs of coastal States.[53] In the Indian Ocean this figure is significantly lower. In the Eastern Indian Ocean high seas catches started to rise significantly in the first half of the 1970s. From a low-point of 3 per cent in 1973, these catches increased to 27 per cent of total catches in Major Fishing Area 57 in 2004.[54] For the Western Indian Ocean the relative weight of high seas catches is still bigger. Since the early 1980s, more than 30 per cent of catches are taken in the high seas, with a peak of 39 per cent in 2003.[55] The role of extra-regional States in high seas catches has diminished over time, but remains significant.[56] For instance, in Major Fishing Area 51, Japan, the Republic of Korea, and Taiwan generally represented more than 50 per cent of landed catches in terms of value until the second half of the 1990s. This figure stood at 30 per cent in 2006.[57]

---

[50] See United Nations Food and Agriculture Organization (FAO), *The State of World Fisheries and Aquaculture 2012* (FAO Rome 2012) 54–5, available at <http://www.fao.org/docrep/016/i2727e/i2727e00.htm> (hereinafter *State of World Fisheries*). The Western and Eastern Indian Ocean are divided by the meridians of 80°E (south of the equator) and 77°E (north of the equator). To the south, their limit coincides with the northern limit of the CAMLR Convention area (see n 5). The western limit of Area 51 and the eastern limit of Area 57 differ to some extent from the western and eastern limit of the Indian Ocean provided by the IHO. For instance, the western limit of Area 51 is set at the meridian of 30° E, whereas the western limit of the Indian Ocean in the IHO definition uses the meridian passing through Cape Agulhas (approximately 20° E). For the definition of Areas 51 and 57, see FAO, Fisheries and Aquaculture Department, *CWH Handbook of Fishery Statistical Standards* (2014), available at <http://www.fao.org/fishery/cwp/handbook/H/en>.

[51] *State of World Fisheries*, n 50, 59.   [52] Ibid.

[53] Ibid, 94. Figures from the Sea Around Us Project up to 2004 show a different division. Between 1992 and 2004 the figure for EEZ catches is around 85 per cent and that for the high seas 15 per cent: Sea Around Us Project, *Percent of Landings in EEZs vs. High Seas*, available at <www.seaaroundus.org/TrophicLevel/PercentEEZHS.aspx?EEZ=000&FAO=0&TypeOut=0&country=EEZ (Global Catch)>.

[54] See Sea Around Us Project, *Percent of Landings Inside EEZs vs. Outside for FAO Area E Indian Ocean*, available at <http://aerlo6.aerl.ubc.ca/TrophicLevel/PercentEEZHS.aspx?EEZ=999&FAO=57&TypeOut=1#>.

[55] See Sea Around Us Project, *Percent of Landings inside EEZs vs. outside for FAO area W Indian Ocean*, available at <http://aerlo6.aerl.ubc.ca/TrophicLevel/PercentEEZHS.aspx?EEZ=999&FAO=51&TypeOut=1#)>.

[56] See Sea Around Us Project, *Real 2000 value (US$) by Fishing Country in High Seas—Indian Ocean, Western*, available at <http://www.seaaroundus.org/highsea/51/14.aspx>, and *Real 2000 Value (US$) by Fishing Country in High Seas—Indian Ocean, Eastern*, available at <http://www.seaaroundus.org/highsea/57/14.aspx>.

[57] See Sea Around Us Project, *Real 2000 Value (US$) by Fishing Country in High Seas—Indian Ocean, Western*, n 56.

The significance of marine capture fisheries for Indian Ocean coastal States varies widely.[58] A number of them, such as Indonesia and India, are among the major fishing nations of the world, while the fisheries in the EEZ of other Indian Ocean coastal States are mainly exploited by distant water fishing nations.[59] Most Indian Ocean coastal States face serious difficulties in managing the fisheries resources in their EEZ, which has resulted in overexploitation.[60] Limited information on catch data generally has resulted in difficulties in monitoring stock status and trends.[61] An assessment of stocks by the Southwest Indian Ocean Fisheries Commission (SWIOFC) for 140 species in the area under its competence—the waters under national jurisdiction of its Member States—indicated that '[o]verall, 65 per cent of fish stocks were estimated to be fully exploited, 29 per cent overexploited, and 6 per cent non-fully exploited in 2009.'[62] It has been submitted that Australia is unique in the Indian Ocean in developing an effective management regime that has resulted in a healthy fisheries industry.[63]

Illegal, unreported, and unregulated (IUU) fishing constitutes a major problem in the Indian Ocean, just as in other ocean areas. One estimate for the period of 2000–2003 indicates that for the Western Indian Ocean the share of IUU fishing was equal to between 11 and 26 per cent of reported catches and that for the Eastern Indian Ocean this figure was between 20 and 43 per cent.[64] According to Hinrichs Oyarce, the issue has been in particular problematical in the Mozambique Channel and the southern part of the Indian Ocean.[65] An assessment of the trends in illegal fishing for the period between 1980 and 2003 indicates that it remained at around the same level in the Eastern Indian Ocean, but significantly declined for the Western Indian Ocean.[66] This decline has been attributed to increased control by coastal States, and a reduction of the unreported catch estimated by the Indian Ocean Tuna Commission (IOTC).[67]

---

[58] For general information on most Indian Ocean coastal States see the Fisheries and Aquaculture Department, *Fishery and Aquaculture Country Profiles* (2014), available at <http://www.fao.org/fishery/countryprofiles/search/en>.

[59] See eg FAO, *Fishery Country Profile; The Republic of Kenya* (FID/CP/KEN) (2007) [3.2] and [4.2], available at <ftp://ftp.fao.org/FI/DOCUMENT/fcp/en/FI_CP_KE.pdf>.

[60] See D Michel, H Fuller, and L Dolan, 'Natural Resources in the Indian Ocean: Fisheries and Minerals' in Michel and Sticklor (eds), n 1, 103, 103–4.

[61] *State of World Fisheries*, n 50, 59.   [62] Ibid.   [63] Michel et al, n 60, 104.

[64] J Hughes, 'The Piracy-Illegal Fishing Nexus in the Western Indian Ocean' in Luke and O'Loughlin (eds), n 3, 41, 42.

[65] X Hinrichs Oyarce, 'Current Ocean Law Issues in the Indian Ocean Region' in HN Scheiber and J Paik (eds), *Regions, Institutions, and Law of the Sea: Studies in Ocean Governance* (Martinus Nijhoff Publishers Leiden 2013) 359, 374.

[66] DJ Agnew et al, 'Estimating the Worldwide Extent of Illegal Fishing' (2009) 4 *Plos ONE* 1, 2 Table 2. For the period 1980–1984, illegal fishing equalled 31 per cent of reported catches in the Western Indian Ocean, and in the period 2000–2003—18 per cent.

[67] Ibid, 3.

The widespread occurrence of IUU fishing has been attributed, among others, to: a lack of effective regional fisheries management;[68] registration of vessels in States that do not participate in such management;[69] lack of enforcement capacities of coastal States;[70] penalties for offences that are too low to discourage illegal practices;[71] and a lack of political will on the part of coastal States.[72] One study on illegal fishing has found 'no significant relationship between illegal fishing and the price of fish or the size of the EEZ or the fishery [concerned], but... did find a significant relationship with World Bank governance indicators'.[73]

Regional fisheries cooperation in the Indian Ocean concerns both bodies that have an advisory role and bodies that are also competent to adopt management measures.[74] The latter are the Meeting of Parties of the Southern Indian Ocean Fisheries Agreement (SIOFA) and two tuna commissions, the IOTC, and the Commission for the Conservation of Southern Bluefin Tuna (CCSBT).

The SIOFA was concluded in 2006 and entered into force on 21 June 2012. Its area of competence is the southern part of Major Fishing Areas 51 and 57 to the west of the meridian of 120° E, excluding areas under national jurisdiction, and it applies to all fisheries resources except for sedentary species of the continental shelf beyond 200 nautical miles and highly migratory stocks as defined in Annex I of the LOSC. Australia, Cook Islands, the European Union, Mauritius, and Seychelles are parties to the SIOFA. There currently is no similar management body for the remaining high seas of Major Fishing Areas 51 and 57. The original focus of the negotiations on the SIOFA on the Southern Indian Ocean seems to be explained by the fact that the members of the Committee for the Development and Management of Fisheries in the South West Indian Ocean that was abolished together with its parent body, the Indian Ocean Fishery Commission, by the FAO Council in June 1999, wished to re-establish a regional fisheries body.[75] The SIOFA takes on board the general principles of fisheries law that have been developed since the adoption of the LOSC. The SIOFA allows fishing entities, ie Taiwan, to participate in it.

The IOTC and the CCSBT both manage tuna fisheries. The CCSBT is only concerned with southern bluefin tuna and its competence extends over all waters where this species is found. This also concerns large parts of the southern Indian Ocean. Its membership originally comprised Australia, Japan, and New Zealand, but was subsequently enlarged with Indonesia and the Republic of Korea. In addition, the CCSBT established an Extended Commission to allow the participation of Taiwan

---

[68] Bateman and Bergin, *Our Western Front*, n 32.
[69] Hinrichs Oyarce, n 65, 374. [70] Ibid, 374–5. [71] Ibid. [72] Hughes, n 64, 41.
[73] Agnew, n 66, 4.
[74] For an overview of these bodies see FAO, *Regional Fishery Bodies (RFB)* (2014) available at <http://www.fao.org/fishery/rfb/search/en>.
[75] FAO, *Final Act of the Conference on the Southern Indian Ocean Fisheries Agreement* (2006), available at <http://www.fao.org/fileadmin/user_upload/legal/docs/035t-e.pdf>.

in management. The European Union, South Africa, and Philippines are currently co-operating non-members.

The IOTC manages tuna and tuna-like species.[76] Its area of competence coincides with Major Fishing Areas 51 and 57, apart from its western boundary, which extends to the meridian of 20° E in order to align that boundary with the area of competence of the International Commission for the Conservation of Atlantic Tunas. Its membership includes the majority of the Indian Ocean coastal States and distant water fishing nations. IOTC's status as an FAO body has prevented the inclusion of Taiwan in its work.

The CCSBT and the IOTC both have their origins in agreements from 1993, which entered into force in respectively 1994 and 1996.[77] The performance of both organizations has been critically appraised as not having been successful in achieving effective management. In both instances, this has in part been attributed to the fact that the treaties that set up both bodies are outdated and do not take into account recent developments in the legal principles for fisheries management.[78] In both cases, the deficiencies in data collection and its consequences for future management have also been pointed out.[79] The fact that Taiwan is prevented from participating in the IOTC is seen as another factor negatively affecting the management of Indian Ocean tuna fisheries.[80] Both the IOTC and the CCSBT are addressing these issues in the light of performance reviews of their work. The IOTC, in considering the recommendation from the Performance Review Panel to either amend the existing Agreement or replace it with a completely renegotiated one, noted that 'the most logical path would be to undertake both paths, in series, i.e. to amend the Agreement...to satisfy some of the recommendations from the Panel, while also undertaking a process to renegotiate the entire Agreement'.[81] The Commission also

---

[76] This includes southern Bluefin tuna, but in practice the IOTC defers to the CCSBT for the management of this species: International Seafood Sustainability Foundation, *Southern Bluefin—Southern Hemisphere* (2014), available at <http://iss-foundation.org/status-of-the-stocks/southern-bluefin-southern-hemisphere/>.

[77] 1993 Convention for the Conservation of Southern Bluefin Tuna; 1993 Agreement for the Establishment of the Indian Ocean Tuna Commission.

[78] For the IOTC, see Bateman and Bergin, *Our Western Front*, n 32, 54; E Franckx and K van den Bossche, 'Regional Issues and Oceans Law: The African Region' in Scheiber and Paik (eds), n 65, 411, 412–21; see Commission for the Conservation of Southern Bluefin Tuna, *Report of the Independent Expert* (2008), available at <http://www.ccsbt.org/userfiles/file/docs_english/meetings/meeting_reports/ccsbt_15/PerformanceReview_IndependentExpertsReport.pdf>.

[79] See Commission for the Conservation of Southern Bluefin Tuna, n 78, 4; Franckx and Van den Bossche, n 78, 412.

[80] WR Edeson, 'An International Legal Extravaganza in the Indian Ocean: Placing the Indian Ocean Tuna Commission outside the Framework of FAO' (2007) 22 *International Journal of Marine and Coastal Law* 485, 486.

[81] Indian Ocean Tuna Commission, *Report of the Seventeenth Session*. Doc IOTC–2013–S17–R[E] (2013) [99], available at <http://iotc.org/sites/default/files/documents/2013/08/IOTC-2013-S17-R%5BE%5D%20-%20FINAL.pdf>.

noted that the institutional links with the FAO inhibited the full involvement of all fleets, ie those of Taiwan, in its work. This contributed to non-compliance, while the Commission had little means at its disposal to deal with it.[82] The CCSBT in the wake of the 2008 Performance Review has developed a Strategic Plan that is intended to address the issues identified by the review.[83] A Second Performance Review is scheduled for 2014. This second review is to evaluate: the performance of the CCSBT; its progress in implementing the recommendations from the Performance Review; and the extent to which modern fisheries management standards have been incorporated into the Commission's work.[84]

4.2.2 Environmental cooperation

Cooperation on the protection and preservation of the marine environment takes place at the global and regional level. As Part XII of the LOSC indicates, this cooperation plays an important role in standard-setting. To give an idea of the participation of Indian Ocean coastal States in global regimes, four randomly selected conventions are considered, namely the Convention on Biological Diversity (CBD), the 1979 Convention on the Conservation of Migratory Species of Wild Animals (CMS) and the 1972 Convention on the Prevention of Marine Pollution by Dumping of Wastes and Other Matter (London Convention) and its 1996 Protocol. All Indian coastal States are parties to the CBD. This level of participation is commensurate with the near universal participation in the Convention. Twenty-three of the 38 Indian Ocean coastal States are parties to the CMS and for the London Convention and its 1996 Protocol these figures are respectively 13 and 6.[85] Especially the latter figure suggests that Indian Ocean coastal States may be lagging in implementing their obligations in relation to the protection and preservation of the marine environment. At the same time, it should be realized that the rate of participation of States from other regions in these instruments is not very dissimilar. The total number of parties to these three instruments stood at 119, 87, and 43, respectively. The rate of participation of Indian Ocean coastal States in

---

[82] Ibid, [100].

[83] Commission for the Conservation of Southern Bluefin Tuna (CCSBT), *Strategic Plan* (2011), available at <http://www.ccsbt.org/userfiles/file/docs_english/operational_resolutions/CCSBT_Strategic_Plan.pdf>.

[84] CCSBT, *Implementation of the CCSBT Strategic Plan* (2013) Attachment A (Draft Terms of Reference for the Second Performance Review of the CCSBT), available at <http://www.ccsbt.org/userfiles/file/docs_english/meetings/meeting_reports/ccsbt_20/report_of_CC8.pdf>. The CCSBT agreed to the draft terms of reference at its 20th Meeting, *Report of the Twentieth Annual Meeting of the Commission* (2013) [81], available at <http://www.ccsbt.org/userfiles/file/docs_english/meetings/meeting_reports/ccsbt_20/report_of_CCSBT20.pdf>.

[85] These figures are based on an assessment by the author of this chapter of 18 November 2013 (on file with the author). Eight Indian Ocean coastal States that are not a party to the CMS are either a party to an agreement or participate in one or more memoranda of understanding concluded in the framework of the Convention.

the CMS is almost the same as that of all parties compared to the membership of the United Nations (respectively, 61 and 62 per cent). For the London Convention and its 1996 Protocol the Indian Ocean compares somewhat unfavourably in this respect, with a rate of participation of 34 and 16 per cent, respectively, as compared against 45 and 22 per cent.

Regional cooperation plays an important role in the protection and preservation of the marine environment. There is no cooperation in this respect spanning the entire Indian Ocean. It can be noted that the same applies for the Pacific and Atlantic Oceans. Cooperation on the protection and preservation of the marine environment is carried out by means of regional seas programs covering five sub-regions of the Indian Ocean: the East African region, including the island States of the south-western Indian Ocean; the Red Sea and the Gulf of Aden; the Persian Gulf and Part of the Arabian Sea; the South Asian Seas; and the East Asian Seas.[86] In the latter two regions' cooperation is based in non-binding action plans and in the first three of these regions cooperation is based in a binding instrument.[87] These conventions all predate developments in environmental law since the second half of the 1980s. Only the Nairobi Convention has been subsequently amended, taking into account these developments.[88]

Most of the maritime zones of the Indian Ocean coastal States are covered by these existing sub-regional cooperative mechanisms, but coverage is not complete. For instance, part of the EEZ and continental shelf of Oman and Yemen is beyond the area of application of the relevant regional conventions. Regional cooperation in general has focussed on areas under national jurisdiction. None of the regional conventions includes the high seas and the Area in their area of application and the focus of the Action Plans is also on areas within national jurisdiction.

Recent developments involving the FAO and the CBD suggest that the interest in the management of areas beyond national jurisdiction (ABNJ) in the Indian Ocean may pick up.[89] These developments also provide an example of the linkages between the global and regional level of implementation of the law of the sea. In July 2012 two workshops on respectively vulnerable marine ecosystems (VMEs) and ecologically

---

[86] The latter area also covers areas beyond the Indian Ocean. Background information on regional cooperation on the marine environment of all these sea areas can be accessed through the website, UNEP, *Regional Seas Programmes*, available at <http://www.unep.org/regionalseas/>.

[87] 1985 Nairobi Convention for the Protection, Management and Development of the Marine and Coastal Environment of the Eastern African Region (hereinafter Nairobi Convention); 1978 Kuwait Regional Convention for Cooperation on the Protection of the Marine Environment from Pollution; 1982 Regional Convention for the Conservation of the Red Sea and Gulf of Aden Environment.

[88] 2010 Amended Nairobi Convention for the Protection, Management and Development of the Marine and Coastal Environment of the Western Indian Ocean (hereinafter Amended Nairobi Convention).

[89] In addition, it can be noted that exploratory activities in relation to mineral resources in the Area are regulated by the ISA. The regulations of the ISA include environmental standards that are based on current principles of international environmental law.

or biologically significant areas (EBSAs) in the Indian Ocean were organized back to back in Mauritius.[90] The workshop on VMEs was jointly organized by the FAO and the IOC and the workshop on EBSAs was convened by the executive secretary of the CBD in collaboration with the Secretariat of the Nairobi Convention and the FAO.[91] Both workshops built on work at the global level and experiences from other regions. The workshop on EBSAs agreed on the descriptions of 39 EBSAs in the Southern Indian Ocean.[92] This also concerns extensive areas in ABNJ.[93] The Workshop on VMEs among others concluded that it:

> ...was successful in raising awareness of VMEs and associated management options, and in explaining the various instruments and pathways necessary to achieve appropriate processes and management decisions. In addition, the workshop was a first step in developing regional networks to support this process.[94]

The Indian Ocean has been designated as one of the priority regions of an FAO program that focuses on capacity development and the implementation of existing agreements and addresses both issues related to VMEs and EBSAs.[95] One interesting aspect of the workshops on VMEs and EBSAs is that they have been actively supported by the Nairobi Convention, but have not attracted involvement from the Action Plans for the South and East Asian Seas.[96] This raises the question what institutions will eventually take part in the management of ABNJ in the Indian Ocean. In that connection it can also be noted that the Meeting of Parties of the SIOFA is competent to deal with VMEs in relation to fisheries, but that there is no body with a similar competence in the northern part of the Indian Ocean.

Another recent development that has a potential to affect regional cooperation in relation to the marine environment concerns the concept of Large Marine Ecosystems (LMEs).[97] The LME concept has been propagated as 'a way forward for advancing ecosystem-based management of coastal and marine resources within a framework of sustainable development'.[98] Experiences with this concept in two

---

[90] See FAO, *Fisheries and Aquaculture Report No. 1030: Report of the Regional Workshop on Vulnerable Marine Ecosystems (VMEs) in the Indian Ocean* (Flic en Flac Mauritius 2012) (hereinafter *VME Report*); *Report of the Southern Indian Ocean Regional Workshop to Facilitate the Description of Ecologically or Biologically Significant Marine Areas* Doc UNEP/CBD/RW/EBSA/SIO/1/4 (2013) (hereinafter *EBSA Report*). Although the latter workshop refers to the Southern Indian Ocean, its geographic scope generally extended up to the meridian of 10° N (see *VME Report*, Annex V).

[91] *VME Report*, n 90, iii; *EBSA Report*, n 90, 2 [5].   [92] *EBSA Report*, n 90, 37.
[93] Ibid, Annex V.   [94] *VME Report*, n 90, 26 [16].   [95] Ibid, 23 [15.1].
[96] Some of the States participating in these Action Plans did attend the workshops.
[97] For further information on the concept, see eg K Sherman and G Hempel (eds), 'Perspectives on Regional Seas and the Large Marine Ecosystem Approach' in *The UNEP Large Marine Ecosystems Report* (2008) 3, available at <http://iwlearn.net/publications/regional-seas-reports/unep-regional-seas-reports-and-studies-no-182/background-report-perspectives-on-regional-seas-and-the-large-marine-ecosystem-approach>. This report also contains information on the LMEs of the Indian Ocean.
[98] Ibid, 5.

parts of the Indian Ocean suggest that its impact may vary greatly depending on the existing framework for regional cooperation. In relation to the Agulhas and Somali current LMEs, which overlap spatially with the area of application of the Nairobi Convention, the Agulhas and Somali Current Large Marine Ecosystems (ASCLME) Project, which runs from 2008 to 2013, has been set up. The Nairobi Convention is a partner in the ASCLME Project and part of its Steering Committee.[99] Due to its focus and set up, the Project is complementary to the activities of the Nairobi Convention and likely providing useful input into the latter.

The Bay of Bengal Large Marine Ecosystem (BOBLME) Project overlaps spatially with the Action Plans for South Asian Seas and East Asian Seas, but not all countries represented in the two Action Plans participate in the BOBLME Project.[100] This makes the interactions with the Action Plans more problematic than in the case of the ASCLME Project for the Nairobi Convention. Moreover, as is observed on the webpage of the BOBLME Project:

Despite the large number of international, regional and sub-regional bodies and programmes operating in the Bay [of Bengal], none have a clear mandate, geographical scope and/or capacity to support a regional initiative that would effectively address the issues confronting the coastal communities of the [Bay of Bengal]. Furthermore, the current existence of many ineffective policies, strategies and legal measures at the National level would likely impede the development of any regional arrangements.[101]

4.2.3 *Maritime security*

Maritime security in its present-day form is a multifaceted concept ranging from the traditional focus over access to the sea and navigational rights and freedoms to modern-day issues such as illegal immigration, IUU fishing, and sub-standard shipping.[102] In the Indian Ocean, traditional maritime security concerns are dominated by the strategic interests of two extra-regional powers, the United States and China, and the major regional player, India.[103] For the law of the sea, a major impact of India's rise as a naval power and its rivalry with China may be that 'India, a recovering champion of coastal State control over the oceans, is realigning its political might and military power to be more in concert with the liberal order of the ocean long promoted by the United States.'[104] At the same time, China's interests

---

[99] For further information on the ASCLME Project, see ASCLME, *Welcome to the ASCLME Project* (2014), available at <http://www.asclme.org/>.

[100] For further information on the BOBLME Project, see BOBLME, *The Bay of Bengal Large Marine Ecosystem Project* (2014), available at <http://www.boblme.org/>.

[101] See BOBLME, *The Bay of Bengal Large Marine Ecosystem Project: About BOBLME, Project Overview* (2014), available at <http://www.boblme.org/project_overview.html>.

[102] For a discussion of the concept of maritime security, see eg DR Rothwell, 'Maritime Security in the Polar Regions' in EJ Molenaar, AG Oude Elferink, and DR Rothwell (eds), *The Law of the Sea and the Polar Regions* (Martinus Nijhoff Publishers Leiden 2013) 367, 370–1.

[103] See further eg Kraska, n 1.   [104] Ibid, 489; see also ibid, 491–2.

in the Indian Ocean also seem to be best served by maintaining the navigational framework contained in the LOSC. China's policy in relation to the seas near its shores is rather based on limiting these rights. To some extent China has tried to manage this tension by arguing the existence of special regimes, allowing a divergence from the LOSC framework, in the latter case. This approach has met with limited success and in the future may require reconsideration in the light of China's broader maritime interests.

Maritime security issues in the Indian Ocean in general have been managed in the existing law of the sea framework, but some approaches to dealing with specific issues have raised questions in this respect. The announcement by Australia in 2004 that it would declare a 1,000-nm maritime identification zone led to concerns of neighbouring States that this would affect their rights.[105] Some doubts about the compatibility of this scheme—implemented as the Australian Maritime Identification System—with the law of the sea have been voiced.[106] More recently, an election promise of the current Australian Government to 'turn back boats [with illegal migrants] where it is safe to do so'[107] has led to questions concerning how such a policy could be implemented within the current law of the sea framework.[108]

One of the main challenges to the current law of the sea, and public international law generally, in the Indian Ocean likely was the surge of maritime piracy in the North-Western Indian Ocean in the wake of the collapse of State authority in Somalia. This implied that pirates could operate with impunity from bases in Somalia and Somalia's territorial sea. Instead of seeking to adjust or bypass international law to address this issue the international community has relied on a mandate of the United Nations Security Council to complement the law of the sea, which only allows addressing piracy beyond the limits of the territorial sea.[109]

Deficiencies in implementation and a lack of capabilities seem to provide a bigger problem for ensuring maritime security than the existing legal framework. For instance, Bateman has pointed out the ineffectiveness of the Indian Ocean Memorandum of Understanding on Port State Control (Indian Ocean MoU). A number of Indian Ocean coastal States (eg Pakistan, Madagascar, and Seychelles)

---

[105] DR Rothwell, 'The Impact of State Practice on the Jurisdictional Framework contained in the LOS Convention: A Commentary' in AG Oude Elferink (ed), *Stability and Change in the Law of the Sea: The Role of the LOS Convention* (Martinus Nijhoff Publishers Leiden 2005) 145, 156.

[106] See DR Rothwell and T Stephens, *The International Law of the Sea* (Hart Publishing Oxford 2010) 96.

[107] The Nationals, *The Coalition's Operation Sovereign Borders Policy* (2013) 5, available at <http://www.nationals.org.au/Portals/0/2013/policy/The%20Coalition%E2%80%99s%20Operation%20Sovereign%20Borders%20Policy.pdf>.

[108] See ABC Fact Check, 'Is it Illegal to Turn Back Boats in International Waters to Indonesia?', *ABC Online* (17 November 2014), available at <http://www.abc.net.au/news/2013-09-26/government-turn-back-boat-policy/4979898>.

[109] See Chapter 37 in this volume.

do not participate in the Indian Ocean MoU. Inspection rates of the MoU are moreover too low.[110]

5 CONCLUSIONS

The practice of Indian Ocean coastal States generally shows a large measure of consistency with the LOSC as regards the extent of maritime zones. A considerable divergence from the LOSC exists in the case of straight baselines, whereas in the case of archipelagic baselines there in general is conformity to the Convention, suggesting that the numerical controls contained in Article 47 have been more effective than the broad language of Article 7. A number of Indian Ocean coastal States has sought to impose restrictions on navigation and overflight that are not in accordance with the Convention's regime. Both as regards this latter issue and straight baselines, divergence from the conventional regime is certainly not unique to the Indian Ocean. The practice of Indian Ocean coastal States in respect of maritime boundary delimitation is similar to that of other regions. The practice of Australia in relation to some maritime security issues suggests that measures that are being considered in this context may lead to tension with the law of the sea. In view of the continued significance of these issues to the Indian Ocean region, they might in the future become a source of instability for certain aspects of the law of the sea.

Notwithstanding some attempts at Indian Ocean-wide cooperation on law of the sea, cooperation centred on specific regions is likely to remain prevalent (for such reasons as geography, larger coherence of these regions as compared to the Indian Ocean as a whole, existing patterns of cooperation, and the likely lack of benefits from moving from regional to Ocean-wide cooperation). Exceptions are only likely to be the case if the object of regulation—such as tuna fisheries—makes Indian Ocean-wide cooperation indispensable. The analysis also points to considerable differences between various regions of the Indian Ocean as regards the impact of existing institutional arrangements on new developments, as is illustrated by the reception of the LME concept in the East African region and the Bay of Bengal and the work on VMEs and EBSAs. The impact of extra-regional actors is among others

---

[110] S Bateman, 'Maritime Security and Port State Control in the Indian Ocean Region' (2012) 8 *Journal of the Indian Ocean Region* 188, 197. See also the review of initiatives to cooperate in combatting piracy in the eastern and western part of the Indian Ocean: N Passas and A Twyman-Ghoshal, 'Controlling Piracy in Southeast Asia—Thinking outside the Box' in RC Beckman and JA Roach (eds), *Piracy and International Crimes in ASEAN* (Edward Elgar Cheltenham 2013) 62, 77; L Cordner, 'Rethinking Maritime Security in the Indian Ocean Region' (2010) 6 *Journal of the Indian Ocean Region* 67, 76.

apparent from their role in high fisheries management and cooperation in combatting piracy off the coast of Somalia.

The analysis of existing cooperation in the field of fisheries, the marine environment and maritime security indicates that the implementation of the law of the sea—and achieving sustainable management of the Indian Ocean—is a work in progress. Many of these regimes need to be updated to bring them in line with the existing global legal framework and participating States oftentimes are lacking in the capacities and resources that are needed in this respect. The differences between the various regions of the Indian Ocean make it likely that they will stay on different trajectories in dealing with the implementation of the law of the sea.

POLAR OCEANS AND LAW OF THE SEA

KAREN N SCOTT AND DAVID L VANDERZWAAG

1 INTRODUCTION

THE Arctic and Antarctic, or 'Poles' as they are more generically referred to, are united by the dominant presence of ice, their particular vulnerability to climate change and other environmental threats and the presence of jurisdictional disputes.* A distinct modern trend in the law of the sea has been to build on these similarities and to attempt to develop common responses to common problems. This trend is particularly noticeable in relation to the safety of shipping where the International Maritime Organization (IMO) is in the process of adopting mandatory global standards of special application to both Polar regions.

However, the similarity between the Arctic and Antarctic can be overstated, not least because the geopolitical realities of the Arctic could hardly be more different than those that operate in the Antarctic. Regional cooperation in the Arctic has

---

* Professor VanderZwaag gratefully acknowledges the research support of the Social Sciences and Humanities Research Council of Canada (SSHRC) under the research project 'Tracking and Envisioning the Future of Arctic Ocean Governance'. The authors would like to thank Donald R Rothwell, Tim Stephens, and Alex Oude Elferink for helpful comments on earlier versions of this chapter. This chapter attempts to be accurate as of 1 December 2014.

largely occurred through the Arctic Council and its soft power approach without an over-arching treaty framework in contrast to the formal institutions and binding instruments developed within the Antarctic Treaty System.[1] The importance of the Arctic to commercial shipping, which is likely to grow as ice cover diminishes as a result of climate change, can be contrasted with the relative isolation of the Antarctic. The current moratorium on the commercial exploitation of mineral resources in the Antarctic is the antithesis of the promotion of mineral and petroleum activities taking place in the Arctic. The Arctic Ocean is surrounded by five coastal States having offshore maritime zones, while the Southern Ocean has no generally recognized coastal or port States.

Defining a boundary for the Arctic Ocean has been more complicated than for the Antarctic. The southernmost boundary of the Arctic Ocean is subject to varying definitions which include the Arctic Circle (an imaginary circle around the globe at 66° 32"N), the 10°C isotherm (the most southerly location where the mean temperature of the warmest month of the year is below 10°C) and varying national delineations, such as Canada's defining Arctic waters to cover those north of 60°N latitude[2] (see Figure 32.1). By contrast, the Southern Ocean, which surrounds Antarctica, is separated by a distinct ecological boundary known as the Antarctic Convergence or the Polar Front, which coincides approximately with the Southern boundary of the Antarctic Circumpolar current[3] (see Figure 32.2).

This chapter explores the commonalities and differences in the law of the sea as it applies to the two Polar oceans, drawing on the disputed sovereignty, environmental vulnerabilities and access to marine resources. Section 2 highlights how the two regions are 'poles together,' sharing some key governance similarities, such as being subject to general law of the sea provisions applicable to maritime safety and environmental protection. Section 3 describes how the regions are 'poles apart' by examining the differing law of the sea contexts and divergent regional approaches and challenges to ocean governance in the Arctic and Antarctic, respectively. Section 4 identifies future challenges for both regions focusing in particular, on institutional developments in the Arctic and on the development of new spatially focused conservation tools in the Antarctic.

---

[1] See T Stephens and DL VanderZwaag, 'Polar oceans governance: shifting seascapes, hazy horizons' in T Stephens and DL VanderZwaag (eds), *Polar Oceans Governance in an Era of Environmental Change* (Edward Elgar Cheltenham 2014) 1.

[2] E Carina, H Keskitalo, T Koivurova, and N Bankes, 'Climate governance in the Arctic: Introduction and Theoretical Framework' in T Koivurova, E Carina, H Keskitalo, and N Bankes (eds), *Climate Governance in the Arctic* (Springer Berlin 2009) 1, 3.

[3] E Fahrbach, 'Stormy and icy seas' in D Walton (ed), *Antarctica. Global Science from a Frozen Continent* (Cambridge University Press Cambridge 2013) 137, 137.

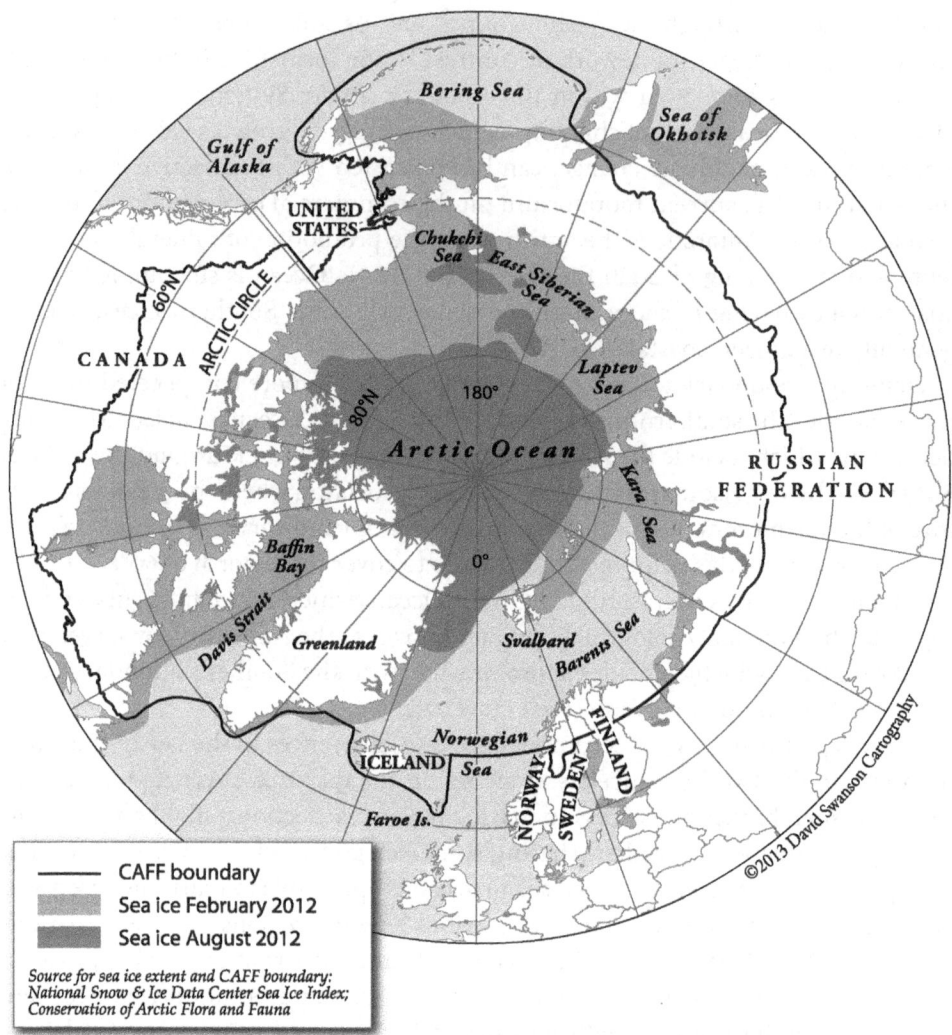

Figure 32.1

2 POLES TOGETHER

The Arctic and Antarctic are similar on three main governance fronts. First, the 1982 United Nations Convention on the Law of the Sea's (LOSC) general provisions govern both regions.[4] For example, the numerous obligations to protect and preserve

---

[4] See DL VanderZwaag, 'Law of the Sea and Governance of Shipping in the Arctic and Antarctic' in N Loukacheva (ed), *Polar Law Textbook* (Nordic Council of Ministers Copenhagen 2010) 45.

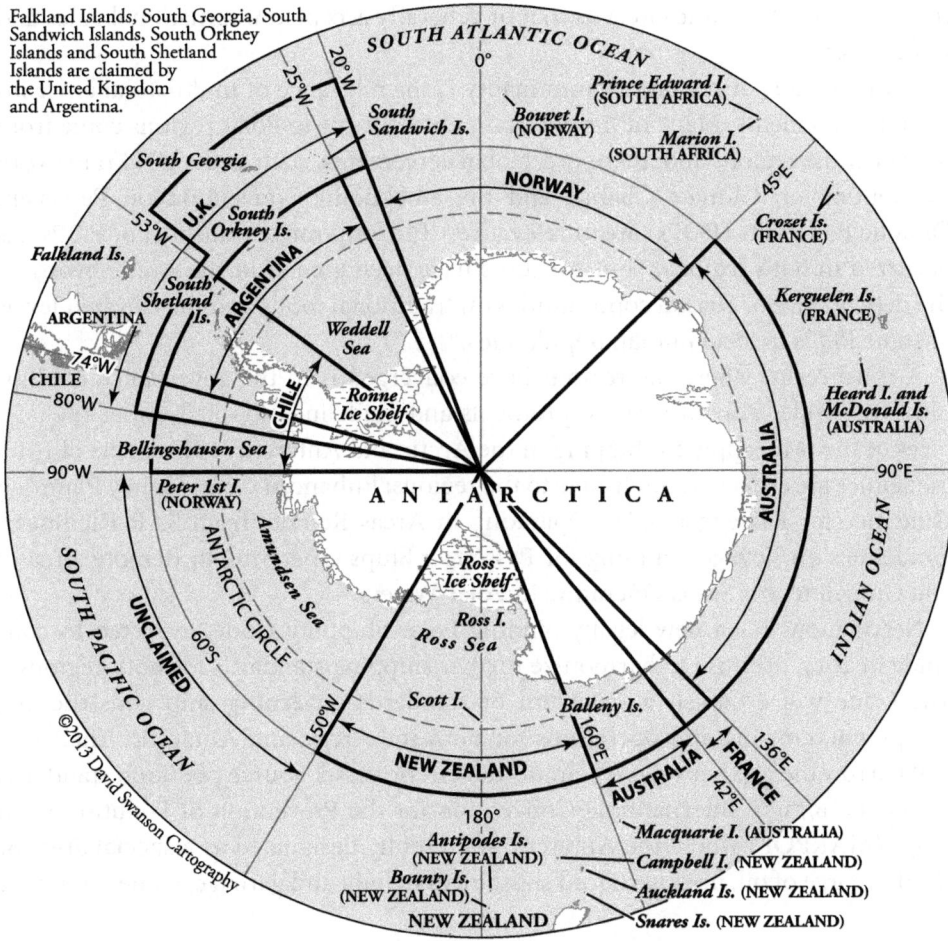

Figure 32.2

the marine environment found in Part XII of the Convention apply, including the need to adopt regional rules and standards for land-based marine pollution, ocean dumping, seabed activities, and atmospheric pollution.[5] The general responsibilities found in Part VII governing the high seas are also common to both regions, including the obligations to cooperate in the conservation and management of marine living resources of the high seas.[6] Flag State responsibilities, among others, include the need to ensure flagged vessels observe applicable international regulation concerning safety at sea[7] and the obligation to adopt laws for vessel-source pollution

---

[5] 1982 United Nations Convention on the Law of the Sea, Arts 207, 210, 208, and 212, respectively (hereinafter LOSC).
[6] Ibid, Arts 117–120.   [7] Ibid, Art 94.

control having the same effect as that of generally accepted international rules and standards.[8]

A second area of regional commonality is the relevance of multilateral environmental agreements. Many of the environmental threats to Polar regions come from outside those regions and, therefore, global agreements, such as the UN Framework Convention on Climate Change and the Stockholm Convention on Persistent Organic Pollutants (POPs) are of relevance.[9] The long-range transport of POPs has occurred in both regions,[10] but concerns have been greater in the Arctic owing to the dependence of coastal communities on traditional foods and the elevated levels of some POPs in local human populations.[11]

A third realm where the regions have converged is in the governance of shipping. The wide array of treaties, protocols and guidelines adopted under the auspices of the IMO apply to shipping in the Arctic and Antarctic.[12] Three sets of IMO guidelines are especially applicable to the regions: Enhanced Contingency Planning Guidance for Passenger Ships Operating in Areas Remote from SAR Facilities;[13] Guidelines on Voyage Planning for Passenger Ships Operating in Remote Areas;[14] and Guidelines for Ships Operating in Polar Waters.[15]

Negotiations for a new legally binding Polar Shipping Code, expected to conclude in 2014, promise to harmonize further shipping standards for both regions.[16] The Code will establish a spectrum of standards governing ship construction, equipment, crewing and operations for both the Arctic and Antarctic. The Code will narrow the gap between Antarctic and Arctic vessel-source pollution standards under the 1973/78 International Convention for the Prevention of Pollution from Ships (MARPOL) where the Antarctic is presently designated as a special area for the discharge of oil, noxious liquid substances in bulk and garbage, while the Arctic

---

[8] Ibid, Art 211.

[9] See T Koivurova, 'Environmental Protection in the Arctic and Antarctic' in Loukacheva (ed), n 4, 22–43.

[10] See D VanderZwaag, R Huebert, and O Hertzman, 'The Arctic Marine Environment: Not a Pristine Pole Apart' in LK Kriwoken et al (eds), *Ocean Law and Policy in the Post-UNCED Era: Australian and Canadian Perspectives* (Kluwer Law International London/The Hague 1996) 351, 376.

[11] See Arctic Monitoring and Assessment Programme (AMAP), *AMAP Assessment 2009: Human Health in the Arctic* (AMAP Oslo 2009).

[12] For a detailed discussion, see DL VanderZwaag, 'The IMO and Arctic marine environmental protection: tangled currents, sea of challenges' in OR Young, JD Kim, and YH Kim (eds), *The Arctic in World Affairs: A North Pacific Dialogue on Arctic Marine Issues* (Korea Maritime Institute and East-West Center Honolulu 2012) 99.

[13] IMO, 'Enhance Contingency Planning Guidance for Passenger Ships Operating in Areas Remote from SAR Facilities', Doc MCS.1/Cir.1184 (31 May 2006).

[14] IMO Assembly Res A.999(25), *Guidelines of Voyage Planning for Passenger Ships Operating in Remote Areas* (29 November 2007).

[15] IMO Assembly Res A.1024(26), *Guidelines for Ships Operating in Polar Waters* (2 December 2009).

[16] For the negotiation background, see VanderZwaag, n 12, 110–13.

is not.[17] The latest draft of the Code available at the time of writing would bring Arctic vessel-source pollution standards much closer to those of the Antarctic with proposed prohibitions on oil and noxious liquid substances discharges and garbage discharges restricted to comminuted or ground food wastes not less than 12 nm from the nearest land, ice shelf, or land-fast ice.[18]

However, not all regulatory standards will be harmonized. For example, while a ban on the use and carriage of heavy fuel oil (HFO) by ships in the Antarctic has been imposed through Regulation 43 of MARPOL Annex I, no such ban will be adopted for the Arctic through the Polar Code.[19]

3 Poles Apart

3.1 Regional developments: the Arctic

Law of the sea developments in the Arctic may be summarized under four themes: ocean boundaries and sovereignty disputes, extended continental shelves, jurisdictional tensions, and regional cooperation.

3.1.1 *Ocean boundary and sovereignty disputes*

Almost all of the ocean boundaries in the Arctic have been settled. Those boundaries include: Norway and the Russian Federation (maritime boundary in the Varanger Fjord Area, 1957 and 2007); Canada and Denmark (Greenland) (continental shelf from Davis Strait to the Lincoln Sea, 1973); Iceland and Norway (Jan Mayen) (continental shelf and fisheries zone, 1981); United States and Russian Federation (territorial sea, 200-nm zones and continental shelf beyond in the Arctic Ocean and Chukchi Sea, 1990); Denmark (Greenland) and Norway (Jan Mayen) (continental shelf and fisheries zone, 1995); Denmark (Greenland) and Iceland (continental shelf and fisheries zone, 1997); Denmark (Greenland) and

---

[17] L Boone, 'International Regulation of Polar Shipping' in EJ Molenaar, AG Oude Elferink, and DR Rothwell (eds), *Law of the Sea and the Polar Regions: Interactions between Global and Regional Regimes* (Martinus Nijhoff Leiden/Boston 2013) 193, 196.

[18] *Report of the Maritime Safety Committee on Its Ninety-Third Session*, MSC 99/22/Add. 3 (30 May 2014) Annex 24.

[19] At the sixty-fifth session of the Marine Environment Protection Committee, the Committee endorsed the view of the majority of delegations that it was premature to regulate the use of HFO on ships operating in Arctic waters. See *Report of the Marine Environment Protection Committee on its Sixty-Fifth Session*, MEPC 65/22 (24 May 2013) [11.53].

Norway (Svalbard) (continental shelf within 200 nm and fisheries zone within 200 nm, 2006); and Denmark (Faroe Islands), Iceland, and Norway (continental shelf beyond 200 nm, 2006).[20] In November 2012, Canada and Denmark reached a tentative agreement on the Lincoln Sea maritime boundary, north of Ellesmere Island, and Greenland, with a treaty text to be prepared based on the negotiations.[21]

In April 2010, Norway and the Russian Federation ended over 30 years of dispute over their exclusive economic zone (EEZ) and continental shelf boundary in the Barents Sea by concluding the 2010 Treaty on Maritime Delimitation and Cooperation in the Barents Sea and the Arctic Ocean.[22] While the Russian Federation had argued for a sector line to delimit the boundary and Norway had relied on a median line, the Treaty essentially splits the difference between the claims[23] and also addresses future cooperation concerning fisheries and possible overlapping hydrocarbon deposits.[24] The parties agreed to apply the precautionary approach to the management of shared stocks, continue application for at least 15 years of previous fisheries agreements, and to continue setting total allowable catches, quotas, and other regulatory measures through the Norwegian-Russian Joint Fisheries Commission.[25] Furthermore, the Parties agreed to negotiate a unitization agreement in case of a transboundary hydrocarbon deposit.[26]

The maritime boundary in the Beaufort Sea remains in dispute between Canada and the United States.[27] Canada claims the maritime boundary is the 141st west meridian with Canada's position being that an 1825 Treaty between Great Britain and Russia set out the meridian not only as a land boundary but also as the maritime boundary.[28] The United States' legal position is that an equidistant line should apply.[29] An area of some 6250 square nm, which may have considerable oil and gas potential, remains in dispute.[30]

---

[20] DL VanderZwaag et al, *Governance of Artic Marine Shipping* (Marine & Environmental Law Institute Dalhousie University Halifax Nova Scotia 2008) Appendix C.

[21] Foreign Affairs, Trade and Development Canada, 'Canada and Kingdom of Denmark Reach Tentative Agreement on Lincoln Sea Boundary', *News Release* (28 November 2012).

[22] An English translation is available at <http://www.regjeringen.no/upload/SMK/Vedlegg/2010/avtale_engelsk.pdf>.

[23] M Byers, *International Law and the Arctic* (Cambridge University Press Cambridge 2013) 42–3.

[24] See T Henriksen and G Alfstein, 'Maritime Delimitation in the Arctic: The Barents Sea Treaty' (2011) 42 *Ocean Development & International Law* 1.

[25] 2010 Treaty between the Kingdom of Norway and the Russian Federation concerning Maritime Delimitation and Cooperation in the Barents Sea and the Arctic Ocean, Art 4 and Annex I.

[26] Ibid, Art 5 and Annex II.

[27] TL McDorman, *Salt Water Neighbours: International Ocean Law Relations between the United States and Canada* (Oxford University Press New York 2009) 181–7.

[28] See TL McDorman and DL VanderZwaag, 'American-Canadian Boundary Disputes and Cooperation' in R Wolfrum (ed), *Max Plank Encyclopedia of International Law* (Oxford University Press Oxford 2010), available at <www.mpepil.com>; and Byers, n 23, 58–9.

[29] JS Baker and M Byers, 'Crossed Lines: The Curious Use of the Beaufort Sea Maritime Boundary Dispute' (2012) 43 *Ocean Development & International Law* 70, 76.

[30] Ibid, 72.

The Beaufort Sea dispute has been generally well managed.[31] Both countries have restrained from authorizing hydrocarbon exploration in the disputed area.[32] The United States has imposed a precautionary moratorium on fisheries in the Beaufort Sea off Alaska,[33] while Canada has placed a similar restriction for potential commercial fisheries in its claimed portion of the Beaufort Sea.[34] Officials from the two countries have met informally to share technical information and viewpoints but without entering into negotiations.

Only one dispute over land territory in the Arctic region persists. Canada and Denmark continue to disagree over the ownership of Hans Island, an uninhabited islet about one kilometre wide located in Nares Strait between Ellesmere Island and Northwest Greenland.[35] When the negotiators of the continental shelf boundary between Greenland and Canada became aware of the differing national opinions, they chose in 1973 to draw the boundary line up to a point near the south side of the island and to continue from a mark close to the north side.[36]

While various flag-raising incidents and protests have occurred over the years,[37] Canada and Denmark have remained good neighbours. In September 2005, the foreign ministers of Canada and Denmark issued a joint statement pledging further discussions towards reaching a long-term peaceful solution to the dispute.[38] The statement also committed each side to inform the other of future activities related to Hans Island without prejudice to respective legal claims and to carry out future contacts with the Island in a low key and restrained manner. Denmark's *Strategy for the Arctic 2011–2020* promises to continue close collaboration with Canada,[39] while Canada's *Statement on Arctic Foreign Policy* sets a priority of working with neighbours to explore the possibility of resolving maritime boundary disputes in accordance with international law.[40]

---

[31] Ibid, 73.   [32] Ibid.

[33] For federal waters beyond the 3 nm territorial sea of Alaska. See North Pacific Fishery Management Council, *Fishery Management Plan for Fish Resources of the Arctic Management Area* (August 2009).

[34] See Memorandum of Understanding between Fisheries and Oceans Canada (DFO) Fisheries Joint Management Committee (FJMC) Inuvialuit Regional Corporation (IRC) and Inuvialuit Game Council (EGC) Regarding the Development of a Beaufort Sea Integrated Fisheries Management Framework (15 April 2011) (copy on file with the authors).

[35] Byers, n 23, 11–12.

[36] A gap of about 875 metres was left in the delimitation line according to Byers, n 23, 14.

[37] Byers, n 23, 13–14.

[38] Government of Canada, 'Canada and Denmark Issue Statement on Hans Island', *News Release No 165* (19 September 2005).

[39] Denmark, Greenland, and the Faroe Islands, *Kingdom of Denmark Strategy for the Arctic 2011–2020* (2011) 54–5, available at <http://www.arctic-council.org/index.php/en/document-archive/category/12-arctic-strategies?download=133:denmarks-strategy-for-the-arctic-in-english>.

[40] Government of Canada, *Statement on Canada's Arctic Foreign Policy: Exercising Sovereignty and Promoting Canada's Northern Strategy Abroad* (2010) 8–9, available at <http://www.international.gc.ca/arctic-arctique/assets/pdfs/canada_arctic_foreign_policy-eng.pdf>.

A further sovereignty-related Arctic issue is the exercise of sovereign rights by Norway in waters off the Svalbard Archipelago located between Greenland (Denmark) and Franz Josef Land (Russian Federation).[41] The 1920 Treaty of Spitsbergen, recognized the sovereignty of Norway over the Archipelago but subjected that sovereignty to various limitations. For example, Article 2 of the Treaty, which applies to territorial waters, confirmed the right of equal access by all ships and nationals of Contracting Parties to fishing and hunting and the right of Norway to impose non-discriminatory conservation measures for marine living resources. The main point of controversy has been whether the non-discriminatory access for Contracting Parties is applicable to maritime zones beyond the territorial sea. Norway's position is that the application of the Treaty ends at the territorial sea and that Norway is entitled to full EEZ and continental shelf rights as recognized under the law of the sea.[42] Other States maintain the Spitsbergen Treaty applies to all maritime zones and places restrictions on Norway's sovereign rights.[43] While Norway has established a 200 nm fisheries protection zone (FPZ) and a continental shelf off Svalbard,[44] Norway has somewhat defused the controversy by allowing fishing access to various states within the FPZ, largely based on their historical fishing in the area.[45]

3.1.2 *Extended continental shelves*

All five coastal States assert entitlements to continental shelves in the Arctic Ocean extending beyond 200 nm, but only Norway has completed the submission process to the Commission on the Limits of the Continental Shelf (CLCS).[46] Norway submitted information on the outer limits of its continental shelf to the CLCS on 27 November 2006 and the Commission issued its recommendations on 27 March 2009.[47] The Russian Federation made its initial submission to the Commission on 20 December 2001, which included a claim up to the North Pole in the central Arctic Ocean (CAO), but the Commission, in 2002, stated it was unable to make a firm determination on the basis of the information provided and a revised submission was recommended.[48] While Denmark has filed submissions for extended

---

[41] See eg DH Anderson, 'The Status under International Law of the Maritime Area around Svalbard' (2009) 40 *Ocean Development & International Law* 373; and T Pedersen and T Henriksen, 'Svalbard's Maritime Zones: The End of Legal Uncertainty?' (2009) 24 *International Journal of Marine and Coastal Law* 141.

[42] EJ Molenaar, 'Fisheries Regulation in the Maritime Zones of Svalbard' (2012) 27 *International Journal of Marine and Coastal Law* 3, 13–17.

[43] Ibid, 17–21.   [44] Ibid, 7.   [45] Ibid, 54.

[46] For a comprehensive review of the claims, see Byers, n 23, 92–127.

[47] Norway, Executive Summary of Submission, 27 November 2006. Submissions to and recommendations of the CLCS are available on the CLCS website, at <http://www.un.org/Depts/los/clcs_new/commission_submissions.htm>.

[48] Russian Federation, Executive Summary of Submission, 20 December 2001, available on the CLCS website, n 47.

shelf areas off Southern Greenland (14 June 2012) and Northeast Greenland (26 November 2013),[49] Denmark on behalf of Greenland has yet to submit data for the area to the northwest of Greenland, with a submission expected in December 2014.[50] Canada made a partial submission to the CLCS on 6 December 2013 for areas of the Atlantic Ocean,[51] but only provided preliminary information concerning its continental shelf in the Arctic Ocean.[52] The United States, while gathering the necessary technical data to substantiate its entitlement to an extended shelf, is not a Party to the LOSC and thus is presently not able to validate its outer limits through the CLCS process.[53]

While the media has often portrayed Arctic coastal States as engaged in a 'mad scramble' to assert extended shelf claims, there has in fact been considerable cooperation at both the regional and bilateral levels. For example, the five littoral States to the Arctic Ocean (the Arctic Five) have met on a periodic basis since 2008 to discuss continental shelf issues among others. The Ilulissat Declaration, issued on 28 May 2008, emphasized that the law of the sea provides the legal framework for delineating the outer limits of the continental shelf and that the five States remain committed to the orderly settlement of any possible overlapping claims.[54] Canada and the United States have conducted joint surveys of the extended continental shelf in the Western Arctic,[55] while Canada and Denmark/Greenland have cooperated in joint expeditions to study the Lomonosov and Alpha Ridges.[56]

Various possible overlapping claims loom on the horizon after the Arctic coastal States have determined the outer limits of their continental shelves beyond 200 nm. Such claims may include Canada and the United States in the Beaufort Sea; Canada and Denmark/Greenland and Russia in the Arctic Basin; and Norway (Svalbard) and Denmark/Greenland.[57]

What areas of the deep seabed will remain beyond national jurisdiction remains to be seen. A prevalent view among authors is that once the outer continental shelves

---

[49] Denmark, Executive Summary of Submission, 14 June 2012 (Southern Greenland) and 26 November 2013 (Northeast Greenland), available on the CLCS website, n 47.

[50] VanderZwaag et al, n 20.

[51] Canada, Executive Summary of Submission, 6 December 2013, available on the CLCS website, n 47.

[52] Canada, 'Preliminary Information concerning the outer limits of the continental shelf of Canada in the Arctic Ocean', available at <http://www.un.org/Depts/los/clcs_new/submissions_files/preliminary/can_pi_en.pdf>.

[53] R Macnab, 'Nationalizing the Arctic Maritime Commons: UNCLOS Article 76 and the Polar Sea' (2010) 2 *Yearbook of Polar Law* 171, 181.

[54] Ilulissat Declaration (28 May 2008) 1, available at <http://www.oceanlaw.org/downloads/arctic/Ilulissat_Declaration.pdf>.

[55] See Foreign Affairs, Trade and Development Canada, 'Third Canada–US Joint Continental Survey to Showcase Scientific Cooperation in the Arctic', News Release No 238 (26 July 2010).

[56] *Kingdom of Denmark Strategy*, n 39, 15.

[57] See TL McDorman, 'The International Legal Regime of Continental Shelf with Special Reference to the Polar Regions' in N Loukacheva (ed), *Polar Law Textbook II* (Nordic Council of Ministers Copenhagen 2013) 77, 89–90.

of the five Arctic coastal States are partitioned, only two relatively small areas will lie beyond national jurisdiction.[58]

3.1.3 *Jurisdictional tensions*

Jurisdictional tensions in the Arctic have revolved around three main issues. The first concerns the validity of internal waters status claimed by Canada within its Arctic Archipelago and by the Russian Federation over parts of the Northern Sea Route. Canada's drawing of straight baselines, effective on 1 January 1986, around the Arctic Archipelago, which clarified Canada's claim to historic internal waters, has been subject to protests by the United States and the European Community (now Union).[59] The United States also contests Russia's claim to internal waters status of the Vil'kitskii, Shokal'skii, Dmitrii Laptev, and Sannikov Straits and the drawing of straight baselines around associated island groups.[60]

A second key issue is whether Russia's Arctic straits and the Northwest Passage are straits used for international navigation.[61] The legal status of the Northwest Passage has been a particular irritant in Canada–United States relations, with the United States continuing to insist that the Passage is an international strait subject to transit passage rights of foreign ships.[62] A key point of controversy is over the functional criterion of international use, and whether actual or potential use is required.[63]

Canada and the United States have managed to quell the dispute through a 1988 Agreement on Arctic Cooperation. Through the Agreement, the United States pledged that future navigation by United States icebreakers within waters claimed by Canada as internal would be undertaken with the consent of Canada and the Parties agreed to disagree over their legal positions in relation to the Northwest Passage.[64]

A third issue concerns the application and interpretation of Article 234 of the LOSC, the provision that bestows special legislative and enforcement jurisdiction on coastal States bordering waters which are ice-covered for most of the year. Key questions surrounding the Article include: what does ice-covered water for most of the year mean? What are the implications of the express applicability to the EEZ? And does the Article apply to international straits?[65] Whether an Arctic coastal

---

[58] See Byers, n 23, 127.   [59] Ibid, 131–9.

[60] Ibid, 144; and S Lalonde and F Lasserre, 'The Position of the United States in the Northwest Passage: Is The Fear of Creating a Precedent Warranted?' (2013) 44 *Ocean Development and International Law* 28, 38–40.

[61] Byers, n 23, 133–7 and 143–6.   [62] See Chapter 6 in this volume.

[63] See DL VanderZwaag, 'Canada and the Governance of the Northwest Passage: Rough Waters, Cooperative Currents, Sea of Challenges' in DD Caron and N Oral (eds), *Navigating Straits: Challenges for International Law* (Brill Nijhoff Leiden/Boston 2013) 87, 101.

[64] See McDorman, n 27, 248–51.

[65] For discussions, see S Lalonde, 'The Arctic Exception and the IMO's PSSA Mechanism: Assessing their Value as Sources of Protection for the Northwest Passage' (2013) 28 *International Journal of*

State may depend on Article 234 to justify mandatory vessel reporting and routeing measures without working through IMO is a further area of tension as Article 234 is focused on the control of marine pollution in ice-covered waters.[66]

3.1.4 *Regional cooperation*

In addition to the 1973 Agreement on the Conservation of Polar Bears,[67] regional cooperation in the Arctic has followed two main avenues. The Arctic Council might be described as the mainstream for cooperation as the Council has served as the central forum for encouraging cooperation in scientific assessments and fostering political discussions.[68] The Arctic Five may be considered a secondary stream as the five littoral States of the central Arctic Ocean have chosen to meet on occasion separately from the Arctic Council to address issues of special concern such as potential for commercial fisheries in the CAO.[69]

3.1.4.1 *The Arctic Council*

The Arctic Council, established pursuant to a non-legally binding declaration in September 1996,[70] has been the main entity for addressing regional issues in the Arctic. The Council has eight Member States (Canada, Denmark/Greenland, Finland, Iceland, Norway, the Russian Federation, Sweden, and the United States); six indigenous organizations as Permanent Participants;[71] and various observers, including 12 non-Arctic States.[72] The Council meets at the ministerial level biennially with the chairing role rotating among the eight Arctic States. The Council has been given a broad mandate to promote cooperation on common Arctic issues

---

Marine and Coastal Law 401; and R D Brubaker, 'The Arctic-Navigational Issues under International Law of the Sea' (2010) 2 *Yearbook of Polar Law* 7, 15–17 and 27–8.

[66] For a discussion of the tussle within the IMO over Canada's reliance on Article 234 to justify its unilateral imposition of a mandatory vessel reporting system, the Northern Canada Vessel Traffic Services Zone (NORDREG) applicable to Arctic waters, see K Bartenstein, 'Navigating the Arctic: The Canadian NORDREG, The International Polar Code and Regional Cooperation' (2011) 54 *German Yearbook of International Law* 77.

[67] For a review of the Convention and other agreements relevant to marine mammal conservation in the Arctic, see N Bankes, 'The Conservation and Utilization of Marine Mammals in the Arctic Region' in Molenaar et al (eds), n 17, 293.

[68] For an overview see T Koivuarova and DL VanderZwaag, 'The Arctic Council at 10 Years: Retrospect and Prospects' (2007) 40 *University of British Columbia Law Review* 121.

[69] For a review of the resultant political tensions, see T Pedersen, 'Debates over the Role of the Arctic Council' (2012) 43 *Ocean Development and International Law* 146.

[70] Joint Communiqué and Declaration on the Establishment of the Arctic Council (19 September 1996) 35 ILM 1382 (hereinafter Declaration on the Arctic Council).

[71] They include the Arctic Athabaskan Council, Aleut International Association, Gwich'in Council, Inuit Circumpolar Council, Russian Association of Indigenous Peoples of the North, and the Saami Council.

[72] Those States are France, Germany, the Netherlands, Poland, Spain, United Kingdom, China, Italy, Japan, Republic of Korea, Singapore, and India. The latter six were admitted as observers in 2013.

including issues of sustainable development and environmental protection, but security matters are excluded from the Council's agenda.[73]

By and large, the Arctic Council has been a forum for study and discussion, with each of its six working groups undertaking numerous assessments and issuing corresponding reports.[74] The working groups include the Arctic Monitoring and Assessment Programme (AMAP); the Arctic Contaminants Action Program; Conservation of Arctic Flora and Fauna (CAFF); Emergency Prevention, Preparedness, and Response; Protection of the Arctic Marine Environment (PAME); and the Sustainable Development Working Group.[75]

However, in recent years, the Arctic Council has transitioned towards policy-shaping and even law-making roles.[76] A key turning point was the Council's *Arctic Marine Shipping Assessment* (AMSA) report published in 2009[77] under the auspices of PAME, which made 17 recommendations for strengthening governance arrangements and measures for Arctic shipping. Recommendations included the need to consider developing an Arctic Search and Rescue instrument and to further develop circumpolar environmental response capabilities possibly through a further agreement or agreements.[78] Subsequently, the Council appointed task forces to negotiate new regional agreements with the Agreement on Cooperation on Aeronautical and Maritime Search and Rescue adopted on 12 May 2011 and the Agreement on Cooperation on Marine Oil Pollution Preparedness and Response in the Arctic concluded on 15 May 2013. While negotiated under Council auspices, the agreements are independent of the Council. The AMSA report and its recommendations continue to be monitored and their implementation subject to periodic reports.[79]

At the eighth Ministerial meeting in May 2013, Ministers decided to establish four other task forces with three promising to be particularly policy relevant.[80] A Task Force on Black Carbon and Methane is mandated to suggest actions to achieve enhanced black carbon and methane emission reductions in the Arctic. A Task Force on Arctic Marine Oil Prevention is required to develop an Arctic

---

[73] Declaration on the Arctic Council, n 70, [1] and [1] n 1.

[74] For a partial review, see DL VanderZwaag, 'The Arctic Council at 15 Years: Edging Forward in a Sea of Governance Challenges' (2012) 54 *German Yearbook of International Law* 281.

[75] Working group publications can be found at Arctic Council, Document Archive, available at <http://www.arctic-council.org/index.php/en/document-archive>.

[76] On the transition, see EJ Molenaar, 'Current and Prospective Roles of the Arctic Council System within the Context of the Law of the Sea' (2012) 27 *International Journal of Marine and Coastal Law* 553.

[77] Arctic Council, *Arctic Marine Shipping Assessment 2009 Report* (2009), available at <http://www.arctic.noaa.gov/detect/documents/AMSA_2009_Report_2nd_print.pdf>.

[78] Ibid, 7 (Recommendation I.E) and 8 (Recommendation III.C).

[79] AMSA progress reports are available for 2013 and 2011 at <http://pame.is/index.php/projects/arctic-marine-shipping/amsa>.

[80] A Task Force to Facilitate the Circumpolar Business Forum was tasked with paving the way for the Arctic Economic Council to foster business development in the Arctic. See 'Arctic Economic Council', available at <http://www.arctic-council.org/index.php/en/about-us/working-groups/aec>.

Council action plan or other arrangement on oil pollution prevention. A Scientific Cooperation Task Force is to work towards an arrangement on improved scientific research cooperation among the eight Arctic States. Reports from the three task forces are to be submitted to the 2015 Ministerial meeting.[81]

The Arctic Council has also been substantially strengthened on the administrative front. A permanent Council secretariat has been established in Tromsø, Norway, and cost-sharing rules for financing the secretariat have been agreed to.[82] An Arctic Observer Manual and updated Rules of Procedure were adopted in May 2013.[83]

3.1.5 *The Arctic Five*

The Arctic Five have on occasion met independently of the Arctic Council, beginning in May 2008 when they adopted the Ililussat Declaration. The Declaration emphasized that the law of the sea provides an appropriate governance framework for the Arctic Ocean and that a new comprehensive international legal regime is not necessary.[84]

A key topic receiving subsequent priority is the possible need to develop interim measures to prevent unregulated commercial fishing in the CAO. Meetings among government officials to discuss potential fisheries in the CAO occurred in Oslo, Norway, in 2010 and Washington, DC, in the spring of 2013, while scientific meetings took place in Anchorage in 2011 and Tromsø, Norway, in October 2013.[85]

The latest policy oriented meeting was held in Nuuk, Greenland, in 24–26 February 2014 where officials agreed on various matters. They decided to continue promoting scientific research on the living marine resources of the Arctic Ocean; to promote cooperation in relevant scientific bodies including the International Council for the Exploration of the Sea (ICES) and the North Pacific Marine Science Organization (PICES); and to hold a third scientific meeting no later than the end of 2015.[86] The meeting reaffirmed that, based on available scientific information, commercial fishing in the high seas of the CAO is unlikely to occur in the near future. Officials also reaffirmed that there is no need at present to develop any additional regional fisheries management organization (RFMO) or arrangement

---

[81] See Arctic Council, 'Task Forces of the Arctic Council', available at <http://www.arctic-council.org/index.php/en/about-us/working-groups/task-forces>.

[82] See *Terms of Reference of the Arctic Council Secretariat DMMO2* (Stockholm 15 May 2012). Norway is to contribute 42.5 per cent of the administrative budget with the balance to be shared equally by all Arctic States.

[83] Available at <http://www.arctic-council.org/index.php/en/document-archive/category/425-main-documents-from-kiruna-ministerial-meeting>.

[84] Ililussat Declaration, n 54, 1–2.

[85] A Håkon Hoel, 'Fish, fisheries and fisheries management in the Arctic Ocean', *Barents Observer* (11 March 2014).

[86] Chairman's Statement, Meeting on Arctic Fisheries (Nuuk Greenland 24–26 February 2014) (copy on file with the authors).

for the area. The meeting agreed on the desirability of developing appropriate interim measures to deter unregulated fishing in the future with application to the high seas parts of the CAO surrounded by waters of the five littoral States. Officials agreed States participating in the interim measures would: authorize their vessels to conduct commercial fishing in the high seas area only pursuant to one or more regional or sub-regional fisheries management organizations or arrangements; establish a joint program of scientific research; coordinate monitoring, control, and surveillance in the area; and encourage other States to take measures for vessels entitled to fly their flags consistent with the interim measures.

The February 2014 meeting also agreed to ways forward.[87] The appropriateness of the Arctic Five taking the lead in developing interim measures was recognized. The meeting agreed to develop a Ministerial Declaration for signature or adoption by the five States. The meeting also recognized the need to engage Arctic residents, particularly indigenous peoples, in moving interim measures ahead and looked forward to a broader process involving additional States. A final outcome could be a binding international agreement. The meeting suggested the possibility of issuing the Declaration in June 2014, but subsequent tensions with the Russian Federation over the annexation of Crimea and events in the Eastern Ukraine have delayed the process.

3.2 Regional developments: the Antarctic

3.2.1 *Applying the LOSC to the Antarctic: political and geographical challenges*

In contrast to the Arctic, disputes over territorial sovereignty in the Antarctic are profound. Seven States maintain claims to the continent of Antarctica, and assert jurisdiction over an associated territorial sea and continental shelf.[88] France and Australia have proclaimed an EEZ off their Antarctic territories,[89] and both Chile and Argentina confirmed in the 1940s and 1960s, respectively, that their maritime claims extend seaward to a limit of 200 nm as measured from the coast.[90] However, neither the terrestrial nor the maritime claims are generally recognized by the international community,[91] and the compromise brokered in Article IV of the 1959

---

[87] Ibid.

[88] Argentina, Australia, Chile, France, New Zealand, Norway, and the United Kingdom.

[89] France claimed an EEZ in 1973 and Australia in 1994. See P Vigni, 'Antarctic Maritime Claims: "Frozen Sovereignty" and the Law of the Sea' in AG Oude Elferink and ER Rothwell (eds), *The Law of the Sea and Polar Maritime Delimitation and Jurisdiction* (Martinus Nijoff The Hague 2001) 85, 104.

[90] PW Quigg, *A Pole Apart: The Emerging Issue of Antarctica* (New Press New York 1983), 173.

[91] Only Australia, France, New Zealand, Norway, and the United Kingdom mutually recognize one another's claims.

Antarctic Treaty, whereby parties agree to disagree over the status of the claims, has set aside rather than resolved the sovereignty dispute. Consequently, the status of the seabed and water column surrounding Antarctica is uncertain.

In practical terms, this has led to a rather mixed implementation of LOSC rights and obligations in the Antarctic. On the one hand, the practical exercise of coastal and port State jurisdiction in Antarctic waters is minimal. This was recently demonstrated by Australia's response to Japanese so-called scientific whaling taking place within what Australia regards as its waters off the coast of the Australian Antarctic Territory. Rather than challenging the whalers under domestic legislation,[92] Australia instead alleged, and in 2014 was successful in proving, that Japan had breached its international obligations under the 1946 International Convention on the Regulation of Whaling by failing to comply with the terms of Article VIII of the Convention.[93]

On the other hand, all seven claimant States have engaged in the process for the delimitation of the outer limits of the continental shelf as provided for under Article 76(8) of the LOSC. Australia, Norway, and Argentina have all provided information on the proposed outer limits of the Antarctic continental shelf to the CLCS.[94] The Commission is however, precluded from examining the Antarctic portion of those claims under its Rules of Procedure, which require the consent of all interested parties to consider any submission subject to a terrestrial or maritime dispute.[95] France,[96] New Zealand,[97] and the United Kingdom[98] have all made partial submissions to the Commission, and have issued clear reservations in respect of

---

[92] Whale sanctuaries in Australian waters are provided for under the Environment Protection and Biodiversity Conservation Act (Aust) 1999. In 2008 an Australian NGO successfully obtained an injunction against Japanese whalers under this Act, but this injunction was never enforced. See *Humane Society International v Kyodo Senpaku Kaisha Ltd* [2004] FCA 15110; [2005] FCA 664; [2006] FCAFC 116; [2008] FCA 3. For a general discussion of this dispute see the special issue of the 11(3) & (4) (2008) *Asia Pacific Journal of Environmental Law*.

[93] *Whaling in the Antarctic (Australia v Japan; New Zealand Intervening)*, Judgment of the International Court of Justice (31 March 2014).

[94] Australia's submission was made in 2004 and the submissions made by Norway and Argentina were finalized in 2009. Information on all submissions to the Commission can be found at the CLCS website, n 47.

[95] CLCS/40/Rev.1, *Rules of Procedure* (17 April 2008) Annex 1, [5]. The Australian and Norwegian submissions in any case requested that the CLCS refrain from considering the Antarctic portion of their claims and Argentina made a similar request during the presentation of its submission.

[96] For its reservation in respect of its Antarctic territories, see Permanent Mission of France to the United Nations, Note No 69 (February 2009), available at <http://www.un.org/depts/los/clcs_new/submissions_files/fra09/fra_note_feb2009e.pdf>.

[97] For its reservation in respect of its Antarctic territories, see New Zealand Permanent Mission to the United Nations, Note No NZ-CLCS-TPN-02 (19 April 2006), available at <http://www.un.org/depts/los/clcs_new/submissions_files/nzl06/nzl_doc_es_attachment.pdf>.

[98] For its reservation in respect of its Antarctic territories, see United Kingdom Mission to the United Nations, Note No 168/08 (9 May 2008), available at <http://www.un.org/depts/los/clcs_new/submissions_files/gbr08/gbr_nv_9may2008.pdf>.

the Antarctic continental shelf with a view to making a final submission to the Commission at a later, as yet undetermined, date. Chile has submitted preliminary information to the Commission and has yet to decide whether to make a full submission to the CLCS or enter a reservation in respect of the Antarctic portion of its claim.[99] The response of the international community to these submissions has been relatively muted,[100] in part because this approach had been informally agreed to by all claimant States and other States party to the 1959 Antarctic Treaty.[101]

More generally, the relationship between the LOSC and the 1959 Antarctic Treaty is equivocal. Article 311(2) of the LOSC preserves the rights and obligations of parties that arise under other agreements provided that those rights and obligations do not affect rights provided for under the Convention. Furthermore, the LOSC also permits States to conclude agreements modifying its operation provided that such modification is not incompatible with the object and purpose of the Convention.[102] The specific obligations developed under the 1959 Antarctic Treaty and the 1991 Environmental Protocol designed to provide for a higher level of environmental protection or to manage scientific research within the Antarctic Treaty area (ATA) would likely be considered compatible with the objects and purposes of the LOSC.

However, it is open to question whether the total ban on minerals activities within the ATA under Article 7 of the 1991 Environmental Protocol can be considered consistent with the object and purpose of Part XI of the LOSC. Further, it should be noted that Article 311(6) of the Convention stipulates that 'States Parties agree that there shall be no amendments to the basic principle relating to the common heritage of mankind set forth in article 136 and that they shall not be party to any agreement in derogation thereof'. Part XI of the LOSC designates the Area—the seabed, ocean floor, and subsoil beyond national jurisdiction[103]—as the common heritage of mankind[104] and establishes a complex regime within which minerals exploitation is permitted subject to environmental controls and on the basis of principles designed to share the benefits of deep-sea mining among all members of the international community.[105] To the extent that the seabed surrounding the continent of Antarctica is not subject to national jurisdiction—a hypothesis accepted by the overwhelming majority of the international community—does it constitute

---

[99] Chile, Preliminary Information Indicative of the outer limits of the Continental Shelf and description of the status of preparation and intended date of making of a submission to the Commission on the Limits of the Continental Shelf, available at <http://www.un.org/Depts/los/clcs_new/submissions_files/preliminary/chl2009preliminaryinformation.pdf>. Preliminary submissions may be made pursuant to Decision SPLOS/183 (2008).

[100] Formal responses filed with the CLCS are made publically available at CLCS website, n 47.

[101] AG Oude Elferink, 'The Outer Limits of the Continental Shelf in the Polar Regions' in Molenaar et al (eds), n 17, 61 and 69.

[102] LOSC, n 5, Art 311(3).   [103] Ibid, Art 1(1).   [104] Ibid, Art 136.

[105] Ibid, Part XI. The 1994 Agreement on the Implementation of Part XI of the Convention has the effect of significantly amending the original provisions in Part XI of the LOSC. For further discussion, see Chapter 11 in this volume.

the Area for the purposes of LOSC? Alternatively, can the 1959 Antarctic Treaty be characterized as having established a *sui generis* regime in respect of the seabed within the ATA? It has been suggested that there was a 'tacit understanding' that Part XI of the LOSC was not intended to apply to the ATA,[106] but it seems improbable that the international community would be willing to relinquish its interest in Antarctic minerals to the seven claimant States or even to the 50 States party to the Antarctic Treaty.[107] While the physical and economic challenges of mining in the Antarctic have largely alleviated any political pressure to reconcile the relationship between the LOSC and the Antarctic Treaty for the time being, this may change should the parties to the LOSC adopt an agreement designed to manage activities, including bioprospecting, located in areas beyond national jurisdiction (ABNJ).[108]

3.2.2 *The Antarctic Treaty system and the law of the sea*

While the Antarctic Treaty system (ATS) does not constitute an archetypal regional seas regime, it nevertheless comprises many of the principles, concepts and institutions that typically provide the foundation of regional oceans management elsewhere. Moreover, the ATS provides the framework for discrete but concomitant instruments focusing on a range of maritime activities including minerals exploitation, coastal infrastructure (such as scientific bases), scientific research, tourism, and the management of fisheries and marine mammals. In theory, the ATS affords an exemplary framework for integrated oceans management in the Antarctic. In practice, however, the sovereignty dispute, which underpins the delicate compromise reached in Article IV of the Antarctic Treaty, continues to undermine efforts for fully integrated cooperation within the region.

Article VI of the Antarctic Treaty applies its provisions to the area south of 60° South Latitude including all ice shelves but stipulates that 'nothing in the present Treaty shall prejudice or in any way affect the rights, or the exercise of the rights, of any State under international law with regard to the high seas within that area'. The 1991 Protocol on Environmental Protection to the Antarctic Treaty similarly applies to the ATA although the overall objective of the Protocol comprises the 'comprehensive protection of the Antarctic environment and *dependent and associated ecosystems*...'.[109] Much debate has surrounded whether the Protocol intended to

---

[106] J Crawford and DR Rothwell, 'Legal Issues Confronting Australia's Antarctica' 13 (1990–1991) *Australian Yearbook of International Law* 53, 86 (citing Gillian Triggs).

[107] Nevertheless, potential preferential access to Antarctic minerals appears to have provided an incentive in respect of recent accessions (such as Malaysia and Pakistan) and for increased activity on the ice and within the Antarctic Treaty forum by existing members such as China and Russia.

[108] The UN Working Group on Marine Biodiversity Beyond National Jurisdiction is currently tasked with exploring prospects for a regulatory regime of application to ABNJ for the purposes of environmental protection and regulating access to genetic resources. Reports of the Working Group can be found at <http://www.un.org/Depts/los/biodiversityworkinggroup/biodiversityworkinggroup.htm>.

[109] Protocol on Environmental Protection to the Antarctic Treaty, Art 2 (emphasis added) (hereinafter Environmental Protocol).

extend the scope of its substantive obligations beyond 60° South Latitude but the practice of States thus far has been to confine initiatives directed at the protection of the Antarctic environment to the ATA.[110] By contrast, the scope of the 1980 Convention on the Conservation of Antarctic Marine Living Resources (CAMLR Convention) extends to the Antarctic Convergence, which lies between 45° and 50°S and, consequently, encompasses the entire Antarctic ecosystem.[111] Notwithstanding the reservation in respect of high seas freedoms provided for in Article VI of the Antarctic Treaty, the members of the ATS have, over the last 60 years, adopted a range of measures that impact on their rights of navigation, scientific research, and fishing within the region as well as their obligation to protect the Antarctic from environmental harm.

The earliest restriction on high seas freedoms can be found in Article I of the Antarctic Treaty, which prohibits, *inter alia*, the carrying out of military manoeuvres and the testing of any type of weapon within the ATA. Provided such activities do not constitute a threat to other States or to the peaceful uses of the seas[112] and are not otherwise prohibited by international law, military manoeuvres and weapons testing are not generally considered incompatible with the law of the sea.[113] The more stringent controls under the Antarctic Treaty were undoubtedly designed to reflect sensitivities associated with the sovereignty disputes within the region. Of a similarly innovative nature are the controls developed in connection with the carrying out of scientific research in the Antarctic.[114] Long before scientific research was specifically identified as a high seas freedom,[115] the freedom of scientific investigation in Antarctica was guaranteed by Article II of the Antarctic Treaty. Under the Antarctic Treaty, State parties have committed to cooperate and share information relating to scientific research activities,[116] foreshadowing, but extending beyond, the principles set out in Part XIII of the LOSC.[117]

Today, States party to the Antarctic Treaty and its associated instruments are obliged to take steps to protect the marine environment and to conserve biological resources within the region and it is these obligations that have had arguably the greatest impact on the evolution of the law of the sea in the Antarctic.

Building on Article V of the Antarctic Treaty, which constitutes the earliest initiative to create a region free from nuclear testing and the disposal of nuclear waste, the

---

[110] But see Resolution 1, *Enhancement of Environmental Protection up to the Antarctic Convergence* (17 April 2009). See also the discussion *infra*.

[111] 1980 Convention on the Conservation of Antarctic Marine Living Resources, Art I (hereinafter CAMLR Convention)

[112] LOSC, n 5, Art 301.   [113] See further Chapter 38 in this volume.

[114] See generally KN Scott, 'Scientific rhetoric and Antarctic security' in AD Hemmings, DR Rothwell, and KN Scott (eds), *Antarctic Security in the Twenty-first Century. Legal and policy perspectives* (Routledge Oxon/New York 2012) 284.

[115] The freedom of scientific research alongside the freedom to construct artificial islands and other installations was officially so-designated in LOSC, n 5, Art 87(1) and added to the list of existing high seas freedoms (navigation, overflight, fishing, and the laying of submarine cables and pipelines).

[116] 1959 Antarctic Treaty, Arts III and VII.   [117] See Chapter 25 in this volume.

parties to the Antarctic Treaty have adopted a range of obligations designed to ensure the protection of the Antarctic environment. For example, all activities other than fishing in the Antarctic Treaty area, including tourism and scientific research, likely to have at least a minor or transitory impact on the environment are subject to the environmental impact assessment (EIA) requirements under Article 8 and Annex I of the 1991 Environmental Protocol. In contrast to Article 206 of the 1982 LOSC, the EIA requirements under the Protocol are relatively comprehensive and, in the case of a Comprehensive Environmental Evaluation—required where the impact on the environment is likely to be more than minor or transitory—subject to a degree of oversight from an international body: the Antarctic Treaty Consultative Meeting (ATCM). More generally, all activities within the ATA must be conducted so as to minimize their detrimental impacts on water quality and the abundance of species under Article 3 of the Protocol. Furthermore, the taking or interference with species not regulated by the 1980 CAMLR Convention, the 1946 International Convention for the Regulation of Whaling (ICRW), and the 1972 Convention for the Conservation of Antarctic Seals (CCAS) is subject to the permitting requirements set out in Annex II of the Protocol. The need to provide special protection of vulnerable ecosystems, highlighted in Article 194(5) of the LOSC, provides the policy parameters of Annex V of the Protocol, which permits the creation of Antarctic specially protected areas (ASPAs) and Antarctic specially managed areas (ASMAs) in order to protect environmental, scientific, historic, aesthetic, or wilderness values.[118] Nevertheless, in common with other regions, protected areas within the marine as opposed to the terrestrial environment are under-represented.[119]

Notwithstanding that shipping is largely regulated at the global level, albeit, as discussed above, with consideration of the special conditions of the Antarctic,[120] the parties to the Antarctic Treaty have been responsible for a number of shipping-focused initiatives, with a particular emphasis on tourist vessels. For example, in 2004, the parties to the Antarctic Treaty adopted and adapted the IMO guidelines for ships operating in the Arctic and recommended that those guidelines be applied to ships operating in the Antarctic.[121] An adapted version of these guidelines—of application to both Poles—was subsequently adopted by the IMO in 2009[122] and a mandatory version is currently under negotiation.[123] In 2005, the ATCM requested that the IMO

---

[118] 1991 Environmental Protocol, n 109, Annex V, Art 2.

[119] To date only five of the 73 ASPAs established so far constitute MPAs although a further five ASPAs comprise a substantial marine component. There is no ASPA of sole application to the marine environment thus far although three of the seven ASMAs include a substantial marine component. Information on protected areas in the Antarctic can be found on the Antarctic Protected Areas Database, available at <http://www.ats.aq/devPH/apa/ep_protected.aspx?lang=e>.

[120] For example, the Antarctic Treaty area is designated a special area for the purposes of 1973 International Convention for the Prevention of Pollution, as modified by the Protocol of 1978, Annexes I, II, and V (hereinafter MARPOL).

[121] ATCM Decision 4, *Guidelines for Ships Operating in Arctic and Antarctic Waters* (2004).

[122] IMO Assembly Res A.1024(26), *Guidelines for Ships Operating in Polar Waters* (2 December 2009).

[123] See the discussion in Section 2 above.

restrict the use of heavy fuel oil by ships operating in the Antarctic[124] and binding international regulations were adopted in 2010.[125] Concern over the introduction of invasive species, particularly in light of the vulnerability of the both the Arctic and Antarctic to climate change, led the ATCM to adopt restrictions on ballast water exchange within the ATA in 2006,[126] prompting the IMO to follow suit in 2007.[127] Finally, and unsurprisingly in light of a series of high profile accidents involving tourist and other vessels in the region, the ATCM has adopted a number of recent resolutions designed to improve search and rescue (SAR) in the region. These initiatives principally focus on information exchange with respect to SAR assets in the Antarctic[128] as well as encouraging tourist vessels to regularly report their positions to relevant Maritime Rescue Coordination Centres (MRCCs).[129] An effort has also been made to develop equipment and operational guidelines in respect of vessels that are excluded from the parameters of global regulation such as yachts[130] and fishing vessels.[131]

The principal challenge to the creation of a regional seas regime in the Antarctic is the implementation and enforcement of regional regulation with respect to vessels registered to States not party to the Antarctic Treaty. The ATCM has attempted to circumvent the limits inherent in any regional regime through effective cooperation with the IMO and the adoption of specialist rules for the Antarctic at the global level.[132] While this strategy has undoubtedly proven successful, it nevertheless also risks opening up the debate on initiatives to a broader range of actors with very different political agendas. This potential to weaken or undermine Antarctic shipping-related proposals has been demonstrated recently by the slow and controversial progress of the Polar Code within the IMO. Moreover, the geographical and political peculiarities of the Antarctic create distinct challenges with respect to the enforcement of both global and regional shipping regulation. Ships operating within the Antarctic are subject to exclusive flag State control[133] and, as noted above, port

---

[124] ATCM Decision 8, *Use of Heavy Fuel* (2008).

[125] Res MEPC.189(60), *Amendments to MARPOL Annex I to add Chapter 9—Special Requirements for the Use or Carriage of Oils in the Antarctic Area* (26 March 2010).

[126] ATCM Res 3 (2006), *Ballast Water Exchange*.

[127] Res MEPC163(56), *Guidelines for Ballast Water Exchange in the Antarctic Treaty Area* (13 July 2007).

[128] ATCM Res 6, *Improving the Coordination of maritime search and rescue in the Antarctic Treaty area* (2010); ATCM Resolution 4, *Improved Collaboration on Search and Rescue (SAR) in Antarctica* (2013).

[129] ATCM Res 6, *Maritime Rescue Coordination Centres and Search and Rescue in the Antarctic Treaty Area* (2008).

[130] ATCM Res 10, *Yachting Guidelines* (2012).

[131] See CCAMLR Res 20/XXII, *Ice-strengthening standards in high latitude fisheries* (2013); CCAMLR Res 23/XXIII, *Safety on board fishing vessels in the Convention area* (2004); and ATCM Res 7, *Vessel Safety in the Antarctic Treaty Area* (2012).

[132] This strategy has been formally endorsed by the ATCM. See ATCM Res 5, *Co-ordination Among Antarctic Treaty Parties on Antarctic Proposals under Consideration in the IMO* (2010).

[133] LOSC, n 5, Art 92.

and coastal State jurisdiction is not exercised in practice within the region. Nevertheless, the Antarctic Treaty does permit representatives of any State party to inspect all ships discharging or embarking cargoes or personnel in Antarctica.[134] However, this power does not appear to extend to the detention of vessels, nor does it create any right of enforcement against vessels. Furthermore, the exercise of port State control over passenger vessels bound for the Antarctic by so-called 'gateway' States—such as Argentina, Chile, South Africa, Australia, and New Zealand—has been endorsed by the ATCM.[135] Under the law of the sea, all States have the right and, increasingly, the obligation to inspect vessels in order to assess their compliance with global standards under the 1974 International Convention for the Safety of Life at Sea (SOLAS), MARPOL, and other IMO instruments. It is less established, however, that port States are entitled to exercise jurisdiction in respect of regional or voluntary standards. Port States are entitled to restrict access to their ports and to establish conditions of entry relating to the construction, design, equipment, and manning of vessels but it is unclear whether those standards must relate to the protection of its own environment and infrastructure or whether they may address safety and other issues in areas beyond national jurisdiction.[136]

The exploitation of marine biological resources within the Antarctic is, with the exception of cetaceans, largely regulated under the 1972 CCAS and the 1980 CAMLR Convention. As commercial sealing has not recommenced following the adoption of the CCAS, it is the CAMLR Convention that constitutes the primary instrument for the management of marine biodiversity in the Antarctic. Incorporating both a precautionary and ecosystem approach to fisheries management, the CAMLR Convention was, and to some extent remains, a pioneer in the field of marine conservation.[137] More than a typical RFMO, CCAMLR seeks to manage the catch of targeted species such as krill or toothfish as well as address issues such as bycatch, the environmental consequences of fishing, and, to a lesser extent, the safety of fishing vessels.[138] Implementation and enforcement of CCAMLR regulations remains a challenge and is exacerbated by the geographical remoteness of the region and the relative absence of port State control. As a consequence, CCAMLR has responded by developing innovative strategies such as the system of international inspection and the catch documentation scheme that applies to the toothfish fishery.[139]

---

[134] Antarctic Treaty, n 116, Art VII.

[135] ATCM Res 7, *Enhancement of Port State Control for passenger vessels bound for the Antarctic Treaty area* (2010).

[136] For further discussion of this issue, see KN Scott, 'Like an Edgar Allen Poe Bride: Safety of Shipping in the Southern Ocean' (2010) 16 *International Journal of Maritime Law* 21. See also Chapter 13 in this volume.

[137] It is beyond the scope of this chapter to provide a history and critique of CCAMLR. For a recent overview, see A Serdy, 'Antarctic Fisheries Management' in Molenaar et al (eds), n 17, 217.

[138] The CCAMLR has adopted over 100 Conservation Measures and Resolutions of application to the CCAMLR area. These are available at <http://www.ccamlr.org/en/conservation-and-management/conservation-measures>.

[139] All CCAMLR conservation measures associated with compliance are available at <http://www.ccamlr.org/en/conservation-and-management/browse-conservation-measures>.

4 POLAR FUTURES

While environmental changes and threats to the polar regions are likely to continue to influence future negotiations and processes under global multilateral environmental agreements, from the 1992 United Nations Framework Convention on Climate Change to the 2001 Stockholm Convention on POPs,[140] the final part of this chapter will highlight key issues and challenges likely to affect the development of the law of the sea at the regional level.

4.1 Future challenges in the Arctic

While three regional challenges are in the process of being addressed by Arctic Council task forces, namely, marine oil pollution prevention, black carbon and methane emissions, and scientific research cooperation, three other ocean governance challenges stand out. They are: future governance of the CAO beyond national jurisdiction; implementing the ecosystem approach; and determining future directions for the Arctic Council.

With the Arctic Five seemingly intent on pushing forward with interim measures to address potential commercial fisheries in the high seas of the CAO, a slate of related challenges have yet to be sorted out. How to engage indigenous organizations is one issue. How the initiative will relate to the Arctic Council and its possible role is a further question. The Arctic Council's *Arctic Ocean Review* (AOR) was quite vague in its recommendation on future fisheries in the CAO, stating that '[f]isheries resources in areas beyond national jurisdiction should be managed based on cooperation in accordance with international law to ensure long term sustainability for fish stocks and ecosystems.'[141] How to bring other States on board for interim measures is another issue with a range of possible ways forward, including informal conferencing, a statement of principles in a UN General Assembly sustainable fisheries resolution,[142] and a multilateral agreement. A possible longer-term governance framework for the CAO has yet to be considered, with one academic suggestion being the establishment of a regional ocean management

---

[140] The Arctic Council's AMAP Working Group is already preparing an updated report on persistent organic pollutants that will include new, emergent POPs that will be considered for inclusion under the Stockholm Convention. See *Final Report, Meeting of Senior Arctic Officials, Whitehorse, Yukon, Canada, 22–23 October 2013* (2013) 9.

[141] PAME, *Arctic Ocean Review Project, Final Report (Phase II 2011–2013), Kiruna, May 2013* (PAME Secretariat Akureyri 2013) 96 (hereinafter AOR Report).

[142] Such resolutions are adopted on an annual basis with the 2013 resolution being UNGA Res A/68/71 (2013).

organization.[143] Whether special shipping measures for the Arctic high seas should be pursued through the IMO is also open to question.[144]

Implementing the ecosystem approach in the Arctic region remains an unmet challenge with the Arctic Council's efforts to date largely aimed at sharing national experiences with ecosystem-based management,[145] further conceptualizing the ecosystem approach, and reviewing integrated ecological assessment methodologies and experiences.[146] The PAME Working Group established an Ecosystem Approach Expert Group in 2007, which has revised a map of Large Marine Ecosystems (LMEs) in the Arctic.[147] Through workshops, it has facilitated understanding on the status of ecological assessments in the region and the challenges in sharing and comparing scientific data.[148] In May 2011, Arctic Council Ministers decided to establish an Expert Group on Arctic Ecosystem-Based Management, and the Expert Group, after meeting three times, issued a report to Ministers in May 2013.[149] The report included a definition of ecosystem-based management (EBM), a set of nine principles and various recommendations suggesting follow-up actions, such as encouraging initiatives between two or more Arctic States to advance EBM implementation and instituting periodic Arctic Council reviews of EBM experiences in the Arctic.[150] The 2013 AOR report included a chapter on ecosystem-based management in the Arctic with a key recommendation also being the periodic convening of Arctic Council-wide meetings on EBM.[151]

Moving from EBM on paper to more concrete commitments and measures is likely to be incremental. Senior Arctic Officials have requested working groups to implement the EBM report's recommendations and have tasked the Arctic Council Secretariat with ensuring a joint report on follow-up activities is prepared for the 2015 Ministerial meeting.[152] The Council's 2004 *Arctic Marine Strategic Plan*, which emphasized the need for an ecosystem approach in marine management,[153] is

---

[143] See R Rayfuse, 'Protecting Marine Biodiversity in Polar Areas Beyond National Jurisdiction' (2008) 17 *Review of European Community and International Environmental Law* 3, 11.

[144] At its meeting in February 2014, the PAME Working Group invited member governments to provide their views to the next PAME meeting on whether, and if so how, protection for the high seas area of the CAO might be pursued by Arctic States at the IMO. PAME, *Record of Decisions and Follow-up Actions, PAME I—2014* (11–13 February 2014) 2.

[145] See A Håkon Hoel (ed), *Best Practices in Ecosystem-based Oceans Management in the Arctic* (Norwegian Polar Institute Tromsø Norway 2009).

[146] For a further discussion, see DL VanderZwaag, 'The Arctic Council and the Future of Arctic Ocean Governance: Edging Forward in a Sea of Challenges' in Stephens and VanderZwaag (eds), n 1, 308, 332–4.

[147] See PAME, *Large Marine Ecosystems (LMEs) in the Arctic area, Revision of the Arctic LME map* (15 May 2013).

[148] See PAME, *Third Ecosystem Approach to Management Working Report* (Reykjavik, Iceland 10–11 June 2013).

[149] Arctic Council, *Ecosystem-Based Management in the Arctic* (May 2013).   [150] Ibid, 5.

[151] AOR Report, n 141, 97.   [152] *Final Report, Senior Arctic Officials*, n 140, 6–7.

[153] Arctic Council, *Arctic Marine Strategic Plan* (2004) 8.

in the process of revision and, when finalized in 2015, can be expected to set out further directions for moving EBM forward.[154] The PAME Working Group has established an Arctic Marine Protected Areas (MPA) Network expert group, co-led by Canada, Norway and the United States, to develop a framework for a pan-Arctic MPA Network but its work has just begun.[155]

A third overall challenge that stands out for the Arctic region is determining future directions for the Arctic Council. An obvious limitation for the Council continues to be the lack of stable and secure funding for Council projects and for Permanent Participant involvement. Development of regional environmental standards has arguably lagged in relation to offshore oil and gas operations[156] and land-based marine pollution.[157] A wide range of possible strengthening measures in relation to the Council have been suggested including giving the Council a treaty-foundation,[158] holding one or more Ministerial meetings at the head of state level, restructuring the working groups and the creation of a broad reporting and monitoring system for ensuring regional guidelines and other commitments are lived up to.[159] Strengthening the Arctic Council remains on the Council's agenda. Ministers at the May 2013 meeting requested Senior Arctic Officials to develop recommendations on ways and means to strengthen the work of the Council with a report to be prepared for the 2015 Ministerial meeting.[160]

4.2 Future challenges in the Antarctic

In the Antarctic, the primary regulatory focus is likely to remain on marine environmental protection. In common with other regions, the need to integrate oceans management across a range of sectors and institutions is increasingly recognized. One important mechanism for implementing integrated and ecosystem management is the marine protected area and Antarctic institutions are in fact leading the vanguard in designating MPAs in ABNJ.[161]

---

[154] The first workshop to consider revision of the Plan included considerable discussion about EBM. See PAME, *Working Report 1st Scoping Workshop for the revision for the 2004 Arctic Marine Strategic Plan* (Reykjavik, Iceland 13–14 June 2013).

[155] *Record of Decisions*, n 144, 3.

[156] The Council has adopted *Arctic Offshore Oil and Gas Guidelines* (2009).

[157] The Council has developed a *Regional Program of Action for the Protection of the Arctic Marine Environment from Land-based Activities* (2009).

[158] See T Koivurova, 'Alternatives for an Arctic Treaty—Evaluation and a New Proposal' (2008) 17 *Review of European Community and International Environmental Law* 14.

[159] See VanderZwaag, n 146, 336–7.

[160] Arctic Council Secretariat, *Kiruna Declaration on the occasion of the Eighth Ministerial Meeting of the Arctic Council* (15 May 2013) 2.

[161] See KN Scott, 'Marine Protected Areas in the Southern Ocean' in Molenaar et al (eds), n 17, 113. In the Northern hemisphere the OSPAR Commission for the Protection of the Marine Environment of the North-East Atlantic (OSPAR Commission) is playing a lead role in establishing MPAs in ABNJ.

In 2009, CCAMLR established what has been described as the first high seas MPA around the South Orkney Islands.[162] The South Orkney Islands Southern Shelf MPA covers just less than 94,000 km^2 of the high seas within which fishing, scientific research associated with fishing and discharges and dumping from fishing vessels are strictly regulated.[163] Nine MPA planning domains were identified by the Commission in 2011[164] and a general framework measure for the designation of MPAs within the CAMLR Convention area was adopted at the same meeting.[165] The General Framework Measure sets out key criteria for the designation of MPAs including: the protection of representative ecosystems, species, and habitats; the establishment of scientific reference areas for long-term monitoring; the protection of vulnerable ecosystems; and the protection of areas to maintain resilience or the ability to adapt the effects of climate change.[166] However, minimal progress has been made since 2011 towards the establishment of a network of representative MPAs within the CAMLR Convention area and some members of the Commission have even questioned CCAMLR's mandate to designate high seas MPAs.[167] MPAs proposed by New Zealand and the United States (in the Ross Sea area) and Australia, France and the EU (in respect of Eastern Antarctica) were controversially but decisively rejected at the Thirty-First Meeting of the CCAMLR in 2012,[168] at the special meeting of the Commission dedicated to MPAs held in Bremerhaven, Germany, in July 2013,[169] and again at the Thirty-Second Meeting of the Commission in October 2013.[170] Russia and Ukraine, in particular, objected not simply to the proposed areas, but also to CCAMLR's legal mandate to designate MPAs and to the legitimacy of high seas MPAs more generally.[171] While it is beyond the scope of this chapter to discuss the legal mandate for the designation of MPAs in ABNJ,[172] it is notable that the overwhelming

---

[162] CCAMLR Conservation Measure 91-03, *Protection of the South Orkney Islands southern shelf* (2009).

[163] Ibid.

[164] *Report of the Thirtieth Meeting of the Commission for the Conservation of Antarctic Marine Living Resources* (Hobart, Australia, 24 October–4 November 2011) [4] (hereainfter CCAMLR—XXX).

[165] CCAMLR Conservation Measure 91-04, *General Framework for the establishment of CCAMLR Marine Protected Areas* (2011).

[166] Ibid, [2(i)]–[2(vi)].

[167] *Report of the Second Special Meeting of the Commission* (Bremerhaven, Germany, 15–16 July 2013) [3.18] and [3.26] (hereinafter CCAMLR— Special Meeting II).

[168] *Report of the Thirty-first Meeting of the Commission for the Conservation of Antarctic Marine Living Resources* (Hobart, Australia, 23 October–1 November 2012) [7.105]–[7.109] (hereinafter CCAMLR—XXXI).

[169] CCAMLR—Special Meeting II, n 167, [3.11].

[170] *Report of the Thirty-second Meeting of the Commission for the Conservation of Antarctic Marine Living Resources* (Hobart Australia 23 October–1 November 2013) [7.32] (hereinafter CCAMLR—XXXII).

[171] CCAMLR—Special Meeting II, n 167, [3.17]–[3.18] and [3.26].

[172] But see Chapters 21 and 33 in this volume.

majority of Commission members did not share Russia and Ukraine's reservations and, globally, the concept of the high seas MPA is gaining traction.

As noted above, the designation of MPAs under Annex V of the 1991 Environmental Protocol is also progressing at a slow rate and, while there is a clear mandate for cooperation between the Committee on Environmental Protection established under the Protocol and the CCAMLR for the protection of the marine environment,[173] collaboration to date is minimal and undoubtedly provides scope for a more integrated approach. Moreover, it might also be argued that the region would benefit from greater cooperation between the ATS and the IMO, in particular, through the designation of another form of MPA, the Particularly Sensitive Sea Area (PSSA), which is designed to manage the impacts of shipping on a vulnerable ecological region.[174] The thirteen PSSAs designated to date are all located within the jurisdiction of coastal States[175] and whether PSSAs can be established in ABNJ has been the subject of much discussion.[176] However, there appears to be no rule that precludes the location of PSSAs on the high seas and a mandate for their designation can arguably be found in several provisions of the LOSC including Articles 192 and 194. PSSAs may only be adopted in conjunction with associated protective measures[177] and it is these measures, rather than the PSSA itself, that have legal implications for the regulation of shipping. Within the Antarctic, there are already a number of measures in place—relating to vessel discharges, the carriage of heavy fuel oil, ballast water management, search and rescue, and construction, equipment, and manning requirements—that could be brought together within the coherency of a PSSA. However, the designation of a PSSA arguably has intrinsic value over and above the collective implications of the associated protective measures,[178] symbolically designating an area as worthy of special protection and requiring the exercise of caution in carrying out shipping activities.

---

[173] See 1991 Environmental Protocol, n 109, Annex V, Art 6; ATCM Decision 9, *Marine Protected Areas and Other Areas of Interest to CCAMLR* (2005); ATCM Resolution 1, *CCAMLR in the Antarctic Treaty System* (2006); and CCAMLR Conservation Measure 91-02, *Protection of the values of Antarctic Specially Managed and Protected Areas* (2012).

[174] IMO Res A.982(24), *Revised Guidelines for the Identification and Designation of Particularly Sensitive Sea Areas*, Annex, [1.2] (1 December 2005).

[175] See IMO, 'Particularly Sensitive Sea Areas', available at <http://www.imo.org/OurWork/Environment/PollutionPrevention/PSSAs/Pages/Default.aspx>.

[176] See KN Scott, n 161, 32–40.   [177] IMO Res A.982(24), n 176.

[178] Julian Roberts et al, 'The Western European PSSA Proposal: A Politically Sensitive Sea Area' (2005) 29 *Marine Policy* 431, 433.

5 Concluding Remarks

Although the presence of ice and the particular vulnerability of the Arctic and the Antarctic to environmental change have led to limited cooperation among States and within the IMO in the application and development of the law of the sea to the regions, for the most part the regions are 'Poles apart' in terms of the economic, political, and environmental challenges they face. The regional responses to these challenges reflect this. The 'agreement to disagree' over the sovereignty of Antarctica permitted States from a very early stage to develop innovative concepts and principles—in relation to military uses of the sea, scientific research, exploitation of resources, and marine environmental protection—of application to the Antarctic. The more traditional jurisdictional disputes in the Arctic have, by contrast, prompted the littoral States to develop a very different regional approach: one largely based on soft power and research and policy development. Nevertheless, the Arctic Council constitutes an innovative international institution in terms of its membership and the role played by indigenous peoples groups. Poles apart they may be, but regional developments within both the Arctic and Antarctic have undoubtedly enriched and contributed to the development of the law of the sea and are likely to continue to do so.[179]

---

[179] For a further discussion, see DR Rothwell, 'Polar Oceans Governance in the 21st Century' (2012) 26 *Ocean Yearbook* 343.

CONSERVING MARINE BIODIVERSITY IN AREAS BEYOND NATIONAL JURISDICTION

CO-EVOLUTION AND INTERACTION WITH THE LAW OF THE SEA

ROBIN M WARNER

1 INTRODUCTION

As global shipping intensifies and technological advances provide more opportunities to access the resources of the high seas and the deep seabed beyond national jurisdiction (ABNJ), the catalogue of threats to the marine environment and its biodiversity increase commensurately.[1] Seaborne trade and

---

[1] H Scheiber, 'Economic Uses of the Oceans and the Impacts on Marine Environments: Past Trends and Challenges Ahead' in D Vidas and PJ Schei (eds), *The World Ocean in Globalisation* (Martinus Nijhoff Leiden 2011) 65, 65–6.

passenger traffic are rapidly expanding and are expected to double over the next two decades.[2] The risks to the marine environment and its biodiversity from intentional and accidental vessel-source discharges including oil and other hazardous substances, noise, and ship strikes on marine mammals, are likely to be compounded with more prevalent high-seas traffic.[3] The deep sea fishing industry is now supported by a battery of technological innovations including global positioning systems, multi-beam sonar, and stronger and more powerful cables and winches. Fishing nets and lines are composed of virtually indestructible synthetic material and may be laid over vast areas of ocean. Heavy bottom trawling gear has already caused substantial damage to vulnerable marine ecosystems.[4] Beyond these threats, new and emerging uses of ABNJ such as more intrusive marine scientific research, bioprospecting, deep seabed mining, and environmental modification activities to mitigate the effects of climate change have the potential to harm the highly interconnected and sensitive ecosystems of the open ocean and the deep seabed, if not sustainably managed now and into the future.[5]

The 1982 United Nations Convention on the Law of the Sea (LOSC) established an expansive framework for protection and preservation of the marine environment in Part XII which purported to cover all areas of ocean space including ABNJ. Article 192 of the LOSC obliges States to protect and preserve the marine environment, and is unlimited in geographical scope. The aspirational provisions of Part XII reflect the need for an integrated system of ocean governance in which global and regional organizations of States would cooperate to craft the international rules, standards, and recommended practices and procedures needed to protect and preserve the marine environment both within and beyond national jurisdiction. The LOSC also recognized that developments in international marine environmental law were already taking place in other international law fora and that this complementary development of international law principles would continue to evolve. Article 237 highlights this complementary relationship between the LOSC and other conventions on the protection and preservation of the marine environment, anticipating and encouraging an on-going reconciliation between the LOSC and other relevant conventions. In practice, implementing governance structures to support an integrated system of environmental protection for ABNJ, including conservation of marine biodiversity, poses considerable challenges in terms of scale and consistency between the two separate trajectories of law of the sea and international marine environmental law. Modern conservation norms, such as environmental impact assessment (EIA), marine protected areas (MPAs), marine spatial planning and development mechanisms

---

[2] Ibid, 87–90.   [3] Ibid, 91–2.   [4] Ibid, 86.
[5] L Reeve, A Rulska-Domino, and K Gjerde, 'The Future of High Seas Marine Protected Areas' (2012) 26 *Ocean Yearbook* 265, 268.

such as technology transfer and capacity-building are under-developed in the legal and institutional framework for ABNJ.[6]

This chapter will explore key normative features of the legal and institutional framework for ABNJ and their applicability to the conservation of marine biodiversity, gaps and disconnects in that framework, and on-going global initiatives to develop more effective governance structures. It will discuss some of the options being considered in the UN Ad Hoc Informal Open-ended Working Group to study issues related to the conservation and sustainable use of marine biodiversity in areas beyond national jurisdiction (BBNJ Working Group) to evolve the legal and institutional framework for conservation and sustainable use of marine biodiversity in ABNJ and their current and future relevance for the law of the sea.

2 Normative Features of the ABNJ Legal and Institutional Framework

The LOSC confirms the customary international law principle that the water column beyond national jurisdiction or the high seas is a global commons, and specifies that freedom of the high seas may be exercised by all States whether coastal or landlocked.[7] The freedom of the high seas encompasses freedoms of navigation and overflight, freedom to lay submarine cables and pipelines, freedom to construct artificial islands and installations, freedom of fishing, and freedom of scientific research.[8] Importantly, the LOSC specifies that the freedoms of the high seas are exercised under the conditions laid down in the LOSC and by other rules of international law.[9] With this qualification, the LOSC recognizes the need to balance the unfettered exercise of high seas freedoms with the discharge of certain international responsibilities. For example, high seas freedoms must be exercised subject to the general obligation to protect and preserve the marine environment in Article 192 of the LOSC. Additionally, a core high seas freedom, the freedom of fishing, is subject to the duty to cooperate in conserving and managing the living resources of the high seas codified in Article 118 of the LOSC. This obligation has been implemented through the 1995 Agreement for the Implementation of the Provisions of the UN Convention on the Law of the Sea relating to the Conservation and Management

---

[6] D Freestone, 'Modern Principles of High Seas Governance: The Legal Underpinnings' (2009) 39 *International Environmental Policy and Law* 44.

[7] 1982 United Nations Convention on the Law of the Sea, Arts 89 and 87 (hereinafter LOSC).

[8] Ibid, Art 87(1).   [9] Ibid, Art 87(2).

of Straddling Fish Stocks and Highly Migratory Fish Stock (Fish Stocks Agreement) and the many conservation and management measures adopted by regional fisheries management organizations that are binding on their Member States. These include measures directed at conserving ecosystems that are associated or dependent on fisheries resources.[10]

The flag State model of jurisdiction has become the predominant method of regulating high seas activities. Linking ships with the nationality of their flag State automatically imports a system of rights and obligations under national and international law into the high seas domain. Part VII of the LOSC specifies certain obligations with which States must comply in relation to their flag vessels. Among the flag State's duties is the requirement to ensure that the master, officers, and crews of its flag vessels are fully conversant with and observe the applicable international regulations concerning the prevention, reduction, and control of marine pollution.[11] These regulations are contained in an array of conventions developed by the International Maritime Organization (IMO) such as the 1973 International Convention for the Prevention of Pollution from Ships, as modified by the Protocol of 1978 (MARPOL) with its detailed technical annexes.[12] Economic and organizational factors in the shipping and maritime transport industry have had a profound impact on the standard of flag State compliance with and enforcement of these obligations particularly as they relate to the protection of the high seas marine environment.[13] In practice, the genuine link between the flag State and the operations of its flag vessels in administrative, technical, and social terms, required under Article 91 of the LOSC, has often been missing. This has led to the continued operation of unsafe and delinquent flag vessels which represent a potent threat to the marine environment both within and beyond national jurisdiction.

Juxtaposed with the high seas regime applicable to the water column in ABNJ, is Part XI of the LOSC which designates the non-living resources of the deep seabed beyond national jurisdiction as the common heritage of mankind and subjects them to a supranational management regime administered by the International Seabed Authority (ISA).[14] The ISA has a circumscribed responsibility under Article 145 of the LOSC to ensure the effective protection of the marine environment from the harmful effects which may arise from activities in the deep seabed beyond national jurisdiction, known as the Area, rather than a comprehensive responsibility to protect the deep sea environment from all threats. For this purpose, it is

---

[10] 1995 Agreement for the Implementation of the Provisions of the United Nations Convention on the Law of the Sea of 10 December 1982 relating to the Conservation and Management of Straddling Fish Stocks and Highly Migratory Fish Stocks, Art 6.

[11] LOSC, n 7, Art 94(4)(c).

[12] Annex I entered into force 2 October 1983, Annex II entered into force 6 April 1987, Annex III entered into force 1 July 1992, Annex IV entered into force 27 September 2003, Annex V entered into force 31 December 1988, and Annex VI entered into force 19 May 2005.

[13] Scheiber, n 1, 90.   [14] LOSC, n 7, Arts 136 and 137(2).

required to adopt appropriate rules, regulations, and procedures for the prevention, reduction, and control of pollution from activities such as drilling, excavation, disposal of waste, construction, and operation or maintenance of installations pipelines and other devices associated with activities in the Area and for the protection and conservation of the natural resources of the Area and flora and fauna of the marine environment.[15] States have a complementary obligation to adopt laws and regulations no less effective than those adopted by the ISA, to prevent, reduce, and control pollution of the marine environment from activities in the Area undertaken by their flag vessels, installations, structures, and other devices under their control.[16] The ISA has so far adopted binding codes for the prospecting and exploration phases of deep seabed mining for three mineral resources (polymetallic nodules, polymetallic sulphides, and cobalt rich crusts) which include detailed environmental safeguards.[17] At every stage of their activities, prospectors and exploration contractors have substantial responsibilities to assess and monitor the effects of their operations on the marine environment. As deep seabed mining activities enter the exploitation phase, further development of the ISA's regulatory framework will be necessary to address the more intrusive impacts of commercial scale mining on the marine environment beyond national jurisdiction.[18]

A substantial body of international law instruments has been developed since the adoption of the LOSC which complements and extends the LOSC framework for protection of the marine environment. Of most import for the conservation of marine biodiversity, is the Convention on Biological Diversity (CBD) adopted in 1992. The CBD introduced the concept of biodiversity into international law, with Article 2 of the Convention defining biodiversity as 'the variability among living organisms from all sources, including, *inter alia*, terrestrial, marine and other aquatic ecosystems and the ecological complexes of which they are part' and including 'diversity within species, between species and of ecosystems'. This comprehensive approach added new dimensions to marine environmental protection which had previously focused on prevention reduction and control of marine pollution and the protection of single species.[19]

---

[15] Ibid, Art 145.   [16] Ibid, Art 209(2).

[17] International Seabed Authority (ISA), Council of the ISA, *Decision Relating to Amendments to the Regulations for Prospecting and Exploration of Polymetallic Nodules* (2013), available at <http://www.isa.org.jm/files/documents/EN/19Sess/Council/ISBA-19C-17.pdf>; ISA, Assembly of the ISA, *Decision Relating to the Regulations for Prospecting and Exploration of Polymetallic Sulphides in the Area* (2010), available at <http://www.isa.org.jm/files/documents/EN/16Sess/Assembly/ISBA-16A-12Rev1.pdf>; ISA, Assembly of the ISA, *Decision Relating to the Regulations for Prospecting and Exploration of Cobalt-rich Ferromanganese Crusts in the Area* (2012), available at <http://www.isa.org.jm/files/documents/EN/18Sess/Assembly/ISBA-18A-11.pdf>.

[18] The deep seabed regime is addressed in Chapter 11 in this volume.

[19] C Joyner, 'Biodiversity in the Marine Environment: Resource Implications for the Law of the Sea' (1995) 28 *Vanderbilt Journal of Transnational Law* 644.

The three broad objectives of the CBD are the conservation of biodiversity, the sustainable use of its components, and the fair and equitable sharing of the benefits arising out of the utilization of genetic resources.[20] For the purpose of allocating substantive rights and obligations under the CBD, however, the components of biodiversity were divided between those within and beyond national jurisdiction. The jurisdictional scope provision in Article 4 of the CBD limits its application to components of biodiversity in areas within the limits of national jurisdiction and to processes and activities related to biodiversity carried out under the jurisdiction or control of Contracting Parties both within and beyond national jurisdiction. Article 5 of the CBD limits the obligations of Contracting Parties in relation to conservation and sustainable use of biodiversity in ABNJ to a duty to cooperate directly or through competent international organizations. There is therefore no direct obligation on Contracting Parties to conserve or sustainably use the components of marine biodiversity in ABNJ.

The 1979 Convention on the Conservation of Migratory Species of Wild Animals (CMS) also plays a role in conserving marine species across ABNJ. The objective of the CMS is to conserve migratory species of wild animals, including certain marine species that migrate through marine areas within and beyond national jurisdiction. Its provisions have direct relevance to many of the seabirds and marine mammals migrating through ABNJ and measures taken by States parties within their national jurisdictions can have a beneficial effect on the relevant species throughout their range. It provides a framework for range States to cooperate in protecting species that migrate across national boundaries through undertaking scientific research, restoring the habitat and removing impediments to the migration of species listed in Appendix I to the Convention as endangered. Agreements may also be concluded between range States to protect migratory species listed in Appendix II to CMS as having unfavourable conservation status. Under the 1996 Agreement on the Conservation of African-Eurasian Migratory Waterbirds (AEWA Agreement) States parties are obliged to take coordinated measures to maintain migratory waterbird species in a favourable conservation status or to restore them to such a status within the limits of their national jurisdiction.[21] Another key CMS agreement for ABNJ is the 2006 Agreement on the Conservation of Albatross and Petrels (ACAP) which obliges States parties to take a variety of conservation measures to enhance the conservation status of albatrosses and petrels including restoring their habitats and developing and implementing measures to prevent, remove, minimize, or mitigate the adverse effects of activities that may influence the conservation status of albatrosses and petrels.[22]

---

[20] 1992 Convention on Biological Diversity, Art 1 (hereinafter CBD).
[21] See also A Trouwbost, 'Migratory Species Conservation in Warming Polar Oceans, With Particular Reference to Seabirds' in E Molenaar, A Oude Elferink, and D Rothwell (eds), *The Law of the Sea and the Polar Regions* (Martinus Nijhoff Leiden 2013) 163.
[22] Ibid.

When viewed together, these normative features of the ABNJ legal and institutional framework represent a fundamentally disjunctive and fragmentary system for the conservation and sustainable use of marine biodiversity in ABNJ. The different legal status of the high seas water column and the deep seabed beyond national jurisdiction complicates the development of a coherent approach to the conservation and sustainable use of biodiversity in ABNJ. Variable compliance standards among flag States with marine pollution obligations and the lack of monitoring and enforcement mechanisms in ABNJ compound the obstacles to achieving an integrated system for conservation and sustainable use of marine biodiversity in these vast areas of the ocean. The separate trajectory of international environmental law instruments such as the CBD has introduced a range of modern conservation norms which have yet to be properly incorporated in the law of the sea framework for protection and preservation of the marine environment.

3 Gaps in Implementation of the ABNJ Legal and Institutional Framework for Conservation and Sustainable Use of Marine Biodiversity

Responsibility for implementing international law obligations to conserve the marine biodiversity of ABNJ is dispersed among a variety of global and regional regimes with no overarching global instrument or institutional focal point to develop best practice standards or to adopt conservation measures for unregulated activities in ABNJ. There are multiple gaps in the geographic coverage of the relevant regulatory instruments and institutions, their incorporation of biodiversity conservation objectives, the effectiveness of their decision making structures and the systems in place to monitor and enforce compliance biodiversity conservation measures in ABNJ. These deficiencies are compounded by a lack of coordination and cooperation between the global, regional, and sectoral organizations which regulate human uses of ABNJ. This section will discuss selected examples from key sectors with responsibility for regulating activities in ABNJ.

3.1 Fisheries

There are 20 existing and prospective Regional Fisheries Management Organizations (RFMOs) with mandates to establish fisheries conservation and management measures.[23] Although tuna and tuna-like species are managed by RFMOs in virtually all the relevant areas of ocean beyond national jurisdiction, there are still significant gaps in the coverage of non-tuna fisheries even though regional collaboration is an essential component in conserving and managing the full range of highly migratory and straddling fish stocks as well as discrete high seas fish stocks. The North East Atlantic Fisheries Commission (NEAFC) and the North-West Atlantic Fisheries Organization (NAFO) cover the North East and North West Atlantic but there is no multilateral body regulating fisheries in the Arctic. The Atlantic south of the NEAFC/NAFO areas of responsibility is only partially covered by the South East Atlantic Fisheries Organization and the Commission for Conservation of Antarctic Marine Living Resources area south of the Antarctic convergence. Until the end of 2009, there were no general fisheries commissions in the Pacific at all to manage non-highly migratory species. The treaty establishing the South Pacific Regional Fisheries Management Organization (SPRFMO) was concluded in November 2009 and entered into force in 2012. Negotiations are still on-going for a North Pacific RFMO. In the Indian Ocean, the Regional Commission for Fisheries (RECOFI) covers the Gulf area and the Southern Indian Ocean Fisheries Agreement (SIOFA), concluded in July 2006, entered into force in June 2012.[24]

Fisheries governance arrangements exhibit considerable diversity and varying rates of progress in their approaches to incorporating environmental protection principles and biodiversity conservation objectives into their management regimes. Recent reviews of RFMO practice at the global level reveal several factors that have limited the effectiveness of RFMOs in implementing fisheries conservation and management measures in an ecologically sustainable manner.[25] These include:

- *Absence of environmental protection principles in the RFMO conventions.* The absence of modern environmental protection principles or guidelines such as the precautionary approach and ecosystem based management in some RFMO conventions concluded prior to the Fish Stocks Agreement means that unless all RFMO members agree, they are not obliged to consider principles of sustainability when adopting conservation and management measures although this is slowly altering with the emerging customary international law status of such principles.

---

[23] Food and Agriculture Organization (FAO), Fisheries and Aquaculture Department, *Regional Fishery Bodies—Fishery Governance Fact Sheets*, available at <http://www.fao.org/fishery/rfb/search/en>.

[24] D Freestone, 'Fisheries Commissions and Organizations' in R Wolfrum (ed), *The Max Planck Encyclopedia of Public International Law* (Oxford University Press Oxford 2008), available at <http://opil.ouplaw.com/home/EPIL>.

[25] Organisation for Economic Co-operation and Development (OECD), Task Force on IUU Fishing on the High Seas, *Closing the Net: Stopping Illegal Fishing on the High Seas* (2006), available at <http://www.oecd.org/sd-roundtable/papersandpublications/39375316.pdf>; MW Lodge et al, *Recommended Best Practices for Regional Fisheries Management Organization* (Chatham House London 2007) x.

- *Ineffective decision-making frameworks.* It is the established practice of RFMOs to take decisions on their conservation and management measures by consensus, even when their instruments may not require it, and to allow for individual objections to conservation and management measures agreed by the majority of member States.[26] This allows objecting RFMO members to take advantage of uncertainties in scientific advice and can lead to a dilution of conservation and management measures even where the precautionary approach and ecosystem based management requirements exist. Many of the RFMOs that were established prior to the conclusion of the Fish Stocks Agreement allow for States to opt out or object to implementing conservation and management measures that have been agreed within the RFMO.
- *Lack of a formal global coordination mechanism.* There is no overarching global coordination mechanism to oversee the conservation and management activities of RFMOs in ABNJ and monitor their performance against best practice standards and ensure cross-sectoral exchange of information. This makes it difficult to address global problems, such as the conservation of highly migratory marine species or illegal, unregulated, and unreported (IUU) fishing, as fishing vessels may move between regions concentrating their fishing effort in areas where conservation and management measures are lax or non-existent. At the regional level, there has been very little consultation and collaboration between RFMOs. The first meeting between the tuna RFMOs, the 'Kobe Process' occurred in 2007.[27]
- *Participation levels.* In many regions, developing States lack the resources and capacity to participate fully in RFMOs and implement their obligations effectively.
- *Failure to deal effectively with non-parties.* Few RFMOs include all the participants in a regional fishery among their members. An RFMO may have agreed on environmentally sound conservation and management measures for fisheries in high seas areas but only those States which have agreed to be bound by the agreement are obliged to apply its measures. The failure to deal effectively with non-parties or 'free riders' undermines the incentives for fishing vessels of RFMO members to adopt restrictive conservation and management measures.

3.2 Regional seas arrangements

Since the early 1970s, a diverse array of binding and non-binding regional arrangements has been negotiated around the globe to engage States in the collaborative protection of their offshore marine environments. Many of the binding regional

---

[26] T McDorman, 'Implementing Existing Tools: Turning Words into Action—Decision-Making Processes of Regional Fisheries Management Organizations' (2005) 20 *International Journal of Marine and Coastal Law* 428.

[27] See Tuna-org, *Meetings Past* (2012), available at <http://www.tuna-org/meetingspast.htm>.

seas arrangements were initiated through the United Nations Environment Programme (UNEP) Regional Seas Programme while others are the result of independent agreements between regional partners.[28] They now cover 18 maritime regions which differ markedly in their character and extent.[29] The UNEP regional seas arrangements, together with the non-UNEP regional marine environmental protection arrangements, involve 149 States, or approximately 95.5 per cent of the world's States.[30] Currently, the areas of responsibility of many of these arrangements are limited to waters within national jurisdiction, and very few of them make provision for consensual environmental protection measures in high seas enclaves and high seas areas adjacent to waters within national jurisdiction.[31] The geographic scope of these arrangements has been determined by political opportunity rather than any systematic scheme to encompass all the oceanic regions of the world.[32] No legally binding conventions have yet been developed for the regional arrangements in the East Asian Seas, South Asian Seas, North-West Pacific, North-East Pacific, or for the Arctic. Moreover, these conventions are primarily groupings of coastal States, and their jurisdiction is generally restricted to their coastal zones, or out to 200 nautical miles (nm). The exceptions are the following: the OSPAR Convention area, which has high-seas areas within its remit; the Mediterranean, where most coastal States have for various reasons not yet claimed EEZs; the South Pacific, which includes within its mandate the 'donut' holes between the EEZs of its members;[33] and the Antarctic Treaty System, consisting of both the Antarctic Treaty and its Protocol on Environmental Protection as well as the CAMLR Convention.[34]

---

[28] A Vallega, 'The Regional Seas in the 21st Century: An Overview' (2002) 45 *Ocean and Coastal Management* 926.

[29] UNEP, Regional Seas Programme, 'About Regional Seas', available at <http://www.unep.org/regional seas/About/default.asp>:

> Today more than 143 countries participate in 13 Regional Seas programmes established under the auspices of UNEP: the Black Sea, Wider Caribbean, East Africa, South East Asia, ROPME Sea Area, Mediterranean, North-East Pacific, North-West Pacific, Red Sea and Gulf of Aden, South Asia, South-East Pacific, Pacific and West and Central Africa. Six of these programmes are directly administered by UNEP. The Regional Seas Programmes function through an Action Plan. In most cases the Action Plan is underpinned with a strong legal framework in the form of a Regional Convention and associated Protocols on specific problems. Furthermore, five partner programmes for the Antarctic, Arctic, Baltic Sea, Caspian Sea and North-East Atlantic Regions are members of the regional seas family.

See also D Freestone, 'International Governance, Responsibility and Management of Areas beyond National Jurisdiction' (2012) 27 *International Journal of Marine and Coastal Law* 196.

[30] Vallega, n 28, 926.   [31] Freestone, n 24, 196–7.

[32] P Sand, 'The Rise of Regional Agreements for Marine Environment Protection' in P Sand, *Transnational Environmental Law: Lessons in Global Change* (Kluwer Law International The Hague 1999) 178, 183; A Boyle, 'Globalism and Regionalism' in D Vidas (ed), *Protecting the Polar Marine Environment* (Cambridge University Press Cambridge 2000) 27.

[33] 1986 Convention for the Protection of the Natural Resources and Environment of the South Pacific Region.

[34] 1959 Antarctic Treaty; 1980 Convention on the Conservation of Antarctic Marine Living Resources (CAMLR Convention); 1991 Protocol on Environmental Protection to the Antarctic Treaty.

The spread of regional arrangements for marine environmental protection has paralleled the negotiation and entry into force of the LOSC and has both reflected and advanced the development of modern environmental protection principles.[35] The early focus of most regional arrangements such as the OSPAR Convention[36] and the Barcelona Convention[37] in the Mediterranean was the control of marine pollution but many have since adopted a more integrated approach to the protection of the marine environment including conservation of its biodiversity and the development of systems of MPAs.[38]

The broadening of their scope in relation to approaches to conservation and targets for conservation intervention has enabled many regional arrangements to assimilate new developments in international environmental law and policy through mechanisms such as protocols and non-binding documents such as programmes for action and strategic plans.[39] The majority of regional agreements are based on framework conventions which depend on implementation by States parties in waters within national jurisdiction. These conventions have been supplemented by Protocols, ministerial-level agreements, and strategy documents which regulate different sources of marine pollution, provide for the protection of threatened and endangered species and the establishment of MPAs to preserve, *inter alia*, rare or fragile ecosystems.[40] In most regions, these binding legal instruments and soft law accords are accompanied by planning documents which define regional priorities for marine environmental protection.[41]

Key factors that have limited the effectiveness of regional seas arrangements in implementing biodiversity conservation in ABNJ include:

- the limiting of their areas of responsibility to waters under national jurisdiction;
- the lack of reference to sustainable development and use of marine biodiversity in their mandates; and
- the absence of specific collaboration provisions or arrangements and mechanisms between regional seas arrangements and RFMOs.

---

[35] T Treves, 'Regional Approaches to the Protection of the Marine Environment' in MH Nordquist, JN Moore, and S Mahmoudi (eds), *The Stockholm Declaration and the Law of the Marine Environment* (Kluwer Law International The Hague 2003) 137, 137–8.

[36] 1992 Convention for the Protection of the Marine Environment of the North-East Atlantic.

[37] 1995 Convention for the Protection for the Marine Environment and the Coastal Region of the Mediterranean.

[38] Sand, n 32, 181.   [39] Ibid, 181–2.   [40] Ibid, 178–82.   [41] Ibid, 181.

3.3 Shipping

Maritime transport, particularly seaborne trade and passenger cruises, constitutes one of the most intensive uses of ABNJ and poses on-going threats to marine biodiversity through the intentional and accidental discharge of pollutants into the sea. The IMO as the focal point for technical expertise and stakeholder interests in international shipping has developed a variety of instruments to reduce and mitigate vessel source pollution across all areas of the ocean including ABNJ. The principal vessel source pollution conventions, including MARPOL, the 1972 London Convention and Protocol[42] and the 2001 Anti-fouling Convention,[43] apply to the flag vessels of member States both within and beyond national jurisdiction. With such a detailed regulatory framework in place, the key gap which arises in connection with conservation of biodiversity in ABNJ is the need to monitor and enforce compliance with the wide array of instruments which have entered into force. This function is still largely the responsibility of individual flag States, particularly in ABNJ, with very little reporting of vessel source pollution and negligible follow up action by flag or port States of high seas pollution incidents.

3.4 Deep seabed mining

The ISA has established a strong framework of environmental safeguards for exploration contractors in the Area. A contractor must submit an assessment of the potential environmental impacts of proposed activities with an application for approval of a plan of work together with a description of proposed measures for the prevention, reduction, and control of possible impacts on the marine environment.[44] The ISA has also issued and revised the 2010 Recommendations for the Guidance of Contractors for the Assessment of the Possible Environmental Impacts Arising from Exploration for Polymetallic Nodules in the Area, which specify the particular activities of exploration contractors that are subject to EIA.[45] The sponsoring State of an exploration contractor is under a due diligence

---

[42] 1972 Convention on the Prevention of Marine Pollution by Dumping of Wastes and Other Matter (hereinafter London Convention); 1996 Protocol to the Convention on the Prevention of Marine Pollution by Dumping of Wastes and Other Matter.

[43] 2001 International Convention on the Control of Harmful Anti-fouling Systems.

[44] 1994 Agreement Relating to the Implementation of Part XI of the United Nations Convention on the Law of the Sea, Annex, [7]; ISA, *Polymetallic Nodules*, n 17, Reg 18(c) and (d).

[45] ISA, Legal and Technical Commission, *Recommendations for the Guidance of Contractors for the Assessment of the Possible Environmental Impacts Arsing from Exploration for Polymetallic Nodules in the Area* (2010) [10], available at <http://www.isa.org.jm/files/documents/EN/16Sess/LTC/ISBA-16LTC-7.pdf>.

obligation to ensure that exploration contractors fulfil all their responsibilities under the ISA's Mining Code.[46] An important element missing from the deep seabed mining environmental protection framework, however, is a collaborative mechanism for monitoring and enforcing compliance involving exploration contractors and ISA representatives. In addition, a code for the exploitation phase of deep seabed mining in the Area has not yet been developed and it may prove more challenging to maintain best practice environmental safeguards once commercial scale activities begin.

4 Global and Regional Initiatives to Develop the Legal and Institutional Framework for Conservation and Sustainable Use of Marine Biodiversity in ABNJ

A number of global and regional initiatives have been taken over the last decade to address some of the gaps and disconnects in the legal and institutional framework for conservation and sustainable use of marine biodiversity in ABNJ. The political centre of gravity for these efforts has been the BBNJ Working Group established by the UNGA in 2004. The CBD has supported these discussions in the BBNJ Working Group with some technical and scientific initiatives related to EIA and the designation of ecologically and biologically significant areas (EBSAs) in the world's oceans including in ABNJ. At the regional level, steps have been taken to designate MPAs and fisheries closure areas with biodiversity conservation components in ABNJ by regional seas arrangements and RFMOs. Governments and non-government organizations with interests in the unique ecosystem of the Sargasso Sea have also launched a special initiative to conserve biodiversity in this ocean area which is largely composed of high seas.

---

[46] *Responsibilities and Obligations of States Sponsoring Persons and Entities with Respect to Activities in the Area*, Advisory Opinion of the Seabed Disputes Chamber of the International Tribunal for the Law of the Sea (1 February 2011) 43–4 [141]–[143]; ISA, *Polymetallic Sulphides*, n 17, Reg 33(6).

4.1 BBNJ Working Group

The main impetus for considering new approaches to strengthen the legal and institutional framework for conservation and sustainable use of biodiversity in ABNJ originated from the United Nations Informal Consultative Process on Oceans and the Law of the Sea (UNICPOLOS) which has discussed a wide range of oceans issues since its inception in 1999. The fifth meeting of UNICPOLOS in 2004 canvassed new and emerging uses of the oceans, highlighting the risks these uses posed to conservation and sustainable use of biodiversity in ABNJ in the absence of environmental protection measures agreed and implemented by the international community.[47] Recommendations from that meeting to the UNGA resulted in the establishment of the BBNJ working group which has now met six times. Some consistent themes have characterized the discussions of the BBNJ Working Group. It has endorsed the fundamental importance of basing decisions on activities in ABNJ on precautionary and ecosystem based approaches and using the best available science and prior EIA to inform such decisions.[48] Participating States have agreed on the need for improved implementation of global and regional agreements relevant to conservation and sustainable use of biodiversity in ABNJ including the LOSC and the CBD.[49] The integral role of sectoral and regional organizations in implementing such agreements has been recognized as has the need to improve the management of these bodies and to develop and strengthen mechanisms for their accountability.[50] Destructive fishing practices have been singled out as one of the major threats to marine biodiversity in ABNJ and it was agreed that these practices should be addressed on an urgent basis by the UNGA, FAO, and RFMOs.[51] IUU fishing was also considered to be a major obstacle to the conservation and sustainable use of marine biodiversity in ABNJ, requiring an integrated and accelerated approach across all relevant fora to address this issue through measures such as enhanced flag State responsibility, port State measures, and more collaborative monitoring and enforcement of compliance with fisheries conservation and management measures.[52] A lack of consensus among participating States on the legal status of marine genetic resources in ABNJ has been a contentious issue throughout the BBNJ meetings. In particular, there has been no consensus on rights of access to, and the sharing of benefits derived from, these resources.[53]

---

[47] UNGA, *Report on the Work of the United Nations Open-ended Informal Consultative Process on Oceans and the Law of the Sea*, 5th Meeting, UN Doc A/59/122 (2004).
[48] UNGA, *Report of the Ad Hoc Open-ended Informal Working Group to Study Issues Relating to the Conservation and Sustainable Use of Marine Biological Diversity Beyond Areas of National Jurisdiction*, UN Doc A/63/79 (2008), Annex I [5].
[49] Ibid, [50] and Annex I [4].   [50] Ibid, Annex I [6].   [51] Ibid, Annex I [7].
[52] Ibid, Annex I [8].
[53] Ibid, Annex I [71] and [72]. This issue is not covered in detail in this chapter, but see further Chapter 36 in this volume.

Although successive reports and recommendations from the BBNJ Working Group have reflected consensus among participating States on the need to promote international cooperation and coordination to achieve better long term conservation and sustainable use of marine biodiversity in ABNJ, there has been no agreement on the legal and institutional mechanisms required to meet this objective and whether this will involve changes to the law of the sea. Suggestions have ranged from maintaining the status quo to the adoption of an implementing or multilateral agreement under the LOSC or even an agreement independent of the LOSC covering conservation and sustainable use of biodiversity in ABNJ including the issues of access to, and distribution of benefits derived from, marine genetic resources. A consensus has now emerged in the BBNJ Working Group around discussing a process to negotiate a multilateral agreement on the conservation and sustainable use of marine biodiversity in ABNJ and the key elements of any potential agreement.

In 2011, the BBNJ Working Group recommended to the UNGA that

> ...a process be initiated...with a view to ensuring that the legal framework for the conservation and sustainable use of marine biodiversity in areas beyond national jurisdiction effectively addresses those issues by identifying gaps and ways forward, including through the implementation of existing instruments and the possible development of a multilateral agreement under [the LOSC].[54]

This process would address 'together and as a whole, marine genetic resources, including questions on the sharing of benefits, measures such as area-based management tools, including marine protected areas, and environmental impact assessments, capacity-building and the transfer of marine technology'.[55]

At Rio + 20, States committed themselves:

> ...to address, on an urgent basis, building on the work of the Ad Hoc Open-ended Informal Working Group and before the end of the sixty-ninth session of the General Assembly, the issue of the conservation and sustainable use of marine biological diversity of areas beyond national jurisdiction, including by taking a decision on the development of an international instrument under the United Nations Convention on the Law of the Sea.[56]

This commitment was recalled by the UNGA in its sixty-seventh session,[57] and reaffirmed in the recommendations to the UNGA developed at the sixth meeting of the BBNJ Working Group in 2013.[58] At the same meeting, the Working Group also proposed to establish a process to make recommendations to the UNGA 'on the scope, parameters and feasibility of an international instrument under the Convention' in order to prepare for the decision to be taken at the sixty-nineth

---

[54] UNGA, *Letter from the Co-Chairs of the* Ad Hoc *Open-ended Informal Working Group to the President of the General Assembly*, 66th session, UN Doc A/66/119 (2011) Annex, Section 1.
[55] Ibid.   [56] UNGA Res 66/288 (27 July 2012) [162].
[57] UNGA Res 67/78 (11 December 2012) [181].
[58] UNGA, *Letter from the Co-Chairs of the* Ad Hoc *Open-ended Informal Working Group to the President of the General Assembly*, 68th session, UN Doc A/68/399 (2013) Annex.

session of the UNGA in 2015, whether to start the negotiation of an international instrument on the conservation and sustainable use of biodiversity in ABNJ.[59] Some potential ramifications of such an instrument for the law of the sea will be discussed in the next section.

4.2 CBD Initiatives

The CBD has laid some of the groundwork for area based management in ABNJ at the regional level through the provision of expert advice on describing marine EBSAs and in addressing biodiversity concerns in sustainable fisheries. In 2008, the Ninth Meeting of the Conference of Parties (COP 9) of the CBD adopted the following scientific criteria for identifying 'ecologically or biologically significant areas in need of protection in open ocean waters and deep sea habitats':

- uniqueness/rarity;
- special importance for life history stages of species;
- importance for threatened, endangered, or declining species and/or habitats;
- vulnerability, fragility, sensitivity, or slow recovery;
- biological productivity;
- biological diversity; and
- naturalness.[60]

This decision also provided scientific guidance for selecting areas to establish a representative network of MPAs including in open ocean waters and deep-sea habitats.[61] The tenth CBD COP in 2010 agreed on a process of regional workshops for the description of EBSAs.[62] The workshop outcomes were designed to inform relevant regional and global organizations. The work was premised on recognition that the application of the EBSA criteria is a scientific and technical exercise, that areas found to meet the criteria may require enhanced conservation and management measures, and that this can be achieved through a variety of means, including MPAs and impact assessments. The CBD also recognized that the identification of EBSAs and the selection of conservation and management measures is a matter for States and competent intergovernmental organizations, in accordance with international law, including the LOSC.[63] Regional workshops on describing EBSAs have been organized covering the North-East Atlantic, the Western South Pacific, the Wider Caribbean and Western Mid-Atlantic, the Western Indian Ocean, and the Eastern Tropical and Temperate Pacific. In addition, areas meeting EBSA

---

[59] Ibid.   [60] CBD COP Decision IX/20, UNEP/CBD/COP/DEC/IX/20 (2008) Annex I.
[61] Ibid, Annex II.
[62] CBD COP Decision X/29, UNEP/CBD/COP/DEC/X/29 (2010) [36].   [63] Ibid, [26].

compatible criteria have been described in the Mediterranean. Preparations are underway for workshops for the North Pacific Region and the South-East Atlantic region, among others.[64] At the CBD COP 11 in Hyderabad in October 2012, it was agreed that the areas described as EBSAs by these workshops and processes, after review by CBD SBSTTA, should be sent to the UN and relevant international organizations.[65]

The Conference of the Parties of the CBD has also been proactive in investigating the scientific and technical aspects of EIA for activities in ABNJ. It convened an Expert Workshop on Scientific and Technical Elements of the CBD EIA Guidelines which focused on ABNJ in November 2009.[66] This highlighted some of the governance and practical challenges related to the implementation of EIA for activities in ABNJ. Some of the practical difficulties associated with conducting EIAs in ABNJ included:

- the industry proposing the activity and the national flag State jurisdiction are often far from the marine area affected;
- the conduct of EIA and management, control, monitoring, surveillance, and follow-up activity were likely to be more costly and may be less effective for a given budget; and
- capacity building needs for EIA in ABNJ would be greater as customs of practice are less established, methodologies less mature, and multiple assessment cultures may converge in the same area.[67]

The complex and fragmentary nature of the law and institutions governing ABNJ were accentuated including:

- the split legal framework for ABNJ—high seas (Part VII of the LOSC) and deep seabed beyond national jurisdiction—the Area (Part XI of the LOSC and 1994 Implementation Agreement);
- the diverse institutional framework for ABNJ including States, non-State actors, and global and regional organizations and the need for cooperation between all these actors to conserve biodiversity;
- the fact that stakeholders are harder to define for ABNJ because communities do not have immediate proximity to these areas; and

---

[64] UNEP, CBD Secretariat, *ESBA Briefing: Organizing Regional Workshops to Describe Ecologically or Biologically Significant Marine Areas (EBSAs)* (2012), available at <http://www.cbd.int/doc/meetings/mar/ebsa-briefing/other/ebsa-briefing-note-en.pdf>.

[65] CBD, *Report of the Eleventh Meeting of the Conference of the Parties to the Convention on Biological Diversity*, UNEP/CBD/COP/11/35 (2012) Annex, Decision XI/17.

[66] CBD, *Report of the Expert Workshop on Scientific and Technical Aspects relevant to Environmental Impact Assessment in Marine Areas beyond National Jurisdiction*, UNEP/CBD/EW-EIAMA/2 (2009).

[67] Ibid, Annex II, [10]–[14].

- the variable standards of compliance among States with environmental assessment obligations in international conventions.[68]

The Workshop's Report was considered by the tenth meeting of the CBD COP in 2010 which endorsed the development of voluntary guidelines for the consideration of biodiversity in EIAs for marine and coastal areas drawing on the guidance from the Workshop.[69] The Guidelines were developed for all marine and coastal areas rather than simply for ABNJ, emphasizing the interconnections between ocean ecosystems across jurisdictional boundaries, and endorsed by the eleventh CBD COP in 2012.[70]

4.3 Regional initiatives

The OSPAR Convention, the non-UNEP regional seas agreement for the North-East Atlantic includes in its area of responsibility waters within and beyond national jurisdiction.[71] At the OSPAR Ministerial meeting in 2010, six MPAs were established in ABNJ.[72] They cover a total area of 287,065 km², protecting a series of seamounts and sections of the Mid-Atlantic Ridge and host a range of vulnerable deep-sea habitats and species.[73] A seventh pelagic high seas MPA, Charlie-Gibbs North (178,094 km²), was designated in 2012 in waters superjacent to an area of the deep seabed included within an Icelandic submission to the Commission on the Limits of the Continental Shelf.[74] Some management provisions are contained in OSPAR Recommendations for each of these areas; however, to date no cross-sectoral management plans have been put in place.

The NEAFC has regulatory competence over three large maritime areas beyond national jurisdiction in the North East Atlantic Ocean and may recommend conservation and management measures for all fisheries resources within its Convention Area with the exception of sea mammals, sedentary species and tuna or tuna-like species.[75] These measures include regulation of fishing gear and size limits for fish, the establishment of closed seasons and closed areas, the establishment of total

---

[68] Ibid, Annex II, [7]–[9].
[69] CBD, *Report of the Tenth Meeting of the Conference of the Parties to the Convention on Biological Diversity*, UNEP/CBD/COP/10/27 (2011) Annex, Decision X/29, [50].
[70] CBD, n 65, Annex, Decision XI/18.
[71] 1992 Convention for the Protection of the Marine Environment of the North-East Atlantic, Art 1(a)(i)–(ii) (hereinafter OSPAR Convention).
[72] OSPAR Commission, *OSPAR Ministerial Meeting 2010* (2014), available at <http://www.ospar.org/content/content.asp?menu=01550108910000_000000_000000>.
[73] Ibid.
[74] Charlie Gibbs Marine Protected Area website, at <http://www.charlie-gibbs.org/>.
[75] 1980 Convention on Future Multilateral Cooperation in North East Atlantic Fisheries, Art 1(1) and (2).

allowable catches and their allocation to Contracting Parties and the regulation of the amount of fishing effort and its allocation to Contracting Parties.[76] NEAFC recognized the vulnerability of some of the deep water habitats within its Regulatory Area by closing five seamount areas and a section of the Reykjanes Ridge on the high seas for three years to bottom trawling and static fishing gear from 2005 to 2007.[77] It also agreed to reduce fishing pressures on a large range of vulnerable species in deep water habitats within the Regulatory Area by 30 per cent for 2005 onwards following International Council for the Exploration of the Sea (ICES) advice.[78] The initial ban on fishing on the Reykjanes Ridge was extended beyond the three year period until new closure measures were adopted based on scientific advice from ICES taking into account FAO's vulnerable marine ecosystem (VME) criteria and consideration by NEAFC's Permanent Committee on Management and Science.

NEAFC's incorporation of biodiversity considerations into its fisheries conservation and management measures has also been facilitated by its close working relationship with OSPAR. OSPAR and NEAFC signed a memorandum of understanding in 2008 and both organizations use ICES as their scientific advisory body.[79] ICES has recommended that a coordinated approach be taken between the two organizations to the protection of VMEs[80] and there has been considerable overlap between areas proposed for protection by OSPAR and those considered for closure to bottom fishing by NEAFC.[81]

A further initiative under the current legal and institutional framework for conserving marine biodiversity in ABNJ is an environmental protection programme being proposed by the Government of Bermuda together with intergovernmental and non-governmental organizations, to introduce conservation and management measures for the Sargasso Sea. The Sargasso Sea, named for the accumulations of holopelagic algae contained within the North Atlantic Subtropical Gyre, is a two million nm^2 ecosystem that is primarily high seas. The OSPAR Secretariat and the Sargasso Sea Alliance have established informal research and information exchange systems and have concluded a Collaboration Arrangement.[82] The Alliance is seeking to use existing sectoral organizations with responsibilities for ABNJ areas—such as the International Commission for the Conservation of Atlantic Tunas (ICCAT),

---

[76] Ibid, Art 7(a)–(c), (e), and (f).

[77] NEAFC, *Report of the 23rd Annual Meeting of the North-East Atlantic Fisheries Commission, 8–12 November 2004*, available at <http://archive.neafc.org/reports/annual-meeting/index.htm>.

[78] Ibid.   [79] Ibid.

[80] The topic of Vulnerable Marine Ecosystems (VMEs) is addressed in Chapter 35 in this volume.

[81] NEAFC, n 77.

[82] OSPAR Commission, Sargasso Sea Alliance, *Collaboration Arrangement between the Secretariats of the OSPAR Commission and the Sargasso Sea Alliance and OSPAR* (2012), available at <http://www.sargassoalliance.org/storage/documents/Collaboration_Arrangement_-_OSPAR_Sargasso_Sea.pdf>.

IMO, and ISA—to put protection measures in place and to convene an inter-governmental meeting to establish a collaborative but non-legally binding protection regime for the Sargasso Sea.[83]

5 Evolving the Legal and Institutional Framework for Conservation of Marine Biodiversity in ABNJ

Efforts by global and regional organizations to evolve and implement the legal and institutional framework for conservation of biodiversity in ABNJ have so far been piecemeal and geographically limited. In addition, the validity under international law of some initiatives such as the OSPAR designation of high seas MPAs has been questioned. A binding agreement under the LOSC on the conservation of biodiversity in ABNJ could provide the basis for a more integrated legal and institutional framework to further implement key provisions of Part XII of the LOSC on the protection and preservation of the marine environment.

5.1 Rationale and objectives for including key biodiversity conservation elements in an agreement under LOSC

The BBNJ Working Group discussions have highlighted multiple reasons and objectives for including area-based management tools in an agreement on conservation of biodiversity in ABNJ under the LOSC. These include 'the fundamental role of area-based management tools, including marine protected areas, in the conservation and sustainable use of marine biodiversity and in ensuring the resilience of marine ecosystems' as well as 'the importance of those tools as part of a range of management options in implementing precautionary and ecosystem approaches to

---

[83] D Freestone and K Killerlain Morrison, 'The Sargasso Sea Alliance' (2012) 27 *International Journal of Marine and Coastal Law* 647; OSPAR Commission, *Sargasso Sea Alliance* (2014), available at <www.sargassoalliance.org>. The CBD COP11 agreed that the Sargasso Sea, among other areas, is to be entered into the CBD Secretariat's repository of EBSAs and transmitted to the United Nations and other relevant competent organizations.

the management of human activities' in ABNJ.[84] The discussions have also emphasized the need to determine a legal basis for designating such MPAs which is consistent with the LOSC.[85] The gap between the scientific process involved in describing EBSAs in ABNJ under the CBD process and the actual designation and endorsement of such areas by a competent global organization was also raised as a reason for including area based management tools in any agreement under the LOSC.[86]

The BBNJ Working Group has also discussed reasons for including EIA as one of the key components in any future Implementing Agreement on the Conservation and Sustainable Use of Marine Biodiversity in Areas beyond National Jurisdiction.[87] A key plank of the rationale for including EIA elements is to capture activities occurring in ABNJ that are not already subject to sectoral EIA processes, in effect, to provide a default EIA system for activities such as bioprospecting and marine geo-engineering. Another reason for including EIA elements is to provide best practice standards for EIA in ABNJ where scientific knowledge of marine biodiversity is still nascent. Developing best practice standards for EIA in ABNJ may entail the incorporation of new elements into the generally accepted components of the EIA process. Rather than perpetuating a situation where EIA is simply a procedural hurdle for the proponents of a particular activity, a best practice standard could require a process that is biodiversity-inclusive, transparent, and subject to international scrutiny with associated powers to impose conditions in the interest of mitigating adverse impacts on the marine environment or to disallow the activity where there is the potential for substantial harm to the marine environment.

5.2 Options for incorporating key biodiversity conservation elements in an implementing agreement

There are a range of options for incorporating a legal and institutional framework for the two key biodiversity conservation elements, area based management tools and EIA, into a multilateral agreement under the LOSC. This section discusses some of the potential options available to States to achieve this objective.

5.2.1 *Area-based management elements*

The multilateral agreement could include as one of its objectives the development of an effectively managed, ecologically representative and well-connected system of MPAs in ABNJ. Specific provisions in the agreement could require States, through regional organizations, to propose areas for designation. The agreement could also define

---

[84] UNGA, *Letter from the Co-Chairs of the Ad Hoc Open-ended Informal Working Group*, 67th Session, UN Doc A/66/119 (2011) Annex, Section II, [23].
[85] Ibid, [24]. [86] Ibid, [28]. [87] Ibid, Section I(a) and (b).

the criteria, conservation objectives and processes for submitting proposals, agreeing management measures and procedures for scientific review and endorsement. It could also oblige States parties to comply with agreed MPA management measures and not to authorize or undertake activities that might be contrary to the objectives for which a MPA was established. An agreement could designate a global scientific body to develop proposals for MPAs which could be approved, kept under review and assisted at the global level and managed through regional processes. A further element of the agreement could be a process for spatial planning designed to foster integrated ecosystem based planning and management which includes the establishment of the system of MPAs in ABNJ. This element of the agreement could require States parties and competent regional and sectoral organizations to coordinate sectoral area-based measures and to integrate their plans to achieve healthy oceans and marine ecosystems with minimal loss of and adverse impacts on marine biodiversity in ABNJ.

5.2.2 *Environmental impact assessment elements*

The EIA elements of a multilateral agreement could include the typical components of an EIA process as they apply to activities in ABNJ including screening, scoping of the terms of reference for an EIA, public notification and consultation, reporting, and post-report decisions on whether to impose conditions on the activity or to disallow it.[88] The threshold of significant effects on the environment as the trigger for subjecting activities to EIA has gained wide acceptance in global and regional instruments including the LOSC.[89] This would appear to be the minimum screening threshold for activities in ABNJ. For activities intended to occur in sensitive areas of the ABNJ environments such as identified vulnerable marine ecosystems and ecologically and biologically significant areas, screening thresholds for EIA could be set at an even lower level such as minor or transitory impacts on the marine environment.

In addition to threshold criteria, many EIA regimes list activities that will automatically be subject to EIAs and criteria to assist in determining which other activities should be subject to EIAs.[90] An indicative list of such activities for ABNJ would include deep sea fishing, aquaculture, dumping of waste, marine geo-engineering, offshore hydrocarbon production, bioprospecting, marine scientific research, laying of submarine cables and pipelines, ballast water exchange, deep-sea tourism expeditions, and ocean energy operations. Criteria to assist States in determining which other activities should be subject to EIAs could be modelled on the CBD Voluntary Guidelines for Biodiversity-Inclusive EIA,[91] particularly as the proposed

---

[88] N Craik, *The International Law of Environmental Impact Assessment* (Cambridge University Press Cambridge 2008) 132.
[89] Ibid, 133.   [90] Ibid, 134–5.
[91] CBD, Commission for Environmental Assessment, Biodiversity in EIA & SEA: Background Document to Decision VIII/28: Voluntary Guidelines on Biodiversity-Inclusive Impact Assessment (2006), available at <https://www.cbd.int/doc/publications/imp-bio-eia-and-sea.pdf>.

international agreement will relate to conservation and sustainable use of biodiversity in ABNJ. These might include whether:

- the proposed activity is located in or close to an area of special environmental sensitivity or representative international importance;
- the intended activity would affect the biophysical environment directly or indirectly in such a manner that it will increase risks of extinction of genotypes, cultivars, varieties, populations of species or increase the chance of loss of habitat or ecosystems;
- the intended activity would surpass the maximum sustainable yield, ie the carrying capacity of a habitat/ecosystem or the maximum allowable disturbance level of a resource, population, or ecosystem;
- the proposed activity would have particularly complex and potentially adverse effects including those giving rise to serious effects on valued species or organisms or those which threaten the existing or potential use of an affected area.

The scoping stage of EIAs for activities in ABNJ could incorporate examination of impacts and alternatives which take into account the shared interests of the international community such as the long term sustainability of marine resources, continuing marine scientific research, and the stability of the global climate. The general obligation to notify and consult affected parties derived from the international law duty to cooperate and found in a variety of hard and soft law instruments could be adapted to activities in ABNJ and reflected in a potential agreement under the LOSC. When information provided as part of an EIA indicates that the environment of ABNJ is likely to be significantly affected by a proposed activity, the proponent of the activity being planned could be required to notify and consult with potentially affected stakeholders and provide them with relevant information. In the ABNJ context, potential stakeholders could include States, members of the public, international and regional organizations, inter-governmental and non-governmental organizations, industry representatives, and corporate entities. Before a decision is made on whether the activity proceeds and on what conditions, these stakeholders should be provided with an opportunity to comment. To assist in this process, States could be encouraged to notify other States and competent international organizations of planned activities under their jurisdiction or control which may have a significant effect on marine biodiversity in ABNJ. There is also the potential for a more enhanced role for the regional seas organizations as dissemination points and consultation hubs on EIAs and as technical advisers on mitigation measures. Under most EIA regimes, the obligation on the final decision-maker is one of due diligence encompassing a full examination of the potential environmental impacts of a particular project and due consideration for the interests of affected parties.[92]

[92] Ibid, 150–1.

The global commons status of biodiversity in ABNJ calls for a more stringent and inclusive standard of decision-making on whether an activity should be allowed to proceed and on what conditions. This could involve developing a further set of criteria related to the permissible levels of impact on marine biodiversity in ABNJ and a decision-making structure which involves a level of international scrutiny over EIAs prepared by proponents of particular activities.

6 Conclusion

The biodiversity conservation elements of any multilateral agreement adopted under the umbrella of the LOSC to conserve and sustainably use biodiversity in ABNJ should be designed to implement the spirit and intent of Part XII provisions of the LOSC, rather than radically changing the basic principles and inherent balance of the law of the sea. Part XII of the LOSC has many open-ended provisions ripe for further evolution and implementation. Given the growing threats and pressures on the marine environment of ABNJ and its biodiversity, it is timely to incorporate and reconcile the modern conservation norms and objectives of international marine environmental law with the law of the sea. The discussions in the BBNJ process and related initiatives in the CBD and at the regional level have demonstrated that a more integrated legal and institutional structure rather than the current patchwork of hard and soft law provisions and disparate institutions is needed to achieve this end. The rationale and objectives for incorporating the biodiversity conservation elements of area-based management tools and EIA in such a legal and institutional structure have been extensively canvassed in the BBNJ Working Group over almost a decade. The time has now arrived to determine the objectives and content of a potential agreement under the LOSC for conservation of biodiversity in ABNJ. These objectives should include the development of an effectively managed, ecologically representative and well-connected system of MPAs in ABNJ and the promulgation of standards and a default system of EIA for all activities not already subject to EIA in ABNJ. The MPA provisions of an agreement should require States, through regional organizations, to propose ABNJ areas for designation. It should also define the criteria, conservation objectives and processes for submitting proposals, agreeing management measures and procedures for scientific review and endorsement. It should also oblige States parties to comply with agreed MPA management measures and not to authorize or undertake activities that might be contrary to the objectives for which a MPA was established. The MPA measures should be supplemented with a system of marine spatial planning in ABNJ designed to foster integrated ecosystem-based planning and management that requires States parties and competent regional and sectoral organizations to coordinate sectoral area-based measures and to integrate their plans to achieve healthy oceans and marine ecosystems. The EIA elements of an agreement should include criteria on the permissible levels of impact on marine biodiversity in ABNJ and a decision-making structure which involves a level of international scrutiny over EIAs prepared by proponents of particular activities. The notification and consultation provisions should reflect the broader scope of stakeholders in ABNJ encompassing relevant State actors as well as international, regional and non-governmental organizations. The political process taking place in the BBNJ Working Group and the UNGA will ultimately determine the shape of any new instrument under the law of the sea and its long term contribution to conserving the biodiversity of the oceans beyond national jurisdiction.

34

WARMING WATERS AND SOURING SEAS

CLIMATE CHANGE AND OCEAN ACIDIFICATION

TIM STEPHENS

1 INTRODUCTION

THE 1982 United Nations Convention on the Law of the Sea (LOSC) was concluded at a time when there was little appreciation of the impacts of anthropogenic global warming on the oceans.[*,1] In 1990, the Intergovernmental Panel on Climate Change (IPCC) published its First Assessment Report (AR1), which included an assessment of sea level rise.[2] In the following decades, there have been major advances in the

---

[*] Thanks are extended to Harrison Grace and Meredith Simons for research assistance. Parts of this chapter draw upon and develop work by the author published elsewhere, including 'Ocean Acidification' in R Rayfuse (ed), *Handbook on Marine Environmental Law* (Edward Elgar Cheltenham forthcoming 2015).

[1] A Boyle, 'Law of the Sea Perspectives on Climate Change' in D Freestone (ed), *The 1982 Law of the Sea Convention At 30: Successes, Challenges and New Agendas* (Martinus Nijhoff Leiden 2013) 157.

[2] Intergovernmental Panel on Climate Change (IPCC), *Climate Change: The IPCC Scientific Assessment* (Cambridge University Press Cambridge 1990) ch 9.

understanding not only of sea level rise but also the marine ecosystem impacts of climate change, and the process of ocean acidification as the oceans absorb carbon dioxide (CO_2) from the atmosphere.

The current state of knowledge is summarized in the IPCC's Fifth Assessment Report (AR5), released in 2013–2014. The AR5 reports that the oceans are undergoing a biophysical transformation that is unprecedented in human history. This process challenges two of the central assumptions upon which the law of the sea is based: that the oceans will continue to provide a predictable and benign environment which allows clear jurisdictional boundaries to be drawn (from stable baselines along the coast), and that the oceans will carry on supporting a range of vital human uses (such as fishing).

This chapter assesses the impacts that the related phenomena of climate change and ocean acidification are having on the oceans, and assesses the implications of these for the international law of the sea. In particular, the chapter evaluates the implications of rising sea levels for territorial sea baselines, the seawards extent of maritime zones, and maritime boundaries. It also considers the restrictions that the LOSC places upon States in pursuing climate mitigation and adaptation policies, such as attempts to 'engineer' the global climate by artificially enhancing the capacity of the oceans to draw CO_2 from the atmosphere. The chapter also provides an analysis of the role that the LOSC may be able to play, alongside other treaty regimes, in addressing the serious threat of ocean acidification.

2 Climate Change and Ocean Acidification: Processes and Impacts

The oceans have a critical role in regulating the Earth's climate. They have significantly slowed global warming, absorbing much of the extra energy that has been trapped in the atmosphere by increasing concentrations of greenhouse gasses (GHGs).[3] As the oceans have absorbed heat, and glaciers and ice sheets have melted, sea levels have risen. Changes in the heat content of the oceans have changed circulation patterns, and impacted upon many marine organisms, and affected the productivity and range of fish species. The oceans have also slowed climate change by acting as a reservoir for GHGs, taking up around a third of all carbon released by humanity into the atmosphere.[4] Ocean acidification, the changing chemistry of

---

[3] GK Vallis, *Climate and the Oceans* (Princeton University Press Princeton, NJ 2012) ch 7.
[4] D Archer, *The Global Carbon Cycle* (Princeton University Press Princeton 2010) 116.

the oceans as they draw down CO_2 from the atmosphere, is one consequence of this process.

From a marine environmental perspective, climate change and ocean acidification are but two of a suite of anthropogenic stressors. A comprehensive review by the International Programme on the State of the Ocean in 2013, in partnership with the International Union for the Conservation of Nature, concluded that 'human activities have led to intense multiple stressors acting together in many marine ecosystems', with the major threats 'arising from overexploitation of biotic resources, climate change effects forming the so-called "deadly trio" (ocean warming, acidification and hypoxia/anoxia[5]) and pollution'.[6] These stressors are producing localized ecosystem decline, and threaten to cause global oceanic ecosystem collapse.[7]

2.1 Sea level rise

In AR5, the IPCC reported that the rate of sea level rise since the 1950s is greater than any rise over the previous 2,000 years.[8] From 1901 until 2010, average sea levels rose by 0.19 m, and the rate of sea level rise increased during this period.[9] Around 75 per cent of the global mean sea level rise is due to the combination of glacier mass loss and thermal expansion of the oceans.[10] There is increased confidence in projections of future sea level rise since the Fourth Assessment Report (AR4) due to better understanding of ice-sheet dynamics.[11] The AR5 projects that sea levels could rise by between 0.26 and 0.55 m by 2100 if GHGs are aggressively mitigated, but by between 0.52 and 0.98 m if there is a continuation of business as usual.[12] These represent mean values, and sea level rise will not be uniform in all places. However, the AR5 concludes that it is very likely that sea levels will rise in more than 95 per cent of the oceans, and around 70 per cent of coastlines globally will experience sea level rises within 20 per cent of the global mean sea level rise projections.[13] Sea level rise will of course not cease in 2100, and it is virtually certain that sea levels will continue to rise due to thermal expansion for many centuries. For very high concentrations of CO_2, sea level rises of almost 4 m by 2300 are possible.[14] The IPCC projections of sea-level rise tend to be conservative, and a recent survey of experts concluded that

---

[5] Hypoxic waters are low in dissolved oxygen, while anoxic waters are completely depleted of oxygen. These conditions can be caused by eutrophication, the influx of nutrients from agricultural run off or sewage which boosts algal growth, and then leads to oxygen being consumed during the subsequent break down of dead algae.

[6] A Rogers and D Laffoley, 'Introduction to the Special Issue: The Global State of the Ocean' (2013) 74 *Marine Pollution Bulletin* 491, 493.

[7] Ibid.

[8] IPCC, *Climate Change 2013: The Physical Science Basis. Contribution of Working Group I to the Fifth Assessment Report of the Intergovernmental Panel on Climate Change* (Cambridge University Press Cambridge 2013) 9.

[9] Ibid.   [10] Ibid.   [11] Ibid, 23.   [12] Ibid.   [13] Ibid, 24.   [14] Ibid, 26.

higher sea-level rises than the AR5 projects are likely (including a real possibility of 2.0 m of sea level rise by AD 2100 under an upper temperature scenario).[15]

2.2 Temperature rise

The AR5 explains the vital importance of the oceans in maintaining the Earth's stable climate, with the oceans absorbing more than 90 per cent of the extra energy accumulated between 1971 and 2010 as a result of heat trapping GHGs.[16] The top 75 m of the oceans warmed by 0.11°C per decade in this period.[17] The deeper oceans have also warmed, but much more slowly.[18] At the ocean surface, increased rates of evaporation and volume of precipitation have both been observed, and this is having flow on impacts on the salinity of the oceans. Regions that are highly saline have become even more so, whereas regions of low salinity have become less so since the 1950s.[19]

The continued warming of the oceans will have a range of impacts, including accelerated warming of high latitude oceans and reductions in the extent of seasonal ice (with the Arctic likely to be ice free in summer within decades), increased stratification of ocean layers which reduces important mixing zones, shifting winds and currents (including changes to the thermohaline circulation), and falling surface water oxygen concentrations.[20] These physical changes will have ecosystem implications, including changes in productivity (decreasing in most places, increasing in some), range shifts and species invasions, changes in abundance of fisheries, increase in diseases among marine organisms, increased extinctions, and increased coral reef mortality.[21]

2.3 Ocean acidification

Ocean acidification and climate change are closely linked. Carbon dioxide is the main GHG by volume, and is also the primary driver of ocean acidification. This means that mitigating global warming by reducing atmospheric concentrations of CO_2 will also address ocean acidification. In the 2009 Copenhagen Accord[22] it was

---

[15] BP Horton et al, 'Expert Assessment of Sea-Level Rise by AD 2100 and AD 2300' (2014) 84 *Quaternary Science Reviews* 1.
[16] IPCC, n 8, 6. [17] Ibid. [18] Ibid. [19] Ibid.
[20] J Bijman, 'Climate Change and the Oceans: What Does the Future Hold?' (2013) 74 *Marine Pollution Bulletin* 495, 498.
[21] IPCC, *Climate Change 2014: Impacts, Adaptation, and Vulnerability, Contribution of Working Group II to the Fifth Assessment Report of the Intergovernmental Panel on Climate Change, Summary for Policymakers* (2014) 16–17, available at <http://ipcc-wg2.gov/AR5/images/uploads/IPCC_WG2AR5_SPM_Approved.pdf>.
[22] Decision 2/CP.15, UN Doc FCCC/CP/2009/11/Add.1 (30 March 2010).

agreed that 'the increase in global temperature should be below 2°C' in order to meet the objective of the 1992 United Nations Framework Convention on Climate Change (UNFCCC) to avoid 'dangerous anthropogenic interference with the climate'. However, there is uncertainty whether the atmospheric CO_2 concentration that this temperature target implies (around 450 parts per million (ppm) CO_2 equivalent) would avoid dangerous ocean acidification. Recognising the potential for ocean acidification to transform the oceans this century, the UN Secretary General devoted the first part of the 2013 Report to the General Assembly on Oceans and the Law of the Sea to the phenomenon.[23]

The 'carbonation' of the world's oceans is leading to unprecedented alterations to their chemistry.[24] While the oceans are slightly alkaline (with a pre-Industrial Revolution pH of around 8.1), oceanic pH is declining rapidly. There has been a 0.1 unit decline in pH over the last century,[25] and the oceans now have a lower pH today than in the previous 20 million years.[26] The pH is projected to decline by 0.2–0.3 units below the pre-industrial level by 2100.[27] If CO_2 emissions are not reduced, then the magnitude of the change to the geochemistry of the world's oceans will be unprecedented in at least the last 300 million years of Earth's history.[28] There is also feedback between ocean acidification and climate change; ocean acidification amplifies climate change by reducing the fluxes of sulphur from the oceans into the atmosphere that help reduce radiative forcing.[29]

Ocean acidification is a more recently identified environmental impact from CO_2 emissions than global warming, and less is known about its effects. Nonetheless, most available evidence indicates that it will have serious and lasting impacts on many marine organisms, and will radically alter biophysical processes in the oceanic environment.[30] It is driving major changes in seawater chemistry (not only pH, but also on nitrogen fixation and other chemical processes), and reducing aragonite and calcite saturation.[31] These changes are reducing the calcification rates of calcifying organisms such as corals (and will eventually erode existing coral structures), placing stress on phytoplankton populations, and are having many other biotic

---

[23] UN Secretary General, *Oceans and the Law of the Sea: Report of the Secretary General to the General Assembly*, UN Doc A/68/71 (2013).

[24] J-P Gattuso and L Hansson, 'Ocean Acidification: Background and History' in J-P Gattuso and L Hansson (eds), *Ocean Acidification* (Oxford University Press Oxford 2011) 1.

[25] T Friedrich et al, 'Detecting Regional Anthropogenic Trends in Ocean Acidification Against Natural Variability. (2012) 2 *Nature Climate Change* 167.

[26] Bijman, n 20, 501.

[27] WR Howard et al, 'Ocean Acidification. Marine Climate Change Impacts and Adaptation Report Card for Australia' (CSIRO Australia 2012).

[28] B Hönisch et al, 'The Geological Record of Ocean Acidification' (2012) 335 *Science* 1058, 1062.

[29] KD Six et al, 'Global Warming Amplified by Reduced Sulphur Fluxes as a Result of Ocean Acidification' (2013) 3 *Nature Climate Change* 975.

[30] Climate Commission, *The Critical Decade 2013: Climate Change, Science, Risks and Responses* (Climate Commission Canberra 2013) 49–51.

[31] Bijman, n 20, 501.

impacts (including affecting photosynthesis and oxygen exchange).[32] When combined with the effects of increased temperature, tropical coral reefs are expected to enter a 'rapid and terminal decline' by 2050.[33] Another recent assessment of corals concluded that if GHG emissions continue unchecked, then no oceans will support coral reef growth by 2100.[34] A disruption of the oceanic food chain as a result of these and other changes would have catastrophic social and economic impacts.[35]

3 THE LAW OF THE SEA AND CLIMATE CHANGE MITIGATION

The impacts of climate change and ocean acidification upon the oceans described in the previous section carry a range of significant implications for the law of the sea. These can be divided into two main categories. First, the extent to which the law of the sea can play a role in *mitigating* climate change and ocean acidification and, second, how the law of the sea provides a framework for *adaptive responses* by coastal and other States to the effects of climate change and ocean acidification. This section considers mitigation options, while the subsequent section assesses how the law of the sea facilitates adaptation.

3.1 Controlling GHGs

Although the LOSC makes no mention of climate change and its impacts upon the marine environment, it does impose wide-ranging obligations to protect and preserve the marine environment and to prevent pollution. The initial question arises as to whether the LOSC requires States to reduce GHGs, or whether this issue is exclusively the province of UNFCCC as the *lex specialis* for controlling climate change.

---

[32] Ibid.   [33] Ibid.
[34] KL Rickie et al, 'Risks to Coral Reefs from Ocean Carbonate Chemistry Changes in Recent Earth System Model Projections' (2013) 8 *Environmental Research Letters* 034003.
[35] R Allan and A Bergin, 'Ocean Acidification: An Emerging Australian Environmental Security Challenge' (2009) 1 *Australian Journal of Maritime and Ocean Affairs* 49; SR Cooley and SC Doney, 'Anticipating Ocean Acidification's Economic Consequences for Commercial Fisheries' (2009) 4 *Environmental Research Letters* 024007.

3.1.1 *LOSC obligations to control GHGs?*

Under Article 192 of the LOSC, States are under an obligation 'to protect and preserve the marine environment', and Article 194(1) requires States to take 'all measures...necessary to prevent, reduce and control pollution of the marine environment from any source'. Article 212(1) makes clear that States must 'prevent, reduce and control pollution of the marine environment from or through the atmosphere'. Moreover, Article 212(3) stipulates that States, acting especially through international organizations or diplomatic conferences, must endeavour to establish rules, standards, and recommended practices to prevent, reduce, and control atmospheric pollution. These provisions, together with the broad definition of 'pollution' in Article 1(1)(4) to include 'substances or energy', impose a due diligence obligation upon States to control and reduce emissions of GHGs that will damage the marine environment causing harm to other States.[36]

However, the provisions of the LOSC are general in character, and obviously do not specify GHG emissions reduction targets or timetables. It is therefore difficult to determine whether a State has or has not met its obligations under the LOSC in taking or failing to take measures to reduce CO_2 emissions. One response to this problem is to rely upon the UNFCCC and instruments adopted under it, most notably the 1997 Kyoto Protocol, which does set prescribed emission reduction or limitation targets for industrialized States, to supply the relevant standard of conduct for the LOSC. However, the Kyoto Protocol in its current form will not deliver the emissions reductions necessary to stabilize atmospheric concentrations of CO_2 at a level that would avoid serious and irreversible damage to the marine environment.[37]

It is therefore difficult to see how States can meet their overriding obligation under Article 192 of the LOSC to 'protect and preserve the marine environment' by satisfying the modest requirements of the Kyoto Protocol. However, it is equally difficult to identify emissions reductions required of individual States in the absence of a global agreement, as action by one or several States will not be effective in isolation to prevent substantial marine environmental damage. Ultimately, therefore, the UNFCCC and implementing agreements under its umbrella remain the primary means to drive mitigation policy that will protect the oceans.[38] If this regime is to be successful in safeguarding the marine environment, it is vital that oceans impacts are more fully considered in the UNFCCC process, including by expressly addressing ocean acidification (which has to date been largely ignored by the UNFCCC).

---

[36] Boyle, n 1.

[37] IPCC, *Climate Change 2014: Impacts, Adaptation, and Vulnerability, Contribution of Working Group II to the Fifth Assessment Report of the Intergovernmental Panel on Climate Change* (2014) ch 6, available at <http://ipcc-wg2.gov/AR5/images/uploads/WGIIAR5-Chap6_FGDall.pdf>.

[38] Boyle, n 1, 161–2.

3.1.2 *Complementary marine environmental regimes*

Although the LOSC does not mandate any specific GHG emission reductions, there are treaties adopted to implement aspects of the LOSC that do seek to place limits on GHG emissions and the storage of GHGs in the marine environment.

The 1972 Convention on the Prevention of Marine Pollution by Dumping of Wastes and Other Matter (London Convention) and the 1996 London Protocol aim to prevent pollution of the oceans by the dumping of materials that could endanger human health or harm the marine environment. Under the regime, dumping at sea of any substance is generally prohibited, unless it can be shown not to damage the marine environment. Any measures to store CO_2 in geological formations under the seabed, on the seabed (at depths at which high pressures will act to condense CO_2), or in the water column, will need to comply with the terms of the dumping regime. Consistent with the 1996 London Protocol's precautionary approach, several measures have been adopted to regulate the active use of the water column as a carbon sink. At the first meeting of the parties in 2006, amendments to the 1996 London Protocol were agreed which permitted the storage of CO_2 under, *but not on or above*, the seabed.[39] The intent of sub-seabed carbon sequestration is that CO_2 streams are retained permanently in undersea geological formations, a technology that the parties to the Protocol endorsed as a strategy both for mitigating climate change and ocean acidification. However, the parties also acknowledged the risks associated with CO_2 sequestration (including the possibility that CO_2 will leak into the water column and exacerbate ocean acidification). To minimize these risks, in 2012, the parties to the London Convention and Protocol adopted detailed 'Specific Guidelines for the Assessment of Carbon Dioxide Streams for Disposal into Sub-Seabed Geological Formations'.[40] Whether or not these will be sufficient to protect the seabed and marine environment is open to question.[41]

The other related development under the London dumping regime is in relation to marine geo-engineering. In 2008, a Resolution of the parties imposed a moratorium on ocean fertilization, except for legitimate scientific research.[42] Ocean fertilization describes processes by which GHG sequestration by the oceans can be enhanced, such as through the introduction of iron, phosphorous or nitrogen compounds to promote the growth of phytoplankton which absorb CO_2. In 2010, the parties adopted Resolution LC-LP.2 (2010) on the 'Assessment Framework for Scientific Research Involving Ocean Fertilization' which guides parties in assessing proposals for ocean fertilization research, and

---

[39] IMO, 'Notification of amendments to Annex 1 to the London Protocol 1996', IMO Doc LC-LP.1/Circ.5 (27 November 2006).
[40] IMO Doc LC 34/15 (2 November 2012) Annex 8.
[41] R Monastersky, 'Seabed Scars Raise Questions Over Carbon-Storage Plan' (2013) 504 *Nature* 339.
[42] Resolution LC-LP.1 (31 October 2008).

includes detailed environmental assessment rules. Subsequently, in Resolution LP.4(8) in 2013, the parties to the London Protocol agreed on a new Article 6bis, which provides that parties shall not allow the placement of matter into the sea from vessels, aircraft, platforms or other man-made structures at sea for marine geo-engineering purposes unless the activity is authorized under a permit. Marine geo-engineering is defined as 'a deliberate intervention in the marine environment to manipulate natural processes, including to counteract anthropogenic climate change' and a new Annex 4 to the London Protocol on marine geo-engineering lists and defines ocean fertilization as 'any activity undertaken by humans with the principal intention of stimulating primary productivity in the oceans'. Ocean fertilization activities can only be permitted if assessed to be legitimate scientific research. These changes are highly significant in acknowledging the potential of the oceans to contribute further to mitigating climate change. However, they also seek to control the negative side effects of marine geo-engineering, including ocean acidification, by limiting the use of some technologies (such as those seeking to enhance upwelling of cold seawater from the depths) that would exacerbate acidification. It must be recognized that these will have limited overall impact in controlling acidification given that its primary driver is the absorption of CO_2 from the atmosphere.[43]

Also of relevance to climate change and ocean acidification mitigation is the 1973 International Convention for the Prevention of Pollution from Ships, as modified by the Protocol of 1978 (MARPOL). MARPOL seeks 'to achieve the complete elimination of intentional pollution of the marine environment by oil and other harmful substances and the minimization of accidental discharge of such substances'.[44] Annex VI of MARPOL addresses the prevention of air pollution from ships, and entered into force in May 2005. In 2011, the International Maritime Organization (IMO) adopted new mandatory technical and operational energy efficiency measures to reduce CO_2 and other GHG emissions from ships, with these entering into force on 1 January 2013. Shipping emissions account for around 2.7 per cent of global CO_2 emissions, and prior to the 2011 amendments being adopted, it was estimated that CO_2 emissions from shipping would increase by up to 300 per cent by 2050.[45] Although the new controls on GHG emissions from ships will have a relatively small effect in mitigating climate change and ocean acidification, they represent a significant development in being the first global GHG controls in any economic sector (by comparison, there are no global limits on GHG emissions from aircraft).

---

[43] P Williamson and C Turley, 'Ocean Acidification in a Geoengineering Context' (2012) 370 *Philosophical Transactions of the Royal Society A* 1974; RA Feely et al, 'Evidence for Upwelling of Corrosive "Acidified" Water onto the Continental Shelf' (2008) 320 *Science* 1490.

[44] 1973 International Convention for the Prevention of Pollution, as modified by the Protocol of 1978, Preamble, 4th Recital (hereinafter MARPOL).

[45] *Oceans and the Law of the Sea: Report of the Secretary-General*, UN Doc A/64/66/Add.1 (2009) [349].

3.1.3 *The climate change regime*

The climate change regime is the primary means through which the international community is seeking to control GHG emissions. However, as currently structured, it has a very limited oceans emphasis, and ignores ocean acidification (indeed the phenomenon is not mentioned in any binding international legal instrument[46]).

Article 2 of the UNFCCC sets out the overall objective of the climate change regime, which is to achieve the stabilization of GHG concentrations in the atmosphere at a level that would prevent dangerous anthropogenic interference with the climate system. The UNFCCC has an obvious and understandable atmospheric rather than oceanic focus. This is emphasized further in the 1997 Kyoto Protocol that sets targets for reducing or limiting emissions on the basis of their impacts upon the atmosphere, rather than the oceans. The Kyoto Protocol bundles together the half-dozen major GHGs (including CO_2) when determining global and national emissions budgets, and establishes no specific obligation to reduce emissions of CO_2, the primary gas causing ocean acidification. Instead States can meet their commitments by limiting their CO_2 *equivalent* emissions of GHGs,[47] and therefore may even *increase* CO_2 emissions, so long as there is a corresponding reduction in other GHGs. Other aspects of the climate regime are in tension with efforts to control ocean acidification, with uptake of atmospheric CO_2 by the oceans presented as a legitimate climate mitigation policy.[48]

Within the climate regime's conferences and meetings of the parties and subsidiary bodies little attention if any has been devoted to ocean acidification, or to climate and oceans issues generally. Galland et al note that this record shows that '[d]espite its significant role in climate regulation and vulnerability to climate change, the ocean is often relegated to footnotes and afterthoughts in the development of climate policy.'[49] They recommend that oceanic threshold data be used (in a manner akin to thresholds of climate sensitivity to GHGs) to design and support emission reduction targets for CO_2 that consider the totality of oceanic impacts from global warming, including sea level rise and ocean acidification, which are having a combined impact upon many marine organisms and ecosystems.[50]

---

[46] UN Secretary General, n 23, 12.
[47] 1997 Kyoto Protocol to the United Nations Framework Convention on Climate Change, Art 3(1) (hereinafter Kyoto Protocol).
[48] See eg 1992 United Nations Framework Convention on Climate Change, Arts 1 and 4(1)(d) (hereinafter UNFCCC).
[49] G Galland, E Harrould-Kolieb, and D Herr, 'The Ocean and Climate Change Policy' (2012) 12 *Climate Policy* 764, 765.
[50] Ibid, 767.

4 THE LAW OF THE SEA AND CLIMATE CHANGE ADAPTATION

It has been seen that law of the sea provides only very general obligations in relation to the prevention of climate change and ocean acidification. In relation to climate change adaptation, defined by the IPCC as 'the adjustment of natural or human systems in response to actual or expected climatic stimuli or their effects, which moderates harm or exploits beneficial opportunities',[51] there are more significant linkages with the law of the sea. This is true both in respect of *physical* adaptation (eg the construction of seawalls) and *legal* adaptation (eg attempts to 'fix' territorial sea baselines despite sea level rise, or to alter rules for fisheries management).

4.1 Sea level rise

Sea levels are rising, and because of momentum in the climate system they will continue to do so for centuries regardless of action taken to reduce GHG emissions. This will result in inevitable changes to coastline geography, particularly in low-lying areas. The landwards shift in the low-water line, and the partial or complete inundation of low-lying territory, including coastal and mid-ocean islands, calls into question the legitimacy of the baselines and basepoints currently adopted by States to set the boundary between internal waters and the territorial sea, and from which coastal States project their maritime zones.

The impact of sea level rise upon baselines has been the subject of significant discussion since the 1990s,[52] when the issue first rose to international prominence with the publication of the IPCC's AR1. However, when the LOSC was negotiated in the 1970s and early 1980s, there was limited awareness of global warming and the associated impacts upon sea levels. After a brief review of the LOSC's baseline provisions, the following discussion assesses the legal implications of sea level rise for the baseline regime.[53]

---

[51] IPCC, *Contribution of Working Group II to the Fourth Assessment Report of the Intergovernmental Panel on Climate Change* (Cambridge University Press Cambridge 2007), 750.

[52] AHA Soons, 'The Effects of a Rising Sea Level on Maritime Limits and Boundaries' (1990) 37 *Netherlands International Law Review* 207; DD Caron, 'When Law Makes Climate Change Worse: Rethinking the Law of Baselines in Light of Rising Sea Level' (1990) 17 *Ecology Law Quarterly* 621.

[53] For detailed discussion of baselines, see Chapter 4 in this volume.

4.1.1 *The LOSC baseline regime*

Bringing to a resolution many decades of controversy, the LOSC sets out a system for delineating baselines to address the wide variety in coastline configuration worldwide. Under the LOSC, a coastal State may determine baselines to suit particular coastline conditions according to the various methods provided.[54]

The LOSC provides that the normal baseline for measuring the breadth of the territorial sea is the low-water line along the coast as marked on large-scale charts officially recognised by the coastal State.[55] There is no definition in the LOSC of the 'low-water line', and States are free to adopt their own approach.[56] In addition, normal baselines may be drawn along the low-water line around low-tide elevations (naturally formed areas of land that are above water at low tide, but submerged at low tide) if these are within the 12 nautical mile (nm) territorial sea.[57] For islands situated on atolls, or islands with fringing reefs, the baseline is the seaward low-water line of the reef, as shown by an appropriate symbol on charts officially recognized by the coastal State.[58]

In several circumstances, it is possible for States to draw straight baselines rather than normal baselines. Where because of a delta or other natural conditions rendering a coastline unstable, the appropriate basepoints may be selected along the furthest seaward extent of the low-water line and remain effective, notwithstanding subsequent regression of the line.[59] Straight lines may be drawn across the mouth of rivers discharging into the sea,[60] and across the mouths of bays that are more than mere curvatures of the coast.[61] Where a coastline is deeply indented and cut into, or if there is a fringe of islands along the coast in its immediate vicinity, then straight baselines may be drawn using appropriate points.[62] These points could include not only positions on the coast, but also low-lying islands, islets, and rocks. However, straight baselines must not be drawn to and from low-tide elevations unless lighthouses or similar installations that are permanently above sea level have been built on them, or such elevations have received general international recognition.[63]

Under the LOSC, archipelagic States may also draw straight archipelagic baselines that are similar to straight baselines along the coastlines of metropolitan States (although the conditions that need to be met are quite distinct). Archipelagic States may draw straight archipelagic baselines joining the outermost points of the outermost islands and drying reefs of the archipelago, so long as certain requirements are satisfied.[64]

---

[54] 1982 United Nations Convention on the Law of the Sea, Art 14 (hereinafter LOSC).
[55] Ibid, Art 5.
[56] DR Rothwell and T Stephens, *The International Law of the Sea* (Hart Oxford 2010) 42. Many States have chosen the lowest astronomical tide: C Schofield, 'Departures from the Coast: Trends in the Application of Territorial Sea Baselines under the Law of the Sea Convention' in Freestone (ed), n 1, 49, 50–1.
[57] LOSC, n 54, Art 13(1).   [58] Ibid, Art 6.   [59] Ibid, Art 7(2).   [60] Ibid, Art 9.
[61] Ibid, Art 10.   [62] Ibid, Art 7(1).   [63] Ibid, Art 7(4).   [64] Ibid, Art 47.

4.1.2 *Baselines and maritime zones: fixed or floating?*

The widely accepted view is that under the LOSC baselines are ambulatory, and move if the land recedes.[65] The corollary to this is that the outer edge of coastal State maritime zones also moves landwards to the same extent (with the exception of the limits of the continental shelf beyond 200 nm, which are set by reference to the physical characteristics of the seafloor). The ambulatory thesis has two variants. The first is that baselines shift with automatic effect as the seas rise. The second is that sea level rise entails an obligation by States to adjust normal and straight baselines in response to changing coastal conditions. However, neither ambulatory theory can draw express support from the text of the LOSC, or any other instrument. And so the argument for the ambulatory approach proceeds from 'negative implication'; that as the LOSC refers to only two situations where baselines or maritime zone limits are fixed, then in all other situations, they must move as the sea engulfs the land.[66] The first reference, in Article 7(2), is to river deltas and other highly unstable coastlines where the coastal State may adopt fixed straight baselines. The second reference, in Article 76(9), is not to a baseline provision, but rather to the outer limits of the physical continental shelf beyond 200 nm which, when set according to the process laid out in Article 76, are 'permanently described'.

An alternative argument to the ambulatory baseline thesis has been advanced by Purcell.[67] She contends that baselines and zonal limits measured from them are not floating, and do not move automatically, in light of 'the clear priority given to coastal State control over national maritime space under the law of the sea'.[68] She is unconvinced by the argument for ambulatory baselines drawn by negative implication. As regards Article 7(2), Purcell argues it could just as well be read as 'an express assurance that the general rule regarding [the] effectiveness [of baselines] will apply even in circumstances of significant coastal change'.[69] Pointing to the emphasis that the LOSC places on stability in ocean affairs, Purcell concludes that it is a matter for individual coastal States, in their discretion, to retain or revise baselines and zonal

---

[65] See R Rayfuse, 'Climate Change and the Law of the Sea' in R Rayfuse and S Scott (eds), *International Law in the Era of Climate Change* (Edward Elgar Cheltenham 2012) 147; M Hayashi, 'Sea-Level Rise and the Law of the Sea: Future Options' in D Vidas and PJ Schei (eds), *The World Ocean in Globalisation* (Martinus Nijhoff Leiden 2011) 187; C Schofield, 'Shifting Limits?: Sea Level Rise and Options to Secure Maritime Jurisdictional Claims' (2009) 4 *Carbon and Climate Law Review* 405; D Freestone, 'International Law and Sea Level Rise' in R Churchill and D Freestone (eds), *International Law and Global Climate Change* (Martinus Nijhoff Leiden 1991) 109; Caron, n 52; Soons, n 52; and the various views contained in International Law Association (ILA), Committee on Baselines Under the International Law of the Sea, *Final Report* (2012), available at <http://www.ila-hq.org/en/committees/index.cfm/cid/1028>.

[66] Rayfuse, n 65, 150.

[67] K Purcell, 'Maritime Jurisdiction in a Changing Climate' in MB Gerrard and K Fischer Kuh (eds), *The Law of Adaptation to Climate Change: United States and International Perspectives* (ABA Chicago 2012) 731.

[68] Ibid, 739.   [69] Ibid, 742.

limits in response to sea level rise. If they are not revised, then they do not shift automatically, and the failure to adjust them can attract no valid protest from other States because there is no legal obligation to move them.[70]

There is significant State practice to support the ambulatory approach, although it is admittedly difficult to draw firm conclusions from the existing practice as States have not needed to respond to significant sea level rise to date, and relatively modest rises are expected during this century. Nonetheless, some States do adopt the position in national legislation that the normal baseline is the physical low-water line along the coast, with no reference to a charted line, with the logical consequence that the baseline will move with the low-water line.[71]

4.1.3 *Implications for coastal States*

As baselines are ambulatory sea level rise will carry implications for many coastal States, particularly those that are low-lying, and most dramatically for some archipelagic and small island States.

The movement of baselines alters the boundary between internal waters and the territorial sea. It also has the effect of moving landwards the limits of the territorial sea, contiguous zone, exclusive economic zone (EEZ), and the 200 nm continental shelf. Adjustments would therefore need to be made to the normal baseline following the coast to bring it landwards. Additionally, low-tide elevations within 12 nm of the coastline that become submerged would no longer generate a territorial sea, or contribute to the outer limits of other maritime zones where relevant.[72] The melting of ice covered areas along coastlines in the Antarctic and Arctic may require special attention, to the extent that States seek to rely upon ice shelf baselines or basepoints that move as the ice contracts.[73] Adjustments would also need to be made to baselines across the mouths of rivers, bays, and along indented coastlines, where the base point becomes submerged at high tide because of sea level rise. In the case of straight baselines along deeply indented coasts or those with fringing islands, these may prove relatively robust in the face of sea level rise as they tend to be drawn to basepoints that are fairly stable.

Insular and archipelagic States may be particularly vulnerable to rising sea levels and ambulatory shifts in baselines and maritime zones. Archipelagic baselines may no longer be able to be drawn if they connect to islands and drying

---

[70] Ibid, 759.

[71] ILA, Committee on Baselines Under the International Law of the Sea, n 65, 16–17. One example given is the *Delimitation of French Territorial Waters*, Law No 71-1060 (1971) Art 1. ('Les lignes de base sont la laisse de basse mer ainsi que les lignes de base droites et les lignes de fermeture des baies qui sont determinés par décret.')

[72] LOSC, n 54, Art 13.

[73] Rayfuse, n 65, 155; DR Rothwell, *The Polar Regions and the Development of International Law* (Cambridge University Press Cambridge 1996) 268–73.

reefs that are permanently submerged.⁷⁴ If sufficient territory of an archipelagic State is inundated then it could mean that the State fails to satisfy the minimum land to water ratio requirement (1:9) or the maximum baseline length rules (normally 100 nm).⁷⁵ However, archipelagic States comprising many islands and drying reefs may fare better than non-archipelagic island States which become submerged or uninhabitable because of effects associated with sea level rise and climate change (such as salt water intrusion, and periodic inundation from storm surges). Article 121(1) LOSC defines an island as a naturally formed area of land surrounded by water, which is above water at high tide. The full suite of maritime zones may be extended from islands, except in the case of 'rocks which cannot sustain human habitation or economic life of their own', which do not have an EEZ or continental shelf.⁷⁶ Although Article 121 is ambiguous, it does suggest that States with islands, or island States, may lose an entitlement to EEZ or continental shelf areas following significant sea level rise. In the case of some States, this will be very significant; a small island may generate an area within the 200 nm zone of 431,014 km², while a rock would generate only a 1,550 km² area of territorial sea.⁷⁷ This means that becoming uninhabitable will be the more serious threat than inundation for some States, as a sea level rise of up to one metre is unlikely to submerge any State completely.⁷⁸

The situation for small island States rendered uninhabitable or completely submerged raises not only law of the sea issues but more fundamental questions concerning the indicia of statehood upon which any assertions of maritime sovereignty and jurisdiction are premised.⁷⁹ The existence of territory and a permanent population are vital requirements for the acquisition of statehood, and the loss of these attributes, certainly if permanent, would appear to deprive an existing State of its status as such.⁸⁰

4.1.4 *Implications for maritime boundaries*

If baselines are ambulatory, then this also raises the question whether maritime boundaries should be adjusted to deal with changing coastal conditions. Legally, this is a more straightforward issue than in respect of baselines, as boundaries (both terrestrial and maritime) are permanent and dispositive, and not susceptible to termination or withdrawal (except on mutually agreed terms), even if there is a fundamental change of circumstances.⁸¹ Moreover, most boundaries are set

---

⁷⁴ LOSC, n 54, Art 47(1).   ⁷⁵ Ibid, Art 47(1) and (2).
⁷⁶ Ibid, Art 121(3).   ⁷⁷ Schofield, n 65, 409.   ⁷⁸ Ibid, 414.
⁷⁹ See, in particular, L Yamamoto and M Esteban, *Atoll States and International Law: Climate Change Displacement and Sovereignty* (Springer Heidelberg 2014); and J McAdam (ed), *Climate Change and Displacement: Multidisciplinary Perspectives* (Hart Oxford 2010).
⁸⁰ E Crawford and R Rayfuse, 'Climate Change and Statehood' in Rayfuse and Scott (eds), n 65, 243.
⁸¹ 1969 Vienna Convention on the Law of Treaties, Art 62(2)(a).

by reference to specific coordinates rather than a method of delimitation that could produce a different boundary if opposite or adjacent coasts are affected differently by sea level rise.[82] Nonetheless, where changing coastal geography has the effect of significantly altering the location of points used as the basis for drawing equidistant or other maritime boundaries, it is conceivable that pressure will be brought to bear by some States to revisit boundary arrangements.[83] This is especially the case if any adjustment would change ownership over natural resources.

4.1.5 *Legal responses: adoption of new baseline rules?*

The initial response by States to sea level rise will be to utilize existing provisions of the LOSC to safeguard baselines and maritime entitlements to the fullest extent possible.[84] Greater use could be made by some States of the straight baseline rules in Article 7 to draw baselines that connect stable features such as rocky points. Indeed, the LOSC itself seeks to promote stability in straight baselines by imposing the requirement that they be drawn to and from low-tide elevations only where there are lighthouses or other similar installations permanently above sea level built upon them.[85]

There are additional opportunities for fixing lines in the sea, entirely consistently with the LOSC as it currently stands. The outer limits of the continental shelf, beyond 200 nm, are established by reference to the actual physical extent of the continental margin, and this is clearly not susceptible to change with sea level rise.[86] While territorial baselines might recede, and with it the various maritime zones, the outer limits of the continental shelf beyond 200 nm would remain, and its breadth would expand.[87] Soons has argued that the same conclusion applies to the 200 nm continental shelf limit, as the provision was designed to fix permanently the boundary between the continental shelf and the Area.

Neither straight baselines, nor permanently described continental shelf limits, will address in a satisfactory or comprehensive way the challenge of sea level rise. It is highly unlikely that States will simply allow maritime space to be lost without a response. Coastal States may decide to declare unilaterally the continued applicability of their baselines to preserve the extent of the maritime estate under coastal State sovereignty and jurisdiction.[88] In the absence of protest by other States this may be effective to maintain the status quo. However, the difficulty remains that there is no clear support in the LOSC for this approach, and the baseline rules as they stand provide an uncertain bulwark against the reality of coastline change.

[82] Rayfuse, n 65, 154.
[83] KJ Houghton et al, 'Maritime Boundaries in a Rising Sea' (2010) 3 *Nature Geoscience* 813, 813–14.
[84] Hayashi, n 65, 191.   [85] LOSC, n 54, Art 7(4).
[86] See further Chapter 9 in this volume.   [87] Soons, n 52, 216–17.   [88] Schofield, n 65, 406.

Uncertainty in the placement of maritime boundaries and breadth of zones is anathema to the modern law of the sea, and for this reason it has been argued by Caron and others that the LOSC should be adjusted to fix baselines at their pre-sea level rise position.

There are sound policy reasons for doing this, and no obvious practical impediments to doing so.[89] Caron has explained that maintaining baselines, maritime zone limits, and agreed maritime boundaries is more equitable than the ambulatory alternative, as it avoids the unfairness inherent in low-lying States losing sovereignty and jurisdiction while giving other States and the international community (as the high seas grow in area) a 'windfall'.[90] Hayashi argues further that allowing a coastal State to retain submerged land as internal waters over which the coastal State has complete sovereignty can be seen as fair compensation for the loss of sovereignty over land territory.[91] Fixing baselines also appears preferable to the rule change suggested by Soons, which is that baselines could be allowed to shift but outer limits of maritime zones could be retained.[92] That would require modification of the rules relating to the breadth of the territorial sea and the EEZ.[93] Fixing baselines is technically feasible (particularly so in the era of sophisticated Geographic Information Systems (GIS)), it would preserve stability and certainty in the law of the sea[94] and it would free States from the wasteful and potentially crippling expenses associated with shoreline reinforcement pursued only to maintain maritime entitlements.[95]

One issue that would need attention in any change to baseline rules would be to select a 'critical date' at which they are fixed. Several possibilities suggest themselves, including the date of conclusion or entry into force of the LOSC, or the date on which a coastal State satisfies the requirements of Article 16(2) by giving 'due publicity' to baseline and base point charts and by depositing a copy of them with the Secretary-General of the UN.[96] It may be prudent to build in the capacity for review of a rule fixing baselines after a specified period, in the event that sea levels rise faster and further than anticipated, radically altering coastal geographies. Another broader practical issue is how any rule change would actually be effected. While consistent and widespread State practice by coastal States over a lengthy period could give rise to a new customary rule recognizing fixed baselines, to avoid uncertainty an amendment of the LOSC, or a new implementing agreement following the model of the 1994 Agreement, would be preferable. An intermediate, and interim, response short of textual amendment may be for the Meeting of States Parties to the LOSC (SPLOS) to adopt a decision on the interpretation and application of the baseline provisions that recognizes the capacity of coastal States to fix their baselines.

---

[89] Caron, n 52, 623. [90] Ibid, 648. [91] Hayashi, n 65, 197. [92] Soons, n 52.
[93] Hayashi, n 65, 196. [94] Caron, n 52, 644. [95] Ibid, 646. [96] Hayashi, n 65, 197–8.

4.1.6 *Physical responses: holding back the tide?*

States enjoy considerable discretion in determining whether and what measures they will implement in response to coastal threats from rising seas and associated risks. However, the LOSC does set some limits on the extent to which coastal States may take physical adaptive steps in responding to climate change in the coastal zone. Article 121(1) of the LOSC provides that '[a]n island is a *naturally* formed area of land, surrounded by water, which is above water at high tide.' Therefore, while an Article 121 island, such as a mainland coast, may be artificially protected, entirely artificial islands, such as Hulhumalé, currently being constructed in the Maldives, are not capable of supporting a territorial sea, contiguous zone, EEZ, or continental shelf.[97] Furthermore, coastal States may not implement coastal engineering works unless there is an assessment of their potential marine environmental effects,[98] and they must adopt laws and regulations to 'prevent, reduce and control pollution of the marine environment from land-based sources'.[99] The *Land Reclamation by Singapore in and Around the Straits of Johor*[100] case has some relevance to coastal works to deal with sea level rise. Implicitly referencing the precautionary principle, ITLOS held that 'prudence and caution' required that Malaysia and Singapore cooperate in assessing and limiting the impact of the land reclamation activities in the strait in order to protect the marine environment. This indicates that the law of the sea requires coastal States to exercise caution when planning coastal adaptation works, and suggests that in the first instance States should investigate adaption options that do not involve substantial physical alteration of the coastal environment.

4.2 Marine resources and ecosystems

Another major arena within the law of sea relevant to climate change adaptation is the body of rules relating to the management and conservation of marine resources and ecosystems. Coastal and fishing States are presented with a number of options to enhance the resilience of marine ecosystems so that they are able to cope, at least for a time, with the stresses associated with climate change and ocean acidification.

Within the territorial sea, a coastal State has broad-ranging capacity to implement rigorous marine environmental protection provisions consistent with its sovereignty over the zone. Hence coastal States may limit fishing or close fisheries,

---

[97] M Gagain 'Climate Change and Sea Level Rise and Artificial Island: Saving the Maldives' Statehood and Maritime Through the 'Constitution of Oceans' (2012) 23 *Colorado Journal of International Environmental Law and Policy* 77, 81–2.

[98] LOSC, n 54, Art 206.   [99] Ibid, Art 207(1).

[100] *Land Reclamation by Singapore In and Around the Straits of Johor (Malaysia v Singapore)* (Provisional Measures) [2003] ITLOS Rep 10.

establish marine protected areas (MPAs) and parks, and impose special protective measures for areas such as reefs. Similarly, within the EEZ, coastal States may implement adaptive measures in relation to resources with little, if any, consideration of the interests of other States. The coastal State is given sole discretion in setting allowable catches for fisheries, taking into account the best scientific evidence, and the responsibility to conserve and manage fisheries so that they are not endangered by overexploitation.[101] Coastal States can therefore take those adaptive measures considered appropriate for fisheries located within the EEZ to respond to climate change and ocean acidification.

In relation to non-living resources, coastal States have a clearly unencumbered right to decide whether and under what circumstances mineral resources are exploited within their continental shelf and EEZ. Article 56(3) of the LOSC provides the rights of coastal States with respect to the seabed and subsoil in the EEZ are made coterminous with those under the provisions of the convention addressing the continental shelf, in Part VI. In essence it is for the coastal State alone to determine whether to explore or exploit the natural resources of the continental shelf, and no other State may undertake such activities without the express consent of the coastal State.[102] As a consequence, coastal States are fully within their rights to include climate change mitigation and adaptation considerations in the planning, assessment, and approvals processes for proposed oil and gas development of the EEZ.

Whereas, in relation to the fisheries and mineral resources of the EEZ and continental shelf, coastal States have wide if not completely unconstrained discretion in taking adaptive measures, the same cannot be said for measures targeting other elements of the marine environment. In relation to marine pollution from vessels, and the risks posed by vessel movements through sensitive marine environments, which remain key concerns for marine environmental protection, coastal States must normally adhere to those international standards adopted under the auspices of the IMO, which are incorporated by reference in the LOSC.[103] However, the IMO regime does allow the designation of certain ecologically vulnerable marine areas as Particularly Sensitive Sea Areas (PSSAs), which in turn allows for the adoption of 'associated protective measures' to prevent, reduce or eliminate the threat posed by international shipping. PSSAs are normally, but need not always be, included within MPAs. MPAs are emerging as a critically important area-based tool for marine conservation in the era of climate change.[104]

---

[101] LOSC, n 54, Art 61.   [102] Ibid, Art 77.   [103] See further Chapter 23 in this volume.
[104] L Kriwoken, J Davidson, and M Lockwood, 'Marine Protected Areas and Transboundary Governance' in R Warner and S Marsden (eds), *Transboundary Environmental Governance: Inland, Coastal and Marine Perspectives* (Ashgate Farnham 2012) 85.

In relating to fisheries and ecosystems that occur across maritime zones of multiple States, or on the high seas, the framework for adapting to climate change and ocean acidification is less robust. Many such fisheries are subject to management by Regional Fisheries Management Organizations (RFMOs), some of which are beginning to consider adaptive responses.[105] Most wild capture fisheries are already under significant pressure, with the Food and Agriculture Organization estimating that 90 per cent of fisheries are being harvested at or beyond their sustainable limits.[106] The performance of RFMOs varies significantly depending upon their membership and institutional dynamics,[107] and given the failure of many RFMOs to manage the stocks under their jurisdiction in a sustainable manner there are reasons to doubt they will respond effectively to climate change. Climate change is affecting not only the productivity of fisheries but also their distribution, which calls for a reconsideration of management approaches and in some RFMOs for a reassessment of an even more fundamental question, namely the legal boundaries of fisheries management set by RFMOs constituent instruments. An example is the 1980 Convention on the Conservation of Antarctic Marine Living Resources (CAMLR Convention). The CAMLR Convention operates south of a saw-toothed circumpolar line that roughly approximates the Antarctic convergence, the oceanic boundary where colder Antarctic waters meet warmer northern waters.[108] All marine ecosystems in the Antarctic are vulnerable to climate change, and key food chain species such as krill are declining as a result of warming waters.[109] Moreover, there is evidence of a southwards shift in the polar ocean front, and Haward and Jabour have noted that if this continues or accelerates then from a management perspective the 30-year-old CAMLR Convention boundary will no longer embrace all relevant Southern Ocean conservation and fisheries interests.[110] Significant change in the productivity and distribution of fisheries poses the risk of radically disrupting cooperative management arrangements that are currently in place. This is likely only to be avoided through better integration of scientific research and ecosystem monitoring in international fisheries management.[111]

---

[105] M Axelrod, 'Climate Change and Global Fisheries Management: Linking Issues to Protect Ecosystems or to Save Political Interests?' (2011) 11 *Global Environmental Politics* 64.

[106] Food and Agriculture Organization (FAO), *The State of World Fisheries and Aquaculture: 2012* (FAO Rome 2012) 56.

[107] See further Chapter 20 in this volume.

[108] 1980 Convention on the Conservation of Antarctic Marine Living Resources, Art 1(4).

[109] PN Trathan and D Agnew, 'Climate Change and the Antarctic Marine Ecosystem: An Essay on Management Implications' (2010) 22 *Antarctic Science* 387, 387.

[110] M Haward and J Jabour, 'Environmental Change and Governance Challenges in the Southern Ocean' in T Stephens and D VanderZwaag (eds), *Polar Oceans Governance in an Era of Environmental Change* (Edward Elgar Cheltenham 2014) 21.

[111] KA Miller et al, 'Governing Marine Fisheries in a Changing Climate: A Game Theoretic Perspective' (2013) 61 *Canadian Journal of Agricultural Economics* 309, 326.

5 CONCLUSION

Until recently, climate change was seen as an 'over the horizon' challenge for the law of the sea. This wait and see approach is no longer appropriate, given the effects that human interference with the carbon cycle is already having on the oceans, and the major impacts that are projected to occur in coming decades and centuries. Many, if not all, areas of the law of the sea are being, or will be, affected by climate change and ocean acidification. As suggested at the outset of this chapter these changes are potentially transformational and require rethinking of the foundations upon which the modern law of the sea has been built.

Rising sea levels carry implications for territorial sea baselines, for maritime zone limits, and for some maritime boundaries. In the case of some small island States, there may be an intersection of both traditional international law questions of territorial sovereignty and statehood and also law of the sea issues relating to the projection of maritime zones. Changing sea conditions, particularly the melting of sea ice, will affect the navigability of certain areas, and may prompt a reconsideration of the status of some waters (the Northwest Passage and the Northeast Passage being obvious examples). Warming waters and souring seas will also have very substantial impacts upon marine biodiversity, including subsistence and commercial fisheries.

In anticipating and responding to these changes, there is a significant role for the LOSC and the constellation of regimes under its aegis. It has been seen in this chapter that the law of the sea has a fairly limited role in mitigating climate change and ocean acidification. As these processes are being driven by GHG emissions, the UNFCCC remains the regime in which an appropriate response will need to be fashioned. But while the LOSC itself is not a strong climate change mitigation regime, it can be used to avoid or ameliorate adverse marine environmental effects from mitigation policies pursued in other fora. This is the case with respect to preventing or moderating geo-engineering schemes that propose radical alteration of marine environmental systems (such as though the deposit of mass quantities of nutrients to promote GHG sequestration through biophysical processes).[112]

There is an urgent need to provide a legal framework for reducing CO_2 emissions that takes into account their acidifying effects on the oceans. While the LOSC has a role to play in setting out general obligations, and some have suggested the desirability of a new LOSC implementing agreement on ocean acidification,[113] the climate change regime remains the most relevant legal mechanism given the linkages between ocean acidification and climate change policy. To this end, it would

---

[112] See generally KN Scott, 'International Law in the Anthropocene: Responding to the Geoengineering Challenge' (2013) 34 *Michigan Journal of International Law* 309.
[113] See eg V González, 'An Alternative Approach for Addressing CO2-Driven Ocean Acidification' (2012) 12 *Sustainable Development Law and Policy* 45.

be desirable to take three main steps within the UNFCCC process to ensure that ocean acidification is appropriately addressed:

- *Enhanced scientific assessment.* The level of scientific knowledge of the rate and effects of ocean acidification needs to be improved.
- *Agreement on a pH threshold.* In a similar way as agreement was reached in the Copenhagen Accord on 2°C as a guardrail beyond which there will be dangerous climate change contrary to the UNFCCC, agreement needs to be reached on an acceptable oceanic pH threshold or range.
- *Amendments to the UNFCCC and Kyoto Protocol.* Key changes needed include the removal of incentives to utilize the oceans as carbon sinks, and, most crucially, placing higher priority upon reducing emissions of CO_2 over other GHGs. Ideally, the climate change regime should include an appropriate atmospheric CO_2 concentration benchmark that addresses both climate change and ocean acidification goals.

By contrast to climate and acidification mitigation (where the UNFCCC rather than the LOSC is the regime of prime importance), the LOSC will be highly relevant to policies of adaptation at national, regional, and global scales, whether these be coastal State measures to fortify coastlines against an 'attacking ocean',[114] or efforts within multilateral institutions such as RFMOs to adjust fishing effort to respond to altered patterns of productivity or fisheries distribution. Despite the growing alarm sounded by scientific assessments, particularly in relation to the effects of ocean acidification on the oceanic food chain, there is little evidence that RFMOs are taking this threat seriously. It should also be recognized that there are limits to adaptation; ocean acidification is occurring rapidly and unlike sea level rise where there are viable adaptation strategies there is little that can be done to ameliorate the complete disappearance of ecosystems.[115] Ocean acidification is a clear instance where the preventive and precautionary principles should be applied, and where the only prudent policy response is to halt (and reverse) the carbonation of the world's oceans by stopping the rise in atmospheric concentrations of CO_2. As Rau et al have noted, 'short of stabilizing if not reducing atmospheric CO_2 there may ultimately be no perfect or even satisfactory conservation options for the ocean, either globally or regionally'.[116]

---

[114] B Fagan, *The Attacking Ocean: The Past, Present and Future of Rising Sea Levels* (Bloomsbury London 2013).

[115] See generally J Verschuuren (ed), *Research Handbook on Climate Adaptation Law* (Edward Elgar Cheltenham 2013).

[116] GH Rau, EL McLeod, and O Hoegh-Guldberg, 'The Need for New Ocean Conservation Strategies in a High-Carbon Dioxide World' (2012) 2 *Nature Climate Change* 720, 723.

35

THREATENED SPECIES AND VULNERABLE MARINE ECOSYSTEMS

EDWARD J GOODWIN

1 INTRODUCTION

EARLY life blossomed in the oceans, which in turn drove the development of conditions capable of supporting ever more diverse and complex life forms.[1] Today, marine ecosystems still abound with life. In 2000, scientists embarked upon a census of marine life. At the end of a decade long survey they had revealed 250,000 confirmed species—20,000 more than initially known.[2] They were convinced in the light of this that there were at least one million species in the ocean but that the total could be greater.[3] This variety of life is not spread evenly. For example, shallow warm water coral reefs are known to account for 100,000 species, including 4,000–5,000 marine fish (40 per cent of the known total) even though reefs only amount to 0.2 per cent of the ocean.[4]

---

[1] See C Roberts, *Ocean of Life: How Our Seas are Changing* (Penguin Books London 2013) ch 1.
[2] JH Ausubel, DT Crist, and PE Waggoner (eds), *First Census of Marine Life 2010: Highlights of a Decade of Discovery* (Census of Marine Life Washington 2010) 11.
[3] Ibid.
[4] M Walser and C Neumann, *The Value of Our Oceans: The Economic Benefits of Marine Biodiversity and Healthy Ecosystems* (World Wildlife Fund Frankfurt 2008) 15.

Maintaining marine biodiversity is important both for conservation objectives and economic development. This is due to a positive relationship between biodiversity, productivity, and stability across all ecosystem levels.[5] Thus healthy, bio-diverse marine ecosystems are best placed to provide maximum long-term benefits for humankind. Placing an accurate economic value on marine ecosystem services[6] is difficult, and, for some, objectionable in principle.[7] Nevertheless much effort continues to be expended in producing figures.[8] One significant study published in 1997 suggested that marine systems accounted for 63 per cent of the service value provided by all ecosystems in their entirety.[9] Destroying or significantly diminishing this service would involve catastrophic implications for humanity.

Yet, as has been regularly noted by the UN Secretary General,[10] humankind's interaction with the oceans and its marine life has already reached a point where impacts are increasing and widely encountered. In particular, over the last 30 years fishing vessels have been fitted with sonar and computer technology to catch fish with ever-greater precision. Except for basic life forms with very short reproductive life cycles, species simply cannot evolve to keep up with this changing environment. Heaving into view is the possibility of a collapse of these ecosystems and the loss of biodiversity on a vast scale. Various threats, acting alone or in concert, have led to nearly 30 per cent of fish stocks being overexploited.[11] Further, because of climate change and ocean acidification, 70 per cent of coral reefs are expected to collapse.[12] Finally, by 2003, between 35 per cent and 86 per cent of mangroves had been lost, principally through clearance for fish farms, urbanization, and coastal landfill.[13]

Two factors make the task of addressing threats particularly difficult. First, much of the damage occurs out of sight. In 1998, 80–90 per cent of coral reefs died in parts of the Indian Ocean due to coral bleaching,[14] yet only marine scientists really raised

---

[5] See B Worm et al, 'Impacts of Biodiversity Loss on Ocean Ecosystem Services' (2006) 314 Science 787.

[6] For the four types of service, see Millennium Ecosystem Assessment, *Ecosystems and Human Wellbeing: A Framework for Assessment* (Island Press Washington 2003) 5.

[7] See A Gillespie, *International Environmental Law, Policy and Ethics* (2nd edn Oxford University Press Oxford 2014).

[8] See eg 'The Economics of Ecosystem Benefits' initiative, available at <http://www.teebweb.org>.

[9] R Costanza et al, 'The Value of the World's Ecosystem Services and Natural Capital' (1997) 387 Nature 253, 259.

[10] See eg UNGA, *Oceans and the Law of the Sea: Report of the Secretary General*, UN Doc A/66/70 (2011).

[11] United Nations Food and Agriculture Organization (FAO), Fisheries and Aquaculture Department, *The State of World Fisheries and Aquaculture 2012* (FAO Rome 2012) 11, available at <http://www.fao.org/docrep/016/i2727e/i2727e00.htm>.

[12] K Frieler et al, 'Limiting Global Warming to 2°C is Unlikely to Save Most Coral Reefs' (2013) 3 Nature Climate Change 165, 165.

[13] NC Duke et al, 'A World Without Mangroves?' (2007) 317 Science 41.

[14] C Wilkinson, 'Executive Summary' in C Wilkinson (ed), *Status of Coral Reefs of the World: 2000* (Australian Institute of Marine Science Cape Ferguson 2000) 11.

the alarm.[15] Second, the current generation tends to forget or overlook the bounty enjoyed by their forebears, and trust only their direct experiences. This shifting baseline means that conservation aims and expectations operate at levels that previous generations would find unacceptable, and even if achieved, leave marine ecosystems in a relatively impoverished State.[16]

Against this background, this chapter therefore examines 'threatened species' and 'vulnerable marine ecosystems' (VME) in the law of the sea. Identifying the former is aided by the International Union for the Conservation of Nature's (IUCN) Red List of Threatened Species.[17] This inventory of species and their conservation status regards 'threatened species' as those in danger of extinction. It divides such species into three sub-categories: (i) critically endangered; (ii) endangered; and (iii) vulnerable to extinction.[18] The database reveals that as at February 2014, 108 marine species are critically endangered, 183 are endangered, and 696 are vulnerable.

When defining VME, a starting point is to note that marine ecosystems are those systems operating by the interaction of a community of living organisms in conjunction with non-living components, one of which must be saltwater.[19] Establishing when such an ecosystem ought to be regarded as vulnerable is harder. The term is predominantly employed for ecosystems found in Areas Beyond National Jurisdiction (ABNJ).[20] Thus the United Nations Food and Agriculture Organization (FAO) defines vulnerability in the context of deep-sea fisheries in the high seas as:

... the likelihood that a population, community, or habitat will experience substantial alteration from short-term or chronic disturbance, and the likelihood that it would recover and in what time frame... VME features may be physically or functionally fragile...[21]

Nevertheless, there is no reason why such vulnerability should be confined to ABNJ. Indeed the United Nations General Assembly (UNGA) recently refused to limit itself in this way.[22] Such jurisdictional division is a human construct rather than one dictated by nature. Furthermore, human disturbance is at least as significant in other maritime zones. Many coastal ecosystems have shown vulnerability to alteration when subjected to anthropogenic disturbances, like over-fishing, or pollution.

---

[15] Roberts, n 1, 2.
[16] See C Roberts, *The Unnatural History of the Sea* (Gaia London 2007).
[17] International Union for Conservation of Nature and Natural Resources, *The IUCN Red List of Threatened Species* (2014), available at <http://www.iucnredlist.org>.
[18] On the distinctions, see International Union for Conservation of Nature and Natural Resources Species Survival Commission, *IUCN Red List Categories and Criteria Version 3.1* (2nd edn IUCN Gland 2012) 16–22.
[19] This definition combines those for 'ecosystem', 'marine ecosystem', and 'saltwater' in C Park and M Allaby, *A Dictionary of Environment and Conservation* (2nd edn Oxford University Press Oxford 2013).
[20] See further Chapter 33 in this volume.
[21] FAO, Fisheries and Aquaculture Department, *International Guidelines for the Management of Deep-Sea Fisheries in the High Seas* (2009) 4, available at <http://www.fao.org/docrep/011/i0816t/i0816t00.HTM>.
[22] UNGA Res 68/70 (9 December 2013) Preamble, [153] and [217].

The extent of anthropogenic threats means that it is difficult to distinguish the vulnerable from the secure. Humankind's imprint is so widespread that there may be no corner of the ocean that is not altered, vulnerable, or threatened. This fact demands wide-reaching broad-spectrum measures to address the underlying drivers. Nevertheless, systems are needed to identify those species and sites that are suffering particularly badly, so that targeted measures can be deployed. Given that the body of law that contributes to the condition of the marine environment is motivated by multiple concerns,[23] this chapter will first, in Section 2, tease out the broad-spectrum responses of international law that tackle the principal anthropogenic threats, these being the want of jurisdiction over marine resources, unsustainable fisheries, pollution, and habitat conservation. Section 3 then extracts rules from within environmental treaties designed to catch emergency cases, where individual species are close to extinction or sites being degraded and disturbed.

2 Broad-Spectrum Action Framed around Threats

The IUCN's Redlist of 'critically endangered' and 'endangered' species suggests[24] that fishing is the principal threat, being cited for 38 per cent of the species listed as critically endangered and 37.5 per cent of those deemed endangered. Illegal, unreported, and unregulated (IUU) fishing rarely receives a separate mention in the records, possibly because it is subsumed within by-catch and targeted fishing effort. Habitat loss, such as through coastal development, is cited in one in five critically endangered species' entries and in over 15 per cent of endangered species' records. Climate change is having a large impact upon species, most notably corals, while land-based sources of pollution (LBSP) are mentioned in many instances. Introduction of species, almost exclusively on land, is also causing widespread population declines, principally among sea birds. These threats also arise as the main threats to ecosystems.[25] How has international law, and the law of the sea in particular, responded?

---

[23] Eg the 1992 Convention on Biological Diversity (hereinafter CBD) addresses multiple concerns including access to biotechnology and the equitable sharing of the benefits from using genetic resources.

[24] This covers approximately 290 entries. Time prevented reviewing the 675+ entries for vulnerable marine species.

[25] Roberts, n 1, 177.

2.1 Want of jurisdiction

Grotius regarded the sea as *res communis*—incapable of private ownership but open to all.[26] In contrast, natural resources such as fish were *res nullius*—capable of private ownership upon appropriation.[27] Consequently, beyond the territorial sea, for much of the twentieth century the model of rights over marine resources was proprietorial.[28] No State had jurisdiction over these resources, only over vessels flying their flag. The ensuing conditions made environmental management difficult, and produced conditions ripe for a 'tragedy of the commons'.[29]

The response has been a transition towards stewardship of natural resources predominantly by coastal States,[30] and a form of resource allocation which no longer fits neatly into the language of *res nullius* or *res communis*. It also reflects a belief that allocating exclusive jurisdiction to one State is more effective in managing natural resources. This can be seen in the 1982 United Nations Convention on the Law of the Sea (LOSC), which employs differential settings concerning the jurisdiction and rights of coastal, land-locked and flag States within the expanded territorial sea, contiguous zone, exclusive economic zone (EEZ), continental shelf, and the Area.[31] For example, after the LOSC, 40 per cent of the ocean fell within the EEZ. The freedom for any nation to fish in these, the most productive, parts of the sea was thereby replaced, so that almost 90 per cent of commercial fisheries fell within single State control.[32] Access to these resources is no longer open to all, but instead to a selected group of States determined by the coastal State, with property allocated on an appropriation basis thereafter. However, the natural resource does not belong to the coastal State, which instead has exclusive competence to manage these fisheries subject to internationally agreed rules and policies.[33] The latter, arguably, reflect the common concern of humankind in marine biological diversity.

The handling of high seas natural resources has also changed. The proprietorial principles of *res nullius* have been restrained through the adoption of agreements concerning highly migratory species and straddling fish stocks, alongside provisions, and other agreements for named high seas species.[34] Conditions for appropriating the remaining high seas species are far less stringent. Nevertheless, the

---

[26] H Grotius, *De Jure Praedae Commentarius* (trans GL Williams) (Oxford University Press Oxford 1950) 231.

[27] Ibid, 232.

[28] AV Lowe, 'Reflections on the Waters: Changing Conceptions of Property Rights in the Law of the Sea' (1986) 1 *International Journal of Estuarine & Coastal Law* 1, 4.

[29] See G Hardin, 'The Tragedy of the Commons' (1968) 162 *Science* 1243.

[30] Lowe, n 28, 9.   [31] See further Chapters 5–11 in this volume.

[32] E Hay, 'The Fisheries Provisions of the LOS Convention' in E Hay (ed), *Developments in International Fisheries Law* (Kluwer Leiden 1999) 27.

[33] Lowe, n 28, 9.

[34] For coverage, see DR Rothwell and T Stephens, *The International Law of the Sea* (Hart Oxford 2010) 303–19.

LOSC is imbued with the language of cooperation and shared responsibility.[35] This all suggests an element of collective common concern for high seas biodiversity, and a transition away from a pure sense of *res nullius*.[36] Nevertheless, with only rudimentary provisions remaining for these high seas resources and in practice poor implementation and enforcement by coastal States, a *de facto* open access regime continues to operate in these waters.[37] Thus open access competition has been concentrated into a smaller area, which has increased the risks to VMEs and threatened species[38] and of a continuing tragedy of the commons.

Despite the developments under the LOSC, doubts about competences within the maritime zones exist, such as those surrounding marine protected areas (MPAs).[39] MPAs are widely regarded as pivotal for the conservation of VMEs and threatened species.[40] Has the LOSC allocated appropriate jurisdiction to deploy them?

In all but the high seas, there appears to be coastal State jurisdiction to introduce MPAs. The territorial sea allocates sovereignty to the coastal State, while LOSC Article 56(1)(b)(iii) grants the same State jurisdiction to protect and preserve the marine environment of the EEZ. Implementing such policies, however, might be hampered by freedoms of other States, such as that of innocent passage through territorial waters, and freedom of navigation in the EEZ. Nevertheless, coastal States can overcome these through powers to regulate the former for reasons linked to, *inter alia*, preservation of the marine environment,[41] and the latter via IMO recognition of a Particularly Sensitive Sea Area (PSSA). On this, IMO may declare PSSAs if a site meets criteria, like being critical habitat for endangered species or because it is fragile and susceptible to degradation.[42]

---

[35] See 1982 United Nations Convention on the Law of the Sea, Art 87(2), Part VII, Section 2 (hereinafter LOSC).

[36] See further Rothwell and Stephens, n 34, ch 19.

[37] R Barnes, 'The Convention on the Law of the Sea: An Effective Framework for Domestic Fisheries Conservation?' in D Freestone, R Barnes, and D Ong (eds), *The Law of the Sea: Progress and Prospects* (Oxford University Press Oxford 2006) 240.

[38] Ibid, 241.

[39] See also the 1946 International Convention for the Regulation of Whaling's authority to set quotas for whales within EEZs; A Gillespie, *Whaling Diplomacy: Defining Issues in International Environmental Law* (Edward Elgar Cheltenham 2005) 289–94.

[40] Roberts, n 16, 377.

[41] Art 21(1)(f); EJ Goodwin, *International Environmental Law and the Conservation of Coral Reef Ecosystems* (Routledge Abingdon 2011) 45–54.

[42] The conditions for establishing a PSSA fall into three categories: (i) ecological, (ii) social, cultural and economic, and (iii) scientific and educational: IMO Assembly Resolution A.982(24), of 1 December 2005, *Revised Guidelines for the Identification and Designation of Particularly Sensitive Areas*. Additional requirements are that it must be vulnerable to damage from international shipping activities and that associated protective measure are available within the competence of IMO. See further MJ Kachel, *Particularly Sensitive Sea Areas* (Springer The Hague 2008) ch 8, and T Henriksen, 'Conservation of Marine Biodiversity and the International Maritime Organisation' in C Voigt (ed), *Rule of Law for Nature* (Cambridge University Press Cambridge 2013) ch 19.

Establishing MPAs in the high seas is more difficult and an important emerging challenge for the law of the sea. Here, MPAs need to be pursued in multilateral settings. Such multilateral efforts fall into two groupings. First, functional groupings: fisheries management under FAO and regional fisheries management organizations (RFMOs); seabed mineral exploitation under the International Seabed Authority (ISA); and conduct of shipping under the IMO. Second, efforts have been channelled through the various regional seas initiatives. However, gaps and problems persist. The regional seas groupings do not cover all regions and rarely areas of the high seas.[43] Even where they do have jurisdiction over high seas, initiatives to declare MPAs may be circumscribed by State consensus to exclude fishing and maritime transport regulation.[44] Therefore under current legal conditions, establishing enclaves in ABNJ requires complex coordination between regional and functional bodies.[45]

Significantly, in 2013, the UNGA resolved to begin work on formulating a proposal on the scope, parameters, and feasibility of an international instrument on the conservation and sustainable use of marine biodiversity in ABNJ.[46] Additionally, the 1992 Convention on Biological Diversity (CBD) has initiated a program for ecologically or biologically significant sea areas in ABNJ aimed at guiding the international community in identifying such sites, thus facilitating designation of MPAs.[47] Two of the criteria for selecting suitable sites for protection are presence of threatened species or VMEs.[48] Both initiatives might ultimately make enclaves in the high seas more practicable.

2.2 Unsustainable Fisheries

Roberts reports that overfishing is:

...one of the biggest soluble environmental problems in the world. We know what must be done and it takes no more than a sentence to say it. We have to fish less, waste less, use less destructive methods to catch what we take, and provide safe havens...So why hasn't it happened?[49]

---

[43] KM Gjerde and A Rulska-Domino, 'Marine Protected Areas Beyond National Jurisdiction: Some Practical Perspectives for Moving Ahead' (2012) 27 *International Journal of Marine and Coastal Law* 351, 356–8.
[44] 1992 Convention for the Protection of the Marine Environment of the North-East Atlantic, Annex 5, Art 4 (hereinafter OSPAR Convention). See further Chapter 29 in this volume.
[45] Ibid; KN Scott, 'Conservation on the High Seas: Developing the Concept of High Seas Marine Protected Areas' (2012) 27 *International Journal of Marine and Coastal Law* 849.
[46] UNGA Res 68/70 (9 December 2013) Preamble, [197]–[201]. See further Chapter 33 in this volume.
[47] Decision VIII/24, UNEP/CBD/COP/DEC/VIII/24 (15 June 2006).
[48] Decision IX/20, UNEP/CBD/COP/DEC/IX/20 (9 October 2008).
[49] Roberts, n 1, 278.

In large measure, it has not happened due to political failures, for example where scientific advice is ignored when setting catch limits[50] in order to appease industry and meet political goals. But criticisms can also be levelled at international law. Given that previous chapters have covered fisheries regulation, and that jurisdiction over marine resources and safe haven policies have been and will be discussed elsewhere herein, the intention is to move swiftly to focus upon two key issues: (i) appropriate total allowable catch (TAC) limits, and (ii) challenging destructive fishing methods.

2.2.1 *Total allowable catch*

The LOSC confirmed a significant realignment of jurisdiction over natural marine resources. It then established the objectives for managing these resources in the EEZ and high seas. Thus in the EEZ and high seas States were to formulate conservation plans or TACs for their vessels that would maintain or return stocks to levels that could support maximum sustainable yield (MSY).[51] This reflected persistence with a well-established concept even though in 1982 MSY was already subject to criticism.[52] Since then, humankind's understanding of the marine environment has developed further. Ecosystem thinking has come to define approaches to biodiversity.[53] Focusing on just the recruitment and mortality rate of a stock of one species is now erroneous as it misses the inter-connected nature of life in the oceans. It ignores the effect on predators, species caught as by-catch, and the knock-on effect for ecosystem functioning and human communities.[54] Moving fisheries regulation away from the narrow focus of MSY has been a challenge.

It might be thought that there is scope within the drafting of the LOSC to introduce ecosystem management of marine fisheries. Article 61(3) qualifies MSY calculations in the EEZ by the inclusion of additional variables, namely 'environmental and economic factors, including economic needs of fishing communities and the special requirements of developing States'. Further, under Article 61(4), the effects on associated or dependent species must be considered. Similar provisions can be found covering high seas stocks.[55] Barnes doubts this, however, since the unconstrained qualifications might justify higher TACS than MSY, and are in any event only to be taken into account suggesting their sub-ordination to use.[56] Ultimately, the Convention remains species-led, rather than guided by the viability of ecosystems.[57]

The ecosystem approach has come to prominence since the adoption of the CBD, and subsequent fisheries agreements and soft-law guidelines reflect this. The 1995 Agreement for the Implementation of the Provisions of the UN Convention on the

---

[50] See Section 3.1.2 in this chapter.
[51] LOSC, n 35, Arts 61(3), 119(1)(a). For a definition of MSY, see P Birnie, A Boyle and C Redgwell, *International Law and the Environment* (3rd edn Oxford University Press Oxford 2009) 590–1.
[52] Ibid.   [53] Decision VII/11, UNEP/CBD/COP/DEC/VII/11 (13 April 2004).
[54] R Hilborn, *Overfishing: What Everyone Needs to Know* (Oxford University Press Oxford 2012) 117.
[55] LOSC, n 35, Art 119.   [56] Barnes, n 37, 243–4.   [57] Ibid.

Law of the Sea relating to the Conservation and Management of Straddling Fish Stocks and Highly Migratory Fish Stock (Fish Stocks Agreement, FSA),[58] while replicating the LOSC measures just described, is credited with injecting a precautionary approach into the management of (predominantly) high seas fish stocks, as well as highlighting the role of excess capacity in overfishing.[59] Ecosystem management is also weaved into the management of fisheries through Article 5 which provides that States 'should adopt, where necessary, conservation and management measures for species belonging to the same ecosystem', although the qualification 'where necessary' seems to subordinate the viability of ecosystems once again.[60]

Of wider relevance, so as to include domestic fisheries, is the non-binding FAO *Code of Conduct for Responsible Fisheries* (1995)[61] (FAO Code of Conduct). It also sets as the goal of management maintaining or restoring stocks to MSY as qualified by environmental and economic factors, while enumerating these factors so as to include: avoiding excess fishing capacity; that economics serve to promote responsible fishing rather than undermine it; duly protecting fishers, habitats, and ecosystems as well as endangered species; and minimizing by-catch and impacts on other species.[62]

While the multilateral fisheries environment is showing awareness of more holistic approaches to TACs, the obvious problem with the current position is that with marine resources being concentrated in the EEZ, no binding arrangements exist beyond the LOSC. Incorporating ecosystem management is thus largely dependent upon either political will or regional agreements.[63]

2.2.2 *Methods*

Trawling and driftnet fishing are well-recorded threats to the survival of species and VMEs. The LOSC's general obligations to protect and preserve the marine environment,[64] and to take measures to protect and preserve rare or fragile ecosystems,[65] when coupled to the above provisions regarding the precautionary and ecosystem approaches,

---

[58] 1995 Agreement for the Implementation of the Provisions of the United Nations Convention on the Law of the Sea of 10 December 1982 Relating to the Conservation and Management of Straddling Fish Stocks and Highly Migratory Fish Stocks (hereainfter FSA).

[59] Barnes, n 37, 247.

[60] Ibid, 248–9; there is some debate as to whether these terms implement the LOSC or amend it, with a bearing upon those States that have not become a party to the FSA.

[61] FAO, Fisheries and Aquaculture Department, *Code of Conduct for Responsible Fisheries* (FAO Rome 1995), available at <http://www.fao.org/docrep/005/v9878e/v9878e00.htm>.

[62] Ibid, Arts 7.2.1 and 7.2.2.

[63] While many RFMOs persist with single species MSY, the 1980 Convention on the Conservation of Antarctic Marine Living Resources pursues rational use rather than MSY and an ecosystem approach to conservation: see MJ Bowman, PGG Davies, and C Redgwell, *Lyster's International Wildlife Law* (2nd edn Cambridge University Press Cambridge 2010) 362 (hereinafter Lyster).

[64] LOSC, n 35, Art 192.   [65] Ibid, Art 194.

form a rudimentary framework for the control of fishing methods. Nevertheless, more detailed directions exist elsewhere.

First the FAO Code of Conduct calls for fishing to be managed so that ecosystems are conserved and endangered species protected, and that by-catch of fish and non-fish species are minimized.[66] The Code goes on to suggest this might include phasing out gear that is inconsistent with responsible fishing, gear restrictions, or closed areas.[67] Worryingly, the positive reviews about the influence of the code do not seem to extend beyond policy development tackling dynamite fishing and poisoning, so as to include trawling.[68]

More specifically, with respect to drift-net fishing, early progress was made with the adoption of the 1989 Convention for the Prohibition of Fishing with Long Driftnets in the South Pacific. Although only regional in extent, the contracting parties agreed to prohibit its national and flagged ships from engaging in such fishing, and to take various measures to prohibit use of driftnets by other nations given access to areas of the sea under their jurisdiction.[69] Encouraged by this, the UNGA adopted by consensus a non-binding resolution calling for States to implement a moratorium on pelagic driftnet fishing across the high seas.[70]

Similar efforts have been made to ban the destructive practice of bottom trawling, particularly in the high seas where seamounts and deep-water coral ecosystems catalyse life. Moves to ban this in the UNGA were blocked in 2006.[71] A resolution adopted in its place reminds States to protect VMEs, including seamounts, hydro-thermal vents, and cold-water corals from destructive fishing methods, and calls upon RFMOs to work on identifying VMEs, assess the impacts of bottom fishing upon them, and to close areas of VMEs on a precautionary basis until suitable management can be introduced.[72]

Without such a ban on trawling, identifying VMEs at risk becomes the priority. Scientific methods need to be developed which are operable by fishing boats. One central approach developed by RFMOs has been closed areas and to introduce move-on rules. For example, the North Atlantic Fishery Organization (NAFO) closed the Newfoundland, New England, and Corner Seamounts in 2006, and a number of coral and sponge protection zones in 2007.[73] Further, a number of

---

[66] FAO, n 61, [7.2.2].   [67] Ibid, [7.6.4] and [7.6.9].
[68] FAO, Fisheries and Aquaculture Department, *Circular No 1038* (2009) 22.
[69] See P Sands and J Peel, *Principles of International Environmental Law* 3rd edn (Cambridge University Press Cambridge 2012) 430–1.
[70] UNGA Res 46/215 (20 December 1991).
[71] 'Ban on Brutal Fishing Blocked', *BBC Online* (24 November 2006), available at <http://news.bbc.co.uk/2/hi/science/nature/6181396.stm>.
[72] UNGA Res 61/105 (8 December 2006) [80], [84]; see also UNGA Res 64/72 (4 December 2009) [112]–[130].
[73] 'Precautionary closure to four seamount areas based on the ecosystem approach to fisheries', NAFO/FC Doc 06/5 (September 2006); 'New CEM Article on interim measures regarding VME—Coral Protection Zone', NAFO/FC Doc 07/18 (September 2007).

RFMOs require fishing boats to stop trawling and move-on 2 nm upon catching 60 kg of corals or 800 kg of sponges.[74] But problems persist. Move-on rules, it has been argued, are set too high and do not reveal soft-bodied species which are pulverized and extruded in nets before reaching the surface.[75] More importantly, the precautionary approach is preferable which demands carefully controlled impact assessment before fully opening an area to fishing.[76]

2.3 Pollution

Responding to concerns about pollution of the sea, the LOSC begins by defining marine pollution as:

... the introduction by man, directly or indirectly, of substances or energy into the marine environment, including estuaries, which results or is likely to result in such deleterious effects...[77]

The principal types of pollution[78] and those most often implicated in ecosystem disturbance and threatening species' survival[79] are: sewage, industrial waste, and agricultural run-off (grouped as LBSP); and carbon dioxide, which is still predominantly of land-based origin, although shipping remains a contributor.[80]

2.3.1 Land-based source pollution

Article 194(1) of the LOSC states contracting parties 'shall take, individually or jointly... all measures... that are necessary to prevent, reduce and control pollution of the marine environment from any source'. Article 207 is more explicit in obliging States to 'adopt laws and regulations to prevent, reduce and control pollution of the marine environment from land-based sources'. This commitment has been pursued primarily through regional initiatives. However, with LBSP still a significant contributor to marine pollution in 1992, Agenda 21 called for the United Nations Environmental Programme (UNEP) to convene an inter-governmental meeting on LBSP.[81] The resulting global conference adopted the 'Global Programme of Action

---

[74] PJ Auster et al, 'Definition and Detection of Vulnerable Marine Ecosystems on the High Seas: Problems with the "Move-On" Rule' (2011) 68 *ICES Journal of Marine Science* 254, 258.
[75] Ibid.   [76] Ibid, 261.   [77] LOSC, n 35, Art 1(4).
[78] Group of Experts on the Scientific Aspects of Marine Environmental Protection, *The State of the Marine Environment: UNEP Regional Seas Reports and Studies No. 115* (UNEP Nairobi 1990) [363].
[79] See n 24.
[80] In 2007, shipping contributed 3.3 per cent of global CO_2 emissions; see IMO, Ø Buhaug et al, *Second IMO GHG Study* (2009) 1, available at <http://www.imo.org/blast/blastDataHelper.asp?data_id=27795>.
[81] UNGA, *Report of the United Nations Conference on Environment and Development*, UNCED A/CONF.151/26 (1992), [17.25] and [17.26].

for the Protection of the Marine Environment from Land-Based Activities' (GPA).[82] The programme is international in scope, but legally non-binding.

Under the GPA, States are encouraged to draw up national action programmes (NAPs) that integrate land-use, river basin and coastal management.[83] A number of recommended actions are set out in the GPA for producing these programmes, including assessing and identifying areas of concern such as vulnerable ecosystems and habitat of threatened species.[84] The GPA then describes the impact of particular types of LBSP, and sets out ways to prevent harm, drawing attention to many VMEs, like mangroves.[85]

Since the GPA's adoption, three inter-governmental meetings have been convened to assess progress and to adopt work plans. These have highlighted mixed progress, a lack of political will on the part of some States, a steady increase in NAP adoption, and, most recently, resistance to calls to set targets for the reduction of nutrient concentrations, which would have helped with monitoring implementation.[86] Given States' evident discomfort with mechanisms that could engender accountability, their preference lies in looser global partnerships for improving water quality where responsibility and success can be shared.[87]

Ultimately, there is little evidence to suggest that the GPA is stemming the negative impacts of LBSP. For instance, sewage is a growing problem as populations increase and sanitation facilities remain prohibitively expensive.[88] In the end, as a non-binding arrangement, the GPA is dependent upon variable political will and this has been more forthcoming regionally, rather than globally.

A handful of regional agreements have been concluded dedicated to LBSP.[89] Of particular note is the protocol on LBSP concluded for the Caribbean region.[90] Similar to most regional LBSP agreements, the Caribbean protocol begins with a general obligation for parties to take appropriate measures to prevent, reduce, and control pollution from LBSP.[91] Thereafter, the protocol differs from the norm. For instance, the agreement envisages that annexes will be developed containing effluent and emissions limits and/or management practices (together with timetables

---

[82] UNEP, *Global Programme Of Action For The Protection Of The Marine Environment From Land-Based Activities*, UNEP(OCA)/LBA/IG.2/7 (1995).

[83] Ibid, [19].   [84] Ibid, [21(e)(i)].   [85] Ibid, [97(b)(iii)], [133], [149], and [152].

[86] See International Institute for Sustainable Development, 'Summary of the Third Intergovernmental Review Meeting on the Implementation of the Global Programme of Action for the Protection of the Marine Environment From Land-Based Activities: 25–26 January 2012' (2012) 25 *Earth Negotiations Bulletin* 1, 1–8.

[87] Ibid, 6–7.

[88] DL VanderZwaag and A Powers, 'The Protection of the Marine Environment From Land-Based Pollution and Activities' (2008) 23 *International Journal of Maritime and Coastal Law* 423, 440.

[89] See eg OSPAR Convention, n 44, Annex I.

[90] 1999 Protocol concerning Pollution from Land-Based Sources and Activities to the Convention for the Protection and Development of the Marine Environment of the Wider Caribbean Region.

[91] Ibid, Art III(1).

for achieving these) for a list of particular sources.[92] These sources are split according to priority of concern within the region.[93] In a reversal of priorities compared to some regions, domestic sewage and agricultural non-point source pollution are specified as a main concern.[94]

Of note are detailed provisions for tackling domestic wastewater, including sewage.[95] The approach is innovative. First, it divides coastal waters likely to be affected by domestic wastewater into two classes. Class I are those containing ecosystems vulnerable to domestic wastewater. This includes coral reefs and areas located within MPAs implemented under the region's enclave protocol.[96] Waters that are not so sensitive fall within Class II. For Class I waters, the Annex commits parties to ensuring that domestic wastewater discharges do not exceed specific concentration levels that are 80 per cent lower than that permitted for Class II waters.[97] Second, these targets are to be achieved according to timescales that vary depending upon the size of the community using the wastewater service.[98] The larger the community, the longer the contracting party has for providing compatible wastewater systems.

The Wider Caribbean protocol on LBSP contains significant commitments from parties for tackling sewage pollution and encourages States to review their agricultural practices. Its innovative approach ought to serve as best practice for many regions.

2.3.2 *Climate change*

Humankind has become reliant upon the burning of fossil fuels to power homes, industry, and transportation. When coupled to cement production, gas flaring, and deforestation, the effect has been anthropogenic increases in the emission of carbon dioxide (CO_2). This causes two dangerous responses. First, large quantities of CO_2 influence the pH of seawater as it is absorbed. This absorption leads to the acidification of seawater with potentially catastrophic effects for calcifying organisms such as corals and shelled marine life.[99] Greater detail on the legal response is provided in Chapter 34.[100] The second consequence is that it is extremely likely that anthropogenic emissions of CO_2, in concert with emissions of methane, nitrous oxide, and a raft of halocarbons, have caused the current warming of the global climate.[101]

---

[92] Ibid, Art IV(1).   [93] Ibid, Annex I.   [94] Ibid.   [95] Ibid, Annex III.
[96] Ibid.   [97] Ibid.   [98] Ibid.

[99] See European Project on Ocean Acidification (EPOCA), D Laffoley and JM Baxter (eds), *Ocean Acidification: The Facts* (2009), available at <http://www.epoca-project.eu/dmdocuments/OA.TF.English.pdf>.

[100] As a short observation, there is a gap in the law. Attempts to deal with ocean acidification under the climate change framework are second rate as it is calibrated and oriented towards the radiative (not acidifying) potential of gases, of which CO_2 is just one. See R Baird, M Simons, and T Stephens, 'Ocean Acidification: A Litmus Test for International Law' (2009) 4 *Carbon and Climate Law Review* 459.

[101] Intergovernmental Panel on Climate Change (IPCC), 'Summary for Policymakers' in TF Stocker et al (eds), *Climate Change 2013: The Physical Science Basis. Contribution of Working Group I to the Fifth Assessment Report of the Intergovernmental Panel on Climate Change* (2013) 11, 15.

As such, CO_2 is often referred to as one of the greenhouse gases (GHGs), capable of having a radiative forcing effect.[102] For the oceans, this affects water temperatures, sea levels, and the number (and intensity) of storms.[103]

The legal regime in place for addressing climate change is also discussed in greater depth in Chapter 34. Its ultimate objective is keeping GHGs in the atmosphere at a level that would 'prevent dangerous anthropogenic interference with the climate system'.[104] Criticisms of the regime are well known, such as the non-participation of the USA—one of the largest emitters of GHGs. Further, while political opinion has coalesced around the view that keeping climate change to a +2°C limit would be in keeping with the objective, the 5 per cent quantifiable emissions reduction target accepted by the group of States subject to mitigation obligations are drastically below what would likely achieve this upper limit.[105] Acceptance of deeper cuts has stalled over concerns that the largest future emitters of GHGs cannot be subject to quantified mitigation targets without diverging from the original agreements' terms. The regime's future is precarious but the Copenhagen Accords[106]—a non-binding arrangement whereby all States gave an indication of the mitigation cuts they would make, and negotiations under the Ad Hoc Working Group on the Durban Platform for Enhanced Action, may lead to further proposals for reinvigorating the system.

For corals and shallow coral reef ecosystems—the most vulnerable and threatened by climate change—the current legal situation remains inadequate. Recommendations from marine biologists are that GHG concentrations of 450 parts per million (ppm) threaten widespread destruction of reefs leaving remnants of greatly reduced diversity in isolated pockets.[107] They are therefore calling for stabilization at 350 ppm, based upon historic concentrations known to have caused negative responses among corals.[108] The Kyoto Protocol commitments are clearly inadequate for this, but even the non-binding Copenhagen Accords only garnered support for 20 per cent cuts in GHGs. According to the Intergovernmental Panel on Climate Change (IPCC), this would produce GHG atmospheric concentrations

---

[102] 'Radiative forcing is a measure of the influence a factor has in altering the balance of incoming and outgoing energy in the Earth-atmosphere system': IPCC, PK Pachauri, and A Reisinger (eds), *Climate Change 2007: Synthesis Report* (2007) 36, available at <http://www.ipcc.ch/pdf/assessment-report/ar4/syr/ar4_syr.pdf>.

[103] IPCC, n 101, 3, 6, 9.

[104] 1992 United Nations Framework Convention on Climate Change, Art 2.

[105] See M Meinshausen, 'What Does a 2°C Target Mean for Greenhouse Gas Concentrations?' in HJ Schellnhuber et al (eds), *Avoiding Dangerous Climate Change* (Cambridge University Press Cambridge 2006) 265.

[106] Decision 2/CP.15, UN Doc FCCC/CP/2009/11/Add.1 (30 March 2010).

[107] JEN Veron et al, 'The Coral Reef Crisis: The Critical Importance of <350ppm CO_2' (2009) 58 *Marine Pollution Bulletin* 1428, 1430.

[108] Ibid.

of approximately 550 ppm.[109] Without significant inflation of State commitments to mitigation, the regime looks 'set fair' to leave coral reefs in a devastated condition.[110]

2.4 Habitat protection and capacity

Many threats to a species or VMEs are varied and cumulative—small incidents that chip away at populations or ecosystem components. Therefore species and VMEs need protection through national measures.[111] This calls for capacity building, in terms of suitable policy development and implementation, appointment of trained personnel, and nurturing channels of communication between stakeholders and governments. This has been an objective of the principal biodiversity treaties, such as the CBD, the 1972 Convention Concerning the Protection of the World Cultural and Natural Heritage (WHC), and the 1971 Convention on the Wetlands of International Importance (Ramsar Convention).[112]

2.4.1 *Convention on Biological Diversity*

The CBD is perhaps the foremost wildlife and habitat treaty for the development of government policy. It provides that States shall 'develop national strategies, plans or programmes for the conservation and sustainable use of biological diversity' (or adapt existing ones) so as to reflect the suggested measures agreed under the convention.[113] Such plans, referred to as National Biodiversity Strategies and Action Plans (NBSAPs), have been drawn up by 92 per cent of parties.[114]

In the marine context, steering the content of NBSAPs is driven by treaty provisions, thematic programmes, and adopting periodic strategic plans. As to the first, the treaty encourages States to pursue *ex situ* conservation measures such as captive breeding programmes,[115] research and training,[116] public education programmes,[117] and community involvement in conservation initiatives.[118] Of particular note is the emphasis on *in situ* conservation, especially Article 8(a) under which

---

[109] IPCC, n 101, 67; see also J Rogelj et al, 'Copenhagen Accord Pledges are Paltry' (2010) 464 *Nature* 1126.

[110] See Goodwin, n 41, ch 9.

[111] It is important to recognize, in contrast to national measures, that the International Seabed Authority, which has jurisdiction over the area and exploitation of the mineral resources found therein, has developed a mining code for prospecting and extraction of these resources, aimed in part to protected VMEs in the area; see International Seabed Authority, *Mining Code* (2013), available at <http://www.isa.org.jm/en/mcode>.

[112] Ramsar is the Iranian town where the Convention text was adopted.

[113] CBD, n 23, Art 6(a).

[114] CBD Secretariat, *National Biodiversity Strategies and Action Plans* (2014), available at <https://www.cbd.int/nbsap/default.shtml>.

[115] CBD, n 23, Art 9. [116] Ibid, Art 12. [117] Ibid, Art 13. [118] Ibid, Art 8(j).

contracting parties shall 'as far as possible and as appropriate' establish a system of protected areas.

The most significant developments, however, have been under the marine and coastal biodiversity programme. At the request of the first plenary meeting, the CBD's scientific committee produced a recommendation for conserving marine and coastal habitats focused around five actions: implementing integrated coastal zone management, establishing and maintaining MPAs, managing living resources in a sustainable manner, ensuring that mariculture is conducted sustainably, and controlling or eradicating harmful alien species.[119] The second Conference of the Parties (COP), in 1995, supported the recommendation, subject to further development, and stated its belief that the recommendation was a solid basis for future action.[120] Such further development has continued with elements added concerning coral reef bleaching[121] and deep sea VMEs.[122]

Strategic plans look to set measurable goals that tie into the thematic programmes. The current plan for 2011–2020 contains what is known as the Aichi Biodiversity Targets.[123] By 2020, the CBD challenges States to, *inter alia*, eliminate or prevent subsidies from affecting biodiversity, halve habitat loss, manage fish stocks sustainably and using an ecosystem approach, and establish MPAs for 10 per cent of coastal and marine areas.[124] Thus the work of the CBD demonstrates a sound understanding of the threats to species and VMEs, while strategic plans move away from mere encouragement of policy formulation towards measurable targets. While much is rightfully left to action at national level, this does bring the international community closer to being able to judge whether the appropriate steps are actually being taken by contracting parties.

2.4.2 *The Ramsar Convention*

The Ramsar Convention's definition of wetlands covers many shallow coastal VMEs like coral reefs,[125] mangroves and sea-grass beds.[126] Some are placed into a sub-set through an inventory of internationally significant wetlands. Wetlands are unilaterally inscribed by States, and qualify for various reasons including that they support 'vulnerable, endangered, or critically endangered species or threatened ecological communities'.[127] State parties are then obliged to formulate and implement plans

---

[119] Recommendation I/8, UNEP/CBD/SBSTTA/1/8 (4 August 1995).
[120] Decision II/10, UNEP/CBD/COP/II/10 (6–17 December 1995).
[121] Decision IV/5, UNEP/CBD/COP/IV/5 (4–15 May 1998).
[122] Decision VIII/21, UNEP/CBD/COP/DEC/VIII/6 (15 June 2006).
[123] Decision X/2, UNEP/CBD/COP/DEC/X/2 (29 October 2010).   [124] Ibid.
[125] Although not obviously; Goodwin, n 41, 147–54.
[126] 1971 Convention on the Wetlands of International Importance, Art 1(1), Recommendation 4.7 (hereinafter Ramsar).
[127] Strategic Framework and Guidelines for the Future Development of the List of Wetlands of International Importance of the Convention on Wetlands, Criterion 2.

that promote the use of all wetlands wisely and to conserve listed wetlands.[128] While these plans might apparently need to aim at different standards, use and interpretation under the regime has assimilated the two, so that wise use and conservation both bear a close relationship to sustainable use, allowing humankind to extract benefit from wetlands provided their ecosystem services are conserved.[129]

In terms of steering appropriate policy, the treaty calls for enclaves to be used, research to be conducted and personnel to be trained.[130] Channels of communication are secured through the National Ramsar Committee initiative whereby governments are encouraged to establish dedicated bodies that can be the focus of national implementation and allow discussions between government departments, individuals, and non-governmental organizations (NGOs).[131] The United Kingdom's equivalent body, for example, allows attendance by the devolved governments, various national departments, and NGOs like Wetlands International.[132] In a developed system, problems with local wetlands can then be addressed nationally. This leaves the plenary meetings under Ramsar to draw attention to threatened wetlands of global significance or as a communication channel for those operating in a State with un-developed national mechanisms for dialogue.

2.4.3 *World Heritage Convention*

The WHC operates under a founding principle that there exists around the world sites of such natural and cultural significance that they need to be preserved for humankind as a whole.[133] Endowed States are then subject to exacting conservation standards[134] designed to maintain and present the outstanding value of these properties. In terms of capacity building, Article 5 demands, for example, that parties conduct research to help conserve their heritage, develop policies that integrate heritage across all planning, and develop bodies responsible for the protection of heritage.

The WHC also maintains an inventory of properties it has verified as of outstanding value. This is the well-known 'World Heritage List'. Admission of a site to the inventory depends upon a variety of criteria being met—the deliberate result being that the list contains only the most outstanding properties.[135] In other words, VMEs

---

[128] Ramsar, n 126, Art 3(1).

[129] Lyster, n 63, 414–16. Although note, wise use of wetlands is qualified by 'as far as possible', unlike the obligation to conserve.

[130] Ramsar, n 126, Art 4.   [131] Ibid, Res 5.7.

[132] EJ Goodwin, 'Delegate Preparation and Participation in Conferences of the Parties to Environmental Treaties' (2013) 15 *International Community Law Review* 45, 59–60.

[133] 1972 Convention on the Protection of the World Cultural and Natural Heritage, Preamble (hereinafter WHC).

[134] EJ Goodwin, 'The World Heritage Convention, the Environment and Compliance' (2009) 20 *Colorado Journal of International Environmental Law and Policy* 157.

[135] UNESCO, *Operational Guidelines for the Implementation of the World Heritage Convention* (July 2013) [52], [77]–[78] (hereinafter WHC Guidelines).

will not necessarily find protection under the convention, since vulnerability is not a criterion. Nevertheless, threatened species may benefit from the strong conservation provisions. Natural heritage includes 'areas which constitute the habitat of threatened species of animals and plants of outstanding universal value from the point of view of science or conservation'.[136] Thirty-three sites containing habitat of threatened marine species have thus been inscribed on the World Heritage List. The threatened species benefiting include Humpback and Blue whales, and various species of coral and sea grass.

Communication channels are more international in this context, perhaps due to the smaller number of sites in comparison to Ramsar. The WHC itself offers a reactive monitoring system to review worsening conditions of heritage sites.[137] It depends upon receipt of information to trigger an investigation, and while this ought to come from the endowed State, non-State actors may make submissions.[138]

3 Responses Framed around Species and Specific Sites

International law has also framed responses around the endangerment of particular species, and ecosystems that have endured anthropogenic pressures such that their vulnerability is both exposed and realized. The following offers an overview of the different responses to these events.

3.1 Species-specific responses

The best-known early response to a species being driven towards extinction concerned the North Pacific Fur Seal colonies on certain islands in the Behring Sea.[139] Conflicts between Canada and the United States led, ultimately, to the agreement of the 1911 Treaty for the Preservation and Protection of Fur Seals. This treaty succeeded in preventing the extinction of these fur seals, and tripled the size of populations, leaving them in excess of two million by 1940.[140] Nevertheless, a number of agreements operate today without such a single species focus, thereby affording greater inclusiveness.

---

[136] WHC, n 133, Art 2.   [137] WHC Guidelines, n 135, IV.A.   [138] Ibid, [174].
[139] For an excellent account, see S Barrett, *Environment and Statecraft: The Strategy of Environmental Treaty-Making* (Oxford University Press Oxford 2003) 19–33.
[140] Ibid, 32.

3.1.1 Whaling

The International Convention for the Regulation of Whaling (ICRW) was agreed in 1946 to manage the whaling industry, and also to secure peaceful interaction between previous enemies.[141] The convention was primarily designed to allow the International Whaling Commission (IWC) to set catch limits for whales.[142] However, with populations continuing to collapse a moratorium on commercial whaling was adopted in 1982. This has offered significant protection for species that were (and often continue) to be regarded as in danger of extinction, namely Right, Bowhead, Grey, Blue, Sei, Humpback, Sperm, Fin, Bryde's, and Minke whales. However, a number of well-known problems in the whaling regime persist.

Foremost is the right of contracting parties to unilaterally issue permits for conducting scientific whaling.[143] While widening scientific understanding should enable ecologically sustainable yields in the future, there is concern that States are using scientific missions as a proxy for commercial whaling.[144] Since the convention demands that whales caught under such permits be processed,[145] an estimated 3,000 tonnes per annum of edible products has been sold in Japan.[146] Significantly, the International Court of Justice (ICJ) recently ruled that Japan's JARPA II research program in the Southern Ocean did not meet the required standards for legitimate scientific research.[147] The ICJ's ruling left Article VIII intact and did not rule out lethal methods for future research programs, but it does raise demands upon Japan to formulate scientifically rigorous methodologies for any future program.

Another key issue relates to the resumption of commercial whaling. Opinion has settled upon the importance of formulating a revised management procedure and management scheme before any resumption.[148] The former was agreed in 1994, with the conservative objective of ensuring stocks reached 72 per cent of their original levels, and with quotas set at zero if levels fall below 54 per cent.[149] The sticking point, however, has been the new management scheme. Arguments continue, *inter alia*, about the coverage of international observers and who will meet the cost of such monitoring.[150] Consequently, many view the ICRW as riven by polarized

---

[141] Lyster, n 63, 153. See also MJ Bowman, '"Normalizing" the International Convention for the Regulation of Whaling' (2008) 29 *Michigan Journal of International Law* 293.

[142] For ambiguity about the whale species covered by the 1946 International Convention for the Regulation of Whaling (hereinafter ICRW), see Gillespie, n 39, 286–9.

[143] ICRW, n 142, Art VIII(1).

[144] See eg PH Sand, 'Japan's "Research Whaling" in the Antarctic Southern Ocean and the North Pacific Ocean in the Face of the Endangered Species Convention (CITES)' (2008) 17 *Review of European Comparative and International Environmental Law* 56.

[145] ICRW, n 142, Art VIII(2).

[146] International Whaling Commission (IWC) Res 2003-2 (7–9 June 2003).

[147] *Whaling in the Antarctic (Australia v Japan; New Zealand intervening)*, Judgment of the International Court of Justice (31 March 2014) [223]–[227].

[148] Lyster, n 63, 166–7.   [149] Ibid.   [150] Ibid, 168.

political positions. There are those who wish to see whaling reintroduced, citing large populations of Minke whale in support, and those who will not contemplate a lifting of the moratorium given popular opposition and concerns that some populations of Blue, Grey, and Bowhead whales remain critically endangered. These divisions threaten the future operation of the agreement and may ultimately lead to pro-whaling States leaving to pursue alternative multi-lateral regimes.[151]

3.1.2 *Tuna*

The genus *Thunnus* contains important commercial species such as Atlantic Bluefin, Bigeye, Albacore, and Yellowfin tuna. Due to overfishing, many are threatened. Indeed, the Southern Bluefin Tuna is regarded as critically endangered with biomass estimated at 7–15 per cent of 1960 levels.[152]

RFMO's aimed at the management of stocks of tuna have been established. These are the International Commission for the Conservation of Atlantic Tuna (ICCAT), the Inter-American Tropical Tuna Commission, the Commission for the Conservation of Southern Bluefin Tuna (CCSBT), the Indian Ocean Tuna Commission (IOTC), and the Commission for the Conservation and Management of Highly Migratory Fish Stocks in the Western and Central Pacific Ocean. Central to their operation is the setting of TACs for regulated species. The majority seek the conservation of these species so as to produce MSY. Meanwhile, CCSBT and IOTC are tasked with conservation which delivers optimum utilization of stocks, suggesting more conservative TACs than would be produced under MSY and more sophisticated calculations incorporating economic, social, and ecological factors.[153]

The success of these bodies is debatable, with ICCAT facing particular criticism. Abundance levels of Atlantic Bluefin tuna have continued to decline since the ICCAT's introduction. Roberts bluntly regards ICCAT as a forum where 'corporate greed has triumphed over human decency' as TACs are set far above levels that allow populations to recover.[154] Webster lends some support to this, charting historic discrepancies between recommended TACs and those adopted.[155] Webster notes that the commission has compounded matters through ineffectiveness in implementing TACs.[156] Dubiously, convulsions of action addressing perceived failings have coincided with attempts to move regulation from ICCAT to the 1973 Convention on International Trade in Endangered Species of Wild Fauna and Flora (CITES).[157]

---

[151] Ibid, 197.

[152] International Union for Conservation of Nature and Natural Resources, B Collette et al, *Thunnus maccoyii. The IUCN Red List of Threatened Species* (2011), available at <http://www.iucnredlist.org/details/21858/0>.

[153] Birnie et al, n 51, 591.   [154] Roberts, n 1, 51.

[155] DG Webster, 'The Irony and the Exclusivity of Atlantic Bluefin Tuna Management' (2011) 35 *Marine Policy* 249.

[156] Ibid, 250.   [157] Ibid, 250–1.

3.1.3 *Convention on International Trade in Edangered Species*

The broad aim of CITES is to control international exports and imports of specimens or products derived from species that are at risk of extinction, or may become endangered because of trade. The regime introduced is deceptively simple. Species that are already threatened with extinction and are, or might be, traded are listed in Appendix I.[158] They are subject to strict regulation effectively banning international trade.[159] CITES also has controls for species that, although not yet threatened with extinction, may become so unless trade is regulated at levels compatible with their survival.[160] These species are listed in Appendix II to the Convention. The main responsibility for them lies with the exporting nation. Upon import a permit must be presented, issued by the management authority of the exporting country. Article IV(2) of CITES provides that these export permits may only be issued once the exporting country's scientific authority confirms that the trade is non-detrimental to the survival of the species.

This system of permits and non-detriment findings is central to CITES' operation.[161] They are supported by the monitoring of, and reporting about, all import and export permits by the UNEP–World Conservation Monitoring Centre, which can in turn trigger the 'Review of Significant Trade' procedure and ultimately suspension of trade recommendations if exports are believed to be unsustainable or in violation of obligations.[162]

Some additional observations are justified in the context of endangered marine species. The meaning of trade includes introducing a specimen from the sea.[163] CITES initially defined this as transporting into a State a specimen that had been taken from the marine environment in ABNJ.[164] Difficulties arose since CITES was concluded before the LOSC confirmed the coastal State's jurisdiction over resources within the EEZ.[165] Clarification was finally provided in Resolution 14.6 that 'introduction from the sea' referred to the landing of marine species captured on the high sea. Thus if a listed specimen is taken from the territorial sea or EEZ and is landed in the coastal State of origin, no permit is required.[166] However, if the listed specimen is landed in the port of another State, this is tantamount to an export[167] and must be accompanied by the appropriate permits. Meanwhile, all listed specimens captured in the high seas must be accompanied

---

[158] 1973 Convention on International Trade in Endangered Species of Wild Fauna and Flora, Art II(1) (CITES).

[159] Ibid, Art III.   [160] Ibid, Art II(2)(a).

[161] See S Aguilar, 'Regulatory Tools for the Management of Fish and Timber Species Through CITES' (2013) 22 *Review of European Comparative & International Environmental Law* 281.

[162] Ibid, 285.   [163] CITES, n 158, Art I(c).   [164] Ibid, Art I(e).

[165] See L Little and MA Orellana, 'Can CITES Play a Role in Solving the Problem of IUU Fishing? The Trouble with Patagonian Toothfish' (2004) 15 *Colorado Journal of International Environmental Law and Policy* 21, 94.

[166] Ibid.   [167] Ibid.

by a certificate issued by the management authority of the State of landing following a non-detriment finding by their scientific authority.[168]

CITES has proved useful in supporting the regulation of some marine species, such as through Appendix I listing of ICRW controlled whales. More often, listing of threatened marine species is patchy. For each success, such as the Napoleon Wrasse and almost all coral species, there are refusals to regulate species with critical population levels, such as the Banggai Cardinal Fish and Atlantic Bluefin Tuna. Two important reasons for this can be advanced.

First, marine species subject to large scale commercial harvesting pose listing problems. The 'Fort Lauderdale Criteria'[169] recommend inclusion in the appendices based on various historical declines in population size. For example, a marked decline is 50 per cent or more from a baseline population figure over a given period.[170] This does not translate easily for marine species. Under modern fisheries management, a reduction in stock size of 50 per cent is close to optimal sustainable utilization levels.[171] The response has been an annotation to the criteria allowing for greater reduction levels for exploited marine species.[172]

Second, some States believe commercial fishing should not be a CITES issue. RFMOs and the FAO are the preferred bodies.[173] In response, closer cooperation has been sought between FAO and CITES, and a Memorandum of Co-operation was signed in 2006.[174] This secured FAO input on the implementation of the Fort Lauderdale Criteria.[175] Furthermore, FAO provides scientific and technical evaluations of proposals for listing.[176] In turn, the Secretariat promises to respect the FAO findings on proposals to the greatest extent possible.[177] This does not guarantee that States will respect FAO advice, with curious results such as the rejection in 2010 of Monaco's proposal to list Atlantic Bluefin Tuna. This proposal was supported by the FAO report, but States considered that ICCAT was the most competent body to manage stocks and economic interests would be unduly affected.[178]

---

[168] CITES, n 158, Arts III(5) and IV(6).
[169] CITES, Res 9.24, CoP15 (7–18 November 1994).   [170] Ibid, Annex 5.
[171] DS Butterworth, 'Possible Interpretation Problems for the Current CITES Listing Criteria in the Context of Marine Fish Species under Commercial Harvest' (2000) 42 *Population Ecology* 29, 30–1.
[172] CITES, Res 9.24, n 169.
[173] CITES, Animals Committee, *Summary Report of Committee I*, COM.I 10.2 (Rev) [28].
[174] MoU Between the Food and Agriculture Organization of the United Nations (FAO) and the Secretariat of the Convention on International Trade in Endangered Species (CITES) (3 October 2006), available at <http://www.cites.org/eng/disc/sec/FAO-CITES-e.pdf>.
[175] CITES, CoP14 Doc 18.1 (3–15 June 2007).
[176] CITES, Animal Committee, n 173, [3]–[4].   [177] Ibid, [6].
[178] See for commentary International Institute for Sustainable Development, 'Summary of the Fifteenth Conference of the Parties to the Convention on International Trade in Endangered Species of Wild Fauna and Flora: 13–25 March 2010' (2010) 21 *Earth Negotiations Bulletin*, 15, 17–18.

3.1.4 *Migratory species*

The 1979 Convention on the Conservation of Migratory Species of Wild Animals (CMS) is principally concerned with protecting endangered migratory species. This revolves around a system of nominating migratory species to appendices under CMS.

Article 1 defines a migratory species as one where a significant proportion of their members 'cyclically and predictably cross one or more national jurisdictional boundary'. This includes most types of migration but will exclude those performed entirely within the jurisdiction of one State or entirely within the high seas.[179] Meanwhile, a species qualifies for nomination and inclusion in Appendix I if they are in danger of extinction throughout all or a significant portion of their range.[180] Interestingly, CMS has looked to align itself with the IUCN Red List's interpretation of endangered status.[181]

Once included in Appendix I, a species benefits from the obligations undertaken by the parties. Principally, according to Article III(5) of CMS, range States shall prohibit the 'taking' of listed species. This includes fishing, 'deliberate killing', and capture[182]—the latter of which, not being qualified by intention, ought to extend to by-catch.[183] In addition, States agree to endeavour to conserve and restore key habitats that are important for removing the species from the danger of extinction.[184]

Two factors hamper CMS's contribution to protecting threatened marine species. First very few migratory marine species are included in Appendix I. Those that are include whales, most marine turtles, basking sharks, African and West Indian manatees, and certain species of spoonbills, petrels, puffins, and albatrosses. Second, CMS has never enjoyed widespread participation from range States. At the time of writing there were 119 contracting parties, but States with significant coastlines like the USA, China, and Brazil have not joined.

Despite this, it is important to note that CMS has catalysed further multilateral arrangements. This occurs because CMS urges the conclusion of agreements for species included in a second appendix. These migratory species should have both an unfavourable conservation status and require international agreements to conserve and manage them, or alternatively benefit from international cooperation.[185] This is not limited to endangered species, although they can be included, nor is it necessary for co-operation to take the form of a binding agreement. Indeed, in relation to the

---

[179] C de Klemm, 'The Problem of Migratory Species in International Law' in HO Bergesen and G Parmann (eds), *Green Globe Yearbook of International Co-operation on Environment and Development* (Oxford University Press Oxford 1994) 67, 70.

[180] 1979 Convention on the Conservation of Migratory Species of Wild Animals, Art I (hereinafter CMS).

[181] Lyster, n 63, 546. [182] CMS, n 180, Art I(1)(i). [183] Lyster, n 63, 548.
[184] CMS, n 180, Art III(4). [185] Ibid, Art IV(1).

latter, only one subsequent arrangement for marine species might be considered binding upon their parties, namely the 2001 Agreement on the Conservation of Albatrosses and Petrels.[186] More coverage is found through non-binding agreements for seals,[187] cetaceans in particular maritime regions,[188] manatees,[189] dugongs,[190] turtles,[191] and sharks.[192]

3.2 Site responses

Emergency response mechanisms also exist for those times where an ecosystem is vulnerable to long term change and the threat that can trigger such change has materialized. These mechanisms principally depend upon inventories and monitoring missions. For example, Ramsar obliges States to inform its bureau about any adverse ecological changes to listed wetlands.[193] A formal list of sites undergoing such change was introduced,[194] now known as the 'Montreux Record', although States must consent to their wetlands being included. Of the 48 wetlands currently on the Montreux Record, 20 contain marine ecosystem elements.[195] The criticism such publicity might imply is counter-acted by prioritizing allocation of Ramsar controlled funding for remediation efforts, while Ramsar Advisory Missions may be sent to sites to provide free assessments and advice for States with limited capacity.[196]

---

[186] The agreement similarly prohibits takings, and has focused attention, *inter alia*, upon reducing mortality as by-catch and loss to introduced species: see generally Lyster, n 63, 232.

[187] See eg CMS, MoU Concerning Conservation Measures for the Eastern Atlantic Populations of the Mediterranean Monk Seal (*Monachus monachus*) (18 October 2007), available at <http://iea.uoregon.edu/pages/view_treaty.php?t=2006-MemorandumUnderstandingProtectionMediterraneanMonkSeal.EN.txt&par=view_treaty_html>.

[188] See eg the 1992 Agreement on the Conservation of Small Cetaceans of the Baltic, North East Atlantic, Irish and North Seas, and the 1996 Agreement on the Conservation of Cetaceans of the Black Sea, Mediterranean Sea and Contiguous Atlantic Area.

[189] CMS, MoU Concerning the Conservation of the Manatee and Small Cetaceans of Western Africa and Macaronesia (3 October 2008), available at <http://www.cms.int/aquatic-mammals/sites/default/files/basic_page_documents/MoU_E.pdf>.

[190] CMS, MoU on the Conservation and Management of Dugongs and their Habitats throughout their Range (31 October 2007), available at <http://www.cms.int/dugong/en/legalinstrument/dugong>.

[191] See eg CMS, MoU on the Conservation and Management of Marine Turtles and their Habitats of the Indian Ocean and South-East Asia (1 September 2001), available at <http://www.cms.int/sites/default/files/document/inf_07_mou_iosea_e_0.pdf>.

[192] CMS, MoU on the Conservation of Migratory Sharks (1 March 2010), available at <http://sharksmou.org/sites/default/files/Migratory_Shark_MoU_English.pdf>.

[193] Ramsar, n 126, Art 3(2).   [194] Ramsar Recommendation 4.8.

[195] Ramsar, *The Montreux Record* (2011), available at <http://www.ramsar.org/cda/en/ramsar-documents-montreux/main/ramsar/1-31-118_4000_0__>.

[196] Lyster, n 63, 445–6.

Similarly, the WHC has always maintained a second list of world heritage properties, these being those regarded as in danger.[197] While inclusion on the Danger List is supposed to be a step towards securing priority in receiving assistance rather than a sanction, in practice inclusion has had a mixed reception. Some States willingly seek listing in order to obtain such assistance and priority attention. Others are less receptive to the list largely because they perceive listing as humiliating and contrary to their best interest.[198]

Four properties have been inscribed on the danger list because of threats impacting upon marine ecosystem components. These are the Belize Barrier Reef Reserve, East Rennell, the Everglades National Park, and the Galapagos Islands. All but the last remain on the list. The Belize site was inscribed principally because of the sale of land within the reserve for tourist development, which led to mangrove cutting and coral dredging. Following a monitoring mission to the property, modest progress was noted on an integrated governmental approach to conservation, and expansion of no-fishing zones, but further development for tourism and oil exploration remained a possibility.[199] The WHC therefore continues to press for a permanent cessation of such activities before removing the property from the danger list.[200]

Unregulated tourist development had also been a factor in the 2007 listing of the Galapagos, along with poor controls over human immigration and introduction of species to a site of high endemism.[201] By 2010 monitoring missions still felt that Ecuador fell short in: implementing proposals to limit points of entry and improve biosecurity measures; empowering the National Park Service; and formulating a tourism plan.[202] Nevertheless the site was removed on the basis of existing progress.[203] Fortunately, progress has continued in the three years since, suggesting the danger listing has kept the Ecuadorian government focused upon the recommended measures to reduce risk to the island's vulnerable ecosystems.

The danger list is an important component in the WHC's set-up that contributes to its ability to pull States towards action for protecting marine sites. However, unlike the potential scope of Ramsar's system, it only affects those few properties that are able to meet the criteria for listing as world heritage.

---

[197] WHC, n 133, Art 11(4); WHC Guidelines, n 135, [180].
[198] Whether a State must consent to inclusion is therefore important; see UNESCO legal advisor's advice in UNESCO, *Summary Record of the 26th Ordinary Session of the World Heritage Committee*, WHC-02/CONF.202/INF.15 (2003) [12.1].
[199] UNESCO, WHC-13/37.COM/7A.Add (2013) 43-6.
[200] UNESCO, WHC Decision 37COM7A (2013) 16.
[201] On the original listing, see Goodwin, n 134, 175-8.
[202] UNESCO, n 199, 35-40.
[203] UNESCO, n 200, 15.

4 Conclusion

It is tempting, when confronted by the complexities of the marine environment, to be reductionist: to reduce the problem of endangered species to a critique of (equally reductionist) calculations of MSY TACs or to regard VMEs as deep-water corals. This chapter has sought to use a more appropriate conception of threatened species and VMEs to expose the many and varied international norms as they currently exist. Coordinating all of these strands, nationally and internationally, deserves due attention, but being aware of them, and drawing many of them together in one place, as this chapter has attempted, is an important step.

The law of the sea clearly has many urgent issues to handle in the future, fishing being at the forefront. Greater deployment of effective protected spaces (like MPAs or PSSAs) is needed to reduce anthropogenic stress upon biodiversity. Also, more gear restrictions—like a ban on bottom trawling—need to be introduced and enforced. Further, it must be recalled that marine waters are significant for food supply, and failure to sustainably manage this source—whether through wild caught or aquaculture—places additional burdens upon terrestrial production and biodiversity. Certainly aquaculture offers much potential, but current practices are having such a negative effect on the marine environment that it is clear remodelling this fishery to ensure optimum sustainability is needed.

Pollution remains a considerable challenge. It undermines conservation measures like MPAs, but while some sources fall within traditional law of the sea competences, others fall outside of marine managers' and ministries' exclusive remits, such as LBSP and CO_2 emissions. Integration of marine concerns across government departments and planning therefore remains a basic tenet of conservation. However, ambitious reductions in GHG emissions, and (somehow) CO_2 in particular, are perhaps the keystones to securing marine biodiversity. All of this requires political will but ultimately this seems to be in short supply. As a result the agreement and implementation of international laws to secure the future of threatened species and VMEs remains of considerable concern.

36

MARINE BIOPROSPECTING

JOANNA MOSSOP

1 INTRODUCTION

MARINE organisms are playing an increasingly important role in the development of biotechnologies in a range of fields including pharmaceuticals, industrial processes, and cosmetics. Bioprospecting is the process of identifying unique characteristics of marine organisms for the purpose of developing them into commercially valuable products. Because the interest in the marine organisms is often in the genetic qualities of the organism, these organisms are often referred to as marine genetic resources.[1]

The legal regime of bioprospecting for marine genetic resources is based on both the 1982 United Nations Convention on the Law of the Sea (LOSC) and the 1992 Convention on Biological Diversity (CBD); however, both Conventions contain ambiguities and gaps that create challenges for regulation. The LOSC does not refer to bioprospecting, and does not include a definition of marine scientific research (MSR) leading to some confusion about the appropriate legal rules that apply to bioprospecting. A further current debate centres around the legal rules that apply to

---

[1] Genetic resources can be defined as 'genetic material of actual or potential value': *Report of the Meeting of the Group of Legal and Technical Experts on Concepts, Terms, Working Definitions and Sectoral Approaches*, UN Doc UNEP/CBD/WG-ABS/7/2 (12 December 2008).

the exploitation of marine genetic resources in areas beyond national jurisdiction, particularly in the Area. The CBD, on the other hand, does contain direction in relation to bioprospecting activities and the use of genetic resources, but its application is primarily limited to areas within national jurisdiction.

This chapter explores the legal regime for bioprospecting marine resources. The emphasis is on identifying the legal rules that apply to bioprospecting and the issues that may require future development. After defining bioprospecting, the chapter broadly covers the LOSC and the CBD before giving more details on the rules applying to marine bioprospecting within and outside areas of national jurisdiction.

2 Bioprospecting

2.1 Definition of bioprospecting

Bioprospecting is part of a process in which commercially useful products are derived from living resources. Generally, samples of living organisms are gathered, returned to the laboratory, and analysed. Potentially useful qualities may then be identified, and ultimately developed into an output such as a drug or other substance. This has been described as occurring in four stages.[2] In stage one, samples are collected. At stage two, scientists will attempt to isolate, characterize, and culture microbes. In stage three, the sample will be screened for useful qualities that may result in a commercial product. Stage four involves the development of the product, including securing intellectual property rights, trials, and sales and marketing. Only an extremely small number of organisms sampled (perhaps 1–2 per cent) will end up as a commercial product.[3] In some cases, the success of a product derived from organisms such as microorganisms will depend on whether the substance can be chemically synthesized in the laboratory as harvesting of sufficient organisms can be difficult.[4]

Bioprospecting is not defined in the LOSC, and it is difficult to locate a universally agreed definition of the activity. One useful definition is 'the scientific investigation

---

[2] See J Jabour-Green and D Nichol, 'Bioprospecting in Areas Outside National Jurisdiction: Antarctica and the Southern Ocean' (2003) 4 *Melbourne Journal of International Law* 76, 85; D Leary, *International Law and the Genetic Resources of the Deep Sea* (Martinus Nijhoff Leiden 2007) 164.

[3] J Jabour-Green, ibid, 87.

[4] JF Imhoff, A Labes, and J Wiese, 'Bio-mining the Microbial Treasures of the Ocean: New Natural Products' (2011) 29 *Biotechnology Advances* 468, 470.

of living organisms for commercially valuable genetic and biochemical resources'.[5] A question that sometimes arises is whether the definition includes the entire process of commercializing a product. The Secretary-General of the UN has suggested that this is not the case.

> ... [T]he term is generally understood, among researchers, as the search for biological compounds of actual or potential value to various applications, in particular commercial applications. This involves a series of value-adding processes, usually spanning several years, from biological inventories requiring accurate taxonomic identification of specimens, to the isolation and characterization of valuable active compounds. As a mere prospecting activity, bioprospecting is only the first step towards possible future exploitation and stops once the desired compound or specific property as been isolated and characterized.[6]

In this chapter, the approach of the Secretary-General will be adopted, and therefore marine bioprospecting is considered to be the process of gathering information from the oceans and seas about genetic resources with the goal of developing new commercial products.[7]

2.2 The commercial value of marine bioprospecting

Marine living resources have become increasingly important to the biotechnology industry as comparatively little of the total marine biodiversity has been explored, compared to terrestrial biodiversity.[8] It has been estimated that the success rate in finding previously undescribed active chemicals in marine organisms is 500 times higher than in terrestrial organisms.[9]

Marine organisms offer unique qualities that are of potential commercial value. One area of focus is microorganisms that survive in extreme conditions of pressure, salinity, and the absence of oxygen and light. These are found at hydrothermal vents and cold seep ecosystems in the deep sea, and are among some of the most genetically diverse ecosystems in the world.[10] However, numerous larger and smaller marine living

---

[5] LA de La Fayette, 'A New Regime for the Conservation and Sustainable Use of Marine Biodiversity and Genetic Resources Beyond the Limits of National Jurisdiction' (2009) 24 *International Journal of Marine and Coastal Law* 221, 228.

[6] UN Secretary General, *Oceans and the Law of the Sea: Report of the Secretary-General*, UN Doc A/62/66 (2007) [150]. This approach is not accepted by all scholars. See eg Leary, n 2, 157.

[7] See T Scovazzi, 'Is the UN Convention on the Law of the Sea the Legal Framework for all Activities in the Sea? The Case of Bioprospecting' in D Vidas (ed), *Law, Technology and Science for Oceans in Globalisation: IUU Fishing, Oil Pollution, Bioprospecting, Outer Continental Shelf* (Martinus Nijhoff Leiden 2010) 309, 310.

[8] D Leary et al, 'Marine Genetic Resources: A Review of Scientific and Commercial Interest' (2009) 33 *Marine Policy* 183, 185.

[9] JM Arrieta, S Arnaud-Haond, and CM Duarte, 'What Lies Underneath: Conserving the Oceans' Genetic Resources' (2010) 107 *Proceedings of the National Academy of Sciences* 18318, 18320.

[10] de La Fayette, n 5, 230; T Koslow, *The Silent Deep: The Discovery, Ecology and Conservation of the Deep Sea* (UNSW Press Sydney 2007) 78. See also *Status and Trends of, and Threats to, Deep*

resources from all areas of the ocean may be the source for commercial biotechnology products. Although the marine biotechnology industry is recognized to be in its relative infancy, the range of products that has already been derived from marine genetic resources is growing.

In a study of applications for patents in relation to genes isolated in marine organisms, it was found that pharmacology and human health represented the largest number, of around 55 per cent of applications.[11] Marine genetic resources have resulted in products that have anti-inflammatory, anti-cancer, or other medical properties.[12] Other uses include cosmetics, agriculture, and enzymes that are used in industrial processes.[13]

Various estimates have been made as to the value of the biotechnology industry based on marine genetic resources. Very broad estimates include USD 2.4 billion for the global market in marine biotechnology in 2004,[14] with double-digit growth expected for the foreseeable future.[15] Another report estimated that worldwide sales of all marine biotechnology-related products was USD 100 billion for the year 2000.[16]

Individual pharmaceuticals can generate revenue in the billions if successful for the treatment of widespread diseases such as cancer. In 1996, the potential market for industrial uses of hyperthemophilic bacteria was estimated at USD 3 billion per year.[17] Inevitably, such figures can only be estimates. However, it is clear that the potential rewards are high, providing incentives for companies to undertake the costly and uncertain process of looking for useful compounds in marine genetic resources.

3 The Legal Framework

Two Conventions provide the main legal framework governing the activity of marine bioprospecting. First, the LOSC establishes the rights States have

Seabed Genetic Resources beyond National Jurisdiction etc, UN Doc UNEP/CBD/SBSTTA/11/11 (22 July 2005) [29]–[44].

[11] Arrieta et al, n 9, 18320.
[12] Leary et al, n 8, 185–6; Imhoff et al, n 4, 471; D Leary 'International Law and the Genetic Resources of the Deep Sea' in Vidas (ed), 353, n 7, 359.
[13] Leary et al, n 8, 191. See also Imhoff et al, n 4.
[14] S Arnaud-Haond, JM Arrieta, and CM Duarte, 'Marine Biodiversity and Gene Patents' (2011) 331 *Science* 1521.
[15] Leary et al, n 8, 190. [16] *Status and Trends*, n 10, [21].
[17] L Glowka, 'The Deepest of Ironies: Genetic Resources, Marine Scientific Research, and the Area' (1996) 12 *Ocean Yearbook* 154, 160.

over natural resources in their maritime zones and sets out a regime for areas beyond national jurisdiction. Second, the CBD is a framework convention that addresses both the sustainable use of biodiversity and States' rights to control access to genetic resources within their jurisdiction. Other legal regimes will also be relevant to the issues surrounding biotechnology. These include international intellectual property treaties because obtaining patents protecting biotechnology developments is an integral part of the process of developing such products. However, the focus of this chapter is on the legal rights governing access to the first part of the process, bioprospecting.

3.1 The Law of the Sea Convention

Three aspects of the LOSC are important to marine bioprospecting. First, the LOSC establishes the rights that each State may exercise in maritime zones from the territorial sea to the high seas. Within national jurisdiction, coastal States exercise significant control over the harvesting of living resources, including marine genetic resources. Beyond national jurisdiction, the prevailing legal principle is that of freedom to exploit the living resources of the high seas, although this is not straight forward and will be elaborated on later in the chapter.

The second important aspect is that the LOSC regulates MSR. Where MSR is directly relevant to the exploitation of living resources, coastal States have a significant level of control over marine scientific projects in their exclusive economic zone and on their continental shelf.[18] Beyond national jurisdiction, MSR is a freedom of the high seas.[19] In the Area, research should encourage international cooperation.[20]

Finally, the LOSC contains provisions requiring States to protect and preserve the marine environment.[21] Although the majority of these provisions focus on the prevention of pollution, there are provisions relating to the protection of the environment generally, including the requirement to conduct prior assessment of activities that may cause significant and harmful changes to the marine environment.[22] Although it is usually accepted that bioprospecting does not generally involve great risks to the marine environment, as the samples taken are small, there may still be some disturbance of the environment which should be evaluated.[23] If the biotechnology process subsequently requires harvesting of marine organisms on a larger scale, the environmental effects of such activity will need to be assessed.

---

[18] 1982 United Nations Convention on the Law of the Sea, Art 246 (hereinafter LOSC).
[19] Ibid, Art 87.   [20] Ibid, Art 143.   [21] Ibid, Art 192.   [22] Ibid, Art 206.
[23] R Warner, 'Protecting the Diversity of the Depths: Environmental Regulation of Bioprospecting and Marine Scientific Regulation beyond National Jurisdiction' (2008) 22 *Ocean Yearbook* 411, 416.

3.2 The 1992 Convention on Biological Diversity and Related Instruments

The CBD is aimed at conserving biological diversity, ensuring the sustainable use of its resources and the fair and equitable sharing of the benefits arising out of the use of genetic resources.[24] The latter objective arose out of developing countries' concerns that they were losing control over genetic resources that were developed by biotechnology companies, with no benefits returned to the country in which the resources were found. Therefore, the CBD confirmed that genetic resources are under the control of the State in which they exist.[25] States have obligations to cooperate for the conservation and sustainable use of biological diversity.[26] States are also obliged to facilitate access to genetic resources by researchers from other States, but such access is to be on mutually agreed terms, based on prior informed consent, and the benefits of commercialization of genetic resources should be shared in a fair and equitable way.[27]

Article 4 of the CBD states that it applies to 'the components of biological diversity, in areas within the limits of [States'] national jurisdiction'. This clearly means that the CBD will apply to marine genetic resources found in the territorial sea, exclusive economic zone, and on the continental shelf. The CBD also applies to processes and activities carried out under the jurisdiction or control of the State whether they are carried out within its national jurisdiction or beyond the limits of national jurisdiction. This means that the CBD has potential application to activities carried out on the high seas or in the Area.

The question of what amounts to facilitation of access, and to fair and equitable benefit sharing, has occupied the Parties to the CBD for many years as States struggled to establish appropriate legislative and regulatory frameworks.[28] A number of attempts to clarify these requirements have been made by working groups established under the Conference of the Parties (COP). In 2002, the COP adopted the voluntary Bonn Guidelines to clarify policies on Access and Benefit Sharing (ABS).[29] These Guidelines established expectations to be fulfilled by countries of origin, users of genetic resources, providers of genetic resources, and user States in relation to prior informed consent, mutually agreed terms, provision of access and benefit sharing. However, it was considered that the Guidelines did not adequately clarify

---

[24] 1992 Convention on Biological Diversity, Art 1 (hereinafter CBD).
[25] Ibid, Arts 3 and 15.   [26] Ibid, Art 5.   [27] Ibid, Art 15.
[28] EC Kamau, B Fedder, and G Winter, 'The Nagoya Protocol on Access to Genetic Resources and Benefit Sharing: What is New and What are the Implications for Provider and User Countries and the Scientific Community?' (2010) 6 *Law, Environment and Development Journal* 246.
[29] See eg B Fedder, *Marine Genetic Resources, Access and Benefit Sharing: Legal and Biological Perspectives* (Routledge London 2013) 46.

the relationship between important concepts and procedures. The non-binding nature of the Guidelines was also criticized.

Soon after the conclusion of the Bonn Guidelines the parties to the CBD agreed to work towards an international treaty on ABS. The Nagoya Protocol was adopted in 2010.[30] It attempts to establish procedures that provide clarity and certainty to those seeking access to genetic resources. Significant recognition is given to the role of holders of traditional knowledge about genetic resources, and the need to involve these communities in decision making and benefit sharing. Parties must cooperate to build capacity in developing countries. As with the CBD, many of the obligations are qualified by such words as 'as far as possible' or 'where applicable'. This has tended to encourage a view that the obligations in the CBD and Nagoya Protocol are not easily enforceable.

The relationship between the CBD and the LOSC is made clear in the CBD. Article 22 of the CBD states that it shall not affect the rights and obligations of any State arising under existing international agreements, 'except where the exercise of those rights and obligations would cause a serious damage or threat to biological diversity'. Contracting parties are instructed to implement the CBD 'consistently with the rights and obligations of States under the law of the sea'. Therefore, if there is an inconsistency between provisions of the CBD and the LOSC, the LOSC will prevail.[31]

3.3 Classification of bioprospecting under the Law of the Sea Convention

A debate has centred around whether marine bioprospecting amounts to MSR. If bioprospecting is considered MSR, then the legal framework for MSR under the LOSC applies.[32] This has implications for the way States can exercise their rights within areas under national jurisdiction but also beyond national jurisdiction. If bioprospecting is not MSR, then the LOSC regime applying to the harvesting of living resources will apply. Probably the key factor inspiring some (particularly developing) countries to argue that bioprospecting is MSR, is the debate surrounding the status of genetic resources in areas beyond national jurisdiction. As will be

---

[30] 2010 Nagoya Protocol on Access to Genetic Resources and the Fair and Equitable Sharing of Benefits Arising from Their Utilization to the Convention on Biological Diversity.

[31] Fedder, n 29, 59; DK Anton, 'Law for the Sea's Biodiversity' (1998) 36 *Columbia Journal of Transnational Law* 341, 357. Not all authors agree: see A Boyle, 'Further Development of the Law of the Sea Convention: Mechanisms for Change' (2005) 54 *International & Comparative Law Quarterly* 563, 579.

[32] See Chapter 25 in this volume.

discussed later, if bioprospecting is MSR, there are certain obligations on States to cooperate in the Area.

It has been suggested that the distinction between bioprospecting and MSR turns on the commercial intent of the researchers. This is because MSR is expected to be transparent and open, with an obligation to disseminate information and data and the subsequent publication of results of the research.[33] Because researchers who intend to seek a patent or other intellectual property rights will not publish the results of their research until such protection is obtained, it is argued that the research cannot be considered part of the MSR regime.[34] Therefore, the intention of the researchers becomes the critical criteria for assessment.[35]

Some commentators have questioned the distinction between bioprospecting and MSR based on intention.[36] Scovazzi argues that MSR includes some research that has direct application to the exploitation of resources—and that this would involve an intention of commercial use.[37] One of the problems is that research trips are expensive, and may be funded by a range of sources. Some research institutions may receive funding from commercial interests for their dives, resulting in a mix of 'commercial' and 'non-commercial' research.[38] In other cases, a research trip with non-commercial intentions may take samples which are later accessed for commercial purposes by other researchers.[39]

Despite these difficulties, it appears that many States are opting to make the distinction between bioprospecting and scientific research based on the intention of the researchers. In both Australia and the Philippines, regulations distinguish between collection of specimens for commercial or non-commercial purposes.[40] In Australia's case, collection for commercial purposes creates obligations to enter into benefit sharing agreements, whereas collection for non-commercial purposes must be accompanied by a declaration outlining the lack of commercial intent and controls on later commercial use.[41] These regulations are primarily driven by

---

[33] LOSC, n 18, Art 244.

[34] *Study of the Relationship between the Convention on Biological Diversity and the United Nations Convention on the Law of the Sea with Regard to the Conservation and Sustainable Use of Genetic Resources on the Deep Seabed*, UN Doc UNEP/CBD/SBSTTA/8/INF/3/Rev.1 (22 February 2003) [39].

[35] See S Arico and C Salpin, *Bioprospecting of Genetic Resources in the Deep Seabed: Scientific, Legal and Policy Aspects* (UNU-IAS 2005) 34, available at <http://moderncms.ecosystemmarketplace.com/repository/moderncms_documents/DeepSeabed.pdf>.

[36] See J Mossop, 'Protecting Marine Biodiversity on the Continental Shelf Beyond 200 Nautical Miles' (2007) 38 Ocean Development and International Law 283, 293.

[37] LOSC, n 18, Art 246; T Scovazzi, 'Mining, Protection of the Environment, Scientific Research and Bioprospecting: Some Considerations on the Role of the International Sea-bed Authority' (2004) 19 *International Journal of Marine and Coastal Law* 383, 402. See also CH Allen, 'Protecting the Oceanic Gardens of Eden: International Law Issues in Deep-Sea Vent Resource Conservation and Management' (2000–1) 13 *Georgetown International Environmental Law Review* 563, 644.

[38] Leary et al, n 8, 184.   [39] Scovazzi, n 37, 403.

[40] H Cohen, 'Some Reflections on Bioprospecting in the Polar Regions' in Vidas (ed), n 7, 339, 342.

[41] Ibid.

the provisions of the CBD rather than the LOSC. Nevertheless, this Chapter will approach bioprospecting on the basis that it does not fall within the regime of MSR under the LOSC.

4 Bioprospecting within National Jurisdiction

The LOSC and the CBD are relevant for States that seek to regulate bioprospecting in areas within national jurisdiction. The CBD applies to components of biological diversity within national jurisdiction; it is the LOSC that determines what living resources are within the national jurisdiction of the coastal State, and the extent of that jurisdiction.

A coastal State has sovereignty over the territorial sea and it is clear that any sort of activity based on taking samples of genetic resources is within its jurisdiction. Article 19 provides that fishing, and the carrying out of research or survey activities, may not be undertaken by vessels exercising innocent passage. In addition, a coastal State can legislate for ships conducting innocent passage in respect of fishing activities, MSR and the conservation of the living resources of the sea.[42] Although bioprospecting is not explicitly mentioned, it would be a valid assumption that a ship engaging in bioprospecting during passage through the territorial sea would be in breach of innocent passage and subject to the coastal State's jurisdiction.

In the exclusive economic zone, coastal States have 'sovereign rights for the purpose of exploring and exploiting, conserving and managing the natural resources, whether living or non-living, of the waters superjacent to the seabed and of the seabed and subsoil'.[43] It is unquestionable that marine genetic resources are included in the category of 'living resources' although the provisions of Part V of the LOSC relating to living resources are written primarily with fisheries as the focus. With this in mind, the coastal State must determine the total allowable catch of the living resources in its exclusive economic zone and share any excess capacity with other States.[44] These obligations have little relevance to marine genetic resources accessed during bioprospecting, as these organisms are harvested for an entirely different purpose than those targeted by fishing interests.[45] However, if marine species were to be later targeted for harvesting for the purposes of the large-scale production of a marine biotechnology product, the obligations may then become relevant.

[42] LOSC, n 18, Art 21(1).   [43] Ibid, Art 56(1)(a).   [44] Ibid, Arts 61 and 62.
[45] Scovazzi, n 37, 400.

However, the coastal State does have obligations to ensure that the marine environment is considered during the bioprospecting process. A coastal State may not allow living resources to be endangered by over-exploitation[46] and has the overall responsibility to protect and preserve the marine environment.[47]

Within the exclusive economic zone, the coastal State has jurisdiction to regulate MSR, although in normal circumstances the coastal State should grant their consent for MSR projects by other States where the research is to increase scientific knowledge of the marine environment for the benefit of all mankind.[48] However, where the project is of the direct significance for the exploration and exploitation of natural resources, the coastal State may refuse consent.[49] This may be relevant if the coastal State is concerned that initially straight forward research involving sampling of organisms could later be used as a basis for commercial activities using those samples.

The regime applicable to the resources of the continental shelf is largely similar to the exclusive economic zone. Sedentary species, which are those living resources that at the harvestable State are either immobile on or under the seabed or are unable to move except in constant physical contact with the seabed, are governed by Part VI of the LOSC.[50] As with the exclusive economic zone, States have sovereign rights over the living and non-living resources of the continental shelf. One important difference is that the regime of the continental shelf can extend beyond the 200 nautical mile (nm) limit of the exclusive economic zone in some circumstances.[51] In that case, a coastal State may have sovereign rights over sedentary species while the adjacent water column is the high seas.[52]

The regime for the regulation of MSR on the continental shelf is also similar to that in relation to the exclusive economic zone, with one important distinction. A coastal State's ability to refuse consent to MSR projects with direct significance for the exploration and exploitation of natural resources is limited in respect of the extended continental shelf beyond 200 nm. On the extended shelf, a coastal State may only refuse consent for such projects if it has designated the area as one in which exploitation or detailed exploratory operations are occurring or will occur within a reasonable period of time.[53] However, this should not prevent a State that wishes to establish a marine protected area on the extended shelf from doing so.[54]

Within these areas of national jurisdiction, the CBD and Nagoya Protocol establish obligations on States—both coastal States (known as provider States in CBD terms) and the States whose nationals wish to access the genetic material (often referred to as user States). First, coastal States have obligations to develop national

---

[46] LOSC, n 18, Art 61(2).   [47] Ibid, Art 192.   [48] Ibid, Art 246(1) and (2).
[49] Ibid, Art 246(5).   [50] Ibid, Art 77.   [51] Ibid, Art 76.
[52] See Mossop, n 36; J Mossop, 'Regulating Uses of Marine Biodiversity on the Outer Continental Shelf' in Vidas (ed), n 7, 319.
[53] LOSC, n 18, Art 246(6).   [54] Mossop, n 36, 291.

strategies for the conservation and sustainable use of biological diversity.[55] This may involve identifying and monitoring biological diversity, and protecting it both *in situ* and *ex situ*.[56] These States must also allow for the prior assessment of the impact of projects on biodiversity, usually through environment impact assessments.[57]

Second, coastal States must 'endeavour to create conditions to facilitate access to genetic resources for environmentally sound uses by other Contracting Parties and not to impose restrictions that run counter' to the objectives of the CBD.[58] Access to resources should be based on the prior informed consent of the parties, and coastal States must take steps to share 'in an equitable way the results of research and development and the benefits arising from the commercial and other utilization of genetic resources with the Contracting Party providing such resources' based on mutually agreed terms.[59]

This second aspect of the CBD has proven most controversial. As already mentioned, the concepts in the CBD are not well defined, and considerable effort has been put into clarifying the role of provider and user States. The Nagoya Protocol is intended to assist States in implementing their obligations under the CBD. Coastal States will be required to identify clearly their domestic access and benefit sharing rules and requirements and specify how to apply for prior informed consent and any required approval by indigenous and local communities.[60] This seeks to improve the ability of foreign researchers to apply for consent to access resources. Legislation or regulation is required to ensure that utilization of genetic resources held by indigenous communities leads to the sharing of benefits with those communities.[61] In addition, each State must designate a national focal point and national authority on access and benefit sharing. These focal points again are intended to facilitate ease of information and access to decision-making procedures within the coastal State. Where genetic resources are found within the territory of more than one State, those States shall endeavour to cooperate to implement the Protocol.[62]

To the extent possible, the legal regime under the LOSC must be reconciled with the CBD. One important difference between the two regimes is that the CBD requires States to facilitate access to genetic resources whereas the LOSC assumes, in relation to the exploitation of living resources, that the coastal State has discretion as to how resources are to be accessed. In the case of MSR, it is arguable that the need for coastal State consent under the LOSC is similar to the requirement for prior informed consent under the CBD. However, the LOSC does not refer to the need for access to be on mutually agreed terms.[63] Ultimately, Fedder suggests that

---

[55] CBD, n 24, Art 6. See Warner, n 23, 425. [56] CBD, Arts 7–10. [57] Ibid, Art 14.
[58] Ibid, Art 15(1). [59] Ibid, Art 15(7).
[60] 2010 Nagoya Protocol on Access to Genetic Resources and the Fair and Equitable Sharing of Benefits Arising from their Utilization, Art 6 (Nagoya Protocol).
[61] Ibid, Art 5. [62] Ibid, Art 11. [63] Fedder, n 29, 56.

the regime under the CBD provides more discretion to determine access to genetic resources if the research is classified as MSR.[64]

5 Bioprospecting beyond National Jurisdiction

The legal regime applicable to bioprospecting beyond national jurisdiction has received considerable attention in recent years. This is because international focus has turned to the deep seabed as a prospective source of genetic material for the biotechnology industry. The varying estimates of enormous profits from marine bioprospecting have led many to believe that the living resources in the high seas and the Area could be the source of considerable wealth in the future.

There are two important legal regimes that apply beyond national jurisdiction in the LOSC: the high seas and the regime for the deep seabed known as the Area. In relation to the high seas, the LOSC stipulates that both fishing and scientific research are freedoms of the high seas, although both are restricted in certain ways.[65] Fishing is subject to the duty of States to adopt measures for the conservation of the living resources of the high seas[66] and to cooperate with each other in conserving and managing these resources.[67] There is also an obligation to determine the total allowable catch based on the best scientific evidence available.[68] As with the regime applicable within national jurisdiction, these provisions are clearly drafted with traditional fisheries interests in mind, however they are applicable to other types of harvesting such as bioprospecting.

The issue is the legal regime that applies to the Area. When Part XI of the LOSC was negotiated, the focus was on the regulation of mineral extraction. Although Article 136 states that the 'Area and its resources are the common heritage of mankind', Article 133 makes it clear that resources means 'all solid, liquid or gaseous mineral resources *in situ* in the Area at or beneath the seabed, including polymetallic nodules'. Some commentators have relied on the broad language of Article 133, and the history of the development of the concept of the common heritage of mankind, to argue that Part XI applies to the living resources of the seabed.[69] The consequence

---

[64] Ibid, 58. [65] LOSC, n 18, Art 87. [66] Ibid, Art 117.
[67] Ibid, Art 118. [68] Ibid, Art 119.
[69] D Tladi, 'Genetic Resources, Benefit Sharing and the Law of the Sea: The Need for Clarity' (2007) 13 *Journal of International Maritime Law* 183; Y Tanaka, 'Reflections on the Conservation and Sustainable Use of Genetic Resources in the Deep Seabed Beyond the Limits of National Jurisdiction' (2008) 39 *Ocean Development and International Law* 129.

of this would be that marine genetic materials in the Area would also be common heritage, with obligations to equitably share the benefits from bioprospecting.

Another argument is based on the argument that bioprospecting is MSR. According to this viewpoint, any bioprospecting in the Area should be conducted according to Part XI of the LOSC. Article 143 requires MSR in the Area to be carried out 'for the benefit of mankind as a whole'. The results of MSR are to be disseminated and there is an obligation to promote international cooperation in MSR. This argument has complicated the debate about the correct categorization of bioprospecting, due to the fact that some States wish to include bioprospecting as MSR because of the consequences for the legal regime applicable to genetic resources in the Area.

These arguments in favour of marine genetic resources being covered by the existing legal regime of the Area are hampered by the clear exclusion of living resources from the resources covered in Part XI. However, the legal question has been thoroughly debated in United Nations fora. In 2004 the General Assembly established an Open-ended Informal Working Group to study issues relating to the conservation and sustainable use of marine biological diversity beyond areas of national jurisdiction. Although the purpose of the Working Group was much wider than the question of genetic resources in the Area, this was a topic that many, particularly developing, countries wished to discuss. There was a strong view that an unregulated access to genetic resources in the Area had serious economic and social implications.[70] The interest of the international community was reflected in the fact that in 2007 marine genetic resources was the topic discussed during the United Nations Open-ended Informal Consultative Process on Oceans and the Law of the Sea.[71]

The positions of States discussing the issue of marine genetic resources in the Area have fallen into three primary positions. First, there is the group that argues that the marine genetic resources of the Area are the common heritage of mankind and governed by Part XI of the LOSC. This group includes the G77 group of nations who are attracted by the benefit sharing consequences of Part XI.[72] Second, many States argue that Part XI does not refer to living resources, and

---

[70] *Recommendations of the Ad Hoc Open-ended Informal Working Group to Study Issues Relating to the Conservation and Sustainable Use of Marine Biological Diversity Beyond Areas of National Jurisdiction and Co-Chairs' Summary of Discussions*, annexed to *Letter Dated 30 June 2011 from the Co-Chairs of the Ad Hoc Open-ended Informal Working Group to the President of the General Assembly*, UN Doc A/66/119 (30 June 2011) [15].

[71] *Report on the Work of the United Nations Open-ended Informal Consultative Process on Oceans and the Law of the Sea at its Eighth Meeting*, UN Doc A/62/169 (30 July 2007).

[72] See eg *Statement on Behalf of the Group of the Group of 77 and China by Minister Diego Limeres, Deputy Permanent Representative of the Permanent Mission of Argentina to the United Nations, at the Ad Hoc Open-ended Informal Working Group to Study Issues Relating to the Conservation and Sustainable Use of Marine Biological Diversity Beyond Areas of National Jurisdiction* (New York 31 May 2011), available at <http://www.g77.org/statement/getstatement.php?id=110531>.

so these are governed by the regime applicable to the high seas. This would result in the conclusion that marine genetic resources are subject to the freedom of the high seas, and open to all States to access freely. Understandably, this group includes developed countries with biotechnology industries, including the United States. Finally, some argue that there is a legal gap and that a new legal instrument should be negotiated. Despite almost ten years of meetings, the divisions in the Ad Hoc Working Group on the appropriate legal regime are still strong.[73]

The General Assembly has agreed that work will begin on exploring the possible development of a multilateral agreement to address the conservation and sustainable use of marine biodiversity in areas beyond national jurisdiction where existing instruments are inadequate.[74] The topics to be discussed include marine genetic resources and the possible sharing of benefits. Therefore, it is possible that in the future the issue of bioprospecting beyond national jurisdiction will be affected by a new treaty.

There are a number of issues that will need to be discussed and resolved in any new treaty. First, it is noteworthy that considerable attention has focused on the genetic resources of the Area but not the high seas. Arguably, the reason is that living resources in the water column are covered by the freedom of the high seas while there is ambiguity about the living resources of the sea floor. However, it seems that the resources of the high seas are, at least in the short term, more likely to result in commercially successful biotechnology products than those from the deep seabed.[75] Some commentators have warned that the predicted bonanza from genetic resources in the Area is overstated.[76]

The primary justification for a distinction between the legal regime that applies to the water column and the seabed in areas beyond national jurisdiction is the development of the common heritage of mankind concept in relation to minerals. Identification of seabed minerals is reasonably straightforward. However, the distinction between the living resources of the seabed and the water column is far harder to make. The only guidelines in the LOSC are based on the 'sedentary species' definition in relation to the continental shelf.[77] It has been pointed out

---

[73] See *Report of the Ad Hoc Open-ended Informal Working Group to study issues relating to the conservation and sustainable use of marine biological diversity beyond areas of national jurisdiction and Co-Chairs' summary of discussions* annexed to *Letter dated 23 September from the Co-Chairs of the Ad Hoc Open-ended Informal Working Group to the President of the General Assembly*, UN Doc A/68/399 (23 September 2013) [17]–[19].

[74] UNGA Res 66/231 (24 December 2011) [168].

[75] United Nations Secretary General, *Oceans and the Law of the Sea: Report of the Secretary-General*, UN Doc A/66/70 (22 March 2011) [63].

[76] See D Leary, 'Moving the Marine Genetic Resources Debate Forward: Some Reflections' (2012) 27 *International Journal of Marine and Coastal Law* 435, 444.

[77] LOSC, n 18, Art 77(4).

that, in relation to bioprospecting and marine genetic resources, the definition of sedentary species is singularly unhelpful.[78] This is because the types of organisms targeted by bioprospecting can range from juvenile to mature organisms, making it problematic to determine when an organism is 'at a harvestable stage'. It may be difficult to fit organisms found at hydrothermal vents into the Article 77(4) model. Leary has suggested that the concept of sedentary species should not be applied in the case of genetic materials on the continental shelf due to the risk of creating a fragmented legal framework.[79] Therefore, if States rely on an idea of sedentary species when creating a regime for the Area, this may lead to further problems.[80]

Another important issue is how to incorporate an access and benefit sharing arrangement for products developed from resources gathered beyond national jurisdiction, and which institution would administer the regime. The International Seabed Authority may be able play a role given its existing role in relation to seabed minerals. However, this is not necessarily possible.[81] The existing LOSC contains no framework for dealing with intellectual property rights or access and benefit sharing that would allow the International Seabed Authority to take on the role without a further legal instrument.

The desire by many States for a robust access and benefit sharing regime has led some to suggest that a possible model is the 2001 FAO International Treaty on Plant Genetic Resources for Food and Agriculture.[82] This treaty is aimed at the conservation and sustainable use of plant genetic resources and the fair and equitable sharing of benefits derived from their use.[83] Under the multilateral system established by the treaty, genetic resources are freely available for the purposes of research, breeding, and training for food and agriculture. Intellectual property rights may be claimed over products incorporating the genetic materials, as long as this does not limit access to the resources or a fixed percentage of the sales is paid. Although the regime applies to materials within national jurisdiction, it is possible that it could form the basis for discussions about a regime that applies to marine genetic resources beyond national jurisdiction.

---

[78] Allen, n 37, 623–4; EJ Molenaar, 'Unregulated Deep-Sea Fisheries: A Need for a Multi-Level Approach' (2004) 19 *International Journal of Marine and Coastal Law* 223, 245; Mossop, n 36, 292.

[79] Leary, n 12, 94.

[80] P Drankier et al, 'Marine Genetic Resources in Areas beyond National Jurisdiction: Access and Benefit Sharing' (2012) 27 *International Journal of Marine and Coastal Law* 375, 406; A Oude Elferink, 'The Regime of the Area: Delineating the Scope of Application of the Common Heritage Principle and Freedom of the High Seas' (2007) 22 *International Journal of Marine and Coastal Law* 143, 151.

[81] Leary, n 2, 223.   [82] Drankier et al, n 80; Leary, n 76.

[83] 2001 FAO International Treaty on Plant Genetic Resources for Food and Agriculture, Art 1.

6 Regional Arrangements

In a few cases regional legal frameworks will have applicability to bioprospecting activities. One significant example is the Antarctic region, where the parties to the 1959 Antarctic Treaty have been grappling with the question of the appropriate legal principles that should apply to bioprospecting since 2002. The species that survive in the extreme conditions that prevail in Antarctica are of considerable interest to researchers and a potential source of biotechnological development.[84] The genetic resources that have been identified as being of interest include anti-freeze proteins from fish found in the Southern Ocean.

The Antarctic Treaty system does not directly regulate bioprospecting, and to date, no agreement has been reached among the Antarctic Treaty Consultative Parties about how this should be done. It has been suggested that the CBD provisions, which are based on national control of genetic resources, are of little assistance under the Antarctic Treaty, which suspends claims to national sovereignty in Antarctica.[85] However, some provisions of the treaties in force in the Antarctic area will be applicable to the activity.

First, the 1959 Antarctic Treaty itself provides for freedom of 'scientific investigation' in Antarctica.[86] To support this goal, information about scientific plans in Antarctica is to be exchanged, and to the extent possible, scientific observations and results from Antarctica shall be exchanged and made freely available.[87] Second, the 1991 Protocol on Environmental Protection to the Antarctic Treaty (Madrid Protocol) establishes a number of environmental principles that are potentially relevant for bioprospecting, including the limitation of adverse environmental impacts and avoiding detrimental impacts on species of fauna and flora.[88] Activities, including scientific research, are subject to the requirement to conduct an environmental impact assessment.[89] Finally, the 1980 Convention on the Conservation of Antarctic Marine Living Resources (CAMLR Convention) applies to marine living resources in the area south of 60° S, and so technically could cover marine bioprospecting. It is unlikely that the collection of marine species for bioprospecting will be at a scale that it will need to be regulated by the Commission for the Conservation of Antarctic Marine Living Resources (CCAMLR). However, the reporting requirements in Article 20 may be relevant.[90]

Bioprospecting in Antarctica has been complicated by the lack of national sovereignty in the area, leading to questions about who owns the resources, who determines

---

[84] D Lohan and S Johnson, *Bioprospecting in Antarctica* (UNU-IAS 2005).
[85] 1959 Antarctic Treaty, Art VI. See Lohan and Johnson, n 84, 28.
[86] Antarctic Treaty, n 85, Art II.   [87] Ibid, Art III(1).
[88] 1991 Protocol on Environmental Protection to the Antarctic Treaty, Art 3.
[89] Ibid, Art 8.   [90] Lohan and Johnson, n 84, 18.

access, and how any benefits should be shared.[91] As this subject is still on the agenda of the Antarctic Treaty Consultative Meeting, there may be future developments that address these questions.

Generally, there is the potential for other regional legal arrangements to have an impact on the law applying to marine biodiversity. Regional seas agreements and regional fisheries management organizations have an interest in the harvesting of marine living resources, although they have not tended to be focused on MSR or bioprospecting. A few countries have adopted regional arrangements for implementing the CBD provisions relating to access and benefit sharing.[92] However, there is little sign at present of a trend towards dealing with marine bioprospecting at a regional level.

7 CONCLUSION

Bioprospecting is a growth industry, and States are beginning to realize the benefits that could flow from accessing the genetic resources of the sea. The LOSC provides a coherent framework for determining States' rights to the resources within national jurisdiction, although it is likely that the question of whether bioprospecting is MSR will continue to cause small issues. The CBD sets out States' rights and obligations in relation to conserving biodiversity and agreeing to access and benefit sharing arrangements. It will take some time to determine whether the Nagoya Protocol will be effective in encouraging States to facilitate access and improve benefit sharing. States would be recommended to have in place clear processes for considering applications to access marine genetic resources in their jurisdiction.

The situation beyond national jurisdiction is uncertain at present. Although some biotechnology products are being developed based on marine genetic resources from beyond national jurisdiction, they remain a very small portion of the total marine biotechnology effort. This is due to the fact that areas within national jurisdiction are still under-explored and are easier to access. However, the interest in

---

[91] CC Joyner, 'Bioprospecting as a Challenge to the Antarctic Treaty' in AD Hemmings, DR Rothwell, and KN Scott (eds), *Antarctic Security in the Twenty-first Century: Legal and Policy Perspectives* (Routledge Oxon 2012) 197, 209.

[92] See eg Nordic Council of Ministers, *Strategy for Genetic Resources in the Fisheries, Agriculture, Forestry and Food Sectors in the Nordic Region 2005–2008* (2004), available at <http://www.cbd.int/doc/measures/abs/msr-abs-nr.3-en.pdf>; Andean Community Commission, Decision 391, Common Regime on Access to Genetic Resources (2 July 1996), available at <http://www.cbd.int/doc/measures/abs/msr-abs-acu-en.pdf>.

extremophiles found at locations such as hydrothermal vents will drive continued interest in remote areas of the oceans.

It is desirable that the international community reach consensus on the appropriate legal framework for bioprospecting and subsequent utilization of genetic resources in areas beyond national jurisdiction. In the absence of agreement, uncertainty tends to stifle exploration of these resources. Unfortunately, to date, the debate has been very slow to progress beyond the entrenched legal positions States have adopted in relation to the legal status of genetic resources in the Area. These positions are influenced by the belief, on the part of many developing States, that because the seabed is considered the common heritage of mankind for mineral resources the same principle should apply to living resources on the seabed. On the other hand, there is sufficient interest in those resources that developed countries wish to protect the potential returns of biotechnology companies operating in the Area. The negotiations for a new international agreement must therefore find a path to accommodate these views.

It is conceivable that a new agreement could establish a mechanism that borrows from the principle of the common heritage of mankind to establish some form of access and benefit sharing in relation to the genetic resources of the Area. The Nagoya Protocol and other work in the CBD may provide some guidance for the future shape of the rights and obligations. However, even such an agreement probably will not resolve a final concern: that the legal regimes for the living resources of the water column and the seabed would be significantly different. It is foreseeable that this will lead to future problems in distinguishing between seabed and water resources.

37
PIRACY

ANNA PETRIG

1 Contemporary Piracy

1.1 Necessity of a counter-piracy legal regime

For many years, piracy was perceived as an outdated 'eighteenth-century concept' of chiefly historical interest. During the drafting of the 1958 Convention on the High Seas (HSC), some delegations even proposed the deletion *in toto* of the provisions on piracy because the phenomenon 'no longer constituted a general problem'. Others argued that devoting eight articles to a specific type of violence at sea, 'which was no longer a very real problem', would be 'out of all proportion' and supported the idea of boiling down the provisions on piracy to a single article.[1] These radical proposals did not meet with success, yet the rather slipshod craftsmanship of the counter-piracy rules in the HSC (which were later borrowed for the 1982 United Nations Convention on the Law of the Sea (LOSC)) are arguably the result of a reluctance to deeply discuss and reflect on the issue of piracy for the purpose of a contemporary codification on the law of the sea.

However, not many years after the adoption of the LOSC the upsurge of violence against ships and their crews in various maritime areas of the world, notably in Southeast Asia, off the coast of Somalia, and in the Gulf of Guinea, brought about a change in attitude regarding the necessity of having a legal regime in place aimed

---

[1] (1958) IV *Official Records of the UN Conference on the Law of the Sea*, Second Committee (High Seas: General Regime), UN Doc A/CONF.13/40 (24 February–27 April 1958) 78–9 and 128.

at the suppression of piracy at sea and on land. The sharp spike in piratical activity in these waters has even provoked calls for additional rules and mechanisms to counter maritime piracy, going so far as to propose the adoption of a convention on piracy or the creation of a universal piracy tribunal.

1.2 Forms of contemporary piracy

Piracy is the single label that has been placed on an entire criminal phenomenon, which is actually quite diverse and to a large extent contingent on the maritime region in which it occurs. Broadly speaking, contemporary piracy takes two forms.

One form of piracy consists of hijacking ships and crews. This may occur for the purpose of negotiating a ransom for their release, which is archetypical for Somali-based piracy.[2] Alternatively, ships are hijacked to be sold after being repainted and renamed—a type of piracy witnessed in Southeast Asia since 2008.[3] Another form of piracy consists of the commission of property offences, which run the gamut from robbing the crew of their valuables—the main form of piracy in Southeast Asia[4]—to stealing the entire cargo, as occurs in the West African part of the Gulf of Guinea during ship-to-ship operations.[5]

1.3 Applicable legal framework and its historical roots

It is the LOSC—notably Articles 100–107 and 110—that sets out the primary legal framework for countering piracy.[6] The largely similar provisions in Articles 14–22 of the HSC are of relevance for the six States currently parties to the HSC but not the LOSC.[7] In addition to the LOSC provisions on piracy, which have attained the status of customary international law,[8] other bodies of international law, most notably

---

[2] The World Bank, *The Pirates of Somalia: Ending the Threat, Rebuilding a Nation* (2013) 1, 92 and 94, available at <http://siteresources.worldbank.org/INTAFRICA/Resources/pirates-of-somalia-main-report-web.pdf>.

[3] R Beckman, 'Piracy and Armed Robbery Against Ships in Southeast Asia' in D Guilfoyle (ed), *Modern Piracy: Legal Challenges and Responses* (Edward Elgar Publishing 2013) 13, 15–16 and 23–25.

[4] Ibid.

[5] United Nations Security Council (UNSC), *Report of the United Nations Assessment Mission on Piracy in the Gulf of Guinea*, UN Doc S/2012/45 (19 January 2012) [5] and [35].

[6] Emphasized in UNSC Res 2125 (18 November 2013) Preamble, [9], and other resolutions concerning Somali-based piracy.

[7] This chapter therefore concentrates on the 1982 United Nations Convention on the Law of the Sea (hereinafter LOSC); however, its findings are generally also valid for the 1958 Convention on the High Seas (hereinafter HSC).

[8] D Guilfoyle, 'Legal Issues Relating to Counter-Piracy Operations off the Coast of Somalia (Written Evidence)' in House of Commons Foreign Affairs Committee (UK), *Tenth Report of Session 2010–12: Piracy off the coast of Somalia* (2012) Ev 80.

international criminal law and human rights law, as well as domestic law, play a role in the suppression of piracy at sea and on land.

The provisions on piracy of the HSC and the LOSC date back to the beginning of the twentieth century. The first attempt to codify counter-piracy rules at the universal level, which took place under the auspices of the League of Nations, was ultimately abandoned in light of doubts as to whether piracy was 'of sufficient real interest in the present state of the world'[9] to be codified.[10] However, the initiative of the League of Nations prompted Harvard Law School to coordinate research on piracy that eventually resulted in the 1932 Harvard Draft Convention on Piracy.[11]

The Harvard Draft Convention on Piracy heavily impacted the work of the International Law Commission (ILC), which built the foundation for the piracy provisions of the HSC that, in turn, strongly influenced the piracy regime of the LOSC. The six provisions on piracy in the draft text by ILC Rapporteur François entitled 'Regime on the High Seas', were simply French translations of the Harvard Draft Convention's provisions.[12] The provisions on piracy adopted by the ILC in 1956 as part of the Draft Articles Concerning the Law of the Sea[13] were also influenced by the Harvard research, which 'the Commission was able to endorse'.[14] Since piracy was perceived as an historical rather than contemporary problem, these provisions did not receive a great deal of attention during the First United Nations Conference on the Law of the Sea in 1958 (UNCLOS I), and they were included, in an amended form, in Articles 14–21 of the HSC. The interest devoted to piracy during the drafting of the LOSC was equally marginal. The counter-piracy provisions of the HSC were—with some minor changes that remain largely unexplained—simply imported into the LOSC.[15]

The following discussion provides an analysis of the scope of counter-piracy enforcement powers (in Section 3) and the legal regime governing the criminal prosecution of alleged pirates (in Section 4), which assumes a holistic approach that goes beyond the law of the sea. Since the notions of 'piracy' and 'pirate ship' are central to both aspects, it is necessary to first elaborate these concepts (Section 2).

---

[9] League of Nations, Doc C.254.1927.V (1928) 22 *American Journal of International Law* Suppl 215, 222.

[10] American Society of International Law (ASIL), 'General Introduction' (1932) 26 *American Journal of International Law* Suppl 1, 1–2; A Rubin, *The Law of Piracy* (2nd edn Transnational Publishers New York 1998) 331–5.

[11] ASIL, n 10, 5, 10, and 12–13; Harvard Draft Convention and Commentary, reprinted in ASIL, 'Codification of International Law: Part IV—Piracy' (1932) 26 *American Journal of International Law* Suppl 739, 743.

[12] Rubin, n 10, 348–9.

[13] ILC, 'Articles Concerning the Law of the Sea with Commentaries' in *Report of the International Law Commission*, 8th session, UN Doc A/3159 (1956).

[14] Ibid, 282.   [15] Rubin, n 10, 216.

2 Piracy Under International Law

2.1 Definition of piracy

Article 101 of the LOSC defines three different offences, all of which are labelled 'piracy'.

2.1.1 *Piracy as defined in Article 101(a) of the LOSC*

Article 101(a) of the LOSC states that piracy consists of 'any illegal acts of violence or detention, or any act of depredation' committed for private ends on the high seas or in a place outside the jurisdiction of any State by the crew or the passengers of a private craft against another vessel or person or property aboard.

This rather broad description of acts amounting to piracy carries with it two ambiguities. First, the meaning of the word 'illegal' preceding 'acts of violence and detention' is unclear. The term could refer to the absence of grounds negating criminal liability despite the use of violence (such as self-defence), or to exceptional situations in which private detention may be lawful (eg in holding a person caught red-handed in the commission of a crime until he is surrendered to law enforcement officials). However, such reference is generally absent from the provisions that define offences, and is indeed missing from Article 101(a) of the LOSC with regard to depredation. What is more, Article 101 of the LOSC is arguably not drafted as a criminal norm.[16] It is debatable whether the element was added with the idea of requiring any qualified illegality,[17] the more likely scenario being that it was slipped into the wording as a result of the shallow examination of the counter-piracy provisions during the drafting of the LOSC.[18] The same may hold true regarding the second ambiguity, which relates to the question whether the words 'acts of violence or detention' require a plurality of acts. A comparison with the remainder of Article 101(a) of the LOSC and sub-paragraphs (b) and (c) of the provision—where the singular 'act' is used—suggests that a single act of violence or detention will suffice.[19]

Moreover, the requirement that the prohibited act must be committed 'for private ends' is fraught with uncertainty and has sparked ample debate in the past.

---

[16] See Section 4.1 below.

[17] D Guilfoyle, *Shipping Interdiction and the Law of the Sea* (Cambridge University Press Cambridge 2009) 43.

[18] Absent in the Harvard Draft Convention, n 11, Art 3, the element was included (without any explanation) in ILC Articles Concerning the Law of the Sea, n 13, Art 39, which resulted in HSC, n 7, Art 15. It was inserted into LOSC, n 7, Art 101 after a brief discussion during which Greece (unsuccessfully) proposed the deletion of the term: *Virginia Commentaries*, Vol III, 200–1.

[19] ILC Articles Concerning the Law of the Sea, n 13, Art 39, refers to a single act throughout the provision.

The interpretative divide is along the dichotomies of 'private/political acts' and 'private/public acts'. Following the first view, the private ends requirement excludes any act that is politically or ideologically motivated from the ambit of piracy.[20] Following this view, maritime terrorism, and violent ecological activism at sea[21] do not amount to piracy because they are politically motivated. If, however, the notion of 'private' is understood as the counterpart to 'public', the subjective motivation of the acting person is irrelevant. As long as an act of violence is lacking State sanction (ie is not authorized or attributable to a State), it is not public but rather undertaken for private ends.[22] Such a reading of the private ends requirement fits best with Article 102 of the LOSC, according to which a warship or a government vessel cannot be a pirate ship unless its crew has mutinied and taken control of it.[23] It was in application of the private/public test that the US 9th Circuit Court of Appeals decided in *Institute of Cetacean Research v Sea Shepherd Conservation Society*, an action brought under the Alien Tort Statute against environmental activists by Japanese researchers hunting whales, that acts of violence committed in pursuit of a political goal can amount to piracy.[24] The same holds true for the decision *Castle John v NV Mabeco* issued by the Belgian Cour de Cassation concerning violent protest by Greenpeace activists against a Dutch vessel in order to publicize its polluting activities.[25] Furthermore, if the subjective motivation is irrelevant, the defence of alleged Somali pirates that their acts are motivated by the political aim to protect the country's natural resources can easily be discarded.

In order to amount to piracy, acts referred to in Article 101(a) of the LOSC must be committed on the 'high seas' or 'in a place outside the jurisdiction of any State'. The geographical limitation to acts committed on the high seas seems at first sight to exclude acts committed in the exclusive economic zone (EEZ). However, Article 58(2) of the LOSC suggests the contrary by stipulating that Articles 88 to 115 LOSC pertaining to the high seas—which include the provisions on piracy—also apply to the EEZ in so far as they are 'not incompatible' with the LOSC's Part V governing that zone. Generally, nothing in Article 56 of the LOSC defining the coastal State's

---

[20] See eg Harvard Draft Convention and Commentary, n 11, 786; C Crockett, 'Toward a Revision of the International Law of Piracy' (1976) 26 *DePaul Law Review* 78, 79–80 (in relation to the HSC, n 7); M Shaw, *International Law* (6th edn Cambridge University Press Cambridge 2008) 615 (in relation to the LOSC, n 7).

[21] See eg *Institute of Cetacean Research v Sea Shepherd Conservation Society* (2012) 860 F.Supp.2d 1216, 1233 (reversed on appeal; see n 24).

[22] M Halberstam, 'Terrorism on the High Seas: The *Achille Lauro*, Piracy and the IMO Convention on Maritime Safety' (1988) 82 *American Journal of International Law* 269, 290; M Bahar, 'Attaining Optimal Deterrence at Sea: A Legal and Strategic Theory for Naval Anti-Piracy Operations' (2007) 40 *Vanderbilt Journal of Transnational Law* 1, 26–37.

[23] Guilfoyle, n 17, 36.

[24] *Institute of Cetacean Research v Sea Shepherd Conservation Society* (2013) 725 F.3d 940 (9th Cir), 943–44; Alien Tort Statute, 28 USC § 1350.

[25] *Castle John v NV Mabeco* (1986) 77 ILR 537 (Court of Cassation, Belgium).

sovereign rights in the EEZ is incompatible with the LOSC provisions on piracy, which therefore apply to all seas *outside* any State's territorial waters.[26]

Article 101(a)(i) of the LOSC further requires that the prohibited acts are committed 'by the crew or the passengers of a private ship' and directed 'against another ship'. This implies that at least two ships must be involved, which excludes crew seizures, mutiny and passenger takeovers from the definition of piracy. The fact that internal seizures, such as the *Achille Lauro* incident, are not piracy under international law prompted the conclusion of the 1988 Convention for the Suppression of Unlawful Acts Against the Safety of Maritime Navigation (SUA Convention) which establishes certain offences without a 'two-ship requirement'.[27] From the wording of Article 101(a) of the LOSC it follows that the victim ship does not necessarily need to be a private ship.[28] Furthermore, the size of the attacked ship is irrelevant and piracy can, for instance, be committed against yachts. However, submarine cables and pipelines or fixed platforms are not ships in the sense of Article 101 of the LOSC.[29] This excludes attacks against oil rigs, as witnessed in the Gulf of Guinea,[30] from the ambit of piracy under international law.[31]

2.1.2 *Piracy as defined in Article 101(b) and (c) of the LOSC*

Article 101 of the LOSC describes two additional situations that amount to piracy under international law.

First, Article 101(b) LOSC qualifies as piracy 'any act of voluntary participation in the operation of a ship... with knowledge of facts making it a pirate ship'. As we will see later in this chapter, a pirate ship is not simply one that has been used for a pirate attack, but also one that is *intended* to be used for such a purpose.[32] Therefore, a person who voluntarily participates in the operation of a ship, in the knowledge that it is intended to be used for a pirate attack, commits piracy under international law as soon as the ship enters the EEZ or high seas.[33] This inchoate offence, which arguably

---

[26] *Virginia Commentaries*, Vol III, 202.   [27] Halberstam, n 22, 270 and 284–7.

[28] See eg *R v Musa Abdullahi Said & Six others* (2009) CR 1184/2009 (Chief Magistrate's Court of Mombasa) qualifying the attempted attack against the supply ship *Spessart* of the German Navy as piracy.

[29] R Lagoni, 'Piraterie und widerrechtliche Handlungen gegen die Sicherheit der Schiffahrt' in J Ipsen and E Schmidt-Jortzig (eds), *Recht-Staat-Gemeinwohl: Festschrift für Dietrich Rauschning* (Carl Heymanns Cologne 2001) 501, 515–16.

[30] UNSC, *Piracy in the Gulf of Guinea*, n 5, [35].

[31] The *Arctic Sunrise* incident (for a summary of the facts, see A Oude Elferink, 'The Arctic Sunrise Incident: A Multi-faceted Law of the Sea Case with a Human Rights Dimension' (2014) 29 *The International Journal of Marine and Coastal Law* 244, 244–51) therefore could not amount to piracy under international law, even if, *arguendo*, violence was used by the Greenpeace activists attempting to board the Russian oil platform.

[32] See Section 2.2 below.

[33] Article 101(b) of the LOSC, n 7, does not explicitly contain a 'high seas requirement'; but its reference to 'pirate ship' as defined in Art 103 of the LOSC, which in turn refers to Art 101(a) of the LOSC containing such a requirement, makes it an implicit element of Art 101(b) of the LOSC.

comes close to the common law concept of conspiracy, was included in Article 3(2) of the Harvard Draft Convention. In the view of the drafters, the provision covering 'piratical roving before any attack has been committed' serves 'as a basis for international police prevention of attacks'.[34] The similar Article 101(b) of the LOSC thus provides a legal basis for the formulation of broad counter-piracy mandates allowing patrolling naval States to intervene at a very early stage. The mandate of the European Union Naval Force countering piracy off the coast of Somalia, for instance, includes the taking of 'measures, including the use of force, to deter, *prevent* and intervene in order to bring to an end acts of piracy'[35] and to 'arrest, detain and transfer persons suspected of *intending*... to commit, committing or having committed acts of piracy'.[36]

Second, by virtue of Article 101(c) of the LOSC, the instigation or facilitation of piratical acts defined in sub-paragraphs (a) and (b) amounts to piracy. Unlike Article 101(a) LOSC, this provision does not contain the geographical limitation 'on the high seas' and does not require that the prohibited acts take place aboard a ship. Hence, it encompasses inciting and intentionally facilitating acts described in Article 101(a) and (b) of the LOSC from ashore, sometimes referred to as 'dry land piracy', or waters subject to a State's jurisdiction.[37]

2.2 Definition of pirate ship

In addition to the concept of piracy, the LOSC defines the term 'pirate ship'. According to Article 103 of the LOSC, two categories of vessels qualify as pirate ships: ships that have been used to commit acts referred to in Article 101 of the LOSC, so long as the ship remains under the control of the persons guilty of that act, and ships intended to be used for the purpose of committing such an act.

The reference found in Article 103 to Article 101 of the LOSC is, *prima facie*, to the provision as a whole, ie the three distinct situations amounting to piracy. This global reference creates several difficulties. First, part of the reference is circular in that Article 101(b) of the LOSC requires involvement in the operation of a 'pirate ship', which Article 103 of the LOSC defines by reference to Article 101 of the LOSC. Second, Article 101(c) of the LOSC includes instigation and facilitation of piratical acts from waters under a State's jurisdiction. This would imply that

---

[34] Harvard Draft Convention and Commentary, n 11, 820.

[35] Council Joint Action 2008/851/CFSP, [2008] OJ L301/33 (10 November 2008) Art 2(d) (emphasis added), as amended several times and latest by Council Decision 2012/174/CFSP [2012] OJ L89/69 (23 March 2012).

[36] Ibid, Art 2(e).

[37] Lagoni, n 29, 520; *US v Ali* (2013) 718 F.3d 929, 936–9; D Guilfoyle, 'Committing Piracy on Dry Land: Liability for Facilitating Piracy', *EJIL Talk!* (26 July 2012), available at <www.ejiltalk.org/committing-piracy-on-dry-land-liability-for-facilitating-piracy/>.

vessels that have been used or are intended to be used for acts of participation or instigation of piracy in the territorial waters or ports of a given State, qualify as pirate ships, and would thus be subject to seizure if later encountered on the high seas. At the same time, a ship that directly engages in acts similar to those defined in Article 101(a) of the LOSC in territorial waters cannot be seized by virtue of Article 105, which is limited to the high seas. This leads to an illogical discrepancy. A possible way out of this circular and arguably too broad reference in Article 103 of the LOSC to the definition of piracy *in toto* is to limit it, by way of a teleological reduction, to acts defined in Article 101(a)(i) of the LOSC.[38] Article 4 of the Harvard Draft Convention defining the concept of 'pirate ship' was limited in such way, while the ILC expanded the reference to all three offences of piracy without further explanation.

In sum, Articles 101 and 103 of the LOSC define the concepts of piracy and pirate ship under *international law*—but not without ambiguity and based on a rather complicated and sometimes circular system of cross-references. The situation is further complicated by the fact that these concepts are at times not distinguished from potentially differing definitions of piracy under municipal law primarily embodied in criminal law provisions. What is more, the term 'piracy' is often (too rashly) used to condemn any kind of violence occurring in the maritime environment,[39] and is frequently not sharply differentiated from the offence of armed robbery at sea.

2.3 Armed robbery at sea—an offence distinct from piracy

A considerable number of violent acts against ships and their crews, the characteristics of which are similar to acts of piracy defined by Article 101(a) of the LOSC, take place in maritime areas other than the high seas and the EEZ and therefore do not fulfil the definition of piracy under international law. Similarly, persons cruising the waters under a State's jurisdiction with the intention of committing piracy-like attacks fall outside the scope of piracy as defined by Article 101(b) of the LOSC. These offences are commonly referred to as 'armed robbery at sea'.

---

[38] R Geiss and A Petrig, *Piracy and Armed Robbery at Sea: The Legal Framework for Counter-Piracy Operations in Somalia and the Gulf of Aden* (Oxford University Press Oxford 2011) 64–5.

[39] The *Mavi Marmara* incident, for example, was qualified in a Security Council debate as 'tantamount to banditry and piracy' and as 'an action that could be described as piracy' (UNSC, Verbatim Record UN Doc S/PV.6325 (31 May 2010) 4, 11–12), even though the acts in question were carried out by the navy (and not by a 'private ship' or a 'warship...whose crew has mutinied') and with State sanction (ie not for 'private ends').

The definitional elements of armed robbery at sea are far from settled under international law.[40] There seems to be general agreement as regards the place of commission of the offence that it can only be within waters under a State's full sovereignty and jurisdiction, that is, *not* the high seas or the EEZ. The offence of armed robbery at sea generally covers acts similar to those mentioned in Article 101(a) of the LOSC. Some definitions also include acts akin to those of Article 101(b) and (c) of the LOSC. Many, but not all, definitions expressly require that the offence of armed robbery at sea be committed 'for private ends'. What remains unclear is whether the definition of armed robbery at sea contains a two-ship requirement. Arguably, the wording 'violence...directed against *a* ship', as it appears in various definitions of armed robbery at sea, can be read as including internal seizures—as opposed to the words 'violence...directed...against *another* ship' used in Article 101(a)(i) of the LOSC.[41]

3 COUNTER-PIRACY ENFORCEMENT POWERS

3.1 The right of visit, seizure, and arrest

To counter piracy at sea, the LOSC grants—as an exception to the generally exclusive enforcement jurisdiction of the flag State on the high seas[42]—certain universal policing powers.

According to Article 110 of the LOSC, a warship or any other duly authorized ship clearly marked and identifiable as being on government service that encounters a foreign ship on the high seas or EEZ is authorized to board that ship if there is reasonable ground for suspecting that it is engaged in piracy. The provision does not specify the meaning of the words 'reasonable ground for suspecting'. What follows from a comparison of Articles 110 and 105 of the LOSC is

---

[40] The following analysis is based on the definitions of armed robbery at sea contained in *Code of Practice for the Investigation of Crimes of Piracy and Armed Robbery Against Ships* IMO Assembly Res A.26/Rs. 1025 (18 January 2010) [2.2] and IMO Assembly Res A.22/Res.922 (22 January 2002) [2.2]; Regional Cooperation Agreement on Combating Piracy and Armed Robbery Against Ships in Asia, Art 1(2), available at <www.recaap.org/AboutReCAAPISC.aspx>; and Djibouti Code of Conduct, IMO Doc C102/14 (3 April 2009) Annex 5, Art 1(2)(a).

[41] Emphasis added. According to the *Virginia Commentaries*, Vol III, 201, Art 101(a)(ii) of the LOSC referring to 'a ship' includes internal seizures.

[42] LOSC, n 7, Art 92(1); *Virginia Commentaries*, Vol III, 213, 238–9, and 244.

that a different degree of probability that a ship is engaged in piracy is required to trigger the respective enforcement powers. Article 105 of the LOSC allows for the seizure of ships and the arrest of suspects aboard, that is, measures that are more intrusive and in greater conflict with the freedom of navigation as compared with those flowing from the right of visit. Consequently, 'reasonable ground for suspecting' that a ship has engaged in piracy is not sufficient to make the enforcement powers of Article 105 of the LOSC available; rather, they are only granted vis-à-vis a vessel identified as 'a pirate ship' as defined in Article 103 of the LOSC. The different standard is in line with the graduation of enforcement powers laid out in these provisions. Further guidance follows from the wording of Article 110 of the LOSC. From its third paragraph ('[i]f the suspicions prove to be unfounded, and provided that the ship boarded has not committed any suspicious act') it follows that an initial suspicion triggering the right of visit may arise even if the ship in question has not committed any suspicious act. This is in line with Article 101(b) of the LOSC defining piracy as the voluntary participation in the operation of a ship knowing that it is a pirate ship, which can be a vessel intended to be used for a future pirate attack. Hence, a reasonable suspicion that a ship is 'cruising with pirate intent' makes it one that is 'engaged in piracy' and triggers the right of visit. Furthermore, the second paragraph of Article 110 of the LOSC also contains a gradual scheme: the initial suspicion justifies verification of the ship's right to fly its flag and only '[i]f suspicion remains' after the document check can the more intrusive examination aboard take place. In sum, the degree of suspicion required to justify a right to inspect the ship's papers (the measure at the bottom of the array of gradually more intrusive enforcement measures) must not be set too high. Indicative criteria, such as the bearing of arms or the use of ships typically involved in pirate attacks seem sufficient, especially in a region prone to piracy. Such an interpretation of the 'reasonable suspicion' criterion is justified in light of the rather temporary interference with the freedom of navigation and the compensation to the ship foreseen in Article 110(3) of the LOSC in cases of unjustified boarding.

The object and purpose of the right of visit is to verify whether a ship is indeed engaged in piracy, which makes the enforcement powers of Article 105 of the LOSC available. To this end, the personnel of a warship may proceed to an examination of the ship's papers, which presupposes a right to stop the suspected vessel. If this does not allay the suspicion that the ship is engaged in piracy, an examination on board may take place.

An initial suspicion can also be substantiated by means others than dispatching a boarding team, notably by identifying a pirate ship from a distance through airborne surveillance by maritime patrol aircrafts and helicopters.[43] Not only is this

---

[43] D Osler, *Operation Atalanta 'Capability Shortfalls' Criticised* (Lloyd's List London 2011).

less of an interference with the liberty of navigation, but it may be more effective in terms of preserving evidence for later criminal proceedings since piracy paraphernalia is often thrown overboard as soon as a law enforcement vessel approaches.[44] If a ship already identified as a pirate ship from a distance is ultimately stopped, the enforcement powers taken against it stem directly from Article 105 rather than from Article 110 of the LOSC.

The first sentence of Article 105 of the LOSC authorizes every State to seize a 'pirate ship' or 'a ship taken by piracy and under the control of pirates', that is, a ship that has become the victim of acts defined in Article 101(a) of the LOSC[45] and has then fallen under the control of persons carrying out these acts, referred to as 'pirates' in the provision but which the LOSC does not specifically define.[46] A fishing vessel hijacked by Somali pirates, who detain the fishermen aboard and use the vessel as a 'mother ship' from which to launch further attacks, is an example of 'a ship taken by piracy and under the control of pirates'.

Article 105 of the LOSC further grants States a right to seize property on board the ships it refers to. Since the second sentence of Article 105 declares the courts of the seizing State competent to determine the action to be taken vis-à-vis seized vessels and property, the seizing State is arguably not permitted to dispose of them summarily. Some commentators suggest that the counter-piracy resolutions authorize the summary disposal of boats and paraphernalia used by alleged Somali pirates.[47] However, the Security Council simply calls upon States to actively fight piracy through, *inter alia*, seizing and disposing of vessels and other piracy equipment in a way that is consistent with the relevant resolutions (which designate the LOSC as the primary legal framework to observe in counter-piracy operations) and international law.[48] Hence, Article 105 of the LOSC remains the governing standard.

Finally, Article 105 of the LOSC allows for the arrest of persons on board a pirate ship or a ship taken by piracy and under the control of pirates. The scope of this right is quite narrow since it does not permit the arrest of persons encountered anywhere other than on board the mentioned ships, such as a person suspected of piracy travelling as a passenger on a non-pirate vessel. At the same time, the provision allows, based on the face of its wording, the arrest of 'persons...on board' the specified ships, without any further requirements. However, an initial suspicion that they have engaged in piracy or intend to commit an act of piracy seems to be necessary.[49]

---

[44] UNSC, *Report of the Monitoring Group on Somalia and Eritrea pursuant to Security Council Resolution 1916 (2010)*, UN Doc S/2011/433 (2011) [94].

[45] A ship can hardly come under the control of pirates by acts defined as piracy in Article 101(b) and (c) of the LOSC, n 7, ie 'conspiracy' and instigation or facilitation of acts of piracy.

[46] Geiss and Petrig, n 38, 66.   [47] Guilfoyle, n 8, Ev 83.

[48] See eg UNSC Res 2125, n 6, [10].   [49] Geiss and Petrig, n 38, 66–7.

3.2 Extension of enforcement powers—the example of Somali-based piracy

While the policing powers that can be taken against piracy are universal, the taking of enforcement measures against persons suspected of armed robbery at sea is within the sole competence of the State that has jurisdiction over the waters in which the offence occurs. However, the respective State can consent to foreign or joint patrols in its waters.[50] For instance, in 2011, Nigeria and Benin agreed to carry out the joint patrol programme 'Operation Prosperity' along the latter's coast to more effectively prevent and suppress attacks against ships and crews.[51]

As regards Somali-based piracy, it was the Security Council—acting at the request and with the consent of the Somali Government—that paved the way for enforcement measures by third States and regional organizations in areas under Somalia's jurisdiction.[52] It did so based on its Chapter VII powers by qualifying the situation in Somalia, one exacerbated by incidents of piracy and armed robbery at sea (rather than the criminal phenomenon alone), as a 'threat to international peace and security in the region'.[53]

By adopting Resolution 1846, the Security Council authorized all States and regional organizations to enter the territorial waters of Somalia for the purpose of repressing acts of piracy and armed robbery at sea and to use 'all necessary means' to do so within that area.[54] Despite this strong wording, the authorization does not go beyond the enforcement measures that are provided by Articles 110 and 105 of the LOSC. This follows from the authorization specifying that enforcement powers are to be exercised 'in a manner consistent with such action permitted on the high seas with respect to piracy under relevant international law'[55] and the repeated emphasis by the Security Council that the LOSC sets out the relevant international law.[56] On the operational level, the call to suppress Somali-based piracy at sea has received a truly international response with States around the globe deploying assets and personnel, as well as three international missions contributing to the naval operations.[57]

---

[50] T Treves, 'Piracy, Law of the Sea, and Use of Force: Developments off the Coast of Somalia' (2009) 20 *European Journal of International Law* 399, 406; S Wolf, 'Territorial Sea' in R Wolfrum (ed), *Max Planck Encyclopedia of Public International Law* (Oxford University Press Oxford 2012) [21] and [43], available at <http://opil.ouplaw.com/home/EPIL>.

[51] UNSC, n 5, [18]–[19].

[52] See Treves, n 50, 406–8, on what the Security Council authorizations add in light of Somalia's consent to enforcement measures in areas under its jurisdiction.

[53] See eg UNSC Res 2125, n 6, Preamble, [34].

[54] UNSC Res 1846 (2 December 2008) [10]; for the latest renewal of this time-limited authorization, see UNSC Res 2125, n 6, [12].

[55] UNSC Res 1846, n 54, [10].   [56] See eg UNSC Res 2125, n 6, Preamble, [9].

[57] On naval activities in 2013, see UNSC, *Report of the Secretary-General on the situation with respect to piracy and armed robbery at sea off the coast of Somalia*, UN Doc S/2013/623 (2013) [37]–[41].

In adopting Resolution 1851, the Security Council authorized States and regional organizations 'to undertake all necessary measures that are appropriate in Somalia, for the purpose of suppressing acts of piracy and armed robbery at sea'.[58] In contrast to Resolution 1846, the enforcement powers authorized by this resolution are not in any way linked to or confined by the type of enforcement measures allowed under the LOSC regime. Rather, in line with the common understanding of the phrase 'all necessary means', a broad range of measures, including military force, are allowed.[59] Except for the singular instance where the European Union Naval Force destroyed piracy logistics on shore (boats and fuel dumps) in May 2012,[60] the authorization has not been used thus far.

3.3 Legal constraints on counter-piracy enforcement powers

The exercise of the far-reaching counter-piracy enforcement powers granted by virtue of the LOSC and HSC implies the use of force and coercion. However, neither treaty indicates the allowable degree of force or coercion. The legal constraints limiting these powers instead emerge from general safeguards applicable to maritime interception operations and human rights law. The rules of international humanitarian law (IHL) governing the conduct of hostilities are, however, inapplicable.

3.3.1 *Inapplicability of international humanitarian law*

The measures for the suppression of piracy authorized or referred to by the law of the sea—notably interdiction, seizure, arrest, and the imposition of penalties—clearly have a law enforcement character. The fact that military means, namely warships and military personnel, are used in order to combat piracy at sea does not entail the application of IHL, which requires the existence of an armed conflict. However, rarely, if ever, will counter-piracy operations meet the threshold of an international or non-international conflict given the actors involved and the level of violence used.[61] The choice of using military means to counter piracy is instead rooted in Article 107 of the LOSC, which designates warships (and other

---

[58] UNSC Res 1851 (16 December 2008) [6]; for the latest renewal of this time-limited authorization, see UNSC Res 2125, n 6, [12].

[59] Geiss and Petrig, n 38, 83.

[60] European Union Naval Force (EUNAVFOR), *Statement by the Spokesperson of EU High Representative Catherine Ashton following the Disruption of Pirate Logistical Dumps in Somalia by EU Naval Force—Operation Atalanta*, A 225/12 (Brussels, 15 May 2012).

[61] On why counter-piracy operations off the coast of Somalia do not amount to an armed conflict, see Geiss and Petrig, n 38, 131–5 and A Murdoch and D Guilfoyle, 'Capture and Disruption Operations: The Use of Force in Counter-Piracy off Somalia' in Guilfoyle (ed), n 3, 147, 155–8.

ships clearly marked and identifiable as being on government service and authorized to that effect) as the only competent vessels to carry out a seizure on account of piracy. This is primarily due to the pragmatic reason that warships navigate the high seas far more frequently than regular police vessels. Furthermore, the limitation on the type of vessels competent to seize alleged pirate ships enhances legal certainty, reduces the risk of abuse of enforcement powers and facilitates the allocation of responsibility in cases of unjustified interferences with the freedom of navigation.[62]

3.3.2 *General safeguards for maritime interception operations*

While IHL is inapplicable to counter-piracy operations, and the law of piracy is silent regarding limits on the use of force and coercion, safeguards must be imported from international case law[63] and treaties[64] applicable to law enforcement at sea pertaining to criminal phenomena other than piracy. In essence, beyond the situation of self-defence, force must be avoided to the extent possible and only used *ultima ratio*. This presupposes a graduated response, whereby resorting to force is preceded by other measures, such as visual and auditory signals to stop and warning shots. Where force is unavoidable, it must not go beyond what is reasonable and necessary in the situation at hand.[65] These principles are, however, quite vague and provide little guidance for specific operations. Furthermore, they presuppose that deployed warships are appropriately equipped and that military personnel specifically trained for law enforcement missions, which differ from the conduct of hostilities. What is more, the safeguards are commonly aimed at protecting ships, their cargo, and the freedom of navigation rather than preserving the individual rights of persons subject to law enforcement measures.[66] Therefore, human rights law is another important source for inferring limits on the exercise of counter-piracy enforcement powers.

---

[62] ILC Articles Concerning the Law of the Sea, n 13, 283; *Virginia Commentaries*, Vol III, 222; liability in cases of unjustified visit or seizure is governed by LOSC, n 7, Arts 110(3) and 106.

[63] See eg SS *'I'm Alone' (Canada/United States)* (1935) III RIAA 1609, 1615 and 1617; *The Red Crusader Case* (1962) 35 ILR 483, 538; *The M/V 'Saiga' (No 2) (Saint Vincent and the Grenadines v Guinea)* (Judgment) [1999] ITLOS Rep 10, [155]–[156].

[64] See eg 1988 Convention for the Suppression of Unlawful Acts against the Safety of Maritime Navigation, Art 8bis(10) (hereinafter SUA Convention), as amended by the 2005 Protocol to the 1988 Convention for the Suppression of Unlawful Acts against the Safety of Maritime Navigation; 1995 Agreement for the Implementation of the Provisions of the United Nations Convention on the Law of the Sea of 10 December 1982 relating to the Conservation and Management of Straddling Fish Stocks and Highly Migratory Fish Stocks, Art 22(1) (FSA).

[65] In more details: Guilfoyle, n 17, 271–94.

[66] UNSC Res 2125, n 6, [15], for example, requests that the use of the authorized enforcement measures 'do not have the practical effect of denying or impairing the right of innocent passage to the ships of any third State'.

3.3.3 *Human rights law*

Patrolling naval States generally exercise counter-piracy enforcement powers in maritime areas not under their sovereignty. The requirements for the extraterritorial application of human rights in a maritime environment are not developed to the same extent as they are for land-based police operations beyond a State's territory.

For enforcement measures taken *on board* a military or government vessel, such as holding an arrested piracy suspect until surrender for prosecution, the human rights obligations of the enforcing State are, first of all, applicable by virtue of the flag State principle.[67] Furthermore, ships in the sense of Article 107 of the LOSC are largely made up of State agents exercising full control over the ship and the suspects held aboard. Therefore, the criterion of 'effective control over persons' by a State beyond its borders—recognized by various human rights bodies as another trigger for the extraterritorial application of human rights[68]—is also fulfilled.[69] While the *applicability* of human rights law on board law enforcement vessels is now generally undisputed, controversial views exist on the content and meaning of certain human rights in the maritime environment. For instance, there are differing views as to whether piracy suspects must be brought promptly before a judge of the seizing State[70] or if it suffices that the legality of their arrest is controlled by a judge of the ultimately prosecuting State and whether the ordinary timelines apply.[71]

As regards enforcement measures, which are *not* taken *on board* the law enforcement vessel itself, but rather when a ship suspected of piracy is pursued, stopped and boarded, and the crew searched and arrested, the most viable basis for the application of human rights law seems to be the 'effective control over persons' criterion. During ship-to-ship operations, the distance between the vessels involved may be quite important and the alleged pirate ship generally tries to evade control by the warship or dispatched craft, yet the use of force in such

---

[67] *Medvedyev and Others v France*, Judgment of the European Court of Human Rights, App No 3394/03 (29 March 2010) [65]; *Hirsi Jamaa and Others v Italy*, Judgment of the European Court of Human Rights, App No 27765/09 (23 February 2012) [75]–[78].

[68] Human Rights Committee, 'General Comment No. 31: The Nature of the General Legal Obligations Imposed on States Parties to the Covenant' in *Compilation of General Comments and General Recommendations Adopted by Human Rights Treaty Bodies: Vol I* (2008) [10]; *Sonko v Spain* (2011) Comm No 368/2008 (Convention Against Torture Committee) [10.3].

[69] A Petrig, 'Human Rights in Counter-Piracy Operations: No Legal Vacuum but Legal Uncertainty' in M Mejia, C Kojima and M Sawyer (eds), *Piracy at Sea* (Springer Berlin 2013) 36–8.

[70] For example by using video-link, see *Re 'MV Elly Mærsk'* (2011) U.2011.3066H, TfK2011.923/1 (Højesteret, Supreme Court of Denmark).

[71] Issues discussed in *Re 'MV Courier'* (2011) 25 K 4280/09 (Verwaltungsgericht Köln, Administrative Court of Cologne, Germany). *In extenso* on arrest and detention of piracy suspects in light of the right to liberty, see A Petrig, *Human Rights and Law Enforcement at Sea: Arrest, Detention and Transfer of Piracy Suspects* (Martinus Nijhoff Leiden 2014) Part 4.

situations can have a considerable impact on the individual concerned. In light of this, it is important to note that recent case law supports the stance that control over persons can be established even before the person is physically in the hands of law enforcement personnel if a close causal link between the act of the State and the sustained injury exists.[72] On the part of the European Court of Human Rights, there is even maritime-specific case law supporting the idea that human rights law applies extraterritorially from the moment a vessel is intercepted and thus prior to boarding.[73] *A fortiori*, control over the persons aboard should be regarded as established when boarding is completed—at the very latest. While the suspects may still try to hinder the establishment of total physical control over them—upon which the criterion is undeniably fulfilled—they have no possibility of fleeing the ship at that moment and find themselves in an inescapable situation.

In sum, international law limits the use of force and coercion in counter-piracy operations. However, the safeguards remain rather vague and, absent a coherently construed legal regime defining the constraints of law enforcement operations at sea, there is a genuine risk of protective gaps.

4 CRIMINAL PROSECUTION OF ALLEGED PIRATES

The criminal prosecution of piracy suspects has traditionally been a matter for domestic courts, which apply domestic criminal norms and procedures. Efforts to overcome or supplement this traditional approach in the case of Somali-based piracy by establishing an international(ized) prosecution model[74] have failed.[75]

---

[72] See eg *Andreou v Turkey*, Judgment of the European Court of Human Rights, App No 45653/99 (27 October 2009) A.3.c. (The Law); *Isaak and Others v Turkey*, Judgment of the European Court of Human Rights, App No 44587/98 (2006) A.2.b. (The Law); *Munaf v Romania* (2009) Comm No 1539/2006 (Human Rights Committee) [14.1]–[14.6].

[73] *Medvedyev and Others v France*, n 67, [87]; in *Women on Waves and Others v Portugal*, Judgment of the European Court of Human Rights, App No 31276/05 (3 February 2009), the Court declared the ECHR applicable simply on the basis that a Portuguese military ship intercepted a Dutch vessel on the high seas off the coast of Portugal (apparently without boarding it) in order to enforce a prohibition on entering Portugal's territorial waters that was previously issued to it.

[74] UNSC, *Report of the Secretary General on Possible Options to Further the Aim of Prosecuting and Imprisoning Persons Responsible for Acts of Piracy and Armed Robbery at Sea off the Coast of Somalia*, UN Doc S/2010/394 (2010).

[75] Petrig, n 71, 25–8.

4.1 The criminal offence of piracy

The criminal prosecution of acts of piracy or armed robbery at sea requires, *inter alia*, the existence of criminal norms defining the prohibited conduct and the applicable penalty.

There are differing views whether Article 101 of the LOSC and Article 15 of the HSC, which define piracy, amount to international crimes based on which a piracy suspect can be prosecuted by domestic penal authorities.[76] It is submitted here that their primary purpose is to define the scope of the *enforcement* jurisdiction the two treaties confer upon States, rather than to criminalize piracy. Piracy suspects must be tried in application of domestic criminal norms[77]. Article 14(2) of the Harvard Draft Convention expressly stipulates that 'the law of the state which exercises such [criminal] jurisdiction defines the crime, governs the procedure and prescribes the penalty'. Nothing in the *travaux préparatoires* for the HSC or the LOSC points to a deviation from the theory of the Harvard Draft Convention, according to which piracy is 'not a crime by the law of nations' but rather the basis of universal enforcement and adjudicative jurisdiction.[78] According to the drafters of the Harvard Draft Convention, '[u]niversal adoption of the draft convention would not make piracy defined by it a legal crime...by force of the convention alone'—a result that would rather 'be reached under the law of a state only through the operation of that state's legal machinery'.[79] The fact that Article 101 of the LOSC or Article of the 15 HSC do not explicitly prohibit the commission of acts of piracy nor state what specific punishment attaches (in not being addressed to individuals, as criminal norms are, but rather to States, as the LOSC generally is[80]) runs counter to the possibility of using them as a basis for domestic criminal prosecutions. To ground criminal charges on municipal rather than international law directly reflects current State practice.[81]

---

[76] Not an international crime: Rubin, n 10, 391–3; Lagoni, n 29, 523; doubts whether an international crime: C Kreβ, 'Universal Jurisdiction over International Crimes and the Institut de Droit international' (2006) 4 *Journal of International Criminal Justice* 561, 569; arguing that it is an international crime: D Guilfoyle, 'Book Review—Robin Geiss and Anna Petrig, Piracy and Armed Robbery at Sea: The Legal Framework for Counter-piracy Operations in Somalia and the Gulf of Aden' (2011) 11 *International Criminal Law Review* 910, 912–13.

[77] MD Fink and RJ Galvin, 'Combating Pirates off the Coast of Somalia: Current Legal Challenges' (2009) 56 *Netherlands International Law Review* 367, 389.

[78] Harvard Draft Convention and Commentary, n 11, Art 2: 'Every state has jurisdiction to...seize and punish persons...because of piracy.'

[79] Harvard Draft Convention and Commentary, n 11, 760.

[80] On the 'difficulty to configure persons as the beneficiaries of rights and the recipient of duties' within the LOSC, n 7, and 'the ensuing uncertain subjectivity of persons under the law of the sea', see I Papanicolopulu, 'The Law of the Sea Convention: No Place for Persons?' (2012) 27 *International Journal of Marine and Coastal Law* 867, 867.

[81] This holds true for all 42 States contributing to the UNSC, *Compilation of Information Received from Member States on Measures they Have Taken to Criminalize Piracy under their Domestic Law and*

The law of the sea, and specifically Article 100 of the LOSC stipulating a duty of all States to cooperate to the fullest extent possible in the repression of piracy, cannot be read as encapsulating an obligation on the part of States to define a specific offence of piracy in their municipal law. In various jurisdictions, such a crime is indeed missing (or was abolished since considered superfluous in 'modern times'[82]). In such cases, suspects can potentially be tried for offences adopted in fulfilment of the obligation to criminalize the acts defined in Article 3 of the SUA Convention[83] or for more general crimes, such as property offences or offences against life, limb, or liberty.[84] The same holds true where the offence of armed robbery at sea[85] is absent from domestic criminal law.

4.2 Criminal jurisdiction over the offence of piracy

The criminal prosecution of an alleged pirate further requires that the State has criminal jurisdiction over the offence(s) with which he is charged.

It is well established that, by virtue of customary international law, any State is competent to try piracy suspects, even absent a link with the respective pirate attack.[86] However, customary international law only provides universal criminal jurisdiction for conduct matching the piracy definition under international law, which delimits the scope of universal enforcement and adjudicative jurisdiction, but not for domestic piracy offences that are defined differently.[87]

Various rationales have been invoked for why piracy constitutes a universally cognizable offence under customary international law. Quite commonly, it is asserted that the heinousness of the crime gives rise to its unique jurisdictional status.[88]

to Support the Prosecution of Individuals Suspected of Piracy off the Coast of Somalia and Imprisonment of Convicted Pirates, UN Doc S/2012/177 (2012).

[82] As France did: L Briand, 'Lutte contre la piraterie maritime: la France renforce son arsenal législatif: À propos de la loi n° 2011-13 du 5 janvier 2011 relative à la lutte contre la piraterie et à l'exercice des pouvoirs de police de l'État en mer' [2011] *Gazette du Palais* 8, 8.

[83] SUA Convention, n 64, Art 5.

[84] In the absence of a specific crime of piracy under domestic law, the Somali men who attacked the German-flagged *Taipan* were convicted for 'attacks against air and maritime traffic' and 'abduction for the purpose of blackmail' (German Criminal Code, §§ 316c and 239a): *German Piracy Trial, Regional Court of Hamburg (Landgericht Hamburg), Germany* (2012), available at <www.internationalcrimesdatabase.org/Case/952/German-Piracy-Trial/>.

[85] Some States recently adopted such offence: see eg Kenyan Merchant Shipping Act 2009, s 371.

[86] *SS 'Lotus' (France v Turkey)* [1927] PCIJ Rep Series A No 10, Dissenting Opinion of Mr Moore, 70; *Arrest Warrant of 11 April 2000 (Democratic Republic of Congo v Belgium)* [2002] ICJ Rep 3, 35 Separate Opinion of President Guillaume, 37; *United States v Shi* (2008) 525 F.3d 709 (9th Cir), 722–4.

[87] This derives quite plainly from Art 9: ASIL, 'Codification of International Law: Part II—Jurisdiction with Respect to Crime' (1935) 29 *American Journal of International Law* Suppl 435 (hereinafter Draft Convention on Jurisdiction with Respect to Crime with Commentary).

[88] *Democratic Republic of Congo v Belgium*, n 86, 63, Joint Separate Opinion of Judges Higgins, Kooijmans, and Buergenthal, 75, 76, and 81.

However, despite the broadness of the spectrum of conduct amounting to piracy and the seriousness of some incidents, piracy generally does not even come close in terms of gravity to that of other universal jurisdiction crimes, such as genocide or crimes against humanity. It is instead comparable to property offences or hostage taking on dry land and thus offences over which customary law does not grant universal criminal jurisdiction.[89] Another explanation is the 'de-nationalization' of pirates and pirate ships as a legal consequence of piracy and the resulting jurisdictional gap.[90] Yet, under the LOSC, this rationale does not apply since the loss or retention of nationality is left to the law of the flag State and not governed by international law.[91] The most convincing explanation for subjecting piracy to universal criminal jurisdiction is the special *locus delicti* of the offence: '[T]he seas where all have an interest in safety of commerce and where no state has territorial jurisdiction.'[92]

Some authors assert that both customary international law and Article 105 of the LOSC provide for universal criminal jurisdiction over the offence of piracy.[93] However, it is difficult to see how the wording of the second sentence of Article 105—'[t]he courts of the *State which carried out the seizure* may decide upon the penalties to be imposed'—can be interpreted as granting universal adjudicative jurisdiction, especially when contrasted with the universal enforcement jurisdiction so clearly expressed in the first sentence of the provision by the words '*every State* may seize a pirate ship... and arrest the persons'. The view held by other commentators that the provision refers to the power of the seizing State to prosecute a piracy suspect (*forum deprehensionis*) can be better reconciled with the wording of the provision.[94] However, the stance taken that the seizing State's adjudicative jurisdiction conferred by Article 105 of the LOSC is *at the exclusion* of any other State—with the consequence that the seizing State is prohibited from surrendering the suspect for prosecution to a third State—seems quite odd.[95] Rather, without limiting universal jurisdiction granted *qua* customary international law, the provision clarifies the factual advantage of the seizing State to bring an alleged pirate to justice if there are competing claims to try a piracy suspect.[96]

In addition to granting universal criminal jurisdiction, customary international law *permits* States to provide for other grounds of extraterritorial criminal

---

[89] Kreβ, n 81, 569.   [90] Harvard Draft Convention and Commentary, n 11, 825–32.
[91] LOSC, n 7, Art 104; see also HSC, n 7, Art 18; ILC Articles Concerning the Law of the Sea, n 13, Art 42.
[92] Draft Convention on Jurisdiction with Respect to Crime with Commentary, n 87, 566, Art 9.
[93] I Shearer, 'Piracy' in Wolfrum (ed), n 50, [18].   [94] Guilfoyle, n 8, Ev 89.
[95] Arguing for exclusivity: E Kontorovich, '"A Guantánamo on the Sea": The Difficulty of Prosecuting Pirates and Terrorists' (2010) 98 *California Law Review* 243, 270; and A Fischer-Lescano and L Kreck, 'Piraterie und Menschenrechte: Rechtsfragen der Bekämpfung der Piraterie im Rahmen der europäischen Operation Atalanta' (2009) 47 *Archiv des Völkerrechts* 481, 514–15 and 521; arguing against Petrig, n 71, 316–19.
[96] Lagoni, n 29, 521.

jurisdiction under their domestic law,[97] notably based on the nationality of the alleged pirate or supposed victim of a pirate attack (active and passive personality principle) or on the flag of the pirate ship or victim vessel (flag State principle). The SUA Convention and the 1979 International Convention Against the Taking of Hostages (Hostages Convention) even *oblige* State Parties to establish their jurisdictions over the offences defined in these treaties and potentially fulfilled by acts of piracy or armed robbery at sea, notably if committed within their territory (including their territorial sea), on board ships flying their flag or by their nationals.[98]

4.3 Bridging policing and criminal prosecution

For the offence of piracy, international law grants both universal policing powers and universal criminal jurisdiction. And yet, despite these comprehensive authorizations, it has proven difficult to implement the basic tenet of every law enforcement operation—to bring apprehended suspects to justice—in the context of Somali-based piracy. Patrolling naval States seizing piracy suspects are often unable or unwilling to prosecute the suspects in their domestic courts. In such cases, the seizing State generally tries to surrender the suspects for prosecution to a third State, mainly located in the region prone to piracy. This implies that with each seizure, the path from policing to prosecution must be paved anew. To facilitate this task, various States, as well as the EU, have entered into transfer agreements with States such as Kenya, the Seychelles, and Mauritius, in which they declare their general willingness to accept piracy suspects for prosecution subject to their consent in each individual case and the fulfilment of specific conditions laid down in the respective agreement.[99] If a prosecuting State can be successfully identified in a specific case, transfers (rather than formal extraditions) are the prevalent means of surrendering the suspects to that State. Current transfer practices, including detention pending transfer, are not unproblematic in terms of human rights law, notably the principle of non-refoulement and the right to liberty.[100] The *Courier* decision, where Germany was held accountable for transferring an alleged Somali pirate to Kenya in breach of the prohibition of refoulement, demonstrated that this concern is not of a purely academic nature.[101]

---

[97] C Ryngaert, *Jurisdiction in International Law* (Oxford University Press Oxford 2008) 21–2.

[98] SUA Convention, n 64, Art 6; 1979 International Convention Against the Taking of Hostages, n 106, Art 5 (hereinafter Hostages Convention).

[99] See eg 2011 Agreement between the European Union and the Republic of Mauritius on the Conditions of Transfer of Suspected Pirates and Associated Seized Property from the European Union-led Naval Force to the Republic of Mauritius and on the Conditions of Suspected Pirates after Transfer [2011] OJ L254/3 (14 July 2011).

[100] See Petrig, n 71, on the mechanics of transfers (Part 2) and their potential incompatibility with human rights law (Parts 4 and 5).

[101] Re 'MV Courier', n 71; the case is pending at the appellate level: Re 'MV Courier' 4 A 2948/11 (Oberverwaltungsgericht Münster).

Despite efforts to bridge policing and prosecution more effectively, a significant number of captured suspects (up to nine out of 10[102]) were released without facing justice despite the availability of evidence suggesting the commission of an offence—a fact over which the Security Council has noted its concern.[103] This catch-and-release practice raises the question whether there is a duty to prosecute or extradite piracy suspects. Article 105 of the LOSC, stipulating that the seizing State 'may' decide upon the penalties to be imposed, does not impose an obligation to try piracy suspects. Article 100 of the LOSC, which urges States to cooperate to the fullest possible extent in the repression of piracy, arguably does not entail a duty to prosecute or extradite either since States shall have 'a certain latitude' in determining the type of cooperation they engage in.[104] A more demanding proposal by Malta—'[a]ll States have the obligation to prevent and *punish* piracy and to fully cooperate in its repression'—was rejected during the drafting of Article 100 of the LOSC.[105] The SUA and Hostages Conventions, which define offences potentially fulfilled by acts of piracy, oblige State Parties 'in the territory of which' the alleged offender is found to submit the case without delay to their competent authorities for the purpose of prosecution if they do not extradite the suspect.[106] However, unless the notion of territory is broadly interpreted—as meaning 'under the jurisdiction' of the respective State—it will be difficult to apply the obligation to a seizing State holding a piracy suspect on board its ship outside its territorial waters.[107]

5 A Mixed Appraisal of the Legal Regime on Piracy

At times, the legal regime on piracy of the HSC and LOSC has been appraised in pessimistic terms. Crocket concluded that '[t]he effect of the 1958 Geneva Convention has been to confuse the law of piracy'.[108] Rubin went a step further, stating that the

---

[102] UNSC, *Report of the Special Adviser to the Secretary-General on Legal Issues Related to Piracy off the Coast of Somalia*, UN Doc S/2011/30 (2011) [14].
[103] See eg UNSC Res 2125, n 6, Preamble, [7].
[104] ILC Articles Concerning the Law of the Sea, n 13, 282 (on a provision similar to Article 100 of the LOSC).
[105] *Virginia Commentaries*, Vol III, 183 (emphasis added).
[106] SUA Convention, n 64, Art 10; Hostages Convention, n 98, Art 8.
[107] Guilfoyle, n 76, 912 (arguing for a textual interpretation); Geiss and Petrig, n 38, 163–4 (arguing for a functional interpretation).
[108] Crockett, n 20, 98.

rules codified in the two treaties 'when read carefully, are incomprehensible and therefore codify nothing'.[109] Yet when tested by the upsurge of what we refer to as 'contemporary piracy', the counter-piracy rules of the HSC and the LOSC proved to be a workable legal framework—despite their ambiguities and limitations.

In terms of enforcement jurisdiction, the LOSC grants an array of universal policing powers against piracy suspects, but they are limited to the high seas and EEZ. As regards Somali-based piracy, the Security Council cured this geographical limitation by authorizing similar enforcement measures in Somali territorial waters. Thereby, the Council relied on the specific situation in Somalia rather than the phenomenon of piracy and armed robbery at sea as such, which would have set a precedent for other States with waters affected by attacks against ships and crews. At the initiative of Indonesia, Resolutions 1846 affirm that the authorizations provided therein, to which Somalia consented, only apply with respect to Somalia and do not affect the rights and obligations of other States under international law and cannot be considered as establishing customary international law.[110] This reflects how jealous States guard their sovereignty over territorial waters and the limited willingness to tamper with the LOSC, which strikes a subtle balance between exclusive flag State jurisdiction and the exceptions to it in order to combat criminal phenomena. Hence, there is little prospect that, *de lege ferenda*, any generally valid rules providing enforcement powers against armed robbery at sea will be enacted. At the same time, the approach taken by the Security Council in the case of Somali-based piracy was arguably unique since it was the 'failed State' situation, rather than piracy, that justified the use of Chapter VII measures. Therefore, it will, as a general rule, remain in the discretion of coastal States affected by armed robbery at sea whether to grant third States any enforcement powers in their territorial seas.

The LOSC rules on piracy are not without ambiguity, especially as regards the definitions of piracy and pirate ship. Furthermore, the LOSC is silent in terms of legal constraints on enforcement powers, and limits inferred from other bodies of law, notably human rights law, remain vague. Also, the applicable human rights standards pertaining to surrender for prosecution of persons intercepted at sea and never brought onto the land territory of the seizing State must be clarified. The need for such clarification is not necessarily because the existing lacuna hampers effective law enforcement, but to ensure that counter-piracy operations adhere to the rule of law and to prevent the ambiguities from resurfacing at a later stage, notably by delaying or impairing the criminal prosecution of piracy suspects.

In sum, any undifferentiated calls for more laws or to radically overcome the avenues currently followed to suppress piracy are not particularly helpful for bolstering the legal framework to counter piracy. Rather, it is essential to understand

---

[109] Rubin, n 10, 393.
[110] UNSC Res 1846, n 54, [13]; affirmed in subsequent resolutions renewing the respective authorization; see eg UNSC Res 2125, n 6, [13].

the complex legal regime governing piracy today and how to properly deploy and articulate the array of available (general and piracy-specific) legal tools. This allows for the identification of gaps in the existing legal framework and for an assessment of the necessity and feasibility of filling them—by way of interpreting existing general rules in the context of counter-piracy operations or by enacting new specific rules.

38

MILITARY OPERATIONS

JAMES KRASKA

1 INTRODUCTION

This chapter focuses on the use of the oceans for military operations and activities, principally during peacetime. The chapter also explores the rules that apply at the seam between peace and war, and how the provisions of the law of naval warfare interact with the law of the sea. The rules and regimes in the 1982 United Nations Convention on the Law of the Sea (LOSC), combined with treaty instruments and customary international law, provide a legal structure for military activities by the armed forces of all States on, over, and under more than 70 per cent of the Earth. Treaty rules, State practice, and associated customary norms of mariners have a symbiotic relationship. Combined, these sources of authority form a coherent regime for military operations throughout the oceans. This regime is formed by 'sets of implicit or explicit principles, norms, rules, and decision-making procedures around which actors' expectations converge' in the maritime dimension of international relations.[1] On the other hand, some of the concepts and provisions in the regime are aging; others are rather opaque. Uncertainty in the regime and inconsistency in its application push the door ajar to disagreement and heightened tension.

The foundation of the regime for military operations at sea is the international law of the sea, which accommodates as well as restricts freedom of action by the

---

[1] SD Krasner, 'Structural Causes and Regime Consequences: Regimes as Intervening Variables' (1982) 36 *International Organization* 185, 186.

armed forces. To the extent the law of the sea is stable and widely accepted, it adds predictability to international relations, builds confidence among suspicious neighbours and far-flung competitors, and helps to avoid interstate conflict. As the principal expression of the law of the sea, the LOSC is the key to a global maritime order. If the provisions in the treaty are open to contending interpretations, subject to disagreement, or fall into desuetude, however, then their stabilizing function erodes. The LOSC contains some rules that are stable and widely recognized, as well as other provisions that are frayed by identity politics and strategic rivalry, particularly in East Asia.

2 THE BASIC FRAMEWORK

Among the positive sources of law that shape naval activities, the LOSC stands paramount. As an 'umbrella' treaty, the LOSC reflects the fundamental legal framework for military operations on, above, or below the oceans. As the centrepiece of oceans governance, the LOSC is the most important framework for global order after the 1945 Charter of the United Nations (UN Charter), and the agreement has profound implications for military operations at sea. The treaty recognizes or assigns freedoms, rights, duties, and jurisdiction, among coastal States, port States, and flag States, to enhance management and governance of the maritime space.

The global maritime regime generally divides legal authority over conduct at sea among flag States, coastal States, and port States. Flag States are those nations that operate ships, submarines, and aircraft under the authority of the State flag, in accordance with rules of national registry, and subject to its sovereignty. Flag States conduct military operations with ships, submarines, and aircraft and other platforms and specialized equipment. Coastal States assert sovereignty, sovereign rights, and jurisdiction over the ocean surface, the water column, the seabed subsoil, and the airspace above the ocean by virtue of their geographic proximity to the sea and in accordance with geopolitical rules derived from the contour of the coastline of the State. Coastal States may enforce security or military prerogative offshore to protect critical infrastructure or pursuant to national defence. Port States are those that authorize and receive into fixed ports, piers, and harbours or roadsteads, vessels registered in other flag States, to facilitate commercial trade, naval engagement, or for other purposes. Because ports serve as a mode of entry into a State, they are subject to law enforcement and national security regulations. After the terrorist attacks of 9/11, the Member States of the International Maritime Organization

(IMO) adopted a comprehensive security regime that standardizes security for international ports and vessels that conduct international voyages.[2]

Each State is accorded special rights, privileges, and duties vis-à-vis other States, and, of course, a single State may simultaneously inure the status, rights, and obligations of all categories. As a network of rules, the maritime regime seeks to balance competing views of State sovereignty and security, promote international seaborne communication, and assure equitable division of the resources of the sea. During periods of armed conflict, the law of naval warfare—derivative of international humanitarian law—also applies to military operations at sea, and it may be thought of as a superimposed layer with its own set of norms and rules. While this chapter touches on some of the major strands of the law of naval warfare, the principle focus is on the peacetime rules of military operations.

2.1 Peaceful purposes

The use of the oceans is reserved for 'peaceful purposes'.[3] As a 'constitutional' principle of the international law of the sea, States shall refrain from the threat or use of force against the territorial integrity or political independence of any other State, or act in a manner inconsistent with international law as reflected in the UN Charter.[4] In particular, the high seas and the exclusive economic zone (EEZ) are reserved for peaceful purposes.[5] Likewise, the Area—the seabed of the ocean beyond areas of national jurisdiction—may be used for peaceful purposes exclusively.[6]

From the outset, the idea that the oceans are reserved for peaceful purposes has given rise to competing interpretation. During negotiations for the LOSC, some developing States sought to shape the requirement for the provision on 'peaceful purposes' to mean that all military operations in the oceans were prohibited.[7] A second group of States suggested that the language prohibits only military activities for 'aggressive purposes', but that approach did not add any additional fidelity to the definition. The core group of major maritime powers disagreed with both positions,

---

[2] IMO Doc SOLAS/CONF.5/31, *SOLAS Diplomatic Conference Final Act* (13 December 2002); Conference Res 1, *Amendments to the 1974 SOLAS Convention* (17 December 2012); Conference Res 2–11, *SPS Code and Conference Resolutions 3 to 11* (17 December 2012); Corrigenda to the Documents Submitted by the Drafting Committee (12 December 2002), reprinted in *IMO Guide to Maritime Security and the ISPS Code* (IMO Sales No IA116E London 2012) 259.

[3] The term 'peaceful purposes' is referenced in the 1982 United Nations Convention on the Law of the Sea, Arts 19, 58(2), 88, 141, 143(1), 147(2)(d), 155(2), 240(a), 242(1), 246(3), and 301 (hereinafter LOSC).

[4] Ibid, Art 301. The Preamble and Art 301 of the LOSC refer to 'peaceful uses', rather than 'peaceful purposes'. The two terms may be read as synonymous. See *Virginia Commentaries*, Vol III, 90.

[5] LOSC, n 3, Arts 58(2) and 88. See also M Hayashi, 'Military and Intelligence Gathering Activities in the EEZ: Definition of Key Terms' (2005) 29 *Marine Policy* 123, 124.

[6] LOSC, n 3, Arts 141, 143(1), 147(2)(d), and 155(2).

[7] *Virginia Commentaries*, Vol III, 88–9.

however, and they maintained that the UN Charter and other obligations of international law determine whether a particular maritime operation is considered peaceful.[8]

A 1985 report by the UN Secretary-General agrees with this position, as it concludes that 'military activities' consistent with the principles of international law embodied in the UN Charter, in particular with Article 2(4) and Article 51, are not prohibited by the LOSC.[9] This finding strongly suggests that the meaning of 'peaceful purposes' does not invite colloquial or elastic applications by States.[10] At the very least, the reference in the LOSC to 'peaceful purposes' does not alter or create new rights or obligations in the law of *jus ad bellum*, and it must be viewed within the context of the UN Charter. In this sense, the 'peaceful purposes' concept encompasses normal maritime diplomacy and activities of warships and routine operations, exercises, and engagement. The line between normal military operations and 'gunboat diplomacy', and the slide toward unlawful threat of force, is especially difficult to locate.

2.2 Military operations

Military operations are permitted, but the LOSC (or more generally, international law, for that matter) does not contain a single and authoritative definition of what constitutes 'military operations'. Consequently, it may be unclear whether intelligence activities, clandestine or para-military operations, or certain law enforcement undertakings constitute 'military operations'.[11] Mission sets vary widely, and include disaster relief and humanitarian assistance, maritime law enforcement, such as counter-drug operations and migrant interdiction, maritime security operations, and constabulary operations, including counter-proliferation of weapons of mass destruction, nuclear deterrence, and naval warfare.[12] As a simplified proposition, it

---

[8] Ibid, 89; *Official Records of the Third United Nations Conference on the Law of the Sea*, Vol V, UN Doc A/CONF.13/41, 62. See also E Rauch, 'Military Uses of the Oceans' (1985) 28 *German Yearbook of International Law* 229, 241–2; B Bocek, 'Peaceful Purposes Provisions of the United Nations Convention on the Law of the Sea' (1989) 8 *Ocean Yearbook* 329, 363–8; BH Oxman, 'The Regime of Warships under the United Nations Convention on the Law of the Sea' (1984) 24 *Virginia Journal of International Law* 809, 829–32.

[9] *Virginia Commentaries*, Vol III, 88–9.

[10] J Kraska, *Maritime Power and Law of the Sea* (Oxford University Press New York 2011) 258.

[11] Interestingly, the Pentagon's dictionary of military terms makes numerous references to 'military operations' as part of other definitions, yet the term 'military operation' is not defined. Department of Defense, *Dictionary of Military and Associated Terms* (Joint Publication 1-02 2010, as amended through 15 November 2013), available at <http://www.dtic.mil/doctrine/new_pubs/jp1_02.pdf>.

[12] Military forces of a handful of nations, including the United States, the United Kingdom, Australia, Germany, and Ecuador, have published manuals to guide their naval operations. See *Commander's Handbook on the Law of Naval Warfare, Naval Warfare Publication 1-14M/COMDTPUB P5800.7* (United States Naval War College Newport 2007); *Handbook on the Law of Maritime Operations: Publication BR 3012* (Ministry of Defence Whitehall London 2005); *The Manual of the Law of Armed Conflict* (Oxford

may be said the military operations normally are conducted by the armed forces of the State—naval forces in the maritime domain.

States operate warships and naval auxiliaries and their associated devices and vehicles on the surface of the ocean, under the water, and in the airspace above it. Manned and unmanned systems and platforms provide *in situ* or extended capability to conduct maritime missions throughout the spectrum of peacetime and war. For naval purposes, one of the key principles of international law is the sovereign immune status under the flag State of these platforms. As widely varied as they are, maritime and naval operations and intelligence activities are inextricably linked to the special status of warships, submarines, and State aircraft.

3 Warships and Naval Auxiliaries

3.1 Definition of warship

Warships, naval auxiliaries, and submarines operate as organs of the State and represent the armed forces of the nation whose flag they fly.[13] These platforms may operate close to the shore or on the high seas, and serve as forward 'sea bases' that maintain an enduring presence and project power far from their homeports and over long periods of extended deployment.

Warships include combatants, such as corvettes, frigates, destroyers, cruisers, aircraft carriers and various types of amphibious assault ships, and submarines. In order to qualify as a warship, vessels must demonstrate four attributes: (a) the ship belongs to the armed forces of a State bearing external markings that distinguish its nationality; (b) is under the command of an office duly commissioned by the government of the State; (c) the name of the vessel appears on the appropriate service list; and, (d) the ship is manned by a crew under armed forces discipline.[14]

Flag States have even asserted authority over sunken warships that have become historic wrecks, although if they are found in waters under another State's

---

University Press London 2005); *Australian Maritime Doctrine, RAN Doctrine 1* (Sea Power Centre Department of Defence Canberra 2010); *Kommandanten-Handbuch—Rechtsgrundlagen für den Einsatz von Seestreitkräften* (*Commander's Handbook: Legal Bases for the Operations of Naval Forces*) (Chief of Staff of the German Navy Berlin 2004); and *Aspectos Importantes del Derecho Internacional Marítimo que Deben Tener Presente los Comandantes de los Buques* (*Important Aspects of International Maritime Law for Commanders of Naval Ships*) (Academia de Guerra Naval Ecuador 1989).

[13] SG Gorshkov, *The Sea Power of the State* (Naval Institute Press Annapolis 1979) 47.

[14] LOSC, n 3, Art 29. The definition is drawn almost verbatim from Article 8(2) of the 1958 Convention on the High Seas (hereinafter HSC).

jurisdiction, that coastal State may control access to the shipwreck.[15] Article 303 of the LOSC recognizes a duty to protect objects of an archaeological or historical nature found at sea.[16]

The definition of 'warship' emerged from the law of naval warfare to enable belligerent and neutral States to distinguish between civilian privateer vessels authorized to conduct warfare pursuant to letters of marque, and mere pirates or brigands. After the conflict in Crimea, the rule was codified by the 1856 Declaration Respecting Maritime Law (Declaration of Paris), which abolished the practice of privateering. The Declaration of Paris also clarified the necessary conditions a State must fulfil to convert a merchant vessel into a warship.[17] The purpose of these rules was to distinguish *bona fide* warships from privateers, which operated from motives of personal gain, by clearly establishing that the warships operated on behalf of a State.[18]

3.2 Sovereign immunity

Warships, coast guard cutters, naval auxiliaries, and naval submarines operate in the maritime domain, and they are imbued with special legal status of sovereign immunity.[19] There are few peacetime legal distinctions between warships and naval auxiliaries.[20] Naval auxiliaries include logistics ships, troop transports, cargo ships, colliers, destroyer and submarine tenders, mine countermeasure vessels, hospital ships, survey ships, tankers, tugboats, and other vessels engaged in non-commercial service that complement warships. The Royal Australian Navy, for example, operates two commissioned surveying ships that conduct hydrographic surveys of

---

[15] President William J Clinton issued the following statement during the last hours of his presidency: 'Pursuant to the property clause of Article IV of the Constitution, the United States retains title indefinitely to its sunken State craft unless title has been abandoned or transferred....': 'Statement on United States Policy for the Protection of Sunken Warships', 37 *Weekly Compilation of Presidential Documents* (GPO Washington, 22 January 2001) 195; see also DJ Bederman, 'Congress Enacts Increased Protections for Sunken Military Craft' (2006) 100 *American Journal of International Law* 649; JR Harris, 'Protecting Sunken Warships as Objects Entitled to Sovereign Immunity' (2002) 33 *University of Miami Inter-American Law Review* 101; and JA Roach, 'France Concedes United States Has Title to CSS Alabama' (1991) 85 *American Journal of International Law* 381.

[16] See also the 2001 Convention on the Protection of Underwater Cultural Heritage.

[17] These latter rules were codified in the 1907 Convention Relating to the Conversion of Merchant Ships into War Ships (hereinafter Hague VII).

[18] *International Law Situations* (United States Naval War College Newport 1912) 160; N Ronzitti (ed), *The Law of Naval Warfare: A Collection of Agreements and Documents with Commentaries* (Martinus Nijhoff Dodrecht 1988) 71.

[19] BH Oxman, 'The Regime of Warships Under the United Nations Convention on the Law of the Sea' (1983–1984) 24 *Virginia Journal of International Law* 809, 820.

[20] Four agreements recognize rights of sovereign immunity for only warships but not for other government vessels. These include the 1926 Washington Convention on Pollution of Navigable Waters; 1965 Convention on Facilitation of International Maritime Traffic, Art 3; 1969 Convention on Tonnage Measurement of Ships, Art 4; 1974 Safety of Life at Sea Convention, Ch V.

the seafloor, as well as two replenishment oilers. Customary international law, as reflected in the *San Remo Manual*, suggests that auxiliaries may be manned entirely by civilians.[21] Military aircraft and other State aircraft are also recognized as sovereign immune craft.[22]

The principle of sovereign immunity renders public vessels and aircraft immune from the legal jurisdiction of other States, including immunity from arrest and seizure, foreign taxation, regulation, and inspection. In short, foreign port State or coastal State authorities may not impose jurisdiction on a foreign warship, submarine, or State aircraft of another nation, irrespective of the geographic location of the ship, such as the territorial sea.

Warship immunity is based on the principle of State sovereignty and legal equality among States.[23] The classic 1812 case US Supreme Court case *The Schooner Exchange* extols the principle of warship sovereign immunity.[24] A schooner owned by John McFaddon and William Greetham had been seized by order of Napoleon Bonaparte on 30 December 1810. The ship was armed and converted into a public vessel and renamed *Balou*. During a deployment to the West Indies in the summer of 1811, *Balou* pulled into port in Philadelphia, and McFaddon and Greetham sought to recover their vessel. The district court dismissed their action in libel on the ground that a public armed vessel of a foreign power at peace with the United States was not subject to the jurisdiction of US courts. The circuit court reversed; on appeal to the Supreme Court, Chief Justice Marshall upheld the district court's order, stating that the 'whole civilized world' concurred in the construction that

> [a warship] constitutes a part of the military force of her nation; acts under the immediate and direct command of the sovereign; is employed by him in national objects. He has many and powerful motives for preventing those objects from being defeated by interference of a foreign state. Such interference cannot take place without affecting his power and his dignity. The implied license, therefore, under which such vessel enters a friendly port, may reasonably be construed, and it seems to the Court, ought to be construed, as containing an exemption from the jurisdiction of the sovereign, within whose territory she claims the rites of hospitality.[25]

The principle of sovereign immunity is recognized in peacetime and during periods of armed conflict. The principle even applies inside another nation's internal waters. In 2012, for example, Ghana held the Argentine three-mast training frigate *ARA Libertad* in port pursuant to satisfaction of a third-party judgment against the

---

[21] L Doswald-Beck (ed), *San Remo Manual on International Law Applicable to Armed Conflicts at Sea* (Cambridge University Press London 1994) [13.22(h)]; R Jennings and A Watts, *Oppenheim's International Law* (9th edn Oxford University Press Oxford 1992) 1170–1. In such case, however, the civilian mariners would not be entitled to combatant immunity under the law of armed conflict.

[22] 1944 Convention on International Civil Aviation, Art 3(a) and (b).

[23] Gorshkov, n 13, 47. [24] *The Schooner Exchange v McFaddon* (1812) 11 US (7 Cranch) 116.

[25] Ibid, 144.

nation of Argentina. Argentina sought to compel Ghana to release the ship by filing suit at the International Tribunal for the Law of the Sea (ITLOS). The Tribunal granted provisional release of the frigate to avoid 'irreparable harm' to Argentina, ruling that because Ghana prevented the ship from getting underway and discharging its duties it violated the sovereign immunity of the ship.[26]

4 Peacetime Maritime Operations

Naval operations span the spectrum of maritime missions, from provision of humanitarian aid and disaster relief to military exercises, engagement, and manoeuvres to strategic deterrence patrols by nuclear-armed ballistic missile submarines. The special legal character and sovereign immune status of warships privileges them to conduct on behalf of the flag State a range of peacetime military tasks, which may be divided into peacetime naval operations, maritime law enforcement, and maritime security operations.

Maritime law enforcement includes protection of fisheries, enforcement of maritime safety rules, and efforts to address crime in the maritime domain. Coast Guard and constabulary forces generally enforce maritime law, although some nations, such as Australia and Thailand, lack dedicated coast guards and therefore may employ armed forces in a constabulary role. Even the United States and the United Kingdom, however, which each have a standing coast guard, use naval forces for particularly challenging law enforcement threats, such as drug-trafficking and piracy.

Maritime security operations lie between simple maritime law enforcement and the conduct of naval warfare, and the division among these categories is far from clear. Maritime security operations may contemplate a greater use of force than law enforcement because the threats are deemed to go beyond mere infractions and harm national interests or affect international stability.[27] These operations include efforts to suppress crimes of universal jurisdiction, such as maritime piracy, human trafficking, illegal migration, and slave trading, international drug trafficking, and maritime counter-terrorism and the interdiction of weapons of mass destruction.

---

[26] *ARA Libertad* (*Argentina v Ghana*), Request for the Prescription of Provisional Measures by the International Tribunal for the Law of the Sea (15 December 2012) [95]; cf ibid, Separate Opinion of Judges R Wolfrum and JP Cot (suggesting the provisions on sovereign immunity in Article 32 of the LOSC apply to the territorial sea only) [45].

[27] J Kraska and R Pedrozo, *International Maritime Security Law* (Martinus Nijhoff Leiden 2013) 7–11.

These maritime security operations also include countering maritime terrorism and proliferation of weapons of mass destruction at sea, and may require a more robust capability than that offered by purely law enforcement forces.

The international response to maritime piracy in the Indian Ocean, for example, overwhelmed law enforcement and required naval capabilities with their extended endurance, firepower, and surveillance assets. Piracy is among the oldest crimes. The English jurist Blackstone, for example, wrote, '[p]iracy consists of the common law, of those acts of depredation and robbery committed on the high seas, which if committed upon the land, would amount to felony there.'[28] Article 94(1) of the LOSC requires flag States adopt adequate criminal laws to prosecute the crime of maritime piracy committed against a ship flying their flag, and under Article 100, all nations have a general duty to cooperate against maritime piracy. Flag State consent is normally required to board a ship flying the flag of another State. Warships also may exercise a right of approach and visit in cases in which reasonable grounds exist for suspicion of maritime piracy, as well as in cases of suspected slave trafficking or illegal broadcast from the sea.[29] States may act in accordance with Article 110 of the LOSC, as well as the right of self defence under Article 2(4) of the UN Charter. Contemporary maritime piracy is defined as:

(a) Any illegal acts of violence or detention, or any act of depredation, committed for private ends by the crew or the passengers of a private ship or private aircraft, and directed—
  (i) On the high seas, against another ship or aircraft, or against persons or property on board such ship or aircraft;
  (ii) Against a ship, aircraft, persons or property in a place outside the jurisdiction of any State;
(b) Any act of voluntary participation in the operation of a ship or of an aircraft with knowledge of the facts making it a pirate ship or aircraft;
(c) Any act of inciting or intentionally facilitating an act described in subparagraph (a) or (b).[30]

For legal purposes, 'piracy' occurs beyond the twelve nautical-mile territorial sea; the same illegal conduct occurring landward of the twelve nautical-mile mark—inside the territorial sea or the internal waters of a coastal State—constitutes 'armed robbery at sea'. 'Armed robbery at sea' is not an international crime, but may be a criminal offense to be punished under the laws of the coastal State.

Article 105 of the LOSC sets forth generalized authority for all nations to assert universal jurisdiction over pirate ships: '[o]n the high seas [or in an exclusive economic zone], or in any other place outside the jurisdiction of any State, every State may seize a pirate ship [or ship taken by piracy] and under the control of pirates, and arrest the persons and seize the property on board.' In the case of

---

[28] W Blackstone and JB Bayly (eds), *Commentaries on the Laws of England* (Saunders & Benning London 1840) 499.
[29] Ibid; LOSC, n 3, Art 110. Warships may exercise the right of visit against civilian ships that fly their flag or that are without nationality or refuse to show a flag.
[30] LOSC, n 3, Art 101.

piracy emanating from the shores of Somalia, however, the UN Security Council has adopted a string of resolutions since 2008 that authorize warships from participating States to conduct counter piracy operations in Somalia's territorial sea and land territory.[31]

Maritime law enforcement and constabulary operations sometimes entail hot pursuit in cases in which they have 'good reason to believe that the ship violated the laws and regulations of that State'.[32] Naval and coast guard forces of a coastal State may pursue a ship from the territorial sea, archipelagic waters, or the contiguous zone onto the high seas when there is reasonable belief the vessel violated the law of that State. If the pursuit begins within the contiguous zone, however, it may be conducted only for violations of the rules pertaining to the contiguous zone, such as customs-related offenses. Likewise, if a foreign ship is suspected of violations of lawful coastal State regulations pertaining to the exclusive economic zone, such as fisheries laws, authorities from the coastal State may initiate pursuit of the vessel onto the high seas. Hot pursuit may not extend into the territorial sea of another State, however, without the permission of the other State.

5 Law of Naval Warfare

The law of naval warfare operates within the context of two monumental treaties—the UN Charter and the LOSC. The Charter outlawed the conduct of aggressive war, and thus has shaped *jus ad bellum*, the law of neutrality and belligerent rights. Although the LOSC is a peacetime convention, it continues to operate as a matter of treaty law among neutrals, and between neutrals and belligerents, in time of armed conflict. That is, States' Parties to the LOSC do not lose their respective rights simply because an armed conflict occurs. The beginning of armed conflict, however, also triggers another set of treaties and customary law: the Law of Naval Warfare (LNW), which contains extensive rules on the conduct of hostilities at sea (*jus in bello*). This body of law exists in conjunction with the LOSC, and supplements the peacetime regime during periods of armed conflict.

Rules on the conduct of naval hostilities are largely codified in treaties and restatements. The 1856 Paris Declaration codified the seventeenth century principle of 'free

---

[31] See eg UNSC Res 1816, UN Doc S/RES/1816 (2 June 2008) and UNSC Res 1851, UN Doc S/RES/1851 (16 December 2008).
[32] LOSC, n 3, Art 111.

ships—free goods', which means that except for contraband of war, enemy goods aboard neutral ships are inviolate.[33] The Hague Conference of 1907 codified much of the law of naval warfare, which is a branch of international humanitarian law.[34] The 1909 London Declaration[35] and 1913 *Oxford Manual of Naval War*[36] are declaratory of customary law. The Washington Naval Conference produced a treaty that restated the illegality of unrestricted submarine attacks against merchant ships. The Convention on Maritime Neutrality declared freedom of commerce in time of war. The 1930 International Treaty for the Limitation and Reduction of Naval Armament (Treaty of London) regulates the use of submarines against merchant vessels. One year later, as the Spanish Civil War was underway, nine States extended the rules in the 1936 *Procès-Verbal* relating to the Rules of Submarine Warfare (London Protocol) to surface ships and aircraft.[37]

Geneva Convention II (1949) on wounded, sick, and shipwrecked members of the armed forces at sea is the most recent codification of sea warfare.[38] Naval war does not feature prominently in the Additional Protocols to the Geneva Conventions, although Additional Protocol I (1977) constrains naval bombardment, as it does land and air attack.[39] Protocol I also protects medical transportation and relief, and these provisions apply to hospital ships and naval warfare more broadly. The Hague and Geneva law predate the LOSC, and there is no single treaty that unifies

---

[33] A corollary of the rule, however, is that neutral goods carried aboard enemy ships may be confiscated.

[34] Much of the law of naval warfare is codified in Hague treaties. See 1899 Hague Convention III for the Adaptation to Maritime Warfare of the Principles of the Geneva Convention; 1905 Convention for the Exemption of Hospital Ships, in Time of War, from The Payment of all Dues and Taxes Imposed for the Benefit of the State; 1907 Status of Enemy Merchant Ships at the Outbreak of Hostilities (hereinafter Hague VI); Hague VII, n 17; 1907 Convention on the Laying of Automatic Submarine Contact Mines (hereinafter Hague VIII); 1907 Convention respecting Bombardment by Naval Forces in Time of War (hereinafter Hague IX); 1907 Convention for the Adaptation to Maritime Warfare of the Principles of the Geneva Convention, produced by the First and revised by the Second Peace Conference (hereinafter Hague X); 1907 Convention Relative to Certain Restrictions on the Exercise of the Right of Capture in Naval War (hereinafter Hague XI); and 1907 Convention concerning the Rights and Duties of Neutral Powers in Naval War (hereinafter Hague XIII).

[35] The parties proposed creation of an international prize court, although it never was established: 1907 Final Protocol to the Naval Conference of London. See also, 1907 Convention Relative to the Creation of an International Prize Court (hereinafter Hague XII) and 1910 Additional Protocol to the Convention Relative to the Establishment of an International Prize Court.

[36] 'Manual of the Laws of Naval War adopted by the Institute of International Law at Its Oxford Session (9 August 1913)' in D Schindler and J Toman (eds), *The Laws of Armed Conflicts: A Collection of Conventions, Resolutions and Other Documents* (Brill Martinus Nijhoff Leiden 1988) 858 (hereinafter *Manual of the Laws of Naval War*).

[37] The 1937 Nyon Agreement. The nine powers are Bulgaria, Egypt, France, Greece, Romania, Russia, Serbia, Turkey, and the United Kingdom. See also the 1937 Agreement Supplementary to The Nyon Agreement (applies to attack by aircraft).

[38] 1949 Geneva Convention for the Amelioration of the Condition of Wounded, Sick and Shipwrecked Members of Armed Forces at Sea, Art 52.

[39] Hague IX, n 34, Arts 1–2 contained a number of military objectives subject to attack.

military operations at sea in wartime and peace.[40] The International Institute of Humanitarian Law, however, convened a group of experts to develop the *San Remo Manual on International Law Applicable to Armed Conflicts at Sea*, which serves as an authoritative restatement of law.[41]

5.1 Belligerent and neutral rights

The terms of LNW apply among belligerent States party to a conflict, or between belligerent States and neutral States, trumping the peacetime rules of the law of the sea insofar as they are inconsistent. Like the peacetime regime, however, LNW provides special status and privileges for warships and naval auxiliaries, so determination of which vessels possess this status is important in time of war as well as peace.

Unlike land warfare, combat at sea is conducted not by individuals, but rather by warships and military aircraft. The definition of a 'warship' is reflected by implication in the 1907 Convention Relating to the Conversion of Merchant Ships into War Ships (Hague VII), and it influenced the definition of 'warship' in the LOSC.[42] Both warships and auxiliaries may be used to perform missions in peacetime operations, but warships alone may exercise belligerent rights.[43] Warships may engage in belligerent military activities during periods of armed conflict, including visit and search of enemy and neutral commercial ships to determine the character of the cargo, blockade against enemy ports and coastlines, interdiction of enemy military forces, and convoy escort of friendly and allied commercial ships.

Auxiliary naval vessels typically are manned by a civilian crew, and therefor cannot take part in hostilities. Similarly, if merchant vessels take part in hostilities, they lose their protection as civilian objects and the crew may be criminally prosecuted.[44] For example, during periods of armed conflict, only warships may

---

[40] HB Robertson, *The 'New' Law of the Sea and the Law of Armed Conflict at Sea* (Naval War College Newport Paper Newport 1992) 16–36.

[41] L Doswald-Beck (ed), *San Remo Manual on International Law Applicable to Armed Conflicts at Sea* (Cambridge University Press London 1994) (hereinafter *San Remo Manual*).

[42] The definition of 'warship' is by implication for the rules established for conversion of merchant ships into warships. Such vessels should bear the external marks denoting nationality, be commanded by a naval officer, carry a crew that served under military discipline, and comply with the laws of war. Furthermore, merchant ships that are converted into warships must be registered in the list of national warships. Hague VII, n 17, Arts 2–6.

[43] D Fleck (ed), *The Handbook of Humanitarian Law in Armed Conflicts* (Oxford University Press Oxford 1995) 415–17, but cf Iranian Revolutionary Guard Corps Navy (IRGCN) military operations during the Iran–Iraq War (1980–88), in which small craft not qualifying as warships conducted naval warfare. The IRGCN is prepared to conduct similar irregular maritime campaigns in the Persian Gulf: AF Krepnievich, *Why AirSea Battle?* (Center for Strategic and Budgetary Assessments Washington 2010) 28–31.

[44] During World War I, some merchant ships rammed enemy submarines. The Germans considered these measures to be unlawful, and executed commanders of ramming vessels. Cf LF Oppenheim and

exercise the belligerent right of visit and search of neutral vessels in order to stop contraband from flowing to the enemy.[45] The right of visit and search in naval warfare is distinct from the peacetime right of approach and visit, which may be conducted by warships and naval auxiliaries.

5.2 Geography of naval warfare

The LOSC did not change how naval warfare could be fought, but it altered (and limited) the geography where belligerents could conduct hostilities by expansion of the territorial sea to 12 nautical miles (nm), and establishment of archipelagic waters. Belligerents may not conduct naval warfare in the internal waters, territorial seas, including waters comprising a strait used for international navigation, or archipelagic waters, of neutral States.[46] Furthermore, belligerents may not carry out hostilities in permanently neutralized waters such as those around Antarctica or the Åaland Islands, situated between Sweden and Finland. In short, naval warfare may not be prosecuted in these areas under the sovereignty of neutral States or that have been neutralized through treaty, unless they become an area of operation for the enemy.

For the purposes of naval warfare, the contiguous zone, the exclusive economic zone, and the continental shelves of neutral States are considered areas of high seas. Even though coastal States enjoy certain sovereign rights or jurisdiction in these areas, they do not unduly restrict combat at sea. Armed conflict at sea can take place anywhere beyond the territorial sea—that is, within the contiguous zone, EEZ or on the continental shelf—of a neutral State.[47]

If hostile actions are conducted in the EEZ of a neutral State, belligerents must 'have due regard for the rights and duties of the coastal State', which are described as, *inter alia*, 'the exploration and exploitation of the economic resources of the [EEZ] and the protection of the marine environment'.[48] Even beyond the conduct of manoeuvre operations and the use of military force in a neutral State's EEZ, belligerents are entitled to lay mines in the EEZ and on the continental shelf, so long as the neutral State is notified of the danger and the size of the minefield and the type of mines laid do not endanger artificial islands, installations, and structures. Like any belligerent activity, however, mine laying operations 'shall avoid so far as practicable interference with the exploration or exploitation of the zone by the neutral State'.[49] The San Remo Manual suggests that if interference is unavoidable, a belligerent

---

H Lauterpacht (ed), *Oppenheim's International Law: Disputes, War and Neutrality* (7th edn Longman and Sons London 1952) 467–8 (defensive ramming by merchant ships of submarines engaged in unrestricted U-boat warfare is not unlawful).

[45] LA Atherly-Jones and HHL Bellot, *Commerce in War* (D Appleton and Co New York 1907) 1.
[46] *San Remo Manual*, n 41, [14]–[15]; *Manual of the Laws of Naval War*, n 36, § 1.
[47] *San Remo Manual*, n 41, [8] and [10].   [48] Ibid, [34].   [49] Ibid, [35].

may inhibit the coastal State's economic prerogatives in the EEZ. This judgment indicates that the rights and jurisdiction relating to the exclusive economic status of the coastal State is subordinate even to distant State belligerent naval activity during periods of armed conflict.

6 Freedom of Navigation in Peace and War

Freedom of movement is one of the principal military uses of the oceans. During antiquity and the middle ages, States depended on oared galleys to project military power at sea. These warships hugged the coastline and typically spent the night ashore. For about two thousand years, little changed in the methods of naval warfare. In the mid-1400s, however, Portugal and then Spain pioneered larger all-sail ships that made possible transcontinental travel. The new ships were larger, able to carry greater supplies and goods for trade, and yet also had a much smaller crew.

As Portugal and Spain encountered the New World and by-passed the land-bound Ottoman Empire to connect Europe to East Asia, they claimed sovereignty over vast tracts of ocean. Later, Anglo-Saxon powers challenged these exclusive claims over the oceans. First Dutch and then English naval forces displaced the Iberian powers, and eventually they established the contemporary model of freedom of the seas.[50] Thus, the rules governing warship operations and access to the world's oceans emerged from the shift in naval technology from oar to sail in the fifteenth century.

In World War I, President Woodrow Wilson included the principle of freedom of the seas as one of his Fourteen Points. Franklin Delano Roosevelt and Sir Winston Churchill followed suit in World War II when they met at Argentia, Newfoundland, to develop war aims for the allied powers, and included the principle of freedom of the seas for all nations in peace and in war.[51] After the war, and with the advent of the nuclear age, States began to adopt new restrictions on unfettered military uses of the oceans. The exclusive claims and restrictions came into conflict with what Bernard H Oxman referred to as 'the sovereign right of communication', or a State's right to use the global commons to maintain links of trade, alliance, politics, and culture, with the world at large.[52]

---

[50] DJ Bederman, 'The Sea' in B Fassbender and A Peters (eds), *The Oxford Handbook of the History of International Law* (Oxford University Press Oxford 2012) 365.
[51] 1941 Declaration of Principles (hereinafter Atlantic Charter).
[52] EL Richardson, 'Power, Mobility, and the Law of the Sea' (1980) 58 *Foreign Affairs* 906.

Naval forces enjoy worldwide mobility, and they are flexible, adaptable, and scalable sea bases able to project air, sea, and ground forces on the water and deep inland. Without the hindrance of legal, political, or logistical challenges of establishing a land base, naval forces may be aggregated and disaggregated and deployed, complemented, or recalled as tailor-made force packages according to political requirements. These qualities make navies particularly attractive instruments of national power, and their lighter footprint and extended loiter time are especially suitable for peacetime endeavour.

Naval forces can be carefully calibrated to convey just the right signal to friends, foes, and competitors. Sea power can be leveraged to achieve political ends without resort to the use of force.[53] Ships, aircraft, and submarines are routinely employed in pursuit of the foreign objectives of the State, and they are flexible instruments in support diplomacy. Maritime diplomacy may be used in the context of international competition or collaboration, or a mixture of both.[54]

Edward Luttwak characterizes two types of 'naval suasion', which may be either latent (routine and undirected), or active (consciously designed to obtain a particular outcome). Similarly, James Cable distinguishes among four kinds of naval force: definitive, purposeful, catalytic, and expressive. Definitive naval diplomacy presents a *fait accompli*, as in the seizure of the USS *Pueblo* by North Korea. The goal of purposeful diplomacy is to persuade nations to change their policy, as in the decision by President Clinton to deploy two aircraft carriers to the Formosa Strait in 1995 after China fired missiles near Taiwan in an effort to intimidate the island during national elections. Catalytic maritime diplomacy is designed to influence events, such as the US Seventh fleet forward deployed in Japan. Finally, expressive naval diplomacy is merely to emphasize a particular attitude or approach, such as US freedom of navigation program that conducts operational challenges against other nations' excessive maritime claims.

While ships of all nations enjoy freedom of navigation on the high seas, by the eighteenth century, it became evident that coastal States enjoyed sovereignty over an offshore area of ocean bound by the contours of the coastline. Yet States disagreed on the breadth of the territorial sea, or the balance of rights and duties between the coastal State and foreign ships that transited the area. A 1930 Hague Conference conducted under the auspices of the League of Nations failed to resolve these issues, as did two UN conferences on the law of the sea held in Geneva in 1958 and 1960. The Third United Nations Conference on the Law of the Sea (UNCLOS III) took

---

[53] See K Booth, *Navies and Foreign Policy* (2nd edn Holmes and Meier Publishers New York 1979); J Cable, *Gunboat Diplomacy* (2nd edn Palgrave Macmillan New York 1981); and E Luttwak, *The Political Uses of Sea Power* (Johns Hopkins University Press Baltimore 1974).

[54] G Till, *Seapower: A Guide for the Twenty-First Century* (3rd edn Routledge Cass Series: Naval Policy and History Florence 2013) 221.

up the issue beginning in 1973, as part of a package of oceans issues that included seabed mining, international straits, archipelagic States, and fisheries.

6.1 Innocent passage in the territorial sea

Importantly, the Conference reached agreement on the breadth of the territorial sea, and the navigational regime that applies within in it, and that determination shaped compromises on other issues. Coastal States were afforded a territorial sea of 12 nm in width and subject to coastal State sovereignty. Foreign vessels are entitled to travel in innocent passage in a coastal State's territorial sea, but proposals to require either notification or authorization of foreign ships were defeated.[55]

Under Article 17 of the LOSC, all States enjoy the right of passage through the territorial sea in accordance with the regime of innocent passage. Article 19 stipulates: 'Passage is innocent so long as it is not prejudicial to the peace, good order, or security of the coastal State.' Passage is considered prejudicial to peace, good order, or security of the coastal State if it engages in the threat or use of force against the sovereignty, territorial integrity, or political independence of the coastal State, or it violates the principles set forth in the UN Charter.[56] The exercise or practice of weapons, collection of information to the prejudice of the coastal State, acts of propaganda designed to affect the defence or security of the coastal State, launch, landing, or recovery of aircraft or 'any military device', acts of 'wilful and serious pollution', and other activities not bearing directly on passage are considered to lie outside of innocent passage.[57] Furthermore, innocent passage is permissible only on the surface of the water, so aircraft are not entitled to innocent passage, and submarines must travel on the surface and show their flag.[58]

States disagree, however, on how the rule on innocent passage of warships in the territorial sea plays out in practice. The mere presence of a foreign warship off the coast of some States may create tension, and the line between innocent passage and 'collection of information' is often hard to determine. The reluctance of even potential adversaries to exercise the right of innocent passage means that often the right is more theoretical than practical.[59]

During the Cold War, for example, the United States and Soviet Union disagreed on the parameters of innocent passage. The United States challenged Soviet laws that purported to restrict the transit of warships in the territorial sea without prior

---

[55] IMO Doc A/CONF.62/WS/37 and Add.1–2, of 8 March 1983, reprinted in (1982) XVII *Official Records of the Third UN Conference on the Law of the Sea* (Plenary Meetings, Summary Records and Verbatim Records, as well as Documents of the Conference, Resumed Eleventh Session and Final Part Eleventh Session and Conclusion) (UN Publication Sales No E.84.V.3) 243–4.

[56] LOSC, n 3, Art 19(2).   [57] Ibid.   [58] Ibid, Art 20.

[59] K Agyeben, 'Theory in Search of Practice: The Right of Innocent Passage in the Territorial Sea' (2005) *Cornell Law School Graduate Papers* Paper 9.

authorization or consent. On 12 February 1988, the USS *Caron* and USS *Yorktown* conducted a freedom of navigation transit through Russia's territorial sea near the port of Sebastopol. In response, the Burevestnik-class frigate *Bezzavetny* shouldered or bumped the *Yorktown* in protest. The Black Sea bumping incident led to negotiations that produced a uniform interpretation of the right of innocent passage in the territorial sea under the rules set forth in the LOSC. The uniform interpretation was signed on 23 September 1989, at a meeting in Jackson Hole, Wyoming.[60] The Jackson Hole Agreement stated that '[a]ll ships, including warships, regardless of cargo, armament or means of propulsion, enjoy the right of innocent passage through the territorial sea... for which neither prior notification nor authorization is required.'[61] The superpowers also agreed that Article 19(2) of the LOSC sets out 'an exhaustive list of activities that would render passage not innocent. A ship passing through the territorial sea that does not engage in any of those activities is in innocent passage.'[62] Although the uniform interpretation does not bind other countries, it carries substantial weight concerning State practice because it reflects the position of the superpowers during the Cold War.

6.2 Straits and archipelagos

The navigational regime of transit passage grew out of the negotiations at LOSC III for a package deal. The right of peacetime transit though straits used for international navigation was recognized by the International Court of Justice (ICJ) in its Corfu Channel decision in 1949.[63] With the expansion of the territorial sea from 3 (or 4 or 6 nm) to 12 nm in the LOSC, it became apparent that more than one hundred straits used for international navigation that previously had high seas corridors through them would fall under coastal State sovereignty. Without a right of transit passage, these straits would be governed by the more restrictive regime of innocent passage, which means that submarines would have to travel on the surface and show their flag, and aircraft in flight had no right of transit.

Generally, the right of transit passage applies to straits that connect one part of the high seas or EEZ and another part of the high seas or EEZ, including strategic straits such as Gibraltar, Bab el Mandeb, Hormuz, Malacca and Singapore, Sunda, Lombok, and the Windward Passage.[64] All ships and aircraft enjoy a right of unimpeded transit passage through such straits in the 'normal mode of operation',[65] which means that submarines can transit submerged, military aircraft can overfly

---

[60] 1989 Union of Soviet Socialist Republics–United States: Joint Statement with Attached Uniform Interpretation of Rules of International Law Governing Innocent Passage.
[61] Ibid, Art 2. [62] Ibid, Art 3.
[63] *Corfu Channel Case (United Kingdom v Albania)* (Merits) [1949] ICJ Rep 4.
[64] LOSC, n 3, Art 37. [65] Ibid, Arts 38 and 39.

in combat formation, and surface ships can transit in a manner consistent with their security, to include formation steaming and launching and recovery of aircraft. Article 44 prohibits States bordering an international strait from suspending transit passage for any purpose, including military exercises. In addition, Article 42(2) prohibits the bordering States from adoption of laws or regulations that have the practical effect of denying, hampering, or impairing the right of transit passage.

A right of non-suspendable innocent passage applies in straits that connect a part of the high seas or EEZ with the territorial sea of a coastal State (ie dead-end straits), as well as to straits that connect one part of the high seas or EEZ and another part of the high seas or EEZ where the strait is formed by an island of a State bordering the strait and its mainland, if there exists seaward of the island a route through the high seas or EEZ of similar convenience with regard to navigation and hydrographic characteristics.[66] There is, however, no right of overflight through such straits.

One of the most interesting and unique creations of UNCLOS was the archipelagic State, which developed in conjunction with the right of Archipelagic Sea Lanes Passage by ships and aircraft.[67] The recognition of the sovereignty over vast ocean spaces by archipelagic States was balanced by a regime of navigational freedom along the shortest routes through archipelagic straits and waters traditionally used for international navigation, or designated by the coastal State and recognized by the International Maritime Organization.

6.3 The exclusive economic zone

Throughout the latter half of the twentieth century, coastal States began to acquire a sense of legal entitlement over offshore areas beyond the territorial sea. The proliferation of advanced radar and naval weapon systems meant that, for the first time, coastal States also developed the capability to enforce their claims. These trends contributed to a series of incidents in which coastal States asserted jurisdiction beyond the territorial sea; in 1968, North Korea seized the USS *Pueblo* (AGER-2) spy ship in international waters, and in 1975, Cambodia captured the SS *Mayaguez* in the Gulf of Thailand.

During UNCLOS III negotiations, the major maritime powers of the Soviet Union, the United States, France, the United Kingdom, and Japan, successfully secured a framework designed to promote freedom of the seas beyond the territorial sea. Article 86, 'Freedom of the High Seas', recognizes that the high seas are open to all States.[68] Nations enjoy an array of rights and freedoms throughout the high seas,

---

[66] Ibid, Arts 45 and 38.

[67] JPA Bernhardt, 'The Right of Archipelagic Sea Lanes Passage: A Primer' (1995) 35 *Virginia Journal of International Law* 719.

[68] Likewise, outer space is regarded as *res communis*, like the high seas, and cannot be appropriated by any State. See the 1967 Treaty on Principles Governing the Activities of States in the Exploration and Use of Outer Space, Including the Moon and Other Celestial Bodies, Art 2.

including the freedom of navigation of ships and submarines, and freedom of overflight over the high seas, and other internationally lawful uses of the sea. The provisions of the high seas apply in the EEZ under Article 58. Some coastal States, however, were never satisfied with the bargains contained in LOSC or disagree on their application, and have continued legal and policy efforts to undermine freedom of navigation. These disagreements have given rise to a number maritime incidents between coastal States and the United States, including naval fighter jet aircraft duels between the United States and Libya in 1981, 1986, and 1989 over the waters of the Gulf of Sirte (Sidra), and between the United States and China in the East China Sea and Yellow Sea.

In 2001, for example, two F-8 Chinese fighter jets intercepted a US EP-3 maritime patrol surveillance (spy) aircraft in the East China Sea. One of the jets collided with the US aircraft, resulting in the loss of the jet and pilot at sea. The damaged US aircraft made an emergency landing on Hainan Island, where the airplane and its crew were detained. Chinese interception of the USNS *Impeccable* (TAGOS-23) military survey ship in the South China Sea in 2009 is just one of the many instances that transits by US military survey ships in China's EEZ were disrupted.[69]

Similarly, on December 5, 2013, the Ticonderoga-class guided missile cruiser USS *Cowpens* (CG-63), was conducting surveillance of naval exercises by the Chinese aircraft carrier *Liaoning* in China's EEZ, when it was approached by a Chinese Navy escort ship and asked to leave the area. The *Cowpens* declined to depart its pattern, at which point a Chinese Amphibious Dock Ship suddenly veered and crossed its bow. The *Cowpens* took evasive action to avoid collision, but the incident underscores the continuing disagreement between the two nations over the right to conduct military activities in the EEZ.

The claims and counter-points pertaining to military activities in the EEZ circulate around a half dozen interlocking arguments.[70] Article 88 of the LOSC, for example, reserves the high seas for 'peaceful purposes', and that provision applies in the EEZ through Article 58(2).[71] The term 'peaceful purposes', however, does not preclude military activities, but only those that are inconsistent with Article 2(4) of the UN Charter.[72] Coastal States shall have 'due regard' for the rights and duties

---

[69] The USNS *Sumner*, USNS *Bowditch*, USNS *Bruce C Heezen*, and USNS *Victorious* have also experienced aggressive interception by Chinese People's Liberation Army (PLA) (navy) ships and Chinese Coast Guard vessels. For comprehensive analysis of the issue of military activities in the EEZ, see R Pedrozo, 'Preserving Navigational Rights and Freedoms: The Right to Conduct Military Activities in China's Exclusive Economic Zone' (2010) 9 *Chinese Journal of International Law* 9; and R Pedrozo, 'Responding to Ms Zhang's Talking Points on the EEZ' (2011) 10 *Chinese Journal of International Law* 207. Cf H Zhang, 'Is It Safeguarding the Freedom of Navigation or Maritime Hegemony of the United States?—Comments on Raul (Pete) Pedrozo's Article on Military Activities in the EEZ' (2010) 9 *Chinese Journal of International Law* 31.
[70] See Kraska, n 10, 257.
[71] The term 'peaceful purposes' is also referenced in LOSC, n 3, Arts 88, 141, 143(1), 147(2), 155(2), 240(a), 242(1), 246(3), and 301.
[72] Kraska, n 10, 257.

of other States operating in their EEZ, while at the same time, other States shall have due regard for the rights and duties of the coastal State.[73] These 'duelling due regards' suggest that the coastal State has a duty not to interfere with freedom of navigation and other internationally lawful uses of the sea, whereas other States, in their use of the EEZ, have a duty to refrain from activity that impinges on coastal State sovereign rights and jurisdiction over the living and non-living resources.[74]

Another point of contention arises from the operation of military survey or oceanographic naval ships in the EEZ.[75] On the one hand, these vessels are sovereign immune ships of the naval service, and they are conducting a military activity under the authority of freedom of navigation and other internationally lawful uses of the sea. Yet some coastal States have suggested that such activities constitute 'marine scientific research', and hence, may be regulated by the jurisdiction of the coastal State.[76] 'Surveys', however, which are mentioned separately in Articles 19, 21, and 40, are a distinct activity from 'marine scientific research'. Whereas the LOSC prescribes coastal State jurisdiction over surveys in the territorial sea and during transit passage through straits used for international navigation, there is no such proscription in the EEZ.

7 Conclusion

The disagreement over military activities in the EEZ is only the latest manifestation of the history of tension between maritime powers and coastal States. The adoption of the LOSC did not entirely quell disagreements over the right to conduct military operations in areas under coastal State sovereignty or jurisdiction. As presciently noted 20 years ago, '[c]oastal states have taken what they could get, waited a decent interval, and then struck out seeking more.'[77] After the LOSC entered into force, coastal States 'control all natural resources to a distance of 200 miles, and to even greater distances on the seabed.... Coastal states seeking more are likely to target military and commercial navigation and overflight.'[78] It is unlikely, however, that the organic dispute resolution mechanisms built into LOSC can ameliorate tension.

Part XV of the LOSC establishes a comprehensive and binding dispute settlement procedure. There are four venues for dispute resolution: the ITLOS, located

---

[73] LOSC, n 3, Arts 56, 58.   [74] Kraska, n 10, 261–9.
[75] Ibid, 270–6.   [76] LOSC, n 3, Art 56(1)(b)(ii).
[77] BH Oxman (Rapporteur), 'United States Interests in the Law of the Sea Convention' (1994) 88 *American Journal of International Law* 167, 170.
[78] Ibid.

in Hamburg, Germany; the ICJ, located in The Hague, the Netherlands; arbitral tribunals constituted under Annex VII; and special arbitral tribunals constituted in accordance with Annex VIII.

States Parties may, however, exclude military activities from dispute settlement jurisdiction under Article 298. The Article specifies that States may make a declaration upon signature ratification, or accession of the LOSC, or any time thereafter, 'that it does not accept any one or more of the procedures', to resolve, '...disputes concerning military activities, including military activities by government vessels and aircraft engaged in non-commercial service, and disputes concerning law enforcement activities....'[79]

Numerous States have invoked Article 298 in declarations that deny an international court or tribunal jurisdiction over their military activities, including Argentina, Belarus, Canada, Cape Verde, Chile, China, France, Germany, Mexico, Republic of Korea, Russia, Tunisia, Ukraine, and the United Kingdom. The United States also intends to make such a declaration if it accedes to the LOSC.[80]

The legal effect of such a declaration is that disputes arising from military activities may be fenced off from dispute settlement. Once removed from review or jurisdiction, military activities are exempt from exposure to arbitration or outside court ruling, or review by a compulsory international panel or other State. It is unclear, however, whether a court or arbitral tribunal would proceed with a case over the objection of a State Party that the dispute at issue involves a 'military activity' that has been removed from jurisdiction pursuant to a declaration by the State. Article 288(4) of the LOSC provides that: 'In the event of a dispute as to whether a court or tribunal has jurisdiction, the matter shall be settled by decision of that court or tribunal.' Thus, if a future tribunal or court determined it could assert jurisdiction over a matter considered to be a 'military activity', the body would have to review its jurisdiction.

For example, on 18 September 2013, Russian Coast Guard officers detained some 30 Greenpeace activists and seized their ship, *Arctic Sunrise*, in response to a protest by the group at the Prirazlomnaya offshore oil platform—a Gazprom installation in Russia's Pechora Sea. The ship is registered in the Netherlands, which brought a suit in the ITLOS against Russia, seeking provisional measures to include release of the ship and persons detained. Russia claims that the arrest was an exercise of its law enforcement rights, as the protesters conducted an unauthorized boarding of an oil platform in the Russian EEZ and intruded into a declared safety zone, and furthermore, that since Russia already selected the optional exclusion from binding settlement processes itemized in Article 298, the matter is one purely of domestic concern. In line with this position, Russia declined to participate in the

---

[79] LOSC, n 3, Art 298.
[80] Committee on Foreign Relations, US Senate, *Senate Executive Report 110-9, Convention on the Law of the Sea, to Accompany Treaty Document 103-39* (United States Senate Washington 2007) 19.

hearings held by the Tribunal. Despite Russia's position, however, ITLOS issued a provision order.[81]

The case of the Arctic Sunrise underscores the dynamic relationship among coastal States, flag States, and international tribunals. Most nations are reluctant to submit military operations to the vagaries of an international tribunal—whether those operations are conducted as part of inshore, homeland security or distant water expeditionary patrols. Although the LOSC established an overall architecture for military operations at sea, disagreement over its interpretation and implementation—and the absence of a tribunal with authority to resolve the disputes—points darkly toward a future of heightened tension and the prospect of naval conflict.

---

[81] *'Arctic Sunrise' Case (Kingdom of the Netherlands v Russian Federation)*, Request for the Prescription of Provisional Measures by the International Tribunal for the Law of the Sea (22 November 2013).

39

CHARTING THE FUTURE FOR THE LAW OF THE SEA

DONALD R ROTHWELL, ALEX G OUDE ELFERINK, KAREN N SCOTT, AND TIM STEPHENS

1 Introduction

In this concluding chapter the future of the law of the sea is assessed in light of the analysis of the past and present development of the law of the sea provided in the preceding chapters.[1] Key themes that emerge from this *Handbook* are considered, with particular attention given to the future of maritime limits and zones, law of the sea actors and institutions, substantive regimes under the law of the sea, and regional oceans management. To conclude, consideration is given to the future of the 1982 United Nations Convention on the Law of the Sea (LOSC), the 'Constitution of the Oceans'.

---

[1] While the authors share collective responsibility for this chapter, Donald R Rothwell was the lead author of Section 2, Karen N Scott of Section 3, Tim Stephens of Section 4, and Alex G Oude Elferink of Sections 5 and 6.

2 Lines in the Sea: The Future for Maritime Limits and Zones

The history of the law of the sea revolves around the competing interests of coastal and flag States (Chapter 1). The twentieth century witnessed adjustments in those relations through, first, the 1958 Geneva Conventions and then the LOSC. However, while the focus in recent decades has been upon the treaties that make up the contemporary law of the sea (Chapter 2), the impact of State practice in the interpretation of law of the sea instruments, and the resulting developments that have occurred in customary international law, should not be overlooked. Together, these sources of international law not only provide the basis for the contemporary law of the sea as they relate to maritime limits and zones, but also provide pointers to how other dimensions of the law of the sea may be developing.

2.1 Spatial definition of maritime zones

One of the most significant achievements of the LOSC was the clarity that it brought to the spatial definition of the six maritime zones recognized under the Convention and the associated limits of internal waters, and archipelagic waters within archipelagic States. The LOSC not only expanded the breadth of the territorial sea, contiguous zone, and continental shelf, but gave recognition to the exclusive economic zone (EEZ) and deep seabed. While the spatial extent of the high seas was reduced under the LOSC compared to its Geneva Convention definition, the impact of the high seas being constrained to the area beyond the 200 nautical mile (nm) limit was lessened by Article 58 and the application of many of the central provisions of the Part VII high seas regime within the EEZ.

As observed in Chapter 4, while Article 7 of the LOSC provides clarity with respect to straight baselines, as derived from the ICJ's judgment in the *Anglo-Norwegian Fisheries* case[2] and the 1958 Convention on the Territorial Sea and Contiguous Zone, some aspects of State practice with respect to straight baselines remain heavily contested. By way of contrast, archipelagic baselines found in Article 47 of the LOSC are, as noted in Chapter 7, a more contemporary development. A total of 22 States have drawn archipelagic baselines in reliance upon Article 47, which in turn triggers the distinctive archipelagic regime provisions of Part IV of the Convention. While there may have been a temptation for certain States to interpret Article 47 liberally, State practice to date has been relatively conservative in this regard.

---

[2] *Fisheries (United Kingdom v Norway)* [1951] ICJ Rep 116 (hereinafter *Anglo-Norwegian Fisheries*).

With this relative clarity in the law with respect to baselines, there has been accompanying certainty in the delimitation of internal waters and the territorial sea, and archipelagic waters and the territorial sea for archipelagic States. Nevertheless, there remain on-going controversies in this area (which the United States highlights via its Freedom of Navigation program[3]) and on-going debates over the status of certain contested waters such as the Northwest Passage (Chapters 6 and 32) and the South China Sea (Chapter 28). In the great majority of instances, there are significant levels of compliance with the LOSC and associated customary rules with respect to recognized limits of the territorial sea, contiguous zone and the EEZ.[4] Continental shelf limits of 200 nm laid down in Article 76 remains subject to coastal State submissions to the Commission on the Limits of the Continental Shelf (CLCS) where the shelf extends beyond that distance (Chapter 9). Owing to the unexpectedly high number of submissions to the Commission and the associated workload and capacity issues this has created, it may now take several decades for there to be a final determination of the outer limits of all coastal State continental shelves. This will have some implications for giving certainty to the Part XI regime of the deep seabed; however, this is only a marginal issue and the vast majority of the 'Area' comprising the deep seabed is defined.

2.2 Substantive regime of maritime zones

The law of the sea under the LOSC has had to reconcile the development of new maritime zones (EEZ and Area), with the juridical expansion in the breadth of some maritime zones (territorial sea, contiguous zone, and continental shelf) and the diminution of the extent of others (high seas). Not surprisingly, this has led to some variations in State practice as to the content of the substantive regimes, especially with respect to the EEZ which is the most 'modern' of the maritime zones over which coastal States exercise sovereign rights and jurisdiction. The Area, while also a LOSC creation, is not a zone within which coastal States exercise sovereign rights and jurisdiction but rather, is an internationalized zone under significant regulatory control by the International Seabed Authority (ISA) (Chapter 11). While the substantive regulatory system within that zone remains under active development, the preparatory work to date of the Authority working with States parties has permitted an orderly development of the Part XI regime for the Area which will increasingly fall under the spotlight as deep seabed mining activities intensify in the coming decade.

---

[3] JA Roach and RW Smith, *Excessive Maritime Claims* (3rd edn Martinus Nijhoff Publishers Leiden 2012) 637–9.

[4] See generally ibid, 136–48, 153–60, and 170–8.

The substantive regimes of the territorial sea, contiguous zone, and continental shelf remain largely identical to those recognized under the Geneva Conventions. Hence, through the combination of long-standing State practice resulting in the development of customary international law, and now conventional law, there has been relative stability in these zones. Navigational rights and freedoms within the territorial sea and international straits have traditionally raised sensitivities, and will continue to do so, as States expand their national security concerns to encompass an ever increasing range of old and new activities (Chapter 26). However, the balance that the law of the sea has traditionally maintained between coastal State sovereignty and navigational rights and freedoms of maritime States (Chapters 6 and 24) has proven to be resilient under the LOSC and should remain so in the future. In comparison to other maritime zones, the contiguous zone has not achieved the same level of coastal State endorsement. This may be due to the narrowly defined maritime enforcement focus of that zone, being limited to customs, fiscal, immigration, and sanitary matters, and the fact that it overlaps with the EEZ and continental shelf. Nevertheless, State practice has highlighted some robust examples of the contiguous zone being utilized to assist in law enforcement.[5] As notions of security continue to expand, coastal States may increasingly also look to the contiguous zone to provide an additional buffer to their sovereign interests in the territorial sea and to enhance their maritime security.

Sovereign rights over the continental shelf are clearly articulated under the LOSC. However, to a degree, the interaction between the EEZ and the continental shelf and the all-encompassing bundle of sovereign rights and jurisdiction granted to coastal States over the water column, seabed, and subsoil, from the outer limit of the territorial sea to the 200-nm limit, through Parts V and VI of the LOSC, mean that coastal States have very extensive substantive rights in this area. Nevertheless, one point of distinction is the continental shelf beyond 200 nm which intersects with the high seas. In this regard, Article 82 of the LOSC and its mechanism anticipating payments and contributions to the States Parties through the International Seabed Authority by coastal States exploiting living resources beyond 200 nm looms as one of the more contentious provisions of the law of the sea.

The substantive regime of the EEZ has been one of the more contested developments arising from the LOSC, no doubt partly due to the way in which the EEZ emerged from State practice framed around claims to exclusive fishing zones and the legacy of this process and the rapidity with which the EEZ was endorsed by States following the conclusion of the LOSC but at a time when the convention had yet to enter into force. Particular challenges have arisen with respect to

---

[5] See for an example of Australia's use of its contiguous zone to interdict vessels carrying asylum seekers en route to Australia: Senate Standing Committee on Foreign Affairs, Defence and Trade (Australia), *Inquiry into the Breach of Indonesian Territorial Waters* (Australian Parliament Canberra 2014).

conformity in EEZ State practice over matters such as coastal State laws regarding fishing and conservation of marine living resources, protection, and management of the EEZ marine environment, and EEZ marine scientific research, which in turn have raised issues with respect to navigational rights and freedoms, and maritime regulation and enforcement (Chapters 8 and 25). Not surprisingly, coastal State regulation and management of the EEZ has featured prominently in cases before the International Tribunal for the Law of the Sea (ITLOS), and there remain on-going concerns over the phenomenon of 'creeping jurisdiction'. While there are legitimate concerns that some coastal States are seeking to extend aspects of territorial sea sovereignty into the adjoining EEZ, these positions have been contested by maritime powers through both actions at sea, and diplomatic and legal means. Given the incentives for the international community to maintain the freedom of navigation within the EEZ, it has to be anticipated that assertions of sovereignty and excessive jurisdiction in the EEZ will continue to be challenged. Nevertheless, creeping jurisdiction remains a legitimate cause for concern as highlighted by the actions of the Russian Federation in the 'Arctic Sunrise' case[6] and China's practices in the South China Sea.

2.3 Interaction of maritime zones

The modern law of the sea under the LOSC provides for different levels of interaction between maritime zones, the most prominent of which are the EEZ/continental shelf, continental shelf beyond 200 nm/high seas, and the Area/high seas. The interaction between the EEZ/continental shelf is already an element in some maritime boundary delimitations (Chapter 12), and also functionally an issue where the Part V and VI regimes intersect (Chapter 8). As exploration and exploitation of the continental shelf beyond 200 nm become more common, the interaction between that regime and the high seas will also become more pronounced than it currently is, and it raises distinctive issues that do not exist where the EEZ and continental shelf are conterminous to 200 nm. A similar dynamic will also arise in the context of operations conducted within the Area and the high seas. This intermingling of maritime zones is a consequence of how the LOSC divides ocean space between coastal States, maritime States and the international community more generally. It adds an additional complexity to the law of the sea that has only gradually begun to be appreciated and has the potential to create future tensions as use of the oceans becomes more congested by multiple users.

---

[6] *'Arctic Sunrise' (Kingdom of the Netherlands v Russian Federation)*, Order of the International Tribunal for the Law of the Sea (22 November 2013).

3 Actors and Institutions: The Future of Ocean Managers

The complexity of oceans governance is, at least in part, a consequence of the diverse and, increasingly, fragmented nature of the actors and institutions responsible for or otherwise involved in oceans governance. As demonstrated in Chapters 13 and 14 of this *Handbook*, the traditional ocean actors—coastal, port, and flag States—continue to maintain primary responsibility for the implementation and enforcement of the law of the sea. Nevertheless, the balance of the power between flag States and coastal/port States has undoubtedly shifted from the former to the latter over the last two decades of the development of the law of the sea and this trend seems set to continue. As discussed in Chapter 13, port State jurisdiction in particular is no longer confined to limited regulatory spheres (such as safety of shipping) but is now more comprehensive in scope, applying to activities associated with fishing and marine pollution, for example. Moreover, port State control in many regions is developing from a right into an obligation, and is increasingly founded on a clear legal mandate, developed in both global and regional instruments (Chapter 13), as well as on existing principles of customary international law. The developments in port State control powers does not, however, diminish the responsibility of flag States for their vessels and an undoubted parallel trend over the same period has been to develop more detailed rules designed to enhance flag State responsibility (Chapter 14). This development has been particularly noticeable in the context of fisheries management following the adoption of the 1995 United Nations Fish Stocks Agreement (FSA), and is likely to be explored further in the pending ITLOS Advisory Opinion on the responsibility of flag States of illegal, unreported, and unregulated (IUU) fishing in the waters of other States (Chapter 14).[7]

As noted in Chapter 14, the binary approach to developing the law of the sea—based on flag State jurisdiction or spatial control—is no longer adequate. Today, a plethora of global and regional organizations and institutions contribute to the development of oceans governance in terms of its substantive content, implementation, and enforcement. The LOSC itself establishes institutions intended to manage the Area (the ISA), the process of extended continental shelf delineation (CLCS) and disputes (ITLOS) (Chapter 17). The latter institution in particular, together with the ICJ and the dispute settlement mechanisms provided for under the LOSC, have notably and substantively contributed to the development of the law of the sea over the last 40 years through international adjudication and arbitration, especially in the

---

[7] Further details on the 2013 *Request for an Advisory Opinion Submitted by the Sub-regional Fisheries Commission (SRFC)* can be found at <http://www.itlos.org/index.php?id=252#c1276>. It should be noted that the jurisdiction of ITLOS has been contested in the case.

areas of maritime delimitation and marine environmental protection (Chapter 18). Nevertheless, while the LOSC permits the UN Secretary General to convene a meeting of the parties,[8] this body does not function as the supreme body of the LOSC regime and there is significant disagreement between the parties as to what role this body should play, particularly with respect to the substantive development of the Convention (Chapter 17). Rather, the UN General Assembly provides oversight of law of the sea matters, including the implementation of the LOSC as is comprehensively described in Chapter 16. In addition to the annual UN Secretary General reports on oceans and the law of the sea and, since the adoption of the FSA, fisheries, and the associated General Assembly resolutions, other subsidiary institutions and processes have been established by the UN in order to further oceans governance. These include the UN Open-ended Informal Consultative Process on the Law of the Sea (established in 1999), the Regular Process (established in 2002), and the Biological Diversity Beyond Areas of National Jurisdiction (BBNJ) Working Group (established in 2004; mandate reviewed in 2011) (Chapter 16). Although the UN General Assembly has quasi-universal participation and thus provides an appropriate global forum for the development of the law of the sea, the detachment of much of the UN's institutional infrastructure from the Convention itself has implications for the evolution of the LOSC as a treaty (Chapter 3). In contrast to other treaties—particularly those operating in the sphere of international environmental law—the LOSC has not been developed through formal amendment or by means of interpretation using decisions and resolutions adopted by the parties. Instead, it is more heavily reliant on State practice and the development of initiatives within UN and other fora (such as the UN conferences on the environment) for its evolution and this inevitably challenges its ability to maintain contemporary relevance. This has proven particularly problematic in the areas of maritime security and marine environmental protection.

Cooperation between the LOSC and other institutions and regimes was provided for in the Convention since its inception and reflects a particularly far-sighted aspect of the regime; one that is now increasingly reflected in other areas of international law, most notably, international environmental law. The LOSC seldom identifies its cooperative partners by name but rather, refers to 'competent international organisations'. The International Maritime Organization (IMO) (Chapter 19) constitutes arguably the most important partner organization but others include the Food and Agriculture Organization (FAO), the UN Security Council, regional seas regimes (see Chapters 27, 29, and 30), regional fisheries management organizations (RFMOs) (Chapter 20), and biodiversity and other conservation-related regimes (Chapter 22). A significant challenge to effective oceans governance is managing the connections between these diverse bodies and ensuring regulatory coherence across

---

[8] 1982 United Nations Convention on the Law of the Sea, Art 319(2)(e) (hereinafter LOSC).

all regimes. In response to this challenge, the UN General Assembly developed two initiatives designed to improve cooperation between bodies with oceans-related mandates: the Oceans and Coastal Areas Network (UN-Oceans) (established in 2002) and the Ocean Compact (established 2012). To date, however, it is unclear that either process has made much progress in providing a platform for collaboration or a mechanism for improving cooperation across regimes.

The law of the sea has long engaged with private actors with respect to its development, implementation and, to a lesser extent, enforcement. These actors range from national maritime law associations to ship owners and operators to private industry bodies associated with shipping standards or insurance. This tradition continues within the LOSC, which provides for rights and obligations in respect of private corporations involved in mining activities in the Area (Chapter 11) including a limited right to directly petition the Disputes Chamber of the ITLOS. More ambiguously, Article 292(2) of the LOSC permits an application for the prompt release of a vessel to be made 'on behalf of the flag State of the vessel' although in practice this right has been limited to permitting a private operator to engage counsel with the permission of the flag State (Chapter 18). The participation of private entities in the law of the sea continues to both enhance and challenge oceans governance. For example, in some areas of fisheries management market based mechanisms relying on private entities are being developed in order to support enforcement of conservation measures and are operating in addition to port State control (Chapter 14). Less positively and of increasing concern is the rise in ship owners and, in some cases (such as Somalia), coastal States engaging private security operators to protect commercial, resource, or other interests to the extent that these operators are, in essence, carrying out security functions traditionally performed by States. Different but equally serious concerns for oceans governance are raised by the activities of private actors in protesting both legitimate and illegitimate activities of States, as exemplified by the activities of Sea Shepherd in respect of Japanese whaling activities in the Southern Ocean[9] and Greenpeace in respect of Russian oil and gas activities in the Arctic.[10] The increasingly direct engagement of private entities with the law of the sea reflects a more general trend in relation to the participation of non-State entities within the international legal system but the fact that these private participants often operate beyond physical and, in some cases, jurisdictional reach of States creates a very particular challenge for effective oceans governance.

---

[9] In 2014, the ICJ found the Southern Ocean Japanese scientific whaling programme to be contrary to the 1946 International Convention on the Regulation of Whaling. See *Whaling in the Antarctic (Australia v Japan: New Zealand Intervening)*, Judgment of the International Court of Justice (31 March 2014).

[10] See *'Arctic Sunrise' Case*, n 6. An Annex VII Tribunal has also been established. See *Arctic Sunrise Arbitration (Netherlands v Russia)* Permanent Court of Arbitration, Case No 2014–02 (pending), available at <http://www.pca-cpa.org/showpage.asp?pag_id=1556>.

During both the negotiations for the 1958 Geneva Conventions and the LOSC the idea of establishing an institution with overall responsibility for all oceans issues was discussed and rejected (see Chapter 18). Concerns were expressed over the practicality of establishing one organization with such a broad mandate and the risk that it would lead to the development of uniform—and potentially inappropriate—standards across diverse sectors. These reservations remain valid today, but the absence of a comprehensive governance body undoubtedly creates challenges for oceans governance and the development of the law of the sea. Issues and activities risk falling through gaps in regulation between regimes or may be subject to multiple—and possibly conflicting—regimes. Geo-engineering and ocean acidification provide current examples of activities/issues that occupy the interstices between oceans and climate regimes. What is needed for twenty-first-century oceans governance is much more active coordination and cooperation between States, organizations, institutions, and private participants in the development, implementation, and enforcement of ocean-related norms.

4 Substantive Regimes: The Future for Global Oceans Management

The LOSC remains a farsighted framework for global oceans management in recognizing that all major oceans issues intersect and need to be addressed in a coordinated way by the international community. The Preamble to the LOSC acknowledges this explicitly, noting that States parties to the LOSC are '[c]onscious that the problems of ocean space are closely interrelated and need to be considered as a whole.'[11] Unlike the terrestrial environment, which, for most management purposes, is two-dimensional and demarcated by defined boundaries, the fluidity, connectivity, and three-dimensionality of the marine environment presents major governance challenges. The remoteness of many ocean areas has also been a management problem throughout the history of the law of the sea, and distinctive responses to particular activities such as piracy (Chapter 37) and pollution (Chapter 23) have had to be developed to ensure that activities well beyond the coast are effectively regulated. Flag, coastal, and port State jurisdiction have all been deployed to assert control over these and other activities, while at the same time safeguarding traditional navigational rights and freedoms (Chapter 24). The extent and validity of these assertions of jurisdiction are of course contingent upon the development and

---

[11] LOSC, n 8, Preamble, Third Recital (emphasis in original).

consolidation of substantive law of the sea regimes across a range of specific oceans issue areas. These main substantive regimes are addressed in Chapters 20 to 26 and 33 to 38 of the *Handbook*, and in respect of each of these areas, it is possible to identify several future challenges for global oceans management.

Regional fisheries management (Chapter 20), and the sustainable and equitable use of marine living resources more generally (Chapter 22), remains an area of unfinished business for the law of the sea, particularly so for high seas fisheries. Global indicators of fisheries sustainability (the proportion of species fully exploited or over exploited) have stubbornly failed to show improvement for well over a decade, and there are many individual species that have particular vulnerabilities (Chapter 35). Yet for all the difficulties encountered by States in managing marine living resources individually and collectively, it must be acknowledged that since the LOSC was concluded there has been a substantial improvement in marine living resource governance. The FSA, and an ever-growing collection of RFMOs, have curbed some of the worst excesses in offshore fisheries. But there remains scant evidence that fisheries managers are anticipating the 'wild card' of climate change, which is raising ocean temperatures, changing circulation patterns, and causing ocean acidification (Chapter 34). Most coastal States and RFMOS remain concerned with immediate and pressing management challenges (including illegal fishing) and while this is understandable there is also a need to prepare for the likelihood of significant disruption to the productivity of some fisheries during this century. This suggests a need for fisheries managers to take seriously the precautionary principle and ecosystem approach.

Describing climate change as a 'wild card' may be accurate in relation to some of its environmental impacts that may occur abruptly, but it is also causing more gradual changes, such as sea level rise. As global sea levels rise by multiple metres over the twenty-first and successive centuries it will be necessary to revisit the LOSC's baseline rules, and probably also the regime applicable to islands (Chapter 34). The LOSC seeks to contribute to 'a just and equitable international economic order',[12] particularly for developing countries, but this objective will be undermined for many States if they lose their existing maritime entitlements.

More so than fisheries, the control of marine pollution (Chapter 23) has been an oceans management domain in which significant success has been achieved in regulating human impacts upon the marine environment. Vessel-source pollutants and the ocean dumping of hazardous wastes, two major environmental issues of the 1970s, have largely been brought under control and subjected to international oversight through the IMO. The IMO (Chapter 19) has demonstrated a capacity to advance legal protection of the marine environment by balancing the interests of States, vessel owners and operators, and insurers, and side-stepping conventional

---

[12] Ibid, Preamble, Fifth Recital.

rules of unanimity in the laying down of stricter international standards. However, while the 1973 International Convention for the Prevention of Pollution, as modified by the Protocol of 1978 (MARPOL) and related pollution control regimes adopted under the auspices of the IMO have been enormously successful in stopping the disposal of hazardous pollutants at sea, they have had no impact upon the largest sources of ocean pollution—those from the atmosphere and the land. The pervasive presence of plastics throughout the marine environment is one of the most visible and intractable manifestations of this problem.

The on-going failure to control land-based and atmospheric pollution of the marine environment illustrates the reality that in the contemporary law of the sea external threats and impacts can undermine the achievements that have been made 'on water' through substantive management regimes applicable to the oceans. This is a hallmark of the Anthropocene, the current geological era defined by the planetary scale of human interference with environmental systems, including the oceans.[13] Addressing extrinsic impacts upon the seas is one of the most significant on-going and future challenges for global oceans governance, and requires much closer coordination between the LOSC and other key global frameworks that have a bearing on oceans issues.

A vital catalyst for greater cooperation and coordination to respond to global ocean threats will be more and better marine scientific research (Chapter 25). This is acknowledged by the on-going United Nations World Ocean Assessment, which seeks 'to improve understanding of the oceans and to develop a global mechanism for delivering science-based information to decision makers and public'.[14] The LOSC seeks to promote scientific understanding of the marine environment that will further the objectives of the Convention including, but not limited to, its environmental protection goals. However, while there could be no objection to this general goal, the marine scientific research regime of the LOSC (Part XIII) has been the subject of some controversy in certain respects. States have for instance taken different views as to what constitutes legitimate marine scientific research within the EEZ (eg whether military surveying of the ocean floor of a coastal State's EEZ is research covered by Part XIII). Another controversial issue is how Part XIII, and the LOSC more generally, accommodates marine bioprospecting (Chapter 36). Particularly uncertain is the status of bioprospecting beyond national jurisdiction, and this is one of the key issues being considered in discussions on a possible LOSC implementing agreement to address the conservation and sustainable use of marine biodiversity in areas beyond national jurisdiction (ABNJ) (Chapter 33).

The most significant response to the realization that oceans issues are closely interrelated (and also intersect with coastal front and land management issues) has

---

[13] Davor Vidas, 'The Anthropocene and the International Law of the Sea' (2011) 369 *Philosophical Transactions of the Royal Society A* 909.

[14] See United Nations World Ocean Assessment website, at <www.worldoceanassessment.org>.

been the development of integrated approaches to oceans governance (Chapter 21). 'Integrated oceans management' takes the key direction of the LOSC Preamble, to address ocean issues holistically, and imbues this abstract principle with real operational meaning. This is achieved through established tools and techniques of environmental management that have been applied to terrestrial and coastal ecosystems, including the designation of protected areas. Marine spatial planning is central to this integrated approach, and seeks to consider and manage the full range of activities taking place within maritime domains demarcated by reference to their ecosystemic characteristics, rather than arbitrary jurisdictional boundaries. Integrated oceans management has in many contexts led to more appropriate regulation of marine spaces, including through the creation of marine protected areas. Importantly, it is also prospective in its orientation, with environmental impact assessment and the precautionary approach requiring decision-makers to anticipate and mitigate the environmental threats from planned activities, rather than seeking to address their consequences after the event.

Although highly desirable in theory, in practice, integrated oceans management has yet to be widely and successfully implemented by States. Moreover, to be truly effective, integrated oceans management needs to be scaled-up from coastal to regional levels, particularly in those ocean spaces that attract the very heaviest use. It is very likely that in the twenty-first century a greater emphasis on integrated oceans management will see the expansion in marine protected areas, from the desultory two per cent of ocean space that they currently embrace. However, these new marine parks will fail to live up to their promise if they are mere 'paper parks' that are not accompanied by robust management systems, or if they are declared over 'residual' areas with limited potential for commercial use.[15]

Better and more integrated assessment and management of pressures upon the marine environment is arguably the predominant theme in the contemporary law of the sea. It is rivalled only by the enduring concern of the law of the sea with security questions. Concerns about maritime security (Chapter 26), which can be defined as 'the protection of a State's land and maritime territory, infrastructure, economy, environment and society from certain harmful acts occurring at sea',[16] have animated many aspects of the LOSC's elaborate regime for jurisdiction and enforcement in coastal State maritime zones. This regime seeks to balance coastal State interests in security along the coastal front with the legitimate interests of other States in the freedom of navigation, including for naval vessels.

Although the LOSC entered into force after the fall of the Berlin Wall, the text was negotiated and concluded against the backdrop of the Cold War in which global

---

[15] BS Halpern, 'Conservation: Making Marine Protected Areas Work' (2014) 506 *Nature* 167.

[16] N Klein, J Mossop, and DR Rothwell, 'Australia, New Zealand and Maritime Security' in N Klein, J Mossop, and DR Rothwell (eds), *Maritime Security: International Law and Policy Perspectives from Australia and New Zealand* (Routledge Oxford 2010) 1, 8.

security issues were relatively well defined and understood. However, contemporary maritime security concerns have taken on new and complex dimensions as a result of the rising power of some non-State terrorist groups and the emergence of 'rogue' States. Military activities by States in the EEZs of other States has also been a flashpoint, as seen in several incidents between China and the United States over the presence of United States naval and air force assets in the Chinese EEZ. Yet, despite these new and evolving security challenges, the LOSC framework has functioned remarkably well, and even developments such as the Proliferation Security Initiative, advanced by the United States following the 9/11 terrorist attacks, have not stepped beyond accepted rules of exclusive flag State jurisdiction.

In sum, the practice within substantive law of the sea regimes has shown that the LOSC has largely operated as it was designed to. It has provided a framework for cooperation and legal innovation, while also limiting the extent to which these developments in the law can exceed the central compromises achieved in 1982.

5 Regional Oceans Management: An Indispensable Instrument with Mixed Results

The implementation of the LOSC and other global instruments first and foremost is a responsibility of individual States. They have to ensure that the rights and obligations contained in these instruments are translated into national legislation and policies. This concerns such critical issues as the definition of the spatial extent of coastal State jurisdiction and the substantive regime applicable to coastal State zones. Boundary delimitation, another issue that is critical to the national interest of coastal States, mostly takes place at the bilateral level. With this caveat in mind, the analysis in Chapters 27 to 32 of the *Handbook* makes clear that the implementation of the law of the sea at the same time is very much dependent on regional cooperation. Owing to the transboundary nature of many activities and processes in the marine environment, these can only be effectively managed where States agree on coordinated responses. To be successful regional cooperation, just like the implementation of the LOSC and other global instruments, depends on follow-up by the participating States.

Apart from looking at regional cooperation, which will be considered subsequently, Chapters 27 to 32 discuss the practice of States in relation to the definition of coastal State jurisdiction. This analysis indicates a chequered pattern. Most coastal States adhere to the jurisdictional framework set out in the LOSC, but there is little indication that this is explained by their participation in regional cooperation on oceans management and the law of the sea. Similarly, divergences from the LOSC regime seem mostly explained by the interests of individual States and not their location in a specific region. There are no markedly regional patterns as regards divergence from the LOSC framework. At least a certain measure of divergence is witnessed in all regions of the world and no region displays a significantly higher level of divergence as compared to the global average. At the same time, the practice of individual States may be affected by their location in a specific region or their participation in a regional regime. For instance, the Antarctic claimant States have coordinated their approach to the implementation of Article 76 of the LOSC because of their common interest in maintaining the stability of the ATS while at the same time avoiding the weakening of their position as claimant States. In the Mediterranean Sea, regional factors explain why most coastal States in the past did not establish an EEZ. The western coast of Latin America, which is not discussed in the regional chapters of this *Handbook*—provides another example of a coordinated approach through the adoption of the 200-nm zone concept in the late 1940s and early 1950s, well in advance of the general acceptance of the EEZ.[17] At the same time, the concordance of interests was not complete as 'the interest related to the freedom of navigation in the zone was different'.[18] However, even States that have substantive cooperation on other issues may not be able to define common positions on the law of the sea. For instance, as is pointed out by Long in Chapter 29, the Member States of the then European Economic Community at the Third United Nations Conference on the Law of the Sea (UNCLOS III) 'had too many divergent interests to forge a strong regional identity on the substantive and procedural matters under negotiation'.

The discussion of bilateral delimitation practice indicates commonalities between the different regions. The (expected) presence of in particular hydrocarbon resources is a significant factor explaining the conclusion of many bilateral delimitation agreements. Bilateral considerations are instrumental to shaping the outcome in individual cases and the regional context in general has little impact on shaping outcomes, apart from instances in which States take into account—or sometimes wilfully disregard—the position and interests of third States in defining the extent of their bilateral boundaries.

Chapters 27 to 32 indicate that coastal geography is a main determinant in shaping the area of application of cooperative mechanisms. In particular, semi-enclosed seas that are only linked to other ocean areas through narrow straits have been a clear focal point for regional cooperation.[19] In the case of sea areas facing the

---

[17] For a discussion, see eg F Orrego Vicuña, *The Exclusive Economic Zone; Regime and Legal Nature under International Law* (Cambridge University Press Cambridge 1989) 3–6.
[18] Ibid, 6.
[19] This approach is also supported by Part IX of the LOSC on enclosed and semi-enclosed seas.

open ocean, the definition of the seaward extent of regional cooperation may be more arbitrary. However, the employment of the Antarctic Convergence in the framework of the 1980 Convention on the Conservation of Antarctic Marine Living Resources (CAMLR Convention) proves that this may not necessarily be the case. The political geography of a region is another major and, in some instances, the primary factor in shaping regional cooperation. The clearest illustration of this point is provided by the Antarctic Treaty System (ATS) that is a result of the diverging views of participating States on the territorial status of Antarctica. The development of this regime has always had to accommodate the opposing views on this question. Other examples are provided by the North-East Atlantic and the South China Sea. In the former case, the European Union's growing involvement in oceans management has had a major role in shaping regional cooperation between its member States and between those member States and third States. In the case of the South China Sea, the disputes over the Paracel Islands, Spratly Islands and Scarborough Reef, and the status and delimitation of the South China Sea, have largely frustrated regional cooperation. The main challenge facing the coastal States in the South China Sea—and this is equally relevant to other regions faced with pervasive maritime disputes—is managing these disputes in such a way that regional cooperation is not largely ineffective.[20]

Chapters 27 to 32 of the *Handbook* illustrate the great variety in regional cooperation as regards institutional set-up and substantive coverage. One fundamental division is between treaty-based cooperation, entailing the existence of legally binding obligations, and cooperation based in action plans or other informal mechanisms. Although the former may lead to a greater compliance-pull, the regional chapters indicate that there is no one on one relationship between institutional set-up and regime effectiveness. The regional chapters indicate that the substantive outputs produced by regional cooperation differ enormously. The 1992 Convention for the Protection of the Marine Environment of the North-East Atlantic (OSPAR Convention) and its Annexes comprehensively cover sea-based activities—with the exception of fisheries and navigation, which are regulated in other international fora—and the OSPAR Commission and its subsidiary bodies have produced a plethora of instruments based on the Convention and its Annexes. Cooperation is less advanced in many other regions. This may be explained by issues such as capacity and the urgency to regulate sea-based activities. Cooperation in many other regions, moreover, is of more recent origin than in the North-East Atlantic. As the analysis in relation to, among others, the Arctic, the Caribbean Sea and the

---

[20] Interestingly, even though ASEAN is a major regional institution it has had little capacity to engage with China on law of the sea matters. This may be explained by the national security focus of these matters in the South China Sea—as opposed to the absence of such a focus in the North-East Atlantic—and the fact that ASEAN's member States have different positions and interests in this respect.

Indian Ocean indicates, there is a continuing development of regional cooperative mechanisms. Those new mechanisms may enhance future cooperation.

Regional cooperation is not necessarily limited to the coastal States of a specific region. For instance, the LOSC's provisions on high seas fisheries indicate that cooperation has to involve all States whose nationals exploit the resources of a given area,[21] whether they come from the region or the other side of the globe. Maritime security is another matter that has led to the involvement of States from outside of the region concerned because of their interests in, for instance, merchant shipping that may be affected. On the other hand, cooperation on the protection of the marine environment in most instances is limited to the coastal and other relevant States of the particular region. The polar regions seem to be outliers in this respect, having attracted more than average interest from extra-regional States. In the case of Antarctica, this can be explained by the absence of undisputed coastal State jurisdiction and the common heritage/common interests characteristics of Antarctica and the ATS. The Arctic is not materially different from other marine regions as far as its political geography and law of the sea is concerned: there are no significant sovereignty disputes and coastal States have extended their jurisdiction in accordance with the law of the sea. The difference in the amount of outside interest in this case is likely explained by the rapid changes the region is facing due to climate change and the opportunities this may offer in terms of shipping and resource development.

One challenge for regional cooperation on the protection and preservation of the marine environment is the growing need for addressing the threats to ABNJ. This will require a larger involvement from extra-regional States and actors such as the ISA. For the moment, no uniform approach exists in this respect. In the future, two options seem to be available: the adoption of an overarching framework at the global level with implementation at the regional level, or, in the absence of agreement at the global level, a piecemeal approach centred on cooperation at the regional level.

The analysis in Chapters 27 to 32 points out that some regional frameworks for cooperation lag behind the development of the law at the global level in both fisheries management and the protection and the preservation of the marine environment. To some extent, this is explained by the fact that it may take considerable time to update a treaty-based regime. This seems to be confirmed by the fact that newly developed instruments in general take into account recent developments at the global level. However, the prolonged reaction time of some regional regimes suggests that the time needed to adjust a constitutive treaty may not be the only explanatory factor.

---

[21] LOSC, n 8, Art 118.

Regional cooperation is bound to remain essential to the effective implementation of the law of the sea and sustainable oceans management. The regional chapters of this *Handbook* point out that this cooperation in many cases is suboptimal. Some improvement may be possible through further guidance developed at the global level and outside assistance to the regions concerned. However, the main factors contributing to the success or failure of regional cooperation are to be found at that level and may include among others the overall political relationship between the States concerned, cultural and socio-economic divergences, the presence or absence of pervasive territorial or maritime disputes, the significance accorded to and prioritizing of oceans management by individual States, the effective implementation of regional instruments by individual States, the nature and extent of sea-based activities and financial resources and capacity.

6 The Law of the Sea Convention: What Future for the Constitution of the Oceans?

The continued relevance of the LOSC will first and foremost be determined by its capacity to deal with new developments relating to the oceans and human activities taking place in them.[22] Chapters 1, 2, and 3, dealing respectively with the history of the law of the sea, the LOSC, and the mechanisms to adapt the LOSC to changed circumstances and regime interaction, paint a distinctly optimistic picture in this respect. In contrast to the four 1958 Geneva Conventions on the law of the sea that preceded the LOSC, the latter is much more comprehensive in nature. Whereas the Geneva Conventions failed to address a number of salient issues in a satisfactory manner, such as the breadth of the territorial sea, the regime of archipelagic waters, and the rights of States over fisheries adjacent to their coasts, the negotiators of the LOSC were successful in addressing all major issues that were on the agenda of UNCLOS III.[23]

---

[22] At a more fundamental level, the future of the LOSC is tied up with the continued relevance of the State-centred organization of the international community. Notwithstanding the increasing relevance of non-State actors, it is submitted that this will not affect the focus on the State as the primary actor under public international law, including the law of the sea, in the foreseeable future.

[23] Admittedly, some unfinished business of the Conference was further considered by the Preparatory Commission for the International Sea Bed Authority and for the International Tribunal for the Law of the Sea that operated from 1983 to 1994 and in two cases a satisfactory solution was only achieved with the adoption of the two implementation agreements to the LOSC on respectively seabed mining and the regime for fisheries of highly migratory and straddling fish stocks in the first half of the 1990s.

The comprehensive nature of the LOSC, taking on board and balancing the interests of many different States, should guarantee that the basic jurisdictional framework it has defined will be resilient. In fact, more than 30 years after the adoption of the Convention and 20 years after its entry into force, there have been only limited and, to date, unsuccessful challenges to this basic framework. Another indicator in this respect is that treaties dealing with specific subjects in general defer to the jurisdictional framework contained in the LOSC. The broad participation in the LOSC, albeit falling short of the near universal participation of some other conventions, is another measure of its success.[24] As the position of the United States, which accepts that most of the LOSC reflects customary law, illustrates, the existence of a significant number of non-parties does not necessarily pose a fundamental challenge to the Convention.

As Chapters 2 and 3 of the *Handbook* indicate, the framework character and incorporation of other regimes through rules of reference make the LOSC flexible and allow it to adapt to changed circumstances without the need to renegotiate the package deal that the Convention represents. Chapter 3, moreover, points out that the Convention has been adapted through subsequent State practice, in this way circumventing the cumbersome amendment procedures of the Convention. The two implementation agreements to the LOSC have also been successful in adapting the Convention without resorting to these procedures.

Another way of looking at the future of the LOSC is considering whether a different comprehensive regime could successfully replace the Convention. There are a number of considerations that indicate that this is not a feasible option. First, as Churchill points out in Chapter 2, '[a]t the present time there appears to be no desire in the international community to replace the LOSC, or even radically to amend it.'

Second, the experience of negotiating the LOSC suggests that the development of an instrument to replace the LOSC would be extremely cumbersome. The negotiations on the LOSC had their inception in the 1960s, leading to the adoption of the LOSC in 1982, but could be argued to have only been completed in 1994 with the Implementation Agreement on seabed mining, which allowed broad participation in the Convention. The current debate on the regime of ABNJ in the framework of the UN General Assembly, which has already lasted for some 10 years without any certainty about the eventual end result, is a further case in point.

---

[24] Still, thirteen coastal States, foremost among them the United States, are not parties to the LOSC. See United Nations Division for Ocean Affairs and the Law of the Sea (DOALOS), *Status of the United Nations Convention on the Law of the Sea, of the Agreement relating to the implementation of Part XI of the Convention and of the Agreement for the implementation of the provisions of the Convention relating to the conservation and management of straddling fish stocks and highly migratory fish stocks; Table recapitulating the status of the Convention and of the related Agreements, as at 10 January 2014*, available at <http://www.un.org/Depts/los/reference_files/status2010.pdf>. In addition, 17 landlocked States are not a party to the LOSC: ibid.

Third, there simply does not seem to be room for a major overhaul of the current jurisdictional framework contained in the LOSC. This point is aptly captured by Treves in Chapter 1:

> With necessary additions, such as the notion of the common heritage, the traditional legal framework and technique could adapt to encompass the coastal States' claims to exclusive rights over broad areas of the sea and combine these claims with the needs of international communication and with those of intensified and more institutionalized cooperation for the exploitation of common resources and the protection of the marine environment which characterize the law of the sea of the final decades of the twentieth century and of today.

The mainstay of the current regime is the compromise between the security and economic interests of coastal States and the needs of international communication. Unless there is a major shift in the forces supporting this compromise, the likelihood of a significantly different regime replacing the LOSC is close to zero. Intensified and further institutionalized cooperation can be accomplished within the current LOSC framework.

Although a radical break with the LOSC regime seems to be beyond our time horizon, piecemeal adaptation of the Convention has been taking place from the time of its adoption. In itself, such adaptation is necessary to ensure the continued relevance of the Convention. As Buga remarks in Chapter 3 in discussing modification by subsequent practice, such adaptation:

> ...helps strike a balance between the core concepts of the LOSC and the contemporary norms that have emerged since its inception, in other treaty regimes and in the realm of custom. If approached with due caution...subsequent practice can contribute to developing the Convention in accordance with the evolving needs of the international community....

A closer look at some of the current developments in relation to the LOSC assists in answering the question whether piecemeal adaptation might in the longer run pose a threat to the effectiveness of the LOSC or some of its specific parts. In this connection, the following topics will be considered: the spatial extent of areas within national jurisdiction, the substantive regime of areas within national jurisdiction, the regime for mining in the Area, the possibility of future implementation agreements to the LOSC and dispute settlement under Part XV of the Convention.

One obvious point of controversy in relation to the spatial extent of maritime zones concerns the practice of many States on straight baselines. The widespread and longstanding practice deviating from Article 7 of the LOSC has drawn protests from both neighbouring States and States with significant maritime interests. States in general seem to have been successful in managing their differences over straight baselines without major conflict. After the 1951 *Anglo-Norwegian Fisheries* case,[25] which settled the general law on this matter, States have not invoked third party

---

[25] *Anglo-Norwegian Fisheries*, n 2.

settlement to address the legality of specific baselines.[26] In that light, it seems likely that the current situation will persist. The continued existence of seemingly inconsistent practice could contribute to fostering doubts about the normative pull of the Convention.

Projected sea-level rise will impact on the location of baselines, negatively affecting the extent of coastal State jurisdiction and, in the case of certain small island, States, may even threaten their very existence. The LOSC, which to a large extent accepts the ambulatory nature of baselines and the resultant outer limits of maritime zones, currently is not equipped to deal with this matter. In the light of the equities that would be involved in protecting the law of the sea interest of in particular small island developing States, this would seem to be an issue that could be successfully addressed without calling into question the broader framework of the LOSC.

The interpretation and application of Article 121(3) of the LOSC, like that of Article 7 on straight baselines, has led to controversy. What is most striking about Article 121(3) of the LOSC is the seeming lack of protest against apparently inconsistent State practice outside of the framework of bilateral boundary delimitations. Apparently, individual States in general have little incentive to raise this issue to prevent encroachments on the commons of the high seas and the Area.[27] The open-textured nature of Article 121(3) moreover makes it difficult for a State to unequivocally argue non-compliance. Whether the current trend in respect of Article 121(3)—practically divesting it of any meaning—is reversible is doubtful.

The implementation of Article 76 of the LOSC has proven to be much more complex than was envisaged during its negotiation at UNCLOS III. Two aspects of the implementation process could eventually prove to be controversial. Coastal States may become dissatisfied with the CLCS, for instance because it is felt that the Commission is arrogating to itself an interpretative power that rests with coastal States. It is conceivable that coastal States in that case might be tempted to seek to circumvent the requirements imposed by Article 76. The reverse could also be the case. States without a continental shelf beyond 200 nm might feel that the Commission gives undue consideration to the interests of broad margin States. Major disagreements concerning the implementation of Article 76 might be more disruptive than some of the other issue areas identified above, due to the perception that Article 76 already has made major inroads into the extent of the Area. On the other hand, the limited interest of most States without a continental shelf beyond 200 nm in the implementation of Article 76 thus far, suggests that concern about encroachment on the Area will not spur States into action.

---

[26] Straight baselines have been in issue in cases concerning the delimitation of maritime boundaries. Courts and tribunals in general have taken care to avoid ruling on the legality of straight baseline claims.

[27] A recent exception is the protest of China and South Korea against Japan's use of Okinotorishima in connection with the determination of the outer limits of its continental shelf beyond 200 nm.

Major change in the law of the sea in general has been the result of coastal States extending their maritime domain. Current trends do not suggest that there will be a major drive by coastal States to erode the balance of interests contained in the LOSC. For one thing, many important coastal States have equally or even more important maritime interests.[28] Second, the continued focus on, in particular, port State measures and cooperative schemes between States to address deficiencies in flag State implementation, attest that States prefer other avenues for resolving deficiencies in flag State enforcement than extending coastal State jurisdiction beyond the scheme contained in the LOSC. Third, major maritime powers can be expected to maintain their categorical rejection of any inroads by coastal States into what they consider to be the LOSC *acquis* concerning military uses of the oceans. Finally, the example of the 2001 UNESCO Convention on Underwater Cultural Heritage indicates that shifts in the balance between the rights of coastal States and other States in one issue area will not necessarily have an impact on other issue areas.[29]

Having fallen short of initial expectations for a long time, exploratory mining activities in the Area in the last decade have significantly increased. The prospect of actual exploitation of mineral resources in the foreseeable future ushers in a new era for the ISA. The supervisory role the ISA will have to assume in this case poses challenges for which the Authority in its present form may not be equipped. The creation of effective supervisory mechanisms will require both funding and capacity building.[30] What these mechanisms will eventually look like will depend on the interests that will be able to shape their future development. Another challenge for the ISA will be the definition of its role under the revenue sharing provisions of Articles 82 and 160(1)(g) of the LOSC. The provisions themselves provide very limited guidance and the coastal States that will have to implement Article 82 seem to have little appetite to give the Authority a significant role. A failure to properly take into account developments after the Convention's adoption in 1982 on such issues as transparency, accountability, and good governance would possibly reflect negatively on the Authority, and potentially, the LOSC itself.

The two implementation agreements to the LOSC of 1994 and 1995 on, respectively, the mining regime of the Area and straddling and highly migratory fish stocks, have been key to further developing and adapting the LOSC to changing

---

[28] The United States is a case in point. Apart from having a global naval projection, it also has the largest EEZ in the world.

[29] See Advisory Committee on Issues of Public International Law, *Advisory Report on the UNESCO Convention on the Protection of the Underwater Cultural Heritage; Translation*, Advisory Report No 21 (The Hague, December 2011) 12, available at <http://cms.webbeat.net/ContentSuite/upload/cav/doc/Report_nr._21_-_UNESCO_Convention_on_the_Protection_of_Under_Water_Cultural_Heritage(2).pdf >.

[30] LOSC, n 8, Arts 153(4) and 153(5) give the Authority significant competencies to supervise mining activities.

circumstances. There have been calls for further implementation agreements, most notably on the regime of ABNJ that is currently being considered in the framework of the UN General Assembly. Scholars have suggested that the law of the sea aspects of sea-level rise might be addressed through an implementation agreement to the LOSC.[31]

Without knowing the contours of possible future implementation agreements, it is difficult to be too specific about their potential impact on the LOSC and the law of the sea more generally. However, it is possible to identify a number of general considerations that are relevant in this respect. The 1994 Implementation Agreement on deep seabed mining might suggest that future implementation agreements could be used to effect significant change to the LOSC. However, the exceptional context of its negotiation—the pending entry into force of the LOSC without the participation of the developed world—indicates that this agreement in that sense does not provide a precedent for future implementation agreements. The FSA could be said to confirm this point. While the 1994 Agreement indicates that it takes precedence over the Convention,[32] the FSA specifies that it 'shall [not] prejudice the rights, jurisdiction and duties of States under the [LOSC]' and that it shall be applied in a manner consistent with the LOSC.[33] At the same time, it should be realized that the FSA is the result of a compromise between sharply diverging interests. Coastal States were looking for a shift in the balance between their rights and those of States fishing on the high seas. The carefully drafted compromise on this point contained in Article 7 of the Agreement might have diverged from the LOSC regime had the interests represented at the negotiations been different.

The extent of participation in an implementation agreement obviously will be an important factor in shaping its impact on the LOSC and the law of the sea generally. The experience with the FSA points to a number of relevant considerations in this respect. Contrary to the LOSC's entry into force requirement of 60 States, the FSA set this figure at 30.[34] Early entry into force of an agreement will prevent prolonged uncertainty about its status and can be expected to enhance its impact. The FSA at the same time indicates that an implementation agreement may have a significant impact even before its entry into force. It has had a major impact on the negotiation or updating of a number of agreements on regional

---

[31] See eg M Hayashi, 'Islands' Sea Areas: Effects of a Rising Sea Level' (10 June 2013) *Review of Island Studies* (translated from 'Shima no kaiiki to kaimen jōshō' (October 2012) 2(1) *Tōsho Kenkyū Journal* 74), available at <http://islandstudies.oprf-info.org/wp/wp-content/uploads/2013/06/a00003.pdf>.

[32] 1994 Agreement Relating to the Implementation of Part XI of the LOSC, Arts 1 and 2 (1994 Implementation Agreement).

[33] 1995 Agreement for the Implementation of the Provisions of the United Nations Convention on the Law of the Sea of 10 December 1982 Relating to the Conservation and Management of Straddling Fish Stocks and Highly Migratory Fish Stocks, Art 4 (hereinafter FSA).

[34] In addition, between 1982 and 1995, there had been a significant increase in the number of States.

fisheries management in the second half of the 1990s and beyond.[35] Obviously, this kind of impact is only possible if the nature of an implementation agreement allows for it. For instance, an implementation agreement on access and benefit sharing in respect of marine genetic resources likely will only be successful if it operates as an effective regime at the global level. To the contrary, in the case of an implementation agreement dealing with the law of the sea aspects of sea level rise unilateral actions of coastal States could have a decisive impact on the way in which the regime would develop. Put in general terms, an agreement setting up a multilateral regime will require broad participation, while an agreement enabling action by specific States may have a significant impact even before its entry into force.

The current participation in the 1994 Implementation Agreement and the FSA is lower than in the LOSC—in the case of the latter less than half of the parties to the LOSC.[36] The conclusion of further implementation agreements is likely to lead to a further diversification of the legal relationships between States. How this will affect the effectiveness of the law of the sea will depend on the considerations set out above.

Finally, it can be asked what the consequences of the absence of an implementation agreement would be in a case in which a significant number of States is interested in adapting or developing the jurisdictional framework of the LOSC. It would seem likely that in this case the States concerned might seek to influence the development of the law through their practice. This could lead to a more fragmented regime than an implementation agreement with limited participation. The latter could act as a focal point of practice, thus avoiding practice going beyond it.

Two recent cases of non-participation in the compulsory dispute settlement procedures of the LOSC—China and the Russian Federation in arbitration procedures started respectively by the Philippines and the Netherlands—might raise the question how this will affect the credibility and stability of the Convention's dispute settlement regime and the Convention generally. Although non-participation in compulsory procedures is not without precedent and, in the case of, for instance, the ICJ has not had a lasting impact on its functioning,[37] in the case of the LOSC the two recent cases of non-participation may point to an underlying problem in this particular case.

---

[35] Admittedly, the FSA operated in a broader political and legal setting, which also propagated the approach contained in the FSA.

[36] The broad participation in the 1994 Implementation Agreement is mostly explained by its specific linkage to the LOSC (see 1994 Implementation Agreement, n 32, Arts 4 and 5). This is not an option for future implementation agreements.

[37] For an overview of non-appearance by respondents before the ICJ, see eg TD Gill (ed), *Rosenne's The World Court; What It Is and How It Works* (6th edn Martinus Nijhoff Publishers Leiden 2003) 78–9.

Acceptance of compulsory dispute settlement as part of the LOSC was a price certain States had to pay to arrive at a generally acceptable compromise. This did not mean that those States renounced their opposition to compulsory dispute settlement. Even though the LOSC allows for significant exceptions to compulsory dispute settlement, the two recent arbitrations involving non-appearance indicate that this does not preclude that cases may be brought that touch on fundamental interests of States. In both these cases, the power disparity between the claimant and respondent is also obvious. These circumstances militate against the acceptability of third party dispute settlement as a viable option:

> When disputants opt for arbitration or adjudication, they must forgo [...] other options [of dispute settlement]. Since States with greater bargaining power are able to guarantee themselves favorable outcomes outside of court, they will be reluctant to submit their claims to arbitration or adjudication unless they can expect a similarly favorable outcome.[38]

These considerations suggest that in the case of the LOSC cases of non-appearance, or disregard for judgments, may prove not to be isolated events. That likelihood may also contribute to dissuading States to initiate compulsory dispute settlement procedures to start with. The perception that the LOSC's system of compulsory dispute settlement can be ignored with impunity may moreover encourage more powerful States to give less weight to the law in determining their policy options.

The current law of the sea to a large extent has been shaped by the interest of the dominant global power—first the United Kingdom and subsequently the United States—in maintaining the freedom of the high seas; in particular the freedom of navigation and, subsequently, also the freedom of overflight. The rise of China, in particular, poses the question whether the interest of dominant global powers in ensuring an order for the oceans in which communicational freedoms are a key factor will be less pronounced in the future. China's posturing in regard of the seas washing its shores might suggest that this might be the case. Certain of China's positions, both in relation to its direct neighbours and the naval presence of the United States in the region, are difficult to reconcile with the LOSC or public international law generally. However, China's broader interests in securing access to global markets and resources rather suggest that China's long term interests will be better served by supporting the current law of the sea regime.

Reliable predictions of the future are only possible after it lies in the past. Still, it is not impossible to draw some general conclusions about the future of the LOSC. There currently do not seem to be major challenges to its jurisdictional framework on the horizon and the Convention thus far has struck a satisfactory balance between stability and adaptability. At the same time, the above analysis identifies a

---

[38] SE Gent, 'The Politics of International Arbitration and Adjudication' (2013) 2 *Penn State Journal of Law & International Affairs* 66, 76.

number of issues that might challenge the effectiveness and stability of the LOSC and there might also be cumulative effects in this respect. It is in any case certain that the LOSC will continue to evolve to address future developments. This may be effected either by the various means available to adapt the Convention to changed circumstances or the development of new customary law. This is likely to be a gradual process with a low probability of a radical breaking of new ground that at least in the short and medium term should be able to ensure the continued effectiveness of the law of the sea.

INDEX

ABNJ *see* areas beyond national jurisdiction (ABNJ)
accession *see* UN Convention on the Law of the Sea 1982 (LOSC 1982), ratification/accession of
Achille Lauro 595, 848
acidification *see* ocean acidification
African Union (AU) 605
Agenda 21 356, 362–3, 365, 465, 487 n.171, 809
Agulhas and Somali Current Large Marine Ecosystems (ASCLME) Project 720
air pollution 525, 526, 531, 783, 785, 898
airspace 91, 96, 186, 538, 549 *see also* overflight, freedom of
Alexander VI, pope 3, 536
Allen, Craig H 421
Alvarez, Alejandro 8
anadromous stocks 167, 443, 668
Anderson, Winston 689
Antarctica, legal regime 738–46
   Antarctic Circumpolar current 725
   Antarctic Convergence/Polar Front 704, 725, 742, 796
   Antarctic Treaty 578, 739–45, 901–3
      Antarctic Treaty Consultative Meeting 743–5
      Antarctic Treaty Consultative Parties 281
      Environmental Protection Protocol 741–3, 750, 761, 840
      South China Sea 642, 644–5
   Antarctic Treaty System 301, 578, 642, 725, 741–5, 761, 840, 902
   areas beyond national jurisdiction 741, 748–50
   biodiversity 761
   bioprospecting 741, 840–1
   boundary delimitations 738–42
   climate change 728, 746, 796, 903
   coastal State jurisdiction 739, 745, 903
   continental shelf 738–40
   dependent and associated ecosystems 741–2
   ecosystem approach 748–9
   enforcement 744–5
   environmental impact assessments 743, 840
   exclusive economic zones 738
   fisheries and living resources 727, 739, 742–6, 749
   flag State jurisdiction 727–8, 744–5
   future challenges 748–50
   geographical challenges 738–41, 744–5
   geopolitics 723–4
   governance of shipping 728–9, 743–4, 750
   high seas 727, 741–2, 749
   IMO 426, 724, 728, 743–5, 750–1
   institutions 748
   integrated oceans management 741, 748
   land-based pollution 527
   marine mammals 739, 743
   Marine Protected Areas 748–50
   MARPOL 728–9, 745
   military operations 742
   multilateral environment agreements 728
   non-living and minerals resources 740–1, 751
   nuclear testing and waste 742–3
   overlapping claims 738–41, 751
   particularly sensitive sea areas 750
   peaceful purposes principle 642
   Polar Shipping Code 426, 728–9, 744
   political challenges 738–41, 744–5
   port State jurisdiction 739, 745
   science 527, 578, 644, 739–42, 749, 751

Antarctica, legal regime (*cont.*)
  search and rescue 744, 750
  South China Sea 642, 644–5
  specially managed areas 743
  specially protected areas 743
  territorial sea 738
  tourism 741, 743
  vessel source pollution 727–9, 743–4
  Whaling Convention 739, 743
applicable law 165–77, 413–14, 636–9
Arab League 605
Arab Spring 605, 623
arbitration 29, 396–400
  arbitrator, agreement on 397
  boundary delimitation 255
  comity 408
  consent 397–9, 406
  constitution 398–9
  Court of Justice 409
  declarations accepting jurisdiction 399
  duty to arbitrate under UN Convention on the Law of the Sea 1982 (LOSC 1982) 397–9
  exclusions 404–6
  experts for arbitration, maintenance of list of 436
  identity of arbitrator, agreement on 397
  IMO 435–6
  International Seabed Authority 249, 399
  investment disputes 395 n.3
  military operations 886
  mixed disputes 400
  party autonomy 397
  provisional measures 399
  related issues 408–9
  South China Sea 640–2
  UNCITRAL Arbitration Rules 249
archaeological and historical objects 108, 607, 609
archipelagic straight baselines 145–7
  archipelagic States, definition of 88, 143–4
  Caribbean Sea and the Gulf of Mexico 155
  climate change 788, 790–1
  customary international law 89–90
  declaration requirement 144

  excessive claims 155
  exclusive economic zones 146
  freedom of navigation 134
  high seas 146
  ILC 88
  implementation 146–7
  Indian Ocean 708, 722
  innocent passage 134
  internal waters 70, 80, 85, 148
  low-tide elevations 73, 143, 146
  North-East Atlantic and North Sea 655
  number of claims 74 n.25
  oceanic archipelagos 155–6
  State practice 138, 155, 889
  territorial sea 88–9, 91, 146, 156
  UNCLOS III 88, 141
archipelagic regime 134–58 *see also* **archipelagic straight baselines**
  archipelagic sea lanes passage (ASLP) 149–54, 157, 538
  archipelagic State, definition of 142–5
  archipelagic status 135
  archipelago, definition of 142–5
  boundary delimitation 135–40, 148
  Caribbean Sea and the Gulf of Mexico 675, 680–1, 693–4
  coastal State jurisdiction 12–13, 16, 294–6
  conflicts of interest 142
  continental or coastal archipelagos 135, 138, 156
  customary international law 156
  declaration requirement 144
  dependent archipelagos belonging to continental States 136, 154–8
  designation procedure 295–6
  development 30, 135–42
  early developments 136–7
  exclusive economic zones 149, 553
  fisheries and living resources 136–7, 149, 498
  freedom of navigation 137, 154, 537–9, 553–4, 557
  General Provisions for the Adoption, Designation and Substitution of Archipelagic Sea Lanes 151–2
  Geneva Conventions 1958 16, 28, 141
  geographical perspective 135–6, 143

Group of Archipelagic States 25
Hague Conference 1930 136–8
high seas 140–1, 205, 553
historical evolution 136
hot pursuit 875
IMO 150–1, 153–4, 418, 433, 554
implementation 135, 144–5, 150–4, 156–7
Indian Ocean 704, 708, 722
Indonesia 138–43
innocent passage 137, 140, 149–51, 154, 295–6, 538, 552–3
interconnecting waters 143
internal waters 140–1, 148
international courts and tribunals 404
islands 28, 554
low-tide elevations 143
marine environment/pollution 153–4
mid-ocean or outlying archipelagos 135–6, 138, 141, 145, 155
military operations 882–3
naval warfare, law of 878
non-navigational rights 148–9
North-East Atlantic and North Sea 651, 655
overflight, freedom of 149–50, 553
Philippines 138–41
physical characteristics 135
reefs 143, 145
scientific research 566–7, 570
sea lanes and traffic separation lanes 150–4, 295, 567, 570, 680–1
sea level, rise in 790–1
State practice 138–40, 155–7, 158
State sovereignty 142, 148
straits 115, 132
submarine cables and pipelines 148–9, 208
territorial sea 8, 95, 136, 138–41, 148–50, 155–6
UNCLOS I 140–1
UNCLOS II 140–1
UNCLOS III 25, 141–2, 148, 154
warships 296, 553
whole territory of states, archipelagos forming 135–6
Arctic Ocean, legal regime 729–38
  Arctic Council 735–7, 746–8, 751
  administration 737
  Arctic Ocean Review (AOR) 746
  ecosystem approach 747–8
  members 735–6, 751
  Polar Bears, Agreement on Conservation of 735
  soft power 725, 751
  working groups 736
Arctic Five 733, 735, 737–8, 746
Arctic Marine Shipping Assessment report 736
areas beyond national jurisdiction 746
baselines 734
black carbon and methane emission reductions 736–7, 746
boundary delimitation 725, 729–32
central Arctic Ocean 732, 735, 737–8, 746–7
climate change 724–5, 746, 903
construction of ships 728
continental shelf 197–8, 372, 729–34
cooperation 735, 751
dispute settlement 371–2
ecosystem approach 746–8
enforcement 734
European Union 734
exclusive economic zones 371–2, 730, 734
fisheries and living resources 460, 729–31, 735, 737–8, 746
flag State jurisdiction 727–8
Framework Climate Change Convention (UN) 728, 746
future challenges 746–8
generally accepted rules and standards 728
geopolitics 723–4
governance of shipping 728–9, 736, 747
high seas 727, 746, 747
Ilulissat Declaration 733, 737
IMO 724, 728, 751
integrated oceans management 474
internal waters 734
interpretation 734–5
islands 731
IUU fishing 737
jurisdictional tensions 734–5
Large Marine Ecosystems 747–8

Arctic Ocean, legal regime (*cont.*)
  Marine Protected Areas 748
  MARPOL 728–9
  media 733
  multilateral environment agreements 728
  non-living and minerals resources 725
  Northwest Passage 120, 131–2, 590, 734, 797, 890
  oil and gas 189, 725, 730–1, 736–7, 748
  overlapping claims 733
  PAME Working Group 747–8
  Polar Shipping Code 426, 728–9
  protect and preserve obligation 726–7
  regional cooperation 735
  regional developments 729–38
  regional fisheries management organization 460, 737–8
  reporting and monitoring 735, 748
  response capabilities 736
  routeing measures 735
  safety 727
  scientific research 737, 746–7
  seabed 733–4
  search and rescue 301, 736
  security 590
  soft power 725
  State sovereignty 729–32
  straits 120, 131–2, 734–5
  sustainable use and management 736, 746
  territorial sea 371–2, 729, 732
  treaties and conventions 728
  vessel source pollution 727–9
M/V Arctic Sunrise incident 173, 187–8, 201, 886–7
Area *see* **international seabed area**
areas beyond national jurisdiction (ABNJ)
  Antarctic 741, 748–50
  Arctic 746
  biodiversity 752–76, 488, 490, 898
  BBNJ Working Group 754, 764–7, 771–2, 775–6, 894
  bioprospecting 826, 838–9
  environmental impact assessments 483–4
  fisheries and living resources 460, 482, 487, 753–4, 758–60
  General Assembly (UN) 905
  Indian Ocean 718–19
  integrated oceans management 466–7, 480–8, 489–90
  marine environment/pollution 368–9, 483–4
  marine spatial planning 485–6
  precautionary approach 482–3
  regional fisheries management organizations 460
  seabed 763–4
  threatened species and VMEs 801–2, 805
armed robbery at sea *see* **piracy and armed robbery at sea**
arrest of ships
  consular notification 105
  crew 105, 505, 851–3, 857, 862–3, 875
  piracy 851–3, 857, 862–3, 875
  ships, of 44, 168–9, 219, 221, 224, 457, 505
artificial islands, installations and structures
  baselines 75
  biodiversity 754
  coastal State jurisdiction 171–3, 297
  construction 171–3, 188
  continental shelf 171, 187–8
  customs, fiscal, health, safety, and immigration laws and regulations 172
  disposal 172, 518
  exclusive economic zones 165, 171–3
  high seas 206
  marine environment/pollution 173, 188, 518, 903
  Mediterranean Sea 611
  mines, laying 878
  naval warfare, law of 878
  piracy 848
  port State jurisdiction 281
  publicity 172
  safety zones 172, 187–8, 431
  scientific research 574
  territorial sea 95
  terrorism 173
  third States, placement by 172
ASEAN (Association of South-East Asian Nations) 341, 636–40, 643, 645, 712
atmospheric pollution 525, 526, 531, 783, 785, 898

atolls 74–5, 143, 788
Australia
   Antarctic 600, 738–9, 745, 749
   archipelagic waters 140–1, 151–2
   ballast water 530
   bioregional planning 468
   bioprospecting 832
   coast guard 873
   compulsory pilotage through Torres Strait 106, 130, 288, 557
   continental shelf 183, 191–2, 198
   Environmental Protection and Biodiversity Act 1999 468
   Great Barrier Reef 106, 288, 468, 513, 627
   Indian Ocean 702–4, 706–7, 710–11, 714–15, 721–2
   integrated oceans management 466–70, 472
   Japan 445, 739, 895
   marine protected areas 468, 513–14
   marine spatial planning 467, 513–14
   multiple use zoning 468
   New Zealand 191–2, 445
   Northern Territory, bioregional planning in 468
   Oceans Policy 468
   particularly sensitive sea areas 130, 288
   port State control 286, 288–9
   regional fisheries management organizations (RFMOs) 445
   scientific research 579, 581
   smuggling of migrants by sea 217, 222, 590–1
   sovereign immunity 871–2
   straight baselines 138
   United States 281
   whaling 511, 577
Axelrod, Mark 461
Azores 3, 143, 155, 649–51, 655–6

Bai Meichu 634
ballast water 525, 530–1, 744, 750, 773
Baltic regional sea regime 465, 473–5
   Baltic Sea Broad-scale Maritime Spatial Planning Principles 475
   Baltic Sea Protected Areas 475
   Bothnian Sea 475
   dumping 519–20
   Helsinki Commission Baltic Sea Action Plan 475, 477
   Helsinki Convention 1992 474–5, 521
   marine environment/pollution 519, 521, 526
   marine spatial planning 470
   Regional Baltic MSP Roadmap 475
   Vision and Strategies around the Baltic Sea Committee 475
Bangladesh and Myanmar delimitation dispute (ITLOS) 184–5, 191–2, 196, 200, 411–12
Bantz, Vincent Cogliati 313
Barnes, Richard 806
Basel Convention on Transboundary Movements of Hazardous Wastes and their Disposal 1989 429
baselines 69–90 *see also* **archipelagic straight baselines; straight baselines**
   ambulatory versus fixed debate 76–7, 87, 89–90, 789–93, 907
   arcs of circle method 95
   Arctic 734
   artificial baselines 73–4
   artificial islands, installations and structures 85
   bays 9, 294
   bilateral process 71
   Caribbean Sea and the Gulf of Mexico 676, 680–1
   changes in coastal geography 76–8, 89–90
   charts, marking on 76–8
   climate change 778
   coast, definition of 69 n.4
   coastal State jurisdiction 70–3, 90, 294, 296–8
   coastal State/maritime State tension 72–3
   contiguous zones 70
   continental shelf 70, 181
   customary international law 90, 793
   developing countries 77
   excessive claims 90
   exclusive economic zones 70
   falsification 78
   fixed versus ambulatory debate 76–7, 87, 89–90, 789–93, 907

baselines (cont.)
function and significance 69–73
Geneva Conventions 1958 14, 73
Hague Conference of 1930 9, 72–3
indentation 93–5
Indian Ocean 707–8, 722
innocent passage, right of 70–1
internal waters 70, 148
islands 9, 71, 74–7
low-tide/sinuosities formulation 73
low-water lines 73–9, 87–90, 95
normal baselines 73–9, 89–90
publicity 793
rocks 74 n.26
sea level, rises in 89–90, 787–93, 897, 907
security 589–90
spatial definition 889–90, 906–7
State practice 72–5, 790, 793
State sovereignty 70–1
territorial sea 70–1, 75, 93–5
warships 70–1
zero mark, as 70
zonal limit delimitation 71
Bateman, Sam 721
Bay of Bengal Large Marine Ecosystem (BOBLME) Project 720
bays
baselines 9
bay-closing lines 82–4
codification 19–20
historic bays 83–4, 294, 406, 607, 641, 655, 681
internal waters 19–20, 82–4
juridical bays 82–4
landlocked States 83 n.68
multi-State bays 83
occupation 4
straight baselines 82–4
Bederman, David J 70
Belgium 471, 555, 647, 651, 655, 847
best available scientific evidence 451, 576–7
best available techniques (BAT) 523
best practicable means 521
biodiversity 752–76
Ad Hoc Working Group 42, 466, 754, 766–7
Antarctic Treaty 761
area-based management elements 772–3
areas beyond national jurisdiction 488, 490, 752–76, 898
artificial islands, installations and structures 754
Biodiversity Convention 484 n.156, 756–7, 775
BBNJ Working Group 764
bioprospecting 825–6, 829–36, 840–2
Conference of Parties 767–9, 814, 830
fisheries 492, 494, 512–14
habitat protection and capacity 813–14
Indian Ocean 717
initiatives 767–9
integrated oceans management 466, 481, 483, 485–6
marine environment/pollution 37
Nagoya Protocol 831, 834–5, 841
objectives 757
regime interaction 62–3
Subsidiary Body on Scientific, Technical and Technological Advice 768
threatened species and VMEs 805–7
Voluntary Guidelines for Biodiversity-Inclusive EIA 773–4
biodiversity, definition of 756
bioprospecting 753, 772–3
BBNJ Working Group 754, 764–7, 771–2, 775–6
Bonn Guidelines on Access and Benefit Sharing 830–1
Caribbean Sea and the Gulf of Mexico 699
climate change 753, 797
Commission on the Limits of the Continental Shelf 769
common heritage of mankind 755–6
cooperation 753, 758, 894
coordination mechanism, lack of a formal global 760
customary international law 754, 759
decision-making 760, 774–6
development of international law 753–4
dumping 763
ecologically and biologically significant areas 764, 767–8, 772

ecosystem approach 512–13, 755–6, 760–2, 765, 771–2, 775–6
endangered species 757
enforcement 758, 764–5
Environment Programme Regional Seas Programme 761
environmental impact assessments 753, 763–4, 766–9, 772–6
exclusive economic zones 761
experts 767
fisheries and living resources 492, 494, 512–14
  areas beyond national jurisdiction 753–4, 758–60
  closure areas 764
  customary international law 759
  Fish Stocks Agreement 502, 754–5, 760
  IUU fishing 760, 765
  marine mammals 769–70
  regional fisheries management organizations 459, 462, 755, 758–60, 764–5
  regional initiatives 769–71
  technological innovations 753
  threatened species and VMEs 806
flag State jurisdiction 755, 763, 765, 768
fragmentation 768
freedom of navigation 754
global initiatives 764–9
habitat protection and capacity 813–14
high seas 754, 763–4, 768
implementation framework 43–4, 758–64, 771–5
Indian Ocean 717
institutions 754–75
integrated oceans management 466, 481, 483, 485–6, 488, 490, 753
International Seabed Authority 755–6, 763
landlocked States and geographically disadvantaged States 345
legal framework, development of 764–75
marine mammals 769–70
marine protected areas 513–14, 662–3, 753, 764, 767–75, 814
marine spatial planning 513–14, 753, 773
MARPOL 755, 763
Mediterranean Sea 761

monitoring 758, 764–5
National Biodiversity Strategies and Action Plans 813–14
North-East Atlantic and North Sea 650, 660–3, 670, 761–2, 769–71
overflight, freedom of 754
port State jurisdiction 302
precautionary approach 760, 765, 771–2
protect and preserve obligation 753–4, 758
regime interaction 62–3
regional fisheries management organizations 459, 462, 755, 758–60, 764–5
regional initiatives 760–2, 764, 769–71
regional organizations 753, 755, 772–6
rules, regulations, and procedures, duty to adopt 755–6
science 53–4, 534, 757, 773–4, 898
seabed 753, 758, 763–4
sectoral organizations 765, 773, 776
South China Sea 628
submarine cables and pipelines 754
sustainable use and management 754, 757–75
targets 484 n.156, 486, 814
threatened species and VMEs 800, 804–7, 824
vessel source pollution 753, 763
vulnerable marine ecosystems 770, 773
bioprospecting *see* **marine genetic resources, bioprospecting**
Blackstone, William 874
boarding and inspection *see also* **visit, right of search and**
Antarctic 745
drug trafficking 221
fisheries and living resources 168, 456–7, 506
flag State jurisdiction 313, 315, 319–21, 557–8
freedom of navigation 557–8
high seas, policing the 219, 221–2, 224
innocent passage 544–5
migrants, smuggling of 217, 222
port State jurisdiction 290
submarine cables and pipelines 208
weapons of mass destruction 223

bottom trawling 458–9, 503–4, 515
boundary delimitation 254–79 *see also*
  baselines; continental shelf
  Antarctic 738–42
  archipelagic regime 135–40, 148
  Arctic 725, 729–32
  bays 406
  bilateral maritime boundaries 71, 191, 196,
    200, 613, 657–8, 901, 907
  Caribbean Sea and the Gulf of
    Mexico 672, 675–81, 687, 692–700
  certainty versus flexibility 278
  climate change 276–7
  contiguous zones 108–9
  Convention on the Territorial Sea and
    Contiguous Zone 1958 255–7
  customary international law 255, 258,
    261–2, 278
  development of the law of the sea 893–4
  dispute settlement 585, 589–90, 602,
    615–16, 693–9
  economic issues 274–6
  elements of the process 266–70
  entitlement, establishing 261–3
  equidistance 259–60, 267–9, 272–4,
    693, 695–6
    equitable principles debate 256–61,
      264–5, 269, 278
    Indian Ocean 709
    islands 273–4
    Mediterranean Sea 612
    North-East Atlantic and North Sea 658
    provisional equidistance line 259–60,
      268–9, 276–7, 696–8
    relevant circumstances rule 258–9
    special circumstances rule 255–9,
      264, 276–7
  equitable principle 256–61, 264–5,
    269–70, 275, 277
  exclusive economic zones 163, 256, 258,
    261–6, 277–9, 892
  geographic factors 269, 274–6
  Indian Ocean 703–9, 722
  interaction of maritime zones 892
  international courts and tribunals 406
  islands 28, 262–3, 269, 271–4,
    612, 613–14

  jurisdictional issues 274–6
  length of coastlines 269–72
  Mediterranean Sea 608–9, 612–16, 624
  natural prolongation 264–5, 269
  North-East Atlantic and North
    Sea 647–8, 651, 657–9
  oil and gas 901
  opposite or adjacent coasts, delimitation
    between States with 254–9, 267,
    269, 272
    median line 257
  outstanding issues 698–9
  overlapping claims 254–62, 265–9, 276,
    585, 612, 698
  pending delimitations 613–14
  preliminary issues 263–6
  primary method, identification of 268
  process of delimitation 261–70
  proportionality 267, 270, 272, 697
  provisional equidistance line 259–60,
    268–9, 276–7, 696–8
  relevant area, identification of 267–72
  sea level, rise in 791–2
  security 585, 589–90, 602
  South China Sea 627–42, 644, 646
  spatial definition 889–90
  stability of boundaries 276–7, 612–13
  State practice 255, 275
  territorial sea 255–7, 259, 261–2, 277
  threats or use of force 695
  three-stage test 259–61, 268, 277,
    615–16, 696–7
  treaties, relationship of UN Convention
    on the Law of the Sea 1982 (LOSC
    1982) to other 36
  unity of a deposit 274–5
  water column 263, 613
Boyle, Alan 30
broadcasting, unauthorized 220, 312, 874
Brundtland Commission 495
Buga, Irina 906
bunkering services 554–5
by-catch and discards
  CMS Convention 821
  Common Fisheries Policy 666
  FAO Code of Conduct 807–8
  General Assembly (UN) 361

IUU fishing 802
marine mammals 508
methods of fishing 503
regional fisheries management
   organizations 450, 457–8
total allowable catch 806–7

Cable, James 880
cables *see* **submarine cables and pipelines**
Canada
   archipelagic States 135, 155
   Arctic 725, 729–31, 733–5, 748
   boundary delimitation 266
   coastal State jurisdiction 303
   continental shelf 186–7, 190–1, 733
   Denmark 730–1, 733
   Eastern Scotian Shelf Integrated Ocean
      Management Plan 469
   federalism 469
   fisheries and living resources 303
   integrated oceans
      management 469–70, 472
   large ocean management areas
      (LOMAs) 469
   marine spatial planning 469
   military operations 886
   National Oceans Action Plan 469
   Northwest Passage 120, 131
   Oceans Act 1996 469
   Oceans Policy 469
   oil and gas 187, 191, 197–9
   port State jurisdiction 286
   scientific research 579
   straits 127, 131
   threatened species 816
   United States 120, 131, 186, 198–9,
      734, 816
cannon-shot rule 5, 92–3, 582 n.1
capacity-building 372, 433–4
   biodiversity 754
   environmental impact assessments 768
   habitat protection and capacity 813
   International Seabed Authority 908
   traditional knowledge 831
   World Heritage Convention 1972 815
Caribbean Sea and the Gulf of
   Mexico 672–700

archipelagic States 675, 680–1, 693–4
Association of Caribbean States 687, 700
background 673–5
Barbados/Trinidad and Tobago
   Arbitration 275, 693–5
baselines 676, 680–1
biodiversity 699
boundary delimitation 672, 675–81, 687,
   692–700
Caribbean Action Plan 687–90
Caribbean Challenge 480
Caribbean Environment Programme 691
Caribbean Large Marine Ecosystem
   Project 689–90
CARICOM 599, 686
Cartagena Convention and
   Protocol 478–9, 688–9
climate change 699
coastal State jurisdiction 681
colonialism 474, 673, 675
Common Fisheries Policy 687
contiguous zones 681
continental shelf 183, 681, 692, 697–9
coral reefs 683–4, 689
cruise ship destination, as 683
developing countries 683
dispute settlement 692–9
distinction between Caribbean and Gulf
   of Mexico 673, 675
drug trafficking 594, 675, 692
ecosystem approach 681, 683–4,
   688–90, 699
enforcement 691–2
equidistance 693, 695–8
exclusive economic zones 681, 697
fisheries and living resources 681,
   683–90, 699
   artisanal fishing 684
   Caribbean Regional Fisheries
      Mechanism 686–7, 691–2
   Fisheries Forum 686–7
   IUU fishing 691–2
   marine environment/pollution 683–90
   regional fisheries bodies, list of 685–6
France 673, 675 n.10, 681, 698
freedom of navigation 682–3
geography 673

Caribbean Sea and the Gulf of
    Mexico (*cont.*)
  high sea areas, lack of 675
  historic bays 681
  IMO 682–3, 770–1
  industrialization 673
  integrated oceans management 465,
      474, 479–80
  islands 676, 684, 693–7
  IUU fishing 691–2
  list of maritime claims 677–9
  main navigation routes 674
  marine environment/pollution 173, 480,
      683–91, 699
    Caribbean Action Plan 687–90
    Caribbean Environment
      Programme 691
    Caribbean Large Marine Ecosystem
      Project 689–90, 700
    Cartagena Convention and
      Protocol 688–9
    fisheries 683–90
    land-based 810–11
    polluter pays principle 688
    precautionary approach 688
    Wider Caribbean Initiative on
      Ship-generated Waste 683
  Maritime and Airspace Security
    Co-operation Agreement 600
  metropolitan powers 673, 675
  Netherlands 673, 675, 687
  Nicaragua v Columbia (ICJ) 45, 260–1,
      265–7, 270–9, 696–9
  Nicaragua v Honduras (ICJ) 256, 268
  non-parties to UN Convention on the Law
    of the Sea 1982 (LOSC 1982) 676
  oceanography 683–4
  OEGS (Organisation of Eastern Caribbean
    States) 686–7
  oil and gas 681, 688, 690–5, 699
  open registries 682–3
  overlapping claims 698
  piracy 691
  port State control 291
  precautionary approach 688
  regional oceans management 902–3
  rocks 697
  sea lanes and traffic separation
    schemes 680–2
  sea level rise 676
  seabed resources 676, 690–1, 693
  security 594, 599–600
  semi-enclosed seas, as 673, 681, 699
  smuggling of migrants 217
  Spain 673
  specially protected areas 479–80, 688–9
  straight baselines 676, 680
  sustainable use and management 687, 689
  territorial sea 681
  Transboundary Diagnostic
    Analysis 689–90
  UNCLOS III 672
  United Kingdom 672, 675, 692
  United States 183, 673–6, 682, 692
  vessel source pollution 683
Caron, David D 793
catadromous species 167, 668–9
CCAMLR Commission 749, 840
**Central America Fisheries and Aquaculture
    Organization (OSPESCA)** 686
charts
  baselines 76–8
  deposit 80
  innocent passage 544
  out-of-date charts 76
  safety 315
chemosynthesis 573
Chile
  Antarctic 738, 740, 745
  boundary delimitation 266
  coastal State jurisdiction 303
  port State control 285–6, 299–300
  straits 127
  Truman Proclamations 11–12
China
  ASEAN 638–40, 645
  China Ocean Agenda 21 644
  dispute settlement,
    non-participation in 910
  exclusive economic zones 175 n.90, 592,
      884, 900
  fisheries and living resources 631
  freedom of navigation 911
  IMO 422

India 175, 342, 701
Indian Ocean 701, 709, 720–1
innocent passage 546
Japan 589, 592
migratory species, conservation of 821
military operations 175 n.90, 546, 592, 880, 884, 886, 900
nuclear weapons 643
Russian Federation 910
scientific research 571, 592
security 589, 720, 911
South China Sea 156, 175, 626–46, 892
straight baselines 155–6
Taiwan 32, 880
territorial sea 546
United States 175 n.90, 592, 641–2, 720, 880, 884, 900
Yellow Sea 644
Chinkin, Christine 30
Churchill, Robin Rolf 156
Churchill, Winston 879
CITES (Convention on International Trade in Endangered Species of Wild Fauna and Flora 1973) 511, 669, 819–20
civil jurisdiction 9, 100, 105, 123–4, 545
climate change 777–99 *see also* **ocean acidification; sea level, rise in**
adaptive responses 782, 787–96, 798
Antarctic 728, 746, 796, 903
Arctic 724–5, 746, 903
atmospheric pollution 783, 785
baselines 778
biodiversity 753, 797
boundary delimitation 276–7
carbon dioxide 778–80, 783–6, 797–8, 811–12, 824
carbon sequestration 784
Caribbean Sea and the Gulf of Mexico 699
complementary marine environmental regimes 784–5
continental shelf 795
Copenhagen Accords 812–13
due diligence 783
dumping 530, 784–5
ecosystem approach 794–6

emission reduction targets 786, 797
exclusive economic zones 795
fertilization of oceans 784–5
fisheries and living resources 451, 459–62, 778, 794–7
Framework Convention on Climate Change 376, 534–5, 728, 746, 782–3, 786
gaps in regulation 896
geo-engineering 784–5, 797, 896
greenhouse gases 778–87, 797, 812, 824
integrated oceans management 471, 487
Intergovernmental Panel on Climate Change 644, 652, 777–87, 812–13
International Programme on the State of the Ocean 779
Kyoto Protocol 783, 786, 812–13
legal adaptation 787
lex specialis 782
localized ecosystem decline 779
marine protected areas 795
mitigation 778–86, 795, 797, 813
natural resources 794–6
non-living and minerals resources 795
North-East Atlantic and North Sea 652, 661, 668, 670
oil and gas 795
particularly sensitive sea areas 795
physical adaptation 787
pollution, definition of 783
processes and impacts 778–83
protect and preserve obligation 782–3
regional fisheries management organizations 451, 459–62, 796, 798
rules, regulations, and standards 783
salinity 780
scientific research 174–5, 566, 573, 784–5, 796
security 594
South China Sea 644
straits 131
temperature rise 780–1, 897
territorial sea 794–5
threatened species and VMEs 800, 802, 811–13, 819–20, 824
Clinton, Bill 880
Cloma, Tomas 633

CLCS *see* **Commission on the Limits of the Continental Shelf (CLCS)**
coastal state jurisdiction 5, 11, 293–301 *see also* **contiguous zone; continental shelf; exclusive economic zone (EEZ); territorial sea**
  Antarctic 281, 301, 739, 745, 903
  archipelagic regime 12–13, 16, 294–6
  artificial islands, installations and structures 171–3, 297
  baselines 12–13, 70–2, 80, 90, 294, 296–8
  biodiversity 769
  bioprospecting 829, 833–42
  concurrent jurisdiction 314
  creeping jurisdiction 28, 178, 294, 302, 892
  criminal offences 71
  definition 280
  expansion of jurisdiction 10–13, 16, 294, 302, 625, 653
  fisheries and living resources 491, 498–500, 505, 514
    expansion 494
    exclusive economic zones 166–9, 298–302
    Fish Stocks Agreement 303
    high seas 207, 301
    IUU fishing 505
    marine spatial planning 514
    regional fisheries management organizations 460–1
    State practice 179
  flag State jurisdiction 294, 304–5, 312, 314, 317–18, 893, 908
  freedom of navigation 11–12, 296, 298, 418, 537–8, 554, 557
  future of the law of the sea 893, 896–7
  historical development 5, 10–13, 16, 22–3
  IMO 418, 428, 430, 432–3, 437
  Indian Ocean 702, 706–10
  innocent passage 540–9
  internal waters 70–1, 294–5
  international courts and tribunals 404–7
  landlocked States and geographically disadvantaged States 326–8, 331–2, 334, 336–7, 343–4
  legal nature of provisions of UN Convention on the Law of the Sea 1982 (LOSC 1982) 30
  marine environment/pollution 71, 176–7, 294, 298, 301
    freedom of navigation 557
    science 518–19, 531–2
  marine mammals 508
  maritime zones 281–3, 294–302
  Mediterranean Sea 607–8, 625
  military operations 867, 880–1, 885–7, 908
  natural resources 10–12
  North-East Atlantic and North Sea 648, 653–7, 671
  occupation 4
  overflight, freedom of 298
  port State jurisdiction 281, 908
  prescriptive jurisdiction 294, 297, 300–1
  regional coastal State cooperation 300–1
  regional fisheries management organizations 301, 460–1
  routeing measures, overseeing and approving requests for 432–3
  rules of reference 300–1
  Santiago Declaration 11–13
  security 584, 586–7, 591–3, 603
  science 173–4, 297, 301, 343, 518–19, 531–2, 560, 562–80
  search and rescue 301
  spatial definition 907–8
  State practice 179, 299, 302–3
  State sovereignty 5, 7, 281, 294–300
  straits 118–19, 296
  submarine cables and pipelines 298
  territorial sea 7, 11–12, 16, 294, 296–7
  threatened species and VMEs 804
  Truman Proclamations 10–12, 13, 16
  UNESCO Cultural Heritage Convention 908
cobalt-rich crusts 228, 241, 243, 246, 385, 756
codes of practice
  FAO Code of Conduct on Responsible Fisheries 482, 486, 497, 807–8
  IMO 420, 426, 428, 530

INDEX   925

International Ship and Port Security
    (ISPS) Code 320, 588, 599, 602–3
Mining Code 66, 241, 244, 319, 756, 764
piracy 601
Polar Shipping Code 426, 728–9, 744
search and rescue 623
security 600
South China Sea 636–7
threatened species and VMEs 807–8
Codex Justinianus 439
codification
    contiguous zones 108
    customary international law 30, 346
    fisheries and living resources 491
    Geneva Conventions 1958 13–16, 30, 37
    Hague Conference of 1930 2, 7–9
    high seas 204, 205
    historical development 2, 7–9, 22
    international courts and tribunals 17–20
    League of Nations 7–9
    naval warfare, law of 875–6
    piracy 845
    progressive development 9, 13, 16, 30
    scholarly works 2
    straits 116
    UNCLOS III 2
    visit, right of 220
    World War II, before 7–9
Cold War 120, 122, 141, 560, 881–2, 899–900
collisions, jurisdiction in
    flag State jurisdiction 210, 218–19
    innocent passage 541
    regime interaction 61
    rules of reference 31
    straits 551
    territorial sea 105
colonialism
    Caribbean Sea and the Gulf of
        Mexico 474, 673, 675
    decolonization 605
    freedom of navigation 537
    Indian Ocean 705
    Mediterranean Sea 605
    North-East Atlantic and North Sea 653
    South China Sea 633–4
Columbus, Christopher 3, 673

Comité Maritime International
    (CMI) 284, 417, 425–6
comity 62, 402, 408, 545
Commission for the Conservation of
    Southern Bluefin Tuna (CCSBT) 442,
    444, 460, 715–17, 818
Commission on the Conservation of
    Antarctic Marine Living Resources
    (CAMLR Commission) 443, 450–2,
    454, 456–60, 759
Commission on the Limits of the
    Continental Shelf (CLCS) 382–5
    allocation of seats 383
    amendment to UN Convention on
        the Law of the Sea 1982 (LOSC
        1982) 43, 385
    Antarctic 739–40
    Arctic 732–3
    artificial islands, installations and
        structures 171
    boundary delimitation 254
    budget and financing 383
    coastal State jurisdiction 298
    common heritage of mankind 411
    composition 195
    customary international law 37–8
    delays 890
    developing countries 383
    development of UN Convention on the
        Law of the Sea 1982 (LOSC 1982) 43,
        47, 893
    dispute settlement 196–7
    DOALOS 353
    elections 383
    experts 195, 382–4
    full-time CLCS, proposal for 384–5
    function 194–5, 382–3
    future of the law of the sea 893
    General Assembly (UN) 358
    geographical representation 383
    independence 383
    Indian Ocean 707, 709 n.27
    interpretation 384
    ITLOS 56, 410–12
    Meeting of States Parties 41, 383–5,
        390, 393

Commission on the Limits of the
    Continental Shelf (CLCS) (*cont.*)
  North-East Atlantic and North Sea 657
  observer, CLCS as 383
  outer continental shelf 39, 190–2, 201,
    382–3, 890
  overlapping claims 411–12
  procedure 195–8
  recommendations 39, 195–6, 198, 201, 298,
    383–4, 411–12
  seabed 411
  South China Sea 635
  spatial definition 890, 907
  subsequent practice, treaty modification
    by 56, 57, 65–6
  Trust Fund 383
  workload 384, 390
common heritage of mankind
  amendment of UN Convention on the
    Law of the Sea 1982 (LOSC 1982) 37
  Antarctic 740
  biodiversity 755–6
  bioprospecting 836–8
  Commission on the Limits of the
    Continental Shelf 411
  continental shelf 190, 202
  developing countries 238
  historical development 22–3
  Implementation Agreement 1994 53
  landlocked States and geographically
    disadvantaged States 335, 344
  seabed 229–30, 238, 332, 755–6, 836–7
  subsequent practice, treaty modification
    by 64, 67
  suspension of UN Convention on the Law
    of the Sea 1982 (LOSC 1982) 37
Comoros 144, 147, 704–5, 707–8, 712
compliance *see* **enforcement and
    compliance**
conciliation 396, 405–6
**Conferences on the Human Environment
    (UN)** 354–7, 368–9
  Charter of UN 355
  environmental impact assessments 483
  Future we want Outcome
    Document 357, 368
  General Assembly (UN) 357

  integrated oceans management 465–6,
    481, 483
  Johannesburg Conference 2002 (World
    Summit) 355, 356–7, 361, 363, 365–6,
    465, 527
  Johannesburg Declaration 356
  relationship between documents and UN
    Convention on the Law of the Sea
    1982 (LOSC 1982) 357
  Rio Conference 1992 355–6, 361–2, 617
  Rio+20 Conference 355, 357, 361, 368,
    465–6, 766
  Rio Declaration on Environment and
    Development 63, 356, 495–6, 512
  Stockholm Conference 1972 28–9, 355
  Stockholm Declaration 28–9, 355, 494
**Conferences on the Law of the
    Sea** *see* **UNCLOS I; UNCLOS II;
    UNCLOS III**
confiscation 169, 504
conservation *see* **Fish Stocks Agreement
    (FSA); fisheries and living resources,
    conservation and management of;
    marine mammals, conservation and
    management of; regional fisheries
    management organizations (RFMOs);
    threatened species and vulnerable
    marine ecosystems (VMEs)**
**Conservation and Management of Pollock
    Resources in the Central Bering Sea
    (CCBSP) Convention** 443
**Conservation Measures for the Eastern
    Atlantic Populations of the
    Mediterranean Monk Seal, MoU
    on** 509
**Conservation of African-Eurasian
    Migratory Waterbirds Agreement
    (AEWA) 1996** 757
**Conservation of Albatross and Petrels
    Agreement 2006 (ACAP)** 757
**Conservation of Anadromous Stocks in
    the North Pacific Ocean Convention
    (NPAFC Convention) 1992** 443
**Conservation of Antarctic Marine
    Living Resources Convention 1980
    (CCAMLR)** 457–60, 704, 742–3, 745,
    749–50, 761, 796, 840, 902

Conservation of Antarctic Seals Convention 1972 (CCAS) 508, 743, 745
Conservation of Cetaceans and their Habitats in the Pacific Islands Region, MoU on 509
Conservation of Cetaceans of the Black Sea, Mediterranean Sea and Contiguous Atlantic Area Agreements 1996 (ACCOBAMS) 509
Conservation of Migratory Species of Wild Animals Convention 1979 (CMS) 717–18, 757
   cooperation 821–2
   definition of migratory species 821
   IUCN Red List 821
   marine mammals 508–9, 821–2
   nomination of species 821
Conservation of Salmon in the North Atlantic Ocean Convention 1982 (NASCO Convention) 668
Conservation of Seals in the Wadden Sea Agreement 1990 509, 670
Conservation of Small Cetaceans of the Baltic and North Seas Agreement 1992 (ASCOBANS) 509, 670
constitution for the oceans, UN Convention on the Law of the Sea 1982 (LOSC 1982) as 44–5, 68, 427
contiguous zones 107–12, 296–7
   baselines 70
   Caribbean Sea and the Gulf of Mexico 681
   coastal State jurisdiction 11, 296–7
   codification 108
   customs, fiscal, health, safety, and immigration laws and regulations 92, 107–8, 110–12, 297, 608, 656, 891
   defensive and fiscal purposes 107 n.118
   enforcement 107–10, 112, 891
   exclusive economic zones 109–11, 112, 891
   expansion of control 110–11, 112
   freedom of navigation 108, 110–11, 537, 554
   Geneva Conventions 1958 14, 92, 95, 104, 108–11, 891
   high seas 108
   hot pursuit 108 n.119, 875
   Mediterranean Sea 608, 625
   naval warfare, law of 878
   North-East Atlantic and North Sea 656
   overlapping claims 891
   sea level, rise in 794
   security 110, 113, 587
   spatial definition 889–90
   State sovereignty 109, 112
   substantive regime of maritime zones 890–1
   territorial sea 92, 95, 104, 107–9
   UNCLOS III 109
continental shelf 181–202, 254–65, 296–8
   see also Commission on the Limits of the Continental Shelf (CLCS); Convention on the Continental Shelf 1958; outer limit of the continental shelf
   airspace 186, 538
   Antarctic 738–40
   applicable law 414
   Arctic 372, 729–34
   artificial islands, installations and structures 187–8
   Bangladesh and Myanmar delimitation dispute (ITLOS) 184–5, 200, 411–12
   Bay of Bengal boundary arbitration 276–8
   baselines 70, 181
   bilateral agreements 182, 200
   bioprospecting 174, 201, 830, 834
   Caribbean Sea and the Gulf of Mexico 183, 681, 692, 697–9
   climate change 795
   coastal State jurisdiction 907
   continental margin 251, 262, 264, 707
   continental rise 182, 193
   continental slope 182, 193–4
   creeping jurisdiction 28
   customary international law 36, 185, 261–2
   declarations 34
   definition 185
   economic and jurisdictional issues 274–6
   enforcement 187–8, 201

continental shelf (*cont.*)
  exclusive economic zones 162, 170, 181, 185–8, 199–200, 265–6, 891–2
  fisheries and living resources 183, 186, 298, 500
  freedom of navigation 184, 186, 201, 538–9
  General Assembly (UN) 358–9
  history 183–4
  inherent rights 185
  IMO 418
  Indian Ocean 706–7, 709, 715, 718
  information, submission of 707
  inherent rights 184–6, 201
  interaction of maritime zones 892
  international courts and tribunals 44, 404–5
  islands 28, 273
  landlocked States and geographically disadvantaged States 332, 336–7
  legal continental shelf 182
  legal regime 184–9
  location 181–2
  low-tide elevations 272–3
  marine environment/pollution 188, 201
  Mediterranean Sea 608, 611–12
  natural prolongation 185–6, 264–5
  natural resources 183–4, 186–9
  naval warfare, law of 878
  non-living and mineral resources 298, 500, 538
  North-East Atlantic and North Sea 653–8
  occupation 184
  oil and gas 183–4, 186–9, 200
  proclamations 184
  regional cooperation 201
  scientific research 207, 563, 567–73, 575, 580
  sea level, rise in 791–2, 794
  seabed 250–1, 539, 907
  seafloor, physical attributes of 181
  security 585–6
  State practice 199
  State sovereignty 184–6
  submarine cables and pipelines 189, 208
  substantive regime of maritime zones 186–9, 890–1
  superjacent waters 200, 538–9
  territorial sea 181
  threatened species and VMEs 803
  title 185
  Truman Proclamation 10–11, 13, 183
  UNCLOS III 185, 907
  water column 162, 181, 184, 200, 891
Convention on the Continental Shelf 1958
  artificial islands, installations, and structures 518
  customary international law 15–16, 21–2
  equidistance-special circumstances rule 21–2
  fisheries and living resources 183
  Indian Ocean 707
  inherent rights 184–5
  marine environment/pollution 518
  North-East Atlantic and North Sea 658
  outer limit 43, 45, 189–90
  ratifications and accessions 14
  reservations 21
  State practice 891
  State sovereignty 15
  substantive rights 186
Convention on the High Seas 1958
  codification 16
  customary international law 36
  freedom of navigation 206
  internal waters 15
  landlocked and geographically disadvantaged States 334–5
  marine environment/pollution 518
  nationality 309
  overflight, freedom of 206
  piracy 843–5, 855, 859, 863–4
  registration of ships 306–10
  scientific research 563
  spatial definition 889
  territorial sea 16
  travaux préparatoires 859
Convention on the Territorial Sea and Contiguous one 1958
  archipelagic regime 28, 141
  baselines 73, 86
  bays 20, 82

boundary delimitation 255-7
coastal State jurisdiction 95, 103
contiguous zones 92, 108-11
freedom of navigation 113
innocent passage 14-15, 98, 540,
   543, 545-6
international courts and tribunals 18-20
landlocked and geographically
   disadvantaged States 334
outer limit 95
ratifications 14
rivers 82
scientific research 563
security 110
spatial definition 889
straits 14-15, 118
substantive regime of maritime zones 891
UNCLOS I 93
cooperation *see also* **regional cooperation**
   Arctic 735, 751
   biodiversity 753, 758, 894
   bioprospecting 829, 835-7
   CMS Convention 1979 821-2
   European Union 661-2
   fisheries and living resources 317-18,
      440-8, 462, 500, 665-70
   flag State jurisdiction 312, 317-18
   future of the law of the sea 894-5, 900-3
   IMO 418-19, 422, 425, 434-5
   Indian Ocean 704, 710-23
   institutions 391-2, 441-2
   integrated oceans management 487
   International Seabed Authority 231, 435
   landlocked States and geographically
      disadvantaged States 339-43
   marine environment/pollution 300-1,
      434-5, 522, 660-1, 717-20, 894
   marine mammals 509
   Mediterranean Sea 616-25
   North-East Atlantic and North Sea 658,
      660-2, 670-1
   Ocean Compact 895
   piracy 369-71, 860
   port State jurisdiction 291-3
   regional fisheries management
      organizations 440-8, 462, 894
   scientific research 565, 573

sectoral cooperation 712-23
Security Council (UN) 369-71, 894
soft norms 31
South China Sea 636-9, 642, 644-6
territorial sea 113
UN-Oceans 895
Cooperation in Research, Conservation
   and Management of Marine Mammals
   in the North Atlantic Agreement
   (NAMMCO Agreement) 1992 510
Coordinating Body of the Seas of East Asia
   (COBSEA) 645
coral reefs
   Caribbean Sea and the Gulf of
      Mexico 683-4, 689
   climate change 812-13
   Coral Triangle Initiative 480
   Great Barrier Reef 106, 288, 468, 513, 627
   habitat protection and capacity 814
   land-based pollution 811
   ocean acidification 781-2
   threatened species and
      VMEs 799-802, 812-13
courts *see* **international courts and**
   tribunals
creeping jurisdiction 28, 111, 112, 178, 294,
   302, 892
criminal offences *see also* **drug trafficking;**
   piracy and armed robbery at sea;
   terrorism
   catch documentation and certification
      schemes 456
   coastal State jurisdiction 71
   drug trafficking 113
   FAO Compliance Agreement,
      breach of 447
   flag State jurisdiction 209-10,
      311-12, 319-21
   fraud 456
   Hague Conference of 1930 9
   innocent passage 100-1, 540, 544
   internal waters 544
   IUU fishing 448, 454-5, 460, 462
   jurisdiction, conflicts of 595-6
   Mediterranean Sea 605-6
   regional fisheries management
      organizations 447-8, 456-7

criminal offences (*cont.*)
  security 584, 586–96, 600–2
  straits 123–4
  technological development 594
  territorial sea 105, 113, 544
criminal jurisdiction, universal
  customary international law 861–2
  military operations 873–4
  piracy 57–9, 691, 860–2, 874–5
cultural heritage
  archaeological and historical objects 108, 571, 607, 609
  Mediterranean Sea 606, 609–10, 622–3
  Syracuse Declaration 623
  underwater cultural heritage 62, 359, 606, 609–10, 616, 622–4, 908
  World Heritage Convention 815–16, 823
  World Heritage List 816, 823
  wrecks 571, 870–1
customary international law
  applicable law 414
  archipelagic regime 89
  baselines 90, 793
  bay-closing lines 83–4
  biodiversity 754, 759
  boundary delimitation 255, 258, 261–2, 278
  codification 30, 346
  continental shelf 36–8, 185, 191, 261–2
  development of LOSC 1982 47
  dispute settlement 38
  due diligence 520
  erga omnes obligations 64
  exclusive economic zones 36, 160–4, 179–80
  fisheries and living resources 167, 503, 759
  flag State jurisdiction 209
  freedom of navigation 537, 539
  future of the law of the sea 905, 912
  General Assembly (UN) 42, 503
  Geneva Conventions 1958 15–16, 21–2, 34–7
  historical development 2, 7, 9, 22
  IMO 422
  innocent passage 113, 117, 537, 545
  international courts and tribunals 17, 19–21
  International Seabed Authority 37
  islands 263, 273
  jus cogens 220
  landlocked States and geographically disadvantaged States 334
  League of Nations 7
  LOSC 1982, relationship to 37–8, 45
  marine environment/pollution 520, 523–4
  military operations 766
  naval warfare, law of 876
  North-East Atlantic and North Sea 653
  piracy 59, 370, 844, 860–2, 864
  port State jurisdiction 283–5, 287, 455, 893
  precautionary approach 482, 497
  scientific research 564
  sea level, rise in 793
  security 598
  South China Sea 639
  spatial definition 889–90
  straight baselines 81
  straits 708–9
  subsequent practice, treaty modification by 47–9, 51, 67–8
  substantive regime of maritime zones 891
  territorial sea 6, 95, 103, 287
  treaties, relationship of LOSC 1982 to other 34–5, 37
  visit, right of 219–20
  warships 545, 872
  water column 754
  weapons 598
customs, fiscal, health, safety, and immigration laws and regulations
  artificial islands, installations, and structures 172
  contiguous zones 92, 107–8, 110–12, 297, 608, 656, 891
  continental shelf 187
  innocent passage 541, 543
  North-East Atlantic and North Sea 656
  port State jurisdiction 282
  security 586–7
Cyprus 605, 608–9, 612 n.29, 613–14

de La Pradelle, Albert 96

deep seabed *see* international seabed area (Area); International Seabed Authority (ISA)
Deepwater Horizon 173, 201, 691
delimitation *see* boundary delimitation
deltas 82, 87, 788–9
Denmark
   archipelagic waters 136, 138, 143, 155, 655
   Arctic 729–33, 735
   baselines 655
   Canada 730–1, 733
   continental shelf 257, 266, 657–8, 732–3
   dispute settlement 286
   European Union 286, 445, 454, 670
   Faroe Islands 155–6, 286, 445, 454, 510, 651, 655–9, 668–70, 730
   fisheries and living resources 266, 519–20
   Greenland 135, 510, 649–51, 655, 659, 668–70, 729–37
   Iceland 659
   marine mammals 669–70
   Netherlands 257
   North-East Atlantic and North Sea 651, 655, 657–9
   Norway 266
   piracy 58
   straits 115, 119 n.37, 127, 649
   territorial sea 138
   WTO 286
dependent archipelagos 154–7
derogations to treaties 52, 56, 64–5
detention of vessels 290, 544
developing countries 26–7, 226–7 *see also* capacity-building; colonialism
   baselines 77
   bioprospecting 837–8, 842
   Caribbean Sea and the Gulf of Mexico 683
   Commission on the Limits of the Continental Shelf 383
   common heritage of mankind 238
   continental shelf 198–9, 383
   exclusive economic zones 161
   fisheries and living resources 362, 515
   IMO 422–4
   Implementation Agreement 1994 226–7
   Indian Ocean 704
   landlocked States and geographically disadvantaged States 328–32, 335–6, 339–40
   MARPOL 683
   Mediterranean Sea 605
   nationality 309
   New International Economic Order 27
   open registries 422–4
   revenue-sharing 192, 198–9, 229–31, 250–2, 891
   scientific research 565
   sea level, rises in 897, 907
   seabed 26, 226–7, 230, 234, 245, 247, 842
      common heritage of mankind 238
      revenue-sharing 192, 198–9, 229–31, 250–2, 891
   security 603
   small arms by sea, proliferation of 224
   traditional knowledge 831
development of international law
   amendment of LOSC 1982 42–5, 893–4
   biodiversity 753–4
   Geneva Conventions 1958 16
   Meeting of States Parties 376–8, 387–90, 393
   North-East Atlantic and North Sea 648
   progressive development 9, 13, 16, 30, 231, 393
      Meeting of States Parties 376–8, 387–90, 393
      North-East Atlantic and North Sea 648
   security 586–601
Dickinson, Edwin D 593
diplomatic immunity 285
diplomatic protection 310, 315, 403
discards *see* by-catch and discards
dispute settlement mechanisms *see also* arbitration; International Court of Justice (ICJ); international courts and tribunals; International Tribunal for the Law of Sea (ITLOS)
   Arctic 371–2
   boundary delimitation 585, 589–90, 602, 692–9
   Caribbean Sea and the Gulf of Mexico 692–9
   compulsory 399–408, 597–8

dispute settlement mechanisms (*cont.*)
    choice of forum 399–401
    exceptions 401, 403–8
    high seas 211
    landlocked States and geographically disadvantaged States 334
    non-participation 910–11
    reservations or exceptions 33
    Seabed Disputes Chamber 247–50
  continental shelf 195–6
  customary international law 38
  development of LOSC 1982 44, 47
  enforcement 39–40
  European Union 661
  exclusive economic zones 212
  fisheries and living resources 39, 167, 445
  Geneva Conventions 1958, Optional Protocol to 14, 16, 29
  high seas 211
  IMO 435–6
  innocent passage 542
  institutionalization 445
  interpretation and application of LOSC 1982 29
  landlocked States and geographically disadvantaged States 334
  Mediterranean Sea 615–16
  military operations 885–6
  non-participation 910–11
  North-East Atlantic and North Sea 651, 658–9, 661
  regime interaction 65
  reservations or exceptions 33
  scientific research 566, 572
  security 597–8
  South China Sea 627–42, 644, 646
  specialized dispute settlements 29
  subsequent practice, treaty modification by 52, 65
  WTO 285–6, 382, 409 n.47, 512
distress, assistance to vessels in
  flag State jurisdiction 316
  freedom of navigation 206
  IMO Guidelines on Places of Refuges for Ships in Need of Assistance 284
  innocent passage 541
  masters 316
  port State jurisdiction 284
  reasonableness 316
Division for Ocean Affairs and the Law of the Sea (DOALOS) (UN) 348, 353–4
  annual reports 353
  Commission on the Limits of the Continental Shelf 353
  duties 353–4
  Fish Stocks Agreement 353–4
  General Assembly 353
  legal and technical services 353
  Legal Counsel (UN) 354
  Meeting of States Parties 353–4, 360
  monitoring 354
  Office of Legal Affairs (UN) 348, 353–4
  open-ended informal consultative process (UN) 353, 365
  Regular Process 367
  research activities 354
  resources 354
  technical assistance 354
Djalal, Hasjim 152
dolphins 442, 457–8, 511, 670, 684
Dominican Republic 144–7, 680, 682, 686, 693
driftnet fishing 42, 361, 443, 503–4, 807–8
drones 593–4
drug trafficking
  arrest of vessels 221
  bilateral agreements 101, 600
  boarding and inspection 221
  Caribbean Sea and the Gulf of Mexico 594, 675, 692
  military operations 873
  security 587, 590, 594, 600
  shiprider agreements 221, 692
  South China Sea 639
  submarines 594
  territorial sea 113
Dubner, Barry Hart 138
due publicity obligations
  artificial islands, installations and structures 172
  baselines 80 n.54
  bioprospecting 832
  charts 80
  dangers 100, 122, 540, 544

geographic coordinates, deposit of 80
innocent passage 18, 100, 540, 544
internal waters 81
Ramsar Convention on Wetlands
    1971 822
sea lanes and traffic separation schemes 128
straight baselines 80
straits 122, 128
dumping *see also* **London Convention**
    adaptive management 530
    Barcelona Convention 1976 528
    Black Sea Convention 1992 528
    climate change 530
    environmental impact assessments 528
    innocent passage 102
    land-based pollution 523
    North-East Atlantic and North
        Sea 528, 660–1
    OSPAR Convention 528
    precautionary approach 525
    radioactive waste 518, 529
    science 519–20, 523, 525, 528–30, 532,
        534–5, 577, 581
    sequestration of carbon dioxide in seabed
        and water column 529–30, 534–5
    vessel source pollution 897
Dutch East India Company 4, 536, 653

East Asian Seas Programme (EAP) 645
East China Sea 155, 589, 633, 884
ecological activism 173, 187–8, 201,
    847, 886–7
ecological protection zones (EPZs) 163,
    299, 607
ecologically and biologically significant
    areas (EBSAs)
    biodiversity 764, 767–8, 772
    Indian Ocean 718–19, 722–3
    Mediterranean Sea 768
    threatened species and VMEs 805
ecosystem approach
    Antarctic 748–9
    Arctic 746–8
    biodiversity 512–13, 755–6, 760–2, 765,
        771–2, 775–6
    Caribbean Sea and the Gulf of
        Mexico 681, 683–4, 688–90, 699

    climate change 794–6
    fisheries and living resources 54, 482, 486,
        501–2, 512–13, 897
    integrated oceans management 464,
        467–8, 471–85, 489, 644, 899
    Mediterranean 478
    North-East Atlantic and North Sea 476,
        648, 651, 660, 667
    ocean acidification 794, 796, 798
    precautionary approach 63
    regional fisheries management
        organizations 449, 450, 457–61
    science 535, 559
    South China Sea 628, 644, 646
    subsequent practice, treaty
        modification by 63
    threatened species and
        VMEs 800–2, 806–9
EEZ *see* **exclusive economic zone (EEZ)**
EIAs *see* **environmental impact**
    assessments (EIAs)
enclosed or semi-enclosed seas or oceans
    Caribbean Sea and Gulf of Mexico 673,
        681, 699
    cooperation 28, 901–2
    IMO 434
    lakes and seas 280–1, 300
    landlocked and geographically
        disadvantaged States 331
    marine spatial planning 486
    Rio Declaration 356
    South China Sea 626, 638
endangered species *see* **threatened**
    species and vulnerable marine
    ecosystems (VMEs)
enforcement and compliance 38–40 *see also*
    dispute settlement mechanisms
    Antarctic 744–5
    Arctic 734
    biodiversity 758, 764–5
    Caribbean Sea and the Gulf of
        Mexico 691–2
    coastal State jurisdiction 297, 300,
        303, 893
    Commission on the Limits of the
        Continental Shelf 39
    contiguous zones 107–10, 112, 891

enforcement and compliance (*cont.*)
  continental shelf 181, 185-8, 199-200
  counter-measures 40
  drug trafficking 101
  exclusive economic zones 170, 178
  fisheries and living resources 168-9,
      504-7, 514-15, 783
    Indian Ocean 715
    military operations 873
    regional fisheries management
      organizations 442-3,
      446-8, 453-7
  flag State jurisdiction 209-10, 304, 311-13,
      316, 505-6, 893
  general international law, mechanisms
      of 39-40
  high seas 219-23, 224, 304, 412
  IMO 430-1
  Indian Ocean 715
  innocent passage 100-2, 543-5
  International Seabed Authority 38-9, 385
  marine environment/pollution 176-7,
      316, 533
  Mediterranean Sea 618, 620-2
  migrants, smuggling of 101
  military operations 869, 873, 883
  piracy 34, 843-5, 849, 850-65, 874
  port State jurisdiction 282-3, 284, 288-91,
      300, 506, 507, 893
  private entities 895
  retorsion 40
  security 596, 599, 601-2
  State sovereignty 34
  straits 123-4, 129-30, 552
  territorial sea 91, 96
entry into force (LOSC 1982) 26-9,
      344, 346-52
  amendment of LOSC 1982 42-3
  Division for Ocean Affairs and the Law of
      the Sea (DOALOS) 348
  future of the law of the sea 905, 909
  General Assembly 348
  Implementation Agreement 1994 349
  institutions 349-52, 374
  Office for Ocean Affairs and the Law of
      the Sea (UN) 347-8
  UNCLOS III 347-8

environment *see* **biodiversity**; climate
    change; environmental impact
    assessments (EIAs); integrated
    oceans management (IOM); marine
    environment/pollution; MARPOL
environmental impact assessments (EIAs)
  Antarctic 743, 840-1
  areas beyond national jurisdiction
      (ABNJ) 483-4
  best practice standards 772
  biodiversity 753, 763-4, 766-9, 772-6
  bioprospecting 835
  capacity-building 768
  dumping 528
  Espoo Convention 522-3
  fisheries and living resources 483
  flag State jurisdiction 768
  integrated oceans management 467-8,
      472, 474, 478, 483-4, 489, 899
  International Seabed Authority 252
  land-based pollution 523
  Mediterranean Sea 619
  Rio Declaration 356
  science 522-3, 528
equidistance 267-9, 272-4
  bisector methodology 256, 260
  Caribbean Sea and the Gulf of
      Mexico 693, 695-8
  continental shelf 256-7, 259
  Convention on the Continental Shelf
      1958 21-2, 256-7
  customary international law 258-9
  equitable principles or equidistance
      debate 256-61, 264-5, 269, 278
  historical and navigational issues 256
  Indian Ocean 709
  islands 273-4
  natural prolongation 264-5, 269
  North-East Atlantic and North Sea 658
  provisional equidistance line 256, 259-60,
      268-9, 276-7, 696-8
  relevant circumstances rule 22, 258-9
  rules and principles, distinction
      between 257
  special circumstances rule 255-9,
      264, 276-7
  territorial sea 255-6, 259

erga omnes obligations 64
European Convention on Human Rights (ECHR) 225, 858
European Union
  Arctic 734
  artificial islands and installations 172 n.74
  bottom trawling 504
  CITES 669
  Common Fisheries Policy 339, 470, 650–1, 665–6, 668–9, 687
  Court of Justice 409, 661
  Eastern Tropical Pacific Seascape 480
  economic development 473–4
  European Marine Regions 473
  fisheries and living resources 650–1, 659–60, 668–9
    Common Fisheries Policy 339, 650–1, 665–6, 668–9
    driftnet fishing 502, 504
    Fish Stocks Agreement 502
    IUU fishing 293
    regional fisheries management organizations 445, 454
    WTO 409 n.47
  free movement of persons, goods, services and capital 338
  GATT 409 n.47, 512
  Habitats Directive 669–70
  Integrated Maritime Policy 473–4
  integrated oceans management 470, 473–4
  international courts and tribunals 408, 412
  landlocked States and geographically disadvantaged States 338–9, 341
  marine environment/pollution 660–1, 664
  marine mammals 511–12, 669–70
  marine spatial planning 474
  Marine Strategy Framework Directive 473, 649, 662–3
  Mediterranean Sea 605, 610, 617
  migrants, smuggling of 222, 590–1
  nationality 306–7
  North East Atlantic and North Sea 648–54, 659–60, 668–9, 671, 902
  participation in LOSC 1982 32, 33
  pilotage 650
  piracy
    Naval Force 849, 855
    transfer agreements 862
  regional cooperation 661–2
  regional fisheries management organizations 445, 454
  State sovereignty 172 n.74
  UNCLOS III 338, 901
  Water Framework Directive 662
  whaling 669–70
  WTO 285–6, 409 n.47, 445, 512
exclusive economic zone (EEZ) 13, 159–80
  Antarctic 738
  applicable law 165–77, 414
  archipelagic regime 146, 149, 553
  Arctic 372, 730, 734
  artificial islands, installations and structures 165, 171–3
  attribution of rights, conflict over 165–6, 178
  balancing of interests 165–6
  baselines 70, 86
  biodiversity 761
  bioprospecting 830, 833–4
  boundary delimitation 163, 256, 258, 261–6, 277–9, 892
  Caribbean Sea and the Gulf of Mexico 681, 697
  CITES 819
  climate change 795
  contiguous zones 109–11, 112, 891
  continental shelf 162, 170, 181, 185–8, 199–200, 265–6, 891–2
  creeping jurisdiction 28, 178, 892
  customary international law 36, 160–4, 179–80
  declarations 34
  designation 164
  developing countries 161
  dispute settlement 212
  due regard obligation 30
  economic resources 170–1
  EEZ minus view 205
  enforcement 170, 178
  evolution of concept 160–4
  exclusivity 165, 171

exclusive economic zone (EEZ) (*cont.*)
   fisheries and living resources 4, 161–3,
      165–70, 177–9, 343
      archipelagic regime 136–7
      coastal State jurisdiction 298–9
      Fish Stocks Agreement 505
      Indian Ocean 706–7
      international courts and
         tribunals 405, 407
      IUU fishing 505
      landlocked and geographically
         disadvantaged States 343
      maximum sustainable yield 498–9
      Mediterranean Sea 607–13
      North-East Atlantic and North
         Sea 656, 659
      precautionary approach 496–7
      regional fisheries management
         organizations 440, 461
      scientific research 563
      shared and highly migratory
         stocks 499–500
   sovereign rights 165
   substantive regime of maritime zones 891–2
   flag State jurisdiction 161, 311, 313
   freedom of navigation 298, 418, 537–9,
      554–5, 557
   applicable law 165
   expansion of jurisdiction 111
   international courts and tribunals 418
   marine environment/pollution 177, 179
   security 179
   substantive regime of maritime zones 892
   freedom of the high seas 162, 171, 180
   functional powers, theory of 161
   future of the law of the sea 178–80, 900
   Hague Conference 1930 160–1
   high seas 165, 205, 208, 212–14
   history and genesis of concept 160–1
   hot pursuit 875
   IMO 418, 430–2
   Indian Ocean 706, 708, 713–15, 718
   inherent rights 296–7
   innocent passage 102
   interaction of maritime zones 892
   international courts and tribunals 44,
      404–5, 407
   interpretation 160, 164, 178
   islands 28, 272
   landlocked and geographically
      disadvantaged States 328–33, 343–4
   legal status 162–3
   limitations 171, 179–80
   marine environment/pollution 165, 171,
      176–80, 533
   freedom of navigation 177, 179
   generally recognized international
      standards 177–8
   IMO 179, 432
   innocent passage 102
   overflight, freedom of 177
   ultra-hazardous cargoes, consent to
      passage of 178
   marine mammals 508
   maximum limit 162–3, 178
   Mediterranean Sea 164, 901
   military operations 178, 213–14, 591–2,
      882–5, 900
   minoris generis/*sui generis* zones 162–4
   naval warfare, law of 878–9
   non-living and minerals resources,
      sovereign rights over 165,
      170–1, 177–8
   North-East Atlantic and North
      Sea 656, 659
   overflight, freedom of 165, 177, 298, 554
   overlapping zones 163, 891
   patrimonial sea, notion of 161
   piracy 847–51, 864
   plastics 533
   port State jurisdiction 289
   proclamations 163–4
   quasi-territorial jurisdiction 289
   rocks 95
   scientific research 173–5, 560, 567–72,
      575, 580–1
      applicable law 165
      high seas 207
      international court and tribunals 407
      landlocked and geographically
         disadvantaged States 337
      State practice 892
      World Ocean Assessment (UN) 898
sea level, rise in 791, 793–4

seabed 161, 170
security 585–7, 591–2, 597
spatial definition 889
State practice 160, 162–3, 171,
    178–80, 891–2
straits 120–1, 126–7, 132, 552, 882–3
submarine cables and pipelines 165,
    177–8, 208, 212–13, 298
subsoil 161, 170
sui generis zones 162–4, 205, 297
superadjacent to seabed, regime of waters
    which are 161
territorial sea 94, 160–2, 164, 892
third States, rights and obligations
    of 165–6, 177–8, 180
threatened species and VMEs 803–4,
    806–7, 819
UNCLOS III 205

Facilitation of International Maritime
    Traffic Convention, amendment
    to 425
failed or failing States 704, 721, 864
Falkland Islands 155, 163 n.24
Fanning, Lucia 683
FAO *see* Food and Agriculture
    Organization (FAO)
Faroe Islands 155–6, 286, 445, 454, 510, 651,
    655–9, 668–70, 730
Fedder, Bevis 835–6
fertilization of oceans 534, 577, 784–5
Finland 127, 135, 138, 475, 735, 878
fiscal laws and regulations *see* customs,
    fiscal, health, safety, and immigration
    laws and regulations
Fish Stocks Agreement (FSA) 167–8, 501–3
    amendment of LOSC 1982 43
    biodiversity 502, 754–5, 760
    boarding and inspection 506
    coastal State jurisdiction 303
    developing countries 362
    development 501–2
    DOALOS 353–4
    ecosystem approach 54, 501–2
    entry into force 909–10
    European Union 502
    FAO report 361–2
    fishing entities, extension to 444–5
    flag State jurisdiction 313, 317–18, 893
    future of the law of the sea 893,
        897, 908–9
    General Assembly (UN) 360–2, 502
    impact 909–10
    integrated oceans management 481–2
    international courts and tribunals 410
    IUU fishing 361–2, 505
    Johannesburg Conference 361
    long-term sustainability 502
    management approach 502–3
    maximum sustainable yield 54
    membership 502
    non-member status 502–3
    non-parties, membership open to
        LOSC 502
    North-East Atlantic and North
        Sea 654–5, 666
    open registries 502
    port State jurisdiction 290, 506
    precautionary approach 54, 63,
        167–8, 501–2
    ratification or accession 168, 361
    regional fisheries bodies 501–3
    regional fisheries management
        arrangements 502
    regional fisheries management
        organizations 54, 167–8, 441, 444–6,
        449–50, 453, 460–1, 501–2
    subsequent practice, treaty modification
        by 52–5, 63
    sustainable use 54, 168, 502
    threatened species and VMEs 806–7
    UNCLOS III 501
**fisheries and living resources, conservation
    and management of** *see also* **by-catch
    and discards; Fish Stocks Agreement
    (FSA); marine mammals, conservation
    and management of; regional fisheries
    management organizations (RFMOs);
    whaling**
    Antarctic 727, 739, 742–3, 745–6, 749
    archipelagic regime 136–7, 149, 498
    Arctic 729–31, 735, 737–8, 746
    areas beyond national jurisdiction 482,
        487, 753–4, 758–60

fisheries and living resources, conservation and management of (*cont.*)
arrest 168–9
artisanal fishing 684
biodiversity 512–15, 753–5, 758–60, 764–5, 769–71, 806
bioprospecting 833, 836, 841
bottom trawling 503–4, 515, 807–9, 824
capture fisheries 712–13
Caribbean Sea and the Gulf of Mexico 681, 683–90, 699
catch documentation schemes 745
CITES 820
climate change 668, 778, 794–7
coastal State jurisdiction 20–1, 207, 298–302, 491, 494, 498–500, 514
Code of Conduct for Responsible Fisheries 482, 486, 497, 807–8
codification 491
Common Fisheries Policy 339, 470, 650–1, 665–6, 668–9, 687
confiscation 169, 504
continental shelf 183, 186, 500
customary international law 167, 503, 759
data collection 716
developing countries 515
dispute settlement 167, 410
driftnet fishing 42, 361, 443, 503–4, 807–8
ecosystem approach 482, 486, 512–13, 897
emerging concepts 512–14
enforcement 168–9, 504–7, 514–15, 715, 873
environmental impact assessments 483
European Union 339, 470, 504, 650–1, 665–6, 668–9, 687
exclusive fishing zones 4, 161–3, 165–70, 177–9, 343, 496–500, 505
  archipelagic regime 136–7
  coastal State jurisdiction 298–9
Indian Ocean 706–7
international courts and tribunals 405, 407
landlocked and geographically disadvantaged States 343
Mediterranean Sea 607–13
North-East Atlantic and North Sea 656, 659
scientific research 563
sovereign rights 165
substantive regime of maritime zones 891–2
fish aggregating devices 172–3
fish, definition of 493
flag State jurisdiction 310, 313–15, 317–18, 321–4, 505–7, 532
flags of convenience/open registries 445–6, 502, 506–7
free riders 760
freedom of navigation 4, 554–5
future of the law of the sea 897
gear, regulation of 503–4, 622, 808
General Assembly (UN) 494, 503–4
Geneva Conventions 1958 14–15, 496
geographically disadvantaged States 167
high seas 500–1, 505, 506
historical development 3–4, 10
Indian Ocean 712–17
information sharing 318
innocent passage 541, 543
inspection 168
integrated oceans management 467, 471, 474, 477, 481–4, 486–7, 489
judicial proceedings 168
landlocked and geographically disadvantaged States 167, 325–6, 330, 333, 339, 343–4
large-scale pelagic driftnet fishing 503
limitations 166
maps 650
marine environment/pollution 494–5, 498, 534, 683–90
market-based mechanisms 895
maximum sustainable yield 496, 498–9, 806–7, 824
Mediterranean Sea 607, 609–11, 621–2, 624–5
methods of fishing, regulation of 503–4, 622, 807–9
military operations 873
move-on rules 809
North-East Atlantic and North Sea 442, 648, 650–6, 659–60, 665–71

ocean acidification 796, 708
OSPAR Commission 467
port State jurisdiction 283, 285–93, 506, 507, 893
precautionary approach 493, 497–8, 513, 514, 897
regulatory regime 166–7
relative stability, principle of 665
scientific research 174–5, 495–7, 559, 563–4, 576–7, 796
security 585, 600
South China Sea 627–9, 638, 644, 646
State practice 168–9
State sovereignty 3, 4, 166, 491, 493–4, 498
statistical information 712–13
Sub-Regional Fisheries Commission 317–18
subsistence fishing 797
subsoil 170
surplus catches 166–7
sustainable use 491–9, 502–5, 512–15, 666, 897
   North-East Atlantic and North Sea 652, 666
   scientific research 576–7
   threatened species and VMEs 805–9
technological innovations 753, 800
third countries 166–7
threatened species and VMEs 803–9
total allowable catch 166–7, 496, 498–500, 806–7, 824
Truman Proclamation 11
UNCLOS II 13
Fitzmaurice, Gerald 118
flag State jurisdiction 214–19, 304–24
   see also **flags of convenience/open registries**
   administrative, technical and social matters, control of 314
   Antarctic 727–8, 744–5
   Arctic 727–8
   assistance at sea 316
   audits 437
   biodiversity 755, 763, 765, 768
   boarding and inspection 313, 315, 319–21, 557–8

broadcasting, unauthorized 312
casualties 316
coastal State jurisdiction 304–5, 312, 314, 317–18, 893, 908
collisions 210, 218–19
concurrent jurisdiction 209–10, 314
conflict of laws 307
constructive presence, doctrine of 312
cooperation 312, 317–18
criminal jurisdiction 209–10, 311–12, 319–21
development 305–6
diplomatic protection 310, 315
distress at sea, assistance for vessels in 316
due diligence 318, 323
effective control 305, 314, 318, 321, 323
enforcement 209–10, 304, 311–13, 316, 505–6, 755, 893
   fisheries and living resources 446–7, 457, 505–6
   high seas 304, 312
   marine environment/pollution 316
environmental impact assessments 768
exclusive economic zones 161, 311, 313
exclusive jurisdiction 209, 311, 313
Fish Stocks Agreement 313, 893
fisheries and living resources 310, 313–15, 317–18, 321–4, 532
   conservation and management 317
   cooperation 317–18
   enforcement 505–6
   FAO Compliance Agreement 507
   Fish Stocks Agreement 317–18
   information sharing 318
   IUU fishing 209–10, 314–15, 318, 321–4, 505, 507, 893
   regional fisheries management organizations 444, 446–8, 453–4, 457
   Sub-Regional Fisheries Commission (SRFC) 317–18
flag State jurisdiction 210, 317
flags of convenience/open registries 446–8
freedom of navigation 210, 313, 556, 557–8

flag State jurisdiction (*cont.*)
  friendship, commerce and navigation bilateral treaties 305
  future of the law of the sea 893, 896–7
  generally accepted international rules and standards (GAIRS) 321–2
  high seas 30, 209–10, 216, 218–19, 224, 304, 312
  hot pursuit 312
  human rights of persons on interdicted vessels 310, 315
  IMO 322–3, 418, 428, 430, 437–8
    Instruments Implementation Code (III Code) 322–3
    Voluntary Member State Audit Scheme 322–3
  international courts and tribunals 17
  ISPS Code 320
  Italian city states 305
  ITLOS 403
  IUU fishing 209–10, 314–15, 318, 321–4, 505, 507, 893
  marine environment/pollution 316, 321–2, 532, 755
  military operations 867, 874
  nationality 306–12, 315, 755
  natural resources 311
  non-living and minerals resources 319
  non-State actors 310
  operation 310–12
  piracy 312, 320–1, 857, 862, 874
  port State jurisdiction 283, 322, 893
  prescriptive jurisdiction 209, 311, 313
  registration 306–10, 317
    conditions 306–10
    maintain, duty to 314
    nationality 306–10
    small vessels 309–10, 314
    stateless or unflagged vessels 314–15
    UN Registration Convention 307
  rights and duties 313–21
  Roman law 305
  rule of reference 321–2
  sanctions 317–18, 320
  scientific research 318
  security 319–21, 588
  Security Council (UN) resolutions 320
  sovereign equality, principle of 321
  standards 312, 315–16, 318, 321–3
  State practice 209, 322
  stateless or unflagged vessels 314–15
  SUA Convention 319
  territorial sea 91–2, 97, 104, 312
  vessel source pollution 532
  visit, right of 220
  warships 312, 870–1
flags of convenience /open registries 216, 306–8
  Caribbean Sea and the Gulf of Mexico 682–3
  developing countries 422–4
  fisheries and living resources 445–6, 502, 506–7
  free riders 445
  IMO 422–4, 437–8, 682–3
  nationality 308
  piercing the corporate veil 447
  regional fisheries management organizations 445–8
Food and Agriculture Organization (FAO)
  biodiversity 765
  Code of Conduct for Responsible Fisheries 482, 486, 497, 807–8
  Compliance Agreement 446–7, 507, 654–5
  Constitution 686
  cooperation 894
  fisheries and living resources 390, 497, 507, 512–13, 805
  Global Record of Fishing Vessels, Refrigerated Transport Vessels and Supply Vessels 454
  Guidelines for Assessing Flag State Performance 446
  nationality 307
  Plan of Action 209–10, 505
  Plant Genetic Resources International Treaty 839
  regional fisheries management organizations 440, 446–7, 455
  Technical Guidelines on the Precautionary Approach to Capture Fisheries 497
  threatened species and VMEs 801–2, 805, 820

force majeure 284, 455, 541
foreign vessels *see* **innocent passage, right of**
fragmentation of international law
   biodiversity 768
   high seas, enforcement on the 224
   institutions 391
   marine environment/pollution 521, 524, 525
   regime interaction 61-2
   State responsibility 224
   subsequent State practice, treaty modification by 48, 61-2, 67-8
France
   baselines 655
   Caribbean Sea 673, 675 n.10, 681, 698
   collisions, jurisdiction in 18, 218
   colonialism 633, 673, 675 n.10, 681, 698
   continental shelf 197, 273, 608, 657-8
   ecological protection zones 610
   exclusive economic zones 176, 213-14
   fisheries and living resources 600
   Indian Ocean 705-6
   international courts and tribunals 18
   marine environment/pollution 176
   marine mammals 670
   Mediterranean Sea 605, 608-10, 612-14, 618
   military operations 213-14
   North-East Atlantic and North Sea 647, 651, 654-8
   nuclear weapons testing 211-12
   piracy 58
   security 276
   South China Sea 631-3
   Spain 613-14
   territorial sea 656
   Turkey 18, 218
   Vietnam 632-4
François, JPA 9, 13, 845
free riders 283, 300, 302, 444-6, 760
freedom of navigation and navigational rights 536-58 *see also* **innocent passage, right of**
   archipelagic waters 137, 154, 537-9, 553-4, 557
   biodiversity 754
   boarding and inspection 557-8
   bunkering services to fishing vessels 554-5
   Caribbean Sea and the Gulf of Mexico 682-3
   coastal State jurisdiction 11-12, 296, 298, 418, 537-8, 554, 557
   colonialism 537
   compulsory pilotage 557
   contiguous zones 108, 110-11, 537, 554
   continental shelf 184, 186, 201, 538-9
   Convention on the High Seas 1958 206
   customary international law 537
   distress, rendering assistance to vessels in 206
   due regard principle 211
   exclusive economic zones 111, 160, 165, 177, 179, 537-9, 554-5, 557, 892
   applicable law 165
   expansion of jurisdiction 111
   international courts and tribunals 418
   marine environment/pollution 177, 179
   security 179
   substantive regime of maritime zones 892
   fisheries and living resources 4, 554-5
   flag State jurisdiction 313, 556, 557-8
   future of the law of the sea 911
   high seas 11, 538-9, 556
   ILC Draft Articles 206
   IMO 418, 427, 432-3
   Indian Ocean 720-2
   internal waters 537-8
   international courts and tribunals 403, 404
   landlocked and geographically disadvantaged States 331-2, 342-3, 556
   marine environment/pollution 177-9, 206, 432, 537, 555, 557
   military operations 211-12, 592, 879-85
   Montreux Convention 296
   North-East Atlantic and North Sea 653-4
   peace, in 879-85
   piracy 844
   seabed 538
   security 179, 557-8, 584, 590, 592-3, 597

freedom of navigation and navigational
    rights (cont.)
  ships, construction, equipment,
      seaworthiness and manning of 206
  South China Sea 646
  straits 121–2, 132–3, 537–9, 549–52
  SUA Protocol 556, 557
  substantive regime of maritime zones 891
  territorial sea 93, 108, 110–11, 538–9, 557
  trade 536–7
  treaties and conventions 557
  Truman Proclamation 11
  UNCLOS III 418, 427
  vessel source pollution 206, 532, 537
  war, in 879–85
  warships 537, 556
  weapons of mass destruction 557
freedom of the high seas see high seas, legal
    regime of the
friendship, commerce and navigation
    (FCN) bilateral treaties 305
Fund Convention 1971 519, 531

Galiani, Ferdinando 5
Galland, Grantly R 786
gas see oil and gas
GATT (General Agreement on Tariffs
    and Trade)
  European Union 409 n.47, 512
  Implementation Agreement 1994 408
  marine mammals 512
  port, conditions for entry into 285–6
  regional fisheries management
      organizations 445
General Assembly (UN)
  annual cycle of review of LOSC
      1982 40–2
  areas beyond national jurisdiction 905
  bioprospecting 837–8
  continental shelf 358–9
  customary international law 42
  fisheries and living resources 360–2,
      493, 502–4
  future of the law of the sea 894
  Future We Want resolution 485–6
  Geneva Conventions 1958 13, 16
  IMO 437

  integrated oceans management 465,
      480–1, 484–9
  International Seabed Authority 250, 358
  marine environment/pollution 359,
      368–9, 484 n.149
  marine protected areas 484–5
  Meeting of States Parties 358, 360, 389–90
  Ocean affairs and law of the sea, annual
      resolution on 41, 353–4, 358, 363–5,
      371, 389, 392, 700
  Ocean Compact 895
  piracy 369
  regional fisheries management
      organizations 443, 458
  Regular Process 366–7, 484 n.149
  resolutions 358–9
    annual cycle of reviews 40–2
    Fish Stocks Agreement 361–2
    future of the law of the sea 894
    integrated oceans
        management 465, 481
    Ocean affairs and law of the sea 41, 353–4,
        358, 363–5, 371, 389, 392, 700
  role 357–9
  scientific research 579
  Secretary-General, role of 358–9, 375–6
  security 599
  threatened species and VMEs 801–2,
      805, 808
  UN-Oceans 362–3, 895
  UNCLOS III 25, 358
General Fisheries Commission for the
    Mediterranean (GFCM) 443
generally accepted international rules and
    standards
  Antarctic 728
  Arctic 728
  collisions 105
  construction, design, equipment, or
      manning 100
  innocent passage 102
  marine environment/
      pollution 102, 176–8
  rules of reference 31
  subsequent practice, treaty
      modification by 66
  territorial sea 105

genetic resources *see* marine genetic resources, bioprospecting
Geneva Conventions on the Law of the Sea 13–16 *see also* Convention on the Continental Shelf 1958; Convention on the High Seas 1958; Convention on the Territorial Sea and Contiguous one 1958
   archipelagic regimes 16, 141
   baselines 14
   codification 13–16, 30, 37
   contiguous zones 14, 891
   continental shelf 891
   Convention on Fishing and Conservation of Living Resources of the High Seas 1958 496
   customary international law 16, 21–2
   General Assembly (UN) 13, 16
   historical development 13–22
   ILC 13–14
   innocent passage 14–15
   international courts and tribunals 18–20, 396
   limitations 904
   oil, discharge of 15
   Optional Protocol on of Signature Concerning the Compulsory Settlement of Disputes 14, 16, 29
   radioactive wastes 15
   ratifications and accessions 14–16
   reservations 14
   scientific research 561, 563–4
   single institution, proposal for 896
   straits 14–15
   UNCLOS II 13
   UNCLOS III 16
Geneva Conventions on the Law of War and Additional Protocols 876–7
geo-engineering 772, 784–5, 797, 896
geographically disadvantaged States *see* landlocked States (LLS) and geographically disadvantaged States (GDS)
Germany
   continental shelf 257
   exclusive economic zones 470
   fisheries and living resources 20
   Iceland 20
   integrated oceans management 470, 472
   ITLOS, seat of 351
   marine protected areas 470–1
   marine spatial planning 470–2
   military operations 213–14
   National Strategy for Integrated Coastal Zone Management 470–1
   piracy 58
   territorial sea 125, 546
   United Kingdom 20
Gibraltar 115, 604–5, 607–8, 656, 882
Gidel, Gilbert 9–10
Global Environment Facility (GEF) 301, 645, 683, 689–90
Global Ocean Observing System 574
global oceans management 896–900
Global Partnership on Marine Litter 534
governance *see* integrated oceans management (IOM)
Great Barrier Reef 106, 288, 468, 513, 627
Greece
   Albania 117, 612 n.30, 613
   Corfu Channel case 117
   Mediterranean Sea 605, 608, 613–14
   territorial sea 608
   Turkey 608, 614
greenhouse gases 778–87, 797, 812, 824
Greenland 135, 510, 649–51, 655, 659, 668–70, 729–37
Grotius, Hugo 4, 114, 203–4, 439, 501, 536, 803
Group of Broad-Shelf States 654
Gulf Cooperation Council (GCC) 712
Gulf of Guinea, piracy in 843–4, 848
Gulf of Mexico *see* Caribbean Sea and the Gulf of Mexico
gulfs 607

habitat protection and capacity 813–16
   Biodiversity Convention 813–14
   Habitats Directive 669–70
   Ramsar Convention on Wetlands 1971 813, 814–15, 816, 822–3
   World Heritage Convention 1972 815–16, 823

Hafner, Gerhard 391
Hague Conference of 1907 876
Hague Conference of 1930 7–9, 13
  archipelagic regime 136–8
  baselines 9, 72–3
  codification 2, 7–9
  criminal jurisdiction 9
  exclusive economic zones 160–1
  hot pursuit 9
  inland and territorial waters, difference between 9
  innocent passage 9, 540
  military operations 880
  straits 9, 116
  territorial sea 93
Hague Conventions on the Law of War 876 n.34, 877
harbour works 85
Harvard Research on International Law 7–8, 136
Haward, Marcus 796
Hayashi, Moritaka 793
hazardous and noxious substances, carriage of
  airspace 549
  archipelagic regime 296
  Basel Convention 1989 429, 548–9
  innocent passage 98–9, 112, 547–9
  territorial sea 548
  ultra-hazardous cargoes, consent to passage of 178
health *see* customs, fiscal, health, safety, and immigration laws and regulations
Hedberg, Hollis D 193–4
heritage *see* cultural heritage
high seas, legal regime of the 203–25
  see also Convention on the High Seas 1958; freedom of navigation; overflight, freedom of
  Antarctic 727, 741–2, 749
  archipelagic regime 140–1, 146, 205, 553
  Arctic 727, 746, 747
  artificial islands, installations and structures 206
  baselines 72, 86
  basic features of high seas 204–8
  battle of the books 4

biodiversity 754, 763–4, 768
bioprospecting 829, 836–8
Caribbean Sea and the Gulf of Mexico 675
challenges 223–5
coastal State jurisdiction 297
codification 204, 205
concurrent jurisdiction 209–10
conflict of rights 212
contiguous zones 108
continental shelf 184
Convention on the High Seas 1958 206
definition 28, 205
dispute settlement 17–19, 211
drug trafficking 556
due regard principle 30, 486 n.164, 556
EEZ minus view 205
enforcement 219–23, 224, 304, 312
exclusive economic zones 162, 165, 171, 180, 205, 208, 212–14
extent 204–8
fisheries and living resources 206, 207, 500–1, 505, 506
flag State jurisdiction 30, 209–10, 216, 218–19, 224, 304, 312
freedom of navigation 11, 538–9, 556
global commons 754
high seas minus view 205
historical development 1–2, 3–5, 7, 22
hot pursuit 875
human rights 224–5
ILC Draft Articles 204, 206, 358
Indian Ocean 709
interaction of maritime zones 892
landlocked and geographically disadvantaged States 335, 556
legal character 208
limitations 206, 556
list of freedoms 206
Mediterranean Sea 611
military operations 883–4
North-East Atlantic and North Sea 649
peaceful purposes, reservation for 210–12
piracy 843–5, 847–50, 855, 864, 874–5
policing the high seas 219–23, 224
reciprocity 64
res communis 203–4

res nullius 203–4
res publica 203–4
scientific research 206, 207, 572
seabed 892
search and rescue operations 224–5
shipping 214–19, 224
spatial extent 205
State sovereignty 1–2, 203–4
stateless vessels 216–18, 224
straits 114, 120, 132
SUA Convention 556
submarine cables and pipelines 206, 207–8, 212–13
territorial sea 7, 18, 93, 205
terrorism 224
threatened species and VMEs 803–4
Truman Proclamation 11
UNCLOS III 205
warships 556
water column 161
highly migratory species *see also* **Fish Stocks Agreement (FSA); migratory/ highly migratory species and straddling stocks**
hijacking ships and crews 844
Hinrichs Oyarce, Ximena 714
Hong Kong Convention on Recycling of Ships 2009 429, 431, 436
hostage-taking 590, 595–6, 861–3
hot pursuit 9, 96, 108 n.119, 188, 312, 875
Hu Jinjie 633
Hu Jintao 643
human rights
crew 104, 310, 315, 857–8, 862, 864
European Convention on Human Rights 225, 858
flag State jurisdiction 310, 315
high seas 224–5
interdicted vessels, persons on 310, 315
liberty and security, right to 169 n.60
piracy 845, 856–8
territorial sea 104, 112
terrorism 224
human trafficking 590–1, 596, 600–1, 606
see also **migrants, smuggling of**
humanitarian assistance 869, 873
hydrocarbons *see* **oil and gas**

hydrothermal vents 1, 572–3, 651, 808, 827, 839, 842

Iceland
archipelagic waters 135, 138
Arctic 729–30, 735
continental shelf 186, 657, 729–30, 769
Denmark 659
European Union 666
fisheries and living resources 186, 500, 510–11, 666, 668
Germany 20
Icelandic Salmon Management Scheme 668
marine mammals 510–11, 669
North-East Atlantic and North Sea 647–8, 650–1, 655–7, 659, 666–70
Norway 500
port State jurisdiction 286
ratifications of LOSC 1982 26
United Kingdom 20
whaling 510–11, 669
ILC *see* **International Law Commission (ILC)**
illegal fishing *see* **IUU fishing (Illegal, Unreported and Unregulated Fishing)**
illegal immigration *see* **migrants, smuggling of**
IMO *see* **International Maritime Organization (IMO)**
immigration *see* **customs, fiscal, health, safety, and immigration laws and regulations; migrants, smuggling of**
immunity 285 *see also* **sovereign immunity**
impact assessments *see* **environmental impact assessments (EIAs)**
Implementation Agreement 1994 27, 226–8
common heritage of mankind 53
consent 227
developed States 226–7
developing countries 226–7
entry into force of LOSC 1982 349
future of the law of the sea 905, 908–9
international courts and tribunals 408, 410
interpretation and application as single instrument 227

946 INDEX

Implementation Agreement 1994 (*cont.*)
  landlocked and geographically
    disadvantaged States 336
  modification or amendment 227 n.6
  Seabed Disputes Chamber 231–2, 236–9,
    241, 243 n.89, 244–6, 250, 252
  spatial definition 908
  State parties 227
  subsequent practice, treaty modification
    by 52–5, 57, 62
implementation agreements *see also*
    Fish Stocks Agreement (FSA);
    Implementation Agreement 1994
  amendment of LOSC 1982 43–4
  areas beyond national jurisdiction
    (ABNJ) 909
  biodiversity 43–4
  bioprospecting 910
  future of the law of the sea 908–9
  North-East Atlantic and North Sea 654
  sea level, rise in 793, 910
  subsequent practice, treaty modification
    by 52–5, 57, 62, 67
implied powers, doctrine of 52, 55
India
  Bangladesh 276–8, 705
  boundary delimitation 276–8
  China 175, 342, 701
  continental shelf 707
  exclusive economic zones 175, 213, 278
  fisheries and living resources 714
  high seas 219
  Indian Ocean 701–2, 704–11, 714, 720
  islands 704
  Pakistan 705
  port State jurisdiction 286, 291–2
  scientific research 571
  security 720
indigenous communities 835
Indian Ocean 701–23
  archipelagic States 704, 708, 722
  Antarctic convergence 704
  areas beyond national jurisdiction
    (ABNJ) 718–19
  ASEAN 712
  baselines 707–8, 722
  Biodiversity Convention 717
  boundary delimitation 703–9, 722
  Chagos Archipelago 163 n.14, 705,
    707 n.18
  China 701, 709, 720–1
  coastal State jurisdiction 702, 706–10
  colonialism 705
  Commission on the Limits of the
    Continental Shelf 707, 709 n.27
  continental shelf 706–7, 709, 715, 718
  cooperation 704, 710–23
  definition and general description 702–6
  developed countries 704
  developing countries 704
  ecologically or biologically significant
    areas (EBSAs) 718–19, 722–3
  economic development 704
  enforcement 715
  equidistance 709
  exclusive economic zones 706, 708,
    713–15, 718
  exclusive fisheries zones 706–7
  fisheries and living
    resources 712–17, 722–3
  France 705–6
  freedom of navigation 720–2
  geostrategic significance 701
  high seas 709
  India 701–2, 704–11, 714, 720
  Indian Ocean Commission 712
  Indian Ocean Marine Affairs
    Co-operation 710
  Indian Ocean Rim-Association for
    Regional Co-operation 710–11
  Indonesia 704, 707–8, 710–11, 714–15
  institutions 710–12
  integrated oceans management 465,
    479, 710
  International Seabed Authority 709
  islands 705–6
  Japan 713, 715
  landlocked and geographically
    disadvantaged States 707
  marine environment/pollution 717–20
  marine protected areas 705
  Nairobi Convention 2010 479, 718–19
  New Zealand 715
  non-parties to LOSC 1982 706

oil and gas 706
overflight, freedom of 722
piracy 219, 702, 721, 723, 874
port State control, MOU on 291, 721–2
regional and sub-regional
    cooperation 704, 710–23, 903
sectoral cooperation 712–23
security 702, 720–2
sustainable use and management 711–12
Taiwan 713, 715–17
territorial sea 706–8, 721
trade 711
tsunamis 560, 574
UNCLOS III 706
United Kingdom 705–7
United States 701, 705, 708, 720
vulnerable marine ecosystems
    (VMEs) 718–19, 722–3
whaling sanctuaries 510
**Indian Ocean Tuna Commission
    (IOTC)** 442, 450, 452, 714–17, 818
Indonesia
    archipelagic regime 13, 135, 138–52,
        157, 295–6
    baselines 12–13, 71
    climate change 471
    Djuanda Declaration 139–40
    fisheries and living resources 149
    freedom of navigation 554
    high seas 217, 222
    Indian Ocean 704, 707–8, 710–11, 714–15
    integrated oceans management 471, 480
    piracy 864
    security 603
    South China Sea 626, 642
    straight baselines 12–13
    straits 123–4
**Informal Consultative Process on Oceans
    and the Law of the Sea (UN)** 65–6
inland waters *see* **internal waters**
innocent passage, right of 98–102, 539–49
    anchoring 541
    archipelagic regime 134, 137, 140, 149–51,
        538, 552–3
    Basel HNS Convention 1989 548–9
    baselines 70–1, 87–8
    bioprospecting 833

boarding and inspection 544–5
charts, publicising 544
civil jurisdiction 100, 545
coastal State jurisdiction 540–9
collisions 541
comity 545
construction, design, equipment, or
    manning (CDEM) 100
continuous and expeditious 103, 428
    n.70, 541
criminal jurisdiction 100–1, 540, 544
customary international law 113, 117,
    537, 545
customs, fiscal, health, safety,
    and immigration laws and
    regulations 541, 543
derogations 65
detention of vessels 544
dispute settlement 18–19, 542
distress, vessels in 541
enforcement 100–2, 543–5
exercise of right 541–2
fisheries and living resources 541, 543
force majeure 541
Geneva Conventions 1958 14–15, 98, 540,
    543, 545–6
geography of territorial sea 98
Hague Conference of 1930 9, 540
hazardous or noxious cargoes, carriage
    of 98–9, 112, 547–9
historical development 3, 5–7, 539–40
hovering, act of 541
ILC 117–18
illegal acts 100–1
IMO 418, 432–3
internal waters 87–8, 537, 540, 544
inward/outward-bound
    passage 540, 545
IUU fishing 543
Jackson Hole Agreement 882
lateral passage 540
manner of passage 541
marine environment/pollution 99, 102,
    544, 547–8
military operations 541, 881–2
navigational aids and facilities,
    protection of 543

innocent passage, right of (*cont.*)
  non-innocence, standards of 98–100, 541–3, 597, 882
  non-suspendable right 537, 552, 557
  notification 112, 881–2
  nuclear weapons, warships carrying 542, 547–9
  overflight, freedom of 98, 540, 553, 881
  peace, good order or security, prejudicial to 541–2, 597, 881
  ports, call at 540, 544
  publicising regulations and dangers 18, 100, 540, 544
  radioactive materials, carriage of 547
  regulations and laws, compliance with 541
  roadsteads 540
  safety 543
  scientific research 541, 543, 567, 570
  scope 98
  sea lanes and traffic separation schemes 544
  security 100, 586, 597
  standards 98–100, 541–2
  State practice 546, 882
  State sovereignty 537, 539
  stopping 541
  straits 18–19, 98, 115–19, 121–2, 127–8, 133, 545
  submarine cables and pipelines 543
  submarines and other underwater vehicles 541, 546, 553, 594, 881
  surveys 541, 543
  suspension 100, 122, 149, 544, 552–3
  territorial sea 5–6, 98–102, 111–13, 538–41, 543–6, 548, 552–3
    criminal jurisdiction 544
    Geneva 14–15, 98, 540, 543, 545–6
    hazardous cargoes 548
    submarines and other underwater vehicles 541
    warships 545–7
  threatened species and VMEs 804
  threats or use of force 541
  warships and other government vessels 18–19, 60, 98–9, 112–13, 542, 545–7
  Yugoslavia, break-up of 106

inspection *see* boarding and inspection; visit, right of search and
installations *see* artificial islands, installations and structures
Institut de Droit International (IDI) 7–8, 116, 136, 632
institutionalization of international law 7, 23
institutions and actors 373–93 *see also* Commission on the Limits of the Continental Shelf (CLCS); Food and Agriculture Organization (UN); General Assembly (UN); international courts and tribunals; International Seabed Authority (ISA); International Tribunal for the Law of the Sea (ITLOS); Meeting of State Parties (SPLOS); Secretary-General (UN)
  Antarctic 748
  biodiversity 754–75
  cooperation and coordination 391–2
  drafting history 374–6
  establishment 231, 349–52
  future of the law of the sea 893–6
  implementation 375, 390–1, 393
  Indian Ocean 710–12
  integrated oceans management 467, 487–8
  international organizations 390–2
  International Seabed Authority 231–2
  marine environment/pollution 390–1
  progressive development of international law 393
  proposals 375
  relationship agreements with UN 392
  single forum, proposal for 375, 391, 896
  South China Sea 636–9
  specialization of international law 391
  specialized agencies (UN) 390
  State practice 393
  system of law of the sea 390–2
  UNCLOS III 374–5, 391
integrated coastal (zone) management (ICM/ICZM) 466, 478–9, 489–90
integrated oceans management (IOM) 463–90 *see also* marine protected areas (MPAs); marine spatial planning (MSP)

acidification 464
Agenda 21 465
Antarctic 741, 748
Arctic 474
areas beyond national jurisdiction
 (ABNJ) 466–7, 480–8, 489–90
Australia 466–9, 470, 472
Baltic regional sea regime 465, 470, 473–5
biodiversity 466, 481, 483, 485–8, 490
Caribbean Sea and the Gulf of Mexico 465, 474, 479–80
Census of Marine Life 464
climate change 471, 487
Conferences on the Human Environment (UN) 465–6, 481, 483
definition 466
ecosystem approach 464, 467–8, 471–85, 489, 644, 899
environmental impact assessment 467–8, 472, 474, 478, 483–4, 489, 899
European Union 470, 473–4, 480
fisheries/living resources 467, 471, 474, 477, 481–9
future of the law of the sea 899
General Assembly (UN) 465, 480–1, 484–5, 487–9
implementation 472, 473–89, 899
Indian Ocean 465, 479, 710
institutional infrastructure, integration of 467, 487–8
integrated coastal (zone) management (ICM/ICZM) 466, 478–9, 489–90
inter-agency working/cooperation 487
interrelationship of oceans 463
littoral states, cooperation amongst 480
marine spatial planning 466–8, 470–7, 485–6, 489, 899
Mediterranean regional sea regime 462, 465–6, 473, 477–8
multi-sectoral policy 465–7
Nairobi Convention 2010 479, 718–19
national implementation 468–72, 487, 489
North-East Atlantic and North Sea 465, 467, 473, 476–7
Oceans Compact (UN) 488
Open-Ended Informal Consultative Process (UN) 465–6, 481
OSPAR Convention 476–7, 484
precautionary approach 467–8, 472, 474–7, 479, 482–3, 489, 899
regional implementation 472, 473–80, 487, 489
regional marine spatial planning (MSP) 472
Rio+20 Conference 465–6
Specially Protected Areas of Mediterranean Importance 477–8
sustainable development 465, 469
tool for marine environmental protection, as 465–7
UN-Oceans 487–8
World Summit on Sustainable Development 465
zonal/sectoral approach 464, 481, 488–9
Inter-American Tropical Tuna Commission (IATTC) 442, 444, 452, 818
Intergovernmental Oceanographic Commission (IOComm) 327, 366–7, 487, 564, 573–4
Intergovernmental Panel on Climate Change (IPCC) 644, 652, 777–87, 812–13
internal waters
archipelagic regime 70, 80, 85, 140–1, 148
Arctic 734
baselines 12, 70, 80–1, 85–8, 148, 537
bays 19–20, 82–4
charts 80
coastal State jurisdiction 11–13, 70–1, 294–5
criminal jurisdiction 537, 540, 544
fisheries and living resources 498
freedom of navigation 537–8
Geneva Conventions 1958 15
innocent passage 87–8, 544
international courts and tribunals 404
Mediterranean Sea 606, 613
naval warfare, law of 878
North-East Atlantic and North Sea 655
publicity 80
Santiago Declaration 11–13
scientific research 566–7

internal waters (cont.)
   sea level, rise in 787, 793
   security 586
   sovereign immunity 872–3
   spatial definition 889–90
   State sovereignty 70, 537
   straight baselines 12, 80–1, 85, 537
   straits 118, 132
   territorial sea 9, 95
International Commission for the Conservation of Atlantic Tunas (ICCAT) 442, 444–5, 452–3, 621, 684–5, 770–1, 818, 820
International Convention for the Conservation of Atlantic Tunas (ICCAT) 667–8
International Council for the Exploration of the Sea (ICES) 450–1, 650, 770
International Court of Justice (ICJ) 16–21, 29, 371
   Commission on the Limits of the Continental Shelf 410–11
   compulsory jurisdiction 16, 641
   consent to jurisdiction 396
   customary international law 37
   declarations accepting jurisdiction 399, 401–2
   development of the law of the sea 893–4
   International Seabed Authority 250
   mixed disputes 400
   non-participation 910
   objective regime, LOSC 1982 as a 45
   salary parity with ITLOS 381
   seat 886
   South China Sea 641–2
   Statute 399
international courts and tribunals 2, 17–22, 394–415 *see also* **arbitration**; **dispute settlement**; **International Court of Justice (ICJ)**; **International Tribunal for the Law of the Sea (ITLOS)**
   advisory opinions 414–15
   applicable law 413–14
   binding decisions 396, 398–9, 401–2, 415
   boundary delimitation 406
   choice of forum for compulsory settlement 399–401
   coastal State jurisdiction 404–7
   codification 17–20
   compulsory dispute settlement 399–408
   conciliation, option to submit to 396, 405–6
   consent to jurisdiction 395–402, 406, 415
   continental shelf 44, 404–5
   customary international law 17, 19–21
   declarations accepting jurisdiction 399, 401–2, 405–8, 886
   duty to arbitrate or adjudicate under LOSC 1982 397–9
   European Union 408, 412
   exclusions from jurisdiction 401, 403–8
   exclusive economic zones 44, 404–5, 407
   fisheries and living resources 168, 410
   freedom of navigation, interference with 403, 404
   Geneva Conventions 1958 18–20, 396
   historical development 2, 17–22
   identity of mediator, conciliator or arbitrator, agreement on 397
   impartiality 396–7
   Implementation Agreement 1994 408, 410
   inconsistent rulings 408
   institutional constraints 408–12
   intergovernmental organizations 395
   internal waters 404
   International Seabed Authority 249–50
   investment disputes, arbitration of 395 n.3
   jurisdiction 394–415
   limitations 401–12
   marine environment/pollution 404
   military operations 406–7, 886–7
   mixed disputes 400
   municipal courts and tribunals 394–5
   nature of dispute 400
   non-State entities 412–13
   overflight, freedom of 404
   overlapping jurisdiction 408
   party autonomy 397
   peacefully, obligation to settle 395–7, 401–3
   political or administrative bodies, relationship with 410

private parties, disputes involving 395 n.3, 412–13
procedural limitations on jurisdiction 401–3
provisional measures 395 n.2, 398–9
regional fisheries management organizations 410
related issues 408–9
reservations or exceptions 405–8
scientific research 405, 407
Security Council (UN) 407–8
self-governing territories and associated States 412
sovereign immunity 395
special agreements 415
State sovereignty 404, 406–7
substantive limitations 403–8
territorial sea 404
treaties and conventions 395
urgent measures 398
use of force 44
International Dolphin Conservation Programme (AIDCP) 442, 458
international humanitarian law (IHL) 103, 855–6, 867, 875–9
International Labour Organization (ILO) 283, 292, 416, 429
International Law Association (ILA) 8
International Law Commission (ILC)
archipelagic regime 88, 137–8, 139
baselines 82, 85
boundary delimitation 255, 256–7
codification 13
Draft Articles on the Law of the Sea
archipelagic regime 137–8, 139
baselines 82, 85
freedom of navigation 206
General Assembly (UN) 357–8
high seas 204, 206
innocent passage 117–18
overflight, freedom of 206
piracy 845
freedom of navigation 206
General Assembly (UN) 357–8
Geneva Conventions 1958 13–14
high seas 204, 206
innocent passage 117–18

international courts and tribunals 18–20
overflight, freedom of 216
piracy 845
regime interaction 61
single forum, proposal for 391
straits 117–18
subsequent practice, treaty modification by 50–1
territorial sea 97, 103
International Maritime Organization (IMO) 390, 416–38 *see also* **MARPOL**
accountability 433
Antarctic 724, 728, 743–5, 750–1
arbitration 435–6
archipelagic regime 150–1, 153–4, 418, 433, 554
Arctic 724, 728, 751
artificial islands, installations and structures, removal of 431
Assembly 417, 421–5
audits of flag States 437
background 417
capacity-building 433–4
Caribbean Sea and the Gulf of Mexico 682–3, 770–1
casualties 436
clearing house for information, as 433
climate change 795
coastal State jurisdiction 418, 428, 430, 432–3, 437
codes and guidelines 420, 428
committees 421–6, 428, 434, 436
competent international organization, as 31 n.37, 105, 150, 176, 301–2, 416–17, 420, 429–30
conferences 422
constitutive instrument 417–21, 424, 427–8, 431, 435
consultative function 420
contiguous zones 92
continental shelf 418
cooperation 418–19, 422, 425, 434–5, 894
Council 421–3
customary international law 422
developing countries 422–4
diplomatic conferences 430
dispute settlement 435–6

International Maritime Organization (IMO) (*cont.*)
documentation 425
dues 423
education and technical programmes 434
enclosed and semi-enclosed areas, cooperation in 434
enforcement 430–1
exclusive competence 429
exclusive economic zones 418, 430–2
expertise 421, 426–7
experts for arbitration, maintenance of list of 436
Facilitation Committee 422, 425
flag State jurisdiction 322–3, 418, 428, 430, 437–8
flags of convenience/open registries 422–4, 437–8
freedom of navigation 418, 427, 432–3
General Assembly (UN) 437
generally accepted international rules and standards 105
geographical representation 423
governance structure 421–7
IMO Convention 1948 417–21, 424, 427–8, 431, 435
importance 416–18
information, exchange of 419, 433
innocent passage 418, 432–3
Instruments Implementation Code (III Code) 322–3
intergovernmental organizations, interaction with and assistance to other 429, 435
Inter-Governmental Maritime Consultative Organization 417
international organizations, other 417, 429
International Seabed Authority 435
landlocked and geographically disadvantaged States 327
Legal Committee 422, 424–5, 426
LOSC 1982, IMO within framework of 427–8
marine environment/pollution 176, 179, 404, 419–37, 577, 663–4, 683
Maritime Conference (UN) 1948 417

Maritime Safety Committee 421–4, 554
Mediterranean Sea 618
nationality discrimination and trade 419
non-State actors 425–7
North-East Atlantic and North Sea 663–4
notification requirements, receiver of 433
number of members 417
observers, NGOs as 425–7
open registries 682–3
particularly sensitive sea areas 804
Polar Code, development of 426
port State enforcement 283, 288, 291–2, 431
private aspects 417
purposes and functions 418–36
quasi-legislative power 421, 429–31
recommendations 419
routeing measures, overseeing and approving requests for 432–3
rules, regulations and procedures 419, 427, 429–32, 434–8
safety 421, 423–4, 426, 429, 429–30, 436
scientific research 429, 435, 576–7
sea lanes and traffic separation schemes 432–3
Secretariat 422
security 588, 599
shipping, governance of 728, 743–4
ship-providing nations and ship-using nations, balance between 422
SOLAS 105–6, 426, 436
South China Sea 645
standards 419–20, 426–38
State parties, duties for 431
straits 418, 883
sub-committees 422, 425–6, 436
tacit acceptance procedure 421–2
technical and operational functions 419–22, 433–4
technical annexes 421
Technical Cooperation Committee 422, 425, 434
technical regulations 426
technical sub-committees, system of 422, 436
technology transfer 433–4
territorial sea 92, 105–6, 418, 432–3

terrorism 867–8
threatened species and VMEs 805
trade 417, 419
travaux préparatoires 426
treaties and conventions 418–22, 425–8, 435–8
trust funds 425
UNCLOS III 418, 427
United Maritime Authority 417
vessel source pollution 897
Voluntary Member State Audit Scheme 322–3
Washington Conference 1889 417
weapons of mass destruction 222–3
World War II 417
International Ocean Space Institution, proposal for 572
international organizations 390–2 *see also particular organizations*
  biodiversity 753
  climate change 783
  intergovernmental organizations 395, 429, 435, 564
  marine mammals 508
  participation in LOSC 1982 32, 33
  scientific research 564, 569–74
  Stockholm Declaration 355
  subsequent practice, treaty modification by 49, 52, 66
  territorial sea 103–7, 112
  territorial sovereignty 105–6
international seabed area 226–53 *see also* **Implementation Agreement 1994**
  administration 28
  aggressive activities, prohibition on use for 230
  Antarctic 740–1
  archipelagic regime 142
  areas beyond national jurisdiction (ABNJ) 763–4
  biodiversity 753, 755–6, 758, 763–4
  bioprospecting 836–8, 842
  Boat Paper Group 349
  Caribbean Sea and the Gulf of Mexico 676, 690–1, 693
  cobalt-rich crusts 228, 241, 243, 246, 385, 756

Commission on the Limits of the Continental Shelf 411
common heritage of mankind 229–30, 332, 836–7
consultation process 227
continental shelf 539, 907
definition 228
developing countries 26, 226–7, 230, 842
development of law 30
due diligence 763–4
enforcement 764
environmental impact assessments 763
exclusive economic zones 161, 170
freedom of navigation 538–9
General Assembly (UN) 358
high seas 892
informal consultations 348–9
interaction of maritime zones 892
landlocked and geographically disadvantaged States 332, 335
legal status 228–30
Mediterranean Sea 608, 611–13
military operations 230
Mining Code 764
North-East Atlantic and North Sea 649
outer limits of continental shelf, fixation of 228–9
peaceful purposes, use for 230
polymetallic nodules 1, 228, 230, 241, 242–3, 385, 709, 756, 763
polymetallic sulphides 228, 241, 243, 246, 385, 573, 709, 756, 836
precautionary approach 482
private entities 895
resources, definition of 230
scientific research 572–3
Seabed Committee 142
sequestration of carbon dioxide 529–30, 534–5
spatial definition 889–90, 908
State sovereignty 229–30
superjacent waters 538
territorial sea 96
threatened species and VMEs 803
water column 838

International Seabed Authority (ISA) 28,
    231–44, 385–7
  advisory opinions 250
  amendment of LOSC 1982, special
      procedure for 385–6
  ancillary functions 231
  approval of plans of work 234–6, 241, 243
  arbitration 249, 399
  Assembly 231–2, 235–8, 336
  autonomous institution, as 385, 387
  biodiversity 755–6, 763
  bioprospecting 839
  budget 232, 234–5, 237
  capacity-building 908
  commercial exploitation 244, 245, 385
  common heritage of mankind 230,
      238, 755–6
  composition 337
  confidentiality 236
  continental shelf 190, 250–1
  cooperation 231, 435
  Council 231–6, 238–40, 243–4,
      250, 336
  developed countries 238–9, 245
  developing countries 230–1, 234, 238, 245,
      247, 251
  development of LOSC 1982 44, 47
  Director-General 232, 238
  dispute settlement 247–50
  due diligence 242, 243 n.89
  Economic Planning Commission 235, 435
  effective control, definition of 247–8
  enforcement 38–9, 385
  Enterprise 231–2, 237–9, 245–7,
      249–50, 253
  establishment 231
  exclusive rights 242
  experts 231
  exploitation, definition of 244
  exploration, definition of 242–3
  Finance Committee 231–2, 234–7
  financial contribution to ITLOS 387
  financial terms and conditions 237
  function 38–9, 228, 231, 240, 385
  General Assembly (UN) 250
  geographic representation 236–7
  ICJ, jurisdiction of 250
  Implementation Agreement 1994 231–2,
      236–9, 241, 243 n.89, 244–6, 250, 252
  Indian Ocean 709
  information, power to request 38–9
  inspectors, power to appoint 38–9
  institutional structure 231–2
  international cooperation, promotion
      of 231, 435
  international courts and tribunals 249–50
  ITLOS, financial contribution to 387
  joint ventures 239, 245–6
  landlocked States and geographically
      disadvantaged States 251, 336–7
  Legal and Technical Commission 231–2,
      234–7, 240–4, 435
  legal personality 385
  licensing 237–8
  location 348, 386, 672
  marine environment/pollution 235,
      242–3, 252–3
  Meeting of States Parties 360, 385–7
  Mining Code 66, 241, 244, 319, 756, 764
  monetary penalties 39
  nationality of ships 248
  Office of Legal Affairs (UN) 348
  organs 231–2
  outer limits of continental shelf 250–1
  payments and contributions 192, 198–9,
      229–31, 250–2, 891
  Preparatory Commission 348
  private entities 237
  progressive development of international
      law 231
  prospecting, definition of 242
  Recommendations for Guidance of
      Contractors 2010 763
  regulation of activities in area 30, 240–3
  reserved areas 245–6
  revenue sharing 192, 198–9, 229–31,
      250–2, 891
  rules, regulations, and procedures 232,
      234–7, 240–2, 248, 252–3, 764–75
  scientific research 573, 581
  Seabed Disputes Chamber
      (ITLOS) 247–50, 387, 399,
      414–15, 497
  Secretariat 231, 239, 385

Secretary-General 231, 234, 239, 386–7
scientific research 231
self-contained regime, as 386, 389
spatial definition 908
special interests, representation of 236–7
sponsorship by States parties 246–8, 250
State entities 237, 240, 250
subsequent practice, treaty modification by 65–6
substantive regime of maritime zones 890, 891
suspension or termination of contracts 40
technology transfer to developing countries 231, 238
threatened species and VMEs 805
travaux préparatoires 247
UNCITRAL Arbitration Rules 249
UNCLOS III 237–8
International Ship and Port Security (ISPS) Code 320, 588, 599, 602–3
international straits *see* **straits used for international navigation**
International Tribunal for the Law of the Sea (ITLOS) 371, 378–82, 885–7
  administration 360
  advisory opinions 250, 414–15
  annual reports by President 381–2
  applicable law 414
  budget and financing 360, 378, 380–1, 387
  comity 402
  Commission on the Limits of the Continental Shelf 56, 410–12
  composition 378–80
  compulsory jurisdiction 400
  consensus 379–80
  continental shelf 184–5, 200, 410–12
  customary international law 37, 497
  damages 403
  declarations accepting jurisdiction 399
  development of LOSC 1982 47, 894
  elections 378–80
  establishment 29
  expenses 380
  fisheries and living resources 169
  flag State jurisdiction, wrongs to 403
  freedom of navigation 555
  geographical representation 379–80
  independence and impartiality 249, 381–2
  judges
    consensus 379–80
    election 378–80
    independence and impartiality 381–2
    pensions 380
    salaries, allowances and compensation 380–1
    security of tenure 381
  Meeting of States Parties 378–82
    annual reports from President of Tribunal 381–2
    budget, approval of 378, 380–1
    consensus 379–80
    judges, election of 360, 378–80, 387
    limits on powers 381
  mixed disputes 413
  Office of Legal Affairs 348
  oversight 381–2
  pensions 380
  political supervision 382
  private entities 895
  prompt release of detained vessel and crew 400
  provisional measures 395 n.2, 398–9
  Seabed Disputes Chamber 247–50, 387, 399, 414–15, 497
  security of tenure 381
  sovereign immunity 395 n.2
Ireland 197–8, 402 n.26, 409, 647–8, 651, 655–9, 661, 668–70
ISA *see* **International Seabed Authority (ISA)**
islands *see also* **archipelagic regime; artificial islands, installations and structures**
  Arctic 731
  baselines 9, 59, 71, 74–7, 87
  boundary delimitation 28, 262–3, 269, 272–4
  Caribbean Sea and the Gulf of Mexico 676, 684, 693–7
  charts 76
  continental shelf 28, 273
  customary international law 263, 273

islands (*cont.*)
  definition 28, 262–3, 272, 791
  equidistance 273–4
  exclusive economic zones 28, 272
  Indian Ocean 705–6
  low-tide elevations 262–3, 272–4
  migrants, smuggling of 104
  North-East Atlantic and North
    Sea 651, 659
  reefs 74–5
  relevant area, identification of 271
  rocks 263, 272
  sea level, rises in 791, 897, 907
  small-island States 78, 790–1, 797, 907
  South China Sea, disputes over 155, 371, 626–7, 629–41, 646
  straits 119–20, 883
  territorial sea 8, 28, 95, 104, 272
Israel 14, 16, 33, 595, 605, 608–9, 613–14, 625, 706
Italy
  ecological protection zones 299, 610
  exclusive economic zones 213–14
  flag State jurisdiction 305
  freedom of navigation 546–7
  innocent passage 127
  internal waters 607
  Italian city states 305
  Mediterranean Sea 605, 607, 609–10, 613–15, 618
  Spain 613–14
  straits 127
ITLOS *see* **International Tribunal for the Law of the Sea (ITLOS)**
IUU fishing (Illegal, Unreported and Unregulated Fishing)
  Arctic 737
  arrest of ships and crew 505
  biodiversity 760, 765
  blacklist approach 507
  Caribbean Sea and the Gulf of Mexico 691–2
  coastal State jurisdiction 505
  definition 504–5
  dispute settlement 39
  enforcement 287–8
  European Union 293
  exclusive economic zones 179, 505
  Fish Stocks Agreement 361–2, 505
  flag State jurisdiction 209–10, 314–15, 318, 321–4, 505, 507, 893
  Indian Ocean 714–15
  innocent passage 543
  inspection 288
  licensing 505
  Mediterranean Sea 605–6, 611, 621–2
  North-East Atlantic and North Sea 666
  open registries/flags of convenience 216
  port State control 283, 287–90, 292–3, 455, 507
  regional fisheries management organizations 448, 454–5, 460, 462
  security 576, 594, 600
  Sub-Regional Fisheries Commission 505
  surveillance 594
  territorial sea 287–8
  threatened species and VMEs 802
  Voluntary Guidelines for Flag State Performance 507

Jabour, Julia 796
Jamaica
  archipelagic States 144, 680
  Caribbean Action Plan 688
  CARICOM 686
  International Seabed Authority 346, 348, 350, 386
  Joint Regime Area with Colombia 693
Japan
  Antarctic 739
  archipelagic States 140, 144, 155
  Australia 445, 739, 895
  China 589, 592
  exclusive economic zones 883
  islands 155
  fisheries and living resources 445, 713, 715
  Indian Ocean 713, 715
  innocent passage 542, 548
  islands 627
  JAPRA II programme 511, 817
  military operations 592, 880
  New Zealand 445, 895
  nuclear waste, carriage of 548

nuclear weapons, carriage of 542
piracy 847
scientific research 561, 577, 581, 739, 817, 895
security 589, 592
South China Sea 589, 626–7, 635
United States 847
whaling 511, 577, 581, 739, 817, 847, 895
Jay, Stephen 485
Johannesburg Conference 2002 (World Summit) 355, 356–7, 361, 363, 365–6, 465, 527
Johannesburg Declaration 356
jurisdiction *see* areas beyond national jurisdiction (ABNJ); coastal State jurisdiction; flag State jurisdiction; port State jurisdiction
jus ad bellum 869, 875
jus cogens 220
jus in bello 875

Kalayaan Islands 633
Kirgis, Frederic L 420
Kissinger, Henry 238, 245
Konig, Doris 307
Kopela, Sophia 155–6
Kraska, James 592
Kyoto Protocol 783, 786, 798, 812–13

landlocked States (LLS) and geographically disadvantaged States (GDS) 28, 325–45
 access to sea 329–30, 334–5
 bays 83 n.68
 biodiversity 345
 coastal State jurisdiction 326–8, 331–2, 334, 336–7, 343–4
 common heritage of mankind 335, 344
 conservation and management 338–9
 continental shelf 332, 336–7
 Convention on the Territorial Sea and Contiguous Zone 1958 334–5
 cooperation 339–43
 customary international law 334
 definition 329
 developing countries 328–32, 335–6, 339–40

 economic integration 338
 emergence of new law of the sea 327–30
 European Union 338–9, 341
 exclusive economic zones 328–33, 343–4
 exclusive rights 326
 fisheries and living resources 167, 325–6, 329–30, 332–3, 339, 343–4
 freedom of navigation 331–2, 342–3, 556
 Group of Coastal States 328, 331
 Group of Landlocked and Geographically Disadvantaged States 25, 328–30, 338
 high seas 335, 556
 Implementation Agreement 1994 336
 Indian Ocean 707
 innocent passage 334
 Intergovernmental Oceanographic Commission 327
 interpretation 334
 landlocked States, definition of 331
 mare clausum, from *mare liberum* to 337
 marine environment/pollution 325–7, 334, 338–9, 345
 most-favoured-nation treatment 334
 national treatment principle 334
 natural resources 325, 329, 345
 non-living and minerals resources 330, 332
 participation in LOSC 1982 33
 piracy 327
 ports, access to 331–2, 343
 Preamble 331–2
 reciprocity 335
 regional economic integration 338–43
 rights of States 338–43
 São Paulo Consensus 339
 scientific research 327, 330, 332, 337, 343
 seabed 251, 332, 335–7
 semi-circle test 82 n.67, 83 n.68
 shelf-locked States 328
 straits 326, 329–35, 339, 341–2, 344
 sub-regions, States belonging to one or more 333–4
 surpluses of living resources 333
 territorial sea 334
 territorialization 328
 Transit Trade Convention 331, 334–5
 UNCLOS III 25, 328–31, 336, 338, 344

large-scale pelagic driftnet fishing 443, 503
Latin American Organization for Fisheries
    Development (OLDEPESCA) 686
law of the sea, future of 888–912
    actors and institutions 893–6
    Antarctic 748–50
    cooperation 894–5, 900–3
    development of the law of the sea 893–4
    flag State jurisdiction 893, 896–7
    global oceans management 896–900
    integrated oceans management 899
    maritime limits and zones 889–92, 906–7
    regional oceans management 900–4
    scientific research 580–1
    security 593–6
    single institution, proposal for 896
    straits 131–2
law of the sea, historical development 1–23
    1493 and end of 19th century, between 3–6
    archipelagic regime 136
    battle of the books 4
    coastal States 5, 10–13, 16, 22–3
    codification 2, 7–9, 13–16, 22
    common heritage of mankind 22–3
    customary international law 2, 7, 9, 22
    Euro/North American centric,
        international law as 22
    exclusive economic zones 160–1
    fisheries and living resources 3–4, 10
    freedom of the seas 1–2, 3–5, 22
    Geneva Conventions on the Law of the
        Sea 13–22
    Hague Conference of 1930 2, 7–9, 13
    innocent passage 3, 5–7, 539–40
    international courts and
        tribunals 2, 17–22
    marine environment/pollution 518–20
    Mediterranean Sea 605
    North-East Atlantic and North Sea 653
    occupation 4–5
    Papal donation 3–4
    piracy 844–5
    scholarly works 2, 4
    State sovereignty 1–2, 3, 5, 7, 9
    straits 116–18
    technology and science, development of 1
    territorial sea 3, 5–9

League of Nations 7–9, 417, 845, 880
Lebanon 605, 613–14, 617 n.47
legal nature of provisions of UN
    Convention on the Law of the Sea 1982
    (LOSC 1982) 9–31
    codification and progressive development,
        mixture of 30
    framework treaty, UN Convention on the
        Law of the Sea 1982 (LOSC 1982) as
        a 31, 66, 68
    norms 30–1, 38
    rules of reference 31, 66
letters of marque 871
lex Rhodia 606
Liberia 422–4
liberty and security, right to 169 n.60
line of sight doctrine 93
living resources *see* fisheries and living
    resources, conservation and
    management of; marine mammals,
    conservation and management of
Llibre de/Consolat de Mar 606
London Declaration concerning the Laws
    of Naval War 1909 876
London Convention
    biodiversity 763
    climate change 784–5
    Guidelines 784
    Indian Ocean 717–18
    Protocol 528–30, 535, 763
    science 520, 528–30, 534–5, 577, 581
London Naval Treaty 1930 876
long-range identification and tracking
    (LRIT) of ships 588, 594, 599
Long, Ronán 901
LOSC, Meeting of States Parties
    (SPLOS) 360, 376–8
    administrative role 55, 388
    ambiguities 377–8
    amendment of UN Convention
        on the Law of the Sea 1982 (LOSC
        1982) 43
    annual cycle of review 40–1
    annual reports of Secretary-General
        (UN) 360, 376, 381–2
    budget and financing 88, 378,
        380–1, 383

Commission on the Limits of the
    Continental Shelf 41, 360, 383–5,
    390, 393
  election of members of 360
  information, receipt of 360
  subsequent practice, treaty
    modification by 56
  workload 390
consensus 55, 378–80, 385
decision-making 55–7, 377–8, 380
development of UN Convention on the
    Law of the Sea 1982 (LOSC 1982) 47
DOALOS 353–4, 360
elections 55–6, 57, 369, 377–80, 383
first meeting 360
frequency 377
functions 41, 360, 377–8, 388–90, 392–3
future of the law of the sea 894
General Assembly (UN) 358–60, 389–90
geographical distribution requirement,
    departure from 56
Implementation Agreement 1994 57
implementation, review of 376, 388, 392
International Seabed
    Authority 360, 385–7
interpretation 55, 56–7, 388–9
ITLOS 55–7, 360, 378–82, 387
limitations 381, 388
nomination of judges 56
observers 383, 386
oversight 389–90
political discussions 389
postponement of election of first members
    of 56, 57
progressive development of UN
    Convention on the Law of the
    Sea 1982 (LOSC 1982) 376–8,
    387–90, 393
review of general developments 387–90
sea level, rise in 793
Secretariat (UN) 377, 380–90
Secretary-General (UN) 360, 376–7, 386–90
State practice 378, 385
subsequent practice, treaty modification
    by 49–50, 55–7, 65
UNCLOS III 378, 388
voting 378

low-tide elevations
  archipelagic regime 73, 143, 146
  baselines 74, 788
  islands 262–3, 272–4
  lighthouses 146
  North-East Atlantic and North Sea 659
  sea level, rise in 788
**low-water line as baseline, see also
    baseline** 73–9, 87–90, 95
Lowe, Alan Vaughan 156
Luttwak, Edward 880

McNair, Arthur 86, 94
Madeira 649, 651, 656
Malaysia
  archipelagic regime 141, 148–9, 156
  Coral Triangle Initiative 480
  high seas 213
  sea level rise 794
  security 603
  South China Sea 626, 629, 633, 635,
    639, 642
  straits 124
management of fisheries see **Fish Stocks
    Agreement (FSA); regional fisheries
    management organizations (RFMOs)**
mare clausum 72, 337
mare liberum 72, 203–4, 337
marine environment/pollution *see also*
    **Antarctic, legal regime of the; Arctic,
    legal regime of the biodiversity;
    climate change; Conferences on the
    Human Environment (UN); dumping;
    environmental impact assessments
    (EIAs); integrated oceans management
    (IOM); marine environment/pollution
    and science; MARPOL; sustainable
    use and management; vessel source
    pollution**
  activism 173, 187–8, 201, 847, 886–7
  archipelagic regime 153–4
  areas beyond national
    jurisdiction 368–9, 903
  artificial islands, installations and
    structures 173, 188
  atmospheric pollution 525, 526, 531, 783,
    785, 898

marine environment/pollution (*cont.*)
bioprospecting 829, 834–5
Bonn Agreement 649–50, 663–4
Caribbean Sea and the Gulf of
  Mexico 173, 480, 683–91, 699
civil liability 419
coastal State jurisdiction 71, 176–7, 294, 298, 301, 557
continental shelf 188, 201
cooperation 522, 300–1, 434–5, 660–1, 717–20, 894
data collection 562
definition 809
developing countries 683
development of the law of the sea 894
enclosed and semi-enclosed areas, cooperation in 434
enforcement 176–7, 316
European Union 617, 650–1, 664
exclusive economic zones 432, 102, 165, 171, 176–80
fisheries and living resources 449–50, 457–8, 494–5, 498
flag State jurisdiction 316, 321–2
freedom of navigation 177–9, 206, 537, 555, 557
future of the law of the sea 894, 896–8
General Assembly (UN) 359, 368–9, 484 n.149
genetic resources 368
generally accepted standards 102, 176–8
IMO 176, 179, 404, 419–37, 577, 663–4, 683
Indian Ocean 717–20
innocent passage 99, 102, 544, 547–8
institutions 390–1
integrated coastal zone management 617, 624
integrated oceans management 899
international courts and tribunals 404
International Seabed Authority 235, 242–3, 252
judiciary powers 176–7
land, pollution from 434, 519, 660–1, 809–11, 824, 898
landlocked and geographically disadvantaged States 325–7, 334, 338–9, 345

large marine ecosystem (LME) mechanisms 301, 719–20
liability fund, development of 253
litter 652
Marine Environment Protection Committee 421–2, 424
marine mammals 508
Mediterranean Sea 610–11, 616–21, 624
noise pollution 652
non-regression principle 65
North-East Atlantic and North Sea 649–54, 660–4, 668, 670
  Bonn Agreement 649–50, 663–4
  OSPAR regime 467, 476–7, 484, 525, 528, 650, 652, 660–1, 670
  Paris Convention 519
oil and gas 188–9
OSPAR regime 467, 476–7, 484, 525, 528, 650, 652, 660–1, 670
Paris Convention 519
overflight, freedom of 177
plastics 898
polluter pays principle 688
port State jurisdiction 283, 285, 302, 893
provisional measures 398
reciprocity 64
refuge, places of 663
Regular Process 366–7, 372, 484 n.149
regulation 176
scientific research 560–2, 565–8, 571, 574–5, 577, 581, 898
security 585, 594–5
South China Sea 636, 638, 644, 645–6
standards 29, 176, 316, 429–35
State intervention, right of 419
Stockholm Declaration and Action Plan 1972 28–9
straits 123–6, 129–32
subsequent practice, treaty modification by 54, 64–8
territorial sea 113
threatened species and VMEs 809–13, 824
treaties and conventions 36–7, 419, 432, 435, 436–7
vulnerable marine ecosystems 718–19

marine environment/pollution and science 516–35
adaptive management 517, 522, 527–8, 530, 532–4
artificial islands, installations and structures, disposal of 518
atmospheric pollution 525, 526, 531
Ballast Water Convention 2004 525
Baltic Area 519, 520–2, 526
best available techniques 523
best practicable means 521
Biodiversity Convention 534
coastal State jurisdiction 518–19, 531–2
cooperation duty 522
current legal regime 520–32
customary international law 520, 523–4
decision-making processes 516–17
dumping 519–20, 523, 525, 528–30, 532, 534–5, 577, 581
ecosystem approach 535
enforcement 533
environmental impact assessments 522–3, 528
fragmentation 521, 524, 535
Fund Convention 1971 519, 531
general obligations 521–5
GESAMP (Joint Group of Experts on the Scientific Aspects of Marine Environment Protection) 366–7, 516
historical development 518–20
Intervention Convention 1969 519
land-based pollution 519, 523–8, 532–3, 535
London Convention 1972 520
noise pollution 535
marine pollution, definition of 516
ocean acidification 798
oil pollution 518, 531
Oslo Dumping Convention 1972 520
OSPAR Convention 525, 528
Paris Convention of Marine Pollution from Land-Based Sources 1974 519, 526
pilot projects 517
plastics 533–4
polluter pays principle 356
precautionary approach 524–5, 533–4
preventive measures 524
radioactive waste, dumping of 518, 529
regulation 516–35
reviews 517
soft law 523–4, 527–8
source-specific obligations 525–32
standards 521–2, 526–8, 531
State responsibility 518, 520, 523
transboundary issues 519
treaties and conventions 520, 523–5, 533–4
vessel source pollution 530–2, 534
marine genetic resources, bioprospecting
access 829–39, 841–2
Antarctic Treaty 741, 840–1
areas beyond national jurisdiction 826, 838–9
benefit sharing 830–1, 835, 837–41, 910
biodiversity 753, 772–3, 825–6, 829–36, 840–2
bioprospecting, definition of 242, 826–7
Bonn Guidelines 830–1
classification under UN Convention on the Law of the Sea 1982 (LOSC 1982) 831–3
coastal State jurisdiction 829, 833–42
commercial value 827–8
common heritage of mankind 836–8
consent 830
continental shelf 174, 201, 830, 834
cooperation 829, 835–7
developing countries 837–8, 842
environmental impact assessments 835
exclusive economic zones 830, 833–4
fisheries and living resources 833, 836, 841
General Assembly (UN) 837–8
high seas 829, 836–8
implementation agreement, proposal for 910
importance 825
indigenous communities 835
information gathering and dissemination 827, 832, 835
legal framework 828–33
marine environment/pollution 368, 829, 834–5

marine genetic resources,
    bioprospecting (cont.)
  patents 828–9, 832, 839
  Plant Genetic Resources International
      Treaty 839
  publicity 832
  regional arrangements 840–1
  regional fisheries management
      organizations 841
  reporting 840
  results, publicising 832
  scientific research 174, 559–60, 580, 829,
      832–7, 841, 898
  seabed 836–9, 842
  sustainable use and
      management 829–30, 835
  territorial sea 833
  total allowable catch 833, 836
  traditional knowledge 831
marine living resources see fisheries and
    living resources, conservation and
    management of
marine mammals, conservation and
    management of 508–12, 580 see also
    seals; whaling
  Antarctic 739, 743
  biodiversity 769–70
  CITES 511
  CMS Convention 508–9, 821–2
  commercial exploitation 508, 510, 580
  endangered species 511, 580
  European Union 511–12, 669–70
  exclusive economic zones 508
  GATT 512
  Habitats Directive 669–70
  international organizations 508
  memoranda of understanding 508–9
  North-East Atlantic and North
      Sea 509, 669–70
  range States 509
  regulation 508–9
  special areas of conservation 670
  trade restrictions 511–12
  treaties and conventions 509, 511
  underwater noise 508
marine protected areas (MPAs)
  Antarctic 748–50
  Arctic 748
  areas beyond national
      jurisdiction 484–5, 662–3
  biodiversity 513–14, 662–3, 753, 764,
      767–75, 814
  climate change 795
  coastal State jurisdiction 514
  designation 472, 489
  ecosystem approach 484
  fisheries and living resources 459, 484–5,
      513–14, 663
  Indian Ocean 705
  integrated oceans management 467–8,
      474–6, 479–85, 899
  marine spatial planning 470–1
  MARPOL 484
  multifunctional MPAs 485
  North-East Atlantic and North
      Sea 476, 662–3
  scientific research 580
  submarine cables and pipelines 189
  threatened species and VMEs 804–5, 811
  vessel source pollution 663–4
  Whaling Convention 484
marine scientific research (MSR) see
    scientific research
marine spatial planning (MSP) 466–8,
    470–7, 489, 899
  areas beyond national jurisdiction 485–6
  biodiversity 753, 773
  ecosystem approach 485
  enclosed or semi-enclosed seas 486
  European Union 474
  Mediterranean 477
  North-East Atlantic and North
      Sea 466, 648
  regional marine spatial planning
      (MSP) 472
maritime boundary delimitation see also
    boundary delimitation; contiguous
    zones; continental shelf; exclusive
    economic zones (EEZs); high seas,
    legal regime of the; internal waters;
    territorial sea
  bilateral maritime boundaries 71, 191, 196,
      200, 613, 657–8, 901, 907
  coastal State jurisdiction 281–3, 294–302

equidistance 267–9, 272–4
  bisector methodology 256, 260
  Caribbean Sea and the Gulf of
    Mexico 693, 695–8
  continental shelf 256–7, 259
  Convention on the Continental Shelf
    1958 21–2, 256–7
  customary international law 258–9
  equitable principles or equidistance
    debate 256–61, 264–5, 269, 278
  historical and navigational issues 256
  Indian Ocean 709
  islands 273–4
  natural prolongation 264–5, 269
  North-East Atlantic and North Sea 658
  provisional equidistance line 256,
    259–60, 268–9, 276–7, 696–8
  relevant circumstances rule 22, 258–9
  rules and principles, distinction
    between 257
  special circumstances rule 255–9,
    264, 276–7
  territorial sea 255–6, 259
future of zones 889–92, 906–7
interaction of maritime zones 892
spatial definition 889–90, 906–8
State practice 889–92
substantive regime of maritime
  zones 890–2
sui generis zones 297, 607, 609–13, 625
Maritime Neutrality Convention 1928 876
maritime security *see* **security**
MARPOL 432, 435, 436–7
  Antarctic 728–9, 745
  Arctic 728–9
  biodiversity 755, 763
  climate change 785
  developing countries 683
  Emission Control Areas 179 n.106
  future of the law of the sea 898
  integrated oceans management 484
  ocean acidification 785
  particularly sensitive sea areas 531
  port State control 285
  regime interaction 66
  territorial sea 106
  vessel source pollution 530, 531

mass destruction, proliferation of
  weapons 557, 873–4
  IMO 222–3, 224
  security 320, 587, 598, 600
Matz, Nele 54
maximum sustainable yield (MSY) 54, 449,
  496, 498–9, 806–7, 824
media 733
Mediterranean Sea 604–25
  archaeological zones 607, 609
  artificial islands, installations and
    structures 611
  Barcelona Convention 1976/1995 477–8,
    616–21, 762
  biodiversity 761
  bordering States 605
  boundary delimitation 608–9,
    612–16, 624
  coastal/marine interface 477–8
  coastal State jurisdiction 607–8, 625
  colonialism of North Africa 605
  common interests 610
  compliance mechanism 618, 620–2
  contiguous zones 608, 625
  continental shelf 608, 611–12
  cooperation 616–25
  criminal offences 605–6
  decolonization 605
  developed countries 605
  developing countries 605
  dispute management 615–16
  ecological and fisheries protection
    zones 607
  ecological protection zones 607, 610
  economic groupings 605
  ecosystem approach 478
  Environment Programme
    (UNEP) 616, 624
  European Union 605, 610, 617
  exclusive economic zones 164, 608,
    610–13, 901
  fisheries and living resources 607, 609–11,
    621–2, 624–5
  forced migration by sea 622, 623
  France 605, 608–10, 612–14, 618
  General Fisheries Commission for the
    Mediterranean (GFCM) 621–2, 624

Mediterranean Sea (*cont.*)
  Greece 605, 608, 613–14, 625
  gulfs and historic bays 607
  historical background 605
  human trafficking 606
  institutionalized
    cooperation 616–23, 624–5
  integrated coastal (zone)
    management 466, 478
  Integrated Coastal Zone Management
    in the Mediterranean (ICZM
    Protocol) 478
  integrated oceans management 465–6,
    473, 477–8, 762
  internal waters 606, 613
  Italy 605, 607, 609–10, 613–15, 618
  IUU fishing 605–6, 611, 621–2
  jurisdictional framework 607–11, 625
  marine environment/pollution 610–11,
    616–21, 624
  marine spatial planning (MSP) 477
  Mediterranean Action Plan 477–8
  migrants, smuggling of 606, 622, 623
  natural resources 614, 615
  oil and gas 614, 615
  overlapping claims 612
  political groupings 605
  port State control 622, 624
  scientific research 610
  seabed 608, 611–13
  search and rescue, regional code on 623
  sedentary species 611
  Spain 605, 608–9, 613–14
  Specially Protected Areas of
    Mediterranean Importance
    (SPAMI) 477–8
  State practice 607
  straight baselines 607–8
  sub-seas 604–5
  subsoil 608, 611–12
  sui generis zones 607, 609–13, 625
  territorial sea 607–9, 612
  underwater cultural heritage 606,
    609–10, 622–3
  United Kingdom 604–5, 607–8, 617,
    656, 882
  water column 608

Micronesia Challenge 480
migrants, smuggling of
  Bali Process 601
  bilateral agreements 101, 222
  boarding and inspection 217, 222
  boat people 104, 112, 222
  Caribbean Sea and the Gulf of
    Mexico 217
  European Union 222, 590–1
  flag State jurisdiction 314
  high seas, enforcement on the 221, 222
  Indian Ocean 721
  islands 104
  Mediterranean Sea 606, 622, 623
  overcrowding 217
  Refugee Convention 104
  rescue, duty of compulsory 217
  sea, by 217, 222, 590–1
  security 590–1, 596, 600–1
  slavery 224
  stateless vessels 217–18
  territorial sea 104, 112
  visit, right of 221, 224
**migratory/highly migratory species and
  straddling stocks** 494, 498–9 *see also*
  Fish Stocks Agreement (FSA)
  CMS Convention 717–18, 757, 821–2
  definition 821
  exclusive economic zones 498–500
  General Assembly (UN) 361
  marine mammals 508
  North-East Atlantic and North Sea 666–8
  regional fisheries management
    organizations 440–2, 460–1
  South China Sea 628
  threatened species and
    VMEs 803–4, 821–2
military operations 866–87
  Antarctic 742
  arbitration 886
  archipelagic waters 882–3
  basic framework 867–70
  Coast Guard 873
  coastal State jurisdiction 867, 880–1,
    885–7, 908
  constabulary forces 873
  criminal jurisdiction, universal 873–4

customary international law 866
definition 869–70
diplomacy 880
disaster relief 869
dispute settlement 406–7, 885–6
drug trafficking 873
enforcement 869, 873, 883
exclusive economic zones 178, 213–14, 591–2, 882–5, 900
flag State jurisdiction 867, 874
freedom of navigation 211–12, 592, 879–85
Hague Conference 1930 880
high seas 883–4
hot pursuit 875
humanitarian assistance 869, 873
identity politics 867
IMO 230
innocent passage 541, 881–2
intelligence, clandestine or para-military operations 869
international courts or tribunals 886–7
international humanitarian law 867
overflight, freedom of 885
peaceful operations 873–5
peaceful purposes 211–12, 868–9, 884–5
piracy 873–4
port States controls 867
radar 883
scientific research 175, 565, 570–2, 581, 885
security 591–3, 596–8, 867, 873–4
South China Sea 643–4
State practice 866
State sovereignty 867–8, 881–3, 885
straits 882–3
strategic rivalry 867
surveillance 593
surveys or oceanographic naval ships 885
territorial sea 880–3
terrorism 867–8, 873–4
treaties and conventions 866
UNCLOS III 880–1, 883–4
use of force 873–4
weapons of mass destruction 873–4
weapons systems 883

Minamata mercury poisoning 518–19, 527–8
mines, laying of 878
Mining Code 241, 244, 319, 756
Moreno-Lax, Violeta 224
most-favoured-nation (MFN) treatment 334
MPAs *see* marine protected areas (MPAs)

Naidu, GVC 711–12
Nairobi International Convention on the Removal of Wrecks 2007 431
Namibia, UN Council for 32
Nandan, Satya N 227, 348–9
Napoleon Bonaparte 872
national treatment principle 334
nationality 248, 595–6
 dual nationality 216, 217
 flag State jurisdiction 306–12, 315, 755
 genuine link 215–16, 306–11
 human trafficking 224
 ships 214–17, 224, 228
NATO (North Atlantic Treaty Organization) 605
Natura Agreement 452
natural action programmes (NAPs) 810
natural prolongation 264–5, 269
natural resources *see also* fisheries and living resources, conservation and management of; international seabed area; International Seabed Authority (ISA); non-living and mineral resources
 climate change 794–6
 coastal State jurisdiction 10–12
 continental shelf 183–4, 186–93, 198, 201–2
 flag State jurisdiction 311
 landlocked and geographically disadvantaged States 325, 329, 345
 Mediterranean Sea 614, 615
 security 585–6, 589
 territorial sea 94
naval auxiliaries *see* warships and naval auxiliaries
naval warfare, law of 875–9
 aggressive war 875

naval warfare, law of (*cont.*)
  belligerent and neutral rights 877–8
  civilian crew 877–8
  codification 875–6
  customary international law 876
  exclusive economic zones 878–9
  Geneva Conventions and Additional
    Protocols 876–7
  geography of naval warfare 878–9
  Hague Conference 1907 876, 877
  London Declaration 1909 876
  London Treaty 1930 876
  Maritime Neutrality Convention 876
  merchant vessels 877–8
  mines, laying 878
  neutral States 878
  Oxford Manual of Naval War 1913 876
  Paris Declaration 1856 875–6
  *San Remo Manual on International
    Law* 877, 878–9
  scientific research 175, 562, 566,
    568–70, 573
  submarines 876
  territorial sea 878
  treaties and conventions 875–7
  visit, right of search and 877–8
  warships and naval auxiliaries 877–8
navigation rights *see* **freedom of navigation;
  innocent passage, right of; straits used
  for international navigation**
neoliberalism 26
Netherlands
  archipelagic regime 139–40
  baselines 655
  Caribbean Sea 673, 675, 687
  coastal State jurisdiction 187–8, 295
  colonialism 139, 673, 675
  continental shelf 257
  Denmark 257
  dispute settlement, compulsory 910
  Dutch East India Company 4, 536, 653
  exclusive economic zones 173, 214
  fisheries and living resources 298
  freedom of navigation 5, 536,
    546–7, 879
  ICJ 886
  integrated oceans management 471–2

  landlocked and
    geographically-disadvantaged
    States 328
  marine spatial planning 471
  North East Atlantic and North Sea 648,
    651, 655
  piracy 58, 847
  Russian Federation 173, 187–8, 399
    n.15, 886–7
  scientific research 580
  South China Seas 631
  territorial sea 92–3, 139
neutrality 584, 875–6, 878
New Strategic Direction for COBSEA 645
New Zealand
  Antarctic 739, 745, 749
  archipelagic States 144
  Australia 191–2, 445
  continental shelf 191–2
  Indian Ocean 715
  Japan 445, 895
  marine protected areas 749
  nuclear warships 70 n.13
  regional fisheries management
    organizations (RFMOs) 445
  whaling 496–7
noise pollution 508, 535
non-living and mineral resources *see
  also* **international seabed area;
  International Seabed Authority (ISA);
  oil and gas**
  Antarctic 740–1, 751
  Arctic 725
  climate change 795
  coastal State jurisdiction 11
  consent 795
  continental shelf 190–3, 198, 201–2, 538
  exclusive economic zones 165,
    170–1, 177–8
  flag State jurisdiction 319
  landlocked and geographically
    disadvantaged States 330, 332
  moratoriums 725
  South China Sea 627–9, 645, 646
  sustainable use 897
non-State parties
  biodiversity 760

Caribbean Sea and the Gulf of
    Mexico 676
Fish Stocks Agreement 502
IMO 425–7
Indian Ocean 706
international courts and tribunals 412–13
regional fisheries management
    organizations 760
security 595
subsequent practice, treaty
    modification by 49
norms 30–1, 38, 62, 65, 68
North Atlantic Salmon Conservation
    Organization (NASCO) 443, 668
North-East Atlantic and North Sea 647–71
    see also **OSPAR regime**
    anadromous stocks 668
    archipelagos 651, 655
    baselines 655
    biodiversity 650, 660–3, 670
    boundary delimitation 647–8, 651, 657–9
    climate change and sea level rise 652, 661,
        668, 670
    coastal geography 650–1
    coastal State jurisdiction 648, 653–7, 671
    colonialism 653
    Commission on the Limits of the
        Continental Shelf 657
    conferences 476
    constituent territories 651
    context 649–52
    contiguous zones 656
    continental shelf 653–8
    Convention on the Continental Shelf
        1958 658
    cooperation 658, 660–2, 670–1
    customary international law 653
    customs, fiscal, health, safety,
        and immigration laws and
        regulations 656
    declarations 476
    Denmark 651, 655, 657–9
    description of area 649–52
    devolved government 651
    dispute settlement 651, 658–9, 661
    dumping 528, 660–1
    economic significance 651–2

ecosystem approach 476, 648, 651,
    660, 667
equidistance principle 658
European Union 648–54, 671, 902
    Common Fisheries Policy 650–1,
        665–6, 668–9
    dispute settlement 661
    fisheries 650–1, 659–60, 668–9
    Habitats Directive 669–70
    marine environment/
        pollution 660–1, 664
    marine mammals 669–70
    Marine Strategy Framework
        Directive 476–7, 649, 662–3
    Water Framework Directive 662
    whaling 669–70
exclusive economic zones 656, 659
FAO Compliance Agreement 654–5
Fish Stocks Agreement 654–5, 666
fisheries and living resources 442, 447,
        648, 650–6, 659–60, 665–71
    anadromous stocks 668
    catadromous species 668–9
    climate change 668
    Common Fisheries Policy 650–1,
        665–6, 668–9
    European Union 659–60, 668–70
    exclusive fisheries zones 656, 659
    Future Multilateral Co-Operation in
        North-East Atlantic Convention
        1980 666
    International Whaling
        Commission 669
    IUU fishing 666
    maps 650
    marine mammals 509, 669–70
    marine protected areas (MPAs) 663
    regional cooperation 665–70
    regional fisheries management
        organizations (RFMOs) 660, 671
    relative stability, principle of 665
    straddling and highly migratory fish
        stocks 666–8
    sustainable use and
        management 652, 666
France 647, 651, 654–8
freedom of navigation 653–4

North-East Atlantic and North Sea (*cont.*)
  geography 649, 650–1, 655–6
  Gothenburg Declaration 2006 476
  high seas 649
  highly migratory fish stocks 666–8
  historic bays 655
  historical background 653
  ICJ 658
  IMO 660, 663–4, 671
  Implementation Agreement 1994 654
  integrated oceans management 465, 467, 473, 476–7
  internal waters 655
  islands 651, 659
  IUU fishing 666
  jurisdictional zones 647–8, 655–7
  low-tide elevations 659
  marine environment/pollution 516, 652, 654, 660–4, 668, 670
    Bonn Agreement 649–50, 663–4
    dumping 528, 660–1
    European Union 650–1, 664
    land-based sources 519, 660–1
    litter 652
    noise pollution 652
    OSPAR regime 467, 476–7, 484, 525, 528, 650, 652, 660–1, 670
    Paris Convention 519
    particularly sensitive sea areas (PSSAs) 664
    refuge, places of 663
  marine mammals 509, 669–70
  marine protected areas 476, 662–4
  marine spatial planning 466, 648
  Marine Strategy Framework Directive 649, 662–3
  Netherlands 648, 651, 655
  North-East Atlantic Environment Strategy 476
  ocean geography 650–1
  oil and gas 653, 658–9, 661, 670–1
  participation in the law of the sea 653–5
  particularly sensitive sea areas (PSSAs) 664
  political geography 650–1
  political stability 651
  port State control 664, 671
  Portugal 648, 651, 655–7
  precautionary approach 476, 648, 660
  progressive development of law of the sea 648
  regions 648, 653–5, 658, 661–71
  seabed 649
  Spain 648–9, 651, 656–8
  State practice 648, 655–6, 663
  State sovereignty 654
  straddling fish stocks 666–8
  straight baselines 655
  straits 654
  sustainable development 648, 652, 666
  territorial sea 653, 655–6, 659
  trade 653, 669
  UNCLOS III 653
  United Kingdom 647
  United States 667–8
  vessel-source pollution, regional measures on 649–50, 663–4
  whaling 669–70
North-East Atlantic Commission 668
North-East Atlantic Fisheries Commission (NEAFC) 442, 445, 452, 454–5, 456, 458–9, 663, 667, 759, 769–70
North Pacific Anadromous Fish Commission (NPAFC) 443, 456
North Pacific Marine Science Organization (PICES) 450–1
North Sea *see* **North-East Atlantic and North Sea**
Northwest Atlantic Fisheries Organization (NAFO) 442, 450–1, 454–5, 456, 458, 759, 808–9
Northwest Passage 120, 131–2, 590, 734, 797, 890
Norway
  archipelagic regime 135–8, 141
  baselines 85–6, 137
  Denmark 266
  exclusive economic zones 176–7, 298
  fisheries and living resources 183, 266, 471
  Iceland 500
  integrated oceans management 471
  skjærgaard 19, 85, 135, 136–7
  straight baselines 85–6, 137

territorial sea 5
United Kingdom 137
nuclear testing 742–3
nuclear waste 742–3
nuclear weapons
  peaceful purposes 210–11
  South China Sea, declaration of nuclear free zone in 643
  Southeast Asia Nuclear Weapon-Free Zone (SEANWFZ) 643
  warships 542, 547–9

ocean acidification 780–2
  adaptive changes 798
  carbon dioxide 778–81, 798
  conferences and meetings of parties 786
  Copenhagen Accord 2009 780–1
  coral reefs 781–2
  ecosystem approach 794, 796, 798
  effects 781–2
  fisheries and living resources 459–61, 796, 798
  Framework Convention on Climate Change (UNFCCC) 781, 783, 797–8
  future of the law of the sea 897
  gaps in regulation 896
  geo-engineering 785
  implementation agreement, proposal for 797
  integrated oceans management 464
  Kyoto Protocol 798
  MARPOL 785
  mitigation 782, 784–6
  pH threshold, agreement on 798
  precautionary approach 798
  regional fisheries management organizations 459–61, 798
  scientific assessment, enhancement of 798
  Secretary-General (UN) 781
  temperature rise 780–1
  threatened species and VMEs 800, 811
Ocean Compact (UN) 488, 895
Oceans and Coastal Areas Network (UN-Oceans) 362–3
  Agenda 21 362–3, 487 n.171
  General Assembly (UN) 362–3
  inter-agency coordination 362

  Johannesburg Plan of Implementation 363
  Rio Summit 1992 362
  Secretary-General (UN) 362–3
  Systems Chief Executives Board (UN) 362
  terms of reference 362–3
O'Connell, Daniel Patrick 184
Office of Legal Affairs (UN) 348, 353–4
offshore installations *see* **artificial islands, installations and structures**
oil and gas *see also* **artificial islands, installations and structures**
  Arctic 189, 725, 730–1, 748
  biodiversity 753
  boundary delimitation 901
  Caribbean Sea and the Gulf of Mexico 681, 688, 690–5, 699
  Civil Liability Convention 1969 519, 531
  climate change 795
  continental shelf 183–4, 186–93, 200–1
  crude oil washing 531
  Fund Convention 1971 519, 531
  Geneva Conventions 1958 15
  Indian Ocean 706
  joint development 645
  liberty and security, right to 169 n.60
  Mediterranean Sea 614, 615
  North-East Atlantic and North Sea 466, 653, 658–9, 661, 670–1
  Oil Pollution Preparedness, Response and Cooperation Convention 1990 189
  pollution
    Arctic 736–7
    biodiversity 753
    Civil Liability Convention 1969 519, 531
    continental shelf 188–9
    Fund Convention 1971 519, 531
    Geneva Conventions 1958 15
    liberty and security, right to 169 n.60
    Oil Pollution Preparedness, Response and Cooperation Convention 1990 189
    OILPOL 518, 531
    science 518

oil and gas (*cont.*)
  science 518
  security 589, 895
  South China Sea 628, 645
  State practice 191
  Truman Proclamation 10–11
open-ended informal consultative process (UN) 353, 363–5
  Agenda 21 365
  annual cycle of review 40–1
  bioprospecting 837
  Division for Sustainable Development of the Department of Economic and Social Affairs 364–5
  DOALOS 353, 365
  future of the law of the sea 894
  General Assembly (UN) 363–5
  integrated oceans management 476–7, 484
  list of items considered 365
  Secretary-General (UN), reports of 364
open registries *see* **flags of convenience/open registries**
opposite or adjacent coasts, delimitation between States with 254–9, 267, 269, 272
OSPAR regime
  biodiversity 761–2, 769–71
  dumping 528
  ecosystem approach 660
  IMO 660
  integrated oceans management 476–7, 484
  marine environment/pollution 525, 528, 652
  marine protected areas 484, 662
  OSPAR Commission 467, 477, 663, 670, 902
  OSPAR Convention 476, 525, 528, 660–1
  precautionary approach 660
  regional oceans management 902
  science 525, 528
  whaling 660
Ottoman Empire 605, 879
outer limit of the continental shelf 189–99, 264–5, 277–8
  Arctic 197–8, 732–4
  Article 76 criteria 190–5, 198, 201

  Bangladesh/Myanmar case 191–2, 196
  bilateral agreements 191–2
  boundary delimitation 196
  Commission on the Limits of the Continental Shelf 39, 56, 190–2, 195–8, 382–3
  composition 195
  dispute resolution 196–7
  expertise 195
  recommendations 195–6, 198, 201
  role 194–5
  spatial definition 890
  common heritage of mankind 190, 202
  Convention on the Continental Shelf 1958 43, 56, 189–90
  customary international law 191
  developing countries, payments and contributions to 198–9
  dispute resolution 195–6
  exclusivity 192, 198
  foot of the slope 193–4, 201
  information, submission of 56, 190, 192, 195–8, 201
  inherent rights 192
  International Seabed Authority 190, 250–1
  Irish formula 193–4
  legal continental shelf 190
  natural prolongation 185–6, 190
  natural resources 189–93, 198, 201–2
  non-living and minerals resources 190–3, 198, 201–2
  oil and gas 190–3, 201
  opposability 192
  procedural requirements 192
  revenue-sharing 192, 198–9, 229
  seabed 228–9
  sedentary species 191
  sediment thickness criterion 193–4
  submarine ridges 194–5, 201
  superjacent waters, depth of 189–90
  territorial sea 95
overflight, freedom of
  archipelagic regime 149–50, 553
  coastal State jurisdiction 298
  Convention on the High Seas 1958 206
  drones 593

exclusive economic zones 165, 177, 298, 554
future of the law of the sea 911
ICAO 124, 551
ILC Draft Articles 206
Indian Ocean 722
innocent passage 98, 540, 553, 881
international courts and tribunals 404
marine environment/pollution 177
military operations 550, 885
radio frequency for distress signals 551
safety 124
straits 124, 550–2
surveillance 594
Oxford Manual of Naval War 1913 876
Oxman, Bernard H 93, 313, 879

pacta tertiis rule 444–5, 447
Palestine 595, 605, 609, 613
Panama 169, 422, 423 n.39, 424, 480, 502, 555, 681–2, 686
Panama Canal 682
Papal donation 3–4
Paracel Islands 155, 627, 629, 632–3, 902
Pardo, Arvid 16
Paris Declaration Respecting Maritime Law 1856 871, 875–6
particularly sensitive sea areas (PSSAs)
  Antarctic 750
  associated protection measures 288
  climate change 795
  IMO 288, 426, 432, 435, 804
  Mediterranean Sea 618
  North-East Atlantic and North Sea 664
  overlapping areas 106
  port State control 228
  threatened species and VMEs 804
patents 828–9, 832, 839
peaceful purposes principle
  Antarctic 642
  developing countries 868
  exclusive economic zones 868
  high seas 210–12, 868
  jus ad bellum 869
  military operations 211–12, 868–9, 884–5
  reciprocity 64
  scientific research 174, 565, 567

seabed 230
Secretary-General (UN) 869
subsequent practice, treaty modification by 64, 67
weapons testing 211–12
Perez de Cuéllar, Javiér 227, 348
persistent organic pollutants (POPs) 526–8, 535, 728, 746
Pharand, Donat 131–2
Philippines
  archipelagic regime 12–13, 138–41, 144–8, 152–3, 156–7
  bioprospecting 832
  climate change 471
  continental shelf 198
  dispute settlement, compulsory 910
  fisheries and living resources 716
  integrated oceans management 471, 480
  Philippine-Vietnam Joint Oceanographic and Marine Scientific Research Expedition (JOMSRE-SCS I to IV) 644
  South China Sea 626, 629, 633, 635–7, 640–5
  straight baselines 13
  United States 641–2
pilotage 129–30, 552, 557, 650
pipelines *see* **submarine cables and pipelines**
piracy and armed robbery at sea 843–65, 896
  airborne surveillance 852–3
  applicable legal framework 844–5
  armed robbery at sea distinguished 844, 850–1, 854–5, 860, 864, 874
    definition 850–1
    two ship requirement 851
  arrest of suspects 851–3, 857, 862–3, 875
  artificial islands, installations and structures 848
  cargo, theft of 844
  Caribbean Sea and the Gulf of Mexico 691
  codification 845
  consent to enforcement action 34
  contemporary piracy 843–5, 874

972   INDEX

piracy and armed robbery at sea (*cont.*)
  Convention on the High Seas 1958 843–5, 855, 859, 863–4
  cooperation 59, 369–71, 860
  criminal jurisdiction, universal 57–9, 691, 860–2, 874–5
  customary international law 59, 370, 844, 860–2, 864
  definition 846–50, 852, 859, 874
  Djibouti Code of Conduct 601
  domestic law, criminalization in 370–1
  dry land piracy 849
  ecological activism 847
  enforcement 34, 843–5, 849, 850–65, 874
  European Convention on Human Rights 858
  European Union
    Naval Force 849, 855
    transfer agreements 862
  evidence, collection of 590
  exclusive economic zones 847–51, 864
  extraterritoriality 857–8, 861–2
  flag State jurisdiction 312, 320–1, 857, 862, 874
  forms of piracy 844
  freedom of navigation 852–3, 856
  General Assembly (UN) 369
  Gulf of Guinea 843–4, 848
  Harvard Draft Convention on Piracy 1932 845, 849, 859
  Harvard Research on International Law 7
  high seas 225, 843–5, 847–50, 855, 864, 874–5
  hijacking ships and crews 844
  historical roots 844–5
  human rights 225, 845, 856–8
  ILC Draft Articles 845
  inchoate offences 848–9
  incitement and facilitation 849–50
  Indian Ocean 219, 702, 721, 723, 874
  international humanitarian law, inapplicability of 855–6
  judge, right to be brought promptly before a 857
  Kenya, prosecution in 57–9
  landlocked and geographically disadvantaged States 327
  League of Nations 845
  limitations on enforcement powers 855–8
  military operations 873–4
  necessity of counter-piracy regime 843–4
  pirate ship, definition of 849–50, 852–3
  political or ideological motivations 847
  private ends, committed for 846–7, 851
  privateering 871
  prosecutions 590, 853, 858–63, 874
    bridging policing and prosecution 862–3
    cooperation 860
    criminal jurisdiction 860–2
    criminal jurisdiction, universal 57–9, 860–2
    criminal offence of piracy 859–60
    customary international law 860–2, 864
    European Union 862
    internationalized model 858
    municipal courts 858
    prosecute or extradite duty 863
    Security Council (UN) 371
    Somalia 858, 862–4
    State practice 859
    transfers 58–9, 862
  ransoms 844
  reasonable suspicion criterion 852
  ReCAAP 599
  safeguards for interception operations 856
  security 587, 590, 593, 599–601
  Security Council (UN) 34, 59, 106–7, 369–71, 590, 721, 854–5, 863–4, 875
  seizure of pirate ships 850–3, 855–6, 861, 874–5
  seizures and mutinies 848
  self-defence 856, 874
  Somalia 590, 601, 701, 843–4, 847, 849, 853–5
    consent to enforcement action 34
    enforcement 34, 225, 854–5
    failed states 864
    political aims 847
    prosecutions 858, 862–4
    Security Council (UN) resolutions 34, 106–7, 369–71, 854–5, 875

State sovereignty 34
  territorial sea 854
South China Sea 639
Southeast Asia 843–5
State practice 58–9
State sovereignty 34
SUA Convention 848, 860, 862–3
submarine cables and pipelines 848
technological development 593
territorial sea 370, 848, 850, 854, 874
terrorism 847
transfers 58–9, 862
two ship requirement 848, 851
UNCLOS I 845
universal policing powers 851, 862, 864
use of force and coercion 855–6
violence requirement 846–7, 850
visit, right of 220, 851–3, 857–8, 874
  warships and government
    vessels 851–2
  warships and government vessels 847,
    851–2, 855–7, 871, 874–5
  yachts 848
**Plant Genetic Resources International
  Treaty (FAO)** 839
plastics 533–4, 898
polar regions *see* Antarctica, legal regime;
  Arctic Ocean, legal regime;
pollution *see* biodiversity; climate
  change; Conferences on the Human
  Environment (UN); environmental
  impact assessments (EIAs); integrated
  oceans management (IOM); marine
  environment/pollution; MARPOL
polymetallic nodules 1, 228, 230, 241, 242–3,
  385, 709, 756, 763
polymetallic sulphides 228, 241, 243, 246,
  385, 573, 709, 756, 836
port State jurisdiction 280–93
  access to port 283–5, 288–9, 331–2, 343,
    455, 745
  airports 284
  Antarctic 739, 745
  artificial islands, installations and
    structures 281
  bilateral agreements 284–5
  biodiversity 302

  boarding and inspection 290, 506
  Caribbean Sea and the Gulf of
    Mexico 291
  coastal State jurisdiction 281, 908
  conditions for entry 285–6, 745
  construction, design, equipment, or
    manning (CDEM) 288
  convenience, ports of 283, 291, 455
  cooperation 291–3
  customary international law 283–5, 287,
    455, 893
  customs 282
  definition 280, 282
  departure State jurisdiction 286–7
  detention 290
  diplomatic immunity 285
  distress, ships in 284
  enforcement 282–3, 284, 288–91, 300,
    506–7, 893
  exclusive economic zones 289
  extraterritoriality 287, 289–91
  fisheries and living resources 283, 285–93,
    506–7, 622, 624, 893
    IUU fishing 455
    quasi-territorial jurisdiction 289
    regional fisheries management
      organizations 453, 455–6
  flag State jurisdiction 283, 322, 893
  force majeure 284, 455
  free riders 283, 302
  freedom of transit 285–6
  future of the law of the sea 893, 896–7
  GATT 285–6
  ICJ 283–4
  illegal activities 282–3,
  ILO 283, 292
  immigration control 282
  IMO 283, 288, 291–2, 431
  Indian Ocean 291, 721–2
  innocent passage 540, 544
  international trade law 285
  IUU fishing 283, 287–90, 292–3,
    455, 507
  landlocked and geographically
    disadvantaged States 331–2, 343
  leaving port, conditions for 286–7
  legal bases 287–93

port State jurisdiction (*cont.*)
  marine environment/pollution 283, 285, 302, 893
  Maritime Ports Convention 284–5
  market-based controls 322
  Mediterranean Sea 622, 624
  memoranda of understanding 282, 291–2, 664
  military operations 867
  monetary penalties 290
  national security 282
  North-East Atlantic and North Sea 664, 671
  outermost permanent harbour works 281
  overlaps in jurisdiction 287
  Paris MOU 664
  Port State Agreement (FAO) 455, 622, 624
  port State control 282, 288–9, 291–2, 893
    fisheries 282
    MOUs 322
    Paris MOU 282, 291–2
    regional arrangements 282
    Tokyo MOU 292
  port State measures 282, 284, 289–90, 292, 302
    fisheries 282
    Model Scheme 292–3
    PSM Agreement 282, 284, 293, 302
  prescriptive jurisdiction 290, 302
  PSM Agreement 282, 284, 293, 302
  quantitative restrictions 285–6
  quasi-territorial jurisdiction 287, 289–91
  regional cooperation 291–3, 302
  regional fisheries management organizations (RFMOs) 283, 290–3
  restrictions on entry 285
  roadsteads 281
  safety and security 283, 302
  sanctions 288–9
  sanitation laws 282
  seaworthiness 287
  sovereign immunity 285
  spatial scope 281
  standards 282, 288, 290, 292–3
  State practice 285
  State sovereignty 283–4
  straits 288–9
  sub-standard ships 664
  territorial jurisdiction 283–4, 287–91
  warships 285
  waste disposal 287
  WTO dispute settlement 285–6
Portugal
  archipelagic States 154–5, 655
  Azores 3, 143, 155, 649–51, 655–6
  baselines 655
  colonialism 3, 673
  continental shelf 657
  exclusive economic zones 548, 656
  freedom of navigation 3, 4, 536, 548
  Madeira 649, 651, 656
  military operations 879
  North-East Atlantic and North Sea 648, 651, 655–7
  piracy 858 n.73
precautionary approach
  areas beyond national jurisdiction 482–3
  ballast water 530
  biodiversity 760, 765, 771–2
  Caribbean Sea and the Gulf of Mexico 688
  customary international law 482, 497
  dumping 525
  ecosystem approach 63
  fisheries and living resources 493, 497–8, 513, 514, 897
    Fish Stocks Agreement 54, 63, 168, 501–2
    regional fisheries management organizations 451, 457, 460–1
  integrated oceans management 467–8, 472, 474–7, 479, 482–3, 489, 899
  North-East Atlantic and North Sea 476, 648, 660
  ocean acidification 798
  regime interaction 63
  Rio Declaration 1992 63, 356
  science 533
  seabed 482
  subsequent practice, treaty modification by 63
  threatened species and VMEs 807–8
  vessel source pollution 530

private entities
  fisheries and living resources 895
  flag State jurisdiction 318
  future of the law of the sea 895
  industry bodies 895
  international courts and tribunals 395 n.3, 412–13
  prompt release 895
  seabed 237, 895
  security 895
  whaling 895
Prohibition of Fishing with Long Drift Nets in the South Pacific Convention 1989 503
Proliferation Security Initiative (PSI) 320, 557, 598, 600–1, 900
prompt release of detained vessels and crew 169, 313, 318, 400, 407, 413, 895
PSSAs *see* particularly sensitive sea areas (PSSAs)
public order 209, 219–21
publicity *see* due publicity obligations
Purcell, Kate 789

Ramsar Convention on Wetlands 1971 813, 814–15, 816, 822–3
Rau, Greg H 798
Reagan, Ronald 26, 580
reciprocity 64–5
Red List of Threatened Species (IUCN) 801–2
reefs *see also* coral reefs
  archipelagic regime 143, 145
  islands 74–5
  sea level, rise in 790–1
  South China Sea 627, 629, 639, 641–2, 902
regime interaction
  future of the law of the sea 904
  relationship of UN Convention on the Law of the Sea 1982 (LOSC 1982) to other treaties 34–7
  subsequent practice, treaty modification by 48, 60–3, 65–6, 904
Regional Commission for Fisheries (RECOFI) 759

regional cooperation *see also* Antarctica, legal regime; Arctic, legal regime; Indian Ocean; Mediterranean Sea; regional fisheries management organizations (RFMOs); North-East Atlantic and North Sea; South China Sea
  biodiversity 753
  coastal State jurisdiction 300–1
  continental shelf 201
  Indian Ocean 704, 710–23, 903
  port State control 291–3, 302
regional fisheries management arrangements (RFMAs) 502
regional fisheries management organizations (RFMOs) 439–62, 504–5
  acidification of oceans 459–61
  advisory function 442
  allocation of fishing opportunity 452–3
  anadromous stocks 443
  annual reports 451
  Arctic 460, 737–8
  areas beyond national jurisdiction (ABNJ) 460
  areas under national jurisdiction (AUNJ) 460–1
  arrest of ships 457
  associated or dependent species 449–50, 457
  at-sea measures 453, 454, 456–7
  best available scientific evidence 451
  biodiversity 459, 462, 755, 758–9, 764–5
  bioprospecting 841
  boarding and inspection 456–7
  bottom fisheries 458–9
  by-catch 457–8
  catch documentation and certification schemes 453, 455–6
  climate change 451, 459–62, 796, 798
  coastal State jurisdiction 167–8, 301, 460–1
  conservation and management measures 442, 444, 447–61
  cooperation 440–8, 462, 894
  criminal offences 447–8, 454–7, 460, 462

regional fisheries management organizations (RFMOs) (*cont.*)
  data and data reporting requirements 442, 444, 450–2, 454, 459, 461
  decision-making 445, 454, 760
  deep-sea fisheries, guidelines on 458
  dispute settlement 410, 445
  due regard duty 441
  ecosystem approach 449, 450, 457–61
  effort, management of fishing 451–2
  enforcement and compliance 442–3, 446–8, 453–7
  European Union 445, 454
  exclusive economic zones 440, 461
  exploratory fisheries 452
  FAO 440, 446–7
    Compliance Agreement 446–7
    criminal offences 447
    Global Record of Fishing Vessels, Refrigerated Transport Vessels and Supply Vessels 454
    Guidelines for Assessing Flag State Performance 446
    Port State Measures Agreement 455
  Fish Stocks Agreement 54, 167–8, 441, 444–6, 449–50, 453, 460–1, 501–2
  flag State jurisdiction 444, 446–8, 453–4, 457
  flags of convenience/open registries 445–8
  fleet capacity limitations 452
  fraud 456
  free riders 444, 445–6
  future of the law of the sea 894, 897
  General Assembly (UN) 443, 458
  general principles of international law 441
  highly migratory species 440–2, 460–1
  institutionalization of conservation 441–3
  investigation and prosecution 456–7
  IUU fishing 448, 454–5, 460, 462
  Kobe Process 442, 760
  large-scale high seas driftnet fishing, moratorium on 443
  legitimacy 440
  limitations 444, 448
  marine environment/pollution 449–50, 457–8
  marine protected areas (MPAs) 459
  'move-on' rules 458
  negative lists of vessels 453–4
  North-East Atlantic and North Sea 660, 671
  objection procedure 445
  observers 443, 444–5, 451, 453, 456, 458
  ocean acidification 798
  opt-out procedure 445
  pacta tertiis rule 444–5, 447
  participation levels 760
  port State control 453, 455–6
  positive lists of vessels 453, 454
  precautionary approach 451, 457, 460–1
  qualified maximum sustainable yield (MSY) 449
  quotas
    allocations 452–3
    exclusive economic zones 461
    loss of quota 454
    total allowable catch (TAC) 445, 450–3
  regulatory measures 442
  sanctions 446–7, 456
  satellite monitoring 456
  scientific committees and bodies 450–1
  scientific evidence 449, 456, 460
  scientific observer programs 451
  scientific research 442, 461
  security 600
  stock assessment 450–1
  straddling species 440–1, 460–1
  sustainable use 440, 449–50, 461–2
  threatened species and VMEs 805, 808–9
  total allowable catch 445, 450–3
  trade-related measures 454, 455
  transhipment bans 453, 454–5
  Vessel Day Scheme 452
  Vessel Monitoring Systems 456
  Vessel Register, restrictions to vessels on 452
regional oceans management 900–4
Regional Programme on Partnerships in Environmental Management for the Seas of East Asia (PEMSEA) 645
Regional Seas Programme (UNEP) 645

registration of ships 217, 248, 306–10, 317
Regular Process (UN) 366–7, 372, 484 n.149
Reisman, W Michael 157
renewable energy 164, 171, 466 *see also* wind farms
res communis 203–4, 803
res nullius 203–4, 803–4
res publica 203–4
reservations or exceptions in treaties and conventions 21, 29, 33–4, 405–8
revenue sharing (ISA) 192, 198–9, 229–31, 250–2, 891
RFMOs *see* regional fisheries management organizations (RFMOs)
Rio Conference 1992 355–6, 361–2, 617
Rio+20 Conference 355, 357, 361, 368, 465–6, 766
Rio Declaration on Environment and Development 63, 356, 495–6, 512
rise in sea level *see* sea level, rise in
rivers 79–82
Roberts, Callum 805, 818
rocks
    baselines 74 n.26
    Caribbean Sea and the Gulf of Mexico 697
    contiguous zones 109
    continental shelf 95
    exclusive economic zones 95
    low-tide elevations 263, 272
    North-East Atlantic and North Sea 659
    sea level, rise in 791
    territorial sea 95
Roman law 305
Roosevelt, Franklin D 879
Rubin, Alfred P 863–4
Russian Federation
    Arctic 729–30, 732–5, 738, 749–50
    Arctic Sunrise, seizure of 173, 187–8, 201, 886–7
    artificial islands, installations and structures 173, 187–8, 201, 886–7
    China 910
    continental shelf 187–8, 197–8, 352
    dispute settlement, compulsory 910
    exclusive economic zones 173

landlocked and geographically disadvantaged States 341
    military operations 882, 886–7
    piracy 58
    regional fisheries management organizations (RFMOs) 445, 453
    straits 132
    territorial sea 882
    whaling 510

safety *see also* customs, fiscal, health, safety, and immigration laws and regulations
    Antarctic 727
    Arctic 727
    artificial islands, installations and structures 172, 187–8, 431
    charts 315
    identification markings 571
    IMO 421, 423–4, 426, 429, 429–30, 436
    innocent passage 543
    long-range identification and tracking (LRIT) of ships 588, 594, 599
    Maritime Safety Committee (IMO) 421–4
    overflight, freedom of 124
    port State control 283, 302
    scientific research 572
    security 596
    SOLAS 105–6, 320, 426, 436, 588, 594, 599, 745
    straits 123–9
    surveys 315
    warning signals 572
San Remo Manual on International Law 877, 878–9
sanitation measures 282
Santiago Declaration 11–13
Sargasso Sea 650, 683–4, 764, 770–1
Sarpi, Paolo 606
satellites
    monitoring of fisheries 456
    remote sensing 562
Scarborough Reef 627, 629, 902
science *see* marine environment/pollution and science; scientific research
scientific research 29, 559–81
    Antarctic 578, 644, 739–42, 749, 751
    applied research 174, 560, 568, 575

scientific research (*cont.*)
   appropriate scientific methods, use of 565
   archipelagic waters 566-7, 570
   Arctic 737, 746-7
   Argo Project 575
   artificial islands, installations and structures 574
   assessments 560
   best scientific evidence available 576-7
   biodiversity 753-4, 757, 773-4, 898
   bioprospecting 569, 580, 829, 832-7, 841, 898
      continental shelf 174
      genetic resources 559-60, 568
   circulation systems 566
   climate change 174-5, 566, 573, 784-5, 796
   coastal State jurisdiction 173-4, 297, 301, 343, 560, 562-80
   commercial oriented research 560, 569
   common heritage of mankind 332
   consent 567-71, 574
   continental shelf 207, 563, 567-73, 575, 580
   cooperation 565, 573
   customary international law 564
   data collection and exchange 560, 562, 570, 574-6, 579
   definition 174, 561-2, 825
   developing countries 565
   development of regime 30, 562-3
   dispute settlement 566, 572
   DOALOS 354
   economic development 565-6
   ecosystem approach 559
   exclusive economic zones 173-5, 560, 567-72, 575, 580-1
      applicable law 165
      high seas 207
      international court and tribunals 407
      landlocked and geographically disadvantaged States 337
      State practice 892
      World Ocean Assessment (UN) 898
   exclusive fishing zones 563
   fees 570
   fisheries and living resources 174-5, 559, 563-4
   climate change 796
   regional fisheries management organizations 442, 461
   sustainable use 576-7
   flag State jurisdiction 318
   floating objects, vehicles and other devices 574-6
   future of the law of the sea 580-1, 898
   General Assembly (UN) 579
   general provisions 564-5
   genetic resources 559-60, 568, 573
   Geneva Conventions 1958 561, 563-4, 568
   geology 560
   geomorphology 560-1
   gliders 574-6
   Global Ocean Observing System 574
   high seas 206, 207, 572
   hydrographic surveying 175, 570-2
   IMO 429, 435, 576-7
   innocent passage 541, 543, 567, 570
   installations and equipment 574-6
   intelligence gathering 175
   interfere with legitimate uses of sea, research must not 565
   intergovernmental organizations 564
   internal waters 566-7
   Intergovernmental Oceanographic Commission (IOComm) 564, 573-6, 579
   International Ocean Carbon Coordination Project 574
   International Oceanographic Data and Information Exchange 574
   international organizations 564, 569-74
   International Seabed Authority 231, 573, 581
   interpretation 562, 571
   landlocked and geographically disadvantaged States 327, 330, 332, 337, 343
   licensing 566
   marine environment/pollution 560-2, 565-8, 571, 574-5, 577, 581, 898
      Antarctic Treaty System 578

data collection 562
 dumping 577, 581
 fertilization of oceans 577
 liability 566
marine protected areas 580
Mediterranean Sea 610
military operations 175, 565, 570–2, 581, 885
municipal laws 579–80
natural resources 175, 562, 566, 568–70, 573
notification of details 569
ocean upwelling pipes 174–5
other regimes, research under 576–8
peace, good order, and security, prejudice to 567
peaceful purposes 174, 565, 567
Preamble of UN Convention on the Law of the Sea 1982 (LOSC 1982) 561
protests 571
pure research 174, 560, 562, 568
regional cooperation 644
results available, making 570
right to conduct research 564
safety 572
sampling 569
satellites, remote sensing from 562
seabed 231, 572–3, 581
Security Council (UN) 565
seismic activity 560
South China Sea 175, 644
State practice 175, 578–9
State sovereignty 566
straits 567, 570
surveillance 571
surveys 175, 567, 570–2, 581
sustainable development 560–1
territorial sea 94, 97, 563, 566–7, 570, 575, 580
UNCLOS III 562, 565, 572, 576
warships 567
whaling 510–11, 561, 577, 581, 817
World Ocean Assessment (UN) 580, 898
wrecks or objects of an archaeological nature 571

sea level, rise in 787–94
 adaptive change 787, 798
 archipelagic States 790–1
 baselines 89–90, 787–93, 897, 907
 basepoints 787
 boundary delimitation 791–2
 Caribbean Sea and the Gulf of Mexico 676
 climate change regime 786
 coastal States, implications for 790–1
 contiguous zones 794
 continental shelf 791–2, 794
 customary international law 793
 developing countries 897, 907
 drying reefs 790–1
 effects of 779–80
 exclusive economic zones 791, 793–4
 experts 779–80
 future of the law of the sea 897
 implementation agreement, proposal for 793, 910
 insular States 790–1
 internal waters 787, 793
 IPCC reports 777–8, 779, 787
 islands 791, 897, 907
 legal responses 792–3
 low-tide elevations 788
 Meeting of States Parties 793
 natural resources, ownership of 792
 North-East Atlantic and North Sea 650–1
 physical responses 794
 rocks 791
 small island states 790–1, 797, 907
 South China Sea 644
 State sovereignty 792–3, 797
 statehood, effect on 294, 791, 797, 907
 straight baselines 788–90, 792
 temperature rise 780
 territorial sea 787, 790, 793–4

sea lanes and traffic separation schemes
 archipelagic regime 149–54, 157, 295, 538, 553–4, 567, 570, 680–1
 Caribbean Sea and the Gulf of Mexico 680–2
 freedom of navigation 553–4
 IMO 432–3
 innocent passage 544
 publicity 128
 South China Sea 627, 629, 646
 straits 128–9, 551
 territorial sea 106

seabed *see* **international seabed area**
seals
  Conservation of Antarctic Seals
    Convention 1972 508, 743, 745
  European Union 511–12
  fur seals 441, 491, 511, 816
  Mediterranean Monk Seals, MoU on 509
  non-binding agreements 822
  special areas of conservation 670
  threatened species and VMEs 816
  trade restrictions 511
  Wadden Sea Agreement 1990 509, 670
search and rescue
  Antarctic 744, 750
  Arctic 301, 736
  coastal State jurisdiction 301
  high seas 224–5
  Maritime Rescue Coordination
    Centres 744
  Mediterranean Sea 623
  migrants, smuggling of 217
  rescue, duty of compulsory 217
  security 596
  South China Sea 639
  territorial sea 103–4
  warships 103–4
Secretary-General (UN) and
  reports 26–7, 375–6
  advice and assistance to States 359
  annual cycle of review 40–1
  bioprospecting 827
  Charter of UN 390
  charts and geographic coordinates,
    facilities for 358
  General Assembly (UN) 359
  Implementation Agreement 1984 359
  information, collection, compilation and
    dissemination of 358–9
  integrated oceans management 465
  ISA 231, 234, 239, 386–7
  Meeting of States Parties 360,
    376–7, 388–90
  ocean acidification 781
  open-ended informal consultative process
    (UN) 364
  Regular Process 366
  threatened species and VMEs 800

  training 359
  UN-Oceans 362–3
security 582–603
  ambiguities, maintenance of 597–8
  archipelagic regime 142
  Arctic 590
  boarding and inspection 320
  borders 582–4
  boundary delimitation 585, 589–90, 602
  Caribbean Sea and the Gulf of
    Mexico 594, 599
  CARICOM Maritime and Airspace
    Security Co-operation
    Agreement 600
  Charter of UN 601
  climate change 594
  coastal State jurisdiction 584, 586–7,
    591–3, 603
  codes of conduct 600
  collective action 588
  contiguous zones 110, 113, 587
  continental shelf 585–6
  criminal offences 584, 586–96, 600–2
  critical issues 589–93
  customary international law 598
  customs, fiscal, health, safety,
    and immigration laws and
    regulations 586–7
  defences of coastal States 591–2
  definition 583
  developing countries 603
  development of law of the sea 596–601
  dispute settlement 597–8
  drug trafficking 587, 590, 594, 600
  economic interests 587–8
  enforcement 596, 599, 601–2
  evolving threats 593–4
  exclusive economic zones 585–7, 591–2,
    597, 900
  fisheries and living resources 585, 600
  flag State jurisdiction 319–21, 588
  freedom of navigation 557–8, 584, 590,
    592–3, 597, 900
  future of the law of the sea 593–6, 894,
    899–900, 903
  General Assembly (UN) 599
  hostage taking 590, 595–6

human dimension 595–6
human trafficking 590–1, 596, 600–1
IMO 588, 599
Indian Ocean 702, 720–2
information gathering 588
innocent passage 100, 586, 597
intelligence gathering 591–3
internal waters 586
International Ship and Port Security (ISPS) Code 320
interpretation 589, 597–8
ISPS Code 588, 599, 602–3
IUU fishing 586, 594, 600
marine environment/pollution 586, 594–5
memoranda of understanding 600
military operations 591–3, 596–8, 867, 873–4
natural resources 585–6, 589
non-State actors 595
oil and gas 589, 895
people smuggling 590–1, 596, 600–1
piracy 320, 587, 590, 593, 599–601
port State control 282–3, 302
private entities 895
Proliferation Security Initiative 320, 557, 598, 600–1, 900
response to threats 586–8
seafarer identification requirements 602
Search and Rescue Region 596
Security Council (UN) 595, 598, 601
South China Sea 589
sovereign immunity 586
State sovereignty 586
straits 122, 585, 597
SUA Convention 591, 599
substantive regime of maritime zones 891
surveillance 593–4, 603
technological development 593–5
territorial sea 107–9, 585–6
terrorism 320, 586, 591, 599, 900
traditional security concerns 582–6
trafficking 590, 594, 596, 600–1
transnational crime 590–4
treaties and conventions 587, 595, 596, 598–601
visit, right to 590, 601

warships and other military/naval vessels 582, 584–5, 591–3, 594, 596–8
weapons 320, 587, 598, 600
Security Council (UN) and resolutions
flag State jurisdiction 320
freedom of navigation 557
international courts and tribunals 407–8
maintenance of international peace and security 106, 133, 320
piracy 34, 59, 106–7, 369–71, 590, 721, 854–5, 863–4, 875
scientific research 565
security 595, 598, 601
straits 133
territorial sea 106
weapons of mass destruction 223
sedentary species
bioprospecting 838–9
continental shelf 183, 186, 191
exclusive economic zones 170
Mediterranean Sea 611
seabed 838–9
Selden, John 4
self-governing territories 32, 33, 230, 251, 412, 651
semi-circle test 82–3
semi-enclosed seas or oceans *see* enclosed or semi-enclosed seas or oceans
Senkaku/Diaoyu Islands 371
Shearer, Ivan A 108
shipping
Antarctic 728–9, 743–4, 750
Arctic 725, 728–9, 736, 747
biodiversity 763
collisions, jurisdiction in 218–19
construction, equipment, equipment and manning 100, 206, 288
flag state jurisdiction 216, 218–19
flag state regulation 214–16, 218–19
flags of convenience/open registries 216
high seas 214–19, 224
illegal, unreported and unregulated (IUU) fishing 216
IMO 728, 743–4
nationality of ships 214–16, 224, 248
registration of ships 217, 248, 306–10, 317

shipping (cont.)
  ship, definition of 311
  small vessels 309–10, 314
  stateless or unflagged vessels 216–18, 224, 314–15
  two or more flags, sailing under 216
shipriders 101, 221, 692
signature of UN Convention on the Law of the Sea 1982 (LOSC 1982) 29
slave trade 220, 224, 312, 871
small arms by sea, proliferation of 223, 224
small-island States 78, 790–1, 797, 907
small vessels 217, 309–10, 314
smuggling 6 see also migrants, smuggling of
SOLAS 105–6, 320, 426, 436, 588, 594, 599, 745
Somalia
  consent to enforcement action 34
  European Union Naval Force 225
  failed State, as 704, 721, 864
  piracy 701, 723, 843–4, 847, 849, 853–5
    consent to enforcement 34
    enforcement 34, 225, 854–5
    political aims 847
    prosecutions 858, 862–4
    security 590, 601
    Security Council (UN) resolutions 34, 369–71, 721, 854–5, 875
    territorial sea 854
  security 895
  Security Council (UN) resolutions 34, 369–71, 721, 854–5, 875
  State sovereignty 34
  territorial sea 854
South Asian Association for Regional Cooperation (SAARC) 712
South China Sea 626–46
  Antarctic Treaty System 642, 644–5
  applicable law 636–9
  arbitration 640–2
  ASEAN 636–40, 643
    Declaration on the Conduct of Parties 2002 629, 637–9, 646
    Declaration on the South China Sea 1992 636–7
    nuclear weapon free zone 643

  Treaty of Amity and Cooperation in Southeast Asia 637
  biodiversity 628
  boundary disputes 155, 371, 627–42, 646, 890
  Charter of UN 631, 636, 638, 642
  China 156, 175, 626–46, 892
  climate change and sea level rise 644
  code of conduct 636–7
  colonialism 633–4
  Commission on the Limits of the Continental Shelf 635
  cooperation 636–9, 642, 644–6, 902
  customary international law 639
  dispute settlement 627–42, 644, 646
  drug trafficking 639
  ecosystem approach 628, 644, 646
  enforcement 636
  estoppel 632
  exclusive economic zones 626, 633, 639
  fisheries and living resources 627–9, 638, 644, 646
  France 631–3
  freedom of navigation 646
  Global Environment Facility (GEF) 645
  historic rights 629
  ICJ 641–2
  Indonesia 626, 642
  institutional arrangements 636–9
  inter-temporal law 632
  islands, disputes over 155, 371, 626–7, 629–41, 646
  Japan 589, 626–7, 635
  Kalayaan Islands 633
  maps 633–5
  marine environment/pollution 636, 638, 644, 645–6
  military operations 643–4
  names of area 633
  Netherlands 631
  non-living and minerals resources 627–9, 645, 646
  nuclear weapons free zone, declaration as 643
  oil and gas 628, 645
  overlapping claims 629, 638

Pacific West Central Region ecosystem (FAO) 628
Paracel Islands 155, 627, 629, 632–3, 902
peaceful means, dispute settlement by 637–8
Philippines 626, 629, 633, 635–7, 640–5
piracy and armed robbery 639
prospects and trends 639–46
reefs 627, 629, 639, 641–2, 902
Scarborough Reef 627, 629, 902
scientific research 175, 644
sea lanes and traffic separation schemes 627, 629, 646
search and rescue, coordination of 639
security 589
semi-enclosed sea, as 626, 638
Senkaku/Diaoyu Islands 371
Spratly Islands 155, 627–9, 632–4, 637, 646, 902
State practice 632
State sovereignty 629–32, 635
straddling and shared stocks, depletion of 628
straight baselines 155
straits 132, 627
Taiwan 627, 629, 633–4
territorial disputes 155, 371, 627–41
territorial sea 626
territorial sovereignty 631–42
trade 627
United Nations Development Programme (UNDP) 645
United States 631, 637, 642
U-shaped line 628–30, 633–6
Vietnam 632–4
World Bank 645
South-East Atlantic Fisheries Organization (SEAFO) 443, 454, 456, 458, 759
South Indian Ocean Fisheries Agreement (SIOFA) 443, 715, 759
South Orkney Islands Southern Shelf MPA 749
South Pacific Regional Fisheries Management Organization (SPRFMO) 443, 445, 453, 759
Southern Africa Development Community (SADC) 712

Southern Bluefin Tuna 396, 402, 415, 442, 445, 460, 667, 715, 818, 820
Southwest Indian Ocean Fisheries Commission (SWIOFC) 714
sovereign equality, principle of 321, 334
sovereign immunity
  internal waters 872–3
  international courts and tribunals 395
  port State control 285
  security 586
  warships 70–1, 129, 395 n.2, 871–3
sovereignty *see* sovereign immunity; State sovereignty
Spain
  archipelagic regime 139, 155
  Caribbean Sea 673
  colonialism 673
  continental shelf 197, 608–9, 657
  fisheries and living resources 299, 285–6, 303, 609–10
  France 613–14
  freedom of navigation 879
  freedom of the seas 3, 4
  Italy 613–14
  marine environment/pollution 124, 169 n.60
  Mediterranean Sea 605, 608–9, 613–14
  military operations 876
  Morocco, enclaves in 613
  North-East Atlantic and North Sea 648–9, 651, 656–8
  straits 124
  United States 139
  WTO dispute settlement procedure 285–6
specialization of international law etc 391
specially managed areas (SMAs) 743
specially protected areas (SPAs) 477–8, 688–9, 743
SPLOS *see* LOSC, Meeting of States Parties (SPLOS)
Spratly Islands 155, 627–9, 632–4, 637, 646, 902
State immunity *see* sovereign immunity
State practice *see also* State practice, treaty modification by subsequent
  archipelagic regime 138–40, 155, 889

State practice (cont.)
  baselines 59, 70–1, 73–5, 790, 793
  boundary delimitation 255, 275
  coastal State jurisdiction 179, 299, 302–3
  concordant, common and consistent requirement 59
  continental shelf 199
  development of the law of the sea 894
  exclusive economic zones 160, 162–3, 171, 178–80, 891–2
  fisheries and living resources 168–9
  flag State jurisdiction 209
  future of maritime limits and zones 889, 906–7
  innocent passage 546, 882
  institutions 393
  internal waters 70
  Mediterranean Sea 607
  Meeting of States Parties 378, 385
  military operations 866
  nationality 306
  North-East Atlantic and North Sea 648, 655–6, 663
  oil and gas 191
  piracy 58–9
  port State control 285
  refuge, places of 663
  regional oceans management 900–1
  scientific research 175, 578–9
  sea level, rise in 792–3, 797
  South China Sea 632
  spatial definition 889, 906–7
  straits 115, 125
  subsequent practice, modification by 47–8, 58–60, 64, 905–6, 910
  substantive regime of maritime zones 890–2
  territorial sea 94–5
  warships 60, 546
State practice, treaty modification by subsequent 46–68
  amendment 47–8
  Commission on the Limits of the Continental Shelf 56, 57, 65–6
  common heritage of mankind 64, 67
  conferral of powers 52
  consensus 55
  consent of parties 47 n.6, 49, 55
  customary international law 48, 49, 51, 67–8
  definition of modification 5
  derogations 52, 56, 64–5
  dispute settlement 52, 65–6
  ecosystem approach 63
  erga omnes obligations 64
  evolutionary provisions of UN Convention on the Law of the Sea 1982 (LOSC 1982) 52, 66
  Fish Stocks Agreement 52–5, 63
  formal amendments 46–8, 50, 54–7, 67
  fragmentation 48, 61–2, 67–8
  future of the law of the sea 905–6, 910
  generally accepted international rules and standards 66
  Implementation Agreement 1994 52–5, 57, 62
  implementation agreements 52–5, 57, 62, 67
  implications for development 64–7
  implied consent 47 n.6
  implied powers, doctrine of 52, 55
  in-built adaptation mechanisms 65–6, 68
  informal character of 47
  Informal Consultative Process on Oceans and the Law of the Sea (UN) 65–6
  international organizations, practice of 49, 52, 66
  International Seabed Authority 65–6
  interpretation 47, 49–52, 55, 56–7, 65–6
  marine environment/pollution 54, 64–8
  Meeting of States Parties 49–50, 55–7, 65
  non-State actors, practice of 49
  norms 62, 65, 68
  peaceful purposes requirement 64, 67
  precautionary principle 63
  procedural provisions 51, 57, 59, 67
  reciprocity 64–5
  regime interaction 48, 60–3, 65–6
  relevant subsequent practice, defining 49–50
  standards 65–6
  State practice 58–60, 64
  straight baselines 59, 66–7
  subsequent agreements 50, 62

substantive or essential
    provisions 51–2, 57
successive treaties 62
tacit modification 48, 51–4, 57–9, 62,
    64, 66, 68
universal jurisdiction over seizure of
    pirate ships or aircraft 57–9
Vienna Convention on the Law of
    Treaties 47, 49–52
State sovereignty see also **territorial**
    sovereignty
Antarctic 840–1
archipelagic regime 142, 148
Arctic 729–32
coastal State jurisdiction 5, 7, 281,
    294–300
contiguous zones 109, 112
continental shelf 184–6
Convention on the Continental Shelf
    1958 15
enforcement, consent to 34
European Union 172 n.74
fisheries and living resources 3, 10, 166,
    491, 493–4, 498
high seas 1–2, 203–4
historical development 1–2, 3, 5, 7
IMO 229–30
innocent passage 537, 539
internal waters 537
international courts and
    tribunals 404, 406–7
military operations 867–8, 881–3, 885
North-East Atlantic and North Sea 654
occupation 5
piracy 34
port State control 283–4
scientific research 566
security 586
South China Sea 629–32, 635
straits 123, 127–8
territorial sea 3–4, 7, 9, 94, 106,
    111–12, 563
stateless or unflagged ships etc 216–18, 224
constructive statelessness 217
dual nationality 216, 217
flag State jurisdiction 314–15
high seas 216–18, 224

nationality 216, 217
presumptive flag state 217
registration 217, 314–15
small vessels 217
smuggling and irregular
    migration 217–18
States parties see **LOSC, Meeting of States**
    Parties (SPLOS)
Stockholm Conference 1972 28–9, 355
Stockholm Convention on Persistent
    Organic Pollutants (POPs) 2001
    (UN) 728, 746
Stockholm Declaration 28–9, 355, 494
straddling fish stocks see **Fish Stocks**
    Agreement (FSA); migratory/
    highly migratory species and
    straddling stocks
straight baselines see also **archipelagic**
    straight baselines
Arctic 734
artificial straight lines 79–89
bay-closing lines 82–4
Caribbean Sea and the Gulf of
    Mexico 676, 680
charts, deposit of 80
coastal State jurisdiction 12–13, 80
Convention on the Territorial Sea and
    Contiguous Zone 1958 85, 87
customary international law 81
deeply indented coastlines 59, 85–7
exceptional coasts 59, 85–6
exclusive economic zones 86
fixed versus ambulatory debate 73
geographic coordinates, deposit of 80
high seas 86
innocent passage 18–19, 87–8
internal waters 80–1, 85, 86–8, 537
interpretation 80–1, 87, 91 n.57
islands 59, 87
low-tide elevations 73–4, 788
Mediterranean Sea 607–8
North-East Atlantic and North Sea 655
number of States 74 n.25
port, closing the waters of 85
publicity 80
rivers 79–82
sea level, rise in 788–90, 792

straight baselines (*cont.*)
  South China Sea 155
  spatial definition 889, 906–7
  State practice 59
  strict interpretation 85–8, 91 n.57
  subsequent practice, treaty modification
    by 59, 66–7
  threshold geographic test 86
  UNCLOS III 66–7
**straits used for international
  navigation** 114–33, 537–8, 549–52, 557
  alternate routes 126
  archipelagic sea lanes navigation 115, 132
  Arctic 120, 131–2, 734–5
  balancing of rights 121–2
  bordering straits, regulation of right
    by 551–2
  channel, use of word 119 n.38
  civil jurisdiction 123–4
  classification of straits 119, 131
  climate change 131
  coastal State jurisdiction 118–19, 296
  codification 116
  Collision Regulations 551
  compulsory pilotage 129–30, 288, 552
  continuous and expeditious
    transit 121, 550
  criminal jurisdiction 123–4
  customary international law 708–9
  delay, proceeding without 550
  developing countries 339
  enforcement 123–4, 129–30, 552
  exclusive economic zones 120–1, 126–7,
    132, 552, 882–3
  financial burdens 123
  force majeure or distress 121, 550
  freedom of navigation 121–2, 132–3,
    537–9, 549–52
  functional element 119–20
  future issues 131–2
  Geneva Conventions 1958 14–15, 118
  geographical element 119, 125
  Hague Conference of 1930 9, 116
  hamper transit, obligation of Strait state
    not to 122–3, 129–30, 883
  high seas 114, 120, 132
  historical development 116–18

  IMO 418, 883
  importance of straits 115
  Indian Ocean 708–9
  inland waters 118, 132
  innocent passage 98, 115–19, 121–2, 127–8,
    133, 545
  inward/outward-bound passage 549–50
  islands 119–20, 883
  landlocked and geographically
    disadvantaged States 326, 329–35,
    339, 341–2, 344
  lateral passage 549–50
  littoral States, mutual rights and interests
    of 115, 126, 128–30, 133
  loss of status as straits 132
  marine environment/
    pollution 123–6, 129–32
  maritime States, mutual rights and
    interests of 115
  military operations 882–3
  Montreux Convention 1936 116, 127
  non-suspendable right 549, 552
  North-East Atlantic and North Sea 654
  occupation 4
  operational issues 124–30
  overflight, right of 124, 550–2
  political changes 132
  port State control 288–9
  proximity of bodies of land 119
  publicity 122, 128
  regulation 549–52
  regulations, procedures and practice 551
  safety 123–9
  scientific research 567, 570
  security 122, 585, 597
  self-defence 123
  South China Sea 132, 627
  State practice 115, 125
  State sovereignty 123, 127–8
  stopping and barring vessels 124, 130
  submarines and other underwater
    vehicles 550, 882–3
  sub-surface navigation 120
  surveys 551
  territorial sea 28, 94, 106, 111–12, 120, 122,
    125–6, 129–30, 132, 550, 552
  threats or use of force 550

tolls and fees 122-3, 129-30
traffic separation schemes and sea
    lanes 128-9, 551
travaux préparatoires 550
treaties and conventions 36, 120
types of navigation 119-20
UNCLOS III 124-5, 882-3
United States 124-5, 131-3
use of force 129
volume of navigation 119-20, 132
warships 116-17, 128-9, 545, 550, 709
width of strait 119
Strategic Action Programme (SAP) for the South China Sea 645
structures *see* **artificial islands, installations and structures**
submarine cables and pipelines
    archipelagic regime 148-9, 208
    biodiversity 754
    coastal State jurisdiction 298
    consent 178, 189
    continental shelf 189, 208
    exclusive economic zones 165, 177-8, 208, 212-13, 298
    high seas 206, 216-18, 224
    inadvertent damage 208
    innocent passage 543
    intentional interference 208
    marine protected areas 189
    piracy 848
    straits 882-3
    surveys 189, 212
    territorial sea 208
submarines and other underwater vehicles
    drug trafficking 594
    innocent passage 541, 546, 553, 594, 881
    naval warfare, law of 876
    security 594
    straits 550
    territorial sea 541
    use of force 541
    warships 546, 870
subsoil 91, 96, 161, 170, 608, 611-12
superjacent waters 161, 189-90, 200, 538-9
Suppression of Unlawful Acts against the Safety of Maritime Navigation (SUA) Convention

flag State jurisdiction 319
freedom of navigation 556, 557
high seas 556
piracy 848, 850, 862-3
terrorism 599
transnational crimes 591
weapons of mass destruction 223
surveillance 571, 593-4, 603
surveys
    hydrographic surveying 175, 270-2
    innocent passage 541, 543
    military operations 885
    safety 315
    scientific research 175, 567, 570-2, 581
    straits 551
    submarine cables and pipelines 189, 212
sustainable use and management
    Agenda 21 356, 362-3, 365, 465, 487 n.171, 809
    Arctic 736, 746
    biodiversity 754, 757-75
    bioprospecting 829-30, 835
    Brundtland Commission 495
    Caribbean Sea and the Gulf of Mexico 687, 689
    fisheries and living resources 491-9, 502-5, 512-15, 652, 666, 897
        Fish Stocks Agreement 168
        regional fisheries management organizations 440, 449-50, 461-2
        scientific research 576-7
    Indian Ocean 711-12
    integrated oceans management 465, 469
    non-living and mineral resources 897
    North-East Atlantic and North Sea 648, 652, 666
    Ramsar Convention on Wetlands 1971 815
    scientific research 560-1, 576-7
    World Summit 2002 355, 356-7
Sweden 5, 127, 135, 183, 475-6, 648, 651, 735, 878

tacit modification of treaties etc 48, 51-4, 57-9, 62, 64, 66, 68
Taiwan
    archipelagic States 155-6

Taiwan (*cont.*)
  China 32, 880
  Chinese Taipei, as 32, 445, 629
  fisheries and living resources 32, 310, 412 n.59, 444–5, 713, 715–17
  flag State jurisdiction 310
  Indian Ocean 713, 715–17
  South China Sea 627, 629, 633–4
  State party to UN Convention on the Law of the Sea 1982 (LOSC 1982), as 32
  straits 115, 627, 733
Tanaka, Yoshifumi 489–90
Tarawa Declaration of the Pacific Forum 1989 503
tax *see* customs, fiscal, health, safety, and immigration laws and regulations
technical assistance 354
technological developments 1, 585–6, 594, 753, 800
technology transfer 30, 231, 238, 433–4, 754
territorial sea 91–107 *see also* Convention on the Territorial Sea and Contiguous Zone 1958
  adjacent or opposite States, boundaries with 95
  airspace 91, 96
  Antarctic 371–2, 738
  archipelagic regime 8, 88–91, 95, 136, 138–41, 146, 148–50, 155–6
  arcs of circle method 95
  Arctic 729, 732
  armed conflict, law of 103
  arrest of people on board foreign vessels 105
  artificial islands and installations 95
  baselines 70–1, 75, 93–5
  below water, natural features 95
  bioprospecting 833
  boat people and migrants, treatment and resettlement of 104, 112
  boundary delimitation 255–7, 259, 261–2, 277
  breadth 92–5
  cannon-shot rule 92–3, 582 n.1
  Caribbean Sea and the Gulf of Mexico 681

  civil jurisdiction 105
  climate change 794–5
  coastal State jurisdiction 7, 11–12, 16, 294, 296–7
  contiguous zones 92, 95, 104, 107–9
  continental shelf 181
  creeping jurisdiction 28
  criminal jurisdiction 105, 113, 537, 544–5
  customary international law 6, 95, 103, 287
  definition 91
  enforcement 91, 96
  exclusive economic zones 94, 160–2, 164, 892
  fisheries and living resources 498
  flag State jurisdiction 91–2, 97, 104, 312
  foreign vessels, jurisdiction over 96
  freedom of navigation 93, 108, 110–11, 538–9, 557
  generally accepted rules and standards 105
  geography 98
  Hague Conference of 1930 93
  Harvard Research in International Law 7–8, 136
  high seas 7, 18, 93, 205
  historical development 3, 5–9
  hot pursuit 96, 875
  human rights 104, 112
  ILC 97, 103, 117–18, 358
  IMO 92, 105–6, 418, 432–3
  innocent passage 98–102, 111–13, 538–41, 543–6, 548, 552–3
  Indian Ocean 706–8, 721
  internal waters 9, 95
  international cooperation 113
  international courts and tribunals 404
  international organizations 103–7, 112
  islands 8, 28, 95, 104, 272
  juridical character 96–7
  line of sight doctrine 93
  location 92–5
  man-made structures 95
  marine environment/pollution 113, 533
  Mediterranean Sea 607–9, 612
  military operations 880–3
  natural resources 94

naval warfare, law of 878
North-East Atlantic and North Sea 653, 655–6, 659
outer limit, method of drawing 95, 533
piracy 370, 848, 850, 854, 874
port State control 283–4, 287–91
proclamations 94–5
regional organizations 106
roadsteads 75, 95 n.26, 656
scholarly writings 95, 96
scientific research 94, 97, 563, 566–7, 570, 575, 580
sea level, rise in 787, 790, 793–4
seabed 96
search and rescue obligations 103–4
South China Sea 626
spatial definition 889–90
State practice 94–5
State sovereignty 7, 9, 91, 96–7, 103, 105–7, 112, 563
straits 28, 94, 106, 111–12, 120, 122, 125–6, 129–30, 132, 550, 552
submarine cables and pipelines 208
subsoil 91, 96
substantive regime of maritime zones 890–1
threatened species and VMEs 803
traffic separation schemes 106
Truman Proclamation 11
UNCLOS I 13, 93, 97, 296
UNCLOS II 93
UNCLOS III 92–4, 105, 113
use of force 103
warships 545–7

territorial sovereignty
Antarctic 738
baselines 69
bays 20
freedom of navigation 538
high seas 17–18
innocent passage 539
international organizations 105–6
port State jurisdiction 283
sea level, rises in 707
South China Sea 631–42

terrorism
artificial islands, installations and structures 173
high seas 224
human rights 224
military operations 867–8, 873–4
piracy 847
security 320, 586, 591, 599, 900
September 11, 2001 terrorist attacks 588, 599, 867–8, 900
war on terror 224

threatened species and vulnerable marine ecosystems (VMEs) 799–824
Agenda 21 809
areas beyond national jurisdiction (ABNJ) 801–2, 805
biodiversity 757, 770, 773, 800, 804–7, 813–14, 824
broad-spectrum action 802–16
Caribbean Sea and the Gulf of Mexico 688–9
CITES 669, 819–20
climate change 800, 802, 811–13, 824
coastal State jurisdiction 804, 819–20
continental shelf 803
coral reefs 799–802, 812–13
ecologically or biologically significant sea areas (EBSAs) 805
ecosystem approach 458–9, 800–2, 806–9
emergency responses 822
exclusive economic zones 803–4, 806–7
exports and imports 819
FAO 801–2, 805, 807–8, 820
fisheries and living resources 803–9, 819
    biodiversity 806
    bottom trawling 807–9, 824
    driftnet fishing 807–8
    FAO 801–2, 805, 807
    gear 808
    highly migratory and straddling stocks 803–4
    maximum sustainable yield 806–7, 824
    methods 807–9
    move-on rules 809
    res nullius 803
    technological development 800
    total allowable catch (TAC) 806–7, 824
    unsustainable 805–9
    vulnerability, definition of 801–2

threatened species and vulnerable marine
    ecosystems (VMEs) (cont.)
  Fort Lauderdale Criteria 820
  General Assembly (UN) 801–2, 805, 808
  habitat protection and capacity 813–16
  high seas 803–4
  IMO 805
  Indian Ocean 718–19, 722–3
  innocent passage 804
  International Seabed Authority 805
  IUCN Red List 821
  IUU fishing 802
  land-based source pollution 809–11
  marine environment/
      pollution 809–13, 824
  marine mammals 511, 580
  marine protected areas 804–5, 811
  migratory species 717–18, 757, 821–2
  monitoring 810, 819
  national action programmes 810
  ocean acidification 800, 811
  particularly sensitive sea areas 804
  permits 819
  precautionary approach 807–8
  protect and preserve obligation 804, 807
  Ramsar Convention on Wetlands 1971
      813, 814–15, 816, 822–3
  regional fisheries management
      organizations 805, 808–9
  regional sea groupings 805
  Red List of Threatened Species 801–2
  seabed 803
  soft law 806–7
  species and specific sites, responses
      framed around 816–23
  specimens 819–20
  territorial sea 803
  total allowable catch 806–7
  tuna 818
  vulnerability, definition of 801–2
  want of jurisdiction 803–5
  Whaling Convention 817–18, 820
  World Heritage Convention 1972 813,
      815–16, 823
threats of force see use or threats of force
Torrey Canyon disaster 419–20, 424, 436,
    519, 531, 663

total allowable catch (TAC) 166–7, 496,
    498–500
  bioprospecting 833, 836
  regional fisheries management
      organizations 445, 450–3
  threatened species and VMEs 806–7, 824
tourism 741, 743, 823
traditional knowledge 831
trafficking see also drug trafficking;
    migrants, smuggling of
  human trafficking 590–1, 596, 600–1, 606
  Mediterranean Sea 606
  nationality 224
  security 590, 594, 596, 600–1
  slave trade 220, 224, 312, 871
  small arms by sea, proliferation
      of 223, 224
  weapons 223, 224, 590, 600
tragedy of the commons 439, 803–4
transit, right of see straits used for
    international navigation
treaties and conventions see also individual
    treaties and conventions
  amendment 421–2, 436
  continental shelf 199
  derogations 52, 56, 64–5
  freedom of navigation 557
  friendship, commerce and navigation
      bilateral treaties 305
  historical development 2
  IMO 418–22, 427–8
  international courts and tribunals 395
  marine environment/pollution 520,
      523–5, 533–4
  marine mammals 509, 511
  military operations 866
  naval warfare, law of 875–7
  regime interaction 66
  rules of reference 31
  security 587, 595, 596, 598–601
  stateless vessels 218
  straits 120
  subsequent practice, amendment
      by 47, 49–52
  treaty-making 419–20, 426
  Vienna Convention on the Law of
      Treaties 34, 61, 66, 199

compliance 47
continental shelf 199
harmonious interpretation 61
regime interaction 66
subsequent practice, amendment by 47, 49–52
visit, right of 221
Treves, Tullio 906
tribunals *see* **international courts and tribunals**
Truman Proclamations 10–12, 13, 16, 183
tuna
  CITES 818
  endangered species 818
  Indian Ocean Tuna Commission 442, 450, 452, 714–17, 818
  Inter-American Tropical Tuna Commission 442, 444, 452, 818
  International Commission for the Conservation of Atlantic Tunas 442, 444–5, 452–3, 621, 684–5, 770–1, 818, 820
  International Convention for the Conservation of Atlantic Tunas 667–8
  maximum sustainable yield 818
  regional fisheries management organizations 818
  Southern Bluefin Tuna 396, 402, 415, 442, 445, 460, 667, 715, 818, 820
  total allowable catch 818
Turkey
  collisions 18, 218
  Cyprus 613
  France 18, 218
  Greece 608, 614
  Mediterranean Sea 605, 608, 613–14, 625
  security 116
  straits 115–16, 127–8
  territorial sea 608

Ukraine 71, 267, 271, 738, 749–50, 886
UN Convention on the Law of the Sea 1982 (LOSC 1982) 24–45
  adoption 25–7, 347
  amendment of UN Convention on the Law of the Sea 1982 (LOSC 1982) 29

Commission on the Limits of the Continental Shelf 43, 385
common heritage of mankind 37
de facto amendments 43
development of UN Convention on the Law of the Sea 1982 (LOSC 1982) 42–3, 45, 894
entry into force of UN Convention on the Law of the Sea 1982 (LOSC 1982) 42–3
Fish Stocks Agreement 43
formal procedures 42–4, 46–8, 50, 54–7, 67, 905
implementation agreements 43–4, 227 n.6
International Seabed Authority 385–6
Meeting of States Parties 43
ratification 42–3
special procedure 385–6
tacit modification 48, 51–4, 57–9, 62, 64, 66, 68
treaties, relationship of UN Convention on the Law of the Sea 1982 (LOSC 1982) to other 36–7
annual cycle of review 40–2
change of circumstances 905
consensus 26
constitution for the oceans, as 44–5, 68, 427
contents, overview of 27–9, 44–5
customary international law, relationship to 37–8, 45
declarations 34
definitions 27, 226–7
developing countries 26–7, 226–7
development 30, 45, 46–8
dominant global powers, interests of 911
durability 373–5
evolutionary provisions 52, 66
final provisions 29
framework treaty, UN Convention on the Law of the Sea 1982 (LOSC 1982) as a 31, 66, 68
future of the law of the sea 904–12
general principles and objectives 36–7
genesis 25–7
importance 24, 373

UN Convention on the Law of the Sea 1982 (LOSC 1982) *(cont.)*
  legal nature of provisions 29–31
  multilateralism 67
  norms 30–1, 38
  objective regime, UN Convention on the Law of the Sea 1982 (LOSC 1982) as a 45
  package deal approach 26, 33, 64, 67–8, 330, 905
  permitted by articles of UN Convention on the Law of the Sea 1982 (LOSC 1982), treaties which are expressly 36
  Preamble 27, 30, 331–2, 494, 561, 896, 899
  preserved by articles of UN Convention on the Law of the Sea 1982 (LOSC 1982), treaties which are expressly 36
  replacement of UN Convention on the Law of the Sea 1982 (LOSC 1982) 905–6
  rules of reference 31, 66
  superiority of UN Convention on the Law of the Sea 1982 (LOSC 1982) 34, 45
  suspension of UN Convention on the Law of the Sea 1982 (LOSC 1982) 36–7
  treaties, relationship to other 34–7
  universal participation, goal of 26, 33, 45, 227, 331, 348, 905
UN Convention on the Law of the Sea 1982 (LOSC 1982), participation in 1–3
  see also **ratification/accession of LOSC 1982**
  coastal States, number of 33
  exclusive economic zones 162–3
  Fish Stocks Agreement 502
  international organizations, transfer of competence to 32, 33
  landlocked States, number of 33
  North-East Atlantic and North Sea 653–5
  number of States 33
  self-governing territories, transfer of competence to 32, 33
  Taiwan (Chinese Taipei) 32
  UN Council for Namibia 32
  universal participation, goal of 26, 33, 45, 227, 331, 348
UN Convention on the Law of the Sea 1982 (LOSC 1982), ratification/accession of 26–9
  amendment of UN Convention on the Law of the Sea 1982 (LOSC 1982) 42–3
  entry into force 349
  exclusive economic zones 213–14
  innocent passage 546
  Johannesburg Declaration 356
  military operations 886
  seabed 227
  straits 124–5
  types of entities 31–2
UN Convention on the Law of the Sea 1982 (LOSC 1982), relationship to other treaties of 34–7
  amendment of UN Convention on the Law of the Sea 1982 (LOSC 1982) 36–7
  Charter of UN, supremacy of 34
  conflict of laws 34
  customary international law 34–5, 37
  derogations 36–7
  Geneva Conventions 34–5
  permitted by articles of UN Convention on the Law of the Sea 1982 (LOSC 1982), treaties which are expressly 36
  preserved by articles of UN Convention on the Law of the Sea 1982 (LOSC 1982), treaties which are expressly 36
  presumption of compatibility 45
  Security Council (UN), resolutions of 34
  superiority of UN Convention on the Law of the Sea 1982 (LOSC 1982) 34, 45
  suspension of UN Convention on the Law of the Sea 1982 (LOSC 1982) 36–7
UNCITRAL (UN Commission on International Trade Law) 249, 416
UNCLOS I
  archipelagic regime 88, 140–1
  decision-making 26
  exclusive economic zones 161

fisheries and living resources 161
ILC draft articles 13, 18–19, 25
institutions 391
Mediterranean Sea 606
piracy 845
territorial sea 13, 93, 97, 296
UNCLOS II
archipelagic regime 141–2
fisheries and living resources 13
territorial sea 93, 296
UNCLOS III 16, 25–6
archipelagic regime 25, 88, 141–2, 148, 154
baselines 59, 66–7
Caribbean Sea and the Gulf of Mexico 672
codification 2
consensus 26
contiguous zones 109
continental shelf 185, 907
creeping jurisdiction 28
developing countries 26
European Union 338, 901
exclusive economic zones 161, 205
fisheries and living resources 161, 501
freedom of navigation 418, 427
future of the law of the sea 904
General Assembly (UN) 25, 358
groups, formation of State 25
high seas 205
IMO 418, 427
Indian Ocean 707–6
institutions 374–5, 391
International Seabed Authority 237–8
landlocked and geographically disadvantaged States 328–31, 336, 338, 344
marine environment/pollution 520
Mediterranean Sea 606
Meeting of States Parties 378, 388
military operations 880–1, 883–4
negotiating texts 25–6
North-East Atlantic and North Sea 653
scientific research 562, 565, 572, 576
straits 124–5, 882–3
territorial sea 92–4, 105, 113
Truman Proclamations 16

UNCTAD (UN Conference on Trade and Development) 416
underwater cultural heritage 62, 359, 606, 609–10, 616, 622–4, 908
UNESCO (United Nations Educational, Scientific and Cultural Organization)
Cultural Heritage Convention 609, 623, 908
Intergovernmental Oceanographic Commission 327, 366–7, 487, 564, 573–4
Regular Process 366
Underwater Cultural Heritage Convention 62, 609, 908
United Kingdom
Albania 18
Antarctic 739
archipelagic regime 137, 140, 144, 147, 155
baselines 85, 137–8, 144, 147
bunkering 555
Caribbean Sea 672, 675, 692
Chagos Archipelago 163 n.14, 705, 707 n.18
Common Fisheries Policy 470
continental shelf 183, 197, 707, 739
customary international law 12, 137
Cyprus 605, 612 n.29
East Inshore and Offshore Areas 470
ecological protection zones 163 n.24
European Union 409
exclusive economic zones 164, 570–2, 883
Falkland Islands 155, 163 n.24
fisheries and living resources 3–4, 164
Germany 20
Gibraltar 115, 604–5, 607–8, 656, 882
high seas 6, 214, 218, 572, 911
historical development 3–6
Iceland 20
IMO 417
Indian Ocean 705–7
infrastructure projects 470
innocent passage 18, 545–6
integrated oceans management 469–70
Ireland 409
Marine and Coastal Access Act 2009 469

United Kingdom (cont.)
  marine environment/pollution 164, 419–20, 424, 436, 519, 531, 663
  Marine Management Organisation 470
  Marine Policy Statement 469
  marine protected areas 470
  Mediterranean Sea 604–5, 607–8, 617, 656, 882
  military operations 873, 883, 886
  North-East Atlantic and North Sea 647
  Norway 137
  piracy 58
  planning areas 469–70
  Ramsar Convention 815
  renewable energy 164
  Santiago Declaration 12
  scholarly works 4
  scientific research 164, 570–2
  smuggling 6
  South Inshore and Offshore Areas 470
  straight baselines 85, 137–8, 147
  straits 125, 129, 138
  sustainable development 469
  territorial sea 5–6, 108
  United States 20
  Venezuela 183
  warships 545–6
  wind farms 470
United Nations (UN) 346–72 *see also* **Conferences on the Human Environment (UN); General Assembly (UN); Security Council (UN)**
  Conferences on the Human Environment 354–7
  Division for Ocean Affairs and the Law of the Sea (DOALOS) 348, 353–4, 360
  entry into force of UN Convention on the Law of the Sea 1982 (LOSC 1982) 346–8, 349–52
  Informal Consultative Process on Oceans and the Law of the Sea 65–6
  institutions, establishment of 349–52
  Legal Counsel 354
  Maritime Safety Committee 421, 423–4
  Meeting of States Parties 353–4, 360
  Oceans Compact 488
  Office of Legal Affairs 348, 353–4
  open-ended informal consultative process 40–1, 353, 363–5, 465–6, 481, 894
  Regular Process 366–7, 372
  relationship agreements with UN 392
  specialized agencies 390
  Systems Chief Executives Board 362
  UN-Oceans 362–3, 487–8
  World Ocean Assessment 580, 898
United States
  archipelagic regime 138–41, 144, 150–2
  Arctic 729–30
  Australia 281
  baselines 83, 890
  bioprospecting 838
  Canada 120, 131, 186, 198–9, 734, 816
  Caribbean Sea and Gulf of Mexico 183, 673–6, 682, 692
  China 175 n.90, 592, 641–2, 720, 880, 884, 900
  coastal State jurisdiction 12, 111
  Convention on the Territorial Sea and Contiguous Zone 1958 113
  continental shelf 11–12, 183, 186, 190, 198
  customary international law 37
  drug trafficking 600, 692
  Federal agencies 471
  fisheries and living resources 11, 288, 502, 731, 733–5, 748–9
  freedom of navigation 542, 546–7, 590, 592, 880, 890, 911
  future of the law of the sea 905
  Geneva Conventions 1958 16
  high seas 214, 217–18
  historical development 6
  IMO 417, 588
  Indian Ocean 701, 705, 708, 720
  innocent passage 112–13, 881–2
  integrated oceans management 471–2
  Interagency Ocean Policy Task Force recommendations 471–2
  Japan 847
  liquor treaties 6
  marine environment/pollution 531, 565
  marine spatial planning 471

military operations 590, 592, 637, 867–8, 872–3, 881–4, 886, 900
National Ocean Council 471
National Ocean Policy Implementation Plan 472
National Oceans Policy 471
non-living and mineral resources 12
North-East Atlantic and North Sea 667–8
oil and gas 183
Philippines 139–40, 641–2
piracy 58
port State jurisdiction 286, 288–9
Regional Marine Planning Handbook 472
Santiago Declaration 12
scientific research 570–2, 580
seabed 227
seals 816
security 588, 590, 592, 595–6, 598–600, 900
September 11, 2001 terrorist attacks 588, 599, 867–8, 900
shipriders 221, 692
South China Sea 631, 637, 642
Spain 139
straits 120, 122, 124–5, 131–3, 138
territorial sea 5–6
terrorism 588, 867–8, 900
treaties, relationship of UN Convention on the Law of the Sea 1982 (LOSC 1982) to other 34, 37
Truman Proclamations 10–12, 13, 16, 183
United Kingdom 20
universal participation, goal of 26, 33, 45, 227, 331, 348
use or threats of force
  arrest of ships 44
  boundary delimitation 695
  innocent passage 541
  military operations 873–4
  piracy 855–6
  straits 129, 550
  submarines and other underwater vehicles 541
  territorial sea 103

van Bynkershoek, Cornelius 5
Vattel, Emmerich de 5, 539–40

Vessel Day Scheme (VDS) 452
Vessel Monitoring Systems (VMSs) 456
vessel source pollution
  Antarctic 727–9, 743–4
  Arctic 727–9
  atmospheric pollution 531, 785
  biodiversity 753, 763
  Caribbean Sea and the Gulf of Mexico 683
  climate change 785, 795
  coastal State jurisdiction 531–2
  flag State jurisdiction 532
  freedom of navigation 206, 532, 537
  IMO 176, 419, 422, 425, 429–30, 432–3, 530, 897
  MARPOL 530, 531
  North-East Atlantic and North Sea 649–50, 663–4
  port State control 283
  precautionary approach 530
  regional measures 649–50, 663–4
  science 530–2, 534
  soft law 530
  Sulphur Emission Control Area 664
  treaties and conventions 530
Vietnam 155–6, 626–9, 632–5, 637–8, 644–5
visit, right of search and
  broadcasting, unauthorized 220
  codification 220
  customary international law 219–20
  flag State jurisdiction 220
  high seas, enforcement on 219–21, 224
  migrants, trafficking of 221, 224
  naval warfare, law of 877–8
  piracy 220, 851–3, 857–8, 874
  sanctions, enforcement of 601
  security 590, 601
  slave trade 220, 224
  statelessness 220
  treaties and conventions 221
  warships 220, 224, 851–2, 874, 877–8
vulnerable marine ecosystems (VMEs) *see* **threatened species and vulnerable marine ecosystems (VMEs)**

war, law of 103, 855–6, 867, 875–9
Warner, Robin 152
warships and naval auxiliaries 870–3
　approach, right of 874
　archipelagic regime 296, 553
　baselines 70–1
　broadcasting, illegal 874
　customary international law 544–5, 872
　definition of warship 870–1, 877
　exclusive economic zones 178
　flag State jurisdiction 312, 870–1
　freedom of navigation 537, 556
　high seas 556
　historic wrecks 870–1
　innocent passage 18–19, 60, 98–9, 112–13, 542, 545–7
　letters of marque 871
　naval warfare, law of 877–8
　nuclear weapons, warships carrying 542, 547–9
　Paris Declaration 1856 871
　piracy 847, 851–2, 855–7, 871, 874–5
　port State control 285
　privateering 871
　scientific research 567
　search and rescue 103–4
　security 582, 584–5, 591–3, 594, 596–8
　slave trafficking 874
　sovereign immunity 70–1, 129, 395 n.2, 871–3
　State practice 60, 546
　straits 116–17, 128–9, 545, 550, 709
　submarines and other underwater vehicles 546, 870
　territorial sea 117, 545–7
　visit, right of search and 220, 224, 851–2, 874, 877–8
　weapons 546
water column
　biodiversity 754, 758
　boundary delimitation 263
　continental shelf 162, 181, 184, 200, 891
　customary international law 754
　exclusive economic zones 161–2
　global commons 754
　Mediterranean Sea 608
　seabed 838

sequestration of carbon dioxide 529–30, 534–5
Water Framework Directive 662
weapons *see also* nuclear weapons
　customary international law 598
　inspection 223
　mass destruction, proliferation of weapons 557, 873–4
　　IMO 222–3, 224
　　security 320, 587, 598, 600
　military operations 873–4, 883
　mines, laying 878
　security 587, 590, 598, 600
　small arms by sea, proliferation of 223, 224
　testing 211–12
　trafficking 223, 224, 590, 600
　warships 546
Webster, Daniel G 818
Weeramantry, Christopher 62–3
Weil, Prosper 69
Wellwood, William 4
Western and Central Pacific Fisheries Commission (WCPFC) 442, 444, 452, 456, 818
Western Central Atlantic Fishery Commission (WECAFC) 686
Westphalia, peace of 305
wetlands 813, 814–15, 816, 822–3
whaling
　aboriginal subsistence whaling 510–11
　Antarctic 739, 743
　CITES 820
　CMS Convention 821
　coastal State jurisdiction 11
　commercial whaling 510–11, 669–70, 817–18
　endangered species, list of 817–18
　European Union 669–70
　Habitats Directive 669–70
　ICJ 817
　Indian Ocean 510
　International Whaling Commission 510, 669, 817
　Japan 511, 577, 581, 739, 817, 847, 895
　JARPA II research program 511, 817
　loopholes 510–11

monitoring 817
moratorium 669–70, 817–18
NAMMCO Commission 510
North-East Atlantic and North Sea 669–70
observers 817
political or ideological methods 847
private entities 895
quotas 509–10
sanctuaries 510
scientific whaling 510–11, 561, 577, 581, 817
subsistence whaling 670
Whaling Convention 484, 491–2, 508, 509–11, 739, 743, 817–20
World Heritage Convention 1972 816
WikiLeaks 288–9
Wilson, Woodrow 879
wind farms 171, 470, 474, 535
Wolfrum, Rüdiger 54, 421, 430
World Bank 645
World Charter for Nature (WCN) 496

World Heritage Convention 1972
Danger List 823
World Heritage List 815–16
World Maritime University 434
World Ocean Assessment (UN) 580, 898
World Summit 2002 355, 356–7, 361, 363, 365–6, 465, 527
World Trade Organization (WTO)
Appellate Body 382, 512
Dispute Settlement Body
European Union 409 n.47
port State control 285–6
reports of panels, adoption of 382
European Union 285–6, 409 n.47, 445, 512
fisheries and living resources 409 n.47
marine mammals 512
port State control 285–6
quantitative restrictions 285–6
wrecks 431, 571, 870–1

Zuleta, Bernardo 348